(Continued inside back cover)

Principles of
Economics

Richard T. Froyen
UNIVERSITY OF NORTH CAROLINA

Douglas F. Greer
SAN JOSE STATE UNIVERSITY

Principles of Economics

MACMILLAN PUBLISHING COMPANY

NEW YORK

Collier Macmillan Publishers

LONDON

Macmillan Publishing Company
866 Third Avenue, New York, New York 10022

Collier Macmillan Canada, Inc.

LIBRARY OF CONGRESS CATALOGING IN PUBLICATION DATA

Froyen, Richard T.
  Principles of economics.

  Includes index.
  1. Economics.   I. Greer, Douglas F.   II. Title.

HB171.5.F77   1989   330   88-13357
ISBN 0-02-339430-7

Preface

There are a number of good introductory economics textbooks. Our book acknowledges their strengths by emulating them in several respects. First, it shares a common purpose with others. We explain how the economy works when functioning freely by markets, as well as when influenced by government policies. Second, our selection of subjects has not strayed from the mainstream. We treat the standard topics: market equilibrium; the Keynesian, monetartist, and new classical models; monetary and fiscal policy; economic growth; oligopoly and other market structures; income distribution; labor relations; and international monetary relations and international trade. In the paperback volumes we cover the standard topics in clusters of micro and macro orientation, as is now customary.

We explain different political and ideological views in an evenhanded manner. We cover the views of both conservatives and liberals.

Features

Why then another principles text? Why try this new offering? An examination of the book will reveal many distinguishing features—matters of content, organization, and exposition.

One significant feature is *logical flow*. The student should not be left with the impression that economics is a loose collection of unconnected topics. We avoid this in several ways. For example, all principles books refer to the basic questions of "what," "how," and "for whom" in the early chapters. We maintain the connection between these basic questions and various aspects of market performance discussed later in the book. In the same vein, we maintain a focus for the student by developing the methodology of two-question logic. For macroeconomics the two questions are "What is expected?" and "What actually happens?"; for microeconomics the questions are "What are the benefits?" and "What are the costs?" Using this two-question logic much hard analysis can be reduced to familiar ways of thinking. The flow of several chapters is smoothed by the use of a run-

ning example. In Chapter 5, for instance, the basic facts of American business are illustrated by a series of discussions concerning General Motors.

A second source of freshness concerns *summaries*. Most texts open each chapter with a preview or outline of the contents and close with a recapitulation. We do this and more. We introduce additional summaries within the chapters. Charts that compare several related diagrams appear throughout the book. "Check your Bearings" reviews within chapters help readers cement their comprehension at intervals shorter than those afforded by end of chapter summaries.

A third characteristic, overlapping the others, is careful presentation. We maintain a logical sequence of topics and develop matters one step at a time. We draw a distinction between *problems* to be solved (for example, what price maximizes profit) and *dilemmas* that require value judgments (for example, the short-run unemployment–inflation tradeoff). We develop alternative macroeconomic models in a clear building-block fashion, with rigor, but without excess complexity.

Finally, dynamics appears in abudance. "What's New" is a basic question we explicitly acknowledge, along with the more traditional key questions. Growth and technological change are central topics in the book. In the same spirit, entrepreneurship is given explicit and extensive coverage as a scarce and valuable resource. Product life cycles are explained in relation to changes in demand and production techniques over time.

Organization

The book is organized as follows.

PART I lays the foundation for the whole volume. Chapter 1 begins with the fundamental concepts of scarcity and choice. In Chapter 2 production possibility frontiers illustrate scarcity in a formal fashion. Opportunity costs naturally follow, and their manipulation leads logically to the development of specialization, market exchange and circular flow. Chapter 3 presents simple market mechanics—demand, supply and their interaction. Chapter 4 covers the market's shortcomings and introduces government as the source of economic policy, recognizing that such intervention may be harmful. Chapter 5 concludes Part I with a glance at basic business realities, such as corporations and stock markets.

PART II begins with a definition and discussion of unemployment and inflation—two key macroeconomic variables—in Chapter 6. Chapter 7 describes the central measures in the National Income Accounts. In Chapter 8 we turn from describing to explaining the behavior of macroeconomic variables. Four macroeconomic models (or systems) are discussed in turn. The starting point is the *Classical* system (Chapter 8). Consideration of the classical system at the start is useful for several reasons. Understanding the classical system provides the background for understanding the *Keynesian revolution.* Moreover, the major modern challenges to Keynesian views are all rooted in classical theory. *Keynesian* economics is presented in Chapters 9–12, building up the complete model in steps. Chapter 13 applies the Keynesian theory to explain the behavior of inflation and unemployment over the past three decades. The next two chapters consider modern alternatives to the Keynesian theory—*monetarism* in Chapter 14 and the *new classical economics* in Chapter 15. Chapter 16 concludes Part II with a summary of the models, examining areas of consensus as well as controversy.

PART III goes into more detail concerning *macroeconomic policy.* Policy questions are discussed in Part II as well, but to keep the initial presentation of macroeconomic models simple, institutional detail and most discussion of actual policy-making procedures are left to Part III. Chapters 17 and 18 consider monetary policy and the banking system. Chapter 19 deals with fiscal policy. In Chapter 20 the focus shifts to the longer run as economic growth and trends in employment and unemployment are discussed. Supply-side economic theories and fiscal policy enter in this discussion in Chapter 20 as well as in Chapter 19.

PART IV, the backbone of the microeconomics part of the book, focuses on product markets. The basics of demand and supply are elaborated upon

with discussions of consumer choice (Chapter 21), elasticity (Chapter 22), and cost conditions (Chapter 23). Chapter 24 then presents an overview of all the main market types—perfect competition, monopoly, oligopoly and monopolistic competition. We stress the fact that market structure determines the firm's view of demand, which in turn determines the firm's revenue experience, which then influences the firm's behavior because revenue experience, along with cost conditions, determine profits—the prime motive behind behavior. Details are presented thereafter. Separate chapters discuss perfect competition and monopoly (Chapters 26 and 27). Oligopoly and monopolistic competition are covered jointly in Chapters 27 and 28, one covering price strategies and the second nonprice strategies. Discussions of regulation, antitrust and information policies round out the analysis, in Chapter 29.

PART V shifts the focus away from product markets toward input markets. Labor, the most important productive input when measured by total household income earnings and overall business expenses, occupies Chapters 30 and 31. Chapter 30 tackles competitive labor markets and explains differences in wages by variations in such things as work conditions and human capital. Chapter 31 covers unions, their economic and institutional aspects. Input markets for resources other than labor—those for land, capital and entrepreneurship, in particular—receive ample attention at the conclusion of Part V in Chapter 32.

PART VI takes up several areas of microeconomics that do not fit neatly elsewhere. In Chapter 33, poverty and discrimination are explained along with the government's attempts to alleviate them. Public choice theory is a topic that has grown to the point of warranting an entire chapter (Chapter 34). Political decision-making is often grounded on economic motives, and public choice theory helps to explain how this relationship affects government inclinations and operations. It will become apparent that the government does not always serve public interests. In Chapter 35, problems with the environment and energy likewise receive attention.

PART VII begins with an analysis of international economics. Chapter 36 recalls international considerations from our earlier discussion. In fact, a number of examples used in the earlier analysis help to emphasize that the U.S. economy functions within a world economy. Now in Chapters 36 and 37 international trade and international monetary relations come to center stage. Chapter 38 closes the volume with a discussion of the developing economies and of nonmarket communist systems. The Soviet economy is used as an example of a nonmarket economy and recent Soviet economic reforms are described.

Learning Aids

The book includes a number of features aimed at increasing reader comprehension. These are:

- Chapter outlines at the beginning of each chapter
- "Check Your Bearings" sections for review at crucial points
- Boxed *Perspectives* that expand on the text discussion
- End-of-chapter summaries
- End-of chapter questions
- Lists of key terms following each chapter
- Glossary with definitions of key terms

Teaching Aids and Supplements

Principles of Economics has a complete set of materials containing the following elements:

1. An *Instructor's Manual,* written by Professor Jack Adams of the University of Arkansas–Little Rock, includes chapter objectives and highlights, suggested instructional strategies, research projects, and complete answers to all end-of-chapter questions and problems.

2. *A Study Guide* by Professor Guy Schick of California State University, Fullerton, will provide students with outstanding self-instructional content. It contains appropriate lists of key terms, succinct summaries of chapters, and a variety of self-tests: multiple choice, true-false, and fill in questions. In addition, graphical and numerical problems are included.

3. The *Test Bank* has a mix of multiple choice, fill-in, true-false, and short essay questions. An additional test bank will contain all multiple choice questions.

4. *Transparencies* will be available upon adoption for those instructors who want overhead projections.

5. *Software* will be provided in a simple "menu-driven" program for students that will contain a series of mini-simulations in which students can make a variety of economic decisions.

Acknowledgments

The authors are grateful to the many reviewers who read all or part of the manuscript and provided many useful comments. These reviewers are:

John D. Abell, University of North Carolina, Charlotte;
Jack E. Adams, University of Arkansas at Little Rock;
Bahram Adrangi, University of Portland;
James T. Bennett, George Mason University;
Michael D. Bradley, The George Washington University;
Ronald Brautigam, Northwestern University;
Byron W. Brown, Michigan State University;
K. Laurence Chang, Case Western Reserve University;
Carl Davidson, Michigan State University;
Larry DeBrock, University of Illinois;
Stephen Gardner, Stephen F. Austin State University;
Otis W. Gilley, Louisiana Tech. University;
Cecil G. Gouke, Ohio State University;
Curtis Harvey, University of Kentucky;
Larry Herman, Ascension College;
Eric Jensen, College of William and Mary;
William Lang, Rutgers University;
Allan Mandelstamm, Virginia Polytechnic and State University;
Walter S. Misiolek, University of Alabama;
Steven M. Rock, Northern Illinois University;
Willard W. Radell, Jr., Indiana University of Pennsylvania;
David I. Rosenbaum, University of Nebraska, Lincoln;
Guy A. Schick, California State University, Fullerton;
Lars G. Sandberg, Ohio State University;

Peter M. Schwarz, University of North Carolina, Charlotte;
Robert W. Thomas, Iowa State University;
Wade L. Thomas, Ithaca College;
C. Gerald Walsh, Villanova University;
Thomas G. Watkins, Eastern Kentucky University;
William C. Wood, Bridgewater College.

We are also grateful to Tony English and Ken MacLeod who, as editors, guided the development of the book at various stages. We have a very great debt to Gerald Lombardi, at Macmillan, who read, commented on, and suggested revisions in the book at every stage. Likewise we are grateful to Linda Froyen who typed the bulk of the macroeconomic section, made editorial changes, suggested revisions, and was still willing to prepare the index. We are grateful to Cheryl Mitchell and Ann Marie Vidovitch for competent and timely typing assistance near the end of the project. Marsha Shelburn did an excellent job helping with end-of-chapter questions and in the process caught some errors in the text. Finally, John Travis was diligent, persistent, and as usual, highly competent as production editor.

With all this help, it is more than normally the case that the authors are at fault for weaknesses or errors that may remain.

R. T. F.
D. F. G.

Contents

I

Introduction

CHAPTER 3

The Market: Desirable Process and Results   53

CHAPTER 4

The Role of Government   83

CHAPTER 5

Basic Facts About American Business 107

II

Macroeconomics: Measurement and Models

CHAPTER 6

Twin Macroeconomic Problems: Unemployment and Inflation 127

CHAPTER 7

The National Income and Product Accounts 141

CHAPTER 11

Money and the Interest Rate   213

CHAPTER 12

The Complete Keynesian System: Aggregate Supply and Demand   229

CHAPTER 13

Inflation and Unemployment: The Keynesian View   245

CHAPTER 14

The Monetarist Counterrevolution   257

CHAPTER 15

The New Classical Economics   275

CHAPTER 16

Macroeconomics: Controversy and Consensus   289

III

Macroeconomic Policy

CHAPTER 17

Money and the Banking System   299

IV

Micro Product Markets

CHAPTER 21

Consumer Choice   *369*

CHAPTER 22

Demand Conditions   *393*

CHAPTER 23

Supply Conditions: Productivity and Costs   *415*

CHAPTER 27

CHAPTER 28

CHAPTER 29

V

Factor Markets

VI

Selected Topics in Microeconomics

VII

International Economics and Comparative Systems

CHAPTER 38

Other Places, Other Systems, Other Problems   793

Glossary

811

Index

823

I
Introduction

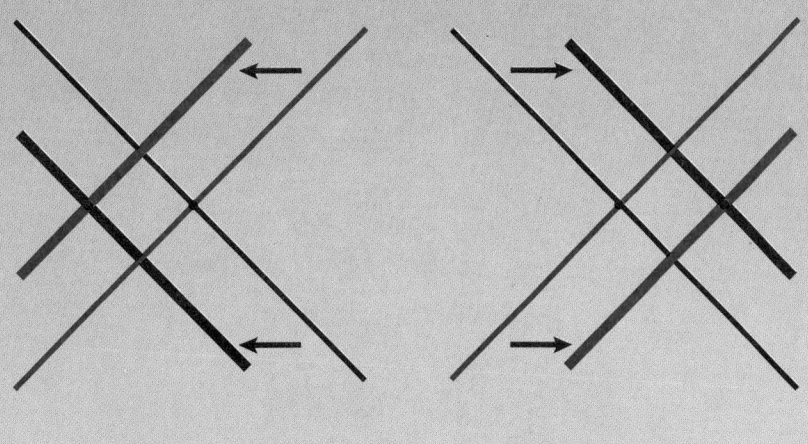

1

The Heart and Soul of Economics

The ideas of economists and political philosophers, both when they are right and when they are wrong, are more powerful than is commonly understood. Indeed, the world is ruled by little else.

—*John Maynard Keynes*

Fourteenth-century Frenchmen believed that brandy worked medical wonders, preserving youth, reviving the heart, repelling the plague, and curing colic, paralysis, and other ailments. To bolster brandy's effect on invalid Charles the Bad in 1387, doctors adopted the idea of wrapping him in a brandy-soaked sheet and sewing the wet bundle tight with needle and thread. Unfortunately, a servant got the idea of cutting the thread with a lit candle, so poor Charles went up like flaming cherries jubilee.

Ideas, wise or stupid, have serious consequences. Stupid economic ideas have especially serious consequences, for they affect momentous economic problems—inflation, unemployment, monopoly power, labor strife, failing industries, environmental pollution, poverty, lagging growth, hazardous products, job discrimination, health care costs, budget deficits, foreign trade deficits, and so on. Who is hit by mistaken economic ideas? Who plays the part of Charles the Bad? All of us.

Consider the possibility that economic ideas are so important that your understanding of them could even improve your self-understanding. In a *Newsweek* poll, thousands of foreigners in six countries were asked how they see Americans. Do you think we were seen as sophisticated, sexy, or friendly? Well, we weren't. We were said to be industrious, energetic, inventive, and self-indulgent—terms that carry obvious economic connotations.[1]

---

[1]"What the World Thinks of America," *Newsweek*, July 11, 1983, pp. 44–52.

I

Scarcity and Economics

A

Scarcity

1. Definition

Goods and services are limited (because productive resources are limited) relative to vast human wants. This is **scarcity.**

Scarcity—this clash between limits and longing—influences each of us individually and all of us as a society. Individually, our incomes cannot fully finance our desires, so our grocery lists are shorter than we would like —our closets less full, our homes smaller, our vacations less exotic. As a society, our individual experiences of shortage add up. Moreover, scarcity also prevents a boundless abundance of defensive weaponry, of schools, hospitals, highways, bridges, parks, and all the soldiers, teachers, doctors, rangers, and other people needed to staff and maintain them.

Scarcity prevails because of two underlying conditions—(1) a physical condition, that is, *limited productive resources,* and (2) a mental condition, that is, *unlimited wants.* If either of these conditions did not hold, scarcity would not hold (and economics would not exist). Let's briefly explore each.

2. Limited Productive Resources Imagine a world in which everyone had an Aladdin's lamp. A rub and a request would then get you anything you wanted—a Porsche, a dozen Porsches, a lobster dinner, an Apple computer, a haircut, a swimming pool . . . you name it, literally anything . . . an MX missile, clean air, whatever. Scarcity disappears in this fantasy because resource limits disappear.

More realistically, goods and services are produced not by magic lamps but by resources, also called *factors of production.* Economists distinguish four main classes of resources: land, labor, capital, and entrepreneurship.

Land is a shorthand term that refers to all of nature's gifts—air, water, sunshine, forests, wildlife, and minerals, as well as soil surfaces.

Consider the air, for example. We use it as a convenient source of oxygen for combustion in cars and also as a convenient place to dispose of the combustion wastes. River water yields fish, floats transport, powers electric generators, irrigates crops. Aside from such productive inputs, nature provides direct services in the form of habitat and amenities. Habitat is simply life support (oxygen to breathe for instance). Amenities are pleasures like swimming, hiking, and skiing.

Labor comprises the physical energy, manual skill, and mental ability that humans apply to the production of goods and services.

A combination of all of these traits is required of some workers—orthopedic surgeons, for instance. Most jobs, though, tend to emphasize just one or two labor characteristics: ditch digging (physical), computer assembly (manual), and electrical engineering (mental).

Capital refers to durable inputs which themselves have been produced in the past. It includes office buildings, factories, machinery, equipment, roads, bridges, trucks, trains, and other such materials used in production.

Capital plays an important and growing part in virtually all production. Familiar references to mechanized farming and computer-assisted engineering design indicate as much. When capital supplants land and labor as an input, economists say that the production process has become more *capital intensive.*

Capital usually embodies a **technology,** *which may be defined as scientific methods and materials designed to achieve industrial or commercial ob-*

jectives. A petroleum refinery obviously embodies technology. A computer does too. Here we run into a hybrid case of productive input, however, because technology almost always has two components: (1) a *hardware* aspect, consisting of the capital equipment that personifies the technology, and (2) a *software* aspect, consisting of the know-how to operate or use the hardware. This software aspect entails labor resources. Thus technology spans both capital and labor categories. And it is through these two categories that technology contributes forcefully to the production of goods and services.

Entrepreneurship is economic leadership and imagination in risk taking, innovating, coordinating, and sometimes financing businesses.

The growth of large corporations headed by managers rather than entrepreneurs has caused many economists to lose sight of entrepreneurship or to lump it with labor, rather than to treat it as a separate resource. But entrepreneurship is enterprise heroism, and as such it is distinct from anything suggested by the term *labor.* It is the source of technological change, economic growth, and other benefits. Without entrepreneurship there would be no Silicon Valley in California, no mass-produced cars, no jet airliners, no Disneyland. Indeed, although entrepreneurship is usually associated with small or medium-sized firms such as Intel and Amdahl Computer, it can often be found in innovative, risk-taking large firms like DuPont.

We have asserted that these resources of land, labor, capital, and entrepreneurship are limited to the point of causing scarcity. And, indeed, proof of their physical limits is easy to find. The numbers measuring them are big, but *not* infinite. The land area of the United States, for example, is only 3.6 million square miles, one-sixth of which is farmable. Roughly 115 million people comprise our total labor force. There are about four dozen steel plants, 300,000 miles of railroad track, 7,000 hospitals, 6 million big trucks, and so on. There are no Aladdin's lamps.

Physical limits alone do *not* establish scarcity in

an economic sense, however; so statistics such as these, though relevant, tell only half the story. The other half—human wants—comes next.

3. *Unlimited Human Wants* Imagine a world populated only by Buddhist monks. You, one among the rest of us, would want nothing more than a small room for space, a robe for raiment, a bowl of rice a day for sustenance, and time to meditate. (If you are a weak prodigal, you might cheat a bit by concealing Nike shoes beneath your robe.) With the wants of everyone so severely limited, those wants would probably not exceed the earth's resource capabilities, thereby greatly alleviating, if not completely eliminating, the problem of scarcity. Scarcity shrinks to insignificance in this case by sheer willpower, not by superabundance. People would simply not want anything they could not have fairly freely.

4. *Conclusion and Definitions*

A good (or service) is a **scarce good** if people want more of it than the amount freely available from nature (at a zero price).

A good is a **free good** if people want less of it than the amount freely available from nature (at a zero price).

These important definitions explain why economists can frequently be heard exclaiming what has almost become their motto: *"There is no such thing as a free lunch."* Moreover, these definitions point to much evidence confirming that, in the real world, scarcity does in fact exist, namely, the fact that *prices* exist.

To illustrate these concepts further, let us note two transformations from *free* to *scarce*. First, surface land. If we set aside complicating details like the Louisiana Purchase and the military conquest of the American Indians, both of which initially put land in the hands of the U.S. government for a price of sorts, it can be argued that land was once so plentiful relative to wants in North America that it was not scarce, but free. During America's first one and a half centuries, Uncle Sam gave millions of acres of land away through homesteading, deeds to states, and grants to railroads and col-

leges. Today, however, land is anything but free. It is scarce, expensively so.

What tarnishes this example a bit is, as suggested, the fact that Uncle Sam actually had to pay some price for it. Thus, though it was indeed free to homesteaders and railroads, it was not, strictly speaking, a free good from society's point of view, the point of view usually adopted in this book. When today the government gives out "free" lunches to school children, those lunches are not free goods. They are scarce goods because they are produced with scarce resources, including land, and are, moreover, paid for by taxpayers. Similarly, you may watch the Super Bowl on the television free of charge. But there are scarce resources consumed by that event, mainly labor and capital, and the auto and beer advertisers are the ones picking up the tab. Goods free of charge to the end user are thus not necessarily free goods in an economic sense.

Our second example is clean air. Clean air was once a free good and free of charge. People could then breathe freely and discharge combustion wastes freely. But the growth of coal and oil combustion, with their discharge of millions of tons of sulfur oxides, hydrocarbons, particulates, and other pollutants, changed all that. Extensive use of the air as a sewage dump caused people to pay a price in the form of ill health, annoyance, and property damage. Conversely, to obtain clean air for breathing and amenities, we must now pay a price through pollution abatement—such as higher prices for cars equipped with pollution control devices and higher electric bills to cover the costs of abatement at power plants.

These examples illustrate the fact that wants usually exceed resource capabilities because of *competing wants* or, stated differently, *competing uses*. Land can be used for farming, ranching, mining, forests, parks, housing, shopping centers, factories, and so on. Air can be used for breathing, combustion discharge, seeing scenic wonders, and so on.

B

Definition of Economics

Scarcity, then, is the central problem of economics. A *short definition of economics* is simply *the study of how society copes with scarcity.* A *long definition* is as follows:

> **Economics** is the study of how people live by producing, distributing, and consuming scarce goods and services.

Scarcity is to the economist what life is to the biologist.

II
The Basic Economic Questions Raised by Scarcity

Hearing of scarcity surprises no one. Contemplating scarcity depresses many. Studying how societies cope with scarcity should intrigue you because societies—including your society—cope by making **choices.** This issue of society and choice adds a personal, even a moral, element not found in the study of, say, chemistry or mathematics. You choose a Spielberg movie over a Hemingway novel. Why? You choose college over swift entry into the workforce. Why? Coca-Cola chooses to use corn syrup instead of sugar in Coke. Why? Uncle Sam chooses to spend additional billions on battleships while cutting back on aid to the poor. Why? Really intriguing value judgments haunt us when we as a society must make choices in life-and-death matters. As expensive technological advances increase the possibility of keeping old and infirm people alive, if only barely alive, with artificial hearts and the like, society will have to decide what volume of resources to devote to this medical effort and who shall receive the care. Economics helps us understand what is gained and what is given up when choices are made.

More generally, scarcity rudely raises five questions for the members of any society: **What?, How?, Who?, What's new?,** and **How stable?** Finding answers necessitates choices.

A
What? (Resource Allocation)

What goods and services shall we produce in what amounts? At first glance, the answer may seem simple and obvious. We need food, clothing, shelter, and transportation. But the answer is not obvious because of the trade-offs scarcity imposes. More food, for example, could mean less clothing as land is shifted from cotton to wheat production. Moving to more detailed decisions, shall it be more Twinkies and less granola, more apartments and fewer single-family dwellings, more sweaters and fewer jackets, more cars and fewer buses? What combination of goods and services is most desirable? In economic jargon, the issue is *resource allocation.*

B
How? (Production Techniques)

How shall goods and services be produced? Many different methods of production are possible for most goods, using different combinations of resources. Cars, for instance, can be made by robots as well as by people. What mixture of the two will it be? Should coal be mined by strip or underground methods? Should electricity be generated by coal or nuclear power? Should wheat be transported by trucks or trains? In short, what combination of resources should be embodied in our *production techniques?*

C
Who? (Distribution)

Who shall get and consume the goods and services we produce? There are two aspects to this question. One aspect relates to *commodity distribution.* Not enough gasoline can be produced for everyone to get as much as they would like at a zero price, for example. Hence that which is available must somehow be distributed among motorists. The other and broader aspect, the main one for our purposes, relates to *income distribution.* What share of our total national income should each household receive? Who, in other words, is to enjoy purchasing power?

D
What's New? (Technological Change and Growth)

What new products and production processes shall we adopt to alter and expand output? Our condition of scarcity is not static, ironclad, or unchanging. Advances in technology and better educational attainments continually expand our productive capabilities, yielding growth in output. Moreover, our outputs change qualitatively as well as quantitatively with changing technologies and tastes. Thus we are confronted with questions of change. Shall we convert to solar energy, automatic bank tellers, personal computers, and cordless telephones? Decisions of acceptance and rejection must continually be made. Our repeated references to these issues later will use the catch-all terms *technological change* and *growth*. In contrast to the first three questions of what, how, and who, each of which concerns a *static* state, this question of What's new? concerns *dynamics*. A lake is static. A river is dynamic.

E
How Stable? (Aggregate Employment and Price Levels)

How can we attain stability for the economy as a whole? Just as rivers sometimes flood or run low, the economy as a whole may exhibit marked instabilities. *Employment level* and *price level* are two matters of particular importance. If overall employment is down, instability prevails and overall output will be down. The problem of scarcity is then aggravated, as those who are unemployed suffer material losses and society's overall output of goods and services is less than it could be. In regard to overall price level, inflation is the biggest form of instability. When prices rise rapidly, people devote their scarce time and other resources to hedges against inflation, just as they would sandbag against a flood. Price stability would be better because resources spent in hedging could then be used in more genuinely productive ways, just as resources gobbled up by sandbagging could, in the event of low water, be used for, say, road building. Hence the question, how can we attain overall employment and price stability? Like the question What's new?, this one has dynamic, as opposed to static, aspects.

Given the pervasiveness of scarcity, these five questions are likewise pervasive, confronting every society. What? How? Who?, What's new?, and How stable? The answers a society devises—the choices we make individually and collectively—

do more than merely intrigue economists. *They determine an entire way of life.* That economists hold these questions and their answers in such very high regard may seem bizarre to you. But we do not exaggerate. Let's take a brief look at a simpler economy than our own to illustrate their importance.

Read Perspective 1A.

In sum, coping with scarcity—the heart of economics—requires that we make momentous choices to answer the five questions of What?, How?, Who?, What's new?, and How stable? Furthermore, as the experience of the Skolt Lapps suggests, a society's answer to one question (e.g., What's new?) can forcefully, even tragically, affect the answers to others.

III
Positive Economics and Normative Economics

In the eyes of pathological optimists, ours is the best of all possible worlds. The real is the ideal, and bliss pervades. But to the rest of us, this is not the best of all possible worlds. Real is not ideal, and bliss is fleeting. To us, a distinction between positive economics and normative economics is essential.

A
Positive Economics (Actualities)

To say of the Skolt Lapps that "the average number of reindeer per household dropped from fifty-two in presnowmobile days, to only twelve in 1971," is to make a positive statement. *A* **positive statement** *discloses factual information—that which is, was, or will be.* To say of our own economy that "The top fifth of the population receives about 43 percent of the income" is to make a positive statement. Another example: The number of women employed outside the home has risen remarkably in the past three decades. Now 60 percent of all women work outside the home, a circumstance that influences births, abortions, marriage, divorce, child care, housing, and pension plans.

Closely related is **positive economic analysis,**

PERSPECTIVE 1A

The Skolt Lapps and the Snowmobile: What, How, Who, What's New?

Prior to the introduction of snowmobiles in 1961, the Skolt Lapps in the Sevettigarvi region of Northern Finland depended upon the herding of semidomesticated reindeer for their livelihood. Along with fish, reindeer meat was the main food. Reindeer sleds were the principal means of transportation, and reindeer hides were used for making clothing and shoes. Surplus meat was sold at trading stores for cash to buy flour, sugar, tea, and other staples. The Lapps saw themselves mainly as reindeer herders, and prestige was accorded men with good strings of draught reindeer. Lapp society was an egalitarian system in which each family had approximately equal numbers of animals. Skolt children received a "first-tooth reindeer," a "name-day reindeer," and gifts on other occasions, including wedding gifts of reindeer, so that a household began with a small herd of the beloved animals. . . .

The rate of adoption of snowmobiles was very rapid among the Lapps. By 1971, ten years after their introduction, almost every one of the seventy-two households in Sevettigarvi had at least one snowmobile. The main advantage of the snowmobile was much faster travel. The round trip to buy staple supplies was reduced from three days by reindeer sled, to five hours by snowmobile. Within a few years of their introduction, snowmobiles completely replaced travel by skis and reindeer sleds in herding reindeers. Unfortunately, the effect of the snowmobiles on the Lapps' reindeer was disastrous. The noise and the smell of the machines drove the reindeer into a near-wild state. The friendly relationships between the Lapps and their animals was disrupted by the high-speed machines. Frightened running by the reindeer decreased the number of reindeer calves born each year. As a result, the average number of

reindeer per household dropped from fifty-two in presnowmobile days, to only twelve in 1971. In fact, this average is misleading because about two-thirds of the Lapp households completely dropped out of reindeer raising as a result of the snowmobile; most could not find other work and were unemployed. On the other hand, one family in Sevettigarvi, which purchased a snowmobile relatively early, built up a large herd, and by 1971 owned one-third of all the reindeer in the community.

Not only did the frightened reindeer have fewer calves, but the precipitous drop in the number of reindeer also occurred because many of the animals were slaughtered for the sale of meat, in order to purchase snowmobiles, gasoline, spare parts, and repairs. A new machine cost about $1,000, and gas and repairs typically cost about $425 per year. Despite this relatively high cost (for the Skolt Lapps, who lived on a subsistence basis), snowmobiles were considered a household necessity, and the motorized herding of reindeer was considered much more prestigious than herding by skis or reindeer sleds. The snowmobile pushed the Skolt Lapps into cash dependency, debt, and unemployment.

So today, their reindeer-centered culture has been severely disrupted. Most families are unemployed and depend upon the Finnish government for subsistence payments. The snowmobile revolution in the arctic led to disastrous consequences for the reindeer and for the Lapps who depended on them for their livelihood.[2]

[2]From Everett M. Rogers, *Diffusion of Innovations*, 3rd ed. (New York: Free Press, 1983), pp. 372–374, which summarizes the work of anthropologist Pertti Pelto, *The Snowmobile Revolution: Technology and Social Change in the Arctic* (Menlo Park, Calif.: Cummings Publishing Co., 1973).

which attempts to determine verifiable relationships among economic variables. Such analysis yields positive statements of *relationships*, such as "If the price of soda pop rises, the quantity of soda people buy will fall" or "If women's wages rise, still more of them will join the labor force." Disputes concerning positive statements and positive analysis can be settled only by consulting facts.

B
Normative Economics (Value Judgments)

Normative statements are quite different. *A* **normative statement** *contains a value judgment about that which ought to be, ought to have been, or ought to become.* A **value judgment,** the key ingredient here, is simply some generalized concept of what is desirable, or, conversely, undesirable. *Welfare* and *happiness*, for example, are desirable in the opinion of most people in our society, so desires for welfare and happiness are value judgments. Other conditions held in high esteem by Americans are *freedom, fairness, justice, equality,* and *progress.* These may be called *ultimate* value judgments because they are very vague, generalized notions. Definitions of them differ among dif-

ferent people, so that, for example, men and women may see fairness differently. Yet these are *supreme* values, worth personal sacrifice to attain and protect.

In practice, these ultimate values are *too* vague to be of day-to-day use. They are therefore applied according to what can be called *proximate* value judgments, which are still generalized concepts of what is desirable, but a bit more concrete. Thus, *welfare* and *happiness* translates into things like *full employment, clean environment,* and *comfortable income levels.* Similarly, *freedom* implies *freedom of choice in consumption and occupation, free enterprise,* and the like. *Equality* is furthered by *equal employment opportunity.* And so on. It is these proximate value judgments that most clearly generate normative statements in economics.

To say that "the Lapps *ought not* to have adopted snowmobiles because they caused inequality," or that "the snowmobile revolution led to *disastrous* consequences," is to make a normative statement. If you believe, with reference to the fact of rising female involvement in our labor force, that there should be publicly funded day-care centers and greater company benefits for maternity leaves, then you are treading on normative grounds. If

	Observed economy (positive economics)	Desired economy (normative economics)
Choice procedures	A 1. *Markets* of all kinds (including monopoly markets) 2. *Governments* of all kinds (including dictatorships)	B 1. *Competitive* markets 2. *Democratic* governments
Choice results	C 1. Answers to *What?* 2. Answers to *How?* 3. Answers to *Who?* 4. Answers to *What's new?* 5. Answers to *How stable?*	D 1. Allocation efficiency 2. Technical efficiency 3. Reduced inequality 4. Growth and progress 5. Full employment with price stability

you think environmental pollution is too severe, then again your thinking is normative rather than positive.

Disputes over normative statements cannot be settled by consulting facts. Unlike positive statements, which are subject to possible falsification, normative statements cannot be disproven because they rest on value judgments. They can be debunked, and pooh-poohed as unwise, wrongheaded, radical, or reactionary, but they cannot be refuted by empirical tests. Nevertheless, normative statements and their underlying value judgments are *extremely* important to economics because they provide the main basis for economic policies. Indeed, in contrast to positive economic analysis, **normative economic analysis** *could, in the main, be considered economic policy analysis. Should* the government increase defense expenditures? *Should* the rich be taxed more heavily than the poor, with the resulting tax proceeds going to the poor?

This is not to say that positive economics has no place in policy analysis. Positive economics contributes immensely to policy by indicating "what is" and "what will be." How could we as a society know that some policy is needed unless we know that "what is" deviates from what we feel "ought to be"? Given some such distinction, how could we make amends through policy unless we knew the probable impacts of policies, namely, "what will be" as a result of policies? This also is the province of positive economics. If, for example, we all agreed that our positive, existing income distribution deviated too much from our normative value judgments of equality, we would need to know the positive impacts of possible corrective policies. What is the economic impact of a hefty income tax on the rich? Of a dole for the poor? How big does the tax bite need to be? How big the dole? And so on. Policy impacts can be complex, hitting unintended targets and causing bad side effects. Good intentions are not enough; good positive analysis is also important.

C
Positive and Normative Economics Plus Procedures and Results

In sum, positive and normative are just jargon distinguishing the *actual* or *observed* economy from the *desired* economy. One further distinction is helpful, namely, that between *choice procedures* and *choice results*. Coping with scarcity, as we have seen, requires that we find answers to the five questions of What?, How?, Who?, What's new?, and How stable? Hence, **choice procedures** are decision-making mechanisms, whereas **choice results** are the decisions themselves.

The distinction between that which is observed (positive) and that which is desired (normative) can be applied to *both* choice procedures and choice results. We can therefore organize our thoughts around the four-part matrix of Figure 1.1, entitled "A four-part division of issues that arise from the necessity of making economic choices." Indeed, Figure 1.1 provides an outline for what follows. Labels A, B, C, and D in the upper-left-hand corners herald the sequence of our ensuing discussion.

IV
Choice Procedures

A
Observed Economy (Positive)

After a Chinese dinner with family or friends, how does your group distribute the fortune cookies? Are the cookies arbitrarily dealt out by whoever pays the bill? Do you self-select cookies at random, or in order of age or seating position? Clearly, the means of choice, the decision-making process itself, can be important to us, quite apart from the results realized. Self-selection of Chinese cookies, for instance, seems to be the preferred procedure for most folks. More pertinent here, societies do not distribute goods and services by random drawings. Nor do they decide what to produce by consulting Ouija boards. These procedures lack appeal as procedures themselves and carry an unacceptable risk of producing wrong results.

How, then, do societies go about answering the key questions of What?, How?, Who?, What's new?, and How stable? Historically, only three basic institutional devices (or answer machines) have evolved—*tradition*, *markets*, and *governments*. Tradition is the procedure typical of most primitive societies, wherein each generation merely emulates its ancestors' pattern of life support. Pre-snowmobile Lapps, for example, closely followed tradition in producing reindeer meat, crafting articles from reindeer hides, and giving gifts of reindeer to equalize the distribution of wealth. Although traces of tradition remain in modern economic systems, (e.g., traditionally secretaries, nurses, and elementary school teachers are women), today's developed economies rely most heavily upon markets and governments. Hence, as indicated in part (A) of Figure 1.1, we shall focus on markets and governments.

1. Markets

> A **market** is an organized process by which buyers and sellers exchange goods and services, usually for money.

Notice that by this definition *every* market has two sides to it—a buyers' side (or *demand* side) and a sellers' side (or *supply* side). Notice also that *every* market entails exchange. As a buyer of this book, for instance, you gave up money and took the book, while the seller gave up the book and took your money. Beyond these universals, markets vary in geographic scope (local to international), in type (e.g., product markets versus labor markets), and in other ways. In particular, markets vary in competitive conditions. Some are controlled by monopoly sellers, in which case buyers must deal with only one seller (as is true of water and electric utilities), or by cartels, in which case sellers may fix prices (as is true of OPEC in petroleum). Other markets tend to be highly competitive (as is true of those for wheat, semiconductors, and lumber).

It is through the interaction of demand and supply that markets decide what is produced, how goods and services are produced, and so on. Later we will have a great deal to say about how markets produce answers to the basic questions. Our present purpose is merely to acknowledge the decision-making task they perform. As a prelude, however, contemplate the market's role in answering only one of the five key questions—What's new. When a new product becomes possible, like the personal computer, how do we decide whether to commit scarce resources to its production? The market decides. On the sellers' side, the market measures the profitability of producing per-

sonal computers. On the buyers' side, the market registers the popularity of purchasing them. If personal computers had not passed the market's test of profitability and popularity, they would have flopped badly.

2. Government

> **Government** is the process within a group for making and enforcing decisions. Public government can claim a monopoly on the legitimate use of physical force within a given territory.

Like markets, governments vary as much as ice cream flavors vary. Broadly speaking, *government* could even include political systems centrally operated by warlords or high priests. (Chairman Mao was a warlord of sorts, and the Ayatollah Khomeini of Iran is a high priest.) More commonly, we tend to place governments on a scale ranging from the totalitarian to the democratic.

Legitimate force is a thread that runs throughout the governmental means of decision making, even in a democracy. For this reason, governments often tend to be coercive. Moreover, governments occasionally display restrictive, centralized, and unfair qualities. Hence our society tends to dislike government. Our revolutionary heritage is, indeed, grounded on skepticism of government as an economic decision-making mechanism.

Despite this skepticism, the government plays a very large part in our economy. We may note briefly, first, that our government is called upon to maintain markets through, for example, the enforcement of contracts. Second, our government is needed where *collective* decision making is required, as in provision for national defense. Third, at its best, a government can possess good qualities. A democratic government is, for example, wonderfully more decentralized than a totalitarian government. The U.S. government is, therefore, quite different from that of the Soviet Union or Elizabethan England.

B
Desired Economy (Normative)

Part (B) of Figure 1.1 identifies competitive markets and democratic governments as the most desirable choice procedures. Competitive markets are deliberately listed first because our society's value judgments seem to favor markets over government, even when government is democratic.

What are the value judgments that guide this selection of ideal choice procedures? Consider the value judgments listed in Table 1.1. We like decision-making procedures that are free, voluntary, decentralized, and fair. We dislike those that are, in contrast, restrictive, coercive, centralized, and unfair. At their competitive best, markets are remarkable for their display of the good qualities and, correspondingly, for their omission of the bad ones. Much the same could be said of democratic governments, but with less conviction. After all, *the distinguishing characteristic of government, even in this ideal form, is its capacity to use force, and force is by definition coercive.*

V

Choice Results

A

Observed Economy (Positive)

Shifting from choice procedures to choice results brings us to part (C) of Figure 1.1, which puts observed choice results in a nutshell by simply noting that they are the actual answers to the basic questions What?, How?, Who?, and so on. Less abstractly and less compactly, you see actual choice results every day all around you—in your home; on the streets; in grocery and department stores; in the length of unemployment lines; in bakeries, breweries, and boutiques; in the air; on the water; literally everywhere.

Figure 1.2 illustrates briefly and broadly our economy's answers to the questions What? and Who?. As regards What?, part (a) of Figure 1.2 is a pie chart showing the breakdown of our gross national product (output). The service sector, which includes financial services like banking and insurance, health services, restaurants, barbering and law and other professions, is the largest sector. Manufacturing—which covers everything from apparel to furniture, boats to autos, and clocks to computers—follows the service sector in overall size. The remaining divisions taken together account for about half of our economic output.

Part (b) of Figure 1.2 illustrates answers to the question Who? by giving the distribution of income in the United States. Arraying the population from most to least prosperous and dividing the array into fifths, the pie chart indicates that income is not equally distributed among the fifths. The top fifth, or 20 percent, of the population receives about 43 percent of the income. At the other extreme, the bottom fifth gets about 5 percent.

TABLE 1.1 Value Judgments Commonly Applied to Assessing Decision-Making Procedures (Normative)

Good Qualities	Bad Qualities
Free (e.g., individual, free choice among alternatives in consumption and occupation)	Restrictive (e.g., individuals lack alternatives, are denied products or a choice of sellers)
Voluntary (e.g., people act on their own volition)	Coercive (e.g., people are forced to act under threat of harm)
Decentralized (e.g., widespread participation by large numbers of people and firms)	Centralized (e.g., few people, agencies, or firms have decision-making power)
Fair (e.g., even-handed treatment of people in similar circumstances, honesty)	Unfair (e.g., arbitrary and disparate treatment, dishonesty)

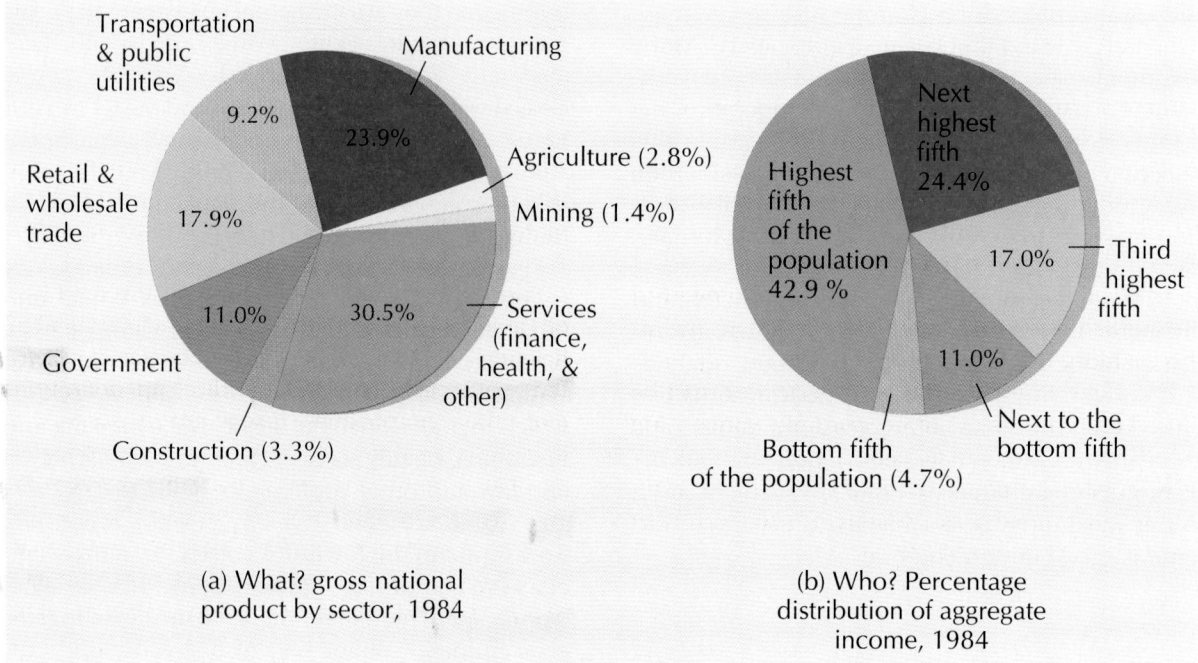

Transportation & public utilities 9.2%

Manufacturing 23.9%

Agriculture (2.8%)

Mining (1.4%)

Retail & wholesale trade 17.9%

Government 11.0%

30.5%

Services (finance, health, & other)

Construction (3.3%)

(a) What? gross national product by sector, 1984

Highest fifth of the population 42.9 %

Next highest fifth 24.4%

17.0% Third highest fifth

11.0%

Next to the bottom fifth

Bottom fifth of the population (4.7%)

(b) Who? Percentage distribution of aggregate income, 1984

FIGURE 1.2 *What and Who in the United States Economy, 1984*

(Source: U.S. Department of Commerce, Statistical Abstract of the United States 1986, *pp. 433, 452.)*

Looking at our answers to the questions What? and Who? in the form of pie charts is a rather dry exercise. Hence Table 1.2 adds life by stating specific examples on the left-hand side. Examples of our economy's answers to the other basic questions—How?, What's new?, and How stable?—are also mentioned. The handiwork of both the market and the government is in evidence.

TABLE 1.2   Outline of Choice Results in Observed and Desired Terms

OBSERVED: The Key Questions and Examples of Actual Answers	**DESIRED: Ideal Answers Based on Value Judgments**
1. *What is produced?* Annually: 2 million dwellings, 7 billion bushels of corn, 8 million cars, 120 million men's trousers, 234 NFL football games, 900,000 college graduations, hundreds of combat aircraft.	1. *Allocation efficiency.* Produce what people want most while being constrained by resource costs. (Later, rigorously, marginal social benefit equals marginal social cost.)
2. *How are goods and services produced?* 29,000 railroad locomotives in service, 240,000 knitting mill workers, beer produced by bottom fermentation.	2. *Technical efficiency.* Lowest-cost methods of production, given the type of product.
3. *Who gets the goods and services?* After accounting for welfare programs, 10 percent of Americans are in poverty. Women and blacks earn lower incomes than white males.	3. *Reduced inequality.* Not well defined. Value judgments greatly differ, preventing consensus.
4. *What's new?* Video games, continuous casting of steel, personal computers, robotic production of autos, ceramic motors, space shuttles, countless chemical products, MX missiles.	4. *Growing real income, longer life, progress.* In the past, the more the better. But value judgments differ, as some pooh-pooh growth and fear some types of technical change.
5. *How stable?* Unemployment exceeded 10% during much of 1982–83. Price inflation soared during the late 1970s.	5. *Full employment with overall price stability.* Views differ on what constitutes full employment. Some say that a little inflation is tolerable.

B

Desired Economy (Normative)

Parallel to these entries for observed results, the right-hand side of Table 1.2 repeats the captions for desired results mentioned earlier in part (D) of Figure 1.1—allocation efficiency, technical efficiency, reduced inequality, growth, and full employment with price stability. If we lived in the best of all possible worlds, there would be no need to distinguish "what is" and "what ought to be" in this fashion. But, alas, we don't.

The gap between reality and perfection can be illustrated with one simple example concerning "How"? and "technical efficiency." Virtually all typewriters and computer keyboards suffer from the terribly inefficient "QWERTY" key arrangement, named after the first six keys in the upper row of letters. QWERTY was designed by one C.L. Sholes in 1873 for the express purpose of slowing typists down. Typists had to be slowed because typewriters in those days had keys that jammed easily. In 1932 Professor A. Dvorak devised a new and much more efficient arrangement, with the most frequently used letters in the home row—*A, E, O, U, I, D, H, T, N,* and *S*. About 70 percent of all typing would be done on Dvorak's home row instead of the 32 percent that is presently done on QWERTY's home row. Yet the old QWERTY keyboard persists. For this reason, studies show that typing now takes twice as long to learn as it should, requires twice the time once learned, and makes us work about 20 times harder than it should.

Several things about the normative right half of Table 1.2 deserve special attention. First, being value judgments, these economic aims remain only *generalized* concepts of what is desirable. They may be more specific than the ultimate value judgments from which they derive—namely, welfare, happiness, equality, and progress. But they are not specific enough to include narrowly stated aims such as "a chicken in every pot" or "unemployment of no more than 4 percent."

Second, this vagueness allows people to differ in their definitions of these aims, both the broad aims as stated and more narrow aims as implied. These differences in definitions create clashes of opinions. To borrow an example from the generation gap, your ideas of desirable developments

under "What's new?" probably differ from the ideas of your parents.

Third, these aims are learned and culture bound, not scientifically determined. We would violate no law of nature if we chose not to pursue allocation efficiency. Regarding equality and progress, the ideals of Skolt Lapps and Buddhist monks differ radically from ideals taught in industrial societies.

Fourth, the several goals listed on the right side of Table 1.2—"allocation efficiency", "technical efficiency", and so on—are not necessarily consistent with each other. Depending on definitions and other complexities, *it may not be possible to make advances toward the achievement of one goal without at the same time detracting from the achievement of another goal.* Among the possible conflicts between goals, none has received greater attention from economists than the potential conflict between allocation efficiency and reduced inequality.

Fifth, given these possible conflicts, and given also the slippery nature of the definitions of aims, it is not surprising that different people assign different *weights or priorities* to these objectives. Conflicts between goals are then resolved within each person's mind according to these subjective weights.

Sixth and lastly, these differing definitions, these conflicts between goals, and these weighted individual resolutions of conflict, in turn, foster irreconcilable conflicts between people. Conservatives do battle with liberals. Right-wing libertarians violently disagree with left-wing socialists. Various "isms" attract followings. And, not to be outdone by others, economists disagree among themselves. In truth, economists have become famous for their tendency to disagree. Will Rogers once quipped that if you put all economists end to end, they wouldn't reach a conclusion.

Most of this disagreement among economists arises in this normative realm. Value judgments, their definitions, and their weights differ between conservative and liberal economists, not to mention the libertarians and socialists. Differences of opinion arise in the positive realm as well because these value judgments color people's interpretations of facts and their perceptions of relationships. Still, by far the biggest disputes occur in this realm of normative economics.

VI
The Methods of Economists

So far, we have acknowledged that economics is the study of how society copes with scarcity, which entails choices in answering the questions What?, How?, Who?, What's new?, and How stable? We have also recognized two levels of that study: (1) a positive level covering _observed_ choice procedures and results, and (2) a normative level covering _desired_ choice procedures and results. Figure 1.1 pictures these divisions.

The _methods_ economists use in their studies vary widely with their tastes and talents. A few conduct controlled experiments, much like those found in psychology. A few rely heavily on introspection, much like that done by philosophers. In the main, however, economists rely on methodologies that differ from those of other disciplines.

A
Positive Economic Analysis

The main approach followed for positive economic analysis is outlined in Figure 1.3. Hypothesis formulation and data gathering start the process.

Which of these two activities comes first varies. Sometimes data are observed that inspire a hypothesis. Sometimes a hypothesis guides the search for relevant data. In either case, it is often difficult to devise measures that correspond exactly to theoretical concepts. Moreover, data usually cannot be generated by controlled experiments, as they can in chemistry. Rather, economists have to take data from real-world observations, such as the price of potatoes or the number of cars sold each year. Because these data emerge from many complex forces, it is difficult to isolate the impact of any one force, the one raised by hypothesis in particular. Economists therefore often have to work with dirty test tubes.

In the next step, the hypothesis is compared with the data for testing. Statistical procedures prevail here, but there is ample room for case studies and even guesswork. Professional judgment influences the testing, and the outcomes are often disputed. Nevertheless, those outcomes constitute various forms of positive economic knowledge, solid or soft knowledge depending on the plausibility of the hypothesis, the accuracy of the data, and so on. As indicated in Figure 1.3, this knowledge emerges as economic "laws," explanations of behavior, and predictions of events.

Read Perspective 1B.

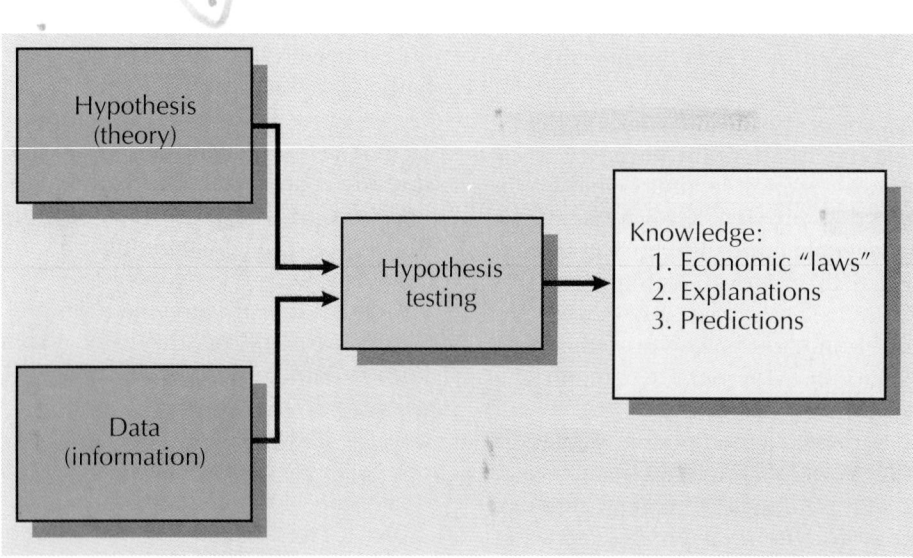

FIGURE 1.3   The Methodology of Positive Economic Analysis

PERSPECTIVE 1B
The Supply of Money and Inflation

An economic hypothesis of vital importance is that excessive growth of the money supply causes inflation. Data on the money supply are available, but in various possible forms. Is the money supply just currency, that is, coins and bills? Is it currency plus checking account deposits? Is it these things plus savings deposits? Data to measure inflation likewise come in various forms. When data for the money supply and inflation are compared to test whether there is a close association between the two variables, economists do find an association, but just how close it is depends on the data, the time period of reference, and so on. Figure 1.4 reproduces a chart used by Professor Milton Friedman in his July 25, 1983, *Newsweek* column, illustrating such as association. The brown line shows the growth of the money supply from one winter quarter to the next winter quarter, one spring quarter to the next spring quarter, and so on for summer and fall, where *money supply* is defined as currency plus all checking account deposits. The red line shows the inflation rate, as measured by the percentage change in the gross national product "deflator" 2 years after the money supply figures. That is to say, the red line has been shifted back 2 years, because Friedman believed that the money supply causes inflation with a time lag of about that long. (Accordingly, the years at the bottom of the chart differ with the data series.) Notice how the two lines move up and down together to a substantial degree, many of the peaks and valleys corresponding rather closely. Moreover, the two series of dots trace the long-term trends in money supply growth and inflation. These trend lines display remarkable unison. From these correspondences and others like them, which constitute tests of the hypothesis, Friedman concluded that money supply growth determines the inflation rate, thereby *explaining* inflation. Moreover, Friedman made *predictions* based on this conviction, predicting in July 1983 that the 1982–83 spurt in money supply growth shown in Figure 1.4 would "mean an upsurge in inflation in 1984 or 1985 at the very latest." He was wrong, but that's a common problem with predictions.

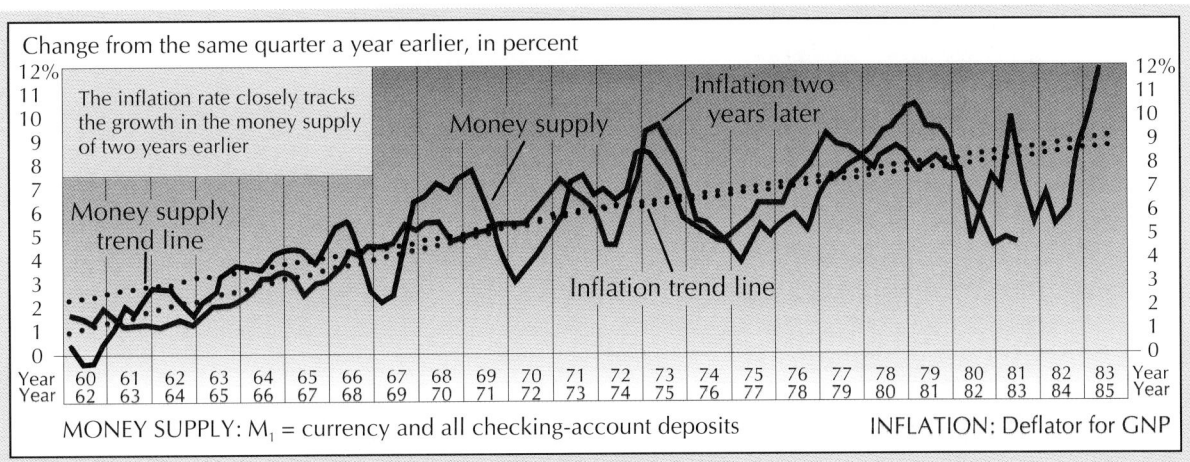

FIGURE 1.4   The Relationship Between Money Supply Growth and Inflation: 1960–1983
(*Source:* Newsweek, July 25, 1983.)

B
Normative Economic Analysis

As shown in Figure 1.5, normative economic analysis uses the knowledge derived from positive economic analysis as a basic building block. That knowledge, which rests on data and verified hypotheses, reflects "what is." When "what is" is compared to "what ought to be," as reflected in our desired aims, problems may then be identified. Once problems are identified, policy proposals follow.

Of course, the policy proposals themselves should be guided by economic knowledge in hopes of finding something that actually works and that does not itself become a problem. Moreover, the policy proposals should be guided by an appreciation of our desired aims (i.e., value judgments). A policy proposal that is sure to advance allocation efficiency may nevertheless be rejected because the policy would, say, crimp freedom or be unfair. Recall that goals often conflict.

Policy proposals usually take one of two forms: (1) the government is called upon to do something, like tax or regulate, in order to correct some perceived problem with the market, or (2) the government is called upon to *stop* doing something and turn matters over to the market.

Read Perspective 1B continued.

VII
Common Pitfalls in Economic Analysis

To employ the methods of economic analysis successfully, we must avoid several common pitfalls that plague it. These pitfalls, or **fallacies,** can be labeled the *fallacy of false cause*, the *fallacy of composition*, and the *fallacy of misplaced blame*. They tend to crop up in economics partly because controlled experiments usually cannot be conducted in this discipline.

A
The Fallacy of False Cause

European peasants of the 1300s believed that a certain herb, if attached to a cord worn around the neck, would be an effective contraceptive. Wade

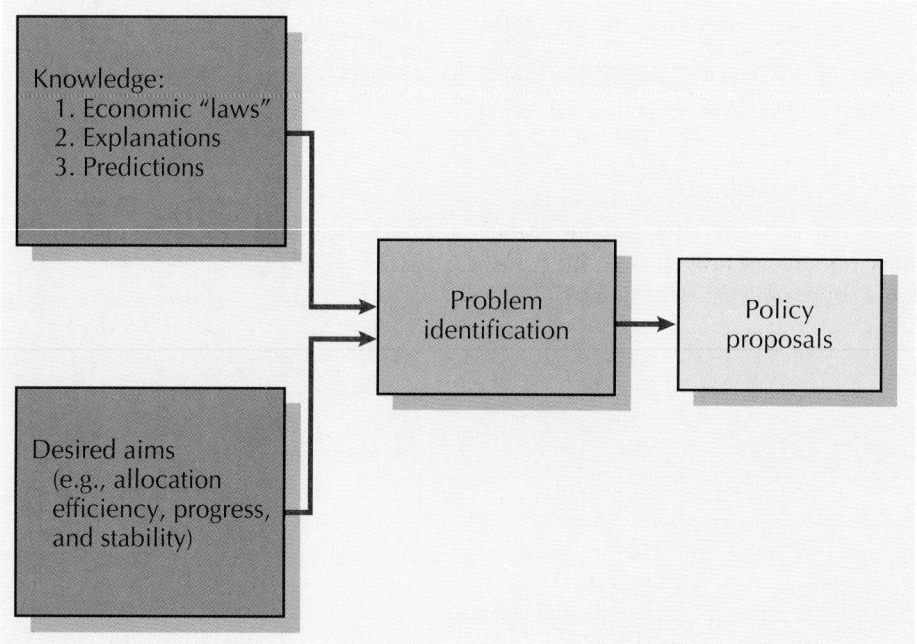

FIGURE 1.5 *The Methodology of Normative Economic Analysis*

PERSPECTIVE 1B CONTINUED
Money Supply and Inflation

Milton Friedman and like-minded economists are convinced that excess money supply growth has caused the inflation we've experienced in the last two decades. Moreover, instability of money supply growth, as shown in the ups and downs of the black line in Figure 1.4, is said to impart serious instability to our economy. Holding these pieces of knowledge up against the desired aim of overall price level stability, Friedman claims to have identified a problem. Moreover, since the money supply is managed by government officials, namely, the Federal Reserve Board of Governors in Washington, D.C., the problem is said to lie with the government itself, government mismanagement in particular. The solution Friedman and others propose is that the Federal Reserve Board should follow a policy of letting the money supply grow at a *slow and constant rate,* regardless of the economic situation. The proposal has not been adopted for reasons that will be taken up later. It is, nevertheless, the interesting and important product of normative economic analysis.

Boggs, an outstanding baseball hitter for the Boston Red Sox during the mid-1980s, ate chicken before each game because early in his career he discovered a correlation between good nights at the plate and visits to the Colonel for buckets of "extra crispy." Countless superstitions such as these arise because people observe that one event, Y, is often preceded by another event, X. As X usually comes before Y, they deduce that X and Y are associated. They reason further that, because X *precedes* Y in this association, X must be the *cause* of Y.

Of course, it is often true that X *does* cause Y. Cold weather does cause leaves to drop. Walking does cause your shoes to wear out. But sequential association does not necessarily prove the presence of cause and effect. Mere coincidence could be at work. If not coincidence, it might be that some third event, say W, is the cause of *both* X and Y, so that although X and Y are *associated,* one is *not causing* the other.

Is the sequential association between the money supply and inflation shown earlier in Figure 1.4 a case of true causality or a case of mere association? Virtually every economist believes that excessive expansion of the money supply does cause inflation. Beyond this generality, however, the answer is disputed. Some economists believe that the money supply is the *only* cause of inflation.

Other economists allow for other possible causes, causes that tend to move the money supply and inflation in mere *association* rather than in a true and sole cause-and-effect relationship. Cause is, in short, often difficult to determine.

> The **fallacy of false cause** occurs when one incorrectly deduces causality from mere association.

B
The Fallacy of Composition

> The **fallacy of composition** occurs when one incorrectly assumes that what is true for an individual is also true for a group.

What is true for an individual is *not* necessarily true for a group. If you stand up while watching a ball game, you get a better view. But if everyone watching stands up, no one gets a better view. If you are a Skolt Lapp, you gain by getting a snowmobile. But if all Skolt Lapps do likewise, they all suffer the loss of their culture.

The fallacy of composition is an especially serious pitfall in learning economics because people new to economics usually do not appreciate the full ramifications of scarcity. If, for example, you get a 100 percent pay raise tomorrow, you will be better off because you can buy 100 percent more goods and services than before. If, however, *everybody* gets a 100 percent pay hike tomorrow through a 100 percent increase in the money supply, is everyone better off because they can buy twice as much as before? No, scarcity intervenes. *Real* goods and services would not become doubly plentiful, only twice as expensive, as prices would rise 100 percent, making no one better off.

C

The Fallacy of Misplaced Blame

Who is to blame for the 50,000 traffic deaths in America each year? Before the mid-1960s, highway carnage was thought to be solely the fault of drivers who were speeding, careless, or drunk. The auto companies were especially adamant about blaming the "nut behind the wheel," the individual driver. Since the mid-1960s, that view has changed. Much research has disclosed that hazardous autos, poorly constructed roads, and high legal speed limits contributed substantially to traffic deaths and injuries. The problem was, in short, redefined to include *system blame* as well as *individual blame*—the entire system of auto design, auto manufacture, traffic regulation, and highway condition.

Unemployment further illustrates individual blame versus system blame. According to some economists, *all* unemployment is a matter of individual blame because people *voluntarily* quit work to relax in leisure, to search for higher-paying jobs, or to retrain for different jobs. According to other economists, *some* unemployment can be blamed on individual choice, but not all, especially not the high unemployment associated with recessions and depressions. They see system blame. According to them, such joblessness is *involuntary*, caused by rigid wage contracts, market imperfections, slack aggregate demand, and other systemic features well beyond the control of individuals. Obviously, the public policy implications of these two views differ radically. Individual blame counsels that nothing be done, that the "problem" is not a problem. System blame counsels that the government intervene in the economy with policies designed to reduce unemployment.

> The **fallacy of misplaced blame** occurs when the individual is blamed for problems that are the fault of the system, or, conversely, when the system is blamed for problems that are the fault of the individual.

Because many problems are actually a *combination* of individual blame and system blame, dodging this fallacy requires fancy footwork (a talent that is, unfortunately, scarce).

SUMMARY

1. Goods and services are scarce because their supplies are limited relative to vast human wants. Their supplies are limited because resources are limited.

2. Land, labor, capital, and entrepreneurship serve as resources. All are scarce. Labor and capital embody technology—the first in the form of software know-how, the second in the form of hardware design.

3. Wants help determine scarcity, because a scarce good is scarce only when people want more of it than is freely available.

4. Economics is, in brief, the study of how societies cope with the problem of scarcity. As such, it is the study of *choices*. Choices must be made to answer five basic questions arising

from scarcity, namely, (a) What goods and services shall be produced in what amounts? (b) How shall goods and services be produced? (c) Who shall get the goods and services? (d) What new products and processes shall we adopt? (e) How stable are overall employment and price levels?

5. Positive economics is the study of actualities, i.e., observable facts and factual relationships. Normative economics covers desirabilities, i.e., things that we think ought to be in light of value judgments.

6. Positive and normative economics can be applied to the study of both choice procedures and choice results (as outlined in Figure 1.1). Economic issues therefore divide into four

different realms: (a) observed choice procedures, (b) desired choice procedures, (c) observed choice results, and (d) desired choice results. (Review Figure 1.1 again.)

7. The principal choice procedure in our economy is the market, which involves systematic exchange between buyers and sellers. Government also plays a big role.

8. Observed and desired choice results are summarized in Table 1.2, which is worthy of careful attention and review.

9. The methods of economists differ depending on the positive–normative division. The positive method essentially involves hypothesis testing to produce knowledge. The normative method centers on problem identification and policy formulation.

10. Several fallacies hamper economic analysis. (a) The fallacy of false cause occurs when one incorrectly deduces causality from mere association. (b) When one incorrectly assumes that what is true for an individual is also true for a group, one is committing a fallacy of composition. (c) To blame individuals for things that are the system's fault, or to blame the system for things that are the individual's fault, is to commit of the fallacy of misplaced blame.

In a nutshell: Scarcity is the problem, the heart of economics. Choice is the issue, the soul of economics—choice mechanisms and results. Fact and fancy both find relevance, each with its own method, while fallacies we hope to avoid.

Appendix
Reading Graphs

"A picture is worth a thousand words." Economists take this old saying seriously. Indeed, to economists, a picture is sometimes worth a million words. The "picture" is not a Van Gogh or Gauguin, however. It is a graph or a two-variable diagram.

Two-Variable Diagrams

Economists rely heavily on two-variable diagrams because they can say a great deal very simply and

clearly. The reason two-variables are used, instead of three or more, is that two variables usually yield the greatest simplicity and clarity. This is so even when, in reality, matters can be so complex as to involve dozens of variables. With two variables depicted, a graph will have two axes radiating from an origin:

1. The *horizontal axis* moves horizontally (right–left) to measure one of the two variables (often the *independent* variable, the variable that is acting on the other).
2. The *vertical axis* moves vertically (up–down) to measure the second variable (often the *dependent* variable, the one that is being acted upon).
3. The *origin* is where these two variables are each equal to zero. *Before analyzing a graph, you should always study the label on each axis so that you know what variable each axis represents. Without this knowledge, you will never understand the graph.*

Figure A on page 22 illustrates these points with two graphs. They depict the costs that a hypothetical sandwich shop might experience for materials that go into its sandwiches—namely, tuna fish, bread, mayonnaise, lettuce, wrapping, and so on. The horizontal axis in each part measures the number of sandwiches produced and sold daily. The vertical axis in part (a) measures the materials cost *per unit*, that is, in this case, *per sandwich*. Assuming that the bread, tuna, mayonnaise, lettuce, wrapping, and other material ingredients cost $1 per sandwich, then the graph of cost per sandwich will be $1 (as read on the vertical axis) at each level of daily output—50 units, or 100 units, or 300 units (as read on the horizontal axis). In this case, variation in the number of sandwiches does not affect the materials cost per unit. It is still $1. The entire line would shift up if, say, the cost of bread rose. But as depicted in Figure A (a), the cost per unit is not a function of the number of sandwiches produced.

In contrast, the vertical axis in Figure A (b) measures the cost of sandwich materials in *total dollar* form—that is, the *total cost* of materials per day. The total cost will be the cost per sandwich ($1) times the number of sandwiches per day. With numbers of sandwiches in the calculation, the total cost of materials *will* be affected by the quan-

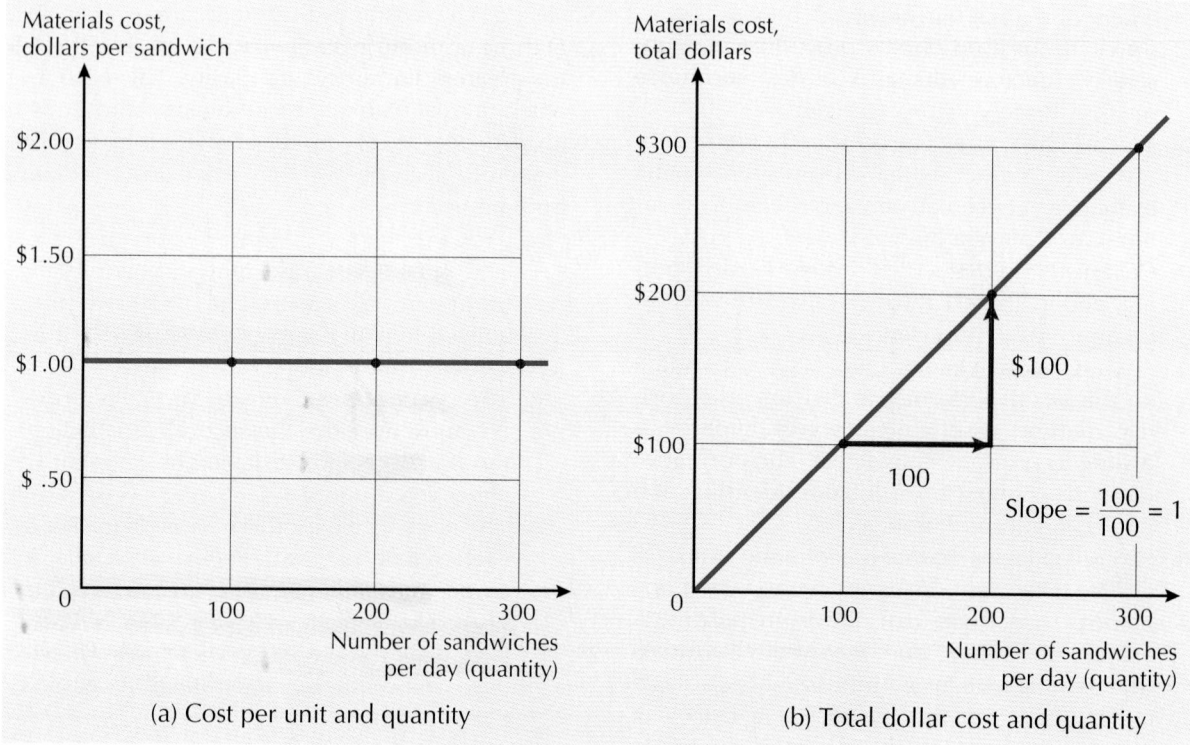

FIGURE A   Graphs Illustrating the Relations Between Variable Costs and Quantity

Part (a) illustrates the cost per sandwich, which is assumed to be $1 for each sandwich produced (the cost of tuna, mayonnaise, two slices of bread, and wrapping). Part (b) illustrates the cost in total dollar form, which is the cost per sandwich ($1) times the number of sandwiches. The total cost of 100 sandwiches is thus $100, that of 200 sandwiches is $200, and so on.

tity. As shown in Figure A(b), zero sandwiches would imply zero cost of materials, 100 sandwiches would cost a total of $100, 200 sandwiches a total of $200, and so on. Because total costs are a function of quantity, the *slope* of the line in part (b) is quite different from the *slope* of the line in part (a).

The Slopes of Lines or Curves

One of the most important features of a two-variable graph is the *slope* of the line (or lines). Simply defined, the slope of a line is the rate at which it rises or falls (as measured by the vertical axis) while moving to the right (along the horizontal axis). In other words, slope measures the extent of a rise (or a fall) associated with a run along the horizontal axis. Defined technically:

The **slope** of a straight line is the ratio of the vertical change to the corresponding horizon-

tal change while moving to the right along the horizontal axis (the ratio of the rise over the run).

Looking again at part (a) of Figure A, you will see that there is *zero vertical change* in the cost per sandwich corresponding to a *positive horizontal change* in the number of sandwiches. The rise is zero for a run of 100 sandwiches between, say, 100 and 200. Hence, the ratio of rise to run in this case is 0/100, for a slope of zero. On the other hand, the slope of Figure A(b) is 1. Total dollar costs always rise vertically by $100 for any corresponding run of 100 sandwiches, yielding a ratio of 100/100 = 1. Between 100 and 200 sandwiches, for instance, total materials costs rise from $100 to $200.

Figure B reinforces these notions by showing what would happen to the cost of sandwiches if the cost of bread were to rise sharply, causing the cost per sandwich to jump from $1.00 to $1.50. The increased cost of ingredients lifts the cost per unit

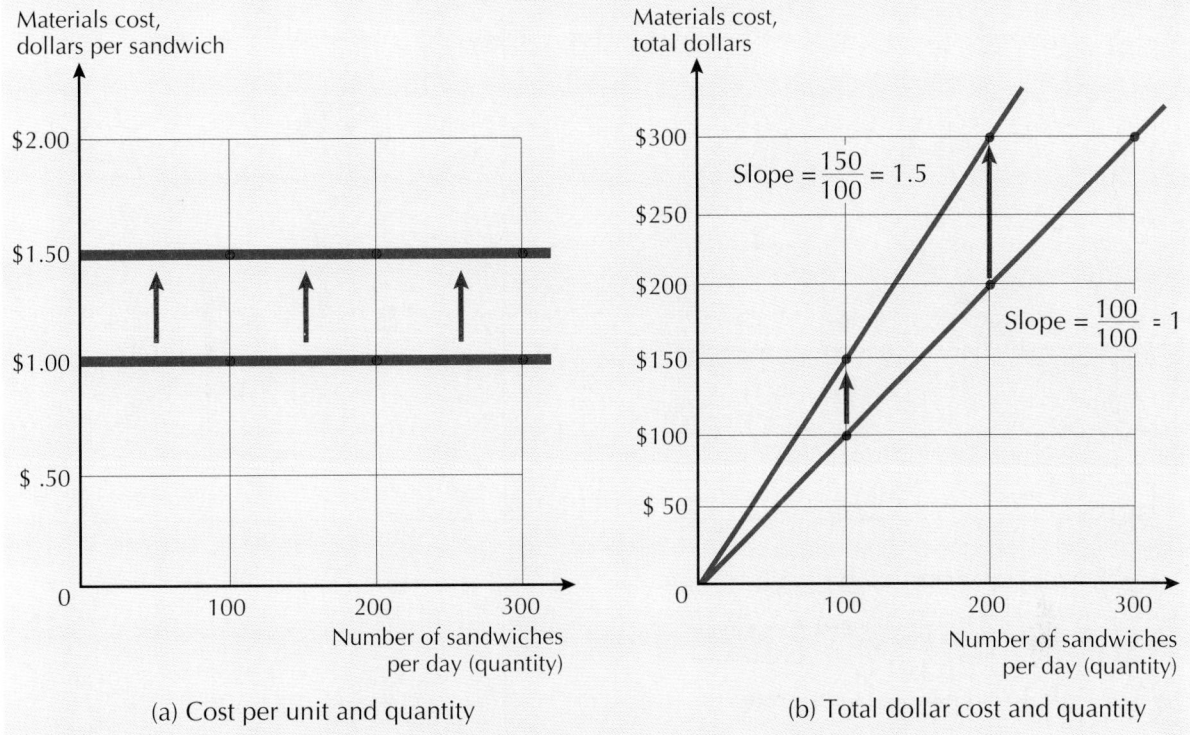

FIGURE B   Changes in the Relations of Cost and Quantity

Here, compared to Figure A, the cost per unit rises to $1.50 per sandwich in part (a). This does not change the slope of the cost per unit line. The slope for the total dollar cost does change, however. It grows steeper, moving from 1 to 1.5.

line in part (a) by 50 cents to $1.50, but the slope of the line remains unchanged at zero. Stated differently, the cost per unit is now higher, but it remains constant _in relation to the quantity produced_ (as indicated by the horizontal axis). In contrast, part (b) shows that the slope of the line for total costs will get steeper. At 100 sandwiches, the total cost for materials is now $150 instead of $100. At 200 sandwiches it's now $300, and so on. A run of 100 in the number of sandwiches, from 100 to 200, thus causes a rise in the total dollar cost from $150 to $300, or $150 (300 − 150). Putting these numbers in ratio form, 150/100, we find that the new slope is 1.5, which is steeper than the old slope of 1.

Figure C illustrates the full range of possibilities for straight lines. Part (a) depicts a positive slope because a positive run on the _x_ axis has a corresponding rise that is also positive. The ratio of two positive numbers will then be positive. Part (b) shows a negative slope. A positive run on _x_ will, in

this case, cause a _negative_ rise in _y_, i.e., a fall. Hence the ratio for the slope will have both positive and negative numbers, yielding a negative slope. The zero slope of part (c) is by now familiar. Finally, part (d) shows what an infinite slope would look like.

The slope of any given _straight line_, such as the one in Figure C (a) or C (b), will be the same at every point on the line. In contrast, the slope of a _curved line_ will change from point to point on the line. This complicates matters, but not too much, as illustrated by the several curved lines of Figure D. The generally positive and negative patterns of parts (a) and (b), respectively, are easy to see, especially when compared to Figure C (a) and (b). The _degree of positive slope_ in Figure D (a) changes at different points on the line, but the slope at each point is positive, (1.5, 1.3, 1.1, etc.). Similarly, the _degree of negative slope_ in Figure D (b) changes, but the slope at each point is always negative (−1.5, −1.3, −1.1, etc.). Figures D (c) and (d) show

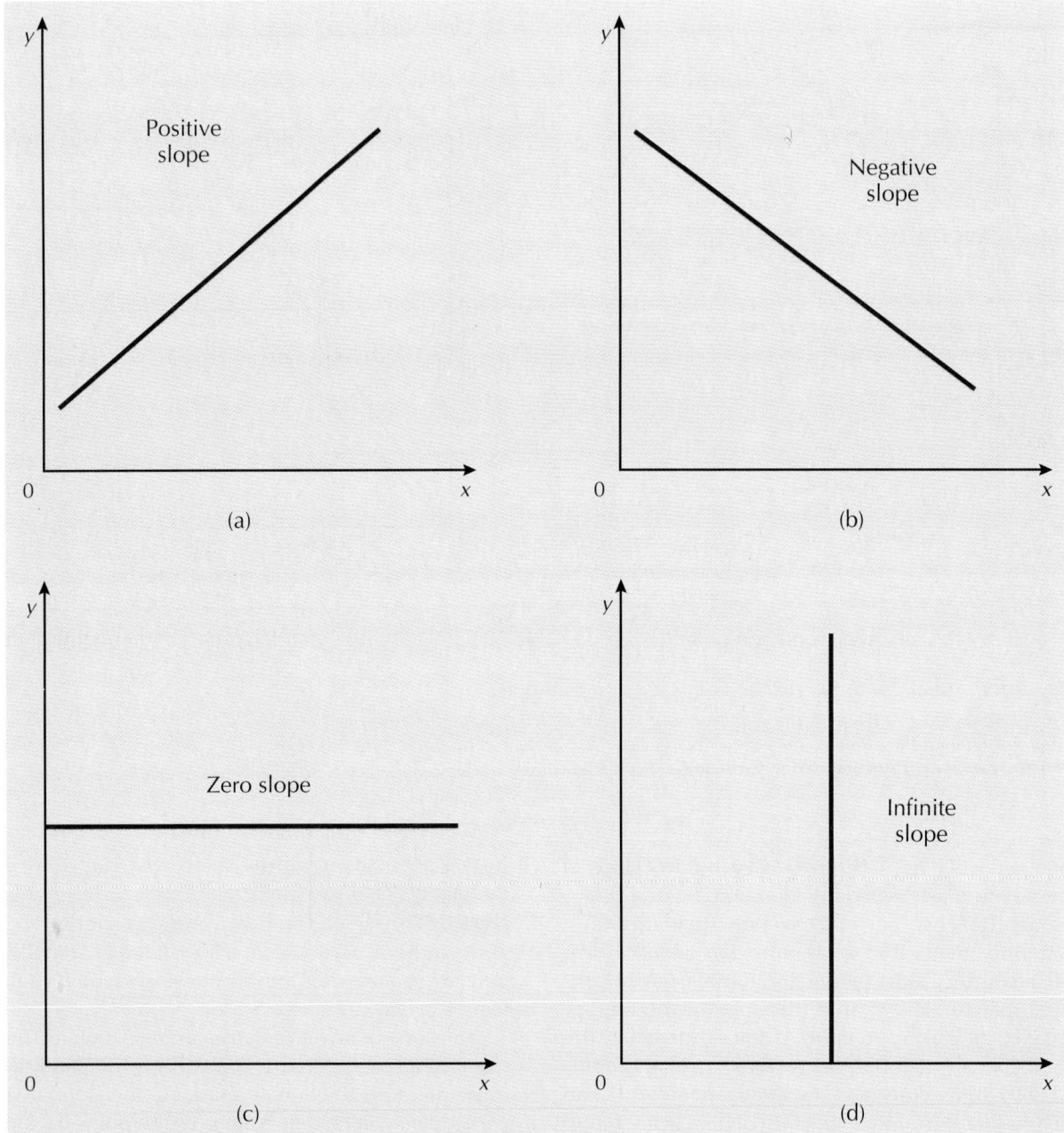

FIGURE C Slopes of Various Straight-Line "Curves"

When both variables, x and y, rise or fall together, as in part (a), the slope is positive. When the two variables move inversely, one rising while the other is falling, the slope is negative. With zero slope, there is no change in y as x changes. With an infinite slope, there is no change in x as y changes.

greater variation. The line in part (c) starts with a negative slope and then becomes positive with rightward movement along the x axis. Conversely, the line in (d) starts with a positive slope and then turns negative with continued horizontal movement to the right.

How, more exactly, is the slope of a curved line calculated? Figure E illustrates this for a curved

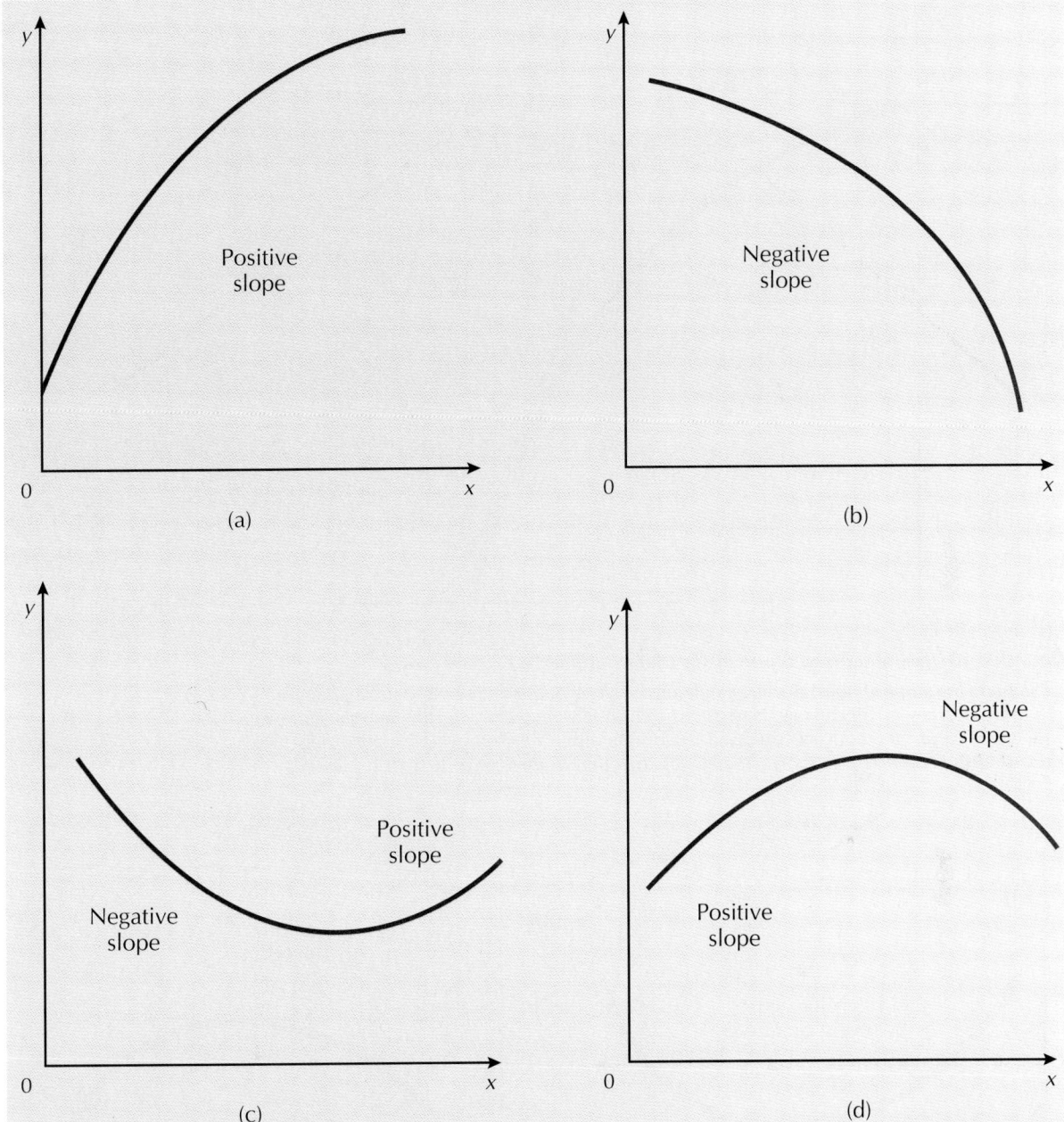

FIGURE D   Slopes in Curved Lines

line that has a negative slope at every point. In essence, the slope at any point is the same as the slope of the tangent line at that point. Because the tangent line is a straight line, the calculation proceeds as it does with straight lines once the tangent line is obtained.

The **slope of a curved line** at a particular point is the same as the slope of the straight line that is tangent to that point.

For example, tangent lines for points A and B are indicated in Figure E. The slope of the tangent line for point A is reflected in the ratio y'/x' because y' is the negative rise associated with the run of x'. Similarly, the slope of the tangent line for point B is

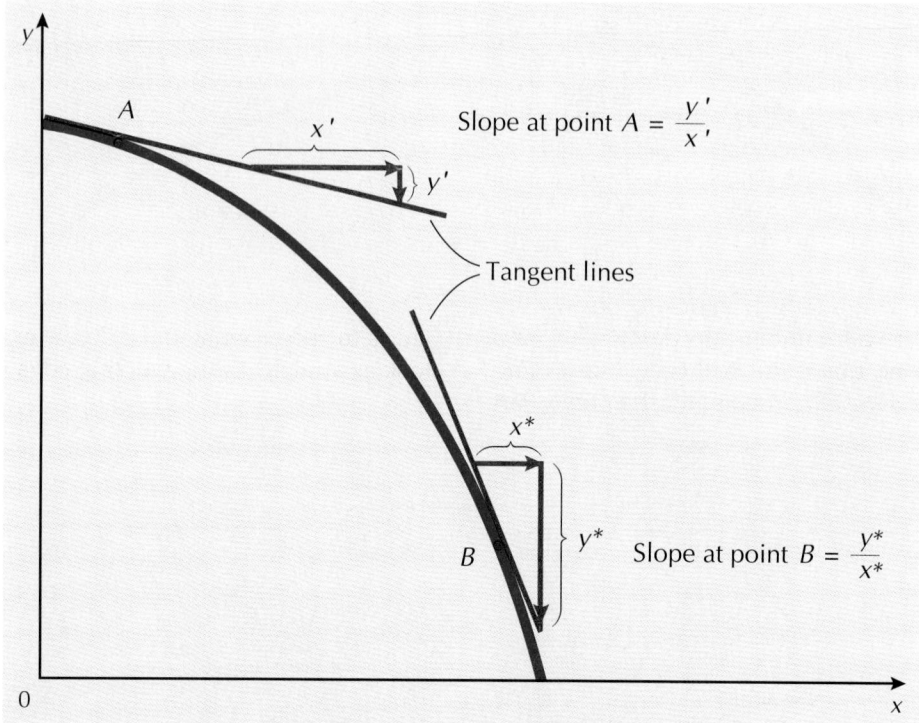

FIGURE E   Determination of Slope at Certain Points on a Curved Line

To calculate the slope at point A, one calculates the slope of the tangent line through point A. Here that slope is y'/x'. Because y' is negative, the slope is negative. To calculate the slope at point B, the same procedure is followed, yielding a slope of y*/x*, which is also negative. Notice that the slope at B is more steeply negative than the slope at A.

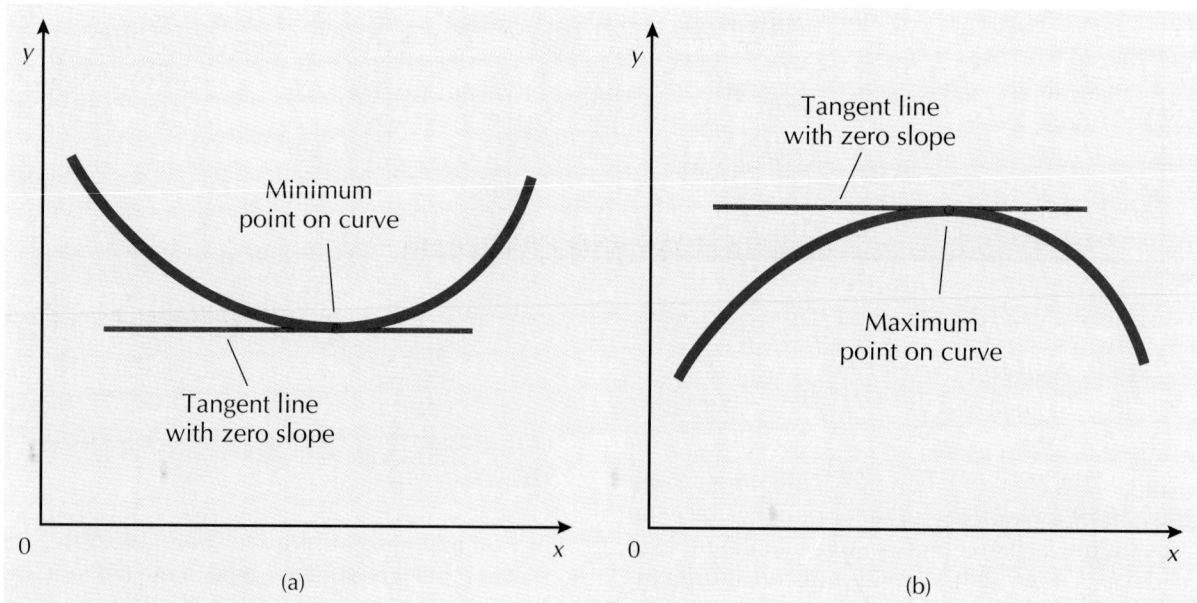

FIGURE F   The Minimum and Maximum Points on Curved Lines That Have Both Positive and Negative Slopes

measured by the ratio y^*/x^*, which will be negative because y^* is negative. Notice that, in very rough approximation, the slope at point A is about -0.23, while the slope at point B is about -2.25. Hence, the slope at B is more steeply negative than the one at A. Or, *in absolute value*, the slope at B is greater than the slope at A (i.e., 2.25 is greater than 0.23).

When a curved line is curved to the extent of switching the slope from negative to positive (or the reverse), it will contain one point with *zero* slope. Moreover, that point will be either a *minimum point* or a *maximum point* on the curve. Part (a) of Figure F illustrates this for the minimum point, while part (b) illustrates it for the maximum point. Familiarity with these two cases of zero slope will occasionally prove useful later in this text.

One final note: Economists have, for some mysterious reason, adopted the habit of calling all lines in graphs *curves*—straight lines as well as those that are really curved. We shall follow this odd practice, so don't be alarmed by our references to curves when the pictures of those curves look as straight as the working edge of a ruler.

KEY TERMS

Scarcity
Choice
Economics
Positive statement (economics)
Normative statement (economics)
Choice procedures
Choice results
Land
Labor
Capital
Technology
Free good
Scarce good
Resources
Positive method
Chapter 1

Normative method
Fallacies
Entrepreneurship
What? question
How? question
Who? question
What's new? question
How stable? question
Market
Value judgment
Government
Positive economic analysis
Normative economic analysis
Slope

QUESTIONS AND PROBLEMS

1. Explain the respective roles of positive economic analysis and of normative economic analysis in economic policy-making.
2. Explain why a lunch may be "free" from the recipient's perspective, but costly from society's perspective.
3. Given that tradition dominates only in very primitive societies, explain the two remaining approaches to answering the key economic questions.
4. Economists in the U.S. and other modern economies generally accept the importance of what five economic goals? Why do economists so often disagree regarding government policies despite their acceptance of the same goals?
5. Can statistical procedures be used to prove that event A caused event B?
6. Define scarcity and discuss its role in society.

From the appendix:
7. Fill in the following blanks:
   (a) When a curve reaches its maximum point, its slope is _____.
   (b) Most often, the _____ variable is measured on the horizontal axis.
   (c) The slope of a straight line is _____.

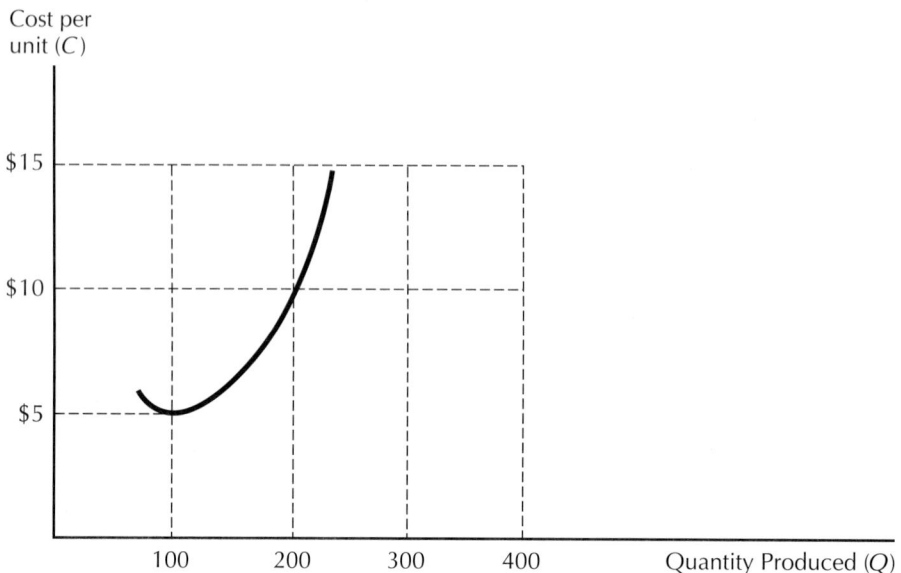

8. Use the graph shown here to fill in the blanks:
   (a) If current production is 100 units, any increase in production will cause costs per unit to _____ (rise, fall, remain constant).
   (b) The slope of the curve between $Q = 100$ and $Q = 200$ is _____ (constant, decreasing, increasing).
   (c) The slope of the curve at $Q = 100$ is _____ (0, greater than 1, less than one).

2

The Ways of Economics: Scarcity Underscored

When the *Endeavour* first sailed into Australia's Botany Bay, carrying Captain James Cook and his crew, the aborigines there tried to ignore it. The large ship drifted to within a few hundred yards of natives fishing from canoes, but they casually continued to fish. The natives on shore also went about their business as if the ship were invisible. "The sight of the *Endeavour*," Alan Moorehead explains, "had apparently meant nothing to these primitives because it was too strange, too monstrous, to be comprehended."[1]

If Chapter 1 was your first glimpse of economics, we hope that it was not "too strange, too monstrous, to be comprehended." This chapter will, as suggested by its outline, ease you further into the subject.

I
Two Ways of Approaching Economics

A
Microeconomics

Microeconomics is the study of economics in the small. It covers personal choice, firm behavior, and individual markets.

If the price of gasoline jumped 50 percent, how would motorists react? How should Xerox price its copy machines to maximize its profit? Do employers discriminate against women? These are the kinds of questions covered by microeconomics.

In terms of the basic questions raised by scarcity, the first three—What?, How?, and Who?—comprise the main province of microeconomics. To a very large degree, these questions concern issues of *mixture*—e.g., more autos versus fewer autos in the mix of all goods and services; or more capital and less labor in the mix of resources producing goods and services; or more income for some families coupled with less for others in the distribution of incomes.

The question What's new? includes issues that likewise qualify as microeconomics, especially issues of technological change. Are giant corporations like General Motors and General Electric the best sources of inventions and innovations? How do patents stimulate research and development? Microeconomics addresses these issues and others like them.

B
Macroeconomics

Macroeconomics is the study of economics in the large. It covers aggregate economic performance.

If federal income tax revenues are cut by $70 billion, what are the consequences for overall employment? If the money supply is expanded at an annual rate of 10 percent, what happens to the overall price level? What causes depressions? These kinds of questions lie in the realm of macroeconomics.

Among the basic economic questions, How stable? is clearly the one most directly addressed by macroeconomics because macroeconomics is concerned with the ups and downs of overall employment, output, and price level. Portions of the question What's new? likewise radiate into macroeconomics because macroeconomics also concerns growth in output.

Whereas microeconomics dissects the economy into parts, macroeconomics treats it as a whole. Markets are aggregated into the *labor market* or the *goods market*. Millions of households are lumped together into masses of *consumers* and *savers*. Government expenditures for missiles, marching boots, typewriters, schools, police cars, and countless other things are treated as one great spending outlay. Macroeconomics focuses on the relationships between these and other aggregate variables.

To be sure, the conduct of the micro parts often influences the macro whole, as when, for example, a leap in the price of oil in 1973 walloped the entire

---

[1] Alan Moorehead, *The Fatal Impact* (New York: Harper & Row, 1966), p. 104.

economy. Conversely, macro developments influence micro behavior. So the micro–macro distinction often blurs, even as it remains useful.

II
Two Ways of Thinking About Economics

Two main modes of thought appear in the ensuing pages. To avoid muddle, we state them here at the outset and then occasionally restate them later. The first is *problem solving*, which deals mainly with positive economics. The second may be called *dilemma addressing*, which serves normative economics.

A
Problem Solving

Here's a problem for you: 2 + 5 = ?. Here's another: If a ship departs Plymouth, England, and sails at a rate of 70 miles per day, it can reach Botany Bay, Australia, in 4 months. How far is Botany Bay from Plymouth harbor by sea?

Problems are simply questions posed for solution. The key to solving problems is understanding the unknown. In math, the unknown usually carries a convenient label, like *x*, so there can be no mistake in identifying the unknown. Story problems are more difficult because the problem solver has to assign the labels and set up the format. Unfortunately, economics is full of storylike problems, so you, the reader, must take special care to understand what the unknown is in each problem-solving situation. Sometimes the unknown will be an obvious, small unknown, such as "What quantity of corn output will maximize a certain farmer's profit?" Sometimes the unknown is huge and abstract, such as "What outputs of an entire economy will achieve allocation efficiency, the ideal answer to the key question 'What?' "?

Once your mind's eye sees the nature of the unknown, the solution itself will remain invisible without the application of logic. And for many very important problems in economics, that logic is **two-question logic**.

1. Micro Two-Question Logic A lucid understanding of microeconomics emerges from repeated application of the following two questions:

What are its benefits?
What are its costs?

The "it" varies with the situation and the decision maker—e.g., an additional wristwatch (your choice), an additional Boeing 747 aircraft (TWA's choice), an additional hamburger cook (McDonalds'), an additional hydroelectric dam (society's choice, taken by Uncle Sam), and so on. Despite these differences, however, the underlying logic is always the same, so understanding it is extremely important.

To ask "What are its benefits?" is to inquire about gains or pluses. To ask "What are its costs?" is to inquire about the losses or minuses of the choice. **Choose whatever is worth more in benefits than what you have to give up in costs. Reject whatever is worth less in benefits than what you have to pay in costs.** The logic is as simple as the logic that should be followed by all speculators: *Buy low and sell high.* Yet it is more powerful because it is more general. The word **benefits** refers broadly to monetary revenues, psychological rewards, efforts saved, and other pluses. **Costs** can include monetary expenditures, mental suffering, efforts spent, and other minuses.

If the choice is your purchase of an additional wristwatch, the benefit would be the psychological pleasure and utility the wristwatch conveyed, while the cost would be the money you pay for it, money that could have been spent on other things. If the benefit exceeds the cost, you buy. If not, you don't. If the choice is TWA's purchase of an additional Boeing 747, then the benefit would be the passenger revenues that the 747 would generate for TWA and the cost would be about $120 million just for the plane. To fill the fuel tanks just once would cost an added $37,000. If the added revenues exceed the added cost, TWA buys. If not, then TWA doesn't buy.

To refer to an "additional" wristwatch or an "additional" 747 is to refer to *marginal units* rather than total units. An airline company might be earning a nice total profit on a fleet of ten 747s taken as a total group. Whether an 11th plane should be added to the fleet depends on the benefits and costs of the 11th plane itself, the marginal unit, not the total profit of the 11-plane fleet taken as a whole. If the benefits of the 11th plane are less than its costs, it should not be bought. An 11-plane fleet might still be profitable despite the 11th plane's losses, but a 10-plane fleet would be *more* profitable. Later we shall have more to say about marginal units in two-question logic as specific problems requiring the logic arise.

> **Marginal** is a term commonly used by economists to mean "additional." For example, if this week you have already had three hamburgers, the benefits of a fourth would be the marginal benefits.

Notice that two-question logic derives directly from the underlying problem of scarcity. Without scarcity, the logic's two questions would not need to be asked or the answers compared for a solution. In a world of Aladdin's lamps, all goods would be free goods, so we would never need to ask "What are its costs?" If, conversely, we were all ascetic monks, we would rarely if ever ask "What are its benefits?" because "it"—the wristwatch, the 747—would be worthless in our eyes. Note also that two-question logic is a *principle* of problem solving that is often difficult to apply in *practice* because we sometimes do not know all the benefits and costs of a choice. Like the maxim "Buy low and sell high," the logic is indisputable, but its application is often difficult.

2. Macro Two-Question Logic Problem solving in macroeconomics also relies frequently on two-question logic, but because the issues in macroeconomics center on the behavior of aggregate variables, the two questions differ from those of microeconomics. The logic of macroeconomics largely hinges on these questions:

> What is expected to happen?
> What actually happens?

When the answers differ—when expectations and actualities diverge—stability can be jeopardized. It's like the tipsy dismay you feel when you expect the elevator to go up and it suddenly goes down. On the other hand, when the answers correspond, macro stability is more likely.

The answers can diverge because our decisions are always based on imperfect information. Especially important in macroeconomics is the fact that gaps between perception and reality arise when one group of people makes decisions that, in the aggregate, differ from those expected by another group. Consumers, for example, may buy less than firms expected when production levels were set, with resulting unsold output.

Differences between expectations and realizations help explain the factors that generate fluctuations in the overall level of economic activity. Firms, households, and government policymakers all change their behavior as they recognize the gap between expectations and outcomes. Macroeconomic stability requires conditions in which expectations are fulfilled. What was expected is what happens.

B
Dilemma Addressing

Problems, as just noted, are mysteries that, in principle, have correct solutions (the stuff of positive economics). *Dilemmas are predicaments that have no fully satisfactory solution.* They are situations that require a choice between unpleasant alternatives. We therefore do not find solutions to dilemmas. Rather, we resign ourselves to compromises. We use value judgments to seek comfortable, not necessarily correct, answers in our choices. Dilemmas thus lie in the domain of normative economics.

1. Microeconomic Dilemmas Many microeconomic situations require a choice between inefficiency and inequity. Taxing the rich to aid the poor may reduce inequity but it probably fosters inefficiency. Taxing rich people limits their incentive to work. Aiding the poor may discourage the able-bodied among them from working. Aside from these disincentives, the government operations involved can be costly, adding further to the inefficiency.

Another broad class of microeconomic dilemmas concerns our society's choice between the market and the government as decision-making mechanisms. When the market limps with imperfections and failures, it is tempting to turn to the government for a cure. But the government likewise suffers serious incapacities, so its intervention may be destructive rather than constructive. When facing the unpleasantries of *both* the market and the government, we must choose the least undesirable of them for the solution.

2. Macroeconomic Dilemmas Macroeconomic dilemmas also plague us. The most prominent one is posed by the trade-off between inflation and unemployment. Short-term gains against inflation can be won only at the expense of greater unemployment. Between 1979 and 1982, for instance, price inflation fell from an annual rate of 13 percent to 4 percent, while unemployment jumped from 6 to 10 percent. Conversely, reduced unemployment aggravates inflation. The nasty dilemma, then, is this: What combination of unemployment and inflation should we accept? Where between this rock and that hard place can we find some comfort? Instead of a "correct" solution, as to the problem 2 + 5 = ?, there are only answers heavily soaked with value judgments.[2]

III
Two Ways of Explaining Economics

Economics is not only challenging because of the subject matter, the micro and macro approaches to the subject, and the mingling of problems with dilemmas. It is also difficult because economists *explain* their subject to outsiders in rather odd ways, odd in comparison to everyday experience and in comparison to other disciplines. Economists rely heavily on *models* and *ceteris paribus* conditions.

A
Models

A model airplane is a representation of the real thing. It shows the essence of a plane. It may have

a motor, so that it swoops overhead. The model may even have dazzling details. Yet, in the end, it is only a representation. It demonstrates how a plane might look and perform. But as a model, it does not actually get you from Denver to Dallas. It is too simplified for that.

Economists rely very heavily on models. These are not physical models. They are conceptual models that can be expressed in words, mathematical expressions, and diagrams. Still, they can serve the same purposes as model planes. *Economic models (1) simplify reality and (2) demonstrate relationships among variables.* In *simplifying reality*, economic models attempt to capture the essence of what is happening in order to obtain basic explanations or predictions. Certain variables get close attention, such as price and quantity. Other variables are ignored, like the religious beliefs of the company's vice-president for marketing. In *demonstrating relationships*, models reveal what happens to one key variable when another one changes—what happens to the quantity of model airplanes sold, for instance, when their price goes up with the rising cost of plastic.

When using models to explain economics, economists often rely on metaphors.[3] Metaphors are turns of phrase in which one thing is spoken of as if it were another. Adam Smith, who lived in the eighteenth century about the time of Captain Cook and who founded economics, referred to the market as an *invisible hand* to explain how it guided and coordinated buyers and sellers in deciding What?, How?, and Who?. As an invisible hand, the market performs automatically, without need of conscious direction from any individual or government. (An appendix on Smith concludes this chapter.)

B
Ceteris paribus Conditions

When explaining economics, economists often preface their remarks with the expression *ceteris paribus*, which means "other things being constant." For example, "Other things being constant, a decline in the price of personal computers will

---

[2]Many economists argue that in the *long run* there is no necessary tradeoff between inflation and unemployment. In this view, price stability and full employment are simultaneously possible given sufficient time. But dilemmas remain even in this rosier perspective because predicaments remain in trying to move from the short run to the long run.

[3]Donald N. McCloskey, "The Rhetoric of Economics," *Journal of Economic Literature* (June 1983), pp. 481–517.

cause buyers to increase their purchases." This assumes that *only* the price of personal computers changes, while other things, like the income of consumers or the price of computer software, remain unchanged. Specifying a *ceteris paribus* condition thus lets us focus on just a few variables, such as the price and quantity of personal computers.

In the real world, with other things changing, a decline in the price of personal computers may or may not be accompanied by increased purchases. If at the same time consumer incomes plummet because of a severe recession, or if the price of software skyrockets, purchases may actually drop rather than rise. To tackle an analysis that simultaneously incorporates all the forces influencing personal computer sales, you would need more than a personal computer. Hence, the *ceteris paribus* assumption permits us to break complexities into simple pieces.

■ CHECK YOUR BEARINGS

To summarize this chapter so far, we have delineated the micro and macro approaches to studying economics, described problem solving and dilemma addressing, and looked at two ways of explaining economics. Your newfound mental perspective is now put to an immediate test as we launch into discussions of production possibilities, exchange possibilities, growth, and circular flow. The *production-possibilities frontier*, for example, is a model built upon *ceteris paribus* conditions. Similarly, to appreciate *exchange possibilities*, one must use the two-question logic of microeconomic problem solving.

IV

Production Possibilities: What?, How?, Who?

A
Scarcity Diagrammed

The production-possibilities frontier nicely illustrates the impact of scarcity. It shows that scarcity compels choices in answering the questions What?, How?, and Who?

Because of scarcity, we can assume (1) limited amounts of productive resources and (2) a given state of current technology. If we assume further that (3) our resources and technology are fully and efficiently employed, then the galaxy of goods and services that we could produce with this utmost effort would form the production-possibilities frontier.

Because the entire range of goods and services our huge economy could produce defies consideration—thousands of gallons of eye drops, billions of hamburgers, millions of TV sets, trillions of aspirin tablets, and so on *ad infinitum*—we shall simplify by considering only two basic commodities of ancient importance, bread (wheat) and apparel (cotton), holding the amounts of other commodities constant. (In Captain Cook's day, bread accounted for as much as 60 percent of people's food budgets and 44 percent of their total income expenditure!) Table 2.1 specifies the amounts of bread and apparel this hypothetical economy could produce, assuming (1) limited resources, (2) given technology, and (3) full and efficient use of resources. These amounts are pictured in Figure 2.1.

Combination *a* indicates that this economy could, at best, produce 35 million pounds of apparel, if it devoted all its resources and technology to the production of apparel and none to the production of bread. Combination *f* is at the opposite extreme. With no apparel production, the utmost possible bread production is 50 million loaves. Combinations in between show outputs of *both* bread and apparel, but limited outputs nevertheless. For instance, point *c* tells us that if 20 million loaves of bread are produced, the maximum possible output of apparel is 27 million pounds. If, instead, 40 million loaves are produced, then the maximum attainable apparel output is given at point *e*, namely, 11 million pounds.

Combinations *outside* the frontier, such as point *k*, would be attractive. But scarcity makes such combinations *impossible* to attain. Conversely, all combinations of apparel and bread *inside* the frontier *are* possible, but since they are not on the outer boundary of possible points (they do not use resources fully and efficiently), they are off the frontier. Point *j* is one such point (15 apparel and 20 bread). Hence:

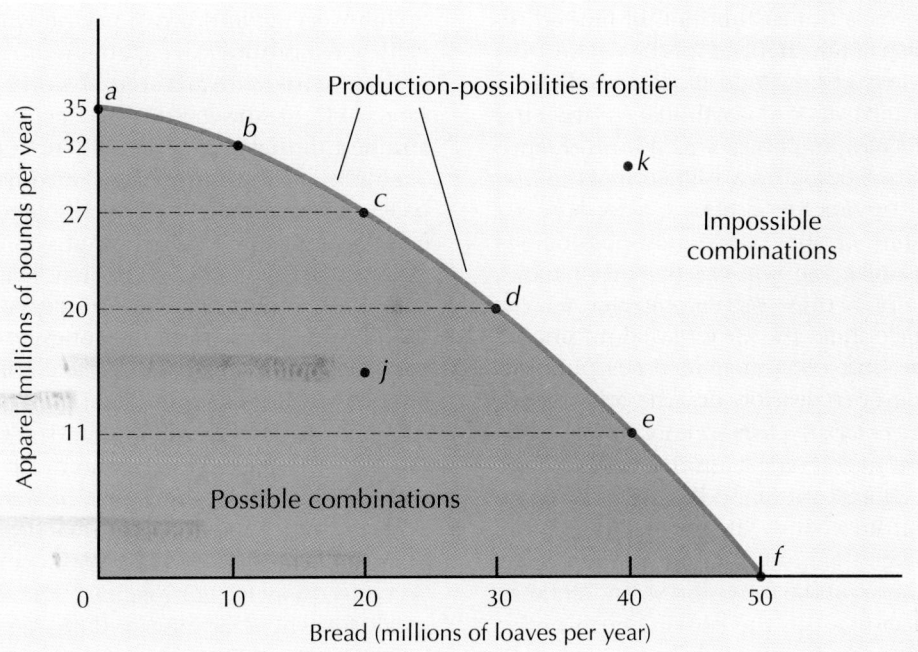

FIGURE 2.1 Production-Possibilities Frontier

Assuming (1) limited resources, (2) a given technology, and (3) full potential use of resources, the production-possibilities frontier shows utmost output combinations. If no bread is produced, the maximum output of apparel is 35 million pounds. If no apparel is produced, 50 million loaves of bread is the maximum. In between are combinations of both apparel and bread, such as 20 million pounds of apparel and 30 million loaves of bread.

TABLE 2.1   Production-Possibilities Data

(1) Combination	(2) Bread (in Millions of Loaves)	(3) Apparel (in Millions of Pounds)	(4) Opportunity Cost of Bread (in Millions of Pounds of Apparel Forgone)
a	0	35	0
b	10	32	3 (35−32)
c	20	27	5 (32−27)
d	30	20	7 (27−20)
e	40	11	9 (20−11)
f	50	0	11 (11−0)

The **production-possibilities frontier** shows the greatest combinations of goods that can be produced with (1) limited resources, (2) given technology, and (3) maximum potential resource use. It shows the choices open to society and those denied by scarcity at a particular point in time.

Several comments are now in order concerning (1)

the assumptions underlying the production-possibilities frontier, (2) the trade-off between goods when on the frontier, and (3) the principle of increasing cost.

1. Assumptions Underlying the Production-Possibilities Frontier The assumptions—(1) limited resources, (2) given technology, and (3) maximum potential resource use—stake out the production-possibilities frontier.

Scarcity compels the assumption of limited resources. If these limits changed for the worse—by, say, a severe loss of land and labor as California slid into the Pacific after an earthquake—then the frontier would have to contract as the productive capacity contracted. Figure 2.2 illustrates the loss of California to our hypothetical economy by showing a shift of the production-possibilities frontier from *abcdef* to *ghi*. On the other hand, changes for the better—better weather, for instance—would shift the frontier out toward *mnp*.

The technology of production is held constant by assuming *ceteris paribus* conditions. This means that cotton and wheat farming methods are fixed; capital equipment embodies a certain state of engineering know-how; the skill level of the labor force is set; the breeds of wheat and cotton are the best known at the time; and so on. All these technological givens pin the possibilities-frontier to points *a* through *f*. Improved but as yet unavailable technologies for cotton and wheat farming or

textile weaving and bread baking would theoretically boost productive capabilities to a degree suggested by the outward shift of *a–f* in Figure 2.2 to *mnp*. Still, at any given time, technology *is* constrained to that which actually exists.

Finally, the assumption of maximum potential usage of resources and technology places the economy *on* the production-possibilities frontier rather than at some point inside it. Movement from point *d* to point *x* in Figure 2.2 demonstrates the pertinence of this assumption.

What could cause a shortfall such as *x*? There are two broad conditions: First, *idle resources* (like unemployed workers, fallow land, and closed bakeries) could cause the economy to languish at some point inside the production-possibilities frontier. In a word, recession or depression. Second, *inefficient* use of resources would have similar consequences. For instance, Kansas is the best locale for wheat farming, and Mississippi is excellent for cotton. But what if we stupidly tried to follow a reverse pattern, with cotton sprouting

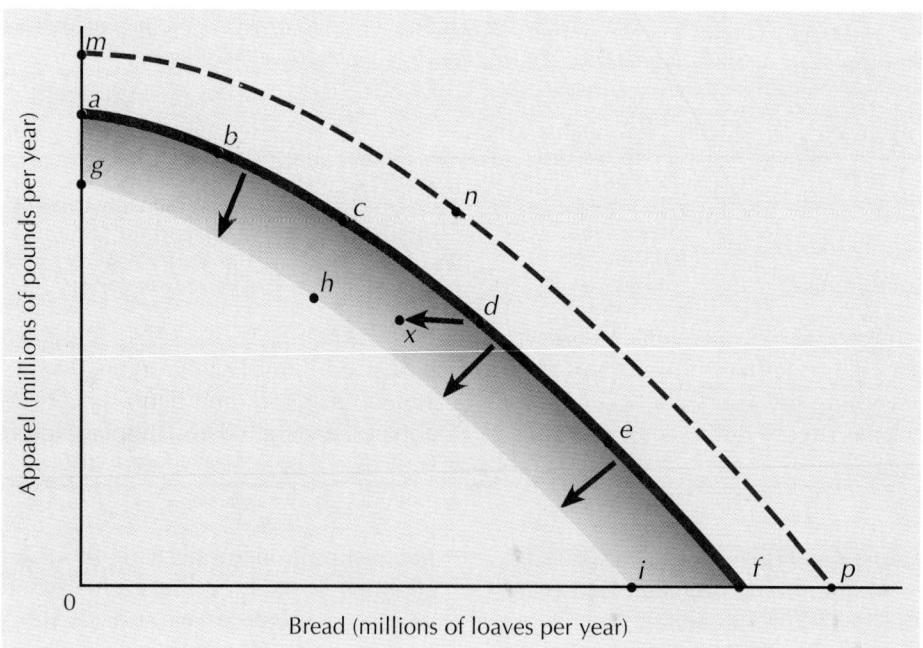

FIGURE 2.2 Changes in Assumptions Underlying the Production-Possibilities Frontier

Altered assumptions alter the frontier. The frontier would shift from abcdef, *for example, to* ghi *if resources were lost to earthquakes or floods. Improved technologies or newly discovered resources would shift the frontier out to* mnp. *Shortfalls, such as recessions, cause the economy to be inside the frontier at points like* x.

only in Kansas and wheat confined to Mississippi? Then we would obviously *not* be producing bread and apparel to our maximum potential.

2. Trade-Offs and Opportunity Costs If the economy is inside the production-possibilities frontier because of idle resources or inefficient use of resources, say at point *j* in Figure 2.1, then the output of *both* bread and apparel could be increased by putting resources to use efficiently. A jump from *j* to *d* would add 10 million loaves of bread and 5 million pounds of apparel. However, once the economy is on the production-possibilities frontier, such twin boosts are impossible. Increased output of one good can occur only with reduced output of the other. Scarcity closes the frontier, forcing a trade-off.

For example, at combination *d* in Table 2.1 and Figure 2.1 (with 30 bread and 20 apparel), an added 10 million loaves of bread can be produced only by sacrificing 9 million pounds of apparel. The plus and the minus move the economy from combination *d* to combination *e*. The plus and minus occur as land and other resources are shifted from apparel to bread production.

Would this move from *d* to *e* be a wise choice? The answer depends on two-question logic: (1) What are its (the added bread's) benefits? (2) What are its costs? The first question cannot be answered without further information. However, the answer to the second question illustrates one of the most fundamental concepts of economics, namely, the *opportunity cost.* What must be given up for the 10 million added loaves of bread in *e* as compared to *d*? Answer: 9 million pounds of apparel as apparel output drops from 20 to 11 million pounds (see column 4 of Table 2.1). Notice that we are not referring to dollar costs, but these are costs nevertheless.

It is scarcity's forced choice that gives rise to such opportunity costs, so such costs are part of every choice. Your choice to study this book at this moment requires you to give up the study of another book or miss out on a movie. Society's use of land for farming means a loss of forest acreage, and so on.

Opportunity cost is, in general, the sacrifice of the next best alternative when a choice is made. The opportunity cost of a product is

the other products given up (e.g., apparel for bread).

3. Increasing Costs The data of column 4 in Table 2.1 and the curvature of the production-possibilities frontier in Figure 2.1 disclose that the opportunity cost of producing additional bread *increases* as more bread and less apparel is produced. Moving from point *a* to point *b*, the first 10 million loaves of bread cost the economy 3 million pounds of apparel. Moving from *b* to *c*, the next 10 million loaves cost 5 million pounds of apparel. From 3 and 5 million pounds the cost then rises to 7, 9, and 11 million pounds for each added 10 million loaves of bread.

The principle of increasing cost says that the opportunity cost rises as more of a particular commodity is produced.

What causes cost to increase? Different resources have different productive capacities for different goods. In the present example, for instance, the resources of Mississippi are best suited for the production of apparel (cotton), while the resources of Kansas are best suited for the production of bread (wheat).This means that at *a*, where *no* bread is produced, Kansas is producing apparel along with Mississippi. Movement from no bread at *a* to 10 million loaves at *b* is achieved at relatively little cost in apparel because it is Kansas's land, labor, and capital that are being shifted to wheat in that first step rather than Mississippi's land, labor, and capital (assuming, as we are, maximum potential use at each step). As more bread is produced, however, resources less and less well suited for bread (and better and better suited for apparel) are shifted from apparel to bread, causing the cost of bread in forgone apparel to rise. The last step, *e* to *f*, is especially costly, as the best remaining apparel resources in Mississippi are, to the last acre, person, and machine, converted from apparel to bread production (the best being saved for last).

The bowed-out shape of the production-possibilities frontier obviously applies to apparel as well as to bread. Hence, reverse movement from *f* toward *a*, for more apparel and less bread, would entail an increasing opportunity cost of apparel by way of forgone bread. As an example of this reverse movement, U.S. acreage in winter wheat declined 18 percent between 1982 and 1983 because of government policy. Yet this 18 percent drop in acreage caused only an 8 percent drop in output because the acreage was not prime wheat land. If it were the *last* 18 percent of wheat acreage, prime acreage, instead of the *first* 18 percent, the loss in output would have been much greater, maybe 30 percent.

B
What? How? Who?

Figure 2.3 illustrates the relationship between the production possibilities frontier and the basic questions What?, How?, and Who?. To answer the question What?, our hypothetical society must choose some combination of bread and apparel output within the realm of possibilities. This choice will depend on people's tastes and preferences, plus the opportunity costs of bread and apparel. People will, in other words, use two-question logic. Let's suppose that the chosen combination is *d*, with 30 million loaves of bread and 20 million pounds of apparel. This, then, would answer What?.

As for How?, combination *d* is *on* the produc-

tion-possibilities frontier instead of inside it, so we know that, with this choice, society is using its resources to maximum potential. Wheat is concentrated in Kansas while cotton is budding mostly in Mississippi. If plantings were contrary, the economy would be held to some smaller combination, such as 26 units of bread and 17 of apparel.

To depict an answer to the question Who?, we might assume that by head count, half the population is rich and the other half is poor. Befitting these labels, Figure 2.3 shows the rich half getting *more* than half of this economy's outputs (20 million loaves of bread and 15 million pounds of apparel), while the poor half gets *less* than half of the outputs (10 million loaves of bread and 5 million pounds of apparel).

V
Exchange Possibilities and Specialization

As it stands, the previous analysis might leave you with the impression that the population of Kansas, though well fed with bread, must work naked in

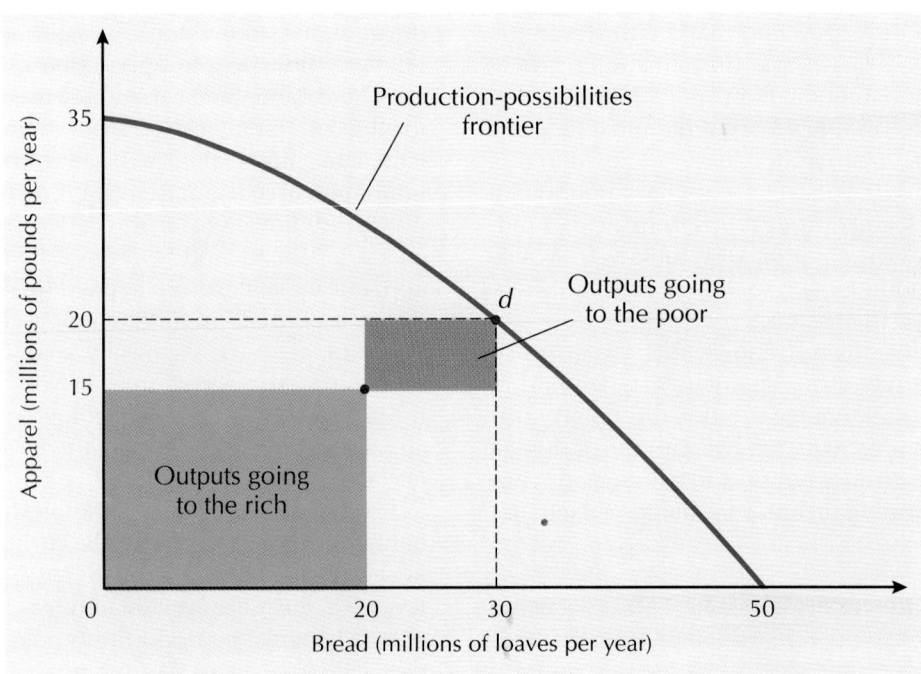

FIGURE 2.3   What, How, and Who in the Production-Possibilities Frontier

their wheat fields, while overdressed and underfed cotton growers populate Mississippi. A silly
thought. One made even sillier by contemplating
state specializations of all sorts—Idaho's potatoes,
Michigan's autos, Nebraska's corn, California's
wine, Florida's oranges, Wisconsin's cheese, Texas's oil, Oregon's lumber, Pennsylvania's steel, and
so on. Although states specialize in *production,*
they obviously do not specialize in *consumption.*
The gap between production and consumption is
bridged by *exchange* (i.e., *trade*), the essence of
market activity. Exchange makes specialization in
production possible. In turn, this specialization
vastly enhances the productivity of resources. We
shall look into exchange possibilities first, and
then explore the marvels of specialization.

A
Exchange Possibilities

Exchange possibilities arise when the opportunity costs of self-supply differ among
those who might engage in exchange.

Individuals engage in exchange, as when the
doctor sets the broken arm of the accountant, who
in turn does the doctor's taxes. *Companies* engage
in exchange, as when the auto company buys steel
and the steel company buys a fleet of autos. *States*
engage in exchange—e.g., Iowa's hogs for Kentucky's coal. *Nations*, too, partake, as when the
United States and Brazil trade computers and coffee.

Exchange becomes an attractive possibility in
each of these instances because independent self-
supply imposes opportunity costs that differ between the parties. With different opportunity
costs, self-supply becomes *more costly* than supply through buying and selling, i.e., market exchange. Wheeling and dealing thus beats complete independence. Differing opportunity costs
push two-question logic into motion toward
trade.

Table 2.2 illustrates exchange possibilities by
giving production-possibilities data for two states,
Mississippi and Kansas, for two goods, wheat and
cotton, with opportunity costs differing between
the states. For simplicity it is assumed that,
although the opportunity costs in Mississippi differ from those in Kansas, the costs within each
state are not increasing, but are instead *constant.*
The data are graphed in Figure 2.4, which displays
straight-line production-possibilities frontiers.

Looking first at Mississippi, we see from its production-possibilities frontier that maximum cotton output is 30 units (wheat then being zero) and
maximum wheat output is 30 units (cotton then
being zero). As more and more cotton is produced,
from 0 to 10 to 20 to 30 units, wheat output falls
from 30 to 20 to 10 to 0 units. The opportunity cost
of *each* added +10 units of cotton is thus a −10
units of wheat, which is shown in Table 2.2 for
Mississippi just below the production-possibilities
data. Conversely, *each* step toward more wheat
and less cotton yields +10 wheat and −10 cotton,
as shown in the last line on Mississippi's side of
Table 2.2. This is what is meant by *constant* cost.

TABLE 2.2 **Annual Production Possibilities and Opportunity Costs for Mississippi and Kansas in the Production of Cotton and Wheat**

Mississippi					Kansas					
Cotton (units)	0	10	20	30	Cotton (units)	0	10	20	30	40
Wheat (units)	30	20	10	0	Wheat (units)	80	60	40	20	0

→ More cotton and less wheat →

Benefit in cotton	+10	+10	+10	Benefit in cotton	+10	+10	+10	+10
Cost in wheat	−10	−10	−10	Cost in wheat	−20	−20	−20	−20

← More wheat and less cotton ←

Cost in cotton	−10	−10	−10	Cost in cotton	−10	−10	−10	−10
Benefit in wheat	+10	+10	+10	Benefit in wheat	+20	+20	+20	+20

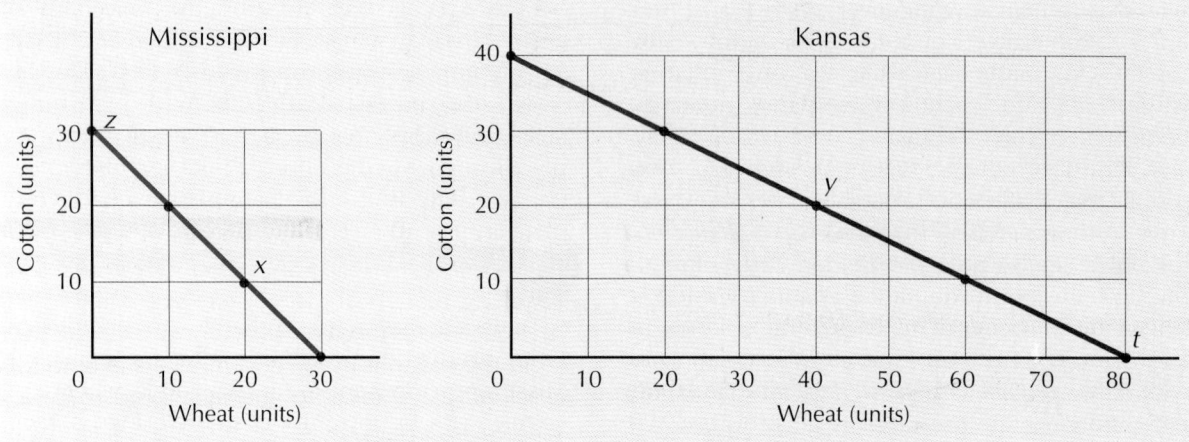

FIGURE 2.4 *Production Possibilities for Mississippi and Kansas, Individually, in Cotton and Wheat*

In Figure 2.4, the straight line with a slope of −10/10, or −1, signals the same.

Looking next at Kansas, we see that maximum cotton output is 40 units (wheat then being zero), while maximum wheat output is 80 units. Thus, at the extremes, it is assumed here that Kansas can produce more cotton than Mississippi (40 versus 30 units) and more wheat (80 versus 30 units). This is called an **absolute advantage** for Kansas. Such an absolute advantage signifies that Kansas is blessed with particularly rich resources in comparison to Mississippi. And it might seem to suggest that Kansas would prefer to go it alone, to operate in isolation without exchange. But this is *not* true. *The opportunity costs of Kansas differ from those of Mississippi, and it is this difference that opens exchange possibilities.*

Moving in the direction of more cotton and less wheat, Kansas experiences a cost of −20 units of wheat for each added +10 units of cotton (see the midsection on the right side of Table 2.2). Moving in the opposite direction of more wheat and less cotton, Kansas gains +20 units of wheat for a cost of −10 units of cotton at each step. The cost ratio of cotton to wheat in Kansas is thus −½, quite different from Mississippi's ratio of −¼. The opportunity cost of 1 added unit of cotton in Kansas is −2 units of wheat; in Mississippi it is −1 unit of wheat. Conversely, the opportunity cost of 1 added unit of wheat in Kansas is −½ unit of cotton; in Mississippi it is −1 unit of cotton. In sum:

Mississippi
cost of 1 cotton = 1 wheat
cost of 1 wheat = 1 cotton
Kansas
cost of 1 cotton = 2 wheat
cost of 1 wheat = ½ cotton

Exchange possibilities arise, then, because of these cost differences. *Cotton is cheaper to produce in Mississippi than in Kansas (1 unit of wheat vs. 2). Wheat is cheaper to produce in Kansas than in Mississippi (½ unit of cotton vs. 1).*

Thus, although Kansas has an *absolute advantage* in both cotton and wheat, it has a *comparative advantage* in wheat. Mississippi, on the other hand, has a *comparative advantage* in cotton. Table 2.2 acknowledges these comparative advantages by shading, while Figure 2.4 shows them with production-possibilities frontiers of differing slopes.

A **comparative advantage** is the ability to produce a good or service relatively cheaply (with a low opportunity cost).

The **law of comparative advantage** states that individuals, companies, regions, or nations can gain by specializing in the production of goods and services that they produce relatively cheaply and exchange them for other goods and services that they produce relatively expensively.

B

Exchange and Specialization

Of course, Mississippi and Kansas could refuse to trade. Let's assume that, without trade, Mississippi would *produce and consume* 10 units of cotton and 20 units of wheat, indicated as point *X* in Figure 2.4. Let's also say that, without trade, Kansas would *produce and consume* 20 units of cotton and 40 units of wheat, placing it at point *Y* in Figure 2.4. Although these might be points of survival, maybe even some comfort for Mississippi and Kansas, *the welfare of these states could be greatly improved* if they converted the exchange possibilities into exchange realities, with Mississippi specializing in cotton and Kansas specializing in wheat. Let's see why **specialization** would be beneficial by applying two-question logic to each state.

Would Mississippi willingly offer 10 units of its cotton in exchange for 16 units of Kansas wheat? In two-question logic:

1. What is the offer worth in benefits? Answer: 16 units of wheat.
2. What does Mississippi give up in cost? Answer: 10 units of cotton, which would cost 10 units of wheat forgone to produce.

The benefit of 16 units of wheat exceeds the cost of 10 units of cotton (= 10 units of wheat lost to produce the cotton). Hence the offer *would* be made.

Would Kansas accept the offer? Its logic must consider two questions:

1. What is the offer worth in benefits? Answer: 10 units of cotton.
2. What must be given up? Answer: 16 units of wheat, which to produce would cost Kansas 8 units of cotton forgone by the shift of resources.

The benefit of 10 units of cotton exceeds the cost of 16 units of wheat (= 8 units of cotton lost to produce the wheat). Hence Kansas *would* accept the offer of cotton for wheat.

In the end, it is in the best interests of both Mississippi and Kansas to specialize and trade. Exchange ensues. Table 2.3 summarizes the results. *Without* trade, they each consume only what they each produce, and their combined total output is 30 units of cotton and 60 units of wheat. *With* trade, they each specialize in production, but not consumption, Mississippi producing 30 units of cotton and Kansas producing 80 units of wheat. The gain from specialization and trade is, therefore, 20 added units of wheat (80 versus 60), which will be shared between the two states to make them *both better off simultaneously*.

Notice that, despite appearances, the gain of 20 units of wheat is a *real* gain. The production-possibilities frontiers did not change, so the gain may seem like a magician's rabbit. But it is real nevertheless, achieved by *movements along* the production-possibilities frontiers, specializations that exploit comparative advantages, plus exchange. The gain is no less real than the gain achieved by, say, better weather or improved technology. Thus, *exchange is productive.* And the market, which by definition is systematic exchange, is truly marvelous at creating economic well-being.

Read Perspective 2A.

TABLE 2.3   Comparison of No-Trade and Trade Cases, Mississippi and Kansas, Based on the Data of Table 2.2

	Without Trade		
	Mississippi	**Kansas**	**Total Combined**
Cotton	10	20	30
Wheat	20	40	60
	With Trade		
	Mississippi	**Kansas**	**Total Combined**
Cotton	30	0	30
Wheat	0	80	80

PERSPECTIVE 2A
Economic Life in Medieval France

Specialization and exchange are, of course, not new. As early as 1268, 130 different crafts had career practitioners in Paris. Among these were shoemakers, furriers, tailors, barbers, locksmiths, ropemakers, water carriers, hatmakers, saddlers, pastry cooks, masons, coopers, jewelers, bakers, wine sellers, laundresses, oil merchants, roofers, doctors, painters, meat butchers, chicken butchers, copyists, blacksmiths, tanners, and plasterers. Exchange is, of course, implied by such specialization. Exchange also flowered in the busy Fairs of Champagne in eastern France, which served as some of the main commodity markets of Western Europe for a century and which were celebrated in medieval song and story. Massive quantities of luxurious fabrics changed hands at these popular gatherings. There were also goods that had to be weighed—like salt from Salins in Franche-Comté, sugar from Syria, wax from Morocco and Tunisia, dyestuffs galore (especially indigo from India), alum from Egypt, and wine and grain from many places. Still other commodities ranged from raw materials to fine handicrafts:

Armorers buy iron from Germany and steel from Spain. Lead, tin, and copper are on hand, from Bohemia, Poland, Hungary, and England. Furs and skins sold by local dealers compete with imports from across the Rhine and even from Scandinavia. Then there are luxury goods from the East, imported by the Italians: camphor, ambergris, musk, rubies, lapis lazuli, diamonds, carpets, pearls, and ivory tusks.[4]

[4] Joseph and Frances Gies, *Life in a Medieval City* (New York: Harper & Row, 1969), p. 217.

VI
Growth and Technological Change: What's New?

A
Introduction and Definitions

The production-possibilities frontier can also illustrate the basic economics of growth, which concerns the question What's new?. The reason for this is simple. The production-possibilities frontier shows feasible *outputs*, and by definition growth refers to outputs.

> **Growth** corresponds to the increasing outputs of goods and services associated with outward shifts of the production-possibilities frontier.

The following identity shows the two main sources of such expanding outputs:

$$\text{Output} = \text{input} \times \frac{\text{output}}{\text{input}}$$

Bursts of output, that is, growth, may thus be obtained either by increasing input or by increasing output/input (or some combination of these two).

Input simply refers to resource inputs, so growth would rise, at least temporarily, if we depleted our nonrenewable resources like coal more rapidly than before, or if we got lucky and discovered vast new reservoirs of oil beneath our lands, or if we raised our capital inputs through investment.

Output/input refers to the amount of output we get from a given amount of resource input, that is, **productivity.** In 1981, for example, the manufacture of one American compact car took about 84 hours of labor. One ton of steel required roughly 1 day of steelworker input. And our wheat output stood at about 32 bushels per acre of wheat land. *Gains* in output/input, or productivity increases, generate greater outputs *without physically increasing inputs.* Today, for instance, we produce nearly twice as much wheat per acre planted in wheat, and three times as much wheat per worker-hour applied to wheat farming, as we did three decades ago. Such gains in output/input can be achieved by capital investment (added farm machinery, for instance), but even more important is the contribution of *technological change* (such as *new types* of farm machinery and hybrid strains of seed).

Technological change thus fosters growth through improved *production processes* and by fashioning entirely *new goods.* Improved production processes boost the output of existing goods, shifting a given production-possibilities frontier outward. New goods, such as video games and radial tires, create entirely new axes for new production-possibilities frontiers. This can be a form of growth. Thus:

Technological change breaks old production-possibilities frontiers with process improvements and revolutionary new products.

We can now consider the two sources of growth—first from capital investment (input) and second from new process technologies (output/input).

B
Capital Investment (Input)

The two commodities depicted in the production-possibilities frontiers of Figure 2.5 are not bread and apparel but rather consumption goods and capital goods. *Consumption goods* are those we use for immediate enjoyment, such as bread and apparel. *Capital goods* are capital resources like factories, machinery, and railroads used to produce other goods. Placing these two goods into a trade-off is warranted not only because of the limits of scarcity, but also because capital goods are created through *investments* financed from

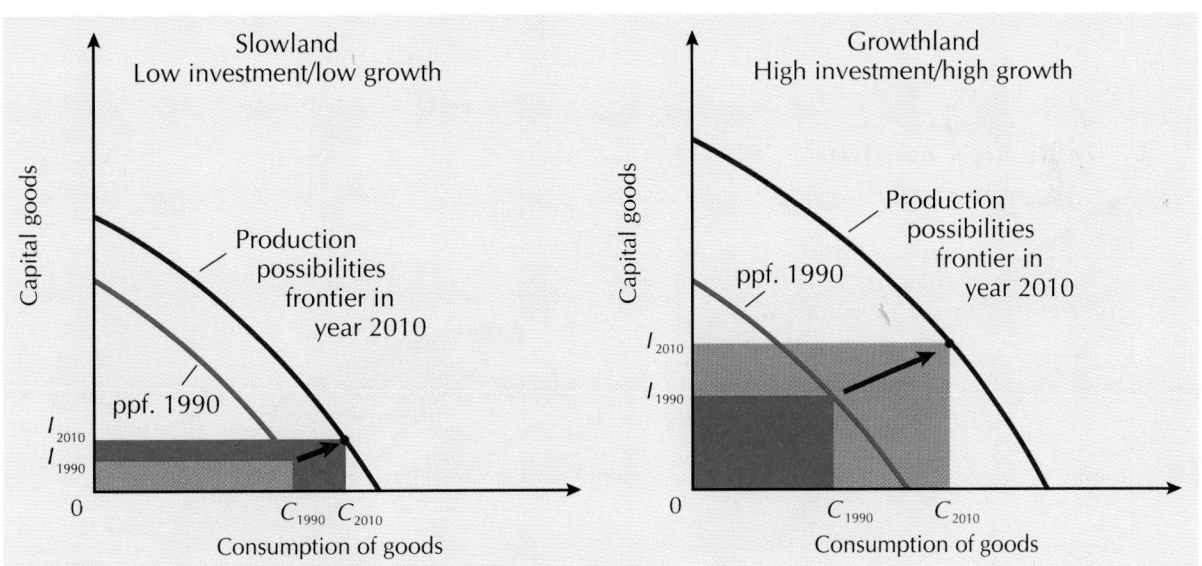

FIGURE 2.5 Capital Investment's Contribution to Growth
Beginning with production-possibilities frontiers that are identical in 1985, these diagrams show different growth depending on the level of investment. The low investment in Slowland (I_{1990} on the left is less than I_{1990} on the right) permits greater current consumption (C_{1990} on the left is greater than C_{1990} on the right). However, the extra investment in Growthland shifts its production-possibilities frontier outward to a greater extent, so that by 2000 Growthland has both greater consumption (C_{2010}) and investment (I_{2010}) than Slowland.

savings of all kinds. These savings must come from curtailed current consumption (just as your current investment in college curbs your current consumption). Two stories are told by Figure 2.5, that of Slowland and that of Growthland. They start with identical production-possibilities frontiers for the year 1990 (labeled *ppf 1990*), but they end up at quite different production-possibilities frontiers in 2010 because of divergent growth rates.

These ending differences occur because Slowland chooses a combination of consumption goods and capital goods that is relatively high in consumption and relatively low in investment compared to Growthland's combination. C_{1990} on the left is *higher* than C_{1990} on the right, while I_{1990} on the left is *lower* than I_{1990} on the right. The greater provision for capital in Growthland during 1990 gives Growthland more inputs during 1991 and later years. Since more inputs mean more potential outputs, its production-possibilities frontier shifts out more rapidly than Slowland's. The reward to Growthland for its continued thrift and investment can be clearly seen by comparing its bountiful production-possibilities frontier for the year 2010 with the more meager picture confronting Slowland. Indeed, Growthland's enhanced productive capacity is so great that in 2010 it has both a higher level of investment in capital *and* a higher consumption level than Slowland.

C
Technological Change (Output/Input)

Technological change is also obtained by investment, but it is investment in research and development rather than in capital accumulation. Hence the easiest way to explain what technological change contributes to growth is to point to how it boosts productivity. As previously mentioned, technological change fosters growth with stunning new *products* as well as marvelous new *production processes.* But for the moment, we must simplify.

Figure 2.6 shows production-possibilities frontiers for bread (wheat) and apparel (cotton) in a single economy once again. Here the frontiers refer to two different time periods, 1950 and 1985, with enough years passing between them to allow for ample new gadgetry, chemistry, or botany. If technological change raises productivity for *both* bread and apparel production, Part (a) of Figure 2.6 suggests the result. Such broad change pushes

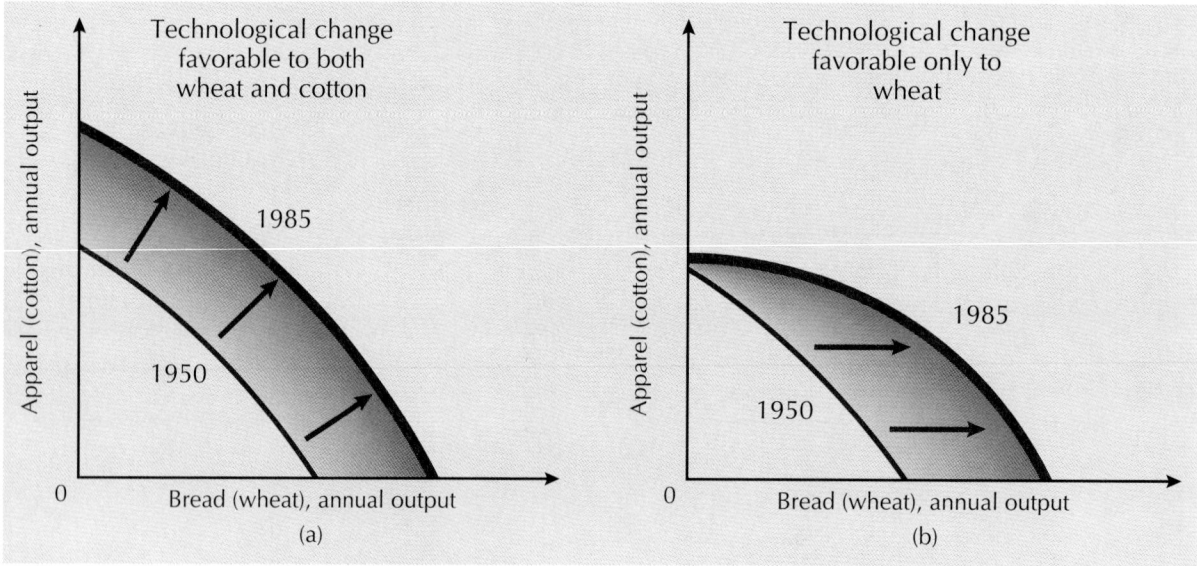

FIGURE 2.6 *Technological Change and Growth*

Broadly favorable technological change (e.g., new fertilizer) would shift the production-possibilities curve out along both axes over time, as shown in part (a). If, however, the change favors only wheat production (e.g., a new hybrid of wheat), the production-possibilities curve shifts out only along the wheat axis.

out the *entire* production-possibilities frontier from 1950 to 1985. This might be the result, for instance, of a new fertilizer that raised yields per acre planted in either wheat or cotton.

If, on the other hand, the technological change affects the productivity of only one good but not the other, the frontier will undergo a lopsided shift. In Figure 2.6 (b), it is assumed that technological change brings forth a new hybrid seed for wheat but leaves cotton horticulture unchanged. The result is vastly improved production possibilities for bread as wheat yields expand, but no change in the case of cotton apparel. In fact, observed changes between 1950 and 1980 in the United States follow a pattern that would be a *blend* of parts (a) and (b). Between 1950 and 1980 the yield per acre in wheat jumped 85 percent, while the yield per acre in cotton rose 59 percent.

Read Perspective 2B.

VII
Circular Flow: How Stable?

"Circular flow" is one of the most useful metaphors in economics. With it, we can leave simple situations involving two traders who barter two commodities and graduate to more complex situations involving many traders, many commodities, and money. From there, we can progress still further to consider the economy as a whole, which brings us finally to the macroeconomic question of How stable?

A
Barter versus Money Exchange

To think of folks in Mississippi and Kansas as directly trading cotton apparel and wheat bread across their borders stretches the imagination. They do not meter pounds and bushels shipped between them, with a balancing of commodity accounts at year's end. That is **barter,** *the direct exchange of goods and services without money.* The main problem with barter, and the reason it is rarely practiced, is that the parties to the exchange must have a double coincidence of wants. Such match-ups scarcely exist in the modern world. To work as a McDonald's counter attendant by barter, for instance, you would have to be willing to exchange your 6 hours of daily labor services for something like 12 Big Macs and 2 Cokes per day every day.

PERSPECTIVE 2B
New Technology in Metallurgy, Power Generation, and Transportation

Separate innovations often reinforce each other in their contribution to productivity and growth. "Metallurgical improvements, for example, were absolutely indispensable to the construction of more efficient steam engines. The steam engine, in turn, was utilized for introducing a hot blast of air into the blast furnace. The hot blast, by improving the efficiency of the combustion process, lowered fuel requirements and thereby reduced the price of iron. Thus, cheaper metal meant cheaper power, and cheaper power was translated into even cheaper metal. Similarly, the availability of cheap iron was essential to the construction of railroads. Once in place, however, the railroads reduced the considerable cost of transporting coal and iron ore to a single location. In this fashion, railroads reduced the cost of making iron. But cheaper iron, in turn, meant cheaper rails; this involved a further lowering of transportation costs which again decreased the cost of producing iron. Thus, part of the secret of the vast productivity improvements associated with the new industrial technology was that the separate innovations were often interrelated and mutually reinforcing."[5]

[5]Nathan Rosenberg, *Inside the Black Box: Technology and Economics* (Cambridge: Cambridge University Press, 1982), p. 246.

Earlier, Mississippi had to have cotton and had to want wheat, while at the same time Kansas had to have wheat and had to want cotton, for exchange to occur. What if this double coincidence did not exist? What if Mississippi wanted wheat, but Kansas did not want cotton? Say Kansas wanted lumber instead. Oregon, which we'll say wants cotton, abounds in lumber and could be brought into a multiparty exchange with the addition of *money*. Figure 2.7 depicts the result. Mississippi can buy wheat from Kansas with money. In turn, Kansas uses its money revenues to buy lumber from Oregon. Oregon completes the sequence by spending its money earnings on cotton from Mississippi (and this was the source of Mississippi's money in the first place, with which it bought wheat). Money flows in a clockwise direction, while commodities flow counterclockwise. The process could obviously be expanded to include many more traders and commodities.

The exchange process can expand, that is, insofar as those who join accept money in exchange for whatever they offer for sale. Money is the key. Money is the *medium* of exchange, as air is the medium of flight. "Money" itself can be almost anything. Primitive societies used shells. The American colonies used tobacco as money. Indeed, during the 1400s, Iceland priced commodities payable in *dried fish*—1 fish for one horse-shoe, 3 for a pair of women's shoes, 100 for a barrel of wine, and so on. Modern monies are issued and regulated by governments (and are therefore less smelly). The important point for exchange is that the seller accepts the "money" of the buyer as payment. The seller will accept it if he, in turn, can pay others with it, others who are likewise receptive because of common acceptance. Thus, "money" is money if it flows. It eliminates the need for a double coincidence of wants.

> **Money** is whatever is commonly accepted as payment in exchange for goods and services (and payment of debts and taxes).

B
Final Goods Markets and Factor Markets

Clearly, money fosters *systems* of exchange and specialization that greatly exceed anything barter could achieve in diversity, intensity, and prosperity. Figure 2.8 acknowledges this marvelous achievement with a simple circular flow diagram of the economy, simple because it excludes the government and other details. On the left are households like yours and ours. On the right are businesses like Coca-Cola, Levi's, and Ford. At the top are final goods markets, like those for soda,

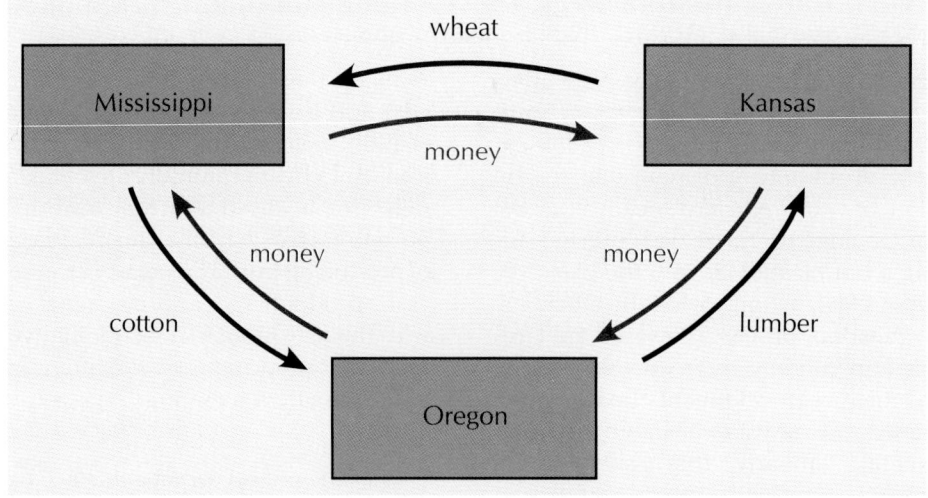

FIGURE 2.7 *Circular Flow of Expanded Exchange with the Introduction of Money*
Barter requires the double coincidence of wants. But money permits exchange without this double coincidence.

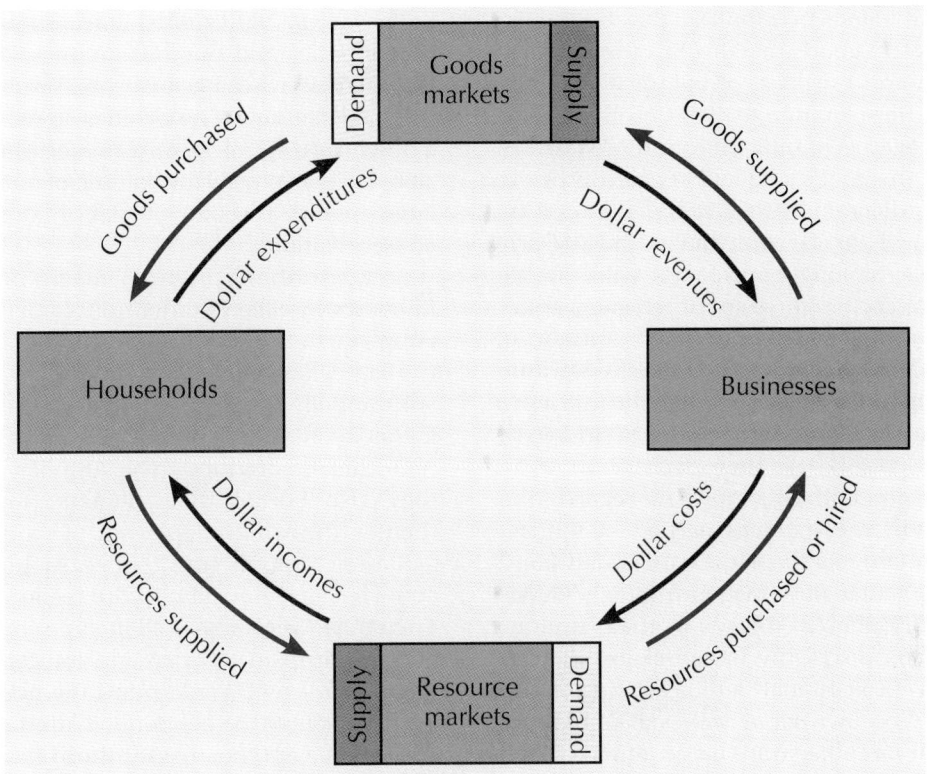

FIGURE 2.8 _Circular Flow of Economic Activity_

Exchange with money creates a circular flow of economic activity. Households, on the left, express their demand for goods with dollar payments. The goods are supplied by businesses, which receive money in exchange. Those receipts are used to purchase and hire resources (labor, land, capital, and entrepreneurship) in the resource markets. These resources are supplied by households, whose reward is various forms of dollar income (wages, profits, rents, etc.).

apparel, and autos. On the bottom are resource markets for labor, land, capital, and entrepreneurship. Note that the goods and resource markets each have a demand side for buyers and a supply side for sellers.

Households, in a manner familiar to us all, make up the demand side of the goods market. They make dollar payments to purchase goods. Those goods are supplied by businesses in exchange for the dollars spent by households. Of course, businesses do not fabricate final goods out of thin air. They produce them by using resources, which create dollar costs when purchased or hired in the resource markets. Those dollar costs pay for labor wages, land rents, capital interest, and entrepreneurial profits. In turn, these payments constitute the income earnings of households, the suppliers of productive resources.

At this point, we have returned to where we started in Figure 2.8—the households. The complete circuit shows money moving in a clockwise direction as it moves from the hands of demanders to the hands of suppliers, who are themselves demanders. In the opposite direction, goods and resources shuffle about as they are exchanged for money in their respective markets.

C
How Stable? (Plus What?, How?, and Who?)

At this point, we also return full circle to microeconomics, macroeconomics, and the fundamental questions raised by scarcity. In terms of Figure 2.8's circular flow, microeconomics is the study of the individual markets woven together by the exchange process—goods markets like those for radios, aspirin, and breakfast cereal, plus resource markets like those for auto workers, crude oil, and capital. The microeconomic question of What? is answered in the goods markets at the top of the circular flow diagram. Goods not demanded by households will not be supplied by businesses. Goods popular among households will, on the other hand, open the purses of purchasers, enticing business suppliers with the resulting revenues. The question How?, is primarily addressed in the lower-right-hand part of the circular flow diagram, where businesses must decide the kinds and combinations of resources they will employ to produce the goods they supply. As regards the question Who?, the incomes earned by households in resource markets (at the lower-left-hand part of the circular flow diagram) largely determine the distribution of income in the economy. Those who possess highly prized skills, such as doctors and professional athletes, those with drive, those who own large real-estate holdings, and those who in other ways can command high compensation from their resources will be rich and will consequently be the most prominent consumers in the goods market (mansions and yachts are goods). Those less well blessed will, accordingly, have to endure thinner and duller slices of the economic pie. The question What's new? receives attention at every turn. Fresh products are introduced to the goods market. New processes and novel labor skills stimulate resource markets.

The circular flow model informs us of both macroeconomics and microeconomics. The question How stable? arises because imbalances may throw the system askew. The circular flow could become a downward spiral, leading to recession or depression. Or, conversely, the volume of money in circulation could, through official actions, swell and cause inflation.

A clue to these unsavory macro-possibilities is found in the different identities of demanders and suppliers in the goods and resource markets. If, in the aggregate, household demand for goods drops substantially, a gap could open in the goods market as business suppliers are caught by surprise. As businesses reduce their supplies in response, they also curtail their demand for resources, thereby throwing people out of work and idling factories. This, in turn, squeezes household income because households are resource suppliers. Then the lower household income could mean yet another drop in the demand for goods, sending another pulse of woe around the circular flow to adversely affect the economy. With the behavior of households and businesses thus out of phase, the economy sputters. The circular flow tends to wobble.

Reversal into a boom may be no better synchronized. Spurts and lunges may then typify the upside of macroeconomic activity. Unsustained boom may then give way to renewed bust. Indeed, the upside and downside instability of the economy is frequent enough to win a special label— *business cycles.*

SUMMARY

1. There are two ways of approaching economics. Microeconomics is the study of individuals, firms, and markets—economics under a microscope. Macroeconomics studies aggregated sectors and variables, like consumer expenditure.

2. When thinking about economics, it helps to know the difference between problem solving (mainly positive) and dilemma addressing (mainly normative). Problems have solutions that may be reached by two-question logic. In microeconomics the two questions are (a) What are its benefits? and (b) What are its costs? For much of macro-

economics they are (a) What's expected? and (b) What happens? Dilemmas, on the other hand, defy easy solution because they arise from conflicting aims. Dilemmas produce compromises influenced by value judgments.

3. Economists lean heavily on models and *ceteris paribus* assumptions when explaining economics. These will help you understand the real world if you realize that they are not literally the real world, only simplifying representations. *Ceteris paribus* means "other things being constant."

4. The production-possibilities frontier is a

useful model built on the assumptions of (a) scarce resources, (b) fixed technology, and (c) full potential resource usage. It shows that scarcity compels choices for What?, How?, and Who? It also illustrates the concept of opportunity cost (what must be given up to get something else). Such costs often increase as more and more of a good is produced.

5. Differing opportunity costs confronting individuals, firms, regions, states, and nations generate exchange possibilities. The differing costs mean that isolated self-supply is more costly (and therefore less rewarding) than specialization and trade. Two-question logic demonstrates the gains. Specialization should correspond to comparative advantage (i. e., low opportunity cost). Do that which you do relatively best. In the end, exchange is productive.

6. Growth derives from the increasing outputs associated with outward shifts of the production-possibilities frontier. Either greater input or greater output/input increases output. Technological change boosts output/input, namely, productivity. The question What's new? may thus receive some exciting answers.

7. Barter is burdened by the need for coincident wants. Money erases this need by acting as a medium of exchange. Indeed, given that exchange is productive, money's aid to exchange is also productive, a tremendous aid to commerce. Money's contribution can best be seen in the concept of circular flow. At the macro-level, the circular flow concept divides the economy in two, with (a) households on the demand side of goods markets and the supply side of resource markets, while (b) businesses supply goods and demand productive resources. Money flows opposite to the flow of real goods and resources, much as air must flow opposite to a flying object. The key question of How stable? arises partly because the activities of households may not blend with those of businesses. Surprises result. Expectations may be assaulted by realities. The circular flow may therefore haltingly expand and contract to cause business cycles.

APPENDIX:
Adam Smith, The Founder of Economics

Adam Smith led a rather uneventful life. A Scotsman, he was born in 1723. Following a normal childhood, he studied at two fine universities, Glasgow and Oxford. Liking the intellectual life, he became a philosopher and college professor. When he died in 1790, his contemporaries held him in high regard, but he was not famous. By all accounts, his personality was bland. For lack of other subjects, legendary tales center on his absentmindedness, one instance in particular. Strolling in his garden one Sunday morning, wearing a dressing gown and deep in thought, he lost track of what he was doing, took a wrong turn, ended up on a country road, and walked 15 miles before his concentration was broken by ringing church bells. This unspectacular life notwithstanding, Adam Smith wrote one of the truly great books of Western civilization, *An Inquiry Into the Nature and Causes of the Wealth of Nations*. With this book, Smith firmly established himself as the founder of modern economics.

England in the age of Smith was filled with individualism and vigor. Captain James Cook's explorations were mentioned previously. More generally, the eighteenth century witnessed many innovations in art, literature, science, mathematics, industry, and agriculture. In politics and commerce, however, individualism was stifled by heavy-handed government intervention. British monarchs ruled with an iron fist. Indeed, these same British monarchs provoked the American colonists into rebellion, and it is pertinent that the *Wealth of Nations* was published in 1776, when the Declaration of Independence launched America's assault on the restrictive economic policies of the British crown. Smith's most enduring contribution was to explain how the invisible hand of the competitive market could replace the iron fist of the government as the basic economic decision-making mechanism of a society.

In essence, Smith argued against *mercantilism*, the prevailing economic and political philosophy of his day. According to mercantilism, the selfish desires of individuals would lead to economic chaos and ruin unless people were tightly regulated and controlled by the state. It was assumed that one person's gain was always another person's loss when personal efforts were left unchecked. Hence, government guidance and regulation was thought necessary to channel personal self-interests in directions beneficial to all. This, the mercantilists argued, would maximize a nation's overall wealth.

Smith recognized that this was basically wrong. He argued that self-interest was a blessing, not a blemish:

> It is not from the benevolence of the butcher, the brewer, or the baker, that we expect our dinner but from their regard to their own interest. We address ourselves, not to their humanity but to their self-love, and never talk to them of our necessities but of their advantages.

According to Smith, the pursuit of personal interest promotes the public interest within a context of individual freedom. The individual

> neither intends to promote the public interest, nor knows how much he is promoting it. . . . He intends only his own security . . . and he is in this, as in many other cases, led by an invisible hand to promote an end which was no part of his intention.

The invisible hand is _competitive market exchange._ It harnesses individual self-interests to bring prosperous order, not chaos. Besides the competitive market, Smith recognized the economic importance of two additional factors—_specialization_ and _capital accumulation._ Specialization emerges from market exchange and capital accumulation fosters economic growth. A noted historian of economic thought summarizes Smith's insights this way:

> Even though each person competed with all others for wealth and profit, their very competition unleashed market forces that led to an orderly increase in the wealth of the nation. The desire for prosperity, coupled with a natural tendency to trade and exchange, led to specialization, investment of capital, and stable economic growth. The free economy served the individual, whose needs and desires were met by the natural tendency of producers to make and sell what consumers desired. The welfare of the community was thereby maximized.[6]

The next chapter explores "market forces" in detail.

[6]Daniel R. Fusfeld, _The Age of the Economist_, 4th ed. (Glenview, Ill.: Scott, Foresman, 1982), p. 31.

KEY TERMS

Microeconomics
Macroeconomics
Two-question logic
Benefits
Costs
Marginal
Production-possibilities frontier
Opportunity cost
Principle of increasing cost
Exchange possibilities

Absolute advantage
Comparative advantage
"Law" of comparative advantage
Specialization
Growth
Productivity
Technological change
Barter
Money

QUESTIONS AND PROBLEMS

1. The cover is torn off a discarded textbook. You pick it up and flip through the pages, glancing at chapter titles and key words. They include: Stabilization Policies, Categories of Federal Spending, Measures of Inflation. Is it a microeconomics text or a macroeconomics text? How do you know?

2. What is the role of value judgments in addressing economic dilemmas? Use at least one example of an economic dilemma in your answer.

3. Explain what the *ceteris paribus* assumption is and why it is often essential in economic models.

4. Explain why some people specialize in teaching economics while others specialize in shoe repair. How have these people applied the law of comparative advantage?

5. Clark Kent III is a medical doctor. Being a male physician, he is quite confident that he could file insurance claims quicker and more accurately than Betty Jones, whom he hires for that task. Nonetheless, he does not fire Betty. Explain why.

6. Sam Smith, excited over fatherhood, has decided to resign his job as a sales representative for Blue Inc. to stay home with the new baby for three years. His wife, Margaret, will continue to work, as before. What are the opportunity costs of this decision by Sam?

7. What two-question logic should Sam Smith have used (in Question 6) to decide whether to resign for full-time fatherhood?

8. Would you expect more rapid economic growth in a modern economy or in an extremely poor country in which few people have even enough to eat? Explain why.

9. Barter economies are primitive economies in which each family relies primarily on its own production to meet its needs. Explain why.

10. Why is a production possibilities frontier well described as a snapshot of existing capabilities?

11. Production possibilities frontiers have often been drawn to explain the "guns versus butter" decision. Compare the values of the Swiss with those of the U.S. and the Soviet Union using production possibilities analysis.

12. If productivity increases, does production necessarily increase? Explain the relationship between the two.

From the appendix:

13. Adam Smith argued that the pursuit of self-interest becomes the pursuit of the common good in a free and competitive market. Can you suggest any weaknesses in his argument? Do these weaknesses justify government intervention?

3

The Market: Desirable Process and Results

Every summer about 60 men climb 4,500 orange trees in Florida to count green, unripened oranges. The trees are only a small sample of the state's 46 million orange trees, and only one branch of each sampled tree is tallied. But the work is brutal. Its perils include 100°F heat, falls, thorns, rattlesnakes, and fire ants. Moreover, visual guesswork will get a counter fired. To avoid missing even one tiny green orange on a selected branch, the climber must feel along its entire length to get the number right. Then his number is crosschecked by a second climber, who gropes his way to a talley.

Why all this painstaking labor just to count green oranges? The U.S. Department of Agriculture runs the count to forecast each October the annual supply of oranges. That supply forecast can mean millions of dollars in profits or losses for commodities traders because supply affects price, the price of orange juice in particular. Indeed, the stakes are so large that the estimate is secret until officially released. Counters face jail and a $1,000 fine for blabbing. Federal officials who compile the data work behind locked doors, drawn shades, and armed guards. During "lockup" day, even their phones are disconnected.[1] The orange juice market is a big one.

Recall that our economy relies mainly on markets to crank out answers to the key questions raised by scarcity. Recall also that markets mean *exchange*, with buyers on the *demand side* and sellers on the *supply side*. This chapter portrays one particular type of market—the *perfectly competitive* market. Looked at in positive economic terms, perfectly competitive markets in the real world cover important chunks of the economy aside from oranges (e.g., agriculture generally, common stocks, and foreign currencies). How they work in terms of demand and supply is both interesting and instructive. (Demand-side mechanics are, in fact, applicable to many markets that are not perfectly competitive.) Looked at in normative economic terms, the perfectly competitive market offers a theoretical ideal of sorts. It is, in brief, a

[1] *Wall Street Journal*, September 14, 1983, pp. 1, 20.

54

decentralized decision-making process that yields allocative efficiency as one of its chief results.

I
Perfect Competition Defined

Put yourself in the dusty shoes of a Florida orange grower. Would the government's crop estimate interest you? Indeed it would. Florida's overall supply of oranges will dramatically affect the price of your crop and therefore your annual income. You don't set the price. The market does. And to learn about the price, you have to check news reports about market developments. If you're a wheat farmer or cattle rancher, the situation is the same. You consult the press for prices. You're a price *taker*.

Now put yourself in the polished shoes of the president of General Motors. Do you read the *Detroit News* or *Wall Street Journal* to find out the price of Chevrolets? No, of course not. The press doesn't tell you the price of your cars. You tell the press what the price is going to be. You're a price *maker*.

A key feature of perfectly competitive markets is that sellers in them are price takers, not price makers. The same applies to buyers. The reason for this is seen in the several conditions that characterize perfectly competitive markets.

In a **perfectly competitive market:**
1. There are many buyers and sellers, who each account for only a small share of the business.
2. The product is standardized, or homogeneous, so that sellers offer identical products.
3. The entry of newcomers into the market is easy.
4. All buyers and sellers are well informed about prices, qualities, product availabilities, and other pertinent facts.

As a whole, these conditions deny individual buyers or sellers any power over price. One tiny seller among a multitude cannot set the price, especially if his or her product is exactly like that of all the others. (There are some 10,000 orange growers in Florida cultivating the standard, juicy Valencia variety.) Easy entry by newcomers and fully informed participants further curb an individual's aspirations for price control in a perfectly competitive market. Entrants are potential competitors. Knowledgeable buyers cannot be fooled by sellers who overcharge, while knowledgeable sellers will not be ripped off by buyers who would like to underpay. Hence the term *price taker* for both buyers and sellers is fitting for such markets.

Most markets are not perfectly competitive because of their failure to meet one or more of these conditions. For example, point by point:

1. There are relatively few sellers of automobiles—General Motors, Ford, Chrysler, and Toyota, plus a handful of others. The extreme opposite of perfect competition in the number of firms is *pure monopoly*, where there is only one seller.
2. The products of auto companies, like those of many manufacturers, are not standardized because each company has its own unique features from brand name to engineering. Products not standardized are said to be *differentiated*.
3. As for ease of entry, many markets have at least moderate barriers against the entry of newcomers. Patents, for instance, pose problems for start-up pharmaceutical companies.
4. Consumers tend to be poorly informed buyers. Studies show that they often buy high-priced brands that are actually lower in quality than low-priced brands.[2]

Where one or more of these several conditions occurs, the market is said to be *imperfectly competitive*.

[2] R. T. Morris and C. S. Bronson, "The Chaos of Competition Indicated by Consumer Reports," *Journal of Marketing* (July 1969), pp. 26–34.

Imperfect competition occurs when there are (1) few sellers or buyers, (2) nonstandardized, differentiated products, (3) barriers to new entry, or (4) poorly informed buyers or sellers.

Price *makers* populate such imperfectly competitive markets because these conditions give them *some* power over the price—not necessarily complete power, only *some* power.

We call attention to imperfections for two reasons. First, they accent the nature of the perfectly competitive market. The absence of these imperfections creates price takers. Second, market imperfections—such as powerful monopoly on the seller's side and ignorance on the buyer's side—help to explain why the perfectly competitive market serves as a normative ideal for desirable choice procedures (see Part (b) of Figure 1.1). That is to say, perfectly competitive conditions suit many of the value judgments our society holds for decision-making procedures. Many buyers and sellers suggest a widely decentralized decision-making process. Free entry implies freedom of enterprise. Full information suggests that no one in a perfectly competitive market can be fooled or treated dishonestly—two signs of unfairness. And so on. (Recall Table 1.1.)

At this point, you may be thinking: Fine. I appreciate that perfect competition might serve as an ideal for both process and results. But if everyone in a perfectly competitive market is a price taker, then how is the price actually determined?

The answer is that the price is determined by the interaction of demand and supply. Let's see how.

II

Demand-Side Mechanics

A

Demand Defined

When economists adopt a word to express some economic notion, its ordinary meaning is often ignored. Such is the case with *demand*. Its everyday meaning—strong request—does not apply here. Moreover, as economic jargon, *demand* is used in three different contexts. First, there is *individual buyer* demand, such as your demand for apples. Second, there is *marketwide* demand, which is the demand that results when all individual buyer demands are added together. Thus, if you are typical, you eat about 20 pounds of fresh apples a year—your contribution to the national, marketwide total of close to 5 billion pounds. Third, and finally, there is demand *as viewed by the individual seller.* Marketwide demand and demand as viewed by the individual seller will be the same only when the seller is a monopolist. Since such a seller is the *sole* seller in the market, his or her view of demand corresponds to marketwide demand. More typically, however, with more than one seller, each seller views his or her demand as if it were some slice of marketwide demand.

The demand of interest to us here is *marketwide demand.* Just how wide the market can be varies geographically. Its scope depends on such things as transportation costs and tariffs. For instance, cement's market is local, with shipments not usually going more than a few hundred miles. Wheat's market spans the nation and in many respects is actually an international market. Marketwide demand is, in short, the demand of all buyers who participate in the market for that product. (Moreover, marketwide demand is not greatly influenced by supply-side imperfections. For this reason, our discussion of marketwide demand typically applied to demand generally—the demand for autos as well as for oranges, for instance.)

In this context, then, *demand* is a quantity–price relationship for some particular good or service:

Demand for a good or service is the set of various quantities buyers would purchase at

various prices during some specified time period (other things being constant).

The key words in this definition are *quantities, prices,* and *time period.* Because quantities and prices are related in a *set,* they may be represented by either a *demand schedule* or a *demand curve.*

Table 3.1 shows a hypothetical *demand schedule* for hamburger. It tells us that if the price of hamburger were $1.50 per pound, consumers would purchase, that is, demand, 10 million pounds per week. If the price were only $1.25 per pound, 15 million pounds of hamburger would be demanded weekly, an amount much greater than the 10 million pounds associated with $1.50. Note the care we take to specify the scales involved—dollars per pound (not cents per ton), millions of pounds (not billions of ounces), and a week (not a year). A change in any scale could yield silly results. (We eat a lot of hamburger in the United States, but not 40 billion tons per week. That would be 200 tons per person per week.)

Any demand schedule becomes a *demand curve* when graphed. Figure 3.1 shows the demand curve for the demand schedule of Table 3.1, with price on the vertical axis and quantity on the horizontal axis. Each point—*a, b, c, d,* and *e*—corresponds to its lettered price–quantity combination in Table 3.1. Point *b* in Figure 3.1, for example, tells us that 15 million pounds of hamburger will be demanded if the price is $1.25 per pound. This price–quantity combination matches that of *b* in Table 3.1.

A **demand schedule** or **demand curve** shows the various quantities of a good or service that buyers would purchase at various possible prices during some time period (ceteris paribus).

TABLE 3.1   Demand Schedule for Hamburger

	Price (Dollars Per Pound)	Quantity Demanded (Millions of Pounds Per Week)
a	$1.50	10
b	1.25	15
c	1.00	20
d	0.75	30
e	0.50	40

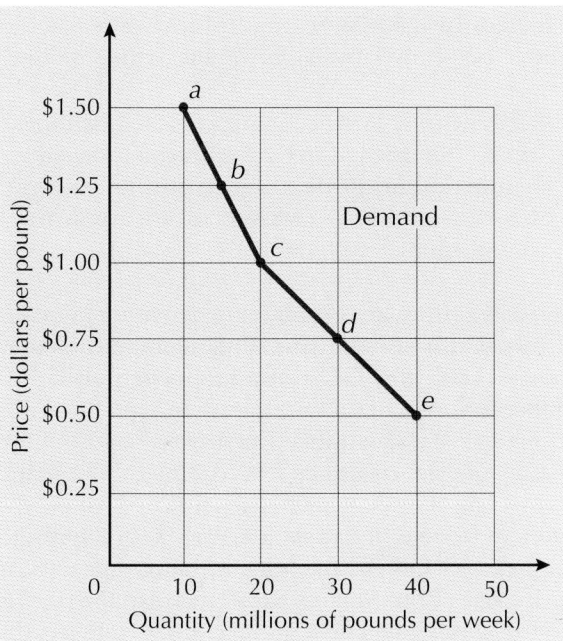

FIGURE 3.1   The Demand Curve for Hamburger

This graph, derived from the data of Table 3.1, shows the various amounts of hamburger that would be purchased at various possible prices during a week's time. When the price is $1.50 a pound, the quantity demanded is 10 million pounds at point a. At lower prices, greater quantities are demanded. At $0.50 a pound, 40 million pounds would be purchased per week (point e). The curve connecting these points is the demand curve for hamburger.

B
The Law of Demand

There is a distinct pattern in the set of price–quantity combinations of Table 3.1 and Figure 3.1. When the price is relatively high, the quantity demanded is relatively low. Conversely, when the price is relatively low, the quantity demanded is relatively high. Thus, if the price falls, the quantity demanded increases. Alternatively, if the price rises, the quantity demanded falls. This negative or inverse pattern occurs so regularly that it has become the *law of demand.*

> The **law of demand** says that the price of a good and the quantity demanded vary inversely (or negatively) when other factors are held constant.

As stated, this inverse or negative relationship assumes that other factors affecting demand, fac-

tors such as consumer income and the prices of other goods, are held constant *(ceteris paribus).* Holding these other factors constant, there are two main reasons why the quantity demanded falls as the price rises. The *first* reason is *substitution.* If the price of hamburger rises while the prices of chicken and pork remain constant, people will buy less hamburger and more chicken and pork, substituting chicken and pork for hamburger. Between 1975 and 1980, supermarket beef prices rose 53 percent (hamburger alone going from 85 cents a pound to nearly $2 a pound). The prices of chicken and pork rose much less rapidly. As a result, annual beef consumption *fell* from 95 to 78 pounds per person during those years, while per capita poultry and pork consumption *rose* 30 percent.[3] If the price of hamburger had fallen, the substitution effect would work in the opposite direction. Virtually all goods have substitutes people can turn to, so virtually all goods abide by the law of demand.

The *second* reason for the inverse relationship is that, as the price rises, people feel poorer. If their income is held constant (by the *ceteris paribus* assumption), the higher price they have to pay for hamburger will reduce their purchasing power of all commodities. Their income does not go as far as it did before the price hike. A family might spend, say, $300 a year on beef priced at $1 a pound. If the price jumped to $2 a pound, the family would then have to spend $600 instead of $300 to purchase the same amount of beef. Hence its income would have to rise $300 to cover the price hike. But without the income boost, the family feels poorer and therefore buys less beef. This is an adverse *income effect.* It, too, contributes to the inverse relationship between price and quantity demanded. (Price reductions produce favorable income effects.)

C
Shifts versus Movements Along the Demand Curve

Pause and reflect. We have now defined demand, reviewed a demand schedule, plotted a demand curve, and acknowledged the law of demand—all

---

[3]*Wall Street Journal,* July 28, 1980, p. 1.

illustrated with the example of hamburger. These several points may be summarized by stating that *the quantity demanded of a good is a negative function of the price of that good, other things held constant.* In illustrating, we have considered *only* the quantity and price of hamburger. Now we can explore the impact of the other factors affecting demand. For, in truth, other things are not always constant in the real world. The demand for a good is a function of the price of that good and *also a function of several other factors.*

These other factors include (1) tastes or preferences, (2) income, (3) the prices of related goods, substitutes and complements in particular, (4) the number of buyers, and (5) buyer expectations. These other factors are taken into account through *shifts* of the demand curve because the only determinant of demand expressely recognized with an axis in Figure 3.1 is the price of the commodity. Changes in the price of hamburger can thus be shown in Figure 3.1 to cause *movements along* the demand curve for hamburger, say from point *c* to point *b* or from *c* to *d*. In contrast,

changes in income or one of these other factors must be shown by *shifts of the entire demand curve.*

> When the price of the good changes, causing a **movement along** the demand curve, the result is called a **change in the quantity demanded.**

> When other factors affecting demand change, causing a **shift** of the entire demand curve, the result is called a **change in demand.**

Figure 3.2 illustrates the several possibilities with specific reference to hamburger. Demand curve *ae* in each part is patterned after the demand curve of Figure 3.1. Part (a) of Figure 3.2 shows changes in the price of hamburger. If the price rises from $1.00 to $1.25, the resulting movement along the curve from *c* to *b* reduces the quantity demanded from 20 to 15 million pounds. Conversely, if the price falls from $1.00 to $0.75 per pound, the quantity demanded rises from 20 to 30

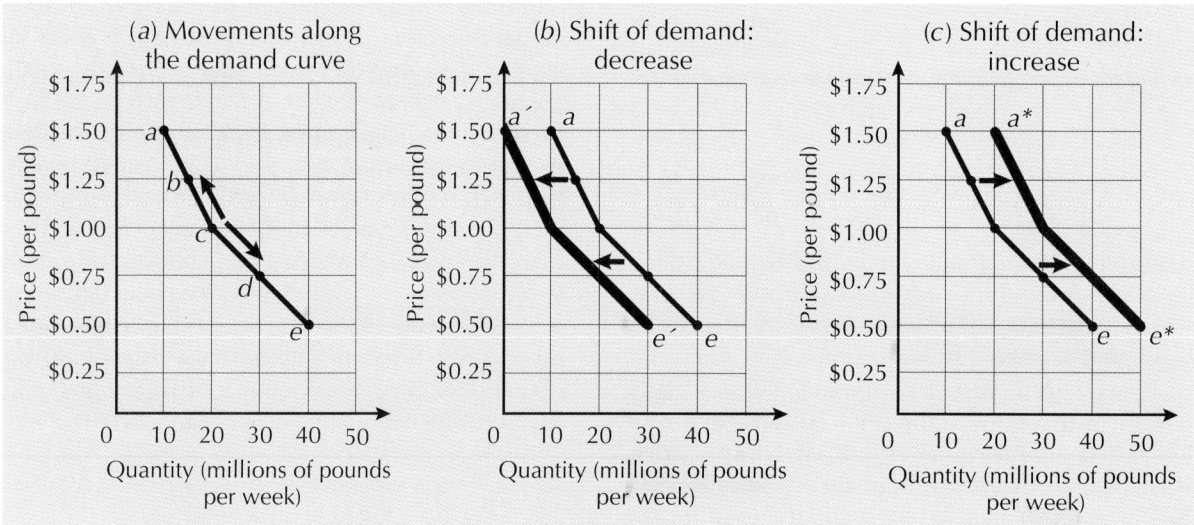

FIGURE 3.2 Movements Along versus Shifts in Demand

(a) Change in quantity demanded. *If the price rises from $1.00 to $1.25, the quantity demanded falls from 20 to 15, with movement along the demand curve from c to b. If the price falls from $1.00 to $.75, the quantity demanded rises from 20 to 30. (b) If the taste for hamburger weakens, or if some other factors cuts consumer willingness to pay, demand decreases, shifting to the left. Less is then demanded at each price. (c) If the taste for hamburger grows, or if some other factor boosts consumer willingness to pay, demand increases, shifting to the right. More is then demanded at each price.*

million pounds, a movement along the curve from *c* to *d*.

Part (b) of Figure 3.2 depicts a *decrease in demand* due to other factors by showing a leftward shift in the entire demand curve from *ae* to *a'e'*. In this event, *less quantity is demanded at each possible price.* At a price of $1.00, for instance, the quantity demanded drops from 20 to 10 million pounds per week. At a price of $0.50, demand falls from 40 to 30 million pounds as a result of the shift.

Finally, Part (c) of Figure 3.2 reports an increase in demand due to other factors, as revealed in a shift to the right. In this case, *more is demanded at each possible price* when demand becomes *a*e** instead of *ae*. At a price of $1.50, for instance, demand doubles from 10 to 20 million pounds. At a price of $0.75, the quantity jumps from 30 to 40 million pounds.

Why do these other factors, like tastes and incomes, cause such shifts in demand? What changes in these factors propel shifts to the left and right? Let's begin with tastes.

1. Tastes (Preferences) People's preferences for commodities change. During the early 1970s, for instance, bicycles became the rage. Sales more than doubled in 3 years, from 6.9 million in 1970 to 15.3 million in 1973. The surge occurred because physical fitness won new popularity among consumers. Millions of adults took up bike riding to trim their flabby waistlines and strengthen their hearts. Favorable swings of preferences such as this shift the demand curve to the right (Figure 3.2c). Conversely, diminishing preferences shift the demand curve to the left (Figure 3.2b).

2. Income The impact of income is fairly obvious. A rise in income causes the demand for most goods to increase, as people enjoy their greater prosperity with greater purchases (Figure 3.2c). Decreases in income foster the opposite and sadder result—a drop in the demand for most goods (Figure 3.2b). We say "most" goods because most goods are *normal goods*, whose demand moves in the same direction—up or down—as changes in income. The positive association is especially pronounced for high-priced durable goods like autos, boats, appliances, and swimming pools.

However, there are a few exceptions. The de-

mand for *inferior goods* actually falls with greater income and rises with lower income. Examples include corn meal, used cars, day-old bread, porridge, washboards, bus rides, and black-and-white TV sets. These items are staples for the poor but are shunned by more fortunate souls. Hence, as income rises, demand for these inferior goods dwindles. As income sags, demand for them perks up.

3. Prices of Related Goods Virtually every good or service has *relations*. When the prices of such related goods change, the demand curve of the good at hand is shifted. There are two kinds of related goods—substitutes and complements.

A **substitute good** *is one that can be used instead of another.* Chicken serves as a substitute for hamburger (and vice versa), gum for candy, and so on. If the price of chicken falls, the demand for hamburger will decrease, shifting to the left, as consumers substitute chicken for hamburger (Figure 3.2b). If the price of chicken rises, the demand for hamburger will increase, shifting to the right. To cite a concrete example, the price of cotton fiber nearly doubled relative to the price of polyester during the 1970s, with the result that the fiber content of clothing changed dramatically, cotton's share falling nearly 22 percent while polyester's share rose.[4]

In contrast, a **complementary good** *is used with another.* Cameras and film are complements. Hamburger and hamburger buns go to together, as do coffee and donuts. Such combinations are countless. And in these instances, demand lurches in directions opposite to those observed for substitutes. If the price of a complement to some good *falls*, the demand for that good *increases* (shifts right), as more of that good is purchased at each possible price (to go with the greater quantity demanded of the complement). If, on the other hand, the price of a complement to some good rises, the demand for that good *decreases* (shifts left), as less of that good is purchased at each possible price (less then being needed to go with the reduced quantity of the complement).

Gasoline complements car tires. Between 1978 and 1980, the price of gasoline nearly doubled,

[4]Organization for Economic Co-operation and Development, *Textile and Clothing Industries* (Paris, 1983), pp. 37–38.

that of regular gas leaping from $0.63 to $1.19 per gallon. This movement up the demand curve for gasoline cut heavily into auto travel, and the average annual mileage per car fell roughly 10 percent from 9,800 to 8,900 miles. In turn, the demand for replacement tires shifted left: 1980 sales were 106.9 million tires, down from 135.2 million in 1978.[5] (Replacement tires are those not sold as original equipment on new cars.)

[5]*Statistical Abstract of the United States 1982–83*, pp. 613, 619, 621.

To summarize for increased prices of related goods:

| If X and Y are substitutes | Then a rise in the price of Y . . . ↑ | Shifts the demand curve for X to the right (see Figure 3.2c) → |
| If M and N are complements | Then a rise in the price of N . . . ↑ | Shifts the demand curve for M to the left (see Figure 3.2b) ← |

---

4. The Number of Buyers What do you suppose happened to the demand for baby food and diapers during the baby boom that followed World War II? There is no mystery here. The demand increased, shifting to the right, as the number of people buying these goods increased dramatically. Later, as birth rates fell and the infant populace dwindled, the demand for baby food and diapers shifted to the left.

The baby boom generation continued to have an

TABLE 3.2   The Influence of Other Factors Affecting Demand, Causing the Demand Curve to Shift

Factor	Influence
Changes in tastes	A decline in preference, such as occurs with dieting, shifts demand left (as in Figure 3.2b). An increase in preference shifts demand to the right (as in Figure 3.2c).
Changes in income	For normal goods, a drop in consumer incomes shifts demand left (Figure 3.2b). A jump in incomes shifts demand to the right (Figure 3.2c).
Changes in the price of substitutes	A drop in the price of chicken shifts demand for hamburger to the left (Figure 3.2b). A rise in the price of chicken shifts demand for hamburger to the right (Figure 3.2c).
Changes in the price of complements	A rise in the price of hamburger buns shifts demand for hamburger to the left (Figure 3.2b). A drop in the price of buns shifts demand for hamburger to the right (Figure 3.2c).
Changes in the number of buyers	A decrease in the number of buyers shifts demand left (Figure 3.2b). A rise in the number of buyers, with population growth, shifts demand right (Figure 3.2c).
Changes in expectations	Expectations of a future price increase shifts demand to the right (Figure 3.2c), as people buy and freeze hamburger for future consumption. Expectations of a future price decline may shift demand left (Figure 3.2b), as consumers postpone purchases.

impact in later years, but the impact affected different products. During the 1970s, for instance, the 21–35 age group grew massively, with the result that beer sales burgeoned at annual rates unknown in recent history.

5. Buyer Expectations If buyers expect the price of a good to fall in the near future, the expectation can shift the demand curve to the left as buyers postpone purchases (Figure 3.2b). Conversely, if buyers expect the price to rise in the near future, demand may shift to the right as buyers decide to purchase now instead of later (Figure 3.2c). Of course, these generalizations apply only to products whose purchase can be delayed or hastened. Durable goods like autos and home computers certainly qualify, as do goods that can be easily stored (canned foods, for instance). These generalizations would not apply to things like electricity or gasoline.

A summary of the demand impact of these several factors—tastes, income, prices of related goods, number of buyers, and expectations—is given in Table 3.2, with specific reference to the example of hamburger. We turn next to the supply side, after a brief perspective on autos.

Read Perspective 3A.

PERSPECTIVE 3A
Auto Demand, 1981–82

The auto market is *not* perfectly competitive, mainly because of supply-side features. In demand, however, it illustrates points common to the demand for many goods. (Recall that market imperfections most commonly arise on the supply side, so that our discussion of demand is broadly applicable.)

When a recession hit the country in 1980, disposable personal income per capita fell (after taking account of inflation). As a consequence, domestic auto producers sold only 6.6 million cars in 1980, down sharply from 8.3 million in 1979 (a leftward shift in demand). Sluggish economic conditions persisted into 1981 and 1982, and auto sales continued to stall. To spark demand during these years, GM, Ford, and Chrysler tried to lure buyers into showrooms with cash rebates, giving customers $500 to $1,000 in price cuts. The price cutting turned into a *series* of campaigns, five in all, during 1981–82, with the results shown in Figure 3.3.

The shaded bands of Figure 3.3 show periods of price cutting during these years, while the vertical axis measures the annual rate of domestic new car sales in millions of units. Sales clearly jumped during the discount campaigns but fell when prices returned upward. This suggests that there was a series of movements along the demand curve for autos, as the quantity varied inversely with the price level.

There is an interesting added factor, however, one that caused shifts of demand in the direction suggested by the sales rate—namely, expectations. As announced, the rebates were *temporary*, so demand during the rebate campaigns was spurred by expectations that prices would soon rise. Moreover, repetition of the discount campaigns led consumers to expect them, depressing demand when the campaigns were off as people waited for the next round of discounting. In September 1982 a vice president of GM admitted this: "We may have just been training the consumer to wait for a rebate, buy, and then hold off." At the same time, GM announced that its future 1983 model prices would be held down in hopes of convincing people that GM cars would be bargain priced without rebates. But the plan backfired. Sales of leftover 1982 cars plummeted as people waited for the low-priced 1983 models. Caught with huge stocks of old 1982 models, the industry kicked off yet another discount campaign in late 1982 (as shown in Figure 3.3).[6]

[6]*Wall Street Journal,* December 15, 1982, pp. 1, 15.

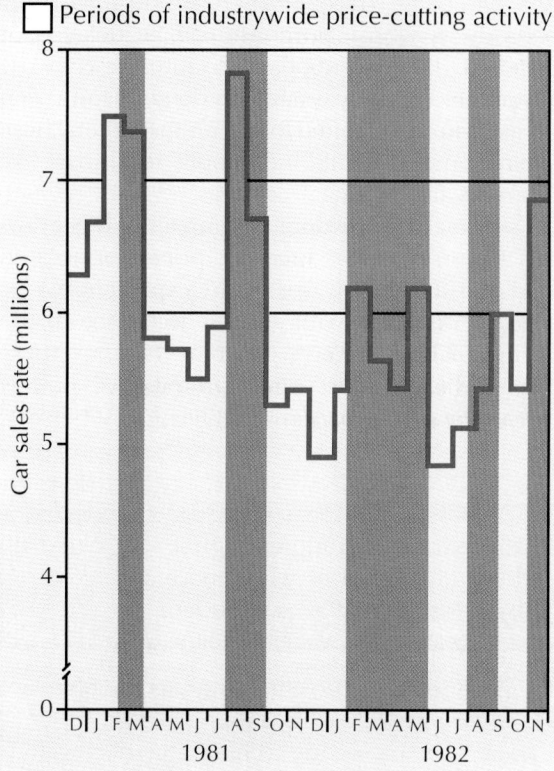

□ Periods of industrywide price-cutting activity

FIGURE 3.3 *Price-Cutting Activity and Domestic Car Sales (in Millions, Seasonally Adjusted Annual Rate)*

During periods of industrywide price-cutting activity, indicated by the shaded bands, domestic auto sales jump. At other times, they stagnate. Two factors are at work here: (1) movements along the demand curve due to price variations and (2) shifts of the demand curve due to expectations; that is, while prices were low people expected them to rise, and while high they were expected to fall. (Source: Wall Street Journal, *December 15, 1982, p. 1.)*

III

Supply-Side Mechanics

The basics of supply in a perfectly competitive market may be covered in steps like those we took for demand—definition of supply, the "law" of supply, and shifts versus movements along the supply curve.

A

Supply Defined

Supply can refer to (1) the supply of an individual seller, (2) marketwide supply, and (3) supply as

viewed by an individual buyer. Here we are interested in *marketwide supply*, just as we were previously occupied by marketwide demand. And the scope of the market here corresponds to the scope of the market on the demand side. It may be local, national, or international, depending on the product.

In this context, supply is another quantity–price relationship:

> **Supply** of a good or service is the set of various quantities sellers would offer for sale at various prices during a specified time period (other things being constant).

Once again, as with demand, quantities, prices, and time period play crucial roles. And once again, quantities and prices are related in a set. The big change here is the identity of the actors. It is *sellers* offering goods for sale rather than buyers making purchases. And the behavior of these sellers may be represented by a *supply schedule* or *supply curve.*

Table 3.3 returns to the example of hamburger by showing a hypothetical *supply schedule.* The set of quantity–price combinations includes the observation that a market price of $1.25 per pound would induce sellers to offer 30 million pounds of hamburger for sale, combination w. At the very low price of $0.50 a pound, sellers would offer no hamburger at all. Supermarket meat counters might still carry pork chops, chicken, and lamb. But, at $0.50 a pound, no hamburger would be offered.

When the data of Table 3.3 are drawn in Figure 3.4, the result is hamburger's *supply curve.* Points v, w, x, y, and z on the curve correspond to the schedule's combinations—labeled v, w, and so on. Thus, at point y in Figure 3.4, you see that a price of $0.75 per pound prompts sellers to offer 10 million

TABLE 3.3   Supply Schedule for Hamburger

	Price (Dollars Per Pound)	Quantity Supplied (Millions of Pounds Per Week)
v	$1.50	35
w	1.25	30
x	1.00	20
y	0.75	10
z	0.50	0

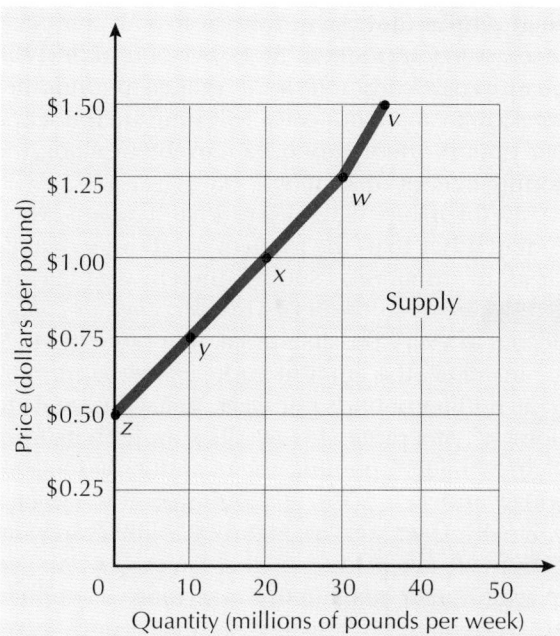

FIGURE 3.4 **The Supply Curve for Hamburger**

This graph, derived from the data of Table 3.3, shows the various amounts of hamburger that would be offered for sale at various possible prices during a week's time. When the price is $1.50, the quantity supplied is 35 million pounds at point v. At lower prices, lesser quantities are supplied. At $0.50 a pound (and prices below $0.50), no hamburger is offered for sale, so point z is on the vertical axis. The curve connecting these points, and w, x, and y, is called the supply curve for hamburger.

pounds of hamburger per week in the market, numbers that match those of combination *y* in Table 3.3.

It follows that:

A **supply schedule** or **supply curve** shows the various quantities of a good or service that sellers would offer for sale at various possible prices during some time period (ceteris paribus).

B
The Law of Supply

There is a distinct pattern to the supply side. When the price is relatively high, the quantity of hamburger supplied is relatively high. When the price is relatively low, the quantity supplied is relatively low (and may even be zero). Thus, if the price falls, the quantity supplied falls. Alternative-

ly, if the price rises, the quantity supplied rises. There is thus a *direct* or *positive* relationship between quantity supplied and price. Such a pattern does not always prevail for supply, but it happens often enough to win recognition in the *law of supply*.

The **law of supply** states that the price of a good and the quantity supplied vary directly (or positively) when other factors are held constant.

As indicated, this direct or positive pattern carries the *ceteris paribus* qualification. When other factors are held constant, the quantity supplied rises as the price rises (and falls as price falls) for one main reason—increasing cost. As stated earlier, the principle of increasing cost says that the opportunity cost rises when more and more of a particular commodity is produced. As the price rises, these higher costs of greater output can be more and more profitably covered, inducing added supply. As the price falls, the higher costs of greater output cannot be profitably covered, so lower prices press the quantity supplied down. The *Wall Street Journal* reported an example in 1980:

> *Vernon Breckenridge has been raising cattle on his ranch near Hennessey, Oklahoma, for 41 years. When times have been bad, he has always just thinned his herd and waited for beef prices to rise. When prices have risen, he has always started building up his herd again.*[7]

Of course, Mr. Breckenridge is only one rancher. Between 1973 and 1975 the retail price of beef rose from $1.40 to $1.55 a pound, and the cattle head count rose by 10 million. Thereafter, from 1975 to 1977, the head count fell by about 9 million as the retail price tumbled.[8]

C
Shifts versus Movements Along the Supply Curve

After 1977, cattlemen continued to thin their herds, from 122.8 million head in 1977 to only 110.9

---

[7]*Wall Street Journal*, July 28, 1980, p. 1.

[8]*Wall Street Journal*, August 29, 1979, p. 1

million in 1979. This seems crazy because during these years the retail price of beef skyrocketed from less than \$1.50 to over \$2.25 a pound. But it was not crazy. The sharp drop in cattle production occurred because the supply curve for beef shifted to the left in response to jolting changes in *other factors* (other than the price of beef). The most significant outside factor was a tremendous increase in the prices cattlemen paid for their inputs, feed prices and interest rates in particular. This raised their costs. The costs of bringing a yearling steer to full slaughter weight rose from \$500 to \$800 between 1977 and 1979, putting a severe crimp in cattlemen's profits. Blistering drought also battered them.

In other words, Figure 3.4 accounts *only* for the quantity and price of hamburger. Other factors are assumed to be constant. Yet the quantity supplied of a good is not a function of only the price of that good. It is *also a function of several other important factors*.

In general, these other factors are (1) changes in the price of inputs, (2) changes in the technology of production, (3) changes in the prices of related goods, (4) changes in the number of sellers, and (5) altered seller expectations. These other factors cause *shifts* of the supply curve because the only cause of quantity supply represented by an axis in a graph of supply is the price of the good supplied (see Figure 3.4 again). Changes in the price of hamburger induce *movements along* the supply curve for hamburger, say from point x to y in Figure 3.4. In contrast, changes in input prices or technology cause a new relationship between price and quantity supplied and must be shown by *shifts of the supply curve.*

When the price of the good changes, causing a **movement along** the supply curve, the result is called a **change in the quantity supplied.**

When other factors affecting supply change, causing a **shift** of the entire supply curve, the result is called a **change in supply.**

Figure 3.5 illustrates the various possibilities for hamburger. In part (a) the price of hamburger changes while all other factors are held constant. The result is movements along the supply curve,

such as the movement from x to w if the price increases from \$1.00 to \$1.25 per pound and the quantity rises from 20 to 30 million pounds per week. If, instead, the price fell from \$1.00 to \$0.75 per pound, there would be movement along the supply curve from x to y.

Part (b) of Figure 3.5 shows what happens when factors other than the price of hamburger change so as to discourage supply, thereby shifting the supply curve to the left. This *decrease in supply* occurs at every possible price. At a price of \$1.25, for instance, the amount supplied drops from 30 to 20 million pounds per week. Point w retreats to point w'. At a price of \$1.50, the supply shifts from 35 to 25 million pounds, the quantities associated with v and v'.

Finally, part (c) of Figure 3.5 illustrates an *increase in supply* due to other factors, as revealed in a shift to the right. In this case, more is supplied at each possible price when the supply curve becomes z*v* instead of zv. At a price of \$0.75, for instance, the supply shifts from 10 to 20 million pounds per week.

One variable causing shifts in supply received previous mention in the example of dwindling beef supplies between 1977 and 1979, namely, input prices. Let's tackle it first.

1. Input Prices (Costs) An increase in the price producers pay for an input—land, labor, or capital—raises their cost, thereby shifting the supply curve to the left. Why does this happen? Given the price of the *output* (e.g., meat), the price of the *inputs* (e.g., cattle feed) becomes critical. There is a clash between these prices if, for a given price of the output, the price of inputs rises. Producers absorb the shock of this clash by reducing their purchases of these now more costly inputs. In turn, reduced inputs implies reduced outputs, so the supply shifts left at each possible price. Alternatively, we could say that a given quantity will now be supplied only if the *output price* rises enough to cover the higher *input price*. Compare points x and w' in Figure 3.5(b), for instance. The quantity is 20 for both points, but the price must rise from \$1.00 to \$1.25 to maintain that output.

A *drop* in the price of an input would have the opposite effect. If labor wage rates fell, or land rents decreased, or capital interest rates receded, the cost of production would diminish. The lower

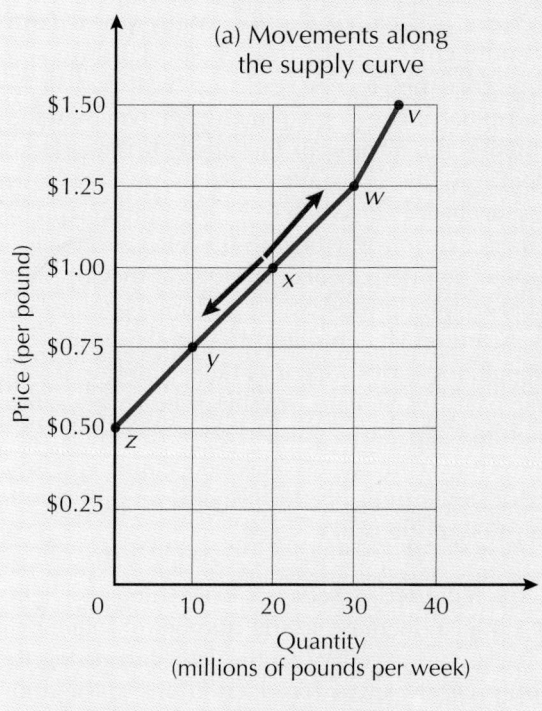

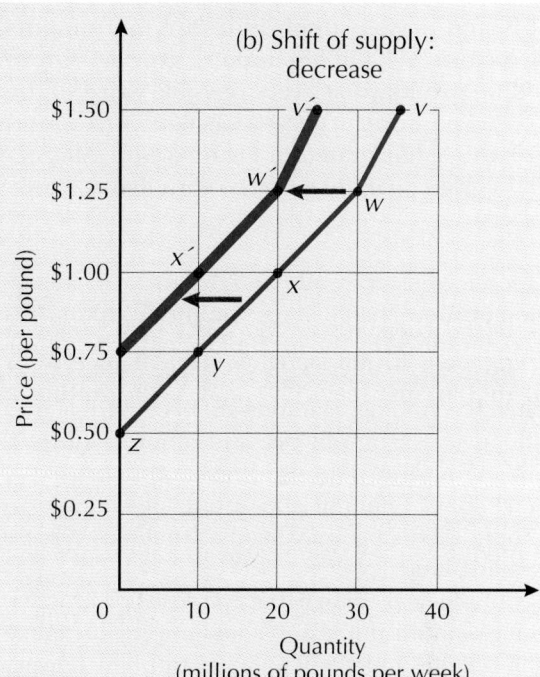

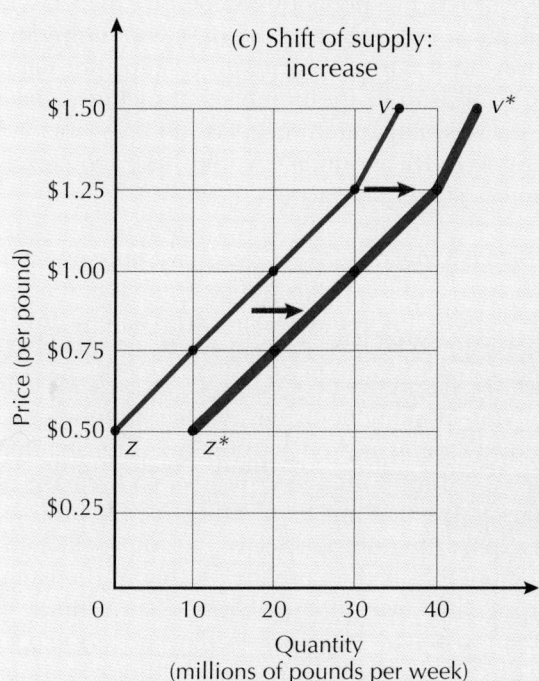

FIGURE 3.5   **_Movements Along versus Shifts of Supply_**

(a) Change in quantity supplied. _If the price rises from $1.00 to $1.25, the quantity supplied rises from 20 to 30 with movement along the supply curve from x to w. If the price falls from $1.00 to $0.75, the quantity supplied falls from 20 to 10._ (b) _If the cost of feed grains rises, or if some other factor cuts cattlemen's willingness to produce, supply shifts to the left. Less is supplied at each possible price as a result._ (c) _If the cost of feed grains falls, or if some other factor boosts cattlemen's willingness to produce, supply shifts to the right. More is supplied at each possible price._

cost would permit suppliers to use more inputs than before. With more inputs, greater output could be produced at every possible price of the output. The supply curve consequently would shift right, as illustrated in Figure 3.5(c). (Alternatively, a given quantity could be supplied at a lower price.)

2. Technology of Production Output is determined by more than just the volume of inputs. It is also determined by the *technology* of those inputs (the "software" know-how and the "hardware" capital). Technology is important because it affects productivity, or output per unit of input (output/input). A hundred pounds of beef output presently require about 1 hour of labor input, for example. In addition, each steer may need as much as 3 acres of grazing land.

Technological change that *increases* productivity (increases output/input) shifts the supply curve to the *right*, as more will then be supplied at every possible output price (Figure 3.5c). Let's assume that an hour of cowboy labor would cost a rancher $5 to hire. If productivity were to increase from 100 pounds of beef per hour of labor to 500 pounds per hour, the labor cost *per pound of beef* would drop dramatically from 5 cents a pound ($5/100) to only 1 cent a pound ($5/500). Lower costs induce greater output.

In fact, technology's contribution to agricultural productivity during this century has been stunning. Special breeding of cows through artificial insemination has more than doubled milk output per cow since 1950, for instance. The U.S. dairy herd now numbers half of what it was in 1950, yet it produces more milk. Scientists say that future technologies, such as embryo engineering, will push the annual milk output of *one* cow from the current 15,000 pounds of milk to nearly 45,000 pounds. That cow would also be as big as an elephant![9] (If we stretched the notion of technology to include changes in the weather—nature's technology—we would unearth another extraneous factor influencing agricultural productivity. Bad weather curbs productivity. Droughts wither pastures and parch corn fields. Reduced yields per acre ensue. By the same token, good weather boosts productivity.)

[9]*Business Week*, June 21, 1982, p. 124.

3. Prices of Related Goods Many wheat farmers could grow corn instead of wheat. Conversely, many corn producers could cultivate wheat instead of corn. The price of each grain will therefore influence the supply of the other. If the price of wheat remains constant while the price of corn rises, farmers will switch from wheat to corn. This shifts the supply of wheat to the left. Conversely, a drop in the price of corn would shift the supply of wheat to the right as wheat farming becomes relatively attractive compared to corn farming.

Ranchers in dry western states cannot plow up their pastures to gain cropland. But midwestern ranchers can. And midwestern ranchers have been known to switch between cattle and soybeans, depending on the price of one relative to the price of the other.

4. The Number of Sellers Everything else being the same, a decrease in the number of sellers will shift the supply curve to the left, decreasing the supply. On the other hand, additions to the number of sellers in a perfectly competitive market will shift the supply curve to the right, increasing the supply. In terms of Figure 3.5's example for hamburger, a drop in the number of ranches or beef feedlots is illustrated in part (b), whereas an increase in their number would have the consequences shown in part (c).

5. Seller Expectations Cows have only one calf each year, and the calf is not fat enough to market as beef until it is about 2 years old. There is thus a maturation period separating the time inputs are committed and the time outputs can be sold. This happens in many fields besides agriculture—e.g., liquor distilling and oil exploration. It means that many producers plan their output on the basis of *expected* price rather than actual price. If producers expect the output price to rise, they will commit more inputs than otherwise, thereby boosting output later even if expectations are ultimately proven wrong by lower prices. If producers expect the output price to fall, they will withdraw inputs, thereby shrinking output later even if expectations are contradicted by robust prices. Shifts of supply, right and left, respectively, may then be the result of these expectations.

Opposite shifts are possible for goods contained in existing stocks or inventories. An owner of a mature stand of timber for example, will tend to hold it off the lumber market if she expects the price of lumber to rise in the future. This would shift the supply left.

Table 3.4 puts these several supply factors in a nutshell.

IV

Demand and Supply Together: Equilibrium

A

Actual Price and Output

So much for _possibilities_—the possible purchases of buyers, the possible sales of suppliers, and the possible prices associated with these possible quantities. What converts these possibilities into _actualities?_ What determines _observed_ prices and quantities? It is neither demand nor supply alone. A market's actual price and quantity emerge from the _interaction_ of demand and supply, from the actual _exchanges_ between buyers and sellers.

In particular, price and quantity will tend toward _equilibrium._ Once at equilibrium, price and quantity will then persist. In a similar sense, our earth and sun exchange gravitational forces to keep the speedy earth in an equilibrium orbit year after year. The earth neither drifts away from nor plummets toward the sun.

Equilibrium price and quantity are pinpointed

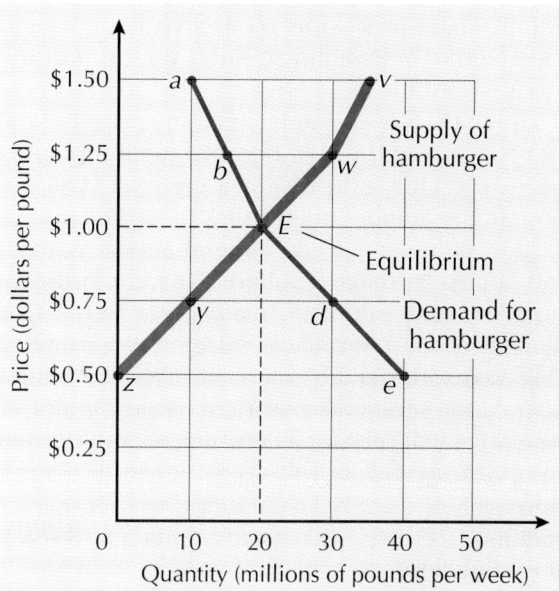

FIGURE 3.6   Demand and Supply Yield Market Equilibrium

Demand from Figure 3.1 and supply from Figure 3.4 are combined for a complete view of the market for hamburger. The actual price and quantity will tend to be the equilibrium price and quantity, which emerge from the intersection of demand and supply at point E. Thus, the equilibrium price is $1.00 a pound. The equilibrium quantity is 20 million pounds per week.

by the _intersection_ of demand and supply. Figure 3.6 illustrates this by presenting the demand curve of Figure 3.1 together with the supply curve of Figure 3.4. (Note that both the vertical axis and the horizontal axis are the same as in each previous

TABLE 3.4   Summary of the Influence of Other Factors Affecting Supply, Causing Supply to Shift

Factor	Influence
Changes in the input price	A rise in the input price, such as a wage hike, shifts supply left (as in Figure 3.5b). A drop in the input price shifts supply right (as in Figure 3.5c).
Changes in technology (productivity)	If productivity slips, supply shifts left. If productivity jumps, supply shifts right.
Changes in prices of related goods	A rise in the price of another good that sellers could produce shifts the supply left. A drop in price shifts supply right.
Changes in the number of sellers	Added sellers add to the supply, for a rightward shift. Fewer sellers have the opposite effect.
Changes in sellers' expectations	Changes in price expectations can cause supply to shift right or left, depending on the circumstances.

graph. These axes—the price of hamburger and the quantity of hamburger—now do further duty in Figure 3.6.)

Equilibrium occurs at point _E_. The price is $1.00 per pound and the quantity is 20 million pounds per week. That is to say, at a price of $1.00 per pound, the amount _buyers_ seek to purchase is 20 million pounds, _and_ the amount _sellers_ wish to sell is also 20 million pounds. The amounts demanded and supplied match precisely. This equality of the quantities demanded and supplied yields equilibrium. The market is _cleared._ Neither buyers nor sellers are surprised or disappointed. The price will remain steady. Buyers will not bid the price up. Sellers will not compete to drive it down.

Equilibrium is a state of balance between conflicting forces. In the market, balance occurs when the quantities demanded and supplied are equal.

Away from equilibrium, surpluses or shortages emerge, as shown in Figure 3.7.

B
Surplus

If the price is initially above the equilibrium price, the quantity supplied will exceed the quantity demanded. In part (a) of Figure 3.7, the price of $1.25 is above the equilibrium price of $1.00, so that the quantity supplied at _w_ is greater than the quantity demanded at _b_, 30 versus 15. A _surplus_ of 15 million pounds (30 - 15) results. The imbalance triggers adjustment, however. To rid themselves of their excess supplies, sellers will trim prices (just as excess supplies of Christmas decorations trigger after-Christmas sales). In turn, the falling price level does two things: (1) it increases the quantity demanded and (2) it decreases the quantity supplied. The price level continues to fall—thereby continuing to encourage purchases and to dis-

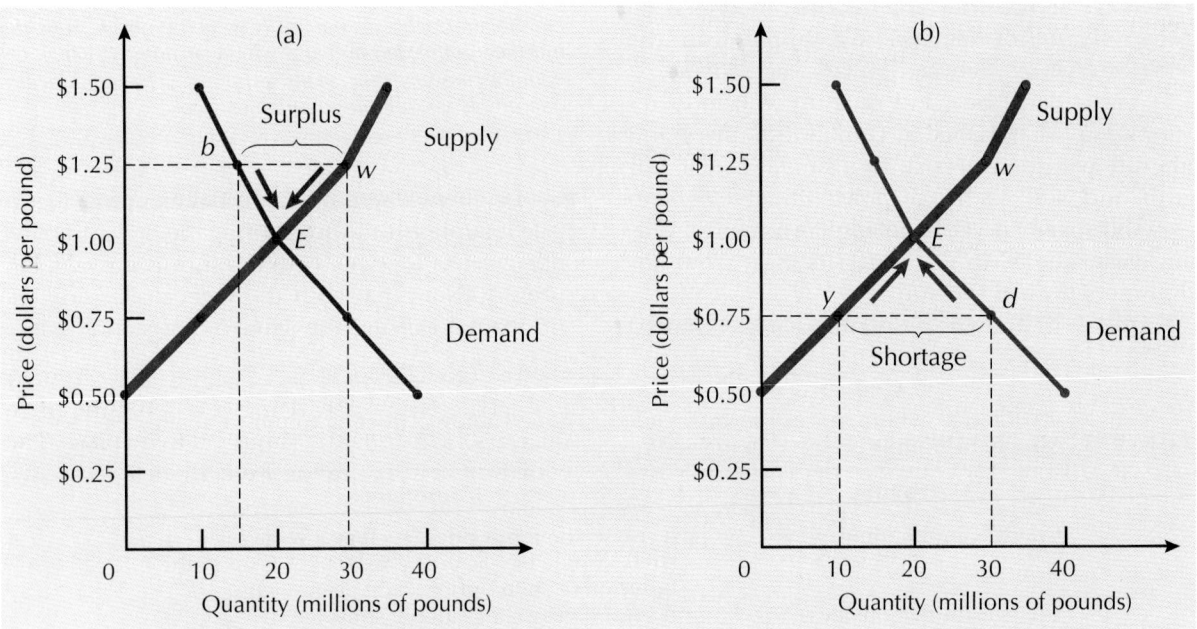

FIGURE 3.7 _Surplus and Shortage_

(a) Surplus: _At a price of $1.25, above equilibrium, the quantity supplied is 30, while the quantity demanded is less at 15. The result is a surplus of 15 (30 - 15). The price will fall, decreasing the quantity supplied and increasing the quantity demanded until equilibrium is attained at E._ (b) Shortage: _At a price of $0.75, below equilibrium, the quantity supplied is 10, while the quantity demanded is greater at 30. A shortage of 20 (30 - 10) occurs. The price will rise, increasing the quantity supplied and decreasing the quantity demanded until equilibrium is reached at E._

courage supplies—until the price settles at the equilibrium level. Once the price reaches the equilibrium level, no further change occurs because the quantities demanded and supplied then match at equilibrium. It was the _surplus_ of supply over demand that pressed the price down. Contraction of the surplus to zero removes the pressure.

C
Shortage

If a surplus is summer, a shortage is winter. They are opposites. In Figure 3.7(b), a _shortage_ arises if the initial price is _below_ the equilibrium level, as $0.75 is below $1.00. The quantity demanded then exceeds the quantity supplied, as point _d_, which is associated with a demand of 30 million pounds, exceeds point _y_, associated with a supply of 10 million pounds. The shortage of 20 (30 − 10) proves frustrating for buyers, who are eager to buy more than is available at that price. They express their eagerness by bidding more than $0.75 per pound, thereby lifting the price. As the price level rises, two responses follow: (1) the quantity demanded contracts, and (2) the quantity supplied expands. These responses dissipate the shortage, but the price continues its upward momentum as long as the quantity demanded exceeds the quantity supplied—as long as some shortage persists. The price won't escalate forever, however, because once it reaches the equilibrium level of $1.00, the shortage disappears completely. Demand and supply then both match 20 million pounds, at point _E_. The skyward trend in price vanishes when the shortage vanishes.

These stories of surplus and shortage are summarized in Table 3.5. When the demand and supply schedules of the previous discussions are placed side by side, you can see that when the price is high, the quantity supplied exceeds the quantity demanded, and the resulting **surplus** pushes the price down. Conversely, when the price is low, the quantity demanded outstrips the quantity supplied, causing a **shortage** that will elevate the price. Only at a price of $1.00 per pound will buyers and sellers have harmonious amounts in mind, 20 and 20, yielding an equilibrium.

Read Perspective 3B.

V
Changes in Equilibrium

We live in a changing world. Markets continually change too. Buffeted by economic booms and busts, by novel technologies, and by countless other forms of flux, markets do not stick to any single equilibrium for long. The resulting changes in equilibrium emerge from (1) shifts in demand, (2) shifts in supply, or (3) shifts in _both_.

A
Shifts in Demand

Figure 3.10, on page 72, shows what happens when demand shifts while supply remains rooted. If demand increases, shifting to the right, as shown by the shift from D_1 to D_2 in Figure 3.10(a), equilibrium will move up the supply curve from E_1 to E_2. The greater new demand will bid the price up, causing the quantity supplied to increase. The equilibrium price jumps from P_1 to P_2 and the

TABLE 3.5   Demand for and Supply of Hamburger Plus Equilibrium

Price*	Quantity Demanded†	Quantity Supplied†	Market Condition	Direction of Price
$1.50	10	35	Surplus $(Q_D < Q_S)$	Down
1.25	15	30	Surplus $(Q_D < Q_S)$	Down
1.00	20	20	Balance $(Q_D = Q_S)$	Equilibrium
0.75	30	10	Shortage $(Q_D > Q_S)$	Up
0.50	40	0	Shortage $(Q_D > Q_S)$	Up

*Dollars per pound.
†Millions of pounds per week.

PERSPECTIVE 3B
Legal Price Ceilings and Floors

The power of the price to equilibrate demand and supply is illustrated most dramatically when that power is drained—when, that is, the price *cannot* adjust in the proper direction because it is constrained by law. Two cases arise: legal *price ceilings* and legal *price floors*.

Price Ceilings When the government imposes a price ceiling, it outlaws any price above a specified maximum. If that maximum is well above the equilibrium level, as P_A is above P_E in Figure 3.8, it will have *no* impact because the observed market price would then be the equilibrium price P_E, which is below that P_A ceiling. Such a high legal ceiling might even be laughable, such as would be a $100,000 price ceiling for new cars. If, on the other hand, the price ceiling lies *below* the equilibrium price, as P_C is below P_E in Figure 3.8, then the maximum packs a real punch. The observed market price then becomes the ceiling price, P_C. Indeed, the punch becomes a pinch because a shortage results. With the price at P_C in Figure 3.8 and unable to rise, the quantity demanded, Q_D, exceeds the quantity supplied by a hefty margin.

Absent the price ceiling, the price would rise and thereby *ration* scarce supplies among competing buyers at equilibrium. Only those willing to pay the higher equilibrium price would persist in their demand. Legally forcing the price down, therefore, results in various forms of *non-price rationing*. The government may issue rationing coupons, as it has done during wartime price ceilings. Buyers may have to form waiting lines, as they did during the gasoline shortages of the 1970s. People new to the market because of youth or emigration may simply be denied *any* opportunity to buy, as occurred during the 1970s when the construction of new natural gas hookups was suspended.

Rent control, which sets maximum rentals on dwellings, is a notable current example. Many cities now have rent control. But the granddad-dy is New York City, which has experienced rent control since 1943. It has also experienced severe housing shortages, long tenant waiting lists, bizarre systems of tenant turnover, and related aberrations. Those benefitting by rent control, namely, tenants of long standing, remain politically powerful. Moreover, they sometimes try to cultivate support for rent controls by making erroneous arguments, such as the one that ceilings are the only means by which rents would ever be held down or fall. Evidence refutes this contention. In 1983, while New York's shortage of rental units continued as usual, a glut of rental units sprang up in the Sun Belt. Vacancy rates ranging from 10 to 30 percent caused rents to *fall* in Phoenix, Atlanta, and places in between. In Houston, West Trails Apartments offered 50 percent discounts.[10]

Price Floors If by law the price cannot fall below some set level, a price floor exists. If the price floor lies beneath the equilibrium price, as P_B lies beneath P_E in Figure 3.9, then the floor would be without bite. A floor for hamburger at 20 cents a pound would produce only chuckles. If, however, the price floor lodges at a level *above* the equilibrium price, as P_F is above P_E in Figure 3.9, then serious consequences follow. P_F becomes the lowest legal price, foiling the market forces that would push it lower. Hence P_F becomes the price actually observed in the market. With P_F the prevailing price, the quantity supplied is Q_S, which exceeds the quantity demanded, Q_D, by an ample margin. The resulting surplus is indicated in Figure 3.9 as the difference between Q_S and Q_D.

The higher price of an effective floor may lead you to doubt that such floors are ever actually imposed by the government. But suppliers frequently benefit by price floors, and they have often swayed the government to act. Indeed, such price floors prop up the price of about 40

[10]*Wall Street Journal*, July 22, 1983, pp. 1, 18.

percent of all farm marketings, thereby allowing this chapter's running example to run on.

First started during the Great Depression of the 1930s, government price supports presently hold up the price of wheat, corn, rice, cotton, tobacco, milk, butter, cheese, and numerous other farm products. Wheat's support price in 1981 was $3.81 a bushel, for example. The government enforces its price floors by, in effect, acting as a buyer of last resort, buying crops at the support price if farmers cannot sell them at a higher price. Stated differently, Uncle Sam keeps the surplus output off the market by buying it. In order to curb the volume of surpluses he has to buy, Uncle Sam also curbs the output of farmers by various gimmicks that restrict supply—limitations on planted acreage in particular. Still, Uncle Sam has accumulated stag-

gering crop surpluses. His relatively moderate inventories of 1981 included 237 million bushels of corn, 191 million bushels of wheat, and 619 million pounds of cheese. The dollar value of these stocks? About $3.6 billion.[11]

It may now be seen that, if the government is going to alter a market's price with a ceiling below the equilibrium price or a floor above the equilibrium price, it must control either demand or supply (or both demand and supply) because these are the forces that determine the price. A price ceiling usually requires some kind of restraint on demand. A price floor is usually achieved by controls on supply.

---

[11]U.S. Department of Agriculture, *Agricultural Statistics 1982,*

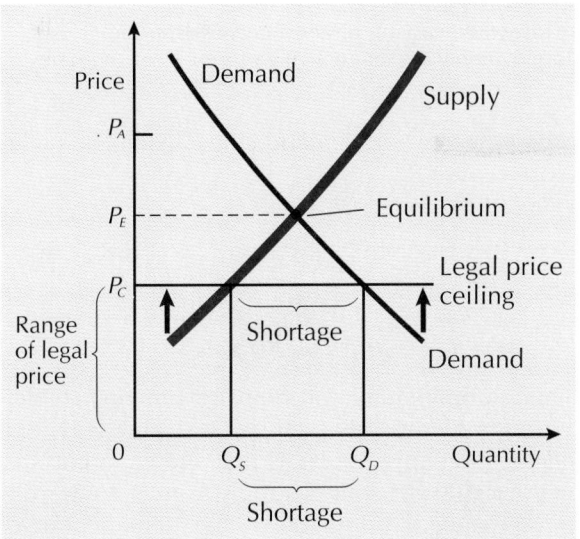

FIGURE 3.8   Legal Price Ceiling and Shortage

A legal price ceiling, P_C, below equilibrium price P_E, prevents the price from rising above P_C despite upward forces. The market price then becomes the highest legal price, P_C. This creates a persistent shortage because quantity demand, Q_D, is greater than quantity supply, Q_S. A legal price ceiling above equilibrium at P_A would have no impact because the market price would then be the equilibrium price, P_E.

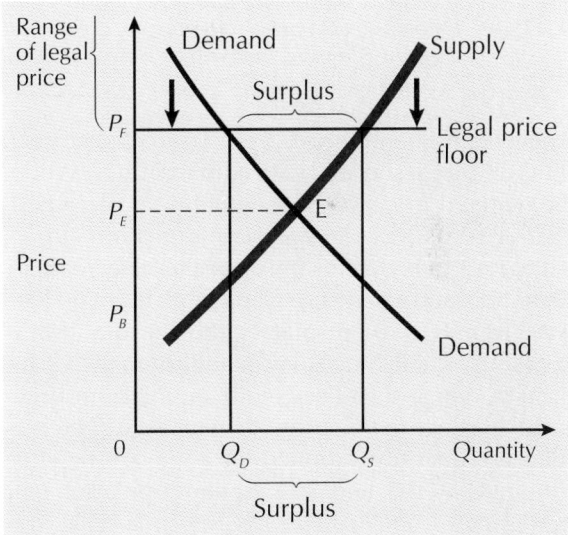

FIGURE 3.9   Legal Price Floor and Surplus

A legal price floor, P_F, above equilibrium price P_E, prevents the price from sinking below P_F despite downward forces. The market price then becomes the lowest legal price, P_F. This creates a persistent surplus because the quantity supplied, Q_S, greatly exceeds the quantity demanded, Q_D. A legal price floor below the equilibrium at, say, P_B would have no impact because the market price would then be the equilibrium price, P_E.

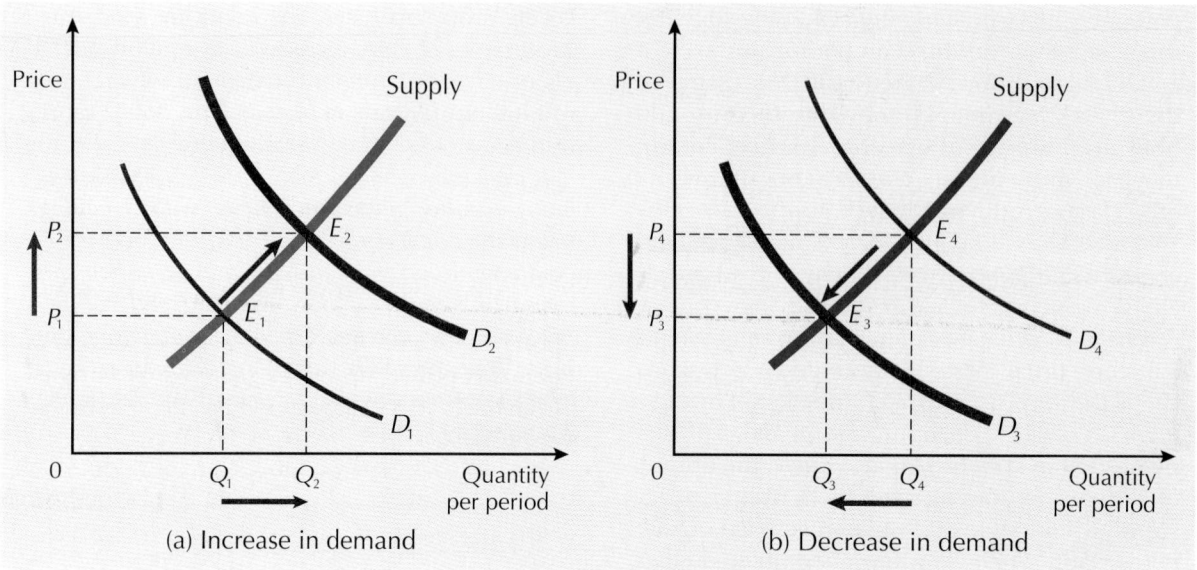

(a) Increase in demand   (b) Decrease in demand

FIGURE 3.10   Shifts of Demand and New Equilibria

If, in part (a), demand is D₁ at the start, an increase in demand from D_1 to D_2 will move the equilibrium up the supply curve from E_1 to E_2. Equilibrium price and quantity both rise, from P_1 and Q_1 to P_2 and Q_2. Conversely, in part (b), a decrease in demand from D_4 down to D_3 would move the equilibrium down the supply curve to E_3 from E_4. Equilibrium price and quantity both fall, from P_4 and Q_4 to P_3 and Q_3. Thus, when demand changes while supply holds steady, price and quantity travel in the same direction, varying directly, because the result is a movement up or down the positively sloped supply curve.

equilibrium quantity rises from Q_1 to Q_2 because Q_2 and P_2 are associated with equilibrium E_2. When the demand increases, the equilibrium price and quantity thus travel in the *same* direction—up.

Figure 3.10(b) depicts the opposite, a decrease in demand. Such a decrease would shift demand leftward from D_4 to D_3, displacing the old equilibrium at E_4 and establishing a new equilibrium at E_3. The drop in demand will cause the equilibrium price to fall because the quantity demanded will be less than the quantity supplied for a short time after the shift. In the end, the equilibrium price will have fallen from P_4 to P_3. As the price falls, the equilibrium quantity supplied likewise tumbles, from Q_4 to Q_3. Price P_3 and quantity Q_3 characterize the new equilibrium at E_3. Both are *below* their E_4 levels.

Notice, then, that *both* price and quantity *rise* when demand increases and *fall* when demand decreases. They move in the *same* direction because the points of equilibrium are moving up and down the steady supply curve, which has a *positive* slope. In short, equilibrium price and quantity

vary *directly* when demand shifts against a stable supply curve.

Read Perspective 3C.

B

Shifts in Supply

When supply shifts and demand remains stable, the outcomes are as pictured in Figure 3.11. An *increase* in supply, such as that shown in part (a) by the rightward shift of supply from S_0 to S_1, will move the equilibrium down the demand curve from E_0 to E_1. With supply briskly up, a temporary glut or surplus is created. This surplus presses the price down, increasing the quantity demanded. Eventually, after E_1 becomes established, the equilibrium price will have *fallen* from P_0 to P_1 and the equilibrium quantity will have *risen* from Q_0 to Q_1.

Figure 3.11(b) illustrates events of an opposite sort. There the supply *decreases*, shifting leftward from S' to S^*. The abrupt displacement of the sup-

PERSPECTIVE 3C

The Popcorn Boom

Popcorn dates back 5,000 years. (Ancient Indians thought that little demons trapped inside the kernels made them pop.) Since the late 1970s, the demand for popcorn has exploded. Sales of unpopped popcorn nearly doubled during these years, reaching about 650 million pounds in 1983. That comes to 10 *billion* quarts after popping, or more than 40 quarts per person annually.

Why the boom? VCRs are bringing movies into living rooms, and movies and popcorn seem to be inseparable complements. Moreover, new cooking equipment—like microwave ovens—now makes popping easier. Popcorn is also one snack that is actually good for you. As if all this were not enough, gourmet popcorn

seems to be the latest craze. The flavors include chocolate, peanut butter, and jalapeño. In brief, tastes and complements have changed.

At the farm level, popcorn is a special breed of corn (not subject to government price supports). Between 1978 and 1982, the explosion in demand puffed up prices received by farmers, from $8.44 to $13.30 per 100 pounds of shelled corn. In response, there was a movement up the supply curve. Land planted in popcorn expanded from 145,000 to 262,000 acres, so the quantity supplied jumped like a hot pot full of popcorn.[12]

[12]Ibid., p. 268, and article by Marsha Kay Seff, *San Jose Mercury News*, November 16, 1983, p. 1F.

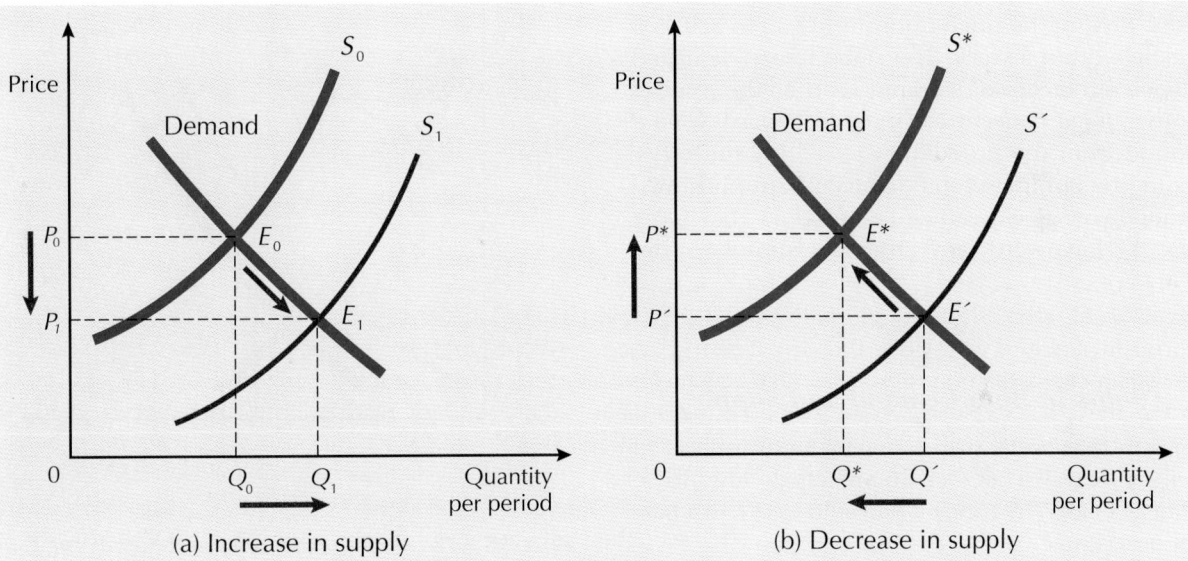

(a) Increase in supply (b) Decrease in supply

FIGURE 3.11 *Shifts of Supply and New Equilibria*

If, in part (a), supply is S_0 originally, an increase in supply from S_0 to S_1 will move the equilibrium down the demand curve from E_0 to E_1. As price falls from P_0 to P_1, the quantity demanded rises from Q_0 to Q_1. Conversely, in part (b), supply starts at S'. A decrease in supply from S' to S^* relocates the equilibrium to E^* from E'. As the price rises from P' to P^* with this movement along the demand curve, the quantity demand falls from Q' to Q^*. Hence, price and quantity vary inversely when the supply curve shifts right or left, while demand remains steady.

ply downward will temporarily cause supply to fall short of demand, producing a shortage. The shortage dissipates, however, as the price is bid up by buyers and the quantity demanded contracts. Hence the equilibrium slides up the demand curve from E' to E^* as a consequence of supply's shift from S' to S^*. The equilibrium price _rises_ from P' to P^* and the equilibrium quantity _falls_ from Q' to Q^*.

In sum, shifts of supply against a given demand curve cause _inverse_ movements in equilibrium price and quantity. One is going _up_ while the other is on its way _down_, and vice versa. The reason for this is simple: The points of equilibrium—such as E_0 and E_1 in Figure 3.11(a)—are points along a given _demand_ curve, which has a _negative_ slope. Trips up or down the demand curve throw price and quantity in opposite directions.

Some of the most commonly observed shifts in supply are visited on agriculture by nasty or pleasant changes in the weather. On the nasty side (leftward supply shifts), beef supplies fell in the late 1970s partly because of drought, pushing the retail price up by $0.75 a pound. Severe frost damaged half of Florida's green bean crop in the winter of 1982, driving the price up from $12.35 to $20.35 a bushel within a week. The same freeze damaged 25 percent of Florida's orange crop, so the price of orange juice concentrate jumped toward $2.00 a pound from the prevailing $1.25.[13] On the other hand, the bumper crops (rightward supply shifts) brought by nice weather create gluts that force prices downward and thereby stimulate demand.

C

Shifts in Both Demand and Supply

Back in 1933 crude oil was selling for as little as 10 _cents_ a barrel! That was an amazingly low price. Shortly before, in 1929, oil had sold for $1.40 a barrel on average.

What caused the price to plummet in 1933? A striking combination of slack demand and burgeoning supply. Demand shifted left as the Great Depression shattered consumer incomes. Factories were also idled, further curbing energy demands. At the same time, petroleum supplies increased after the discovery of the massive East Texas Field in 1930 and the drilling of thousands of relatively low-cost wells. The dramatic effect of these combined forces is suggested by Figure 3.12. There D_{1929} and S_{1929} symbolize U.S. demand and supply in 1929, while E_{1929} is their equilibrium point. Demand then shifts left to D_{1933}, which represents demand in 1933 during the depths of the Depression. Supply shifts right to S_{1933} as production from the gigantic East Texas Field comes onstream. Equilibrium therefore plunges to E_{1933}, with the price much lower at P_{1933} and the quantity down slightly at Q_{1933}. Equilibrium price is bound to fall under such circumstances, but quantity can rise, fall, or remain unchanged depending on the relative extent to which demand and supply each shift. In fact, U.S. crude oil consumption in 1933 was 845 million barrels, down from 1929's 953 million barrels. Hence it appears that the shift in the demand curve overwhelmed the shift in the supply curve, so Figure 3.12 has been drawn accordingly.

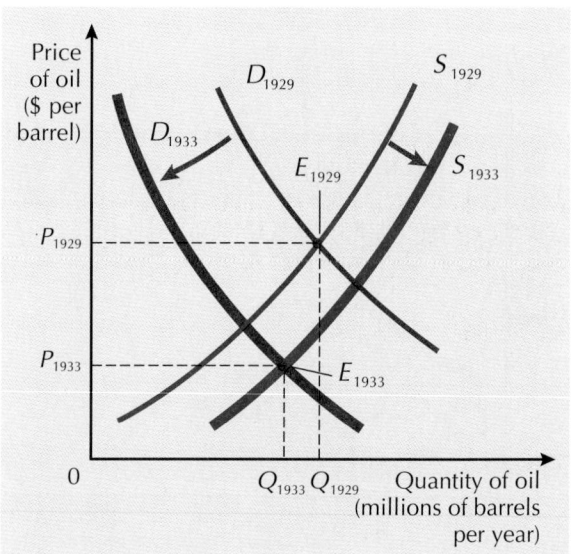

FIGURE 3.12   _Shifts of Demand and Supply for U.S. Crude Oil, 1929–1933_

In 1929, demand D_{1929} and supply S_{1929} yielded an equilibrium in crude oil symbolized by E_{1929}. Price is P_{1929} and quantity is Q_{1929}. Thereafter, demand shifted left because of the Great Depression, and supply shifted right because of the discovery and extensive drilling of the immense East Texas Field. By 1933, the price was as low as 10 cents a barrel in some areas. Output was down only slightly, despite the rock bottom price level.

---

[13]_Wall Street Journal_, January 13, 1982, p. 38.

To obtain a sweeping summary of the changes in the equilibrium price and quantity that follow shifts in both demand and supply, study Figure 3.13. Part (a) shows the same situation just depic-

ted in Figure 3.12. Demand falls as supply rises, driving the equilibrium price down. Part (b) shows demand rising as supply falls, with the opposite results for the equilibrium price. In both parts (a)

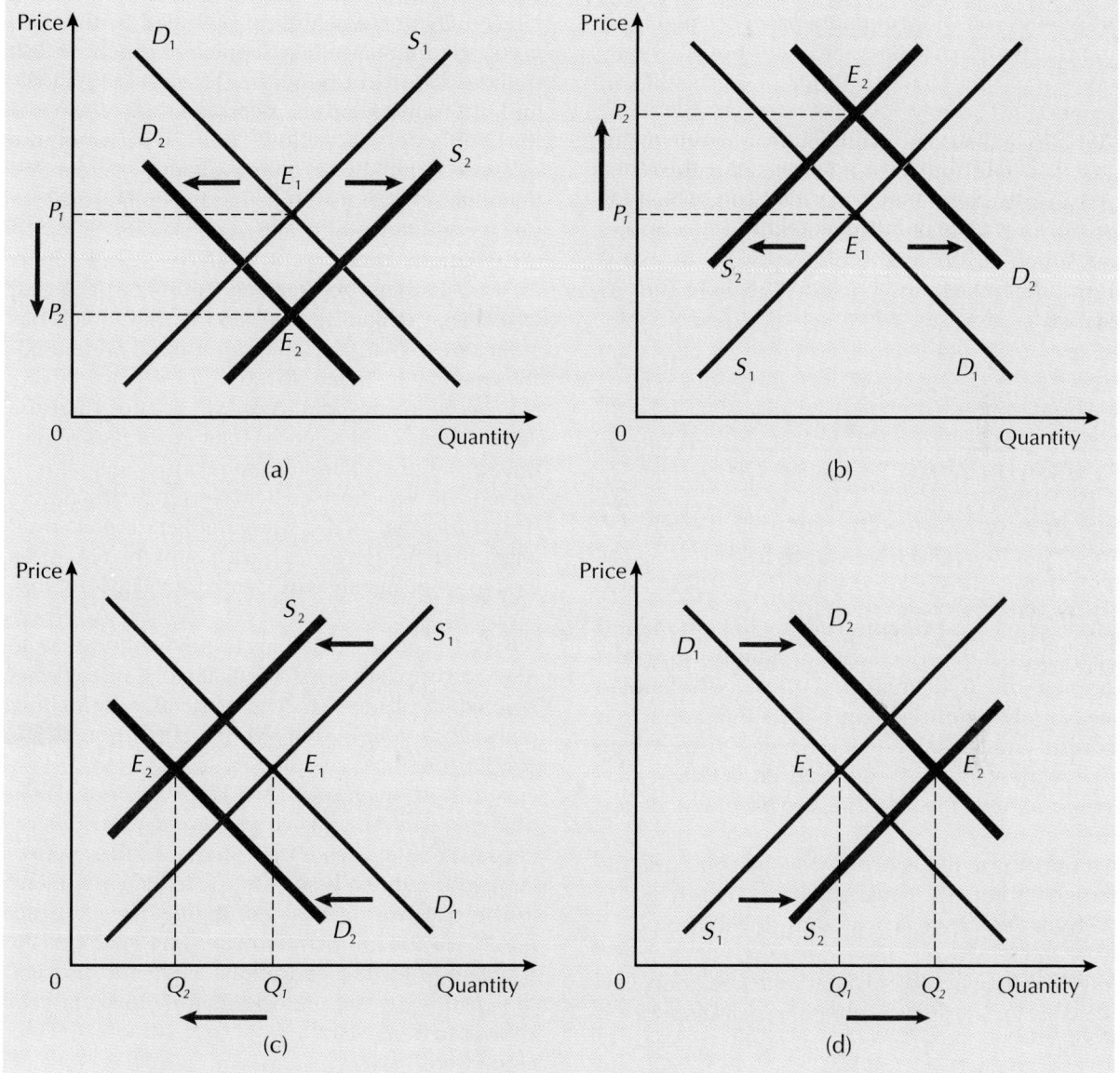

FIGURE 3.13   *Summary of Price and Quantity Changes When Both Demand and Supply Shift*

(a) When demand falls (shifts left) and supply rises (shifts right), the equilibrium price is certain to fall. Equilibrium quantity can remain unchanged, or rise, or fall. (b) When demand increases and supply falls, the equilibrium price will rise. Equilibrium quantity can remain unchanged, or rise, or fall. (c) When demand and supply both fall (shift left), equilibrium quantity is bound to fall. Equilibrium price can remain unchanged, or rise, or fall. (d) When demand and supply both rise, equilibrium quantity will rise. Equilibrium price may remain unchanged, or rise, or fall.

and (b), equilibrium quantity is shown to be unchanged, but imbalance in these shifts could cause equilibrium quantity to rise or fall instead. Parts (c) and (d) show what happens when demand and supply shift in the same direction. When both fall, equilibrium quantity falls. When both rise, equilibrium quantity rises. The equilibrium price is shown to be unchanged, but it actually depends on the relative weights of these shifts in demand and supply.

Whatever the point occupied by a new equilibrium, the new equilibrium will be established by the same market forces that established the old equilibrium—namely, the quantities demanded and supplied. When the price adjusts to marry these quantities in equality, equilibrium is reached.

VI

Competitive Market Results: What? How? Who? What's New? and How Stable?

This chapter has presented market definitions and mechanics. It described the conditions for perfect competition. It defined and displayed demand and supply. And it explored their interactions in terms of equilibrium and its changes. In short, you have witnessed what a perfectly competitive market is and how it works. Both are *positive economics*.

It remains to be seen, however, just *how well* the perfectly competitive market works. We rely extensively on markets to answer those questions posed by scarcity—What?, How?, Who?, What's new?, and How stable?. It is only natural to ask, then, *how well does the perfectly competitive market perform this job?* Do the *answers* attained by this sort of market match our society's value judgments of goodness as opposed to badness, our *normative standards?*

Later we shall address this issue at length. Right now, we can only give a brief overview. This summary identifies the competitive market's answers to the five basic questions and then compares those answers to the ideals outlined on page 14. Let's begin with the questions What?.

A
What?

What is produced in what amounts? You have now seen the perfectly competitive market's answer to this question. In the abstract, the answer was labeled Q_E, for equilibrium quantity. In the concrete, genuine numbers appeared, such as 650 million pounds of popcorn at farm level in 1983, and 953 million barrels of crude oil in 1929. Thus the perfectly competitive market answers the question What? by bringing quantity demanded and quantity supplied together in equilibrium (under the guidance of price).

At bottom, there are actually two issues here. First is whether a good or service will be produced at all. That which is produced is that which has sufficient demand relative to supply. Sometimes there is *in*sufficiency. If the highest price buyers are willing to pay is in no case greater than the price sellers need to cover their costs plus a minimal profit, then *none* of the product will be produced. Do you find garlic-flavored toothpaste in drugstores? No. Is there any market for male mud wrestling? No. Here you have two of the countless examples of insufficient demand relative to supply.

Second, given a demand sufficiently great to reward suppliers with a satisfactory price, what *amount* is produced? The perfectly competitive market's answer is: that amount corresponding to equilibrium, no more and no less.

Is this observed result the ideal result of *allocation efficiency?* In theory, yes. We say "in theory" because some further conditions besides perfect competition must be met for us to be certain. And in the real world, these conditions are often not met.[14] For the moment, however, we shall put the problem of further conditions aside and proceed to explain why the perfectly competitive market's answer to the question What? is, in theory, the ideal answer.

The explanation unravels from an application of two-question logic. Buyers and sellers each apply two-question logic in the market. But in the present context, we want to apply two-question logic from the point of view of *society as a whole,*

---

[14]These conditions are, in brief, an absence of *external costs, external benefits,* and *public goods.* These cause a problem of *market failure,* despite perfectly competitive conditions.

including buyers, sellers, and the rest of us. Further relying on the example of hamburger, the two questions are:

1. How does society benefit by producing some added hamburger (marginal social benefit)?
2. What does society have to give up in cost to get that added hamburger (marginal social cost)?

If the amount of benefit in the first question is *greater* than the cost in the second question, logic then suggests that added hamburger be produced. The added social benefits *exceed* the added social costs, so we should do it. Conversely, if the amount of benefit in the first question is *less* than the cost in the second question, then logic indicates that more hamburger *not* be produced. The added social benefit *falls short* of the added social cost.

Diagrammatically, the logic is adapted to the demand and supply curves of Figure 3.14. The answer to the first question—What is the benefit

of added hamburger?—is shown by the demand curve. Recall the definition of demand. The demand curve indicates how much people will purchase at each possible price. Stated differently, it shows how much value people place on each additional pound of hamburger (reading up, vertically, from the Q axis). At low quantities, each pound is worth a lot, such as $4. At abundant quantities, each added pound is worth very little, say 20 cents. In Figure 3.14, the worth of a pound at Q_{TL} is the vertical distance to B_1, which is much greater than the vertical distance to B_2, for a pound at Q_{TM}. In economic jargon, each point on the demand curve shows the *marginal social benefit* of each added pound of hamburger.

The answer to the second question—What does each pound of hamburger cost?—is shown by the supply curve. Recall now the meaning of supply. The prices in the set of supplier's prices must cover the cost of producing each pound plus a profit. For example, if these costs shift, supply shifts. Looking behind these costs, the wages paid to cowboys and meat cutters who produce hamburger must be high enough to attract them away from

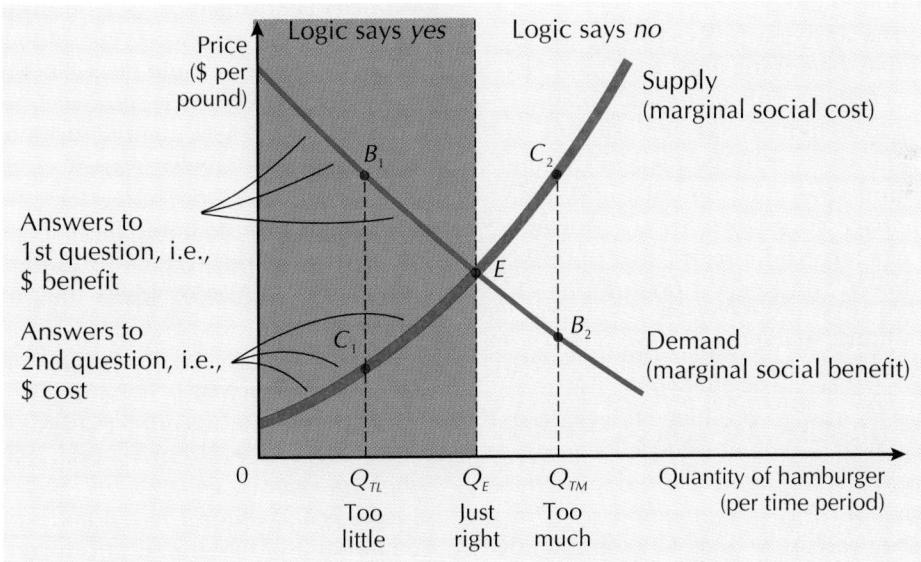

FIGURE 3.14 What? Allocation Efficiency Under Perfect Competition

The demand curve indicates the benefit *or worth of each pound of hamburger (depending on how many pounds precede each one). The supply curve indicates what society must give up in* cost *to get each pound. When the added benefit exceeds the added cost of a pound, as B₁ is greater than C₁ at quantity Q_{TL}, that quantity should be produced, and more, as then there is too little hamburger. Conversely, when the added benefit is less than the added cost of a pound, as it is at Q_{TM}, that quantity should not be produced. Less should be, because there is too much. At Q_E, the amount is just right. There is allocation efficiency.*

other jobs where they would produce other goods like wheat or poultry. So too, the rents paid for pasture land must be great enough to keep that land in pasture instead of converting to, say, corn fields or housing tracts. The profits earned by cattlemen must be generous enough to keep them in cattle ranching instead of switching to soybeans or apples. In other words, the supply curve's values reflect hamburger's *opportunity cost* in forgoing whatever is the next best use for these resources. (Recall in the previous chapter that the cost of cotton was the wheat given up.) This being the case, the price at each point on the supply curve is an index of what society *gives up* when less of these other things is produced in order to produce more hamburger. In economic jargon, it is the *marginal social cost.*

Moreover, as more and more hamburger is produced, more and more of these other things must be given up. Marginal social cost rises. To produce a pound of hamburger at Q_{TL} in Figure 3.14, the value of what is given up is indicated by the vertical dollar value at C_1. As hamburger output increases to Q_E, value given up for a pound at Q_E is vertical distance E. In turn, value C_2 is higher still for an added pound at Q_{TM}.

Comparing the answers to the two questions, then, we find that, beginning at zero output, *benefit gained exceeds cost given up for each pound of hamburger up to output Q_E*, as, for example, B_1 exceeds C_1. Logic says yes to the issue of whether to produce pound 1, pound 2, pound 3, and so on, *up to the poundage symbolized by Q_E*. However, logic says no when considering the first pound of hamburger *after Q_E*, the second pound after Q_E, the third pound after, and so on. The data tell us that *no* resources should be used to produce hamburger beyond Q_E because, thereafter, those resources should be used to produce other outputs like corn and wheat, which at that point become relatively more valuable. For amounts greater than Q_E, hamburger's *worth in benefit falls short of the cost given up for each pound*, as for example, C_2 exceeds B_2.

Output Q_E is, then, the ideal. And perfect competition attains the ideal by achieving the Q_E result. The perfectly competitive market allocates scarce resources to produce just the right amount of hamburger. Not too little, not too much. At Q_E there is *allocation efficiency.*

Allocation efficiency requires that marginal social benefit equal marginal social cost. If too little is produced, marginal social benefit exceeds marginal social cost and there is an underallocation of resources to the commodity. If too much is produced, marginal social benefit is less than marginal social cost and there is an overallocation of resources to the commodity.

These principles for coping with scarcity are so important that they are worth rephrasing:

1. What is the value of using scarce resources *here*, in this market, to produce hamburger?
2. What is the value of using scarce resources *elsewhere*, in other markets, to produce other worthy goods like bread?

The *demand curve* provides an index of *value here* for each pound of hamburger. Simultaneously, the *supply curve* provides an index of *value elsewhere*. At any output to the *left* of Q_E in Figure 3.14, *value here exceeds value elsewhere*. Logic says "yes," produce here instead of elsewhere. Indeed, output here should be *expanded*. Too little is being produced. Resources should be reallocated from elsewhere to here, where the resources are more highly valued. *Conversely*, at any output to the *right* of Q_E in Figure 3.14, *value elsewhere exceeds value here*. Logic says "no," do not produce. Once beyond Q_E, output should be *reduced* toward Q_E. Too much is being produced. Resources should go from here to elsewhere, where they are more highly valued.

At Q_E, the value of the resources as they are used *here*, to produce hamburger, just *matches* the value of the resources used *elsewhere* to produce bread and other goods. *With value here equal to value elsewhere, no reshuffling of resources is necessary. There is allocation efficiency.* The amount of hamburger produced is just right. Such is the achievement of perfect competition.

Finally, note that this market handles *changes* very nicely. If demand for hamburger shifts right, signaling that resources are now more valuable here than before, hamburger output increases, but not too much (just up to the new equilibrium). If supply shifts right, signaling that resources have become less valued elsewhere, output here again jumps. Conversely, altered tastes might shift demand leftward, reflecting lower value here than before, and that lowered value here will be followed by lower output here as resources move elsewhere. A leftward shift of supply, indicating increased value of the resources elsewhere, also triggers a shift of resources to elsewhere, but not too much of a shift.

Table 3.6 summarizes for this question What?

B
How?

How shall goods and services be produced? Many different methods of production are possible for most goods, using different combinations of resources. The beef in hamburger may be raised on ranches or in feedlots. The processing of that beef may be highly mechanized or labor intensive. And so on. The ideal is _technical efficiency._

Technical efficiency requires that a given output be produced at the lowest cost possible. This implies no wasted resources, no wasted motion, and no use of obsolete technology. Also, the resource combination used is most economic.

Whereas _allocation_ efficiency identifies the ideal quantities of each commodity produced, _technical_ efficiency specifies that each of those quantities be produced as cheaply as possible, with care, good management, a wise combinations of resources, and diligent effort. This does not necessarily mean that all producers of some commodity operate exactly alike. The conditions they confront may vary, and they should act accordingly. Where land is relatively scarce, for example, its rental value, or price, will be high, causing cattlemen to choose feedlot operations. Where instead land is plentiful and cheap, with few alternative uses, cattlemen will choose to graze their herds in open pastures.

When interviewed in 1983, over 300 U.S. business executives said that "goldbricking" was very common among their employees. If this survey is accurate, the typical worker loafs about 4 hours and 15 minutes a week, wasting company time by chatting, reading newspapers, and so on. The estimated cost to the economy of this loafing? About $137 billion annually.[15] It would thus appear that most American markets do not live up to the ideal aim of technical efficiency. Still, extensive research reveals that competitive markets are more technically efficient than noncompetitive markets.[16] Competition apparently _forces_ firms to be efficient. Those who fail to be technically efficient fail to remain in business. Thus, in general, the perfectly competitive market seems to answer the question How? very well.

(There is a major exception, however. In some industries, large firms are more technically efficient than small firms because of economies of scale.)

C
Who?

Who shall get and consume the goods and services produced? This question is answered by markets

[15]Employment consultant Robert Haft conducted the survey. _San Jose Mercury News_ (UPI), November 17, 1983, p. 1F.

[16]For a survey of the evidence, see D. F. Greer, _Industrial Organization and Public Policy_ (New York: Macmillan, 1984), pp. 425–428.

TABLE 3.6   Summary of Answers to the Question What?

	Allocation Efficiency (Just Right)	Under-allocation (Too Little)	Over-allocation (Too Much)
General requirement	$MSB = MSC$	$MSB > MSC$	$MSB < MSC$
English translation	Value here = value elsewhere	Value here > value elsewhere	Value here < value elsewhere

MSB = marginal social benefit.
MSC = marginal social cost.

at two levels—final good markets and resource markets (the top and bottom of Figure 2.8). Regarding final goods, the question is, "Who shall get the hamburger that's produced?" Or the gasoline, or any other good. The answer is, "Those who are willing and able to pay the equilibrium price." Thus, each person decides. If you are willing and able to pay the price, you get hamburger. If you are not willing and able to pay, then you do not get any hamburger. Maybe you're a vegetarian. Maybe you're too poor.

Allusion to the possibility that poverty could have an influence brings us to the second level, that of resource markets. A Rockefeller can buy more hamburger than you can because a Rockefeller's income is much greater. Hence the question of Who? ultimately depends on income distribution. Those who are rich get more goods and services than those who are poor. Those in between get less than the rich but more than the poor. Under a market system, people's incomes are determined in resource markets by the amount of various resources they own and the price at which each resource sells. Those who own highly valued resources in abundance—oil tycoons, real estate barons, brain surgeons, and the like—will garner high incomes. Those less fortunate will be less well off.

Unfortunately there is no clearly defined ideal answer to this question of Who?. There is no consensus among economists, or politicians, or any other group on the "fairest" or most "equitable" distribution of income. At one extreme are those who argue for some sort of perfect equality. At the other extreme are those who have little sympathy for anyone disadvantaged. In between, ambiguities abound.

One need not look far for the source of this confusion. When it comes to Who?, there is a dilemma. *Given scarcity, and given also efficiency in What? and How?,* the only way to improve the lot of the poor is to take from the rich. There is thus a *trade-off.* The needy can gain only at the expense of the not so needy. Hence no distribution satisfies everyone, and value judgments run rife.

Still, despite the diversity of opinion, most people tend to favor *reduced inequality* to provide for orphans, the seriously disabled, the unemployed, and other classes of unfortunates. Reduced inequality does not imply income equality.

How well does the perfectly competitive market perform in this light? A very wide variety of income distributions are consistent with perfectly competitive markets. This indeterminancy, plus the absence of any specific ideal distribution, prevents economists from saying with certainty whether the perfectly competitive market is good or bad in this respect.

D
What's New?

What new products and production processes will be adopted to alter and expand output? The perfectly competitive market's answer to this question is rather limited. A central problem here is that the model of perfect competition is *static* rather than *dynamic.* Once equilibrium is reached, for instance, nothing changes. Such a situation may be fine for defining allocation efficiency, but new products and new processes and growth obviously imply continuing change—that is, *dynamic* developments.

Although perfectly competitive markets offer little in theory or in practice regarding What's new?, markets in general can handle the question. Will jalapeño popcorn be a hit? The market decides. What about wristwatch radios or VCRs? The market again decides. Although perfect competition may not furnish the ideal here, monopoly doesn't either. We shall see later that to some degree, *imperfect* competition may be best in this respect.

E
How Stable?

How can we attain stability for the economy as a whole? Since this is a macroeconomic question, perfect competition would have to prevail throughout the economy for us to answer it. *In theory,* various schools of thought, some quite old, argue that perfect competition in this respect would assure stability or minimize instability. It would preclude the possibility of involuntary unemployment. Or so it is argued.

In fact, there is no sure way to test this theory because perfect competition has never permeated the economy and never will. The observed behavior of highly competitive sectors like agriculture suggests to many economists that competition is indeed helpful in achieving stability. As a consequence, many theories of inflation and unemployment are based on some perceived market "imperfection" such as downward price and wage rigidity. These theories are interesting but too difficult to test or implement in the complex, real world.

There are, moreover, contrary theories.

In sum, the question of How stable? lacks solid answers in fact and theory. There are no clear, universally accepted ideals. There is no consensus on the market's role.

SUMMARY

1. Markets are the major economic choice mechanism in our society. Perfectly competitive markets have some nice features of form and performance. In form, they embody (a) many buyers and sellers, (b) standardized products, (c) easy entry, and (d) well-informed buyers and sellers.
2. Marketwide demand is the set of various quantities buyers would purchase at various prices during some period. Typically, these prices and quantities are inversely related by the law of demand. Changes in the commodity's price cause movements along the demand curve. Changes in other variables, like income, cause shifts of the entire demand curve. Table 3.2 summarizes the impact of these other variables.
3. Marketwide supply is the set of various quantities sellers would offer at various prices during some period. If supply conforms to the law of supply, these prices and quantities form a positive curve. Whereas changes in the price of the commodity prompt movements along the supply curve, changes in other variables shift the entire supply curve. See Table 3.4 for an overview.
4. Markets embody a combination of demand and supply. The forces of demand and supply combine to determine a market's price and output. At the equilibrium price, the quantity demanded equals the quantity supplied, and the market comes to rest.

A legal price ceiling below the equilibrium price will prevent the price from rising to equilibrium level, thereby causing a continual shortage. Conversely, a legal price floor above equilibrium level lifts the price above equilibrium, creating surpluses. Nonmarket measures must then cope with these shortages and surpluses.
5. Changes in equilibrium follow shifts in demand or supply or both. Equilibrium price and quantity rise and fall together when demand shifts against a stable supply curve. Equilibrium price and quantity move inversely when supply moves against a fixed demand curve. When both supply and demand lurch about, the possibilities are varied.
6. As for results, the perfectly competitive market answers the question What? with allocation efficiency. The question How? is answered well by technical efficiency (but economies of scale sometimes undercut this result). Regarding Who?, perfect competition is compatible with diverse results. Problems arise for What's new?, however. Some imperfections seem to work best in a dynamic context. The ambiguity becomes greater in regard to the macroeconomic question How stable? Still, it can once again be said that competition, though not necessarily perfect competition, is probably favorable.

KEY TERMS

Perfectly competitive market
Imperfect competition
Demand

Law of supply
Movement along the supply curve
Change in the quantity supplied

Demand schedule (curve)
Law of demand
Movement along the demand curve
Change in the quantity demanded
Shift of the demand curve
Change in demand
Substitute good
Complementary good
Supply
Supply schedule (curve)

Shift of the supply curve
Change in supply
Equilibrium
Price ceiling
Price floor
Allocation efficiency
Technical efficiency
Surplus
Shortage

QUESTIONS AND PROBLEMS

1. Explain why the market-wide demand curve for any product will slope down (two reasons).

2. A market analyst in 1978 suggested that "petroleum demand would exceed supply by the year 1984." Could demand for any product ever exceed supply? Explain.

3. Discuss the relationship between the market price and the equilibrium price for a product. When will they be the same? When will the market price be above the equilibrium price? What will market analysts predict about market prices when they believe that the equilibrium price is rising? Why?

4. We have reviewed factors that may shift demand and supply curves. Considering these factors, equilibrium is best thought of as a short-lived state of balance between quantity demanded and quantity supplied. Name some products whose equilibrium prices and quantities are subject to very dramatic and/or frequent change and explain why.

5. If you go to three retail stores and find that an item they normally stock has sold out (the shelf is empty), you can be assured that your inability to purchase the item is temporary unless the government has imposed price or quantity restrictions. You may be justified, however, in worrying that when the item returns to the shelf it will have a higher price tag. Use graphs to explain why the item will soon return to the shelf and why the price tag may be higher.

6. An important function of prices in a market economy is to ration goods and services. If government refuses to allow prices to ration a particular product, it must be rationed some other way. History provides examples of rationing methods that have been used: (a) first-come, first-served; (b) favorite customers only; (c) ration coupons. Compare price rationing to these alternatives, noting the implications of each for allocation efficiency and for equity.

7. Periodically, rumors have circulated that a particular food product contains some harmful or distasteful ingredient. The producers of these food products have naturally been most anxious to squelch the rumors. Explain graphically the cause for their concern.

8. An excise tax is a tax imposed on a particular product. The producer is required to forward the tax revenue to the government, perhaps $1.00 for each unit of the product sold. Sometimes an excise tax is called a "vice tax" because it is imposed on a product such as cigarettes or liquor. Use supply and demand curve analysis to show why society might approve such a "vice tax."

9. Price ceilings on a product discourage production and encourage consumption. Show these effects graphically.

10. Each spring, a prestigious professional golf tournament is held on the same luxurious golf course. If your name is on "the list," you have the privilege of purchasing a ticket for $75.00. If your name is not on "the list," you cannot purchase a ticket from tournament authorities. Local residents are accustomed to the question "Know anyone who wants to sell tickets?" Many tickets are resold at much higher prices despite the fact that tournament authorities discourage resales and "scalping" is illegal in the state. (Scalping is defined as reselling a ticket at a price higher than you paid.) Discuss:
    (a) What can be said about the equilibrium ticket price?
    (b) Why would tournament authorities keep the ticket price at about $75.00 year after year?
    (c) What are the positive economic results of scalping?
    (d) How does scalping affect the answer to Who?
    (e) Combine positive economic analysis with normative analysis to decide whether scalping should be legalized.

4

The Role of Government

Markets are wonderful, but . . . Sulfanilamide, the first modern "wonder drug," won worldwide glory when introduced in 1936. To cash in on its popularity, drug companies rushed to market a vast array of derivative products, one of which was a liquid called Elixir Sulfanilamide. Unfortunately, sulfanilamide does not dissolve in water, alcohol, or any other common medical solvent, but it does dissolve in diethylene glycol. Upon discovering this, the makers of Elixir Sulfanilamide used diethylene glycol for their solvent. As a result, 108 people died painfully, and the Food, Drug, and Cosmetic Act of 1938 was enacted.

The deaths were not the sole reason for the legislation, but they demonstrated a problem. Other examples abound:

1. The Cuyahoga River in Cleveland, Ohio, became so polluted that in 1969 it caught fire. Stiff water pollution controls were passed by Congress in 1972.
2. In 1905 the State of New York established one of the nation's first public utility commissions after discovering that the New York Gas and Electric Light Company was selling electricity at a price that ran as high as 15 cents per kilowatt-hour. The company's cost was only 3.6 cents.
3. The economy crumbled during the Great Depression. One-fourth of all workers lost their jobs and the nation's total output dropped by a third. Thereafter, the Employment Act of 1946 authorized federal action in aggregate economic affairs.

In the jargon of Chapter 1, these are examples of problem identification and policy proposal. The role of government could be studied by sifting through a variety of such examples, but that would be confusing. Instead, this chapter splits into parts that deal separately with problems and policies: problems of procedure; problems of results; policy responses; and problems with government.

Earlier, Figure 1.1 outlined the two broad economic issues at stake—choice procedures and choice results. We will follow that division here by first looking at problems of procedure and then at problems of results. The same division will apply to policy responses. Finally, in the last section, we explain that government may often be the problem, not the solution.

I

Problems of Procedure: Market Maintenance

A

Basic Upkeep

Your car will sputter without basic upkeep. The same is true of the market system. Markets could be based on barter but they work best with *money*. Moreover, dried fish could serve as money, but experience and common sense argue that official coin and currency work better, so the government issues and regulates money.

Besides money, markets are greatly improved by a legal device—namely, the **contract.** In essence, a contract is the binding element of any market exchange. *It is a commercial promise that the government will enforce.* Commercial promises can be enforced by other means, such as threat of bodily harm. But in our society such primitive enforcement procedures have been abandoned. Contracts lubricate the market system because they serve two functions: (1) They allow people to determine their own terms in exchanges and (2) they move us beyond a day-to-day, willy-nilly existence to long-run reliances.

Private property further facilitates the market process. Indeed, assorted chunks of private property are the things that are exchanged in many markets. Thus your private-property money becomes your private-property stereo through exchange. By simple definition, *private property is a* *bundle of rights and liberties.* These rights and liberties need not relate to anything material, like land, though they commonly do. They may concern intangibles—like the franchise for the New York Yankees or patent number 3,476,112. Delineation and defense of these rights and liberties have fallen to the government rather than to vigilante gangs or religious institutions. Private property also serves two functions: (1) It provides incentive for people to work hard and (2) it helps make decentralized decision making possible (in markets and in government).

Bolstering the market system with contract and private property yields an *economic system* called *capitalism* (or the free enterprise system).

> **Capitalism** is an economic system in which the means of production are privately owned and operated for profit. In addition, the economic activities of people and businesses are coordinated by free markets through contractual exchanges.

Under pure capitalism, the market system would be *completely* free of government intervention except for matters of money, contract, and private property. Perhaps a few other tasks of basic economic upkeep could also be assigned the government, such as the standardization of weights and measures. But not much more would be permitted to government under pure capitalism—certainly nothing greatly altering economic results. Only that which provides a procedural, legal framework.

In fact, however, we live under a system of *mixed capitalism.*

> Under **mixed capitalism** the government is quite active, owning large amounts of public property, correcting market imperfections, and influencing answers to the basic questions What?, How?, Who?, What's new?, and How stable?.

Hence we may now move beyond the matter of basic upkeep. Aside from the basic questions and their ultimate answers, our government addresses a further class of procedural problems that arise from market imperfections.

B
Correction of Market Imperfections

The conditions for perfect competition—many participants, a standardized product, easy entry, and full information—are usually not met in real markets. Imperfections abound. Most of these deviations from perfection pose no serious problems. Reducing the number of sellers in a market from 3,000 to 40, for example, may not lessen competition at all, especially when competition is defined so as to include rivalry. Still, imperfections can become serious, leading to problems of both procedure and results. Two such imperfections—monopoly power and consumer misinformation—are especially common.

1. Monopoly Power

> With **pure monopoly,** there is just one seller and high barriers to entry.

That single seller can raise the price *above* what it would be with competition by restricting the supply *below* what it would be with competition. A monopoly controls the supply because it is the sole source of supply.

Such restrictions of output are often possible even when the monopoly is less than pure—when, that is, there is a dominant seller or just a few sellers. These firms have some degree of "monopoly power" despite the absence of pure monopoly. That monopoly power can likewise raise the price and curb output, especially when the firms collude to form cartels.

Aristotle observed monopolistic behavior centuries ago, and it can still be seen today. It causes problems for both the What? and the Who? questions. Regarding What?, the monopolist typically produces a *smaller* quantity of output than would be produced under competition—*too little* compared to the amount that would yield allocation efficiency. Regarding Who?, the monopolist may garner excessively high profits, which could enrich the wealthy owners of the monopoly at the expense of poor consumers.

Moreover, there are adverse *procedural* implications of monopoly. Would you like it if there were only one or two auto companies to deal with? Or petroleum companies? Probably not. Our society likes having many options. We also like decentralized decision making. This is a procedural blessing economically. It is also desirable politically because political power is often grounded on economic power.

2. Consumer Misinformation Consumer misinformation is another market imperfection that raises problems for both procedures and results. Ill-informed consumers buy the wrong product or the wrong brand. They favor one seller's offering more than they should, and favor another's less than they should. The result is that they buy _too much_ of some things and _not enough_ of others. Markets therefore can be seriously flawed when answering the questions What? and What's new?.

Setting these faulty results aside for the moment, let's stick to the issue of choice procedure. Why are consumers ill informed? Why do they err? One reason is advertising, _persuasive_ advertising in particular. Advertising can be helpfully _informative_, as when supermarkets advertise their weekly grocery specials in newspapers. On the other hand, much of it, maybe even most of it, is largely persuasive, exhorting consumers with endorsements from ex-athletes (light beer), with fearsome house fires (insurance), with sexy models (cosmetics), with catchy jingles (soda pop), with all kinds of tactics that are extensively tested by marketing researchers for their sales potency. These pitches seem to foster faulty buying behavior. Consumers themselves say so. From 70 to 80 percent of all people polled agree that "advertising leads people to buy things they don't need or can't afford."[1]

Deceptive advertising is especially troublesome. Firestone advertised that its Super Sports Wide Oval tires could stop 25 percent quicker, when in fact they couldn't. Listerine spent tens of millions of dollars over several decades persuading people that its mouthwash helped prevent colds and lessened their severity, when in fact it didn't. Campbell Soup Company formerly put marbles in the bottom of its televised bowls of soup, so that the

vegetables and other solid parts of the soup would appear abundantly above the surface.

Is this behavior fair to consumers? Is it fair to the competitors of those who deceive? Probably not. Yet it is a commonplace imperfection of the free market.

II
Problems Regarding Results

What happens when the economy misses the mark for normative standards of What?, How?, Who?, What's new?, and How stable? There is, to put it dryly, a problem regarding results.

As just seen, these problems can be due to market imperfections. The problems we turn to now, however, are not simply problems of imperfection. With imperfections, faith in the free market is staunchly held. The basic idea is that the free market _is capable_ of serving society if certain repairs are made, just as a car is capable of getting someone from St. Louis to Chicago if in good repair. In contrast, the present section takes up problems stemming from perceptions that the free market _is not capable_, not even if it is free of imperfections. An auto is not capable of transporting someone from Los Angeles to Honolulu. An auto is not capable of giving comfortable housing. Complete substitution is called for. Boats and dwellings must be pressed into service. Similarly, the economic problems of the present section, which are outlined in Table 4.1, warrant government policies that _modify_, _override_, or _supplant_ the market system.

A
Allocation Problems (Re: What? and a Bit of How?)

The major achievement of the perfectly competitive market is, as you have seen, allocation efficiency. It produces the "just right" amount. It equates marginal social benefit with marginal social cost. This applies to many goods. This does _not_ apply, however, to _public goods_. Freely competitive mar-

---

[1]R. A. Bauer and S. A. Greyser, _Advertising in America: The Consumer View_ (Boston: Division of Research, Graduate School of Business Administration, Harvard University, 1968), pp. 175–183.

TABLE 4.1   Problems Regarding Results: Free Market Incapabilities

Nature of the Problem	Value Judgment Applied	Examples
Allocation problems (re: What? and a bit of How?)	Efficiency	Pollution, education, defense
Distribution problems (re: Who?)	Equity	Poverty, discrimination
Promotion problems (re: What's New?)	Progress	Slow growth, little innovation
Stabilization problems (re: How stable?)	Stability	High unemployment, inflation

kets fail for them. These goods are analogous to the Los Angeles–Honolulu trip in the auto metaphor. Moreover, freely competitive markets also fail to achieve allocation efficiency when *externalities* are present. Hence, public goods and externalities are referred to as *market failures* (instead of mere imperfections).

> Public goods and externalities create misallocations of resources, even if markets are perfectly competitive. They are therefore instances of **market failure.**

1. Public Goods   Ponder coffee, a *private good.* You might drink seven cups a day, while a friend drinks none. Moreover, when you drink a certain cup of coffee, no one else drinks that same coffee. You consume it *individually.* The same is true of sweaters, eyeglasses, and hamburgers. Indeed, given scarcity, it is remotely true that the more you have of these things, the less will be available to others.

Such is not true of *public goods* because they are consumed *collectively* by many people simultaneously. National defense is the classic example of a public good because everyone in the country enjoys its protective umbrella, babies as well as grownups, westerners as well as easterners, doctors and patients alike. Moreover, national defense cannot be parceled out in small pieces, permitting a lot more to hawks than to doves. More for hawks also means more for doves. Whatever the defense budget comes to—$213 billion or $327 billion— that is exactly the amount *each* of us gets.

> A **public good** benefits everyone. Excluding people from it is either impossible or too expensive.

Free markets fail to provide enough of a public good. There is too little of it. Why? Ponder once again the contrast with coffee, a market-supplied good. If you want to get some, you pay for it, and you get it. If you don't want any coffee, you don't pay for it, and you don't get it. Paying and getting are inseparably linked, and the market can respond to each individual's strength of demand.

In contrast, there is for public goods a chasm between paying and getting in the free market. If you pay, you might not get it. If you don't pay, you might get it anyway. Two-question logic collapses, and you don't pay. You fear getting nothing for something and hope to get something for nothing, thereby becoming a **free rider.** Others are in the same boat, so with no one paying, the market collapses.

Imagine, for example, a city of 1 million families. If each family contributes, say, $50 per year, the city could obtain the ideal amount of fire-fighting protection. Modern trucks, ample equipment, and expert fire fighters could be strategically located in fire stations throughout the city so that no burning home would be more than 5 minutes away from rescue following an alarm call. Does this mean that the Smith family (or any other family) would eagerly and voluntarily pay its $50 each year for fire fighting? Probably not. Two possibilities deflate their motivation: (1) the possibility that the Smiths pay their $50 but hardly anyone else does, in which case they have paid for first-class, 5-minute fire protection but actually get third-rate, 30-minute protection, or (2) the possibility that even though they do not pay $50, nearly everyone else does, in which case they have a close approximation to first-class, 5-minute protection without paying a dime. Hence the Smiths do not pay. Neither do most others. With few people paying, the market provides _too little_ of this public good.

2. Externalities Production and consumption often create _externalities,_ also called _spillovers,_ that help or harm bystanders, neighbors, or others not directly involved. When these spillovers are good, they are _external benefits._ If they are bad, they constitute _external costs._

Stated in terms of two-question logic, free markets run on the experiences of market participants, on their private benefits and costs—the first and second values of the two-question values _they themselves_ confront. Free markets work fine when market participants receive first-question benefits that are the same as society's first-question benefits and when they also incur second-question costs that match society's second-question costs. However, this is often _not_ the case.

External Benefits and Too Little: When you pay for a vaccination against polio, you get protection against polio. Moreover, those around you also benefit because your vaccination severs a possible link in the chain of communicating polio to others.

Education, especially through high school, likewise illustrates external benefits. You benefit from your education because your mind is your mental living room and you like it well furnished. Schooling also boosts your income prospects. _Others_ also benefit because you are more couth as a neighbor, more intelligent as a fellow voter, more articulate as a partner in conversation, more discerning as a shopper. Society as a whole thus gains by your basic academic attainments. Conversely, you benefit from good schools anywhere in the country.

Markets for vaccinations and education would surely exist without government prompting. Unlike public goods, such goods _can_ be parceled out individually. When you pay as a purchaser, you _do_ get the benefit you pay for. It's just that _others also benefit,_ so society's benefit is not measured by yours alone. And for this reason, private free-market provision of such goods is _too little_ as compared to the social ideal.

Figure 4.1 illustrates this situation. The supply curve, as before, reflects both marginal _private_ cost _and_ marginal _social_ costs. That is to say, the market's private participants face a second question in two-question logic that is the same as society's. The demand curve is different, however. Viewed vertically from the horizontal axis, it measures _only the private benefits_ of purchasers. It's their first-question values. Thus, when purchasers exercise their two-question logic, market output stops at Q_{FM}. This free market output brings marginal private benefit into equality with marginal private cost at point E. But this is _too little_ from society's point of view because society's marginal benefit at that output is much higher at point B, higher by the amount of the external benefit, _EB._ Marginal social benefit is marginal private benefit _plus_ external benefit. With social benefit greater than social cost for Q_{FM}, output should be _increased_ to level Q_G. But the free market fails to budge beyond Q_{FM}.

> **External benefits** are benefits gained by people other than those directly involved in some production or consumption activity.

External Costs and Too Much: Pollution is the classic example of external cost. When producers and consumers pollute, they are not shouldering the costs of their waste disposal but rather forcing those costs onto others. When borne by others, these costs take several forms—costs of avoidance (air conditioning, moving out of town), of repair (painting, medical treatment), and of raw damage (death, noxious air). If people suffering from these problems could bill polluters for their losses, these costs would be _internalized._ Polluters would then see these external costs in the same light they see their regular costs, and thereby would be induced to reduce their pollution. But this doesn't happen in the free market. External costs thus cause problems of _too much_—too much pollution and too much of the products and processes that pollute.

Figure 4.2 shows the free market equilibrium at E, where demand meets supply. Without external benefits, demand reflects both private and social benefits. This time the problem lies with the _sup-_

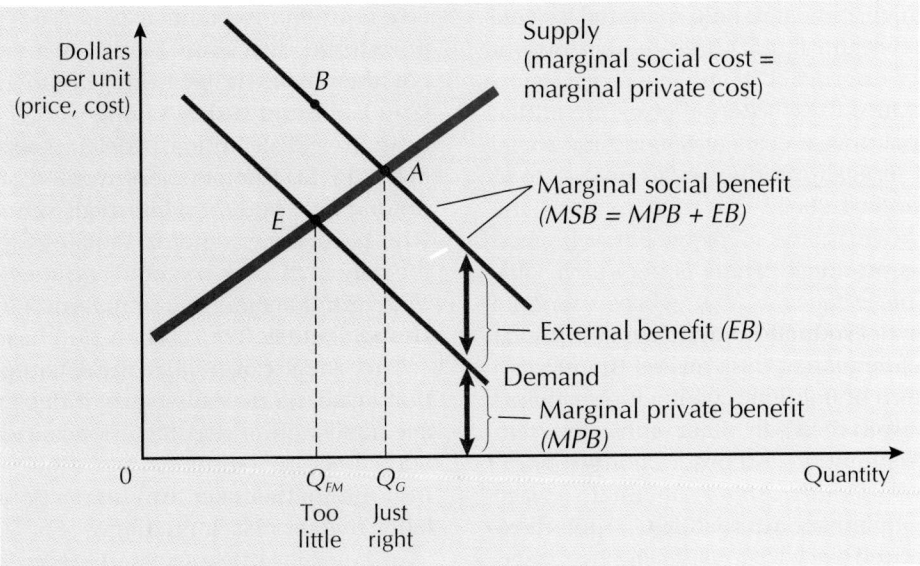

FIGURE 4.1 *External Benefits: A Market Failure*

The free market works with the private benefits and costs of the participants. Here the private costs match the social costs, but social benefits are greater than private benefits because external benefits occur. The free market reaches equilibrium E, with output Q_{FM}. This is too little, however. Marginal social benefit, the vertical distance to B, exceeds marginal social cost, the vertical distance to E, by amount EB (the external benefit). Output should be increased to level Q_G, so marginal social benefit and cost match at A.

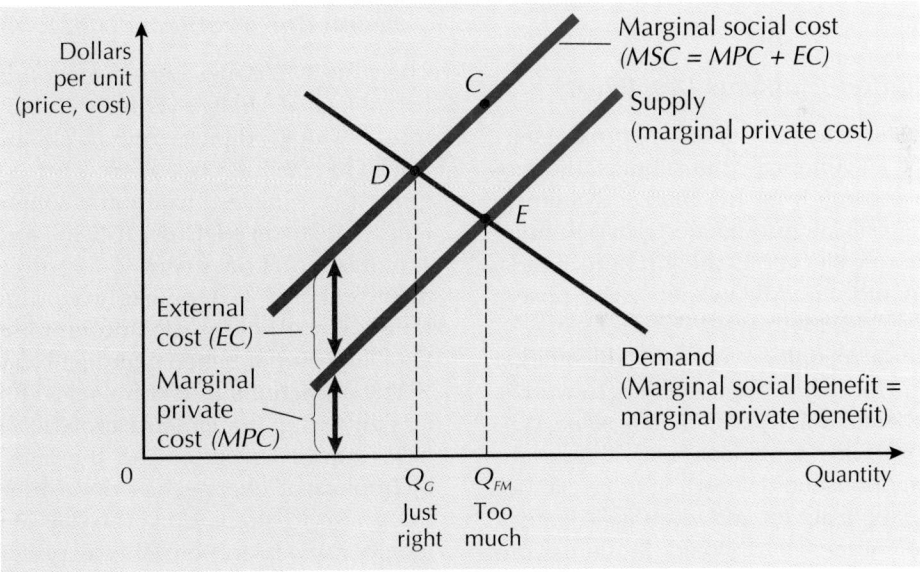

FIGURE 4.2 *External Costs: A Market Failure*

The free market works with private benefits and costs of the participants. The free market reaches equilibrium E, with output Q_{FM}. Here the private costs match the private benefits, but too much is being produced. Marginal social cost, the vertical distance to C, exceeds marginal social benefit, the vertical distance to E, by amount EC (the external cost). Output should be reduced to level Q_G so that marginal social benefit and cost match at D.

ply curve, which indicates _only_ marginal _private_ costs. At equilibrium _E_, with free market output Q_{FM}, there are external costs indicated by vertical distance _EC_. Once these external costs are added to the marginal private costs at _E_, marginal social cost extends vertically all the way from Q_{FM} to _C_. Thus the marginal social cost at _C_ exceeds the demand curve's marginal social benefit at _E_ when output Q_{FM} is produced. There is _too much_. Output should be _reduced_ to Q_G, where marginal social benefit does equal marginal social cost at point _D_. The free market thus misses the mark.

External costs of pollution, which if unchecked would probably exceed $40 billion annually, stem from both consumption and production. Pop bottle litter, auto exhaust, and residential sewage illustrate consumption externalities. Sulfur dioxide from coal-fired electricity plants and hydrocarbons from petroleum refineries illustrate the problems in production. Because production processes are involved here, the question How? is involved as well as the question What?

> **External costs** are costs borne by people other than those directly involved in some production or consumption activity.

B
Distribution Problems (Re: Who?)

During the 1970s and early 1980s, approximately 24 percent of all American households did not earn enough income from the market system to rise above the officially designated poverty line.[2] This amounts to well over 15 million households, and the many more people in them, who pose a _poverty_ problem for the market system.

Who are these people? Why can't the market system provide for them? Their inability to work is a big part of the answer. _Approximately 60 percent_ of these households have low market incomes because their household head simply cannot work. These people are too old (over age 65), crippled, blind, or otherwise disabled. Students and single women with children under 6 also have trouble working and account for another _12 percent_ of those with market earnings below the pov-

erty line. The remaining _28 percent_ of those impoverished earn some market income from work, but their work is part-time or poorly paid (e.g., farm labor and dish washing).[3]

Another distribution problem is _discrimination._ Men do far better than women, for instance. Among able-bodied white high school graduates who headed households, females experienced an incidence of poor market earnings nearly _eight times greater_ than that of males, 24.9 percent versus 3.2 in 1978.

This statistic _overstates_ the extent of discrimination against females because it does not take into account such added factors as work experience and career interruptions. Nevertheless, other data indicate that females and blacks do indeed suffer labor market discrimination.

In sum, it appears that there are at least two distribution problems—(1) poverty in general and (2) substantial discrimination against women and nonwhites in the labor market. These problems apparently offend our society's sense of equity because our government has been called upon to respond with wide-ranging remedies.

C
Promotion Problems (Re: What's New?)

There are two issues here—_economic growth_ and _technological change_. The desirability of growth most obviously derives from its ability to boost our standard of living. Less obvious is the contribution growth can make to softening some of the problems just surveyed. Growth helps reduce poverty. It builds industrial might to improve our national defense. Some economists even argue that economic growth eases the burden of treating problems of external benefits and external costs.

The attractions of technological change are no less glittering. It augments growth. Also, from the first squawky telephone to the latest microchip, technological change has done more than anything else to shape our everyday life. Innovation lengthens lives and enriches experiences.

The question is, then, do free markets provide the right amounts of economic growth and technological change? This question has no easy an-

---

[2]In 1987, the officially defined poverty line for a four-person family was $11,000.

[3]Peter D. McClelland (ed.), _Introductory Macroeconomics 1983–1984_ (Ithaca, N.Y.: Cornell University Press, 1983), p. 177.

swer because another key question lacks any solid answer, namely, What are the "right" amounts of growth and technological change?

The absence of a clear answer to the question "What are the right amounts?" is perhaps most clearly demonstrated by the sharp disparity of opinions voiced about observed rates of growth and technological change. By some value judgments, America does not have enough. By others, America has too much. Let's note just one argument that the free market provides too little technological change.

Those who believe that the free market provides _too little_ technological change often contend that the free market offers too little reward to inventors and innovators relative to society's gains from their efforts. Short on reward, pioneers will lack sufficient incentive. The problem is similar to the problem of a public good. Use of a body of knowledge by someone does not mean that less knowledge is then available to others. Knowledge can be used once or a million times, by a few or by many, without suffering wear and tear, without ever being used up. Thus it can be collectively used, and it is often difficult to exclude users. An inventor or innovator therefore sees the situation much like the little boy who climbs and shakes the apple tree, only to find out that his buddies on the ground have run off with most of the loot before he can get down. Imitators and others reduce the pioneer's rewards. With rewards not commensurate with their costs, pioneers will produce less new knowledge than is desirable. By this argument, government intervention is needed to get more.

Without well-defined, widely accepted standards, we cannot be certain whether the market errs in these respects. However, if the history of actual policies is any guide, the market seems to provide too little growth and technological change. Substantial government policies promoting these developments have existed in America since its founding.

D

Stabilization Problems (Re: How Stable?)

Periodically, the economy is engulfed by _depression_ or _recession_, more colorfully called _panic_ or _collapse_. The depression of 1873, our first as an industrial society, was notable for its violence:

> At the blackest period of the depression the country was swarming with "tramps," who were usually factory or farm hands looking vainly for a livelihood and drifting into gang life. Here and there bands of these men allied with professional criminals, drinking, stealing, raping, and murdering.[4]

Subsequent depressions, such as those of 1882–85 and 1893–97, produced their own tales of woe, but none was worse than the Great Depression of the 1930s. The value of all corporate stocks on the New York Stock Exchange plunged from $89.6 billion to $15.6 billion between September 1, 1929, and July 1, 1932. Eighty-five thousand businesses failed. Residential construction tumbled by 90 percent. Thousands of banks failed. Unemployment reached 25 percent in 1933.

More recently, 1981–82 witnessed the worst recession since the Great Depression.

A second major indicator of aggregate instability is inflation, or the annual percentage rate of change in price level. During the period since 1958, the inflation rate has ranged from a low of 0.7 percent in 1961 to a high of 13.3 percent in 1979. The inflation rate thus seems quite unruly.

There is no universally accepted yardstick for measuring the seriousness of the stability problem. Some economists argue that the economy is not gravely injured by even moderately high rates of inflation. Others make light of the problem of unemployment unless the jobless rate exceeds 7 percent or so. Still, even by these lenient standards of price and employment performance, the economy has frequently broken the scales of constancy. This is true both historically and recently.

■ CHECK YOUR BEARINGS

The economic functions we call on government to perform are many and varied. Yet the main ones fall into two broad categories and six subcategories.

First, several of the government's activities facilitate or strengthen the market system:

1. Provision of a healthy financial and legal

---

[4]Eric F. Goldman, _Rendezvous with Destiny_ (New York: Vintage Books, 1956), p. 25.

framework— money supply, private property, and contract.

2. Reduction of market imperfections, which helps to keep sellers competitive and buyers informed.

Second, many government activities modify or supplant the market system to address problems with results:

3. Allocation: the allocation of resources is altered in order to increase some outputs and reduce others.

4. Distribution: incomes are redistributed and discrimination is curbed.

5. Promotion: economic growth and technological change are encouraged.

6. Stability: excessive unemployment and inflation prompt policy efforts.

III
Government Policies

The government's toolbox of economic policies overflows with gadgetry. Government can manipulate the monetary and legal framework by, for example, expanding or contracting the money supply or by altering the property rights of patents. Government can guarantee bank loans. It can own and operate enterprises, such as the U.S. Postal Service and the Tennessee Valley Authority. The list is lengthy.

For the present, however, we must limit the list to just three broad types of tools—(1) taxation, (2) spending, and (3) regulation. Several other instruments are important enough to be mentioned below, but taxation, spending, and regulation predominate. We begin by identifying each, as summarized in Table 4.2. We then proceed to match problems with policies.

A
Overview: Basic Tools

1. Taxation The grand total tax take for all governments—federal, state, and local combined—easily exceeds $1 trillion annually. A trillion is one thousand billion, and a billion is a very big number

in its own right—1,000,000,000. One billion _hours_ ago, people were living in caves. Still, when viewed in _relative_ terms, this aggregate government tax burden is less awesome. It amounts to somewhat more than $4,000 per person.

A **tax** is a compulsory government levy on some activity or asset.

The main purpose of taxes is to raise general revenues for the government. George Washington had to be paid a salary. The local police force doesn't donate its services. Military suppliers like Lockheed and General Dynamics make profits as well as weapons, so they too must be paid. Thus, general revenue is the first purpose of taxes listed in Table 4.2 together with some chief examples, namely, income taxes, sales taxes, and property taxes.

Figure 4.3 reveals the vast magnitude of these taxes. Individual income taxes alone have accounted for nearly 40 percent of the government's total tax revenue of late, counting federal, state, and local levels combined. Taxes on corporate income, general sales, and private property bring in another 30 percent or so.

Other taxes likewise raise government revenue but also accomplish other purposes. The largest of these other taxes—as suggested in Table 4.2 and Figure 4.3—are designed to redistribute income. Thus, Social Security payroll taxes are taken from people who are working and given to those who are retired or disabled. Inheritance, or death, taxes chip away at wealthy estates, thereby also redistributing income.

Still other taxes are collected to finance specific government services. The motor fuel tax, which funds highway construction and maintenance, is perhaps the best example.

2. Spending In recent years, total **government spending**—federal, state, and local together—has also topped $1 trillion. And there are, as suggested in Table 4.2, three main types of government outlay: (1) purchases of goods and services, (2) transfer payments, and (3) subsidies.

The government _purchases goods_ when it buys things like submarines, traffic lights, and copying machines. The government _purchases services_

TABLE 4.2   Basic Government Economic Policies

1. TAX—COMPULSORY LEVY

Main purposes
a. Raise general revenues

b. Redistribute income
c. Finance specific services
d. Alter economic behavior

Examples
a. Income taxes, sales taxes, property taxes
b. Social Security taxes, inheritance taxes
c. Gasoline tax for highway construction
d. Cigarette and liquor taxes, import tariffs, investment tax credits

2. SPEND—GOVERNMENT OUTLAY

Main purposes
a. Purchase goods and services provided to the public
b. Transfer income to certain citizens
c. Subsidize or encourage behavior

Examples
a. Hire judges and clerks, purchase missiles and desks
b. Social Security, welfare spending

c. Student loans, transportation subsidies

3. REGULATE—RULES AND CONTROLS

Main purposes
a. Antitrust, i.e., maintenance of competition
b. Information regulations
c. Price level regulations

d. Social regulation

Examples
a. Bans against cartels and monopolization
b. Labeling laws, grade ratings
c. Public utility regulation, minimum wage law
d. Safety, health, and antidiscrimination regulations

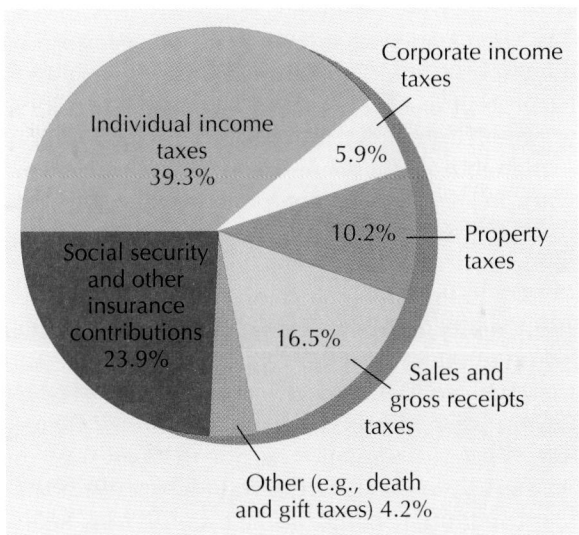

FIGURE 4.3   Federal, State, and Local Government Tax Revenues by Type, 1983

Note: Excludes revenues from public enterprises such as the postal service and higher education. (Source: Statistical Abstract of the United States 1986, pp. 266, 306.)

when it hires fire fighters, school teachers, and forest rangers, not to mention desk-bound bureaucrats. One distinctive feature of these **purchases** is that, in making them, *the government is making a direct claim on the productive capacity of the nation.* It is snaring a share of our scarce resources and channeling those resources toward governmental ends and away from private ends. A submarine, for instance, embodies materials that could be used to produce microwave ovens. An air force pilot flies the government's bombers instead of United's passenger planes.

Government **transfer payments** are different. These include welfare payments and Social Security checks. Those who receive these payments *give the government nothing in return.* To be sure, the recipients must meet certain qualifications. They must be old and retired, for instance. But the basic purpose of these payments is kindness rather than compensation. As such, transfer payments *do not* divert resources from the private sector to the public sector, as do purchase payments. Rather, they redistribute resources among different pockets and purses in the private sector, from the young to the old, for instance, or from the rich to the poor.

Finally, **government subsidies** lie somewhere between purchases and transfers in both character and effect. In simplest form, the government subsidizes _by paying part of the cost of some favored private sector's production or consumption activity_. For example, the federal government pays half the cost of constructing merchant ships in U.S. shipyards. Likewise, the federal government pays part of the cost of Amtrak's passenger train operations. The government's payments sometimes take convoluted forms—low-interest loans (e.g., to college students), services sold at discount prices (e.g., low postage rates for books and magazines), and tax breaks (e.g., tax credits for solar energy equipment). Nevertheless, all of these are subsidies.

Note that, with a subsidy, the government is _not_ always directly transferring resources from the private to the public sector, as it does with a purchase. By the same token, a subsidy is _not_ a simple handout, or transfer, because those receiving the subsidy do perform productively—building ships, buying solar equipment, attending college, and so on. Nevertheless, since subsidies share many of the characteristics of both purchases and transfers, they overlap these other categories. Moreover, their economic effect falls between those of purchases and transfers. Subsidies divert resources from unfavored toward favored activities, but the favored activities are not necessarily public ones.

> **Government spending** refers to government outlays for purchases, transfer payments, and subsidies.

The overlaps among purchases, transfers, and subsidies make it difficult to determine exactly how much the government is actually spending on each category. No official breakdown is available. By rough approximation, however, purchases of goods and services take the lion's share, something over 60 percent of all government outlays. Transfers account for most of the rest, followed by subsidies.

3. Regulation The two main features of **regulation** are _standard setting_ and _enforcement by monitoring and remedies._

Table 4.2 mentions four major types of government regulations. The first two—_antitrust and information policies_—affect the market system only slightly. Their purpose is not to overthrow or replace the market's results, but rather to correct procedural imperfections. The last two—_price level regulation and social regulation_—are much more intrusive. With these, the government becomes involved in the daily affairs of businesses. Moreover, the government must establish large bureaucracies to set and enforce standards of intricate complexity, immense variety, and vast quantity. Accordingly, the examples of such regulation are endless. Here are two: (1) The price you pay for electricity is regulated by a public utility commission (unless your electric utility happens to be among the 20 percent that are government owned and operated). (2) Since 1984, all cars sold in the United States must not emit more than 0.41 grams of hydrocarbons per mile traveled.

B

Specifics: Problems and Policies Together

Tax, spend, and regulate—the list of basic government tools is thus short. The list of key problems is likewise brief—problems of imperfection, allocation, redistribution, promotion, and stabilization. It therefore might seem easy to match problems with policies. But it's not, partly because any one problem can be treated by several policy options.

Take pollution, for instance. The government's main policy weapon against pollution is regulation. Polluters are given standards to meet and then policed. Detected violations prompt product recalls, plant closures, fines, and other regulatory remedies. Yet regulation is not the only way, or necessarily even the best way, to secure abatement. Pollution could also be curbed by taxing emissions or by purchasing abatement equipment and services. In fact, real-life examples of pollution taxes and abatement purchases presently exist. Buyers of soda pop and beer in several states must pay a tax-like deposit of 5 or 10 cents per bottle, which they get back if they don't pollute (i.e., return the bottle) or which they actually pay if they do pollute (i.e., discard the bottle). As for purchases, all levels of government spent over $40 billion between 1972 and 1983 on sewage treatment facilities. Still, regulation remains the main policy approach to pollution control.

Hence, a word of warning: The following review only highlights problem/policy pairings.

1. _Market Imperfection Policies_   To combat anticompetitive conditions, the United States has the world's oldest and largest body of _antitrust laws_, which are regulations of a sort. Born in 1890 with the Sherman Act, this body of laws has grown through subsequent legislation and thousands of court cases to become this nation's mainstay in maintaining competition. Three offenses receive most of the enforcement effort and news coverage:

1. _Collusion_ among rivals to rig prices or otherwise stifle competition. The federal government took action against 551 such restraints of trade during 1963–82.
2. _Mergers_ among rivals that may lessen competition. Nearly 20 cases a year have been brought since 1963.
3. _Monopolization_ of a market, unless achieved by efficiency, innovation, or other laudable economic advantage. These cases are big cases. The most notorious one of late ended with the breakup of AT&T.

Regulations to keep consumers informed divide into two categories—those _encouraging disclosure_ and those _prohibiting misrepresentation._ Regulations encouraging disclosure force sellers to reveal information helpful to wise shopping, such as the contents of canned goods, the fiber composition of textiles, and the interest rates on loans. In contrast, regulations prohibiting misrepresentation ban misleading advertising and control high-pressure door-to-door salespeople.

2. _Allocation Policies (What? and a Bit of How?)_
The problems of public goods and external bene-

fits are met primarily by government purchases of goods and services or government subsidies. Figure 4.4 offers a sweeping view of government activity in these areas by showing government purchases of goods and services (which include some subsidies) as a percentage of total national output. Before 1930, official purchases were comparatively low—less than 10 percent of national output. The Great Depression brought some escalation as the government initiated public works projects like dam building. Thereafter a big bulge occurred for World War II. Finally, total government outlays settled at about 20 percent of America's total economic output, beginning in the early 1950s and remaining there, with some fluctuations, for the past three decades. The composition of that 20 percent total has shifted—with the federal government losing share and state and local governments gaining share—but the overall total has been remarkably immobile.

Regarding specifics, the profound impact of national defense expenditures on the federal government's total, both up and down, emerges quite clearly in Figure 4.4. Not shown is education, the biggest single item of state and local government expenditure. And highways, hospitals, and police protection also burden state and local budgets considerably.

The free market's problem with public goods and external benefits is one of producing too little. So it is fitting that the foregoing activities _increase_ outputs above free market levels. Market misallocations of the opposite sort—too much due to external costs, for instance—are handled primarily by _regulation_. The regulations _reduce_ pollution, product hazards, workplace dangers, and other unsavory risks.

Such regulation began long ago, with food and drug legislation in 1906. Official activity then jumped a bit during the 1930s. But the biggest expansion occurred during the 1960s and 1970s when a series of crises erupted, contaminating the air, crippling babies, and killing motorists. Popular books, such as Rachel Carson's _Silent Spring_ and Ralph Nader's _Unsafe at Any Speed_, broadcast the bad news. The names of the main federal agencies created or vastly expanded during this period reveal the nature and scope of the regulatory effort

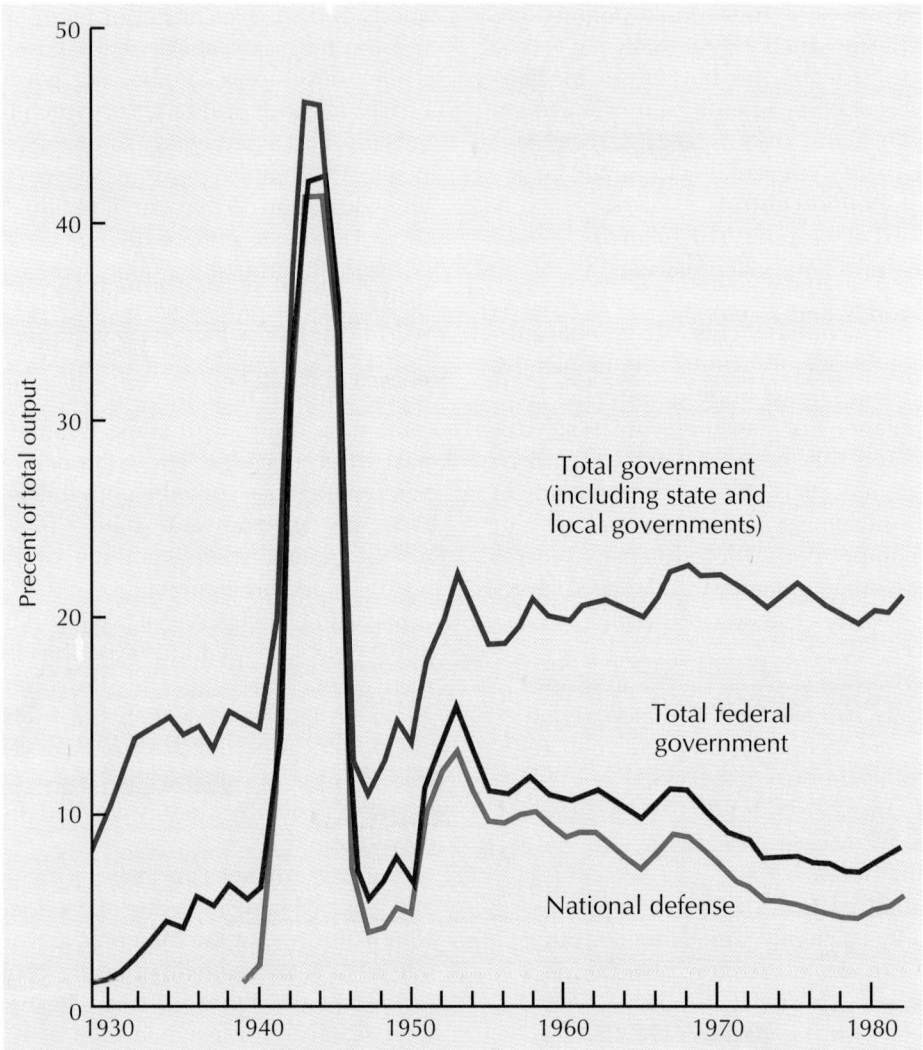

FIGURE 4.4 *Government Purchases of Goods and Services as a Percentage of Total National Output*

(*Source:* Economic Report of the President, *various years.*)

by the federal government:

Food and Drug Administration (FDA)
National Highway Traffic Safety Administration (NHTSA)
Consumer Product Safety Commission (CPSC)
Mine Safety and Health Administration (MSHA)
Occupational Safety and Health Administration (OSHA)
Environmental Protection Agency (EPA)

During 1970–81, airborne particulate emissions fell 53 percent and sulfur oxide pollutants fell 21 percent, illustrating that these regulations have pushed things in the right direction. Still, they are costly, and the main costs are shouldered by producers and consumers—costs of safety equipment and pollution abatement technicians, for instance. Estimated compliance costs for 1983 were about $60 billion.[5] Aghast at the high costs and

[5]*Survey of Current Business,* March 1985, pp. 18–22.

ideologically opposed to such regulation, the Reagan administration cut back on these efforts but did not abandon them.

Overall, government efforts at reallocation have grown markedly during the last three decades. However, the trend has not been fueled by government purchases, which have held fairly steady at about 20 percent of total output since 1950. Rather, the trend has been lofted by burgeoning regulations that have dramatically altered private sector purchases of goods and services.

3. Distribution Policies (Who?) Taxation and transfer payments are the kernel of the government's redistribution effort. As shown in Figure 4.5, which depicts government transfer payments as a percent of total personal income in the United States, transfers were relatively tiny before 1930. The Great Depression of the 1930s produced a bulge because the hard times fostered new programs like unemployment compensation. A second bulge arose during the late 1940s because of World War II veterans' benefits. Basic transfers for many hard-core welfare cases, like the disabled, were thus generally in place by 1950. Since 1950, however, transfers have erupted. Moving from less than 5 percent of personal income in 1950 to over 15 percent in 1982, total transfers have bounded upward mainly by the historic ascent of just two related programs—Social Security and government employee retirement. By 1980, 95 percent of all people over age 65 received government transfer payments.

Besides transfer payments, the government supplies *in-kind* goods and services to those who would otherwise be left poor by the market system. The in-kind benefits include medical care, housing, and special educational services. These too have grown substantially since 1950.

The problem of *discrimination* has been treated by regulation. Prompted by massive demonstrations and violent riots, the Civil Rights Act was passed in 1964. Under the act, firms, unions, apprenticeship programs, and employment agencies are prohibited from discriminating against anyone on the basis of race, color, sex, or national origin. Subsequent amendments by Congress and enforcement actions by the Equal Employment Opportunity Commission have expanded this effort.

4. Promotion Policies (What's New?) Given that growth has many sources—capital investment, education, and research and development among them—many government policies promote growth. *Tax subsidies to promote capital formation are probably the most important.* A tax subsidy is a tax break that wins for its beneficiary a lower tax bill than would otherwise be paid. In many ways it is equivalent to an expenditure subsidy, except that it works through the tax side of the government's budget instead of the expenditure side. Linking these tax breaks to business purchases of capital equipment—like machinery and tools—spurs capital formation and growth. An example is the investment tax credit, which, if pegged at 30 percent, would reduce a firm's tax bill by \$3 million for every \$10 million of qualifying equipment purchased. In effect, then, the equipment is \$3 million cheaper to buy.

Just about every president since Eisenhower has urged tax breaks to promote investment and growth. Tax credits have been a favorite method. Recently the Reagan administration endorsed existing credits and went further to obtain accelerated depreciation.

Nontax policies promote invention and innovation by encouraging research and development (R&D). This the government does in three main ways. First, *patents* give inventors legal monopoly rights for 17 years, with the prospect of fantastic profits, thereby promoting private R&D efforts. Second, the government itself spends tens of billions of dollars annually on R&D. Finally, the government often goes out of its way to buy the new goods produced by industrial innovation. The government made a market for the first computers and semiconductor devices. Now it is making a market for super, fifth-generation computers.[6]

5. Stabilization Policies (How Stable?) Because stabilization is a *macro*economic task, only *federal* policies are of importance here. Moreover, federal policies are especially important in their *aggregates* rather than their particulars. Thus, federal taxes and spending come into play once again, but here their overall sizes are more important than

[6]Richard R. Nelson (ed.) *Government and Technical Progress* (New York: Pergamon Press, 1982).

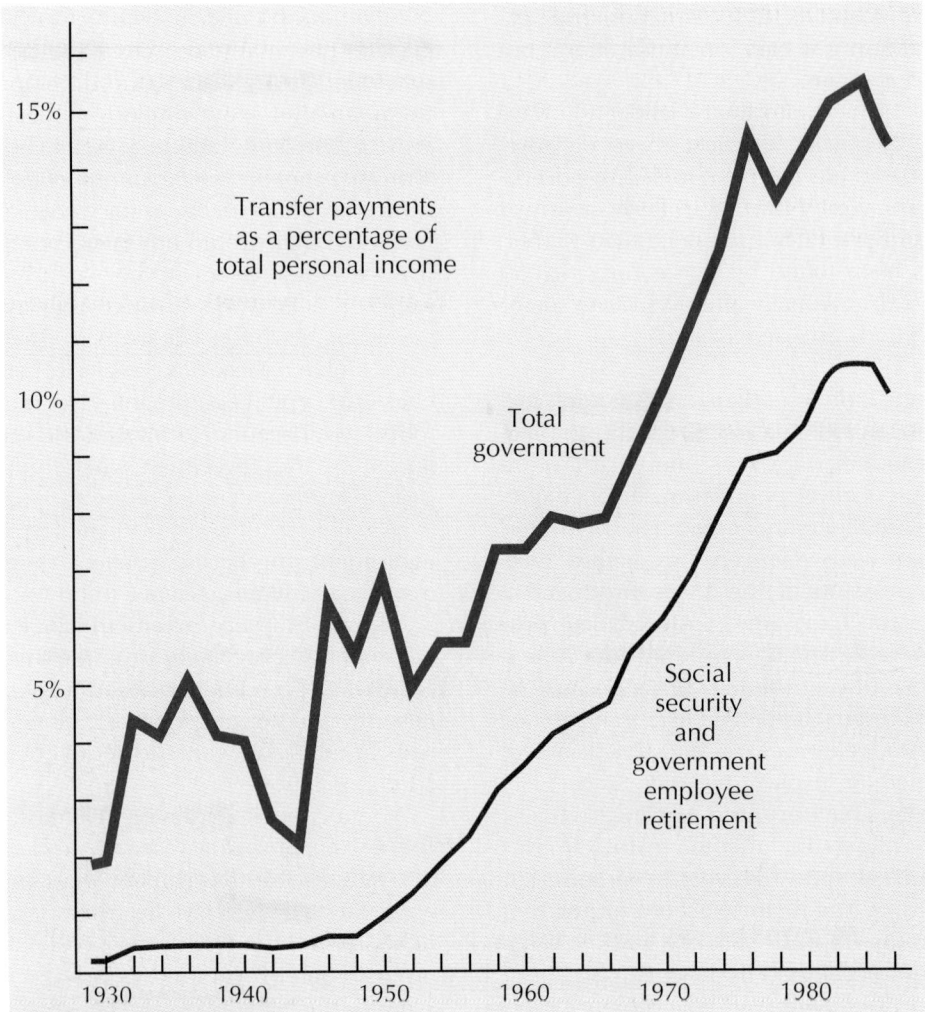

FIGURE 4.5 *Government Transfer Payments as a Percentage of Total Personal Income (Less Social Insurance Contributions)*

(*Source:* Economic Report of the President, *various years.*)

their composition. Manipulation of the overall levels of taxes and spending to control the level of economic activity is called *fiscal stabilization policy.*

Conventional wisdom holds that federal tax cuts or expenditure increases stimulate the economy. So if the economy is skidding badly, with employment falling and factories closing, tax cuts or expenditure boosts are supposed to help it recover. Conversely, if the economy is overheating from too much vigor, with shortages emerging and inflation raging, tax increases or expenditure reductions are called for.

Problem	Policy
Recession or depression	Stimulate with tax cuts or spending boosts
Overheated boom	Dampen with tax boosts or spending cuts

With aggregate tax receipts and expenditure outlays each going their own way, they need not match. When tax receipts exceed expenditure outlays, there is a budget *surplus.* Conversely, when tax receipts fall short of expenditure outlays, there is a budget *deficit.* Figure 4.6 shows the arithmetic in historical perspective. Of late, outlays have exceeded receipts, thereby producing a pattern of very large deficits.

A third tool of stabilization policy, besides aggregate revenues and expenditures, is *monetary policy*—the government's control over the money supply. Government can expand or contract the supply of money. Expansion of money tends to stimulate the economy, whereas contraction dampens it.

IV

Problems With Government

Finding problems with the market system is easy. Imagining ideal government solutions is also easy. All that's needed, it might seem, is to tax a bit, spend somewhat, and regulate in the public interest. There is a temptation to conclude, then, that government *should* always intervene to remedy things. But the temptation should be stoutly resisted. Government, too, is seriously flawed. Its intervention may make a bad situation worse.

Let's tackle several prominent government problems. We begin with imperfections and then proceed to cover mistakes concerning allocation, distribution, promotion, and stabilization.

A

Imperfections: Monopoly and Ignorance

1. Monopoly Power First, and most obviously, government is by nature a monopolist. It is not goaded by competition to be lean, productive, or competent. Were this monopoly a monopoly over

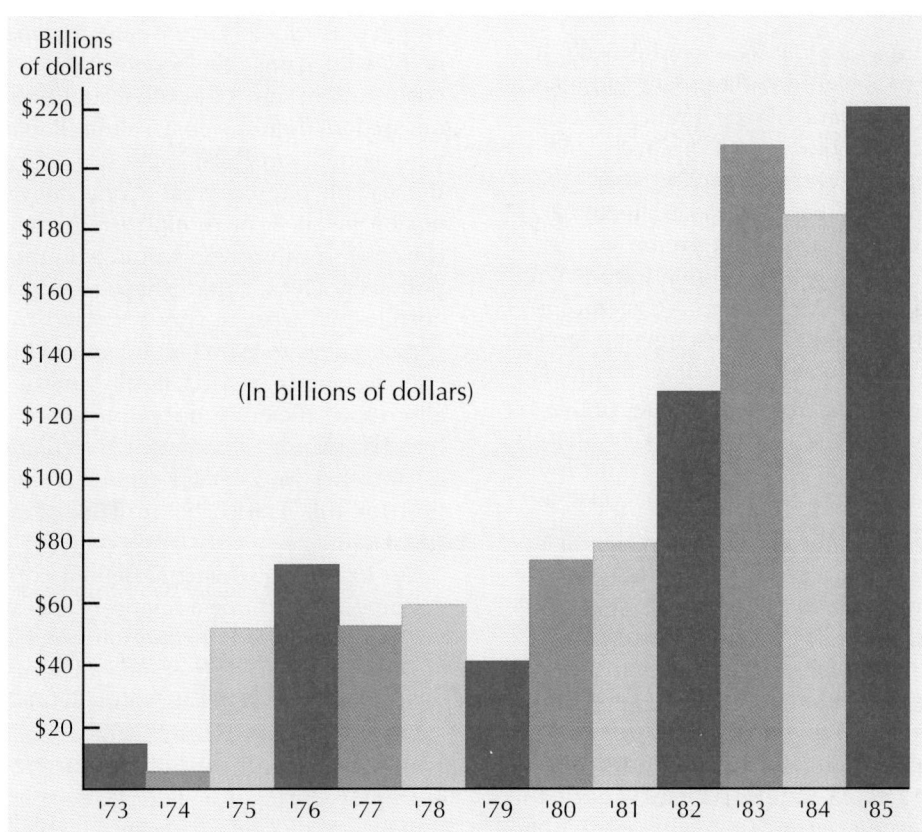

FIGURE 4.6   Federal Budget Deficits, 1973–85

A deficit occurs when outlays exceed receipts. (Source: Statistical Abstract of the United States 1986, *p. 305.)*

bubble gum, the economic implications might be trivial. But *the government has a monopoly on the legitimate use of force in our society.* Its actions are therefore coercive. Actions to tax, spend, and regulate are all, in the end, backed by coercion. Individual freedom may suffer as a consequence.

2. *Government Ignorance* The government can be just as ignorant as consumers. Authority and wisdom are not necessarily identical.

Part of this official ignorance stems from voter ignorance. To the extent that democratic government responds to people's wishes, and to the extent that those wishes are ill informed, the government's actions will be misplaced.

The problem runs deeper, however, as may be illustrated by some questions about taxes, spending, and regulation:

1. If corporate income taxes were raised 10 percent, who would end up paying the tax increase? Owners of corporations? Customers of corporations? Employees? The government doesn't know for sure. The economic reactions of all those affected are simply too complex to determine.
2. As regards government spending, what amounts would be necessary just to correct for the market's failures in such areas as education, police protection, and mass transit? The answer is unclear.
3. Finally, what about regulation? How many lives would be saved annually if the government required passive restraints like air bags in all new cars? Two thousand? Twenty thousand?

The government often lacks sound knowledge because *everyone* lacks sound knowledge —economists, sociologists, engineers, and other "experts," as well as the government. The complex ways in which people react to policies muddy the waters. For example, if cars are made safer by regulations, many people might drive more carelessly than before. Safer cars would thus *add* to highway safety, but less caution among drivers would *subtract*, leaving the net change uncertain.

B
Allocation Problems

The market cannot cope well with public goods and externalities. But government is not necessarily always the best remedy. Indeed, government itself is a flagrant source of external costs, pollution in particular. Government dams, irrigation projects, and canals have seriously polluted waterways in the western United States. Government also ravages the environment with toxic chemicals.

Read Perspective 4A.

C
Distribution Problems

The government frequently *mis*allocates resources because its actions are often guided not by comparisons of society's overall benefits and costs, which enter society's two-question logic, but rather by *who* gains the benefits and *who* pays the costs. Action may be taken even though the benefits are less than the costs, a misallocation, if those who benefit are politically more powerful than those who pay the cost. Conversely, action may *not* be taken even though the benefits outweigh the costs, if those who would gain the benefits are politically weaker than those who would pay the cost.

References to Who? may seem to imply that the government is serving equity at the expense of allocation efficiency, but *political power* is the key here. Much public policy furthers *neither* economic efficiency *nor* greater equity. A major explanation for this failure lies in *special interest politics.*

For example, when the benefits of a policy are concentrated among a relatively few, and the costs are widely spread throughout society, then the special interests who benefit will be able to muster well-organized, vocal support, while apathy will silence the many who will bear the cost. Tariffs and other restrictions on imports are a classic example. During the late 1970s, restrictions on imports of color television sets, textiles, shoes, sugar, and CB radios benefited the relatively few domestic producers and workers in these industries by about $281 million annually. At the same time, the restrictions cost all U.S. consumers about

---

PERSPECTIVE 4A
Government Toxic Waste Pollution

By some estimates, U.S. government facilities spew out more hazardous chemicals than the three largest chemical companies combined. Part of the problem lies in a double standard: Regulations for the federal government are more lenient than those facing private industry. The results are disturbing. (1) For 20 years before 1983, thousands of tons of toxic solvents, paint residues, and heavy metals were routinely dumped carelessly into the ground around the Air Force's missile plant in Tuscon, Arizona. Now the chemicals seriously threaten Tuscon's sole source of drinking water. (2) At the government's Oak Ridge laboratory in Tennessee, 2.4 million pounds of toxic mercury used in weapons production leaked into surrounding groundwater and surfacewater from 1950 to 1980. The State of Tennessee complains that some discharges were 3,000 times above legally permitted levels. (3) The cost of cleaning up the Army's Rocky Mountain Arsenal near Denver could run as high as $2 billion. The Army has made nerve gas and pesticides at the site. It has been discovered that the toxic pollution spreads underground over 25 square miles.[7]

[7]*Wall Street Journal*, July 22, 1983, p. 19.

$2 billion annually.[8] So many consumers paid, however, that they each paid only a tiny part of the $2 billion.

These snafus may even turn equity upside down, the results being inequitable. Rich farmers have, for instance, gained more government aid than poor farmers. A 1983 survey of 708 farms in nine states found that they were each averaging $175,000 in aid from the U.S. Department of Agriculture. Seven of these farms were payed more than $2 million each.[9]

D

Promotion Problems

Can government efforts to promote growth and technological change occasionally go wrong? Indeed they can. Consider civilian nuclear power for electricity. By funding research and development, by building experimental reactors, by subsidizing the production of nuclear fuel, and by other means, the government was instrumental in creating the nuclear energy industry, at an estimated cost of between $13 billion and $37 billion during 1950–80. By 1974 over 200 nuclear power plants had been built or were on order. Since then, however, the nation's electric utility industry has canceled nearly half of the nuclear capacity it ordered. The costs of dropping partially completed projects are expected to run anywhere from $35 to $55 billion. Why the massive cancellations? Nuclear energy turned out to be more expensive than anticipated, despite government subsidies. Growth of energy demand proved less rapid than anticipated, mainly in response to higher prices for all kinds of energy, oil and coal as well as nuclear energy.[10]

E

Stabilization Problems

People tend to put more weight on the present than the future. Such shortsightedness often creates problems when the costs and benefits of some action do not match up in time. When someone tries to stop smoking, for instance, the costs in agony are immediate and the benefits of better health far off. Quitting smoking is therefore diffi-

[8]*Wall Street Journal*, July 25, 1980, p. 2.

[9]*Washington Post National Weekly Edition*, November 21, 1983, p. 36.

[10]U.S. Department of Energy, *Federal Support for Nuclear Power: Reactor Design and the Fuel Cycle* (1981); C. Komanoff, "Assessing the High Costs of New Nuclear Power Plants," *Public Utilities Fortnightly* (October 11, 1984) pp. 33–38.

cult. Delay and postponement pervade. Conversely, benefits are sometimes immediate, while the costs arise later. Such situations induce hasty action when abstinence is best.

Shortsightedness often infects government. When it does, the government's macroeconomic policies can be destabilizing rather than stabilizing. For example, During 1983–84, the Reagan administration was running enormous, record budget deficits approaching $200 billion dollars annually. Moreover, projections showed that the deficits would persist into 1988, menacing the economy unless taxes were raised to stem the flood of red ink. Prominent economists inside and outside government warned of various economic calamities unless action was taken quickly. Yet corrective action was put off. The benefits of stability were too distant, the costs of the action too close to the 1984 presidential election.

■ CHECK YOUR BEARINGS

Upon close inspection, the government is not the savior it might at first seem to be. It suffers imperfections of monopolization and ignorance. It has been known to inflict external costs, thereby creating misallocations rather than correcting them. Problems of distribution arise because of interest group effects—i.e., small but politically powerful interest groups often tilt the public treasury to their benefit at the expense of most other people. Government often overpromotes or incorrectly promotes. Finally, government actions may be *de*stabilizing rather than stabilizing.

Still, the market might do worse. Waste in the military, for instance, is a perennial problem, but turning national defense over to the free market could prove disastrous. Thus a main implication, of the previous discussion is not that government ought to be abolished, but rather that society must choose between two faulty mechanisms—the market and the government. Care is therefore required to choose the least imperfect in each instance of need. This is dilemma addressing, not problem solving. And, overall, some mix of the market and government seems best, depending on the situation.

Read Perspective 4B.

PERSPECTIVE 4B
Conservatives and Liberals

No discussion of government would be complete without reviewing two philosophies that influence economists' attitudes toward government—**conservative** and **liberal.** Moderates occupy the ground between conservatives and liberals, so our outline of conservative and liberal beliefs will also tell you something about moderates.

Given the range of value judgments in economics (e.g., efficiency and equity), given also the good and bad aspects of both the market and the government, it's no surprise that economists and other people hold diverse philosophies. Conservatives and liberals differ in their value judgments, their regard for the market, and their confidence in government. Before grappling with these differences, however, we should note their different views on human nature. Our review is, of necessity, oversimplified.

Human Nature To conservatives, all men and women are (1) inherently materialistic and (2) completely rational or enlightened in pursuing their own self-interest. The descriptive label is *Homo economicus,* or economic man. The main implication of this notion is individualism. Satisfaction of individual wants is or should be the main objective of any social order, and individuals themselves are the best judges of the worth of those wants and the means of fulfilling them.

Liberals reject *Homo economicus* as unrealistically cold and calculating. Their view of human nature makes room for needs, for cooperation, and for fallibility. To quote John Maynard Keynes: "It is *not* a correct deduction from the Principles of Economics that enlightened self-interest always operates in the public interest. Nor is it true that self-interest generally *is* enlightened; more often individuals acting separately to promote their own ends are too ignorant or too weak to attain even these."[11] The implication is that liberals sometimes display paternalistic attitudes. As they see it, people often need care and protection.

Value Judgments Conservatives stress freedom. Any conflict with other value judgments such as equality or fairness is usually resolved in favor of freedom. Thus, Milton Friedman, a leading spokesman for conservatives and a Nobel laureate in economics, writes, "We take freedom of the individual, or perhaps the family, as our ultimate goal in judging social arrangements."[12] Further, when it comes to defining freedom, conservatives usually mean freedom from government.

Liberals ardently defend freedom, even the freedom to do foolish things. But they deny that freedom should be defined as freedom from government. Paul Samuelson, also a Nobel laureate in economics, put it this way: "Traffic lights coerce me and limit my freedom. Yet in the midst of a traffic jam on the unopen road, was I really 'free' before there were lights? . . . Stop lights, you know, are also go lights."[13] Thus, to liberals, freedom includes freedom from seriously hazardous products, oppressively long work hours, stock fraud, stifling pollution, and biting poverty. Moreover, liberals value equity much more than conservatives do.

Regard for Market Conservatives have great faith in free markets. The market is efficient,

even equitable. None of the free market's trappings cause most conservatives to flinch in their faith. Advertising, for instance, is praised by many as a pure blessing, informing consumers rather than persuading them, gently guiding consumers to their best buys rather than manipulating them.[14] Monopoly, too, is no problem in the eyes of some conservatives.[15]

Liberals hold the free market in very high regard. They admire its potential for efficiency, fairness, progress, and so on. But liberals readily find flaws—the imperfections, failures, and other problems surveyed earlier. They seem particularly concerned that the market system is inequitable to people suffering disadvantages and discrimination.

Regard for Government If the free market is the conservatives' delight, government is their despair. They often couple government with allusions to despotism or tyranny.[16] Further, government not only endangers freedom, its efforts rarely improve economic conditions and usually make matters worse.

As liberals see it, government can strengthen the operation of markets where they produce desirable results. Government can also modify markets or completely overturn them with good results. Indeed, some liberals seem to think that government can do almost anything well. They thus place more confidence in officialdom than conservatives do. Still, some liberals have developed, especially in recent years, an appreciation for the government's blemishes. For example, liberals recently spearheaded the effort to *de*regulate the airlines, trucking, and telecommunications.

In brief, normative economics has no single norm. There are norms to the right and left—conservative and liberal—among American economists.

[11]John M. Keynes, "The End of Laissez Faire," in *Essays in Persuasion* (New York: Norton, 1963), p. 312.

[12]Milton Friedman, *Capitalism and Freedom* (Chicago: University of Chicago Press, 1962), p. 12.

[13]Paul Samuelson, "Personal Freedoms and Economic Freedoms in the Mixed Economy," in E. F. Cheit (ed.), *The Business Establishment* (New York: Wiley, 1964), pp. 218–219.

[14]Dean A. Worcester, Jr., *Welfare Gains from Advertising* (Washington, D.C.: American Enterprise Institute, 1978).

[15]Dominick T. Armentano, *Antitrust and Monopoly* (New York: Wiley, 1982).

[16]Friedman, op. cit., p. 13.

SUMMARY

1. The market is a marvelous servant of society. Left free of government, its choice procedures and results shine attractively. Yet the market is an incomplete, often clumsy, servant. As regards _choice procedures:_

   a. The market needs a healthy financial and legal framework within which to function. Money needs to be issued and regulated. Private property needs defending. And contracts require enforcement.

   b. The market is susceptible to imperfections like seller monopoly and buyer ignorance. Hence measures to maintain competition and enhance information are warranted.

2. As regards _choice results_, the market's problems run the range of basic questions from What? to How stable?:

   c. Allocation: The free market produces too little when public goods or external benefits are involved. Conversely, the free market produces too much in the event of external costs.

   d. Distribution: The zero or very low labor market earnings of many people press them into poverty. Discrimination is also a problem.

   e. Promotion: In the judgment of many, growth and technological change need special encouragement.

   f. Stability: Recurrent recessions and an occasional depression rock the economy.

3. Enter the government, which also serves society. Among the government's many tools for service, the three outlined in Table 4.2 stand out—(1) taxation, (2) spending, and (3) regulation. Taxation is mainly a source of general revenue, but it also serves to redistribute income, finance services, and alter behavior. Spending takes the form of purchases, transfers, and subsidies. Regulation entails standard setting and enforcement.

4. The problem of market imperfections is treated by limited forms of regulation, such as antitrust policy and information policy. Reallocations for public goods and external benefits are carried out most massively by government taxation and purchase spending, with spending amounting to 20 percent or so of total U.S. output since 1950. Reallocation to address external costs like pollution is managed by regulation. Such regulation has grown substantially of late.

5. Taxes and transfer payments to achieve aims of income redistribution have likewise risen remarkably in recent decades, the main push coming from Social Security. The problem of discrimination has, in contrast, been the focus of many new regulations.

6. Subsidies are a favorite way of encouraging growth and technological change. Tax breaks boost capital investment for growth. Government R&D funding, along with patents, help technological progress.

7. As for stabilization, overall levels of federal taxing and spending play a major role. Money supply variations are also important.

8. Our government servant often bungles the job, however. Imperfections of monopoly and ignorance blemish government action. Moreover, the government perpetrates problems of allocation, distribution, promotion, and stabilization. Occasionally, officialdom may be the problem, not the solution.

9. In sum, one finds defects in both markets and government. Society has no perfect servant. But tasks must nevertheless be assigned. The trick is to find what's right for the clumsy butler and what's right for the bungling maid.

KEY TERMS

Contract	Government purchases
Private property	Transfer payment
Capitalism	Government subsidies
Mixed capitalism	Regulation
Pure monopoly	Market imperfection
Market failure	Budget deficit
Public goods	External costs
Free rider	External benefits
Tax	Conservative
Government spending	Liberal

QUESTIONS AND PROBLEMS

1. The label "Capitalists" has often been used to express disgust for Americans. Is the U.S. economy capitalistic? One who rejects "Capitalists" and their economic system apparently favors what alternative?

2. "Pure" capitalism has been judged unacceptable by American citizens, presumably because free markets fail to answer certain economic questions in a satisfactory manner. Describe ways in which government in the U.S. acts to alter free market outcomes. In each case, explain briefly why society might deem the free market outcome unacceptable.

3. There are communities in the U.S. in which fire-fighting protection is *not* provided using tax revenues. Residents have the option of paying an annual fee for coverage by a privately-owned fire-fighting company. Some people in these communities are outraged when the fire-fighting company is called by a non-member household, comes to the scene of the fire to protect surrounding houses of members, and watches the non-member's house burn. Explain why such apparently insensitive behavior is necessary to the survival of the private company. Can you think of a better way for the private company to operate?

4. A generally accepted regulatory goal of the federal government is the promotion of competition. How does the government do this?

5. Discuss the importance of informed consumers in a market economy. Are there certain markets in which it is quite difficult for consumers to obtain accurate information regarding variables relevant to their decision-making? What are the implications of consumer ignorance for answers to the questions What?, How?, and Who?

6. List the three main types of government outlays, explaining each. Does the government make a direct claim on society's limited resources with each dollar it spends?

7. Some people are reluctant to turn over to the government any economic task that could be performed by the private sector. Are there logical reasons for such reluctance?

5

Basic Facts About American Business

Which corporation made history by being the first to top $100 billion in annual sales? General Motors, the colossal auto company, did it in 1986. This implied greatness. In the same year, however, GM's management was sharply criticized by H. Ross Perot, a member of GM's board of directors and a legendary U.S. businessman who owned over $1 billion in stocks, bonds, and other investments. He launched a one-man crusade to change the huge corporation because its market share was slipping and its costs were soaring. His plan? "Revitalizing GM is like teaching an elephant to tap dance," he said. "You find the sensitive spots and start poking."[1]

Mr. Perot found the sensitive spots and started poking, but the results were unexpected. Within a few months of the preceding statement, GM's management bought all of Mr. Perot's GM stock for $742 million, a price well above its prevailing market value. In exchange, Mr. Perot resigned from GM's board of directors and agreed never to criticize GM's management publicly again (slips of the tongue being punishable by "fines" of up to $7.5 million). The battle between Perot and GM's management, especially GM's chairman, Roger B. Smith, was described by GM insiders as "more exciting than 'Dallas,' 'Dynasty,' and 'Knots Landing'."[2] Mr. Perot's departure stunned stockholders, causing the price of GM shares to tumble.

Note some of the key terms in this story—*board of directors, chairman, stock market value, bonds, management, stockholders,* and *shares.* Gaining an understanding of these terms and others like them is a main task of this chapter. Another task is to identify the basic forms of business organization prevailing in the United States—namely, sole proprietorships, partnerships, and corporations.

This focus on basic facts about American *businesses* is not meant to slight two other major groups in our economy—*households* and *governments.* Compared to households and governments, however, businesses are relatively unknown entities. You already known about house-

[1]*Business Week,* October 6, 1986, p. 60.

[2]*The Wall Street Journal,* December 2, 1986, p. 3.

holds from personal experience. And you know about governments—federal, state, and local— through your studies of civics. However, when it comes to businesses—their diverse types, their sources of funding, and so on—your familiarity is perhaps limited to ownership and operation of a lemonade stand when you were 8 or 9 years old.

To move a bit beyond that lemonade stand, let's conclude this introduction with a few more words of background on GM, which will often serve as an example in this chapter.

Read Perspective 5A.

I

Firms versus Establishments

A
Basic Definitions

To avoid confusion, it is important to understand the difference between *firms* and *establishments.* Often they are virtually the same. However, in many instances, they are different.

*An **establishment** is a physical place of business activity.* It can be a factory, assembly plant, retail store, warehouse, office building, or some other facility. The basic idea is that establishments are places where goods are made or stored or processed, or where services are performed. Most small businesses have only one establishment, as is probably true of your local shoe repair shop or dentist's office. On the other hand, most large businesses are composed of numerous establishments, giving rise to the useful notion of *firm.*

*A **firm** is a business organization that owns and/ or operates one or more establishments.* Other general labels frequently used include *company, enterprise,* and *business venture.* To continue the example of GM, that is a firm having many establishments, including engine plants, metal stamping plants, assembly plants, finance offices, and research laboratores. Indeed, GM has so many establishments that its 1986 announcement of

PERSPECTIVE 5A

General Motors Corporation

General Motors is the largest corporation in the world when measured by sales or number of employees or assets. Figures for 1986 are as follows:

Sales	$102,813,700,000
Assets	$ 72,593,000,000
Profits	$ 2,944,700,000
Employees	876,000

Formed shortly after the turn of the century, when a swarm of small companies populated the auto industry, GM's early growth came about by mergers among many formerly independent auto companies (e.g., Buick, Cadillac, Oldsmobile, Oakland, and Chevrolet). From 1913 through the early 1920's GM's arch-rival, Ford, was the leading producer because of the immense success of Ford's low-priced Model T and Model A. In 1921, for instance, Ford's market share was 55 percent. However, GM nudged Ford out of the top spot for a few years in the late 1920s. Ford resumed leadership briefly. Then in 1931 GM took the lead and has held it ever since. Two keys to GM's early success were (1) its diversity of price classes and styles, ranging from inexpensive Chevrolets to costly Cadil-

lacs, and (2) its policy of making annual model changes, sometimes rather dramatic changes, in order to spur sales by planned obsolescence. From the mid-1950s to the mid-1980s, GM's share of U.S. auto production never fell below 50 percent. If imports are included in the figures for a share of total U.S. sales, GM's share ranged from 44 to 50 percent over the period 1950–84. Indicative of its recent troubles, its share of total sales fell from 46 percent in 1979 to 42 percent in 1986.

GM began its association with H. Ross Perot in 1984 when it acquired EDS Corporation through an exchange of stock worth $2.5 billion. EDS was founded and run by Perot, and after its acquisition by GM, Perot became GM's largest single shareholder, with 0.8 percent of its total stock outstanding. It was this ownership stake that placed Perot on GM's board of directors and that GM bought back to rid itself of his pesky criticism. Incidentally, EDS was a computer services firm, having very little to do with autos before its acquisition, and much of Perot's criticism concerned another multi-billion dollar-deal involving another nonauto company that GM purchased in 1985—Hughes Aircraft.

nine plant closings, involving nearly 30,000 jobs, was barely noticed by the news media.

B

The Biggest Firms

Table 5.1 lists some of the largest American firms, ranked by sales in 1986. Note how many of them are primarily in the business of producing oil and gasoline or motor vehicles. Nine of the top 15 are in one of these two industries, which illustrates the tremendous economic influence of the automobile—its manufacture and operation. Note also

that the sales volumes of these companies are so huge that it is hard to imagine that any of them could operate out of just one establishment, and of course, they don't. Each has many.

The numerous establishments that any firm may operate can be classified into _horizontal, vertical,_ or _conglomerate_ combinations (and the firms in Table 5.1 are combinations of these three). A _horizontal_ combination occurs when the firm has a number of establishments at the _same stage_ of the production-distribution process. For example, each of the oil companies mentioned in Table 5.1 owns numerous petroleum refineries. In comparison, a _vertical_ combination of establishments oc-

TABLE 5.1   Some of the Largest American Firms, 1986

Rank	Company	Main Line of Business	Sales (Billions)
1.	General Motors	Motor vehicles	$102.8
2.	Exxon	Oil and gasoline	69.9
3.	Ford Motor	Motor vehicles	62.7
4.	IBM	Computers	51.3
5.	Mobil	Oil and gasoline	44.9
6.	General Electric	Electronics	35.2
7.	American Tel. & Tel.	Telecommunications	34.1
8.	Texaco	Oil and gasoline	31.6
9.	DuPont	Chemicals	27.1
10.	Chevron	Oil and gasoline	24.4
11.	Chrysler	Motor vehicles	22.5
12.	Philip Morris (Gen. foods)	Tobacco and foods	20.7
13.	Amoco	Oil and gasoline	18.3
14.	RJR Nabisco	Tobacco and foods	17.0
15.	Shell Oil	Oil and gasoline	16.8
16.	Boeing	Airplanes	16.3
18.	Procter & Gamble	Detergents	15.4
22.	USX (U.S. Steel)	Steel	14.0
26.	Eastman Kodak	Photo supplies	11.6
29.	Goodyear	Tires and rubber	10.4

curs when a single enterprise owns establishments that operate at _different stages_ of the production-distribution process. For example, in addition to owning numerous petroleum refineries, each of the leading oil companies engages in a full range of related petroleum operations that occur both before and after petroleum refining—namely, crude oil exploration and extraction, crude oil transportation, petroleum product transportation, wholesale marketing, and retail marketing.

Finally, _conglomerate_ combinations bring together under common ownership establishments that have _nothing or very little in common._ USX, for instance, is identified in Table 5.1 as primarily a steel producer. But USX also owns the Marathon Oil Company, one of the largest oil companies in the country, plus several chemical operations and diverse other businesses. Indeed, in recent years, the company became so diversely conglomerated that in 1986, after steel no longer accounted for a majority of its revenues, the firm changed its name from U.S. Steel to USX. Another example of conglomeracy in Table 5.1 has already been mentioned, namely, GM's acquisition of a computer services firm (EDS) and an aerospace firm (Hughes Aircraft).

C
Smaller Firms

The largest firms, such as those in Table 5.1, have an enormous impact on the economy. Overall, there are millions of firms in the American economy. But relatively few of them, the very largest, carry disproportionate weight. The 200 largest manufacturing corporations hold over 60 percent of all manufacturing assets. The Fortune 500 companies account for well over 50 percent of all industrial activity when measured by sales.

Still, smaller firms are also extremely important, and in many ways even more important than the largest. Medium-sized and small firms, for instance, usually account for more _new employment_ than large firms because they seem to be especially adroit at job creation.

Moreover, in certain crucial sectors of the economy, medium-sized and small firms outweigh their larger brethren in sales, assets, and other measures of economic activity. Figure 5.1 shows that medium-sized and small firms (those with fewer than 500 employees) account for over 50 percent of industry sales revenues in agriculture, construction, wholesale trade, retail trade, and services.

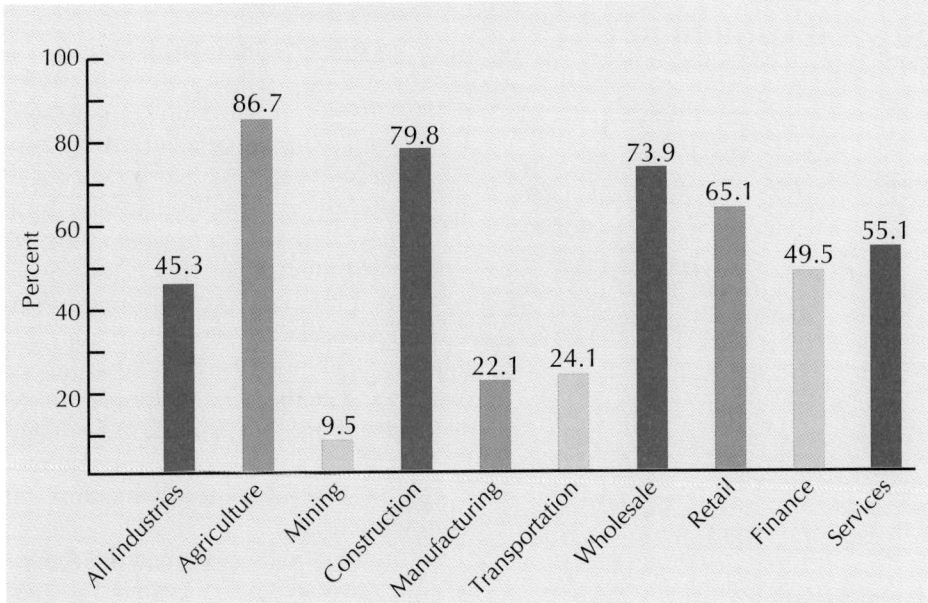

FIGURE 5.1 *Percentage of Industry Sales by Firms with Fewer Than 500 Employees, 1980*

(*Source:* The State of Small Business: A Report of the President, *March 1983, p. 53.*)

Finally, small and medium-sized firms should be credited with much of the entrepreneurial activity in our economy. This entrepreneurial spirit may be measured in several ways. In the area of technological change, for instance, a very substantial number of major inventions and innovations come from small or medium-sized enterprises. Past examples include xerographic copy machines, home computers, jet engines, catalytic cracking of petroleum, and airplanes.

Alternatively, one can look to new business formations, which by definition tend to be small firms entailing a great deal of entrepreneurial activity. Figure 5.2 shows that new incorporations are quite numerous, running well over 500,000 per year. Of course, many of these new incorporations do not succeed. So Figure 5.2 also reports the annual rate of bankruptcies in the United States from 1970 to 1985. As is easily seen, bankruptcies run in the tens of thousands annually. The especially sharp rise in bankruptcies from 1980 to 1983 was due to the most severe recession in U.S. history since the Great Depression of the 1930s. Taken together, these numerous new incorporations and bankruptcies indicate that a substantial turnover

of business enterprises regularly occurs in our economy, at least among small and medium-sized firms. This is as it should be because economic efficiency requires that poor management, ill-conceived products, and other failings should be punished, while at the same time good management, attractive products, and other successes should be rewarded.

Saying that the numbers in Figure 5.2 are for incorporations suggests the existence of alternative forms of business. Recognition that businesses can, and frequently do, fail also raises the question of who is responsible for the debts or liabilities of a bankrupt company. We turn next to these and related issues.

II

Business Types

Firms can be one of three basic types—*sole proprietorship, partnership,* or *corporation.* Each has certain advantages and disadvantages, many of

New business incorporations . . .

(in thousands)

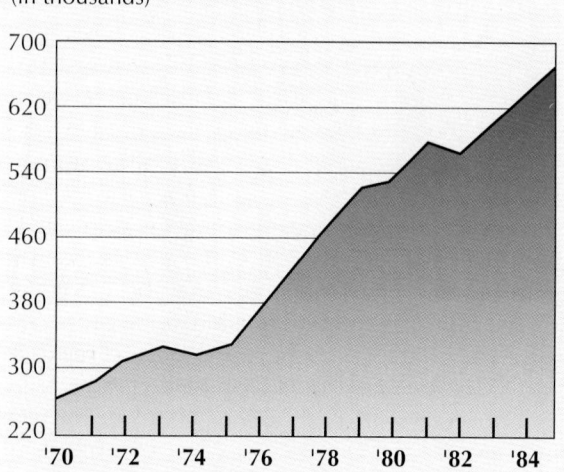

. . . and bankruptcies

(in thousands)

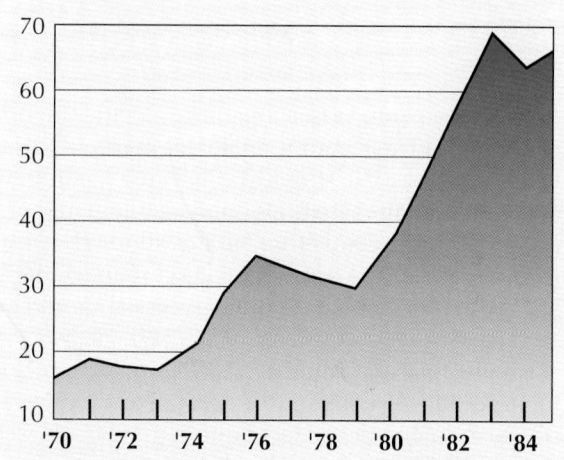

FIGURE 5.2 *New Business Incorporations and Bankruptcies, 1970–85*

(Source: Dunn & Bradstreet Corp., 1986; Administrative Office of the U.S. Courts, 1986; as reported in The Wall Street Journal, *May 19, 1986, p. 5D.)*

which relate to the problem just mentioned, namely, liability in the event of bankruptcy. Let's tackle each ownership type in turn.

A
Sole Proprietorships

A **sole proprietorship** is a business firm owned directly by one person (without the legal device of incorporation).

A sole proprietorship is the most common type of ownership for small firms, like tiny retail shops, farms, and repair services. One reason for its popularity among small businesses is the great ease with which sole proprietorships can be set up. Complicated paperwork can be avoided and legal costs minimized. Aside from the registrations and licenses that are typically required of many businesses, all one needs to do in this case is start to work. A barber, for instance, once licensed, can begin barbering. Another advantage is related to this one: A sole proprietor has complete control of his or her business. Ownership and control go together.

Among the disadvantages of the sole proprietorship, two are most noteworthy. First, these businesses often tend to suffer from shortages of financial capital, which restricts their size. Sole proprietorships cannot issue shares of common stock, as corporations do, to raise financial capital. Their main source of funds therefore tends to be whatever the owner can borrow from local banks (as well as borrow from friends and relatives). For example, Nolan Bushnell started Atari with only a few hundred dollars of his own money plus several hundred more from friends. He later incorporated and sold out to Warner Communications, Inc., for about $17 million, but starting out was tricky.

The second disadvantage relates to the liability the owner has to any of these lenders in the event of business failure. That liability is said to be *unlimited* because the firm's lenders may collect their due from the owner's private property (houses, cars, personal bank accounts, etc.), as well as any business assets (such as office furniture or manufacturing equipment). This obviously puts the proprietor in a risky position.

In summary, *advantages* of the sole proprietorship include:

1. Simple legal creation.
2. Complete control in the hands of the owner.

Disadvantages include:

1. Limited access to financial capital.

2. Unlimited liability for the owner if failure occurs.

B
Partnerships

A **partnership** is a firm whose ownership is shared by a fixed number of proprietors.

A proprietorship is very similar to a sole proprietorship, but it has more than one owner. Given multiple ownership, partnerships are based on legal agreements that specify the ownership shares and duties of each partner. For example, two partners might contribute equal amounts of financial capital, but one of the two, the *managing partner*, might have full responsibility for the daily operations of the firm. Law firms are perhaps the most common example of partnerships. As for size, some of the very largest partnerships are found in investment banking. All in all, most partnerships tend to be fairly small firms dealing in services of various kinds.

Because partnerships share many legal similarities with sole proprietorships, their advantages and disadvantages are also similar to those of sole proprietorships. One advantage of a partnership is the relative ease with which it can be set up. Compared to corporations, which often require complicated legal structures, partnerships are not difficult to establish once mutual agreement is achieved among all the partners involved. A second advantage of a partnership arises in comparison with a sole proprietorship. A partnership can raise more financial and managerial inputs than a proprietorship because it has more owners from whom to draw those inputs. Regarding financial inputs, partnerships are better than sole proprietorships because the wealth and borrowing capacities of more than one person are involved. Regarding managerial inputs, partnerships allow greater specialization than can typically be achieved in sole proprietorships. For example, one partner might specialize in manufacturing, while another has exceptional talents in marketing.

Among the disadvantages of a partnership, three are particularly noteworthy. First, although partnerships have easier access to financial capital than sole proprietorships, their ability to raise financial capital is restricted in comparison to that of a corporation. The ability of the partnership to raise financial capital is bounded by the amount of money the partners can raise from their personal wealth and by borrowing. Second, partners have unlimited liability for the debts of the partnership. If the partnership fails, each partner could lose his or her personal assets to meet the obligations of the firm. Third, partnerships suffer from some special legal complications. The partnership agreement itself may be difficult to devise because the contributions of the partners may be wildly diverse, leading to great dissension among the partners about business responsibilities and rewards. Moreover, the partnership agreement often cannot cope very well with changes that occur over time.

In summary, *advantages* of the partnership include:

1. Ease of legal creation.
2. Access to more financial and managerial inputs (compared to sole proprietorships).

Disadvantages include:

1. Limited access to financial capital (compared to corporations).
2. Unlimited liability of each partner for the debt obligations of the firm.
3. Certain legal complexities that cause problems for perpetuation of the partnership in the event of ownership changes.

C
Corporations

A **corporation** is a firm created by a government charter. The law grants certain powers, privileges, and liabilities separate from those of the individual stockholder-owners.

The corporate form of business organization evolved as a means of overcoming the disadvantages associated with sole proprietorships and partnerships. Most important, a corporation has tremendous freedom because it has the legal status of a person and is thereby capable of acting as a person under the law—to enter into contracts, to hire workers, to raise capital, and so on, all separate from direct involvement by the owners of the corporation. As indicated in Figure 5.3, which presents the standard structure of corporate organizations, the *stockholder-owners* have the highest status, but they are largely separate from the rest of the organization. The stockholders elect a *board of directors* to represent their views to management, a board that meets only occasionally, such as once a month. In turn, management, headed by a president and assisted by various vice-presidents, serves at the pleasure of the board and is responsible for the daily operations of the firm. In small corporations, these several layers of power and responsibility often rest with the same

individuals. But in large corporations, they are almost always separated.

Stated differently, incorporation provides a legal foundation that permits the firm to grow to immense size and last for an indefinite period. The importance of the corporate form to the creation of large firms is illustrated in Table 5.2. In terms of the *number of firms*, sole proprietorships are by far the most common type of business organization. As indicated in the first two columns of Table 5.2, there are more than 10 million (nonfarm) sole proprietorships, and they account for nearly 70 percent of all business entities. Corporations are much less numerous, amounting to just 20 percent of the total number of firms. However, as measured by *sales revenues*, which are shown in the

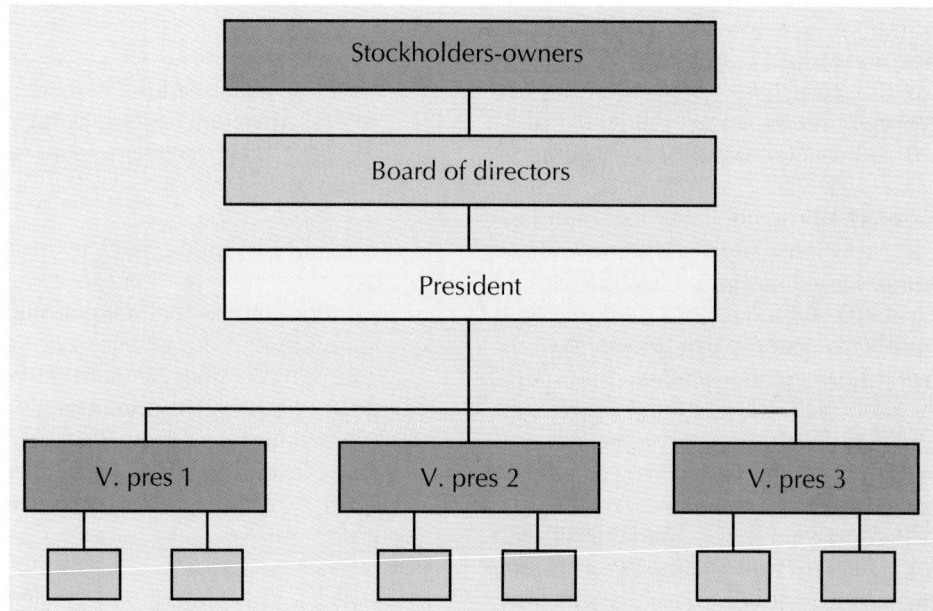

FIGURE 5.3   Standard Corporate Organizational Structure

TABLE 5.2   Types of Firm Ownership in Numbers and Revenues, 1982

Firm Type	Number of Firms		Sales Revenues	
	In Thousands	Percent of Total	Billions of Dollars	Percent of Total
Sole proprietorships*	10,106	69.5%	$ 434	5.6%
Partnerships	1,514	10.4	297	3.8
Corporations	2,926	20.1	7,024	90.6
Totals	14,546	100%	$7,775	100%

*Excludes farm proprietorships.
Source: Statistical Abstract of the United States 1986, p. 517.

last two columns of Table 5.2, corporations are by far the biggest sort of firm. Collectively they account for over $7 trillion in business receipts, or about 90 percent of the total. Stated differently, the data of Table 5.2 indicate that the average size of a corporation in annual sales revenues is about $2,400,547, while the average size of a partnership is $196,169 and that of a sole proprietorship is $42,944. Measured by something other than an average, say a median, the size of corporations would be even more impressive relative to that of sole proprietorships and partnerships. Nearly all of the largest firms in the economy, say the top 1,000, are corporations.

The advantages of the corporate form center on (1) vastly greater accessibility to financial capital compared to either proprietorships or partnerships, (2) limited liability for owners, and (3) unlimited potential life. First, as regards access to financial capital, corporations can tap a source of funds not open to proprietorships or partnerships. They can sell *shares* of company ownership in the form of *common stock* or *preferred stock*. To the extent that a person buys these shares, that person becomes an owner of the corporation. For example, H. Ross Perot was the largest single stockholder in General Motors before he sold out. He owned 11.4 million shares, or 0.8 percent of the total shares outstanding, meaning that he owned 0.8 percent of the company. This stake, worth hundreds of millions of dollars, was small in percentage terms because GM is so immense, with a total ownership value running into the tens of billions of dollars. Millions of stockholders own pieces of that huge value, illustrating the vast potential of the corporate form of ownership. Whereas the sources of ownership capital for sole proprietorships and partnerships are limited to the single or several owners of those types of businesses, corporations can elicit ownership capital from literally millions of owner-investors, millions who may have no connection to the corporation other than ownership of some shares of stock. (Corporations can also be *closely held* or *privately held*, which means that most or all of the corporation's stock is in the hands of a few owners, usually those who also manage the firm.)

Aside from its much greater ability to raise financial capital from people who become owners of the firm, a corporation also has substantial advantages in raising debt capital. The corporation may sell *bonds*, which have a stated schedule of interest payments going to their purchasers plus repayment of the amount loaned (after some fixed number of years). In addition, the corporation may borrow money from banks. Such corporate borrowings from banks are very similar to those by sole proprietorships and partnerships, but corporations generally obtain better terms and conditions plus larger lines of credit than do these alternative business types. Hence corporations typically have greater access to financial capital because of their unique sources and their unique status in dealing with nonunique sources. (We shall have more to say about stocks and bonds shortly.)

The second major advantage of corporations, and in many ways the single most important advantage, is the limited liability of its owners.

With **limited liability** the amount an owner-shareholder of a corporation can lose in the event of bankruptcy is limited to the amount paid to purchase an ownership stake in the corporation.

If you pay $1,000 to purchase ownership in a corporation that makes garlic-flavored toothpaste, the *most* you could lose if the corporation went belly-up would be that $1,000. The corporation might have borrowed extensively from banks and it might owe millions to garlic farmers. If the assets of the corporation are not sufficiently large to cover these liabilities, you need not worry. The banks and garlic farmers will not be able to collect the amounts owed to them by going after your car, your savings account, or your home. Legally your liability is strictly limited to the $1,000 you paid for your stock ownership.

A third advantage of the corporation is that its legal life is independent of its owners' lives. This makes it possible for the corporation to last indefinitely, even hundreds of years. Still, corporate life is not necessarily unlimited. Corporations cease to operate because of bankruptcies and mergers. But the main point is that their life spans are not directly linked to those of their owners, as is true of sole proprietorships and partnerships.

Regarding the disadvantages of the corporate form of business organization, two features raise potential problems. First, it is often said that, from the viewpoint of owners, corporate profits are subject to _double taxation_ to the extent that those profits are paid out to owners as dividends. For example, imagine a corporation that earns $10 million in profits and has 1 million shares outstanding. The $10 million profit is taxed at the corporate tax rate, which for purposes of illustration can be assumed to be 20 percent. That leaves $8 million in corporate profit after taxes. If this $8 million is then paid out to stockholders, each stockholder will earn $8 per share, (which is calculated by dividing the $8 million after-tax profit by the number of shares outstanding, 1 million). This $8 per share is then taxed as the personal income of the shareholder, and the dividend may in the end be worth no more than about $6 per share after this second round of taxes. This $6 is obviously far below the original corporate earnings of $10 per share.

There are several qualifications that lighten the blow of this double taxation, however. Notice, for instance, that in the foregoing example we assume that _all_ the corporate profits were paid out to stockholders. When some or all of the corporate profits are held as _retained earnings_ rather than paid out, the burden of double taxation is eased. Earnings that are retained can be invested in new plants and equipment, financing the growth of the corporation. As the corporation grows, the value of the corporation increases, so the price of each share of its stock also grows. Stockholders then experience **capital gains,** because the market value of what they hold has appreciated. Such capital gains are taxed, but only after some delay in comparison to dividend taxes; further, in some cases, they were taxed at a lower rate than income earnings. Another qualification is needed to point out that investors in corporations will not, on the average, make less than investors in sole proprietorships. In order to attract investors, corporations must reward them at after-tax rates that compare favorably with rates of return on noncorporate investments, like partnerships or real estate. How can corporations do this given the problem of double taxation? Corporations can provide attractive after-tax rewards by earning higher pretax profits than they would earn without the double taxation. Hence, double taxation tends to keep corporate businesses out of economic activities that offer relatively limited profit opportunities.

Aside from double taxation, corporations may suffer a disadvantage because their managers may operate so independently of the owners that, to some degree, they run the corporation in a way that is contrary to the interests of the owners. This problem is called _separation of ownership and control_, and it is especially noteworthy among the very largest corporations. Large corporations, like those listed in Table 5.1, typically have tens of hundreds of thousands of stockholders. With such widespread ownership, individual owners cannot have much of an influence on the daily operations of the corporation. As a result, the corporation's managers have leeway to buy an excessive number of Lear jets, pay themselves excessive salaries, and in other ways operate in a fashion that is less than fully efficient. It might be argued, to the contrary, that stockholders need not be close to the daily operations of the firm in order to have their interests served because the board of directors can ride herd on management. This is the theory behind the corporate structure of Figure 5.3. There may be some truth to this, but only some. Managers play a large role in the selection of the people who serve on the board of directors, so boards often serve management's interests more thoroughly than those of the owners. Remember the story of H. Ross Perot. Here was a man with a $750 million ownership stake _and_ a seat on the board of directors. Yet his efforts to influence GM were rebuffed.

All of this is not to say that stockholder-owners have no influence on corporate management. Disappointed stockholders can sell their shares of stock. Such selling will tend to lower the price of the shares, and this in turn will make it more difficult for management to raise financial capital, thereby penalizing management. Even more dramatically and immediately, a reduced price per share of common stock increases the possibility that the corporation will be acquired by another corporation. This would put ownership in the hands of a relatively few, and those few could oust the wayward managers of the acquired corporation and replace them with managers who are more responsive to the owners' wishes.

In summary, _advantages_ of the corporation include:

1. A vast capability to raise financial capital.

2. Limited liability of the owners in the event of bankruptcy.
3. Unlimited potential life span.

Disadvantages include;

1. Double taxation.
2. Separation of ownership from managerial control.

III

Corporate Finance: Stocks and Bonds

Corporations raise money in two ways common to all business firms (proprietorships and partnerships included). They accumulate savings from after-tax profits (retained earnings), and they borrow directly from banks, often establishing a *line of credit* that can be drawn upon automatically in case of need (somewhat like the line of credit a Visa card gives you). As just suggested, however, corporations are an especially strong form of business organization because of their unique ability to raise money, and that ability centers on three main types of securities: (1) common stocks, (2) preferred stocks, and (3) bonds. Each of these securities has special characteristics of importance to both the corporations that issue them and the investors who purchase them.

A

Common Stock

Common stock is the chief certificate of ownership for a corporation. One *share* of common stock represents a certain share of ownership. Hence, collectively, all the holders of common stock are the owners of the corporation. Each share gives the holder a share of the firm's profits and a share of the voting power in matters decided by shareholder elections. Profit payments on these shares are called *dividends*.

A **common stock** of a corporation is a piece of paper that gives an ownership share in the company.

For example, if a corporation issues 1 million shares of common stock (and no preferred stock), then a person holding 100,000 shares will own 10 percent of the company. The dollar dividends that are paid by the corporation are variable, perhaps even falling to zero, but someone with a 10 percent stake would consistently receive 10 percent of the profits paid out in dividends. A total dividend payout of, say, $10 million in the first quarter of the year would result in $1 million going to the person with a 10 percent stake, an amount that would equal $10 per share.

B

Preferred Stock

Preferred stock is another type of ownership certificate that corporations sometimes issue in addition to common stock. Preferred stock is similar to common stock in that it too grants an ownership share, and payments from profits are again called *dividends*. However, preferred stock is quite different from common stock in a number of other respects. The dividend for preferred stock is not variable, as in the case of common stock. Rather, the dividend is fixed at some stated amount, such as $1.5 per share per year. This reduces the risk to the shareholder that a low or zero dividend per share will be paid. And to ensure that this risk is in fact reduced, corporations have a policy of paying no dividends to holders of common stock until the dividend commitments to preferred stockholders have been met. Indeed, this priority for the dividends on preferred stock is what gives the stock its *preferred* name. Another difference is that preferred stock carries no voting rights.

A **preferred stock** grants a fixed prior claim on profits (ahead of common stock).

C

Bonds

Bonds are quite different from common stock or preferred stock. Whereas stocks grant ownership shares rewarded by dividends, bonds are not ownership instruments and they do not pay dividends. Bonds are debt obligations of the corporation that pay a set interest return to the investor, as well as provide for repayment of the original amount lent (called *principal*).

Corporate bonds are formal IOUs that require the corporation to pay a fixed sum of money annually until maturity (interest payment) and then, at maturity, a fixed sum of money to repay the initial amount borrowed (principal).

For example, in early 1987 the Chrysler Financial Corporation raised $90 million by issuing bonds that paid 8.375 percent interest and matured in 1997. Let's assume that you had purchased one of these bonds, worth $1,000 at face value. You would now be obtaining annual interest payments of $83.75, and on February 1, 1997, you will be able to collect the $1,000 principal.

Payments of interest and principal are *binding* obligations of the firm. If these payments are missed because the firm is losing money, the firm may be forced into bankruptcy, in which case bondholders will likely suffer some losses, getting only part of their principal back and probably losing out on some interest payments. The firm's obligations to bondholders are reflected in the fact that the claims of bondholders come before the claims of stockholders. The corporation will always pay its interest obligations before it pays dividends to stockholders.

Capital Gains and Losses The preceding discussion focuses on the annual rates of return associated with stocks and bonds. There is, in addition, a second way investors can make or lose money from stocks and bonds, namely, *capital gains or losses*. From the investors' perspective, these securities are financial assets that can be sold—sold for a price greater or less than the price originally paid. If the asset can be sold for *more* than the original purchase price, the result is a capital *gain*. If the asset can be sold only for *less* than the original purchase price, the result is a capital *loss*.

A **capital gain** is the increase in the market value of any asset above the price originally paid. The capital gain is realized when the asset is actually sold.

A **capital loss** is the decrease in the market value of any asset below the price originally paid. The capital loss is realized when the asset is actually sold.

For common stock, a simple example is easy. Assume that you purchased 1,000 shares of the JKL corporation for $6 apiece when they were first issued 5 years ago. You originally paid a total of $6,000 for the lot. Now, 5 years later, you can sell them for $10 each, or $10,000 total, thereby realizing a capital gain of $4,000 ($10,000 − $6,000) in addition to any dividends that were paid out while you owned the shares. What would cause such capital gains? A big jump in the profit prospects of the corporation would be the main explanation.

Bonds can also experience capital gains and losses. These experiences are, however, a bit more complicated than those involving stocks. The main cause of capital gains or losses in already issued bonds is variation in the interest earned on newly issued bonds. For an example involving a capital loss, let's assume that you purchased a $1,000 bond 3 years ago at 8.375 percent interest, so it pays $83.75 annually. If you wanted to sell that bond today in order to get some cash, you would not be able to sell it for $1,000 if the interest rates on newly issued bonds is now much higher—say, 13 percent. Prospective buyers of your bond could get $130 a year for their $1,000 instead of the $83.75 per year your bond offers. Prospective buyers would buy your bond *only* if its price were substantially discounted below $1,000, which would mean a hefty capital loss for you. Thus, *in general, a rise in the interest rate on newly issued bonds will lower the price on already issued bonds, while a decline in the interest rate on newly issued bonds will raise the price of already issued bonds.*

IV

The Stock Market

Over 40 million Americans invest in common stocks. The vast majority of them do not buy freshly issued shares of common stock offered by corporations seeking to raise financial capital. Instead, they buy and sell shares of common stock that were issued some time ago. Indeed, the buying and selling of existing shares, which occurs in the *stock market,* dwarfs the amount of business done in new issues. The New York Stock Exchange, the largest and most famous of all the stock exchanges in the stock market, regularly sees over 140 million shares of stocks changing hands daily. If you wanted to participate in the stock market, all you would need is money and some instructions for a stockbroker on what stocks you would like to buy at what price.

Read Perspective 5B.

The oldest and most widely cited index of how the stock market is doing is the Dow Jones Industrial Average. Dating back to 1896, when the prices of just 12 stocks on the New York Stock Exchange were included in the index, the Dow Jones Industrial Average currently includes 30 blue-chip stocks in industries ranging from oil to computers.

Figure 5.4 shows the history of the Dow Jones Industrial Average from 1928 until the first days of 1987, when it closed above 2000 for the first time. Each annual entry in the diagram shows the range of the Dow Jones average over the course of the year (by the vertical expanse of band) and the closing price of the year's last day of trading (the tab). For example, during 1928 the Dow ranged from a low of about 200 to a high of about 300, closing the year at the latter figure. Shortly thereafter, the index registers the dramatic events of the Great Crash. After climbing steadily during the 1920s, the Dow peaked at 381 on September 1, 1929, fed by feverish speculation. The index then sank to a low of 41 on June 8, 1932. Thus the index lost 90 percent of its value in less than 3 years. It was not until 1945 that the index reached 200 again. Later, the 1950s as a whole were very good to the stock mar-

PERSPECTIVE 5B
Reading the Stock Listings

Basic information about the stocks traded on the New York Stock Exchange may be found in your local newspaper or _The Wall Street Journal_. To illustrate the latter source, let's look briefly at the _Journal_'s listing for General Motors' common stock on February 5, 1987.

The first two entries indicate the high price and the low price of the stock during the previous year. The stock is then identified as that of General Motors with the abbreviation _GMot_. (General Motors had several other listings besides this one, two for different issues of preferred stock indicated by a _pf_ after the _GMot_.) Next is the annual dividend per share ($5.00), followed by the percentage yield (6.3 percent), which is the dividend as a percent of the closing price. _P-E Ratio_ stands for _price-earnings ratio_ (8). This is the price per share divided by the company's profit earnings in the previous year, including retained earnings as well as earnings paid out in dividends. The P-E ratio is often used as an index of whether the current

price of the stock overvalues or undervalues the corporation, but interpretation of the index can vary depending on the circumstances. For example, a P-E ratio of 16 may seem bad compared to the 8 of General Motors. However, if the 16 is for a new, rapidly growing firm whose earnings are currently pinched by heavy research and development expenditures that promise fantastic future innovations, then the 16 may actually signal a better bargain than GM's 8. The next number (56721) indicates the number of shares that were traded during the day in hundreds (5,672,100). As you might guess, GM is one of the most actively traded stocks on the market. Three prices for the stock then follow: the highest price per share during the day ($81), the lowest price ($77.63), and the price at the close of trading ($80). Finally, the change in price from the previous day's close (+1.63) shows whether the current trend is up or down.

52 Weeks										
High	Low	Stock	Div.	Yld %	P-E Ratio	Sales 100s	High	Low	Close	Net Chg.
88 5/8	65 7/8	GMot	5.00	6.3	8	56721	81	77 5/8	80	+1 5/8

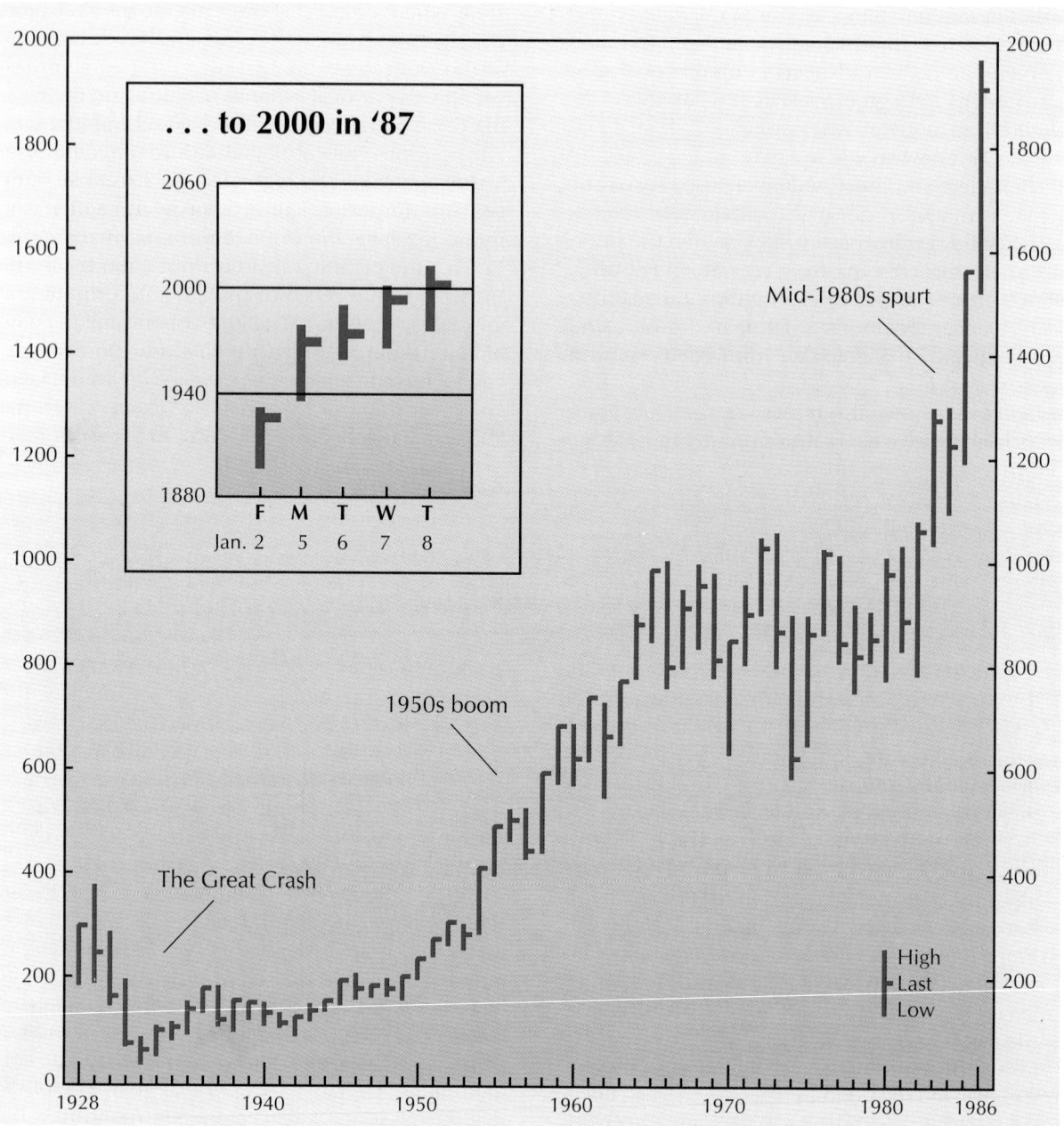

FIGURE 5.4 The Dow Jones Industrial Average: From 300 in 1928 . . .
(*Source:* The Wall Street Journal, *January 9, 1987, p. 23.*)

ket, as the Dow opened that decade at around 200 and closed it at more than 600, a threefold jump. Subsequently, from the mid-1960s through the first few years of the 1980s, the market fluctuated rather widely, while at the same time making no substantial overall progress. Then in the mid-1980s the market took off, lifting the Dow Jones index from 1000 to 2000 in just a few years. January 1987 typified the explosion. During that month alone, something on the order of $300 billion in capital gains were made in the stock market.

Except for the Great Crash of the late 1920s and early 1930s, Figure 5.4 may make a rather favorable impression. It may prompt you to withdraw your bank savings and find a stockbroker, hopeful that you can get rich quick by playing or even beating the stock market. However, you should resist the temptation at least long enough to ponder the following two qualifications.

First, the Dow Jones average may be misleading about how easy it is to get rich quickly. For example, as presented in Figure 5.4, the Dow Jones index is not adjusted for inflation, and prices of stocks will rise simply because of price inflation generally, even when there has been no real inflation-adjusted gain for investors on average. During the two decades from the end of 1966 to the end of 1986, the Dow Jones index rose about 150 percent, from 785 to 1940. At the same time, however, consumer prices tripled, which means that, after adjusting for inflation, no capital gains were earned on average. (Things look better if the dividends paid on the Dow Jones stocks are assumed to have been reinvested for the purchase of additional stock. Adjusting for both inflation and an assumed reinvestment of dividends over the 1966–86 period results in a real annual return of 2.9 percent for an investment portfolio that would match the stocks in the Dow Jones index.)[3]

The second pin to puncture your dreams of getting rich quickly may be introduced by citing the wildly diverse predictions that stock market experts were making after the Dow Jones average pushed through the 2000 mark. According to Monte Gordon, director of research for the Dreyfus Corporation, the market would follow that historic feat by experiencing a significant contraction, dropping the Dow to 1850 or 1875 during the following year. On the other hand, Elaine Garzarelli, a market strategist for Shearson Lehman Brothers, optimistically forecast that the Dow would continue to rise throughout 1987, hitting 2300 or 2400 by year's end. This wide disparity in stock market forecasts always prevails. The market has a large *random* element to its ups and downs, making predictions of its course highly speculative. In particular, the market can be said to behave randomly in *two* ways, both of which frustrate efforts to get rich quickly.

First, when gauged by its *overall average*, as measured by indexes like the Dow Jones Industrial Average, the stock market has a large random component. The stock market generally has a slightly positive long-term trend, but aside from this, it is impossible to predict what the market will do tomorrow, next month, or next year simply on the basis of where it is today or what has happened to it in the recent past. It is like flipping a coin. Each flip is independent of any other, so you cannot reasonably expect tails simply because your coin has come up heads five times in a row.

Second, the behavior of *individual stocks* also tends to be largely random. If you chose six stocks to purchase by throwing darts at the listings in the *Wall Street Journal*, the performance of those six stocks would, on average, probably be about as good (or bad) as the performance of six stocks you chose after arduous study. This statement is made possible by the fact that dart throwing has actually been tried and found to be as effective as more sophisticated methods. Moreover, it has been shown that professional stock market money managers, those who are richly paid to select stocks for pension funds and wealthy clients, cannot do better, on average, than the market as a whole. For example, compared with Standard & Poor's 500-stock index over the decade 1975–85, 44 percent of all money managers did better, while 56 percent, a solid majority, did worse.[4]

The reason it is so difficult to get rich quickly, or to beat the stock market, is that the stock market is highly **efficient.** As new information affecting the value of stocks becomes publicly available, the prices of stocks change quickly to reflect that new information because competition between sophisticated investors causes that information to be widely disseminated and acted upon with buy and sell orders. In short, stock prices *are* usually where they *should be* in light of publicly available information. Being where they should be, those prices then afford no real bargains, except those discovered by blind luck. There is an old saying that "the early bird gets the worm." Knowing this,

---

[3]*The Wall Street Journal*, January 9, 1987, p. 23.

[4]*Business Week*, February 4, 1985, pp. 58–59.

all sophisticated investors try to become early birds. As a consequence, only the *lucky* early bird gets the worm.

Note that, in light of these principles, there is only one sure way to get rich quickly or beat the stock market. If you could get *insider information* about a firm's prospective performance, that would be the ticket. Information that the firm has found a massive oil field, or that it is about to be acquired by GM for a handsome premium above the market price, would be highly valuable because you would know that, once it is made public, it will drive the stock price skyward. With insid-

er information you could buy low and later sell high. The chief problem with trading on insider information is that it is illegal. In 1985, in the largest case against insider trading ever tackled by the U.S. Securities and Exchange Commission, Ivan Boesky was fined $100 million. This penalty was apparently just a fraction of the total profits Mr. Boesky made on the basis of insider information, but it is sufficiently large to leave you with the proper impression that insider trading is seriously frowned upon by the authorities.

Read Perspective 5C.

PERSPECTIVE 5C

The Panic of '87

Nothing illustrates these points better than the stock market's behavior during 1987. The Dow Jones Industrial Average (DJIA) made history by passing the 2000 mark in early January 1987, and the reactions of forecasters at that time have been noted. Some predicted that the DJIA would rise above 2400 by year's end. Others said that it would fall back to 1850. Amazingly, *both* predictions were right. Indeed, the market outdid them both. After January, the DJIA rose fairly steadily until, as shown in Figure 5.5, it surpassed 2700 in late August. Then, after wobbling around a bit in September, the stock market plunged as if it were falling off a cliff. Figure 5.5 shows that the week ending October 23, 1987, was the worst. In those 5 days of trading the DJIA fell below 2000, losing 13 percent of its value. Monday of that week is now called *Black*

Monday because on that day alone the Dow dropped 508 points, a loss of 22.61 percent. This shattered the old record for a single-day loss, the previous record being −12.82 percent on October 28, 1929, which triggered the Great Crash of 1929. Two days after Black Monday, with its record drop, the market rebounded with considerable force. The DJIA jumped 10.15 percent on Wednesday, October 21, 1987, the fourth highest percentage rise in 1 day ever recorded for the Dow.

In sum, the events of 1987 displayed great volatility. Many individuals experienced capital gains *and* losses running into hundreds of millions of dollars. And, as shown in Figure 5.5, the DJIA finished 1987 almost exactly where it started the year—a shade below 2000.

SUMMARY

1. Commercial establishments are places where business activities are conducted. A firm is an enterprise that owns and/or operates one or more establishments. Each of the largest firms in the economy has numerous establishments in horizontal, verti-

cal, or conglomerate relationship to each other.

2. Relatively few large firms (e.g., the largest 500) account for the bulk of all business activity. At the same time, however, small

and medium-sized firms are notable for their dominance of several lines of business (like agriculture and construction) and for their significant contributions to new employment and entrepreneurship.

3. Sole proprietorships, which have direct one-person ownership, are simple to create and control. However, they suffer from limited access to financial capital and unlimited liability.

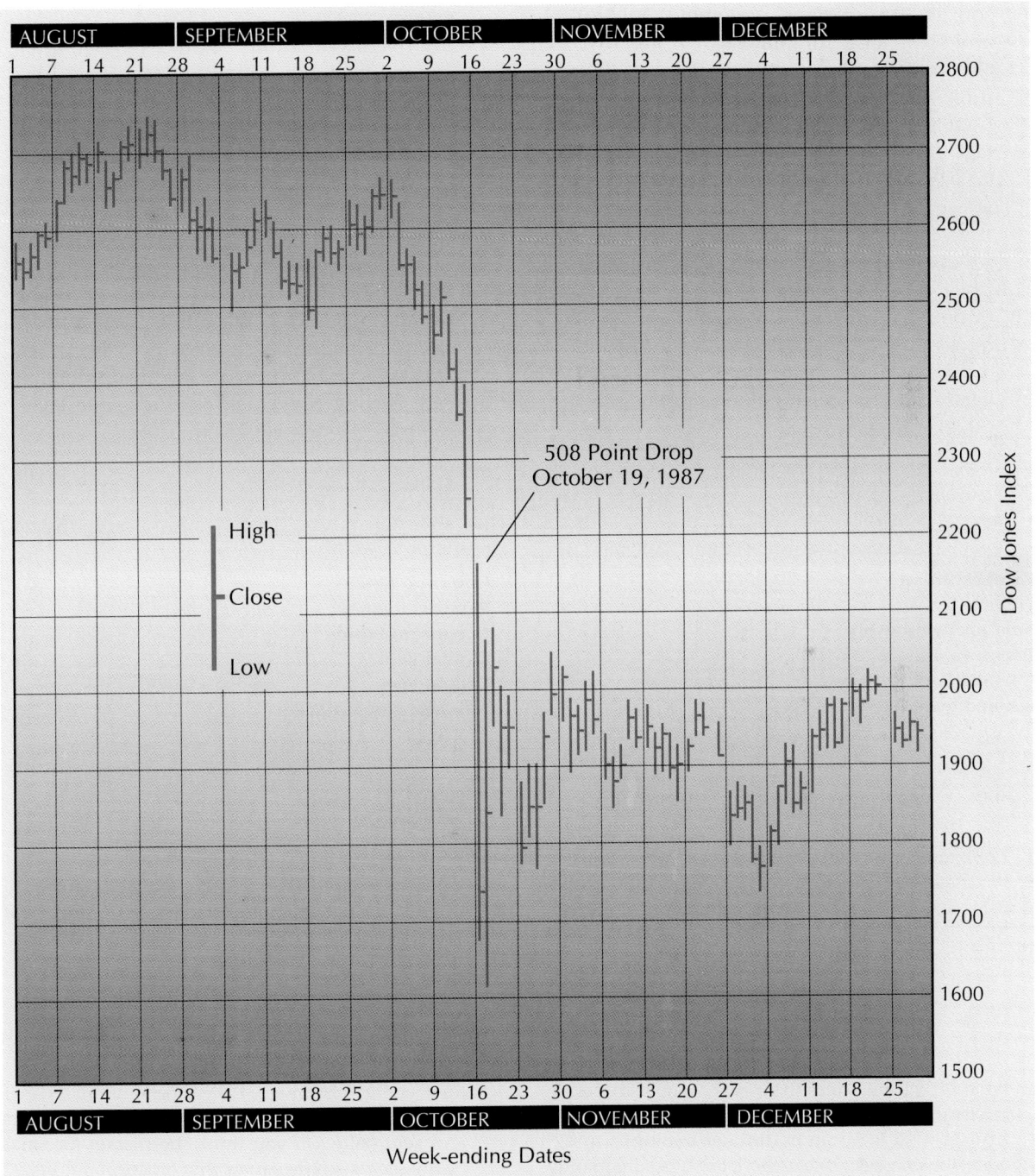

FIGURE 5.5 *The Dow Jones Industrial Average During the Last Five Months of 1987.*

(*Source:* The Wall Street Journal, *January 4, 1988, p. 18.)*

4. Partnerships are, in effect, multiperson proprietorships. Easy to establish and superior to sole proprietorships in their access to financial capital, partnerships nevertheless have several disadvantages: limited access to financial capital in comparison to corporations, unlimited liability, and some legal complexities.

5. Corporations are autonomous legal creatures chartered by states. Their status as legal persons helps to give them advantages, such as a vast capacity to raise financial capital, limited liability, and a lasting life span. On the other hand, corporations have problems with double taxation and separation between ownership and control.

6. Common stocks and preferred stocks grant ownership shares with variable and fixed dividends, respectively. Bonds are debt obligations of the corporation that pay interest to investors.

7. The stock market, as epitomized by the New York Stock Exchange and other major exchanges, is home to the massive trading that occurs for existing stocks. Historic events include the Great Crash of 1929–32 and the Dow Jones Industrial Average passing 2000 in January 1987.

8. Two considerations should temper anyone's dreams of getting rich quickly by beating the stock market. First, after adjustment for inflation, the rising raw values of stock market indexes, like the Dow Jones Industrial Average, are not as attractive as they first appear. Second, the stock market is extremely efficient. Stock prices are usually what they should be because competition among sophisticated investors quickly adjusts prices according to the latest public information. With efficiency, the prospects for hefty profits are largely randomized, leaving only luck as the major legal source of stock market treasure.

KEY TERMS

Establishment	Common stock
Firm	Preferred stock
Sole proprietorship	Corporate bonds
Partnership	Capital gain
Corporation	Capital loss
Limited liability	Efficient stock market

QUESTIONS AND PROBLEMS

1. Compare corporations and sole proprietorships.
2. What causes "capital gains" in stocks? in bonds?
3. Sales figures show that large corporations dominate American industry. Nonetheless, small firms are vital to our economy. Explain why.
4. Explain the information contained in the following Union Carbide common stock listing from the *Wall Street Journal* for October 14, 1987:

52 Weeks				Yld	P-E	Sales				Net
High	Low	Stock	Div.	%	Ratio	100s	High	Low	Close	Chg
32½	20⅝	U Carb	1.5	5.0	8	9547	30⅝	29½	29⅞	−1

5. What is the Dow Jones Industrial Average? Describe briefly the history of the Dow Jones since 1928.
6. Explain what is meant by "insider trading."
7. Small businesses (sole proprietorships) frequently change hands, as owners retire, die, or decide to use their energy elsewhere. Large corporations change hands very gradually as shares of stock are bought and sold daily. Do you think the market for small businesses is as efficient as that for corporate stock? Explain.

II

Macroeconomics: Measurement and Models

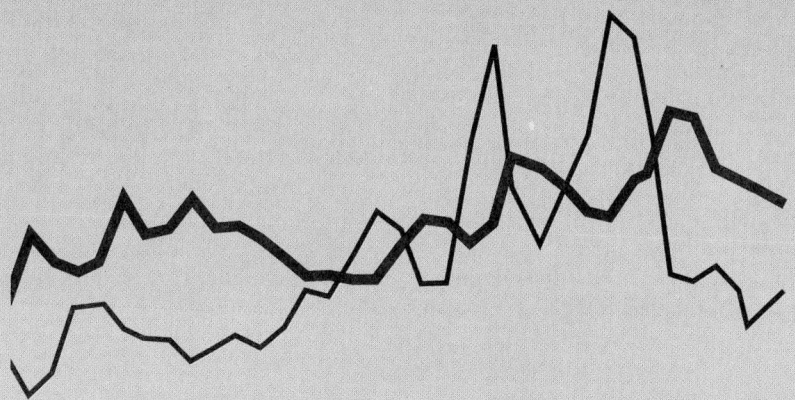

6

Twin Macroeconomic Problems: Unemployment and Inflation

In 1933 the United States was struggling with what we now call the Great Depression. Unemployment had risen from 3.2 percent in 1929 to 25.2 percent (or one out of every four workers) in 1933. Output had plunged 30 percent from the 1929 level. The financial system was in shambles; between 1929 and 1933, 9,000 banks had failed. In 1933, stocks listed on the New York Stock Exchange were worth less than 20 percent of their 1929 value.

The causes of this terrible economic collapse and, alternatively, the conditions that yield prosperity are the subject matter of *macroeconomics*. Microeconomics focuses on individual decision makers and individual markets, while macroeconomics tackles the economy as a whole.

Unemployment, inflation, output, and interest rates are some of the variables studied in macroeconomics. These are what we will call *aggregate economic variables*, *aggregate* because they are measured for the economy as a whole, *variables* because they take on different values over time. In fact, our interest is in *why* these aggregates take on the values they do. What determines whether the rate of unemployment or inflation is high or low? What, for example, caused millions to lose their jobs almost overnight during the Great Depression?

In this chapter we consider two of these variables: the levels of unemployment and inflation. High employment (a low unemployment rate) and price stability (a low inflation rate) are goals of government policymakers in all countries. We examine these goals and the costs of failure to achieve them. The next chapter defines output for the economy as a whole—the *gross national product* (GNP)—and examines some related concepts. The remaining chapters in this part of the book turn to the more challenging task of explaining, rather than simply describing, these central macroeconomic variables.

I

Unemployment

Each month the Bureau of Labor Statistics surveys 60,000 households to check the employment status of household members. Those who are employed, actively seeking employment, or waiting to report to a new job or for recall to a previous job (within 30 days) are counted in the civilian labor force. In 1987 there were 119.8 million people in the civilian labor force. Of these, 112.4 million were employed. The other 7.4 million, who were without jobs but who were either seeking employment or waiting to begin or return to a job, were counted as unemployed.

> The **unemployment rate** expresses the number of unemployed persons as a percent of the labor force.

For 1987,

$$\text{Unemployment rate (1987)} = \frac{7.4}{119.8} \times 100 = 6.2\%$$

In addition to those officially counted as unemployed, there are some who are not actively seeking work, and therefore *not* counted as unemployed (or in the labor force), who would like to work. They do not seek employment because they do not think they can find a job. These *discouraged workers*, while not counted in the statistics, are a significant part of the unemployment problem.

A

The Costs of Unemployment

The costs associated with unemployment make high employment a policy goal. One way of looking at these costs is in terms of the output not produced because individuals are unemployed. Total output of goods and services in the economy is measured by the GNP. When labor, as well as plant and equipment that combine with labor to produce output, are utilized at certain benchmark high levels, the economy is said to be operating at the level of *potential GNP*. A high level of unemployment means that actual GNP is falling far short of potential GNP. The economy is operating inside the production-possibilities frontier described in Chapter 2. For example, actual GNP was about $130 billion below potential GNP in the recession year 1975. In 1982, during the deepest post–World War II recession, actual GNP fell over $300 billion below potential GNP.

Besides forgone output, social and personal costs also accompany high unemployment rates in our society, where ideas of self-worth are closely tied to the ability to work. Unemployment has severe psychological costs. Rising unemployment is linked to increases in crime, alcoholism, mental disorders, and suicide. While the costs of unemployment are high, the personal cost to the unemployed varies greatly among individuals and across demographic groups. For most people, "spells" of unemployment are short, lasting only a few months. For some, unemployment insurance cushions the financial effects of these periods. The increasing number of two-income families has eased unemployment's impact when only one

person in the family is unemployed. Still, the human costs of unemployment are great for many. As Table 6.1 indicates, unemployment and therefore the costs of unemployment affect different demographic groups very unevenly. The unemployment rate of blacks is substantially higher than that of whites. The unemployment rate of teenagers is much higher than that of other age groups.

A further cost of unemployment is that unemployed people lose the opportunity to learn skills on the job and, especially important for younger workers, to develop a stable record of work experience. This, in turn, makes it more difficult to find stable employment in the future. Current unemployment therefore makes future unemployment more likely.

B
Types of Unemployment

Given these costs of unemployment, the government is committed to high employment. But by how much can the unemployment rate be reduced through public policies? This is a central and highly controversial question in our later analysis. To help sort out the issues, it is useful to distinguish different categories of unemployment according to the causes of each.

1. Frictional Unemployment Some unemployment is due to the time workers spend between jobs, or to the search time entrants or reentrants to the labor force need to find jobs. This is termed **frictional unemployment.** Some such unemployment is unavoidable and not socially unproductive. To the degree that policymakers want to reduce frictional unemployment, they proceed with policies to improve the efficiency of the labor market. Better job counseling or improved dissemination of job information are examples of such policies.

2. Structural Unemployment Like frictional unemployment, **structural unemployment** originates in the dynamic nature of the product and job mix in the economy, but structural unemployment lasts longer. It results from a mismatch between the skills and/or location of workers and

TABLE 6.1   Unemployment Rates by Demographic Groups (1987)

	Demographic Group	Percent Unemployed
	ALL civilian workers	6.2
Males	Total	6.2
	16–19 years	17.8
	20 years and older	5.4
Females	Total	6.2
	16–19 years	15.9
	20 years and older	5.4
Black	Total	13.0
White	Total	5.3

Source: Economic Report of the President, 1988.

the existing opportunities for employment. When industries decline—as happened recently, for example, with some "smokestack" industries such as steel and automobiles in the Midwest—workers are displaced. These workers cannot move easily into industries that are growing quickly—high-tech industries in Massachusetts, for example. Structural unemployment also results when teenagers leave school with few marketable skills.

Unlike frictional unemployment, structural unemployment is *not* socially productive. Policies advocated to eliminate it include retraining and relocating workers. More broadly, the structural unemployment that results as industries decline is an element in the case made for some type of overall government *industrial policy*. Industrial policy is a very general term for a government plan to influence the structure of the economy. Such a plan would aim to improve compatibility between the skill mix and location of the labor force and the employment opportunities in industry. Possible ways to do this include subsidies to declining industries tied to worker retraining programs, and government investment policies aimed at using the existing skill and location mix of the labor force.

3. Cyclical Unemployment

Cyclical unemployment results from fluctuations in the level of economic activity and consequent fluctuations in industry demand for workers. Most rapid changes in unemployment result from cyclical fluctuations in economic activity. When the downturn in economic activity began in July 1981, the unemployment rate stood at 7.0 percent. By December 1982, it had risen to 10.8 percent. Approximately 4.5 million more persons had become unemployed.

The obvious remedy for cyclical unemployment is to eliminate severe fluctuations in the level of economic activity. Policies aimed at this objective are called *macroeconomic stabilization policies.* We will see that there is sharp disagreement among economists about the best way for government to design policies to achieve macroeconomic stability.

What does our discussion of the various types of unemployment reveal about how low we might drive the unemployment rate? Because there will always be frictional unemployment, zero unem-

ployment is not feasible. There is also structural unemployment that, while we might like to eliminate it in the long run, is not amenable to short-run policies. With these considerations in mind, macroeconomic policymakers in the 1960s adopted 4 percent as a goal for the unemployment rate. Unemployment in excess of 4 percent was viewed as cyclical unemployment. At 4 percent unemployment the economy was presumed to be at its potential output (GNP) level.

During the 1970s, policymakers and economists began to believe that changes in the composition of the labor force had made a 4 percent target too optimistic. Specifically, young workers and female workers had increased relative to older male workers as a proportion of the labor force. Since the former groups contain more new entrants or reentrants to the labor force and tend to change jobs more frequently, they would be expected to have more frequent episodes of frictional unemployment. By 1975, therefore, 5 percent was being used as a high-employment benchmark by the President's Council of Economic Advisors.

This benchmark was revised again in the late 1970s and early 1980s, when an unemployment rate of 6 percent came to be regarded as a high-employment level. Growing structural unemployment in several basic industries was one reason given for the upward revision. A further argument was that an improved combination of unemployment insurance, food stamps, and welfare benefits increased the target unemployment rate, even if the economy was operating near capacity. The argument is that these benefits reduced the incentive to take jobs, especially low-paying ones. These factors led not only to an increase in the perceived benchmark for unemployment but also to greater uncertainty about any specific benchmark.

C
Unemployment: The Historical Record

Figure 6.1 shows the annual unemployment rate from 1929 to 1987. A striking feature of the figure is the exceptionally high unemployment level during 1929–39—the period of the Great Depression. By 1939 the unemployment rate was still very high at 17.2 percent. High unemployment in the 1930s

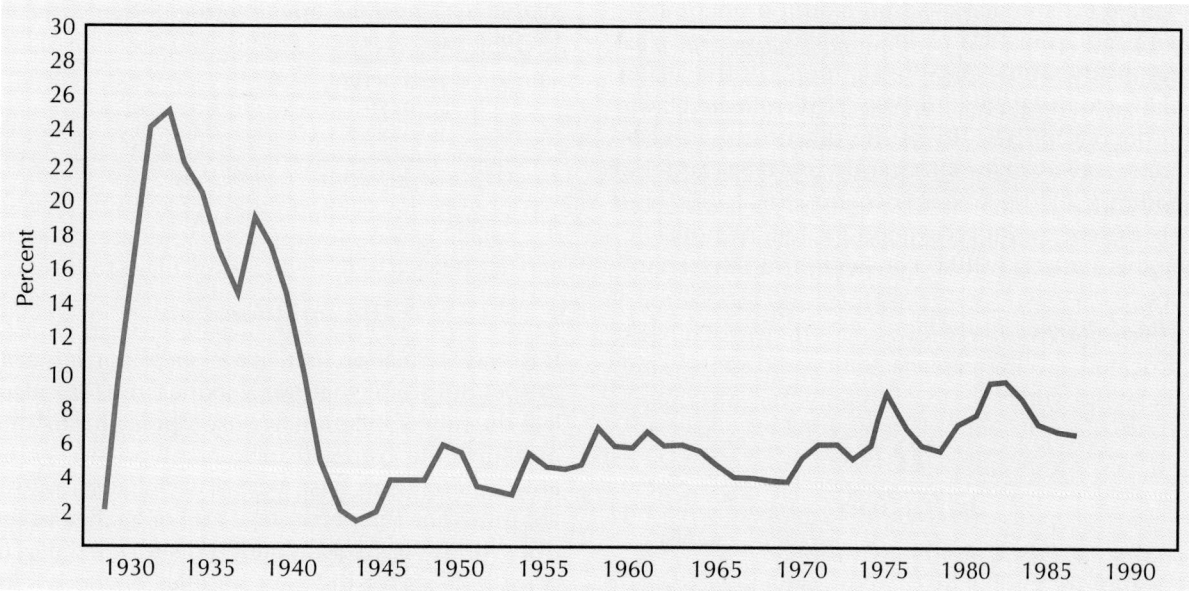

FIGURE 6.1   U.S. Unemployment Rate, 1929–87

was not unique to the United States, but was an experience shared by other industrialized countries.

The Depression finally ended with the military buildup during World War II. Unemployment fell to 4.7 percent in 1942 and to only 1.2 percent by 1944. This latter figure is below what we would view as normal frictional unemployment, or put differently, the unemployment rate during 1944 was lower than the benchmark rate for defining potential output. During a major war, resources are so fully mobilized that the economy can perform above normal peacetime capacity.

Fortunately, the post–World War II period did not see unemployment return to the levels of the Great Depression, but cyclical fluctuations in economic activity and resulting cyclical unemployment did resume. Unemployment rates of 5.9 percent in 1949, 5.5 percent in 1954, 6.8 percent in 1958, and 6.7 percent in 1961 corresponded to postwar *recessions.*

A **recession** is a period when economic activity declines significantly relative to potential output, but less severely than in a depression such as that of the 1930s.

The period 1961–69 was a time of steady expansion in the economy and steady decline in the unemployment rate. By 1968, during the Vietnam War, the unemployment rate declined to 3.6 percent. Relative to the 4 percent benchmark for potential output, the economy, which was already near capacity, was pressed above it by increased military expenditures.

The unemployment rate rose to 5.9 percent in 1971 during a mild drop in economic activity. In 1975 unemployment reached 8.5 percent during the recession that followed the sharp rise in the price of oil by the Organization of Petroleum Exporting Countries (OPEC). The unemployment rate then fell to 5.8 percent by 1979, after which another drop in the level of economic activity pushed it back up to 7.1 percent in 1980. Before unemployment could decline again, the next recession began in 1981. The unemployment rate rose to a postwar high of 9.7 percent in 1982 (10.8 percent in December of that year). Unemployment then declined gradually, but still averaged 9.6 percent for 1983, 7.5 percent for 1984, and 7.0 percent by 1986. As the economic recovery continued in 1987, the unemployment rate fell to 6.2 percent, the lowest level since 1979.

Table 6.2 summarizes trends in the unemployment rate from 1953 to 1987. Unemployment was high in the 1970s and during much of the 1980s relative to the 1950s and 1960s. This reflected both the increasing severity of the downturns in economic activity in the 1970s and early 1980s and the tendency of the unemployment rate to decline less during recent recoveries. Factors responsible for this pattern will be considered in later chapters.

Read Perspective 6A.

TABLE 6.2   Average Unemployment Rate, Selected Periods

1953–69	4.8%
1970–79	6.2%
1980–87	7.7%

Source: Economic Report of the President, 1988.

II

Inflation

Inflation is an increase in the general level of prices.

At any time, the prices of some products are falling while the prices of others are rising. When inflation occurs, however, prices on average are rising. Price stability, which in practice means a low rate of inflation, is the second major goal of macroeconomic policy.

A

The Inflation Rate

It is said of inflation that, like an elephant, it is easy to spot but somewhat tricky to measure. To calculate the rate of inflation, we use a **price index** that measures the aggregate (or general) price level relative to a chosen base year. The inflation rate is computed as the percentage rate of change in the price index over a given period. There are different price indexes for different bundles of goods. Our discussion here will focus on the *consumer price index (CPI)*, with other price indexes considered in the next chapter.

The CPI measures the retail prices of a fixed "market basket" of several thousand goods and services purchased by households. Each of the goods and services is given a weight in the index in proportion to its importance in the market basket.

PERSPECTIVE 6A
Employment and Output

As explained in this section, it is primarily cyclical unemployment that macroeconomic stabilization policy seeks to eliminate. Cyclical unemployment results from fluctuations in the level of economic activity and consequently in employment. Our central measure of economic activity, to be described in more detail in Chapter 7, is real gross national product, current production of goods and services—what we will term *output*.

Figure 6.2 illustrates the relationship between percentage changes in output and percentage changes in employment in the 1980s.

There was a brief, but sharp, fall in output in 1980, and employment also fell for two quarters. After a few quarters of recovery the recession of 1981–82 began, and there are several quarters in which the changes in both output and employment were negative. Output and employment both then recovered in 1983–84 and settled into patterns of slower growth in 1985, 1986, and 1987.

It is the close relationship between fluctuations in output and those in employment that lead policymakers to try to stabilize employment growth by stabilizing growth in output.

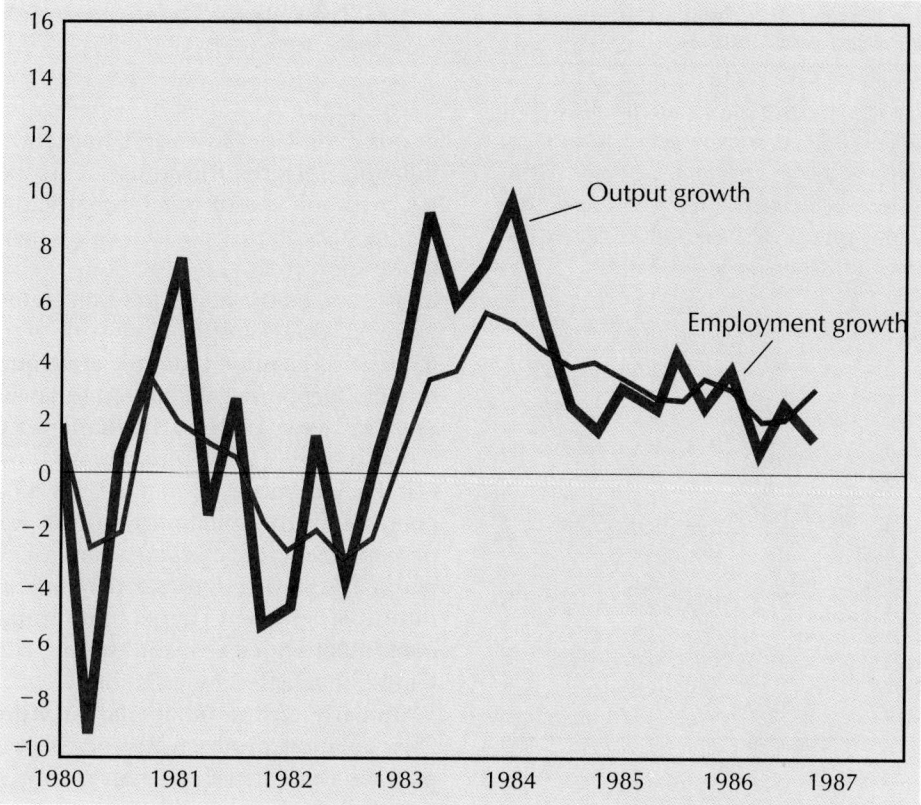

FIGURE 6.2   *Output and Employment in Recession and Recovery*

Food, for example, is weighted much more heavily than hatpins. The goal is to measure the cost of living for a representative household. The consumer price index for 1967–87 is given in column (1) of Table 6.3.

The base year for the series is 1967 = 100. Movements in the CPI show changes in the overall level of prices. For example, from the table we can see that a market basket of goods purchased in 1978 cost nearly twice as much (195.4/100 = 1.954) as in 1967. The inflation rate for a given year *(t)* relative to the previous year *(t − 1)* is computed as

$$\text{Inflation Rate } (t) = \frac{\text{CPI } (t) - \text{CPI } (t-1)}{\text{CPI } (t-1)} \times 100$$

that is, the change in the CPI from one year to the next expressed as a proportion of the previous year's CPI, then multiplied by 100 to form a percentage change. For example, the inflation rate for 1987, relative to 1986 using CPI figures from Table 6.3, is

$$\begin{aligned} \text{Inflation rate} \atop (1987) \ &= \frac{\text{CPI}(1987) - \text{CPI}(1986)}{\text{CPI}(1986)} \times 100 \\ &= \frac{(340.4 - 328.4)}{328.4} \times 100 \\ &= 3.7\% \end{aligned}$$

B
The Costs of Inflation

As with unemployment, low rates of inflation are a policy goal because inflation is costly to society. What are these costs? It is not as simple as saying that with inflation we must pay more for the things we buy and, therefore, we are less well off. Overall, our incomes, as well as our expenditures, rise with inflation.

However, while people seem to view increasing prices as a cost of inflation, they feel that they have *earned* their increased incomes, even though these increases may be, in fact, inflation related. They then perceive inflation as depriving them of

TABLE 6.3   The Level and Percentage Increase in the Consumer Price Index, 1967–87

	(1) CPI	(2) Inflation Rate (Percentage Increase in the CPI)
1967	100.0	2.9
1968	104.2	4.2
1969	109.8	5.4
1970	116.3	5.9
1971	121.3	4.3
1972	125.3	3.3
1973	133.1	6.2
1974	147.7	11.0
1975	161.2	9.1
1976	170.5	5.8
1977	181.5	6.5
1978	195.4	7.7
1979	217.4	11.3
1980	246.8	13.5
1981	272.4	10.4
1982	289.1	6.1
1983	298.4	3.2
1984	311.1	4.3
1985	322.2	3.6
1986	328.4	1.9
1987	340.4	3.7

Source: Economic Report of the President, 1988.

these gains. But other costs of inflation are not just a result of how things are perceived. To understand these costs, two features of the inflation experience of the United States and other developed countries must be kept in mind:

1. Higher inflation has led to more variable and uncertain inflation. For example, in the 1950s the inflation rate averaged only about 2 percent and varied relatively little from year to year. In the 1970s, it was harder to predict whether inflation for the next year might be 4 percent or 12 percent. Many of the costs of inflation are associated with the gap between what is expected and what actually happens—one example of the two-question logic of macroeconomics.

2. Many of our institutions, which were designed when there was little inflation, turn out to be ill-suited to a more inflationary environment. Thus, old labor market practices and regulations in financial markets both functioned poorly in the inflationary 1970s.

To see the relationship between these features of our experience with inflation and the costs of inflation, consider the adjustments that would occur without institutional constraints if inflation were a smooth process that could be predicted far in advance. In financial markets, we would expect interest rates to reflect fully the rate of inflation. Suppose, for example, that with zero inflation a bank would lend you money at an annual interest rate of 2 percent. A dollar lent today would return $1.02 in 1 year. With no inflation, this would mean a *real* return of 2 percent, a 2 percent increase in purchasing power. If, instead, it was correctly expected that the inflation rate was going to be 10 percent over the coming year, the interest rate could be adjusted to 12 percent, again, a real return of 2 percent (12 percent minus the 10 percent inflation rate). Neither the bank nor you would be affected by inflation.

Similarly, in the labor market, if in a world of zero inflation productivity increases justified a 2 percent wage increase, then with a correctly expected inflation rate of 10 percent, wages could rise 12 percent. Thus, in real (inflation-adjusted) terms the increase in the wage would be 2 percent.

In actuality, where inflation is variable and only imperfectly foreseen, the preceding adjustments take place only partially, if at all. The resulting costs appear as scrambled income distribution (Who?), inefficiencies (What? and How?), and assorted social strains.

1. Income Distribution (Who?) In financial markets, many contracts are based on misperceptions of future inflation. To the degree that existing contracts are based on *under*predicting inflation, the interest rate will be lower than with inflation perfectly foreseen; debtors will gain and lenders will lose. The reverse will be true if market participants *over*predict inflation. In labor markets, in real terms, workers will lose (gain) depending on whether labor contracts are based on underpredicting (overpredicting) the inflation rate.

Institutions could be designed to adjust for even unanticipated changes in the inflation rate. Financial market arrangements and labor contracts can be *indexed* to the inflation rate and, therefore, continuously adjusted depending on the actual rate of inflation. An indexed labor contract might, for example, call for a 2 percent increase in purchasing power and, therefore, a 7 percent increase in the current dollar wage if the inflation rate were 5 percent, a 12 percent increase if the inflation rate were 10 percent, etc. In the real world, such indexing is partial and does not exist at all for many types of contracts.

Thus, inflation has real effects in financial and labor markets. Among such effects are redistributions of income and wealth, as we have seen, between borrowers and lenders and between workers and firms. There is an element of randomness and unfairness to these redistributions. Some people hit the jackpot. Others lose. These random distribution effects are one of the main costs of inflation.

2. Inefficiencies (What? and How?) A second cost of variable and uncertain inflation, given our existing institutions, is that it distorts resource allocation. One direct distortion occurs when firms and individuals devote resources to devising ways of protecting themselves from the effects of inflation. These resources are diverted from more productive uses.

A more general distortion caused by high and variable inflation is the reduction in the efficiency of the price system as a mechanism for coordinating economic activity. Prices transmit the information people use to solve the problems of what to produce and how to produce. Such price information is central to resource allocation in our economy. During a period of high and uncertain inflation, observed prices start to provide misleading signals. A business manager sees the price of tennis shoes rising quickly. Does this reflect increased interest in the sport and a growing market for the shoes? Or is overall inflation just speeding up? In such inflationary times "the broadcast about relative prices is, as it were, being jammed by the noise coming from the inflation broadcast."[1] The efficiency of the price system in allocating resources declines.

[1]Milton Friedman, "Inflation and Unemployment," *Journal of Political Economy*, 85 (June 1977), 451–472.

3. Social Strains A final cost of inflation is the loss of political and social cohesion. Inflation leads to a search for the villains behind it. Few are likely to see themselves as benefiting from inflation. But many believe that someone must be: Greedy trade unions? Profiteers in industry? Unproductive speculators? Bankers? Inflation breeds distrust, which extends to the public's view of government; policymakers promise to end inflation but fail. Changing the policymakers often does no good. How far inflation must proceed before such a loss of social and political cohesion becomes significant is hard to determine, but such a loss is potentially the most serious cost of sustained inflation.

Read Perspective 6B.

C
Inflation: The Historical Record

Figure 6.3 shows the U.S. inflation rate as measured by the CPI for 1929–87. During the 1929–33 period, the early part of the Great Depression, the price level was falling, as evidenced by the negative rate of inflation. The price level rose during the recovery period from 1934 to 1937, then fell again with a new period of recession that began in 1937–38. The inflation rate rose sharply with the U.S. entry into World War II near the end of 1941. In response, direct government controls on prices and wages were set up. After controls were removed, inflation rose again in the 1946–48 period. Price and wage controls were resumed in 1951 during the Korean War.

The behavior of the inflation rate over the post–Korean War period can be broken down into four stages, as shown in Table 6.5. Over the 1953–65 period, inflation was low, averaging only 1.3 percent. A second stage began during the late 1960s with an acceleration in the inflation rate, which rose from 1.7 percent in 1965 to 5.9 percent by 1970. This increase coincided with the sharp rise in economic activity during the Vietnam War. The average inflation rate for the 1966–72 period was 4.1 percent.

The 1973–81 period saw a further increase in the inflation rate, which averaged 9.1 percent. Inflation reached 11.0 percent in 1974 and 13.5 per-

PERSPECTIVE 6B

The German Hyperinflation

Hyperinflation occurs when inflation reaches astronomical proportions. The most famous example of this phenomenon occurred in Germany in the early 1920s. Table 6.4 shows the value of a price index for Germany from the beginning of World War I through the period of hyperinflation. The price level rose steadily during the war and then quite rapidly in the first few years after the war. By 1921, the price level was approximately 20 times higher than in 1914. Yet this was *before* the worst of the hyperinflation. During 1922 and 1923, the price level simply exploded. From August 1922 to November 1923, the average *monthly* inflation rate was 322 percent. The value of the price level at the end of the hyperinflation was 126 trillion (compared to 100 in the base year 1913)!

The German hyperinflation illustrates the costs of inflation in the extreme. Random effects on income distribution were everywhere. Fortunes based on bank deposits or other financial assets were destroyed as astronomical prices made money valueless. By the end of the hyperinflation, the whole of the German money supply in 1918 wouldn't have purchased a ride on a Berlin streetcar. But some industrialists, recognizing that the value of debt would also be destroyed, built fortunes by borrowing heavily to buy factories and other tangible assets. Inefficiencies were also pervasive. Firms had to devote manpower to endlessly complex calculations of new prices, wages, and taxes. Workers had to be paid several times per day and were forced to spend their money quickly before it became valueless.

With regard to the social strains that resulted, an economist who studied the period described the costs of the hyperinflation as follows:[2]

It provoked a serious revolution in social classes, a few people accumulating wealth . . . whilst millions of individuals were thrown into poverty. It was a distressing preoccupation and constant torment of innumerable families; it poisoned the German people by spreading among all classes the spirit of speculation and by diverting them from proper and regular work, and it was the cause of incessant political and moral disturbance. It is indeed easy enough to understand why the record of the sad years 1919–23 always weighs like a nightmare on the German people.

TABLE 6.4 The Price Level in Germany, 1914–24 (Base Year 1913 = 100)

1914		105.3
1915		141.5
1916		152.5
1917		178.8
1918		216.8
1919		416.2
1920		1,488.3
1921		2,296.0
1922	January	3,670.0
	February	4,100.0
	March	5,430.0
	April	6,360.0
	May	6,460.0
	June	7,030.0
	July	10,160.0
	August	19,200.0
	September	28,700.0
	October	56,600.0
	November	115,100.0
	December	147,480.0
1923	January	278,500.0
	February	588,500.0
	March	488,800.0
	April	521,100.0
	May	817,000.0
	June	1,938,500.0
	July	7,478,700.0
	August	94,404,100.0
	September	2,394,889,300.0
	October	709,480,000,000.0
	November	72,570,000,000,000.0
	December	126,160,000,000,000.0

[2]Constantino Bresciani-Turroni, *The Economics of Inflation* (London: Allen and Unwin, 1937), p. 404.

Source: Thomas Sargent, "The Ends of Four Big Inflations," in Robert Hall (ed.), *Inflation* (Chicago: University of Chicago Press, 1982).

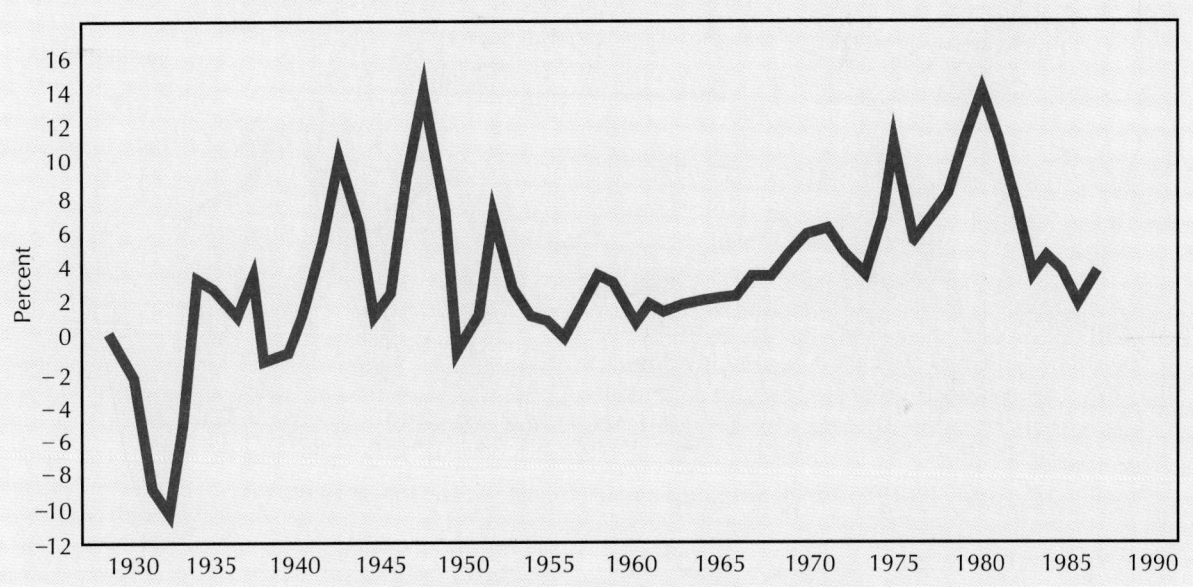

FIGURE 6.3   Annual Inflation Rate (CPI), 1929–87

TABLE 6.5   Average Inflation Rate, Selected Periods (Percentage Increase in the CPI)

1953–65	1.3%
1966–72	4.1%
1973–81	9.1%
1982–87	3.8%

cent in 1980. Both spurts followed disruptions of the world petroleum market, which boosted energy prices sharply. Finally, as can be seen from the last line of Table 6.5, the inflation rate dropped substantially beginning in 1982.

III
Inflation and Unemployment

Figure 6.4 shows annual inflation and unemployment rates for 1953–87. Note the inverse relationship between inflation and unemployment from 1953 to about 1969. When the unemployment rate was high, the inflation rate tended to be low, and vice versa. But as we have seen in our separate discussions of inflation and unemployment, the 1970s saw *both* unemployment and inflation rise. The distressing combination of high inflation and high unemployment came to be termed *stagflation.* The early 1980s show a return to the pattern of the 1950s and 1960s in that the unemployment rate rose while the inflation rate fell, though the level of unemployment was substantially higher in the early 1980s than at similar inflation rates in the 1950s and 1960s. Then in the mid-1980s, the inflation rate remained low while the unemployment rate steadily declined.

Why did the relationship between inflation and unemployment change in the late 1960s? What explains the disheartening developments of the 1970s, when inflation and unemployment rose simultaneously? Why did the early 1980s show a return to the inflation–unemployment relationship of the 1950s and 1960s? How will inflation and unemployment be related as we move into the 1990s? Seeking answers to such questions is an important part of macroeconomics.

Read Perspective 6C.

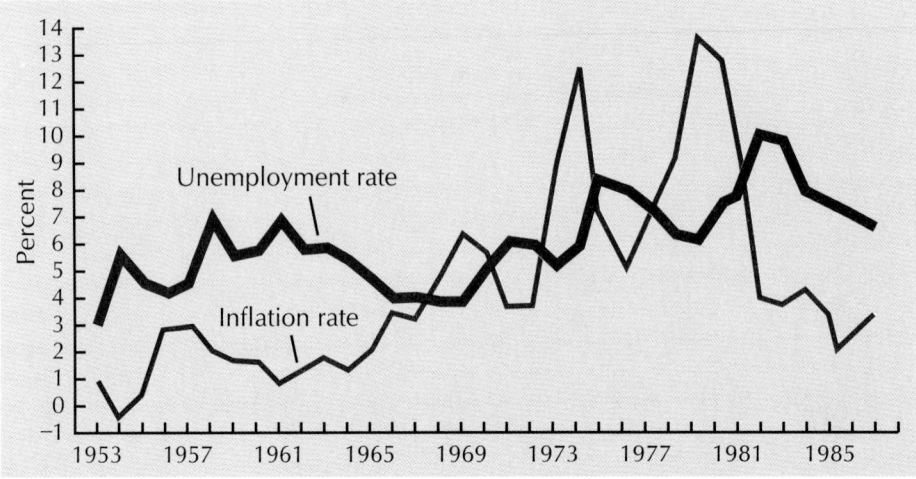

FIGURE 6.4 *U.S. Inflation and Unemployment Rates, 1953–87*

PERSPECTIVE 6C

Inflation and Unemployment: International Comparisons

For a long time, the foreign economic relations of the United States were considered so insignificant that macroeconomic analysis proceeded, for the most part, as if the United States was a *closed* economy, one having no economic dealings with the rest of the world. Our international economic relations have, however, grown to great importance over time. In 1961, the volume of imports (purchases of products from abroad) was equal to 3 percent of our GNP. By 1986, imports totaled nearly 12 percent of the GNP. The disruption of U.S. economic activity in 1974 and again in 1979, when foreign supplies of crude oil became uncertain, is one dramatic illustration of the growing interdependence of the United States and other economies.

Figure 6.5 illustrates common developments in the world economy, as well as some differences across countries. The figure compares average unemployment (part a) and inflation (part b) rates for nine industrialized countries for 1963–70, 1971–81, and 1982–86.

There are distinctive features in the experience of individual countries, such as the exceptionally low rate of unemployment in Japan and the especially high inflation rate in Italy in the 1970s. Yet the data reveal significant common trends. The average inflation rate for these countries in the 1971–81 period (9.5 percent) was more than double that of the earlier (1963–70) period (4.0 percent). The average unemployment rate for the later period (5.2 percent) was double that of the earlier period (2.6 percent). Note that not only did the average values across countries for the variables move in these directions, but in *every one* of the countries, the unemployment rate and the inflation rate rose between these periods. Figure 6.5 indicates that the acceleration in inflation accompanied by rising unemployment—the stagflation of the 1970s—was not confined to the United States, but was common to the industrialized countries.

During the 1982–86 period, the inflation rate fell in all nine countries while unemployment rose. The rise in unemployment was especially severe in several European countries (Belgium, the Netherlands, the United Kingdom), but was common to all. The *disinflation* and especially high unemployment in the 1980s were also part of the common experience of industrialized countries.

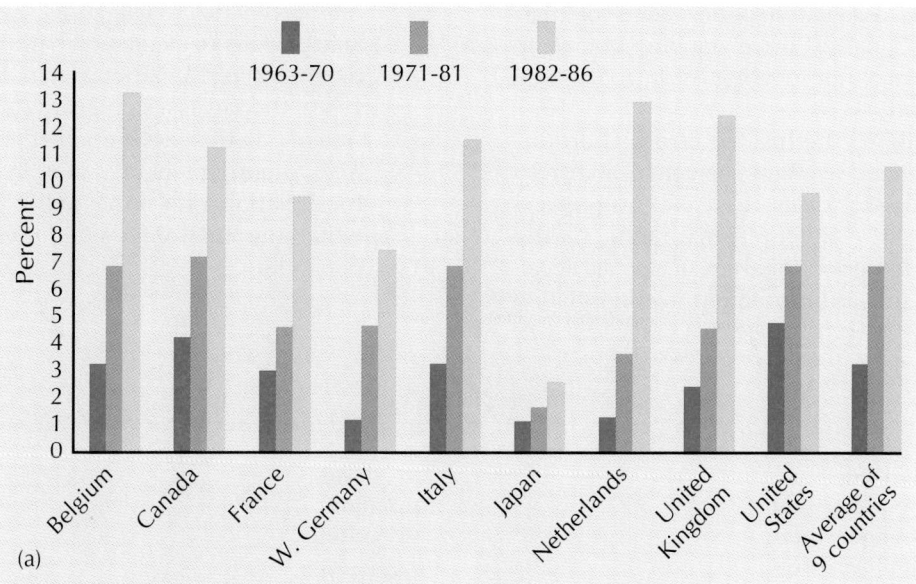

FIGURE 6.5   Inflation and Unemployment, Selected Countries
(a) Average unemployment rate, 1963–70, 1971–81, 1982–86.

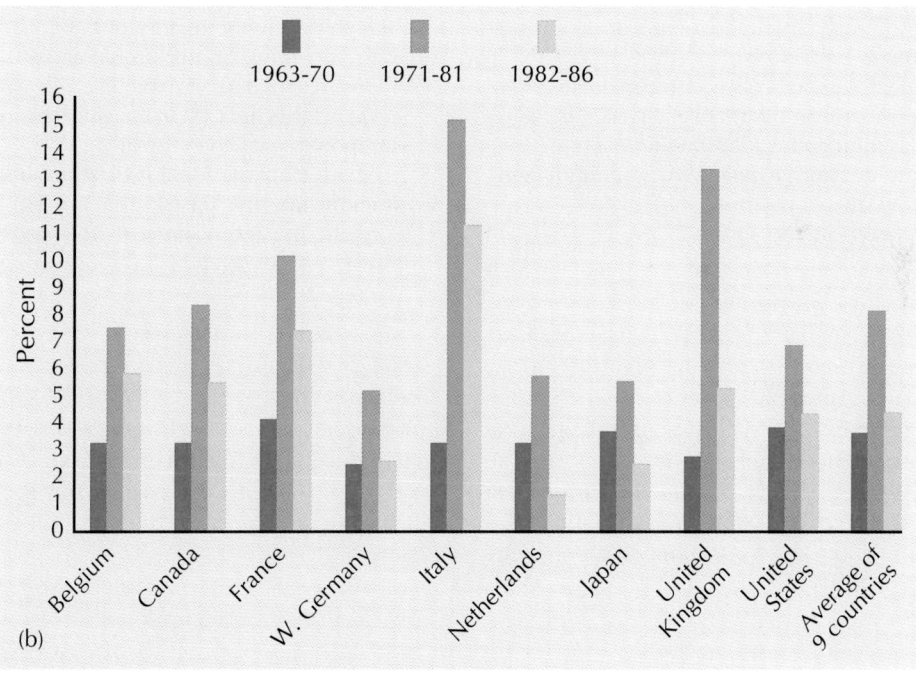

FIGURE 6.5   (b) Average inflation rates, 1963–70, 1971–81, 1982–86.

SUMMARY

1. This chapter has sought to raise questions rather than answer them. We began by considering *unemployment* and *inflation*, two central problems in macroeconomics,

with the associated policy goals of high employment and price stability. The costs to society of not meeting these goals were explained.

2. In examining the historical record on unemployment, we have seen that relative to the 1950s and 1960s, there was an upward trend in the unemployment rate in the post-1970 period. There was also an accelerating upward movement in the inflation rate in the 1970s. The 1970s saw considerable periods of stagflation with high unemployment and inflation. Then, in the early 1980s, there was a significant decline in the rate of inflation, accompanied, however, by high unemployment. Later in the 1980s, the inflation rate remained relatively low, while the unemployment rate gradually declined.

KEY TERMS

Unemployment rate
Frictional unemployment
Structural unemployment
Cyclical unemployment

Recession
Inflation
Price index

QUESTIONS AND PROBLEMS

1. Explain why a high unemployment rate is considered a problem.
2. Unemployment can be broken into three categories based on its cause. List the three categories, explaining causes and potential solutions for each.
3. Is "high employment" a near-zero unemployment rate? Explain why or why not.
4. Why is inflation costly to society?
5. Sketch briefly the history of U.S. inflation.
6. Can you think of any problems with using a price index calculated via the fixed market basket approach (as is the CPI) to measure the loss of purchasing power over the years?
7. In 1981, Congressional legislation indexed personal income tax brackets in the U.S. for the first time. Explain the importance of this legislation for the American taxpayer.

7

The National Income and Product Accounts

Now what I want is, Facts. Teach these boys and girls nothing but Facts. Facts alone are wanted in life. Plant nothing else, and root out everything else. You can only form the minds of reasoning animals upon Facts; nothing else will ever be of any service to them. . . . Stick to the Facts, sir![1]

So spoke the character Thomas Gradgrind in Dickens's *Hard Times*. This chapter may lead the reader to fear that we have adopted Gradgrind's educational philosophy, for it deals only with facts and definitions. But take heart, the remaining chapters will deal with theories that try to explain the behavior of major macroeconomic variables. To understand these theories, however, it is best to begin by carefully defining the real-world variables that the theories seek to explain and looking briefly at how these variables have behaved in the past. So, in this chapter, we "stick to the facts."

The *facts* we look at are the main items in the U.S. *national income and product accounts.* Every business firm has a set of accounts that measure the output of the firm and the sales of that output on one side of the ledger and payments by the firm for wages, interest, rent, and other expenses on the other. The national income and product accounts are the analogous set of accounts for the nation as a whole. On the one side, production and sales are measured—the product side—while on the other, the distribution of proceeds is measured—the income side. The latter is so named because proceeds from sales of the nation's production form the source of the nation's income.[2]

---

[1]Charles Dickens, *Hard Times* (New York: Norton, 1966), p. 1.

[2]Simon Kuznets (winner of the 1971 Nobel Prize in economics) and Richard Stone (winner of the 1984 prize) played a pioneering role in the development of techniques for national income accounting. During World War II the U.S. Commerce Department took on the task of maintaining the national income accounts. National income accounts data are published in the *Survey of Current Business.* Historical series for the national income accounts can be found in the Commerce Department's publication *The National Income and Product Accounts for the United States, 1929–82: Statistical Tables.*

The summary measures from each side, *gross national product (GNP)* and *national income*, will be central variables in our later analysis. We begin our discussion with the product side of the national income accounts.

I
Gross National Product

The summary measure on the product side is *gross national product.*

Gross National product (GNP) is a measure of all currently produced final goods and services.

Remember that what we are after is a measure of total national output. GNP includes only goods produced in the current period. GNP for 1987, for example, includes only goods produced in that year. Note also that GNP includes only *final* goods and services, which means only goods and services sold to the final purchasers. This excludes intermediate products—goods purchased to be used in the production of other goods. Flour purchases to be used in making bread and steel to be used in making automobiles are examples of intermediate products. The flour and steel are taken account of in GNP by counting the bread and automobiles. To count intermediate products separately would be double counting.

All currently produced final goods and services are valued in GNP at their *current market prices.* This is the trick to adding numbers of autos plus tons of steel plus pounds of grapes plus gallons of milk, and so on. We measure all these diverse goods in dollars and say that for 1987 the GNP is $4,486.2 billion. But measuring all GNP goods and services at current market prices does create problems. First, most goods and services not sold on a market are excluded, such as the output of home gardens and the services of homemakers. The value of some services not sold on markets is estimated (or imputed) by the Commerce Department, however. For example, services of owner-occupied homes are estimated on the basis of rental values.

Second, since GNP is measured in *current* market prices, it changes when prices change, even if the amount of goods actually produced remains unchanged. This is unfortunate because we want GNP to be a measure of the quantity of the nation's output. To correct for the effect of price changes, the national income accountants calculate *real* GNP, which is the value of the nation's production in terms of constant prices from a base year. The way in which this calculation is made is discussed in Section VI. To distinguish it from real GNP, GNP in current prices is called *nominal* (or *money*) *GNP*.

II
The Components of GNP

GNP can be broken down into the components shown in Table 7.1. The values of each component for selected years are also given. The data in the table suggest a number of trends and patterns that will be of interest to us later.

A
Consumption

The **consumption** component of GNP in Table 7.1 consists of the part of current production purchased by the household sector.

Consumption can be further broken down into consumer durable goods (autos, televisions, refrigerators, etc.), nondurable consumption goods (food, beverages, clothing, etc.), and consumer services (medical services, haircuts, legal fees, etc.). Consumption is the largest component of GNP, between 60 and 67 percent of GNP in recent years.

B
Investment

The next component of GNP in Table 7.1 is *investment*.

> **Investment** is the part of GNP purchased by the business sector plus residential construction.

Investment consists of three subcomponents. The first and largest of these is *business fixed investment*, which consists of the business firms' purchases of plant and equipment. If General Motors builds an automobile factory in Tennessee, the cost of the structure (plant) and machines (equipment) would be counted as business fixed investment. Business fixed investment is the business sector's purchases of what are called *capital goods*.

The other part of investment expenditure by firms is *inventory investment*. This is the *change in* business inventories, which are stocks on hand of raw materials and finished goods. If General Motors increases its inventory of unsold cars, this would be counted as inventory investment. Only changes in business inventories represent *produc-

TABLE 7.1   Nominal GNP and Its Components, Selected Years (Billions of Dollars)*

Year	GNP	Consumption	Investment	Government Purchases	Net Exports
1929	103.9	77.3	16.7	8.9	1.1
1933	56.0	45.8	1.6	8.3	0.4
1939	91.3	67.0	9.5	13.6	1.2
1945	213.4	119.6	11.3	83.0	−0.5
1950	288.3	192.1	55.1	38.8	2.2
1970	1,015.5	640.0	148.8	218.2	8.5
1987	4,486.2	2966.0	716.4	923.8	−119.9

*Components may not sum to total due to rounding error.
Source: Economic Report of the President, 1988.

tion in the current period and are counted in GNP. Should inventories fall, inventory investment will be negative, reflecting the fact that some goods sold were not produced but were sold out of inventories and should not be counted in current output (GNP).

The last component of investment is *residential construction,* the building of single- and multi-family housing units.

Over the years covered by the table, investment was a volatile component of GNP, ranging from 2.5 percent in 1933 to 18.8 percent in 1950. This instability of investment plays an important role in some of the macroeconomic theories considered in later chapters.

C
Government Spending

The next component of GNP in Table 7.1 is *government purchases of goods and services.*

> **Government purchases of good and services** are the part of current output that goes to the government sector—the federal government as well as state and local governments.

This component includes such things as federal government purchases of aircraft and the services of government employees, construction of new government buildings, and, at the state and local government levels, items such as expenditures on schools, police, firemen, and trash collection.

It is important to note that not all expenditures of the government sector are part of GNP. This is because not all expenditures are purchases of currently produced goods and services. Many government expenditures are *transfer payments,* such as Social Security payments, veterans' pensions, and food stamp subsidies. None of these involves a direct purchase of goods and services by the government but is simply a transfer of funds from one source (e.g., taxing the public) to some group in the population (e.g., veterans). Another category of government expenditure that is *not* in GNP is interest payments that the government makes to holders of government bonds (interest on the national debt).

From Table 7.1, it can be seen that government's share of GNP has increased in the post–World War II period relative to the prewar period. In 1929, government purchases of goods and services were 8.5 percent of GNP. Not surprisingly, in 1945 the government component of GNP, swollen by the wartime military budget, had risen to 39 percent. But in the postwar period the government sector did not return to its prewar size. Government purchases of goods and services were approximately 20 percent of GNP in both 1970 and 1987.

D
Net Exports

The final component of GNP given in Table 7.1 is *net exports.*

> **Net exports** equals total (gross) exports minus imports.

These items represent the direct contribution of the foreign sector to GNP. Gross exports are currently produced goods and services sold to foreign buyers. They are a part of GNP. Imports are purchases by domestic buyers of goods and services produced abroad and should not be counted in GNP. Imported goods and services are, however, included in the consumption, investment, and government spending totals in GNP. Therefore, we need to subtract the value of imports to arrive at the total of domestically produced goods and services. Net exports remain as the (net) direct effect of foreign sector transactions on GNP. As can be seen from the table, net exports were strongly negative in 1987, reflecting the large excess of imports relative to exports.

Before turning from the product to the income side of the national income accounts, it should be noted that the breakdown of GNP into consumption, investment, government purchases, and net exports (exports minus imports) results from the attempt to group purchases by type of buyer rather than, for example, by type of product. This is done with an eye toward explaining the levels of such components by isolating the factors that motivate each group of purchasers. Consumers would be expected to be influenced by household incomes, businesses by profit opportunities, and the government by macroeconomic policy.

PERSPECTIVE 7
What GNP Is Not

GNP is the most comprehensive measure of a nation's economic activity. Policymakers in industrialized countries use GNP figures to monitor short-run fluctuations in economic activity as well as long-run growth trends. For less developed countries, GNP figures are used as a measure of their stage in the development process. There are, however, some important limitations of the GNP concept.

Nonmarket Productive Activities Are Left Out
Because goods and services are evaluated at market prices in GNP, nonmarket production is left out. (As noted earlier, for instance, homemaker services are left out.) Cross-country comparisons of GNP overstate the gap in production between highly industrialized countries and less developed nations where largely agrarian nonmarket production is of greater importance.

The Underground Economy Is Left Out Also left out of GNP are illegal forms of economic activity and legal activities that are not reported to avoid paying taxes, the *underground economy*. Gambling and the drug trade are examples of the former. Activities not reported for purposes of tax avoidance take many forms; for example, repairmen who are paid in cash for services may underreport or fail to report the income. It is hard to estimate the size of the underground economy for obvious reasons. Rough estimates for the United States range from 5 to 15 percent of GNP. For countries where tax evasion is more widespread—Italy is often cited as an example—estimates of the underground economy are 25 percent of GNP or more.

GNP Is Not a Welfare Measure   GNP measures production of goods and services; it is not a measure of welfare or even of material well-being. For one thing, GNP gives no weight to leisure. If we all began to work 60-hour weeks, GNP would increase, yet would we be better off?

GNP also fails to subtract for some welfare costs to production. If, for example, production of electricity causes acid rain, and consequently water pollution and dying forests, we count the production of electricity in GNP but do not subtract the economic loss from the pollution. In fact, if the government spends money to try to clean up the pollution, we count that too!

GNP is a useful measure of the overall level of economic activity, not of welfare.

III
National Income

We turn now to the income side of the national income and product accounts. For the nation as a whole, as for the individual firm, production and sales generate income. The income is used to pay for the *factors of production* (productive resources) used to produce output.

National income is the sum of the earnings of all factors of production that come from current production. The factors of production are labor, land, capital, and entrepreneurship.

Since each dollar of GNP is one dollar of final sales, if there were no charges against GNP other than payments to factors of production, GNP and national income would be equal. If $4,000 billion came in from sales, $4,000 billion would be paid out to labor, land, and capital. There are, however, some other charges against GNP that cause national income to diverge from GNP, but the two concepts are still closely related. See Table 7.2.

The first charge against GNP not included in national income is *depreciation*, the portion of the capital stock that wears out each year. This must be subtracted from final sales (GNP) in computing national income because depreciation represents a cost of production rather than funds available to pay factors of production. (To simply maintain the capital stock, the firm must replace this portion of its plant and equipment.) We must also subtract *indirect business taxes*, which are general sales taxes and excise taxes.[3] An indirect business tax such as a sales tax is a part of the total proceeds from sales (the amount entered in GNP) that must be paid to the government. It is not part of payment to factors of production and is not counted in national income. There are a few other minor adjustments to GNP that must be made in calculating national income. These are included in the item "other" in Table 7.2.[4] In 1987 the net effect of these adjustments was that national income amounted to $3,635.9 billion compared to a GNP of $4,486.2 billion.

IV

The Components of National Income

National income is composed of payments to factors of production. Table 7.3 shows the breakdown of these payments.

A

Compensation of Employees

Compensation of employees is the largest element of national income, 72.8 percent in 1987. It is the payment to labor and includes wages and salaries,

---

[3] The taxes are called *indirect* because they are not directly levied on individuals or firms but on products. An excise tax is a per unit tax on a particular good. A sales tax is a percentage tax on sales revenues.

[4] An example of the type of item included in the "other" category is bad debts to the business sector. Since such debts are uncollected, they are not factor earnings, yet they represent sales included in GNP.

TABLE 7.2 Relationship of GNP and National Income, 1987 (Billions of Dollars)

GNP	4486.2
Minus: Depreciation	479.4
Indirect taxes and other	370.9
National income	3635.9

Source: Economic Report of the President, 1988.

as well as supplementary benefits (e.g., free health insurance).

B

Corporate Profits

Corporate profits, as well as the next two items in Table 7.3 (net interest and rental income of persons), represent joint factor payments to capital and land. Corporate profits were 8.4 percent of national income in 1987. Part of these profits were paid to shareholders in the firms as stock dividends. The rest were either paid as taxes or retained by the firm for investment.

C

Net Interest and Rental Income of Persons

Net interest consists of interest payments by businesses minus the interest paid to them. In 1987 this component amounted to 9.3 percent of national income. Rental income of persons accounted for less than 1 percent of national income in 1987.

D

Proprietors' Income

Proprietors' income, which was 9.0 percent of national income in 1987, is the income of unincorpo-

TABLE 7.3 Components of National Income, 1987 (Billions of Dollars)

Compensation of employees	2,647.5
Corporate profits	305.3
Net interest	336.8
Rental income of persons	18.5
Proprietors' Income	327.8
	3,635.9

Source: Economic Report of the President, 1988.

rated businesses. As such, it represents factor payments to capital, land, entrepreneurial services, and, to some extent, labor (that of the owners) in the unincorporated sector.

We have looked separately at the production and income sides of our national accounts. Before we go on to some related concepts, consider for a moment the relationship between these two sides, a relationship referred to as the *circular flow of income*. Production generates sales and therefore revenue for the firms. This, in turn, generates income as the firms pay out their revenue (minus the other charges in Table 7.2) to factors of production; this is national income. It is out of income that households buy output—and it is here that the circularity arises. National income generates sales, which spur production (GNP).

We will return to this interrelationship between income and output later when we consider how the levels of these variables are determined.

V

Personal Income and Personal Disposable Income

National income is a measure of income earned from current production of goods and services. For some purposes, however, it is useful to have a measure of income received by *persons* regardless of the source. For example, we noted that consumption expenditures by households are influenced by income. The relevant income concept is one of all income received by persons. Also, we want a measure of income after deducting personal tax payments, since income needed to make tax payments cannot be used to finance consumption.

> **Personal income** is the national income accounts measure of the income received by persons from all sources. When we subtract personal tax payments from personal income, we get a measure of **disposable (after-tax) personal income.**

In order to go from national income to personal income, we have to subtract elements of national income that are not received by persons and add income of persons from sources other than current production of goods and services. The necessary adjustments are shown in Table 7.4. The first items subtracted from national income are the portions of the corporate profits item in the national income accounts that are not paid out as dividends to persons. This includes corporate profits tax payments and undistributed profits (retained earnings). Also subtracted from national income in computing personal income are contributions to Social Security by the employer and employee. Such *payroll taxes* are included in the employee compensation term in national income but go to the government, not directly to persons.

The items added in going from national income to personal income are payments to persons that are not in return for current production of goods and services. The first of these are *transfer pay-*

TABLE 7.4   Relationship of National Income, Personal Income, and Disposable Income, 1987 (Billions of Dollars)

National income	3,635.9
less	
corporate profits tax payments, undistributed profits	217.8
contributions to Social Security	394.4
plus	
transfer payments to persons	543.0
personal interest income	179.1
Personal income	3,745.8
less	
personal taxes	564.7
Personal disposable income	3,181.1

Source: Economic Report of the President, 1988.

ments to persons. These are predominantly government transfer payments such as Social Security payments, veterans' pensions, and payments to retired federal government workers. There are also a relatively small amount of business transfers to persons that, in the national income accounts, include gifts to charities. The other item to be added in going from national income to personal income is personal interest income—mostly interest payments by the government to persons. Government interest payments are made on bonds previously issued by federal, state, and local governments. Personal interest payments here do *not* include interest payments by corporations. These are considered to be payments for factor services and, as we noted, were included in national income. With these adjustments we can calculate personal income, which in 1987 equaled $3,745.8 billion. We then subtract personal taxes to get personal disposable income, which was $3,181.1 billion in 1987.

Table 7.5 shows how we used our disposable income in 1987. Most of it, $2966.0 billion, was spent for consumption, the household sector's purchases of goods and services. There were two other expenditures. The first was interest paid to business (installment credit and credit card interest). The second, a very small component of personal expenditures, was transfers to foreigners (e.g., gifts to foreign relatives).

Personal savings is the part of personal disposable income that is not spent. In 1987 personal saving was $120.1 billion or 3.8 percent of personal disposable income, the lowest rate since the late 1940s, when households were buying heavily to make up for rationing during World War II. In 1980 the saving rate had been 7.1 percent. Later we will consider the implications of the low U.S. personal saving rate.

TABLE 7.5 Disposition of Personal Disposable Income, 1987 (Billions of Dollars)

Personal disposable income	3,181.1
less	
personal consumption expenditures	2,966.0
interest paid to business	93.5
personal transfer payments to foreigners (net)	1.5
Personal saving	120.1

Source: Economic Report of the President, 1988.

VI
Real versus Nominal GNP

So far, the figures we have been discussing are for *nominal* GNP, which is the output of currently produced goods and services evaluated at current market prices or in current dollar terms. Since GNP is the value of currently produced goods and services measured in market prices, it will change when there is a change in the overall price level, as well as when the actual volume of production changes. For many purposes, we want a measure of output that varies only with the quantity of goods produced. Such a measure is, for example, most closely related to the level of employment; more workers are not needed to produce a given volume of output simply because it is sold at a higher price. To construct a measure of output that changes only when quantities and not prices change, what is termed **real GNP,** we measure output in terms of constant prices or constant-valued dollars from a base year. Using 1982 as a base year, for example, we can compute the value of GNP in 1929, 1975, or 1987 *in terms of the price level or value of the dollar in 1982.* Changes in GNP in 1982-valued dollars then measure quantity changes between these years.

Column (1) of Table 7.6 shows the nominal GNP for the same years as those given in Table 7.1, as well as for some additional years. Column (2) shows the value of real GNP as measured in 1982 prices for each of these years. In 1982 real and nominal income are the same, of course, since base-year prices are current prices. In prior years, when current prices were lower than 1982 prices, real GNP is higher than nominal GNP. Conversely, in the years after 1982, when prices were higher, nominal GNP exceeds real GNP.

Table 7.6 shows that real GNP often behaved quite differently from nominal GNP. Nominal GNP changes whenever the quantity of goods produced changes *or* when the market price of those goods changes; real GNP changes only when production changes. It is therefore when prices are changing dramatically that the movements of the two measures diverge sharply. The decline in real GNP between 1929 and 1933, for example, was much less than the decline in nominal GNP, although it

TABLE 7.6   Nominal GNP, Real GNP, and Implicit Price Deflator, Selected Years

Year	(1) Nominal GNP (Billions of current dollars)	(2) Real GNP (Billions of 1982 dollars)	(3) Implicit GNP Deflator (Column 1 ÷ Column 2 × 100)
1929	103.9	709.6	14.6
1933	56.0	498.5	11.2
1945	213.4	1,354.8	15.8
1950	288.3	1,203.7	24.0
1970	1,015.5	2,416.2	42.0
1971	1,102.7	2,484.8	44.4
1972	1,212.8	2,605.5	46.5
1973	1,359.3	2,744.1	49.5
1974	1,472.8	2,729.3	54.0
1975	1,598.4	2,695.0	59.3
1976	1,782.8	2,826.7	63.1
1977	1,990.5	2,958.6	67.3
1978	2,249.7	3,115.2	72.2
1979	2,508.2	3,192.4	78.6
1980	2,732.0	3,187.1	85.7
1982	3,166.0	3,166.0	100.0
1984	3,772.2	3,279.1	107.7
1986	4,235.0	3,713.3	114.1
1987	4,486.2	3,819.6	117.5

measure of price level

Source: Economic Report of the President, 1988.

was still large (30 percent). The nominal GNP decline was larger (46 percent) because prices were falling during these years.

More recently, it can be seen from the table that while nominal GNP rose by over $200 billion from 1973 to 1975, real GNP actually declined between those 2 years. Again, between 1979 and 1980 there was a rapid increase in nominal GNP but a fall in real GNP. In both periods, real GNP declined because the actual production level of goods and services declined. Prices, however, rose rapidly enough in these inflationary years to make nominal GNP rise. At such times, the distinction between real and nominal figures is especially important.

Now consider the numbers in column (3) of Table 7.6, which gives the ratio of nominal GNP to real GNP (nominal GNP ÷ real GNP), where the ratio is multiplied by 100 (following the procedure in the national income accounts). The ratio of nominal GNP to real GNP is a measure of the value of current production in current prices (e.g., in 1987) relative to the value of the _same_ goods and services in prices for the base year (1982). Since the same goods and services appear at the top and

bottom, the ratio of nominal GNP to real GNP is just the ratio of the current price level of goods and services relative to the price level in the base year. It is a measure of the aggregate (or overall) price level—which in the previous chapter we called a _price index_. This index of the prices of goods and services in GNP is called the _implicit GNP deflator._

We measure changes in the aggregate price level by comparing values of the implicit GNP deflator in different years. First, consider a comparison of the implicit price deflator between the base year, 1982, and 1987. In the base year, real and nominal GNP are the same and the implicit price deflator has a value of 100. In 1987 the value of the implicit price deflator was 117.5 (1987 nominal GNP ÷ 1987 real GNP = 1.175). This means that GNP at current prices in 1987 (nominal GNP) was 17.5 percent greater than the same goods and services at 1982 prices. The aggregate price level, as measured by the GNP deflator, rose 17.5 percent between 1982 and 1987.

We can also use the implicit GNP deflator to measure price changes between 2 years, neither of which is the base year. Between 1986 and 1987, for example, the implicit GNP deflator rose from 114.1 to 117.5. As measured by this index, the percentage rise in the aggregate price level (or rate of inflation) between 1986 and 1987 was

$$[(117.5 - 114.1) \div 114.1] \times 100 = 3.0\%$$

Before going on, consider how the GNP deflator got its name. The ratio of nominal to real GNP is termed a *deflator* because we can divide nominal GNP by this ratio to correct for the effect of inflation on GNP—to deflate GNP. This is obvious since

$$\text{GNP deflator} = \frac{\text{nominal GNP}}{\text{real GNP}}$$

$$\text{real GNP} = \frac{\text{nominal GNP}}{\text{GNP deflator}}$$

Less obvious is why the adjective *implicit* is attached to the name of this price index. The GNP deflator is an implicit price index in that we first construct a quantity measure, real GNP, and then compare the movement in GNP in current and constant dollars to gauge the changes in prices. We do not try, directly or explicitly, to measure the average movement in price. The **consumer price index (CPI),** discussed in Chapter 6, which tracks the retail prices of a representative market basket of consumer goods, is, for example, a direct or explicit price index.

VII

Alternative Price Measures

We have now considered two measures of the aggregate price level: the implicit GNP deflator and (in Chapter 6) the CPI. There is a third price index that is widely reported, the **producer price index (PPI),** which measures wholesale prices of approximately 2,800 goods. Like the CPI, the PPI directly measures prices, but at the stage when producers sell the items to retailers, wholesalers, or other producers.

Since we have three measures of aggregate price level, we can measure the inflation rate in three different ways. In Chapter 6, using the CPI, we found that for 1987 the inflation rate was 3.7 percent. In the previous section, using the implicit GNP deflator, we found the inflation rate to be 3.0 percent. Calculating the inflation rate for 1987 using the PPI, we get 2.1 percent.

Figure 7.1 shows the inflation rate calculated using each of the three price indexes (CPI, GNP deflator, and PPI) since the 1960s. One can see substantial differences in inflation rates for a number of years. Still, for broad trends in inflation, all the indices are in agreement. By each measure, inflation rose in the late 1960s, with the upward trend accelerating in the 1970s. Each series also shows the marked slowdown in inflation in the 1980s. The differences in the series reflect their different compositions. The PPI, for example, does not measure the prices of services (doctors' fees, haircuts) that are not sold at the wholesale level, nor does it measure retailer margins. The PPI therefore gives a proportionately greater weight to raw materials. When raw materials prices (e.g., for crude oil) rose rapidly in the mid-1970s, the PPI was pushed up most rapidly. Conversely, when raw materials prices fell in the early to mid-1980s, the inflation rate as measured by the PPI fell the most.

No one of the three measures of inflation is obviously superior. Each has its use. The GNP deflator is the most comprehensive measure of inflation because it measures changes in the prices of all currently produced goods and services. The CPI is, however, the one most closely related to the price of goods that households buy. For that reason, many pensions and wage agreements are *indexed* to the CPI, meaning that their levels rise depending on movements in the CPI. The PPI, since it includes raw materials prices and prices of semifinished goods, is a signal of future price movements at the retail level. The CPI and PPI have the advantage that each is reported monthly, while figures for the GNP deflator are reported only quarterly.

Well, we told you that measuring inflation was tricky. To keep things simple in the remaining chapters of this part, unless otherwise stated, when we refer to the *aggregate price level* we will mean the GNP deflator.

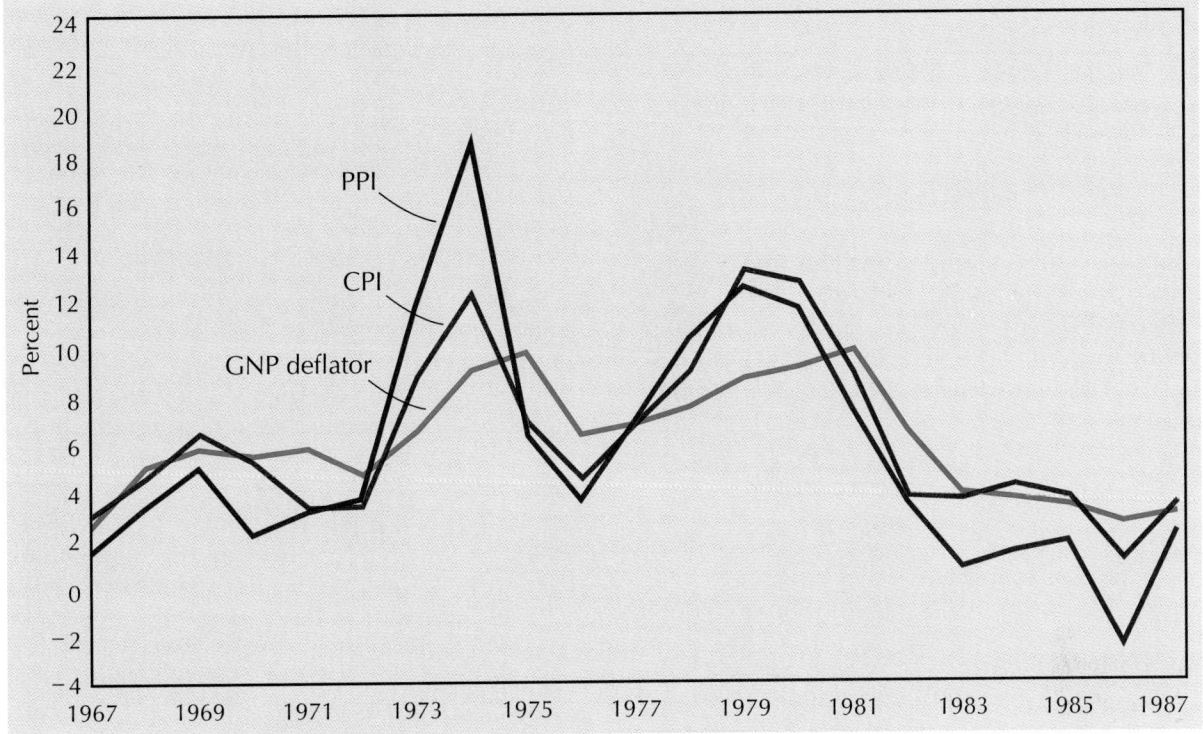

FIGURE 7.1 *Three Measures of the Inflation Rate*

VIII

Cyclical Movements in Output

Most of the macroeconomic analysis to follow focuses on short-run or cyclical movements in output and employment. By *cyclical movements* in output we mean the fluctuations in actual output, measured by *real* GNP, around the level of potential output.

Potential GNP (output) is the level that would be reached if productive resources (labor and capital) were being used at benchmark high levels.

Potential GNP is not the level that could be produced if the capacity of the nation's plants were strained and every available adult was put to work, as in a wartime situation. It is just the level that would be produced at high *normal* levels of resource utilization.

Potential output grows over time as the size and skill level of the labor force grow, as more capital goods are added to the capital stock, and as technological advances are made. In the long run—for example, over periods of several decades—growth in the economy comes predominantly from such growth in potential output. In the short run, over a period of a few years, sharp changes in output growth consist of changes in utilization rates of capital and labor. These output movements are fluctuations in actual output around the level of potential output.

As was pointed out in the previous chapter, economists disagree over which unemployment rate should be used in computing potential output. Figure 7.2 shows annual values of actual real GNP and two measures of potential output. The first is shown by the line marked "Trend GNP." This measure does not use any benchmark unemployment rate to represent high employment, but simply assumes that potential GNP grew throughout the period at the trend (or average) rate of growth of real output. The second measure, the

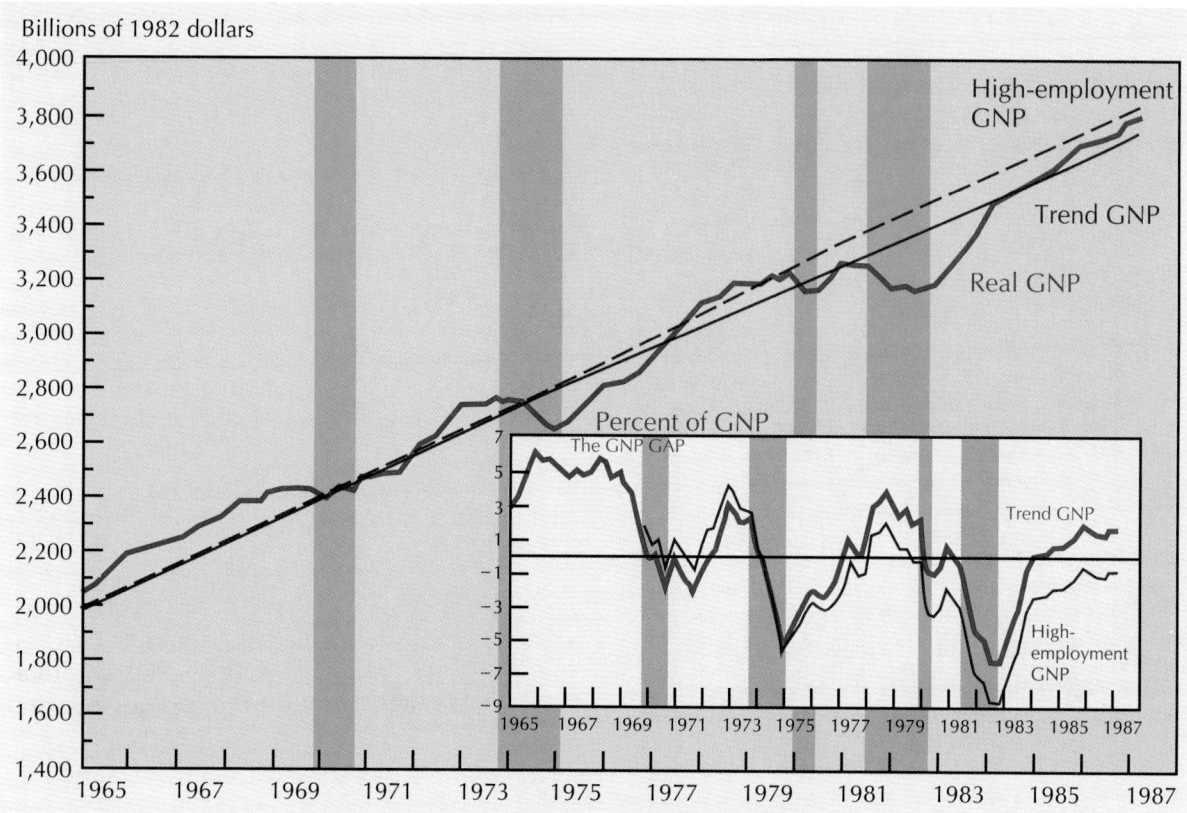

Billions of 1982 dollars

FIGURE 7.2 Potential and Actual Real GNP

dotted line marked "High-employment GNP," uses 6 percent as the high-employment benchmark unemployment rate. Shaded areas in the graph represent recessions when the level of economic activity was declining. The inset in the lower-right-hand corner of the graph shows the _GNP gap_, the amount by which actual GNP fell short of potential GNP (negative numbers) or exceeded potential GNP (positive numbers), measured as a percentage of potential GNP.

Looking at the figure, one can trace the cyclical course of output. In the late 1960s the economy was overheated, with actual GNP above potential GNP. This was the period of high Vietnam War expenditures imposed on an economy already operating at high resource utilization rates. The result was to push employment above a sustainable

rate for the long run.[5] Another result was an accelerating inflation rate as demand exceeded capacity.

In the wake of restrictive policies, the boom conditions of the late 1960s gave way to a mild recession in 1970, followed by a strong expansion that again pushed actual GNP above potential GNP by 1973. Then came the severe recession of 1974–75 when, as the graph of the GNP gap shows, actual GNP fell over 5 percent below potential GNP.

After a recovery in the late 1970s, GNP again fell below potential GNP in the recession of 1980, and before a sustained recovery occurred, another re-

[5]During this period, the unemployment rate was not only below the 6 percent benchmark used for the figure, but also below the 4 percent benchmark used at that time.

cession began in 1981. This most recent recession was the most severe of the post–World War II period, with the GNP gap reaching 9 percent of potential GNP (measured on the high-employment GNP line). A long period of expansion then began at the end of 1982.

These fluctuations in actual output around the level of potential output, as illustrated in Figure 7.2, together with the associated variations in other important macroeconomic aggregates, such as employment, prices, and interest rates, form the subject matter for much of the analysis to come.

SUMMARY

We have now examined the real-world counterparts to most of the macroeconomic variables we will meet in the coming chapters. We have the *facts* we need to begin the more challenging task of explaining the way these important economic variables behave. From this chapter, the key points to keep in mind are as follows:

1. The gross national product is a measure of all currently produced final goods and services evaluated at market prices. GNP evaluated at current market prices is called *nominal* (or *money*) GNP. GNP evaluated at constant prices from a base year (e.g. 1982) is called *real* GNP.
2. GNP is composed of consumption, investment, government spending, and net exports (exports minus imports).
3. National income is the sum of the earnings of all factors of production. The components of national income are compensation of employees, corporate profits, net interest, rental income, and proprietors' income.

4. Personal income is all income paid to persons regardless of the source. It does not include the part of national income not paid out to persons (e.g., undistributed corporate profits) but does include income that is not a payment for current production (e.g., government transfer payments).
5. The implicit GNP deflator is a price index that measures the prices of all the goods and services included in GNP. Two other widely reported price indexes are the consumer price index (CPI), which measures prices at the retail level, and the producer price index (PPI), which measures prices at the wholesale level.
6. Cyclical fluctuations in GNP are movements of output around the level of potential (capacity) output. Most of the short-run variation in output is due to cyclical fluctuation. Cyclical movements in output and associated macroeconomic variables, such as the level of employment and unemployment, are the focal point for much of the analysis to come.

KEY TERMS

Gross national product (GNP)
Consumption
Investment
Government purchases of goods and services
Net exports
National income
Personal income

Disposable (after-tax) personal income
Real GNP
Implicit GNP deflator
Consumer price index (CPI)
Producer price index (PPI)
Potential GNP

QUESTIONS AND PROBLEMS

1. What four groups buy goods and services produced in the U.S.? What do we call their respective purchases?

2. If a car is produced in 1986, but not sold until 1987, which year does it count in GNP? Explain.

3. GNP is not a perfect measure of a nation's economic activity. Briefly describe flaws in its calculation.

4. This chapter explains that if all revenues from the sale of final goods and services went to pay factors of production, then GNP would equal National Income. (That is, the dollar value of output would equal the dollar value of income earned in producing that output.) However, GNP and National Income are not equal. Explain why.

5. Why is income received by households during the year *not* equal to income earned by households during the year?

6. Though both are used to measure inflation, the Consumer Price Index and the GNP deflator are calculated differently. Explain.

7. Will real GNP for a given year ever be smaller than nominal GNP for that year?

8. Explain the relationship between potential GNP and actual GNP. Is potential GNP always larger? Why or why not?

9. How does product innovation and improvement distort comparisons of output levels over time? Consider in your analysis the contribution to real GNP in 1973 of a basic $(+, -, \times, /,$ functions only) hand calculator priced at $75.00 versus the contribution in 1985 of a financial hand calculator (functions include $+, -, \times, /, \ln x, e^x, y^x$, PV, and many others) priced at $35.00.

8

Getting Started: the Classical Macroeconomics

This and the following chapters trace the development of several competing macroeconomic theories. It would be simpler and more appealing if we could just present *the* macroeconomic theory. But we cannot. There are many areas of controversy in macroeconomics that should not be ignored. There are also areas of agreement, as we will see. This chapter takes up *classical* macroeconomics. Chapters 9–13 examine *Keynesian* macroeconomic theory. Chapter 14 considers *monetarism* and Chapter 15 examines the *new classical* macroeconomics. Chapter 16 summarizes our discussion of competing macroeconomic theories.

I
The Keynesian Revolution

In a letter to George Bernard Shaw in 1935, John Maynard Keynes wrote:

> I believe myself to be writing a book on economic theory which will revolutionize—not, I suppose, all at once but in the course of the next ten years—the way the world thinks about economic problems.

The next year, Keynes (rhymes with *rains*) published *The General Theory of Money, Interest and Employment*. The revolution the book engendered is call the *Keynesian revolution.*

The backdrop to the Keynesian revolution was the world depression of the 1930s. In Chapter 6 we saw how widespread unemployment was in the United States during this period (25.2 percent in 1933). Unemployment was similarly high in all the European countries. To Keynes, the existing theory failed to explain adequately both the causes and cures for such massive unemployment. The nature of the Keynesian revolution in economic thinking is best understood by examining pre-Keynesian macroeconomic theory, what Keynes called *classical economics.* First, however, we consider some general features of macroeconomic models.

II
Aggregate Supply and Demand

Variables such as real GNP, the aggregate price level, the inflation rate, and the unemployment rate are important. We would like to know how these variables are determined and how they can be affected by policy actions. But the level of U.S. real GNP, for example, depends on the actions of over 200 million people. How can we describe the process that caused U.S. real GNP to fall by 1.9 percent in 1982 or grow by 6.9 percent in 1984? Clearly, we cannot describe the behavior of each of the participants in the process.

What is feasible, instead, is to develop a *macroeconomic model* (or models) of GNP determination. *Macroeconomic models are simplified representations of the economy that attempt to capture the important factors determining aggregate variables such as GNP, employment, and the price level.* Elements of the models are hypothesized relationships among these variables. The key simplification is the omission of *microeconomic* detail; only the behavior of the aggregates is considered. We analyze the factors that determine the level of aggregate output (real GNP) without considering the composition of GNP among automobiles, televisions, clothing, groceries, haircuts, etc.

Keeping in mind that we are dealing with economywide aggregates, let us develop the central relationships of a macroeconomic model by a comparison with the model of supply and demand for a single market developed in Chapter 3. In that model, the price *(P)* and quantity *(Q)* of a single good were determined by the forces of supply and demand. As illustrated in Figure 8.1, equilibrium in the market occurs where supply and demand are equal. The equilibrium price and quantity are given by P_0 and Q_0, respectively. [1]

---

[1]At certain times in our analysis, we will use a symbol with a subscript (e.g., P_0 and Q_0) to denote a value of a variable *(P* and *Q)*. At other times, we will give numerical examples. We often use the symbols not to be abstract (or confusing) but simply because when we are not using a numerical example the choice of a number (e.g., $P_0 = 5$) is arbitrary.

Suppose we reinterpret price *(P)* as the *aggregate* price level measured, for example, by the GNP deflator discussed in Chapter 7. Similarly, suppose we reinterpret quantity *(Q)* as *aggregate* output measured by the level of the real GNP. We again assume that equilibrium levels of price and output, now aggregate price and aggregate output, are those that equate supply and demand, in this case *aggregate supply* and *aggregate demand*. What would these aggregate supply and demand curves look like? How would they differ from the market supply and demand curves in Figure 8.1?

A
Aggregate Supply

First, consider the *aggregate supply curve*.

The aggregate supply curve is the macroeconomic analogue to the individual market supply curve, which shows the output forthcoming at each level of product price (the *S* curve in Figure 8.1). The aggregate supply curve shows the amount of *overall* output

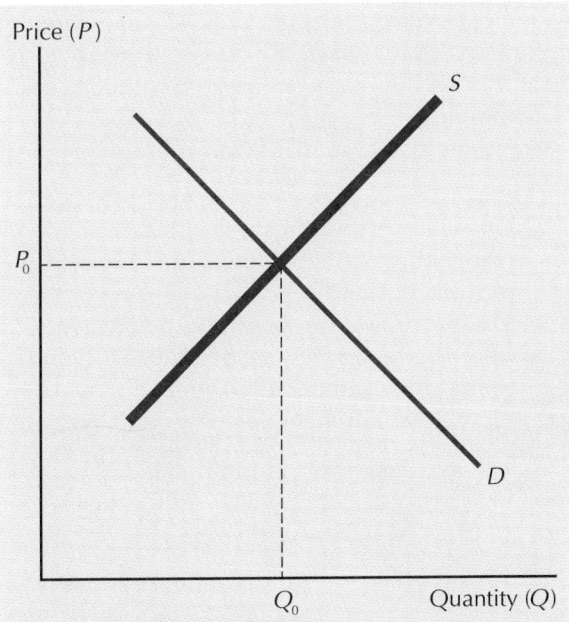

Price *(P)*

S

P_0

D

Q_0 Quantity *(Q)*

FIGURE 8.1 Price and Output Determination in a Single Market

The market supply curve shows the amount firms will produce at each price level. The demand curve shows the amount consumers will purchase at each level of product price. The intersection of the two curves determines the equilibrium price (P$_0$) and quantity (Q$_0$).

firms choose to produce at each value of the aggregate price level.

The assumption underlying construction of the single-market supply curve is that the cost of purchasing inputs for the production of the good is fixed. As firms hire more labor and use additional quantities of material inputs, the prices of these *factors of production* are assumed not to rise. (Wages remain unchanged, and so on.) Consequently, an increase in product price with input prices constant provides an incentive for firms to increase output; the individual market supply curve is upward sloping.

In constructing the aggregate supply curve, we cannot assume that as the product price rises, attempts by firms in the aggregate to increase output will not put upward pressure on the price of inputs. Consider the market for labor. As firms throughout the economy try to increase output, they must hire more workers. This increased demand for workers would be expected to cause a rise in the wage level as firms try to attract workers from other firms and induce more people to enter the labor force.

Before determining the form of the aggregate supply curve, we must examine the nature of the adjustments that take place in the labor market as firms try to change their output levels. We will find that in some of the models the aggregate supply curve is upward sloping, like the individual market supply curve in Figure 8.1, but in one model, the classical model considered later in this chapter, the aggregate supply curve is vertical.

B
Aggregate Demand

Now consider the *aggregate demand curve*. The individual market demand curve shows how the quantity demanded of some product varies as the price of the product changes, while influences such as consumer incomes and the prices of other products are held constant.

The aggregate demand curve measures the demand for total output at each value of the aggregate price level.

As the aggregate price level changes, consumer incomes change by definition because the amount paid for aggregate output generates aggregate income (sales receipts are paid to factors of production). Also, of course, because we are considering different values of the *aggregate* price level, we are not holding *other* prices constant. Therefore, we cannot rely on the simple intuition behind the downward-sloping market demand curve—namely, that as the price of a given product declines, consumers will buy more of the product—to explain the downward slope of the aggregate demand curve. We will see that the aggregate demand curve *is* downward sloping in each of the models we examine, but the reasons for this will be explained later.

C
Macroeconomic Equilibrium

Despite these important differences between supply and demand curves in an individual market and in the aggregate economy, the individual market model is a good starting point for our discussion of macroeconomic models. In aggregate analysis, as with the individual market, we divide the factors that influence output into those that influence supply—*supply-side factors*, and those that affect demand—*demand-side factors*.

On the supply side of our models we find firms making production decisions. Interrelated decisions on how much labor to employ in the production process bring the labor market into the supply side. On the demand side we find consumers, firms, and government sectors making decisions about the quantities of aggregate output they wish to purchase.

Taken together, the actions of firms on the supply side (with the resulting adjustments in the labor market) and the actions of purchasers of aggregate output on the demand side will determine aggregate supply and demand. Equilibrium aggregate price and output in our models will be reached when supply equals demand. The differences among the models we consider can be interpreted in terms of differing conclusions about the slopes of the aggregate supply or demand curves, as well as in terms of different views about what factors shift these two curves. By comparing the graphs of the aggregate supply and demand curves for the given models, we can summarize the differences and similarities among the various theories.

With this background, let's now consider the *classical* macroeconomic model.

III
The Classical Model

Keynes used the term **classical economics** to refer to the theories of late-eighteenth-, nineteenth-, and early twentieth-century British economists. The luminaries were Adam Smith (*Wealth of Nations*, 1776), David Ricardo (*Principles of Political Economy*, 1817), Alfred Marshall (*Principles of Economics*, 1890), and A. C. Pigou (*The Theory of Unemployment*, 1933).

There are no classical economists today, although many economists take classical economics as a starting point for their theories. There are no classical economists now largely because of Keynes's attack on the classical theory. Still, the *monetarists* and *new classical* economists of today have updated parts of the classical analysis to form a basis for their modern models. In addition and more recently, a group called the *supply-side* economists have proposed policies supported by arguments drawn from the classical theory. Classical theory, therefore, is crucial to modern macroeconomics.

There are two essential features of the classical theory:

1. Output is determined solely by its supply (with employment thereby also being determined).
2. The price level is determined solely by the level of the money supply, which determines aggregate demand.

To explain these features, we need to develop the classical aggregate supply and demand curves. Next, we consider the policy conclusions that emerge from the classical theory.

IV
The Classical Theory of Supply

Two potential sets of factors may affect output: supply factors and demand factors. This is true both for individual markets (see Figure 8.1) and for the overall economy. In the classical theory only one set, supply factors, actually determine (real) output. Let us see why.

Supply influences on output include the actions of the firm in producing output and, for this purpose, hiring labor in the labor market, as well as households in supplying labor. First, consider households supplying labor. Labor is a major input, indeed the most important input, for producing output. Hence when households vary their supply of labor, they greatly influence aggregate output. Consider next the firm. Our focus, as in all the chapters in this part, is on the *short run.* For the short run, we assume that the available stock of capital and the state of technology cannot be changed. A firm has an existing stock of plant and equipment. The firm can vary the level of output it produces only by changing the level of labor employed (and raw materials purchased). Put differently, once the firm chooses a level of labor to employ, it has determined the level of output supplied.

Therefore, once we determine the level of employment in the classical model, we have fixed the level of output. The level of employment in the classical model is determined by the forces of supply and demand in the *labor market*—supply by households and demand by firms.

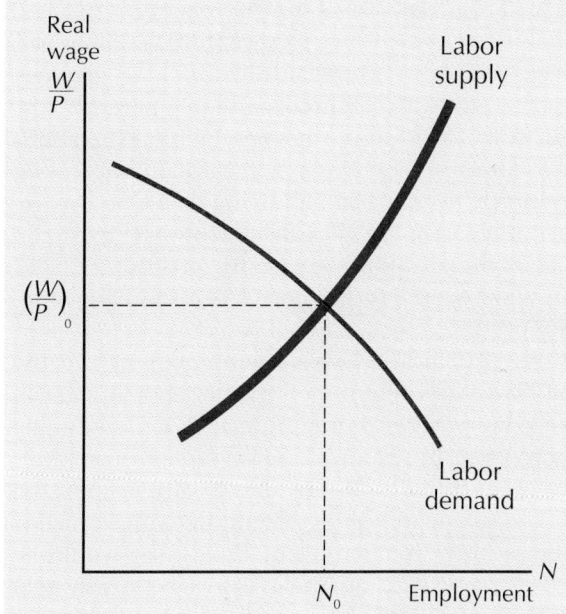

FIGURE 8.2   *The Classical Labor Market*

The quantity of labor supplied depends positively on the real wage, which is the return to the laborer. The quantity of labor demanded depends negatively on the real wage, which is the cost of labor to the firm. The equilibrium value of the real wage and the equilibrium level of employment are determined at the intersection of the two curves where supply equals demand.

A

The Classical Labor Market

Avoiding microeconomic detail for the labor market means ignoring the many different types of labor services that actually exist in the economy. Here and in later models we assume that there is simply one type of labor service. The labor market is the market where this service is purchased (demanded) by firms and sold (supplied) by households.

The classical labor market is depicted in Figure 8.2. The figure shows supply and demand curves plotted with the *real wage* on the vertical axis. The real wage is equal to the money wage divided by the aggregate price level *(W/P)*. The money wage is simply the number of dollars paid per unit of labor, e.g., $5 per hour. The purpose of dividing by the aggregate price level is to "deflate" the money wage in just the same way as we deflated money GNP (using the GNP deflator) to find real GNP in Chapter 7. The money wage divided by the price

level expresses the wage in real or constant purchasing power terms. If, for instance, between two points in time the money wage rose from $5 to $10 per hour and the aggregate price level, expressed as an index, went from 1.0 to 2.0, the real wage would remain unchanged $(5/1 = 10/2)$.[2]

In the classical view, both labor demand and labor supply depend on the real wage. The labor demand curve is downward sloping, plotted against the real wage. A smaller quantity of labor is demanded at higher levels of the real wage because the real wage represents the price of the labor input *(W)* relative to the product price *(P)* the firm receives for its output. As this relative price of labor rises, profits are pinched and firms therefore demand less labor.

On the other side of the market, the supply curve for labor is upward sloping when plotted

---

[2]Price indexes are discussed in Section II of Chapter 6 and Section VI of Chapter 7. The indexes discussed there are measured with the base year equal to 100. Here the price level is an index with base 1.

against the real wage. To the workers, the real wage is the return they receive for their labor services (W) relative to the average price (P) they pay for the goods they purchase. Put differently, the real wage represents the command over goods and services that workers receive in return for shunning leisure and supplying labor. As this return increases, the classical economists assumed that workers would increase the quantity of labor supplied (would forgo more leisure to earn more money).

The equilibrium levels of employment and the real wage are determined in the labor market at the point where labor supply and demand equal each other. In Figure 8.2, these equilibrium levels are N_0 and $(W/P)_0$. Notice that at any level of the real wage below $(W/P)_0$, labor demand exceeds labor supply. In such a situation, there would be upward pressure on the real wage. At any real wage above $(W/P)_0$, there would be an excess supply of labor, with consequent downward pressure on the level of the real wage. In the classical view, the labor market functions just like the perfectly competitive product markets described in Chapter 3. Equilibrium price (the real wage) and quantity (employment) are determined by the forces of supply and demand. *The wage is assumed to be perfectly flexible and to move immediately to the equilibrium value.* Also, workers are all assumed to observe changes in the aggregate price level. They always know the real wage.

A final point to note about the classical labor market is that the equilibrium level of employment is a *full*-employment level, meaning that all those supplying labor at wage $(W/P)_0$ find jobs. There is no unemployment in the sense of an excess of labor supply relative to demand. Those who are unemployed *choose* to be unemployed. There is no *involuntary* unemployment.

B

The Classical Aggregate Supply Curve

We see, then, that the level of employment is determined by supply and demand in the labor market. Once the level of employment is determined, the level of output is fixed. This follows because, as explained previously, firms can change output only by changing the amount of labor employed.

The employment level N_0, for example, corresponds to some level of output y_0. With this background, we can now construct the classical aggregate supply curve.

The *aggregate supply curve* shows the amount of overall output firms choose to produce at each value of the aggregate price level. To see how output supplied varies in the classical system as we move to different values of the aggregate price level, consider the adjustments in the labor market that take place when the aggregate price level doubles, beginning at a value P_0 and increasing to $P_1 = 2P_0$. These adjustments are illustrated in Figure 8.3.

Initially, the labor market is in equilibrium at a level of employment N_0 and a real wage (W_0/P_0), which is composed of a money wage W_0 divided by the initial price level P_0 (e.g., $W_0/P_0 = \frac{5}{1} = 5$). If, instead, the price level were P_1, which is double

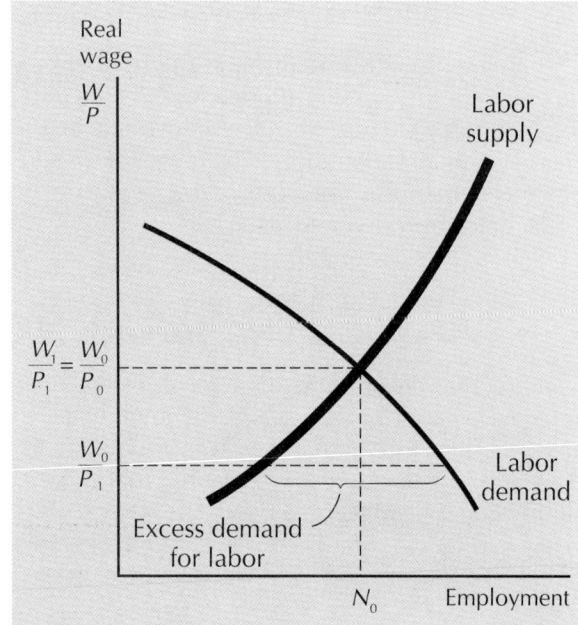

FIGURE 8.3   Labor Market Adjustment to a Change in the Aggregate Price Level

A rise in the price level from P_0 to P_1 lowers the real wage from W_0/P_0 to W_0/P_1. At this lower real wage, firms demand more labor, but workers supply less. There is therefore an excess demand for labor, which results in a rise in the money wage. In the classical model, equilibrium is restored only when the money wage has risen to W_1, where the initial real wage is restored $(W_1/P_1 = W_0/P_0)$. With the real wage back to at its initial level, equilibrium employment is at N_0.

the price level P_0, the real wage would be cut in half to a level shown on the figure as (W_0/P_1) (e.g., $\frac{5}{2} = 2.5$). At this lower real wage, firms would demand more labor, while workers would supply less labor. There would be an *excess demand* for labor and, consequently, upward pressure on the real wage. The process at work here would be one in which firms observe the higher selling price for their product and respond by attempting to expand employment and, therefore, production. To expand employment, they offer higher money wages to workers. As the aggregate money wage consequently rises, the real wage moves up. This process will stop only when the money wage has risen enough to make labor supply again equal to labor demand. This requires that the money wage rise enough to restore the initial real wage because, at any real wage below the initial level, labor demand will exceed labor supply somewhat and there will still be upward pressure on the money wage. In Figure 8.3, the money wage must double, from W_0 to W_1 $(= 2W_0)$, so that the initial real wage is restored with the price level double its initial value $(W_1/P_1 = W_0/P_0)$.

With the real wage back at its initial level, the level of employment will also return to its initial level (N_0). With employment back at N_0, the level of *output* will have returned to its initial level (assumed to be y_0). The important point here is that the amount of output firms produce at the price level P_1 is the same as the amount they produce at the lower price level.

If we consider a still higher price level, say P_2, which is double P_1, we would again find that labor market equilibrium requires a proportionately higher money wage but no change in the level of output. The level of output firms will supply in the classical system does *not* depend on the value of the aggregate price level. Equilibrium forces in the labor market adjust money wage levels to match any change in the price level, leaving the real wage (W/P) and employment unchanged. With employment unchanged by price level variations *the classical aggregate supply curve is vertical, as shown in Figure 8.4.*

A higher price level results in a higher level of output supplied *only* if the higher price level is *not* matched by a proportionate increase in the money wage, as is the case in a single market where the supply curve is constructed on the assumption of

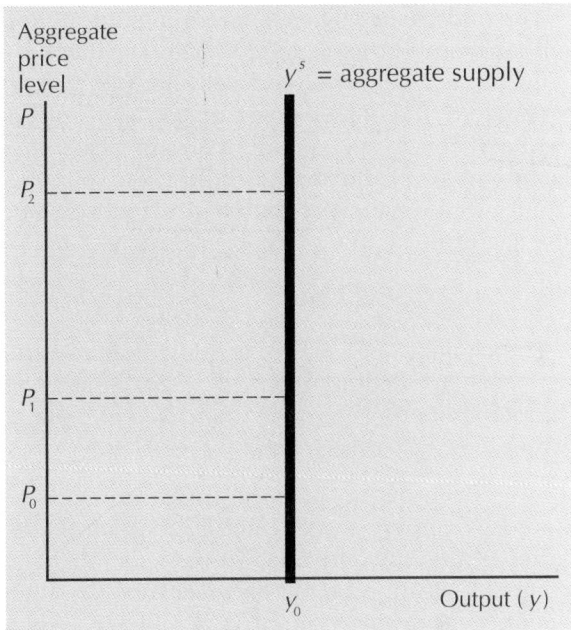

FIGURE 8.4 The Classical Aggregate Supply Curve
The vertical classical aggregate supply curve illustrates the fact that output is completely supply determined in the classical model.

a fixed or constant money wage level (see Figure 8.1). In the aggregate, as we have noted, we cannot assume that the money wage is unaffected by the attempt of all firms to increase employment and output. Such an attempt would boost the money wage as all firms bid for added labor. Given the assumptions made by the classical economists, equilibrium in the labor market *requires* the money wage to rise proportionately with the aggregate price level to restore the unique equilibrium real wage. But once the money wage does rise proportionately with the price level, firms have no incentive to expand production.

The vertical aggregate supply curve illustrated in Figure 8.4 is a distinctive feature of the classical model. *The vertical supply curve means that equilibrium output and, therefore, employment are completely determined by (output) supply-side factors in the classical system.* Whatever the theory of output demand and, consequently, the form of the aggregate demand curve we add to Figure 8.4, equilibrium output must be at y_0, determined by the position of the vertical aggregate supply curve, which in turn is anchored to the level of employment set by labor market equilibrium.

The underlying factors determining output and employment in the classical system are therefore only those with supply-side effects. Changes in technology and changes over time in the stock of capital increase the amount of output per unit of labor employed and shift the supply curve in Figure 8.4 to the right. Population growth also shifts the aggregate supply curve rightward.

V
The Classical Theory of Money and Prices

Generally, supply and demand factors jointly determine quantity and price in markets. The first distinctive feature of the classical model is that quantity (aggregate output) is completely determined by supply; aggregate demand determines only the aggregate price level. The second distinctive feature of the classical model is that the level of aggregate demand, and hence the price level, are determined by the quantity of money in the economy.

This classical theory of aggregate demand is termed the **quantity theory of money.**

A
The Equation of Exchange

The starting point for the classical quantity theory of money is the equation of exchange, which can be written as

$$M \times V = P \times y \qquad (8.1)$$

In this equation $P \times y$ is the product of the aggregate price level *(P)* times the level of real output *(y)*. This equals money GNP.[3]

The symbol *M* denotes the quantity of money in the economy. *Money* is defined as the collection of assets that serve as the means of payment in the economy, those assets that are used for

transactions. One measure of the money supply in the U.S. economy is currency (e.g., $10 bills) plus deposits on which one can write checks and, hence, use for transaction purposes. We will see in later chapters that money has several uses other than as a medium of exchange, and that there are difficulties in defining those assets that we want to include in the definition of money. For now, however, we regard money as simply currency plus checkable deposits.

The remaining item in the equation of exchange, *V*, is the *velocity of money*.

The **velocity of money** is the rate at which money *turns over* in GNP transactions during a given period, i.e., the average number of times each dollar is used in GNP transactions.

This can be seen by rearranging the equation of exchange, so that velocity appears on the left-hand side equal to the ratio of money GNP to the money supply.

$$V = \frac{P \times y}{M} \qquad (8.2)$$

For example, suppose that for a given year, money GNP $(P \times y)$ is $4,000 billion and the money supply is $500 billion. Then the velocity, or turnover rate, of money is

$$V = \frac{4,000}{500} = 8$$

The $500 billion in the money supply were used, on average, eight times in GNP transactions during that year.

The key assumption in the classical theory is that *for short-run analysis, velocity can be taken as a constant.* Classical economists believed that the velocity of money was determined by the payment habits and technology of the economy, by institutional factors that would change only slowly over time. Factors such as the average length of the pay period for workers (e.g., daily, weekly, or monthly) and the use of charge accounts, bank credit cards, or overdraft facilities would influence the velocity of money. Greater use of charge cards, for example, would increase the turnover rate (velocity) of

---

[3]Money, or nominal, GNP is GNP in current dollars. We will use the term *money GNP* rather than *nominal GNP* because it denotes current money values more clearly. Real GNP is output valued in dollars of a base year or constant valued dollars.

money. This follows because in charge card transactions money (currency or checkable bank deposits) need only be used occasionally to settle charge card balances and, as a consequence, a given money supply can support a larger flow of transactions.

Recall from the previous section that real output, *y*, in the equation of exchange is determined totally by supply-side factors. As a result, in the quantity theory of money, real output is taken as fixed—given from the supply side. We have just seen that velocity is also assumed to be fixed in the short run. Thus, *the equation of exchange becomes a relationship between the quantity of money and the aggregate price level.*

To see this clearly, we rewrite the equation of exchange (from equation 8.1) as

$$P = \frac{\overline{V}}{\overline{y}} \times M \qquad (8.3)$$

The bars over *V* and *y* indicate that they are fixed: $(\overline{V}/\overline{y})$ is simply a constant. Therefore, equation (8.3) states that *P* (the price level) is a constant $(\overline{V}/\overline{y})$ times *M* (the quantity of money). *The aggregate price level is proportionate to the quantity of money.* This implies that the price level always changes proportionately with the change in the quantity of money. If the quantity of money jumps by 10 percent, then the price level also jumps by 10 percent. If the quantity of money doubles, the price level doubles.

To illustrate, let $\overline{V}$ be 8 and let *M* be $500 billion as before. Imagine further that *y* is 4,000 billion pounds of output (total output for a simple economy producing only one product) priced at *P* = $1 a pound, which is why we begin with *P* × *y* = $4,000 billion. Plugging these values into equation (8.3), we have

$$\$1 \text{ per pound} = \frac{8}{4,000 \text{ billion}} \times \$500 \text{ billion}$$

$$\$1 \text{ per pound} = \frac{8 \times \$500 \text{ billion}}{4,000 \text{ billion}}$$

$$\$1 \text{ per pound} = \frac{\$4,000 \text{ billion}}{4,000 \text{ billion}}$$

Doubling *M* from $500 billion to $1,000 billion would double the price level if 8/4,000 billion is

held constant (velocity and real output are unchanged):

$$\$2 \text{ per pound} = \frac{8}{4,000 \text{ billion}} \times \$1000 \text{ billion}$$

It is easy to see mathematically, from equation (8.3) and this example, that the price level will always change proportionately with the money supply, but what economic process produces this result? Classical economists believed that money was held for use in transactions. Beginning from a point of equilibrium, an increase in the quantity of money raises the amount of money above what people need for transactions. According to the classical view, people would use these excess money balances to demand (try to buy) more goods. As a result, classical economists believed that there would be "too much money chasing too few goods." People would want to spend their excess money to buy more goods, but no more goods would be made available to buy. Remember that the level of output (overall quantity of goods) is fixed by supply-side factors. As people try to rid themselves of excess money, they bid up the aggregate price level.

The price level stops rising when it has increased in the same proportion as the quantity of money. To return to our earlier example, if the money supply doubles, then the price level doubles. At that point, the money value of transactions (*P* × $\overline{y}$ = money GNP) has doubled and people need all the new money to carry out transactions. They stop trying to buy more goods and stop bidding up the price level.

B

The Classical Aggregate Demand Curve

These linkages between the quantity of money and the aggregate price level are illustrated in Figure 8.5. The same linkages can be illustrated within the aggregate supply–aggregate demand framework, as shown in Figure 8.6. The classical quantity theory of money implies that the *quantity of money determines the level of aggregate demand.* This means that setting the quantity of money fixes the position of the aggregate demand curve. In Figure 8.6, for example, if the quantity of money

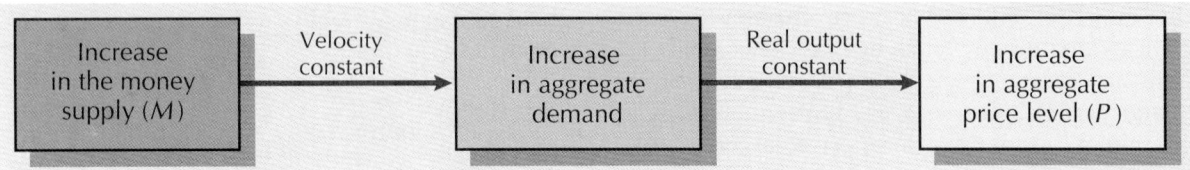

FIGURE 8.5   Money and Prices in the Classical Model

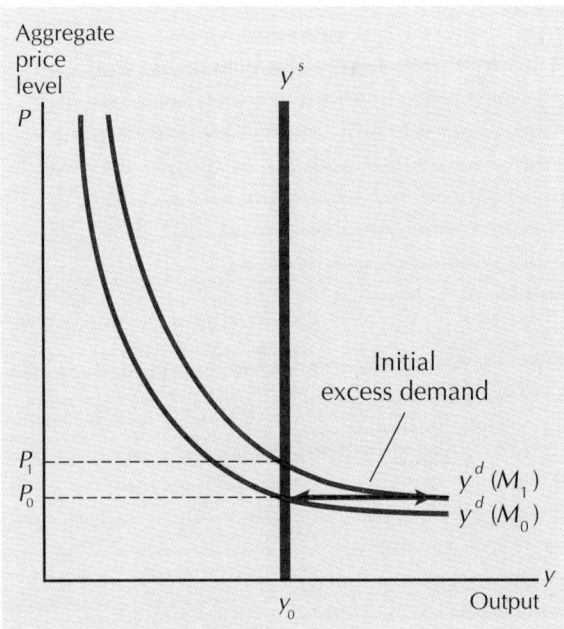

FIGURE 8.6   Aggregate Demand and the Price Level in the Classical Model

The level of aggregate demand determines the price level in the classical model. If the aggregate demand curve is y_0^d, the price level is P_0. If aggregate demand is higher at y_1^d, the price level be at the higher value P_1. The level of output (y_0) is unaffected by changes in demand.

is M_0, the classical aggregate demand curve is $y^d(M_0)$. As just discussed, changes in the quantity of money will change the demand for goods. An increase in the quantity of money raises the demand for goods *at a given price level*. At the given price level, with the higher money supply, we just saw that people have more money balances than they need for transactions, so they demand more goods. In terms of the classical aggregate demand curve, an increase in the quantity of money, from M_0 to M_1 in Figure 8.6, shifts the aggregate demand curve to the right, from $y^d(M_0)$ to $y^d(M_1)$. At the initial price level, there is now an excess of

demand above the fixed supply (too much money chasing too few goods). The price level consequently rises to P_1.

To summarize, in the classical theory, the quantity of money determines the level of aggregate demand. With output completely supply determined, demand determines the aggregate price level.

VI
Stabilization Policy in the Classical System

We saw in Chapter 4 that one of the roles of government was macroeconomic stabilization policy. Stabilization policy takes two forms: *monetary policy*, which consists of government actions to control the supply of money, and *fiscal policy*, which is the use of government spending and tax policies to affect the level of economic activity.

Classical economists believed that the economy was self-adjusting to full employment. There was little need for macroeconomic stabilization policy. In the labor market, the money wage adjusted to equate labor demand and supply. This meant that there was no involuntary unemployment, which would imply an excess supply of labor, and thus no need for government policies to combat unemployment. The factors influencing growth in output and employment—technological change, capital formation, and population growth—were not amenable to short-run macroeconomic control. Classical economists also believed that over the longer run, growth would be best promoted by a *laissez-faire* or free market system.

What are the implications of this *noninterventionist* position for the classical view of monetary and fiscal policy?

PERSPECTIVE 8A
Money in the German Hyperinflation

In Chapter 6 we looked at the price explosion that occurred in Germany in the early 1920s. The relationship between the quantity of money and the price level stands out strikingly in such periods of *hyperinflation*. In Germany, between August, 1922 and November, 1923, the price level rose by 322 percent per month. Over the same period, the money stock grew by 314 percent *per month!* This relationship between the rise in the money stock and the rise in the price level is illustrated in Figure 8.7.

Hyperinflation is clearly a case of too much money chasing too few goods. With such rapid growth in the money stock (in Germany in October 1923, over 99 percent of all money had been printed within the previous 30 days), any effect on output is swamped. Indeed, output is constrained to the extent that people use their time to cope with inflation instead of working. More money simply pushes up the price level.

A
Monetary Policy

Since the aggregate price level depends on the quantity of money, monetary policy *is* important in the classical system. The classical economists believed that either inflation or deflation (a fall in aggregate price level) would disrupt the economic system. Therefore the task for monetary policy was to provide a stable price level. Over time, real output would grow due to supply-side factors (population growth, capital formation, and technological change). To provide a stable price level would require money growth proportional to the growth in real output. Suppose, for example, real output (y) grew over time at 2 percent per year. If the money supply also grew at 2 percent per year, by the equation of exchange, $M\bar{V}$ and, consequently, Py would grow at 2 percent per year. The price level would thus be constant. (Py grows only 2 percent due to the growth in y.)

During the nineteenth and early twentieth centuries, governments in the United States, Great Britain, and other industrialized countries attempted to gear monetary policies to provide price stability. Frequently, however, the aggregate price level moved sharply up or down. These movements were generally associated with booms and recessions in economic activity and with financial crises and bank panics. Even before the Great Depression of the 1930s, during which the classical theory came to be questioned, stable money and, hence, stable prices had been more the goal than the reality.

B
Fiscal Policy

There was little role for fiscal policy in the classical model. The classical economists did not believe that actions such as increasing government spending or cutting income taxes would seriously affect aggregate supply or demand. Therefore such fiscal policy actions would not affect price or output (and thus employment).

1. Supply-Side Effects of Fiscal Policy Modern *supply-side* economists, whose beliefs are based on classical economics, *do* believe that tax rates have important effects on aggregate supply. Income tax rates, for example, form a *wedge* between a worker's earnings and what he or she takes home. If the size of the wedge is reduced (the tax is lowered), the labor supply and, therefore, the supply of output will rise. We will examine such supply-side effects of taxes later. These effects did not play an important role in the original classical model because when the classical economists wrote, tax rates were low and were applied to only

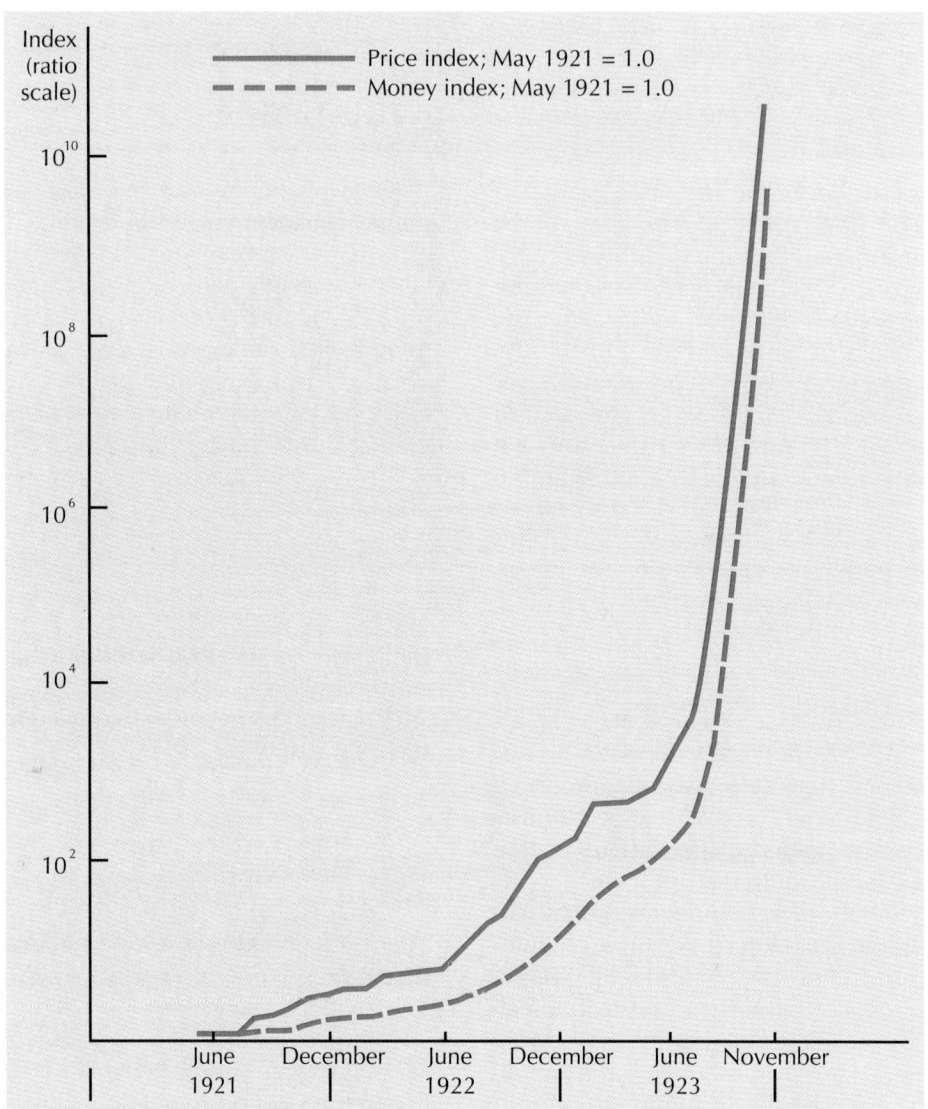

FIGURE 8.7 *Money and Prices During the German Hyperinflation*
(Source: William Poole, Money and the Economy: A Monetarist View, *p. 12.)*

a relatively small (high-income) proportion of the population.

2. Demand-Side Effects of Fiscal Policy The major issue for the classical economists was whether increased government spending could increase aggregate demand and stimulate employment. The classical economists said that it could not. If the government spent more on public projects like buildings and highways, for example, it would have to fund the increased spending. The

government can raise funds in three ways: by raising taxes; by borrowing money from the public, which means selling bonds to the public; or by printing money.[4]

Consider the classical view of the effects of increases in government spending financed in each of these ways.

[4]In modern financial systems, when government spending is financed by an increase in the money supply, the process is more sophisticated than simply cranking up the printing press. This process is discussed in Chapter 19.

Tax Financing: If the government increased taxes to finance increased spending, the classical economists expected that the two actions would cancel each other out. Aggregate demand would rise because the government spent more. On the other hand, those paying the increased taxes would spend less by approximately the same amount.

Bond Financing: Suppose, instead, that the government sold bonds to the public (borrowed money). The classical economists believed that the government would then compete with private borrowers for available funds and push up the interest rate. The higher interest rate would discourage investment spending by firms because firms have to borrow to finance investment.[5] Increased spending by the government, if financed by selling bonds to the public, would **crowd out** private spending, primarily investment spending by firms,

by pushing up the interest rate. Total demand for output would therefore not increase in this case either.

Money Financing: But what if the increased gov-

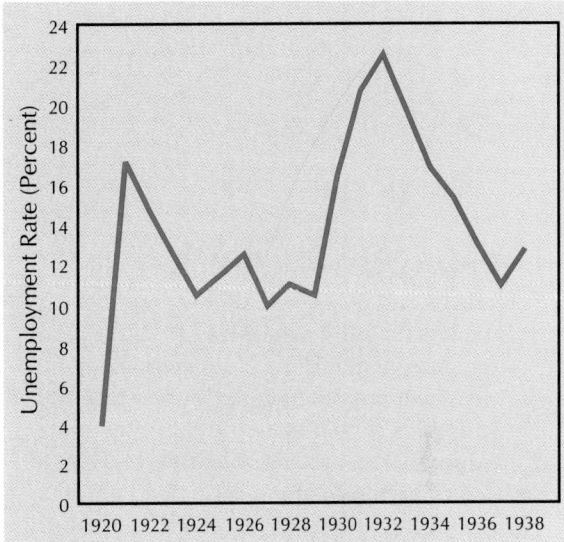

FIGURE 8.8 *British Unemployment Rate, 1920–38*

[5]Recall here that *investment* refers to the business sector's demand for plant, equipment, and inventories. To finance such projects, firms borrow in capital markets. At higher interest rates, firms find fewer projects profitable, and investment spending declines.

PERSPECTIVE 8B

British Unemployment in the 1920s

In the 1920s this question of whether an increase in government spending could generate increased employment held more than academic interest. As can be seen from Figure 8.8, Great Britain had very high rates of unemployment during the 1920s. There was an intense policy debate over whether increased public expenditures would increase output and thus alleviate the problem. The Conservative Party, in power for most of this period, held the *Treasury position*, which was an expression of the classical view just discussed. Winston Churchill, then Chancellor of the Exchequer (in U.S. terms, Secretary of the Treasury), expressed this view as follows: "It is the orthodox Treasury dogma, steadfastly held, that whatever might be the political or social advantages, very little

employment can, in fact, as a general rule, be created by state borrowing and state expenditure."

Keynes and others, including the leader of the Liberal Party, David Lloyd George, disagreed. They argued that increased public expenditure *would* increase aggregate demand. Not only would increased government expenditure add directly to demand, but, by increasing the incomes of those who were employed in producing the goods and services sold to the government, such expenditure would *stimulate* private expenditure, adding indirectly to aggregate demand as well. Keynes's task was to provide a theoretical framework to support his "heretical" policy position.

ernment expenditure were to be financed by printing money? In the classical view, the increase in the money supply would lead to an increase in aggregate demand and in the price level, as illustrated in Figure 8.6. This increase in aggregate demand would be due, however, simply to the increase in the money stock—due to *monetary* policy. The fiscal policy action, the increased gov-

ernment spending, would itself have no effect on aggregate demand. As the classical economist R.G. Hawtrey wrote in 1925, "The public works are merely a piece of ritual, convenient to people who want to be able to say that they are doing something, but otherwise irrelevant."

Overall, the classical economists did not view fiscal policy as a useful stabilization policy tool.

SUMMARY

1. The classical model has several striking features and distinctive policy conclusions. Output is supply determined. The level of aggregate demand and, consequently, the price level are determined by the quantity of money. In terms of policy issues, the economy is assumed to be self-adjusting to full employment. There is no need for macroeconomic policies to stabilize output and employment. The role of monetary policy is to ensure price stability. Fiscal policy has no stabilization role.

2. Before going on to the Keynesian attack on the classical view, it is useful to make explicit several assumptions that are essential to these classical results. We will see in later chapters that other models reach conclusions that differ from those of the classical economists to the degree that they *do not* accept these assumptions.

3. *On the supply side* of the economy, the two key classical assumptions are as follows:

   1. The money wage rate and the price level are perfectly flexible.
   2. Market participants have perfect information about all market prices.

The first assumption is important because the price level and the money wage rate must adjust to equate supply and demand in the labor and output markets. Particularly important is that the money wage adjusts quickly to equate supply and demand in the labor market. Flexibility of the money wage is crucial to the assumed self-adjusting property of the classical model.

The second assumption, that market participants have perfect information about all market prices, also has important implications for the labor market. Both labor suppliers and demanders are assumed to know the real wage. For labor suppliers (workers), this means that when making their employment decision, they know the purchasing power of the money wage they will receive; they know the value of the aggregate price level for the time period when they spend their earnings.

These classical supply-side assumptions can be looked at in terms of the two-question logic of macroeconomics. In the classical model, what is expected *is* what happens. Markets work. There are no surprises. The classical system is the application to macroeconomics of the perfectly competitive supply and demand model of Chapter 3. In this ideal setting, there is little role for government policy.

4. *On the demand side*, the key classical assumption is that the velocity of money is constant, or at least quite stable in the short run. If velocity is constant, then the quantity of money fixes the level of total monetary transactions $(P \times y)$. The quantity of money determines the position of the aggregate demand curve. If velocity were not constant, to find the level of aggregate demand, we would need to know the factors that determine velocity. Money would not be the only variable determining the level of aggregate demand.

   The Keynesian theory, to which we now turn, is an attack on these classical assumptions.

KEY TERMS

Aggregate demand curve
Classical economics
Aggregate supply curve

Quantity theory of money
Velocity of money
Crowding out of private expenditures

QUESTIONS AND PROBLEMS

1. In what economic context did John Maynard Keynes write his *General Theory?*
2. Explain the concept of an aggregate demand curve and of an aggregate supply curve.
3. Explain why there is no cyclical unemployment in the classical model.
4. Why is the demand for labor schedule in the classical model downward sloping when plotted with the real wage on the vertical axis?
5. Why is the aggregate supply curve vertical in classical analysis?
6. Define the "velocity" of money and explain why the classical economists considered it a constant.
7. How is the aggregate price level determined in the classical model?
8. What is macroeconomic stabilization policy and why did classical economists consider it unnecessary?
9. Classical economists considered what monetary rule appropriate? Why?
10. What are the three ways that a government can fund additional spending? According to classical economists, did the impact of government spending vary according to how it was financed?

9

The Keynesian Theory of Aggregate Demand

We turn now to the second of the four macro models we will consider—the model constructed by John Maynard Keynes. Keynes attacked the classical view that the economy was self-adjusting to full employment within a reasonable period of time. Instead, he believed that

it is an outstanding characteristic of the economic system in which we live that, whilst it is subject to severe fluctuations in respect to output and employment, it is not violently unstable. Indeed it seems capable of remaining in a chronic condition of subnormal activity for a considerable period without any marked tendency either toward recovery or toward complete collapse. Moreover, the evidence indicates that full, or even approximately full, employment is of rare and short-lived occurrence.

The classical theory dealt only with a special case—full employment.[1]

Moreover, the characteristics of the special case assumed by the classical theory happen not to be those of the economic society in which we actually live, with the result that its teaching is misleading and disastrous if we attempt to apply it to the facts of experience.

Keynes believed he had constructed a *General Theory* that described both the special case of full employment and the more prevalent case of less than full employment. From this theory he derived policy prescriptions that he considered more applicable to "the society in which we actually live," which to Keynes was the Depression-ridden economy of the 1930s.

Keynes's theory, as amended by his followers,

will occupy our attention over the next five chapters. In this chapter we will explain Keynes's theory of aggregate demand, his view of how the economy settles at a position of less than full employment. To simplify this initial analysis, we will not bring the government sector into the model we construct. This means that we cannot discuss monetary and fiscal policy. Here we can describe the macroeconomic problem as Keynes saw it, but not his solution to the problem. In Chapter 10 we will consider how changes in fiscal policy variables cause changes in output. There we will see the potential for fiscal stabilization policies in Keynes's model. Chapter 11 considers monetary policy and, more generally, the role of money in the Keynesian system. In all these analyses, we concentrate on the *demand* side of the economy. In Chapter 12 we will extend the model to consider aggregate *supply*. Until we bring in the supply side there, we will be assuming that the aggregate price level is fixed. Thus, for the moment, we are assuming that *output varies, but the price level does not.*

■ *Check Your Bearings*

Since the next three chapters concentrate only on the Keynesian theory of aggregate demand, we will not be using the full aggregate supply–aggregate demand curve framework. Still, for future reference, it is useful to interpret what we are doing within that framework.

When we assume that price is given and output is determined totally by demand, we are assuming that supply is no constraint. In this case, we must be on the horizontal range of the aggregate supply curve, as shown in Figure 9.1. Over this range, it is the level of demand (the position of the y^d schedule) that determines output. This presumes that the economy is operating below potential output, where, in Figure 9.1, supply would constrain output. The more complete Keynesian model, which is presented in Chapter 12, allows a role for the supply side even before the level of potential output is reached.

---

[1]In the classical model, full employment was a situation where all those wishing to work at the going real wage were able to find employment. In that simple model, there was no allowance for *frictions* that exist in the real economy (it must take some time to find a job after entering the labor force) or for *structural* unemployment. In the real economy, full employment can be thought of as a situation where there is no *cyclical* unemployment; the unemployment rate is at the benchmark high-employment rate where the economy is at its potential output.

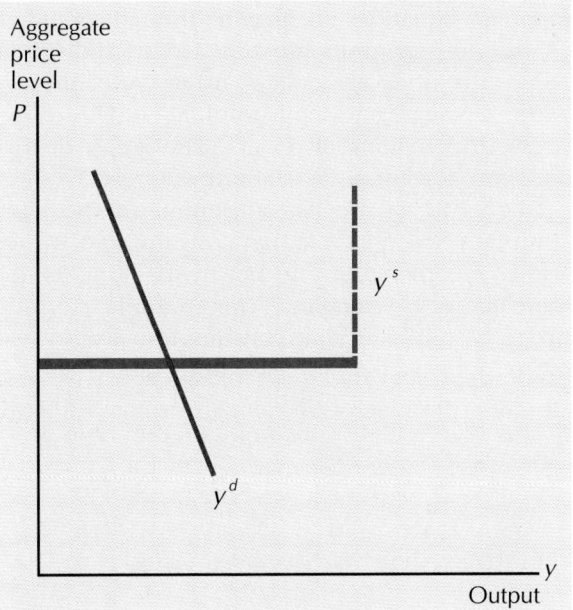

FIGURE 9.1 _Aggregate Demand and Supply in the Fixed-Price Keynesian Model_

I

The Keynesian Income–Expenditure Approach

Contrary to the classical model, in which output is strictly supply determined, the _simple_ Keynesian model focuses only on the role of aggregate demand in determining output. In the more complete version of the Keynesian system, which we examine in Chapter 12, both supply and demand factors have important effects on output and employment. Still, the most novel aspects of Keynesian theory are the development of a theory of aggregate demand and the explanation of the role of aggregate demand in determining output. The simple model of this chapter highlights these essential elements.

It is easy to see why Keynes would focus on demand-side factors in the midst of the Great Depression. In the United States, where 25.2 percent of the labor force was unemployed in 1933, the nation's factories had huge unused capacity; supply did not appear to be a constraint on output. Moreover, supply-side factors could not ex-

plain the large drop in the level of economic activity from 1929 to 1933.

The Keynesian approach to output determination has been termed the **income–expenditure approach.** The essence of this approach is illustrated in Figure 9.2. Production of output generates income for factors of production. Income stimulates expenditures on output (aggregate demand), which, in turn, stimulates production.

> An _equilibrium_ level of output occurs when the income generated by that level of output produces a level of aggregate demand just equal to the level of output—_when output equals aggregate demand._

We begin the discussion of income determination by examining this income–expenditure linkage.

II

The Components of Aggregate Demand

Aggregate demand is the sum of the demands for current output by each of the buying sectors of the economy: households, businesses, the government, and foreign purchasers of exports.

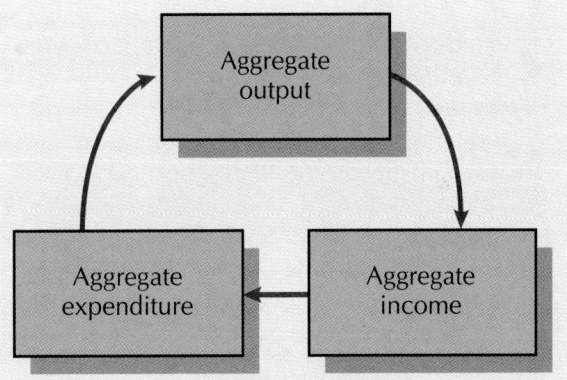

FIGURE 9.2 _The Keynesian Income–Expenditure Linkage_

Aggregate output generates aggregate income as firms make payments to factors of production. This income, in turn, generates a demand for output.

In this chapter we will consider only the household and business sectors. *Consumption* is the household sector's demand for output for current use. *Investment* is the business sector's demand for plant and equipment, plus the change in business inventories. Investment also includes expenditures on residential construction, which are a form of investment by households. We will look at the determinants of each of these components of aggregate demand. We will also consider the saving decisions of households, which are closely related to consumption decisions.

A
Consumption

Consumption expenditures consist of purchases of durable goods (e.g., autos and televisions), non-durable goods (e.g., food and newspapers), and services (e.g., haircuts and taxi rides). In 1987, consumption expenditures totaled $2966.0 billion, or approximately 65 percent of GNP.

1. The Consumption–Income Relationship Keynes expressed his view of consumption as follows:

> The fundamental psychological law on which we are entitled to depend with great confidence . . . is that men are disposed, as a rule and on the average, to increase their consumption as their income increases, but not by as much as the increase in their income.

Consumption expenditures depend positively on household income.

The relationship between consumption and income posited in Keynes's "psychological law" is termed the Keynesian **consumption function.**

This consumption function is the heart of the Keynesian linkage between income and consumer expenditure.

Consider the following numerical example:

$$C = 50 + 0.75Y, \qquad (9.1)$$

where C is the symbol for consumption and Y for

income.[2] Equation (9.1) may be thought of either as the consumption function for an individual where the units are dollars, or as the economy-wide or *aggregate* consumption function expressed in billions of dollars. The graph of this consumption function is shown in Fig. 9.3.

One property Keynes attributed to the consumption function was that consumption would rise as income rose, "but not by as much as the increase in . . . income." Our example has this property, implying that consumption would rise by $0.75 for each $1 increase in income.

The increase in consumption per unit increase in income is what Keynes called the **marginal propensity to consume** *(MPC).*

In the symbols we have been using,[3]

[2]The relevant income measure in the consumption function is disposable income, household income less taxes. In this chapter, because there is no government sector in the model, there are no taxes and we need not distinguish between total income and disposable income.

[3]The differencing symbol Δ denotes the change in the variable it precedes; ΔC, for example, is the change in consumption expenditures.

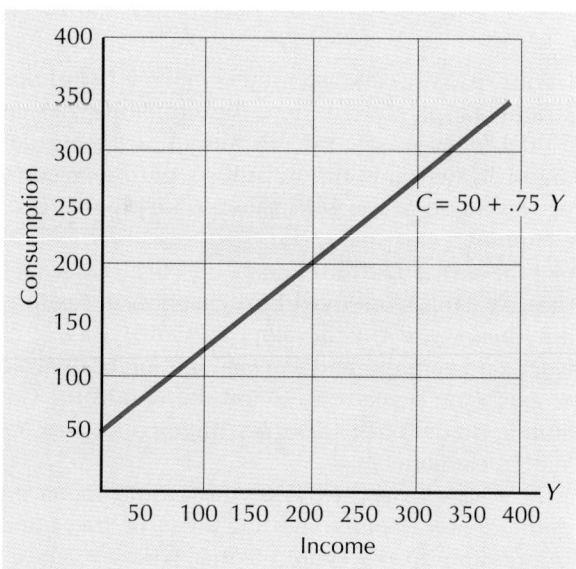

FIGURE 9.3   A Numerical Example of the Consumption Function

The Keynesian consumption function shows the level of consumption at each level of income.

$$MPC = \frac{\Delta C}{\Delta Y} = 0.75$$

The marginal propensity to consume is illustrated in Table 9.1, which shows the levels of consumption at various levels of income as calculated from our example of a consumption function. For example, with an income of $400, consumption will be $50 + 0.75(\$400) = 50 + 300 = 350$. The increase in consumption is always 0.75 *(MPC)* times the increase in income. Consumption rises by $75 for every $100 increase in income.

2. The Saving–Income Relationship   The saving and consumption decisions are closely linked because any part of income that is not consumed is saved; given our present assumption of no taxes, saving plus consumption is, by definition, equal to income.[4] The consumption decision, therefore, necessarily implies a saving decision.

Consider our numerical example:

$$C = 50 + 0.75Y$$

According to this relationship, consumption would be 50 (dollars or billions of dollars in the aggregate) at a zero level of income. Consumption plus saving is, by definition, equal to income:[5]

[4]When taxes are included later, we must modify this condition to say that saving plus consumption, by definition, equals *disposable* income (income less taxes).

[5]It is important to distinguish identities such as (9.2), which are indicated by the three-bar symbol (≡), and equations, which are indicated by the usual equal sign (=). Identities are relationships that follow from accounting or other definitions and therefore hold for any and all values of the variables.

$$C + S \equiv Y \tag{9.2}$$

or

$$S \equiv Y - C \tag{9.3}$$

Consequently, at zero income,

$$S \equiv Y - C$$
$$= 0 - 50 = -50$$

Saving would be negative (-50). This means that consumption is being financed by depleting past savings or by borrowing.

Now consider how saving changes as income changes. In our numerical example, consumption rises by $0.75 per $1 increase in income. This implies that saving rises by $0.25 per $1 increase in income because the increase in income is either consumed or saved.

We can, therefore, define the **marginal propensity to save** *(MPS)* as the increase in saving per dollar increase in income.

$$MPS = \frac{\Delta S}{\Delta Y}$$

In our example the *MPS* equals 0.25. By definition,

$$\frac{\Delta C}{\Delta Y} + \frac{\Delta S}{\Delta Y} = MPC + MPS \equiv 1$$

In our example $0.75 + 0.25 = 1.0$.

TABLE 9.1   Income, Consumption, and the Marginal Propensity to Consume

Income (Y)	Consumption (C)	Change in Income	×	MPC	=	Change in Consumption
400	350					
		100	×	0.75	=	75
500	425					
		100	×	0.75	=	75
600	500					
		100	×	0.75	=	75
700	575					
		100	×	0.75	=	75
800	650					
		200	×	0.75	=	150
1,000	800					

In defining the consumption–income relationship (the consumption function), we have thus also implicitly defined a saving–income relationship—a **saving function.** Gathering the results previously found ($S = -50$ at $Y = 0$; $\Delta S/\Delta Y = 0.25$), we can write this as

$$S = -50 + 0.25Y \qquad (9.4)$$

This saving function is plotted in Fig. 9.4. Table 9.2 illustrates how saving and consumption vary as income changes. Note that in each case the changes in saving and consumption sum to the total of the change in income.

3. Nonincome Influences on Consumption and Saving

In the Keynesian theory, income is the dominant determinant of consumption. This does not mean that there are no other influences on consumption behavior. Here we examine several factors that change the level of consumption for a given level of income.

Wealth: We would expect consumption expenditure to increase with higher wealth. For example, if during a period of economic expansion the value of stocks and bonds held by households increased sharply, we would expect this increase in wealth to stimulate consumption.

Such **wealth effects** mean that changes in the price level will affect *real* consumption *for a given level of real income.* This follows because the value of many assets such as currency, bank deposits, and government and corporate bonds is fixed in nominal (money) terms. A $10,000 bank certificate of deposit is, for instance, worth $10,000 regardless of the price level. As the price level rises, the real value of these *financial assets* is eroded. Household wealth declines, and we would expect consumption to decline as well. For a given level of real income, consumption would thus be negatively affected by increases in the price level.[6]

Inflationary Expectations: The effect just discussed is one of actual price changes on consumption. Some theories also link the level of consumption to expected future inflation, but the direction of the effect of *inflationary expectations* on consumption is uncertain. On the one hand, expected future inflation might lead consumers to

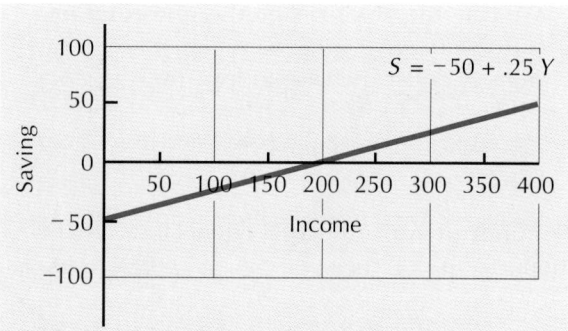

FIGURE 9.4   The Keynesian Saving Function

The Keynesian saving function shows the level of saving at each level of income.

[6]Increases in the price level can, of course, increase the value of some *real* assets such as gold, land, and residential property if the price of these assets rises faster than the general price level. On balance, however, the wealth effect from increases in the price level is likely to be negative.

TABLE 9.2   Income, Consumption, and Saving

Income	Consumption	Change in Income	× MPC	=	Change in Consumption	Saving	Change in Income	× MPS	=	Change in Saving
400	350					50				
		100	0.75		75		100	0.25		25
500	425					75				
		100	0.75		75		100	0.25		25
600	500					100				
		100	0.75		75		100	0.25		25
700	575					125				
		100	0.75		75		100	0.25		25
800	650					150				
		200	0.75		150		200	0.25		50
1,000	800					200				

increase current expenditures, as they attempt to buy before the expected price increases take place. Such behavior would lead to a *positive* relationship between current consumption and expected future inflation.

On the other hand, expected future inflation leads households to expect a decline in the value of their wealth because, as just discussed, price increases reduce the real value of financial assets held by households. Further, inflationary expectations may lead to increased uncertainty about the future economic environment. The expected decline in real wealth and increased uncertainty resulting from increased inflationary expectations could *negatively* affect consumption. Since there are influences in both directions, the overall effect on consumption of an increase in inflationary expectations is uncertain.

4. The Proper Income Concept for the Consumption Function   The income measure in the original Keynesian consumption function was simply current income. Post-Keynesian theoretical and empirical research on the consumption function suggests that the income concept most relevant for consumption is average expected lifetime income, not simply current income. There is a *persistence* in consumption patterns, meaning that, once established, households will try to maintain a given living standard. If, for example, the Smith household suffers a sudden temporary loss in income, the Smiths would, to an extent, maintain their consumption pattern by cutting back on current saving or by spending previous savings (taking money out of their bank account).

For most of our analysis, the distinction between actual current income and expected lifetime income will not be important. This distinction will be needed only when considering *transitory* changes in income that are not expected to continue in the future, such as a one-time tax rebate or a temporary income tax surcharge. Since the income effects of such changes in tax policy are brief, the consumption effects should be smaller than those of permanent changes in tax policy. Such transitory changes in income should have a smaller effect on consumption because they will *not* also affect average future expected income.

B
Investment

Investment, while a much smaller component of GNP than consumption spending, also plays a central role in Keynes's theory. Investment in the national income accounts includes both business spending on plant and equipment (fixed business investment) and the change in business inventories (inventory investment).[7] Investment in the national income accounts also includes expenditures for residential construction.

We have seen that consumption expenditures depend predominantly on income. These expenditures are, for the most part, what we will term *induced expenditures*.

Induced expenditures are expenditures that are determined primarily by current income.

Consumption expenditures will vary over time *as a result of* fluctuations in income.

Investment, by contrast, is an important category of *autonomous expenditures*.

Autonomous expenditures are expenditures which are largely determined by factors other than current income.

According to Keynes's theory, variations in autonomous expenditures, particularly in investment, *are responsible for* the instability in income. Too low a level of investment spending, in Keynes's view, was the reason for the low level of economic activity during the Great Depression. In the United States, gross business investment, $16.7 billion in 1929, had plummeted to just $1.6 billion by 1933. Net investment, which equals gross investment minus depreciation (the portion of capital stock that wears out in each period), was actually negative (−$6.0 billion) in 1933. Businesses failed even to replace worn-out plant and equipment. While not as unstable as in Keynes's time, investment spending since World War II has also varied considerably.

Read Perspective 9A.

---

[7]As explained in Chapter 7, firms hold stocks (inventories) of both raw materials to be used in the production process and finished goods awaiting sale. Changes in these stocks are an investment by the firm.

PERSPECTIVE 9A

The Cyclical Variability of Investment

While not as volatile as earlier in the century, cyclical fluctuation in investment has been considerable since World War II. Figure 9.5 shows total investment as a percent of GNP for the years 1973–86. Note the sharp drops in investment in 1974–75 and again in 1982 as the economy sank into deep recessions. Investment spending dropped less severely during the short recession in 1980.

The numbers plotted in the graph are for total investment. Fixed business investment, the autonomous expenditure component on which Keynes focused, is one component of total investment. Remember, however, that total investment also includes residential construction and the change in business inventories. These additional investment categories have shown considerable cyclical instability in this period and are an important element in the modern Keynesian analysis of business cycles.

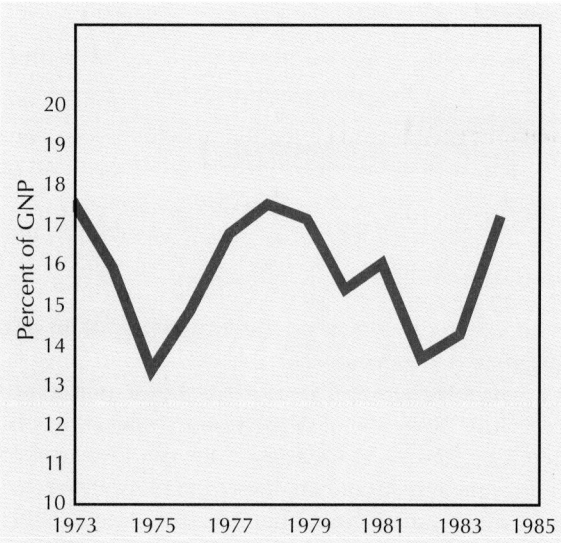

FIGURE 9.5   *Investment as a Percentage of GNP, 1973–85*

If, as Keynes believed, investment is the most variable component of autonomous expenditures, and if variation in autonomous expenditures is important for explaining business cycles, the next question is, what determines the level of investment?

Consider how you, as a business manager, would decide about an investment project such as the construction of a plant. First, you would be interested in the returns from the project—its profitability. Profits, however, will be realized only in the future, and the future is uncertain. You would have to base your decision on *expectations* about future profits. Second, you would want to know the cost of financing the project—the interest rate at which you can borrow money to pay for the plant. You would be led to consider the same two variables considered by Keynes:

1. Business expectations about the future profitability of investment projects.
2. The rate of interest.

1. The State of Business Expectations   Keynes believed that changes in business managers' expectations about the future profitability of investment projects were the prime cause of the instability of investment: "The outstanding fact is the extreme precariousness of the basis of knowledge on which our estimates of prospective yield have to be made." Consider what a business manager needs to know to gauge accurately the future profitability of an oil refinery, automobile plant, or textile plant over its prospective lifetime of 20, 30, or more years. He or she would need to know, among other things, the future demand for the product, the state of future competition, production costs, and tax laws. Keynes stressed the extreme uncertainty surrounding such long-term forecasts. Nonetheless, investment decisions are made every day.

In Keynes's view, because investment decisions are based "on so flimsy a foundation," business expectations are subject to "sudden and violent" changes. With drastic revisions in the state of confidence of business managers come sharp swings in investment expenditure.

2. The Rate of Interest Depending upon the state of business expectations, a firm would be able to calculate an *expected rate of return* on various investment projects. The expected rate of return is the expected profit rate, expressed as a percent of the project's cost. The firm could then compare the expected rate of return with the market rate of interest to assess the profitability of a given investment project. The market rate of interest—for example, the interest rate the firm must pay on bonds—is the cost of borrowing the money to pay for the project.[8] Here is an example of micro two-question logic. What is the investment worth?—the rate of return. What must be given up?—the interest rate on the money borrowed. If the rate of return exceeds the interest cost, the investment is profitable.

At successively lower market interest rates (lower borrowing costs), successively more projects would have expected returns high enough to be considered profitable. (More projects would be profitable at a 10 percent interest rate than at a rate of 15 percent.) Keynes therefore believed that *the level of investment would be negatively related to the market rate of interest.*

III
Equilibrium Output

Here we bring together the relationships discussed so far and explain the requirements for equilibrium in this simple Keynesian model. (Re-

call that the model has only a household and a business sector. When we add a government sector to the model in Chapter 10, the expressions derived here will have to be changed. Also, recall that the price level is assumed to be fixed; we will relax this assumption in Chapter 12.)

Equilibrium in the Keynesian model requires that output (Y) be equal to aggregate demand (AD). For the model of households and firms (no government sector), the Keynesian condition for equilibrium output is

$$Y = AD = C + I \qquad (9.5)$$

The level of output must equal the sum of the two components of aggregate demand: consumption (C) plus investment (I).

Before going on, further explanation of the variables in equation (9.5) is needed. As explained in Chapter 7, if there were no charges against GNP other than factor earnings, then GNP (final sales of goods and services) would equal national income (factor incomes from current production). Each dollar of GNP would be a dollar of sales receipts to the firm, and the whole dollar could be paid out to factors of production. There are, in fact, some charges against GNP in addition to earnings of factors of production, the most important of which are depreciation (of the capital stock) and indirect business taxes. In the model here, however, we are neglecting depreciation, indirect business taxes, and the other minor items that cause national output (GNP) and national income to diverge; *aggregate output and aggregate income are equal, and the terms output and income are used interchangeably in the discussion that follows.* This is very important to keep in mind as we proceed.

Also, investment must be interpreted as *planned* investment. Only planned or desired investment constitutes a demand for output. Planned investment may deviate from *realized* investment, which is the number recorded in the GNP accounts. The GNP accountant computes business investment as the total volume of business spending on plant and equipment, plus actual inventory investment (the increase or decline in business inventories). For expenditure on plant and equipment, we may assume that actual and planned spending are equal. It is in the last category, inventory investment, that desired and realized totals may differ.

[8]All investment projects are not financed by borrowing. Some are financed from business saving (or internal funds). If the firm finances a project with internal funds, a comparison between the expected rate of return on the project and the market rate of interest is still relevant. This follows because the available funds could be lent out at the market rate of interest as an alternative to the investment project. The market rate of interest represents the *opportunity cost* of using the funds for investment projects. (Opportunity cost is discussed in Chapter 2.)

The actual or realized total, as computed by the GNP accountant, includes all goods that are produced but not sold as inventory investment—*whether such investment was desired or not.* Aggregate demand contains only planned changes in inventories. Unintended inventory changes do enter the process of GNP determination. As we will see, the effects of such unintended inventory changes can be interpreted in terms of macro two-question logic.—What was expected? What actually happens?—and the effects of the discrepancy between the two. For now, however, simply keep in mind that *I is planned investment.*

A

Interpreting the Condition for Equilibrium Output

Figure 9.6 is a flow chart of income and output in our simplified economy. Each of the magnitudes in the chart (each of the items in equation 9.5) is a *flow* variable measured in dollars per period. In the lower part of the chart is the flow marked national income (Y) that runs from the business sector to households. This flow consists of payments for factor services: wages paid to labor, rents on land, and interest and dividends. These payments also sum to the total value of output produced because we assume that every dollar

firms receive from the sale of output is paid out to households in return for factor services.[9]

Households spend part of their income on consumption expenditures (C), which is shown as a flow back to the business sector as a demand for output. This is the income–expenditure mechanism described in Figure 9.2. Firms produce output (Y), which generates an equal income to the households, which, in turn, generates a demand for output (C).

National income that is not consumed consists of household saving. If we think of the inner loop in our flow chart as the central output expenditure linkage between firms and households, saving is a **leakage** from this loop. This saving leakage goes into financial markets, as each dollar saved is held by households in the form of some financial asset (currency, bank deposits, bonds, corporate equities).

Because each dollar of output generates a dollar of income to households, and because only a portion of that income is spent on consumption, consumption expenditures will be less than total output. This is true as long as there is a positive saving leakage from the inner loop of our flow diagram. This does *not* mean that total aggregate demand necessarily falls short of output produced. There

[9]The model omits corporate retained earnings and the tax on corporate profits.

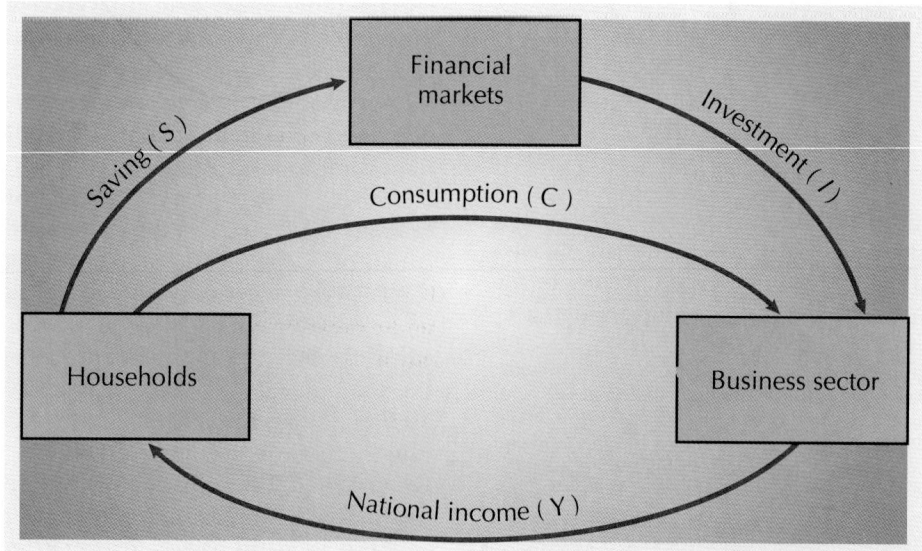

FIGURE 9.6 *The Circular Flow of Income and Output: Firms and Households*

is also investment demand for output on the part of the business sector. In other words, while it is true that some output is not demanded by households, investment expenditures by firms are a separate, additional source of demand. In terms of the circular flow diagram, investment spending by firms is an **injection** into the central loop. This investment injection is shown as a flow from financial markets to the business sector. The purchases of the investment goods are made by the firms in the business sector, but these purchases must be financed by borrowing in financial markets. Thus, the dollar amount of investment expenditures by firms is balanced by an equivalent dollar flow from the financial sector to the business sector.

Now look at the condition for equilibrium among the flow variables in our model, as expressed by equation (9.5). A level of output (Y) generates an equivalent level of national income. Via the Keynesian income–expenditure relationship embodied in the consumption function (e.g., $C = 50 + 0.75Y$), this level of income generates a demand for output (C). A level of output will be an *equilibrium level* if, when this induced consumption demand (C) is added to the *desired* investment expenditures of firms (I), this total aggregate demand (AD) is just equal to output

$$Y = AD = C + I \qquad (9.5)$$

Note from the flow chart that there is another way of looking at equilibrium. Equilibrium occurs

---

[10]Equation (9.6) is, in fact, equivalent to our earlier form of the equilibrium condition (9.5). This can be seen as follows. National income in our simple economy is all paid out to households and must either be consumed or saved. That is,

$$C + S \equiv Y \qquad (9.7)$$

For equilibrium, according to equation (9.5), we must have

$$Y = AD = C + I \qquad (9.5)$$

Putting (9.5) together with (9.7), we have, in equilibrium,

$$C + S \equiv Y = C + I$$

Subtracting C from both sides, we get

$$S = I$$

which is equation (9.6).

when saving, the leakage from the central loop of the circular flow, is just balanced by desired investment, the injection into that central loop. When the injection just balances the leakage, output, the flow in the central loop, will remain constant. Therefore, another way of stating this equilibrium condition is that saving (the leakage) must equal desired investment (the injection):[10]

$$S = I \qquad (9.6)$$

Equilibrium output in the Keynesian system can then be described in two ways. Output must equal aggregate demand $(Y = AD = C + I)$. Equivalently, the saving leakage, which is the portion of output not purchased by households $(S = Y - C)$, must be equal to the investment injection (I), which is the portion of output that firms desire to buy, and which also ensures that total aggregate demand just equals output.

B

The Tendency Toward Equilibrium

The condition for equilibrium output in the Keynesian system can be better understood by considering the forces that lead to a change in output when this condition is *not* met.

Consider the situation when output exceeds aggregate demand $(Y > AD = C + I)$. The excess of output above demand is unsold output, that is, output added to inventories. This increment to inventories is in addition to any planned inventory investment, which is included in aggregate demand; it is *unintended inventory accumulation.*

If $Y > AD$, $Y - AD$ = unintended inventory accumulation

If, at a given level of output, firms are accumulating undesired inventories, there will be a tendency for output to fall. Firms will cut production levels to prevent further undesired inventory accumulation. If, to consider one sector of the economy, auto sales fall short of production, inventories of unsold cars pile up on storage lots. Production cuts soon follow.

Conversely, suppose that aggregate demand exceeds output $(C + I = AD > Y)$. As orders above the level of production are filled out of existing inventories, there will be an *unintended inventory shortfall.*

If $Y < AD$, $AD - Y =$ unintended inventory shortfall

In this situation, there will be a tendency for the level of output to increase. Firms will raise production levels to prevent a further undesired fall in inventories. Returning to the example of automobiles, if demand exceeds production, inventories of autos run low, backlogs of orders accumulate, and auto makers increase output.

Only when output is equal to aggregate demand $(Y = AD = C + I)$ *will there be neither an unintended inventory buildup nor a shortfall. Consequently, only at this level of output will there be no tendency for output to change. This is what is meant by equilibrium.* In terms of macro two-question logic, when output equals aggregate demand, the expectations of firms are met. What was expected happens. Equilibrium results. When expectation differs from realization (output is not equal to aggregate demand and, hence, there is either an unintended inventory accumulation or a shortfall), we are out of equilibrium.

IV
Equilibrium Output: A Numerical Example

Here we construct a numerical example of equilibrium output determination in our simple Keynesian model.

In our previous example, the level of consumption *(C)* was given by the consumption function,

$$C = 50 + 0.75Y \qquad (9.8)$$

The level of investment depends on the state of expectations concerning future profits and on the rate of interest. The state of expectations is an autonomous or *exogenous* factor, meaning that it is not determined within the model we construct here; rather, it is determined outside of or independently of the model. For now, we will also take

the interest rate as being given exogenously, though this assumption will be dropped when we later consider monetary policy in the Keynesian model. With these assumptions, all the determinants of investment are exogenous to the model. We can take the level of *desired* investment as being fixed for a moment in time. Let us suppose that this fixed level of desired investment is $100 billion per year.

Using the consumption function given by equation (9.8) and the assumption that desired investment is fixed at $100 billion, we can compute the level of aggregate demand corresponding to a given level of output. This is done in Table 9.3 for output levels from $200 to $1,000 billion.

The output levels are given in column (1) of the table. The consumption total (computed from equation 9.8) is in column (2) (e.g., if $Y = 500$, $C = 50 + 0.75 (500) = 50 + 375 = 425$). The level of saving could be computed from the saving function given in Section II. More simply, saving is just equal to output (income) minus consumption expenditures $(S = Y - C)$. This level of saving is shown in column (3). The level of desired investment expenditures, shown in column (4), is fixed at $100 billion at each level of output. The level of aggregate demand (AD) is equal to consumption expenditures by households plus desired investment expenditures by firms $(AD = C + I)$, as shown in column (5).

Note that aggregate demand exceeds output at each output level below $600 billion. When we add the amount of consumption generated by each of these output (income) levels to the fixed amount of desired investment, total demand exceeds production. Consequently, for each of these output levels below $600 billion, there is an inventory *shortfall,* as indicated by the negative entries in column (6). Note also that at each of these output levels below $600 billion, investment exceeds saving. In terms of our circular flow diagram, injections exceed leakages.

At each of the output levels above $600 billion, the situation is reversed. Aggregate demand falls short of output; the saving leakage from the circular flow exceeds the investment injection, and there is undesired inventory *accumulation.*

At output levels below $600 billion, there will be a tendency for output to increase as firms try to end the rundown in inventory stocks. At output

TABLE 9.3 Equilibrium Output: A Numerical Example

(1) Output Y	(2) Consumption C	(3) Saving S = Y − C	(4) Investment I	(5) Aggregate Demand AD = C + I	(6) Unintended Inventory Shortfall (−) or Accumulation (+) (Y − AD)
200	200	0	100	300	−100
300	275	25	100	375	−75
400	350	50	100	450	−50
500	425	75	100	525	−25
600	500	100	100	600	0
700	575	125	100	675	25
800	650	150	100	750	50
1,000	800	200	100	900	100

Compare for equilibrium

levels above $600 billion, there will be a tendency for output to fall as firms try to stop the undesired accumulation of inventories.

The equilibrium point is at an output level of $600 billion. The level of consumption generated by this level of output (income) $(C = 50 + 0.75 (600) = 500)$ plus desired investment expenditures (100) is equal to output $(Y = C + I = 600)$. Also, at a level of output of $600 billion, the saving leakage is balanced by an equal investment injection $(S = I)$; the portion of output not purchased by consumers $(Y − C = S)$ is equal to the portion that firms wish to purchase. At an output level of $600 billion, there is no undesired accumulation or shortfall of inventories. In terms of macro two-question logic, expectations are equal to realizations.

V

Equilibrium Output: A Graphic Illustration

The mechanics of output determination in the Keynesian system are illustrated in Figure 9.7. Output (Y) is measured along the horizontal axis. Consumption (C) and investment (I), the components of aggregate demand, are measured on the vertical axis. The sum of consumption plus investment is shown by the aggregate demand schedule $(AD = C + I)$ also measured on the vertical axis.

The 45° line is drawn to split the positive quadrant in half, that is, to run right through the middle of the area between the axis. This line contains all the points having the property that the value of the variable measured on the vertical axis is just equal to the value of the variable measured on the horizontal axis. The 45° line, therefore, contains all the points where aggregate demand $(C + I)$ is just equal to output, that is, all possible points of equilibrium. At points above the 45° line, the value of the variable measured on the vertical axis (aggregate demand) exceeds the value of the variable measured on the horizontal axis (output). At points below the 45° line, the value of the variable measured on the horizontal axis (output) exceeds the value of the variable measured on the vertical axis (aggregate demand).

> Points above the 45° line are points of *excess demand;* points below the 45° line are points of *excess supply;* points on the 45° line are potential *equilibrium points.*

In Figure 9.7, we continue to use the numerical example from the previous section. We have plotted the consumption function $(C = 50 + 0.75Y)$. The consumption function slopes upward, reflecting the positive consumption–income relationship. The slope of the C schedule is equal to the marginal propensity to consume, 0.75 in this case. The aggregate demand or $C + I$ schedule lies above the C schedule by the amount of invest-

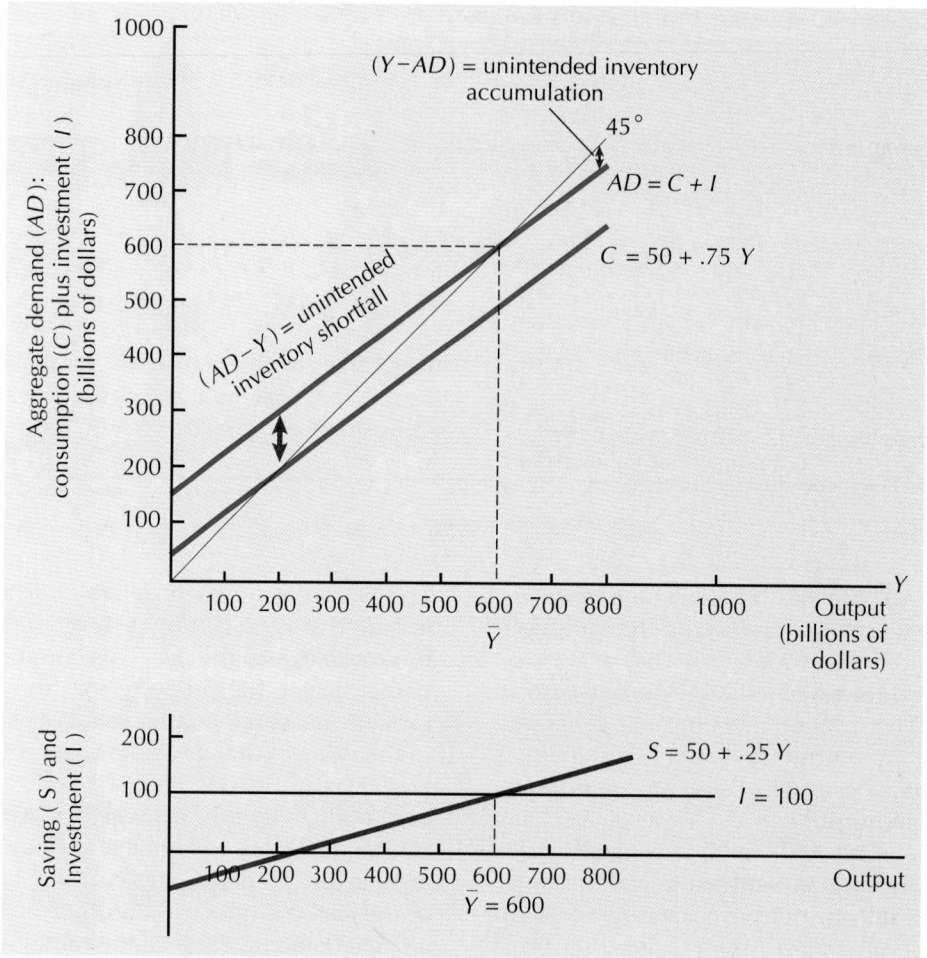

FIGURE 9.7   Equilibrium Output: A Graphic Example

Equilibrium output is at $600 billion. At this level, output equals aggregate demand (Y = AD) and leakages equal injections (S = I).

ment, $100 billion in the figure. The investment and saving schedules are plotted on the lower part of the graph. The I schedule is horizontal because investment is assumed not to vary with income. The saving schedule ($S = -50 + 0.25Y$) is positively sloped because saving depends positively on income. The slope of the saving function is equal to the marginal propensity to save, 0.25 in our example.

The equilibrium level of output (or income) in Figure 9.7 is at $600 billion, the point at which the $AD = C + I$ schedule crosses the 45° line, indicating that aggregate demand is equal to output. This output level is also the point where saving ($100 billion) is just equal to the fixed level of desired

investment.

At all levels of output *above* (to the right of) $600 billion on the horizontal axis, the $AD = C + I$ schedule is below the 45° line, indicating that aggregate demand (the variable measured on the vertical axis) is below output (the variable measured on the horizontal axis). As we saw in Table 9.3, over this range of output levels, there is undesired inventory accumulation and, thus, a tendency for output to fall toward the $600 billion equilibrium level. Also, over this range, the saving function is above the investment function, indicating that the saving leakage exceeds the investment injection into the circular flow of income.

At output levels below $600 billion on the horizontal axis, the $AD = C + I$ schedule is above the 45° line, indicating that aggregate demand exceeds current output. Here we have an undesired inventory shortfall, and there is a tendency for output to rise toward the $600 billion equilibrium level. Over this range of output levels, the investment schedule is above the saving schedule; the investment injection exceeds the saving leakage.

VI

Keynes versus the Classics: A First Look

Numerical examples are helpful in understanding the details of output determination in the Keynesian system. But the details should not be allowed to obscure the larger picture. The central message of Keynes's *General Theory* was that aggregate demand was an important determinant of output. Output was not supply determined at a full-employment level, as the classical economists believed. For a level of output to be an equilibrium level, output must equal aggregate demand.

Moreover, nothing guarantees that the level of equilibrium output in the Keynesian system will be a *full-employment level*. The full employment level of output was to Keynes just one special case of his *General Theory*. As the quotation at the beginning of this chapter indicated, Keynes believed that the economy was "capable of remaining in a chronic condition of subnormal activity for a considerable period without any marked tendency either toward recovery or toward complete collapse." Such a situation is illustrated in Figure 9.8.

Suppose that, as in our previous example, *equilibrium* output (Y) is $600 billion but *full-employment* output (Y_f) is $800 billion. As we have seen, at any level of output above $600 billion, aggregate demand will fall short of output; there will be

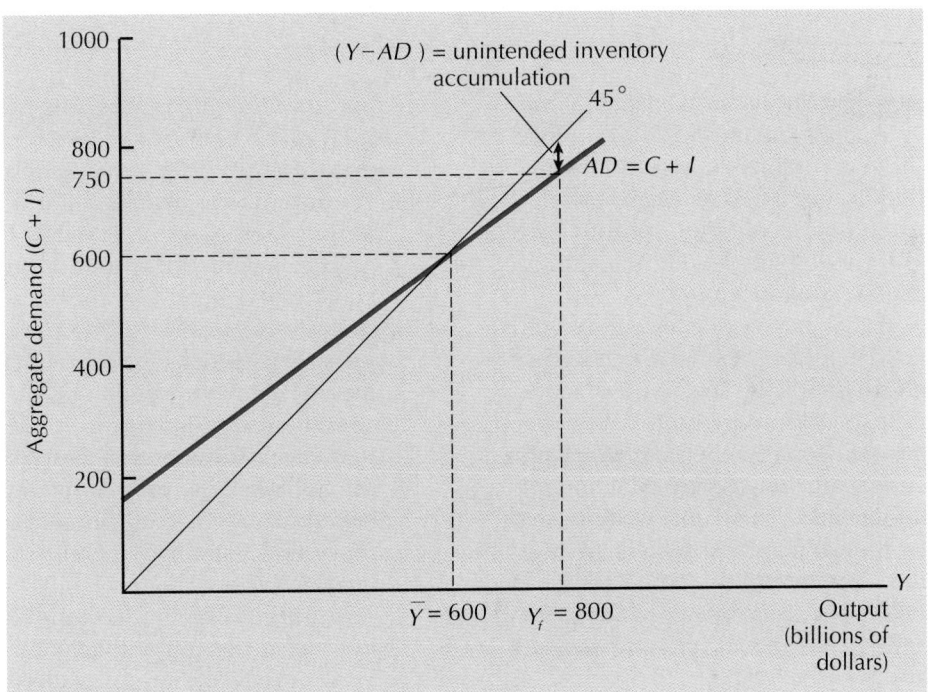

FIGURE 9.8 A Less Than Full-Employment Equilibrium

Equilibrium out ($\bar{y}$), where aggregate demand (AD = C + I) is equal to output, is at 600 units. At the full-employment level of output (y_1), aggregate demand falls short of output. At the full-employment level of output there is unintended inventory accumulation (y − AD) and, therefore, a tendency for output to fall.

undesired inventory accumulation and, therefore, a tendency for the level of output to fall. At the full-employment level of $800 billion, for example, consumption would be $650 billion ($50 + 0.75 \times 800$), which, added to $100 billion of desired investment expenditures, would make aggregate demand equal to $750 billion. Unintended inventory accumulation would be $50 billion. Aggregate demand is too low to support the full-employment level of output.

The saving equals investment $(S = I)$ form of the condition for equilibrium output makes clear the reason why the full-employment output level of $800 billion is not sustainable. At an income level of $800 billion, saving will be $150 billion ($Y - C = 800 - 650 = 150$), while investment is fixed at $100 billion. Saving, which in our simple model is the portion of income not spent on output and,

hence, the portion of output not purchased by households ($150 billion), exceeds the portion of output the firms want to buy, given by desired investment ($100 billion). This excess becomes undesired inventory accumulation ($50 billion), prompting output to fall toward $600 billion.

The level of consumption will rise with the level of income (at $600 billion, $C = $500 billion; at $800 billion, $C = $650 billion) because consumption is what we termed *induced expenditure*. Investment, however, is *autonomous* expenditure, which *does not vary with income*. The investment level of $100 billion is too low to sustain the full-employment output level of $800 billion. *Too low a level of such autonomous expenditures was Keynes's explanation of why the economy could sink into and remain at a "chronic condition of subnormal activity."*

SUMMARY

1. Keynes attacked the classical belief that the economy is self-adjusting to full employment within a reasonable period of time. He argued instead that if aggregate demand is too low, equilibrium output can fall far short of full employment, resulting in substantial unemployment.

2. In this first look at the Keynesian system, aggregate demand consists of consumption plus investment. The level of consumption expenditure by households depends primarily on income. Consumption expenditures are an *induced* element of aggregate demand. This consumption–income relationship is expressed in the Keynesian *consumption function,* the change in consumption per unit change in income being measured by the *marginal propensity to consume.*

3. Desired investment expenditures by firms depend on the state of expectations about the future profitability of investment projects and the rate of interest—two fac-

tors that *do not* vary directly with current level of income. Investment is an *autonomous* component of aggregate demand.

4. For output to be at an equilibrium level, the output level must be equal to the level of aggregate demand. In the simplified model constructed here, this means that output must be equal to consumption expenditures plus *desired* investment ($Y = C + I$).

5. An alternative expression of the Keynesian condition for equilibrium in this model is that saving, which reflects a leakage from the circular flow of income, must be just balanced by desired investment, which represents an injection into the circular flow ($S = I$).

6. Any output level above the equilibrium level (e.g., the full-employment level, if it exceeds the equilibrium level) is unsustainable due to undesired inventory accumulation. Aggregate demand is thus central to output determination in the Keynesian theory.

Appendix:

Equilibrium in the Keynesian System: An Algebraic Interpretation

Here we provide an algebraic interpretation of the determination of equilibrium income in the Keynesian system. As with the numerical and graphic examples, the aim of the exercise is to aid in the understanding of the condition for equilibrium income in the Keynesian system.

The condition for equilibrium was that output equals aggregate demand:

$$Y = AD = C + I \qquad (9.5)$$

The level of consumption (C) was assumed to be given by

$$C = 50 + 0.75Y, \qquad (9.1)$$

where Y was income. Equation (9.1) can be written in more general form as

$$C = a + bY \qquad (A.1)$$

$$a > 0$$
$$0 < b < 1$$

The intercept of the consumption function, a, is assumed to be positive, meaning that consumption would be at some positive level (e.g., 50 in equation 9.1) even if income were zero. The marginal propensity to consume is given by b and is assumed to be between 0 and 1.

Desired investment was assumed to be given at a fixed level of 100. In our algebraic example, we simply denote the fixed value of investment as I.

By substituting equation (A.1) for C in the equilibrium condition (9.5), we can write an expression for equilibrium output as follows:

$$Y = C + I$$
$$Y = a + bY + I$$
$$Y - bY = a + I$$
$$(1 - b)Y = a + I$$
$$\bar{Y} = \frac{1}{1 - b}(a + I) \qquad (A.2)$$

where the bar over the Y indicates an equilibrium value of output.

The level of equilibrium output can be computed from equation (A.2) for given values of a, b, and I. In the numerical example in the chapter we had

$$a = 50$$
$$b = 0.75$$
$$I = 100$$

using these values in equation (A.2) we find that

$$Y = \frac{1}{1 - b} \times (a + I)$$

$$Y = \frac{1}{1 - 0.75} \times (50 + 100)$$

$$Y = \frac{1}{0.25} \times (150)$$

$$\bar{Y} = 4 \times (150) = 600$$

the value of equilibrium income in Table 9.3.

Now suppose we substitute a value of $I = 150$, making no change in a or b. We then have

$$Y = \frac{1}{1 - b} \times (a + I)$$

$$Y = \frac{1}{0.25} \times (200)$$

$$\bar{Y} = 800$$

Note that the level of equilibrium output rises by 200 units when the level of desired investment increases by only 50 units; equilibrium output rises by a *multiple* of the increase in investment. We see why this happens in the next chapter.

Key Terms

Keynesian income–expenditure approach
Aggregate demand
Consumption function
Marginal propensity to consume
Marginal propensity to save
Saving function

Wealth effects
Induced expenditures
Autonomous expenditures
Leakages and injections

QUESTIONS AND PROBLEMS

1. Explain Keynes's concept of the *marginal propensity to consume*.
2. Explain Keynes's *saving function*. Give a numerical example of the saving function.
3. Carefully explain the difference between *desired* and *realized* investment. In which component of investment does the discrepancy between the two occur?
4. Explain the distinction between *induced* expenditures and *autonomous* expenditures.
5. Why is investment an unstable component of aggregate demand?
6. Carefully explain the condition that must be met for a level of output to be an equilibrium level in the Keynesian model.

7. Data on inventory levels in U.S. industry are often reported and analyzed as an indicator of the future path of the economy. Are changes in inventories valid economic indicators? Why or why not?
8. If consumption in an economy were described by $C = 20 + 0.80Y$ and if planned investment were 125, what would the equilibrium level of income be? Demonstrate this in a schedule with columns to show output, consumption, saving, investment, aggregate demand, and unintended changes in inventory. (See Table 9.3)
9. Convert the data in Question 8 to graphical form, as in Figure 9.7, marking the equilibrium output level.
10. What is significant about a 45 degree line drawn on a graph in the positive quadrant?

10

The Government Sector, the Multiplier Concept, and Fiscal Policy

A Keynesian macroeconomic model without a government sector is like Shakespeare's *Hamlet* without the Prince of Denmark. Keynes believed that the government had a necessary role in stabilizing the economy and should be bold enough to exercise it. He was a policy activist in a broad sense, believing that

There is no reason why we should not feel ourselves free to be bold, to be open, to experiment, to take action, to try the possibilities of things. And over against us, standing in the path, there is nothing but a few old gentlemen tightly buttoned-up in their frock coats, who need only to be treated with a little friendly disrespect and bowled over like ninepins. Quite likely they will enjoy it themselves once they have got over the shock.[1]

To Keynes a free enterprise capitalist system provided the most satisfactory answers to the important microeconomic questions of What? and How? However, Keynes did not believe that a private enterprise system could provide macroeconomic stability on its own. Here he saw a necessary role for government policy.

In this chapter, we begin to examine the role of government policy in the Keynesian system. First, we extend our model of households and firms to include a government sector that spends and collects taxes. With this extension, we again examine the conditions required for equilibrium output. Then we consider the factors that cause income to change. Among these factors are variables responsible for the cyclical instability of output, as well as variables that are potential tools for government stabilization policy. This chapter is restricted to potential fiscal policy variables. Monetary policy is discussed in the next chapter.

[1]John M. Keynes, "Can Lloyd George Do It?" in *Essays in Persuasion*, (Cambridge: Cambridge University Press, 1984), p. 125.

I

A Model with a Government Sector

The government sector affects aggregate demand via *fiscal policy*—its spending and taxing decisions. Government spending means the government sector's purchases of goods and services (e.g., tanks and aircraft for defense, the postal service, construction of new government office buildings). Government spending is an element of *autonomous* expenditures. The level of government spending is controlled by fiscal policymakers, ultimately by the executive and legislative branches of the federal government. As with investment, changes in government spending are a *cause* of changes in total output (GNP). Changes in government spending are therefore a potential tool for stabilization policy or, if mismanaged, a source of instability.

Tax policy is the second fiscal policy tool. At this point, we assume that only one tax is levied on households and that the policymaker controls actual tax receipts. Later we will make the more realistic assumption that the policymaker merely sets a tax rate as a percentage of income and that tax receipts then depend on the level of income.

Taxes are a *wedge* that causes disposable income (income less taxes) to diverge from national income. Any increase in taxes paid by households reduces the income they have available to spend (disposable income) and consequently lowers household consumption spending. Tax cuts increase disposable income and stimulate consumption. The link between taxes and aggregate demand in the Keynesian model is this effect of tax changes on disposable income, and therefore on consumption.

A
Equilibrium Output with a Government Sector

Figure 10.1 extends the circular flow chart in Figure 9.6 to include the government sector. The lowest arrow in the figure shows the flow of national income (Y) from the business sector to the household sector. This flow is paid out by households in three flows: consumption (C), saving (S), and tax payments (T). Tax payments are a money flow from the household sector to the government sector. In relation to the inner loop, which is the central output expenditure linkage, tax payments represent a *leakage* from the circular flow of income.

There is also a flow payment from the govern-

ment to households in the form of *transfer payments* such as Social Security benefits, welfare payments, veterans' benefits, etc. The tax payment should, therefore, be considered net of (or after subtracting) transfers:

$$T = \text{taxes} - \text{transfer payments}$$

This means, for example, that when we consider the effect of an increase in taxes, *it is the same as that of a decrease in transfer payments of an equal amount.* Both actions reduce disposable income. We return to this point later but keep in mind: T is **net taxes**.

Government spending (G) is shown as a flow from the government sector to the business sector, from which the government purchases goods and

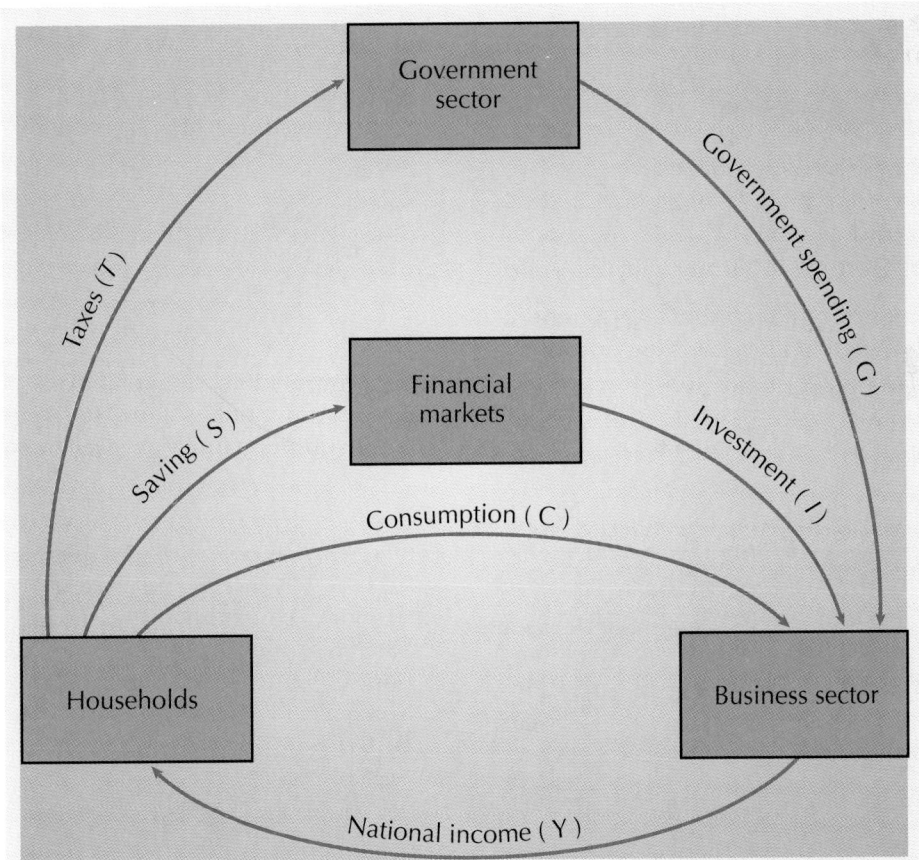

FIGURE 10.1   Circular Flow of Output and Income

services. In relation to the inner loop of our circular flow diagram, government purchases are an *injection* into the circular flow of income.

With the government sector included, aggregate demand equals consumption plus desired investment plus government spending. Our equilibrium condition, which specifies that output must equal aggregate demand, now becomes

$$Y = AD = C + I + G \qquad (10.1)$$

The second form of the condition for a level of equilibrium output in the Keynesian system is that leakages from the circular flow of income must be balanced by injections into that flow. In the model with households and firms, this means that saving must equal desired investment $(S = I)$. With the addition of the government sector, there is an additional leakage, tax payments, and an additional injection, government spending. The expanded version of the equilibrium condition becomes

$$\begin{aligned} \text{leakages} &= \text{injections} \\ S + T &= I + G \end{aligned} \qquad (10.2)$$

B

Equilibrium Output: A Numerical Example

To see more concretely how the government affects the determination of equilibrium output, we extend the numerical example from the previous chapter to include a government sector. We assume that the consumption function is

$$C = 50 + 0.75Y_D \qquad (10.3)$$

In Chapter 9, where there were no tax payments, we did not distinguish between national income (Y) and disposable income (Y_D), which in the model equals national income less taxes $(Y_D = Y - T)$, because the two were equal $(T = 0)$. But consumption depends on disposable income, that is, the income households actually have to spend. To make this distinction clear and to make explicit the negative relationship between consumption and tax payments, we rewrite the consumption function as

$$C = 50 + 0.75(Y - T) \qquad (10.4)$$

We continue to assume that desired investment (I) is \$100 billion. To find equilibrium output, we need to make some assumption about the levels of government spending (G) and tax payments (T). For our example, we assume that fiscal policymakers set government spending at \$125 billion and set tax payments at \$100 billion.

Taken together, our assumptions are as follows:

$$\begin{aligned} C &= 50 + 0.75Y_D = 50 + 0.75(Y - T) \\ I &= 100 \\ G &= 125 \\ T &= 100 \end{aligned}$$

The computation of equilibrium output under these assumptions is shown in Table 10.1. Using the consumption function given by equation (10.4),

TABLE 10.1   Equilibrium Output with a Government Sector

(1)	(2)	(3)	(4)	(5)	(6)	(7)	(8)
Output	Taxes	Disposable Income	Consumption	Investment	Government Spending	Aggregate Demand	Unintended Inventory Accumulation(+) or Shortfall(−)
(Y)	(T)	$Y_D = Y - T$	(C)	(I)	(G)	$(AD = C + I + G)$	$(Y - AD)$
500	100	400	350	100	125	575	−75
600	100	500	425	100	125	650	−50
700	100	600	500	100	125	725	−25
800	100	700	575	100	125	800	0
900	100	800	650	100	125	875	25
1,000	100	900	725	100	125	950	50

Compare for equilibrium

we compute consumption at each level of output. To do so, we first subtract tax payments (T) in column (2) from output (Y) in column (1) to compute disposable income (Y_D) in column (3). Consumption is then calculated in column (4). Columns (5) and (6) show the fixed levels of desired investment expenditures (I) and government expenditures (G). The level of aggregate demand, as shown in column (7), is computed by adding consumption plus investment plus government spending.

The equilibrium point is an output level of $800 billion. At that point, aggregate demand (AD = C + I + G) equals output (Y). At levels of output below $800 billion, aggregate demand exceeds output; there are unintended shortfalls in inventories, as can be seen in column (8) (Y − AD < O), and a consequent tendency for output to rise. Conversely, at output levels above $800 billion, aggregate demand falls short of output; there is unintended inventory accumulation (Y − AD > O) and a tendency for output to fall. Only at an output level of $800 billion does aggregate demand equal output, with no shortfall or undesired accumulation of inventories and therefore no tendency for output to change.

Table 10.2 takes a different view of the same example. It illustrates that at the equilibrium level of output where aggregate demand equals output, leakages from the circular flow of output are just balanced by injections. This means that saving plus taxes (the leakages) are just balanced by desired investment plus government spending (the injections).

Output (Y) is shown in column (1) of the table. Disposable income (Y_D) is computed in column (3)

by subtracting the fixed level of tax payments (T) in column (2) from each output level. Column (4) gives the level of saving (S) at each level of disposable income. Saving levels can be computed using the saving function, which for our example is

$$S = -50 + 0.25Y_D$$

or, more simply, as the difference between disposable income and the level of consumption shown in column (4) of Table 10.1. Column (5) shows total leakages equal to saving plus taxes (S + T). Columns (6) and (7) show the fixed level of desired investment (I) and government spending (G), respectively. These totals are added together to derive total injections (I + G) in column (8).

Leakages from the circular flow of output and income (S + T) reflect income paid to households that does not come back to the business sector as demand for output by the household sector. In equilibrium, such leakages must be balanced by injections of demand from the other sectors, here the business and government sectors. If injections (I + G) exceed leakages (S + T), there will be a shortfall of inventories equal to the amount of this excess [(I + G) − (S + T)] as total demand exceeds output; this is the situation at Y less than 800. If leakages exceed injections, there will be an equal amount [(S + T) − (I + G)] of undesired inventory accumulation as output exceeds aggregate demand; this is what happens at Y greater than 800. At Y equals 800, leakages equal injections, which implies that aggregate demand and output are equal, as can be verified from Table 10.1.

TABLE 10.2   Equilibrium Output: Leakages equal Injections

(1) Output (Y)	(2) Taxes (T)	(3) Disposable Income $Y_D = Y - T$	(4) Saving (S)	(5) Saving plus Taxes (S + T)	(6) Investment (I)	(7) Government Spending (G)	(8) Investment plus Government Spending (I + G)
500	100	400	50	150	100	125	225
600	100	500	75	175	100	125	225
700	100	600	100	200	100	125	225
800	100	700	125	225	100	125	225
900	100	800	150	250	100	125	225
1,000	100	900	175	275	100	125	225

Compare for equilibrium

C
Equilibrium Output: A Graphic Illustration

Figure 10.2 illustrates the determination of equilibrium output with the addition of the government sector. This figure may be compared to Figure 9.7 for the model with only households and firms.

As before, the consumption schedule (C) is upward sloping; consumption rises with income. The aggregate demand schedule $(AD = C + I + G)$ now lies above the C schedule by the amount of investment plus government spending, which together are fixed at 225 units $(I = 100; G = 125)$. The $I + G$ schedule is plotted separately and is horizontal because neither investment nor govern-

ment spending is assumed to vary with output. The final schedule, labeled $S + T$, plots the level of saving plus taxes. It slopes upward because saving increases as income (output) increases.

The equilibrium level of output is shown at $800 billion where the aggregate demand schedule crosses the 45° line. At that point, the value of the variable measured on the horizontal axis (Y) is equal to the value of the variable measured on the vertical axis $(AD = C + I + G)$. The equilibrium condition in equation (10.1) is met. At that point, from the lower portion of the figure, it can also be seen that the $S + T$ schedule intersects the horizontal $I + G$ schedule $(S + T = I + G)$.

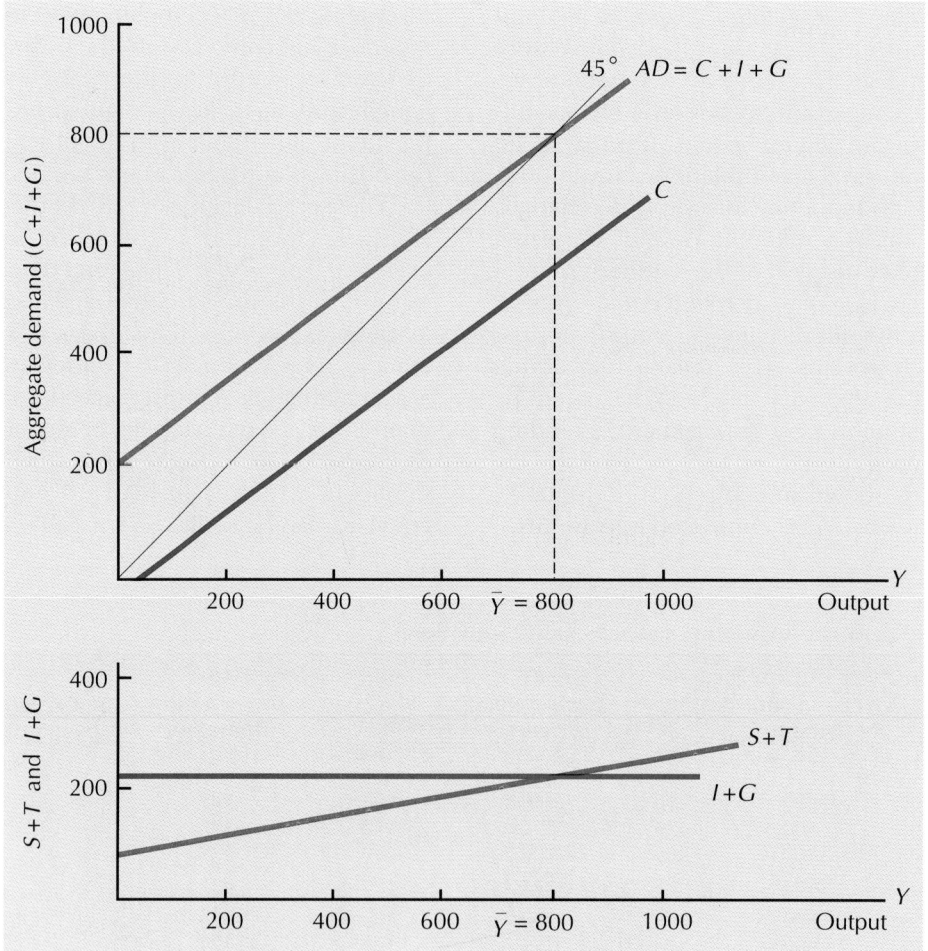

FIGURE 10.2 *Equilibrium Output in a Model with a Government Sector*
Equilibrium output is at $800 billion. At this level, output equals aggregate demand (Y = C + I + G) and leakages equal injections (S + T = I + G).

II

Factors That Cause Changes in Equilibrium Output

We have examined how equilibrium output is determined in the Keynesian system. In this section, we consider the factors that cause *changes* in equilibrium output. These factors can explain the cyclical variations in output and provide potential instruments for government policies to stabilize the economy.

In the simple Keynesian model, equilibrium output is determined by aggregate demand. To explain *changes* in equilibrium output, we must find the factors that cause *changes* in aggregate demand. The consumption component of aggregate demand is primarily *induced* expenditure, that is, expenditure that depends directly on the level of income. This income–expenditure linkage is important in the process by which income varies but, for the most part, consumption changes in response to changes in output rather than output changing in response to a change in consumption.

To explain the cause of changes in aggregate demand, we look to the *autonomous* elements of aggregate demand. These are the components that are determined, for the most part, independently of the current level of output. Changes in the levels of the autonomous components of aggregate demand cause output to vary. Keynes's own theory of the business cycle stressed the highly variable

nature of investment demand. As explained in Chapter 9, Keynes believed that investment demand was unstable because of sudden shifts in business managers' expectations concerning the future profitability of investment projects. Such sudden shifts in expectations were, in turn, the result of the high level of economic uncertainty and the resulting precarious foundation of such expectations. Keynes believed that instability in the investment component of aggregate demand was the primary cause of instability in output. To begin our analysis of changes in equilibrium output, let us consider the effects of a change in investment demand within our model.

A

The Change in Equilibrium Output with a Change in Investment

Suppose that, due to a favorable change in expectations concerning the future profitability of investment projects, the level of investment rises. In terms of our numerical example, suppose that the level of desired investment spending rises from $100 billion to $200 billion.

Table 10.3 recomputes the level of equilibrium output for an investment level of $200 billion. The levels of government spending (G), tax payments (T), and the form of the consumption function ($C = 50 + 0.75Y_D$) are unchanged from Table 10.1. As can be seen in the new table, at the former level of equilibrium output (800), aggregate demand (900) now exceeds output. At that former level of output, with the higher investment level of $200

TABLE 10.3   The Change in Equilibrium Output with an Increase in Investment

(1)	(2)	(3)	(4)	(5)	(6)	(7)	(8)	(9)
Output	Taxes	Disposable Income	Saving	Consumption	Investment	Government Spending	Aggregate Demand	Unintended Inventory Accumulation(+) or Shortfall(−)
(Y)	(T)	($Y_D = Y - T$)	(S)	(C)	(I)	(G)	($AD = C + I + G$)	($Y - AD$)
800	100	700	125	575	200	125	900	−100
900	100	800	150	650	200	125	975	−75
1,000	100	900	175	725	200	125	1,050	−50
1,100	100	1,000	200	800	200	125	1,125	−25
1,200	100	1,100	225	875	200	125	1,200	0
1,300	100	1,200	250	950	200	125	1,275	+25

Compare for equilibrium

billion, there would be an unintended inventory shortfall of $100 billion and a consequent tendency for output to rise. It can also be seen in Table 10.3 that at the old equilibrium level of output (800), injections ($I + G = 325$) exceed leakages ($S + T = 225$). In terms of macro two-question logic (what happens versus what was expected), realized demand differs from output; equilibrium is displaced, and a new equilibrium output must be reached.

Equilibrium output corresponding to the higher investment total of $200 billion can be seen from the table to be at $1,200 billion. At this higher level, output and aggregate demand are equal. Also, leakages balance injections ($I + G = S + T = 325$). There is no unintended inventory accumulation or shortfall.

The change in the level of equilibrium output as a result of a change in autonomous investment expenditures is illustrated in Figure 10.3. We denote the original level of investment expenditures of $100 billion as I_0. Initially, the aggregate demand schedule is $AD_0 = C + I_0 + G$ and the $I + G$ schedule is $I_0 + G$. Equilibrium output (Y_0) is $800 billion.

The new higher-level investment expenditure of 200 is denoted by I_1 in the graph. The increase in investment causes the aggregate demand schedule to shift upward from $AD_0 = C + I_0 + G$ to $AD_1 = C + I_1 + G$. The distance of this upward shift in the aggregate demand schedule is just equal to the amount of the increase in I. In this example, $I_1 - I_0 = 200 - 100 = 100$. The $I + G$ schedule also shifts upward by just the amount of the rise in investment $I_1 - I_0 = \$100$ billion. The new level of equilibrium output (Y_1) is at $1,200 billion, where the higher aggregate demand schedule crosses the 45° line and where the higher $I + G$ schedule intersects the $S + T$ schedule.

B

The Autonomous Expenditure Multiplier

1. The Concept of the Multiplier From Table 10.3 and Figure 10.3 we see that a rise in autonomous investment expenditures from 100 to 200, a rise of $100 billion, causes equilibrium output to increase from $800 billion to $1,200 billion, a rise of $400 billion. The rise in equilibrium output is a *multiple* of the rise in investment. This is a general

feature of the Keynesian model. A given change in autonomous expenditures causes output to change by a multiple of the original change in autonomous expenditures. This multiple is called the Keynesian **autonomous expenditure multiplier.**

In our example, equilibrium output rises by $4 for each $1 change in autonomous investment expenditure. The value of the autonomous expenditure multiplier is 4. Why does income change by a multiple of the change in investment?

The explanation of the process behind the multiplier concept is quite simple. The initial increase in investment expenditures is both an increase in aggregate *output* and, correspondingly, an increase in national *income*. As this initial increase in output generates additional income for households, there is an *induced* increase in consumption demand for output, with a consequent further increase in output. As with the initial increase in investment demand and, hence, output, this increased output of consumption goods generates increased income for households, so there is yet a further induced increase in consumption. (One person's expenditure is another person's income, which becomes the basis for more expenditure— and, in turn, more income.) The resulting total increase in equilibrium output will be equal to the initial *autonomous* increase in investment *plus* the sum of *induced* increases in consumption as the income generation process proceeds through successive rounds.

In our example, the initial increase in investment is $100 billion. As output increases by $100 billion, the payments to households for factor services also increase by $100 billion. Because tax payments are constant, this is an increase in disposable income of $100 billion. From the consumption function, we see that this leads to an induced increase in consumption expenditures of $75 billion; $MPC = 0.75$. This is round 1 of the induced increase in consumption expenditures. But the process does not stop here.

The consumption component of national output has increased by $75 billion. This increase in the output of consumption goods generates additional increased national income to households of $75 billion. With an MPC of 0.75, this increase in household disposable income generates a round 2 increase in consumption expenditures of $56.25

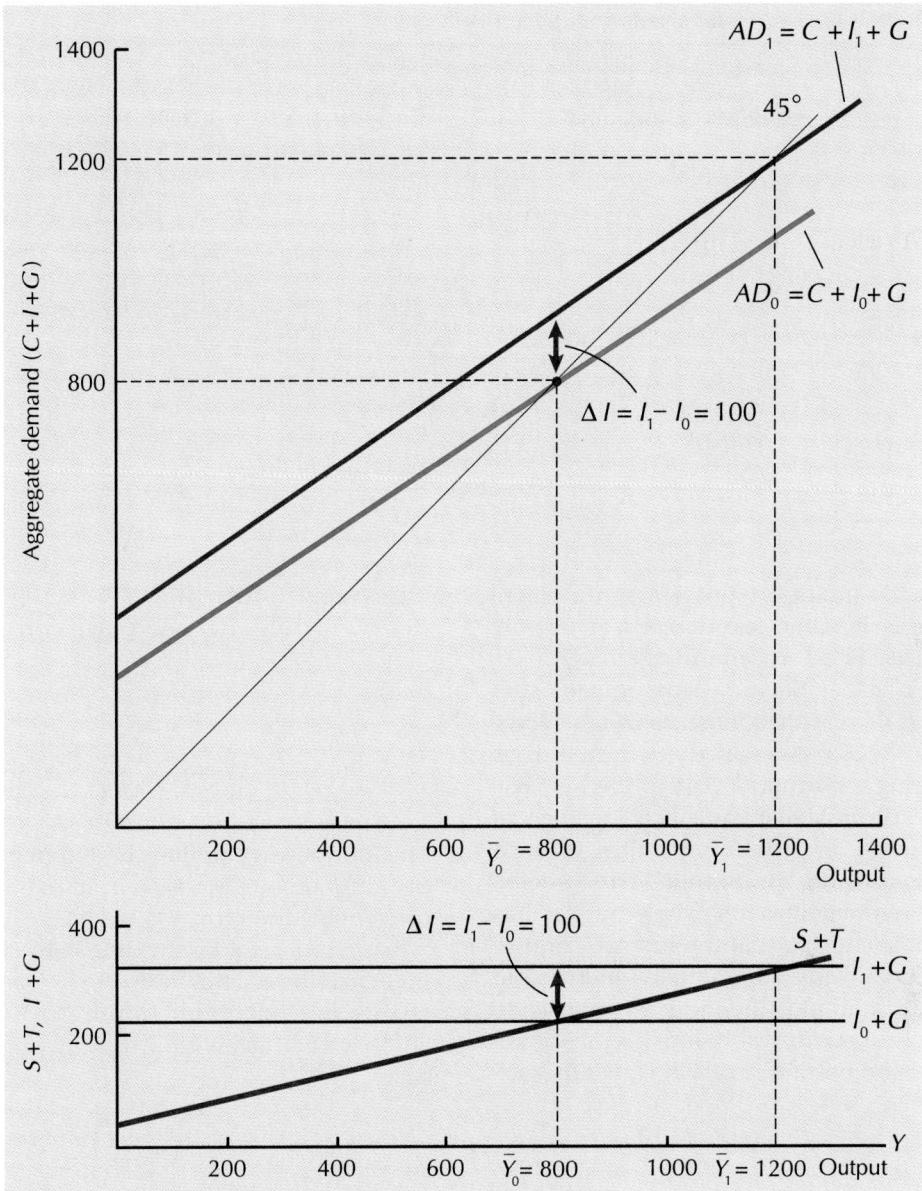

FIGURE 10.3 _The Effect of an Increase in Investment_

An increase in investment, from I_0 to I_1, shifts the aggregate demand schedule upward, from AD_0 to AD_1. The $I + G$ schedule also shifts upward, from $I_0 + G$ to $I_1 + G$.

billion (0.75×75). Round 2 will be followed by round 3, where the $56.25 billion of new output of consumption goods generates an equal increment to household income with a further induced increase in consumption ($42.19 = 0.75 \times 56.25$), and on into further rounds.

The multiplier process for a $100 billion in-

crease in investment is spelled out in detail in Table 10.4 over 15 rounds. Note that at each round the induced increase in consumption diminishes. The process eventually settles down at the new equilibrium, which, as we have seen in Table 10.3, occurs when output has increased by $400 billion.

TABLE 10.4   Details of the Multiplier Process

		Initial autonomous increase in investment	100 units
Induced increase in consumption	Round 1	$(100 \times 0.75) =$	75
	Round 2	$(75 \times 0.75) =$	56.25
	3	$(56.25 \times 0.75) =$	42.19
	4	$(42.19 \times 0.75) =$	31.64
	5	$(31.64 \times 0.75) =$	23.73
	6	$(23.73 \times 0.75) =$	17.80
	7	$(17.80 \times 0.75) =$	13.35
	8	$(13.35 \times 0.75) =$	10.01
	10	$\cdot$ $=$	5.63
	15	$\cdot$ $=$	1.34
	$\cdot$	$\cdot$ $=$	$\cdot$
	$\cdot$	$\cdot$ $=$	$\cdot$
	$\cdot$	$\cdot$ $=$	$\cdot$
	Total increase in output		400

Why does the multiplier process settle down, and why, precisely, when output has risen by $400 billion or $4 per $1 increase in investment?

The process settles down because in each successive round the induced increase in consumption demand becomes smaller. In turn, this is because, during each round, part of the increase in household disposable income becomes part of the saving leakage and does not return to businesses as a demand for output. The process comes to a new equilibrium when output has increased sufficiently so that the increase in output is just equal to the autonomous increase in investment demand plus the induced increase in consumption expenditures. At this point, aggregate demand and output are again equal. In symbols.

$$\Delta Y = \Delta C + \Delta I \qquad (10.5)$$

We know from the consumption function that the induced increase in consumption equals the marginal propensity to consume times the increase in income, that is,

$$\Delta C = MPC \times \Delta Y$$

So we can rewrite equation (10.5) as

$$\Delta Y = MPC \times \Delta Y + \Delta I$$

Then, gathering ΔY terms, we can write

$$\Delta Y - MPC \times \Delta Y = \Delta I$$
$$(1 - MPC)\Delta Y = \Delta I$$

or

$$\Delta Y = \frac{1}{1 - MPC} \times \Delta I \qquad (10.6)$$

The increase in equilibrium output equals the initial autonomous increase in investment expenditures times the term $1/(1 - MPC)$.

As can be seen by dividing both sides of equation (10.6) by ΔI, this term $(1/(1 - MPC))$ gives the change in equilibrium output per unit change in autonomous expenditures, investment in this case.

$$\frac{\Delta Y}{\Delta I} = \frac{1}{1 - MPC} \qquad (10.7)$$

This term $(1/(1 - MPC))$ is the Keynesian *autonomous expenditure multiplier.*

Since the marginal propensity to save is equal to one minus the marginal propensity to consume ($MPS = 1 - MPC$), we can also write the autonomous expenditure multiplier as

$$\frac{\Delta Y}{\Delta I} = \frac{1}{MPS} \qquad (10.8)$$

2. Numerical Examples   In our example, the marginal propensity to consume was 0.75. The marginal propensity to save $(1 - 0.75)$ was 0.25. We have, therefore,

$$\frac{\Delta Y}{\Delta I} = \frac{1}{1 - MPC} = \frac{1}{MPS} = \frac{1}{0.25} = 4$$

This agrees with the result in Table 10.3, where equilibrium output rose $400 billion with a $100 billion increase in investment, or by $4 per $1 increase in investment,

$$\Delta Y = \frac{1}{1 - MPC} \times \Delta I$$

$$= \frac{1}{1 - 0.75} \times 100$$

$$= \frac{1}{0.25} \times 100$$

$$\Delta Y = 4 \times 100 = 400$$

Table 10.5 shows the value of the autonomous expenditure multiplier corresponding to various values of the marginal propensity to consume and the marginal propensity to save. It can be seen that the higher the marginal propensity to consume, (the lower the marginal propensity to save), the higher the value of the autonomous expenditure multiplier. Recall that the reason there is a multiplier at all is that the initial increase in investment,

via the income–expenditure link in the Keynesian system, leads to increases in consumption. The higher the marginal propensity to consume (the lower the marginal propensity to save), the larger the induced increase in consumption expenditures at each round in the multiplier process and, consequently, the larger the rise in equilibrium output as a result of any increase in autonomous expenditures.

3. The Importance of the Multiplier Concept
The multiplier concept was central to Keynes's theory of the business cycle because it explained how shifts in the unstable investment component of demand could cause instability in the general level of economic activity.

Our examples have used an *increase* in autonomous investment expenditures, but clearly the multiplier also works in *reverse*. A *fall* in investment due, for example, to an unfavorable shift in business expectations would lead to a downward multiplier process. Here the initial autonomous decline in investment would be compounded by induced declines in consumption. If we reverse our shock to a decline in investment from $200 billion to $100 billion, we find that equilibrium output falls by $400 billion (still assuming the marginal propensity to consume to be 0.75 and, therefore, the value of the autonomous expenditure multiplier to be 4). The $100 billion decline in

TABLE 10.5   Numerical Examples of the Autonomous Expenditure Multiplier

Marginal Propensity to Consume (*MPC*)	Marginal Propensity to Save (*MPS*)	Autonomous Expenditure Multiplier $\frac{1}{1 - MPC} = \frac{1}{MPS}$
0.9	0.1	$\frac{1}{1 - 0.9} = \frac{1}{0.1} = 10$
0.8	0.2	$\frac{1}{1 - 0.8} = \frac{1}{0.2} = 5$
0.75	0.25	$\frac{1}{1 - 0.75} = \frac{1}{0.25} = 4$
0.6	0.4	$\frac{1}{1 - 0.6} = \frac{1}{0.4} = 2.5$
0.5	0.5	$\frac{1}{1 - 0.5} = \frac{1}{0.5} = 2$
0.4	0.6	$\frac{1}{1 - 0.4} = \frac{1}{0.6} = 1.67$

investment plus a $300 billion induced decline in consumption expenditures produce a combined drop of $400 billion. Autonomous increases or decreases in investment were Keynes's explanation for most booms and recessions, including the Great Depression of the 1930s.

Keynes's theory also implied that other components of autonomous expenditures have multiplier effects similar to those of investment. We will see in the next section how policymakers might stabilize aggregate demand through fiscal policy changes.

III
Fiscal Policy

Without a government stabilization policy, Keynes expected private sector aggregate demand and, therefore, output to be unstable. Unlike classical economists, who stressed the self-equilibrating tendencies of the private sector left free of government interference, Keynes stressed the need for government policies to stabilize aggregate demand. The classical economists were *noninterventionist;* Keynes was a policy *activist.*

Keynes believed that policymakers could use both fiscal and monetary policy to stabilize aggregate demand. We will analyze monetary policy in the next chapter. Here we consider **fiscal stabilization policy.**

A
The Effect of a Change in Government Spending

Fiscal policy tools available to policymakers in our simple version of the Keynesian model are the levels of government spending and tax collections. We begin by considering the effects of government spending on equilibrium output.

Let us return to our numerical example *before* the autonomous rise in investment expenditure considered in Table 10.3. That is, we return to the situation described in Tables 10.1 and 10.2. Investment is fixed at $100 billion, government spending is at $125 billion, and tax collections are fixed at $100 billion. The consumption function continues to be that given in equation (10.3) ($C = 50 + 0.75$ Y_D). The level of equilibrium output is $800 billion, as shown in Table 10.1. Now consider the effect of an increase in government spending from $125 billion to $225 billion, an increase of $100 billion.

The new level of equilibrium output is computed in Table 10.6. At the old equilibrium output level of $800 billion, with the higher level of government spending, aggregate demand ($900 billion) exceeds output. Equivalently, at an output level of $800 billion, injections into the circular flow of income ($I + G = 325$) exceed leakages ($S + T = 225$). There is an unintended inventory shortfall of $100 billion and a tendency for output to rise. Again, in terms of our macro two-question logic, what happens diverges from what was expected. We are thrown out of equilibrium. Output must adjust.

TABLE 10.6   The Change in Equilibrium Output with an Increase in Government Spending

(1)	(2)	(3)	(4)	(5)	(6)	(7)	(8)	(9)
Output	Taxes	Disposable Income	Saving	Consumption	Investment	Government Spending	Aggregate Demand	Unintended Inventory Accumulation(+) or Shortfall(−)
(Y)	(T)	(Y_D)	(S)	(C)	(I)	(G)	($AD = C + I + G$)	($Y − AD$)
800	100	700	125	575	100	225	900	−100
900	100	800	150	650	100	225	975	−75
1,000	100	900	175	725	100	225	1,050	−50
1,100	100	1,000	200	800	100	225	1,125	−25
1,200	100	1,100	225	875	100	225	1,200	0
1,300	100	1,200	250	950	100	225	1,275	25

Compare for equilibrium

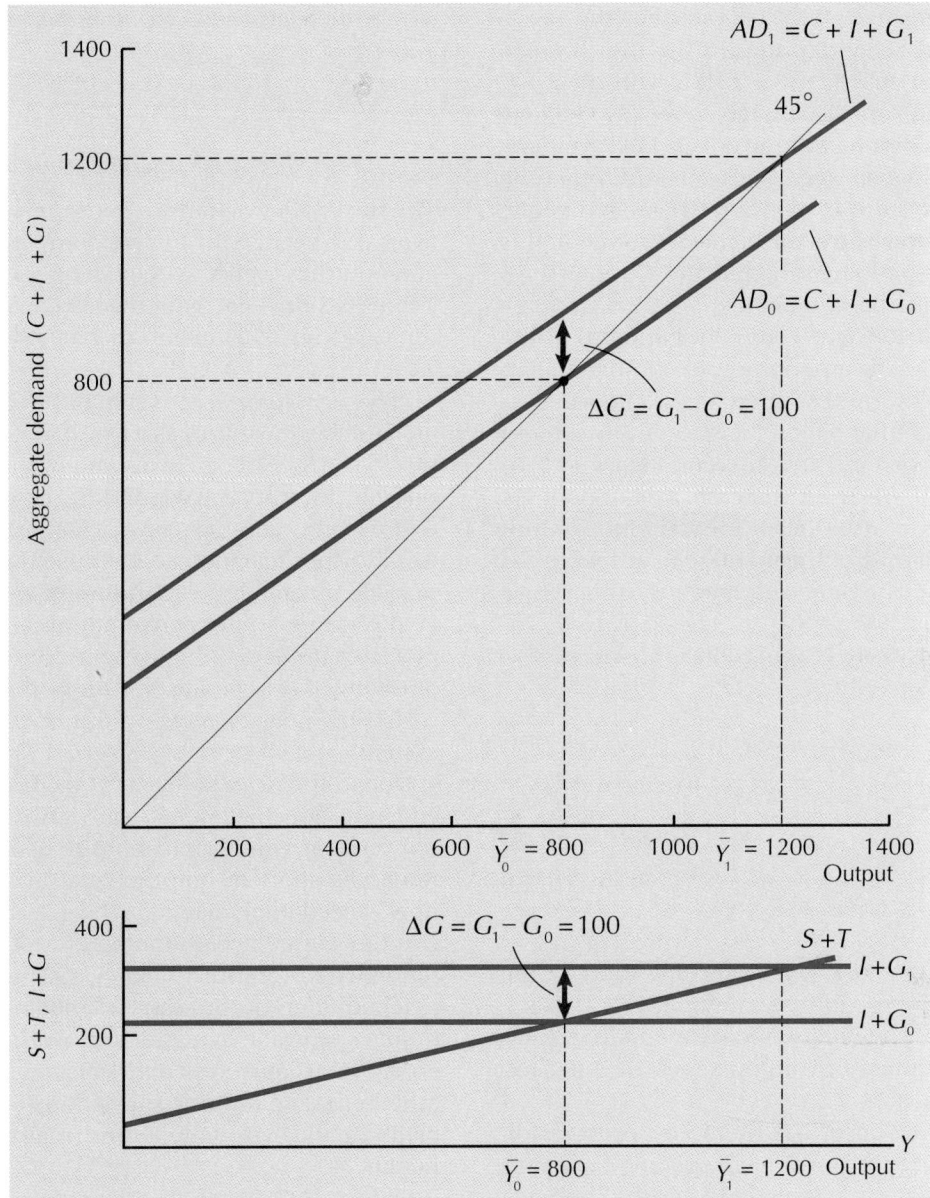

FIGURE 10.4 **The Effect of an Increase in Government Spending**

An increase of 100 units in government spending causes the equilibrium level of output to rise by 400 units, from 800 to 1200.

The new equilibrium output level is $1,200 billion, where aggregate demand is again equated with output. Injections equal leakages ($I + G = 325 = S + T$), and there is no undesired inventory shortfall or accumulation. Expectations then match realizations.

This adjustment of equilibrium output to a higher level of government expenditures is illus-

trated in Figure 10.4. The *initial* level of government spending of $125 billion is represented by G_0; the *higher* level of government spending of $225 billion is represented by G_1. Initially, the aggregate demand schedule is $AD_0 = C + I + G_0$, and investment plus government spending is given in the lower portion of the figure by $I + G_0$. Equilibrium output (Y_0) is $800 billion. The increase in government spending to G_1 ($225 billion) shifts the aggregate demand schedule upward (by the distance $G_1 - G_0 = 100$) to $AD_1 = C + I + G_1$, and the $I + G$ schedule shifts up (also by 100) to $I + G_1$. The new level of equilibrium output (Y_1) is $1,200 billion, where the higher aggregate demand schedule (AD_1) intersects the 45° line and where, in the lower portion of the figure, the higher investment plus government spending schedule $(I + G_1)$ intersects the saving plus taxes schedule $(S + T)$.

Both Table 10.6 and Figure 10.4 show that the effect on equilibrium output of a $100 billion increase in government spending is the same as the effect of a $100 billion increase in investment that we analyzed in Table 10.3 and Figure 10.3. In both cases, there is an increase in autonomous expenditures of $100 billion. Equilibrium output rises by a multiple of the increase in autonomous expenditures. The same autonomous expenditure multiplier that we applied in considering an increase in investment is applicable to an increase in government spending:

$$\Delta Y = \left(\frac{1}{1 - MPC}\right)\Delta G \qquad (10.9)$$

or

$$\frac{\Delta Y}{\Delta G} = \frac{1}{1 - MPC} \qquad (10.10)$$

In our example, $MPC = 0.75$ and the value of the autonomous expenditure multiplier is $4(1/(1 - 0.75))$. With a $100 billion increase in government spending, equilibrium output rises by $400 billion.

The explanation of the multiplier process following a change in government spending parallels that for a change in investment; only the source of the initial shock is different. Suppose that the increase in government spending comes in the form of increased purchases for national defense. The government begins to buy more tanks, ships, and aircraft from the business sector. As with an increase in investment expenditures, the increase in autonomous spending generates additional income, which is paid out to households, in this case, as payments for factor services to the defense-producing industries. Household disposable income rises. This induces an increase in consumption and begins the multiplier process,

which then proceeds as described previously in Table 10.4.

B
The Effect of a Change in Taxes

The next policy action we consider is a change in taxes. We begin with the economy in equilibrium at an output level of $1,200 billion, as described in Table 10.6. Now consider the effects of an *increase* in taxes from $100 billion to $200 billion.

1. The Tax Multiplier Table 10.7 shows the effect on equilibrium output as a result of the increase in taxes. The increase in taxes *lowers* the level of disposable income corresponding to each level of GNP; we now subtract 200 instead of 100 from GNP to get disposable income. Because the level of disposable income corresponding to each GNP level is lower, the level of consumption and, therefore, of aggregate demand corresponding to each level of GNP will also be lower. This is the channel by which tax policy affects output in the Keynesian system.

Due to the negative effect of the tax increase on consumption, the level of aggregate demand at the old level of equilibrium output of $1,200 billion now falls short of output. Total leakages $(S + T)$ now exceed total injections $(I + G)$. There is undesired inventory accumulation of $75 billion and a tendency for output to fall. A new equilibrium is reached at an output level of $900 billion. At this point, aggregate demand and output are again equal; total injections and leakages are equated; and there is no undesired inventory accumulation or shortfall. Expectations and realizations again match.

Figure 10.5 illustrates the effects of the tax increase. The initial level of tax collections of $100 billion is represented by T_0 in the graph and the new higher level by T_1. The increase in taxes shifts the consumption function downward from $C = 50 + 0.75(Y - T_0)$ to $C = 50 + 0.75(Y - T_1)$. Consequently, the aggregate demand schedule will also shift downward, from $AD_0 = (C + I + G)_0$ to $AD_1 = (C + I + G)_1$. The intersection of the aggregate demand schedule and the 45° line is moved to the left to the lower output level of $900 billion.

Comparing the effects on equilibrium output of

TABLE 10.7   The Change in Equilibrium Output with an Increase in Taxes

(1)	(2)	(3)	(4)	(5)	(6)	(7)	(8)	(9)
Output	Taxes	Disposable Income	Saving	Consumption	Investment	Government Spending	Aggregate Demand	Unintended Inventory Accumulation(+) or Shortfall(−)
(Y)	(T)	(Y_D)	(S)	(C)	(I)	(G)	$(AD = C + I + G)$	$(Y - AD)$
800	200	600	100	500	100	225	825	−25
900	200	700	125	575	100	225	900	0
1,000	200	800	150	650	100	225	975	25
1,100	200	900	175	725	100	225	1,050	50
1,200	200	1,000	200	800	100	225	1,125	75

Compare for equilibrium

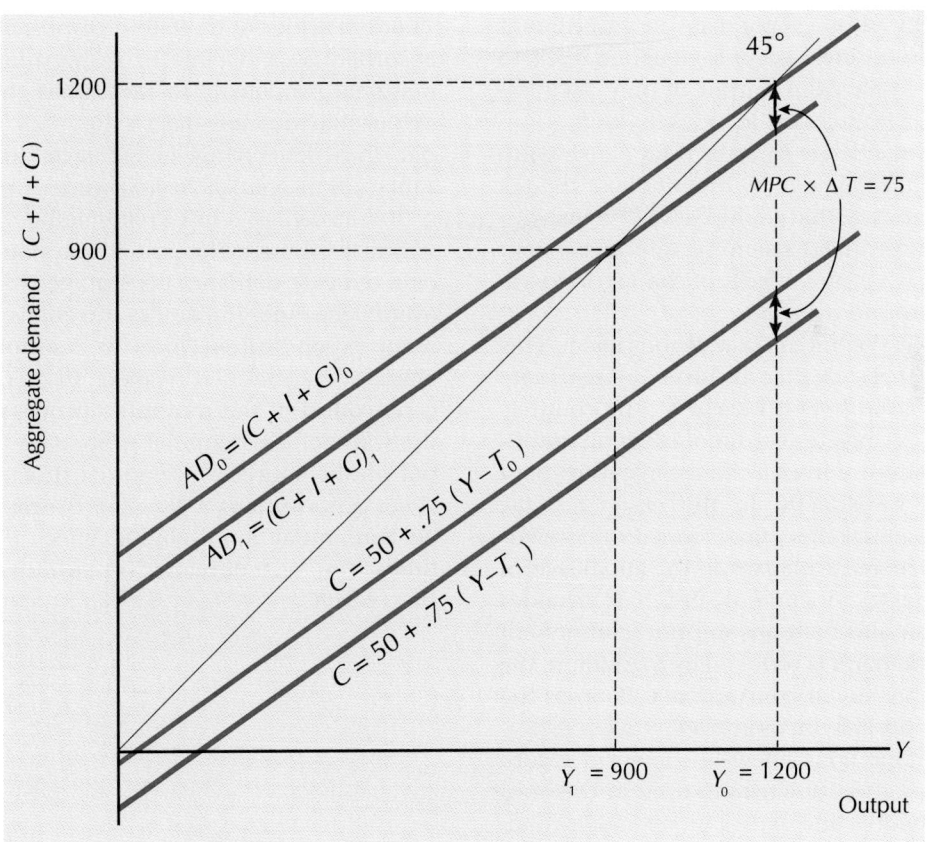

FIGURE 10.5   The Effects of an Increase in Taxes

An increase in taxes shifts the consumption function down from C = 50 + 0.75 (Y − T_0) to C = 50 + 0.75 (Y − T_1). The aggregate demand schedule consequently shifts down from AD_0 to AD_1. The level of equilibrium output falls from 1200 to 900 units.

a $100 billion increase in taxes with the effects of a $100 billion increase in government spending, as analyzed in the previous subsection, there are two differences. First, the tax increase causes equilibrium output to *decline*, whereas the increase in government spending causes equilibrium output to *rise*. The reason for this difference is obvious. The tax increase is a *restrictive* policy action because it reduces the level of disposable income and, hence, the level of consumption demand corresponding to a given level of GNP. The rise in government spending is an *expansionary* policy action that causes aggregate demand to increase.

The second difference between the effects of a $100 billion increase in taxes and an equal increase in government spending is that, per dollar, the government spending increase has a larger effect on equilibrium output than does the tax increase. The $100 billion increase in government spending causes equilibrium output to rise by $400 billion, or $4 per $1 increase in government spending. The tax increase of $100 billion leads to a decline in equilibrium output of only $300 billion, or $3 per $1 increase in taxes.

Note that the change in taxes *does* cause equilibrium output to change by a *multiple* of the tax change; in this case, that multiple was −3. As with changes in government spending and investment considered earlier, the effects of the tax increase can be broken into two parts.

First, there is the initial autonomous effect. This is the effect of the change in taxes on aggregate demand *at a given level of output (Y)*, the counterpart for a tax change to the direct effect on autonomous expenditures from a change in government spending or investment. In the case of a tax increase, this initial effect is on consumption. For a $100 billion increase in taxes, at the initial level of GNP (Y), disposable income ($Y_D = Y - T$) declines by $100 billion and the consumption component of aggregate demand is reduced by $75 billion, the marginal propensity to consume of 0.75 times the change in disposable income ($MPC \times \Delta T = 0.75 \times 100$). This autonomous effect is shown in Figure 10.5 as the negative (downward) shift in the consumption schedule and aggregate demand schedule of ($-MPC \times \Delta T$).

Besides this initial autonomous drop in consumption, there is the second effect—an *induced* decline. The initial drop in consumption causes

output to fall and, consequently, the national income flow to households declines. This additional drop in disposable income causes the further decline in consumption. This is the first round in the same type of multiplier process that occurs with changes in government spending and investment. In Figure 10.5 this adjustment is the movement down the consumption function as we go to the new equilibrium output level of $900 billion. Equilibrium output changes by a multiple of the change in taxes.

The reason the multiple by which output changes for a given change in taxes is smaller than for an equal change in government spending (or investment) is that *the initial autonomous change in aggregate demand is smaller*. An increase in taxes of $100 billion causes disposable income to fall by an equal amount, but the decline in consumption that results *directly* will be equal only to $MPC \times 100$, in this case $75 billion ($0.75 \times 100$). The remainder of the fall in disposable income is absorbed by a decline in saving that equals the marginal propensity to save times the decline in disposable income—$0.25 \times 100 = 25$, in our example. The initial change in aggregate demand with a $100 billion change in government expenditures or investment is a full $100 billion.

Due to the smaller initial autonomous impact on aggregate demand, tax changes have a smaller overall effect per dollar than do changes in government expenditures. Once we compute the initial change, the induced changes in consumption at each round of the multiplier process depend on the value of the marginal propensity to consume, not on the source of the initial shock. The overall effect on output as a result of the tax change will be the initial autonomous effect ($-MPC \times \Delta T$) times the autonomous expenditure multiplier ($1/(1 - MPC)$).

$$\Delta Y = (-MPC \times \Delta T) \times \frac{1}{1 - MPC}$$

or

$$\Delta Y = \frac{-MPC}{1 - MPC} \times \Delta T \qquad (10.11)$$

In the numerical example here we have

$$\Delta Y = \frac{-MPC}{1 - MPC} \times \Delta T$$

$$= \frac{-0.75}{1 - 0.75} \times 100$$

$$= -3 \times 100$$

$$\Delta Y = -300$$

This is the change in equilibrium output shown in Table 10.7, where output fell from $1,200 billion to $900 billion.

We can rewrite equation (10.11) as a **tax multiplier** that gives the change in equilibrium output per unit change in taxes:

$$\frac{\Delta Y}{\Delta T} = \frac{-MPC}{1 - MPC} \qquad (10.12)$$

In our example with $MPC = 0.75$, we have

$$\frac{\Delta Y}{\Delta T} = \frac{-0.75}{1 - 0.75} = -3$$

2. Government Transfer Payments   In Section I we defined disposable income Y_D as

$$Y_D = Y - T$$

where $Y = $ GNP
and $T = $ taxes − transfer payments

T is *net* taxes, with transfer payments subtracted. Net taxes is the net flow of payments that households make to the government.

Suppose, for example, that GNP equals $4,000 billion; (gross) tax payments are $900 billion, but households also receive $400 billion in transfer payments (Social Security payments, veterans' benefits, farm price supports, etc.). Net taxes would then be $500 billion and disposable income would be $3,500 billion (4,000 − 900 + 400). This net flow of payments by households to the government would change whenever tax payments varied *or* if the level of transfer payments varied. In this numerical example, net taxes would rise from $500 billion to $600 billion if either tax payments rose from $900 billion to $1,000 billion ($T = 1,000 − 400 = 600$) or transfer payments declined from $400 billion to $300 billion ($T = 900 − 300 = 600$).

It follows, then, that our (net) tax multiplier ($\Delta Y/\Delta T$) gives the effects of either an increase in tax payments or a *decrease* in transfer payments. Both are restrictive policy actions that reduce disposable income and therefore consumption. Conversely, decreases in taxes or increases in transfer payments are expansionary actions.

C

The Balanced Budget Multiplier

Table 10.8 compares the value of the autonomous expenditure multiplier, which gives the change in equilibrium output per unit change in govern-

TABLE 10.8   The Autonomous Expenditure Multiplier and the Tax Multiplier: Numerical Examples

Marginal Propensity to Consume (*MPC*)	Autonomous Expenditure Multiplier $1/(1 - MPC)$	Tax Multiplier $-MPC/(1 - MPC)$
0.9	$\dfrac{1}{1 - 0.9} = 10$	$\dfrac{-0.9}{1 - 0.9} = -9$
0.8	$\dfrac{1}{1 - 0.8} = 5$	$\dfrac{-0.8}{1 - 0.8} = -4$
0.75	$\dfrac{1}{1 - 0.75} = 4$	$\dfrac{-0.75}{1 - 0.75} = -3$
0.6	$\dfrac{1}{1 - 0.6} = 2.5$	$\dfrac{-0.6}{1 - 0.6} = -1.5$
0.5	$\dfrac{1}{1 - 0.5} = 2$	$\dfrac{-0.5}{1 - 0.5} = -1$

ment spending (or investment), and the tax multiplier ($\Delta Y/\Delta T$) for various values of the marginal propensity to consume. It can be seen that in each case the tax multiplier is opposite in sign to the autonomous expenditure multiplier and exactly one less in absolute value. Thus, in our example, with $MPC = 0.75$, the autonomous expenditure multiplier was $+4$ and the tax multiplier was -3. This relationship between the two multipliers gives rise to an interesting result when we consider the effects of an increase in government spending accompanied by an equal increase in taxes, *a balanced budget increase*. To find the effect of a 1-unit increase in government spending together with a 1-unit increase in taxes, we combine the two multipliers, $\Delta Y/\Delta G$ and $\Delta Y/\Delta T$, as follows

$$\frac{\Delta Y}{\Delta G} + \frac{\Delta Y}{\Delta T} = \frac{1}{1 - MPC} + \left(\frac{-MPC}{1 - MPC}\right)$$

$$= \frac{1 - MPC}{1 - MPC} = 1$$

The combination of a \$1 billion increase in government spending and a \$1 billion increase in taxes causes equilibrium output to rise by \$1 billion. This expression is called the **balanced budget multiplier.** The balanced budget multiplier is 1 because the tax multiplier is smaller in absolute value than the government expenditure multiplier by 1 unit.[2]

We see an example of the effects of an increase in government spending accompanied by an equal increase in taxes by putting together the results in Table 10.6 and 10.7. Table 10.6 shows the effects of a \$100 billion increase in government spending. Equilibrium output rises from \$800 billion to \$1,200 billion, a total of \$400 billion, or \$4 per \$1 increase in government spending. Table 10.7 shows that an equal increase of \$100 billion in taxes causes equilibrium output to fall from \$1,200 billion to \$900 billion, a total of \$300 billion, or \$3 per \$1 increase in taxes. The effect of the combination of policies is that a balanced budget increase of \$100 billion results in a \$100 billion

---

[2]Note that the term *balanced budget multiplier* is used because we are considering a change in government spending (G) just *balanced* by a change in taxes (T). This will leave the budget deficit (G − T) unchanged. The deficit, however, need not be zero, that is, we need not have a balanced budget in that sense (G = T).

increase in equilibrium output, from \$800 billion to \$900 billion, or by precisely \$1 per \$1 balanced increase in the budget.

In more complicated models, the precise relationship between the size of the autonomous expenditure ($\Delta Y/\Delta G$) and tax ($\Delta Y/\Delta T$) multipliers will not hold, so the balanced budget multiplier will not continue to be 1. The result that tax changes affect aggregate demand by less per dollar than do changes in government spending is, however, a quite general one. Consequently, balanced increases in the budget causes equilibrium output to rise; balanced decreases in the budget cause equilibrium output to fall.

■ *CHECK YOUR BEARINGS*

The preceding two subsections have examined how changes in certain variables affect the level of equilibrium output. In each case, the change in equilibrium output per unit change in the variable is given by a multiplier. These multipliers are summarized in Table 10.9.

IV

Fiscal Stabilization Policy in the Keynesian Model

We have seen that shifts in the unstable investment component of aggregate demand cause instability in the general level of economic activity via the multiplier process. Fiscal policy instruments, namely, the levels of government spending and taxes, also have multiplier effects on the level of aggregate output in the Keynesian model. In the model, fiscal stabilization policy uses these instruments to stabilize aggregate demand by *offsetting* shifts in the unstable investment component.

Suppose, for example, that the economy is running at a level of activity that provides reasonably full employment, but the government predicts a decline in investment spending of \$75 billion for the coming year. If, as in our example, $MPC = 0.75$ and the autonomous expenditure multiplier was therefore equal to 4, this decline in autonomous expenditure would cause output to fall by \$300 billion (4×75). An undesirable rise in unemploy-

TABLE 10.9 Summary of Multipliers Determining ΔY (The Unit Change in Output Per Unit Change in I, G, or T)

English Label	Symbolic Form	Numerical Example	Comments
Autonomous expenditure multiplier	$\dfrac{1}{1 - MPC}$ or $\dfrac{1}{MPS}$	$\dfrac{1}{1 - 0.75} = 4$ or $\dfrac{1}{0.25} = 4$	Applies to ΔG or ΔI
Tax multiplier	$\dfrac{-MPC}{1 - MPC}$	$\dfrac{-0.75}{1 - 0.75} = -3$	Applies to ΔT and is negative
Balanced budget multiplier	$\dfrac{1 - MPC}{1 - MPC} = 1$	$\dfrac{1 - 0.75}{1 - 0.75} = 1$	This is the combination of ΔG and ΔT multipliers: $\dfrac{1}{1 - MPC} - \dfrac{MPC}{1 - MPC} = \dfrac{1 - MPC}{1 - MPC}$

ment would result because less output means less employment.

Policymakers could, by taking the proper expansionary fiscal policy action, offset the decline in investment, maintain the initial level of aggregate demand, and prevent the rise in unemployment. This could be accomplished by a $75 billion increase in government spending. Because, dollar for dollar, changes in government spending and investment have the same effect on equilibrium output ($\Delta Y/\Delta G = \Delta Y/\Delta I = 1/(1 - MPC)$), the increase of $75 billion in the level of government spending would offset the effect of the decline in investment.

Alternatively, policymakers could cut taxes. Because, dollar for dollar, changes in taxes have smaller effects on equilibrium output than changes in investment, offsetting the effect of the decline in investment would require a tax cut of more than $75 billion. In our example ($MPC = 0.75$), the $75 billion decline in investment, without any fiscal policy action, would cause equilibrium output to fall by $300 billion because the autonomous expenditure multiplier equals 4. A tax cut of $100 billion would offset the effects of the decline in investment because, for this case, the tax multiplier is -3 ($-3 \times -100 = +300$).

Whether by a tax cut or an increase in government spending, the role of fiscal policy is to offset undesirable changes in private sector aggregate demand and, therefore, to stabilize equilibrium output at a high-employment level.

Read Perspective 10.

SUMMARY

1. We extended our analysis of the Keynesian model to include a government sector. We then examined the factors that cause equilibrium output to change in the Keynesian model. Changes in the unstable investment component of aggregate demand were seen to cause changes in the overall level of economic activity via the multiplier process. An autonomous change in investment causes equilibrium output to change by a multiple of the change in investment, the value of that multiple being the Keynesian autonomous expenditure multiplier ($1/(1 - MPC)$).

2. Changes in the level of government expenditures have the same multiplier effects on the level of equilibrium output as changes in investment ($\Delta Y/\Delta G = \Delta Y/\Delta I = 1/(1 - MPC)$).

3. Changes in taxes also have multiplier effects. Such effects are in the opposite direction to those of changes in investment or government spending. Increases in taxes cause equilibrium output to fall, for example, while increases in

---

PERSPECTIVE 10
Fiscal Policy in Practice

An example of fiscal stabilization policy within the Keynesian framework is the Kennedy-Johnson tax cut of 1964. There had been a serious recession in 1958 during which the unemployment rate had risen from 4.3 percent (in 1957) to 6.8 percent. There had only been a short-lived recovery from this recession in 1959. In 1960 the economy sank back into a recession, which many believe cost Richard Nixon the presidency that year in his first try for the office. The Kennedy administration came into office in 1961 with a program to get the economy moving again through the application of Keynesian theory to macroeconomic policy. Their program—called the *new economics*—entailed a large cut in both personal and business taxes.

Kennedy's economic advisers believed that aggregate demand was too low for the economy to operate at a high-employment level. The unemployment rate in 1961, for example, was 6.7 percent, compared to the 4.0 percent then considered to be "full" employment. In terms of Figure 10.5, the tax *cut* was intended to shift the consumption schedule, and therefore the ag-

gregate demand schedule, upward sufficiently to increase output up to potential output.

Nonetheless, the Kennedy administration could not persuade Congress to enact the tax cut, mainly because congressional leaders worried over the budget deficit that the tax cut would create. After Kennedy's assassination, however, President Lyndon Johnson persuaded Congress to enact a tax cut of 20 percent for persons and 10 percent for businesses early in 1964. Output and employment then grew rapidly; the unemployment rate fell to 4.8 percent by the first half of 1965 and to 3.8 percent in 1966. This was the high point of influence for the Keynesian theory of fiscal policy.

As U.S. involvement in the Vietnam War grew in the 1966–68 period, however, government spending on defense increased rapidly. This increase in aggregate demand, with the economy already at potential output, generated inflationary pressures. The 1960s demonstrated that, in practice, fiscal policy could destabilize as well as stabilize the economy.

---

government spending or in investment cause equilibrium output to rise. Tax increases are restrictive policy actions. By reducing disposable income, they lower consumption. Per unit, changes in taxes have smaller effects on output than do changes in investment or government spending; the tax multiplier ($\Delta Y/\Delta T = -MPC/(1 - MPC)$) is smaller than the autonomous expenditure multiplier ($1/(1 - MPC)$).

4. In the Keynesian model, because changes in government spending and taxes affect equilibrium output, there is a role for fiscal stabilization policies. Fiscal policy should stabilize aggregate demand, offsetting the effects of changes in unstable investment demand.

5. The analysis here and in Chapter 9 highlights some of the main features of the Keynesian revolution within a very simple model. Keynes believed that aggregate demand was very impor-

tant in determining the level of equilibrium output. The model constructed here illustrates the way in which aggregate demand affects the level of equilibrium output.

6. The simple and incomplete nature of the model in these chapters must, however, be kept in mind. Not only are supply factors omitted, but we have not yet brought the monetary sector into the model. Even when these additions are made, we will be left with only a highly simplified, highly aggregate model that attempts to capture some important features of the real economy. The implications and results of the model provide insights into the real economy, but they cannot be taken too literally. For example, our description of the effects of fiscal policy actions, if taken literally, implies a much too mechanical working of the economy; a $100 billion change in government spending results in a

$400 billion change in income, etc. If policymakers could act with such certainty, their jobs would be much simpler than they are in reality. The later chapters on economic policies add more real-world features to our models and, we hope, suggest the complications as well as the potential for stabilization policy.

Appendix

An Algebraic Interpretation of the Simple Keynesian Model

In the appendix to Chapter 9, we provide an algebraic treatment of income determination in the Keynesian model containing firms and households. Here we extend the model to include the government sector, as was done in the graphic and numerical examples in this chapter. We also provide an algebraic interpretation of the Keynesian autonomous expenditure multiplier.

The Simple Keynesian Model with a Government Sector

With the addition of a government sector, the condition for equilibrium output in the Keynesian model becomes

$$Y = AD = C + I + G \qquad (10.1)$$

The consumption function is

$$C = a + b\,Y_D \qquad (A.1)$$
$$a > 0$$
$$0 < b < 1$$

where $Y_D = Y - T$. Relative to the appendix in Chapter 9, we have added the government spending component (G) to aggregate demand in equation (10.1), and we now must subtract taxes (T) from GNP (Y) to get disposable income (Y_D), the income concept relevant for consumption expenditures.

Substituting equation (A.1) into equation (10.1), and using the definition of disposable income ($Y_D = Y - T$), we can write the following expressions for equilibrium output:

$$
\begin{aligned}
Y &= C + I + G \\
&= a + bY_D + I + G \\
&= a + b(Y - T) + I + G \\
&= a + bY - bT + I + G \\
(Y - bY) &= a - bT + I + G \\
(1 - b)Y &= a - bT + I + G \\
\bar{Y} &= \frac{1}{1 - b}(a - bT + I + G), \qquad (A.2)
\end{aligned}
$$

where, as in the appendix to Chapter 9, the bar over Y indicates an equilibrium value for output.

We can use equation (A.2) to compute the level of equilibrium output with given values of I, G, and T and for assumed values of the parameters of the consumption function, a and b. In Section I we had

$$I = 100$$
$$G = 125$$
$$T = 100$$

The consumption function was

$$C = 50 + 0.75Y_D,$$

so we had

$$a = 50$$
$$b = 0.75$$

Putting these values into equation (A.2), we find

$$
\begin{aligned}
Y &= \frac{1}{1 - b}(a - bT + I + G) \\
&= \frac{1}{1 - 0.75} \times (50 - 0.75 \times 100 + 100 + 125) \\
&= 4(200) \\
&= 800,
\end{aligned}
$$

which is the result we found in Table 10.1.

The Autonomous Expenditure Multiplier

Equation (A.2) can be broken into two parts as follows:

$$Y = \underbrace{\frac{1}{1 - b}}_{\text{(autonomous expenditure } \times \text{ multiplier)}} \underbrace{(a - bT + I + G)}_{\text{(autonomous expenditures)}}$$

$$Y = \begin{array}{c}\text{(autonomous} \\ \text{expenditure} \times \\ \text{multiplier)}\end{array} \qquad (A.3)$$

The first term $1/(1 - b) = 1/(1 - MPC)$ is the autonomous expenditure multiplier explained in Section II. The second term is the sum of the components of autonomous expenditures: government spending (G), investment spending (I), the element of consumption expenditure that does not depend on income (a), and the effect of taxes on consumption $(-bT)$.

Now consider the effect of a change in any of these elements of autonomous expenditures. First, let investment change, holding constant the other terms in parenthesis in equation (A.2). We then have

$$\Delta Y = \frac{1}{1 - b}(\Delta I)$$

or

$$\frac{\Delta Y}{\Delta I} = \frac{1}{1 - b} = \frac{1}{1 - MPC}$$

As we found in the chapter, the change in equilibrium income equals the change in autonomous expenditures (ΔI) times the autonomous expenditure multiplier $(1/(1 - b) = 1/(1 - MPC))$. Similarly, we can let G vary and find

$$\frac{\Delta Y}{\Delta G} = \frac{1}{1 - b}$$

For a change in taxes, we have

$$\Delta Y = \frac{1}{1 - b}(-b\Delta T) = \frac{-b}{1 - b}\Delta T$$

$$\frac{\Delta Y}{\Delta T} = \frac{-b}{1 - b}$$

As taxes change, autonomous expenditures decline by b dollars per \$1 change in taxes. The change in equilibrium income per unit change in taxes is $-b$ (the change in autonomous expenditures) times the autonomous expenditure multiplier $(1/(1 - b))$.

In the chapter, the value of $MPC(b)$ was 0.75. We had therefore

$$\frac{\Delta Y}{\Delta I} = \frac{\Delta Y}{\Delta G} = \frac{1}{1 - b} = \frac{1}{1 - 0.75} = 4$$

$$\frac{\Delta Y}{\Delta T} = \frac{-b}{1 - b} = \frac{-0.75}{1 - 0.75} = -3$$

The final multiplier concept discussed in the chapter is the balanced budget multiplier, which gives the effect of a change in government spending (ΔG) financed by a change of equal magnitude in taxes (ΔT). From equation (A.2) we can compute the effect of such a balanced budget change as

$$\Delta Y = \frac{1}{1 - b}(\Delta G - b\Delta T)$$

Since $\Delta G = \Delta T$, by assumption, we can rewrite this expression as

$$\Delta Y = \frac{1}{1 - b}(\Delta G - b\Delta G)$$

$$\Delta Y = \frac{1 - b}{1 - b}\Delta G = \Delta G$$

Equilibrium output rises by precisely the amount of the increase in G; the balanced budget multiplier is 1. This follows for any value of the $MPC(b)$. The fact that the balanced budget multiplier is always 1 reflects the fact that the tax multiplier is smaller in absolute value than the government spending multiplier by just 1 unit for each value of the MPC. In the preceding examples, with $MPC = 0.75$, for example, the government spending multiplier is 4 and the tax multiplier is -3.

KEY TERMS

Net taxes
Autonomous expenditure multiplier
Keynesian fiscal stabilization policy

Tax multiplier
Balanced budget multiplier

QUESTIONS AND PROBLEMS

1. What is fiscal policy?
2. What are transfer payments? When did they appear in the model developed in this chapter?
3. Using the following information, make a table which shows the equilibrium income level:

   $C = 20 + 0.80\,Y_D$
   $I = 125$
   $G = 100$
   $T = 75$

4. Confirm the result in Question 3 using a graph (as in Figure 10.2).
5. Suppose that business forecasts turn gloomy and desired investment drops from $125 billion to $75 billion as a result. If no other autonomous change occurs, how will the drop in investment alter the equilibrium income level of Question 3? Show this graphically and in table form.
6. One way to describe the multiplier process which is triggered by an autonomous change in investment is by use of a flowchart such as this:

$$\Delta I \;\rightarrow\; \Delta Y \rightarrow \Delta C \;\rightarrow\; \Delta Y \rightarrow \Delta C \;\rightarrow\; \Delta Y \rightarrow \Delta C \;\rightarrow\; \dots$$
$$\searrow \Delta S \qquad\quad \searrow \Delta S \qquad\quad \searrow \Delta S$$

Using the same data as in Question 3 and the change in investment of − $50 billion described in Question 5, fill in the amounts of each change shown in the flowchart (for 3 rounds of the multiplier process), beginning with $\Delta I =$ − $50 billion.

7. According to Keynes, what caused the Great Depression?
8. In the Keynesian model, which will have a greater expansionary impact on equilibrium output, a $75 billion government expenditures increase or a $75 billion tax decrease? Explain why.
9. To rid the economy of a recession (high unemployment), a Keynesian economist would recommend what fiscal policy actions?

11

Money and the Interest Rate

Between 1929 and 1933 the U.S. money supply fell by one third. Over 9,000 banks failed. The decline in the money supply was one important cause (some economists would argue, *the* cause) of the Great Depression. Proper control of money and of the financial system via monetary policy is clearly crucial to economic stability. In this chapter, we consider the role of money and monetary policy in the Keynesian system. As a part of this analysis, we examine the factors that determine the interest rate and, additionally, the relationship between the interest rate and aggregate demand. Before getting on with these tasks, however, we need to answer the question *What is money?*

I

The Definition of Money

A

The Functions of Money

The standard way to define money is as whatever performs monetary functions, and there are three widely accepted functions of money:

Means of exchange—money serves as a medium for transactions. You can buy goods or services with money. You receive money for sales of goods or services. We don't often think about it, but this function of money contributes greatly to economic efficiency. Exchange without money would mean swaps of goods for goods—what is called *barter*. Some barter transactions exist even in a monetary economy. You might trade babysitting services for a free room in a house near campus, for example.

But barter as the predominant means of trade is very inefficient. The problem is that barter transactions require a *double coincidence of wants*. Ms. Jones wants to buy shoes and sell jewelry. Ms. Smith wants to sell shoes but wants to buy a computer. No trade takes place, and both must take time to look for trading partners whose buying *and* selling desires coincide with theirs. In a monetary economy, Ms. Jones buys the shoes from Ms. Smith with money. Ms. Smith can then use the money to buy a computer from *anyone* selling one. Ms. Jones needs only to find someone who wants to buy jewelry (without necessarily wanting to sell shoes).

Store of value—money functions as a store for wealth, a way to save for future spending. Money is one type of financial asset (see Perspective 11A). Other stores of value (e.g., a corporate or government bond) are not money because they do not perform the other monetary functions. They cannot be used as a means of exchange or as a unit of account, the third central function of money.

Unit of account—prices are measured in terms of money. In Albania prices (and debts) are measured in terms of the lek, in Poland the zloty, in Britain the pound. In the United States, you already know that prices and debts are measured in dollars and cents. As with the means of exchange function, money provides great convenience as a unit of account. Merchants, for example, simply post one price in dollars (or leks), not in terms of each possible commodity that might be traded for their goods.

B

Components of the Money Supply

The money supply is composed of those financial assets that serve the preceding functions. Which assets are these in the United States? This question is harder to answer than it might at first appear. In fact, there are several different measures of the money supply. All are composed of currency and deposits at commercial banks and other depository institutions (e.g., savings and loan associations).

One measure, called **M1**, is the narrowest of the money measures in the United States. It consists of currency plus *checkable* deposits.

214

Checkable deposits are those on which you can write checks, that is, those on which you can direct the bank in writing to make payments to another party.[1] Currency clearly fulfills the three monetary functions previously discussed.[2] So do bank deposits as long as you can write checks on them. Checks on deposits can be used to buy things (means of exchange function); the deposits are a store of value, and currency or deposits are a unit of account.

Two other measures, **M2** and **M3**, are broader. They include all the components of M1 plus some additional bank deposits that have no or only limited provisions for checks.

M2, for example, includes money market mutual fund accounts, which allow only checks for amounts above some minimum (e.g. $500), and also regular savings and time deposits on which no checks can be written.[3] M3 is an even broader measure of money that includes large deposits, termed _certificates of deposit_ (CDs), on which no checks can be written. Details of the composition of each of these measures of money, as well as figures for the level of these measures for September 1987, are given in Table 11.1.

The rationale for the broader money measures is that the additional deposit categories included in them relative to M1 are very similar to checkable deposits or easily converted to checkable deposits. Balances in regular saving accounts, for example, can be converted into checkable deposits (or currency) simply by going to the bank. If these additional deposit types are sufficiently close substitutes for checkable deposits and currency, we may want to consider them as money.

---

[1]Another small item included in M1 is travelers' checks. Our discussion here ignores a number of small items in the different definitions of money. For detailed definitions, see the footnote to Table 11.1.

[2]Often in the discussion it is convenient to refer to deposits as _bank_ deposits, but keep in mind that other institutions such as savings and loan associations and credit unions, which are not strictly banks, provide some of these deposit accounts.

[3]Balances in regular savings accounts are, in practice, available on demand. Time deposits, however, are for a specified time period (e.g., 1 year), and there may be penalties for early withdrawal.

TABLE 11.1 Money Supply Measures (Billions of Dollars), September 1987*

M1	$ 760.7
M2	2,893.3
M3	3,650.3

*The composition of the money stock measures is as follows: M1: averages of daily figures for (1) currency outside the Treasury, Federal Reserve Banks, and the vaults of commercial banks; (2) travelers' checks on nonbank issuers; (3) demand deposits at all commercial banks other than those due to domestic banks, the U.S. government, and foreign banks and official institutions less cash items in the process of collection and Federal Reserve float; and (4) negotiable order of withdrawal (NOW) and automatic transfer service (ATS) accounts at banks and thrift institutions, credit union share draft accounts (CUSD), and demand deposits at mutual savings banks.
M2: M1 plus savings and small-denomination time deposits at all depository institutions, overnight repurchase agreements at commercial banks, overnight Eurodollars held by U.S. residents other than banks at Caribbean branches of member banks, money market mutual fund shares, and money market deposit accounts (MMDAs).
M3: M2 plus large-denomination time deposits at all depository institutions and term repurchase agreements at commercial banks and savings and loan associations.

C
Who Controls the Money Supply?

What determines the level of the money supply? Why, for example, was the M1 measure of money $760.7 billion in September 1987? In modern industrialized countries, _central banks_ have an important role in determining the level of the money supply. Central banks are government agencies that regulate financial markets and conduct monetary policy.

The U.S. central banking system is the **Federal Reserve System**. The Federal Reserve System (Federal Reserve for short) is composed of 12 regional Federal Reserve banks and the Board of Governors located in Washington, D.C.

In the chapters that follow we will, for simplicity, assume that the central bank, the Federal Reserve, alone controls the money stock. However, as we will see in Chapter 17, financial institutions and the nonbank public also have a potential role in determining the money supply.

How does the Federal Reserve control the money supply? It controls currency directly, since currency is issued by the Federal Reserve System; the bills in your pocket or purse are Federal Reserve notes (check the top of one).

How the Federal Reserve controls the volume of bank deposits is more complex and is discussed in detail in Chapter 17. For now, it is enough to know that the Federal Reserve requires banks to hold *legal reserve* assets equal to a portion of their deposits. Assets that qualify as legal reserves are currency and funds deposited at the regional Federal Reserve banks. The Federal Reserve controls the quantity of these assets in order to control, in turn, the level of the money supply. If the Federal Reserve wants to expand the money supply, it makes more legal reserves available to back up deposits; to contract the money supply, it reduces the quantity of legal reserves. How the Federal Reserve controls bank reserves is also explained in Chapter 17. For now, simply keep in mind the general process of money supply control, as illustrated in Figure 11.1.

We have seen what money does and what money is. In the rest of the chapter, we will examine the Keynesian view of the role of money in the macroeconomy. How does the quantity of money affect important macroeconomic variables such as output, employment, and the aggregate price level?

II

The Role of Money: Keynes versus the Classics

In the classical view, the quantity of money determined aggregate demand and, consequently, the price level. This was the *quantity theory of money.* Classical economists stressed the direct link between changes in the quantity of *money* (the money supply) and changes in the demand for *goods* (aggregate demand). If the money supply increased, the supply would exceed the amount of money demanded by the public. The excess of money supplied over money demanded would *spill over* to the goods market as an excess demand for goods, causing the price level to rise. When the price level had risen proportionately with the quantity of money, the demand for money would also have increased proportionately with the quantity of money. Because of the higher price level, proportionately more money balances would be needed for transactions. This follows because the turnover rate of money, its *velocity*, was assumed to be constant in the short run.[4]

Keynes questioned the importance of the direct, almost mechanical, link in the quantity theory between changes in the quantity of money and the demand for output. Such a relationship did characterize European nations in the sixteenth century, when gold and silver from the Americas came into their economies and drove up commodity prices. But in the industralized nations of the twentieth century, money was put into the system by the central bank, for the most part, via the banking system (see Figure 11.1). The major effect of such infusions of money via the banking system, Keynes believed, was to make credit available at a lower cost—*to lower the rate of interest.* In Keynes's view, the rate of interest was the key link between changes in the money supply and the level of aggregate demand.

In the Keynesian view, an increase in the money supply would lower the interest rate. As discussed in Chapter 9, the level of investment varies inversely with the level of the interest rate—lower interest

---

[4]Recall from Chapter 8 that velocity is, by the equation of exchange, equal to the ratio of income to the money supply ($MV = Py$; thus, $V = Py/M$). Constant velocity therefore means that income (Py) must change proportionately with the money supply (M).

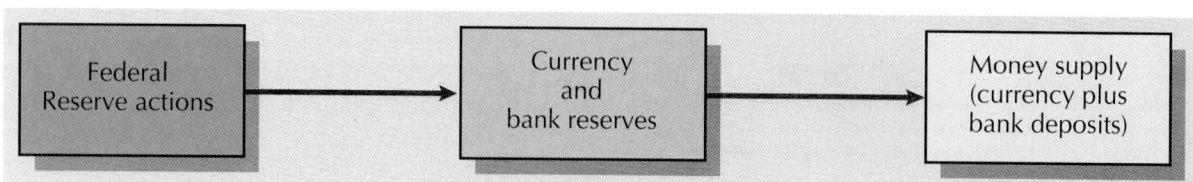

FIGURE 11.1 Money Supply Control

rate, higher investment (or higher interest rate, lower investment). Therefore, according to Keynes, as the interest rate fell, investment would increase, with a consequent multiplier effect on aggregate demand. Equilibrium output would rise. This sequence is illustrated in Figure 11.2. Conversely, a decline in the quantity of money would lead to a rise in the rate of interest, as banks tightened credit, and to falls in investment, aggregate demand, and equilibrium output.

III
The Keynesian View of the Money Market

Figure 11.3(a) depicts the money market from a Keynesian viewpoint. The quantity of money (M) is measured on the horizontal axis and the rate of

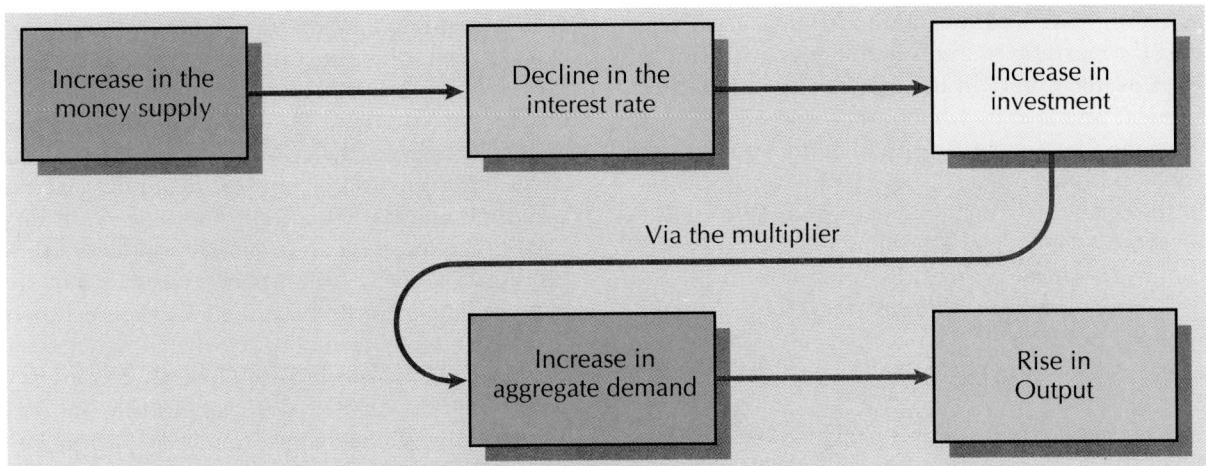

FIGURE 11.2   *The Effects of an Expansionary Monetary Policy: A Keynesian View*

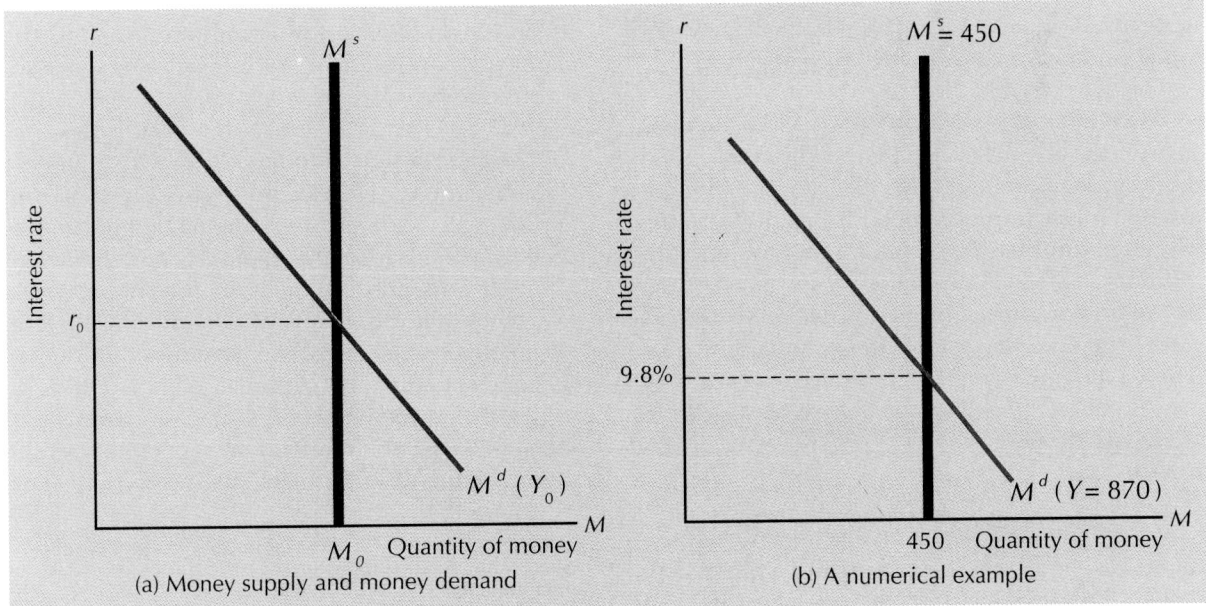

FIGURE 11.3   *A Keynesian View of the Money Market*

interest (r) is measured on the vertical axis. We assume that the Federal Reserve controls the money supply, measured, for example, by the M1 definition (currency plus checkable deposits). Consequently, the money supply schedule (M^s) is a vertical line at the Federal Reserve's set level of the money supply. The money supply is independent of the interest rate (r). But the money supply schedule can shift to the right or left, depending on Federal Reserve policy.

For reasons to be discussed shortly, the money demand function (M^d) is a downward-sloping schedule when plotted against the interest rate, and the position of the schedule depends on the level of income, Y_0 in the figure. The equilibrium interest rate is at r_0, where money demand is just equal to the money supply. Figure 11.3(b) illustrates a numerical example of equilibrium in the money market. The money supply is assumed to be set at $450 billion. The money demand schedule is drawn for an income level of $870 billion. The equilibrium interest rate in this case is shown as 9.8 percent.

A

Keynes's Theory of Money Demand

The money demand schedule in Figure 11.3(a) reflects Keynes's theory of the demand for money. In Keynes's theory, the demand for money depends on income and on the interest rate.

1. Money Demand and Income As in classical theory, Keynes believed that individuals hold money to use in transactions. The amount of money held for this purpose depends positively on the volume of transactions, meaning that the amount of money held for transactions rises (falls) when the volume of transactions rises (falls). Keynes, as well as the classical economists, assumed income to be a good measure of the volume of transactions and, therefore, *the demand for money was assumed to depend positively on the level of income.*

2. Money Demand and the Interest Rate The Keynesian theory of money demand, while recognizing the demand for money for use in transactions, also recognized that there was an

opportunity cost associated with holding money. To see this, consider an individual with a given amount of wealth, say $20,000. He has the choice of holding his wealth in money (e.g., currency plus checkable deposits) or other, **nonmonetary assets** such as stocks and bonds. We will refer to all these nonmonetary assests simply as *bonds* (see Perspective 11A for a description of some real-world nonmonetary assets). By holding money, the individual foregoes the interest payments that would be earned if all his wealth were invested in bonds.[5] This opportunity cost affects demand. As the interest rate paid on bonds (or other nonmonetary assets) rises, people economize on transactions balances to take advantage of the higher interest rate. *The quantity of money demanded depends negatively on the level of the interest rate* (paid on bonds), meaning that the amount of money demanded rises (falls) with a fall (rise) in the interest rate. Classical economists had not systematically considered this effect of the interest rate on money demand. In classical theory, money demand depended solely on income. If the demand for money depends on the interest rate as well as on the level of income, then velocity, which is the ratio of income to money, will *not* be a constant. This follows because, for a given level of income, people will hold differing amounts of money depending on the level of the interest rate. Keynes's theory of money demand therefore was an attack on the central assumption behind the classical quantity theory of money—the constancy of velocity.

3. The Keynesian Money Demand Schedule Consider the money demand schedule shown in Figure 11.3(a) or 11.3(b). The schedule slopes downward because the quantity of money demanded depends inversely on the interest rate. The demand for money also depends on the level of income. This is why we draw the money demand schedule for a given level of income, Y_0 in the figure. At a given interest rate, an increase in income causes the demand for money to rise; the money demand schedule shifts to the right. This

---

[5]Some components of M1 (e.g., Super NOW accounts) do pay interest, but at lower rates than can be earned on bonds or other nonmonetary assets. The opportunity cost of holding such deposits is the difference between their deposit rate and the higher rate on the nonmonetary asset.

follows because at a higher level of income more money is needed for a higher level of transactions. Conversely, a fall in income shifts the money demand schedule to the left. For example, in Figure 11.4 we see how a rise in income from $870 billion to $920 billion shifts the money demand schedule to the right.

B

The Money Supply and the Interest Rate

Consider the effect in the money market of an increase in the money supply from the level M_0^s to a higher level, M_1^s, as shown in Figure 11.5. At the initial equilibrium interest rate, r_0, there is now an _excess supply of money;_ money supply exceeds money demand. The excess supply of money puts downward pressure on the rate of interest. The Federal Reserve has increased the money supply, but at the initial interest rate the public does not want to increase its money holdings. Corresponding to the excess supply of money is an _excess demand for bonds_ (our term for all nonmonetary financial assets). The public will attempt to exchange the new money for bonds. As the public

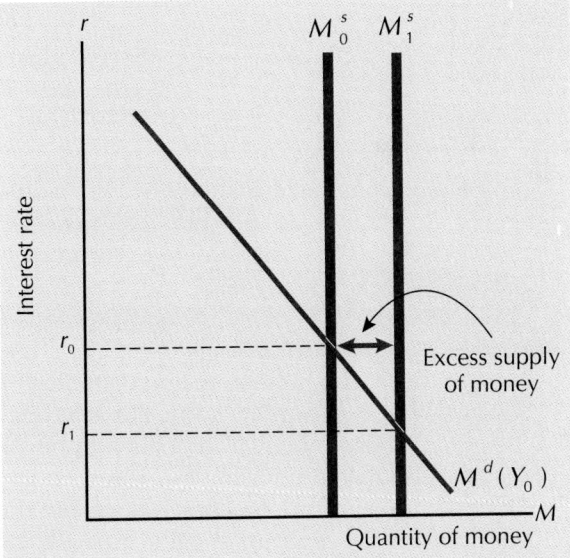

FIGURE 11.5 _The Money Stock and the Interest Rate_

An increase in the money supply from M_0^s to M_1^s creates an excess of money supply relative to money demand at the initial interest rate r_0. The interest rate falls to r_1, where money supply and money demand are again equal.

tries to buy more bonds, the terms on which the sellers of bonds, borrowers such as firms and the government, can raise funds will improve; _the interest rate falls._ The fall in the interest rate increases the quantity of money demanded. A new equilibrium is reached at r_1, where the interest rate has fallen enough to increase the quantity of money demanded up to the higher level of the money supply (M_1^s).

IV

The Interest Rate, Aggregate Demand, and Equilibrium Output

Now we are ready to tackle the key difference between the Keynesian system and the classical system where money is concerned. Recall that in the classical system, variations in the money supply had _no_ effect on aggregate _output._ Money supply changes pushed the price level up or pressed it

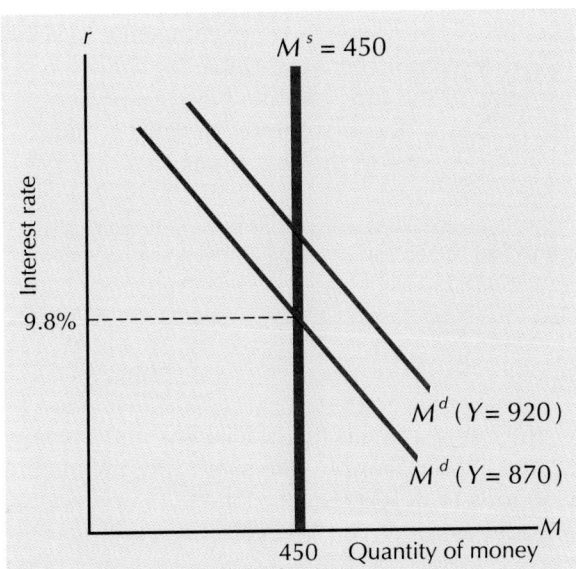

FIGURE 11.4 _The Effect on Money Demand of an Increase in Income_

An increase in income from $870 billion to $920 billion shifts the Keynesian money demand schedule rightward from $M^d (Y = 870)$ to $M^d (Y = 920)$.

PERSPECTIVE 11A
Nonmonetary Financial Assets

Some financial assets are alternatives to holding money, what we call *nonmonetary financial assets*. These assets fall into two categories: *debt instruments* and *equities*.

Debt instruments are claims against money income at a specified interest rate. They are assets to those who hold them and liabilities to those who issue (or supply) them. For example, when you borrow money from a bank to buy a car, the bank holds the loan you "issue," a liability as you see it, and the bank has a claim on your income for repayment plus interest. Of greater relevance here are debt instruments issued by the government and corporations and held by investors—generally people and banks. These debt instruments have different maturities, where *maturity* refers to the amount of time before the *principal*, or amount of the debt, is repaid. An example of a *short-term debt instrument* is a 3-month U.S. Treasury bill. Here the issuer is the U.S. government and the maturity is in 3 months. Commercial paper is another type of short-term debt instrument. In this case, the issuer is a corporation and the maturity is typically 3 or 6 months. Examples of *long-term debt instruments* are 30-year corporate or U.S. government bonds. For example, the Ford Motor Company might issue a corporate bond for which the holder would receive quarterly interest payments, with the principal returned in 30 years.

Equities, or shares of stock, are claims against variable streams of income. You might, for example, invest in shares of the IBM corporation, for which you will receive dividend payments quarterly. IBM does not, however, guarantee a particular dividend rate for as long as you hold the shares. Your dividends depend on the firm's profits, among other things.[6]

In our discussion, we do not consider the choice among these alternatives to holding money as an asset, such as commercial paper versus government bonds versus common stocks. This is an interesting and important question, especially to investors, but not our question. Our concern is with the choice between money and nonmonetary assets generally. Therefore, it does no harm, for our purposes, to assume at times that all nonmonetary assets can be represented by one composite asset called, for simplicity, *bonds*. Also for simplicity, we refer to *the* interest rate, which represents an average of the many interest rates *on nonmonetary assets* in the real economy.

[6]For more details concerning the markets for debt instruments and equities, see Sections III and IV of Chapter 5.

down proportionately, but output was determined solely by supply-side factors, mainly equilibrium in the labor market. What did Keynes argue in attacking the classicals on this point? What role did he see for money supply as a determinant of output? The answer lies in his perception of a chain running from the money supply to the interest rate, to investment, to aggregate demand, and thereby eventually to equilibrium output.

The interest rate is the crucial link in this chain, as the money supply affects it and investment responds to it. Investment depends negatively on the interest rate. The interest rate represents the cost of borrowing to finance investment projects.[7] Given the expected profitability of possible invest-

[7] Be sure to keep in mind that firms' *investment* refers to the purchase of plant, equipment and inventories. The term *investment* does *not* refer to purchases of financial assets (e.g., bonds).

PERSPECTIVE 11B
Monetary Expansion, 1982–83

In November 1982, the unemployment rate had risen to 10.8 percent, and the U.S. economy was in the midst of its most severe post–World War II recession. During 1982, the Federal Reserve switched from a restrictive policy, which it had been following since 1980 as an anti-inflationary measure, to a more expansionary policy.

Figure 11.6 shows the rate of growth in the money supply (MI) and the level of the interest rate (on a short-term government debt instrument called a *Treasury bill*) for 1981, 1982, and 1983. It can be seen that, as the money supply growth spurted upward, from 6.4 to 8.5 percent and then to 9.0 percent the interest rate on Treasury bills tumbled from 14.0 to 10.7 percent and then to 8.6 percent.

ment projects, business managers find more projects sufficiently profitable to actually launch if the interest rate is lower. An increase in the money supply lowers the interest rate and therefore leads to increased investment. An increase in investment, via the multiplier process described in the previous chapter, in turn causes an increase in the general level of economic activity (see Figure 11.2 again).

Figure 11.7 illustrates this chain of events. Part (a) simply replicates Figure 11.5. An increase in the money supply from M_0^s to M_1^s causes a decline in the interest rate from r_0 to r_1. Part (b) shows how this fall in the interest rate affects equilibrium output. Initially, with the rate of interest at r_0, investment is given by $I(r_0)$. The aggregate demand schedule is $AD_0 = C + I(r_0) + G$. Equilibrium output is initially at level Y_0 on the horizontal axis. The

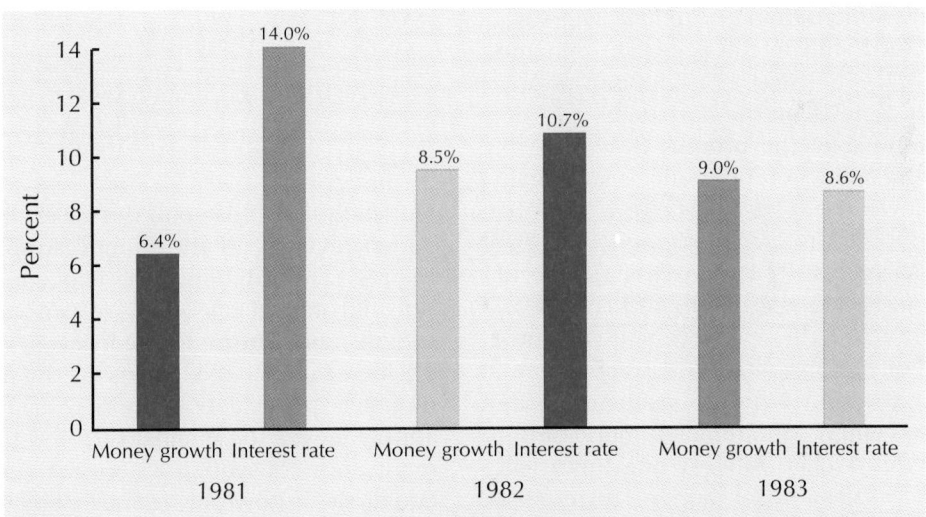

Money growth = percentage change in M_1 (currency plus deposits on which checks may be written)
Interest rate = the rate paid on 3-month Treasury securities commonly call *Treasury bills*

FIGURE 11.6 *Money Growth and the Interest Rate, 1981–83*

As the money supply grew more rapidly in 1982 and 1983, the rate of interest declined.

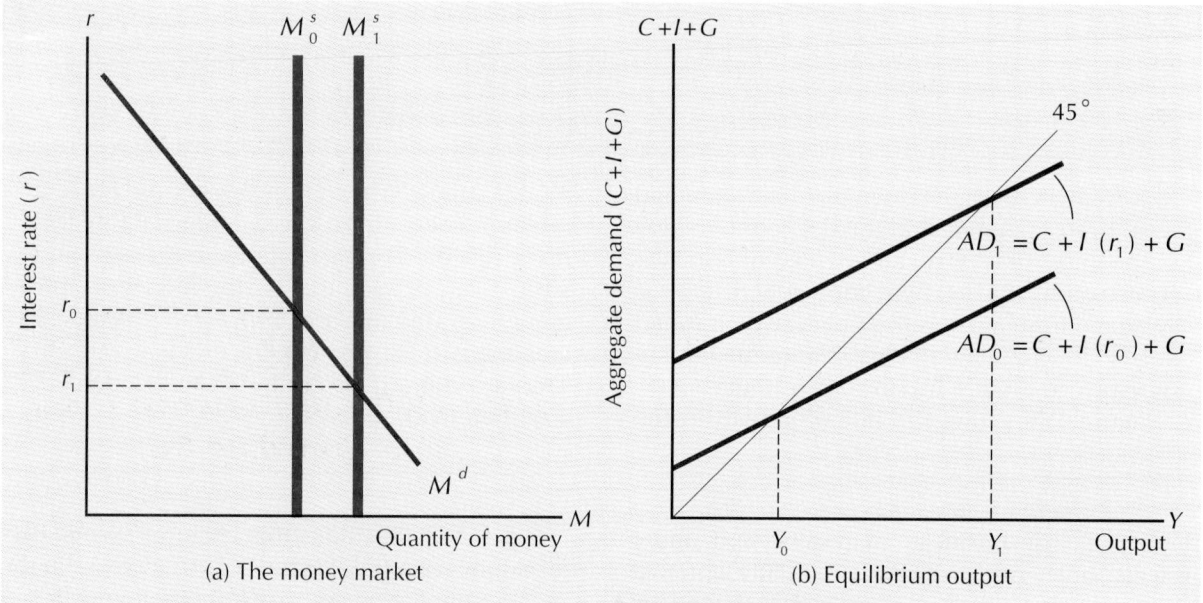

FIGURE 11.7 *The Effects of an Increase in the Money Supply*

In part (a), an increase in the money stock from M_0^S to M_1^S lowers the equilibrium interest rate from r_0 to r_1. The decline in the interest rate increases investment. In part (b), this increase in investment is shown to shift the aggregate demand schedule from $AD_0 = C + I(r_0) + G$ to $AD_1 = C + I(r_1) + G$. Equilibrium output rises from Y_0 to Y_1.

decline in the interest rate from r_0 to r_1 causes an increase in investment from $I(r_0)$ to $I(r_1)$. There is a resulting upward shift in the aggregate demand schedule to $AD_1 = C + I(r_1) + G$. Equilibrium output rises from Y_0 to Y_1 on the horizontal axis.

We can summarize the process by which an increase in the money supply affects aggregate output as follows. The injection of money into the economy increases the money supply above the level of money demand. This excess supply of money causes the interest rate to fall. The fall in the interest rate stimulates investment demand, and the level of equilibrium output rises.

A decline in the money supply has the opposite effects. As the central bank removes money from the economy, at a given interest rate there will then be an excess demand for money. The interest rate will rise. The rise in the interest rate causes investment demand to decline. Via the multiplier process, the level of equilibrium output falls.

In short, money does matter—it can influence output markedly. This is the main point regarding money distinguishing Keynes from classical economists.

V

Feedback Effects from Output to the Interest Rate

Our analysis to this point describes the process by which changes in the money supply affect the interest rate and then the level of equilibrium output, but it neglects what we can call **feedback effects from output to the interest rate.** Consider, for example, the effects of an expansionary monetary policy action. An increase in the money supply lowers the interest rate and boosts investment and, consequently, output. As output (income) rises, however, money demand increases for, as we explained previously, transactions purposes. In terms of Figure 11.7, the M^d schedule in part (a) shifts to the right, causing the interest rate to rise somewhat above level r_1. The rise in the interest rate due to this feedback effect somewhat dampens the expansion.

To clarify this point, consider an analogy to the

benefits of exercise in a weight loss program. While exercise burns off calories, which is its purpose, it also stimulates the appetite. Eating more will lessen the weight lost from (dampen the effect of) the exercise program. In fact, you could eat so much more that you might actually gain weight. Could there be a similar result in monetary policy? For example, could faster money growth so stimulate the economy that the interest rate actually rises? Keynesian economists do not think so. In their view, the feedback effect from output to the interest rate only partially offsets the direct effect that the increase in the money supply has on the interest rate.

VI
Monetary Policy in the Keynesian System

The role of *fiscal* policy in the Keynesian model is to stabilize aggregate demand and, therefore, output in the face of shifts in the investment component of demand. For example, policymakers could offset the effects of a downward shift in investment demand by cutting taxes or increasing government spending. Monetary policy gives policymakers an additional means of stabilizing aggregate demand.

Suppose, for example, that the economy is initially at a satisfactory level of employment and equilibrium output, but because of an unfavorable shift in business managers' expectations, the level of investment declines. Without any monetary or fiscal policy action, the level of aggregate demand and equilibrium output would fall, and there would be an undesirable rise in unemployment.

The monetary authority could offset the effect of the decline in investment by increasing the money supply. This could drive the interest rate down enough so that an increase in investment demand would just counterbalance the expectations-induced decline in investment demand. With investment demand restored to the initial level, aggregate demand and, therefore, equilibrium output would also again be at their initial levels.

As this example indicates, monetary policy within the Keynesian framework is an effective

alternative to fiscal policy as a means of stabilizing aggregate demand in response to shocks to the unstable elements of private sector investment. This means that both monetary *and* fiscal policy are believed to have strong, predictable effects on equilibrium output. The choice of the appropriate *mix* of monetary and fiscal policy is discussed in the next section.

VII
Fiscal Policy, the Interest Rate, and Crowding Out

When discussing what we called the *feedback effect* of output on the interest rate, we saw that as output rises following an increase in the money supply, the demand for money increases. This increase in the demand for money leads to an increase in the rate of interest, which, in turn, dampens the overall effects of the expansionary monetary policy.[8] Note, however, that it is not only an expansion in output due to monetary policy that causes money demand to increase and puts upward pressure on the rate of interest. *Any* expansion has this effect. In particular, an increase in output caused by an *expansionary fiscal policy* action will put upward pressure on the interest rate, with a resulting adverse effect on investment spending.

> This is the **crowding-out effect;** expansionary fiscal policy actions cause interest rates to rise and crowd (or push) private borrowers out of the credit market. Investment spending falls.

An illustration of *crowding out* is provided in Figure 11.8. Assume that initially the economy is at an equilibrium level of output Y_0. In part (a) of the figure, the demand for money is therefore given by $M^d(Y_0)$. With the money supply at M_0^s, the initial equilibrium interest rate is r_0. In part (b), the aggregate demand schedule is initially given by $AD_0 = C + I(r_0) + G_0$.

[8]Recall that the increase in the money supply causes the interest rate to *fall*. The resulting expansion causes the interest rate to *rise* back toward (but not to) its initial level.

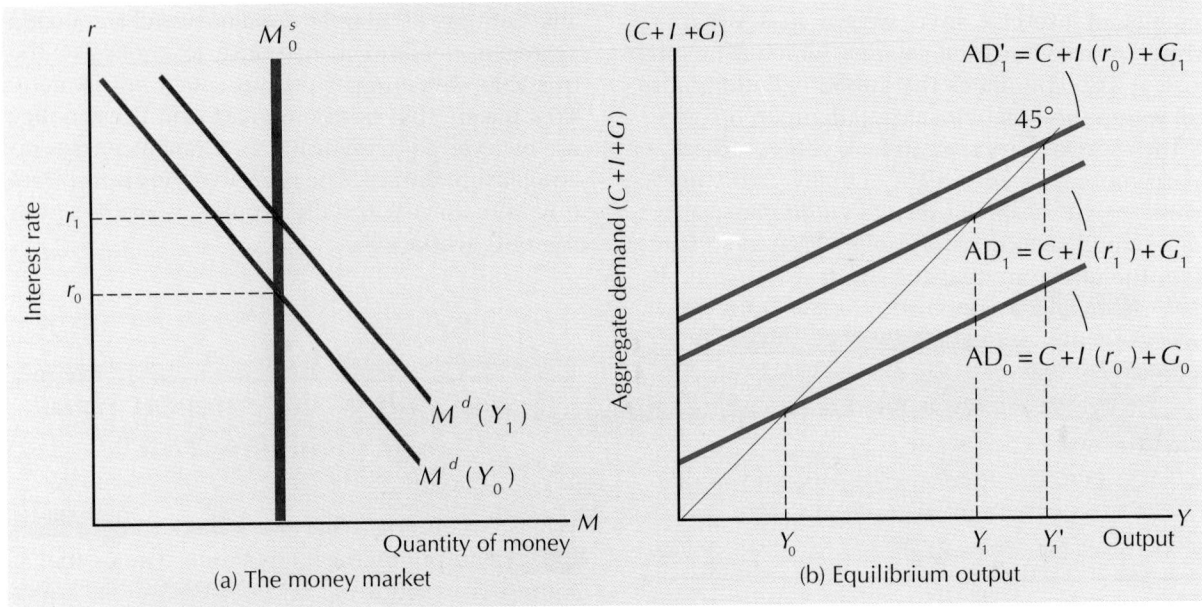

FIGURE 11.8   *Crowding Out in the Keynesian Model*

An increase in government spending, from G_0 to G_1, shifts the aggregate demand schedule from AD_0 to AD_1'. Output rises, causing money demand and thus the interest rate to rise (from r_0 to r_1). The resulting crowding out *of investment shifts the aggregate demand schedule downward from AD_1' to AD_1.*

Now suppose that policymakers increase the level of government spending from G_0 to a higher level, G_1. The increase in government spending shifts the aggregate demand schedule upward from AD_0 to $AD_1' = C + I(r_0) + G_1$. The increase in aggregate demand causes output to rise from Y_0 to Y_1' on the horizontal axis. This is as far as we carried the analysis of a fiscal policy shift in Chapter 10 because we had not introduced the money market into our analysis. Note, however, that the increase in income from Y_0 to Y_1' increases the demand for money, shifting the money demand schedule to the right and causing the interest rate to rise if the supply of money is fixed. As this happens, investment demand falls. The aggregate demand schedule shifts downward somewhat.

In Figure 11.8(a), the fiscal policy induced expansion is shown to shift the demand for money schedule from $M^d(Y_0)$ to $M^d(Y_1)$. The equilibrium interest rate rises from r_0 to r_1. This rise in the interest rate causes investment to decline from $I(r_0)$ to $I(r_1)$. The final position of the aggregate demand schedule in (b) is at $AD_1' = C + I(r_1) + G_1$.

Equilibrium output is at Y_1 below Y_1'; *the crowding-out effect thus dampens the expansionary effect of the increase in government spending.*

How serious is such crowding out of investment expenditures? In Chapter 8 we examined the classical view on this issue, which was that crowding out was virtually complete. In the classical view, the decline in private investment due to the rise in the interest rate cancels out the *entire* expansionary effect of a fiscal policy action. Fiscal policy has *no* effect on output. When we examine the monetarists' position in Chapter 14, we will see that they also believe that crowding out is serious enough to make fiscal policy ineffective. Keynesian economists, however, do not agree.

Keynesians believe that even after taking account of the decline in investment caused by the fiscal policy-induced rise in the interest rate, expansionary fiscal policy actions still have strong effects on output. They believe that the crowding out of investment is a harmful side effect of an expansionary fiscal policy. By lowering the level of investment, both the rate of growth in the capital stock and, consequently, the _future_ potential growth in output are diminished.

Their concern about potential crowding out of private investment has led Keynesian economists to favor a relatively "tight" or restrictive fiscal policy together with a relatively "easy" or expansionary monetary policy. This policy mix, they believe, will provide enough stimulus in the short run and keep interest rates low enough to encourage investment and capital formation. Many Keynesian economists were critical of President Ronald Reagan's economic policies in 1981, which they interpreted as an easy fiscal policy (tax cuts) combined with a tight monetary policy (slowing the rate of growth in the money supply) to keep aggregate demand from growing excessively. They argued that short-run gains would be coupled with damaging long-run costs.

PERSPECTIVE 11C

The Monetary–Fiscal Policy Mix

We have seen that in the Keynesian view either monetary or fiscal policy can affect income. But the effects of each policy on the interest rate and, therefore, on investment are quite different. In the case of expansionary monetary policy, the interest rate declines and investment increases. With an expansionary fiscal policy— an income tax cut, for example—the interest rate rises and investment declines. This is a significant difference because the level of investment determines the rate of capital formation and is important to long-term growth of the economy.

This explains the Keynesian preference for a policy _mix_ of relatively tight fiscal policy and easy monetary policy in order to keep the interest rate low and encourage investment. Moreover, whenever fiscal policy actions such as increases in government spending or income tax cuts are used to expand the economy, the Keynesians often like to see an _accommodating_ monetary policy—an accompanying increase in the money supply that will prevent the interest rate from rising and thus prevent the crowding out of investment. Such a monetary–fiscal policy combination is illustrated in Figure 11.9.

An increase in government spending from G_0 to the higher level G_1 shifts the aggregate demand curve in part (b) up from $AD_0 = C + I(r_0) + G_0$ to $AD_1 = C + I(r_0) + G_1$. As income rises to Y_1, the money demand schedule in part (a) shifts rightward from $M^d(Y_0)$ to $M^d(Y_1)$. If the money supply remained constant at the initial level M_0^s, there would be upward pressure on the interest rate, pushing it to r_1'. Investment would decline and crowding out would occur. But if the Federal Reserve _accommodates_ the expansionary fiscal policy by increasing the money supply to M_1^s, the interest rate will remain at r_0. In this case, there will be no crowding out of investment, which remains at $I(r_0)$ in part (b) of the figure. There is no dampening of the expansion.

As an example of such a coordinated expansion, the Keynesians point to the tax cut of 1964 and the accompanying increase in money supply growth. The tax cut was 20 percent for individuals and 10 percent for businesses. Growth in the money supply increased to 4.7 percent over the 1964–65 period compared to 3.7 percent in 1963. The result was a GNP growth of 5.4 percent in 1964 and 5.5 percent in 1965 (rates well above the growth in potential output). As a result of this accommodating monetary policy, the interest rate (corporate bond rate) rose only slightly, from 4.0 percent in 1963 to 4.3 percent in 1965. The business tax reductions included in the 1964 tax cut were also aimed at preventing any decline in investment. In fact, fixed business investment increased from 9.0 to 10.5 percent of GNP between 1963 and 1965.

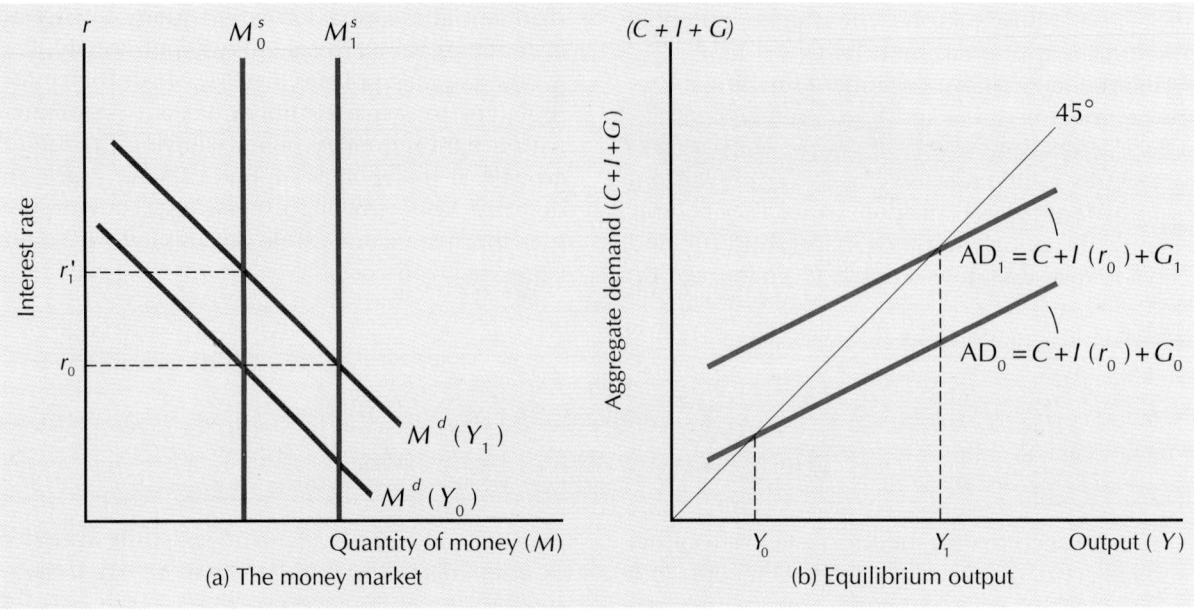

FIGURE 11.9 *Fiscal Policy with Monetary Accommodation*

SUMMARY

1. This chapter began by defining money and considering the functions of money in the economy. The three main functions of money are to serve as a means of exchange, a store of value, and a unit of account.

2. For the U.S. economy, we examined three measures of the money supply: M1, M2, and M3. All include currency. They differ in the range of bank deposits they include. M1 is the narrowest measure, including only checkable deposits. As we go from M1 to M2 to M3, progressively more categories of deposits are added.

3. We then analyzed the role of money and monetary policy in the Keynesian system. In Keynes's view, changes in the money supply affect the level of the interest rate, which, in turn, affects aggregate demand. An expansionary monetary policy, for example, increases the money supply, causes the interest rate to decline, and stimulates the investment component of aggregate demand.

4. Consideration of the effects of changes in the interest rate on the level of aggregate demand leads to a modification of the relationship between fiscal policy and aggregate demand. As expansionary fiscal policies raise the level of output (income), the demand for money for use in transactions increases. With the money supply unchanged, this increase in money demand causes the interest rate to rise. The rise in the interest rate, in turn, causes the level of investment to decline. Expansionary fiscal policy actions crowd out private investment spending. The decline in investment spending dampens the expansionary effect of the fiscal policy action.

5. Even after accounting for such crowding out, Keynesian economists believe that fiscal policy actions have significant effects on the level of economic activity—that fiscal policy *is* an effective stabilization tool. Keynesians also believe that monetary policy will have a significant effect on equilibrium output. To them, monetary and fiscal policies are alternative means of stabilizing aggregate demand.

KEY TERMS

M1, M2, M3
Federal Reserve System
Nonmonetary financial assets

Feedback effects from output to the interest rate
Monetary–fiscal policy mix
Crowding-out effect

QUESTIONS AND PROBLEMS

1. Barter serves as the principal means of exchange only in very primitive economies where households are largely self-sufficient. Why is barter not the dominant means of exchange in any highly developed economies?

2. When the person-on-the-street says "money," he or she usually means coins and currency only. Explain why checkable deposits at financial institutions should be included.

3. What are M1, M2, and M3?

4. Contrast Keynes's ideas on the demand for money with those of the classical economists.

5. Briefly describe two categories of *nonmonetary* financial assets.

6. Explain the "feedback effect" of expansionary monetary policy.

7. Explain the "crowding out" effect of fiscal policy and why it is considered harmful. How significant was the "crowding out" effect in classical theory? in Keynesian theory?

8. Keynesian economists generally favor what monetary/fiscal policy mix? Why?

9. What is an *accommodating* monetary policy?

10. Using graphs of the sort in Figure 11.7, trace the impacts of a *decrease* in the money supply.

12

The Complete Keynesian System: Aggregate Supply and Demand

British economist Alfred Marshall once compared supply and demand to the two blades of a scissors. Both were necessary, he said. Expressing the same idea, American economist James Tobin has remarked that God gave us two eyes so that we could watch both supply and demand. Until now, we have been discussing only one-eyed models of real output determination: the classical model, in which output was supply determined, and the simple Keynesian model of the previous three chapters, in which output was determined solely by demand. It is time to extend the Keynesian model to take account of the supply side—to add the second blade to Marshall's scissors.

I

The Aggregate Demand Curve

So far, we have considered the Keynesian system under the assumption that the price level is fixed. The essential notion in the simple Keynesian model is that, in equilibrium, output must equal aggregate demand. In assuming that the price level is fixed, the only condition that must be met for equilibrium is that output equals *demand*. We have been assuming that as long as we are below the level of potential output (y_p), *supply* is no constraint.[1] That is to say, as much output as is demanded will be supplied at the going price level. This assumption is illustrated in Figure 12.1.

Recent years, however, have not been characterized by a constant price level, even though the economy has generally been below potential output. We have been assuming that the price level is constant simply because the fixed-price version of the Keynesian model highlights Keynes's theory of aggregate demand. Indeed, *the* distinctive feature of the Keynesian system is the importance of aggregate demand as a determinant of equilibrium output. Keynesian economists, however, do not

[1]Recall from Chapter 6 that potential output is the output level that would be reached if labor and capital were employed at benchmark, high-employment levels.

230

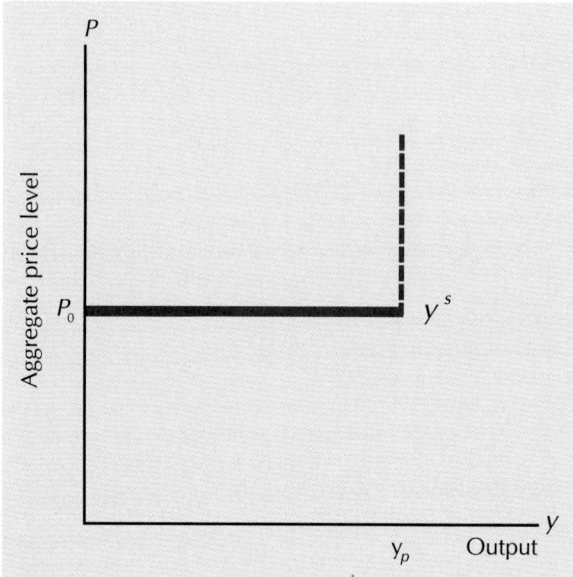

FIGURE 12.1 The Aggregate Supply Curve in the Fixed-Price Keynesian Model

So far in our discussion of the Keynesian model, we have assumed that the price level was fixed and output was determined by aggregate demand. We have been assuming that the aggregate supply curve was horizontal. Whatever level of output was demanded would be forthcoming at the existing price level. The previous analysis assumed that the economy was operating below potential output (y_p).

deny that supply factors are also crucial. To allow for supply factors and to take account of changes in the aggregate price level, we must develop the Keynesian view of aggregate supply.

First, however, we should examine how changes in the price level affect the level of aggregate demand. Up to this point, with the supply curve as drawn in Figure 12.1 and a given price level (P_0 in the figure), we simply had to find the level of aggregate demand to determine output on the horizontal axis. If, instead, the price level varies, we must construct a *Keynesian aggregate demand curve*.

The **Keynesian aggregate demand curve** gives the different levels of output demanded for different values of the aggregate price level.

Later in the chapter, we put this aggregate demand curve together with a Keynesian aggregate supply curve to see how price and output are *jointly* determined in the Keynesian system.

One point concerning notation should be observed. So far in our treatment of the Keynesian model, it has not been necessary to distinguish between real and money (or current dollar) GNP because the price level was assumed to be fixed. All changes in money GNP were changes in real GNP. *Because we will allow for changes in the price level from this point on, this distinction is important; we denote real GNP by a lowercase y and money GNP by a capital Y.*

A

The Slope of the Aggregate Demand Curve

How is the level of aggregate demand affected by changes in the price level? Another way of asking this question is: What is the slope of the aggregate demand curve when plotted with the price level on the vertical axis? In the Keynesian model, the aggregate demand curve is downward sloping, as illustrated in Figure 12.2. Aggregate demand for output is negatively related to the aggregate price level. Why? The answer is *not* the same as that for individual product markets, such as that for soda pop. As the price of soda pop rises *while all other prices remain constant*, the quantity demanded falls because of substitution effects, among other things. Beer, for instance, is substituted for soda pop as the price of soda pop escalates *relative* to the price of beer. Such substitution doesn't occur in this aggregate context, however, because *overall* price levels are at issue here, not relative prices. Hence, we must tread carefully now.

The *first factor* that explains the decline in aggregate demand as the aggregate *price level* rises is the effect of the price increase on the demand for money and hence on the rate of interest, which in turn influences *output* by its impact on investment. Hence there is an indirect tie between price level and output, the two variables of Figure 12.2. One motive for holding money, in the Keynesian view, is for use in transactions. The amount of money held for this purpose depends

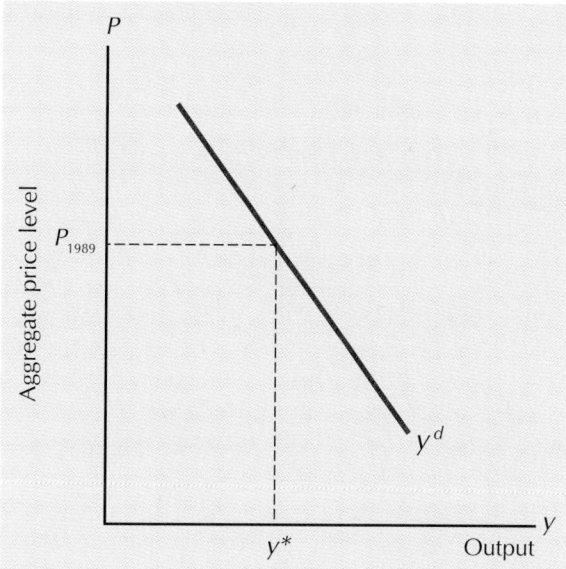

FIGURE 12.2 The Keynesian Aggregate Demand Curve

The Keynesian aggregate demand curve (y^d) is downward sloping. Less output will be demanded at higher aggregate price levels.

on the volume of transactions. GNP (national output or income) was taken as a good measure of the volume of transactions. Therefore, the transactions demand for money was assumed to vary positively with GNP. If money demand is measured simply in terms of *current dollars*, such as those now in your pocket or purse, the appropriate measure of income is money, or *current dollar* GNP. As money GNP rises, the volume of transactions increases and the demand for current dollar money rises. (By a crude analogy, big spenders need to carry more money than small spenders.)

An increase in the price level causes money GNP to rise and thereby increases the demand for money. This is illustrated in Figure 12.3, for a rise in the price level from an initial level, P_0, to a higher P_1. When money GNP increases from $Y_0 = P_0 y$ to $Y_1 = P_1 y$, where y is real income, the money demand schedule shifts to the right. With the money *supply* fixed by the central bank, there is an excess demand for money and the interest rate rises from r_0 to r_1. The rise in the interest rate causes investment and, therefore, aggregate demand to decline. This *interest rate effect* is one way a higher price

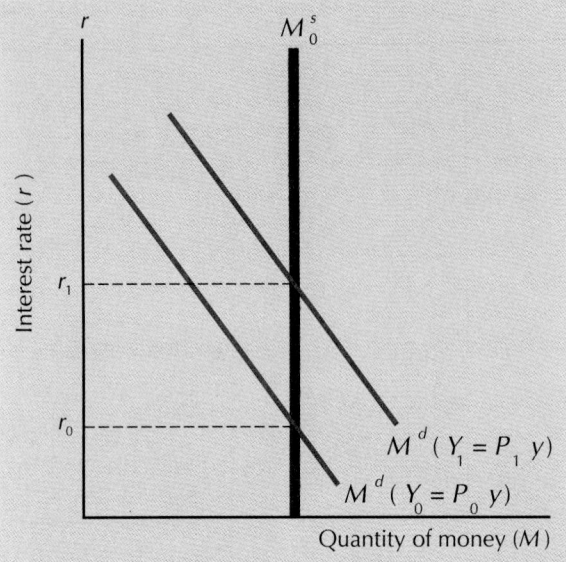

FIGURE 12.3   The Price Level and the Interest Rate

An increase in the price level from P_0 to P_1 raises the money GNP from Y_0 to Y_1. The rise in money GNP increases the transactions demand for money. The money demand schedule shifts rightward from $M^d(Y_0 = P_0 y)$ to $M^d(Y_1 = P_1 y)$. The equilibrium interest rate rises from r_0 to r_1.

level causes lower aggregate demand, as in Figure 12.3.

The *second factor* leading to a decline in aggregate demand as the aggregate price level rises is the effect that the rise in the price level has on household *wealth*. As the aggregate price level rises, the *real* value of many financial assets held by households declines. Financial assets, such as currency, bank deposits, and bonds, have fixed current dollar values, and a rise in the price level means that they are worth less in real or constant-valued dollars. For example, suppose you put $1,000 into a savings account a year ago. If the price level has risen 10 percent since then, the money in your account will buy 10 percent less today—less food, less apparel, less auto insurance, whatever. In our discussion of consumption behavior, we pointed out that wealth is one of the variables other than income that affects aggregate consumption. As the *real value* of wealth declines with a rising price level (e.g., the value of your savings account balance falls), households are less well off. In *real* terms, consumption expenditures

then fall, and consequently so too the aggregate demand for output, as shown in Figure 12.2.

To summarize, an increase in the price level causes a decline in aggregate demand via two channels:

> The **interest rate effect:** An increase in the price level will cause an increase in the demand for money to use in transactions. The increase in the demand for money causes the interest rate to rise. The rise in the interest rate causes the investment component of aggregate demand to fall.

> The **wealth effect:** An increase in the price level reduces the real value of many financial assets held by households. This decline in the real wealth of households lowers the consumption component of aggregate demand.

B

Shifts in the Aggregate Demand Curve

Next, consider factors that determine the *position* of the aggregate demand curve. Changes in these factors shift the curve. Fortunately, no new analysis is required. We simply use the aggregate demand curve to summarize our previous analysis of the factors that determine aggregate demand in the simple Keynesian model.

In that model we asked, "What determines the level of aggregate demand for a given price level?" The necessary condition for a level of output to be an *equilibrium level* was that output equal aggregate demand. Thus, once we determined demand $(C + I + G)$, we found equilibrium output. In finding the level of demand *for a given value of the aggregate price level*, we were determining the position of the aggregate demand curve. Refer back to Figure 12.2 for an example. Given the price level in 1989, we were determining the level of real output on the horizontal axis to be y^*.

Now we again consider how aggregate demand changes. However, demand is now represented as an aggregate demand *curve* showing the level of demand for real output y associated with *each possible price level*. Factors that previously changed aggregate demand at a fixed price level now shift the aggregate demand curve, i.e., *they change the level of demand at each value of the price level.* Let's consider some examples.

In the simple Keynesian model, an increase in government spending stimulates aggregate demand and causes equilibrium output to rise. The effect of this expansionary fiscal policy action is illustrated in Figure 12.4.

Figure 12.4(a) repeats our previous illustration of how an increase in government spending increases aggregate demand at a given price level.

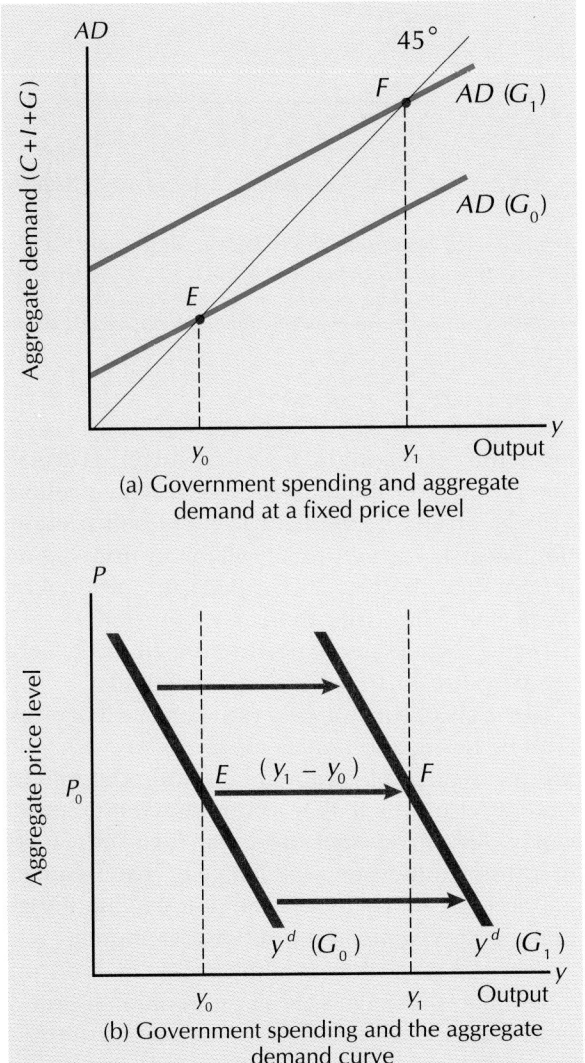

(a) Government spending and aggregate demand at a fixed price level

(b) Government spending and the aggregate demand curve

FIGURE 12.4 *An Increase in Government Spending Shifts the Aggregate Demand Curve*

Suppose that this price level is P_0 in Figure 12.4(b). The rise in government spending from G_0 to G_1 can be seen, from part (a), to increase equilibrium output *for the given price level,* P_0, from y_0 to y_1 on the horizontal axis; the equilibrium point moves from E to F. In Figure 12.4(b), this corresponds to the rightward shift in the aggregate demand curve from $y^d(G_0)$ to $y^d(G_1)$. Output demanded increases by the amount $(y_1 - y_0)$ at price level P_0 *or at any other price level.* The increase in government spending shifts the aggregate demand curve to the right.

A tax cut or an increase in autonomous investment also shifts the aggregate demand curve rightward because these changes increase the level of aggregate demand for a given value of the aggregate price level. Conversely, a decline in government spending, a tax increase, or an autonomous fall in investment demand each causes the level of aggregate demand at a given price level to fall. Each of these changes shifts the aggregate demand curve to the left.

Changes in monetary policy also shift the aggregate demand curve. An increase in the money supply causes a decline in the interest rate and, therefore, an increase in investment demand. The aggregate demand curve consequently shifts to the right. Conversely, a decline in the money supply shifts the aggregate demand curve to the left.

Notice that results from our simple Keynesian model are used to determine how various factors change the level of aggregate demand *at a given price level.* The simple model determines the shift that will take place in the aggregate demand curve when there is a change in one of the underlying determinants of aggregate demand. If the price level were truly constant, this change in demand would directly determine the change in equilibrium output, as in the numerical and graphic examples considered previously. If the price level is not fixed, knowing the shift in the aggregate demand curve is not sufficient to determine the change in output. To see how the effects of a given shift in the demand curve are distributed between a change in output and a change in price, we need to know the nature of the supply curve along which the demand curve is shifting. If the price level varies, we need both blades of Marshall's scissors.

II
The Keynesian Theory of Aggregate Supply

Quadrupling oil prices and disruption of oil supplies in the wake of the 1973 Mideast war demonstrated the economic importance of supply-side factors. This first oil price shock of the 1970s led to a severe recession in the United States and other major oil-importing nations. In this section we examine the Keynesian view of the economy's supply side.

To repeat, we have been assuming that in the Keynesian system supply is no constraint on output. This assumption was made in drawing the horizontal aggregate supply curve in Figure 12.1. Such an assumption would be realistic, if at all, only in an economy operating far below potential output, with abundant supplies of idle capital and labor. In more normal circumstances, Keynesian economists believe the aggregate supply curve to be *upward sloping*. The level of output that firms will produce rises only with an increase in the aggregate price level.

The **Keynesian aggregate supply curve** is shown in Figure 12.5. At very low output levels, the curve is flat, reflecting the absence of a supply constraint. Over the range of output levels where the economy would normally operate, however, the curve slopes upward to the right.

The upward-sloping segment of the aggregate supply curve indicates that firms supply an increasing amount of output as the aggregate price level rises. To see why, consider the reaction of an individual firm to a jump in the price of its product.

A
Rising Cost as Output Rises

The aim of the firm is to maximize its total profit, which is total revenue minus total cost. An increase in product price increases the revenue from the sale of each additional unit of the prod-

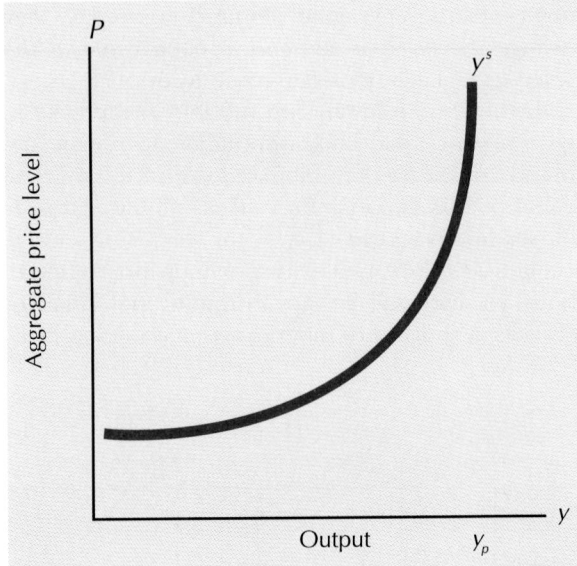

FIGURE 12.5 The Keynesian Aggregate Supply Curve

At low levels of output, the Keynesian aggregate supply curve is flat, reflecting the absence of a supply constraint. At higher levels of output the curve slopes upward to the right, becoming steeper as we approach potential output (y_p).

uct. If the cost of producing each additional unit of the product is unchanged, the rise in product price is clearly a stimulant to increased production because higher profits will follow from higher production. But what happens to production costs as the firm tries to increase output? Does it actually remain unchanged? Probably not. Let's see why.

In the short run, the firm can increase its output level by hiring additional employees to work with the fixed stock of capital (plant and equipment). One effect of this is that as additional employees work with a fixed stock of capital, the productivity of these employees will fall (e.g., two workers cooperating to use a machine produce more than one working alone, but not twice as much).

The cost of producing additional units of output is equal to the wage paid to an additional unit of labor divided by the number of units of output produced by that unit of labor, which is productivity. For example, if an additional worker, hired for $75 per day, would increase production by three transistor radios, the unit cost of the additional radios is $25 ($75/3). For a given wage, therefore, as labor productivity falls, the cost of producing each additional unit of output (unit cost) rises. This is one reason why the aggregate supply curve is upward sloping; because *unit cost rises as the level of output increases, firms supply more units of output only at a higher price.*

This analysis of the firm assumes that additional units of labor input can be hired at an unchanged wage level, a reasonable assumption for individual firms. Each firm is presumed to be small enough so that, in its attempt to hire additional units of labor, it does not appreciably tighten conditions in the labor market and put upward pressure on the wage level. When we consider firms in the aggregate, however, we cannot neglect the effect on labor market conditions of an attempt by firms to increase output. As firms *in general* increase output, the demand for labor increases, putting upward pressure on the wage rate. *Any increase in the wage rate contributes to the rise in unit cost as output increases. This is another reason why firms increase output supplied only as the price level rises.*

B
But Cost Rises Less Than Price

What keeps the wage rate from rising proportionately with the price level, thereby negating the incentive for firms to increase their output at all? In other words, how do we know that the Keynesian aggregate supply curve is not vertical? Recall that the classical aggregate supply curve *is* vertical; to maintain labor market equilibrium when the aggregate price level increases in the classical model, the money wage must rise *proportionately*—10 percent for one means 10 percent for the other. Since the money wage does rise proportionately with the price level in the classical system, firms have no incentive to expand production. Unit cost rises proportionately with product price. Profit does not rise. The classical aggregate supply curve is vertical.

Keynes reached a different conclusion because he did not accept the two key assumptions made by classical economists concerning the labor market:

1. The money wage rate is perfectly flexible.

2. Labor market participants have perfect information about the real wage.

Let's explore each assumption in turn.

1. Money Wage Inflexibility The first assumption was important because if the money wage is inflexible, it cannot rise proportionately with the product price. The Keynesian model assumes that in the short run the money wage is neither completely flexible nor completely rigid. As explained previously, when firms expand output following a rise in product price, labor market conditions tighten and the wage rate rises. According to the Keynesian view, however, in the short run this adjustment is *less* than proportional to the rise in the price level.

Keynesian economists provide several explanations for this "stickiness" in the money wage. One is the existence of contracts of 2 or 3 years' duration that fix the levels of money wages over the contract's life. Consequently, the money wage does not respond to changes in labor market conditions over the term of the contract. Such *explicit* long-term contracts exist in the unionized sector of the labor market, but even in segments where there are no explicit contracts, there are often *implicit* agreements between employers and employees that fix the money wage over some period of time. The wage is changed only once per year, for example. Such explicit and implicit labor contracts are cited by Keynesian economists as sources of short-run money wage inflexibility.

2. Imperfect Information An additional reason for the less than proportionate change in the money wage relative to a change in product price derives from the Keynesian attack on the second classical labor market proposition—the assumption that all market participants, including the workers who supply labor, *know* the real wage (the money wage divided by the aggregate price level). Keynesians argue that because the labor bargain is in terms of the *money* wage, such as $9.80 an hour, the worker knows the money wage (W) but not the price level (P), and thus not the real wage (W/P). Through implicit or explicit contracts, the worker agrees to provide labor services over some period of time. However, he or she does not know what the value of the aggregate price level will be over that period.

The worker must base the money wage demand on an *expectation* of the future behavior of the price level. Keynesians believe that wage demands based on this expectation impart a stickiness to money wages because such an expectation reflects, for the most part, the *past* behavior of the aggregate price level. In the Keynesian view, price expectations are primarily *backward looking*. If the price level changes, workers are fooled for a while; they evaluate current money wage offers on the basis of the past level of prices. It takes time for their expectations to reflect the new price level. In the meantime, the wage level does not adjust completely.

In short, Keynesian economists believe that rigidities due to labor contracts and backward-looking price expectations cause the money wage to rise less than proportionately with increases in the product price. Consequently, firms supply a larger quantity of output as the product price rises in the short run. This explains the upward-sloping segment of the Keynesian aggregate supply curve in Figure 12.5.

A final feature of the Keynesian aggregate supply curve, as drawn in Figure 12.5, is that the curve becomes steeper as the economy approaches potential output (y_p). Labor market conditions are tight over this range, with shortages of certain types of workers and intense use of the capital stock. Under these conditions, the cost of increased units of production will be rising sharply due to upward pressure on wages and diminishing productivity of additional units of labor.

III

Macroequilibrium in the Keynesian System

In Figure 12.6 the Keynesian aggregate supply curve is put together with the aggregate demand curve of Section I to determine the equilibrium output level and the price level. Points along the aggregate demand curve show the level of aggregate demand for each price level indicated on the vertical axis. Points along the aggregate supply curve give the overall output level that firms are

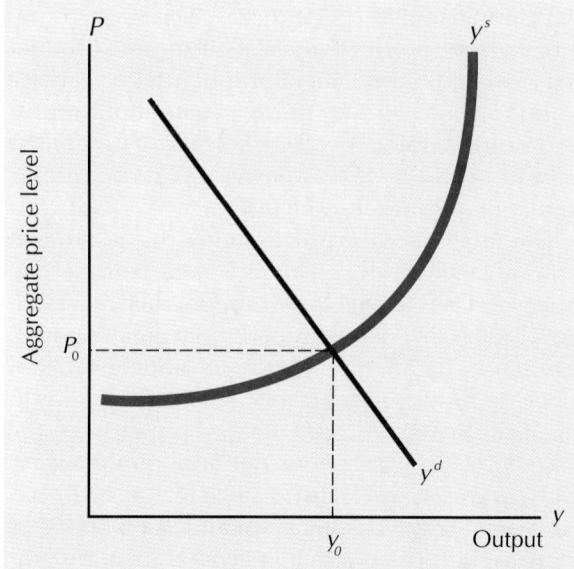

FIGURE 12.6   Equilibrium in the Keynesian Model
Macroequilibrium in the Keynesian system is a price (P_0) and output (y_0) combination that equates aggregate supply and demand.

willing to produce at each price level. At price level P_0, aggregate demand and aggregate supply both equal y_0. This point of intersection is the point of macroequilibrium given these curves.

In the Keynesian system, the factors that determine the levels of aggregate price and output are the factors that determine the positions of the aggregate demand and supply curves. Let us examine how output and the aggregate price level are affected by changes in some of these demand- and supply-side influences.

A

Shifts in the Aggregate Demand Curve

In Section I we discovered how changes in monetary and fiscal policy, as well as autonomous shifts in investment, affect the aggregate demand curve. Expansionary changes shift the aggregate demand curve to the right, while contractionary changes shift the curve to the left. We can now see how such changes affect the equilibrium levels of price and output in the complete (variable-price) Keynesian model.

The effects of an increase in government spending are illustrated in Figure 12.7. Assume that the initial level of government spending was G_0 and that, after the increase, the new higher spending level is G_1. This expansionary fiscal policy action shifts the aggregate demand curve to the right from $y^d(G_0)$ to $y^d(G_1)$. The level of real output rises from y_0 to y_1 and the aggregate price level rises from P_0 to P_1.

As in the simple Keynesian model, the increase in government spending stimulates aggregate demand, causing the level of output to rise. Note, however, that the level of output rises *less* than it would have if the price level had remained constant. If supply had been no constraint, the supply curve would have been horizontal and output would have risen by the full distance of the horizontal shift in the aggregate demand curve, to level y_1' on the horizontal axis in Figure 12.7. But supply *is*, in general, a constraint. The price level must rise to provide an incentive for firms to increase output, given that an increase in output will increase the firms' unit production costs. The rise in the price level somewhat dampens the increase

in aggregate demand due to the interest rate and wealth effects explained in Section I. As a result, real output rises not all the way to y_1', but only to y_1.

A tax cut, an increase in the money supply, or an autonomous increase in investment also causes the aggregate demand curve to shift to the right and therefore causes aggregate price and real output to rise. As with the increase in government spending, the expansionary effect on output from each of these changes is dampened somewhat by the accompanying rise in the aggregate price level. Conversely, a decline in government spending, a tax increase, a fall in the money supply, or an autonomous drop in investment causes the aggregate demand curve to shift to the left. The levels of aggregate price and real output then both decline.

From a policymaking standpoint, one important consideration is the portion of a change in aggregate demand that is reflected in a change in real output compared to the portion reflected in a change in the aggregate price level. For example, a policymaker evaluating the merits of an expansionary monetary policy would want to know the relative degree to which the policy action would cause real output and price to rise. The positive effect on real output would be a benefit, while the rise in price would be a cost.

An increase in the money stock shifts the aggregate demand curve to the right along the aggregate supply curve. The relative degree to which equilibrium price and output change depends on the slope of the aggregate supply curve. The steeper the aggregate supply curve, the larger the rise in price and the smaller the rise in real output. Our discussion in the previous section indicates that the aggregate supply curve becomes progressively steeper as we approach full potential output—as the economy comes nearer to operating at full capacity. This implies that the output effects of expansionary aggregate demand policies are relatively large and the price effects are relatively small if the economy is well below potential output. As full-capacity output is approached, the gains in terms of increased real output grow smaller relative to the costs in terms of an increased aggregate price level.

Read Perspective 12A.

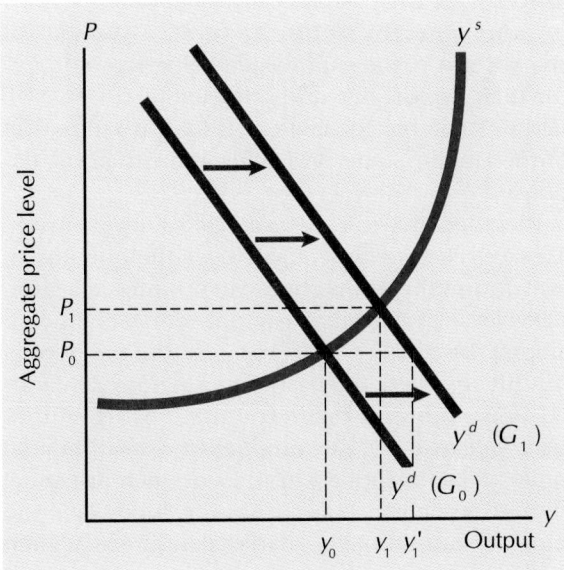

FIGURE 12.7   *The Effect on Price and Output of an Increase in Government Spending*

An increase in government spending shifts the aggregate demand curve rightward from $y^d(G_0)$ to $y^d(G_1)$. Output rises from y_0 to y_1 and the aggregate price level rises from P_0 to P_1.

PERSPECTIVE 12A

Aggregate Demand in the Great Depression

In the Keynesian view, the Great Depression of 1929–33 was the result of a collapse in aggregate demand. In terms of the Keynesian aggregate demand–aggregate supply curves, the Depression resulted from a large leftward shift in the aggregate demand curve, as illustrated in Figure 12.8. Real output (1982 constant dollars) fell by 30 percent (from $709.6 billion to $498.5 billion). The aggregate price level fell by 23 percent (from 14.6 to 11.2). The unemployment rate rose from 3.2 percent in 1929 to 24.9 percent in 1933.

The tremendous drop in aggregate demand was the result of several factors. Following a boom in the 1920s, construction expenditures (business and residential construction) fell in 1929. The stock market crash of 1929 reduced household wealth and, consequently, consumption demand. The crash also, most likely, dampened business managers' future expectations about profits, lowering investment demand. Finally, the disintegration of the world payments system and growing barriers to international trade led to a fall in export demand. In the Keynesian view, all of these factors contributed to the collapse in aggregate demand. The fact that the Federal Reserve allowed the money supply to fall by over 25 percent during 1929–33 greatly aggravated this decline in demand.

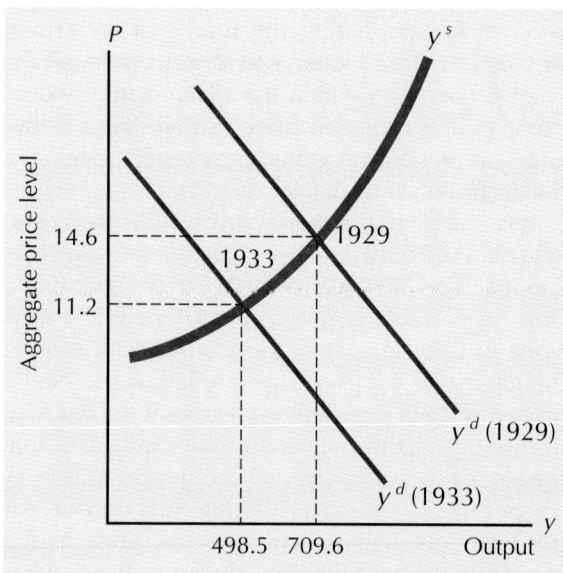

FIGURE 12.8 The Collapse in Aggregate Demand, 1929–33

change. During the 1950s and 1960s, there was little variation in supply-side factors. Demand-side factors were the primary causes of cyclical swings in output. In the 1970s, however, a number of sharp shifts in the supply-side influences, such as the quadrupling of world crude oil prices in 1974, had unfavorable consequences for the economies of the United States and other industrialized nations.

What factors shift the aggregate supply curve?[2] The aggregate supply curve gives the quantity of real output that firms choose to produce at a given price level. The aggregate supply curve is upward sloping because as firms increase the quantity of output supplied, the cost of producing each added unit of output rises. The unit cost of output rises because (1) the productivity of additional units of labor applied to a fixed stock of capital diminishes and (2) as firms hire more labor to increase output, labor market conditions tighten and the money wage rises. Consequently, firms

B

Shifts in the Aggregate Supply Curve

Supply-side factors also affect aggregate price and real output. Shifts in the aggregate supply curve cause output and the aggregate price level to

[2]Over long periods of time, the supply curve shifts outward due to growth in factors of production, labor and capital, and due to technological change. These influences on the supply curve are neglected here because we are only considering the short-run behavior of output.

must receive higher prices before they will expand output (supply a larger quantity of goods).

Now consider a shift in the aggregate supply curve, for example, an upward shift from y^s_0 to y^s_1, as illustrated in Fig. 12.9. After an upward shift in the aggregate supply curve, firms produce less output at each possible price level (y^* as opposed to y_0 at price P_0, for instance). Put differently, firms will continue to produce the same output, only at a higher price (P^* as opposed to P_0 for output y_0). Events that cause such a shift are those that change the unit cost of production *at a given level of output*. For example, any event that increases unit cost at a given level of output causes an *upward* shift in the aggregate supply curve. To continue to produce the same level of output with higher unit costs, firms require a higher product price. Conversely, any change that reduces the unit cost of producing a given level of output shifts the aggregate supply curve *downward*. After the downward change, firms require a lower price to produce the given level of output.

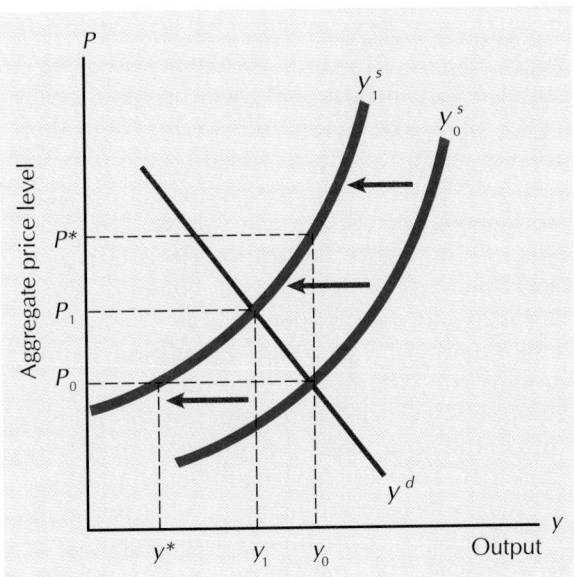

FIGURE 12.9 *An Unfavorable Shift in the Aggregate Supply Curve*

An unfavorable supply shock (e.g., an autonomous rise in energy prices) shifts the aggregate supply schedule from y^s_0 to y^s_1. Output falls from y_0 to y_1 and the aggregate price level rises from P_0 to P_1.

IV

Factors that Shift the Aggregate Supply Curve

What factors would cause the unit cost of production at a given level of output to change? Such factors are often called **cost push** factors because they affect price independently of the level of demand by shifting the aggregate supply curve.

A

Changes in Inflationary Expectations

One set of cost push factors affects the money wage demands of workers at a given level of output. We have already seen that as we get closer to potential output and conditions in the labor market tighten, in the sense that the unemployment rate becomes low, there will be upward pressure on the money wage. This is embodied in the slope of the aggregate supply curve and is *not* a shift in the curve. If, however, labor's money wage demands increase for a given level of output, then to the degree that those demands are met by management, the money wage and, therefore, the unit cost for a given level of output would rise.

One important factor that increases labor's money wage demands at a given output level is an expectation of higher future prices. With higher future price level expectations, workers seek money wage increases to protect their real wage levels. For example, if workers expect 3 percent inflation next year, they may then demand a 5 percent increase in their money wage to secure a real wage increase of 2 percent ($5 - 3 = 2$). If instead they expect 10 percent inflation next year, they must get a money wage increase of 12 percent to secure a 2 percent increase in their real wage ($12 - 10 = 2$). The faster the expected increase in the aggregate price level (the higher the expected inflation rate), the higher percentage money wage increases labor demands. Such increases in *inflationary expectations* produce leftward shifts in the aggregate supply curve. Conversely, if expectations of inflation decline, the money wage demands of labor decline and the aggregate supply curve shifts to the right.

In the Keynesian model, price expectations are _backward looking_. Expectations about the future behavior of the price level depend heavily on the past behavior of prices. Therefore, increases in cost push pressure from increased wage demands are most important when past inflation rates have been high. Workers have been fooled for a time, and they are now trying to protect themselves against future erosion of their real earnings. This increase in wage demands due to past increases in the price level is an important element in the Keynesian explanation of the unemployment–inflation trade-off discussed in Chapter 13.

B

Supply Shocks

To keep our analysis simple, we have assumed that the only factor inputs are capital and labor. In the real world, however, there are also raw material and energy inputs. Unit costs are composed of labor, raw materials, and energy costs. It follows that any autonomous change in materials prices or energy prices, changes often referred to as **supply shocks,** also changes the unit cost of producing a given level of output. Hence, supply shocks are cost push factors as well. Autonomous _increases_ in the price of these inputs, unfavorable supply shocks, also increase the unit cost of producing a given output and shift the aggregate supply curve upward to the left, as in Figure 12.9. Unfavorable supply shocks cause output to decline and the aggregate price level to rise. Autonomous _declines_ in raw material or energy prices have just the opposite effects. Such favorable supply shocks cause the aggregate supply curve to shift rightward; the level of output rises and the aggregate price level declines.

Read Perspective 12B.

PERSPECTIVE 12B

The Oil Price Shock of 1973–74

The massive increase in the price of oil in late 1973 and early 1974 is an example of a large and unfavorable supply shock. The Organization of Petroleum Exporting Countries (OPEC) raised the price of oil sold to industrialized countries (and for a time after the Mideast war in 1973, the Arab states refused to export any oil to the United States). The price of OPEC oil increased by 270 percent between September 1973 and January 1974. Overall, the price of this oil skyrocketed by 422 percent, more than a fourfold increase, during the 1973–75 period. The result was a decline in output in oil-importing countries and a rise in their aggregate price levels.

In the United States, real GNP fell by 1.8 percent ($49.1 billion) from 1973 to 1975. The aggregate price level rose by 19.8 percent. The unemployment rate rose from 4.9 percent in 1973 to 8.5 percent in 1975; 3.6 million workers were added to the ranks of the unemployed.

While not all elements have been captured, the overall effects of the OPEC oil price shock can be illustrated within the Keynesian aggregate demand and supply framework, as shown in Fig. 12.10. The autonomous increase in the price of oil, in this case caused by the pricing decisions of OPEC, increased the unit cost of production. The supply curve shifted left from y^s (1973) to y^s (1975). Output declined from $2,744 billion in 1973 to $2,695 billion in 1975. The aggregate price level rose from 49.5 in 1973 to 59.3 in 1975 (1982 = 100). As output fell, unemployment rose.

Supply shocks need not be unfavorable, however. In the early 1980s, the price of oil began to fall as new sources were developed and as the OPEC cartel fell into disarray. By 1986, the price of oil had fallen approximately 50 percent from its 1980 level. The effect of this was to shift the aggregate supply curve outward. Favorable developments (for consumers) in the oil market were one factor contributing to the recovery from the sharp recession that occurred in industrialized countries during the early 1980s.

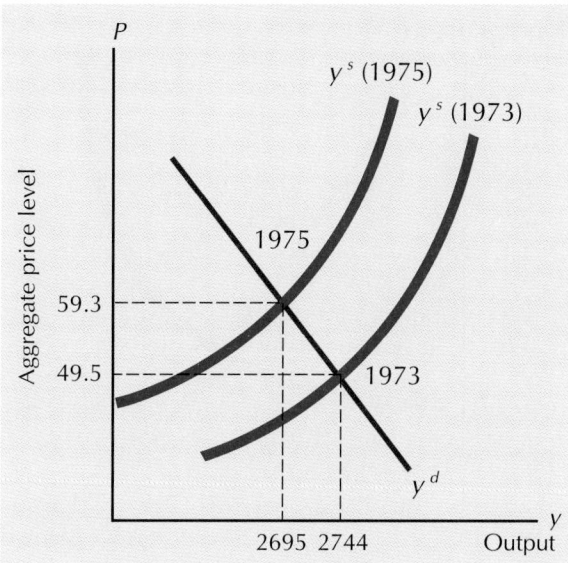

FIGURE 12.10 Effect of the OPEC Oil Price Increase

changes in government spending or taxes (fiscal policy variables), changes in the money supply, and autonomous changes in investment. Expansionary changes (increases in government spending or the money supply, tax cuts, and autonomous increases in investment) shift the aggregate demand curve to the right. Output and the aggregate price level both rise. Changes in the opposite direction in these demand-side factors shift the aggregate demand curve to the left. Output and the aggregate price level both fall.

Supply-side influences shift the aggregate supply curve. Those we have considered include changes in workers' expectations about inflation and autonomous changes in energy or raw materials prices. Unfavorable changes in these variables (increases in inflationary expectations or autonomous increases in energy or raw materials prices) shift the aggregate supply curve to the left. Output falls and the aggregate price level rises. Favorable changes in these supply-side factors (declines in inflationary expectations and autonomous declines in energy or raw material prices) shift the aggregate supply curve to the right. Output rises and the aggregate price level falls.

Note that changes in *demand-side* factors cause price and output to move in the *same* direction (both rise or both fall). Changes in *supply-side* factors cause output and price to move in *opposite* directions.

■ CHECK YOUR BEARINGS

Let us stop and review our findings about the variables that affect output determination in the Keynesian system.

Demand-side influences shift the aggregate demand curve. Those we have considered include

SUMMARY: Keynes Versus the Classics

How does the Keynesian theory that we have considered in the preceding four chapters differ from the classical theory? In other words, what are the central elements of the Keynesian revolution? The classical aggregate demand and supply curves which summarize the central elements of the classical system are reproduced as Figure 12.11 (a). We have seen in this chapter how the Keynesian model can be represented in terms of alternative aggregate supply and demand curves, as in Figure 12.11 (b). A convenient way to summarize the differences between the two theories is to examine the difference between the respective aggregate supply and demand relationships in the two models. We can then consider the differences between the theories in the broader sense of the *visions* of the

economy embodied in the classical and Keynesian theories.

1. *Aggregate supply.* On the supply side, the key difference between the classical and Keynesian theories is the slope of the aggregate supply curve. The classical aggregate supply curve is vertical. This reflects the fact that output and, therefore, employment are completely supply determined in this model. That is to say, the classical labor market was self-adjusting to the full-employment level. This full-employment level of labor, plus the level of the fixed capital stock and the state of technology, determined how much output was produced. Aggregate demand had *no* role in output determination in the classical system.

The Keynesians deny that the money wage ad-

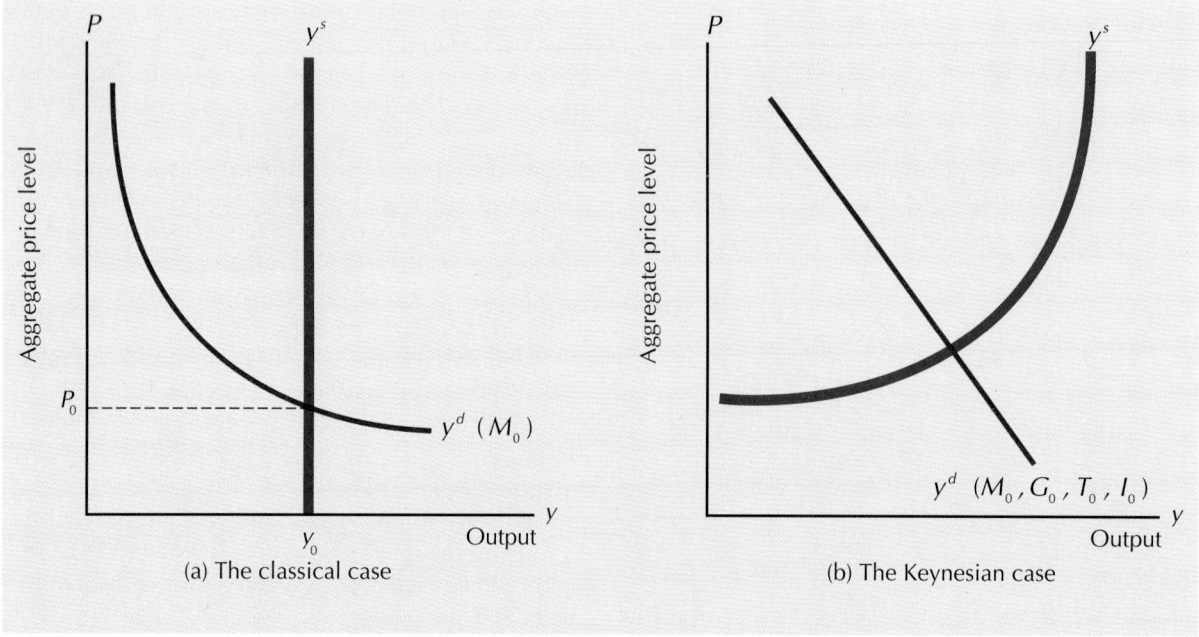

FIGURE 12.11   The Classical and Keynesian Models

justs quickly enough in the short run to maintain full employment. Indeed, when employment is quite low (unemployment high), the Keynesian aggregate supply curve is flat, with no slope. Here aggregate demand alone determines aggregate output. Beyond this flat range, the aggregate supply curve in the Keynesian model slopes upward to the right. Shifts in the aggregate demand curve move the economy along the upward-sloping supply function, causing output to change. Here output is not completely demand determined; aggregate supply is important in determining the levels of output and employment. But supply is not independently predominant, as in the classical system.

2. *Aggregate demand.* The classical aggregate demand curve was derived from the quantity theory of money. The key classical assumption was that the velocity of money is fixed, or at least relatively stable in the short run. If velocity is fixed, then fixing the quantity of money will, via the equation of exchange ($MV = Py$), fix the total nominal demand for output. The position of the aggregate demand curve will depend solely on the quantity of money—higher quantity, greater demand (shift right); lower quantity, lesser demand (shift left).

Keynes attacked the quantity theory of money.

In the Keynesian theory, to find the level of aggregate demand, we need to consider directly the determinants of desired consumption, investment, and government spending. As we have seen in this chapter, the Keynesian aggregate demand curve shifts with changes in the factors that influence each of these components of aggregate demand. These factors include the money stock (M_O), which affects the interest rate; fiscal policy variables such as the levels of government spending (G_O) and taxes (T_O); and the level of autonomous investment (I_O).

In the Keynesian view, private-sector aggregate demand is unstable. To keep aggregate demand and, consequently, output stable in the face of unstable private-sector demand requires appropriate monetary and fiscal policies. Due to their theory of aggregate demand, Keynesians reach *activist* policy conclusions. On the other hand, due to their theory of the self-adjusting nature of the economy, classical economists reach nonactivist or *noninterventionist* policy conclusions. Their model has no need for, or possibility of, aggregate demand policies to stabilize output and employment. These variables are determined by supply and only supply. Moreover, involuntary unemployment is impossible in their system.

3. *A broader perspective.* During the Great De-

pression, Keynes was asked whether there had ever been anything like it in the past. "Yes," he replied. "It was called the Dark Ages, and it lasted four hundred years." Such was the background against which Keynesian economics developed. Not surprisingly, Keynes focused on the sources of instability in the macroeconomy.

As we have seen, by "instability" Keynes meant that the economy,

whilst it is subject to severe fluctuations in respect to output and employment, it is not violently unstable. Indeed it seems capable of remaining in a chronic condition of subnormal activity for a considerable period without any marked tendency toward either recovery or toward complete collapse.

Keynes had seen the unemployment resulting from this "chronic condition of subnormal activity" lead to the fall of the Weimar Republic and the subsequent rise of Hitler in Germany, as well as to growing political instability in other Western democracies. Failure to provide high employment was a potentially fatal flaw in the capitalist free-enterprise system. To Keynes and his followers, activist aggregate demand policies for stability were a middle ground between the laissez-faire, noninterventionist position of the classical economists and the command-type policies advocated by the fascists and communists of the 1930s.

What is the relevance of Keynes's vision to the world economy of the 1980s? Modern Keynesians accept what economist Franco Modigliani terms the *fundamental practical message* of Keynes's work:

that a private enterprise economy using an intangible money needs to be stabilized, can be stabilized, and therefore, should be stabilized by appropriate monetary and fiscal policies.

Stated differently, modern Keynesians believe that active monetary and fiscal policies are *necessary*, *feasible*, and *desirable*. They are *necessary* because the economy suffers serious instabilities from an aggregate demand that lurches about and an aggregate supply rocked at times by violent shocks. Big gaps naturally open between expectations and realizations. Moreover, these policies are *feasible* because they can push aggregate demand in a favorable direction in timely fashion. Finally, they are *desirable* because the economy's natural instabilities generate tremendous costs—economic costs in lost output and human costs in lost employment.

The 1980s are, in the view of the neo-Keynesians, dissimilar to the 1930s in many respects, some of which require extensions and modifications of the Keynesian theory and policy prescriptions. However, Keynes's vision remains applicable.

There are, however, skeptics. Their positions are examined in Chapters 14 and 15.

KEY TERMS

Keynesian aggregate demand curve
Interest rate effect
Wealth effect

Keynesian aggregate supply curve
Cost push factors
Supply shocks

QUESTIONS AND PROBLEMS

1. Draw a Keynesian aggregate demand schedule. Carefully explain why it slopes downward.
2. Explain the transactions demand for money.
3. How would the Keynesian aggregate demand curve be affected by a tax increase? By a decrease in the money supply?

4. Explain why an increase in output will, in the short run, mean higher unit costs for the typical firm. How is this reflected in the Keynesian aggregate supply curve?
5. The Keynesian model assumes that money wages are "sticky." What does this mean? What explana-

tions are offered for this "stickiness"?

6. What is "cost push" inflation and why does it happen?

7. Summarize key differences in the economic theories of Keynes and the classical economists using aggregate supply, aggregate demand analysis.

8. Summarize key differences in the policy conclusions of Keynes and the classical economists.

13

Inflation and Unemployment: The Keynesian View

Before turning to critics of the Keynesian model, let us put the model to work. Specifically, in this chapter, we see how the behavior of inflation and unemployment—the key macroeconomic goal variables—are explained by the Keynesian theory.

In Chapter 6 we observed a negative relationship between inflation and unemployment from the early 1950s through the late 1960s. In these years, when the unemployment rate was high the inflation rate was low, and vice versa. The 1970s, however, brought both rising unemployment and rising inflation, a nasty combination that was called **stagflation.** The early 1980s showed a return to the pattern of the 1950s and 1960s: As the inflation rate fell, the unemployment rate moved up (even though the unemployment rate for the first half of the 1980s was substantially higher than at similar inflation rates in the 1950s and 1960s). In the mid-1980s, the inflation rate remained low and the unemployment rate slowly declined.

How can these patterns of unemployment and inflation be explained in the Keynesian system? Taken together, they seem quite odd. Explaining them all is a tough test for the Keynesian system (or any other one).

I
Inflation and the Unemployment–Inflation Tradeoff

In the previous chapter, we discussed the factors that determine the aggregate price *level* (as well as the level of output). Here we switch our focus to inflation, which is the *rate* at which the aggregate price level is rising.[1]

The factors that determine the rate of inflation in the Keynesian theory are also those that determine the rates at which the aggregate supply and demand curves are shifting over time. Since the aggregate demand and supply curves jointly de-

termine price and output, the rate of change in output is related to the rate of inflation. The rate of growth in output is, in turn, related to the levels of employment and unemployment in the economy. When the economy grows rapidly enough to operate near potential (or full-capacity) output, growth in employment keeps up with growth in the labor force and the unemployment rate is low. If growth in the economy is slow or the level of economic activity declines, growth in employment lags behind growth in the labor force, and at times employment falls, causing the unemployment rate to rise. Inflation, real output changes, and the level of unemployment are all determined jointly.

A
Inflation and Aggregate Demand

To begin, we neglect shifts in the aggregate supply curve and focus on the relationship between aggregate demand and the rate of inflation.

Figure 13.1 illustrates how the price level increases as the aggregate demand curve shifts outward. Given the position of the aggregate supply curve, the more rapidly the aggregate demand curve shifts to the right, the more quickly the price level rises. This means that the more rapid the growth in aggregate demand, the higher the inflation rate. Note also that the rise in the price level for a given rightward shift in the aggregate demand curve is larger when the economy is already close to potential output. In Figure 13.1, the rise in the price level (from P_0 to P_1) as the demand curve shifts from y_0^d to y_1^d is small relative to the rise in the price level (from P_2 to P_3) as the aggregate demand curve shifts from y_2^d to y_3^d when output is closer to y_P, the level of potential output.

Faster growth in aggregate demand causes the price level to rise more rapidly but also causes output to rise more quickly. Therefore, given supply-side conditions, more rapid growth in aggregate demand leads to higher employment and to a lower rate of unemployment in the Keynesian system.

Because more rapid growth in aggregate de-

[1] If the aggregate price level is falling, we refer to this as a negative inflation rate, or *deflation.*

246

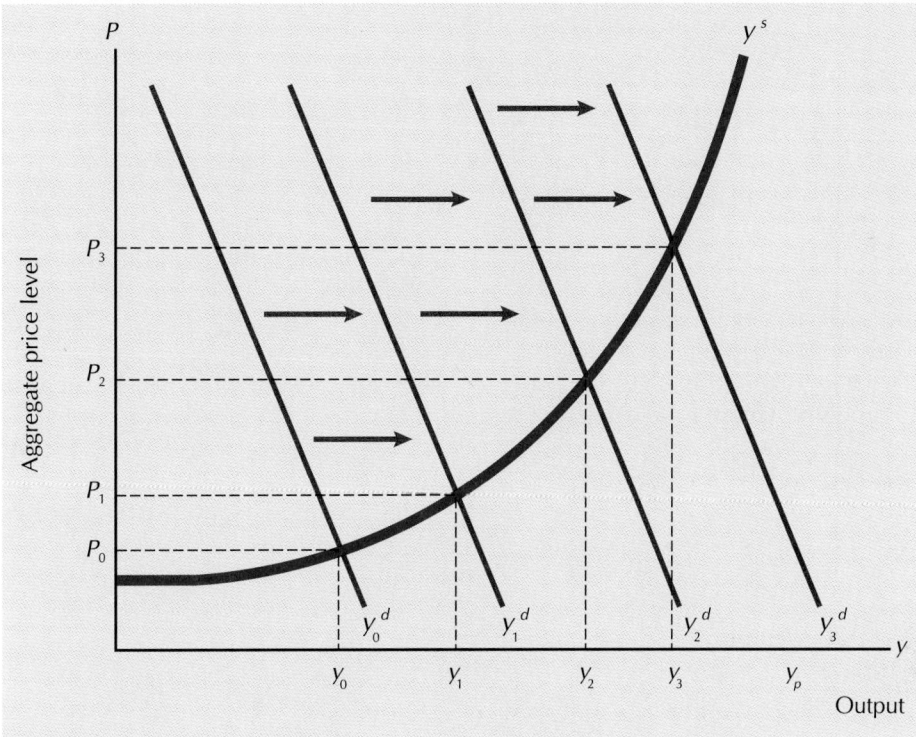

FIGURE 13.1   The Rise in Price and Output as Aggregate Demand Grows

As the aggregate demand curve shifts successively to the right, output and the price level both rise. As output approaches the level of potential output (y_p), increases in demand are reflected more in rising prices than in increased output.

mand leads to a higher inflation rate but a lower unemployment rate, the Keynesian model implies that *for given supply-side conditions* there is a *negative* relationship between unemployment and inflation, such as was observed in the 1950s and 1960s in the United States.

The schedule showing this negative relationship between the unemployment and inflation rates has been termed an economy's **Phillips curve,** named after the British economist A. W. H. Phillips, who was an early student of the tradeoff between unemployment and inflation.

An example of a Phillips curve is plotted in Figure 13.2. Along the curve, lower rates of unemployment correspond to higher rates of inflation, both being the result of higher rates of growth in aggregate demand. Moreover, the Phillips curve becomes steeper as the unemployment rate be-

comes lower. Low rates of unemployment correspond to levels of output near potential output. When output is in this range, increases in demand go mostly into increases in the aggregate price level, with little increase in output. Therefore, over this range the Phillips curve is steep, indicating that the gain in output, and hence the reduction in unemployment, are small for a given increase in inflation.

The negative relationship between unemployment and inflation in the Keynesian model implies that there is a tradeoff between the macroeconomic policy goals of low unemployment and low inflation. Policymakers can, through expansionary monetary and fiscal actions, cause aggregate demand to increase rapidly. Such policies would cause unemployment to decline as we move up the Phillips curve, but the cost of such policies would be an increase in the inflation rate. If this is correct, it poses a serious dilemma because the goals of price stability and low unemployment

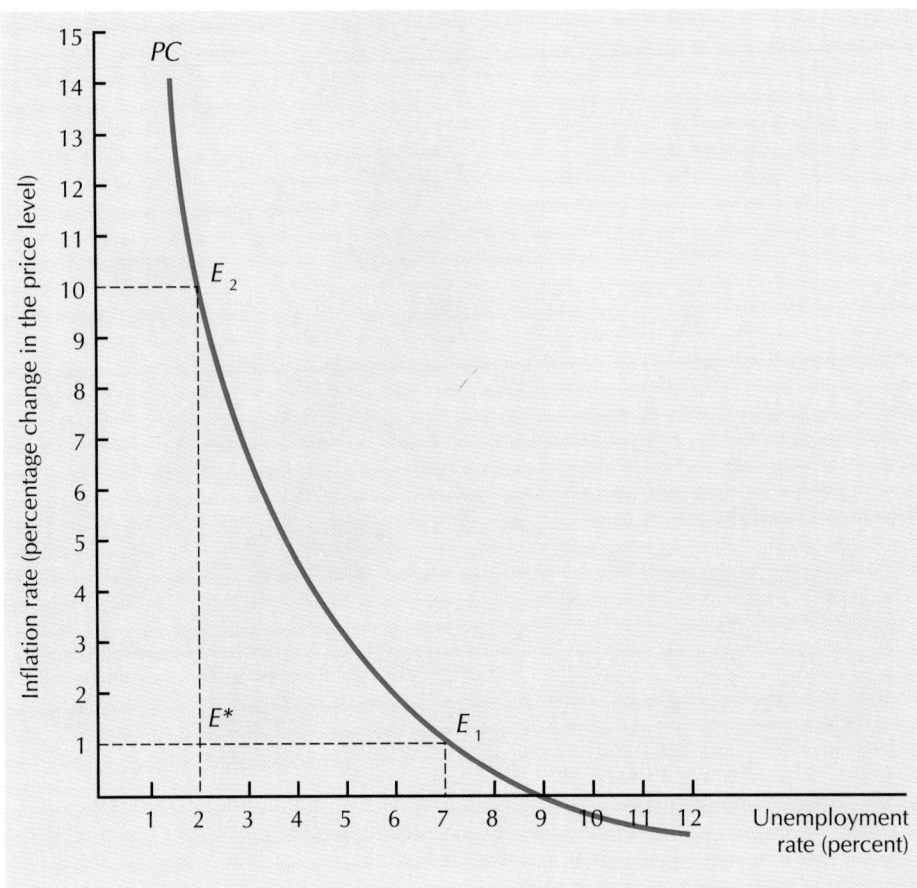

FIGURE 13.2   The Phillips Curve

The Phillips curve depicts the tradeoff between inflation and unemployment. Along the Phillips curve, lower rates of unemployment correspond to higher rates of inflation, both the result of more rapid growth of aggregate demand.

conflict. In Figure 13.2, for example, policymakers could move the economy to a point such as E_1, with a high unemployment rate of 7 percent and a low inflation rate of 1 percent; or to E_2, with a low unemployment rate of 2 percent and a high inflation rate of 10 percent. They could not use monetary and fiscal policy to reach a point like E^*, with low unemployment *and* low inflation.

B
Supply-Side Factors, Inflation, and the Unemployment–Inflation Tradeoff

In the preceding analysis, we considered the effect of demand factors, holding constant supply-side factors. In reality, of course, supply-side as well as

demand-side factors vary, with consequent effects on unemployment and inflation. In Section IV of Chapter 12 we analyzed how shifts in the aggregate supply curve affect the levels of aggregate price and output. Such shifts consequently also affect the rates of inflation and unemployment.

Consider, for example, the effects of unfavorable supply shocks such as the large rises in energy prices in the United States and other industrialized countries in the mid-1970s. These supply shocks caused shifts to the left in the aggregate supply curve, as illustrated in Figure 13.3. The resulting increases in the price level (from P_0 to P_1, P_2, and P_3 in the figure) meant an increased inflation rate during the supply shocks. The shifts to the left in the aggregate supply curve also caused

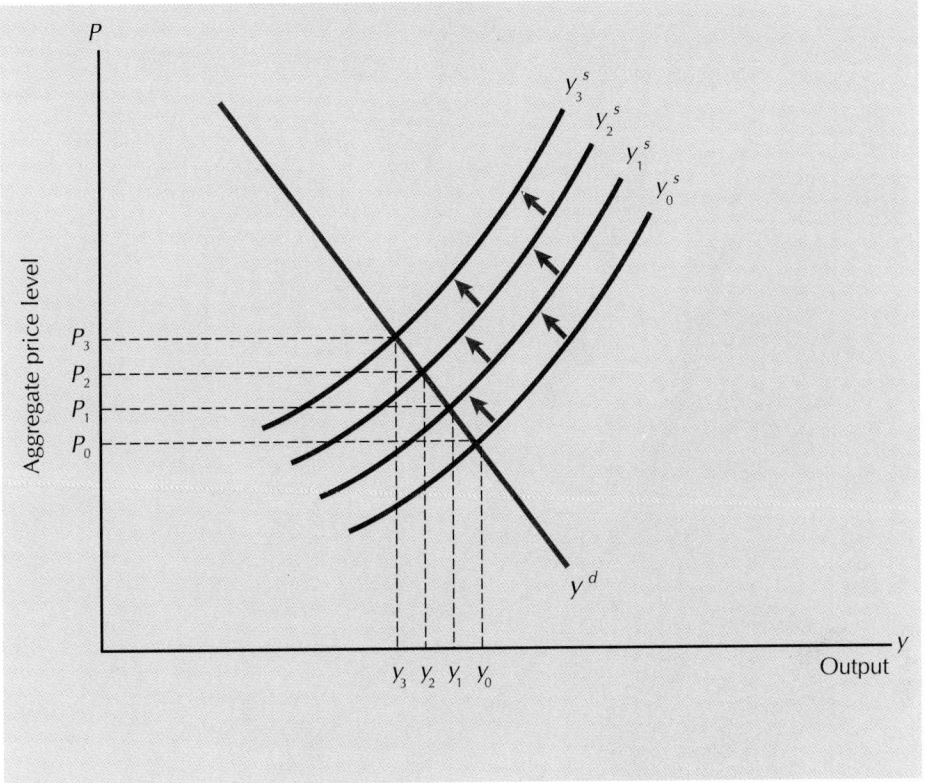

FIGURE 13.3 *The Price and Output Effects of Unfavorable Supply Shocks*

A series of unfavorable supply shocks shift the aggregate supply curve upward to the left. As the supply shocks occur, the price level rises. These price level increases are, in the short run, reflected in a higher rate of inflation.

declines in output (from y_0 to y_1, y_2, and y_3 in the figure). Employment falls, so the unemployment rate rises.

In terms of the Phillips curve diagram, the curve shifts upward, as illustrated in Figure 13.4. The initial Phillips curve is PC_0, and we assume that the economy is operating at point *A* along this curve, with unemployment at 5 percent and inflation running at 3.5 percent. The energy price shocks shift the Phillips curve to the right, to a new position such as PC_1. The economy moves to a point such as *B* along the new Phillips curve, with *both* a higher unemployment rate (7 percent) *and* a higher inflation rate (5 percent).

The energy sector was an important source of supply shocks during the 1970s, but, as suggested previously, other factors may also shift the aggregate supply curve. These factors also cause the Phillips curve to shift. Important among them are changes in the wage demands of labor due to changes in workers' expectations concerning future inflation. An increase in the expected inflation rate, for example, increases money wage demands of labor. This upward pressure on wages shifts the aggregate supply curve upward to the left. Just as was the case with unfavorable energy price shocks, the shift to the left in the aggregate supply curve causes a decline in output (and employment) and a rise in price. During a period of increasing inflationary expectations, therefore, we would observe increased inflation corresponding to any unemployment rate. If this is depicted by the Phillips curve, the curve shifts outward to the right, just as in Figure 13.4. Inflation and unemployment rates both rise.

We see, then, that unfavorable supply shocks such as increases in energy prices (or other raw material prices), as well as increases in workers' inflationary expectations, shift the Phillips curve outward to the right. In Figure 13.4 we showed the

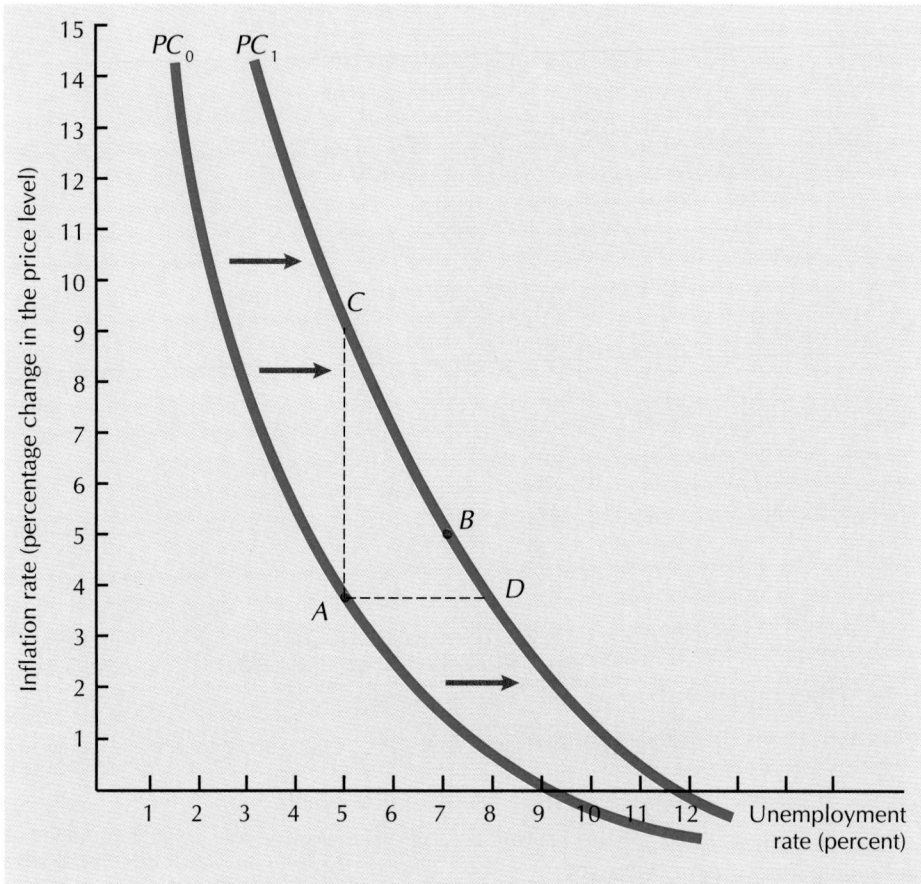

FIGURE 13-4. *Unfavorable Supply Shocks and the Phillips Curve*

A series of unfavorable supply shocks will shift the Phillips curve out to the right from PC$_0$ *to* PC$_1$. *The economy will move from a point such as* A *to a point such as* B, *where both the unemployment and inflation rates are higher.*

economy moving to a position of higher inflation and higher unemployment (from *A* to *B*) as a result of the shift. That the economy must move to *some* point along the new Phillips curve is clear, but what determines the precise point? What determines in Figure 13.4, for example, whether the economy moves to point *B*, to points *C* or *D*, or to some other point along PC$_1$?

In the Keynesian model, the point to which the economy moves depends on how policymakers adjust the level of aggregate demand in response to supply shocks. Suppose that aggregate demand policy does not change in response to the supply shock. This was the assumption made in Figure 13.3, where the aggregate demand curve remains fixed as the aggregate supply curve shifts. In this case, output *must* fall and inflation *must* rise as the

supply curve shifts leftward, as shown in the figure. The economy would move from point *A* to a point such as *B* in Figure 13.4.

But policymakers may not leave the level of aggregate demand unchanged. After all, they observe increases in both inflation and unemployment, while the goals they pursue are *low* inflation and *low* unemployment. Suppose, for example, that policymakers are especially concerned by the fall in output and the consequent rise in unemployment that results from supply shocks. Through monetary or fiscal policies, they could expand aggregate demand. By increasing aggregate demand, they attempt to offset the unfavorable output and employment effects of the supply shocks.

Figure 13.5 illustrates this type of aggregate de-

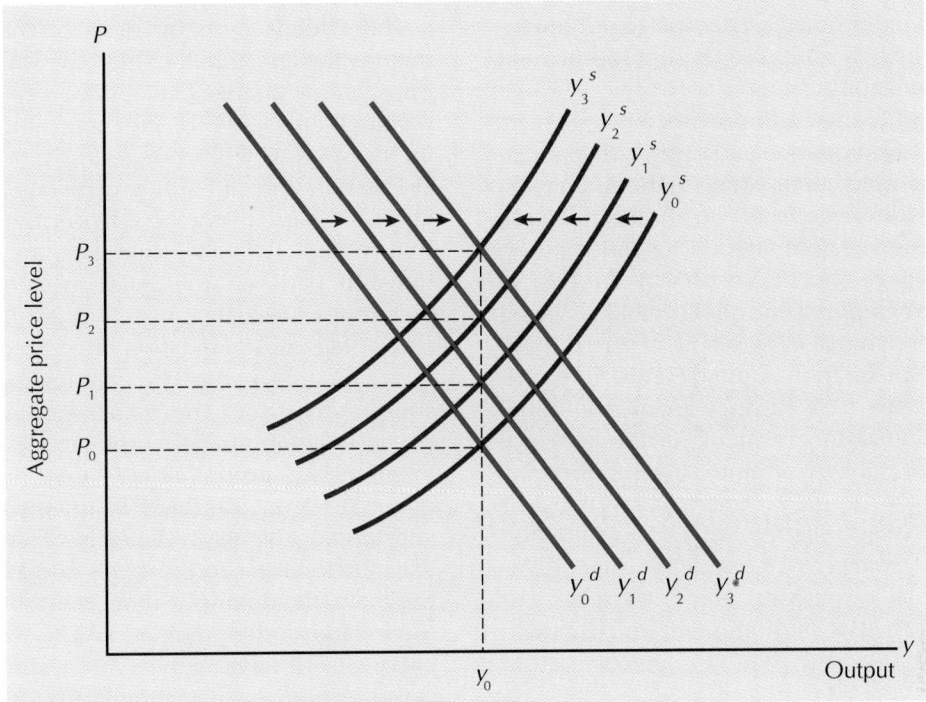

FIGURE 13.5 *Accommodation of Supply Shocks*

By increasing demand, for example through expansionary monetary policy, policymakers could keep output at y_0, even though the aggregate supply curve is shifting to the left.

mand response to unfavorable supply shocks. Policymakers, through expansionary policies (for example, increases in the money supply), cause the aggregate demand curve to shift from y_0^d to y_1^d, y_2^d, and then y_3^d so that output remains at y_0 even as the supply curve shifts leftward (from y_0^s to y_1^s, y_2^s, and y_3^s). Policymakers in this case can be said to *accommodate* the supply shock in the sense that they increase aggregate demand sufficiently so that even at the higher prices caused by the supply shocks, the public still demands the original output level (y_0) on the horizontal axis.

In terms of the Phillips curve, such a complete accommodation of supply shocks would result in the economy moving from point *A* in Figure 13.4 to point *C*. This follows because if the initial output level (y_0 in Figure 13.5) is preserved, the initial level of unemployment will also be maintained.

Such complete accommodation of supply shocks, in the short run, offsets the adverse employment effects of the shocks, but consider the implications of such a policy for the inflation rate. As we move vertically to point *C* in Figure 13.4, the inflation rate rises to a rate not only higher than at

point *A*, the inflation rate before the supply shock, but also higher than at point *B* (9 percent compared to 5 percent), the inflation rate that would result from the supply shocks without any policymaker response. In alleviating the unemployment effects of the supply shocks, the policymaker worsens the adverse inflationary effect.

Alternatively, the policymaker's initial primary concern may have been the inflation caused by the supply shocks. Such concern would lead to restrictive monetary and fiscal policies, such as lowering the money supply, raising taxes, or cutting government spending, in order to lower aggregate demand sufficiently to restore the initial inflation rate. In terms of Figure 13.4, the economy would move from point *A* to point *D*. Note that while the restrictive aggregate demand policy can eliminate the inflationary effects of supply shocks, such a policy makes the unemployment rate worse. At point *D*, the unemployment rate (on the horizontal axis) has risen to a higher rate than at point *B* (8 percent compared to 7 percent), the point the economy moves to without any policymaker response to the supply shock. The restrictive aggregate demand policy itself causes increased unemployment, which is added to the unemployment caused by the supply shocks.

Adverse supply shocks thus cause a nasty policy dilemma. Accommodation of supply shocks can offset the unemployment effects only by increasing their inflationary effects. On the other hand, restrictive aggregate demand policies reduce their inflationary effects, but do so only at the cost of worsening unemployment. Policymakers faced just such a dilemma as a result of the supply shocks of the 1970s. In the United States, for example, following the 1974 oil price shock, the initial concern was inflation. President Ford urged fiscal and monetary policy restraint. To symbolize the anti-inflationary campaign, Americans were asked to wear WIN (Whip Inflation Now) buttons. By the spring of 1975, concern had swung to rising unemployment (over 10 percent) and a large tax cut was enacted. The WIN buttons went into the trash basket.

II
The Changing Nature of the Unemployment–Inflation Tradeoff

The analysis in the previous section leads to the following two conclusions:

1. Changes in the rate of growth in aggregate demand cause the unemployment and inflation rates to move in *opposite* directions. *Such demand-side factors give rise to the negatively sloped Phillips curve.*
2. *Changes in supply-side factors cause unemployment and inflation to move in the same direction.* Supply-side factors result in shifts in the Phillips curve. Unfavorable supply shocks such as the energy price increases of the 1970s shift the Phillips curve upward to the right, increasing *both* inflation and unemployment. Favorable supply developments from 1982 to 1986 contributed to declines in both inflation and unemployment during that period, causing the Phillips curve to shift downward.

The Phillips curve analysis of the unemployment–inflation relationship answers the questions about changes that have occurred in the relationship between inflation and unemployment. Figure 13.6 reproduces the plot of the annual inflation and unemployment rates for 1953–87 given in Chapter 6. As noted, over the early part of that period (1953–69), there was an inverse relationship between the inflation and unemployment rates. The data points for the 1970s, however, show high rates of inflation often accompanied by high unemployment. The data for the early 1980s show a return to the negative relationship between inflation and unemployment, as declining inflation was accompanied by rising unemployment. However, the level of unemployment was substantially higher in the early 1980s than at similar inflation rates in the 1950s and 1960s. Later in the 1980s, the unemployment rate fell slowly while the inflation rate remained low.

Consistent with conclusions 1 and 2 above, we can interpret the data points for 1953–69 as the result of a period when *changes in aggregate demand* were the primary cause of changes in unemployment and inflation. Figure 13.7 plots the annual unemployment and inflation rates for this period. The points for 1953–69 represent movements along a quite stable downward-sloping Phillips curve. The reasons for such stability of the Phillips curve during this period were two. The first was the absence of major supply shocks. The second, and related, reason was that the 1953–65 period was one of low and stable inflation rates. In that environment, workers' inflationary expectations were stable; changes in inflationary expectations were not a factor causing the Phillips curve to shift.

Figure 13.8 shows the unemployment–inflation rate combinations for 1970–87, as compared to the 1953–69 Phillips curve. Here *changes in aggregate supply* come into play. Note that *all* the points for 1970–87 lie above the Phillips curve for the earlier period. Moreover, they do not lie on any one curve but rather indicate the presence of several shifts in the Phillips curve during this period. Already in 1970 and 1971, there was evidence of an upward shift. This shift is attributable to a rise in workers' expected rate of inflation. With the beginning of the Vietnam War in 1965, government spending on national defense rose rapidly. This increased spending was only partially (and belatedly) fi-

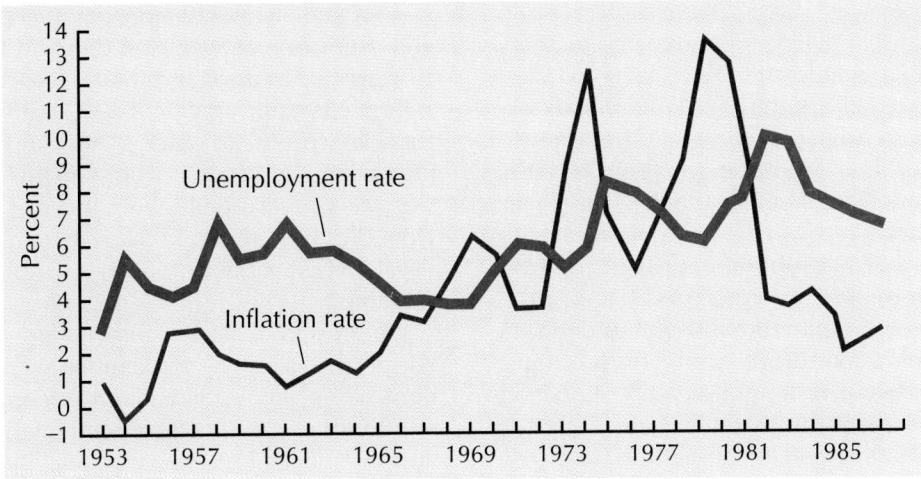

FIGURE 13.6 *U.S. Inflation and Unemployment Rates, 1953–87*

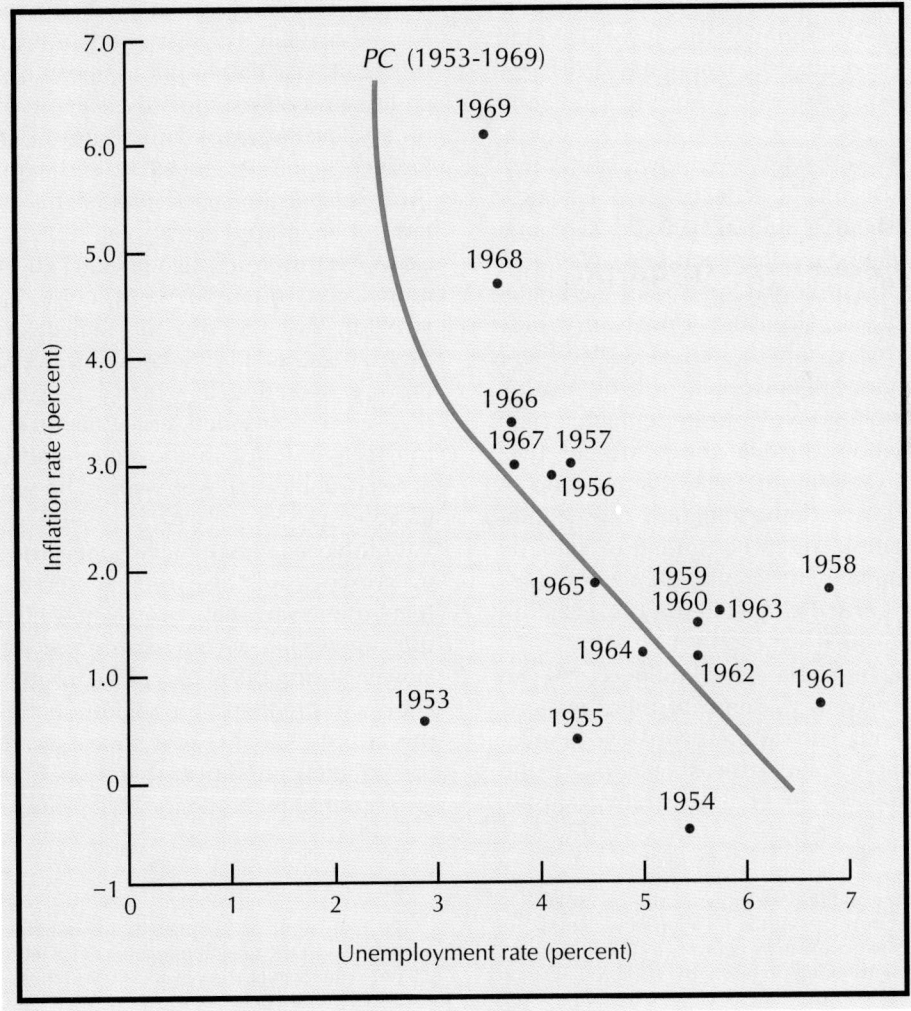

FIGURE 13.7 *The U.S. Phillips Curve, 1953–69*

nanced by increased taxes. The result was an expansionary fiscal policy applied to an economy already at a high employment level. The inflation rate climbed steadily, and by 1970 inflationary expectations had adjusted upward. The consequence was an upward shift in the Phillips curve, as indicated by the position of the data points for 1970 and 1971.[2]

Beginning in 1973, supply shocks also became a factor shifting the Phillips curve upward. In 1973, the supply shocks came from the agricultural sector. Unfavorable harvests both in the United States and abroad resulted in shortages that pushed food prices up 15 percent during the first nine months of the year. In 1974 and then again in 1979, the shocks occurred in the petroleum market, where the price of a barrel of crude oil *quadrupled* in 1974 and *tripled* in 1979. As the inflation rate rose due to these supply shocks, inflationary expectations of workers increased, reinforcing the upward shift in the Phillips curve during the rest of the 1970s (see, for example, the points for 1974 and 1979 in Figure 13.8).

By 1981, these unfavorable supply shocks had ceased. There was a *fall* in energy prices in 1982–86. The Phillips curve shifted back down somewhat. But inflationary expectations, well entrenched after the prolonged period of high inflation in the 1970s, adjusted downward only gradually. For this reason, though we will see later that other factors were at work as well, by historic standards the unemployment rate remained high for a given inflation rate (see the points for 1982 and 1983, for example). In 1986, a large drop in energy prices lowered the inflation rate significantly and unemployment continued to fall. The inflation–unemployment combinations for 1986 and 1987 had returned almost to the 1953–69 Phillips curve.

The Keynesian analysis of the Phillips curve can then provide answers to some of the questions raised in Chapter 6. The simultaneous rise in inflation and unemployment—the *stagflation* of the 1970s—was the result of unfavorable supply shocks and rising inflationary expectations. What about the role of aggregate demand policies over this period? In the United States, government budget deficits were larger in the 1970s and early 1980s than in the 1950s and 1960s. Annual rates of growth in the money supply in this later period were also substantially above those of earlier years. How did these different patterns of monetary and fiscal policy variables affect unemployment and inflation?

We saw in the previous section that adverse supply shocks pose a dilemma for policymakers controlling aggregate demand. *Accommodation* of supply shocks offsets the unemployment effects of supply shocks but worsens their inflationary effects; *restrictive* policies reduce inflationary effects only at the cost of worsening unemployment. The unfavorable supply shocks of the 1970s presented policymakers with difficult choices. In the Keynesian view, the increased government deficits reflect, in part, attempts to accommodate supply shocks and offset some of their unfavorable effects on the level of employment. But in large part, the budget deficits of the 1970s and early 1980s were the *result* of the recessions of the period. As the level of economic activity fell during these recessions, tax revenues also fell and government payments for unemployment compensation rose, swelling the government deficit.[3] Later in the 1980s, the deficit remained large even as the economy recovered. The expansionary fiscal policies that led to continued large deficits contributed to the recovery, but in the Keynesian view created other problems as well—an issue we return to in Chapter 19.

In the case of monetary policy, the higher money growth rates also represented a response to high unemployment over much of the 1970s. In the Keynesian view, had money growth been slower during the recessions caused by the supply shocks of the 1970s, the unemployment caused by the supply shocks would have been higher and the inflation rate lower than was, in fact, the case. A tightening of monetary policy between 1979 and

---

[2]In August 1971 mandatory wage and price controls were enacted. These controls slowed the inflation rate in 1971 and 1972. The end of most mandatory controls in December 1972 was also a factor contributing to the sharp rise in the inflation rate in 1973.

[3]In Section III of Chapter 19, we attempt to unravel the movements in the federal budget deficit that result from cyclical movements in economic activity and those that result from discretionary shifts in fiscal policy.

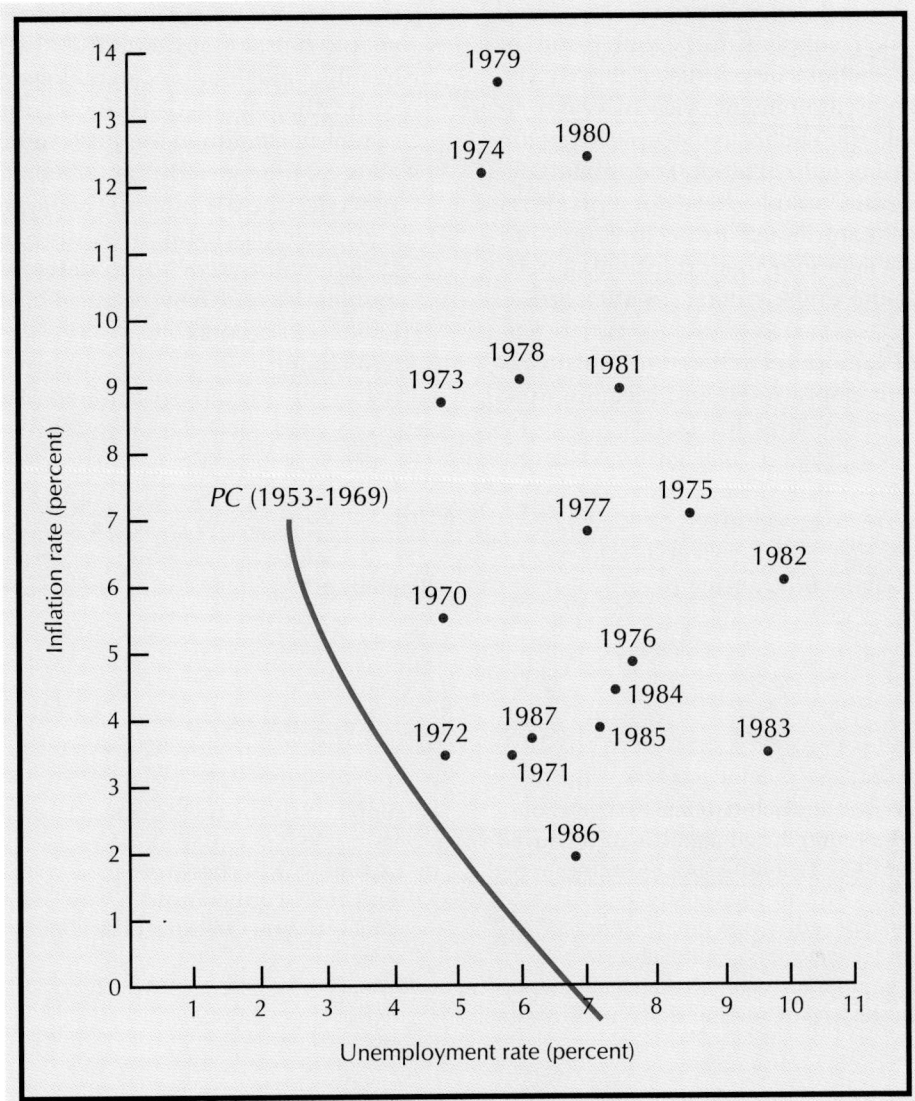

FIGURE 13.8   A Shifting Unemployment–Inflation Tradeoff, 1970–87

1982, in the Keynesian view, was the primary cause of the recession during that period (although money growth rates remained high relative to those of the 1950s and 1960s). A more expansionary monetary policy beginning in late 1982 contributed to the recovery that followed.

SUMMARY

1. The Keynesian model implies that changes in the rate of growth in aggregate demand cause the unemployment and inflation rates to move in *opposite* directions. Such demand-side factors give rise to a negatively sloped Phillips curve. This negatively sloped Phillips curve characterizes the 1953–69 period.

2. Changes in supply-side factors cause unem-

ployment and inflation to move in the *same* direction. Such supply-side factors result in shifts in the Phillips curve. Unfavorable supply shocks such as the energy price increases in the 1970s shift the Phillips curve upward to the right, increasing *both* inflation and unemployment. Favorable supply developments from 1982 to 1986 contributed to declines in both inflation and unemployment during that period, causing the Phillips curve to shift downward.

3. The Keynesian model can therefore explain the behavior of unemployment and inflation from

the 1960s to the 1970s and into the 1980s. It should be said, however, that this explanation has the benefit of hindsight. Keynesians, along with other economists, found the phenomenon of stagflation in the 1970s much more puzzling as it occurred than when seen in retrospect. In fact, the puzzling behavior of inflation and unemployment over the course of the 1970s contributed to the development of the monetarist and new classical critiques of the Keynesian model that we consider in the next two chapters.

KEY TERMS

Unemployment–inflation tradeoff
Phillips curve

Stagflation

QUESTIONS AND PROBLEMS

1. Do policymakers at any point in time have to choose between the goals of reduced inflation and reduced unemployment? Use aggregate supply, aggregate demand analysis to explain your answer.

2. What is *stagflation* and why did it occur in the 1970's? Illustrate *stagflation* graphically.

3. What are the appropriate demand management policy actions in the face of adverse shifts in aggregate

supply? Explain any dilemmas faced by policymakers.

4. Explain why Keynesian analysis gives rise to a Phillips Curve. Further, explain why Keynesian analysis would lead one to expect the Phillips Curve to shift sometimes.

5. What is the difference between increasing prices and increasing inflation?

14

The Monetarist Counterrevolution

Describing the reception that Keynesian economics received from the new generation of economists in the 1930s, Nobel Prize winner Paul Samuelson wrote:

> *The General Theory caught most economists under the age of thirty-five with the unexpected virulence of a disease first attacking and decimating an isolated tribe of South Sea islanders.*[1]

Milton Friedman, though only 24 in 1936, was among those with an immunity to the Keynesian influence. By the late 1940s, he had become the central figure in the development of **monetarism**, the first of the modern challenges to Keynesian economics. For many years while enthusiasm for Keynesian economics remained strong, Friedman felt as if he were "preaching in the wilderness." A turning point came in the 1970s, however, when many blamed the poor performance of the economy on the failure of Keynesian economic policies. Friedman's wilderness became more populated, and today monetarism is embraced by an influential minority of economists. In this chapter, we examine the basic elements of the monetarist counterrevolution. We also consider the Keynesian response to the monetarists.

Read Perspective 14A.

I
Central Monetarist Themes

Our discussion of monetarism is organized around the following three major themes:

1. Monetarists stress the longer-run self-stabilizing properties of the economy.
2. Monetarists believe that the quantity of money is the dominant factor in determining the level of money GNP.

3. Monetarists favor a noninterventionist approach to macroeconomic policy.

These views should have a familiar ring. Each echoes a classical economic view and, in fact, monetarism is a modernization of parts of the classical economics. Our discussion will show the classical roots of monetarism and point out areas where monetarists modify the classical view. We begin by considering each of the three monetarist themes in turn.

II
Longer-Run Self-Stabilizing Properties

Keynes criticized the classical economists for not addressing short-run macroeconomic problems. To Keynes, merely explaining the long-run equilibrium point to which the economy might move was "too easy, too useless a task." Keynes's focus was on the short-run or cyclical problems and on policies to solve them. For the longer-run course of the economy, Keynes had less concern. "In the long run," he noted, "we are all dead."

Friedman believes that Keynes shifted the focus of macroeconomics too far toward the short run.

> *Economists now tend to concentrate on cyclical movements, to act and talk as if any improvement, however slight, in control of the cycle justified any sacrifice, however large, in long-run efficiency, or prospects for growth, of the economic system.*[2]

Taking a longer perspective, Friedman believes that a private enterprise system left free of destabilizing government policies provides the most favorable climate for economic progress. Also, if left free of government intervention, the economy will

[1] Paul Samuelson, "The General Theory," in Robert Lekachman (ed.), *The General Theory: Reports of Three Decades* (New York: St. Martin's, 1964), p. 315.

[2] Milton Friedman, "A Monetary and Fiscal Framework for Economic Stability," in Milton Friedman, *Essays in Positive Economics* (Chicago: University of Chicago Press, 1953), p. 133.

PERSPECTIVE 14A
Why Economists Disagree

Here and in Chapter 15, we will consider *schools* of macroeconomists that reject the Keynesian vision—just as Keynes rejected the classical vision. Macroeconomics would be simpler if disagreement did not exist, if there were a unified consensus model. But important macroeconomic controversies *do* exist and we have to sort them out.

Discussing why economists disagree, Milton Friedman wrote:

> The true test of a scientific theory—of a set of propositions about a class of observable phenomena—is whether it works, whether it correctly predicts the consequences of changes in conditions. But this is not an easy test to apply in any field and certainly not in economics. Controlled experiments permitting near isolation of one or a few forces are virtually impossible. We must test our propositions by observing uncontrolled experience that involves a large number of people, numerous economic variables, frequent changes in other circumstances, and, at that, is imperfectly recorded. The interpre-

tation of the experience is further complicated because the experience affects directly many of the observers, often giving them reasons, irrelevant from a scientific view, to prefer one rather than another interpretation of the complex and ever-changing course of events.[3]

As Keynes had noted 30 years before, "In economics you cannot *convict* your opponent of error—you can only *convince* him of it."[4]

Since we cannot perform controlled laboratory experiments, we must deal with differing interpretations of macroeconomic reality. But as we will see in the next two chapters, there are also substantial areas of agreement among macroeconomists. In Chapter 16 we will pull our analysis together and identify areas of consensus as well as controversy.

[3]Milton Friedman, "Why Economists Disagree," in Milton Friedman, *Dollars and Deficits* (Englewood Cliffs, N.J.; Prentice-Hall; 1968), pp.15–16.
[4]Paul Davidson, *Money and the Real World* (New York: Wiley, 1978), p. ix.

---

tend toward *natural rates* of output and unemployment. The private sector of the economy is essentially *shock absorbing* or *self-stabilizing*.

This view runs counter to the Keynesian view that private sector demand, particularly investment demand, is *unstable*. Although his theory is closer to the classical view, Friedman differs from classical economists by recognizing that shocks to the economy will in the *short run* cause output and employment to deviate from their natural rates. Only in the longer run will stability prevail.

Why not, then, pursue activist Keynesian policies to ensure desirable short-run performance of the economy? Friedman's objections to such policies can be better understood after we consider the second of the monetarist tenets—the importance of money.

III
Money Determines Money GNP

Monetarists believe that the quantity of money is the dominant factor determining the level of economic activity measured in current dollars. *Money determines money GNP.* Recall that

$$\text{Money GNP} = Y = P \times y \qquad (14.1)$$

That is, money (or nominal) GNP (Y) is equal to real GNP (y) multiplied by the aggregate price level (P). It is the value of this product ($P \times y$) that in the monetarist view is determined by the money supply. The monetarist theory of the relationship between money and GNP is a modern version of the classical **quantity theory**, which, as Friedman puts it, "fell into disrepute after the crash of 1929 and the subsequent Great Depression."[5]

Central to the classical quantity theory was the equation of exchange:

$$M \times V = P \times y \qquad (14.2)$$

The money supply (M) times the velocity of money (V), the average number of times each dollar is used in a GNP transaction during a period (e.g., a year), must be equal to money GNP ($P \times y$).

In the classical theory, the velocity of money (V) was determined by institutional factors and assumed to be constant in the short run. Real GNP (real output, y) was determined completely by supply-side factors. Changes in the money supply (M) would cause changes in only the price level term (P) in equation (14.2). The price level would change proportionately with a change in the quantity of money.

Monetarists do not believe that velocity is constant, but they do believe that movements in velocity play only a minor role in explaining short-run changes in economic activity. Movements in the V term on the left-hand side of equation (14.2) are secondary to changes in the M (money supply) term in causing changes in money GNP ($P \times y$ on the right-hand side).

Monetarists part company with classical quantity theorists in a more substantive manner over the determinants of real output. They do not believe that output is totally supply determined in the short run. Rather, they believe that changes in the quantity of money will have strong effects on real output in the short run. The y (real output) term as well as the P (price level) term in equation (14.2) will change when the money supply changes. Therefore, in the hands of the monetarists, the quantity theory becomes a theory of money GNP ($P \times y$) rather than a theory of the price level alone. *Changes in the quantity of money cause approximately proportional changes in money GNP.*

The monetarist model is represented graphically in Figure 14.1. The aggregate demand curve, y^d,

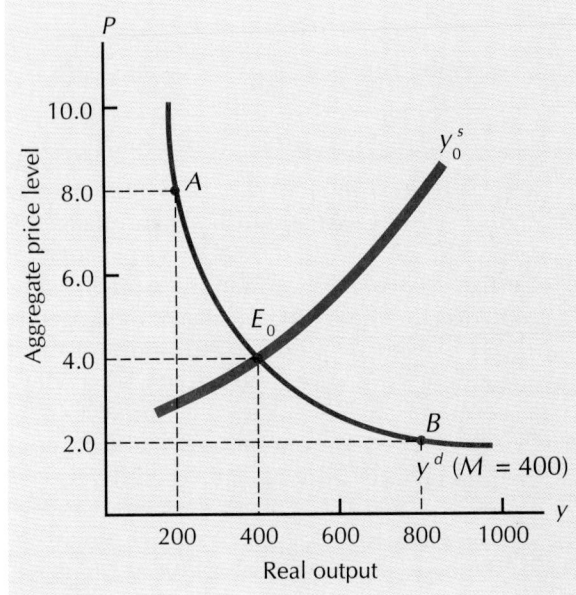

FIGURE 14.1   The Monetarist Model

is drawn so that the quantity measured on the vertical axis times the quantity measured on the horizontal axis ($P \times y$ = money GNP), is 1,600 at all points along the curve. Points such as $P = 8.0$, $y = 200$ (point A), and $P = 2.0$, $y = 800$ (point B) lie on the curve. The position of the aggregate demand curve ($M = 400$) depends on the level of the money supply, assumed to be 400 for this example. Fixing the money supply at 400 units therefore fixes money GNP at 1,600 units. The money supply determines money GNP.[6]

The monetarist aggregate supply curve, like the Keynesian aggregate supply curve, slopes upward to the right. As explained previously, monetarists do not believe that output is completely supply determined. On this issue, they agree with the Keynesians that both supply and demand are important in determining short-run output. Equilibrium output will be where aggregate supply and demand are equal. This occurs at point E_0 in Figure 14.1, an output level of 400 and a value of 4.0 for the price level.

Figure 14.2 illustrates the effects of increasing

---

[5]Milton Friedman, *The Counter-revolution in Monetary Theory* (London: Institute of Economic Affairs, 1970). p. 11.

[6]We are therefore assuming that velocity is 4.0. This can be seen from equation (14.2), where $V = (P \times y)/M$. In our example, $V = 1,600/400 = 4$.

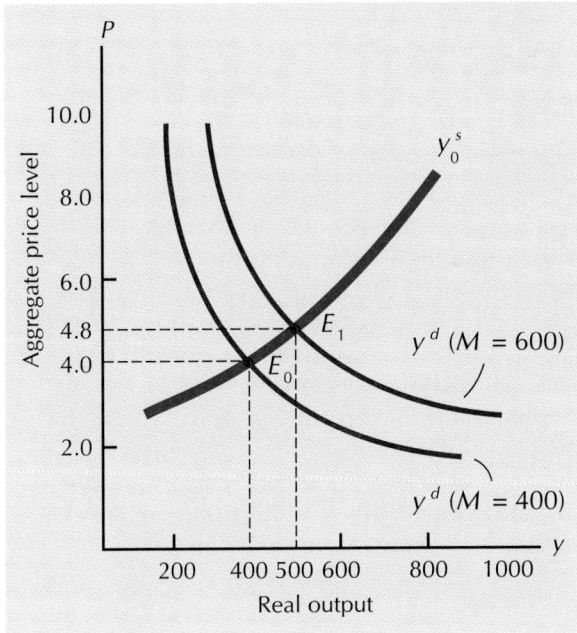

FIGURE 14.2 *The Effects of an Increase in the Money Supply in the Monetarist Model*

In the monetarist model, an increase in the money supply causes a proportionate increase in money GNP. What determines the degree to which this rise in money GNP ($P \times y$) occurs as a rise in real output (y) or a rise in the price level (P)? In terms of our example, output rose from 400 to 500 units, while the price level rose from 4.0 to 4.8. What factors determine these proportions?

To begin, we ask why output rises at all: Why is the monetarist aggregate supply curve not vertical, as in the classical model? The explanation is the same as the explanation of why the Keynesian aggregate supply schedule is not vertical. As the price level rises, in the short run money wages are assumed not to rise in proportion. The rise in the price level, because it is not matched by an equal rise in (labor) costs, stimulates production. The reasons why money wages do not rise in proportion to the rise in the aggregate price level in the monetarist analysis parallel those given by Keynesians (see Section II in Chapter 12). First, fixed money wage contracts tie down many workers' wages in the short run. Second, it will take time before workers recognize that prices are rising and hence demand higher money wages. As in the Keynesian system, price expectations in the monetarist model are *backward looking*.

In the short run, output and the price level both rise in response to an increase in the money supply. Friedman, in the late 1960s, believed that the output response would be strong, with the price level rising only a little in the first few years of an expansionary monetary policy. In recent years he has become less certain of this. However, even if there is a strong output response to an expansionary monetary policy, the essential point for the monetarists is that this is a *temporary* effect. Over the longer run, the period of greater interest to the monetarists, Friedman believes that output and employment move to what he calls their *natural rates*. These natural rates are not affected by the money supply.

the quantity of money from 400 to 600, an increase of 50 percent. The increase in the money supply shifts the aggregate demand curve out to the right from y^d ($M = 400$) to y^d ($M = 600$). The new aggregate demand curve intersects the aggregate supply curve at E_1, where the output level is 500 and the value of the aggregate price level is 4.8. Note that the new level of money GNP is $4.8 \times 500 = 2400$. Money GNP ($P \times y$) rises from 1600 (4.0×400) to 2400 (4.8×500), an increase of 50 percent, equal to the percentage increase in the money supply.

Just as our numerical and graphic examples made relationships in the Keynesian model appear overly mechanical, so is the case here. Monetarists would not expect money GNP to rise by *precisely* 50 percent if the money supply rose by 50 percent. Nor would monetarists argue that the money supply is the only factor that influences aggregate demand. But Figures 14.1 and 14.2 do reflect the central monetarist view that the money supply is the *dominant systematic influence* on money GNP.

Read Perspective 14B.

PERSPECTIVE 14B
The Monetarist Explanation of the Great Depression

The Great Depression of the 1930s had a profound effect on macroeconomic thinking. It led to the downfall of the classical economics and the rise of Keynesian economics as a new orthodoxy. Milton Friedman and other monetarists do not deny that the experience of the 1930s contradicts the classical view of the labor market, where the money wage adjusts quickly to maintain full employment. After all, the U.S. unemployment rate never fell below 12 percent during the 1930s and reached 25 percent in 1933. Monetarists do not believe that real output is supply determined at the full-employment level, as it is in the classical model.

Friedman and other monetarists do, however, deny that the Great Depression disproved the other central part of classical economics—the quantity theory of money. In fact, they believe that the sharp decline in economic activity in the United States was *caused* by a decline in the money supply, as predicted by the quantity theory.

Table 14.1 shows the level of several macroeconomic aggregates in 1929, the start of the Depression, compared with their level in 1933, the low point of the slump. The table indicates that money GNP fell 46.1 percent and real GNP fell 29.6 percent. The rest of the drop in money GNP is accounted for by a fall in the aggregate price level. The narrowly defined money stock,

M1 (currency plus checkable deposits), fell by 26.5 percent between 1929 and 1933. The M2 measure of the money supply, which includes other bank deposits, fell by 33.3 percent. Monetarists conclude that the decline in the money supply caused the bulk of the fall in both money and real GNP between 1929 and 1933.

Keynesians dispute this monetary explanation of the Depression. They do believe that if the Federal Reserve had been able to prevent a decline in the money supply during the 1929–33 period, the Depression would have been less severe than it was. They believe, however, that the primary causes of the Depression were autonomous declines in several components of aggregate demand—consumption, investment, and exports—caused, in turn, by factors such as the stock market crash in 1929, overbuilding in the construction sector in the late 1920s, and the breakdown of the international monetary system. This has been called the *spending hypothesis* in contrast to the *money hypothesis* advanced by Friedman and other monetarists.[7]

[7]For Friedman's analysis, see Milton Friedman and Anna J. Schwartz, *The Great Contraction* (Princeton, N. J.: Princeton University Press, 1965). Also on the subject of the causes of the Great Depression see Peter Temin, *Did Monetary Forces Cause the Great Depression?* (New York: Norton, 1976), and the papers in Karl Brunner (ed.), *The Great Depression Revisited* (Boston: Martinus Nijhoff, 1981).

TABLE 14.1   Selected Macroeconomic Aggregates, 1929 and 1933

	Money GNP (*Y*)	Real GNP (*y*) (in 1982 Dollars)	M1	M2
1929	$103.9 billion	$708.6 billion	26.4	46.2
1933	$ 56.0 billion	$498.5 billion	19.4	30.8
Percentage decline (1929–33)	46.1%	29.6%	26.5%	33.3%

Natural rates of output, employment, and therefore unemployment, in the monetarist model are determined by *real* supply-side factors: the capital stock, the size of the labor force, and the level of technology. In our simple model, the natural rates of output, employment, and unemployment are the classical equilibrium levels of these variables (unemployment being confined to frictional and structural forms).

Friedman differs from the classical economists in that he does not argue that the economy necessarily moves to these natural rates in the short run.

A
Effects of an Increase in Money Growth

To analyze how the economy can be moved away from natural rates of output, employment, and unemployment in the short run but not in the longer run, consider the effects of a change in the *rate of growth* of the money supply. This is a switch from analysis of a one-time change in the money supply, as in Figure 14.2, to a change in the rate of growth in the money supply. The switch will facilitate comparison with the Keynesian Phillips curve that we discussed in Chapter 13.

Suppose that all variables are initially at their natural rates and that the money supply is growing at 5 percent per year. Let us assume that real output is growing at 3 percent per year, i.e., the natural rate of output grows at 3 percent per year, due to growth in the capital stock, labor force, and technological change. In the monetarist view, money GNP $(P \times y)$ in this situation would be growing by approximately the 5 percent growth in the money supply. With real output growing at 3 percent, initially the inflation rate is 2 percent. Let us also assume that we are initially at a natural unemployment rate of 6 percent. These initial conditions are summarized in column 1 of Table 14.2.

Figure 14.3 shows this initial position of the economy as point *A*, an unemployment rate of 6 percent and an inflation rate of 2 percent. The figure shows point *A* as one point along the downward-sloping Phillips curve, PC_0. In the short run,

TABLE 14.2 **The Effects of an Increase in the Growth Rate in the Money Supply**

	(1) Initial	(2) Short Run	(3) Longer Run
Money supply growth	5%	7%	7%
Real growth rate	3%	4%	3%
Unemployment rate	6%	5%	6%
Inflation rate	2%	3%	4%

as we move down the Phillips curve, we are considering lower rates of growth in the money supply. Lower rates of growth in the money supply mean lower rates of growth in money GNP, which are reflected in lower rates of increase in prices and real output. The lower rate of increase in prices is, of course, a lower inflation rate. The lower rate of growth in output leads to slower growth in employment and, therefore, to higher unemployment. The monetarist *short-run* Phillips curve is downward sloping, as in the Keynesian case.

Now consider the effects of an increase in the rate of money growth, for example, from 5 percent

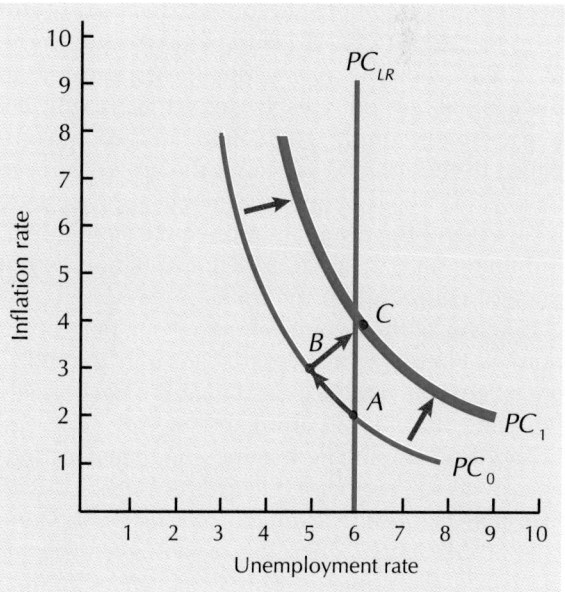

FIGURE 14.3 *The Monetarist Phillips Curve*

to 7 percent per year. The growth rate in money GNP would also rise from 5 percent to approximately 7 percent. The inflation rate would increase. The growth rate in real output would also increase and, therefore, the unemployment rate would fall. In terms of Figure 14.3, we move from point *A* to point *B*, where the inflation rate has increased from 2 percent to 3 percent and the unemployment rate has fallen from 6 percent to 5 percent. Economic conditions at this new short-run position (point *B*) are summarized in column (2) of Table 14.2.

But Friedman and other monetarists stress that this is only the *short-run* adjustment of the economy. In the *longer run*, as workers see that the inflation rate has risen, they will demand a higher rate of increase in money wages. As a consequence, a higher rate of inflation will now correspond to any given unemployment rate. This means that the Phillips curve will shift out from PC_0 to a position such as PC_1. As in the Keynesian analysis, an increase in inflationary expectations on the part of workers shifts the Phillips curve to the right. When this longer-run adjustment is complete, the economy will be at point *C* in Figure 14.3. The economic situation will be as summarized in column 3 of Table 14.2.

At the new longer-run equilibrium point, workers have restored their initial real wage level. Thus, there will no longer be an incentive for firms to maintain employment and output above the natural rate. Output growth, employment, and, therefore, the unemployment rate have returned to their initial natural rates. Because the growth rate in the money supply is still higher (7 percent compared to the initial 5 percent), the growth rate in *money* GNP is permanently higher at approximately 7 percent. However, all of the increased growth in money GNP is due to a higher inflation rate, 4 percent compared to the initial 2 percent.

In terms of the two-question logic of macroeconomics, Friedman believes that it is only the difference between what is expected and what actually happens that affects output and employment. The output and employment gains due to faster money growth are temporary. *Once the longer-run adjustment has been made and the higher inflation rate is fully anticipated, the only result of faster growth in the money supply is a higher inflation rate.*

B
Policy Implications

The monetarists use the theory of natural rates of unemployment and output to explain the upward spiral in inflation in many industrialized countries during the late 1960s and throughout the 1970s. Policymakers, in the monetarist view, pursued short-run gains in output and employment that were paid for by progressively higher inflation rates. This type of inflationary spiral is illustrated in Figure 14.4.

Suppose that policymakers pursue a target unemployment rate of 4 percent because they believe that this is in some sense a desirable (or politically popular) rate. As in our example, assume, however, that the natural rate is actually 6 percent and begin with the same initial conditions as in Figure 14.3 and Table 14.2.

As in Figure 14.3, a policy to lower the unemployment rate below 6 percent toward the 4 percent goal could begin with an increase in the rate of growth in the money supply—in the example, from 5 percent to 7 percent. The policy would work at first. The economy goes from point *A* to point *B*. After perhaps a year or two, however, the economy has moved to point *C*. In the monetarist view, the policy fails to lower unemployment per-

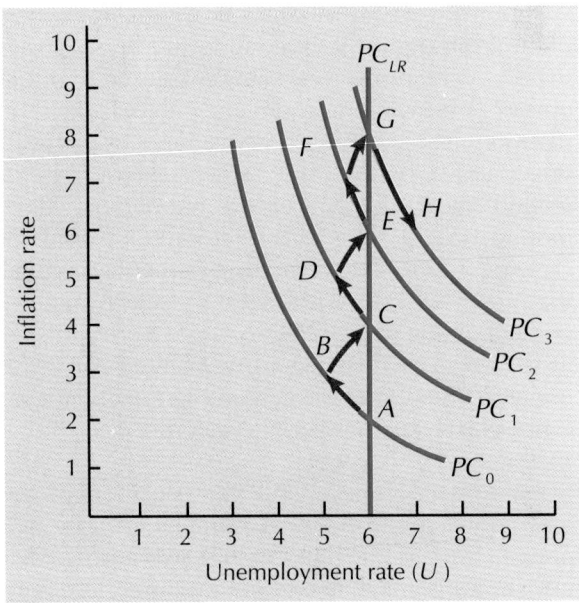

FIGURE 14.4 An Inflationary Spiral

manently. At this point, if policymakers still pursue the unemployment target, they must raise the rate of growth in the money supply to stimulate the economy further, for example, from 7 percent to 9 percent. In the short run we go to a point such as D, but as the new, even higher inflation rate is perceived, the economy adjusts back to the natural rate at point E. Onward and upward this process might go to points such as F and G.

This is the core of the monetarist explanation for the way inflation accelerated between 1969 and 1980. But what about the higher unemployment during these years? At times, inflation came to be regarded as a more pressing problem than unemployment. Policymakers temporarily abandoned the pursuit of arbitrary unemployment rate targets, and growth rates in the money supply were reduced, often drastically. When we hit the monetary brakes in a climate of high inflationary expectations, the monetarists believe that we will move from a point such as G to a point such as H in Figure 14.4, where we have *both* high inflation and high unemployment.

Because workers expect a high inflation rate following a period of rapid growth in the money supply, growth in money wages does not slow down quickly when there is a switch to an anti-inflation policy. The economy has to move along a very unfavorable Phillips curve such as PC_3 in Figure 14.4. Such an anti-inflation policy was followed by the Nixon administration in 1969 and by the Ford administration in 1974. The switch to a more restrictive policy by the Reagan administration (and by the Federal Reserve) in the early 1980s lasted longer. In the monetarist view, the 1980s saw downward shifts in the Phillips curve (from PC_3 to PC_2, for example). Workers came to expect lower inflation rates, and, therefore, reduced money wage demands.

V

Noninterventionist Policy Conclusions

By pulling together elements of the monetarist position discussed so far, we can see the basis for the noninterventionist policy conclusions that the monetarists reach. Monetarists take a longer view of the economy than do Keynesians. Over this longer time horizon, they stress the self-stabilizing properties of the economy, its tendency to return to natural rates of output and employment.

Friedman argues that the differing time perspective has an important influence on the policy stance economists take. He also believes that the choice of time perspective is related to one's overall view of the role of government: "The person who gives primacy to freedom and believes in limited government tends to take the long view, to put major emphasis on the ultimate and permanent consequences of policies rather than on the immediate and possibly transitory consequences."[8] In part, the monetarists' noninterventionist policy conclusion is an expression of faith in the free market system, faith that, left to itself, the economy will produce macroeconomic stability if given a reasonable amount of time.

A

Monetary Policy

One area where Friedman believes that the government must have responsibility is in control of the money supply. Because monetarists believe that the money supply is the dominant influence on money GNP ($P \times y$), this is a crucial responsibility. As Friedman has said innumerable times, "Inflation is always and everywhere a monetary phenomenon."[9] Changes in the money supply also, as we have seen, have important short-run effects on *real* output. How can the monetary authority, the Federal Reserve System in the United States, best conduct monetary policy?

Monetarists believe that the Federal Reserve should provide stable growth in the money supply. Because of the close link between the money supply and money income, the monetarists believe that stable growth in the money supply will go far toward providing stable growth in economic activity.

Friedman and many other monetarists believe that the best way to provide stable growth in the money supply is via a **constant money growth**

[8]Friedman, "Why Economists Disagree," p. 7.

[9]Friedman, "Inflation: Causes and Consequences," in *Dollars and Deficits*, p. 18.

rate rule. Criticizing the Federal Reserve for past instability in money growth, Friedman describes his view as follows:

> My own prescription is still that the monetary authority go all the way in avoiding such swings by adopting publicly the policy of achieving a specified rate of growth in a specified monetary total. The precise rate of growth, like the precise monetary total, is less important than the adoption of some stated and known rate.[10]

While Friedman recognizes that to establish a specified growth rate, the Federal Reserve must choose from among three measures of money supply to control (M1, M2, or M3), and select a specific target rate of growth for this measure, these decisions are less important than that the specified rate should remain constant—that year after year the Federal Reserve should pursue the *same* target. In contrast to the activist policies favored by the Keynesians, there would be *no* discretionary countercyclical monetary policy action. Monetarists favor putting money growth on "automatic pilot." Friedman would go so far as to write the constant money growth rule into the U.S. Constitution.

Why, given the importance monetarists attach to changes in the money supply, would they not favor variations in money growth to counteract the short-run effects of shocks to the economy? Friedman opposes such policy actions because he believes that we cannot forecast the magnitude of such shocks precisely enough to design policies to counteract them. Of importance here is the fact that while Friedman believes that changes in the money supply are the dominant factors causing changes in money GNP, he believes that the money supply affects money GNP *with a lag* of several months. Friedman does not believe that we can forecast shocks to the economy far enough in advance to offset them by changing money supply growth.

Moreover, as we saw in the previous section, attempts to achieve short-run gains in output and employment can set off an inflationary spiral. Policymakers may believe that they are stabilizing the economy when, in fact, they are the source of the instability. As Friedman states:

> There is a saying that the best is often the enemy of the good, which seems highly relevant. The goal of an extremely high degree of economic stability is certainly a splendid one; our ability to attain it, however, is limited."[11]

The constant money growth rate rule would eliminate extreme and prolonged fluctuations in economic activity. To Friedman, with his longer-run viewpoint, that is sufficient.

B
Fiscal Policy

The monetarist view of fiscal policy is similar to the classical view examined in Chapter 8. Monetarists do not believe that fiscal policy (changes in government spending and taxes) is an effective stabilization tool. To illustrate why, let us consider the effects of an increase in government spending, for example, increased spending on national defense.

The government must somehow raise funds to increase spending. If the spending increase is financed by a tax increase or a sale of government bonds to the public, then monetarists argue, as did the classical economists, that the increased government spending would crowd out or replace an approximately equivalent amount of private sector spending. In the monetarist view, if the spending increase is financed by new taxes, then those paying these taxes will spend less, primarily on consumer goods. If the government borrows from the public by selling bonds, the government will compete with private sector borrowers, primarily businesses borrowing to finance investment. The interest rate will be pushed up, and in this case, investment expenditures will be crowded out because investment declines when the interest rate rises. In either case, due to crowding out of private expenditures, monetarists do not believe that the increase in government spending would have significant and sustained effects on output or employment. To quote Friedman, the effects of fiscal policy changes are "certain to be temporary and likely to be minor."

[10]Milton Friedman, "The Role of Monetary Policy," *American Economic Review*, 58 (March 1968), p. 16.

[11]Milton Friedman, "The Supply of Money and Changes in Prices and Output," reprinted in Milton Friedman, *The Optimum Quantity of Money* (Chicago: Aldine Publishing Company, 1969), p. 187.

It is important to recognize that when monetarists speak of fiscal policy being ineffective, they refer to changes in the government budget *for a given level of the money supply.* The government can finance increased spending by creating new money, rather than by raising funds by taxing or borrowing money from the public. In this case, the monetarists would expect the increase in the money supply to have strong effects on the price level and also, in the short run, on output and employment. But these effects are due mainly to the increased money supply—a monetary policy action—not to the change in fiscal policy.

If fiscal policy is not to be used for stabilization, on what grounds should government budget decisions be made? Friedman and some other monetarists favor a rule for fiscal policy just as they favor a rule for monetary policy.

The rule favored by Friedman would force the government to balance the federal budget except in cases of national emergency. Federal government budget deficits, such as the huge ones of recent years, would not be allowed. Friedman supports a constitutional amendment to enforce the **balanced budget rule.**[12]

Not all those who support such an amendment are monetarists and not all monetarists support such an amendment, but the general monetarist position is compatible with it. Since the private enterprise economy is stable over the long run, we do not need changes in government spending and taxation, with possible resulting deficits, for stabilization purposes. In any case, as we saw, monetarists regard fiscal policy as ineffective. Further, the balanced budget amendment conforms well to Friedman's desire to limit the size and role of government. He believes that elected officials will spend less if all spending must be financed by taxes, which are unpopular, instead of by deficits.

Moreover, monetarists believe that deficits pressure the Federal Reserve to increase the money supply too rapidly. Thus, unstable fiscal policy can destabilize monetary policy. This might happen as follows: If the government finances the deficit by borrowing, interest rates will rise. Higher interest rates are unpopular, so elected officials will pressure the Federal Reserve to increase the money supply because making more money available will

drive the interest rate back down, at least for a time.

The relationship between fiscal and monetary policy and its political implications were apparent shortly before the 1984 election, when the government deficit was large and interest rates rose sharply. Members of the incumbent Reagan administration began what journalists termed *Fed bashing*, blaming the rise in interest rates on the overly restrictive policy of then Federal Reserve Board Chairman Paul Volcker. A Reagan campaign strategist was quoted in the *Wall Street Journal* as threatening:

> It's vital to let Volcker know that if his shenanigans foul up this economy, the White House is prepared to stick his bald, cigar-chomping head before the American people and say, "Here he is, folks."

If the Federal Reserve increases the money supply to prevent a deficit-caused rise in interest rates, monetarists believe that inflation will result. Thus, if deficits were avoided in the first place, the problem of inflation would be avoided.

To summarize, monetarists who favor a constitutional amendment to balance the federal budget do so because:

1. They favor noninterventionist policies.
2. They believe that fiscal policy is an ineffective stabilization tool.
3. They believe that the balanced budget amendment will limit the growth of government spending.
4. They believe that the balanced budget amendment will keep fiscal policy from interfering with the proper conduct of monetary policy.

Overall, monetarists favor policymaking by fixed rules, not by the discretion of policymakers.

VI
Monetarists versus Keynesians

To compare and evaluate the monetarist and Keynesian positions, we consider the Keynesian view on each of the monetarist themes presented

---

[12]The precise form of Friedman's proposed rule is explained in Chapter 19.

in this chapter. Then we look at some data on the behavior of the economy to help evaluate the monetarist and Keynesian positions.

A
Longer-Run Self-Stabilizing Properties of the Economy

Keynes, while not believing the economy to be wildly unstable, did believe that it would settle for considerable periods at positions far below full employment. Modern Keynesians agree that the economy, left to itself, will not produce a satisfactory level of macroeconomic stability. From the vantage point of the Great Depression, Keynes doubted even the long-run self-stabilizing ability of capitalist economies. He stressed the instability of private sector aggregate demand.

Modern Keynesians are more optimistic about the long-run stability of the economy, but they see no reason to suffer the short-run costs of economic instability. They also believe that, without a stabilization policy, aggregate demand will be unstable. Fixed business investment, business inventory investment, residential construction investment, and consumer purchases of durable goods such

as autos are subject to substantial destabilizing swings. Supply shocks such as the energy price shocks of the 1970s are another source of instability.

What about Friedman's theory of the natural rates of unemployment and inflation? To many Keynesians, the existence of natural rates is only a "theoretic *curiosum*." The job of stabilization policy is to *stabilize*, to keep the level of economic activity near potential output. The fact that, left to itself, the economy would approach potential output in the long run does not eliminate the need for short-run stabilization policies. This view reflects the short-run horizon of the Keynesians in contrast to the longer-run view of the monetarists.

Read Perspective 14C.

B
Money as the Dominant Influence on Money GNP

Friedman stresses the dominant influence of the money supply on money GNP. Changes in the money supply result in approximately proportional changes in GNP. The Keynesians believe that the

---

PERSPECTIVE 14C
Keynes on Capitalism

Since we have touched on Friedman's more general view on the performance of the capitalist system and the role of government in the economy, we should also consider Keynes's view on these matters. In 1926, when Great Britain was already in an economic slump, but before the Great Depression, Keynes wrote, "For my part I think that capitalism, wisely managed, can probably be made more efficient for attaining economic ends than any alternative system yet in sight, but that in itself it is in many ways extremely objectionable."[13] Keynes believed that the capitalist system allocated resources

with tolerable efficiency (satisfactory answers to the question of What?) and that inequality of income was necessary to provide incentives to individuals in a free market system. However, he criticized the degree of inequality in the society of his day (unsatisfactory answers to the question of Who?). As we have seen, he also felt that capitalism failed to provide macroeconomic stability. Keynes, then, gives "one cheer for capitalism" and emphasizes the need for the government to manage the system wisely.

[13]John M. Keynes, "The End of Laissez-Faire," in *Essays in Persuasion* (London: Macmillan, 1972), p. 294.

money supply is *an* important determinant of money GNP, but they believe there are others. Changes in variables such as government spending, taxes, autonomous investment, and, for open economies, imports and exports also cause substantial changes in money GNP. In the Keynesian view, these other variables may cause money GNP to be unstable even if growth in the money supply is stable.

Stable or even constant money growth will *not*, in the Keynesian view, guarantee stability in economic activity. Thus, the rationale for the monetarist constant money growth rate rule is weakened considerably because greater economic stability may be achievable by varying the money supply growth to offset changes in these other influences on money GNP.

What explains the divergent view of the monetarists and Keynesians on the closeness of the money–money GNP relationship? This question can be answered in terms of their respective views on the *velocity of money*. Recall the equation of exchange that was central to the monetarist theory:

$$M \times V = P \times y \qquad (14.2)$$

The velocity of money (V), the number of times each dollar is used in GNP transactions per period, is the ratio of money GNP ($P \times y$) to the money supply (M):

$$V = \frac{P \times y}{M}$$

If V is constant or if changes in V are small, then $P \times y$ and M move proportionately (e.g., if M doubles, $P \times y$ will double). This is the monetarist case.

If, however, changes in V are substantial, then the relationship between money GNP and money supply will *not* be proportional or even close to it. In terms of equation (14.2), in the Keynesian view, other variables influence velocity. While monetarists do not regard velocity as a constant, they believe that changes in the money supply (M) are much more important to the behavior of money GNP ($P \times y$) than changes in velocity (V).

C
Monetarist Noninterventionist Policy Conclusions

Just as the belief in noninterventionist policy rules follows from the other elements of the monetarist position, the rejection of such rules follows from the Keynesian refusal to accept these other elements of monetarism. Because the Keynesians have a more short-run focus and because they believe that the private sector is inherently unstable, they reject the monetarists' noninterventionist position. Because they believe that the money–money GNP relationship is much less close than the monetarists believe, they oppose the constant money growth rate rule of the monetarists.

The Keynesians favor the use of activist (or discretionary) monetary and fiscal policies to stabilize output, employment, and the price level. Rules such as constitutional amendments requiring a balanced federal budget or mandating the constant money growth rate rule are seen by the Keynesians as detrimental because they leave policymakers without the tools they need (changes in government spending, in the tax rate, in the growth rate of the money supply) to stabilize an otherwise unstable economy.

D
The Monetarist–Keynesian Controversy: Evidence from the U.S. Experience

Before leaving the monetarist–Keynesian controversy, let us consider what light some data on money and money GNP shed on the issues. Figure 14.5 plots quarterly percentage changes (at annual rates) in both the money supply and the money GNP from the third quarter of 1979 to the first quarter of 1984. This was an especially interesting period because the Federal Reserve adopted an anti-inflationary program in the third quarter of 1979 that called for closer control over the money supply. Let's look at the results. As the figure shows, this was a turbulent period with a lot of variation in both variables. While that was not good for the economy, it enables us to evaluate whether the large movements in each series behaved as either monetarists or Keynesians would predict. Did money GNP move more or less in pro-

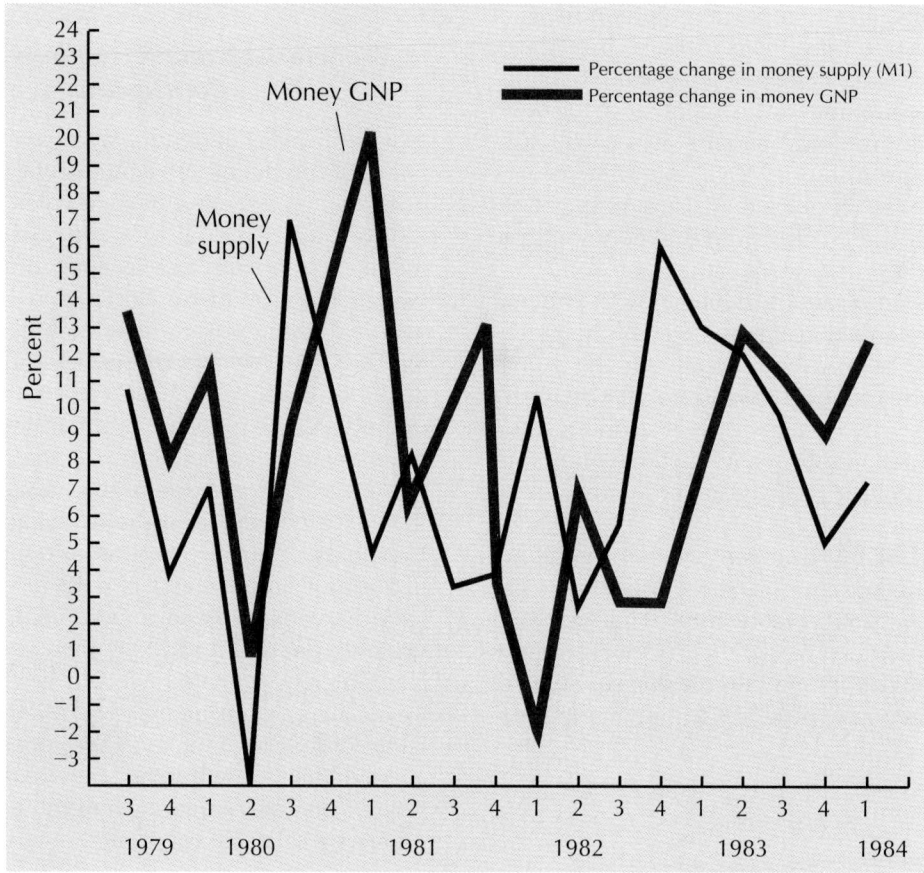

FIGURE 14-5. *Percentage Changes in the Money Supply and in Money GNP*

portion with changes in the money supply? Did the money supply appear to be the dominant influence on money GNP over this period?

There were times during this period when the money supply and the money GNP moved in similar fashion. Look at the points for late 1979 and then the similar drop in both series during the brief recession of 1980. At other times, however, the movements are quite dissimilar. In early 1981 money supply growth *fell* sharply, but the rate of growth of money GNP *rose* sharply. The opposite occurred in early 1982. Overall, the data seem to leave room for other influences on money GNP. Quarterly movements in the two series don't seem all that close. From Figure 14.5 it would appear that the data support the Keynesian more than the monetarist position.

Figure 14.6, which shows the quarterly percentage change in velocity (again at annual rates) over this same period, also seems to support the Keynesian position. According to the monetarists, changes in velocity should be only a minor factor in changes in money GNP. If the money supply and the money GNP move closely together, velocity, which is the ratio of the two variables ($V = (P \times y)/M$), will be quite stable. Velocity, as can be seen from the figure, was anything but stable over this period.

On the basis of this U.S. experience, many non-monetarists have argued that monetarism was discredited. But the issue is not so easily resolved in favor of the Keynesians.

How would Milton Friedman interpret these data on growth in money GNP and the money supply? Fortunately, we don't need to speculate on this question because Friedman has analyzed these data. He argues that in looking at the money–income relationship, we must recognize that changes in the money supply cause changes in income *with a lag*. Earlier Friedman had argued

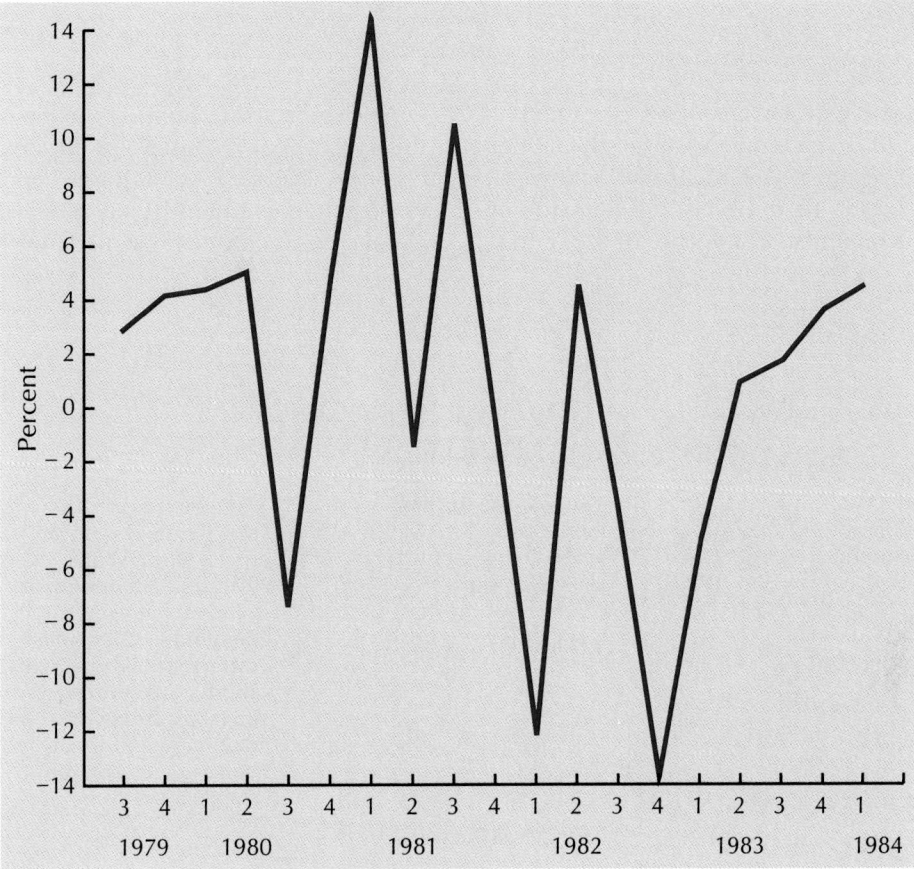

FIGURE 14.6 Percentage Changes in Velocity

that this lag was long and variable, but he believes it is now shorter, approximately one calendar quarter. Therefore, when Friedman plots money supply growth and growth in money GNP, the money growth is one quarter previous to the money GNP growth. Friedman's graph, reproduced in Figure 14.7, shows a much closer association between money growth and growth in money GNP.

The issue, then, is not resolved by the data. Economists have more sophisticated tools than these simple charts to analyze relationships among economic variables and many other historical periods have been examined, but even these tools and additional data do not enable the monetarists or Keynesians to, in Keynes's words, "convict their opponent of error." As noted in our discussion of why economists disagree, we cannot test theories with controlled laboratory experiments. The economist's laboratory is the economy itself. Data from this laboratory are often inconclusive.

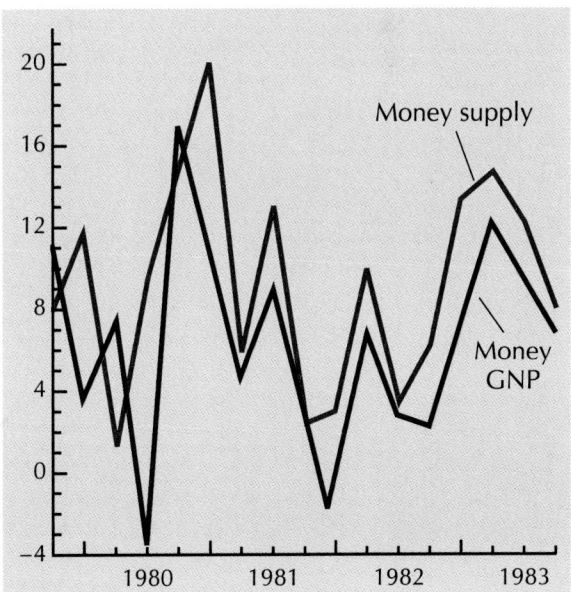

FIGURE 14.7 Friedman's View of the Money–Income Relationship, 1979–84

SUMMARY

Monetarist and Keynesian positions are summarized in Table 14.3. The monetarists are the first of two *schools* of economists who attack the Keynesian position, basing their attacks on elements of the classical economics. In the case of the monetarists, the starting point is the classical quantity theory of money. The group we next turn to are the *new classical* economists. Their attack on Keynesian economics has as its starting point the classical view of the labor market.

TABLE 14.3   The Monetarist and Keynesian Positions Compared

	Monetarist Position	Keynesian Position
Self-stabilizing properties of the economy	The focus is on the longer run. The government sector is viewed as the primary source of instabilities.	The focus is on the short run. The private sector is viewed as unstable. Autonomous elements of aggregate demand (e.g., business investment) and supply shocks are sources of instability. Activist monetary and fiscal policies are required to stabilize the economy.
Relationship between money supply and money GNP	The money supply is the dominant influence on money GNP. Changes in the money supply result in proportionate changes in money GNP.	The money supply is one important variable that affects the level of money GNP. There are, however, other variables, including government spending, taxes, and autonomous investment, that have significant effects on money GNP.
Proper conduct of macroeconomic policy	Policy should be conducted by rules, not by discretion. The optimal monetary policy is a constant money growth rate rule. For fiscal policy, some monetarists favor a constitutional amendment to balance the budget. Macroeconomic policy should be noninterventionist.	Policy should be conducted by discretion, not by rules that tie the hands of policymakers. Activist monetary and fiscal policies are required to stabilize an otherwise unstable economy.

KEY TERMS

Monetarism
Quantity theory
Natural rate of output

Natural rates of output and employment
Constant money growth rate rule
Balanced budget rule

QUESTIONS AND PROBLEMS

1. Milton Friedman argues that economists should not focus on the short run to the exclusion of the long run. Doing so, he argues, will tend to yield what result?
2. Compare monetarist economic theory and classical theory.
3. Compare Keynesian and monetarist explanations of why the Great Depression happened.
4. What is the "natural" rate of unemployment? What determines it? What is the relationship between the actual unemployment rate at any point in time and the natural rate?
5. Why does Milton Friedman argue in favor of a constant money growth rate?
6. Compare the monetarist and Keynesian views of the way that fiscal policy should be conducted.
7. Is there a tradeoff between unemployment and inflation in the monetarist model? Explain.
8. Compare the monetarist and Keynesian views concerning the velocity of money. Which seems more consistent with recent U.S. experience?
9. Within the monetarist framework, analyze the effect of a fall in the rate of growth in the money supply (e.g. from 10 percent to 5 percent per year).

15

The New Classical Economics

The poor performance of the U.S. economy and the economies of other industrialized nations in the 1970s led to widespread dissatisfaction with the prevailing Keynesian orthodoxy. The contrast between the 1960s, the high point of Keynesian influence on both economists and policymakers, and the 1970s can be seen in Figure 15.1. The 1960s was a decade of unbroken economic growth. In the 1970s growth was more erratic and, in several years, the level of output actually declined. What had gone wrong?

One by-product of dissatisfaction with Keynesian theory, as noted in the previous chapter, was an increased interest in the views of Milton Friedman and other monetarists. But not all of those dissatisfied with Keynesian economics were ready to embrace monetarism. A new school of macroeconomics, the **new classical economics,** developed in the 1970s as an alternative to both the Keynesian and monetarist positions, though much more sharply opposed to the former than the latter.

Robert Lucas, the founder of the new classical

economics, argues that "what went wrong, in brief, is that Keynesian macroeconomic theory failed."[1] In an article setting out the new classical position, Lucas and Thomas Sargent, another important contributor to the new classical economics, termed aspects of Keynesian macroeconomics a "spectacular recent failure" and "fatally flawed." They identified the task of modern students of macroeconomics as "that of sorting through the wreckage, determining which features of that remarkable intellectual event called the Keynesian Revolution can be salvaged and put to good use, and which others must be discarded."[2]

As with the attack of the monetarists, the new classical attack brought forth a counterattack by

[1]Robert E. Lucas, "On a Report to the OECD," in *Studies in Business Cycle Theory* Cambridge (Cambridge, Mass.: MIT Press, 1981), p. 265.

[2]This and the previous quotation are from Robert E. Lucas and Thomas Sargent, "After Keynesian Macroeconomics," in *After the Phillips Curve: Persistence of High Inflation and High Unemployment* (Boston: Federal Reserve Bank of Boston, 1978).

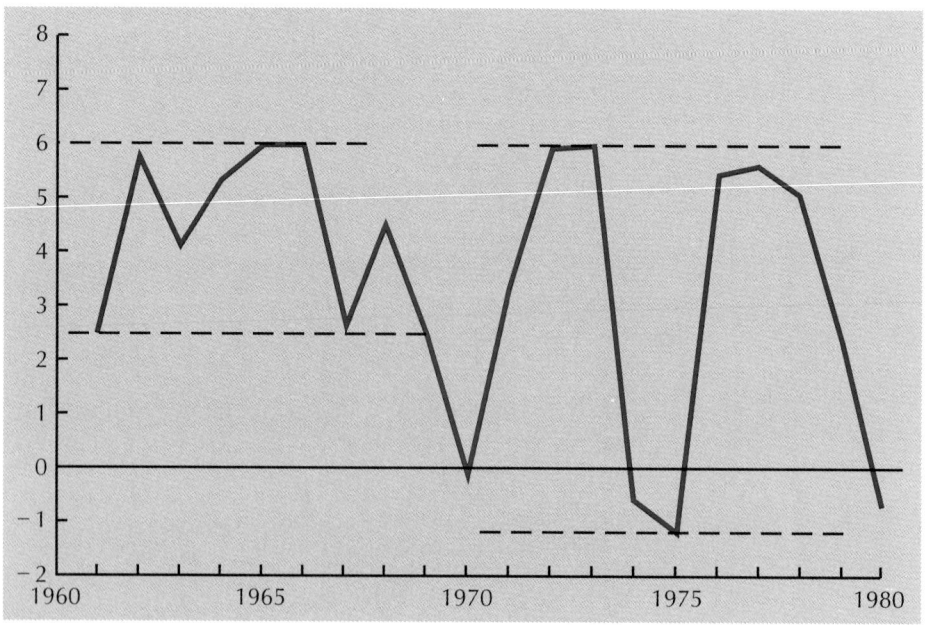

FIGURE 15.1   Percentage Growth in Real GNP, 1961–80

the Keynesians, often in terms as strong as those of the opposition. Robert Gordon, for example, argued that a central feature of Lucas's new classical economics "should be relegated to the same scrap heap of discarded ideas where lie the earlier classical models of perfect market clearing laid to rest by Keynes forty years ago."[3]

In this chapter we will examine the central elements of the new classical economics. As with monetarism, we will see that the new classical economics has its starting point in aspects of the original classical model presented in Chapter 8. We will then examine the Keynesian response to this new challenge. In the final section of the chapter, as we did with monetarism, we will see how some recent evidence bears on the issues separating the views of Keynesian and new classical economists.

I

Rational Expectations and the New Classical View of the Labor Market

A

A Review of the Classical Labor Market Assumptions

Let us start by recalling the way in which the labor market functioned in the classical model, as explained in Section IV of Chapter 8. Assumptions made by classical economists concerning the labor market were crucial to their results. Because of these assumptions, output was completely supply determined at the full-employment level. Demand-side shocks or policies didn't affect output or employment.

Consider the adjustments that take place in the classical labor market following an increase in the money supply.

The increase in the money supply would push up the price level as it led to an increased demand for goods. In the labor market, both suppliers (workers) and demanders (firms) would observe

[3]Robert J. Gordon, "The Theory of Domestic Inflation," *American Economic Review*, 67 (February 1977), p. 132.

the rise in the price level and see it as a decline in the real wage paid to labor. (Recall that the real wage is the money wage, current-valued dollars per hour, divided by the price level.) At a lower real wage, firms demand more labor. Workers supply less. When the real wage falls, firms demand more labor because the real wage represents the real (inflation-adjusted) cost of labor. Workers supply less when the real wage falls because their real (inflation-adjusted) payment for working is lower.

With demand *higher* and supply *lower*, we have an excess demand for labor that puts upward pressure on the *money* wage. In the classical system, the money wage rises in proportion to the price level. For example, if the increase in the money supply is 10 percent, the price level rises by 10 percent. To restore equilibrium in the labor market, the money wage must also rise by 10 percent.

If the money wage rises proportionately to the price level, there is no incentive for the firm to change its output level. Product price and cost of production have gone up together. This is why, in the classical model, an increase in the money supply does not affect output or employment.

The classical results followed from two assumptions about the labor market:

1. The money wage rate and the price level are perfectly flexible.
2. Firms and workers have perfect information about all market prices.

The first guarantees that the money wage is free to move, not fixed by formal or informal contracts. The second assures that workers properly perceive the price changes taking place. In terms of our previous example, the workers are assumed to know that the money supply, and therefore the price level, has risen by 10 percent, so that they demand a 10 percent increase in the money wage.

B

The Keynesian and Monetarist Objections

In the Keynesian and monetarist views, the money wage is not perfectly flexible in the short run. In modern labor markets, they believe that the money wage is likely to be set for some time in the future either by a formal written contract, often for 3 years' duration, or by an informal contract between the employer and employee. Hence the first classical assumption is incorrect. In addition, Keynesians and monetarists argue that when workers negotiate such contracts, they do not know what the price level will be over the future term of the contract. They do not have perfect information about all market prices. Hence the second classical assumption is incorrect. Workers must base their wage demands on *expectations* of future price levels. Moreover, Keynesians and monetarists assume that such expectations concerning future price levels are *backward looking*, based for the most part on the *past* behavior of the price level. If prices have been stable for a long while, workers will expect them to be stable in the future; if there has been a high rate of inflation in the past, workers will expect prices to rise rapidly in the future.

Consider the previous example, an increase in the money supply of perhaps 10 percent—this time from a Keynesian *or* monetarist standpoint. The increase in the money supply will increase aggregate demand and the price level will rise. The money wage, however, will not rise proportionately with the price level. This is because the fixed money wage contracts make money wages sticky in the short run. Also, it will take some time before the backward-looking expectations of labor suppliers adjust to the new situation. Since the money wage does not rise as much as the price level, firms have an incentive to produce more and employ more workers. The increase in the money supply increases output and employment in the Keynesian and monetarist frameworks.

C

The New Classical View

The new classical conception of the labor market is much closer to the classical than to the Keynesian or monetarist view, though new classical economists modify the classical analysis in one fundamental way.

Consider the two preceding classical assumptions.

1. Flexibility of the Money Wage In the new classical view, while the money wage is not pre-

sumed to be perfectly flexible, markets, including labor markets, are assumed to work well; *markets clear*. New classical economists do not believe that labor contracts are so rigid as to prevent adjustments in the money wage in response to changes in labor market conditions. Robert Barro, another new classical economist, writes in this regard, "it is hard to see how the ability to contract could lessen the private economy's ability to deal with disturbances and thereby enhance the case for Keynesian macropolicies."[4] The new classical economists are much closer to the classical position that money wages are flexible than to the monetarist or Keynesian view that money wages are sticky.

2. Perfect Information Concerning Market Prices The new classical economists do not, however, assume that workers have perfect information concerning market prices. They agree with the Keynesians and monetarists that labor supply decisions must be based on *expectations* of future price levels. They are critical, however, of the assumption made by the monetarists and Keynesians that expectations of future price levels are backward-looking, based for the most part on the past behavior of the price level. The new classical economists assume that economic agents will form what they call *rational expectations*.

> **Rational expectations** are expectations formed on the basis of all available relevant information concerning the variable being predicted. Moreover, economic agents are assumed to use available information intelligently; that is, they understand the relationships between the variables they observe and the variables they are trying to predict.

If expectations are indeed formed rationally, then in making predictions about future price levels, workers will use *all* relevant current or past information, including information they have about the behavior of policy variables. Furthermore, in assuming that workers predicting future price levels form rational expectations, the new classical economists assume that workers under-

[4]Robert Barro, "Rational Expectations and Macroeconomics in 1984," *American Economic Review*, 74 (May 1984), p. 180.

stand the relationship between policy variables and the behavior of the price level; they use available information intelligently. Rational expectations are _forward-looking_ in that they take account of any information available today which has implications for the future. For example, consider the policy action previously discussed, where there was a 10 percent increase in the money supply. If information concerning this policy action was available, workers would recognize that the price level would rise as a result of the increase in the money supply. They would take this into account in forming their expectation of future price levels that determined their money wage demands. The fact that changes in policy variables that can be predicted on the basis of available information will affect rationally formed expectations has very important implications for the effectiveness of such policy actions, as we will see.

■ CHECK YOUR BEARINGS

Before going on, however, we stop here to review the differing labor market assumptions made in the classical, Keynesian, monetarist, and new classical theories. These assumptions are summarized in Table 15.1. The different assumptions are crucial to the conclusions reached by each school of economists concerning the ability of policy variables to affect real variables such as the levels of output and employment.

II
Policy Implications of Rational Expectations

To see the policy implications of rational expectations, consider the policy action previously discussed, a 10 percent increase in the money sup-

ply. In the Keynesian or monetarist models, such an expansionary monetary policy action would lead to an increase in both price and output. This is illustrated in Figure 15.2. Initially the money supply is at M_0 and the aggregate demand curve is $y^d(M_0)$. Equilibrium price and output are at P_0 and y_0. After the 10 percent increase, the money supply is M_1 and the corresponding aggregate demand curve is $y^d(M_1)$. The increase in the money supply shifts the aggregate demand schedule to the right along the fixed aggregate supply curve. Equilibrium price and output rise to P_1 and y_1. The increase in output leads to an increase in employment.

What is important here is that the supply curve is fixed. Nothing occurs as a result of the increase in the money supply that changes the cost to the firm of producing a given output. Such changes would shift the supply curve.

Now consider the effect of the same policy action within the new classical framework. As ex-

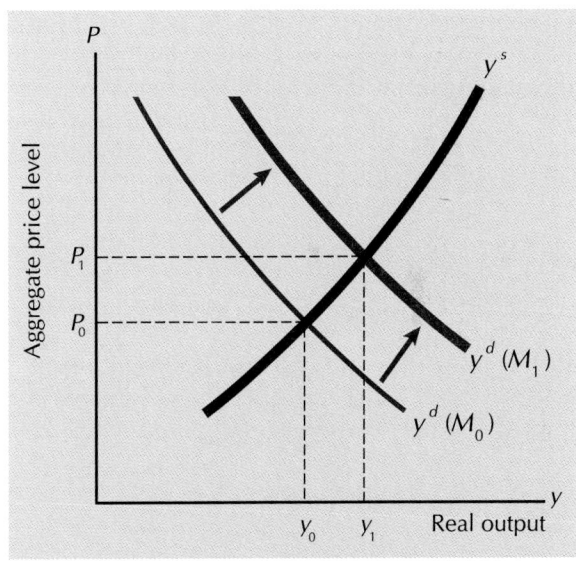

FIGURE 15.2 *Effect of an Increase in the Money Supply: A Keynesian or Monetarist View*

TABLE 15.1 Labor Market Assumptions

	Money Wages	Workers' Information About the Price Level
Classical	Flexible	Perfect information
Keynesian or monetarist	Sticky	Backward-looking expectations
New classical	Flexible	Rational (forward-looking) expectations

plained previously, the workers' money wage demands depend on their expectations of future values of the price level. *If expectations are formed rationally*, these expectations depend on the level of policy variables and, therefore, change with predictable changes in policy variables. Consequently, in looking at the effects of a change in the money supply, we need to specify whether the policy action was predictable or a surprise. This is important because we need to know whether the price level expectations of workers, and hence their money wage demands, are affected by the policy action. To start, assume that the policy was predictable. For example, the central bank may have announced the change beforehand.

A
Effects of a Predictable Increase in the Money Supply

The effect of this preannounced 10 percent increase in the money supply in the new classical model is illustrated in Figure 15.3. As in the Keynesian or monetarist analysis, the increase in the money supply (from M_0 to M_1) shifts the aggregate demand curve to the right from $y^d(M_0)$ to

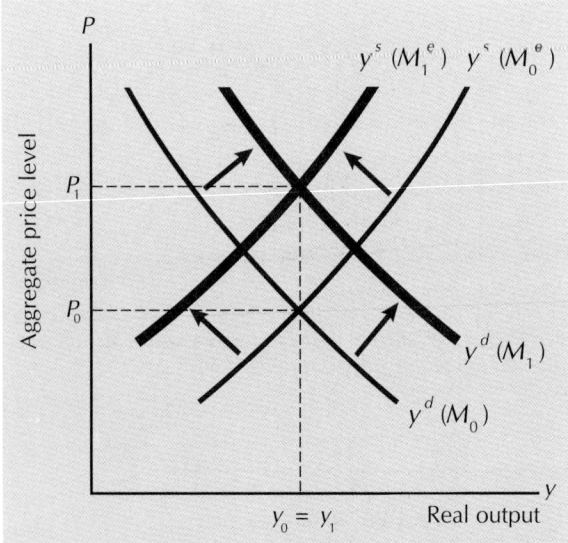

FIGURE 15.3 *Effect of a Preannounced Increase in the Money Supply: A New Classical View*

$y^d(M_1)$. In the new classical model, however, *the aggregate supply curve also shifts*. The initial level of the aggregate supply curve is $y^s(M_0^e)$, where M_0^e is the initial expected level of the money supply (the letter *e* now indicating expectations). The position of the aggregate supply curve depends on the expected level of the money supply because the expected level of the money supply influences the workers' rational expectations about future values of the price level. These price level expectations, in turn, affect the money wage that workers demand and therefore firms' cost of production.

Because the increase in the money supply from M_0 to M_1 is assumed to be preannounced, the workers' expectation of the money supply also rises by 10 percent from M_0^e to M_1^e. The effect of this is that workers now expect the price level to be higher; they are assumed to understand fully the positive relationship between the money supply and the price level. Expecting the price level to be higher, they demand higher money wages. This results in an upward shift in the supply curve. Higher money wages increase the cost of producing a given output and, consequently, the price level at which firms will produce a given output. In Figure 15.3, the aggregate supply curve shifts from $y^s(M_0^e)$ to $y^s(M_1^e)$.

In the new classical view, workers rationally predict the price level increase that will result from the preannounced increase in the money supply and demand a proportionately higher money wage. Put differently, the same supply of labor will be available to firms only if the money wage is raised proportionately. *If the money wage rises proportionately with the price level, the price increase provides no incentive for firms to increase output.* In Figure 15.3 this is why, taking account of the shift in the supply curve, the new equilibrium output level (y_1) is the same as the initial output level. *The only effect of the increase in the money supply is to raise the equilibrium price level to P_1.*

To summarize, in the new classical model an increase in the money supply increases aggregate demand, as in the Keynesian and monetarist frameworks. By itself, this increase in demand would cause output and the price level to rise (the effect of the shift of the y^d curve in Figure 15.3). If the increase in the money supply is predictable (e.g., preannounced), then it will also increase workers' expectations concerning the price level. This will push up the money wage and increase firms' cost of production, eliminating the incentive to increase output (the effect of the shift in the y^s curve in Figure 15.3). *The effect of a predictable increase in the money supply will be to increase the price level with output unchanged.*

What explains the difference between the Keynesian or monetarist analyses and the new classical analysis? *Rational expectations.* In the Keynesian or monetarist model the workers' price expectations, and hence their money wage demands, are not assumed to be affected significantly by changes in current policy variables. Workers' expectations are assumed to be dependent mostly on the past behavior of prices themselves—*backward-looking expectations.* Labor contracts are also important. Even if workers do predict that an increase in the money stock will cause prices to rise, in the short run this will not put upward pressure on money wages if money wages are set by preexisting contracts.

In the Keynesian or monetarist model, the supply effect (the shift to the left in the y^s schedule) is absent, as can be seen by comparison of Figures 15.2 and 15.3. In the Keynesian or monetarist model there is only the demand effect, which will increase output as well as price.

B
Effects of a Monetary Surprise

Now consider the case where the increase in the money supply could not have been predicted. The Federal Reserve (the U.S. central bank) changes course in a way the public cannot predict, *even though the public is assumed to form rational expectations.* What are the effects of such a **monetary surprise** in the new classical model?

The important point to note here is that since there is no way for workers to predict the increase in the money supply, this policy shift can have no effect on their price level expectations. Therefore, the policy shift has no effect on workers' money wage demands. The supply-side effect (the shift in the y^s schedule in Figure 15.3) is absent in this case. For a monetary surprise in the new classical model, we are left with only the demand-side

effect (the outward shift in the y^d schedule in Figure 15.3 or 15.2). *This increase in demand will increase both equilibrium price and output. For an unpredictable increase in the money supply, the new classical model yields the same result as the monetarist or Keynesian framework.*

C
Real-World Policy: Predictable or Surprising?

The new classical economists believe that actual monetary policy is composed of both predictable policy actions and surprises. Useful stabilization policies must, however, be *systematic* and therefore, to a large extent, will be predictable if expectations are in fact formed rationally. For example, if monetary policy is aimed at achieving a high level of employment and output, then *systematically* when employment and output begin to fall substantially below the potential levels of the economy, the Federal Reserve should step in and increase the money supply. But if the Federal Reserve acts in such a predictable manner, the public forming rational expectations will be able to predict the increase in the money supply by watching the levels of employment and output. If the increases are predictable, then in the new classical view, they won't affect output or employment. *The policy won't work!*

This example illustrates the basic problem the new classical analysis poses for macroeconomic stabilization policy. To be effective, policy must be systematic. But if policy is systematic, it will be *predictable*, and if it is predictable, it will not affect real variables such as output and employment. We have focused on monetary policy, but the new classical analysis applies to any aggregate demand policy. For example, changes in government spending and taxes that change the level of aggregate demand will affect output only if they are not predictable—if they are fiscal surprises. In fact, the analysis extends to any class of demand-side shocks—for example, autonomous changes in private investment. If such changes can be predicted in advance, they will not affect output or employment in the short run. If they are unpredictable, they will.

III

New Classical Policy Prescriptions

What, then, is the role of monetary and fiscal policy in the new classical model? Economist Bennett McCallum describes it as follows:

> The clear implication is that . . . monetary and fiscal policies should be designed to yield the sequence of price levels (or inflation rates) that is regarded as most desirable. In other words, the Federal Reserve and the Treasury should concentrate their attention on the prevention or reduction (if such is desired) of inflation, not of unemployment. There is no point in focusing policy choices upon variables, no matter how great their intrinsic importance, that cannot be systematically affected by these choices.[5]

The new classical economists argue that monetary and fiscal policies cannot be used to stabilize output and employment and, therefore, the unemployment rate. Systematic policies will result in predictable changes in aggregate demand that will leave these *real* variables unaltered.

But systematic monetary and fiscal policies *will* affect the price level. For example, the preannounced 10 percent increase in the money supply considered previously resulted in a permanent increase in the price level. New classical economists conclude that aggregate demand policies should be aimed at desirable behavior of the price level, and therefore the inflation rate, over time. In practice, desirable behavior means a low, stable rate of inflation.

What monetary and fiscal policies would be likely to achieve this goal? For monetary policy, many new classical economists favor the constant money growth rate rule policy recommended by Milton Friedman and other monetarists. The Federal Reserve would simply announce in advance that the money supply would be increased at a specified percentage rate. The rate chosen would not affect output and employment, since it would be completely predictable. If a low rate was chosen, a low inflation rate would be achieved.

[5]Bennett McCallum, "The Significance of Rational Expectations Theory," *Challenge Magazine*, (January–February 1980), p. 43.

For fiscal policy, the new classical economists also want to achieve stability; consequently, many favor some type of set rule. They want to avoid large, erratic budget deficits for reasons similar to those of the monetarists; they believe that large budget deficits will make it difficult for the Federal Reserve to keep money growth stable, since pressures will develop to help finance the deficits by increasing the money supply. New classical economists such as Lucas and Sargent were, for example, critical of the large deficits that resulted from President Reagan's fiscal policies. One rule, favored by some new classical economists, is that the federal budget be balanced *on average* over the course of the business cycle, though not for each and every year. (Deficits in recessions would, for example, have to be offset with surpluses in prosperous years.) While this is a more flexible rule than Milton Friedman's proposal examined in the previous chapter, it still severely limits the government's ability to conduct an activist fiscal stabilization policy.

Overall, the new classical economists' policy prescription is reasonably close to that of the monetarists or the original classical economists. They favor *noninterventionist* rules for policies. Their position is in opposition to the Keynesian position, which favors *activist* stabilization policies.

IV

The Keynesian Countercritique

Keynesian economists are unconvinced by the arguments of the new classical economists. They criticize the new classical economists for making unrealistic assumptions both about the public's ability to understand the economy (the assumption of rational expectations) and, more important, about the way the labor market works. We consider each of the points in turn.

A

The Realism of Rational Expectations

Many Keynesian economists believe that the rational expectations assumption overstates the ability of the public to predict economic events. Keynesians criticize the assumption that workers entering into labor market contracts use all or even most of the available relevant information. Such an assumption ignores the cost of gathering and processing information.

The rational expectations assumption also presumes that individuals use available information intelligently. They know the relationships that link observed variables with the variables they are trying to predict. The public is also presumed to be able to estimate the systematic parts of policy actions. In our examples, the public was assumed to understand the relationship between the money supply and the price level, and to figure out any pattern of policymaker responses to variables such as unemployment. Many Keynesian economists deny that workers possess such knowledge of the way the economy works.

If information is costly to gather, and if it is hard to figure out what to make of it once available, workers may fall back on looking at the past behavior of prices when predicting future price level. Thus the _backward-looking_ assumption made by the Keynesians.

If expectations are formed in this backward-looking fashion, they will not respond much to current information, including the behavior of monetary and fiscal policies. Systematic stabilization policies will not be predicted by the public, and therefore such policies _will_ affect output and employment. If expectations are for the most part backward looking, there is a role for activist stabilization policies, and because the Keynesians believe that the private sector is unstable if left to itself, there is a need for such policies.

Differing views of how expectations are formed—the rational expectations view of the new classical economists versus the backward-looking assumption of the Keynesians—are one reason for the different policy conclusions reached by these groups.

Read Perspective 15A.

B
The Role of Labor Market Contracts

Just as in the original classical model, the assumption that the money wage adjusts rapidly to clear the labor market is central to the new classical

analysis. Keynesians believe that this assumption is fundamentally _wrong_. They deny that the money wage is set to clear the labor market in the short run. The Keynesians believe that money wages are sticky, meaning that they are not fixed but adjust only slowly over time.

The Keynesian view of the labor market is a **contractual** one. Long-term arrangements exist between buyers (firms) and sellers (workers), and long-term relationships develop between _particular_ buyers and sellers. Generally, the form of such relationships has been to fix the money wage while leaving the firm free to adjust employment. Thus, Keynesians argue that changes in aggregate demand, predictable or not, result in changes in employment in the short run, _not_ in adjustments in the money wage. Declines in the demand for output cause layoffs, as firms need fewer workers. Increases in demand, caused, for example, by expansionary monetary and fiscal policies, cause increases in employment.

In the longer run, Keynesians and monetarists, who also accept this contractual view of the labor market, believe that money wages will adjust. Contracts eventually expire, and new ones are made reflecting current conditions. In the long run, expansionary monetary policies will not, for example, affect output and employment in the Keynesian or monetarist framework. In terms of our discussion in Chapter 14, these variables will tend toward their natural rates. But in the short run, both the Keynesians and the monetarists believe that changes in aggregate demand _will_ have real effects, _whether such changes are predictable or not_.

V
The New Classical–Keynesian Controversy: Some Evidence from the U.S. Experience

As discussed in Chapter 14, in late 1979 the Federal Reserve _announced_ a switch to a restrictive anti-inflation policy with tighter control of the money supply. The 1980–83 period was one of disinflation, a dramatic slowdown in the inflation rate

PERSPECTIVE 15A
A Test of the Rational Expectations Hypothesis

Given its important policy implications, there have been many tests of the rational expectations hypothesis. One such test by Arlington Williams involved 146 college students from Indiana University and the University of Arizona.[6]

Students participated in an artificial market where they bought and sold a fictitious commodity, making trades on linked computer terminals. They were given financial incentives to buy (sell) at a lower (higher) price than the true cost (or value of the commodity determined by the experiment's designer). Experiments were conducted over a sequence of market periods. After each period, the students were asked to forecast the average price for trades that would be made in the next period.

The students had a rich set of information about the market, including such data as their own cost (or value) for the next period (supplied by the experimentor), the actual average price and their forecasts from all past periods, and the number of offers to buy and sell in previous periods. What happened?

[6]Arlington Williams, "The Formation of Price Forecasts in Experimental Markets," *Journal of Money, Credit and Banking*, 19 (February 1987), pp. 1–18.

Analysis of the students' forecasts did not support the rational expectations assumption. For one thing, students made systematic errors in their forecasts, meaning that their errors did not average out close to zero. This indicates that some relevent information was not used, a violation of the rational expectations assumption. Another problem was that forecast errors in one period were related to errors in the past. This is also contrary to rational expectations theory, which assumes that people learn from a pattern of errors and adjust their forecasts accordingly.

The students' forecasts were more supportive of the Keynesian or monetarist backward-looking price expectations hypothesis. Students seemed to use *adaptive* behavior, modifying their *forecasts* in each period on the basis of their observations of the *actual* average price level from the previous period.

No one study of the rational expectations assumption is definitive. Other studies have analyzed the forecasts of consumers and businessmen. To date, the number of studies favorable to rational expectations falls short of the number of unfavorable ones. But research on the subject continues.

(from 13.5 percent in 1980 to 3.2 percent in 1983), caused by a dramatic slowdown in the rate of growth in aggregate demand—the result of the more restrictive monetary policy. Let's examine the degree to which the decline in the growth rate of aggregate demand over these years resulted in a decline in the growth rate in money wages versus the degree to which employment fell and unemployment rose.

Figure 15.4 plots the quarterly unemployment rate and the quarterly rate of change in the money wage rate from the first quarter of 1980 to the first quarter of 1984. The data indicate that the rate of growth in the money wage did gradually decline,

from an annual rate of 10.5 percent in 1980 to 9.7 percent in 1981, 7.8 percent in 1982, and 5.2 percent in 1983. The unemployment series shows, however, that the decline in the money wage growth rate was not rapid enough to prevent an immense increase in unemployment as aggregate demand fell. From 6.2 percent in the first quarter of 1980, the unemployment rate rose to a post–World War II record high of 10.8 percent in the fourth quarter of 1982. Conversely, as aggregate demand rose rapidly during the expansion that began in 1983, the unemployment rate declined sharply.

The disinflation of 1980–83 was an extremely

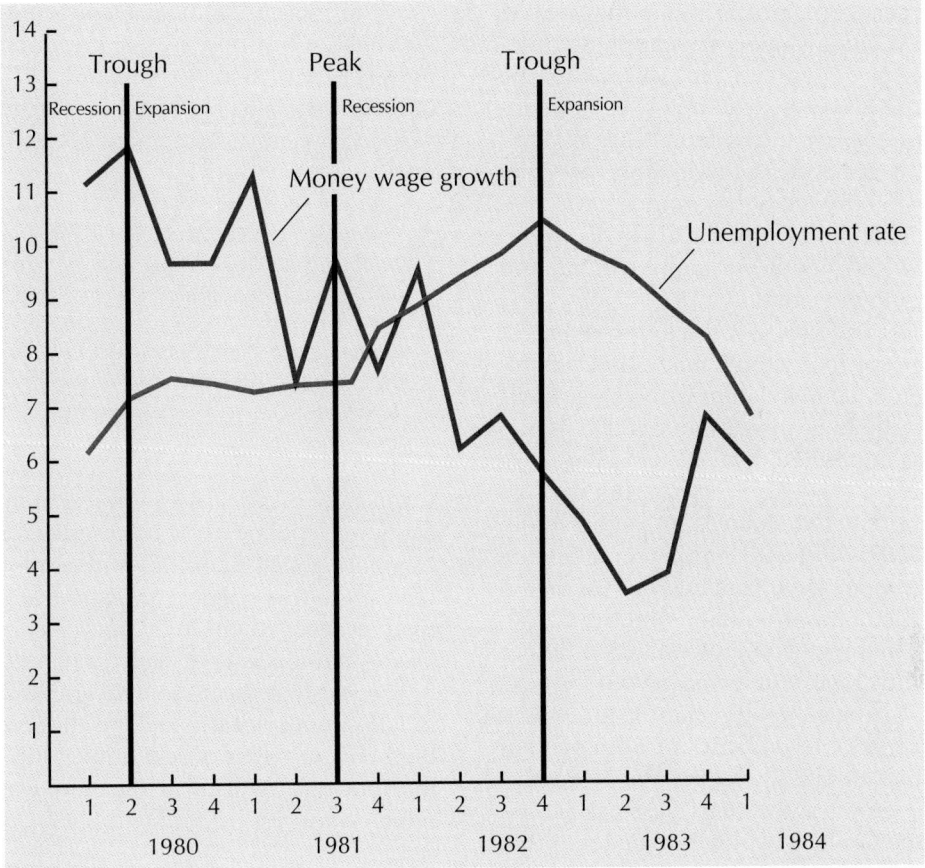

FIGURE 15.4 *U.S. Unemployment Rates and Growth Rates in Money Wages, 1980:1–1984:1*

costly one—costly in terms of real output, which fell approximately 10 percent below potential output; and costly in terms of unemployment, with 12 million workers idled by December 1982.

A
A Keynesian or Monetarist Explanation of the Data

The data in Figure 15.4 conform well to the Keynesian or monetarist explanations. Both groups of economists would expect a restrictive monetary policy to lower output and employment in the short run. They would also expect that as the inflation rate fell, and enough time passed for workers to perceive the lower inflation rate, money wage demands would decline. But Keynesian and monetarist economists would not have expected

the decline in money wage growth to be fast enough to avoid a substantial rise in unemployment. Economists from both of these groups did, in fact, predict beforehand that lowering the U.S. inflation rate quickly in the early 1980s would mean bearing high costs in terms of unemployment and foregone output.

B
A New Classical Explanation of the Data

The data in Figure 15.4 are more difficult to explain in a manner compatible with the new classical model. Clearly, if the restrictive monetary policy was predictable, the disinflation of the early 1980s should not have had a high cost in terms of lost output and employment if the new classical view is correct. Predictable changes in aggregate demand should affect only prices and money wages, not output and employment. This applies to declines in aggregate demand, as well as to the increases in the preceding examples. In the context of the early 1980s, if the Federal Reserve's shift to a restrictive policy was predictable, workers forming rational expectations would have predicted lower inflation. Money wage growth would have dropped sufficiently for employment and output to remain the same.

If the new classical view is correct, the decline in output and the rise in unemployment that accompanied the reduction in inflation in the early 1980s must have resulted because the restrictive monetary policy was unpredicted. The Federal Reserve's policy shift was a *monetary surprise*. As we saw previously, unpredicted changes in aggregate demand *do* affect output and employment in the new classical model. If workers had not predicted the shift in Federal Reserve policy, and the consequent decline in the inflation rate, they would not have been willing to accept lower growth in money wages. In this case, as the rate of growth in aggregate demand fell, output and employment would have had to fall. Even after the restrictive policy was in effect, some new classical economists argue, the public may not have believed that the Federal Reserve would maintain it. Workers did not want to accept drastically reduced growth in money wages and then see the Federal Reserve

revert to more inflationary money growth.

Critics of the new classical economics do not, however, find these explanations of the 1980–83 period as the effects of a restrictive *monetary surprise* convincing. As Benjamin Friedman of Harvard University puts it:

> *Although the initial change in monetary policy in October 1979 may well have caught the public unaware, the continuation of that policy from late 1980 onward was hardly a surprise. Especially in the context of the 1980 general election, the tight monetary policy during this period was probably about as well anticipated as such a policy is ever likely to be.*

If the new classical view that systematic macroeconomic policy will be predictable, and will therefore not affect output and employment, is not relevant to this episode of restrictive policy, Friedman argues "then it is not clear when—or if ever—that analysis is likely to be relevant."[7]

The fact that the systematic, preannounced disinflation policy of the Federal Reserve had such a high cost in terms of real output has led many to question the realism of the new classical policy conclusions.

[7]Benjamin Friedman, "Recent Perspectives in and on Macroeconomics," Research Working Paper No. 1208. Cambridge, MA. National Bureau of Economic Research, September 1983.

SUMMARY

1. The conflict between new classical economists and Keynesians centers on the same disagreement about how the labor market works that separated Keynesians from classical economists. Classical economists assumed that (a) money wages are flexible up and down and (b) workers have perfect information about *real* wages. Keynesians argued that (a) money wages are sticky, especially on the down side, and (b) workers form highly imperfect, backward-looking expectations about the price level and, therefore, the real wage.

   New classical economists are much closer to classical economists than to Keynes-

   ians on the issue of money wage flexibility. They base their model on the idea that the labor market clears—supply and demand are equated—which requires flexibility of the money wage.

2. On the question of the information available to workers when making money wage demands, new classical economists are also closer to the classical economists. They do not, however, assume that workers have perfect information. They assume that workers form rational expectations; workers use all available relevant information to predict the price level and hence form an expectation of the real wage. More-

over, they understand the workings of the economy well enough to use information intelligently.

3. Because in the new classical model the money wage will adjust to clear the labor market and because expectations are rational, predictable changes in aggregate demand, including changes in policy variables, result in adjustment in wages and prices *but not in output and employment.* Policies to stabilize output and employment must be systematic and thus predictable under the rational expectations hypothesis. Therefore, in the new classical framework, such policies don't work.

4. Macroeconomic policy in the new classical view should instead be directed toward achieving a low, stable inflation rate. This leads the new classical economists to favor noninterventionist rules for monetary and fiscal policy.

5. In the Keynesian or monetarist framework, with sticky money wages and workers' slowly adjusting price expectations, changes in aggregate demand, predictable or not, affect real output and employment. With a fall in aggregate demand, the money wage does not fall sufficiently in the short run to clear the labor market. Rising unemployment and reduced output result.

6. The evidence from the U.S. experience during the disinflation of the early 1980s seems to favor the monetarist or Keynesian view. The disinflation, engineered largely by a systematic (therefore, seemingly predictable) restrictive monetary policy, still had huge costs in terms of output and employment. This experience has led many to doubt the realism of new classical policy conclusions, at least if these conclusions are taken literally. The implications of the new classical view for policy formation are still important, and the way in which they have influenced even Keynesian opinion on this subject is discussed in the next chapter.

KEY TERMS

New classical economics
Rational expectations

Monetary surprise
Contractual view of the labor market

QUESTIONS AND PROBLEMS

1. Review the two key assumptions of the classical economists regarding the labor market. What are their implications?

2. Review the Keynesian and monetarist objections to the two key classical assumptions regarding the labor market.

3. Explain the difference between the assumption that expectations are rational and the assumption of perfect information.

4. The impacts on the economy of changes in monetary policy, according to new classical economists, will depend on whether the policy changes are predictable or not. Show graphically the new classical view of the different impacts of a) a predictable decrease in the money supply and b) a surprise decrease in the money supply.

5. How do the new classical economists believe monetary policy should be conducted? Why?

6. Would an anticipated increase in the money supply affect the price level in the new classical model? Why or why not?

16

Macroeconomics: Controversy and Consensus

This chapter summarizes our analysis of competing macroeconomic theories. Our aim is to show that the issues that divide macroeconomists into different groups are a number of well-defined differences in their theoretical models and empirical views concerning the economy. The different policy conclusions reached by the various schools of economists are shown to follow naturally from these theoretical and empirical differences. Such matters occupy Sections I and II. In Section III we consider areas where substantial agreement among macroeconomists exists. We see that there is consensus as well as controversy in macroeconomics.

I

The Models in Pictures

Figure 16.1 shows the aggregate demand and supply curves for each of the four models we have considered. To analyze the differences between these models, let us focus first on aggregate supply and then on aggregate demand.

A

Aggregate Supply

In the classical model, the aggregate supply curve is vertical. Output is therefore *completely* supply determined. Changes in aggregate demand, including those caused by monetary and fiscal policy actions, have no effect on output. Such changes in demand affect only the aggregate price level.

In the Keynesian or monetarist model, the aggregate supply curve is upward sloping. Output is determined by *both* supply and demand. Changes in aggregate demand affect both output and the price level in the short run.

In the new classical model, the aggregate supply curve also slopes upward to the right, but notice that it is drawn for given values of the *expected* money stock (M^e), levels of government expenditures

tures (G^e), taxes (T^e), and autonomous investment ($\bar{I}^e$). Changes in the expected values of these variables shift the new classical aggregate supply curve. If there is an unexpected change in aggregate demand (an unexpected change in the money supply, for example), then the aggregate supply curve does not shift (M^e is unchanged). The aggregate demand curve does shift, and output as well as price is affected. Output is affected by supply factors and unexpected changes in demand in the new classical model.

Expected changes in aggregate demand shift the new classical aggregate supply curve, as well as the aggregate demand curve. An expected increase in the money supply (an increase in M and M^e), for example, causes the aggregate supply and demand curves to shift upward proportionately, as we saw in the previous chapter (see Figure 15.3). The price level rises but output is unchanged. *Expected* changes in aggregate demand do *not* affect output in the new classical model.

The differences among the aggregate supply curves in the four models reflect different assumptions about labor markets. In the classical model, wages are perfectly flexible and workers have perfect information about the real wage. As an increase in aggregate demand pushes the price level upward, the money wage rises proportionately and there is no incentive for firms to increase employment and therefore output.

In the Keynesian or monetarist model, money wages are *sticky* due to explicit and implicit labor contracts that fix the level of the money wage. Moreover, workers don't have perfect information about the price level that will prevail over the life of the contract; therefore, they don't know the real wage. Workers are assumed to try to predict the future behavior of the price level primarily on the basis of its past behavior. They have backward-looking price expectations. Consequently, in the Keynesian or monetarist model, as an increase in aggregate demand causes the price level to rise, the money wage rises less than proportionately. The real wage falls and firms have an incentive to increase employment and output.

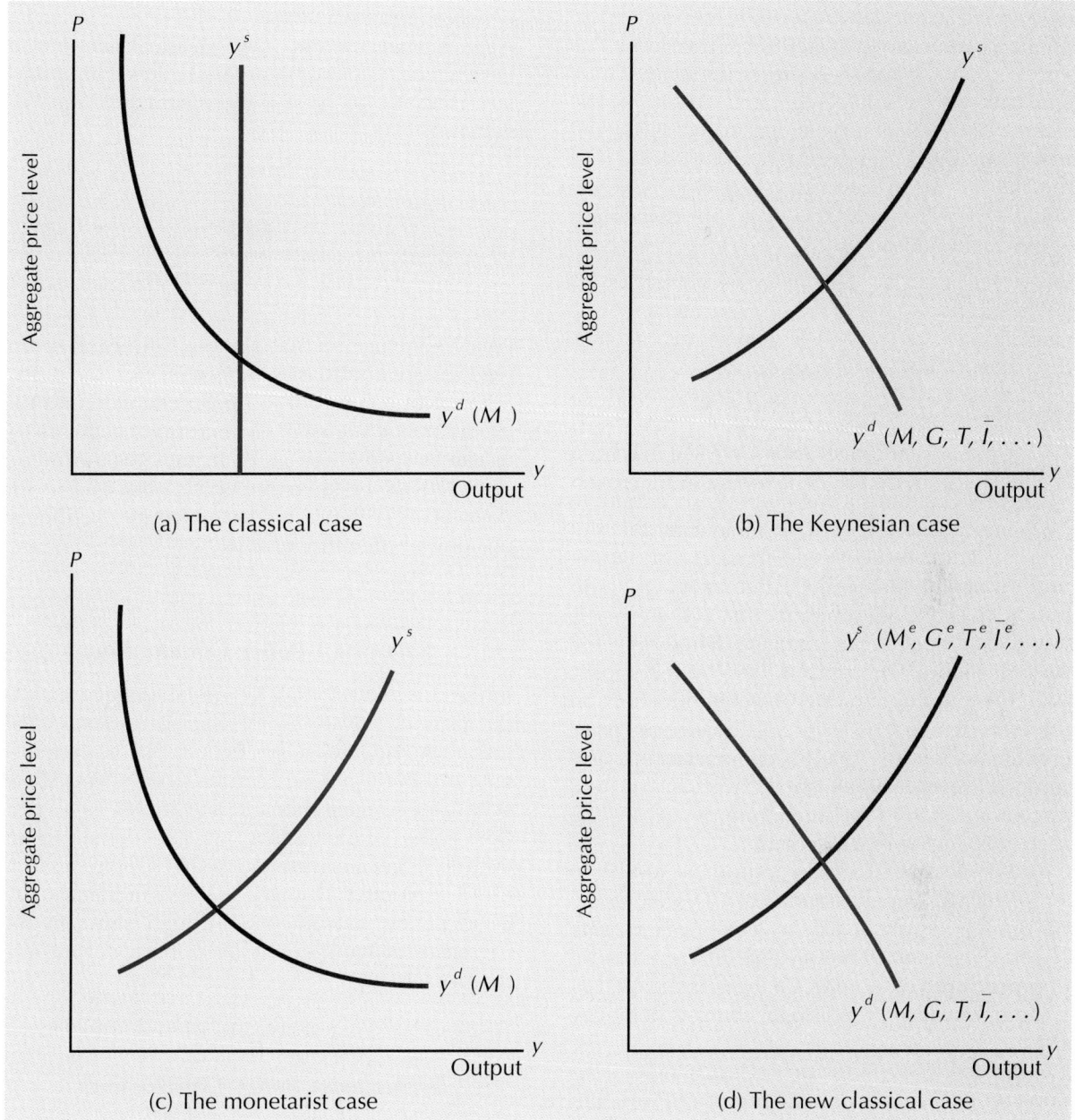

FIGURE 16.1 *Aggregate Supply and Demand Curves from Four Macroeconomic Models*

Explaining the roles of supply-side and demand-side variables in these four models is the task of the chapters in this part.

In the new classical model, the money wage is assumed to be flexible, much as in the classical case. Workers are not, however, assumed to have perfect information about the price level. Instead they are assumed to form forward-looking *rational expectations* about the price level, and thus the real wage, by using all relevant information intelligently. An *expected* increase in aggregate demand, for example, leads workers forming rational expectations to expect an increase in the price level. The flexible money wage rises proportionately. There is no increase in employment and output. In the case of an unexpected change in aggregate demand, workers do not expect the price level to rise. The money wage does not rise proportionately with the price level, and there is a spur to increase employment and output.

B
Aggregate Demand

On the demand side, the issue that divides macroeconomists is the realism of the quantity theory of money.

Classical economists and monetarists adhere to the quantity theory, though in somewhat different forms. As the labeling of the classical and monetarist aggregate demand curves indicates, both groups of economists believe that money is the dominant influence on aggregate demand. In the classical model, with output fixed by the supply side, the quantity of money, through its effect on aggregate demand, determines the aggregate price level. Changes in the quantity of money cause proportional changes in the aggregate price level (a 10 percent increase in the money supply causes the price level to rise by 10 percent).

In the monetarist model, output is not fixed completely by supply-side factors. In this model the money supply, again by affecting aggregate demand, determines money GNP ($P \times y$)—the total expenditure on output. Changes in the quantity of money cause proportional changes in money GNP.

In the Keynesian or the new classical model, the money supply is only one of a number of variables affecting aggregate demand. Other important influences on demand include fiscal policy variables such as the levels of government spending and taxes, as well as the level of autonomous investment spending. Changes in any of these affect the level of aggregate demand *for a given level of the money supply*. Neither money GNP nor the price level is proportional to the money supply.

In short, classical economists and monetarists have a monetary theory of aggregate demand in which the money supply is the dominant influence. Keynesians and new classical economists have a more general theory that allows nonmonetary variables to have a significant influence on demand.

II
Policy Conclusions

Policy conclusions that emerge from each of the theories are summarized in Table 16.1.

The first column of the table characterizes the overall policy stance of each group of economists. As can be seen, there are really only two positions. The activist or interventionist position of the Keynesians is contrasted to the noninterventionist position of the other groups.

A
Keynesian Policy Conclusions

Important to the overall Keynesian policy stance is the view of private sector aggregate demand as unstable. The Keynesians believe that both monetary and fiscal policies can be used effectively to stabilize aggregate demand and therefore output. Both types of policy affect aggregate demand. Furthermore, because the aggregate supply curve is upward sloping, changes in both monetary and fiscal policy instruments, through shifts in the aggregate demand curve, affect both output and the price level.

B
Monetarist Policy Conclusions

In contrast to the Keynesians, monetarists see the private sector as relatively self-stabilizing and shock absorbing, with the government sector as the primary source of destabilizing shocks. At least this is their view of the behavior of the economy over the longer time horizon that they believe to be of interest. Major government policy actions that destabilize the economy are erratic swings in the growth rate of the money supply. Thus, the best way to prevent swings in money growth is to man-

TABLE 16.1   Policy Positions of Major Schools of Macroeconomists

	Overall Policy	Monetary Policy	Fiscal Policy
Keynesian	Activist (interventionist). Policy by discretion, not rules.	Affects both price and output in the short run.	Affects both price and output.
Monetarist	Noninterventionist. Policy by rules, not discretion.	Affects both price and output in the short run.	Little effect on price or output.
New classical	Noninterventionist. Policy by rules, not discretion.	Unpredictable changes in the money supply (money surprises) affect both price and output in the short run. Predictable changes affect only the price level.	Unpredictable changes in government spending and taxes affect both price and output. Predictable changes affect only the price level.
Classical	Noninterventionist. Policy by rules, not discretion.	Affects only the price level.	Little effect on price or output.

date a constant growth rate for the money supply. Money growth is of primary importance because the money supply is the dominant influence on aggregate demand.

Fiscal policy is of little independent importance because changes in the money supply are the primary determinant of aggregate demand. Budget deficits, however, may be destabilizing if they put pressure on the Federal Reserve to increase the money supply as a means of financing the deficit. Therefore Milton Friedman and some other monetarists favor a rule for fiscal policy that would mandate balancing the federal budget.

C
New Classical Policy Conclusions

The new classical economists come to the same noninterventionist policy position as the monetarists. Useful stabilization policies must involve *systematic* movements in monetary and fiscal variables over the business cycle. Stimulus is necessary as recessions approach; restraint is necessary when the economy expands too rapidly. Such sys-

tematic policy actions will be predictable and, in the new classical view, they will not affect output and employment. Stabilization policy therefore should not be directed at these real variables but instead should be directed at maintaining a stable, low rate of inflation. This can best be achieved, in the new classical view, by rules for monetary and fiscal policy, as the monetarists believe.

D
Classical Policy Conclusions

Both the monetarist and new classical models are rooted in the original classical model. Not surprisingly, all three frameworks share the same noninterventionist policy stance. With output and employment determined by supply-side factors, in the classical model there is no role for policies to stabilize these variables. The rate of change in the quantity of money determines the inflation rate. A low, constant money growth rate ensures a low, stable inflation rate. Fiscal policy has little effect on either price or output. Balancing the budget each year represents sound government finance to the classical economists.

III

Areas of Consensus

The title of this chapter indicates that macroeconomics is characterized by both controversy and consensus. By now it is apparent that there are significant questions on which economists disagree—areas of controversy. These disagreements have made it necessary for us to describe and contrast the different models that macroeconomists have developed. In contrasting these models, however, we should not lose sight of the areas where there is general agreement among economists—areas of consensus. The cliche "Ask five economists a question and you will get six different answers" is applicable to some but not all questions. Let us consider a number of areas of consensus.

1. *Sustained high rates of inflation are possible only if they are accommodated by rapid money supply growth.*

Economists generally believe in what can be called the *valid core of the quantity theory.* Sustained high rates of inflation cannot occur without accompanying high rates of growth in the money supply. An extreme illustration of this relationship is the astronomical rate of growth in the money supply that accompanies hyperinflation. In Hungary, for example, during 1945 and 1946, when the inflation rate was 19,800 percent *per month*, the money supply grew by 12,200 percent *per month.* (See also the example of the German hyperinflation in Perspective 8A.) But the relationship between money growth and sustained inflation does not require such extreme conditions. Few, if any, economists, for example, would expect that an inflation rate of 10 percent could be maintained for 3 years if the money stock grew at a constant annual rate of 3 percent. To the monetarist Milton Friedman, "Inflation is always and everywhere a monetary phenomenon." A Keynesian would disagree. Both, however, agree that rapid money growth is a necessary precondition for *rapid, sustained* inflation.

2. *The level of aggregate demand does affect output and employment.*

A look at Table 16.1 shows that Keynesians, monetarists, and new classical economists *all* attribute some role to demand-side factors in determining output and therefore employment. This may be called the *valid core of the Keynesian revolution.* Few modern economists subscribe to the pure form of the classical model presented in Chapter 8. That model was useful to introduce the novel element of the Keynesian model and was the starting point for the monetarist and new classical models. The Great Depression of the 1930s, however, disproved a completely supply-side theory of real output and employment. In the United States from 1929 to 1933, real output fell by 30 percent. The unemployment rate rose from 3.2 to 25.2 percent. There were no rapid changes in supply-side conditions during this period that can explain this economic collapse.

3. *Supply-side factors are dominant in determining real output over longer periods.*

The importance of aggregate demand in determining output in the short run should not obscure the importance of supply-side factors over longer periods of time. The classical emphasis on the supply side is valid when applied to the long run. Over the long run, growth in factor supplies (capital and labor) and technological changes are the dominant influences on the growth rate of output and employment. In recent years, all groups of macroeconomists have emphasized the need for policies that create a favorable climate for such long-run growth—policies to promote saving in order to finance capital formation and to encourage investment; policies to promote job training and hence labor productivity; and policies to encourage research and development. There is disagreement on how to achieve these goals but agreement on the goals themselves.

4. *Expectations matter for policy effectiveness.*

Here perhaps we might lose a hard-line Keynesian or two, but most economists would, we think, agree that public expectations significantly influence policy effectiveness. We have seen that the Keynesians and monetarists do not believe that the public forms completely rational expectations. Most would agree, however, that as the economy became more turbulent during the 1970s and 1980s, the public began to watch policy more closely. As the Keynesian economist Robert Solow remarked, "It is possible that what happened between the 1960s and 1970s is a kind of loss of virginity with respect to inflationary expectations."[1] The public refused to believe any longer that inflation was delivered by the stork and started looking around for its real causes. Economic reporting on television and in the newspapers became much more detailed. Public awareness of changes in Federal Reserve policy and federal budget policy increased substantially. Public awareness of macroeconomic policy limits its effectiveness along the lines suggested by the new classical economists. That policy effectiveness depends, at least in part, on whether the policy is predictable or not is what we would call the *valid core of the new classical economics.*

Keynesians would argue that due to labor contracts and consequently sticky money wages, even a completely anticipated monetary or fiscal policy action would affect output and employment. Most would not deny, though, that the effect of a given policy action would be less in a world where the public watches the actions of policymakers carefully than in one where it does not.

[1]Robert Solow, "Summary and Evaluation," in *After the Phillips Curve: Persistence of High Inflation and High Unemployment* (Boston: Federal Reserve Bank of Boston) 1978.

SUMMARY

There are important areas of consensus in macroeconomics. There are important questions on which macroeconomists agree. The areas of agreement, however, do not extend to most issues concerning stabilization policy in the short run. Consequently, as we consider such policy questions in the chapters in the next part, we return to areas of controversy.

QUESTIONS AND PROBLEMS

1. Compare the classical, Keynesian, monetarist, and new classical assumptions regarding:
   (a) wage flexibility
   (b) information flows in the labor market
   (c) formation of expectations
   (d) the possibility of periods of significant unemployment
   (e) variables influencing aggregate demand.
2. Explain why the Keynesians are the only group who advocate government intervention in the form of monetary and fiscal policy actions designed to stabilize the economy.
3. List four areas of consensus among macroeconomists.
4. Explain how the improvement and growth in television and newspaper reporting may have altered the effectiveness of monetary and fiscal policies.
5. Which of the frameworks we have considered do you view as providing the best explanation of how the economy really works? Defend your choice.

III

Macroeconomic Policy

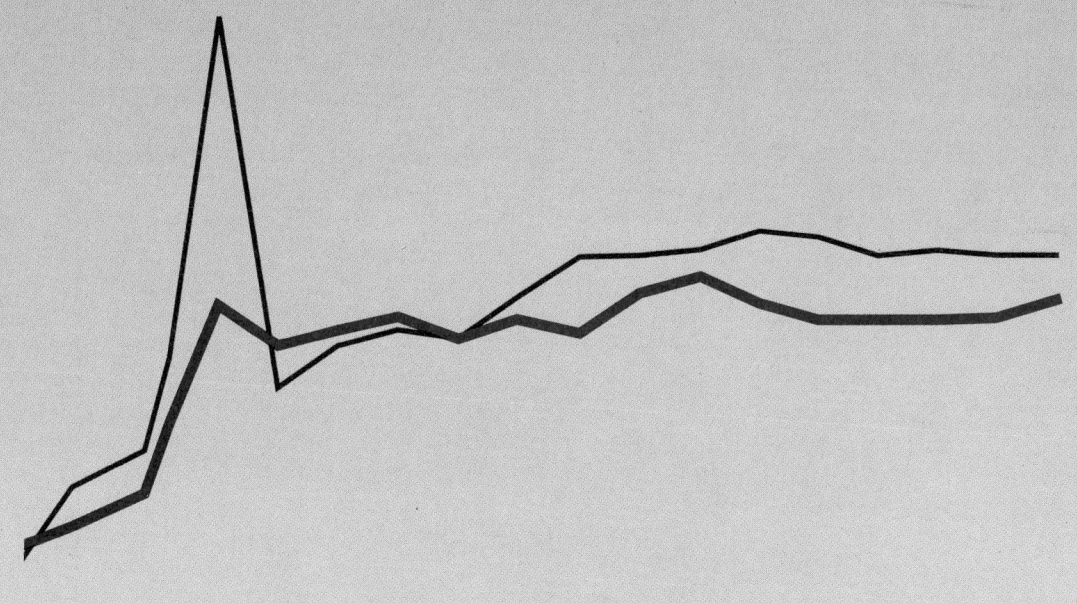

17

Money and the Banking System

The chapters in this part consider macroeconomic policy. We examined policy questions as we developed the different macroeconomic models, but here we go into more detail. We discuss the actual processes by which policy decisions are made and consider how policy *should* be conducted. We start in this chapter with *monetary policy*.

In surveys of businessmen in the mid-1980s, Paul Volcker, then Chairman of the Federal Reserve Board, was often ranked the second most influential man in the United States. (President Reagan was ranked first.) This ranking reflected the importance businessmen attach to the conduct of monetary policy, which is the job of the Federal Reserve. As explained in Chapter 11, the Federal Reserve System is the U.S. *central bank*.

The U.S. system of central banking was established by the Federal Reserve Act of 1913. Unlike European countries, which have a single central bank, the United States has a system of Federal Reserve Banks, one for each of 12 Federal Reserve Districts. Each Federal Reserve Bank is named for the city in which it is located: the Federal Reserve Bank of New York, the Federal Reserve Bank of Chicago, the Federal Reserve Bank of Atlanta, the Federal Reserve Bank of San Francisco, and so forth.

In this chapter we examine the way in which the Federal Reserve can control the supply of money in the U.S. economy. As discussed in Chapter 11, the different measures of the money supply (M1, M2, M3), the *monetary aggregates*, consist of currency plus various categories of bank deposits. Consequently, the relationship between the Federal Reserve and the banking system will be central to our discussion. Section I focuses on the tools the Federal Reserve uses to control the money supply. In Section II the focus shifts to the banking system's role in the money supply process. Chapter 18 will consider how the Federal Reserve should conduct monetary policy. What is the best way to use the tools it has?

I

Federal Reserve Control of the Money Supply

Decisions on monetary policy are made by two groups within the Federal Reserve. The first of these is the *Board of Governors of the Federal Reserve*.

The **Board of Governors of the Federal Reserve** is composed of seven members (governors) appointed by the President of the United States with the advice and consent of the Senate for a term of 14 years. One member of the board is appointed chairman.

Forceful chairmen such as Arthur Burns for much of the 1970s and Paul Volcker in the 1980s have dominated monetary policy.

The second monetary policymaking body is the *Open Market Committee*.

The **Open Market Committee** is composed of 12 voting members: the 7 members of the Board of Governors and 5 of the presidents of regional Federal Reserve Banks. Presidents of the regional banks serve on a rotating basis, with the exception of the president of the Federal Reserve Bank of New York, who is vice chairman and a permanent voting member of the committee.

The New York bank president's special status is due to the central role that the bank plays in the committee's function, as explained later.
Read Perspective 17A.

A

The Control Process

The money supply consists of currency plus certain categories of bank deposits. To simplify our

PERSPECTIVE 17A
The Regional Federal Reserve Banks

Figure 17.1 shows the location of each Federal Reserve Bank and the boundaries of each Federal Reserve District. The Federal Reserve Act of 1913 was essentially a compromise between those who wanted a centrally controlled banking system and those who feared that a single central bank would fall under the control of eastern (especially Wall Street) influences. The regional banks were intended to diffuse power within the system.

Today the regional banks perform several functions. They issue currency (Federal Reserve notes) and replace it as necessary. They provide check clearing (processing) services, collect data on the economy of their regions, and do economic research. Also, it is the regional banks that supervise loans that the Federal Reserve makes to banks, as explained later. Finally, as noted previously, the regional bank presidents serve on the Open Market Committee on a rotating basis.

---

discussion, let us assume that there is only one type of deposit, a *transactions* deposit, which represents all deposits on which checks may be written. The money supply concept we consider then corresponds to the narrow M1 definition.

Currency in the United States consists primarily of Federal Reserve notes—paper money issued by the Federal Reserve, as you can verify by checking the heading on the bills in your wallet. (Each is also marked by the regional Federal Reserve Bank that issued it.) The Federal Reserve can therefore control the supply of currency directly. Federal Reserve control of the deposit component of the money supply is more complex.

To control the quantity of bank deposits, the Federal Reserve sets *legal reserve requirements.*

Legal reserve requirements specify that banks must hold a certain percentage (fraction) of deposits either in the form of vault cash (currency) or as deposits at regional Federal Reserve Banks. They are what are called *fractional reserve requirements.*

For example, suppose the legal reserve requirement is set at 10 percent. If the Old Reliable Bank and Trust Company has $20 million on deposit (meaning that the public has deposits of $20 million in that bank), it must hold $2 million in vault cash and deposits at a regional Federal Reserve Bank. Having set legal reserve requirements, the Federal Reserve can control the money supply by regulating the supply of legal reserves.

Technically, setting legal reserve requirements and fixing the level of reserves only sets a ceiling on the level of deposits. With a 10 percent legal reserve requirement, for example, if the Federal Reserve sets reserves at $60 billion, then the maximum quantity of deposits would be $600 billion. In fact, since legal reserves (currency in the vault and deposits at regional Federal Reserve Banks) pay no interest, banks will hold few reserves beyond those required by the Federal Reserve. Thus the actual level of deposits will be close to the ceiling. In the preceding example, with $60 billion in reserves and a 10 percent legal reserve requirement, the *actual level of deposits will not fall far short of $600 billion.*

B
Tools of Federal Reserve Control

But how does the Federal Reserve set (or control) the level of legal bank reserves? There are three major tools that the Federal Reserve uses to control banks' reserve positions: *open market opera-*

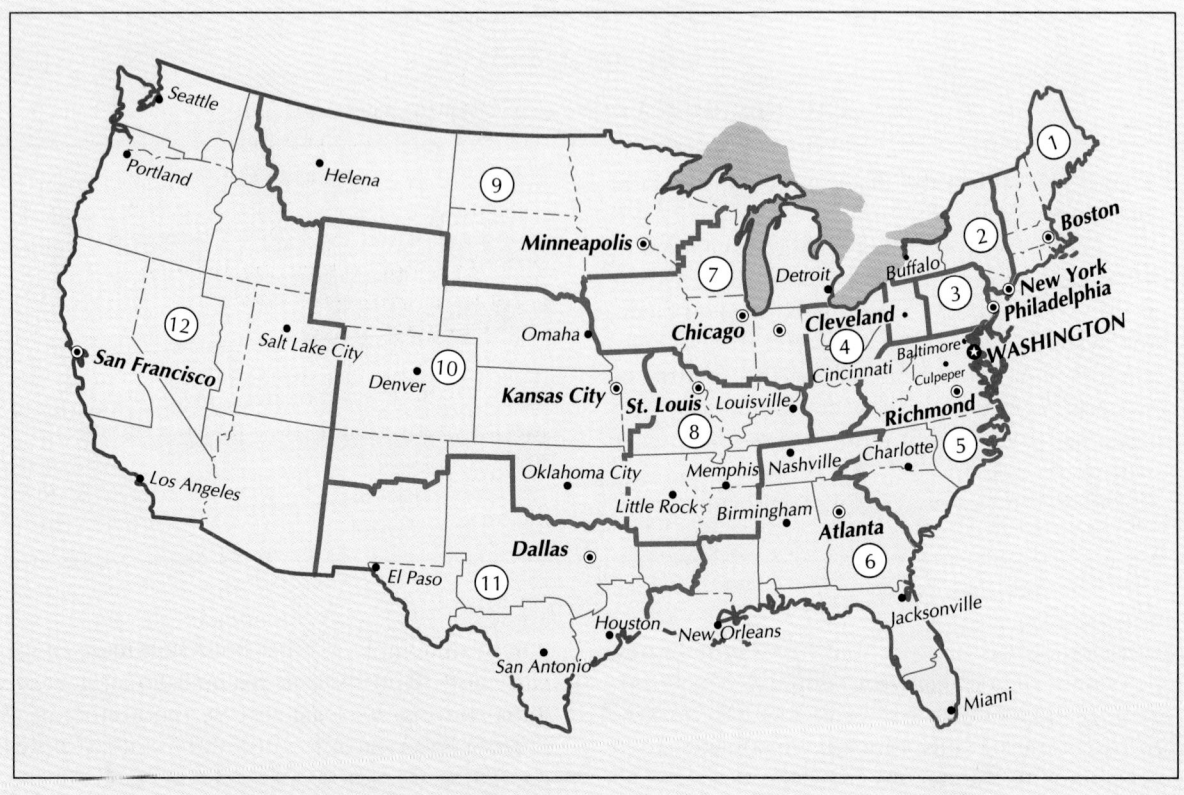

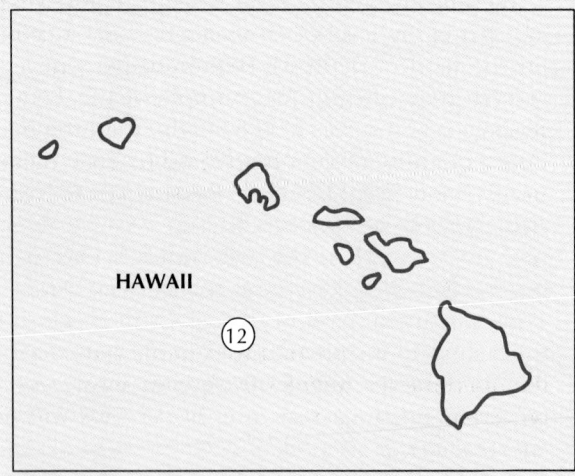

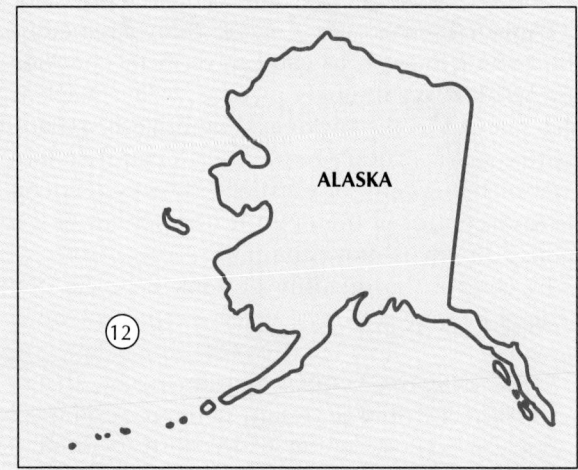

Legend

— Boundaries of Federal Reserve districts

— Boundaries of Federal Reserve branch territories

⊗ Board of governors of the Federal Reserve System

⊙ Federal Reserve bank cities

• Federal Reserve branch cities

• Federal Reserve bank facility

FIGURE 17.1   The Federal Reserve System

Boundaries of Federal Reserve districts and their branch territories tions, the *discount rate,* and the *required reserve ratio.*

1. Open Market Operations

The *open market* is the market of dealers in government securities in New York City. Government securities are interest-bearing debt instruments issued by the U.S. Treasury.[1] They come in maturities ranging from 3 months to 30 years, where the *maturity* of a bond is the time from when it is issued until the time the amount borrowed must be repaid. These government securities are traded in the open market. A possible transaction might be as follows: A life insurance company purchases a $10,000 U.S. Treasury bond in 1988 that matures in the year 2008. In 1989 the company decides to sell the security and invest the funds in another way (buy shares of General Motors stock). Because most Treasury securities are *marketable,* meaning that their ownership is transferable,[2] the life insurance company goes to a government security dealer, who sells the bond in the open market.

Where does the Federal Reserve come into this process? Not at all for many open market transactions. For example, if the buyer in the preceding transaction is an individual or company wanting to increase holdings of government securities, the transaction would be a simple asset swap. However, when the Federal Reserve does enter the open market to buy and sell securities, such transactions have broad implications.

Federal Reserve purchases and sales of government securities are called **Open Market Operations.** They are supervised by the Open Market Committee.

Open market operations have important effects on bank reserves and therefore on bank deposits and the money supply. To see the link between open market operations and bank reserves, suppose that in the preceding example the Federal Reserve bought the security sold by the life insur-

ance company—a $10,000 Federal Reserve open market *purchase.*

The Federal Reserve Bank of New York acts as the Open Market Committee's agent in carrying out open market operations. To buy the $10,000 security, the manager of the *open market desk* at the New York bank writes a check. A key point to note here is that the Federal Reserve Bank of New York does not reduce the balance in any other account by writing the check. The Federal Reserve simply creates a new liability against itself. Once the life insurance company receives the check (through its security dealer), it will be deposited in the company's bank account, at Citibank in New York, for example.

Citibank will then present the check to the Federal Reserve Bank of New York for payment. The Federal Reserve will credit Citibank's account balance at the New York Federal Reserve Bank with $10,000. But remember, deposits at regional Federal Reserve banks are legal reserves. *The open market purchase results in an increase of an equal amount in bank legal reserves.*

To keep track of the effects of Federal Reserve actions here and in the next section (when we look at changes in deposits), we record the changes in balance sheets caused by the policy action. A balance sheet is simply a listing of assets (on the left side) and of liabilities, or claims against the institution (on the right side).

The effects of open market purchases on the balance sheet of the Federal Reserve are shown in Table 17.1. On the asset side the Federal Reserve has $10,000 more in government securities, while on the liability side, bank reserve deposits are $10,000 higher.[3]

Conversely, a *sale* of government securities in the open market *reduces bank reserve deposits by an equal amount.* For example, if the Federal Reserve sold a $10,000 security to a firm, they

---

[1]Short-term (less than 1 year) Treasury obligations are called *Treasury bills.* Long-term obligations are referred to as *bonds. Securities* is a general term for debt obligations of any maturity.

[2]Some series of *savings bonds* sold by the Treasury are not marketable.

[3]Hereafter we drop the adjective *legal* when referring to bank reserve assets that satisfy reserve requirements.

TABLE 17.1 Effect on the Federal Reserve's Balance Sheet of a $10,000 Open Market Purchase

Assets		Liabilities	
Government securities	+10,000	Bank reserve deposits	+10,000

would receive a check, drawn on the firm's bank for $10,000. They would then *reduce* that bank's deposit balance at a regional Federal Reserve Bank by $10,000. The plus items in Table 17.1 would be replaced with minuses. Bank reserves would be lower by $10,000.

Open market purchases and sales of government securities provide a flexible means of controlling bank reserves and are the most important of the Federal Reserve's tools for control of the money supply.

2. *The Discount Rate* The Open Market Committee oversees open market operations. The remaining tools of monetary control are administered by the Board of Governors of the Federal Reserve System. The first of these is the Federal Reserve *discount rate*. The Federal Reserve makes loans to banks at what are called **discount windows** at each of the regional Federal Reserve Banks.

> The **discount rate** is the interest rate charged to banks on loans. The Federal Reserve raises or lowers this rate to regulate the volume of such loans to banks.

To see the effect on bank reserve deposits of changes in the volume of loans from the Federal Reserve, consider the effect of a $10,000 loan from the Federal Reserve to a bank. The effects on the Federal Reserve's balance sheet are shown in Table 17.2.

The asset item "loans to banks" increases by $10,000. Proceeds from the loan are credited to the account of the borrowing bank at the Federal Reserve. At this point, bank reserve deposits increase by $10,000. By lowering the discount rate, the Federal Reserve can encourage banks to borrow and increase the borrowed component of bank reserves. Raising the discount rate has the opposite effect.

Because our concern is control of the money supply, our focus has been on the relationship between bank borrowing at the discount window and the level of bank reserves. The discount window, however, has another important function. One of a central bank's responsibilities is to stabilize the banking system. It must stand ready to act as the *lender of last resort* for banks that are in trouble and might otherwise fail. The Federal Reserve fulfills this function by arranging loans for problem banks through the discount window. Why banks become problem banks will be discussed later (see Perspective 17C).

3. *The Required Reserve Ratio* The third tool used by the Federal Reserve to control banks' reserve positions, and therefore the quantity of deposits, is the *required reserve ratio*.

> The **required reserve ratio** is the percentage of deposits banks must hold as reserves.

While changes in this ratio do not affect the level of total bank reserves, they do affect the quantity of deposits that can be supported by a given level of reserves. Increases in the required reserve ratio reduce the quantity of deposits that can be supported by a given amount of reserves.

Consider our previous example, where reserves were set at $60 billion. With a 10 percent reserve requirement, the maximum level for deposits was $600 billion. If the required reserve ratio were increased to 12 percent, the maximum level of deposits, with reserves unchanged at $60 billion, would be $500 billion $(0.12 \times 500 = 60)$. The increase in the required reserve ratio from 10 percent to 12 percent would have the same effect as a reduction in reserves (e.g., via an open market sale of securities) from $60 billion to $50 billion $(50 = 0.10 \times 500)$.

In general, increases in the required reserve ratio decrease the maximum quantity of bank de-

TABLE 17.2   Effect on the Federal Reserve's Balance Sheet of a $10,000 Loan to a Bank

Assets		Liabilities	
Loans to banks	+10,000	Bank reserve deposits	+10,000

posits, while reductions have the opposite effect. In practice, however, changes in reserve requirements are not often used as a policy tool by the Federal Reserve. One reason for this is the accounting and administrative costs to banks of frequent changes in required reserve ratios.

II
The Banking System and the Money Supply

We have examined the way in which the Federal Reserve can control bank reserves. In this section we explain the relationship between bank reserves and bank deposits—the largest component of the money supply. As background for this discussion, we consider some general features of the U.S. banking system.

A
Banks as Depository Institutions

We all know what banks are, but what exactly do they do? We have been using *banks* as a term to describe *depository institutions*—institutions whose liabilities are included in the monetary aggregates. These depository institutions include *commercial banks, savings and loan associations, mutual savings banks,* and *credit unions.*

All of these institutions accept checkable deposits and savings deposits. Deposits are their major liability, i.e., their major source of funds. They use deposits to make loans and buy securities. Loans and securities are their assets, i.e., their major uses

of funds. Today the major difference among the classes of depository institutions is the mix of these assets. The principal assets held by each of these types of depository institutions are listed in Table 17.3. The table also shows the total assets held by each type of institution as a measure of relative size. To keep the discussion simple, we will call all depository institutions *banks* and focus our attention on the commercial banking system. Keep in mind, however, that our analysis also pertains to other depository institutions.
Read Perspective 17B.

B
Bank Deposits and Bank Reserves

Section I examined the way the Federal Reserve can use open market operations, changes in the discount rate, and changes in the required reserve ratio on deposits to affect the reserve position of banks. Next we consider the process whereby changes in reserves affect the level of deposits in the banking system and, thus, the money supply. A convenient starting point for this analysis is the balance sheet listing assets and liabilities of commercial banks. A simplified version of the consolidated balance sheet for all commercial banks is shown in Table 17.4. Assets are listed on the left and liabilities on the right.

On the asset side, the first item is cash assets of commercial banks. Reserves (vault cash plus deposits at the Federal Reserve) come under this category, but other items are also included (e.g., bank deposits at other banks). Reserves as of the time period for which the table was compiled (January 1986) totaled $48.0 billion, of which all but $1.1 billion were required reserves. As explained previ-

TABLE 17.3 Assets of Depository Institutions

Institution	Primary Assets	Total Assets (Billions of Dollars, January 1986)
Commercial banks	Business and consumer loans U.S. government and municipal bonds	$2,443
Savings and loan associations	Mortgages	1,070
Mutual savings banks	Mortgages	216
Credit unions	Consumer loans	119

Source: Federal Reserve Bulletin, May 1986.

PERSPECTIVE 17B

Financial Intermediation

Depository institutions are examples of **financial intermediaries.** To understand the role of such institutions, consider the graphic representation of the financial sector in Figure 17.2.

The lower arrow shows direct loans from original lenders (savers) to ultimate borrowers (spenders). Households, for example, may be the savers lending directly to business or government by buying bonds issued by a corporation such as Exxon or by the U.S. Treasury. This is an example of direct financing. However, suppose the borrower is a small business, Sal's Soccer Supplies, or an individual, Alice Smith, who wants to buy a new car. Prospects for floating a bond issue would be bleak. Or consider a saver, Andrea, who would be very happy to invest in Exxon or the U.S. Treasury, but being 14, she can invest only $10 per month. Buying a $1,000 or $10,000 bond is not a possibility for her.

Enter financial intermediaries. As shown by the top arrow of the figure, these institutions take deposits from savers and lend them to borrowers to finance spending for investment or consumption. Financial intermediaries make profits out of the difference between their lending and deposit rates.

Financial intermediaries reduce *transactions costs* for borrowers and lenders. Alice, for example, simply goes to the bank rather than having to advertise that she is looking for a lender. *Information costs* are reduced for savers (lenders) because the bank will have already checked Alice Smith's credit rating or the prospects for Sal's soccer business. Also, financial intermediaries make possible pooling of funds from savers of small amounts (e.g., Andrea with $10 per month) to make larger investments.

In addition to the depository institutions listed in Table 17.3, financial intermediaries include life insurance companies, fire and casualty insurance companies, and pension funds. These other financial intermediaries also channel funds (e.g., pension contributions or life insurance premiums) from ultimate savers (or insurance buyers) to ultimate borrowers. But they do not accept deposits that can be withdrawn or transferred. What makes depository institutions of special interest is that their primary liabilities (deposits) are an important part of our payment system. They are *money*.

---

ously, banks hold few excess reserves, since reserve assets do not pay interest. The other major items on the asset side of the ledger are loans by the commercial banks, which include loans to consumers and businesses, and the banks' holding of both government and corporate securities.

TABLE 17.4   Consolidated Balance Sheet for the Commercial Banking System, January 1986 (Billions of Dollars)

Assets		Liabilities	
Cash assets, including reserves	188.1	Transactions deposits	488.2
Loans	1,600.6	Time and savings deposits	1,241.3
U.S. Treasury securities	249.0	Other liabilities and capital	694.5
Other securities	178.3		
Other assets, including cash assets in process of collection	208.0		
Total assets	2,424.0	Total liabilities and capital	2,424.0

Source: Federal Reserve Bulletin, May 1986.

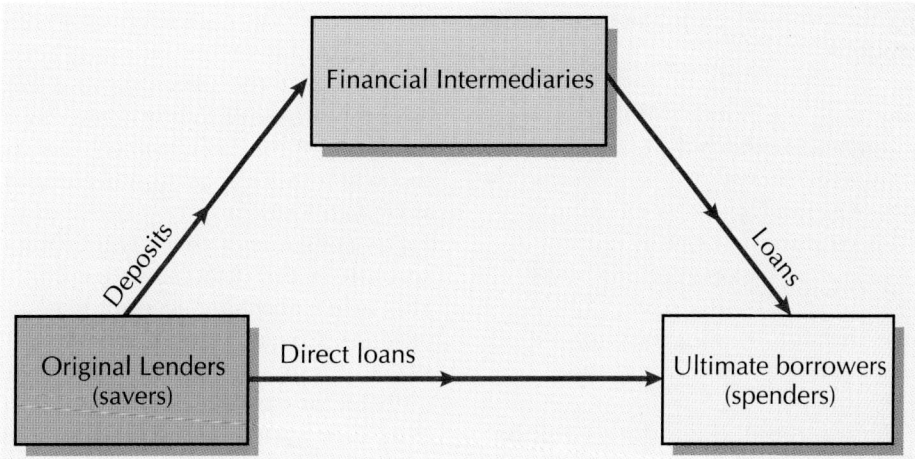

FIGURE 17.2 *Financial Market Flows*

The major liabilities of the commercial banks are deposits, both transactions (checkable) and savings.[4]

C
A Simple Model of Deposit Creation

Now consider the effect on the banking system of an increase in reserves. Let us return to our previous example, where the increase in reserves was the result of an open market purchase by the Federal Reserve. Recall our assumption that the Federal Reserve had purchased a $10,000 U.S. government security from a life insurance company, making payment with a check drawn on the Federal Reserve Bank of New York. The life insurance company deposited the check in an account at Citibank. When the check is presented for pay-

ment at the Federal Reserve Bank of New York, Citibank's reserve deposits at that Federal Reserve Bank increase by $10,000. To this point, the effects on Citibank's balance sheet as a result of the open market purchase are as shown in Table 17.5. Transactions deposits and reserves have both increased by $10,000. With a 10 percent required reserve ratio, required reserves will increase by $1,000 (0.10 × 10,000). Citibank will then have increased excess reserves of $9,000, excess reserves being those above the reserve requirement.

The situation depicted in Table 17.5 will not be the final position for Citibank's balance sheet because the bank will not, in general, wish to increase *excess* reserves. Since reserves do not pay interest, the bank will convert the excess reserves, which are in the form of deposits at the New York Federal Reserve Bank, into interest-earning assets. In doing so, a process of *deposit creation* will be set in motion whereby the initial increase in reserves of $10,000 causes deposits to increase by a multiple of that initial increase.

---

[4]*Savings* and *time deposits* both refer to noncheckable deposits. Unlike savings deposits, time deposits are invested for a specified time period—3 months, 1 year, etc.—generally with a penalty for early withdrawal.

TABLE 17.5 **Initial Effect on Citibank's Balance Sheet From a $10,000 Open Market Purchase**

Assets			Liabilities	
Reserves		+10,000	Transactions deposits	+10,000
Required reserves	+1,000			
Excess reserves	+9,000			
Total assets		+10,000	Total liabilities	+10,000

In describing the process, we make some simplifying assumptions:

1. We assume that the public's holdings of currency remain unchanged. None of the additional increase in reserves is converted to currency (e.g., the life insurance company does not withdraw $1,000 in currency from Citibank after making the initial deposit).
2. We assume that the banking system's *desired* level of excess reserves is constant.

The effect of altering these assumptions will be examined in the next section. Throughout, we will deal only with the case involving just one type of deposit, a transactions account. (To consider other types of deposits would add complications not central to an understanding of the deposit creation process.)

Having made these assumptions, we are ready to describe the process of deposit creation. Citibank in our example has $9,000 in excess reserves that it wants to convert into interest-earning assets. The bank can do this by either increasing loans or purchasing additional securities. Neither of these actions will produce any lasting effect on the level of Citibank's deposits. Buying a new security clearly does not change deposits. If the bank makes a loan, it may temporarily credit the amount of the loan to the checking (transactions) account of the customer, and this would increase

deposits. But the customer would not borrow just to increase his or her checking account balance. Suppose that the loan was to a consumer who used the proceeds to buy a new car. The consumer pays for the car with a check drawn on Citibank, and when this transaction is completed, deposits at Citibank return to their preloan level.

The consumer's check will be deposited in the account of the dealership that sold him the car. This firm's checking account balance, let us suppose at Chase Manhattan Bank, increases by $9,000. Chase Manhattan presents the check to Citibank for payment. The check *clears* the Federal Reserve System, which means simply that Citibank honors the check by transferring $9,000 from its own account to Chase Manhattan's account at the Federal Reserve Bank of New York. At this point, the $9,000 in excess reserves are eliminated from Citibank's balance sheet; the bank's reserve deposits have declined by $9,000. Citibank's balance sheet is now at its final position, where the effects of the open market operation are shown in Table 17.6. On the liability side, deposits are higher by the $10,000 deposit of the company that originally sold a U.S. government security to the Federal Reserve. Required reserves are higher by $1,000 (0.10 × 10,000). Earning assets of the bank, loans in our example, have risen by $9,000.

Although we are now finished with Citibank's balance sheet, the process of deposit creation is not complete. Table 17.7 shows the effects on Chase Manhattan's balance sheet to this point.

TABLE 17.6 Final Effects on Citibank's Balance Sheet From a $10,000 Open Market Purchase

Assets		Liabilities	
Reserves	+1,000	Transactions deposits	+10,000
Required reserves	+1,000		
Loans	+9,000		
Total assets	+10,000	Total liabilities	+10,000

TABLE 17.7 Initial Effects on Chase Manhattan's Balance Sheet

Assets		Liabilities	
Reserves	+9,000	Transactions deposits	+9,000
Required reserves	+900		
Excess reserves	+8,100		
Total assets	+9,000	Total liabilities	+9,000

Because of the deposit by the car dealership, deposits are up by $9,000. After the check clears through the Federal Reserve System, $9,000 has been transferred to Chase Manhattan's reserve account. Thus reserves are increased by $9,000, of which only $900 (0.10 × 9,000) is required to back the increase in deposits. Chase Manhattan, finding itself with $8,100 (9,000 − 900) of excess reserves, will attempt to convert it into interest-earning assets by proceeding in the same manner as did Citibank. The bank will increase its volume of loans or buy additional securities.

Suppose the bank uses the $8,100 of excess reserves to buy a corporate bond, for example, a bond issued by General Motors Corporation. The final position of Chase Manhattan is as shown in Table 17.8. Deposits remain up by $9,000, increasing required reserves by $900. As soon as Chase Manhattan pays for the bond with a check drawn

upon itself and that check clears the Federal Reserve System, the bank's excess reserves will be zero. Earning assets will be increased by $8,100.

The process of deposit creation continues beyond this point, however, because the individual who sold the corporate bond to Chase Manhattan has deposited the proceeds of the check he received for $8,100 in his deposit account at some other commercial bank. That bank now has excess reserves of $7,290, the $8,100 minus the $810 of reserves required to back the deposit. Another round of deposit creation will begin.

The initial increase of $10,000 in reserves began a process of deposit creation whereby deposits of $10,000, then $9,000, then $8,100, then $7,290, and so forth were used to convert what were initially excess reserves into interest-earning assets. Table 17.9 traces the deposit process through several more stages. The individual bank, attempting to

TABLE 17.8 Final Effects on Chase Manhattan's Balance Sheet

Assets		Liabilities	
Reserves	+900	Transactions deposits	+9,000
Required reserves +900			
Securities	+8,100		
Total assets	+9,000	Total liabilities	+9,000

TABLE 17.9 Deposit Creation: An Example

An original open market purchase of $10,000 results in the first-stage increase of $10,000 in reserves

Stage	Bank	Initial Change in Reserves	Change in Deposits	Final Change in Reserves (= 0.10 × Deposits)
1	Citibank, N.Y.	$10,000	$ 10,000	$1,000
2	Chase Manhattan Bank	9,000	9,000	900
3	Mellon Bank, Pa.	8,100	8,100	810
4	First Chicago, Ill.	7,290	7,290	729
5	NCNB, N.C.	6,561	6,561	656.1
6	Bob's Bank, Minn.	5,904.9	5,904.9	590.49
7	.	5,314.41	5,314.41	531.441
8	.	4,782.969	4,782.969	478.2969
9	.			
10	.			
Total			$100,000	$10,000

rid itself of excess reserves, under the assumptions made to this point, simply transfers the reserves to another bank and creates a deposit at that bank. The newly created deposit increases required reserves by 10 percent of the increase in deposits; thus, at each round in the process, the newly created deposit is 10 percent smaller than that of the previous round. The process will stop when all the new reserves have been absorbed by required reserves. With a $10,000 increase in reserves and a required reserve ratio of 10 percent, the new equilibrium will be reached when the quantity of transactions deposits has increased by $100,000 ($10,000 = 0.10 \times 100,000$). At that point, required reserves will have increased by $10,000. There will no longer be any excess reserves in the system. The expansion of bank credit and the resulting creation of new bank deposits will come to an end.

More generally, an increase in reserves (R) of ΔR will cause deposits to increase until required reserves have increased by an equal amount. The increase in required reserves is equal to the increase in deposits times the required reserve ratio on deposits; that is,

$$\text{Increase in required reserves} = rr_d \times \Delta D, \quad (17.1)$$

where rr_d is the required reserve ratio and ΔD is the increase in deposits. Deposit creation will stop when

$$\begin{array}{c}\text{Increase in reserves} = \text{increase} \\ \text{in required reserves}\end{array} \quad (17.2)$$

$$\Delta R = rr_d \times \Delta D \quad (17.3)$$

Therefore, the increase in deposits is

$$\Delta D = \frac{1}{rr_d} \times \Delta R \quad (17.4)$$

The increase in deposits will be a multiple $(1/rr_d)$ of the increase in reserves. In our previous example, with ΔR equal to 10,000 and rr_d equal to 0.1 (a 10 percent reserve requirement), we have, from equation (17.4),

$$\Delta D = \frac{1}{0.1} \times (10,000) = 100,000 \quad (17.5)$$

the result reached previously.

III
Deposit and Money Multipliers

A
The Deposit Multiplier

From equation (17.4) we can define a **deposit multiplier,** giving the increase in deposits per unit increase in bank reserves:

$$\frac{\Delta D}{\Delta R} = \frac{1}{rr_d} \quad (17.6)$$

The deposit multiplier for the simple case considered so far is the reciprocal of the required reserve ratio on deposits. For rr_d equal to 0.1 in our example, the deposit multiplier is 10. Deposits increase by 10 dollars for each $1 increase in reserves.

This simple form of the deposit multiplier results from the simplifying assumptions made previously and will have to be modified when we drop those assumptions. What follows generally is that given the system of fractional legal reserve requirements, an increase in reserves will cause deposits to increase by a multiple of the reserve increase. A similar process of deposit creation would result from a reduction in the Federal Reserve discount rate, which would increase borrowed reserves, or from a lowering of reserve requirements, which, although it would not change total reserves, would create excess reserves in the banking system at the initial level of deposits. The balance sheet changes for such policy actions would be somewhat different than those shown in Tables 17.5 to 17.8, but the general effect would be the same. Both of these alternative expansionary policies would cause both bank credit and bank deposits to increase.

Also, note that all of our analyses can be reversed to consider the effects of an open market *sale* of securities, which will lower bank reserves and begin a process of deposit *contraction*. Suppose, for example, the Federal Reserve had initially *sold* a $10,000 security to a life insurance company, which paid for it with a check drawn on Citibank. Citibank would find its deposits *and reserves* lowered by $10,000. Required reserves would have fallen only $1,000 ($0.10 \times 10,000$). Citibank would have to sell securities or reduce its loans by $9,000 to increase reserves back to the required level. As individuals pay for securities that Citibank sells, or pay off loans to Citibank, deposits at other banks fall. This process of deposit contraction will proceed until deposits for the whole banking system have *fallen* by $100,000. At that point *required* reserves would have fallen by $10,000, the amount of the initial reserve decline. Increases in the discount rate or the required reserve ratio also lead to deposit contractions.

B

The Money Multiplier

The relationship just derived between reserves and deposits can be restated as a relationship between the *monetary base* (*MB*) and the money supply (*M^s*).

The **monetary base** is equal to currency held by the public plus bank reserves.

Thus far, we have assumed that currency holdings of the public are constant, so that the change in the monetary base equals the change in reserves ($\Delta MB = \Delta R$). The change in the *money supply* will in this case be just equal to the change in bank deposits, again since currency held by the public is held constant ($\Delta D = \Delta M^s$). As a consequence, we can write a **money multiplier,** giving the increase in the money supply per unit increase in the monetary base:

$$\frac{\Delta M^s}{\Delta MB} = \frac{\Delta D}{\Delta R} = \frac{1}{rr_d}, \quad (17.7)$$

which in this simple case is just equal to the deposit multiplier. This expression will also require modification when we drop some of our simplifying assumptions, and generally the money multiplier will *not* be equal in value to the deposit multiplier. In general, however, a given increase in the monetary base will cause the money supply to rise by a multiple of the increase in the base.

As described so far, the process of deposit or money creation must seem very mechanical. New doses of reserves are converted via simple multipliers into new deposits, and the money supply increases. Simple models such as the one developed in this section are helpful in explaining the close relationship between bank deposits and

bank reserves but tell us little about the economic processes behind deposit and money creation. Before going on to describe more complex models of deposit creation, it is worthwhile to stop and consider the nature of these processes.

When banks find themselves with excess reserves following a Federal Reserve open market purchase of securities, they attempt to convert those excess reserves into interest-earning assets. They attempt to expand bank credit by making more loans and purchasing securities. To increase their volume of lending, banks offer lower interest rates on loans and perhaps adopt lower standards of creditworthiness. By increasing their demand for securities as interest-earning assets, commercial banks are increasing the overall demand for securities. This has the effect of reducing the interest rate that borrowers, such as corporations and the U.S. government, have to pay to find enough buyers for their securities. Also among the interest-earning assets banks buy are mortgages; thus, in times of credit expansion, mortgage interest rates also fall. Federal Reserve open market purchases, as well as other expansionary policy actions that increase bank reserves, will therefore lead to *credit expansion* and a general decline in interest rates. This is the other side of the process of deposit and money creation.

Read Perspective 17C.

C

Deposit Creation: More Complex Cases

The description of deposit creation in the previous subsection was kept simple by making two restrictive assumptions:

1. Currency held by the public did not change.
2. Banks' *desired* excess reserves were constant.

For more general cases where these assumptions do not hold, the deposit and money multipliers will be *smaller* than $1/rr_d$, the reciprocal of the required reserve ratio. More important, it will be difficult for the Federal Reserve to predict the precise value of the deposit or money multipliers. It will thus be difficult to know the change in deposits, and therefore in the money supply, which will result from a given open market operation.

PERSPECTIVE 17C

The Federal Reserve as the Lender of Last Resort

Having examined the fractional reserve nature of commercial banking, we can spell out the Federal Reserve's role as the *lender of last resort*. Recall that this was referred to previously as an additional role served by the discount window, where the Federal Reserve lends to banks.

Banks keep a fraction of their deposits and invest the rest in interest-earning assets. If the depositors come to doubt the quality of those investments, perhaps because they hear that some of the bank's loans have been made to now-bankrupt firms, they will worry about whether they can get back the money they deposited in the bank. This can lead to a *run* on the bank whereby many depositors simultaneously withdraw their money. Even if the bulk of its investments are sound, the bank cannot immediately convert many of them (consumer or business loans, for example) to cash. Even potentially sound banks may fail because of a run if they do not have a source from which to borrow. Bank failures and depositor panics were especially prevalent during the Great Depression of the 1930s, when poor economic conditions cast doubt on the value of loans and other investments banks had made. Between 1929 and 1933, 9,000 commercial banks failed.

To help prevent bank runs, federal insurance of deposits was instituted. With deposit insurance, the worst thing that can happen in the event of the bank's failure is that depositors will experience some inconvenience in collecting

their money from the Federal Deposit Insurance Corporation (FDIC). Depositors are therefore less likely to become worried about the bank's investments, making bank runs less likely. But bank runs have not been completely eradicated. In May 1984, for example, there was what amounted to a run on the Continental Illinois National Bank and Trust, at that time the ninth largest bank in the United States. Depositors had grown concerned about the number of nonperforming loans (loans on which interest payments are 90 days overdue), particularly loans to corporations in the energy sector. They were also concerned about Continental's large loans to several debt-ridden Latin American countries.

Small deposits are protected by deposit insurance, but deposits over $100,000 are not. Between May and July, Continental lost an estimated $20 billion in deposits. The bank's first response was to borrow $4.5 billion from a group of other large banks. When this proved insufficient to allow the bank to pay off depositors and continue operating, the Federal Reserve Bank of Chicago began to lend to Continental. These loans eventually reached $7.5 billion. In this case, the central bank was serving its function as the lender of last resort. Continental continued to operate while the FDIC worked out a plan to take over some of Continental's old loans and reorganize the bank as an essentially new institution.

1. Changes in Currency Holdings First, consider the effect of modifying our assumption that currency holdings of the public are constant throughout the process of deposit creation. Instead assume, as seems likely, that currency holdings rise along with the increase in deposits. As individual money holdings rise, part of the increase will be in deposits, part in currency. In this case, some of the

increase in the monetary base (currency held by the public plus bank reserves) as a result of an open market purchase will end up not as increased bank reserves but as an increase in currency.

Suppose that the public holds a fixed ratio of currency to deposits, for example, $1 in currency per $4 in deposits. Returning to our example of a

$10,000 open market purchase, the life insurance company that sold the security to the Federal Reserve would now have deposited only $8,000 in its account at Citibank, keeping $2,000 in currency (2,000/8,000 = 1/4). Deposit and reserve creation at the first stage would only be $8,000. Also, at each of the other stages of deposit creation in Table 17.9, there would be a further _leakage_ into currency. The increase in total deposits would fall short of $100,000. A simple way to see this is to note that because reserves increase by less than $10,000 (due to the leakage into currency), deposits _must_ increase by less than $100,000 for banks to be able to satisfy a 10 percent reserve requirement.

With the public increasing its currency holdings, however, the increase in the money supply (deposits plus currency) will exceed the increase in deposits. Still, the increase in the money supply per unit increase in the monetary base (the money multiplier) will be smaller than for the case where currency holdings were constant. This follows because each dollar that the public holds as currency simply counts as $1 in the money supply, while each dollar held as reserves allows the deposit component to be higher by a multiple number of dollars—$10 in our example, where the required reserve ratio is 10 percent. The maximum increase in the money supply as the result of an open market operation will therefore come when all the resulting increase in the monetary base occurs in reserves, i.e., when currency holdings of the public are constant.

2. Changes in Banks' Desired Excess Reserves
Relaxing our assumption that banks do not change their desired holdings of excess reserves provides an additional reason to expect that the expression derived in the preceding subsection ($1/rr_d$) is an overstatement of the true deposit and money multipliers. It appears likely that as deposits rise, banks will increase their excess reserves. Excess reserves are held as a buffer against unexpected deposit flows (e.g., unexpected levels of withdrawals). As deposits increase, so does the potential volume of such deposit flows. Additionally, as we have discussed, the process of deposit expansion leads to a drop in the level of interest rates. The cost of holding excess reserves is the interest forgone by not using these funds to purchase interest-bearing assets (an example of an opportunity cost). As the interest rate falls, this cost becomes lower. Banks are likely to respond by holding more excess reserves.

If some of the increase in bank reserves ends up as new excess reserves, the quantity of deposits created by a given increase in reserves will be smaller than when excess reserves are constant. For example, in our case of a $10,000 open market purchase, if excess reserves rose by $500, then only $9,500 could possibly end up as required reserves. With a 10 percent required reserve ratio, the maximum increase in deposits would be $95,000 compared to $100,000 with excess reserves constant.

IV

The Precision of Money Supply Control

It was stated in the previous section that not only would the money multiplier ($\Delta M^s/\Delta MB$) become smaller, it would also be subject to greater uncertainty in the more general case where currency holdings and excess reserves were allowed to vary. The Federal Reserve _knows_ the required reserve ratio (rr_d); therefore, in the more restrictive case, the money (or deposit) multiplier ($1/rr_d$) is also known. In the more general case, the value of the multiplier depends on the _leakages_ into currency and desired changes in banks' holdings of excess reserves, as discussed previously. The Federal Reserve has no way of knowing exactly how large these leakages will be and can therefore only predict the size of the money multiplier.

Precise money supply control is further complicated by the banks' ability to borrow reserves through the discount window. Our previous example assumed that the Federal Reserve had complete control of the monetary base (bank reserves plus currency held by the public). But the monetary base includes borrowed reserves. Although the Federal Reserve can influence bank borrowing by changing the discount rate, and can offset any undesired changes in borrowed reserves through open market operations, there will be some time lags before such adjustments are made. As a consequence, month-to-month movements in the monetary base will depend to some extent on the borrowing behavior of commercial banks.

Given the difficulty of predicting the money multiplier and even of controlling the monetary base, how closely can we expect the Federal Reserve to control the money supply? The answer to this question depends on the time frame considered. For a short period of time, 1 or 2 months, for example, the previously discussed difficulties appear to make precise money supply control very difficult. Although no one denies that Federal Reserve actions are an important influence on money supply growth from month to month, expecting policymakers to hit precise targets (e.g., keep money growth between 5 and 6 percent for January) is unrealistic.

For a longer period, 6 months to 1 year, for example, difficulties in money supply control due to uncertainty about the money multiplier or level of bank borrowing become less serious. Although the Federal Reserve might not achieve a target level of money supply growth in each month, policymakers can monitor the month-to-month behavior of the money supply and use open market operations to achieve the desired *average* rate of growth over longer periods such as a year.

Suppose the target for 1989 was 5 to 7 percent growth in the money supply. If in January growth were 3 percent, the Federal Reserve would increase the volume of open market purchases or lower the discount rate to speed money growth. If money growth increased above 7 percent later in the year, they could reverse gears with an open market sale or a rise in the discount rate. If the Federal Reserve concentrated solely on control of the money supply, they could achieve or come very close to a range such as 5 to 7 percent for money supply growth.

Yet in actual experience, the Federal Reserve has announced money growth targets for 6- to 12-month periods and ended up wide of the mark. For example, the money growth target range for 1985 (M1 definition) was 4 to 7 percent. Actual money growth was 11.9 percent. If, as argued previously, the Federal Reserve *can* control the money supply with reasonable precision, what explains the failure of the Federal Reserve to hit its own preannounced money growth targets? Why in practice has the Federal Reserve often not closely controlled the money supply?

We previously assumed that the Federal Reserve controlled the monetary base and *concentrated its policy actions* on achieving a money supply target. Monetary growth targets are not achieved in practice simply because the Federal Reserve is unwilling to concentrate all its efforts on this one policy goal. The Federal Reserve has also been interested in the behavior of other financial market variables, the most important being interest rates. Conflicts arise between hitting target levels of money supply growth and achieving desirable behavior of these other variables. When such conflicts arise, the Federal Reserve has sometimes chosen to miss money growth targets rather than accept what is viewed as the cost of hitting such targets: the resulting undesirable behavior of interest rates. We consider this choice between money targets and interest rate targets in Chapter 18.

SUMMARY

This chapter has analyzed the way in which the Federal Reserve can control the money supply.

1. The Federal Reserve System is the U.S. central bank. Its key policymaking bodies are the Board of Governors of the Federal Reserve and the Open Market Committee.
2. The Federal Reserve has several tools that it uses to control bank reserves and the monetary base (the sum of bank reserves plus currency held by the public). The most important of these are *open market operations,* which are purchases or sales of government securities in the open market. Such purchases (sales) by the Federal Reserve lead to increases (decreases) in bank reserves and the monetary base.
3. The other tools the Federal Reserve has are changes in the discount rate (the interest rate on loans it makes to banks) and in the required reserved ratio. Reductions (increases) in the discount rate result in in-

creases (decreases) in borrowed reserves and therefore in the monetary base. Increases (decreases) in the required reserve ratio decrease (increase) the quantity of deposits that can be supported by a given level of bank reserves.

4. Changes in bank reserves cause bank deposits to change by a multiple of the change in reserves. This multiple is called *the deposit multiplier*. The reserve–deposit relationship can also be stated as relationship between the monetary base and the money supply. Changes in the monetary base cause the money supply to change by

a multiple of the change in the base. This multiple is called the *money multiplier*.

5. By controlling bank reserves and the monetary base, the Federal Reserve can monitor the month-to-month behavior of the money supply and, by appropriate adjustments of the base, achieve desired *average* (e.g., annual) rates of *growth* in the money supply. Over periods such as 6 to 12 months, when the Federal Reserve misses targets for money supply growth, it is because it is concentrating on other policy goals.

KEY TERMS

Board of Governors of the Federal Reserve
Open Market Committee
Legal reserve requirements
Open market operations
Discount rate
Discount window

Required reserve ratio
Financial intermediaries
Deposit multiplier
Monetary base
Money multiplier

QUESTIONS AND PROBLEMS

1. What agency is responsible for controlling the money supply to the U.S.? List the three tools available for use in that effort and indicate the most important of the three.
2. How are central banks different from commercial banks?
3. Explain what legal reserve requirements are. What two categories of commercial bank assets are considered legal reserves?
4. Answer the following questions about open market operations:
   (a) What is the "open market?"
   (b) What is bought by whom in an open market purchase?
   (c) Through what channel would an open market purchase affect the money supply?
5. What is the discount window? Why is it important to commercial banks? Why are movements in the discount rate an indicator of the direction of monetary policy?

6. Why do savers and borrowers use financial intermediaries?
7. How do financial intermediaries make profits?
8. What are excess reserves? Why do banks hold so few? What can they do with their excess reserves?
9. Trace through the first five stages in Table 17.9 assuming that the original open market purchase was $20,000 and the legal reserve requirement was 12%. Then use the deposit multiplier formula to compute the total change in deposits throughout the commercial banking system as a result of this open market purchase.
10. Explain how and why the level of interest rates is affected by open market purchases by the Federal Reserve.
11. Suppose that the public increases its demand for currency relative to bank deposits (its currency-deposit ratio). How would such a shift affect the money multiplier and the money supply?

18
Monetary Policy

Open market operations, the central policy actions taken by the Federal Reserve on a day-to-day basis, are decided upon by the Federal Open Market Committee (FOMC). The setting for the Committee's meetings is as follows:

> The FOMC's regular meetings take place in the boardroom of the Board of Governors in Washington. The seven governors and 12 Reserve Bank presidents gather around a long conference table under a high ceiling. Also seated around the table are the secretary of the FOMC, senior advisers to the FOMC, and the managers for foreign exchange and domestic operations. Senior research officers of the Reserve Banks, other senior Board officials, and an officer from the New York Reserve Bank's domestic trading desk sit around the side of the room, available to their principals if needed.[1]

What should they do? The task of the committee is to formulate a directive to the Open Market Desk at the Federal Reserve Bank of New York, which will actually carry out open market operations. The directive will tell the Desk manager what to do over the coming month. How should the directive be worded?

The question of the *optimal* way to conduct monetary policy is the central focus of this chapter. We first discuss the Federal Reserve's goals in Section I. Section II explains the monetary policy strategy followed by the Federal Reserve in recent years. Section III considers proposed alternative strategies. Section IV evaluates the relative merits of these different ways to conduct monetary policy.

I

Federal Reserve Policy Goals

Throughout Part II, we assumed that policymakers pursue macroeconomic goals of price stability, low unemployment, and steady economic growth.

Policymakers, acting as agents for the public, pursue the public welfare. This view has not, however, gone unquestioned. Critics argue that rather than pursuing the public good, government officials (bureaucrats) who formulate macroeconomic policy attempt to maximize their own welfare. As Gordon Tullock put it, "Bureaucrats are like other men. . . . If bureaucrats are ordinary men, they will make most (not all) of their decisions in terms of what benefits them, not society as a whole."[2] Tullock espouses the *public choice* view of macroeconomic policymaking.

> **Public choice,** in this context, simply means the application to macroeconomic policymaking of the microeconomic theory of how decisions are made.

In microeconomics it is generally assumed that each individual maximizes his or her own welfare. Applied to elected public officials, the public choice view implies that these officials will try to maximize votes for their parties and themselves. That is the way to stay in office.

Advocates of the public choice view worry that policies designed to gain votes will not be in the public interest. Policymakers may overstimulate the economy, for example, to create seemingly prosperous conditions in order to gain votes. The long-range inflationary consequences are ignored, since they occur after the election. When the consequences have to be faced after an election victory, a restrictive policy is put in place to slow the inflation and a recession follows. Advocates of the public choice view argue that this is how *political business cycles* arise: Periods of inflation and recession are caused by politicians seeking votes, not by an underlying instability in the private economy.

What implications does the public choice view of macroeconomic policymaking have for Federal Reserve policy? The Board of Governors and regional Federal Reserve Bank presidents are not elected by the public, so they have no direct incen-

---

[1]Paul Meek, *U.S. Monetary Policy and Financial Markets* (New York: Federal Reserve Bank of New York, 1982), p. 88.

[2]Gordon Tullock, *The Vote Motive* (London: London Institute of Economic Affairs, 1976), p. 26.

tive to try to influence votes. If the Federal Reserve acts to affect votes, it is responding to pressures from Congress and the executive branch. How susceptible is the Federal Reserve to such pressures?

A distinctive feature of the U.S. central banking system is the considerable degree of independence given to the Federal Reserve. As pointed out in the previous chapter, members of the Board of Governors serve 14-year terms and cannot be reappointed, which provides considerable insulation from the political process. The Chairman of the Board of Governors is appointed for a 4-year term, but it is not concurrent with that of the President of the United States. Therefore, an incoming President does not immediately get to choose a chairman. The regional Federal Reserve Bank presidents are appointed by the directors of the regional banks with the approval of the Board of Governors. A President who disagrees with Federal Reserve policy can say so, but can take little direct action in the short run to change it.

In the 1970s, Congress passed legislation requiring periodic reports from the Federal Reserve on the conduct of policy, but monetary policy decisions such as the target growth rate in the money supply or the target level for interest rates are not subjects on which Congress legislates. These decisions are made by the Open Market Committee. Further, the Federal Reserve has a degree of independence from the budget appropriations process because its expenses are paid by its interest earnings on holdings of government securities.

All this is not to say that the Federal Reserve is completely autonomous or that monetary policy is conducted in an apolitical setting. The Chairman of the Board of Governors comes up for reappointment (as Chairman) during the course of a President's term. For example, President Carter declined to reappoint Arthur Burns as Chairman in 1978, replacing him with G. William Miller. In 1983 President Reagan did reappoint Paul Volcker (who was appointed by Carter in 1979 when Miller became Secretary of the Treasury), but only after much speculation that Reagan would prefer his own nominee. In 1987, when Volcker asked not to be considered for a third term as Chairman and was replaced by Alan Greenspan, there was speculation that he did so because President Reagan failed to signal directly that he wanted Volcker to stay. Also, since board members often resign be-

fore the end of their terms, a President can sometimes make several appointments to the board and, therefore, perhaps change the course of monetary policy. By 1987 President Reagan had appointed _all_ the members of the board.

Given this institutional setup, it is sensible to assume that month-to-month monetary policy decisions rest with the members of the Open Market Committee; they are not simply handmaidens of the administration or Congress. In appropriate cases, though, we must consider political pressures that may affect their decisions.

But what are the goals of Open Market Committee members? They are Tullock's bureaucrats, after all. Do their interests diverge from the public interest in economic stabilization? Some economists believe they do. Milton Friedman, for example, believes that the Federal Reserve resists his suggestion of a constant money growth rate rule because of bureaucratic self-interest. "If the Fed [Federal Reserve] gave up discretion," he asked, "would any poll show the chairman of the Fed as the second most important man in the country? The Fed would be a minor institution."

Friedman's statement and other related arguments about the bureaucratic goals of monetary policy are hard to evaluate because they concern the unobserved motivations for people's actions. We will continue to consider the Federal Reserve's goals as those of the public: price stability, low unemployment, and stable economic growth. As we examine the record of their actions, the reader should remain open to other interpretations. We will return to the public choice view of policymaker's behavior when we consider fiscal policy in Chapter 19.

II
Monetary Policy Strategies

We begin our analysis of the optimal conduct of monetary policy by examining the strategy followed by the Federal Reserve between October 1979 and the fall of 1982. Later we will see that current monetary policy is a modified version of that strategy.

A

Federal Reserve Policy: 1979–82

Federal Reserve policy for 1979–82 closely resembled the description of the monetary policy process in Part II. The process was depicted in Figures 11.1 and 11.2, which are reprinted here as Figures 18.1 and 18.2. Figure 18.1 illustrates the Federal Reserve's control of currency plus bank reserves—defined as the *monetary base*—in order to control the money supply. In Chapter 17, we examined the tools used by the Federal Reserve to control the monetary base: open market operations, changes in the discount rate, and changes in the required reserve ratio. These are the Federal Reserve actions referred to in the first box in Figure 18.1.

The Federal Reserve wants to control the money supply because, as depicted in Figure 18.2 (for the case of an expansionary policy), changes in the money supply affect the interest rate and eventually aggregate demand and output. The money supply is an *intermediate target*, a variable the pol-

icymakers control because they believe it is closely related to their *ultimate target*, which in this case is output—the variable the Federal Reserve really cares about. The money supply is controlled because the policymaker believes that changes in the money supply are important in determining the behavior of output (real GNP).

Figure 18.2 was taken from Chapter 11 before we had allowed for a varying price level. When prices vary, inflation becomes a second ultimate target. Here again control of money is thought useful because of the relationship between money supply growth and inflation. In fact, it was because of the perceived relationship between money growth and inflation that the Federal Reserve adopted the strategy of intermediate targeting on money late in 1979. At that time the inflation rate was over 12 percent per year. By slowing money supply growth, monetary policymakers hoped to slow inflation.

The strategy of targeting on the money supply is implemented in the following way. At its annual meeting in February, the Open Market Committee

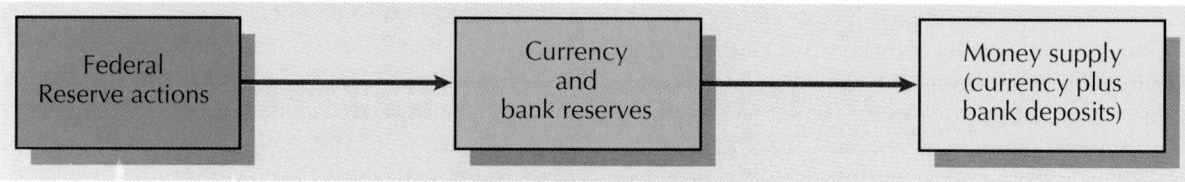

FIGURE 18.1 *Money Supply Control*

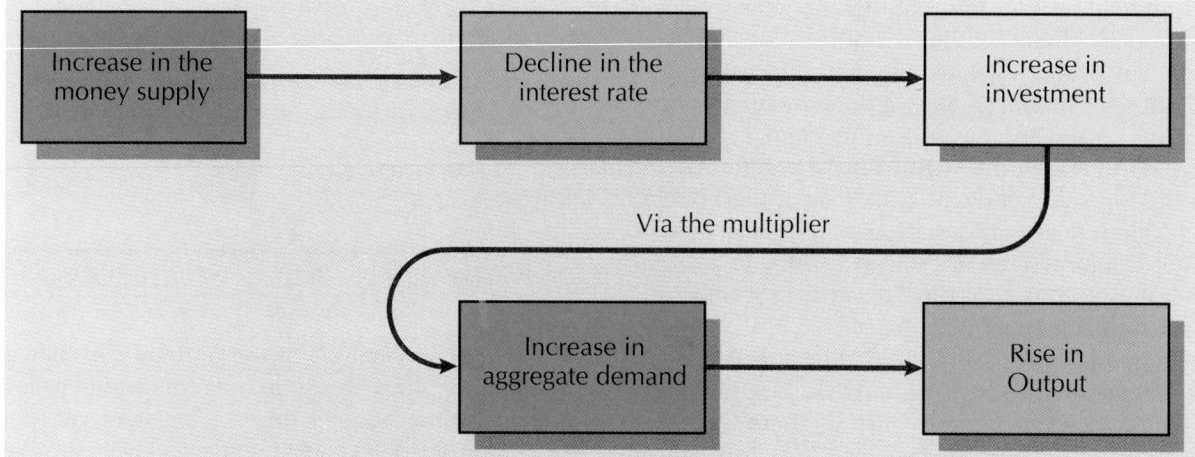

FIGURE 18.2 *The Effects of an Expansionary Monetary Policy: A Keynesian View*

sets target ranges for growth in each of the money supply measures—M1, M2, and M3 (see the definitions of these terms in Table 11.1). These target ranges are set in annual percentage terms, e.g., a range of 5 to 7 percent annual growth in M1.

The directive is sent to the Open Market Desk to carry out open market operations so that growth in bank reserves will lead to money supply growth within the specified ranges. As we saw in Chapter 17, the manager of the Open Market Desk cannot always control the money supply with sufficient precision to stay within the target ranges on a month-to-month basis, but he will try to hit the targets on average over the year.

The Open Market Committee will meet seven other times during the year. It may change the target ranges at any one of these meetings in response to economic conditions. The onset of a recession, for example, might lead it to raise the target ranges for money supply growth.

B

Federal Reserve Policy 1982–88

During the summer of 1982, the Federal Reserve became concerned about distortions in money growth figures resulting from innovations in the banking industry. New types of deposits were being offered, and as the public shifted funds from one type of deposit to another or from other assets into deposits, money supply numbers were affected. The Open Market Desk manager could offset these changes via open market operations and still hit money supply targets, but should he?

Such changes in the money supply did not reflect changes in underlying economic conditions. Recall that the strategy of intermediate targeting on the money supply rested on the existence of a close relationship between the money supply and the ultimate policy targets (inflation rate, level of unemployment, level of economic growth). This relationship was becoming less close due to financial market innovations (see Perspective 18A). The Federal Reserve reacted by formally suspending intermediate targeting on the money supply in October 1982.

Targeting on monetary aggregates was resumed in 1983, but in a less mechanical and more discretionary way compared to the 1979–82 period. Directives from the Open Market Committee still specified target ranges for money supply measures, but they contained a qualifier such as the following:

> The Committee understood that policy implementation would require continuing appraisal of the relationships not only among the various measures of money and credit but also between those aggregates and nominal GNP.[3]

In other words, before adjusting growth in bank reserves to try to keep money growth rates on track, the Federal Reserve considered whether there were any reasons to believe that special developments in financial markets were causing aberrations in the money–income relationship. The monetary policy response to movements in the money supply has become much more judgmental.

III

Alternatives to Targeting on the Money Supply

Because of the recent instability in the money–income relationship, there has been an increased interest in alternative strategies for monetary policy. What are the other possibilities?

Recall from Chapter 17 that the process of deposit creation set in motion by a Federal Reserve open market purchase of bonds had another side to it. At the same time that bank deposits were increasing, on the asset side banks were making loans and buying securities. In the process, they were improving the terms on which individuals and businesses could borrow money. The other side of deposit creation is *expansion of credit and lowering of interest rates*. The strategy of intermediate targeting on money focuses open market operations on the deposit side, so that deposits and, consequently, the money supply stay within target ranges. Alternative strategies focus wholly or partly on the effects of open market operations on interest rates and credit.

[3]*Federal Reserve Bulletin*, 70 (August 1984), p. 649.

A
Targeting on the Interest Rate

One alternative strategy is for the Federal Reserve to focus on the level of the interest rate. The Open Market Committee would set a target range for a representative interest rate and the Open Market Desk would be instructed to keep the rate within the range.

1. Interest Rate Targeting in Practice An example may help to clarify how such a strategy would work. The Open Market Committee could set a range for the coming month of 5 to 6 percent for the rate on 3-month Treasury bills. As with money supply targets, the range for the target interest rate would be chosen to hit the ultimate policy targets (inflation rate, unemployment rate, and growth rate of the economy). The interest rate would replace the money supply as an *intermediate target*.

Once the target range was set, the Open Market Desk would monitor the market where Treasury bills trade, which is part of the open market. If the interest rate on Treasury bills rose above the 6 percent ceiling of the target range, the Desk manager would begin open market purchases. These could involve Treasury bills or other government securities. The effect of open market purchases, as we have seen, is to expand credit and lower interest rates. The Desk would carry out enough open market purchases to reduce the Treasury bill rate below 6 percent.

Alternatively, if the Treasury bill rate temporarily fell below 5 percent, the Open Market Desk would begin to *sell* securities in the open market—reducing bank reserves, restricting credit, and raising interest rates—until the Treasury bill rate rose back above 5 percent.

Thus, the Open Market Desk would keep the average Treasury bill rate between 5 and 6 percent for the month.

2. Implications for the Money Supply Note that in carrying out open market purchases or sales, the Open Market Desk increases or decreases bank reserves, bank deposits, and therefore the money supply. For example, keeping the interest rate in the target range might require large open market purchases or sales and, therefore, large changes in the money supply. This might well conflict with any specified money supply target. Keeping the interest rate within narrow bounds, such as the 1 percent range we have been discussing, will, in general, not be compatible with achieving target growth rates for the money supply.

The last point can be illustrated using the graph of money market equilibrium where money supply equals money demand, as shown in Figure 18.3. A strategy of rigidly targeting on the money supply is depicted in Figure 18.3(a). Here we ignore the range and consider the extreme case where there is simply a target level for the money supply (M^*).[4] Rigidly targeting on the money supply would make the money supply schedule vertical, as given by M_0^s. Regardless of the demand for money (M_0^d, M_1^d, M_2^d), the Open Market Desk would carry out open market operations to keep $M^s = M^*$. Note that with this strategy the interest rate must fluctuate (between r_0 and r_2); the Federal Reserve cannot also hit an interest rate target.

A policy strategy of rigidly targeting the interest rate is illustrated in Figure 18.3(b). To keep the interest rate equal to the target level r^* (where again we ignore a range around the target), the Open Market Desk manager must be willing to let the money supply go to whatever level the public demands $(M_0^d, M_1^d, M_2^d$ in the figure). He must carry out whatever level of open market operations are required to create market equilibrium at r^*. This has the effect of making the money supply schedule horizontal. Through these open market operations, the Federal Reserve must supply whatever amount of money is required to keep the interest at r^*.

Clearly the Federal Reserve cannot make the money supply schedule vertical (independent of money demand) and horizontal (completely passive in response to money demand) at the same time. *Given a sufficiently long period, the Federal Reserve can hit money supply or the interest rate targets but, in general, not both.*

This is not to say that the Federal Reserve cannot try to *influence* both variables, perhaps paying more or less attention to one or the other, depending on the circumstances. The more it emphasizes one target, however, the less it em-

---

[4]For example, if the target growth rate was 5 percent and last period's money supply was $500 billion, then M^* for the current period would be $525 billion ($500 + 0.05 \times 500$).

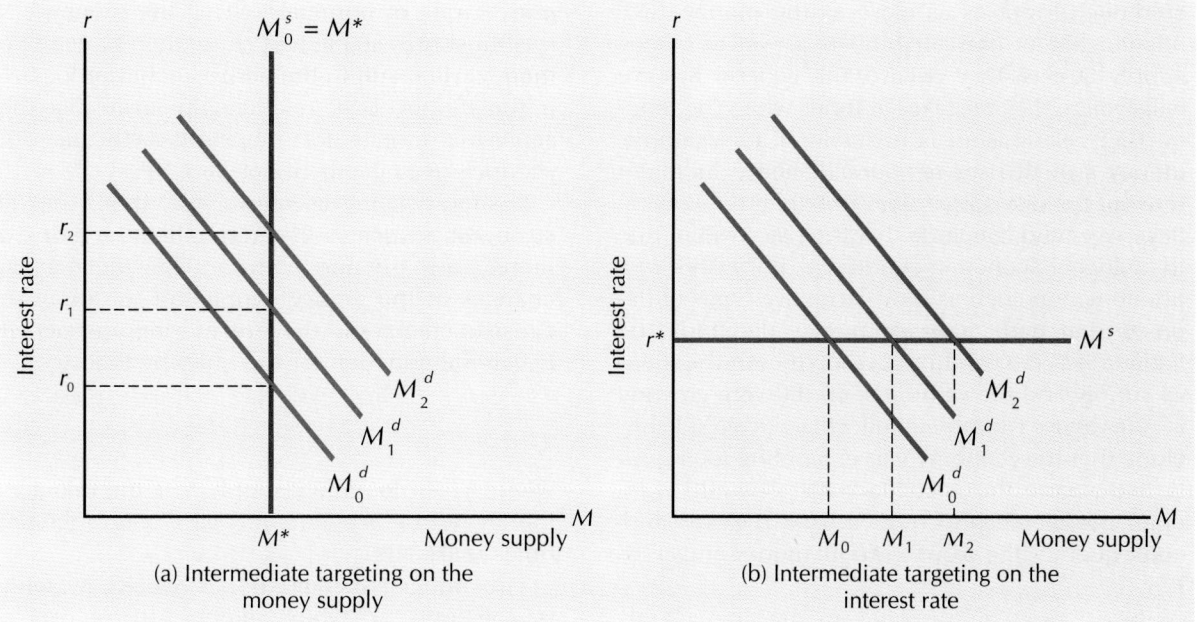

FIGURE 18.3   _Money Supply versus Interest Rate Targets_

In part (a), open market operations are carried out to hit the money supply target. The interest rate must adjust to whatever level (r_0, r_1, r_2) will equate money demand to the target money supply. In part (b), open market operations are carried out to keep the interest rate at the target level, r^*. The money supply must adjust to the level demanded (M_0, M_1, M_2) at the target interest rate.

phasizes the other. This is a fundamental tension in monetary policymaking.

In the 1970s, Federal Reserve policy on a month-to-month basis focused on the interest rate, keeping it within narrow target ranges. Money supply targets were also set, but these were on an annual basis and the targets were often missed. The move in 1979 to intermediate targeting on the money supply was a move away from close control of the interest rate. The move in 1982 toward less rigidity in targeting on the money supply was not a move back to rigid targeting the interest rate, but it did allow movements in interest rates to have more influence on Federal Reserve actions.

B

Targeting on Credit or Debt

An open market operation increases bank reserves and therefore banks' demand for interest-bearing assets (loans and securities): this is a credit expansion or, looked at from the borrowers' perspective,

an increase in debt. One proposal for Federal Reserve strategy is to try to control the growth of credit, or equivalently, debt. The particular credit aggregate proposed as a target is the total outstanding credit (debt) extended to the government, households, and nonfinancial corporations (corporate bonds; federal, state, and local government bonds; consumer and business loans; mortgages; etc.). This excludes the debts of financial intermediaries, which are viewed as a link in the chain connecting savers with ultimate borrowers (see Perspective 17B). The proposal most recently advanced has been to use this credit aggregate as an additional intermediate target while retaining a money supply target.[5]

Advocates of a credit target argue that the total

[5]The use of a credit (or debt) target was proposed in a number of papers by Professor Benjamin Friedman of Harvard University. See, for example, "Using a Credit Aggregate Target to Implement Monetary Policy in the Financial Environment of the Future," in _Monetary Policy Issues in the 1980s_ (Kansas City: Federal Reserve Bank of Kansas City, 1982).

credit–GNP ratio is as close as the money–GNP relationship. By trying to hit debt as well as money supply targets, they believe, the Federal Reserve will avoid policy mistakes at times when the money–GNP relationship is unstable. If, for example, money growth rises _temporarily_ above its target rate but the debt target does not, then the Federal Reserve would conclude that the rise was not due to changing economic conditions, but rather to a phenomenon such as new, attractive types of deposits that had increased money demand. The Federal Reserve would not react. If both the money supply and the volume of credit were growing at rates above the target, policymakers would conclude that the economy was expanding too rapidly. In that case, the Open Market Desk would begin open market sales to reduce bank reserves and, consequently, the growth of _both_ money and credit.

IV
Which Strategy Is Best?

We have examined several alternative strategies for the conduct of monetary policy. Which one should the Federal Reserve choose? The answer depends to an extent on how you believe the economy works, in other words, on which of the theories from Part II you adopt (Keynesian, monetarist, etc.). Though as with other questions there are areas of agreement as well as controversy; there is general agreement at least on what the issues are. In this section we consider the strengths and weaknesses of each of the proposed strategies.

A
Intermediate Targeting on the Money Supply

The rationale behind intermediate targeting on the money supply is that by controlling money, one will control the level of economic activity. Crucial to this belief is the existence of a stable relationship between the quantity of money and the level of economic activity, or, expressed in terms of growth rates, between the rate of growth in a money supply measure such as M1 or M2 and the

growth rate of nominal GNP. If the money–GNP relationship is stable and close, then targeting on money will result in the desired behavior for GNP. If the money–GNP relationship is erratic, then achieving targets for money growth may not produce desirable behavior for GNP.

It should come as no suprise, then, that the strongest advocates of intermediate targeting on money are the monetarists. They believe that changes in the money supply are the dominant cause of changes in the level of economic activity. Recall the equation for the quantity theory:

$$M \times V = P \times y, \tag{18.1}$$

where M is the money supply; V is the velocity of money, and $P \times y$ is money GNP (the price level times real GNP).

The monetarists believe that velocity (V), which is the rate at which money turns over in transactions (number of times the average dollar is used in GNP transactions during some time period), is relatively stable over time. They believe that stable money growth is the key to stable growth in money GNP. Monetarists are staunch supporters of controlling bank reserves to, in turn, target on money growth. In fact, they go one step further, favoring a constant money growth rate rule—a special form of targeting.

But intermediate targeting on the money supply has advantages that also appeal to _some_ nonmonetarists. One is that it is a simple quantifiable strategy, thereby increasing Federal Reserve _credibility_. In other words, the Federal Reserve can announce target ranges for the different money supply measures, and the public (and Congress) can then evaluate the Federal Reserve's performance. If the Federal Reserve continually hits the targets, monetary policy gains credibility; the public starts to believe that the Federal Reserve will carry out announced policies. This creates a stable environment where the public can form reliable expectations of variables such as the inflation rate. Many new classical economists favor targeting on the money supply for this reason. Monetary surprises that cause output to deviate from its natural rate will be minimized.

Another advantage of targeting on the money supply is that control of inflation over medium-term periods (e.g., 3 to 5 years) is virtually assured by a strong commitment to hitting target rates for money supply growth. Recall from Chapter 16 that all economists believe that sustained high inflation requires accommodating money supply growth. There will be no double-digit inflation for 5 years with money growth at 3 percent per year. Strict adherence to money supply targets severely limits monetary accommodation unless the target growth rates are themselves high. The latter is unlikely, at least in the current U.S. environment. A Federal Reserve chairman would have rough going explaining to Congress why the target money growth for 1989 was 15 percent!

Objections to intermediate targeting on the money supply arise when the money–income relationship is unstable. In terms of equation (18.1), these are times when velocity behaves erratically. At these times, keeping the money supply growing at a steady rate will lead to instability in the growth of GNP.

In recent years, innovations in financial markets have led to instability in the money–income relationship. In particular, new types of deposits offered by banks have caused sudden changes in the public's demand for money *at given levels of income*. For example, money market deposit accounts (see Perspective 18A) were first introduced at the beginning of 1983. By April the public had deposited $350 billion in such accounts. Much of this simply came out of other accounts, but some funds represented a shift away from nonmoney assets—an increase in the demand for money. With such instability of money demand, stable growth in the money supply is no guarantee of stable growth in GNP.

Read Perspective 18A.

PERSPECTIVE 18A

Financial Market Innovations and the Demand for Money

At a number of points in our discussion, we have referred to problems caused by innovations in the financial sector and the resulting instabilty of money demand. Here we examine the nature of some of these innovations.

At the beginning of the 1970s, the rates that banks and other depository institutions could pay depositors were constrained by law. No interest could be paid on checking deposits, and there were also ceiling rates on saving and time deposits. As interest rates rose in the 1970s, these ceiling rates began to lag far behind market rates for other assets such as Treasury bills. Also, new competition developed for banks in the form of *money market funds* that sold shares on which some checks could be written. The money market funds were not subject to interest rate ceilings. They therefore paid much higher interest rates in the late 1970s and lured many deposits away from the regulated depository institutions.

In response to these developments, Congress passed the Depository Institutions Deregula- tion and Monetary Control Act of 1980, which set in motion a process of relaxing and eventually eliminating the ceilings on the interest rates for most deposits. Table 18.1 shows the steps in eliminating deposit rate ceilings, which are called *Regulation Q ceilings*, after the Federal Reserve regulation that established them. By 1986 the only deposit rate ceiling remaining was the prohibition (ceiling of 0 percent) of interest on regular checking accounts, the abolition of which would require additional legislation.

As can be seen from the table, the elimination of deposit rate ceilings has been accomplished, in part, by allowing banks to offer new kinds of deposits not subject to as low a ceiling rate or, in some cases, subject to no ceiling rate at all. As the public shifts money among different types of deposits and shifts funds into new deposits and out of nonmoney assets (e.g., Treasury bills or bonds), the demand for the various monetary aggregates (M1, M2, M3) becomes unstable.

TABLE 18.1   Steps in the Phase-Out of Regulation Q

Effective Date of Change	Nature of change
June 1, 1978	MMCs established, with minimum denomination of $10,000 and maturities of 26 weeks. The floating ceiling rates for each week were set at the discount yield on six-month Treasury bills at S&Ls and MSBs, 25 basis points less at CBs.
November 1, 1978	CBs authorized to offer ATS accounts, allowing funds to be transferred automatically from savings to checking accounts as needed to avoid overdrafts. The ceiling rate on ATS accounts was set at 5.25 percent, the same as the ceiling rate on regular savings accounts at CBs.
July 1, 1979	SSCs established with no minimum denomination, maturity of 30 months or more and floating ceiling rates based on the yield on 2 1/2-year Treasury securities, but 25 basis points higher at S&Ls and MSBs. Maximums of 11.75 percent at CBs and 12 percent at S&Ls and MSBs.
June 2, 1980	The floating ceiling rates on SSCs raised 50 basis points relative to the yield on 2 1/2-year Treasury securities at S&Ls and MSBs and at CBs. The maximum ceiling rates set in June 1979 were retained.
June 5, 1980	New floating ceiling rates on MMCs. All depository institutions may pay the discount yeild on 6-month Treasury bills plus 25 basis points when the bill rate is 8.75 percent or higher. The ceiling rate will be no lower than 7.75 percent. A rate differential of up to 25 basis points favors S&Ls and MSBs if the bill rate is between 7.75 percent and 8.75 percent.
December 31, 1980	NOW accounts permitted nationwide at all depository institutions. Ceiling rates on NOW and ATS accounts set at 5.25 percent.
August 1, 1981	Caps on SSCs of 11.75 percent at CBs and 12 percent at S&Ls and MSBs eliminated. Ceiling rates float with the yeild on 2 1/2-year Treasury securities.
October 1, 1981	Adopted rules for the All Savers Certificate specified in the Economic Recovery Act of 1981.
November 1, 1981	Floating ceiling rates on MMCs each week changed to the higher of the 6-month Treasury bill rate in the previous week or the average over the previous four weeks.
December 1, 1981	New category of IRA/Keogh accounts created with minimum maturity of 1-1/2 years, no regulated interest rate ceiling and no minimum denomination.
May 1, 1982	New time deposit created with no interest rate ceiling, no minimum denomination and an initial minimum maturity of 3-1/2 years. New short-term deposit instrument created with $7,500 minimum denomination and 91-day maturity. The floating ceiling rate is equal to the discount yield on 91-day Treasury bills for S&Ls and MSBs, 25 basis points less for CBs. Maturity range of SSCs adjusted to 30-42 months.

SOURCE: R. Alton Gilbert and A. Steven Holland, "Has the Deregulation of Deposit Interest Rates Raised Mortgage Rates" Federal Reserve Bank of St. Louis *Review,* 66 (May 1984), p. 6.

B

Interest Rate Targeting

Interest rate targeting is likely to be desirable just when targeting on the money supply is not desirable—when the public's demand for money and therefore the money–income relationship are unstable. Note from Figure 18.2 that the interest rate is the channel through which changes in the financial sector (an increase in the money supply in the figure) influence aggregate demand and therefore output. If the Federal Reserve targets on the interest rate, aggregate demand will be *insulated* from instability in the financial sector—including unstable money demand. This insulation from instability in financial markets is the most important advantage of interest rate targeting.

However, interest rate targeting lacks one important advantage of targeting on the money supply: it does not provide the credible anti-inflation-

TABLE 18.1   Steps in the Phase-Out of Regulation Q—continued

Effective Date of Change	Nature of change
September 1, 1982	New deposit account created with a minimum denomination of $20,000 and maturity of 7 to 31 days. The floating ceiling rate is equal to the discount yield on 91-day Treasury bills for S&Ls and MSBs, 25 basis points less for CBs. These ceiling rates are suspended if the 91-day Treasury bill rate falls below 9 percent for four consecutive Treasury bill auctions.
December 14, 1982	MMDAs authorized with minimum balance of not less than $2,500, no interest ceiling, no minimum maturity, up to six transfers per month (no more than three by draft), and unlimited withdrawals by mail, messenger or in person.
January 5, 1983	Super NOW accounts authorized with same features as the MMDAs, except that unlimited transfers are permitted.
	Interest rate ceiling eliminated and minimum denomination reduced to $2,500 on 7- to 31-day accounts.
	Minimum denomination reduced to $2,500 on 91-day accounts and MMCs of less than $100,000.
April 1, 1983	Minimum maturity on SSCs reduced to 18 months.
October 1, 1983	All interest rate ceilings eliminated except those on passbook savings and regular NOW accounts. Minimum denomination of $2,500 established for time deposits with maturities of 31 days or less (below this minimum, passbook savings rates apply).
January 1, 1984	Rate differential between commercial banks and thrifts on passbook savings accounts and 7- to 31-day time deposits of less than $2,500 eliminated. All depository institutions may pay a maximum of 5.50 percent.
January 1, 1985	Minimum denominations on MMDAs, Super Nows and 7- to 31-day ceiling-free time deposits reduced to $1,000.
January 1, 1986	Minimum denominations on MMDAs, Super NOWs and 7- to 31-day ceiling-free time deposits eliminated.
March 31, 1986	All interest rate ceilings eliminated, except for the requirement that no interest be paid on demanded deposits.

Terms:

S&Ls—savings and loan associations	SSCs—small saver certificates
MSBs—mutual savings banks	ATS accounts—automatic transfer service accounts
CBs—commercial banks	NOW accounts—negotiable order of withdrawal accounts
MMCs—money market certificates	MMDAs—money market deposit accounts

SOURCE: R. Alton Gilbert and A. Steven Holland, "Has the Deregulation of Deposit Interest Rates Raised Mortgage Rates" Federal Reserve Bank of St. Louis *Review*, 66 (May 1984), p. 6.

ary policy that strict adherence to money supply targets does. In fact, targeting on the interest rate can lead the Federal Reserve to fuel inflationary pressure unwittingly by allowing excessive monetary growth.

To see how this might happen, consider Figure 18.4, which shows the graph of the money market for the case of interest rate targeting. The money supply schedule is horizontal, as in Figure 18.3(b), because the Federal Reserve will supply enough money to keep the interest rate at the target level (r^*). (As earlier, the Federal Reserve does not directly supply or print money, but it carries on whatever volume of open market operations is required to keep r at r^*.)

Now consider what happens if an inflationary boom begins, due to a sharp increase in private sector demand for goods. The boom results in higher nominal income ($P \times y$) as the price level (P) and real output (y) rise. The rise in nominal

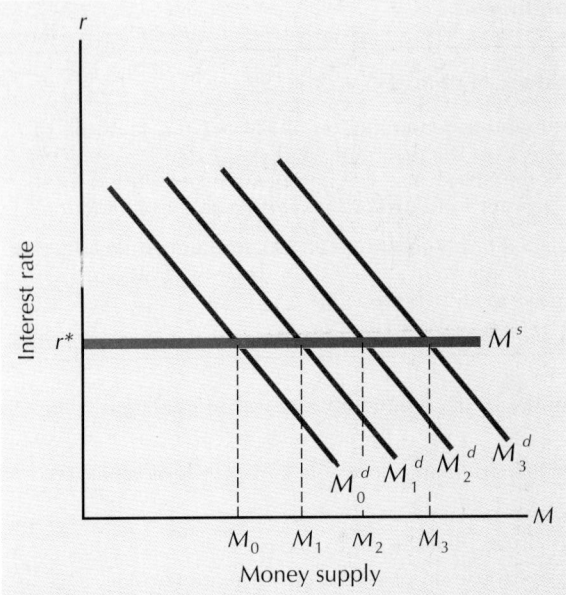

FIGURE 18.4   _Inflationary Accommodation of Money_
Demand

Inflationary growth in money GNP causes money de-
mand to increase (from M_0^d to M_1^d to M_2^d to M_3^d). To keep
the interest rate at the target level (r^*), the Federal
Reserve must expand the money supply (from M_0 to M_1
_to M_2 to M_3)._

income increases the demand for money for use in
transactions. In Figure 18.4 we assume that as the
boom proceeds, the money demand schedule
shifts from M_0^d to M_1^d to M_2^d to M_3^d. To keep the
interest rate at r^*, the Federal Reserve must
increase the money supply (from M_0 to M_1 to M_2 to
M_3) each time the demand rises. The Federal
Reserve must _accommodate_ the rise in money
demand. But such accommodation fuels inflation.
Instead of becoming more restrictive, in this exam-

ple the Federal Reserve allows _faster_ money
growth.

This is _not_ to say that targeting on the interest
rate _must_ result in inflation. If the Federal Reserve
recognizes the inflationary pressures, it will raise
the interest rate target. A higher interest rate will
slow the inflationary growth in aggregate demand.
During inflationary periods, however, it is hard for
the monetary authority to know how much the
interest rate target needs to be increased. Moreover, there is sometimes a lag before policymakers
recognize the presence of inflationary pressures.
Therefore, at times, such as during the middle to
late 1970s, when preventing inflation became the
primary goal, central bankers here and in Europe
began to move away from targeting on the interest
rate toward targeting on the money supply. As
inflation abated in the early 1980s, central bankers
adhered less rigidly to money supply targets and
gave more weight to interest rates in making monetary policy decisions.

Read Perspective 18B.

■ _Check Your Bearings_

This is a good point at which to stop and review
the relative merits of targeting on the money supply versus targeting on the interest rate, as summarized in Table 18.3. See if you can explain why
each strategy has the advantages and disadvantages listed in the table.

C
A Credit Target

Use of a credit target, or what is the same thing, a
debt target, has been proposed not as a separate
strategy, but as an adjunct to intermediate target-

TABLE 18.2   Short-Term Interest Rates and Money Supply Growth in 1979

	Short-Term Interest Rate (3-Month Treasury Bills, Percent)	**Money Supply Growth (Percent Change in M1, Annual Rate)**
June	9.04%	16.1%
July	9.26	10.4
August	9.45	6.8
September	10.18	11.5
October	11.50	2.5
November	11.90	1.6

PERSPECTIVE 18B

The Federal Reserve's Policy Shift in 1979

During the 1970s, on a month-to-month basis, the Federal Reserve targeted on the interest rate, keeping short-term rates within very narrow ranges. This did not mean that the money supply was neglected completely. The Federal Reserve moved the target interest rate up or down to try to keep money supply growth within *annual* target ranges. But often the attempt failed. In October 1979 the Federal Reserve shifted from control of the interest rate to closer control of bank reserves and the money supply.

This shift occurred because the Federal Reserve realized that by targeting the interest rate, it was accommodating rapid growth in money demand in a manner similar to that illustrated in Figure 18.4. Actually, the situation was not quite as bad as that in Figure 18.4, because the Federal Reserve had been increasing the target interest rate since the spring of 1979, as can be seen from Table 18.2, which charts the behavior of a representative short-term interest rate and of the money supply from June to November 1979. But as can also be seen from the table, the interest rate did not rise sufficiently to stop the rapid growth in the money supply until the policy shift in October. The cost, however, of gaining control of the money supply was a sharp rise in short-term interest rates. The 3-month Treasury bill rate, for example, averaged 11.5 percent in 1980 and 14.5 percent in 1981.

ing on the money supply. The role of the credit target, as discussed previously, is to indicate times when the money–income relationship is unstable due to instability of money demand. Presumably, at such times, for example, when new types of deposits are introduced, the growth in credit would not be affected. This would indicate to the Federal Reserve that no policy action was needed.

Beginning in 1982, when monetary policymak-

TABLE 18.3   Relative Merits of Targeting on the Money Supply versus the Interest Rate

	Target on:	
	Money Supply	**Interest Rate**
Advantages	If the money–income relationship is stable, growth in money GNP will be reasonably stable.	Insulates the rest of the economy from instability in financial markets.
	Strict adherence to money growth target will provide a *credible* anti-inflation policy.	
Disadvantages	If the money–income relationship is unstable, due to unstable money demand, for example, adherence to strict money supply targets will lead to unstable growth in money GNP.	May result in the Federal Reserve unwittingly accommodating inflationary growth in money demand.

ers began to use more discretion in the process of intermediate targeting on the money supply, they began to set credit targets.

Monetarists are the main critics of a credit target. They believe that use of a credit target must dilute the emphasis given to the money supply. Also, when a credit target and a money supply target are both in use, a certain amount of discretion is inevitable in monetary policy formulation. The policymaker must decide which target to respond to when the targets give conflicting signals. For example, money supply growth may be in the target range, while credit is growing faster than its target range. What does the policymaker do? The monetarists want to eliminate discretion by instituting a hard-and-fast constant money growth rule. They do not want the Federal Reserve to give any weight to credit (or to interest rates) in formulating monetary policy.

SUMMARY

1. The Federal Reserve can choose from among several possible strategies, each having strengths and weaknesses. In the 1970s, Federal Reserve policy focused on short-term interest rates, though annual growth targets for the money supply received some weight. In 1979, the Federal Reserve switched to a strategy that deemphasized interest rates and placed more weight on the money supply. The switch was an attempt to slow the rapid inflation of the late 1970s by slowing money supply growth. Over the 1979–82 period, monetary policy was characterized by our description of intermediate targeting on the money supply.

2. In 1982, however, the Federal Reserve became convinced that innovations in financial markets were making the money–income relationship unstable. Also, economic conditions had changed. Inflation was under control, but the unemployment rate had reached a post–World War II record level. The Federal Reserve continued to target on the money supply, but much less mechanically. Growth in a credit aggregate and the level of the interest rate received more weight.

3. Current Federal Reserve strategy continues formally to be one of intermediate targeting on the money supply, but discretion is used in deciding when to let money supply growth stay outside the target ranges and when to act to keep growth within these ranges. Former Chairman Volcker explained the rationale for this strategy:

The uncertainties surrounding M1, and to a lesser extent the other aggregates, in themselves imply the need for a considerable degree of judgment rather than precise rules in the current conduct of monetary policy—a need that, in my thinking, is reinforced by the strong crosscurrents and imbalances in the economy and in the financial markets. That may not be an ideal situation for either the central bank or for those exercising oversight—certainly the forces that give rise to it are not happy. But it is the world in which, for the time being, we find ourselves.[6]

One of the imbalances he refers to is the fiscal policy imbalance, as evidenced by the huge federal government deficits, the subject to which we now turn.

[6]*Federal Reserve Bulletin*, September 1985, p. 694.

KEY TERMS

Public choice   **Financial market innovations**

QUESTIONS AND PROBLEMS

1. What group decides the magnitude of open market operations? Where are the open market operations actually done?

2. Explain the *public choice* view of macroeconomic policymaking.

3. What are *political business cycles?*

4. How and why are Federal Reserve Board members partially insulated from politics? In what ways is the Board still linked to politics?

5. From 1979–82, the Federal Reserve sought to control the money supply because of its ultimate impacts on real output and inflation. What tool did the Federal Reserve use in attempting to keep money supply measures within target ranges? Explain how this process works.

6. Why did the Federal Reserve stop targeting the money stock for a period beginning October 1982?

7. Can the Federal Reserve keep both interest rates and money supply measures within specified target ranges? If so, how? If not, why not?

8. What arguments support the use of the total credit to GNP ratio as a target by the Federal Reserve?

9. Provide arguments for and against the use of a money supply target by the Federal Reserve.

10. Provide arguments for and against the use of interest rate targeting by the Federal Reserve.

11. Discuss the policy change adopted by the Federal Reserve in October 1979. What prompted the change and what were its effects?

19

Fiscal Policy

Fiscal policy consists of federal government budget decisions—decisions on expenditures and taxes.[1] In the mid-1980s the fiscal policy process was in a terrible muddle. Spending ran way ahead of tax revenues so huge budget deficits resulted, at times exceeding $200 billion per year. In despair, Congress passed the Balanced Budget and Emergency Deficit Reduction Control Act of 1985, called the **Gramm-Rudman Act** after its sponsors, Senators Philip Gramm and Charles Rudman. The Gramm-Rudman Act mandated a move to a balanced budget in steps over 5 years, by *automatic* spending cuts if Congress failed to balance the budget by legislation. Supporters of the bill thought this approach an undesirable but necessary last resort (Senator Rudman called the bill "a bad idea whose time has come".) One critic, Keynesian economist Walter Heller (Chairman of the Council of Economic Advisors in the Kennedy administration), called Gramm-Rudman "economically capricious, socially unfair, militarily risky, constitutionally questionable, politically irresponsible, procedurally perverse and administratively outlandish." As we examine the fiscal policy process, perhaps we will find the source of the muddle.

Because fiscal policy concerns federal budget decisions, we begin in Section I by examining the federal budget. Sections II–IV examine the issue of how best to conduct fiscal policy. These sections consider fiscal policy from a Keynesian perspective. In Section V we explore the different views of monetarist and new classical economists. Section VI examines the view of yet another group that was influential in forming fiscal policy during the Reagan administration—the supply-side economists. We conclude with a discussion of the current fiscal situation.

---

[1]State and local governments also make spending and tax decisions, but the federal budget is the main instrument for fiscal policy at the macroeconomic level.

I
The Federal Budget

Table 19.1 gives figures for total federal government receipts and outlays (expenditures) and for the federal deficit (receipts minus outlays). The figures reveal rapid growth in both outlays and revenues, as well as rapid growth in the deficit in recent years. But the economy has been growing as well. Figure 19.1 shows some budget items expressed as percentages of GNP. There you see a clearer picture of how the government has grown relative to the economy as a whole.

In 1929 the federal government was quite small as a portion of the economy. Total federal outlays were less than 3 percent of GNP. Fiscal policy changes typically represented minor budget adjustments and were of little significance to the overall economy. Both outlays and revenues rose modestly during the 1930s. Outlays rose more than revenues, with a resulting budget deficit. World War II brought a huge expansion in government military spending, only partly paid for with increasing tax revenues. Budget deficits in the early 1940s rose as high as 25 percent of GNP, the equivalent of a deficit of over $1,000 billion in terms of GNP in the late 1980s. These huge wartime deficits were financed by massive sales of bonds to the public.

After the war, both expenditures and tax revenues declined as proportions of GNP. Yet federal government outlays did not sink back to the insignificant level of the 1920s. By the mid-1950s, both outlays and revenues were about 17–18 percent of GNP. The federal government had taken on a number of new domestic functions in the 1930s: regulatory agencies, the Social Security system, price supports for agricultural products, and rural electrification, among others. Also, with the onset of the cold war in the late 1940s, defense spending remained high even in peacetime.

From Figure 19.1, it can be seen that over the last

TABLE 19.1   Receipts and Outlays of the Federal Government (Billions of Dollars at an Annual Rate), Selected Years*

	Receipts	Outlays	Surplus or Deficit (−) (Receipts − Outlays)
1929	3.8	2.7	1.2
1933	2.7	4.0	−1.3
1939	6.8	9.0	−2.2
1941	15.5	20.5	−5.1
1945	42.7	84.7	−42.1
1950	50.4	41.2	9.2
1955	93.1	88.6	4.4
1960	96.9	93.9	3.0
1965	125.8	125.3	0.5
1970	195.4	207.8	−12.4
1975	294.9	364.2	−69.4
1980	553.8	615.1	−61.3
1981	639.5	703.3	−63.8
1982	635.3	781.2	−145.9
1983	659.9	835.9	−176.0
1984	726.0	895.6	−169.6
1985	788.6	984.6	−196.0
1986	827.4	1,032.0	−204.7
1987	916.5	1,069.1	−152.6

*Figures may not sum to the total due to rounding.

Source: _Economic Report of the President,_ 1988.

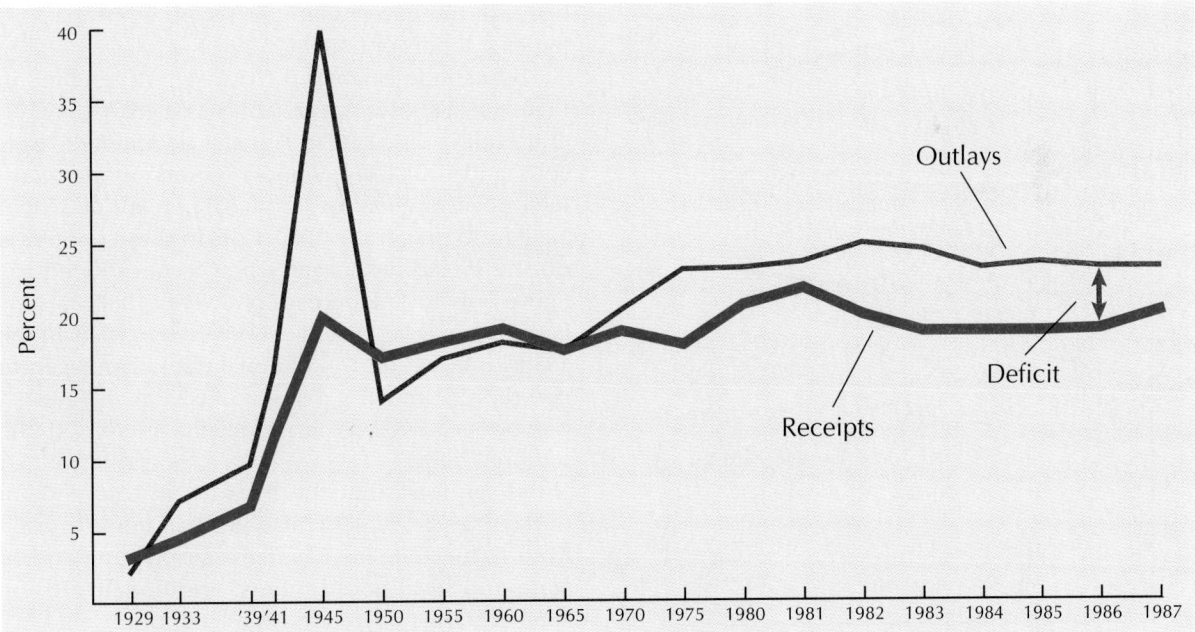

FIGURE 19.1   _Receipts and Outlays of the Federal Government as a Percentage of GNP, Selected Years_

three decades government outlays have grown as a proportion of GNP, from 17 percent in 1955 to 24 percent in 1987. Tax revenues rose as well (as a percentage of GNP), but beginning in the late 1960s, growth in spending outpaced revenue growth and resulted in a persistent budget deficit. The budget deficit grew rapidly during the first half of the 1980s as the general upward trend in outlays continued, while revenues declined slightly as a percentage of GNP. In 1986 the budget deficit was roughly 5 percent of GNP ($204.7 billion). In 1987 the deficit declined to 3.4 percent of GNP ($152.6 billion), still very high relative to pre-1980 U.S. experience.

The causes of the growing federal budget deficit can be traced more precisely by considering data for several expenditure categories shown in Figure 19.2. Each is a percent of GNP.

The schedule marked "Federal Government Purchases of Goods and Services" is a narrower category than total federal government outlays. Federal government purchases of goods and services include only purchases of currently produced output. This is the government spending

variable that appears in the national income accounts and in the macroeconomic models of Part II. Total federal outlays include, in addition to purchases of current output, transfer payments to persons (Social Security payments, veterans' benefits, food stamps, aid to families with dependent children, etc.), transfer payments (grants) to state and local governments, and interest payments on the government debt (securities issued to finance previous deficits).

From the graph, it can be seen that federal purchases of goods and services have not been rising as a proportion of GNP over recent decades. Looking at the schedule marked "Defense Spending," one sees that the pattern of overall purchases has closely followed the pattern of purchases for national defense. That pattern was generally downward (as a percent of GNP) over the years from 1960 to 1980, with one upward interruption in the late 1960s during the Vietnam War. In the post-1980 period, defense spending has risen as a percent of GNP, and as a consequence, overall purchases have also risen. Still, in 1987 overall federal government purchases totaled only 8.4 percent of GNP compared to 10.6 percent in 1960. Growth in *total* federal government outlays has *not* come because the government sector now purchases a larger fraction of GNP.

The schedule marked "Transfer Payments" in Figure 19.2 shows the area of fastest growth in federal outlays since 1960. Transfer payments to persons and transfer payments (grants) to state and local governments rose from 5.5 percent of GNP in 1960 to 13 percent in 1980. Cuts in these programs during President Reagan's first term reduced the figure only to 11.2 percent of GNP by 1987, 5.7 percent higher as a portion of GNP than in 1960. In the 1980s, interest on the national debt also began to rise rapidly from 1.3 percent of GNP in 1980 to 3.4 percent in 1987, as large deficits increased the national debt.

We see then that the increase in total federal outlays (as a percent of GNP) has come mostly from rising transfer payments to persons and to state and local governments. Additionally, in the 1980s, interest payments on the national debt have risen rapidly. Tax revenues have not kept pace. Revenues as a share of GNP have actually fallen slightly in the post-1980 period, resulting in gov-

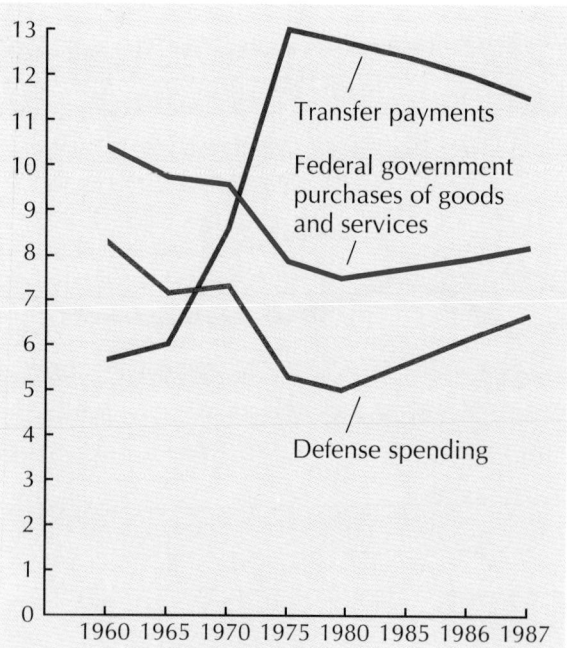

FIGURE 19.2   Selected Categories of Federal Expenditures as a Percentage of GNP

ernment deficits that by the mid-1980s were very large compared to previous U.S. peacetime experience.

Read Perspective 19A.

II
Roles and Rules for Fiscal Policy

What should be the goals for fiscal policy? How should fiscal policy be conducted? These are controversial issues subject to heated debate. The Gramm-Rudman Act, discussed at the beginning of this chapter, set rigid deficit reduction targets for each year through 1991, with the budget to be balanced thereafter. This is one form of a rule for fiscal policy. Should fiscal policy be conducted by a balanced-budget rule or should spending and tax decisions, and therefore the size of the government deficit, be left to the discretion of Congress and the President?

In this and the following two sections, we consider the Keynesian view on the role of fiscal policy and the desirability of rules to govern fiscal policy actions. Sections V and VI take up contrasting views on these issues derived from the alternative macroeconomic theories considered in Part II.

Fiscal policy in the Keynesian system has three goals:[2] allocation, distribution, and stabilization. Let us consider each goal in turn.

A
Allocation: The Federal Government's Say About What Is Produced

The allocation role of fiscal policy is the decision on how much to spend on public consumption, and as a result, how many resources remain to produce privately consumed goods. Public consumption includes items such as national defense,

---

[2]A pathbreaking treatment of the Keynesian view of fiscal policy is Richard Musgrave, *A Theory of Public Finance* (New York: McGraw-Hill, 1959). See especially Chapter 1.

PERSPECTIVE 19A
Financing the Government Deficit

Because the government deficit has been the center of much fiscal policy discussion, it is useful to review what the deficit is and how it is financed. The federal deficit results from an excess of expenditures over revenues collected by taxation. From Table 19.1 we see, for example, that for 1986 expenditures exceeded tax revenues by $204.7 billion.

Since this $204.7 billion was not financed by revenues raised through taxation, it must have come from other sources. The government must have money to finance its outlays (e.g., checks to Social Security recipients or defense contractors). The Treasury gets this money by borrowing from the public through the sale of securites. It borrows both short-term (e.g., bills for 3 or 6 months) and long-term (e.g., bonds for

20 or 30 years). Those purchasing Treasury securities and thereby lending to the government include individual and institutional investors, both in the United States and abroad. Table 19.2 shows the value of the outstanding privately held government debt at the end of recent years. Additionally, some government debt is held by the Federal Reserve and other government agencies. As can be seen in the table, larger government deficits have resulted in rapid growth in government debt during the 1980s. The table also shows the amount of federal government debt held by foreign investors. While still a relatively small fraction of the total debt, foreign holdings of our debt have grown rapidly since 1980.

TABLE 19.2 Federal Government Debt Held by Private and Foreign Investors, December 1978–December 1987 (Billions of Dollars)

	Federal Debt Held by Private Investors	Federal Debt Held by Foreign Investors
1978	506.5	132.1
1980	614.7	128.5
1981	693.0	135.4
1982	846.9	148.2
1983	1,018.7	165.2
1984	1,206.6	191.8
1985	1,409.2	211.7
1986	1,592.3	250.7
1987	1,734.8	287.0

interstate highways, the federal court system, and various regulatory agencies. These are what were termed _public goods_ in Chapter 4. The benefits of these goods are available to all, and it is difficult, if not impossible, to have people pay individually and fairly for the benefits they receive. Therefore, decisions on how much to spend on such activities are reached collectively and financed (collectively) through taxes.

A second potential role of allocation, also discussed in Chapter 4, is the financing of activities that offer external benefits to society in addition to benefits for individuals—what we termed _externalities_. For example, free or subsidized education benefits individual students, and society is better off for having more educated citizens (as voters or consumers, for example). Consequently, the public may collectively want to subsidize education and also finance the expenditure collectively via tax revenues.

The allocation goal is met by setting government spending on current goods and services at a level that produces the optimum allocation between public and private consumption. Note that if allocation were the only goal of fiscal policy, the federal budget should be balanced. Resources used for public consumption require that resources be withdrawn from private consumption. It is fair, then, that we be taxed to finance them.[3]

[3]The budget should, however, separate capital good purchases from current public consumption, which the current federal budget does not. Capital good purchases such as spending on highways and bridges provide services in the future, and it would not be unfair to finance them by borrowing. Future taxpayers would then pay taxes to repay the borrowed funds, but they would also benefit from the highways and bridges.

B
Distribution: The Federal Government's Say About Who Gets What

The federal government, through taxes and transfer payments, influences the _distribution_ of income. In an economy with no government, ownership of resources and skills would lead to a certain distribution of wealth and income. The government, by determining who pays taxes and who receives transfer payments, can modify this free market distribution.

Most people agree that the government should make some adjustments to the income distribution that would result from market processes alone. We agree that children should not be allowed to starve and the sick should have medical care regardless of their private incomes. How far the federal government should go in redistributing income is an important, controversial, but _microeconomic_ issue, which we need not address here. The relevant point here is simply that we collectively (via the political process) arrive at some degree of income redistribution through tax and transfer decisions—through fiscal policy.

With government spending on goods and services set to achieve the allocation goal, the distribution goal is met by additional expenditures on transfer payments such as aid to dependent children, food stamps, and old age and disability pensions. The structure of tax rates also affects income distribution. For example, with a _progressive_ income tax structure, tax rates rise with the level of income. The goal is to collect a larger fraction of income in taxes from higher-income individuals, thereby making after-tax income less unequal than pretax incomes.

Note that, like the allocation goal, the distribution goal should be achieved with a balanced budget. If we want to transfer income to some people and give them the ability to purchase goods and services, others should pay the necessary taxes and forego consumption.

C

The Stabilization Goal: The Federal Government's Say About Macrostability

A *stabilization* role for fiscal policy was central to the Keynesian revolution. Changes in government expenditures and taxes were tools by which policy makers could stabilize aggregate demand. Unlike the allocation or distribution goals, the stabilization goal generally requires deviations from a balanced budget. In some circumstances, the stabilization goal dictates that there *should* be a deficit in the federal budget.

Such a situation is illustrated in Figure 19.3. Given all other influences on aggregate demand, with

a balanced budget such that government spending (G) is equal to tax collections (T), the aggregate demand schedule would be at $y^d(G - T = 0)$. Equilibrium income would be at y_0, which is below potential output, shown as y_p in the graph. If the policymakers' goal is to move the economy to potential output, then an expansionary fiscal policy is called for. A spending increase or tax cut shifts the aggregate demand curve to the right. In the graph, for example, suppose that a tax cut that results in a deficit of $50 billion shifts the curve out to $y^d(G - T = 50)$ and thereby achieves the level of potential output.

A deficit is not always required to maintain potential output. Indeed if excessive aggregate demand is the problem, a surplus may be necessary. Still, it is the stabilization role of fiscal policy in Keynesian theory that creates a conflict with the rule of balancing the budget. In the Keynesian view, the overall federal budget should be set to provide the proper degree of stimulus or restraint to aggregate demand. This will generally imply an *unbalanced* budget.

D

Can Fiscal Policy Do All This?

We have outlined an ambitious agenda for fiscal policy, helping the economy arrive at optimal answers to the What?, Who?, and How stable? questions. Can fiscal policy accomplish all this? Critics of the Keynesian view think not, as we will see. Do even Keynesians believe that fiscal policy can simultaneously achieve all of the goals discussed previously? They do in theory—if, that is, the budget need not be balanced.

The allocation goal is met by setting government spending *on goods and services*. The distribution goal is met by setting the amount of transfer payments and the structure of tax rates (progressive or not? how progressive?). Once the *structure* of tax rates is set, the *level* of tax rates is still free for use in pursuing the stabilization goal. For example, if the allocation and distribution goals are met and aggregate demand is too low, the overall level of income tax rates can be cut to increase aggregate demand but leave distribution unchanged.

Additionally, policymakers have some flexibility in varying government spending on goods and ser-

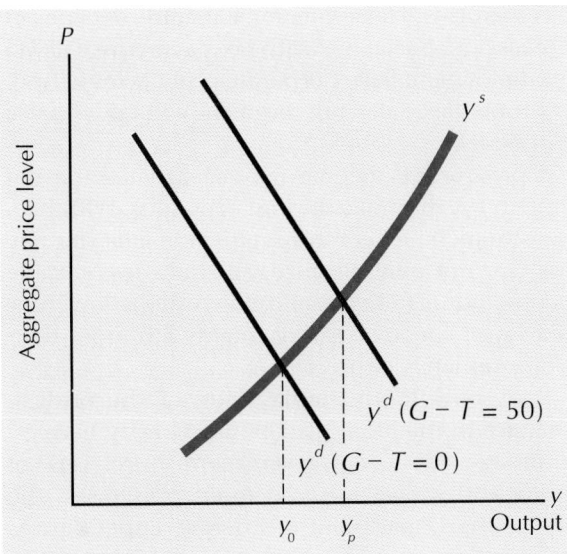

FIGURE 19.3 Stabilization Policy Requiring a Budget Deficit

With a balanced budget, the aggregate demand curve is $y^d(G + T = 0)$. The level of output will be at y_0, which is below the level of potential output, y_p. An increase in spending or a tax cut that results in a $50 billion will shift the aggregate demand curve to $y^d(G - T = 50)$ and increase output to the level of potential output (y_p).

vices as well as transfer payments for stabilization purposes. For example, government construction projects undertaken to meet the allocation goal can be timed to promote the stabilization goal. Projects would be speeded up in recessions to absorb unemployed resources and slowed down in boom periods for the opposite reason. Some changes in transfer payments might be similarly coordinated with the level of economic activity, though with obvious limitations.

Cuts or increases in overall income tax levels, together with some adjustments in government expenditures, provide sufficient flexibility to achieve the stabilization goal while also meeting the allocation and distribution goals. However, when decisions on the level of taxes and expenditures are made with an eye to meeting these goals, the budget will generally not balance.

Even if fiscal policy *can* accomplish these goals in theory, *will it in practice?* The type of process the preceding analysis brings to mind is one where the heads of the allocation, distribution, and stabilization branches of the fiscal policy authority meet, ready with decisions on their aspects of the budget (all heavily influenced by wise economists!). Together these officials set government expenditure and the structure and level of taxes to meet fiscal policy goals. The real-world fiscal policy process, however, is far different. Fiscal policy decisions are made by Congress and the President in a political setting. Elected officials are under pressure from many groups. What ensures that real-world decisions will correspond to optimal fiscal policy?

Nothing, of course. And many critics of the Keynesian view favor *rules* for fiscal policy—such as a balanced budget rule—precisely because they believe that elected officials, left to their own discretion, will make very undesirable choices. This is the *public choice* view explained in Chapter 18. Keynesian economists are not blind to the impact of political pressures on fiscal policy, but they view the likely results of policy by a rule such as a balanced budget requirement as worse than those of policy by discretion, even if flawed by political pressures. A further reason for the Keynesians' preference for policy by discretion rather than rules will emerge in the next section.

Read Perspective 19B.

III
Automatic Fiscal Stabilizers

So far, we have focused on how spending and tax decisions affect the economy. Now let us reverse the question and ask how the level of economic activity affects the budget. In answering this question, we will see how changes in the federal budget caused by changes in economic activity limit the extent of the changes in economic activity. Changes in the budget work as **automatic stabilizers.**

A
Cyclical Changes in Tax Revenues and Transfer Payments

Consider what happens to the federal budget when the economy goes into a recession. First, look at the tax side. In the simple models of Part II, we assumed tax collections were set at some total dollar amount. But tax revenues actually depend on the level of economic activity. Personal income tax receipts will fall as personal income declines in a recession. Social Security tax payments will fall as employment falls. Corporate profit taxes will fall as profits fall. Sales tax revenues will fall as sales volume falls.

A progressive income tax accentuates the decline in tax revenues during recessions. With progressive income tax rates, as income falls you pay less tax, not only because you have less taxable income but also because the tax *rate* is lower for that lower income. Tax payments fall more than proportionately with income.

Turn now to the outlay side of the budget. Changes in the level of economic activity have no automatic effect on government purchases of goods and services (e.g., defense purchases, the size of the Department of Energy). Expenditures for transfer payments are, however, affected. The most direct effect will be on payments for unemployment compensation, which rise as the number of unemployed persons rises. Payments by other programs such as food stamps, aid to families with dependent children, and general welfare also increase during recessions as private incomes

PERSPECTIVE 19B
Fiscal Policy by Discretion: Some Historical Examples

Past fiscal policy decisions have been made by discretion, not rules. Here we look at some historical examples of stabilization policy to evaluate how successful policy by discretion has been. We concentrate on the post-1960 period, because after 1961, with the advent of the Kennedy administration, the stabilization role for fiscal policy was more systematically pursued.

One example of successful stabilization policy often cited by advocates of activist fiscal policy is the income tax cut of 1964 (see Perspective 10). The tax cut, 20 percent for individuals and 10 percent for businesses, strengthened the sluggish recovery from the 1960–61 recession. The tax cut required that the government budget go into deficit, moving from a surplus of $0.3 billion in 1963 to a deficit of $3.3 in 1964. In retrospect, 1964 represents the high point of the Keynesian influence on fiscal policy.

On the negative side of the ledger, fiscal policy was clearly overly expansionary later in the 1960s. With the beginning of the Vietnam War, military spending rose by over $20 billion between 1965 and 1967. Since this increase was not financed by higher taxes, the federal deficit rose by approximately $14 billion over this period. With the economy already at potential output (the unemployment rate was 3.8 percent by 1966), the overexpansionary fiscal policy increased inflation. An income tax surcharge was passed in 1968. This was a temporary additional tax, at first equal to 10 percent of an individual's or corporation's tax liability, later reduced to 5 percent. But this was too little and too late to stem the inflationary pressure in the late 1960s.

Returning to the plus side of the ledger, in the 1970s there was a well-timed tax cut just at the trough of the 1974–75 recession, which aided the recovery. Then in the early 1980s, the Reagan administration's income tax cuts added up to a total reduction of 23 percent in personal income taxes and substantial business tax cuts as well. During the recession of 1981–82, Keynesian economists believed that tax cuts provided needed stimulus for the economy. After the recovery was well underway in 1984 and 1985, however, many Keynesian economists were critical of the Reagan administration's fiscal policy. They believed that the large deficits, caused in part by the tax cuts, were having adverse effects on the economy by keeping interest rates high (the *crowding-out* effect explained in Section VII of Chapter 11).

All in all, from the Keynesian viewpoint, the record of discretionary fiscal policy is a mixed one, with some successes and some failures. Keynesians do not believe that the discretionary fiscal policy record is so bad that we should move to policy governed by fixed rules.

fall. Together, the fall in taxes and the rise in transfer payments cause *disposable personal income* (roughly, national income after taxes but including transfers) to be affected much less by recession than is GNP. The fact that disposable personal income is *cushioned* by the changes in taxes and transfer payments makes the recession less severe. This follows because consumption expenditures, which depend on personal disposal income, are less affected. *Changes in taxes and transfer payments automatically contribute to the stability of the economy.*

The cushioning effect on disposable income is evident in Figure 19.4, which shows personal disposable income as a percent of GNP ($\frac{Y_D}{Y} \times 100$) during each quarter from 1981 to 1985.

During the recession of 1981–82, personal dis-

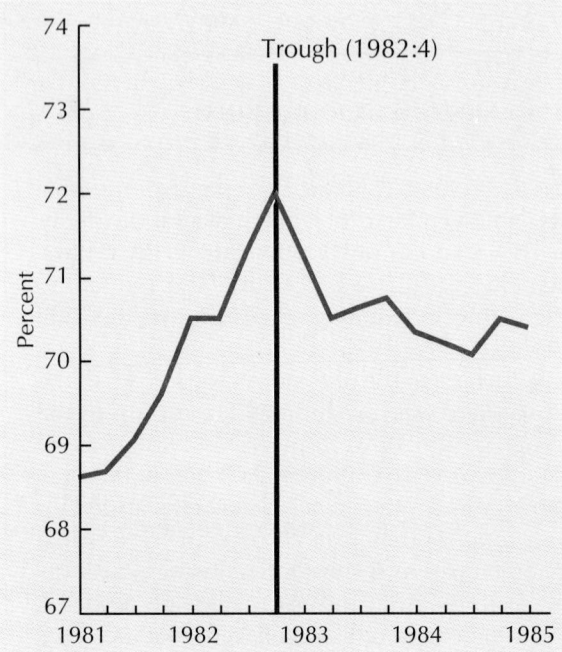

FIGURE 19.4   *Personal Disposable Income as a Percentage of GNP* ($Y_D/Y \times 100$)

posable income rose from 68.6 percent of GNP in the first quarter of 1981 to 72 percent of GNP during the trough of the recession in the fourth quarter of 1982. This reflected the fact that while real GNP *fell* by $35.7 billion between these two quarters, real personal disposable income *rose* by $25.1 billion. While this difference reflects, in part, the effects of tax cuts in late 1981 and mid-1982, automatic stabilizers (falling tax revenues and rising transfers) were also important. As the recovery proceeded from 1983 through 1985, disposable personal income fell as a percent of GNP, as tax revenues recovered and transfer payments fell.

B
Automatic Stabilizers versus a Balanced Budget

As with discretionary changes in fiscal stabilization policy (e.g., a cut in tax rates), the working of the budget as an automatic stabilizer generally *requires* an unbalanced budget. During the 1981–82 recession, for example, due to the effects of automatic stabilizers and discretionary tax cuts, the federal budget deficit increased from $61.3 bil-

lion in 1980 to $145.9 in 1982. While Keynesian economists were critical of the large budget deficits later in the 1980s, this was not the case during the recession.

Suppose that a law (or constitutional amendment) requiring a balanced budget had been in effect in the early 1980s. Then, as tax revenues fell during the recession and transfer payments rose, either an increase in tax *rates* or cuts in other spending categories would have been required— these being the only ways to keep the budget in balance. Fiscal policy during the Great Depression provides an example of such a situation. Although there was no law requiring policymakers to balance the budget, doing so was considered sound budget policy at the time. With the onset of the Depression, the federal budget had moved into deficit in 1930 and 1931 due to lost tax revenues. To eliminate the deficit, President Hoover proposed and Congress passed a substantial *increase* in income tax rates in 1932 *at a time when the unemployment rate was 24 percent*. In the Keynesian view, the tax increase made the Depression even more severe. In fact, the tax increase failed to balance the budget in part because the increase in tax *rates* further lowered income (and thus tax *revenues*). Keynesian economists do not believe that efforts to balance the budget will cause a modern counterpart to the Great Depression. There is, after all, still monetary policy to use for stabilization (assuming there are no rules that constrain it). Keynesians do believe that a balanced-budget rule would make the overall stabilization task more difficult, especially because of the "shut-off" of the automatic stabilizers discussed in this section.

IV
But What About the Deficit?

We began this chapter with a discussion of the large federal budget deficits that emerged in the 1980s with fiscal policy governed by discretion rather than rules. How do the Keynesians view such deficits?

A
Cyclical versus Structural Deficits

We have seen that the federal budget deficit depends in part on the level of economic activity.

> The **cyclical deficit** is the portion of the deficit that results from the economy being at a low level of economic activity.

Cyclical deficits that reflect the working of automatic stabilizers are desirable.

> The portion of the deficit that would exist even if the economy were at its potential level of output is called the **structural deficit.** A structural deficit is not directly attributable to the behavior of the economy and is the part of the deficit for which policymakers are directly responsible.

In other words, the structural deficit is the result of decisions policymakers have made about tax rates, the level of government spending, and benefit levels for transfer programs.

To break the deficit into cyclical and structural components, we need a measure of potential output—the level of output achieved when both capital and labor are utilized at their highest sustainable rates. We can then compute the changes in tax revenues and transfer payments that would have taken place if the economy had moved from

actual to potential output. Using these figures, we can find the structural deficit. To give an example, suppose the actual deficit is $100 billion but the economy is far below potential output. If the level of economic activity increased to the potential level, tax revenues would rise, let us assume by $30 billion. Transfer payments would fall, say by $10 billion, because unemployment compensation payments would decline as employment rose. The structural deficit—the deficit at potential output—is then $60 billion (100 − 30 − 10). As discussed in Chapter 7, to compute the level of potential output requires choosing a benchmark *high-employment* unemployment rate. As also discussed there, considerable disagreement has arisen in recent years concerning the appropriate level for this benchmark rate. Table 19.3 shows the breakdown of federal government deficits for selected recent years into cyclical and structural components using 6 percent for the benchmark high employment rate—a figure proposed by a number of economists and government officials.

Note that during periods of recession such as 1975, 1980, and 1981–82, a substantial fraction of the deficit was cyclical. But note that by the mid-1980s the federal deficit had become mostly structural. By 1987, with the unemployment rate down almost to the 6 percent benchmark, virtually the *whole* deficit was structural. This means that the deficit was due to policymakers' decisions concerning tax rates, spending levels, and benefit levels for transfer payments.

TABLE 19.3 Cyclical and Structural Federal Budget Deficits, Selected Years

	Actual Deficit	Structural Deficit	Cyclical Deficit
1974	−11.6	−10.4	−1.2
1975	−69.4	−43.0	−26.4
1976	−53.5	−33.5	−20.0
1977	−46.0	−34.7	−11.3
1980	−61.3	−37.4	−23.9
1981	−63.8	−27.9	−35.9
1982	−145.9	−60.7	−85.2
1983	−176.0	−101.6	−75.4
1984	−169.6	−142.3	−27.3
1985	−196.0	−172.0	−24.0
1986	−204.7	−187.9	−16.8
1987	−152.6	−147.6	−5.0

Sources: *Economic Report of the President,* 1988 and *Survey of Current Business,* various issues.

B
Are Structural Deficits Bad?

In the Keynesian view, there is no reason to think that the budget should even be balanced when the economy is at potential output. In fact, a structural deficit may be required to keep the economy operating at potential output. In Figure 19.3, for example, to keep aggregate demand high enough to maintain potential output requires a $50 billion deficit at y_p—a structural deficit of $50 billion. In the Keynesian view, the proper level of the structural deficit is determined on stabilization grounds, not to fulfill *any* particular accounting principle.

To say that deficits, even structural ones, are not necessarily bad is not to say that all deficits are good. Keynesian economists have been critical of the larger structural deficits that have resulted from fiscal policy decisions during the Reagan administration. Why?

C
Easy-Fiscal, Tight-Monetary Policy

Other things being equal, an excessively expansionary fiscal policy, one that causes an excessively high structural deficit (too much spending, too low tax rates), will result in excessive aggregate demand. Excessive aggregate demand will in turn lead to inflation. This is a major reason to limit the structural deficit, so that it provides enough *but not too much* demand to maintain potential output.

Other things need not, however, be equal. Even with an overly expansionary fiscal policy, which in the Keynesian view is what we had for much of the 1980s, inflationary pressure need not build up if *monetary* policy is sufficiently restrictive. Fiscal policy can push demand up quickly, but monetary policy provides restraint. Keynesians believe that such a situation existed during much of the Reagan administration, though at some points when the private sector was sluggish, monetary policy was also expansionary.

If a restrictive monetary policy can offset inflationary pressures generated by expansionary fiscal policy, as was the case during much of the 1980s, why worry about large structural deficits? Keynesians believe that the problem with this mix

of a tight (restrictive) monetary policy and an easy (expansionary) fiscal policy is that it causes high interest rates. We have seen how expansionary fiscal policy causes the interest rate to rise, with the resulting *crowding-out* effect on investment spending. Restrictive monetary policy reinforces the upward pressure on interest rates, further retarding investment spending. Low investment today means a smaller capital stock and less output in future years. In this sense, large deficits impose a burden on future generations, who will inherit a smaller capital stock and thus a less productive economy.

D
Budget Deficits and Trade Deficits

Keynesian economists have advanced a second criticism of the *policy mix* in the Reagan administration that also concerns the resulting *composition* of output. We have just examined their first criticism, namely that a policy mix consisting of easy fiscal and tight monetary policy will result in high interest rates and consequently will discourage investment. The Keynesians also believe that such a policy mix will affect the composition of output by encouraging imports of foreign goods and discouraging U.S. exports. They believe that the easy-fiscal, tight-monetary policy of the Reagan administration contributed to the record U.S. foreign **trade deficits** of the 1980s—the trade deficit being the excess of imports over exports.

That there is a link between the government budget deficit (the result of expansionary fiscal policy) and the trade deficit is suggested by the data in Table 19.4, which show both deficits rising sharply in the mid-1980s. The link between the budget deficit and the trade deficit is the level of U.S. interest rates.

In the Keynesian view, expansionary fiscal policies that produced the budget deficits, together with a relatively tight monetary policy, caused U.S. interest rates to be high over the first half of the 1980s. In turn, the high interest rates caused foreign investors to buy our securities—government bonds and bills and private bonds. To buy U.S. securities, however, foreign investors had to exchange their currency for U.S. dollars. For example, a German resident who wanted to buy a U.S. Treasury bond first exchanged German marks for

TABLE 19.4   Federal Government Budget Deficit and Foreign Trade Deficit (Billions of Dollars)

	Federal Government Budget Deficit	Foreign Trade Deficit
1980	−61.3	−25.5
1981	−63.8	−28.0
1982	−145.9	−36.4
1983	−176.0	−57.6
1984	−169.6	−107.9
1985	−196.0	−133.6
1986	−204.7	−156.2
1987	−152.6	−171.2

Source: *Economic Report of the President, 1988.*

dollars and then used the dollars to buy the bond.

This demand for U.S. dollars to purchase U.S. securities pushes up the value of the dollar relative to other currencies (e.g., the mark, the British pound, etc.). The Keynesians believe that the demand for dollars by foreign investors was the main cause for the rise of over 50 percent in the value of the dollar (relative to an average of foreign currencies) that took place between 1980 and 1985.

The rise in the value of the dollar makes U.S. goods (exports) expensive to foreigners. If the dollar rises in value in relation to the German mark, for example, German residents must pay more marks to buy U.S. goods. Due to this price rise, the demand for U.S. exports falls. On the other hand, the rising value of the dollar means that U.S. residents can buy foreign currencies and therefore foreign goods more cheaply. Our demand for imports will rise. The fall in exports and the rise in imports show up as a U.S. foreign trade deficit—an excess of imports over exports. As can be seen in Table 19.4, in 1987 the trade deficit reached $171.2 billion.

Figure 19.5 summarizes the linkages between the policy mix and the trade deficit that we have discussed.

Since the rising value of the dollar makes imported goods cheaper to U.S. residents while making our export goods more expensive to foreigners, there were clearly benefits and costs as a result of the rise in the value of the dollar over the first half of the 1980s. The Keynesians believe, however, that the costs in terms of loss of jobs and excess capacity in many basic U.S. export industries and industries that compete with imports outweighed the benefits of cheaper imports and foreign travel.

In 1986, as U.S. economic growth became sluggish, monetary policy became less restrictive and the dollar began to fall in value. Also, as we will see in Chapter 22, policymakers both here and abroad took actions aimed at lowering the value of the dollar. By mid-1988, the value of the dollar had fallen back to the level of 1981, but the reduction in our trade deficit proved to be a slow process.

V

Monetarist and New Classical Fiscal Policy Views

Given the choice, over the first half of the 1980s, Keynesians would have opted for a policy mix consisting of a more restrictive fiscal policy which would have permitted a more expansionary monetary policy. This Keynesian prescription was essentially Walter Mondale's economic platform in 1984 when he advocated a tax increase to reduce the deficit. Since Mondale carried only the state of Minnesota and the District of Columbia, other arguments must have proved persuasive to voters. Let us see what they were.

Monetarist and new classical economists reach conclusions about fiscal policy that are quite dif-

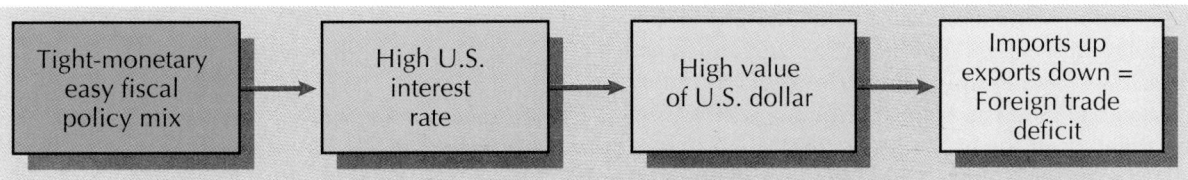

FIGURE 19.5   The Policy Mix and Trade Deficit

ferent from those of the Keynesians. Most important is the fact that neither monetarist nor new classical economists envision a stabilization role for fiscal policy. Recall that it was the stabilization role that required an unbalanced government budget. It is the need to use fiscal policy as a stabilization tool that leads Keynesians to oppose balanced-budget rules. Monetarist and new classical economists tend to view such rules in a more favorable light.

A

Monetarist and New Classical Views of the Deficits of the 1980s

Both monetarist and new classical economists agree with the Keynesians that federal budget deficits in the 1980s have been too high. Milton Friedman and other monetarist economists believe that the deficits have financed too high a level of government spending. Monetarists also believe that large government deficits and resulting high interest rates put pressure on the Federal Reserve to follow overly expansionary monetary policies, i.e., to expand the money supply too rapidly in an attempt to bring down interest rates. Though the Federal Reserve under Paul Volcker resisted such pressure in the early 1980s, in 1985 monetarists were critical of the Federal Reserve for letting M1 grow at an annual rate of nearly 12 percent.

The new classical economists also believe that the large budget deficits of the early and mid-1980s destroyed the *credibility* of restrictive monetary policy. They believe that the Federal Reserve followed a restrictive economic policy over the first part of the 1980s. But the public, seeing the large federal government budget deficits, expected the Federal Reserve to increase money growth eventually in order to keep the deficit from pushing up interest rates.

As a consequence of the federal budget deficits and the resulting lack of credibility of Federal Reserve policy, the public was slow to lower its expectation of inflation over the medium term (the next several years). Workers were reluctant to accept lower money wage increases. This, the new classical economists believe, explains why lowering inflation in the eary 1980s caused high unemployment. Recall that in the new classical model an anticipated restrictive monetary policy would

reduce inflation without causing lower output growth and higher unemployment, but this would occur only if the policy is *credible*—if people believe that it will be continued for the foreseeable future. Restrictive monetary policies will not be credible if they are accompanied by large and increasing budget deficits. In the words of one new classical economist, "the idea of coupling a very loose fiscal policy with a very tight monetary policy is a big mistake."[4]

B

Fiscal Policy Rules: Monetarist and New Classical Views

Neither monetarist nor new classical economists see a role for discretionary fiscal stabilization policy. Consequently, they are more favorably disposed toward fiscal policy rules than are Keynesians. What they perceive as harmful large deficits in recent years lead monetarists and new classical economists to favor rules that limit the government's ability to run deficits.

Milton Friedman and some other monetarist economists favor a constitutional amendment that would force Congress and the President to balance the budget. A key section of the amendment Friedman favors reads as follows:

Prior to each fiscal year, the Congress shall adopt a statement of receipts and outlays for that year in which total outlays are not greater than total receipts. The Congress may amend such statement provided revised outlays are no greater than revised receipts. Whenever three-fifths of the whole number of both houses deem it necessary, Congress in such statement may provide for a specific excess of outlays over receipts by a vote directed solely to that subject. The Congress and the President shall pursuant to legislation or through exercise of their powers under the first and second articles, ensure that actual outlays do not exceed outlays set forth in such statement.[5]

[4]Thomas Sargent, quoted from an interview in Arjo Klamer, *Conversations with Economists* (Totowa, N.J.: Rowman and Allenheld, 1983), p. 70.

[5]Milton and Rose Friedman, *Tyranny of the Status Quo* (New York: Harcourt Brace Jovanovich, 1984), p. 56.

The amendment requires that Congress and the President plan for a balanced budget. On the spending side of the budget, they must also see that the plan is realized. But on the receipts side, they do not have this responsibility. This is deliberate. Friedman wants the amendment to allow revenues to respond to economic conditions. "Let a boom develop, actual receipts will exceed planned receipts; let a recession develop, receipts will drop."[6] There would then still be some room for automatic fiscal stabilizers to work even with the balanced budget amendment in effect.

New classical economists have been less involved than monetarists and Keynesians in the debate about fiscal policy rules. A number of new classical economists have, however, expressed a preference for a balanced-budget rule (or another type of rule) rather than discretion in fiscal policy-making.

VI
The Supply-Side View of Fiscal Policy: A First Look at Reaganomics

To complete the fiscal policy picture, we must examine the views of one other group who were very influential during Ronald Reagan's presidency—the **supply-side economists.** The views of supply-side economists are grounded in the tradition of classical economics (see Chapter 8). The popularity of supply-side views concerning fiscal policy first developed during the 1970s in what one supporter has called "the supply-side revolution."[7] These views were embodied in the Reagan administration's fiscal policies—part of a package that came to be called "Reaganomics."

The essence of the supply-side view is simply stated in President Reagan's 1986 economic report to Congress:

> The Federal government cannot provide prosperity or generate economic growth; it can only

[6]Ibid., p. 57.

[7]Paul Craig Roberts, *The Supply-Side Revolution* (Cambridge, Mass.: Harvard University Press, 1984).

encourage private initiative, innovation, and entrepreneurial activity that produces economic opportunities.[8]

The role of fiscal policy is to encourage—or at least not to discourage—*private* initiative. In terms of tax and spending decisions, this means, first and foremost, that tax rates should be kept low. Spending must also be kept relatively low if large budget deficits are to be avoided.

Let us consider in turn supply-side views on tax rates, government expenditures, and the deficit.

A
Marginal Tax Rates

The supply-side view focuses on the *incentive* effects of tax rates. The relevant tax rate is the **marginal** tax rate, the rate paid on each *additional* dollar earned from an activity. This marginal tax rate forms what supply-side economists call a *wedge* between the actual return to an activity (e.g., working) and the *after-tax* return to that activity. High marginal tax rates are disincentives to productive activities. In the supply-side view, high marginal tax rates discourage the private initiative that President Reagan cites as a spur toward growth.

The supply-side view implies that marginal tax rates on both individual and corporate income should be reduced to their feasible minimums. Some supply-side economists believe that such tax reduction should be accompanied by a move away from taxing income toward taxing consumption. Sales taxes, for example, would replace the income tax, which is a disincentive to providing labor services. Other proposals are efforts to expand the tax *base* through the elimination of deductions, so that the tax *rate* can be lowered. The most extreme proposal to accomplish the latter objective calls for a *flat tax*, in which all income would be taxed with no deductions. With such a large base, the tax rate would be fairly low.

To lower marginal income taxes, President Reagan's Economic Recovery Act of 1981 lowered personal tax rates in three stages by 23 percent. There were also changes in the provisions that substantially lowered the rate at which corporate income was taxed. Much of this decrease, some estimate

[8]*Economic Report of the President*, 1986, p. 6.

all, was reversed by a substantial increase in Social Security (payroll) tax rates in 1983 and adjustment in the measures to lower business taxes in 1982. In the second Reagan administration, the emphasis was on broadening the tax base and lowering, as well as simplifying, the rate structure. The details of the resulting tax reform act of 1986 will be discussed in Chapter 20.

B
Government Expenditures

Many supply-side economists agree with monetarists such as Milton Friedman, who concludes that "There is nothing wrong with the United States that a dose of smaller and less obtrusive government will not cure."[9] Still, as can be seen from Table 19.1, and especially from Figure 19.1, the Reagan administration, though influenced by the supply-side economists, was unable to reduce the size of government spending.

In part, the failure to reduce government expenditure stemmed from the Reagan administration's belief that one area of spending, namely defense spending, needed to be increased substantially. The military buildup during President Reagan's first term boosted defense spending from $142.7 (5.2 percent of GNP) in 1980 to $262.2 (6.6 percent of GNP) in 1986. Congress was unwilling to cut nondefense spending by an amount sufficient to reduce overall spending, given the defense buildup.

C
The Deficit

The supply-side economists share the free market view of the classical economists. They do not favor activist government policies to stabilize the economy. In particular, they do not favor discretionary fiscal stabilization policies. As echoed in the statement by President Reagan quoted earlier, the role of fiscal policy is to create the proper climate for private initiative, not to try to provide prosperity itself.

It was the stabilization role of fiscal policy that, in the Keynesian view, necessitated an unbal-

[9]Friedman and Friedman, *Tyranny of the Status Quo*, p. 168.

anced budget. Seeing no such role for fiscal policy, the supply-siders, like the monetarists and new classical economists, have no clear reason to oppose a balanced-budget amendment such as the one discussed in the previous section. Many supply-side economists do, in fact, support the amendment, believing that it will help reduce the size of government and restrain government spending. President Reagan has long supported such a constitutional amendment. The key feature in the supply-side view of a balanced-budget amendment or of deficit reduction in a series of steps, as specified in the Gramm-Rudman Act, is that budget balance must be achieved by spending cuts, *not by tax increases*. This follows because increases in tax rates have, in the supply-side economists' view, such harmful disincentive effects. This supply-side view has also been the Reagan administration's position.

VII
The Current Fiscal Policy Situation

In 1987 the Supreme Court ruled that a key provision of the Gramm-Rudman act was unconstitutional. The provision that "triggered" the automatic spending cuts called on the General Accounting Office, a congressional agency, to stipulate the cuts that needed to be made. The Supreme Court ruled that this violated the *separation of powers* between the legislative and executive branches; Congress was in effect ordering the executive branch to reduce spending. By 1987, it was also clear that Congress would not legislate spending cuts to meet the Gramm-Rudman deficit targets, nor would the President approve tax increases for that purpose.

In late 1987, reacting to instability in financial markets, which had been made jittery by continuing trade deficits, the falling dollar, and rising interest rates, Congress and the President did reach a compromise. This compromise, embodied in the Deficit Control Act of 1987, reduced spending and increased revenue by totals of $30 billion for 1988 and $46 billion for 1989. Current projections call for deficits of $125 billion for 1988 and

$117 billion for 1989. Deficit projections have, however, been very unreliable in the past.

In the absence of a recession which would produce a *cyclical* deficit, a return to deficits of the magnitude of those in 1985 and 1986 is unlikely. It is probable, however, that Congress will be wrestling with deficit reductions for several years to come.

SUMMARY

Fiscal policy consists of decisions about the federal budget—decisions about expenditures and taxes.

1. Federal government outlays (expenditures) and revenues have grown as a share of GNP over the years since World War II. In the 1960s, outlays began to grow more rapidly than revenues, with resulting persistent federal budget deficits. The size of these deficits skyrocketed in the 1980s.

2. In the Keynesian view, fiscal policy has an allocation goal, a distribution goal, and a stabilization goal. The first two can be achieved with a balanced budget. The stabilization goal, however, generally requires an unbalanced budget. This leads Keynesians to oppose legislated rules or constitutional amendments that require a balanced federal budget.

3. Changes in taxes and transfer payments that result from changes in economic activity work as *automatic stabilizers*. They cushion disposable personal income from the full effects of the changes in economic activity. The functioning of automatic fiscal stabilizers also requires that, in general, the budget not be balanced.

4. The actual federal budget deficit can be broken into two parts: *structural* and *cyclical* deficits. The structural deficit is the portion of the deficit that would still exist if the economy were operating at potential output. The cyclical deficit is the portion of the deficit that results when the economy operates below potential output.

5. The Keynesians were critical of the high structural deficits run by the Reagan administration in the mid-1980s. They believed that these large deficits resulted in high interest rates, which discouraged investment. They also believed that the high interest rates resulted in a high value of the dollar (relative to foreign currencies) during the 1981–85 period, which discouraged exports and encouraged imports.

6. Monetarist and new classical economists have also been critical of the large deficits of the 1980s. Milton Friedman and some other monetarists favor a constitutional amendment that would require a balanced federal budget. New classical economists are also sympathetic to rules rather than discretion in fiscal policymaking.

7. The supply-side economists were influential in shaping fiscal policy during the Reagan administration. Supply-side economists favor low tax rates as incentives to private initiative. Thus, the thrust of fiscal policy during the Reagan years was toward tax cuts. Many supply-side economists, as well as Reagan himself, favor a balanced-budget rule, but they believe that a balanced budget must be achieved by spending cuts, not tax increases.

KEY TERMS

Gramm-Rudman Act
Federal government purchases of goods and
  services
Transfer payments
Automatic stabilizers

Cyclical deficit
Structural deficit
Trade deficit
Supply-side economists
Marginal tax rate

QUESTIONS AND PROBLEMS

1. Give a brief history of federal tax revenues and outlays as a percentage of GNP, indicating periods of deficit and surplus.

2. What components of federal government outlays have been responsible for the growing federal budget deficits in recent years?

3. Who purchases the Treasury securities that are sold to finance deficit spending?

4. Keynesian economists would argue that fiscal policy decisions should be made in view of what three fiscal policy goals? Explain each goal briefly.

5. Which of the three Keynesian fiscal policy goals would justify deficit spending? Explain.

6. Evaluate the historical record of discretionary fiscal policy actions since 1960.

7. Explain how certain components of the federal budget act as automatic stabilizers once the economy goes into a recession.

8. Explain why Keynesian economists oppose balanced budget laws.

9. Distinguish the cyclical component of a federal budget deficit from the structural component. Do Keynesian economists consider structural deficits unacceptable? Explain.

10. When, in Keynesian analysis, is a budget deficit too large?

11. Use Keynesian analysis to explain how large federal budget deficits in the 1980s caused large U.S. trade deficits.

12. Have federal budget deficits been too high in the 1980s? Explain why from the perspectives of (a) Keynesians, (b) monetarists, and (c) new classical economists.

13. Explain why some economists today favor balanced budget amendments or laws.

14. Supply-side economists focus on what side effects of tax laws?

20

Economic Growth

"Do We Live As Well As We Used To?" This was the title of a *Fortune* magazine cover story in 1987. According to results of a poll reported there, "fewer Americans were satisfied with their economic circumstances in 1986 than in 1956."[1] Are Americans worse off today than 30 years ago? Or is it just that, as comedian Jackie Gleason said, "The past remembers better than it lived." In this chapter we will see that Americans' incomes are higher today than they were 30 years ago. But the *rate* at which incomes are growing has slowed in the past two decades. This slowdown in U.S. economic growth may be the source of the dissatisfaction the *Fortune* pollsters found.

Up to this point, our predominant concern has been the *cyclical* or short-run behavior of the economy. We now examine the economy over a longer time frame. How have the key macroeconomic variables behaved over periods of several decades (e.g. 1956–86)? What are the recent trends in important variables such as the rate of economic growth and the levels of employment and unemployment? How can government policies be used to achieve desirable behavior of the economy over this longer time frame?

The dominant feature of the U.S. economy over the long run is growth. Figure 20.1, a time path of real GNP, illustrates the dimensions of U.S. economic growth over this century. The average annual growth rate of real GNP was 3.1 percent, with the result that by 1986 real GNP was over *14 times* its level in 1900. While the U.S. population has also grown during this period, more than tripling since 1900, real GNP per person has grown by a factor of four to five.

Unfortunately, when we break the U.S. growth experience into shorter time intervals, we see that the growth rate has declined in recent years. As noted in Chapter 6, for example, the average annual rate of growth in real GNP was 3.6 percent for the years 1953–69, but only 2.7 for 1970–87.

An upward trend in unemployment has accompanied this slowdown in economic growth. We have analyzed how unemployment rises during recessions and then falls during a subsequent

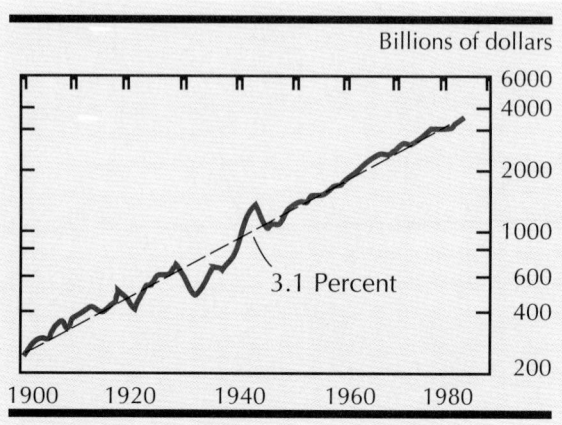

FIGURE 20.1   GNP, Constant 1982 Dollars

recovery. Recently, the rise in unemployment during recessions has been greater and its subsequent fall during recoveries has been less than in earlier decades. For example, the unemployment rate in mid-1986, after 3.5 years of recovery from the 1981–82 recession, was 7.1 percent. This is higher than the highest level reached *during any recession* in the 1950–70 period. By mid-1988, the unemployment rate had fallen to 5.5 percent, but was still high in comparison to average unemployment rates in the 1950s or 1960s.

To see why U.S. economic growth has slowed, we look at the sources of growth—the economic processes that generate growth—in Section I. Then in Section II we examine the changes in the growth-producing process that led to the slowdown since 1970. In Section III we consider some additional factors that contributed to the rising unemployment rate. Finally, in Section IV, we examine the policy response to slower U.S. economic growth.

I

Sources of Economic Growth

Economist Edward Denison has carefully studied economic growth in the United States. Table 20.1 summarizes his findings concerning the sources

---

[1]*Fortune* Magazine, September 14, 1987, p. 32.

TABLE 20.1 Sources of U.S. Economic Growth, 1929–82

Annual growth rate of output (percent)	2.9
Percent of growth due to:	
Growth in labor input	32
Growth in labor productivity	
Education per worker	14
Capital	19
Technological change	28
Economies of scale	9
Other factors	−2

Source: Edward F. Denison, *Trends in American Economic Growth. 1929–82* (Washington, D.C.: The Brookings Institution, 1985), p. 30.

of growth in U.S. output for 1929–82. As the table indicates, real output grew at an *annual* rate of 2.9 percent over this period.[2] The other numbers in the table show the percentage (proportion of the total) contribution to the growth rate of a number of factors. These factors are broken into two groups.

The first group, containing one factor, is growth in labor input. This is simply growth in output due to the increase in the quantity of labor. We have seen that, in the short run, firms can increase output by hiring more labor. The same process goes on over longer periods such as the one covered by the table. Over the longer run, however, growth in the labor input comes primarily from growth in the population and, therefore, the labor force. The labor force may also change due to changes in *labor force participation ratios*, which are the proportions of different groups in the population that are members of the labor force. In the 1960s and 1970s, for example, the proportion of women in the labor force rose rapidly, contributing to growth in the labor input. Overall, Dension estimates that 32 percent, approximately one third, of the growth in output between 1929 and 1982 came from this source.

The other sources of growth are factors that increase the amount of output per unit of labor input (e.g., per hour of labor), factors that increase **labor productivity.** Let's consider each in turn.

[2]This figure is somewhat below the trend for the twentieth century (3.1 percent, as shown in Figure 20.1), primarily due to the zero growth decade of the 1930s, the period of the Great Depression. This period gets a higher weight in the average when the shorter 1929–82 period is considered. Also, the earlier 1900–28 period was one in which growth averaged above the overall trend for 1900–87.

A
Education Per Worker

The first of these other sources of growth listed in Table 20.1 is education per worker. As explained by Denison:[3]

> *Educational background decisively conditions both the types of work an individual is able to perform and his proficiency in any particular occupation. The distribution of American workers by highest school grade completed has shifted upward continuously and massively, and this shift has been a major growth source.*

Dension estimates that 14 percent of U.S. economic growth is due to increased education of the labor force.

B
Capital

The term *capital* refers to plant and equipment used in the production process. Growth in the stock of plant and equipment is called **capital formation.** As capital formation takes place, more and better capital is used together with labor. As a result, output per unit of labor increases. Denison estimates that increased capital formation was responsible for 19 percent, just less than one fifth, of U.S. economic growth between 1929 and 1982.

C
Technological Change

The next factor in Table 20.1 is **technological change.** This includes changes in technological knowledge (e.g., ways to employ robots in the production process), as well as new knowledge about how to organize businesses (managerial strategies). In Denison's estimates, technological change accounts for 28 percent of growth and is the most important influence on labor productivity.

D
Economies of Scale

The scale (or size) of the economy also influences growth, according to Denison's estimates. As the

[3]Edward F. Denison, *Trends in American Economic Growth 1929–82* (Washington, D.C.: The Brookings Institution, 1985), p. 15.

U.S. economy became larger, enterprises could serve larger markets, enabling them to specialize more and use mass production techniques. The resulting efficiencies in production, what are called **economies of scale,** increase the productivity of both labor and capital. Denison estimates that 9 percent of U.S. growth results from this source.

E
Other Factors

Denison considers a number of other factors that either stimulate or retard the growth process (e.g., changes in allocation of resources across industries, effects of weather on farm output, work stoppages). Taken together, these factors had a net negative effect equal to 2 percent of economic growth.

Overall, Denison's estimates indicate that the main sources of U.S. growth from 1929 to 1982 were *growth in the quantity of the labor input* and four other factors that cause labor productivity to grow: *education per worker, capital formation, technological change,* and *economies of scale.*

II
Causes of the Growth Slowdown

The decline in the rate of growth in U.S. output most likely began in 1973. According to Denison's estimates, the U.S. economic growth rate was 1.2

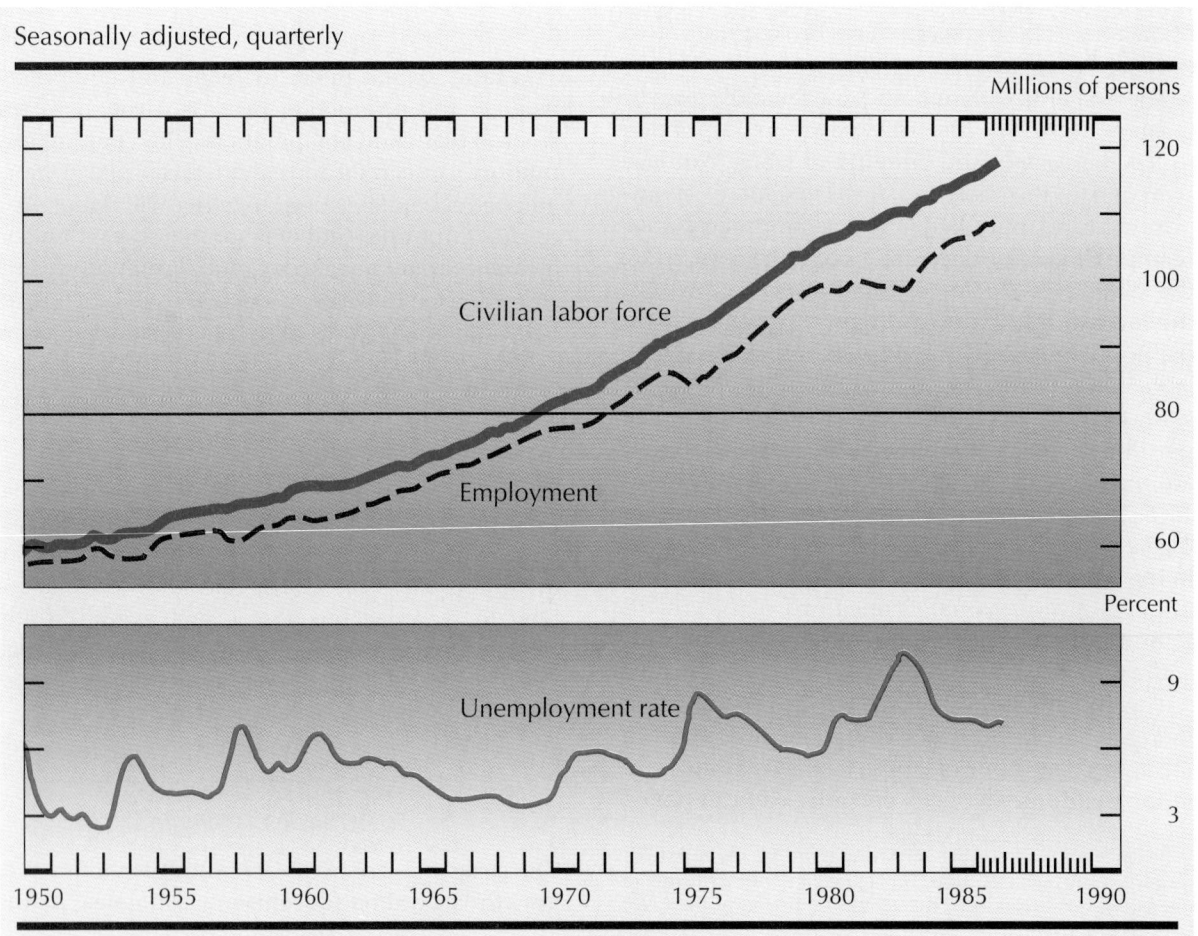

FIGURE 20.2   *Labor Force, Employment, and Unemployment*

percent lower in 1974–82 than in the earlier post–World War II period of 1948–73. Extending the later period to 1974–87, and again in comparison to 1948–73, the decline is 1.5 percentage points , from a growth rate of 3.9 for 1948–76 to 2.4 percent for 1974–87.

Figure 20.2 charts the growth of the labor input, one major source of output growth since 1950. There is no apparent slowdown in labor force growth. In fact, the labor force began to grow more rapidly in the mid-1960s as the many babies born in the immediate post–World War II years (the baby boom generation) reached working age. The increase in the female labor force participation rate over the 1960s and 1970s also speeded up growth in the labor force.

It is, of course, only employed labor that produces output, but as Figure 20.2 indicates, employment growth also showed no sign of slowing in the post-1970 period. There were interruptions during recessions, but no general downward trend. However, employment growth was not sufficient to absorb the more rapid growth in the labor force, and therefore, as can be seen from the bottom panel of the figure, the unemployment rate tended to rise in the 1970s and into the 1980s.

Looking at the overall trends in labor force and employment growth, changes in growth in labor input do not appear to have contributed to the slowdown in output growth. This has led researchers to focus on changing growth in *labor productivity* (output per hour of labor input) as the culprit in the economic growth slowdown. Figure 20.3 shows the annual percentage rate of growth in labor productivity for each year since 1948. While there is a good deal of year-to-year fluctuation in productivity growth, clearly the fluctuations are around a lower average (or trend) growth

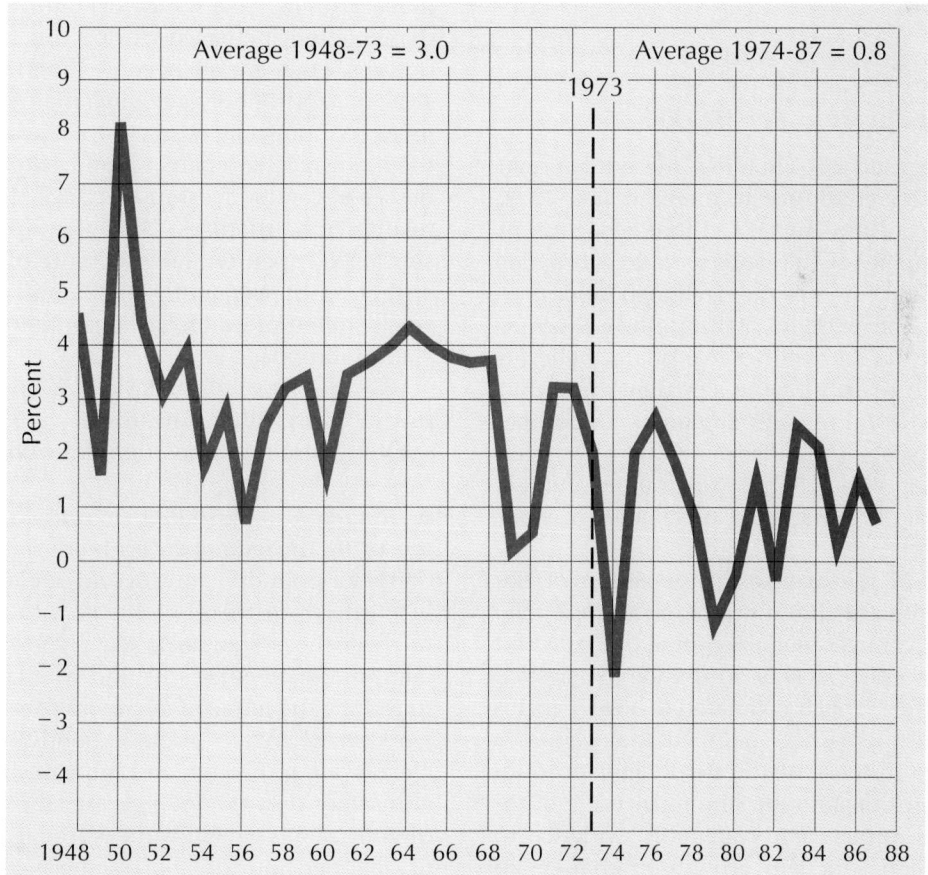

FIGURE 20.3   Growth Rate in U.S. Labor Productivity

rate in productivity in the post-1973 years. Productivity growth averaged 3 percent per year for 1948–73 compared with 0.8 percent for 1974–87, a fall of 2.2 percentage points. During 4 of the 14 years from 1974 to 1987, labor productivity actually fell, something that did not happen in *any* year in the earlier period.

If the source of the growth slowdown is slower growth in labor productivity, we are led to consider changes in the behavior of the factors responsible for growth in labor productivity—educational level of workers, capital formation, technological change, and economies of scale—as the ultimate causes of the growth slowdown. How much of the 2.2 percentage point drop in labor productivity growth can be attributed to the different behavior of these factors in the post-1973 period relative to the earlier post–World War II years?

To begin with the last, there seem to have been no drastic changes in the nature of economies of scale. So we concentrate on the other three factors.

A
Education Per Worker

Measured in years of schooling, the educational level of workers continued to increase after 1973. Some, however, have suggested that a decline in the overall quality of the work force in a broader sense has contributed to the decline in labor productivity. In the extreme, Arthur Burns, former Chairman of the Federal Reserve Board, believed that the main reason for the slowdown was that "people don't want to work anymore." Of course, for over 100 years, the older generation has been saying this about the younger generation, and it is not clear that 1973 marked a breakpoint in work intensity.

A change in the age–sex composition of the labor force toward the entrance of more female workers and younger workers overall probably did reduce the average level of on-the-job experience of the workforce. This is estimated to have contributed about 0.2 percentage points of the overall 2.2 percent drop in the growth rate of labor productivity. Beyond this amount, one must rely on impressionistic rather than systematic evidence to blame slower productivity growth on changes in the quality of the labor force.

B
Capital Formation

Capital formation takes place through investment. Firms buy structures and equipment to add to their stock of capital goods. So, to see if lagging capital formation is the source of lagging productivity growth, a starting point is investment data. The data reveal that investment, expressed either as a percent of GNP or as a percent of the capital stock, has *not* declined since 1970. Looking at several aspects of the performance of investment over recent years, however, there are three reasons for believing that changes in the *pattern* of capital formation were a factor in the slower growth of labor productivity: *rising depreciation, regulation-mandated investment, and labor–capital substitution.*

1. Rising Depreciation New investment contributes to capital formation, but depreciation, the portion of the capital stock that becomes obsolete, must also be taken into account. This rate of depreciation increased during the 1970s for two reasons. First, energy became much more expensive, making energy-guzzling plants and equipment economically obsolete well before the end of their normal life span. Second, after 1970, businesses began to invest more heavily in equipment relative to structures. Since equipment has a shorter life span on average, more of it wears out each year. Consequently, as the mix of the capital stock shifted more toward equipment, the depreciation rate rose.

With a relatively stable flow of investment, the rise in depreciation lowers *net* capital formation (new investment minus depreciation).

2. Regulation-Mandated Investment During the 1970s, the federal government set stricter standards for pollution control and worker safety. Part of a firm's investment had to go into expenditures to meet these standards (e.g., smokestack scrubbers to reduce emissions and ventilation systems to reduce the levels of chemical substances in the workplace). While such expenditures produce cleaner air and water, and improve worker health and safety, they do not increase labor productivity directly as it is generally measured (e.g., more tons of steel per hour of labor services). To the degree that more investment has gone to meet federal regulatory standards, less has been available for the type of capital formation that increases labor productivity.

3. Labor–Capital Substitution While investment did not decline (as a percent of GNP) in the 1970s, it also did not increase to allow growth in the capital stock to match the increased rate of growth in the labor force. Consequently, the rate at which capital per hour of labor or per employee was growing declined in the 1970s. The growth rate in capital per hour of labor services fell from 3.2 percent over 1950–70 to 1.9 percent for the decade of the 1970s. With capital per worker (or per worker hour) growing more slowly, labor productivity also grew more slowly.

A mid-range, perhaps somewhat conservative, estimate is that changes in capital formation, including energy price effects on obsolescence and effects of regulation, explain about 0.5 percentage points, or nearly one fourth, of the drop in the growth rate in labor productivity.

C
Technological Change

Technological change accounted for the largest proportion of the growth in labor productivity over the 1929–82 period. Did the rate of technological advancement slow after 1973, and if so, why? These are difficult questions to answer because we do not measure technological change directly, as we do, for example, the quantity of labor input. We simply attribute growth in output over and above growth explained by increases in the quantity and quality of factors of production, and other measurable factors, to improvements in organization and technique—technological change.

The effect of technological change is therefore a *residual*. Consequently, when growth in labor productivity declines more than appears explainable from other sources, this *may* indicate that the pace of technological change has slowed. Or it may mean that something else has happened that we have failed to measure (e.g., maybe, as Arthur Burns suggests, people really don't want to work anymore or perhaps, as others have suggested, top management in the United States has failed to manage).

D
Cyclical Factors

An additional influence on labor productivity growth, not important for Denison's long period, 1929–82, but potentially important for a relatively short period such as 1974–87, is the *business cycle*. The growth rate in labor productivity typically falls in recessions. Note in Figure 20.3 that 3 of the 4 years when labor productivity fell in absolute terms were recession years (1974, 1980, 1982). This happens because, while firms lay off workers during recessions, they do so less than in proportion to the drop in output. A 10 percent drop in output might, for example, be accompanied by a 7 percent drop in employment. As a result, as output falls during recessions the ratio of output to labor input (labor productivity) falls. Why do firms do this? Firms risk losing workers on layoffs to other jobs, which means retraining costs for new workers at the end of the recession. This causes them, at least temporarily, to hold on to some workers, especially skilled ones, even if they are not needed at current production levels.

If labor productivity declines in recessions, then at least part of the decline in productivity growth during 1974–87 was due to the three recessions in that period, two of which were prolonged and severe. This compares to 1961–72, for example, during which there was one mild recession. The poorer cyclical performance of the economy is estimated to be the cause of 0.5 percentage points or almost one fourth of the total drop in the labor productivity growth rate.[4]

■ *CHECK YOUR BEARINGS*

Table 20.2 summarizes our conclusions on the sources of the post-1973 fall in the growth rate of U.S. labor productivity. Changes in labor quality, the rate and mix of capital formation, and cyclical factors explain about one half of the drop. The rest may be due to a decline in the rate of technological change or to some other factor we have failed to take into account. One group of economists, the supply-siders, blame high taxes and government

---

[4]This estimate is from Barry Bosworth, *Tax Incentives and Economic Growth* (Washington, D.C.: The Brookings Institution, 1984). See Bosworth's book for a detailed survey of the literature on the issues discussed in this section.

TABLE 20.2   Estimate of Sources of Decline in the Growth Rate of Labor Productivity

Sources	Annual Percentage Change
Decline in labor quality	0.2
Change in the rate and mix of net capital formation	0.4
Cyclical factors	0.5
Technological change or other residual factors	<u>1.1</u>
Decline in the growth rate in labor productivity	2.2

regulation for this residual. Their views are discussed in Section IV in the context of the policy response to the growth slowdown. Before turning to that topic, however, we consider another aspect of the slowing growth rate in output and productivity—the upward trend in the unemployment rate.

Read Perspective 20A.

III

Additional Causes of Rising Unemployment

As noted in Chapter 6 and at the beginning of this chapter, rising unemployment has accompanied slower growth in output in the 1970s and 1980s.

This upward trend in the unemployment rate is apparent in Figure 20.2. To an extent, slower output growth has caused the trend in the unemployment rate. The economy has not grown fast enough to generate new jobs for all those entering the labor force. But there have also been some additional influences on the unemployment rate.

A

Demographic Factors

There is general agreement that changes in the age–sex composition of the labor force are responsible for part of the rise in unemployment in the post-1970 period. Specifically, the numbers of young workers and female workers have increased relative to older male workers. The rise in younger workers came as the post-World War II baby boom generation entered the labor force, beginning in the late 1960s. The higher proportion of women in the labor force reflected the fact that while about one third of adult women were in the labor force in the early 1950s, over one half were in the labor force in the early 1980s.

Younger workers and women reentering the labor force have periods of unemployment before they find a job. Also, workers in these groups tend to change jobs more frequently and to combine periods of employment with periods of attending school or working in the home. Consequently, these groups have more *spells* of what in Chapter 6 we called *frictional* unemployment. As the proportion of these workers in the labor force increased

PERSPECTIVE 20A
Growth and Productivity in Other Industrialized Countries

Table 20.3 shows growth rates in output and labor productivity for Canada, Japan, and several European countries. Annual growth rates for 1960–73, 1973–79 and 1979–85 are given. Note that during the 1973–79 period growth in output and labor productivity declined substantially in each country. The mid-1970s began

a period of slower growth for virtually all industrialized countries.

In the post-1979 period, there was little evidence of a general reversal of the trend toward slower growth in both output and labor productivity. The first half of the 1980s was a period of recession followed by only a sluggish recovery for these countries.

TABLE 20.3 The Worldwide Growth Slowdown

Country	Growth Rate in Output			Growth Rate in Labor Productivity		
	1960–73	1973–79	1979–85	1960–73	1973–79	1979–85
Canada	5.4	4.2	2.3	2.6	1.3	1.0
Japan	9.6	3.6	4.0	8.2	2.9	3.0
West Germany	4.4	2.3	1.3	4.2	2.9	1.6
France	5.6	3.1	1.1	4.8	2.8	1.4
Italy	5.3	2.6	1.4	5.8	1.7	1.0
United Kingdom	3.1	1.5	1.2	2.8	1.3	1.8
Sweden	4.1	1.8	1.8	3.5	0.5	1.3

Source: OECO *Historical Statistics,* p. 44, p. 47.

relative to that of older males, who have low rates of frictional unemployment, the overall unemployment rate also increased.

Estimates indicate that changes in the age–sex composition were responsible for about a 2 percentage point rise in the unemployment rate between the late 1950s and late 1970s. The effect in the mid-1980s (again, relative to the late 1950s) is only about 1 percentage point because the bulk of the baby boomers are no longer young workers. By 1990 this age–sex composition effect should be negligible. Still, as of 1987, it meant that an unemployment rate of 7 percent was roughly comparable to one of 6 percent in the 1950s.

B
Transfer Payment Effects

While general agreement exists concerning the effect of the changing age–sex composition on unemployment, the other factors we consider are more controversial. The first is the effect of government transfer payment programs. Some argue that growth in these programs has contributed substantially to the upward trend in the unemployment rate. Among the programs cited in this regard the most important is unemployment compensation.

Because workers receive unemployment benefits, they are under less pressure to find new employment quickly after a layoff or when they quit a job. Moreover, the existence of unemploy-

ment benefits may make employers more likely to adjust their work force by means of temporary layoffs. Employers know that workers can collect unemployment benefits—increasing the likelihood that they will not accept alternative jobs and will be available for recall when the firm later wants to increase its work force.

Thus, it is argued, by increasing the number of workers covered by unemployment insurance over the past two decades, the government has contributed to the rise in unemployment. It should be pointed out, however, that even if this is true, we would not necessarily want to take any policy action to reverse it. Society provides unemployment insurance for a purpose—to prevent undue hardship for the unemployed.

C
Growing Structural Unemployment

Along different lines, some have attributed the upward trend in unemployment to rising *structural* unemployment. Structural unemployment is due to a mismatch of the skills and locations of workers with those required for available jobs. The growth in structural unemployment is blamed, in turn, on the decline of basic U.S. industries such as steel and autos, partly as a result of foreign competition, and on the difficulty of retraining and relocating displaced workers for employment in the growing service and high-tech industries.

Read Perspective 20B.

PERSPECTIVE 20B

High European Unemployment

Like the slowdown in growth and productivity, the rising trend in unemployment has not been confined to the United States. Figure 20.4 plots the average annual unemployment rate for seven European countries (West Germany, France, the United Kingdom, Italy, Belgium, the Netherlands and Spain) for the years since 1970. During the 1960s and the early 1970s, these countries had very low rates of unemployment, in the range of 1 to 3 percent. The upward trend since the mid-1970s and especially in the early 1980s was sharper than in the United States, with the average unemployment rate reaching 11.4 percent by 1986.

As in the United States, high unemployment in Europe cannot be explained solely by cyclical factors. There was a recession in Europe in 1981–82, but by 1986 the recovery was well into its fourth year. Still, employment, particularly in manufacturing, did not grow fast enough to absorb the growth in the labor force. In some cases, employment actually fell even though output grew.

The growth slowdown in Europe that began in the mid-1970s is, as in the United States, one cause of the rising trend in European unemployment. But as in the United States, other factors are also at work.

In some European countries the number of young workers in the labor force was increasing rapidly in the late 1970s, reflecting the high birth rate of the 1960s. Since, as discussed earlier, young workers typically have high rates of frictional unemployment, this *age composition* effect may have resulted in a modest rise in unemployment.

Transfer payments such as unemployment insurance and other welfare programs, which are more liberal in many European countries than in the United States, have also been blamed for rising unemployment. But the levels of such benefits have not been rising, and in some countries have been falling in real (inflation-adjusted) terms.

One Keynesian explanation of high European unemployment is that these countries have simply followed overly restrictive aggregate demand policies after being frightened by the inflation of the 1970s. If this were true, the remedy would be simple—move to more expansionary monetary and fiscal policies. On the other hand, if inadequate demand is not the cause of the high unemployment, European governments fear that a move to expansionary policies may rekindle inflation. The proper way to deal with what for many countries are record post–World War II levels of unemployment is the key economic policy issue in Europe in the late 1980s.

D

Future Employment Trends?

It is possible, however, to end our discussion of the higher unemployment rates of the 1970s and 1980s on a note of *cautious* optimism. By mid-1988 the unemployment rate had fallen to 5.5 percent, a 14 year low (though still above average rates for the 1950s and 1960s). This drop reflected steady employment growth over a period of more than 5 years. Also, as noted above, the demographic factors that increased frictional unemployment in the 1970s and 1980s will be unimportant by 1990. There is then reason for optimism with regard to the future trend in the U.S. unemployment rate.

There are, however, reasons for caution in taking this view. Maintaining a relatively low unemployment rate will require avoidance of recession. Will the economy be able to continue the long expansion that began in 1983? Related to this is a point concerning the nature of many of the new jobs created in the 1980s. Relative to earlier decades, more new jobs in the 1980s were part-time jobs and more were with small newly created

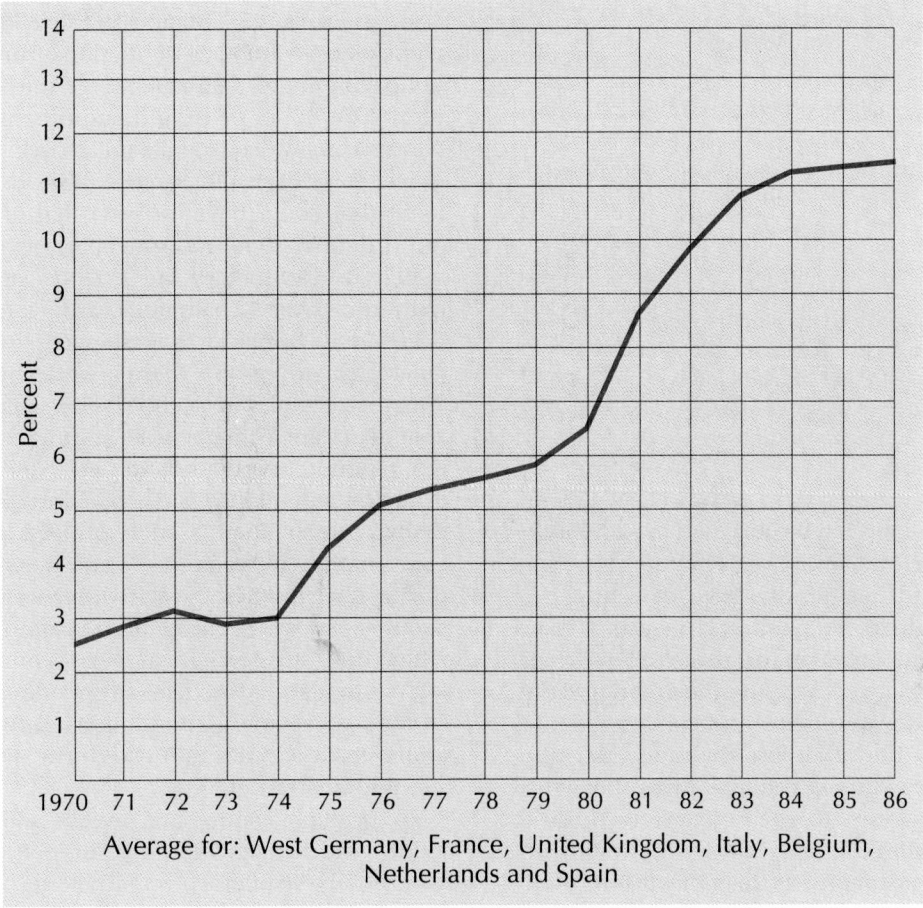

Average for: West Germany, France, United Kingdom, Italy, Belgium, Netherlands and Spain

FIGURE 20.4 *Average Unemployment Rate for Seven European Countries*

firms. There is the fear that these jobs may be particularly vulnerable should a recession occur. Finally, it should be noted that Europe has not generally shared the improving unemployment performance. Unemployment, while still very high, has declined in some countries (e.g. United Kingdom), but continues on the rise in others (e.g. Italy).

IV

The Policy Response

In the summer of 1979, amid double-digit inflation and slackening economic growth, President Carter went up to Camp David and called in numerous advisors from his and former administrations. He came down from the mountains and announced that America was suffering from a *malaise.*

Especially after the continuous growth of the 1960s, the economic performance of the 1970s was disappointing. In 1980 the electorate decided to try another tack and elected Ronald Reagan. Reagan's platform contained a number of ideas that had been advocated by the *supply-side economists.* The policies that grew out of their ideas—which became known as *Reaganomics*—were aimed at reversing the growth and productivity slowdown and at generating more employment to reverse the rising trend in unemployment. In this section, we will look at the elements and criticisms of the macroeconomic side of Reaganomics.

A

Reaganomics

The rationale for the Reagan administration's supply-side policies was touched on in Chapter 19. In

President Reagan's words:

> *The Federal government cannot provide prosperity or generate economic growth; it can only encourage private initiative, innovation, and entrepreneurial activity that produces economic opportunities.*

Moreover,

> *An overly active government actually hinders economic progress. Federal spending absorbs resources, many of which could be better used by the private sector. Excessive taxation distorts relative prices and relative rates of return.*

With this view, the way to go was clear. Government regulation was to be curtailed to avoid interfering with private initiative. Tax rates for both individuals and business were to be reduced to increase incentives to work and invest. The tax rates that are important in this regard are *marginal* tax rates. These are tax rates on the additional dollar earned by corporations or individuals (tax rates at the margin), and therefore the rates that influence incentives. Among the incentives that President Reagan wanted to encourage were those to save and invest, so a number of additional programs were designed with this objective in mind.

Further, government spending should be reduced to free resources for use in the private sector. An exception, however, was defense spending, which the Reagan administration believed needed to be increased substantially for national security.

B
First-Term Legislation

Although no President's program is enacted in its entirety, a large portion of President Reagan's economic program did become law during his first term in office. Individual tax rates were reduced in three stages by a total of 23 percent. The top tax bracket for nonlabor income (e.g., interest earnings or rental income) was lowered from 70 to 50 percent.

The first Reagan administration's tax legislation also had several features to encourage business investment in plant and equipment. The most important of these was the *accelerated cost recovery system (ACRS)*. Businesses take depreciation allowances, which are deductions from corporate tax payments to take account of the wearing out (depreciation) of plant and equipment. The ACRS allowed businesses to take these deductions more quickly. For example, a piece of industrial equipment that could have been written off (its whole value deducted for tax purposes) over approximately 9 years before the 1981 tax act could be written off over 5 years afterward.

President Reagan was less successful in cutting federal spending and therefore freeing resources for use in the private sector. In some areas, he was able to cut spending or at least reduce the growth in spending. In real (inflation-adjusted) terms, for example, federal grants to state and local governments, which finance such projects as housing construction, water projects, and mass transit, fell during Reagan's first term. In other areas, however, such as Social Security and veterans' benefits, which have strong political constituencies, spending was not cut. Also, defense spending increased. Overall, government spending as a proportion of total output was not reduced during the first Reagan administration.

To protect against an "overly active government," the Reagan administration tried to curb government regulatory activity in several sectors. Expenditures by regulatory agencies such as the Environmental Protection Agency (EPA) and the Occupational Safety and Health Administration (OSHA) were trimmed. An attempt was made to abolish the departments of Energy and Education (but Congress would not agree). The energy and communications industries were deregulated. Airline and financial market deregulation, which had begun during the Carter administration, was continued.

C
The Second Term

On the spending side, the second Reagan administration continued the policy of the first with attempts to increase defense expenditures and reduce nondefense expenditures. As in the first term, many politically popular domestic programs proved impossible to cut. Moreover, as huge deficits continued, Congress became reluctant to increase defense spending substantially.

On the tax side, the centerpiece was _tax reform_—touted by President Reagan as a "second American Revolution." The aims of tax reform were, first, to broaden the tax _base_ by eliminating many deductible items and, second, to reduce _marginal tax rates_. The combination of these actions was to be offsetting, so that total revenues would neither rise nor fall. Lower marginal tax rates would, however, improve incentives for labor supply, saving, and investment. According to the supply-side view, this would significantly increase growth in output and labor productivity.

Congress passed a tax reform act in August 1986 that reflected not only the President's wishes but also the goals of tax reformers in Congress from both political parties. The act lowered the highest tax rate from 50 percent to 28 percent—the lowest top rate since 1931. Moreover, it created only two tax rates, 15 percent (on income up to approximately $30,000 on a joint return) and 28 percent.[5] The act also raised personal exemptions so that approximately 6 million low-income recipients were removed from the tax rolls. To keep tax reform from reducing tax revenues, the act removed many deductions and eliminated a number of tax shelters. It also increased corporate income tax payments.

D

Critics of Reaganomics

Reaganomics was a sharp departure from previous economic policies, which were primarily based on Keynesian principles. Not surprisingly, the most vocal critics of Reaganomics have been Keynesian economists (although, as we saw in Chapter 19, monetarists and new classical economists were also critical of the Reagan administration's fiscal policies). The focus of President Reagan and the supply-side economists (whose ideas were embodied in the novel features of his program) was, of course, on the supply side. Keynesian economists do not ignore the supply side and the need to provide incentives for the private sector, but they have been critical of Reaganomics for

focusing exclusively on supply and neglecting _aggregate demand_. They have also been critical of the programs by which the Reagan administration sought to stimulate the supply side.

We have already examined one criticism that Keynesian economists had of the Reagan program. They objected to the _policy mix_ over the first 5 years of the Reagan presidency, which in practice was an expansionary fiscal policy, with a resulting large structural budget deficit coupled with a relatively restrictive monetary policy. They criticized this policy mix because it discouraged investment (via generally high interest rates) and exports (via a high value of the dollar, relative to foreign currencies, over much of this period).

Concentrating only on fiscal policy, Keynesians did not believe that cuts in marginal income tax rates would have much effect on labor supply and therefore on economic growth, as the supply-siders argued. Keynesians simply did not believe that workers' decisions on whether to enter the labor force or how much to work were influenced very much by tax rates. Moreover, they pointed out that the growth slowdown was not caused by slower growth in the labor force.

Keynesian economists were not opposed to tax cuts to stimulate saving and investment. In fact, the idea of an investment tax credit, where a certain fraction of investment expenditure can be used as a credit against corporate income taxes, originated with President Kennedy's Keynesian advisors in the early 1960s. Keynesians did, however, question the effectiveness of some of the specific measures to improve the incentives for saving and investment. In any case, they believed that higher saving and investment would affect output growth only over a long-run horizon, and they rejected the rosy predictions that supply-siders made for the economy during President Reagan's first term.

Fundamentally, the Reagan administration's fiscal policy, with its concentration on tax cuts _and_ reductions in government spending, did not make sense to the Keynesians. They saw fiscal policy effects primarily from the aggregate demand side. The tax cuts could stimulate demand, but the spending cuts would curtail demand. On balance, they believed that the program would be _neutral_ in effect and would not stimulate economic growth.

[5]There was, in effect, a third marginal rate of 33 percent on incomes between $43,000 and $90,000 due to a phase-out of the benefits of personal exemptions over this income range.

E

The Record to Date

Who was correct—the supply-side economists, whose ideas inspired much of Reaganomics, or Keynesian (and other) critics of the program? It seems clear that Reagan administration officials promised too much. According to administration public forecasts in 1981, inflation was supposed to decline without a recession. Growth in real GNP in 1982, for example, was forecast to be 4.2 percent; actual growth turned out to be _minus_ 2.5 percent. The federal budget was supposed to be balanced by 1985; the actual budget deficit was just short of $200 billion in that year.

But the fact that Reaganomics was oversold at its inception does not mean that the program was a failure. Nor was the Reagan administration unique in promising more than could be achieved. Perhaps the question to be asked is whether the program produced better results than plausible alternatives—for example, the policies of a second Carter–Mondale administration. Since we can't observe the economy under any alternative programs for these years, we fall back on a comparison of the performance of the economy under the first 7 years of the Reagan administration (1981–87) to that of the actual Carter administration (1977–80). Keep in mind, however, that factors other than each President's policies influenced the behavior of the economy during each of these periods.

Table 20.4 compares various aspects of economic performance in the two administrations. Looking at the first five rows of the table, which focus on real growth in the economy and the related measure of productivity growth, unemployment, saving, and investment, it is striking how little change there has been. Output growth, saving, and investment have behaved virtually the same in the two periods. The growth in labor productivity during the Reagan years has exceeded that in the Carter years but is still quite low compared to the U.S.

TABLE 20.4 The Carter and Reagan Years, Various Statistics

	Carter Administration (1977–80)	Reagan Administration (1981–87)
1. Output growth (percent)	3.1	2.7
2. Productivity growth (percent)	0.3	1.5
3. Unemployment rate (percent)	6.4	7.8
4. Saving rate (percent of GNP)	6.9	5.5
5. Investment (percent of GNP)	11.6	10.9
6. Government spending (percent of GNP)	21.5	24.1
7. Taxes (percent of GNP)	19.9	19.8
8. Budget deficit (percent of GNP)	1.6	4.2
9. Inflation rate (percent)	9.8	4.7
10. Money wage growth (percent)	8.2	4.6

experience since World War II. Unemployment has been somewhat higher on average during the Reagan administration.

Turning to the government budget in lines 6–8 of the table, we see that, as noted previously, the Reagan administration has failed to cut government spending (as a percent of GNP). Cuts in nondefense spending have been insufficient to finance the defense buildup, and spending actually rose from 21.5 to 24.1 percent of GNP. Taxes fell very slightly as a percent of GNP. The income tax cuts of 1981 were nearly balanced by later increases in payroll taxes and the reversal of some business tax cuts in 1982. With spending rising and taxes falling slightly as fractions of GNP, the budget deficit rose from 1.6 percent of GNP during the Carter years to 4.2 percent during the Reagan years.

It is in the last two rows that a sharp contrast between the two periods emerges. The inflation rate and the rate of increase in wages both fell sharply over the first half of the 1980s. Even supporters of Reaganomics, however, would attribute much of the disinflation of the early 1980s to restrictive Federal Reserve monetary policy rather than to supply-side fiscal policies.

Overall the data in Table 20.4 do not show that Reaganomics has reversed the U.S. growth slowdown. Supporters of President Reagan's supply-side approach argue that his programs have provided a noninflationary climate that will ultimately lead to faster economic growth. Moreover, they point out that the economic recovery that began in the last quarter of 1982 is the longest continuous peace time expansion for the U.S. economy in the post-World War II period.

SUMMARY

1. Growth in real output and labor productivity slowed markedly after 1973. Slower growth was accompanied by an upward trend in unemployment.

2. To see why the U.S. growth rate has fallen, we first examined the sources of economic growth. Key among these are growth in the quantity of the labor input and several other factors that cause labor productivity to grow: improvements in education per worker, capital formation, technological change, and economies of scale.

3. The factors that cause labor productivity to grow are the key ones to examine for an explanation of the U.S. growth slowdown. Changes in the growth rates in the quality of labor, the rate and mix of capital formation, and cyclical factors (more recessions) can explain perhaps half of the drop in productivity growth and, consequently, output growth. The rest may be due to a decline in the rate of technological change, which is difficult to measure, or to other factors we have not taken into account.

4. Higher unemployment after 1973 was in part the result of slower output growth. Changes in the age–sex composition of the labor force, primarily the high number of new workers that had to be absorbed into the work force, also contributed to rising unemployment. In addition, some blame growing government transfer payment programs and others growing structural unemployment for the upward trend in the unemployment rate.

5. The policy response to the growth slowdown was Reaganomics, a series of tax cuts and tax reforms aimed at reducing marginal tax rates and improving economic incentives for both individuals and corporations. Reductions in government regulation of business and reductions in nondefense government spending were other elements of the program. Examination of the record to date does not indicate that Reaganomics has reversed the U.S. growth slowdown, though a substantial disinflation was accomplished over the first half of the 1980s.

IV
Micro Product Markets

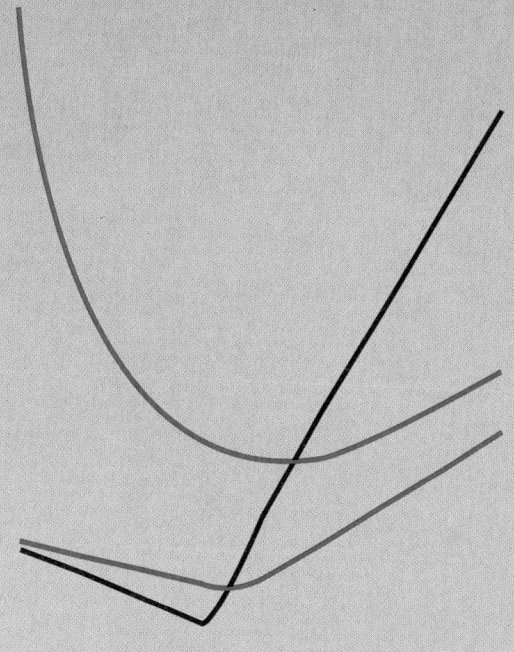

21

Consumer Choice

It's called *BehaviorScan*. Seven supermarkets in Marion, Indiana, have computerized scanners that record every grocery purchase of 2,500 families. Moreover, whenever these families watch their TVs, microcomputers record every program and every advertisement. The marketing researchers who run BehaviorScan can therefore study in detail the sales influence of TV advertising. Researchers can even conduct controlled experiments, cutting into TV broadcasts to replace regular commercials with test commercials, then monitoring the buying behavior of those families exposed to the test commercials. BehaviorScan thus seems to invade the privacy of human guinea pigs. But the voluntary cooperation of these Indiana families, and over 12,000 others, is bought by offerings of merchandise and prizes. This expensive research is paid for by firms with a keen interest in understanding consumer behavior—namely, those who manufacture supermarket products, like Campbell Soup, General Foods, Procter & Gamble, and Ralston Purina.[1]

Economists are likewise interested in consumer behavior. This chapter covers basic economic views of consumer behavior, with a special focus on individual and marketwide demand curves. Individual demand curves are those of individual consumers or families. Each curve shows the amounts of a good that the *individual* will buy at various possible prices during some time period. When these individual demands for some good are added together, they create a marketwide demand curve. This shows the marketwide quantities of a good that will be bought at various possible prices.

Of course, individual demands differ immensely. Some people adore cheeseburgers. Others prize pizza. Some spend heavily on phonograph records, while others attend countless movies. Much the same could be said of marketwide demands. The marketwide demand for strawberries differs from that of autos. Of necessity, then, the main messages in this chapter are sweeping

generalizations. One important generalization is that quantity and price are inversely related. That is, the individual demand curves slope downward. Marketwide demand curves also slope downward because they represent collections of individual demands.

I
Actual Consumption Patterns

A sweeping scan of consumer behavior, more sweeping than that of BehaviorScan, is a good place to start. There are nearly 85 million households in the United States. During the early 1980s, median income per household was just over $20,000 annually. Taxes and saving bit into this income, so not all of it could be spent on consumption. That which was spent on consumption financed the purchase of tens of thousands of goods and services (hereafter, simply goods). Broad classes of these expenditures, each as a percentage of total consumer expenditures, are shown in Figure 21.1 for 1984. Food and drink accounted for 18.9 percent of all consumer spending. Housing, which includes household furniture and equipment, took another big share—24.0 percent. Nourishment and shelter thus seem to be most important, followed by transportation, medical care, and apparel.

Figure 21.1 also shows changes in the composition of U.S. consumer spending over time. Today, as just indicated, food and drink take a large chunk of our household budgets—roughly 19%. But in the past they accounted for a lot more: 28 percent in 1960 and 40 percent in 1935. In 1900 *over half* of all spending went for nutrition. (Retreating still further to 1800 and shifting to Berlin, Germany, we find that a mason's family of five spent 73 percent of its budget on food and drink, with 44 percent for bread alone.[2])

---

[1] *Wall Street Journal*, September 25, 1981, p. 29; *Fortune*, July 25, 1983, p.72.

[2] Fernand Braudel, *Capitalism and Material Life 1400–1800* (New York: Harper & Row, 1975), p.90.

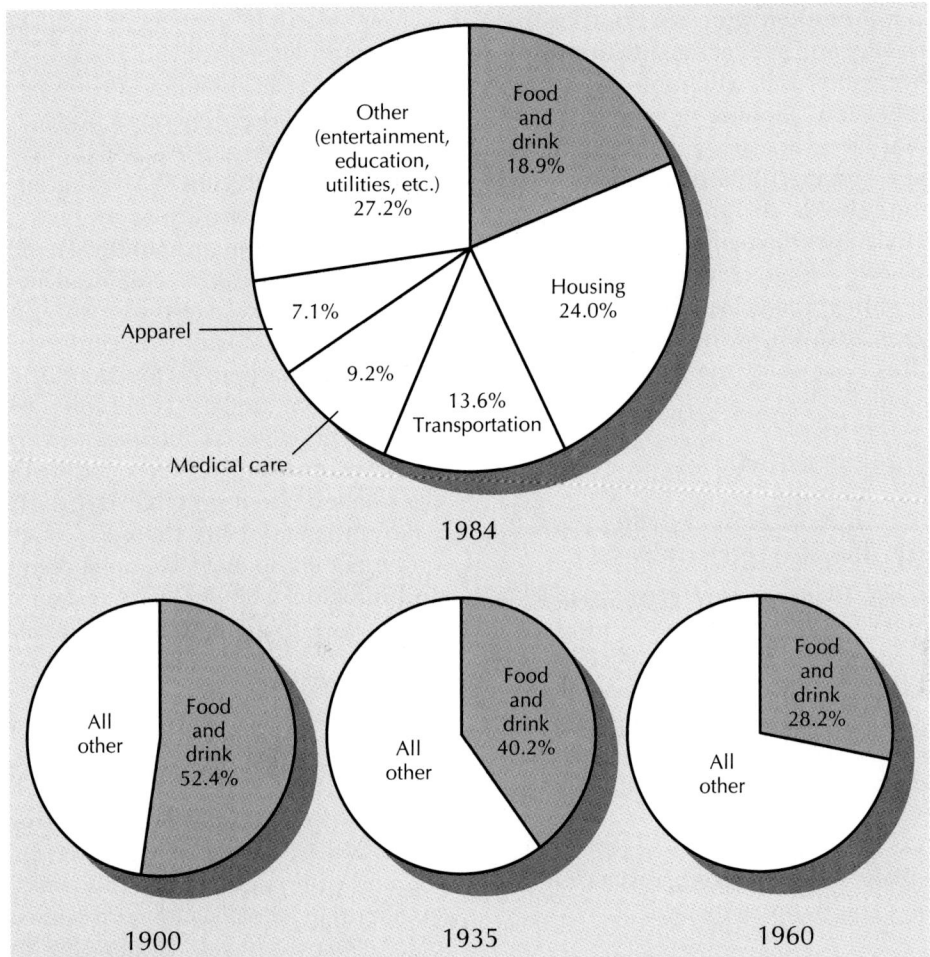

FIGURE 21.1 _The Composition of Consumer Expenditures, United States, 1900–84_
(_Sources:_ Handbook of Labor Statistics 1975—Reference Edition, _p. 362;_ Statistical Abstract of the United States 1986, _pp. 97, 435._)

The main explanation for these remarkable changes in the composition of consumption is the ballooning real income that economic growth has given us. Food and drink are bare necessities. Our preindustrial economy of over a century ago could do little more than provide incomes and outputs that just met the basic biological needs of most Americans. Food and drink were very expensive relative to household earnings. A typical day's wage bought relatively little bread, so a large fraction of a day's wage was spent on bread simply to stay alive. Now a typical day's wage can buy much more bread, but much more bread is not needed for survival. Much more bread is likewise not very satisfying in comparison to the books, phono-

graph records, telephone calls, and the many other items that today's higher household income can buy. Hence bread is still bought, and household _dollar_ spending on food and drink is greater than what it was 100 years ago, but the _fraction_ of spending accounted for by these basics has fallen.

Consumer expenditures also change for other reasons. Demographics change. As the percentage of the population over age 65 rises, demand for medical care rises. Tastes likewise change. Sales of cigarettes are falling, while sales of exercise equipment are skyrocketing.

Despite all the changes and individual differences, systematic patterns do emerge. Consumer spending is not a random process. Priorities for necessities like food and shelter emerge from their behavior. Other goods gain attention as income and price levels allow. Probing more deeply, we confront several basic questions: How are these consumer choices made? How do consumers, be they family households or individuals on their own, allocate their spending among broad classes of goods (like food versus clothing) and among specific goods within broad classes (like hamburgers versus pizza)? Answers to these questions are found in the theory of utility maximization.

II

Utility Maximization: An Economic Theory Of Rational Choice

The theory of utility maximization dates back to the time when over half of all consumer expenditures were for food. _Utility_ has a simple definition:

Utility is the satisfaction people feel as a result of consuming goods and services.

The theory of utility maximization would explain Figure 21.1 by referring to an _objective, a constraint, and a decision rule._

1. _Objective:_ Everyone tries to get the most out of his or her budget. That is, they try to maximize the overall utility (or satisfaction) derived from their consumption spending.
2. _Constraint:_ Because budgets are limited, those maximums are likewise limited. Consumption spending is limited by one's income relative to the prices one must pay for goods.
3. _Decision rule:_ Given that budget dollars are scarce, they will be spent in an orderly fashion. The first dollar spent will boost one's utility by the greatest amount possible. The next dollar spent will boost utility by the next greatest amount possible. And

so on, until all budget dollars are spent. Getting the most utility out of each added dollar spent results in the highest overall utility allowed by one's budget.

Looking back to Figure 21.1, we could say that consumers' first dollars are spent on food and drink because of the immense utility they bestow—they support life. Moving beyond these first dollars, and consequently moving beyond eating as a necessity into the realm of eating as gluttony, the utility of further dollars spent on food and drink falls below the utility of dollars spent on other desirable things. Therefore, as incomes (and budgets) rise, the fraction spent on food and drink falls, while the fraction spent on other things rises.

To understand the theory of utility maximization more completely, we must define total utility and marginal utility, clearly restate the objective, underscore the constraint, and explain the decision rule.

A

Total and Marginal Utility

You feel nourished by a wholesome meal, refreshed by a cold drink, comforted by warm clothing, and entertained by a rock concert. In brief, you obtain utility or satisfaction from the consumption of goods and services. Utility cannot be quantitatively measured because it is subjective and personal. BehaviorScan might record that the Smith family of Marion, Indiana, bought three bottles of Heinz ketchup during the month of August 1986, but BehaviorScan cannot record the amount of utility the Smiths may have enjoyed from the ketchup. Fortunately for economics, exact measurement of utility is not necessary to a theory of consumer choice that centers on utility maximization. Still, to _explain_ such a theory at this introductory level, it is convenient to _assume_ that utility _can_ be measured by units of utility—call them _utils_. We might imagine, for instance, that those three bottles of ketchup gave the Smith family 17 utils of utility during the month of August. Similarly, all their August purchases might have given them 9,211 utils of utility.

It is important to distinguish between _total_ utility and _marginal_ utility, a distinction best explained by an example. Imagine, if you will, that the utility data of Table 21.1 are your own. When graphed, your data would look like Figure 21.2. According to these data, the *total* utility you would get from eating one pizza per week would be 6 utils. The *total* utility you would get from eating three pizzas per week would be 12 utils. In other words, total utility is a measure of the *overall* satisfaction you gain by eating a certain number of pizzas per week.

> The **total utility** of a good is the overall, entire satisfaction one derives from consuming that good.

In contrast, *marginal* utility measures the *additional* satisfaction you get from an *additional* pizza per week. The first pizza brings you 6 added utils of utility over and above what you would get from no pizza, which would be 0 utils. A second pizza adds 4 utils of utility. A third pizza adds 2 utils. A fourth pizza adds 1 util. Finally, a fifth pizza would add no further satisfaction at all. Notice the con-

trast at this point: five pizzas per week yield a *total* utility of 13 utils but zero *marginal* utility. After four pizzas per week, you've had your fill. (After five pizzas, you might even begin to experience

TABLE 21.1 Total Utility and Marginal Utility Derived from Your Consumption of Various Numbers of Pizzas Per Week*

Number of Pizzas	Total Utility (in Utils)	Marginal Utility (in Utils)
0	0	—
1st	6	6 (= 6 − 0)
2nd	10	4 (= 10 − 6)
3rd	12	2 (= 12 − 10)
4th	13	1 (= 13 − 12)
5th	13	0 (= 13 − 13)

*This table illustrates total and marginal utility. Total utility rises with added consumption of pizzas. Marginal utility, which is the added utility from each added pizza, falls because of the law of diminishing marginal utility.

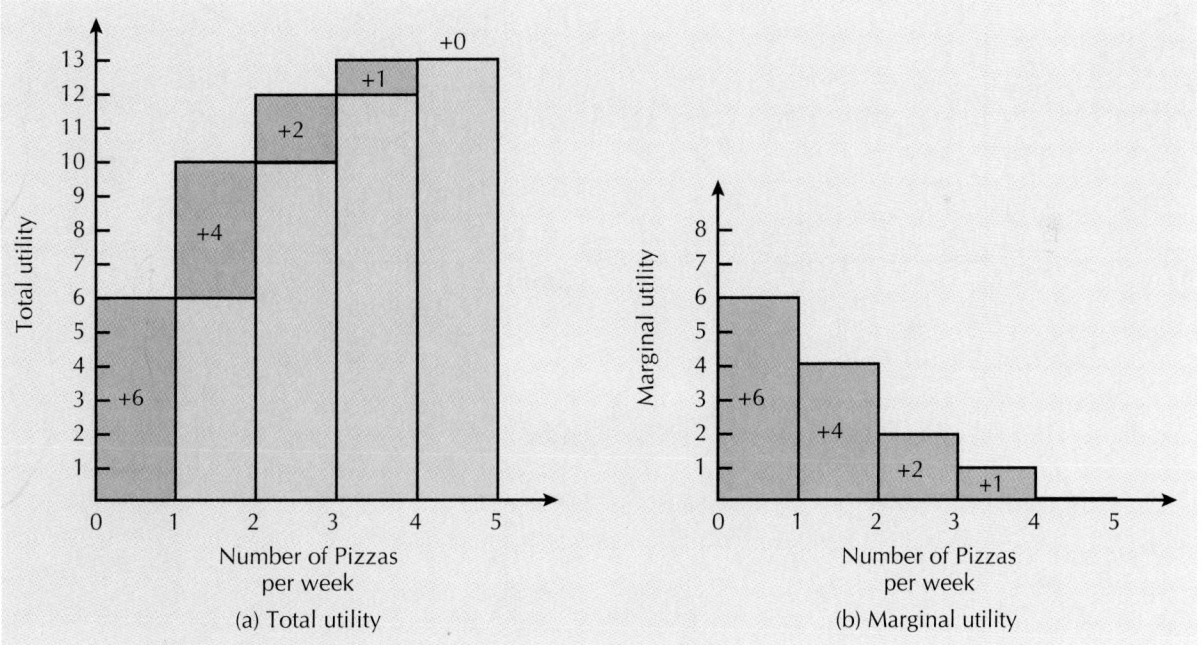

FIGURE 21.2 *Total and Marginal Utility from Pizza, Per Week (Data from Table 21.1)*

In part (a), total utility rises with added consumption of pizza, so that the total utility derived from four pizzas per week is 13 utils. Total utility rises at a decreasing rate, so, in part (b), marginal utility falls. The first pizza gave 6 utils, the second 4 utils, the third 2 utils, and so on.

negative marginal utility, which would imply a falling, though still positive, total utility. The *disutility* beyond five might be due to a weight problem that causes you worry and discomfort). Note also that the *sum* of the marginal utilities, or the *area* under the marginal utility curve, matches the total utility at some given number of pizzas. The sum of marginal utilities for three pizzas in Figure 21.2(b) is 6 + 4 + 2 = 12, which corresponds to the height of the total utility curve in Figure 21.2(a), as read off the vertical axis.

> The **marginal utility** of a good is the additional satisfaction a consumer derives from consuming one additional unit of that good.

Our example shows the marginal utility of pizza falling. This is typical. The first several units consumed of some commodity typically give greater satisfaction than later units of the same commodity. If a baseball star owns several dozen cars, the

marginal utility he gets from his first car is undoubtedly greater than the marginal utility he gets from his last one. Economists have generalized this common experience into the *law of diminishing marginal utility*.

> The **law of diminishing marginal utility** states that, as a person consumes more and more of a given commodity, the marginal utility of the commodity eventually declines.

This does not say that all people exerience the same marginal utilities. It merely says that a consumer's marginal utility will eventually fall. Figure 21.3 presents several hypothetical marginal utility curves to illustrate this point, curves that have been smoothed out. Each refers to an individual's consumption of hamburgers per week, and each is downward sloping in accord with the law of diminishing marginal utility, yet each is quite different from the others because of different tastes

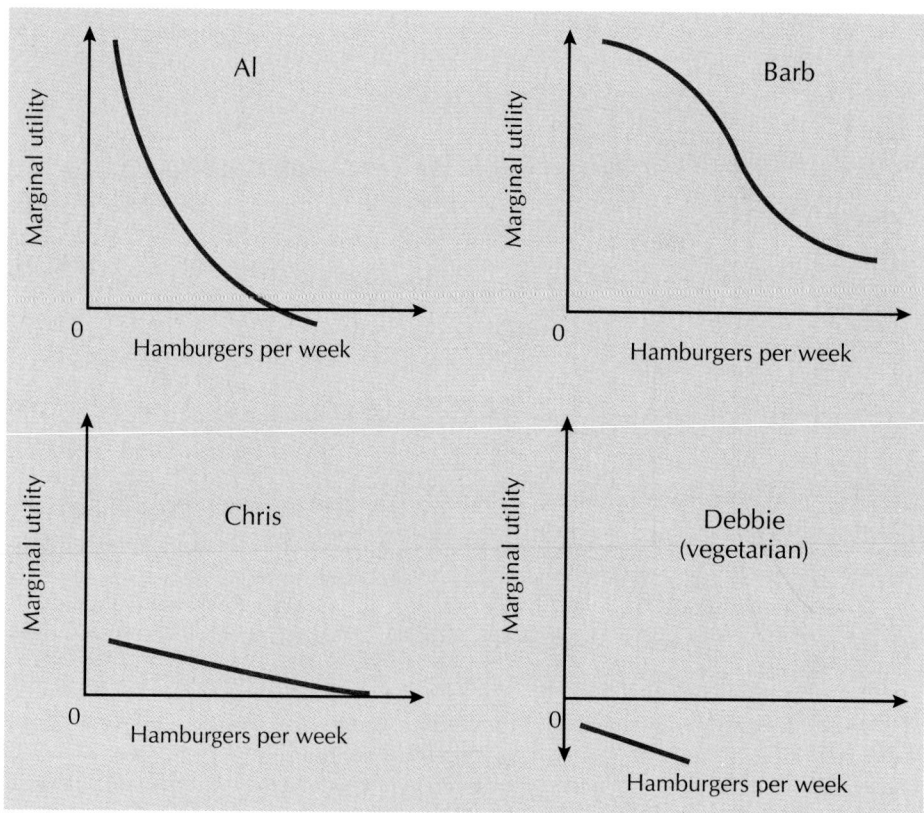

FIGURE 21.3 *Different Illustrative Marginal Utility Curves for Hamburgers Per Week (Hypothetical)*

or preferences. The most distinctive marginal utility curve is that of Debbie, who experiences disutility from her very first hamburger because she is a vegetarian.

B
Consumer Objective

As stated previously, the objective of consumers is to get the most satisfaction out of whatever budget they have. The objective is *not* to get the highest total utility out of pizza, or hamburger, or water. It is, rather, *to obtain the highest total utility possible from one's total dollar spending*.

To appreciate this objective, you must realize that dollar spending acquires goods, and that those goods, as we have seen, generate utility. Accordingly, we can speak of the total utility and marginal utility that derive from the *dollars* in a consumer's weekly or yearly budget, just as we earlier referred to the total utility and marginal utility that you might get from eating pizzas. Those *dollars* buy pizza and other desirable things.

The **total utility** of a consumer's budget is the overall, entire satisfaction derived from that budget. The **marginal utility** of a budget dollar is the additional satisfaction a consumer derives from spending one additional dollar.

Figure 21.4 illustrates these concepts using $100 increments in a consumer's weekly budget (the $100 increments being most convenient pictorially, even though $1 increments would be most accurate definitionally). As the weekly budget rises from $100 to $200 to $300 and so on, total utility rises at a decreasing rate and marginal utility falls. The objective, then, is to move up the total utility scale as high as possible, as indicated by the arrow in Figure 21.4(a). Stated differently, the objective is to move out the marginal utility function in Figure 21.4(b) as far as possible, spending one's dollars in such an order so as to obtain the greatest marginal utility per dollar at first, followed by lower levels of marginal utility per dollar. Necessities like food and drink will receive priority over luxuries like diamonds. The idea is similar to what a manager of a baseball team has in mind when he puts his best hitters first in the batting order and his weakest hitters last. That way, the best hitters will make the most plate appearances during the nine innings "budgeted."

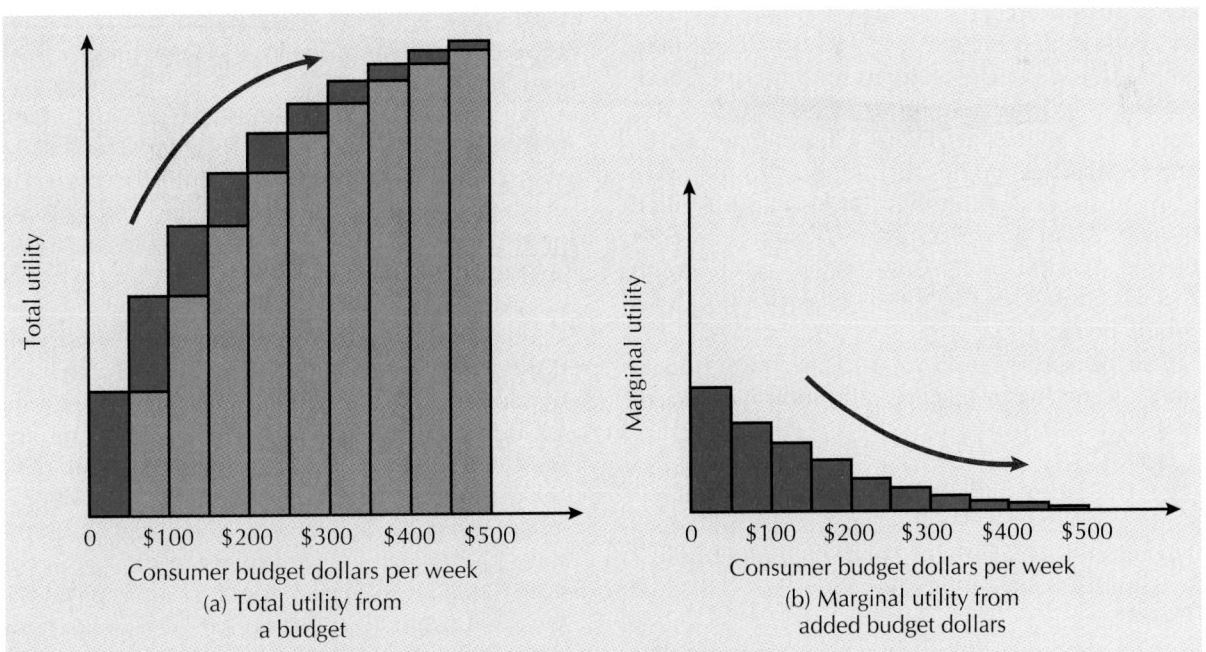

FIGURE 21.4   Total and Marginal Utility from Consumer Spending

C
Budget Constraint

Alas, as we all know too well, this maximization of total budget utility is subject to a budget constraint. The hypothetical consumer depicted in Figure 21.4 cannot climb to ever greater heights of total utility indefinitely. If that consumer's budget is limited to $300 per week, then the highest level of total utility achievable is that level associated with $300 per week in part (a). Similarly, the marginal utility associated with a budget of $300 per week is that level in the ordering of marginal utilities associated with $300 per week. At higher budget levels, say $400, total utility would be higher.

D
Decision Rule: Commodity Specific

Thus far, we have seen the total and marginal utility derived from specific commodities, such as pizza. We have also observed the total and marginal utility embedded in budget dollars, assuming those dollars are spent rationally, so as to maximize total budget utility. The next step is to connect utility as it applies to quantities of *specific commodities* with utility as it applies to *dollar spending*. We now know that dollar spending should be ordered, so that marginal utility per dollar spent is highest at first, followed by lower marginal utilities per dollar spent until the total budget is gone. This is a good decision rule. But it needs to be translated into a form that can be applied to commodities themselves. Given that we want to maximize the total utility in our limited budget, when do we stop buying pizza and start buying hamburgers? How many phonograph records should we buy versus books versus shoes versus pens?

The decision rule for maximizing total budget utility at the level of specific commodity purchases is· this:

> **Maximum satisfaction** requires that the marginal utility per extra dollar spent on any good be the same as the marginal utility per extra dollar on every other good.

More concretely, the marginal utility per dollar spent on hamburger must equal the marginal utility per dollar spent on soda pop, on shoes, and on every other item in the budget. What is the marginal utility per dollar spent on, say, hamburgers? It is the marginal utility of an additional hamburger divided by the price of the hamburger, namely, *MU/P*.

For example, if the marginal utility of an added hamburger is 16 utils and the price is $2, then the marginal utility of an extra dollar spent on hamburgers is 16/2 = 8. An extra dollar of spending on hamburgers adds 8 utils. Now we can see clearly where *prices* come into the story, along with utilities (preferences) and budgets (incomes). Moreover, we can now restate the decision rule in more technical terms:

> **Maximum satisfaction** requires that the consumer allocates spending on goods such that
>
> $$\frac{\text{Marginal utility of good 1}}{\text{Price of good 1}} = \frac{\text{marginal utility of good 2}}{\text{price of good 2}} =$$
>
> $$\frac{\text{marginal utility of good 3}}{\text{price of good 3}} = ... = \frac{\text{marginal utility of good } z}{\text{price of good } z}$$

Once this condition is reached, **consumer equilibrium** is achieved. Satisfaction cannot be improved by spending less on one good and more on another.

We thus have two related decision rules. First, budget dollars should be spent in declining order of marginal utility per dollar until the budget is exhausted (from Figure 21.4). Second, the consumer should equalize the marginal utility of dollars spent on different goods (from the previous discussion).

Tables 21.2 and 21.3 show that these rules yield the *same* result. We simplify by assuming that our hypothetical consumer, Sawyer, has a hankering for only two goods—milkshakes and hamburgers—and has a budget of only $11. With milkshakes priced at $1 each, the marginal utility *per dollar spent* on milkshakes in column (3) is the same as the marginal utility per milkshake in column (2). For example, the first milkshake has $MU_M = 12$ and $P_M = \$1$, so $MU_M/P_M = 12$. Hamburgers, on the other hand, are priced at $2 each, so marginal utility *per dollar spent* on hamburgers

TABLE 21.2   Sawyer's Hypothetical Data for Utility Maximization with Two Goods and a Budget of $11

Milkshakes: Price = $1			Hamburgers: Price = $2		
Unit of Good (1)	Marginal Utility, Utils, MU_M (2)	Marginal Utility Per Dollar, MU_M/P_M (3)	Unit of Good (4)	Marginal Utility, Utils, MU_H (5)	Marginal Utility Per Dollar, MU_H/P_H (6)
1st	12	12	1st	26	13
2nd	10	10	2nd	22	11
3rd	8	8	3rd	18	9
4th	6	6	4th	16	8
5th	5	5	5th	12	6
6th	4	4	6th	10	5

TABLE 21.3   Sawyer's Steps to Achieve Maximum Satisfaction (Consumer Equilibrium) with Data of Table 21.2

Step	Choices	Decision (Highest MU/P)	Budget Remaining
1st purchase	1st milkshake: $MU_M/P_M = 12$ 1st hamburger: $MU_H/P_H = 13$	Buy 1st hamburger	$11 − $2 = $9
2nd purchase	1st milkshake: $MU_M/P_M = 12$ 2nd hamburger: $MU_H/P_H = 11$	Buy 1st milkshake	$9 − $1 = $8
3rd purchase	2nd milkshake: $MU_M/P_M = 10$ 2nd hamburger: $MU_H/P_H = 11$	Buy 2nd hamburger	$8 − $2 = $6
4th purchase	2nd milkshake: $MU_M/P_M = 10$ 3rd hamburger: $MU_H/P_H = 8$	Buy 2nd milkshake	$6 − $1 = $5
5th purchase	3rd milkshake: $MU_M/P_M = 8$ 3rd hamburger: $MU_H/P_H = 9$	Buy 3rd hamburger	$5 − $2 = $3
6th and 7th purchases	3rd milkshake: $MU_M/P_M = 8$ 4th hamburger: $MU_H/P_H = 8$	Buy both	$3 − $3 = 0

in column (6) is obtained by dividing the marginal utilities of hamburger in column (5) by the price of $2. Thus it is the comparison of columns (3) and (6) in Table 21.2 that really counts for Sawyer, because they report her marginal utility *per dollar spent* on these two commodities.

Table 21.3 shows the decision steps Sawyer takes in light of these data. Following the rule that money should first be spent to obtain the highest marginal utility per dollar, followed thereafter by lower marginal utilities per dollar, she first spends $2 on a hamburger ($MU$ per dollar = $MU_H/P_H = 13$). She next spends $1 on a milkshake ($MU$ per dollar = $MU_M/P_M = 12$), and so on, until her budget of $11 is gone. Sawyer's budget is exhausted at the point of purchasing three milk-

shakes ($3) and four hamburgers ($8). Moreover, it may be noted from Table 21.2 that at this point $MU_M/P_M = MU_H/P_H$, which meets the decision rule for specific commodity spending.

The resulting consumer equilibrium can also be understood in terms of two-question logic, i.e., by considering benefits and costs. Starting from this situation of three milkshakes and four hamburgers, we can consider the consequences of Sawyer's buying one more hamburger, a move that would force her to stop buying two milkshakes because of the budget constraint ($11) and the prices ($P_M = $1, P_H = 2).

Question 1: What are the benefits of a fifth hamburger? *Answer*: 12 additional utils (6 utils per dollar spent)

Question 2: What does it cost to get that fifth hamburger? *Answer:* 18 utils (8 from loss of the third milkshake and 10 from loss of the second milkshake)

Comparing the 12 utils gained to the 18 utils lost, it's obvious that two-question logic says, "No, Sawyer, don't buy a fifth burger at the expense of two shakes." A "no" would also result from considering the purchase of more milkshakes and fewer hamburgers. Given these data, Sawyer is thus at equilibrium with three shakes and four burgers.

■ CHECK YOUR BEARINGS

We have scanned the composition of consumer spending back to 1900. To explain patterns of consumer behavior, economists theorize that consumers maximize the total satisfaction, or *utility*, allowed by their limited budgets and observed prices. To meet this objective while coping with the rude constraints of reality, consumers follow two decision rules that, in the end, yield the same results. The first rule is simple: Consumers order their spending, beginning with purchases yielding the highest marginal utility per dollar, followed by ever lower marginal utilities per dollar until the money runs out. The second rule is more com-

plex, but it refers to specific goods and explicitly introduces prices: The marginal utility per dollar spent on good A should equal that of good B and all other goods. That is, $MU_A/P_A = MU_B/P_B = MU_C/P_C = \ldots$ and so on. From this foundation, we can derive individual and marketwide demand curves.

Read Perspective 21A.

III

Individual Demand Curves

A

Derivation and Pattern

Individual demand reflects the quantities a person would buy at various possible prices. Returning to the data of Table 21.2, we can calculate how many milkshakes Sawyer would buy at various possible prices.

We already know that she will buy three milkshakes when they are priced at $1 (holding other prices and income constant). This, then, is one point on Sawyer's demand curve for milkshakes, point *X* in Figure 21.5.

If the price of milkshakes were to fall to $0.50, the marginal utility *per dollar spent* on milkshakes would rise twofold. The values of column (3) in

---

PERSPECTIVE 21A:

The Diamond–Water Paradox

Perfect diamonds sell for thousands of dollars a carat, while water sells for only a few cents per gallon. Such gaping disparities in the value of diamonds and water have held for centuries. And for centuries people had no satisfactory explanation for them. Diamonds are only adornment, while water is essential for life. Why are diamonds considered more valuable than water? The answer, we now know, is found in an understanding of total utility, marginal utili-

ty, and the law of diminishing marginal utility. The *total* utility of water to the typical consumer is indeed immense, but water is so abundant that its *marginal* utility is low. At the margin, it is used to wash sidewalks. On the other hand, diamonds generate relatively little total utility for the typical consumer, much less than water, but diamonds are so scarce that their *marginal* utility is relatively high. Indeed, many people have yet to obtain their first diamond.

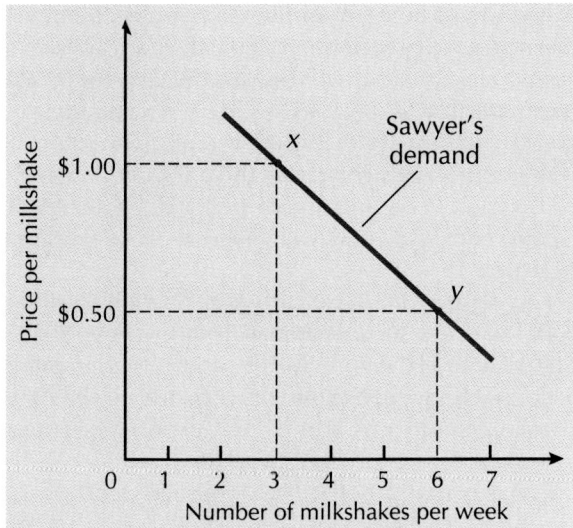

FIGURE 21.5 *Sawyer's Demand for Milkshakes*

Sawyer's individual demand curve is derived from her utilities (preferences), budget (income), and the prices she must pay. Point x shows a demand of three shakes when the price is $1 per shake, a result taken directly from Table 21.2. Point y shows a demand of six shakes when the price drops to $0.50 per shake because the lower price doubles the marginal utility per dollar spent on shakes.

Table 21.2 would therefore double. Before, with a price of $1, MU_M/P_M for the first shake was 12/$1 = 12. Now, with a price of $0.50, MU_M/P_M becomes 12/$0.50 = 24. Doubling all values of MU_M/P_M means that the sixth milkshake now yields a marginal utility per dollar spent of 8. The new equilibrium for Sawyer, still with an $11 budget, will consequently be six milkshakes ($3) and four hamburgers ($8). Sawyer's demand for six shakes when the price is $0.50 is plotted in Figure 21.5 as point Y. Thus declining marginal utility produces a downward sloping individual demand curve.

The connection between marginal utility and individual demand is underscored by part (a) of Figure 21.6. There it may be seen that a consumer's demand will be very steeply sloped when extra units of the good are associated with rapidly falling marginal utility. Conversely, a consumer's demand will decline very slowly when extra units of the good are associated with slowly falling marginal utility.

Figure 21.6(b) shows the influence of an increase in income while the price is constant. An increase in income eases the budget constraint, typically encouraging the consumer to buy more of the

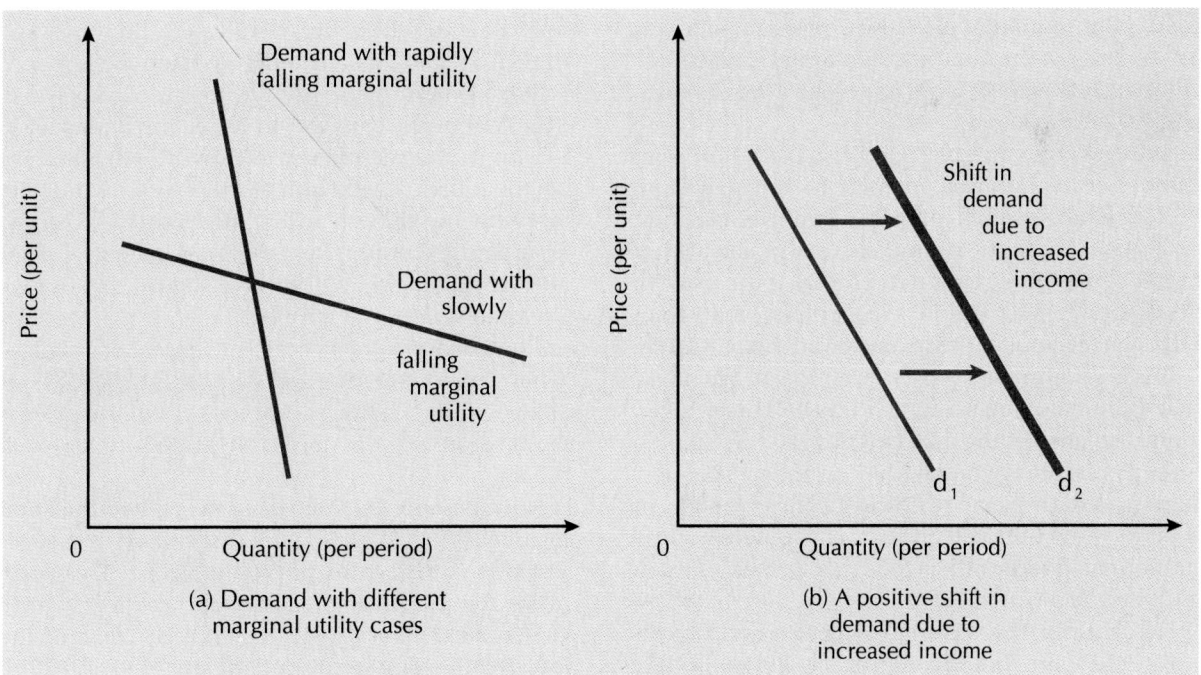

FIGURE 21.6 *Individual Consumer Demands Under Different Conditions of Underlying Marginal Utility and Income*

good than before at each possible price. This is shown by the shift from demand d_1 to demand d_2 in Figure 21.6(b).

B

Substitution and Income Effects Cause Downward-Sloping Demand Curves

Demand curves typically slope downward because a price change produces two effects—a *substitution effect* and an *income effect*. To see this, let's consider a price reduction. Let's also state these effects in a general way in order to illustrate the point that precise measurement of utility is not necessary to explain why individual demands slope downward.

A drop in the price of a good has a **substitution effect** because that good then becomes cheaper relative to other goods (whose prices remain unchanged). Once it becomes cheaper, that good yields more satisfaction per dollar than before, so consumers will buy more of it than before, obtaining the money to do so by reducing their expenditures on other goods. If, for example, the price of milkshakes falls, consumers will tend to substitute milkshakes for other beverages and even for other foods. Consequently, the lower price encourages an increase in the quantity demanded. The substitution effect *always* contributes to a downward-sloping demand.

A drop in the price of a good also has an **income effect** because it gives consumers an increase in real income. Recall the mason's family in Berlin in 1800 for a clear-cut example. Nearly half of that family's income was spent on bread. If the price of bread fell by half, the mason's family could then buy just as much bread as it did before while spending half as much money on bread. Spending half as much on bread, which was half the budget, would be like getting a 25 percent raise in income (the .5 price cut times the .5 budget proportion = .25 improvement). Thus the income effect of a price reduction will induce consumers to buy more of all goods, other goods as well as the one with the lower price.

Demand for the cheapened good need not always rise with this income effect, however. The demand for *inferior goods* falls as income rises.

Bread might be an example. As people's incomes rise, they can get their needed calories from more savory fare. In contrast, the substitution effect of a price decline *always* works in the direction of greater quantity demanded. Overall, then, a price reduction usually increases the quantity demanded through a *combination* of the substitution effect (always positive) and the income effect (usually positive).

For a price *increase*, the substitution and income effects usually cause a *decline* in the quantity demanded. People buy less at a higher price because (1) they *substitute* other goods for the now more expensive one and (2) they experience a loss in real *income*, a loss that provokes a cutback in all purchases not only the higher-priced good.

C

Consumer Surplus: Individual Demand

A concept that will come in handy later is the concept of *consumer surplus*. It emerges directly from knowledge of individual demand and an application of two-question logic. Suppose the demand curve in Figure 21.7 represents your monthly demand for phonograph record albums. That demand curve reflects answers to the first question in two-question logic, namely, what is each record worth to you in benefits? The first record is worth $10. That means you would be willing to pay up to $10 for it. The second record is worth $9, the third $8, the fourth $7, the fifth $6, and so on. These are *marginal* benefits, so adding them up at some given quantity would reflect the *total* benefits, just as adding the marginal utilities of Figure 21.2(b) gave the total utility in Figure 21.2(a).

The second question in two-question logic—What must you give up to get a record?—is answered by the price you must pay. If the price is $6.50, that is what must be given up for each record.

Now, comparing the two answers, two-question logic tells you, "Yes, buy the first record; it's worth $10 but you have to pay only $6.50." This logic urges the purchase of the second record also ($9 versus $6.50), the third ($8 versus $6.50), and the fourth ($7 versus $6.50), but *not* any more. The fifth record is worth $6 to you, which is *less* than the

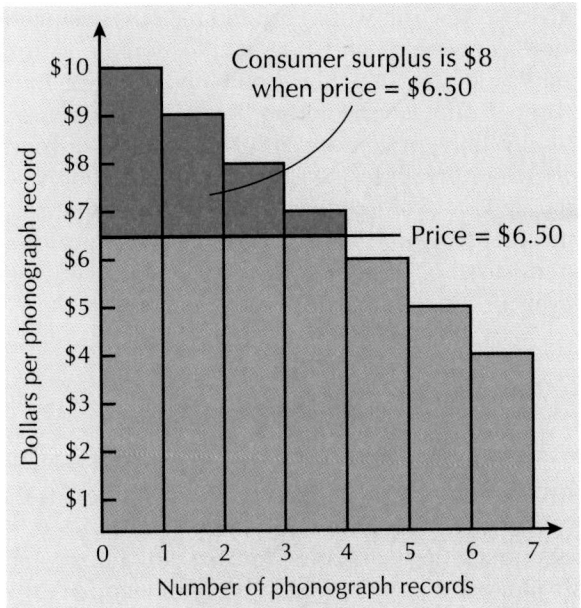

FIGURE 21.7 *Consumer Surplus*

Consumer surplus is the amount the consumer would be willing to pay for his or her purchases less the amount actually paid. At a price of $6.50, four records are purchased and the consumer surplus of $8 ($3.50 on the first record, $2.50 on the second, $1.50 on the third, and $0.50 on the fourth).

$6.50 price you would have to pay. Consumer surplus emerges from a comparison of the answers in two-question logic to the extent that the logic leads you to make purchases. It is called *surplus* because it represents a plus, or a bonus, for you as a consumer. Your surplus on the first record is $10 (what it's worth to you) minus $6.50 (what you actually pay), or $3.50. Your surplus on the second is $9 − $6.50 = $2.50; on the third, $8 − $6.50 = $1.50; and on the fourth, $7 − $6.50 = $.50. The total surplus, your *consumer surplus* in this case, is then $8 ($3.50 + $2.50 + $1.50 + $0.50). You do not buy the fifth record *precisely because* there is *no* surplus with that purchase.

Stated differently, your consumer surplus is the difference between the total amount you would be willing to pay for all the records you purchase and the total amount you actually pay. You would be *willing* to pay $34 for the records—that is, $10 + $9 + $8 + $7. You *actually* pay $26 ($6.50 + $6.50 +

$6.50 + $6.50). Your surplus is therefore $34 − $26 = $8. Diagrammatically, this is the area under the demand curve and above the price line.

> For an individual, **consumer surplus** is the difference between the amount one is willing to pay and the amount one actually pays.

Notice what would happen if records went on sale during June for $4.50 instead of $6.50. Would you run down to Tower Records or Sears and buy 57,213 records for your collection? Obviously not. Declining marginal utility tilts your demand curve downward, so according to Figure 21.7, you would buy only two more records than your usual four (at $6.50). Your two-question logic compares the *worth* of the added records ($6 for the fifth and $5 for the sixth) to your cost (price = $4.50) and approves the added purchase of only two more. Now you should be able to see that, because of the discount price, your consumer surplus for June has increased from $8 to $18, a gain of $10. The gain of $10 results from a gain of $2 on each of the four records you would have purchased anyway and now purchase for $4.50 apiece, plus $1.50 on the fifth record ($6 − $4.50) and $0.50 on the sixth record ($5 − $4.50).

Consumer surplus may seem unreal, a phantom phenomenon, but it's not. It is so genuine that it can easily be made to materialize. To materialize a portion of the consumer surplus in Figure 21.7, let's return to the case where the price is $6.50 per record and you purchase four albums. If a sales tax of 6.15 percent were imposed by the state, you would have to pay 40 cents in tax on each record in addition to the $6.50 price. You would now have to pay $6.90 per record. Given that the fourth record is worth $7.00 to you, you still buy four records. The amount you pay for sales tax, $1.60 (= 4 × $0.40), thus comes directly from your consumer surplus. The state then gets it, not you. Your surplus falls from $8 to $6.40, a material drop once the $1.60 materializes.

The concept of consumer surplus can also be applied to marketwide demand curves. But first, we must generate the marketwide demand from individual demands.

IV
Marketwide Demand

A
Derivation

Individual demand curves are downward sloping because of the law of diminishing marginal utility, which when combined with price changes results in substitution and income effects. It is only natural to expect, then, that marketwide demand curves likewise slope downward. Fine, you say. But how, precisely, are individual demands and marketwide demand related?

Marketwide demand is the summation of the individual demands for some good. It is the addition of the quantities individuals demand at each possible price.

Ordinarily, there will be thousands, even millions, of consumers in a given market. Full representation of them here would be impossible. However, if we assume that there are only three consumers, we can devise a simplified illustration of how individual demands add up to form marketwide demand. Figure 21.8, which smooths out the demand curves, is the result.

Figure 21.8 shows the monthly demand for pineapples of three hypothetical characters— Carlson, Dow, and Edison. It is assumed that the price per pineapple is set competitively in the marketplace, so each of these people sees exactly the same price as measured on the vertical axes. If it's $1.80 per pineapple, each would have to pay $1.80 per pineapple. Although the price is the same to each, the quantities each would buy at a given price are different. Because quantities are registered on the horizontal axes, the marketwide demand curve is obtained by taking the *horizontal* summation of the individual demand curves at each possible price.

Figure 21.8 illustrates this for the prices of $3, $2, and $1. At a price of $3 per pineapple, Carlson, who apparently likes pineapple more than most people, would buy two pineapples. Dow and Edison, however, would buy none. If the price were to

fall to $2, Carlson would expand his purchasing to three pineapples and Dow would now be in the market, buying 1. Their combined total of four (three + one) is reflected at the marketwide level. Finally, if the price were to fall as low as $1 (a good price for pineapples), Carlson would buy still more at four, Dow would expand his purchases to three, and Edison would now be carting two home, for a grand total of nine pineapples at the marketwide level.

B
Consumer Surplus Again

Consumer surplus at the marketwide level is simply the summation of the consumer surpluses of those individuals in the market. In Figure 21.8, it is easy to see that only Carlson has any consumer surplus when the price is $3 per pineapple, and that this would then be the only consumer surplus at the marketwide level. As the price falls, consumer surplus at the marketwide level would expand with the expansion of Carlson's surplus and the appearance of surpluses for Dow as well as for Edison.

More generally, Figure 21.9 depicts consumer surplus marketwide at two different price levels— $2.00 and $1.25. When the price is $2.00, as it is in Figure 21.9(a), the quantity purchased is Q_1. Using two-question logic, we may ask, first, What is Q_1 worth to consumers? The answer is area ABQ_10, which is the entire area under the demand curve. We ask, second, What is paid to buy quantity Q_1? The answer is area CBQ_10, which is the price ($2) times quantity Q_1. Consumer surplus, then, is the difference between these two values, or area ABC.

$$\text{Consumer surplus} = ABQ_10 - CBQ_10 = ABC$$

Stated in English, *consumer surplus is the amount people would be willing to pay for some market quantity minus the amount they actually pay.*

A drop in the price to $1.25, shown in part (b) of Figure 21.9, more than doubles the size of the consumer surplus (if it was, say, $387 million before, it would be more than $800 million after). The *addition* to consumer surplus is indicated by the area $CBJK$. Hence, overall, area AJK is the consumer

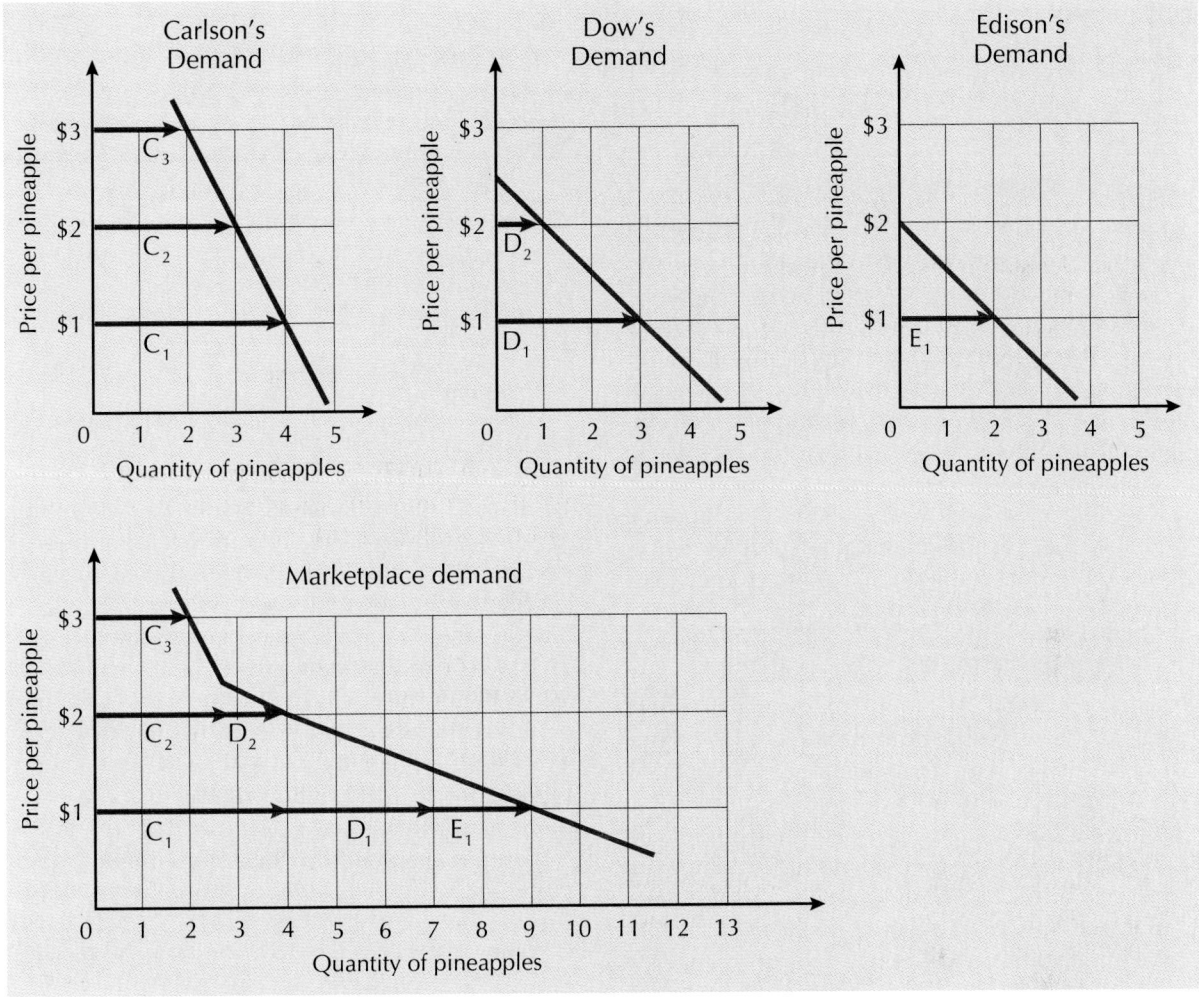

FIGURE 21.8   Individual Demand Curves and Marketwide Demand

Marketwide demand derives from the horizontal summation of the individual demand curves at each possible price. For example, at a price of $1 per pineapple, Carlson's demand is four pineapples, Dow's is three pineapples, and Edison's is two pineapples. Adding these up yields a market demand of nine pineapples ($C_1 + D_1 + E_1$).

surplus when the price is $1.25.

Read Perspective 21B.

■ CHECK YOUR BEARINGS

The theory of utility maximization yields an explanation of why individual demand curves slope downward. Price changes, when combined with diminishing marginal utility, produce substitution and income effects, causing an inverse relationship between price and quantity most of the time. When individual demand curves are added horizontally, the result is a marketwide demand curve that shares the same property. Consumer surplus, which is the difference between the amount consumers are willing to pay and the amount they actually pay, arises at both individual and marketwide levels. It emerges because demands slope downward while prices are commonly fairly uniform across all quantities and all consumers. The gap between demand and actual price bestows surplus.

PERSPECTIVE 21B:

Consumer Surplus and TV Viewing

When the price of a good or service is zero, the entire area under the demand curve would then be consumer surplus. Many goods, though costly to produce, are provided free of charge—e.g., highways, radio broadcasts, and TV broadcasts. These illustrate the law of diminishing marginal utility very nicely. If their utility to us did not decline at the margin, we'd all be spending *all* of our time out on the highways, simultaneously listening to our radios and watching free TV. Quite a sight! This doesn't happen because their marginal utilities to us become zero at some point, a point of small use for some people, great use for others.

Estimation of consumer surplus when goods are supplied freely is a tricky business, but economists Noll, Peck, and McGowan estimated consumer surplus for free broadcast TV during the late 1960s. We can update their estimates by using the broad numbers mentioned earlier—there are now roughly 85 million households in the United States with a median income of $20,000 annually. These numbers and the estimates of Noll, Peck, and McGowan yield the following estimates of annual surplus for TV broadcasting:

Number of Stations	Total Surplus	Marginal Surplus
1st network station	$44.2 billion	$44.2 billion
2nd network station	$69.0 billion	$24.8 billion
3rd network station	$86.2 billion	$17.2 billion
1st independent station	$97.6 billion	$11.4 billion

This says that Americans would be willing to pay $44.2 billion annually in order to have one network TV station instead of none at all. Having a second network station as opposed to just the first is valued at $24.8 billion *more* annually, so the two together generate a total surplus of $69.0 billion annually. Three network stations and one independent station (which was the typical TV availability in 1968) yield a total surplus close to $100 billion. Because more stations are available today than in 1968, the total consumer surplus from TV entertainment may now exceed $100 billion annually, a hefty sum.[3]

[3]Roger G. Noll, Merton J. Peck, and John J. McGowan, *Economic Aspects of Television Regulation* (Washington, D.C.: Brookings Institution, 1973), pp. 28–29, 288.

V

Problems with Utility Maximization Theory: New Alternatives

Downward-sloping demand curves are a well-established fact, empirically verified time and again. Consumer surplus is also well established. But what about the theory of utility maximization? To this point, we have been careful to refer to it as theory rather than fact. Now it is time to ask, as many leading economists increasingly ask, is utility maximization a fact? Is that how consumers actually behave?

The theory of utility maximization is essentially a theory of what consumers *ought* to do. They *ought* to spend so as to achieve the equilibrium $MU_A/P_A = MU_B/P_B = \ldots MU_Z/P_Z$ for the thousands of goods they buy. That would maximize the utility of their budget. But do people *actually* behave in that cold, calculating way? Many economists believe that they do. Many others are skeptical. Let's briefly review this interesting debate.

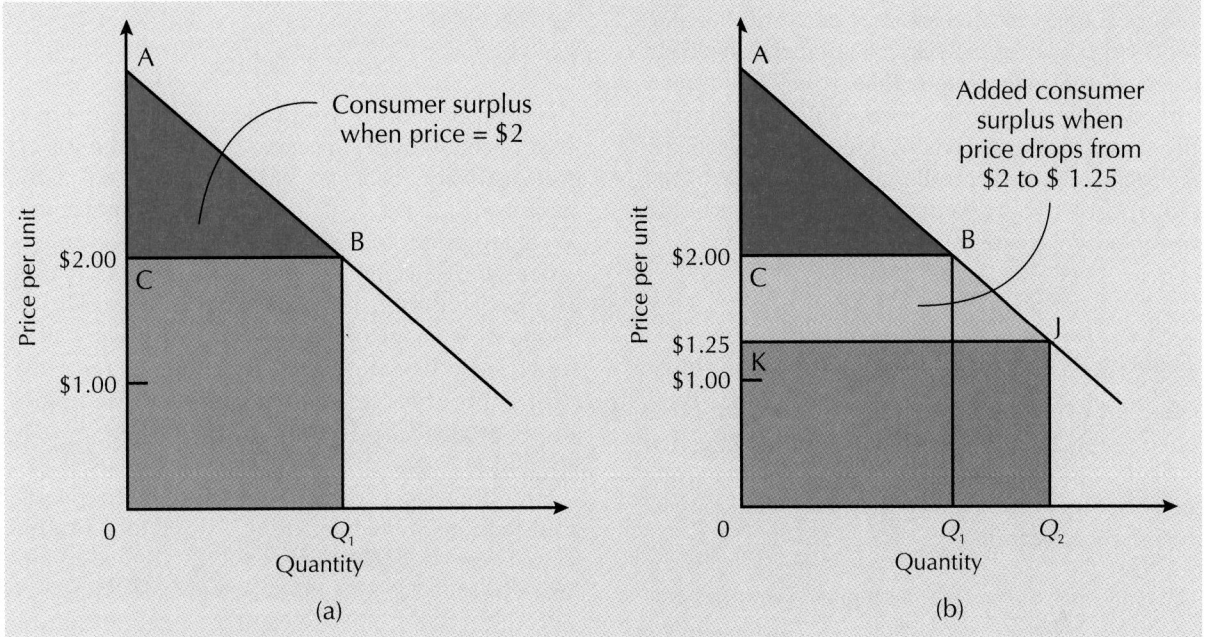

FIGURE 21.9 *Marketwide Demand and Consumer Surplus*

At the market level, consumer surplus is the area beneath the marketwide demand curve and above the price line. In part (a) this is area ABC. In part (b) consumer surplus is increased as the price falls from $2.00 to $1.25. The added surplus is indicated as area CBJK. The total then becomes area AJK.

A

Critical Arguments and Observations

One possible criticism of the theory of utility maximization is that consumer decision making simply does not work that way. Who could possibly be expected to juggle all the marginal utilities per dollar? Indeed, which economist can personally claim to follow the theory's rules? Given the thousands of goods and services that confront consumers and given the bewildering complexities of some of those goods (like VCRs and home computers), no one could be expected to buy in this way. Indeed, studies show that households typically do *not* follow plans that would guide their spending across expenditure categories. They are forced into many purchases (e.g., auto insurance and college textbooks). They spend a great deal on impulsive purchases. And they gather very little information about price or utility before purchasing even major items like cars, TVs, furniture, and carpet-

ing. In short, many, perhaps even most, purchases are preceded by *no deliberate decision-making process.*[4]

A second criticism states that consumer preferences are *unstable* and *easily manipulated.* If preferences are unstable, then marginal utilities will also be unstable. Consumers cannot aim their spending through the gunsights of marginal utility because those sights are shaky. Moreover, if preferences are easily manipulated by the exhortative advertising of sellers, how do we know that consumers are really acting in their own best interests? They may be acting in the best interests of those who manufacture soda pop or cigarettes, rather than moving up their total utility functions as high as their budgets permit.[5] An interesting

[4]Richard W. Olshavsky and Donald H. Granbois, "Consumer Decision Making—Fact or Fiction?" *Journal of Consumer Research* (September 1979), pp. 93–100.

[5]John Kenneth Galbraith has been a great champion of this view. See, e.g., *The New Industrial State* (Boston: Houghton Mifflin, 1967), pp. 198–218.

example concerns diamonds. For centuries diamond rings played no part in Japanese marriage customs. But beginning in 1968, when less than 5 percent of Japan's brides wore diamonds, a carefully conceived and lavishly financed advertising campaign changed a millennium of tradition. By 1981, approximately 60 percent were converted to the American custom.[6]

B
Defenders' Arguments and Observations

Defenders of conventional utility theory admit that consumers do not consciously and diligently abide by utility-maximizing theory. But they argue that consumers behave *as if* they were following its precepts *instinctively*:

> No consumer will actually use [utility] concepts and diagrams to make consumer choices. For the same reason, no bluejay needs to study aeronautical engineering to fly. Bluejays can fly without advanced training, and consumers can make reasonably wise decisions.[7]

More bluntly put, "The mass of consumers usually reach choices that are much the same *as if* they were applying the precise analysis of utility."[8]

As for the problems of changing and apparently manipulated preferences, defenders of utility theory say that, *properly defined*, preferences are stable and not manipulated. Properly defined, preferences are desires for certain *broad services*, such as nourishment, transportation, shelter, and entertainment. Consumers want the broad services that goods provide rather than the goods themselves. They want nourishment, not McDonald's hamburgers. They want transportation, not Ford autos. Hence a switch from fish to chicken, or from autos to airplanes, may give the appearance of shifting preferences, but no such shift actually takes place.

C
Hard Evidence

The defenders of conventional utility theory are at least partially right. Grocery shoppers *do not* load their grocery baskets haphazardly (by taking something off the shelf at every 3 feet of movement down supermarket aisles or by some other aimless process). Moreover, people *do* behave as if they experience diminishing marginal utilities, and so demand curves usually do slope downward. Consumer surpluses follow as well. But being *partly* right is not the same as being *entirely* right. And ample evidence indicates that consumers probably *do not precisely maximize their total utility.*

First, there is evidence that, quite often, people couldn't maximize their utility even if they wanted to because of a *lack of knowledge.* They are ignorant not only of product characteristics that provide utilities but also of product prices. Without adequate knowledge of the utilities provided or the prices charged, consumers often "miss the boat."[9]

Second, with respect to specific commodities, consumers frequently buy brands that are inferior in quality to other brands and pay *more* in price despite the lower quality. Purchase of low-quality merchandise fits nicely into utility maximization theory only when the lower quality is priced lower. When the low quality is priced higher, consumers cannot be maximizing utility.[10]

Third, consumers often knowingly act *against* their own self-interest. Thirty-five percent of the U.S. adult population is hooked on cigarettes. Ten percent consume enough alcohol to have a drinking problem. Four million Americans suffer cocaine dependency. Many people gamble to the point of endangering their health, not to mention

[6]Edward Jay Epstein, *The Rise and Fall of Diamonds* (New York: Simon & Schuster, 1982), pp. 10–11.

[7]W.H. Locke Anderson, A. Putallaz, and W.G. Shepherd, *Economics* (Englewood Cliffs, N.J.: Prentice-Hall, 1983), p. 107.

[8]Ibid.

[9]F.E. Brown and A.R. Oxenfeldt, *Misperceptions of Economic Phenomena* (New York: Sperr & Douth, 1972); E.S. Maynes and T. Assum, "Informationally Imperfect Consumer Markets: Empirical Findings and Policy Implications," *Journal of Consumer Affairs* (Summer 1982), pp 62–87. More generally, see R. Nisbett and L. Ross, *Human Inference* (Englewood Cliffs, N.J.: Prentice-Hall, 1980).

[10]C. Hjorth-Anderson, "Lancaster's Principle of Efficient Choice," *International Journal of Industrial Organization* (September 1983), pp. 287–295; P. Riesz, "Price–Quality Correlations for Package Food Products," *Journal of Consumer Affairs* (Winter 1979), pp. 236–247.

their pocketbooks. The typical cases of Dr. Donald Scheurer, a specialist in "Casino Medicine" in Atlantic City, illustrate the point:

> He regularly prescribes anti-inflammatory drugs to relieve "slot-machine elbow." He also treats cuts and bruises that frustrated gamblers sustain when they slug the slot machines, and he gives medication to gamblers who linger too long in the casino and develop cystitis, or . . . "blackjack bladder."[11]

People who delight in such self-destruction pose no problem for utility maximization theory. The problems are created by those who _unsuccessfully resist,_ who act against their will.[12]

An earlier point now needs repeating. Although these kinds of evidence cast doubt on the theory of utility maximization, they do not necessarily undermine the law of diminishing marginal utility or the principle of downward-sloping demand curves. Alternative theories of consumer behavior retain these tenets while discarding the notion of utility maximization.

For example, one alternative theory is that consumers _satisfice_ rather than maximize. This theory argues that consumers typically do not weigh all possible options, selecting the best, or the optimal one, from among them. Instead, it is argued that they simply reach "satisfactory" results through "satisfactory" procedures. Those procedures usually exclude deliberation in favor of custom, habit, training, rearing, and even whim. When people do deliberate, their deliberations are limited. Such behavior suffices, except when things go too far wrong (as when, for instance, one's overly expensive car is repossessed).[13]

[11]_Wall Street Journal,_ February 22, 1984, p. 1.

[12]T.C. Schelling, "Self-Command in Practice, in Policy, and in a Theory of Rational Choice," _American Economic Review_ (May 1984), pp. 1–11.

[13]H.A. Simon, _Models of Man_ (New York: Wiley, 1957); H. Leibenstein, _Beyond Economic Man_ (Cambridge: Harvard, 1976).

SUMMARY

1. Observed consumption patterns reveal certain broad regularities in consumer spending. As income rises, the fraction spent on necessities like food and drink falls, while the fraction spent on luxuries like diamonds and vacation trips rises. Moreover, individual demand curves and marketwide demand curves typically slope downward. If they didn't, we would observe many oddities, such as people spending all of their income on radishes if radishes went on sale.

2. The theory of utility maximization is the oldest economic theory of consumer behavior. _Utility_ is the satisfaction people feel from consuming goods and services. _Marginal_ utility is the _added_ satisfaction from consuming _added_ quantities. A key ingredient of the theory is the _law of diminishing marginal utility,_ which states that as a person consumes more and more of a given commodity, the marginal utility of the commodity eventually declines.

3. From these building blocks, the theory of utility maximization shifts to dollar spending and posits an _objective_ of getting the greatest utility possible, a _constraint_ imposed by budget limitations and prices, and a _decision rule_ that may be stated in one of two equivalent ways: (a) in terms of budget dollars, the consumer should spend in an orderly way so as to obtain the greatest marginal utility per dollar first, followed by ever lower marginal utilities per dollar; (b) in terms of specific commodities, maximum satisfaction requires _consumer equilibrium,_ which holds when $MU_A/P_A = MU_B/P_B = MU_C/P_C = \ldots$ for all commodities, where MU is marginal utility and P is price per unit.

4. Downward-sloping individual demand curves emerge from this theory. Substitution effects and income effects usually create the downward slope. In turn, that downward slope contributes to the existence of individual consumer surplus,

which is the difference between the amount one is willing to pay and the amount one actually pays for a certain quantity.

5. The horizontal addition of individual demand curves yields the downward-sloping marketwide demand curve. At this marketwide level, consumer surplus is collectively the amount people would be willing to pay for some market quantity minus the amount they actually pay.

6. Critics of the conventional economic theory of consumer behavior do not question the existence of general tendencies, like the priorities given to necessities in budget allocation and downward-sloping de-

mands. They also accept in principle the law of diminishing marginal utility and the notion of consumer surplus. They doubt, however, that consumers *maximize* utility, a doubt based in part on an observed lack of consumer deliberation and on arguments that preferences are unstable and easily manipulated. Defenders reply (a) by substituting instinct for conscious deliberation and (b) by redefining preferences.

7. What do consumers do if they don't maximize utility? One alternative theory argues that they *satisfice*. Guided by habit, whim, and broad rules of thumb, consumers reach satisfactory results rather than an optimal equilibrium.

KEY TERMS

Utility
Total utility
Marginal utility
Law of diminishing marginal utility
Consumer equilibrium

Substitution effect
Consumer surplus
Marketwide demand
Income effect

QUESTIONS AND PROBLEMS

1. List major categories of consumption for households in the U.S. Describe some factors that tend to alter the composition of expenditures over time.

2. John is eating potato chips. He has already eaten ten chips and is popping the eleventh into his mouth. Sam is eating his first chip now.
   (a) Which is greater, John's total utility from the eleven chips or his marginal utility from the eleventh chip? How do you know?
   (b) Which will be greater, John's marginal utility from the eleventh chip or the marginal utility that he got from the third chip? How do you know?

3. Gertrude and Sue both like coffee. Gertrude drinks ten cups per day on the average. Sue averages only two cups per day. Explain this difference in coffee consumption. How is the law of diminishing marginal utility involved here?

4. With a progressive tax, by definition, the tax rate rises as the individual's income rises. Advocates of progressive taxes can justify their position using the marginal utility concept. Explain how.

5. Use the hypothetical data below to decide how Sam should spend $220, assuming that the two goods shown are his only choices.

Clothing Price = $40 per Item		Recreation Price = $20 per Activity	
Units of Good	Total Utility	Units of Good	Total Utility
1	100	1	60
2	160	2	100
3	200	3	120
4	230	4	125

6. If the price of cheese rises, the quantity of cheese demanded by consumers will fall due to the substitution and income effects. Explain each.

7. (a) You buy a sweater at $30.00. You liked it so much that you would have paid $60 if necessary. What does this indicate about the consumer surplus that you received from the sweater?

(b) You meet a neighbor at a party who is wearing an identical sweater. Even if the neighbor paid the same price, he/she probably did not receive the same amount of consumer surplus. What factors determine the magnitude of an individual's consumer surplus, given the product price?

8. Have you ever bought a product, thinking that it would be worth more to you than you paid, then wished later that you had never purchased the item? If so, does this mean that you have unstable wants? If not, what accounts for your behavior?

From the appendix:

9. Using indifference curve analysis, show how changes in consumer buying patterns can result from changes in tastes, incomes, and relative prices.

Appendix:

Indifference Curves and Consumer Demand

A theory of consumer behavior that does not assume that satisfaction can be measured in precise units such as utils focuses on indifference curves. To be *indifferent* is to regard two or more alternatives as equals. You don't care which of the several alternatives you might actually obtain. This is the foundation for an elaborate theory of individual demand.

The Indifference Curve Figure A demonstrates the principle of indifference as it might apply to an individual buying two goods—paperback books and record albums—during the course of a typical month. Each point on the *indifference curve*, including *v*, *w*, *x*, *y*, and *z* in particular, depicts some combination of books and records. Point *v*, for instance, represents eight books and one record per month. Point *w* is a combination of five books

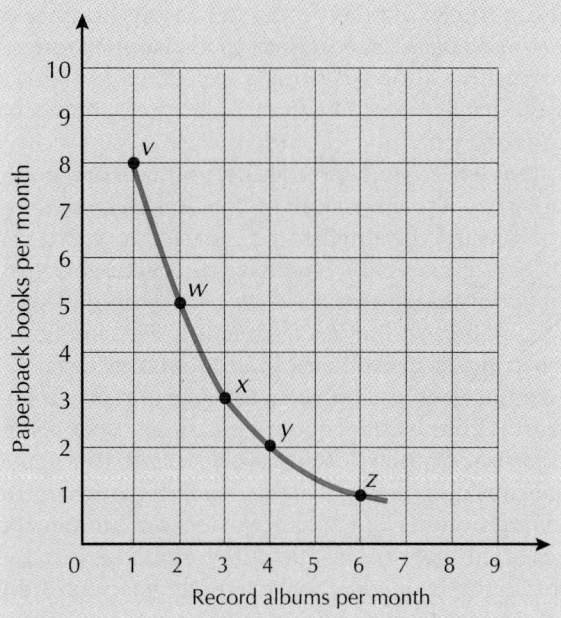

FIGURE A *An Indifference Curve*

Each point on this curve shows a combination of records and books that yields equal satisfaction to every other combination on the curve. A combination of eight books and one record (point v*) would be just as satisfying as three books and three records (point* x*), or one book and six records (point* z*), all on a monthly basis.*

and two records per month. *Each of these points gives the individual consumer the same level of utility or satisfaction* (a level not precisely quantified). Hence combination *v* is just as rewarding as *w* or *x* or *y* or *z*, and each of these latter combinations of books and records is as rewarding as any other. Thus, an indifference curve shows every combination of two goods that is equally pleasing to a consumer.

The goods selected for this example were arbitrarily chosen. Any two other goods could serve just as well. Books and records simply illustrate a *general* theory. Moreover, Figure A illustrates the two main characteristics of indifference curves in general—their downward slope and their curved shape.

Downward Slope: Note that the indifference curve of Figure A plots an inverse or negative relationship. As the number of records rises, the number of books falls. This downward slope is necessary if indifference is to be maintained over all depicted combinations. To maintain indifference, the number of books must fall as the number of records rises. A rise in *both* goods would produce a positive, upward-sloping relationship and it would make the consumer better off, shattering indifference.

Curved Slope: Note that the indifference curve of Figure A is not a straight line. It is curved, bowing toward the origin (so as to be convex to the origin). This general characteristic occurs because of *diminishing marginal utility,* something we discussed earlier. Moving from left to right, retaining fewer books and obtaining additional records, the marginal utility of books rises while that of records falls. With the utility of each remaining book rising and that of each added record falling, more and more added records will be needed relative to the falling number of books in order to maintain the constant level of overall utility embodied in the indifference curve. For example, compare the movement from x to y and from y to z. One book is lost in each movement. The first movement, from x to y, is compensated for by gaining one record (the fourth), while the second movement, from y to z, is compensated for by gaining two records (the fifth and sixth).

Sets of Indifference Curves

These general characteristics of indifference curves might be more fully appreciated once it is recognized that any single indifference curve is just one of many possible indifference curves for any two commodities. Hence the curve for Figure A is only one of an infinite number possible for books and records. Figure B shows two others as well. The curve of Figure A (v, w, x, y, and z) is labeled I_1 in Figure B, while the two new indifference curves are labeled I_2 and I_3. Each of the new indifference curves has a downward slope and is bowed toward the origin, just like the original indifference curve, I_1. What distinguishes these new curves is that they lie farther out in the space of possible combinations of books and records. They depict possible combinations of *greater magnitude* and therefore *greater satisfaction* as compared to the original indifference curve, I_1. In particular, each combination on I_2 in Figure B is preferred to each combination on I_1. In turn, each combination on I_3 is preferred to each combination on I_2 (and I_1). Compare points v, m, and n, for instance. Each has eight books. However, m is preferred to v because it has three records instead of one. Next, n is preferred to m

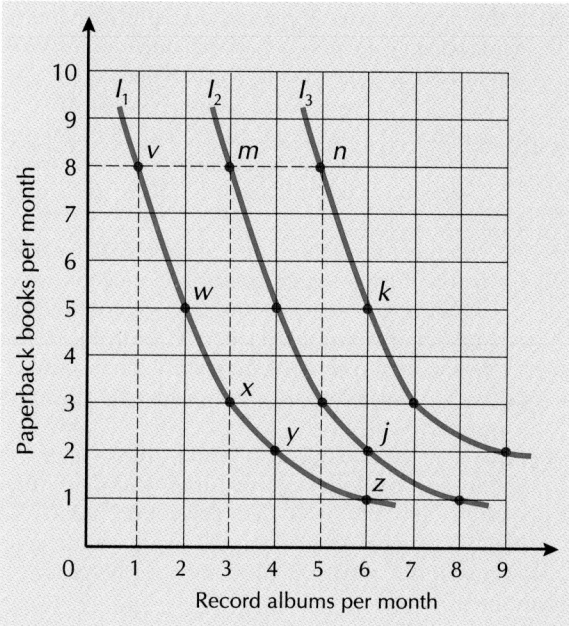

FIGURE B   A Set of Indifference Curves

An infinite number of indifference curves are possible. Here is a set of three to illustrate, identified by I_1, I_2, and I_3. I_2 represents greater satisfaction than I_1, and I_3 represents greater satisfaction than I_2. Note points x, y, and z, for instance. The number of albums rises from one to three to five, while the number of books remains constant at eight. Points z, j, and k show books increasing, with albums constant. Point k on I_3 shows more books and albums compared to point x on I_1.

because it has five records instead of three. To hold the number of records constant while considering greater numbers of books, compare points z, j, and k. Note also that I_3 can offer a greater combination of *both* goods simultaneously in comparison to I_2 or I_1. Compare points k and x for a specific instance of this situation.

The Budget Constraint

Alas, people are not free to choose from among infinitely large combinations of goods because they must contend with a budget constraint, as set by income limits. A formal analysis could deal with a consumer's entire income. We shall simplify by assuming that some fixed portion of the monthly income is budgeted for paperback books and record albums. The results, when translated into the commodity space we have been working with, may be seen in Figure C. Budget line *R* represents the situation when $18 is the monthly budget coupled with prices of $3 apiece for paperback books and $6 apiece for record albums. If the entire $18 is spent on books in this case, six books can be bought ($18/$3). If the entire $18 is spent on records, three records can be bought ($18/$6). Intermediate combinations, like two books and two records, lie on the straight budget line R connecting these two extremes. Budget line S shows what happens when the price of records falls by half from $6 to $3 (while the $18 total budget and the $3 price for books remain unchanged). As the price of records falls, the same budget will now buy more records, so the budget line fans out along the record axis from a maximum of three (for R) to a maximum of six (for S). If, in contrast, the price of records rises, the budget line swings in the opposite direction. It collapses toward the origin along the record axis, allowing fewer possible record albums compared to budget R.

Assume now that the prices of budget S hold—namely, $3 apiece for either a book or a record album. The $18 total of this budget would buy either six books or six records or some combination of the two. A higher total, such as $27, would buy more of _both_ goods, shifting the budget line from S to T in Figure C. With books and records priced at $3 apiece, a monthly budget of $27 could support purchases of nine books, or nine records, or some intermediate combination, such as seven and two, or five and four.

Consumer Maximization   Given a budget constraint, including the prices of these goods as well as the total amount that can possibly be spent on them, what purchases of these goods would maximize the consumer's satisfaction? Conceptually, the answer is easy. _The consumer should purchase that combination of goods that places him or her on the highest indifference curve possible, given the budget constraint._

This is illustrated for our example of books and records in Figure D. Given the budget line depicted in Figure D, our consumer could purchase combination v, or w, or any other previously identified combination on indifference curve I_1. But moving to higher indifference curves is possible and wise (such as the indifference curves lying between I_1 and I_2). The _best_ combination of books and records that can be obtained is at point H on I_2, which has three books and five records. The budget constraint stands in the way of reaching

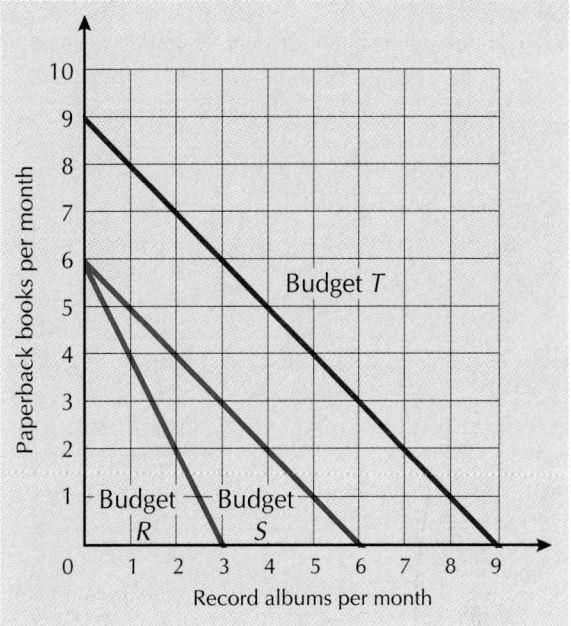

FIGURE C   Budget Constraints

Budget constraints vary with prices and income levels. Budget R would occur if your income allowed a monthly expenditure of $18 on books or records and books were priced at $3 apiece, while records were priced at $6 apiece.

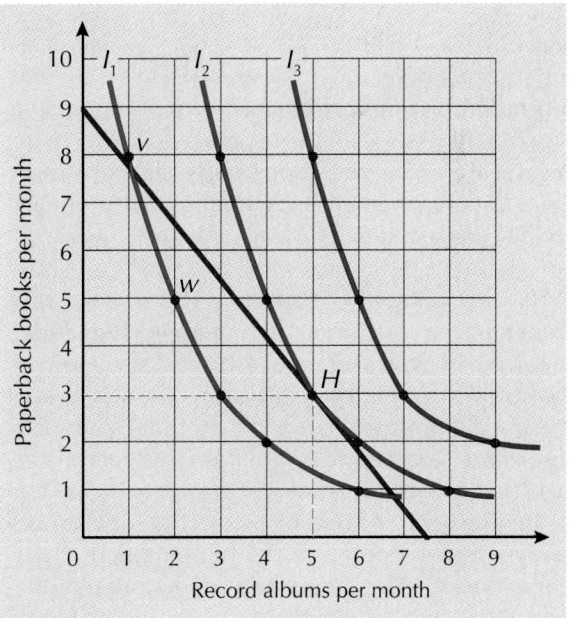

FIGURE D   Consumer Optimization

The consumer will maximize satisfaction in this case by purchasing a combination of three books and five records per month, as indicated at point H. This places the consumer on the highest indifference possible (I_2), given the straight-line budget constraint depicted.

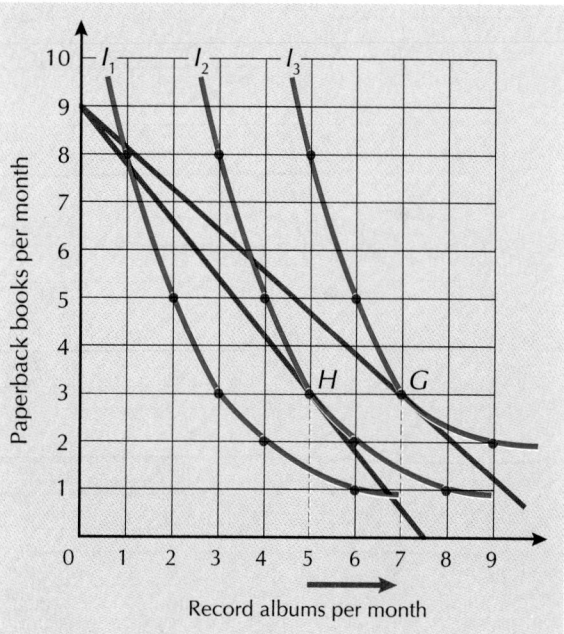

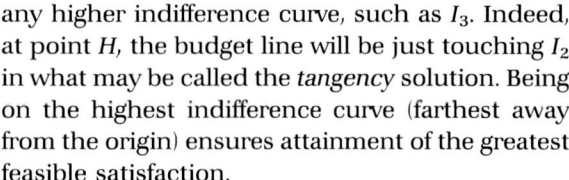

FIGURE E   Price Reduction

A reduction in the price of records, which shifts the budget line outward, will cause the number of records purchased to increase from five (at point H) to seven (at point G). This is the relationship that holds for a demand curve, where price and quantity move inversely.

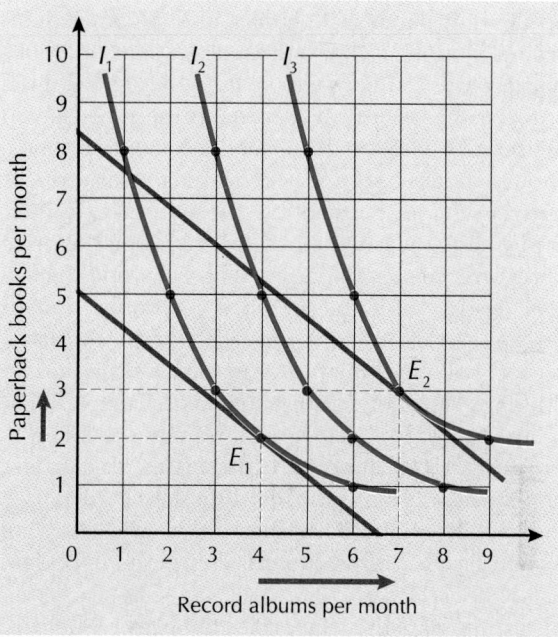

FIGURE F   Budget Increase

Increased budget limits shift the budget line out, away from the origin. This allows the consumer to buy greater combinations of both books and records.

any higher indifference curve, such as I_3. Indeed, at point H, the budget line will be just touching I_2 in what may be called the *tangency* solution. Being on the highest indifference curve (farthest away from the origin) ensures attainment of the greatest feasible satisfaction.

Price Changes and Demand   The inverse relationship between price and quantity demanded (as seen in typical demand curves) can now be demonstrated. Figure E has this task. Recall that the budget line associated with optimal solution H embodies certain prices for books and records. As we know from our earlier discussion of Figure C, a reduction in the price of records will cause the budget line to fan out to the right along the horizontal axis. Figure E contains such a price reduction. This shifts the consumer from point H to a new optimal solution at point G. Note the consequences of this change for the quantity of records purchased per month. As the price of records falls,

the quantity purchased rises from five to seven. This would produce a negative, downward slope to a demand curve for records. In general, lower prices result in higher quantities demanded for a good.

Income Changes and Demand   Finally, Figure F demonstrates the impact of a budget increase (as would follow from an income increase). Recall that budget increases shift the budget line away from the origin. This allows greater consumption of each good singly and of both goods simultaneously. In Figure F the consumer moves from an initial optimum at point E_1 to a new optimum at point E_2. The greater budget results in more books (two to three) and more records (four to seven) being purchased than before. This obviously implies that a higher level of satisfaction is reached by the budget boost. This is borne out pictorially in Figure F by the fact that E_1 is on indifference curve I_1, while E_2 is on higher indifference curve I_3.

22

Demand Conditions

Approximately 594 billion cigarettes were sold in the United States during 1983. That sounds like a lot, but sales were down 28.7 billion, or 4.6 percent, from the previous year, so the cigarette companies grumbled. Their major lament was a rise in excise taxes on cigarettes, which had pushed prices up steeply from an average of 73 cents to 93 cents a pack, a jump of 27 percent. S. P. Pollack, President of Philip Morris (Marlboro), berated legislators, saying that "this industry isn't a tomato that can be squeezed endlessly."

Aside from higher taxes, the cigarette industry has been suffering signs of decline from other causes—namely, continued health scares, regulations on smoking in public, and changing consumer tastes. The response of the cigarette companies has been to diversify by acquiring companies in industries experiencing greater growth, such as soda pop, insurance, and pet food.[1]

The main message of this story is simple: Demand conditions play a decisive role in the fortunes of markets and firms. Until now we have barely scratched the surface of understanding demand conditions. Most important, past chapters have established the "law" that demand curves slope downward, explored shifts in demand (as opposed to movements along the demand curve), and explained how, under competitive conditions, demand and supply interact to determine equilibrium prices and quantities. This chapter probes demand conditions still further, as indicated in this chapter's outline.

I

Price Elasticity of Demand (Marketwide)

A

Elasticity Defined

So far, you have learned directions but not distances. You know from the law of demand that a price increase will curb the quantity demanded.

[1]*Business Week*, December 19, 1983, pp. 62–63.

You're also aware that changes in other variables, like income, cause shifts in demand. These directions are of course critical, but they do not reveal distances. *How much* does demand change with these changes? Such magnitudes of response are very important.

Elasticity measures the magnitude of change in demand. It shows the responsiveness of the quantity demanded to changes in the price of the good, or to changes in other variables determining demand, such as income or the prices of related goods. Here we consider *price elasticity of demand*, saving other types of elasticity for later discussion.

> **Price elasticity of demand** measures the responsiveness of the quantity demanded to changes in the price of the good. In particular, it is the percentage change in quantity divided by the percentage change in price.

If E_d symbolizes price elasticity of demand, this definition can be represented by a ratio:

$$E_d = \frac{\text{percentage change in quantity demanded}}{\text{percentage change in price of the good}}$$

In the case of cigarettes during 1982–83, the quantity demanded fell 4.6 percent, while the price rose 27.0 percent. Thus, according to these numbers, the price elasticity of demand for cigarettes is -0.17:

$$E_d = \frac{4.6\% \text{ decline in cigarettes demanded}}{27.0\% \text{ increase in price of cigarettes}}$$
$$= -0.17$$

The minus sign stems from the demand curve's negative slope. Because all demand curves slope downward, economists typically drop the minus sign as excess baggage. This permits economists to refer to "high" elasticities and "low" elasticities as high and low *absolute* values. We too will ignore the negative sign.

Figure 22.1 illustrates the three main divisions of magnitude for price elasticity of demand—*inelas-*

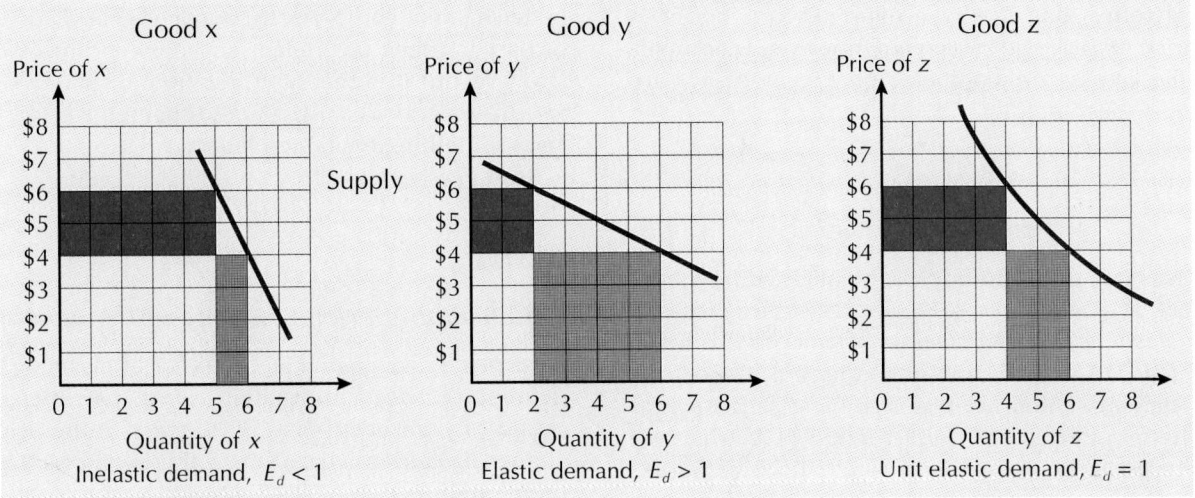

FIGURE 22.1

The size of the price increase is exactly the same in each of these instances, rising from $4 to $6. The initial quantity is likewise the same—six units. However, the responses in quantity change are quite different. For good X, the decline in quantity demanded is small compared to the increase in price, so the demand is inelastic. _For good Y, the decline in quantity demanded is very large relative to the price increase, so the demand is_ elastic. _For good Z, quantity declines in the same proportion as price increases, so the demand for Z is_ unit elastic.

tic, _elastic,_ and _unit elastic_ demand. The percentage change in price is the same for all three parts of Figure 22.1, as the price is assumed to increase from $4 to $6 in each. The different elasticities thus show up clearly in the substantially different responses of quantity demanded relative to identical increases in price. Part (a) shows the quantity of good _x_ falling only slightly relative to the price increase. Dividing the percentage change in quantity by the percentage change in price would yield a low elasticity of _less than 1_. This is said to be _inelastic_ demand. Cigarettes, with $E_d = 0.17$, fall into this category. In contrast, the quantity demanded of good _Y_ in part (b) falls dramatically as the price of _Y_ jumps from $4 to $6. When the percentage change in quantity demanded exceeds the percentage change in price, as it does in the case of _Y_, the resulting ratio is _greater than 1._ Such goods have an _elastic_ demand. Finally, part (c) illustrates the third category. As the price of good _z_ rises, the quantity demanded falls by an equivalent degree. When the percentage change in quantity matches the percentage change in price, the price elasticity of demand for _z_ will exactly _equal 1_, a situation labeled _unit elastic._ To summarize:

Condition	Label	Numerical Value
Percentage change in quantity is less than percentage change in price.	Inelastic	$E_d < 1$
Percentage change in quantity equals percentage change in price.	Unit Elastic	$E_d = 1$
Percentage change in quantity is more than percentage change in price.	Elastic	$E_d > 1$

It must be stressed that elasticity deals in _percentage_ changes, such as 4.6 percent and 27.0 percent for cigarettes, instead of the 28.4 billion drop in the number of cigarettes and the 20-cent hike in price. The reason for this is simple but important. Expressing the changes as percentages allows easy comparisons across commodities. It standardizes the measure of responsiveness. A price increase of 20 cents, for instance, is economically much more significant when applied to a pack of cigarettes than it is when applied to a TV set. A price increase of 4.6 percent, however, is comparable across commodities. Hence percentages are most meaningful.

B
Extremes of Elasticity

Measures of magnitude are highlighted by a brief look at extreme cases. Figure 22.2 shows *perfectly inelastic* and *perfectly elastic* demands. The perfectly inelastic demand of part (a) is a vertical line parallel to the price axis, signifying *zero* responsiveness in quantity demanded as price changes. The perfectly elastic demand of part (b) is a horizontal line running parallel to the quantity axis. This signifies that quantity demanded is *infinitely* responsive to changes in price.

Neither of these extremes holds for the market-wide demand of any real-world commodity, although *portions* of some demand curves might approach them. The demand for heroin, for example, may approach the perfectly inelastic form of Figure 22.2(a), but the availability of substitute drugs like crack probably keeps the demand for heroin from matching that extreme. Enormous increases in the price of heroin can move dope addicts toward alternative dependency (or toward

better habits). The perfectly elastic demand curve of part (b) does not reflect any commodities we know of, but it is this type of demand that *firms* would experience in perfectly competitive markets (something explained later).

Read Perspective 22A.

C
Calculating Price Elasticity of Demand

Percentage changes lie at the heart of elasticity's definition. The computation of a percentage change is normally easy. It is some numerical change divided by a base for comparison, which is then multiplied by 100. Take, for example, the price increase from $4 to $6 found in Figure 22.1. Using the initial price of $4 as the base, we have:

$$\text{Numerical change} = \$6 - \$4 = \$2, \text{ base} = \$4$$
$$\text{Percent change} = \frac{\$2}{\$4} \times 100 = 0.5 \times 100 = 50\%$$

There is a problem, however, with this base of $4. If it were a price *decrease* from $6 to $4, instead of a price increase from $4 to $6, this approach would alter the percentage change merely because the base would change from an initial price of $4 to an

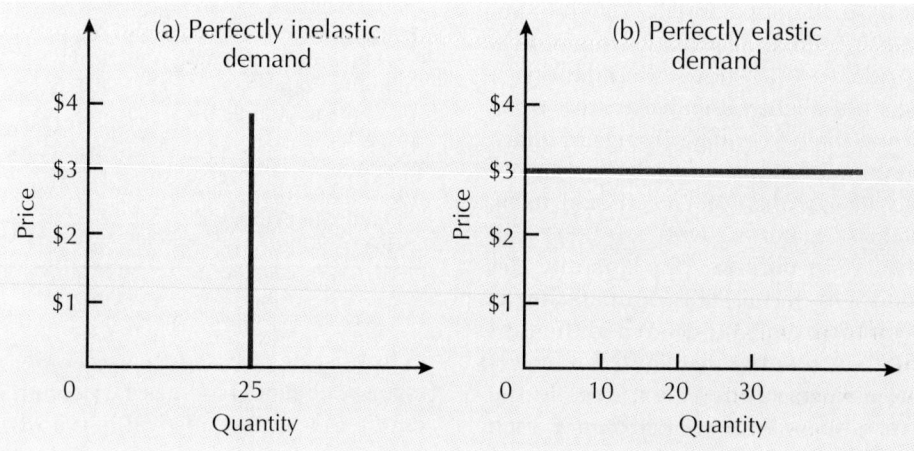

FIGURE 22.2   Extremes in Elasticity of Demand

At one extreme, in part (a), the quantity demanded would be utterly unresponsive to changes in price. It would be fixed at, say, 25 units per time period. This would be a perfectly inelastic demand. At the other extreme, in part (b), demand is a horizontal line. Sales could be very small or very large at the price of $3; they would be zero at $3.01. A perfectly elastic demand describes this extreme.

PERSPECTIVE 22A
The Importance of Price Elasticity of Demand

During the 1970s and early 1980s, the price elasticity of demand for energy became a matter of national importance. From 1973 to 1982, the price of gasoline to U.S. consumers rose 51 percent, natural gas delivered to homes rose 139 percent, and residential electricity jumped 23 percent (all relative to prices of other goods). Contributing substantially to these changes was a series of price hikes in the international petroleum market engineered by the Organization of Petroleum Exporting Countries (OPEC). OPEC prices rose a whopping 300 percent from $3 to $12 a barrel in late 1973. Several increases of 5 to 10 percent followed from 1975 through 1978. Then a final big jump of more than 100 percent came during 1979. If the demand for energy were highly elastic, well above 1, these shocks would have posed relatively few problems. Consumers could have reduced their demand sharply in response to the higher prices without much trouble. If, on the other hand, the demand for energy were inelastic, well below 1,

then these price escalations would have created serious difficulties. In order to pay much higher prices for about the same quantities, consumers would have had to pay much larger portions of their income for energy, leaving substantially less income for food, clothing, housing, and other very desirable goods. Energy is, after all, a big chunk of a consumer's budget. In fact, the price elasticity of demand for energy at the consumer level is estimated to be less than 1, but not critically close to 0. It is in the range of about 0.5 to 0.9, which means that energy demand could be pictured by blending parts (a) and (c) of Figure 22.1, because they depict inelastic and unit elastic demands. Between the years 1973 and 1982, U.S. consumption of energy per dollar of GNP declined 17.5 percent.[2]

[2]J. L. Sweeny, "The Response of Energy Demand to Higher Prices: What Have We Learned?" *American Economic Review* (May 1984), pp. 31–37; *Statistical Abstract of the United States, 1982–83*, p. 572.

---

initial price of $6. The *numerical change* would be the same $2, but the base would become $6:

Numerical change = $2, base = $6

$$\text{Percent change} = \frac{\$2}{\$6} \times 100 = 0.33 \times 100 = 33\%$$

Thus the problem is this: Which should be used to calculate elasticity in this case, 50 percent or 33 percent? The problem of a shifting base also muddles the calculation of percentage change in quantity. Yet the price elasticity of demand should not vary with the direction of movement. It refers only to *one* segment of the demand curve.

To solve this problem, the formula for computing price elasticity of demand uses an *average* of the two prices for the base in calculating percentage change in price, and an *average* of the two quantities for the base in calculating percentage

change in quantity. The result, in absolute values, is the *midpoint formula:*

$$E_d = \frac{\text{percentage change in quantity}}{\text{percentage change in price}}$$

$$= \left| \frac{\dfrac{\text{change in quantity}}{\text{average of quantities}} \times 100}{\dfrac{\text{change in price}}{\text{average of prices}} \times 100} \right|$$

When written in symbols, final adjustments can be made to reflect the fact that the 100s on top and bottom cancel out. Moreover, the brackets for absolute value can be dropped, it being understood that the negative sign is ignored. Let P_1 and P_2 be the first and second prices, and let q_1 and q_2 be the first and second quantities associated with those prices. Then

$$E_d = \frac{q_1 - q_2}{(q_1 + q_2)/2} \Big/ \frac{P_1 - P_2}{(P_1 + P_2)/2}$$

The data in part (a) for good X of Figure 22.1 would fit this formula as follows:

q_1 = initial quantity = 6 units
q_2 = ending quantity = 5 units
p_1 = initial price = \$4
p_2 = ending price = \$6

$$E_d = \frac{6 - 5}{(5 + 6)/2} \Big/ \frac{4 - 6}{(4 + 6)/2}$$

$$= \frac{1}{5.5} \Big/ \frac{-2}{5}$$

$$= \frac{1}{5.5} \times \frac{5}{-2} = -\frac{5}{11} = -0.45 = 0.45$$

Being less than 1, this result confirms that the demand for good X is price inelastic. Check the formula using the data of Figure 22.1(b). Your answer should be $E_d = 2.5$, which confirms the elastic label for good Y.

D

Demand, Elasticity, and Total Revenue

Quite often, neither the demand curve nor its elasticity is of primary concern. Instead, the main interest lies in the implications for total revenue that they have.

The threesome of demand, price elasticity, and total revenue are closely, even intimately, related members of the same family because the *same* two variables—*price* and *quantity*—determine each. (1) Demand relates price and quantity in a schedule. It could be looked upon as a *per unit* form. From the buyer's viewpoint, it is *expenditure per unit* (like \$1.23 per jar of jam). From the seller's viewpoint, it is *revenue per unit* (again, \$1.23 per jar). (2) The definition of price elasticity is, as we've just seen, percentage change in quantity divided by percentage change in price. (3) The definition of total revenue is price times quantity (like \$1.23 × 2,000,000 jars of jam = \$2,460,000). It could also be called, from the buyers' perspective, total expenditure.

The **total revenue** of sellers in a market (or the **total expenditure** of buyers) is obtained by multiplying price times quantity.

A compact summary of the threesome is:

1. Demand—dollar revenue per unit of quantity.
2. Price elasticity—ratio of percentage changes in quantity and price.
3. Total revenue—total dollar revenue for a given total quantity.

Let's link demand and total revenue first, then bring in price elasticity.

Consider the market for phonograph records in a university community. If, when records are priced at \$8 each, 3,000 are demanded monthly, then the total revenue of record shops would be \$8 × 3,000 = \$24,000 a month. Changing the example to incorporate a bit more reality does not damage the basic definition. If rock records were priced at \$8 while country and western albums went for \$6, then these prices would be multiplied by their respective quantities and summed:

\$8 × 2,000 = \$16,000 (rock revenue)
\$6 × 1,000 = \$ 6,000 (c & w revenue)
Sum \$22,000 (total revenue)

Resisting reality for the sake of simplicity, the \$8 × 3,000 = \$24,000 would be one combination of demand and total revenue. More generally, *each* point on a demand curve for records (or any commodity) will represent a *different* total revenue, because each point joins a different price–quantity combination, and total revenue is price times quantity.

Table 22.1 and Figure 22.3 illustrate this, using further hypothetical data for record demand. The price–quantity combinations for demand are given in columns (1) and (2) of Table 22.1 and pictured in the *upper* part of Figure 22.3. The corresponding total revenue data are presented in column (3) of Table 22.1 and pictured in the *lower* part of Figure 22.3 (note the axes' labels). Combinations A, B, C, and D of Table 22.1 are labeled as points on the demand curve of Figure 22.3. Corresponding combinations A*, B*, C*, and D* are shown on the total revenue curve.

TABLE 22.1 Demand Data and Total Revenue, Market for Records (Hypothetical Data)

(1) Price (in Dollars)		(2) Quantity (in Albums)		(3) Total Revenue (in Dollars)
$11		0		$ 0
10		1,000		10,000
9	—A—	2,000	—A*—	18,000
8	—B—	3,000	—B*—	24,000
7		4,000		28,000
6		5,000		30,000
5		6,000		30,000
4		7,000		28,000
3	—C—	8,000	—C*—	24,000
2	—D—	9,000	—D*—	18,000
1		10,000		10,000
0		11,000		0

When each price observation in column (1) of Table 22.1 is multiplied by its quantity observation in column (2), the result is the total revenue in column (3). Pair _A_, for example, shows a price of $9 per record associated with sales of 2,000 records for a total revenue of $18,000. Pair _B_, with $8 and 3,000 records, yields a total revenue of $24,000. Note that when the price is so high that _no_ records are sold, or so low as to be $0, total revenue will be zero.

In the _upper_ portion of Figure 22.3, total revenue is the _area_ of the rectangle created by joining price and quantity on the demand curve. That area is price times quantity. When the price is $9 and the quantity is 2,000 records, pair _A_, the corners of the rectangle, are points 0, 9, _A_, and 2. Hence the total revenue associated with pair _A_ is area 09A2. Pair B generates a total revenue represented by area 08B3 in the upper portion of Figure 22.3. Because the vertical axis of the upper portion measures dollars _per unit_, total revenue can find expression from a demand curve only in these rectangular areas.

The vertical axis of the _lower_ portion of Figure 22.3 measures _total dollars_, so total revenue is explicitly depicted there. Moreover, the horizontal axis of the lower portion is _exactly the same_ as that of the upper portion—quantity of records in thousands per month—so there is a direct tie-in between the lower portion and the upper portion. In other words, the upper and lower portions of Figure 22.3 contain essentially the same information viewed differently—first in dollars per unit (upper)

and second in total dollar revenue (lower). The total revenue associated with pair _A_ in the upper portion (area 09A2) is shown in the lower portion as the _vertical distance_ to point A*, or $18,000. Similarly, the total revenue associated with pair _B_ in the upper portion (area 08B3) is shown in the lower portion as the vertical distance to point B*, or $24,000.

Now, in order to link price elasticity of demand with total revenue, note that price elasticity _varies_ across different segments of a straight-line demand curve. Segments in the _top_ half of a straight-line demand curve are elastic ($E_d > 1$), while segments in the _bottom_ half of such a demand curve are _inelastic_ ($E_d < 1$). Finally, with elasticity greater and lesser than 1 at each end, justice is served when elasticity equals 1 in the middle of the demand curve. Specifically, if the midpoint formula is applied to demand segment _AB_, price elasticity is revealed to be 3.4.[3] Demand segment _CD_ has a price elasticity of 0.29.[4] And around point _M_ the formula produces $E_d = 1$.[5]

$$^3E_d = \frac{1,000}{2,500} \Big/ \frac{1}{8.5} = \frac{1}{2.5} \Big/ \frac{1}{8.5} = \frac{8.5}{2.5} = 3.4$$

$$^4E_d = \frac{1,000}{8,500} \Big/ \frac{1}{2.5} = \frac{1}{8.5} \Big/ \frac{1}{2.5} = \frac{2.5}{8.5} = .29$$

[5]Using prices of $6 and $5 with quantities of 5,000 and 6,000 yields $E_d = 1$.

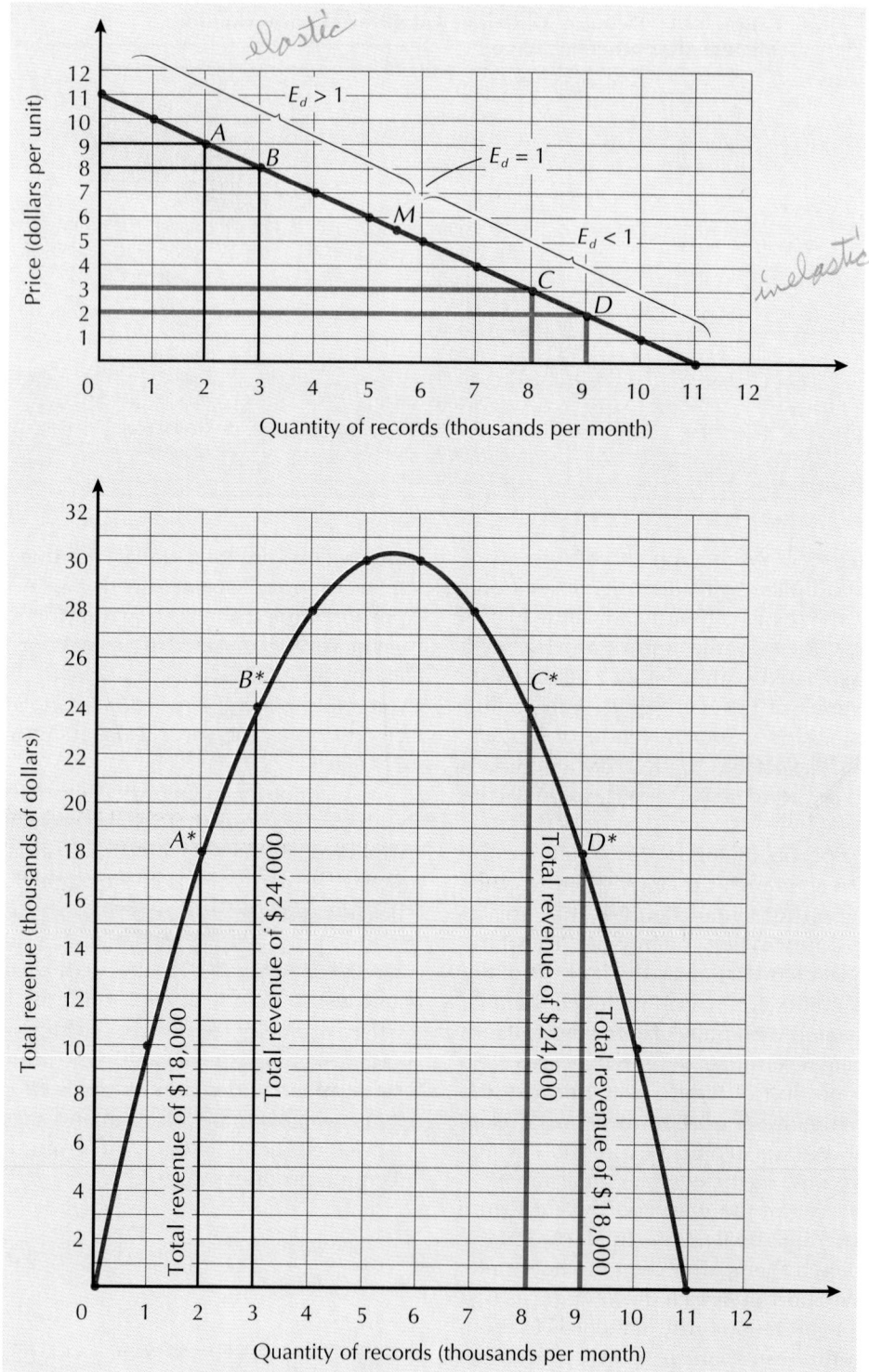

FIGURE 22.3 _The Relationship Between Price Elasticity and Total Revenue for a Down-ward-Sloping, Straight-Line Demand Curve_

The fact that elasticity varies along a straight-line, downward-sloping demand curve illustrates that elasticity does *not* depend solely on the slope of the demand curve, as the slope of the demand curve in Figure 22.3 is the same throughout. It depends, rather, on the slope *and* location on the curve. Earlier, in Figure 22.1, we were able to label the demand for good X as inelastic because only the bottom end of a longer demand curve was represented. Likewise, we were safe in saying that the demand for good Y was elastic because only the top end of its demand curve was pictured.

Thus, it may be seen that, when demand is price *elastic*, a drop in price *increases* total revenue. In Figure 22.3, a price cut from $9 to $8 increases the quantity from 2,000 to 3,000 units—a movement down an elastic segment of the demand curve from A to B. In turn, total revenue rises from $18,000 to $24,000, as indicated by movement up the total revenue curve from A^* to B^*. However, when demand is price *inelastic*, a drop in price will decrease total revenue. A price cut from $3 to $2 lifts the quantity from 8,000 to 9,000 records, resulting in movement down the demand curve from C to D. Total revenue at C is $24,000, while at D it is $18,000. Hence the price cut represented by travel from C to D causes total revenue to fall, sliding from C^* to D^*.

Intuitively, these results make sense. When the price level drops, it has a *negative* force on total revenue. But total revenue is price times quantity, and the resulting increase in quantity will have a *positive* force on total revenue. Whether the negative or the positive force dominates depends on price elasticity of demand, which, in a way, represents a ratio of these forces. If demand is *elastic*, the negative force of the price decline is outweighed by the bigger positive force of the quantity increase, causing total revenue to rise. If, on the other hand, demand is inelastic, the negative force of the price cut is not outweighed by the positive force of the quantity increase because the quantity increase will be relatively slight. Total revenue then declines with the price cut.

Price *increases*, with their consequent movements up the demand curve, foster opposite changes in total revenue, depending on price elasticity. Consider first a price increase from $2 to $3 in Figure 22.3. Because demand there is inelastic, quantity demanded falls relatively little, from 9,000 to 8,000 records (about 12 percent), despite the relatively large jump in price (about 40 percent). The journey from D to C embodies an increase in total revenue from $18,000 to $24,000, symbolized by a change from D^* to C^*.

Consider next a price increase from $8 to $9 per album, a jump of about 12 percent. Because demand is elastic in this price range, the quantity demanded drops rather drastically (by about 30 percent) from 3,000 to 2,000 records. This relatively large drop in quantity dents total revenue considerably, causing it to fall. Hence the trip up the demand curve from B to A fuels a trip down the total revenue curve from B^* to A^*.

To appreciate these impacts of price increases, we can continue the reasoning applied to price decreases. Here, however, the positive force on total revenue stems from the price increase, while the negative force derives from the decline in quantity. When $E_d<1$, the positive force of the price increase dominates the negative force of the drop in quantity, so total revenue rises. When $E_d>1$, the positive force of the price increase shrinks beside the larger negative force of declining quantity, so total revenue takes a tumble.

Finally, when price elasticity equals 1, changes in price, either up or down, leave total revenue unchanged. The numerator and denominator of the elasticity formula match each other. Hence, for a price cut, the negative influence of the price decline will be just matched by the positive influence of the increased quantity. For a price hike, the positive influence of the price increase will be offset by the negative influence of the reduced quantity. Notice, for instance, that in Table 22.1 and Figure 22.3 a price reduction from $6 to $5, or the reverse, an increase from $5 to $6, leaves total revenue unchanged at $30,000. This is because either change in price spans the segment of the demand curve that is unit elastic.

These several relationships between price changes, elasticity, and total revenue acquire tremendous importance later. Figure 22.4 therefore provides a summary that fits easily into one's memory bank.

Read Perspective 22B.

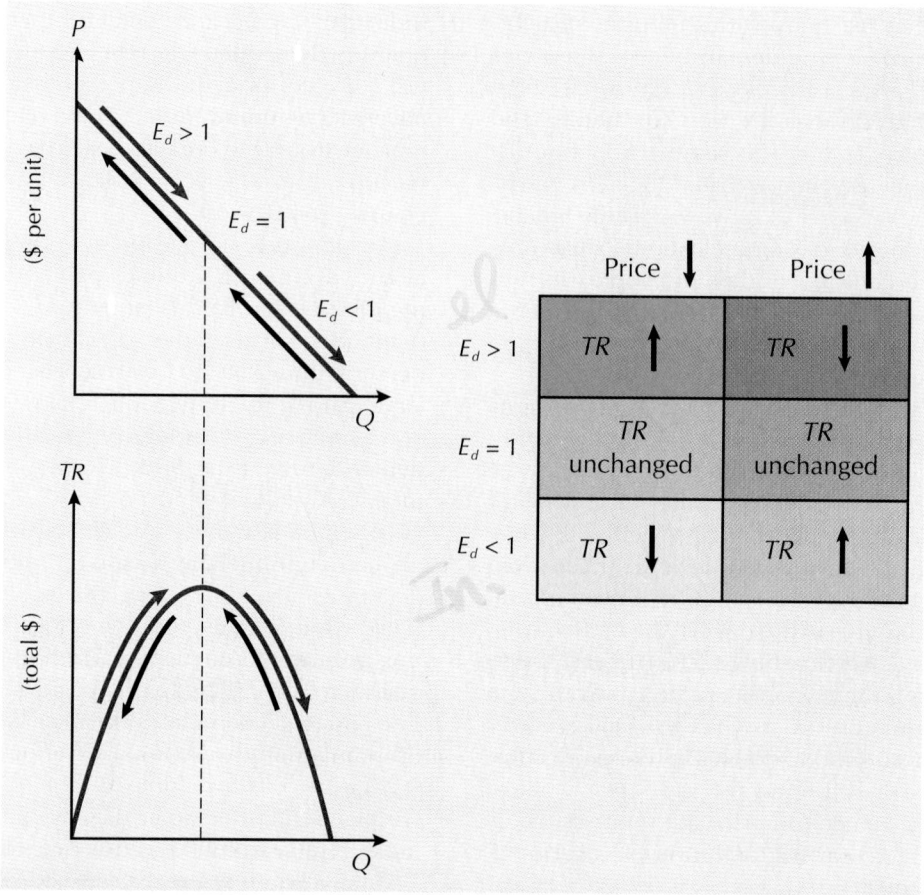

FIGURE 22.4   Summary of the Relationships Linking Price (P) Changes, Price Elasticity of Demand (E_d), and Total Revenue (TR)

E
The Determinants of Price Elasticity

Although price elasticity of demand hinges on location on a commodity's demand curve, it is possible to attribute various price elasticities to various commodities in general. As we have seen, price elasticity is typically low for cigarettes, energy, and mass transit. By comparison, it tends to be quite high for strawberries, vacation travel, and restaurant meals. Why is quantity highly responsive to price in some cases but not others?

Several factors determine whether a commodity will have a low or high price elasticity. We shall review three: (1) the availability of close substitutes for the commodity; (2) the portion of the consumer's budget spent on the good; and (3) time.

1. The Availability of Substitutes As a general rule, *the abundant availability of close substitutes causes price elasticity of demand to be high.* Plums, nectarines, pears, and other fruits serve as fairly close substitutes for peaches. An increase in the price of peaches will consequently cause a relatively large drop in the quantity of peaches demanded as consumers shift from peaches to other fruits. If, on the other hand, the price of peaches falls, consumers readily switch from those alternatives to peaches, again a highly responsive result. In fact, the price elasticity of demand for peaches is estimated to be about 1.5, which is elastic.[6]

[6]Karl A. Fox, *The Analysis of Demand for Farm Products*, U.S. Dept. of Agriculture Technical Bulletin No. 1081, September 1953.

PERSPECTIVE 22B
Elasticity and Mass Transit Revenues

John Kramer, head of Chicago's Transportation Authority, made news in early 1984 when he reduced fares to help revive the region's troubled mass-transit system. Commuter train riders were promised savings of $49 to $228 a year in lower fares. Rush hour bus fares were dropped from 90 to 60 cents. As _The Wall Street Journal_ put it, these cuts represented a _"radical idea."_ Why radical? Because the price elasticity of demand for mass-transit service is low (less than 1), the typical approach to raising revenues in this market is to _raise_ fares, not slash them. Indeed, during the 5 years before Mr. Kramer's "radical" reductions for Chicago, mass-transit fares rose 65 percent on average nationwide. One exception to this upward pattern occurred in Los Angeles, but that exception proved the point. In 1980 the basic bus fare was cut from 85 to 50 cents, a drop of about 52 percent (using the midpoint formula). That increased ridership during the 2 following years, but only by about 30 percent. As a result, total revenues in Los Angeles slumped more than 35 percent. Are Mr. Kramer and Chicago ignorant of the basic economics here? Are they crazy? No. When it announced the cuts, Chicago's Transit Authority estimated that revenue losses of $9 million annually _would_ ensue. Mr. Kramer admitted that the fare cuts would cost the system money. Still, he favored them as one step among many to convert Chicago to a "place where mass transit can be made to work."[7]

[7]_Wall Street Journal_, January 17, 1984, pp. 33, 41.

Conversely, _an absence of close substitutes typically produces a low price elasticity of demand._ Consider milk. Are soda pop, beer, tomato juice, or vodka close substitutes for milk? For most purposes the answer is clearly "no." (Have you ever tried tomato juice on your breakfast cereal?) Thus, the estimated price elasticity of demand for milk is quite low—somewhere in the inelastic range of 0.2 to 0.5.[8]

2. Proportion of Income   Other factors being the same, _price elasticity will be higher, the greater the proportion of consumer income that is spent on the commodity._ Items that bulk large in the budget respond relatively highly to price changes because _income effects_ will typically then be larger. A doubling of the price of toothpicks or paper clips would not even be noticed by most consumers, but a doubling of the price of electricity or housing would injure most budgets enough to force greater responsiveness in demand.

[8]_Ibid._

Local phone service illustrates the point more precisely. In 1980 the price of basic local telephone service was, aside from some regional variations, quite similar for all families. This meant that poor families spent a larger share of their budget on local phone service than rich families. A study of how various families would respond to the rise in local phone rates after 1983 revealed that the poor would indeed be more responsive to price hikes than the rich. The results are summarized in Table 22.2.

3. Time   Consumers cannot, as a rule, react instantaneously to a change in price. It takes time for people to adjust their expenditures—time for them to learn about a price change, time to alter their consumption habits, and time to scrap durable goods. Thus, _the price elasticity of demand for many goods is higher in the long run, when there is ample time to adjust, than in the short run, when responses are crimped by abruptness._

Examples abound, none better than the response of consumers to higher gasoline prices

TABLE 22.2   Estimated Responsiveness of Consumers of Different Income Levels to a $10 Increase in the Monthly Price of Local Phone Service, Early 1980s

| Income Level | Percentage of Households Subscribing to Local Phone Service | | Change in Percentage Points |
	Before Price Increase (%)	After Price Increase (%)	
Under $3,500	80.5%	71.4%	−9.1
About $20,000	96.6	94.0	−2.6
Over $45,000	99.0	98.0	−1.0

Source: Estimates of National Economic Research Associates, as reported in the *Wall Street Journal*, December 12, 1983, p. 2.

during the 1970s. As gasoline prices shot up after the crude oil price escalations of OPEC, motorists could do very little immediately. They could not quickly move closer to work to save on gasoline burned up by commuting. They could not hastily dump their gas-guzzling old cars for fuel-efficient new ones. About all they could do in the short run was to cut down on discretionary driving, e.g., consolidate their shopping trips and drop Sunday drives. With time, however, these short-term measures were augmented by many long-term actions to produce a much larger eventual response. In particular, new cars sold in 1983 were 39 percent more fuel-efficient than new cars sold 10 years earlier, when they got only 13 miles per gallon on the average. Estimates of price elasticity for gasoline vary accordingly. The *short-run* elasticity, based only on motorists' reduced driving, is only about *0.2,* while the *long-run* elasticity, allowing for improved auto efficiency, is far higher, about *0.8*[9].

The selected examples of elasticity in Table 22.3 give further voice to the influence of time. There are exceptions, but duration usually aids consumer responsiveness to price changes. Table 22.3 also illustrates, though only crudely, the influence of the other factors—substitutability and budget share. Compare water with motion pictures, for instance. Notice, too, the relatively low price elasticity of phonograph records. At existing prices, records apparently have few substitutes in the eyes of their buyers.

II
Cross-Price Elasticity of Demand

The quantity demanded of a good reacts not only to changes in its *own* price but also to changes in the prices of *other* goods. The demand for gasoline responds to the price of gasoline and *also* to the prices of autos, tires, and airplane travel. Changes in the prices of these other goods *shift* gasoline's demand curve, thereby changing the quantity of gasoline sold. The direction of the shift and its magnitude are measured by the *cross-price elasticity of demand.* A definition with respect to commodities *J* and *K* is:

The **cross-price elasticity of demand** for J with respect to K is the percentage change in the quantity of J divided by the percentage change in the price of related good K.

Or, more compactly:

$$E_{JK} = \frac{\text{percent change in the quantity of } J}{\text{percent change in the price of } K}$$

A midpoint formula could apply once again.[10]

Although the "own" price elasticity that we discussed earlier will always be negative, this cross-

[9]Sweeny, *op. cit.,* p. 37.

[10]$E_{JK} = \dfrac{(q_1^J - q_2^J)}{(q_1^J + q_2^J)/2} \bigg/ \dfrac{(p_1^K - p_2^K)}{(p_1^K + p_2^K)/2}$

TABLE 22.3   Selected Estimates of Price Elasticity of Demand

Commodity	Short-Run Elasticity	Long-Run Elasticity
Tobacco products	0.46	1.89
Water	0.20	0.14
Medical care	0.31	0.92
Auto repairs	0.40	0.38
Gasoline	0.15	0.78
Toilet articles	0.20	3.04
Motion pictures	0.87	3.67
China and glassware	1.55	2.55
Milk	0.40	N.A.
Apples	1.30	N.A.
Chicken	1.15	N.A.
Phonograph records	0.52	N.A.

N.A. = not available.
Sources: H.S. Houthakker and L.D. Taylor, *Consumer Demand in the United States*, 2nd ed. (Cambridge, Mass.: Harvard University Press, 1970); L.W. Weiss, *Case Studies in American Industry*, 3rd ed. (New York: Wiley, 1980), pp. 52–53; A. Belinfante and R.R. Davis, Jr., "Estimating the Demand for Record Albums," *Review of Business and Economic Research* (Winter 1978–79), pp. 47–53.

price elasticity can be either negative or positive, so its sign cannot be ignored. Which sign holds is of significance because it depends on whether the two goods are substitutes or complements.

If *J* and *K* are *substitutes,* then a 10 percent *increase* in the price of *K* would cause an *increase* in the demand for *J* as buyers switched from *K* to *J*. Were *J*'s quantity to rise, say 15 percent, in response to this 10 percent increase, then

$$E_{JK} = \frac{+15}{+10} = +1.5$$

The resulting cross-elasticity is positive. Running in reverse, a *drop* in the price of *K* would prompt a *drop* in the quantity of *J*. With negatives above and below, E_{JK} is again positive. A general principle thus emerges:

The cross-elasticity of demand will be positive if the two goods involved are substitutes.

Natural gas, for example, can substitute for electricity in many home uses—heating hot water, drying laundry, and cooking dinner. Residential demand for electricity could then be expected to vary positively with changes in the price of natural

gas. And indeed it does. The cross-price elasticity of home demand for electricity with respect to the price of natural gas has been estimated to be about +0.31.[11]

Complements conspire to yield an opposite sign. If goods *J* and *L* are used jointly, then a 10 percent *increase* in the price of *L* would produce a *decrease* in the demand for *J*, say −20 percent, as buyers curtailed their consumption of both *L* and *J*. Plugging these numbers into the formula:

$$E_{JL} = \frac{-20}{+10} = -2$$

Clearly, the resulting cross-price elasticity is negative. If the price of *L* fell instead of rose, this outcome would still hold: $E_{JL} = +20/-10 = -2$.

The cross-elasticity of demand will be negative if the two goods involved are complements.

Electricity is a complementary good for electric home appliances. Thus the demand for home ap-

[11]John W. Wilson, "Residential Demand for Electricity," *Quarterly Review of Economics and Business* (Spring 1971), pp. 7–22.

pliances should, if well behaved, reflect the implication that the price of electricity has a negative impact. Measuring quantity demand by the percentage of homes with certain appliances, an economist estimated the cross-elasticity of demand for electric dryers to be −1.8; food freezers, −0.9; and electric ranges, −1.9.[12] Thus the empirical evidence supports the principle.

■ *CHECK YOUR BEARINGS*

A major demand condition is the responsiveness of quantity to changes in the price of the commodity, or price elasticity of demand, E_d. It is the percentage change in quantity divided by the percentage change in price. Ignoring the ever-present negative sign, demand is price elastic if $E_d > 1$, inelastic if $E_d < 1$, and unit elastic if $E_d = 1$. Because price and quantity are the ingredients of elasticity, and because total revenue is price times quantity, elasticity and total revenue intertwine. When $E_d > 1$, price and total revenue move in opposite directions, one up and the other down. When $E_d < 1$, price and total revenue move in the same direction. When $E_d = 1$, price changes leave total revenue unchanged. Price elasticity varies widely across commodities. In general, it is higher when (1) close substitutes are available; (2) the good takes a large share of consumer budgets; and (3) a long time is allowed for the quantity to adjust. Finally, cross-price elasticity of demand is the percentage change in the quantity of one good divided by the percentage change in the price of another.

III

Dynamic Demand Conditions

Time dominates dynamics. Conditions of price elasticity and cross-price elasticity can be understood with little reference to time. For other, more dynamic influences, time is of the essence.

Music illustrates the point because music is, by its very nature, a dynamic phenomenon. Absent

[12] *Ibid.*

time, music collapses to a single note, or at best a single chord.

Adding time to our consideration of a commodity's demand condition raises several intriguing questions. What happens to demand as economic growth lifts household incomes? Does it make any difference whether a commodity has been around a long time or is fairly new? When are substitution and complementarity influenced by time?

This section is devoted to demand dynamics. It begins with income growth, moves on to the life cycle of commodities, and concludes with remarks on several miscellaneous influences.

A

Income Growth and Demand

On the whole, time has been good to Americans. We have had bad experiences with short-run recessions and occasional depressions, but over the long haul our incomes have grown generously. For example, median family income *doubled* during the three decades between 1950 and 1980. This excludes the counterfeit effects of inflation, so it's a real doubling. The rise in real income, off and on though it may be, gives rise to a question: How does demand for individual commodities respond to income changes, both long-term rises and short-term fluctuations?

The *income elasticity of demand* is a handy measure of the impact of income change on quantity demanded. It resembles the earlier elasticities in concept but has its own definition:

> The **income elasticity of demand** is the percentage change in the quantity of a good demanded divided by the percentage change in consumer income (holding all prices constant).

If, for instance, consumer income rose 6 percent and the quantity of television sets demanded rose 9 percent, then the income elasticity of demand for TVs would be $+9/+6 = +1.5$.[13] The changes can be registered over long or short time periods.

[13]The midpoints formula, with I indicating income, would be $\dfrac{(q_1 - q_2)}{(q_1 + q_2)/2} \bigg/ \dfrac{(I_1 - I_2)}{(I_1 + I_2)/2}$

(Note: the impact of income is to shift the demand curve rather than to move along it.)

Income elasticity of demand is almost always positive, as greater income means greater spending on most goods. The positive trajectory can be high or low, however. A ratio *above 1*, which is *elastic*, indicates that mounting income lifts quantity sales disproportionately. With sales rising more rapidly than income, the *share* of income spent on these goods will rise. Luxuries like boats, recreation vehicles, and VCRs illustrate this class of commodities. Conversely, a ratio *below 1* reflects an *inelastic* response to income growth. Sales rise but by less, in percentage terms, than income. The *share* of income spent on these goods will therefore fall as income rises. Necessities fit this description, with food offering a classic example. Food is income inelastic, so its share of consumer spending has been shrinking over time. (However, certain foods—like veal and lobster—are luxuries, with income elasticities greater than 1.)

B
Product Life Cycle

Countless commonplace products are fairly new. Video games, VCRs, granola bars, and home computers come readily to mind. Looking back a little further, we find innovations that have burrowed deeply into our daily lives—electricity, autos, telephones, TVs, movies, antibiotics, airplanes, and zippers, to name but a few wonders of the modern world. Quite clearly, products vary in age. Some have been around for a few months, others for many decades. How do the dynamics of product aging influence demand?

A simplified answer is found in the theory of **product life cycles.** According to this theory, products pass through four distinct phases as time elapses—introduction, growth, maturity, and decline. Figure 22.5 summarizes these phases by showing annual industry sales as a function of time, while Figure 22.6 summarizes several main characteristics often attributed to each of the four phases:

Introduction is the phase during which the product is just getting off the ground. Sales growth may be slow at first, as buyers must learn about the innovation and overcome their hesitancy about buying a product that may need "debugging." The market will typically be small at this stage. The innovator—like Atari in video games or Apple in personal computers—may enjoy a brief period of market dominance, partly because of its head start on rivals and partly because of the undersized market.

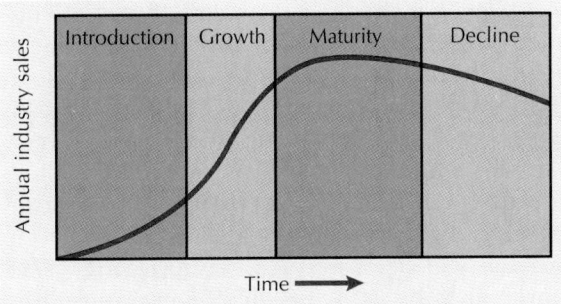

FIGURE 22.5 *Product Life Cycle Over Time*

Phase	Introduction	Growth	Maturity	Decline
Market rate	Slow	Rapid	Slow-level	Negative
Market size	Small	Medium-level	Large	Contracting
Competition	Dominance by innovator, few firms	Entry, many competitors, shifting shares	Solidified shares, stability	Exits, price competition

FIGURE 22.6 *Product Life Cycle Characteristics*

Growth describes the next phase, when demand expands rapidly. As the product's novelty wears off, buyers relax their skepticism, perk up their interest, and open their purses. First-time buyers flock to the market. As the market becomes ever larger, competition among sellers takes the form of new entry, new innovations, and new marketing promotions. Atari was challenged by Coleco and others during this phase, while Apple witnessed a flood of new entrants in personal computers, IBM and AT&T included.

Maturity settles in when growth subsides. Here the market reaches its largest dimensions, with demand solidly established. First-time purchasing dwindles relative to replacement buying. Competition at this stage is typically less chaotic than it is during growth. The market shares of firms tend to stabilize after what is called a *shakeout*, a period that bridges growth and maturity, with the demise of the market's weakest firms. As this is written, the market for video games has reached maturity. The personal computer market remains one of growth.

Decline, if it occurs, is a period of market contraction. Demand dwindles, perhaps even to the point of disappearing. A major cause of such decline is the new appearance of preferred substitute products, which enter their growth phase partly by attracting consumers away from the old, now declining products, as refrigerators displaced iceboxes. Competition among firms in declining markets often centers on price level and costs. Moreover, firms leave the market because of the depressed circumstances.

Changes in price elasticity and income elasticity may also characterize a product's life cycle, but less clearly and less assuredly than those features just itemized. Broadly speaking, many products tend to have high price and income elasticities during introduction and growth. Later, during the maturity phase, their price and income elasticities tend to fall, often becoming inelastic. Autos, telephone service, radios, and refrigerators illustrate the transformation. Their price and income elasticities are probably much lower now than they were during the first half of this century.

The main problem with the four-phase theory of product life cycles is that it fits many real markets only very loosely and others not at all. The duration of the phases varies widely across products.

Moreover, some products skip a phase or two, moving, for example, from growth to decline without pausing for a stretch of maturity. Other products, like shoes, never experience decline. Indeed, decline can sometimes be postponed indefinitely by innovations that periodically revive the market. Prerecorded music technologies, for instance, have gone from the old 78s, to LPs and 45s, to cassettes, to the present wonder—compact laser disks. Still, the theory is often useful.

Read Perspective 22C.

C

Other Dynamic Influences on Demand

Many dynamic forces affect demand, thereby nurturing a product through a standard life cycle or causing deviations from the four phases.[14] We shall focus on just three forces with influences related to factors discussed previously—(1) complementary innovations, (2) substitute innovations, and (3) buyer segmentation.

1. Complementary Innovations The dynamic expansion or contraction of a product's demand can often be caused by complementary linkage to another product experiencing expansion or contraction. Computer software highlights the case of expansion. During the early 1980s, the booming sales of personal computers fostered an enormous expansion in the market for personal computer software. From humble beginnings as a relatively tiny industry in 1979, personal computer software sales grew at an astounding 44 percent annual rate to exceed $2 billion in 1984. Sales may be about $8 billion in 1989, which implies a rate of sales growth exceeding that of personal computers themselves.

2. Substitute Innovations The innovation and growth of new products that serve as substitutes for old products can cause those old products to age more rapidly than otherwise. Maturity may then come prematurely. Decline could then be quickened. This is, of course, what happened to the horse and buggy after the advent of the auto-

---

[14]Michael E. Porter, *Competitive Strategy* (New York: Free Press, 1980), pp. 162–88.

PERSPECTIVE 22C:
U.S. Auto Sales, 1900–85

The strengths and weaknesses of the product life cycle theory can be seen in Figure 22.7, which shows new car sales in the United States from 1900 to 1985. To smooth year-to-year fluctuations, the data are presented as averages of annual sales during 5-year intervals. Except for the two decades of the 1930s and 1940s, which can justifiably be set aside, the data fit the theory fairly well, but obviously not precisely. During the 1930s, the United States languished in the Great Depression and the auto industry suffered severely, along with most other industries. During the early 1940s, World War II forced a very sharp curtailment in auto production as the industry's resources were turned to the manufacture of war vehicles like tanks, trucks, and jeeps. There were, for example, only 139 new cars sold in the United States during 1943. Aside from the economic traumas of these two decades, though, there are several periods that seem patterned on the phases of product life cycle theory. First, the years 1900 through 1915 display characteristics of introduction. Second, the ensuing 15 years, from 1915 to 1930, appear to qualify as a growth stage. Annual auto sales multiplied stupendously during that era, doubling and redoubling until sales in 1929 were *five times* greater than they were in 1915. Third, it can be argued that the 1950s and 1960s represent an age of transition between growth and maturity. Sales expanded briskly, but nowhere near the high percentage rate of expansion over 1915–1930. Finally, possibly since the late 1960s and certainly since the early 1970s, the auto market has shown signs of maturity. Annual sales have, on the whole, stagnated at around 9 to 10 million. Hence, on the basis of present data, it seems safe to say that the U.S. auto market is now in a phase of maturity and has been for two decades or so.

---

mobile. Iceboxes provide another good example. Icebox sales chilled rapidly after electric refrigerators were introduced in the late 1920s.

Substitute innovations need not always push rival products into an early grave. However, even when they do not, they may sharply alter the evolution of the old product's demand, thereby prompting suppliers of the old product to innovate in self-defense. The motion picture industry has, for instance, weathered several storms from substitute innovations—television and VCRs most obviously. It has survived, and by some measures continued to grow, by following two broad strategies that have retained a large following of buyers. First, motion pictures exhibited in theaters have been improved by such innovations as Cinemascope and Dolby sound. Second, the industry branched out to take part in the markets for substitute products, producing films for television and packaging films for VCR replay. The industry followed its demand to new pastures, so to speak,

adapting to technological change rather than succumbing to it.

3. Buyer Segmentation Henry Ford's Model T had a great deal to do with lifting the auto industry out of its introduction phase into explosive growth. Priced below average per capita income at only $450, it became the industry's standard of what a car should be. And standard it was, fixed in one simple style for nearly 20 years from 1908 to 1925 and available in only one color—black. Had cars remained patterned on the Model T Ford, the industry might not have reached its present-day prominence. But the growth spurt of the 1920s can be credited in part to a growing diversity of product offerings. For prices under $1,000, buyers had only 3 cars to choose from in 1920 but 27 to choose from by 1926. A leader in developing a diversity of autos was General Motors, which foresaw that a *range* of model offerings, spanning a *range* of price categories and styles, would stimulate demand

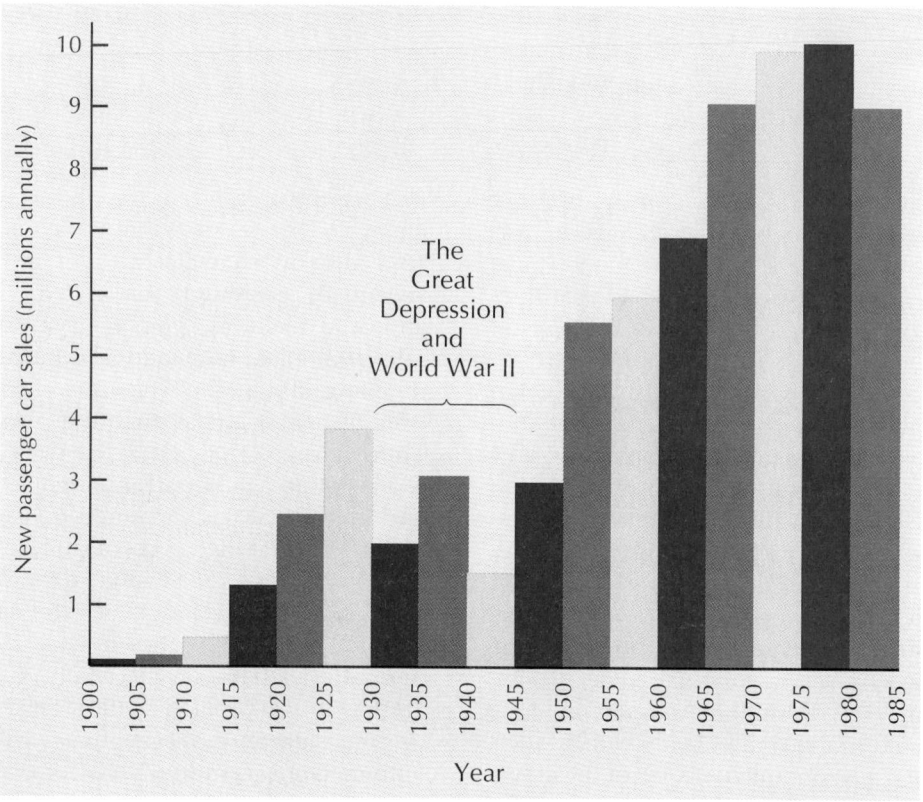

FIGURE 22.7 U.S. Passenger Car Sales in Millions, Five-Year Averages of Annual Rates

(*Source: A. D. Chandler, Jr.*, Giant Enterprise. *New York: Harcourt, Brace, 1964, p. 4*; Statistical Abstract of the United States).

appreciably by serving different segments of the consuming population. The result was Chevrolet in the low-priced segment and Cadillac in the high-priced segment, with Pontiac, Buick, and Oldsmobile in between. Ford and Chrysler followed with their own families of cars. Now that the auto industry is in its maturity, segmentation goes beyond price range to include substantial variations in size, seating capacity, mechanical capability, and sports styling.

Such product segmentation occurs because buyers can be segmented by features that affect their demand—in particular, income level and a number of factors that influence tastes (e.g., age, sex, geographic location, and ethnic origin). Moreover, buyer segmentation often seems to grow as products advance through stages of their life cycle, at least into maturity. Decline often prompts a decline in segmentation. A main reason for this is that market size varies with life cycle, and a large market can support greater segmentation than a small market.

SUMMARY

There is more to demand than meets the eye. The relationship between price and quantity is rich:

1. Price elasticity of demand measures the responsiveness of quantity to price variations. Defined as the percentage change in quantity divided by percentage change in price, it is *elastic* if greater than 1, *inelastic* if less than 1, and *unit elastic* if equal to 1.

The midpoint formula yields consistent computation.

2. Total revenue is price times quantity, so its genealogy likewise lies in demand. Moreover, total revenue and price elasticity share intimacies. When $E_d > 1$, price and total revenue move in *opposite* directions, one up and the other down. When $E_d < 1$, price and total revenue move in the same direction. When $E_d = 1$, price changes leave total revenue undisturbed.

3. Price elasticity varies across commodities. In general, it is higher when (a) close substitutes are available; (b) the good takes a large share of consumer budgets; and (c) a long time is allowed for quantity to adjust.

4. Cross-price elasticity of demand results from the ratio of the percentage change in the quantity of one good over the percentage change in the price of another. A positive price-cross elasticity holds for substitutes, a negative one for complements.

5. Dynamic conditions influence demand over time. (a) With changes in income—usually upward changes over time—the income elasticity of demand gains importance. It is the percentage change in quantity divided by the percentage change in consumer income. (b) A product's life cycle often, though not always, follows a four-phase pattern of introduction, growth, maturity, and decline. (c) Real-world dynamics include the influence of complementary innovations, substitute innovations, and buyer segmentation. These influences can be positive, negative, or mixed.

KEY TERMS

Price elasticity of demand
Total revenue
Total expenditure
Cross-price elasticity of demand

Income elasticity of demand
Product life cycles
Price elasticity of supply (in appendix)

QUESTIONS AND PROBLEMS

1. Schmoos were priced at $10.00 in May and the manufacturer was selling 2000 per week. In June, the price tag was raised to $11.00 and sales dropped to 1800 per week. Assuming that no other considerations other than price were involved in the decline in sales, compute the price elasticity of demand for schmoos. Is schmoo demand elastic, inelastic, or unit elastic?

2. Compare the formulas by which you compute the slope of a straight line demand curve and the price elasticity of a straight line demand curve. Which terms cause the price elasticity to vary along the curve, while the slope is constant?

3. If a monopolist (controlling an entire market) wanted to maximize its total revenue, it would price its product in such a way that a certain price elasticity of demand would be experienced. What would that price elasticity be? (Hint: Refer to Figure 22.4.)

4. How could the owners of a small family business estimate the price elasticity of demand for their product? Do you think most small business owners would be very interested in the price elasticity of demand for their product? Why or why not?

5. Individual consumers differ in their demands for any given product. In particular, some will be more responsive to price cuts than others. In view of this, can you explain why a local clothing store might choose to have a heavily advertised one-day sale every month rather than to reduce prices for the entire month?

6. Describe the four phases suggested by the product life cycle theory. What implications might this theory have for a company deciding whether to market a new product?

7. Would the demand curve for insulin by diabetics be perfectly inelastic? Why or why not?

8. As standards of living rise over the years, some sectors of an economy will decline in importance

while others gain. For example, agricultural output typically declines as a percentage of total output. Explain why.

9. List some factors that determine the price elasticity of demand for a given commodity and explain their impacts.

From the appendix:

10. Distinguish between the immediate run, the short run, and the long run (both graphically and verbally).

Appendix:

Elasticity of Supply

The concept of elasticity can be applied to supply as well as demand. Whereas price elasticity of demand measures the responsiveness of *buyers* to changes in price, price elasticity of supply measures the responsiveness of *sellers* to price changes. The price elasticity of supply is calculated in the same way as the price elasticity of demand, except that quantity, or *q*, now refers to quantity *supplied*, not quantity demanded.

> **Price elasticity of supply,** E_s, is the percentage change in quantity supplied divided by the percentage change in price.

The midpoint formula would again apply. Let p_1 and p_2 be the first and second prices, and let q_1 and q_2 be the first and second quantities supplied by firms in the market. Then

$$E_S = \frac{q_1 - q_2}{(q_1 + q_2)/2} \Big/ \frac{p_1 - p_2}{(p_1 + p_2)/2}$$

As with price elasticity of demand, the E_s numbers fall into three classes:

$E_s > 1$ (elastic)
$E_s = 1$ (unitary elastic)
$E_s < 1$ (inelastic)

When $E_s > 1$, quantity supplied is highly responsive to price changes. When $E_s = 1$, quantity supply and price level move proportionately. A 10 percent price hike induces a 10 percent rise in supply. When $E_s < 1$, quantity supplied tends to be *unresponsive* to changes in price.

Figure A highlights the range of possible responsiveness by showing *perfectly elastic* and *perfectly inelastic* supplies. If supply is perfectly elastic, E_s is infinite and any amount can be offered by suppliers at the going price, say $2.00. If, in contrast, the supply is perfectly inelastic, E_s is 0 and variations in price lead to no changes in the quantity supplied.

What factors determine elasticity of supply? There are some special circumstances. The supply of genuine Rembrandt paintings can only be perfectly inelastic, given the Dutch master's inability to produce more. Sidestepping such special circumstances, cost conditions play a major role, and the element of time sharply influences costs. *In general, the longer period of time producers have to vary their output in response to price changes, the greater the elasticity of supply.*

Economists conventionally distinguish three time periods in which producers can respond to a given change in prices—the immediate run, the short run, and the long run. *The immediate run is a time period so short that the quantity supplied cannot change at all.* This is an instantaneous situation, also called the *market period* or *momentary period.* All that can be supplied is that which is already offered for sale. The result is a perfectly

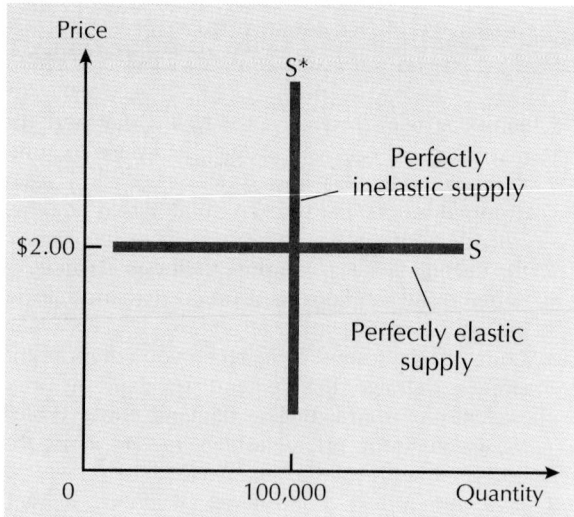

FIGURE A *Perfectly Elastic and Perfectly Inelastic Supply Curves*

If supply is perfectly elastic, $E_s = \infty$. At a price of $2.00, any amount can be supplied by sellers. If supply is perfectly inelastic, $E_s = 0$. Here 100,000 units of output will be offered by sellers regardless of price level.

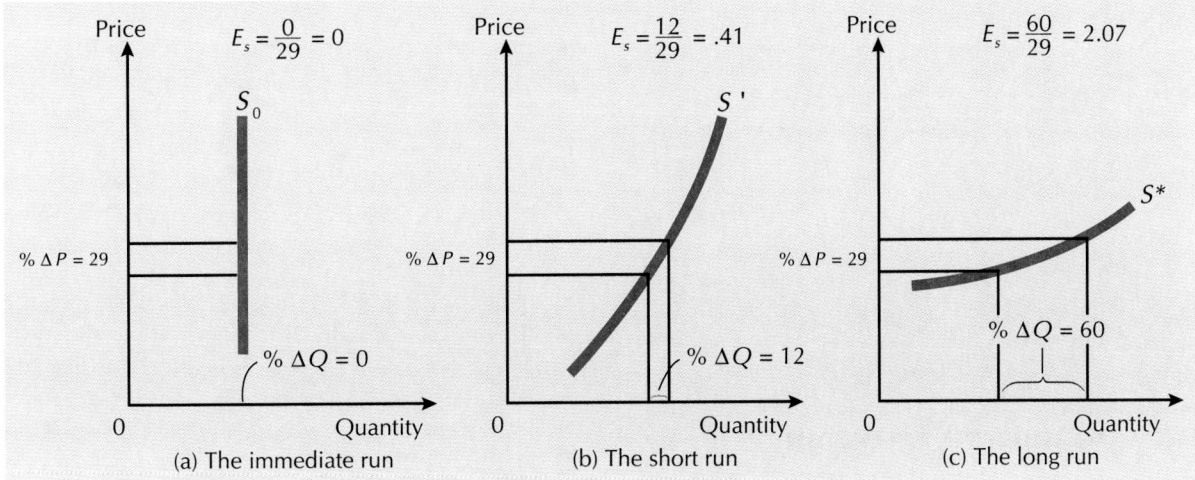

FIGURE B _The Price Elasticity of Supply as Determined by Time Period_

(a) In the immediate run, time is so short that the only supplies offered will be those already produced, a fixed amount. (b) In the short run, output can be varied only within the limits permitted by fixed inputs like plant and equipment. (c) In the long run, supply can be highly responsive to price changes because all inputs can vary. Additional plants can be built and additional equipment purchased, adding productive capacity.

inelastic supply curve such as the one pictured in part (a) of Figure B. A 29 percent price change is indicated, but the quantity supplied cannot change.

The short run is a period of time long enough to allow existing firms to vary their output by varying capacity use, but not long enough for them to change their capacity or long enough for firms to enter or exit the market. Inputs that are variable in the short run can be increased or decreased, but fixed inputs remain fixed. Thus firms respond to price increases by putting employees on overtime, adding night shifts, purchasing more materials,

burning more fuel, and the like. Output can increase, but only at much higher cost per unit as capacity is pressed to the limit. The marketwide result is an inelastic supply curve such as that shown in Figure B(b). The 29 percent jump in price coaxes the supply to increase, but only by about 12 percent, an inelastic result.

The long run is a period of time long enough to allow existing firms to expand their capacity and new firms to enter the market (or to allow contraction of capacity and exits). The long run grants more flexibility to producers, as Figure B(c) illustrates.

23

Supply Conditions: Productivity and Costs

A few cost figures are worth a thousand words. The Japanese auto industry has been gaining on the U.S. auto industry in a battle that has raged since the 1960s. At stake are hundreds of thousands of jobs and tens of billions of dollars in car sales. Aside from quality differences, the Japanese have had a tremendous advantage in terms of lower costs per car. As of 1983, for instance, the Japanese could produce and ship a subcompact car at a cost running $1,600 to $2,000 less than U.S. costs.

Why the huge cost difference? Two factors explain most of it. First, labor _productivity_ in Japan was about 2.5 times greater than that in the United States. Second, labor _costs_ per hour were $8 higher in the United States. These two factors combined caused a U.S. subcompact car to cost about $1,600 more than the Japanese product in 1983.[1]

What is productivity? What are costs? What is the arithmetic behind these momentous numbers? These comprise the key questions of this chapter. You will learn about:

1. Economic concepts of costs derived from opportunity costs.
2. The factors influencing costs—productivity and input prices in particular.
3. Productivity as a function of input levels.
4. Costs as a function of output levels.
5. Costs as a function of input prices and technology.

I

Costs and Profits: Basic Concepts

A

Opportunity Costs

Scarcity is the central focus of economics. Moreover, scarcity gives rise to opportunity costs. It's therefore fitting that when economists speak of

[1]_Fortune_, June 25, 1984, p. 23.

costs, opportunity costs are what they usually have in mind.

Defined earlier as the sacrifice of the next best alternative when a choice is made, opportunity costs loom at every level of economic activity. Your opportunity cost of an album might be a forgone steak dinner. America's opportunity cost of building missiles might be many forgone VCRs and microwave ovens. Business firms likewise face opportunity costs.

> The **opportunity cost** of an action is the value of the best forgone alternative.

A firm's opportunity costs fall into two categories—_explicit costs_ and _implicit costs_. To see where the division lies, imagine that the Chrysler Corporation has a plant presently capable of producing 200,000 cars a year and occupying part of a vast tract of land. Suppose Chrysler purchased the land and built the plant 50 years ago, so that it owns them both outright. Now the firm is planning a modern addition that will take up 60 of its unused acres. What are the opportunity costs of the plant expansion?

Some will be _explicit costs_ because they entail explicit payments to resource suppliers—payments to purchase building materials, to acquire equipment, to hire workers, and the like. Chrysler writes checks to cover these obligations. The explicit costs reflect opportunity costs because Chrysler will have to pay enough to attract these resources away from their alternative uses. The building materials could be used to construct bakeries, breweries, or other plants, so Chrysler must pay enough to compensate suppliers for those forgone alternatives. The workers Chrysler hires could be employed elsewhere, so they must be paid a wage high enough to attract them away from alternative jobs. In sum, a firm's explicit costs are essentially the same as its _accounting costs_, the costs accountants record for raw materials, labor, energy, and the like. The explicit costs also reflect opportunity costs.

Consider next the cost of the idle 60-acre parcel covered by the plant expansion. Is it correct to say that it costs nothing because Chrysler, having long-term ownership, need not pay one penny to purchase the land? No. There is an *implicit cost*. Using the land for this plant expansion means that it cannot be used by Chrysler for some other purpose, such as a warehouse, and cannot be sold to another firm, which would use it for, say, an amusement park. The value of the land in its next best alternative use is the opportunity cost of the land, a cost that would not show up on Chrysler's accounting books, but a cost nonetheless—an implicit cost.

> An **explicit cost** (or accounting cost) is incurred when the firm makes an actual payment. An **implicit cost** is incurred when a valued alternative is forgone. Explicit costs plus implicit costs equal the firm's overall opportunity costs.

The most important implicit costs typically do not relate to land, which usually incurs explicit costs, but rather to less tangible items. Entrepreneurial compensation is one such item. If you were the owner-operator of a one-cab taxi service, you might not pay yourself a wage for your hourly time, choosing instead to take whatever accounting profit you could claim for the business. Your time has an implicit cost, however, a cost reflected in the best income you could earn by working for wages (as an auto assembler, perhaps). Another important implicit cost relates to financial capital. If you spend $10,000 of your savings to buy a taxi cab, you forgo the opportunity of earning the best alternative return. Your money could earn interest in a savings account or dividends from stock ownership. In November 1983, Lee Iacocca, chairman of Chrysler, disclosed the importance of this implicit cost when discussing $600 million in cash that his company was holding. He announced that Chrysler might cancel plans to spend the $600 million to develop a new small car, and use the money to buy a bank instead. "I'm thinking seriously about getting the hell out," he said, because "the profit margin is higher in the banking business than in automobiles." (When asked to elaborate by reporters, Iacocca went on to say that the small-car business threatens to become unprofitable for

U.S. manufacturers because a Japanese car had a $2,000 cost advantage.)[2]

B
Economic Profits

Iacocca's comments raise a further issue—namely, the distinction between *accounting profits* and *economic profits*. To understand, imagine what Iacocca might say if Chrysler's chief accountant reported happily to him that Chrysler had made not a loss but a tidy profit in, say, 1982. Upon entering Iacocca's office, the accountant gleefully states that subtracting total accounting costs from total sales revenues yields a profit of $11,347. Would Iacocca be pleased? Certainly not. He might shout, "This corporation has $6.3 billion in assets! A profit of $11,347 is no real profit at all!" In economic jargon, this accounting profit of $11,347 is not an *economic* profit because it ignores implicit, nonaccounting opportunity costs such as the opportunity cost of Chrysler's capital.

> **Accounting profit** is the firm's revenues less explicit accounting costs. (If negative, it's an accounting loss.) **Economic profit** is the firm's revenues less total opportunity costs. (If negative, it's an economic loss.)

The examples in Table 23.1 illustrate these definitions. The accounting approach of the first example looks only at the difference between total revenue and explicit costs, yielding an accounting profit of $20 million. The economic approach of the second example subtracts *all* opportunity costs from total revenue, implicit as well as explicit. The result yields a positive economic profit of $10 million. The third example, which assumes a revenue of $85 million instead of the $100 million in the first two examples, illustrates a case in which accounting profit would be positive ($85 − $80 = $5) while economic profit is negative, a loss of $5 million.

The data of Table 23.1 tell us one thing more. Given explicit costs of $80 million and implicit costs of $10, total opportunity costs are $90 million. If revenues were $90, equalling this cost total, economic profit would be zero. A condition of zero

[2]*San Jose Mercury News*, November 17, 1983, p. 1F.

TABLE 23.1   Hypothetical Examples of Cost Concepts (in Millions)

1. Accounting Approach		2. Economic Approach (with Economic Profit)		3. Economic Approach (with Economic Loss)	
Revenue:	$100	Revenue:	$100	Revenue:	$ 85
Less accounting costs:		Less opportunity costs:		Less opportunity costs:	
Explicit costs	$ 80	Explicit costs	$ 80	Explicit costs	$ 80
		Implicit costs	$ 10	Implicit costs	$ 10
Accounting profit	$ 20	Economic profit	$ 10	Economic loss	($5)

economic profit has special meaning in economics. It is a significant threshold for those who would be suffering economic losses *below* the zero threshold or enjoying economic profits *above* the zero threshold. Who might these people be? They would *not* be those on the receiving end of explicit costs, like materials suppliers or wage earners, because they are paid explicitly according to contractual commitments, "on the spot" so to speak. Rather, they would be those people rewarded without contractual assurances, namely the entrepreneur whose time has an implicit opportunity cost (as a salaried worker elsewhere) and the owners whose capital investment has an implicit opportunity cost (the return that could be earned if the funds were invested elsewhere). If economic profits are *less than zero* (*negative*), it does not matter that accounting profits might be positive (like the hypothetical $11,347 reported to Iacocca). These owners and entrepreneurs will disappointedly pull up stakes, fold their tents, and divert their resources to the more promising alternative opportunities reflected in the implicit opportunity costs. Conversely, if economic profits are *greater than zero* (*positive*), these owners and entrepreneurs will be delighted because their rewards will then exceed those expected of their next best alternative opportunities. Indeed, positive excess profits would attract additional entrepreneurial and capital commitments from outsiders who want to get a piece of the highly profitable action. In between, with economic profit *equal to zero*, entrepreneurs and owners will simply be content to maintain their positions. At zero, the signal sent by economic profit is neither negatively repellent nor positively magnetic.

Stated bluntly, economic profits and losses trigger the expansion and contraction of firms and industries. The prospect of positive economic profits encourages risk taking, including innova-

tion. The prospect of negative economic profits discourages investment. This signal thus plays a key role in guiding the market system toward answers to the basic economic questions of What?, How?, and What's new?

A situation of zero economic profit goes by another name that is more compact and perhaps more descriptive—*normal profit*. When a firm earns a normal profit, there is enough accounting profit to cover the opportunity costs of entrepreneurial services and ownership capital, no more and no less. Such is also the case when economic profit is zero. If profit is not normal, it is either above or below normal. Above-normal profit (or excess profit) attracts added resource commitments. Below-normal profit acts as a repellent, causing owners and entrepreneurs to depart for greener pastures.

> A **normal profit** is compensation for entrepreneurial skill and financial capital that is just enough to keep that skill and capital from leaving a firm and going into other productive activities. It is the opportunity cost of a firm's owners.

Unless stated otherwise, future references to a firm's costs include a normal profit as a cost because it is, after all, an opportunity cost.

II

Basic Determinants of Costs

A

Identification

Figure 23.1 illustrates that there are two main determinants of cost per unit of output, such as cost per car or cost per can of chili. First, and most

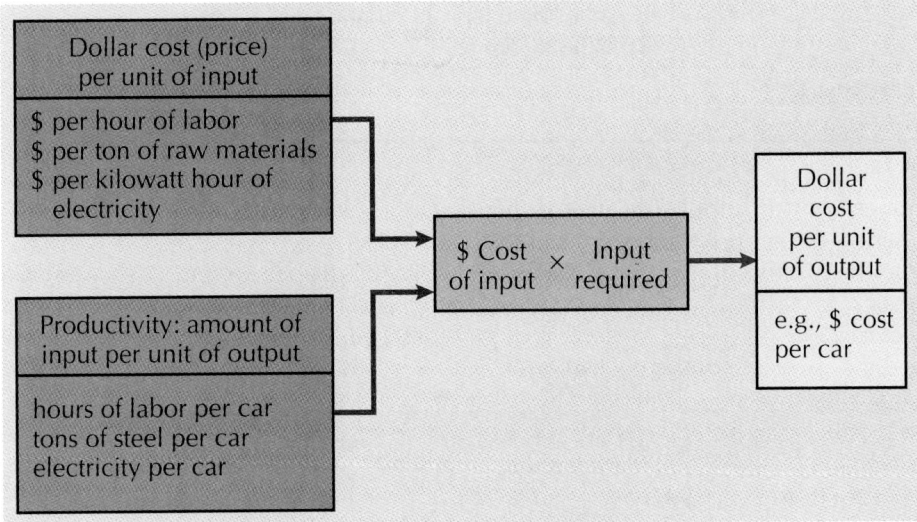

FIGURE 23.1 *Basic Determinants of Cost Per Unit (e.g., Per Car)*

obvious, is the dollar outlay that must be made to purchase each unit of resource input, resources such as labor, raw materials, and energy. For example, the price paid, or cost, for an hour of labor in the U.S. auto industry was about $22 in 1983. This included fringe benefits like health insurance, as well as the hourly wage rate. The comparable cost in Japan was about $14 per hour of labor.

The second basic determinant of cost per unit of output is input productivity. For present purposes, this is most easily expressed as the number of units of each input required to produce a unit of output. In our example of 1983 automobile production, it took roughly 91 hours of labor time to assemble a subcompact car in the United States, whereas in Japan it took approximately 32 hours. These numbers for labor tell the most about the advantages that the Japanese auto industry had over its U.S. counterpart because the productivity of other inputs in the two countries was much more closely comparable. The amounts of steel and glass in Japanese and U.S. subcompacts, for instance, were essentially the same. Indeed, it is interesting to note that the number of labor hours embodied in the auto *parts* of these two subcompacts (as distinct from the assembly of those parts into autos) were about the same: around 50 hours.

Productivity can also be expressed as the amount of output per unit of some input. This is simply the *inverse* of productivity expressed as input requirement per unit of output. Oversimplified, output per unit of input is output/input, while the input requirement per unit of output is input/output. If, for example, 91 hours of labor time are required to assemble one car (input/output = 91/1), then car output per hour of labor input is the inverse, 0.011 car per hour (output/input = 1/91).

> **Productivity** refers to the relation between resource inputs and product outputs. It is expressed as inputs required per unit of output (input/output) or outputs per unit of input (output/input).

Productivity expressed as input requirements is most convenient for present purposes because, as shown in Figure 23.1, it may be *multiplied* by the dollar cost per unit of input to yield the *dollar cost per unit of output*. It is a simple recipe combining (1) the dollar cost of each unit of input and (2) the number of input units needed for each unit of output. To wrap up our example of labor cost per subcompact car, we can compute the multiplication for the United States and Japan using the data already revealed:

	$ per Hour Cost of Assembly Labor	×	Hours of Assembly Labor per Car	=	Labor Cost per Car
United States	$22	×	91 hours	=	$2,002
Japan	$14	×	32 hours	=	$ 448

Using output per unit of input (the inverse of input requirements), the same results are reached by *division*. For the United States, for instance, $22 ÷ 1/91 = $2,002.

Read Perspective 23A.

B
Variations

Digging deeper, we must ask, what causes the dollar outlay per unit of input to vary? And what determines input productivity? Knowing that the

---

PERSPECTIVE 23A
The Cost of Steel

Like the U.S. auto industry, the U.S. steel industry has been battered by Japanese competition over the past two decades. Here, too, the crux of the competition lies in costs. Table 23.2 gives the average operating costs (excluding capital and administrative costs) of producing a ton of cold-rolled sheet steel in the United States in 1980. The first two columns present data for the two elements of cost outlined in Figure 23.1, namely, (1) dollar outlay per unit of input and (2) the amount of input required per ton of steel output. Multiplying these two columns yields the cost per ton of cold-rolled sheet in column (3). Thus, labor cost per ton is $135, and iron ore cost per ton of steel is $58. Adding all the inputs gives an overall cost of $374 per ton. Comparable data for the Japanese

steel industry indicate that their operating costs per ton were $88 lower—that is, $286 per ton of steel. Which of the inputs of Table 23.2 was most to blame for this $88 difference? Labor. Japanese labor costs of $64 per ton of steel were $71 less than the U.S. figure of $135, less by more than half of the U.S. figure. The final question is, which element of labor was to blame for the labor cost differential, hourly outlay or productivity? It turns out that *both* were to blame, but the wage rate differences were most striking. The wage-cost-times-labor-input equation for Japan, by comparable data, was $11 per hour × 5.8 hours = $64 per ton of cold-rolled sheet. Chilling numbers if your livelihood hinges on the fortunes of the U.S. steel industry.

TABLE 23.2 The Operating Costs of Producing 1 Ton of Cold-Rolled Sheet Steel in the United States, 1980

Input	(1) Cost of Input (per Unit of Input)		(2) Input Required (Number of Units)		(3) Cost per Ton of Steel
Labor	$18.80 per hour	×	7.20 hours		= $135
Iron ore	$36.00 per ton	×	1.59 tons		= $ 58
Purchased scrap	$89.50 per ton	×	0.16 ton		= $ 14
Coking coal (energy)	$52.50 per ton	×	0.85 ton		= $ 45
Other	—		—		$122
	Total operating costs per ton				$374

Source: D.F. Barnett and L. Schorsch, *Steel: Upheaval in a Basic Industry* (Cambridge, Mass.: Ballinger, 1983), p. 64.

cost and productivity of inputs combine to determine the cost of output is not enough. What influences them?

1. The Cost (or Price) of Inputs The cost (or price) of each input—like an hour of labor—depends on opportunity costs. A firm must pay each input a rate high enough to entice it away from alternative opportunities. That is the basic idea. Elaboration on this basic idea would require discussion of the demand for and supply of resources, consideration of institutional factors like labor unions, and discussion of official regulations governing resource markets. These topics would take us too far afield right now. Hence, this elaboration is saved for later chapters.

Setting this issue of resource prices aside, then, the remainder of this chapter focuses chiefly on variations in productivity. In general, we assume that input prices are constant.

2. The Productivity of Inputs If input requirements rise, cost per unit of output also rises. If input requirements fall, cost per unit of output also falls. So, what causes input requirements per unit of output to rise or fall?

Several interrelated elements are at work—(1) capacity utilization, (2) scale of capacity, (3) time, and (4) technology. These elements are best explained with reference to the productivity of a single input, namely, labor, an input that, overall, accounts for most of the costs of production in our economy and an input subject to wide variations in productivity.

First, variations in *capacity utilization* affect labor productivity. Once built, a plant can be operated more or less intensively over a range that at the low end would imply shutdown and at the high end would imply full-capacity use. Similarly, a farm of a given size could be worked by 1 person, or 3, or 30, or any other number of farm hands with varying degrees of intensity. Measured in *output* rather than input, capacity utilization is often expressed as a percentage. It is a plant's observed output as a percentage of potential, full-capacity output. In 1982, for instance, auto plants in the United States were operating at less than 80 percent capacity utilization.

Labor requirements per unit of output often fall as capacity use rises from low levels. This reduces

the labor cost per unit of output. However, as capacity use rises to the saturation point or beyond, labor requirements per unit eventually rise, causing the labor cost per unit to rise as well. The main reason for these variations in input/output is that resource mix varies as capacity use varies. Less or more labor is being employed in an existing plant of fixed configuration and size, so the resource mix is less or more labor intensive.

Scale of capacity is a second condition influencing labor requirements per unit. A *given, established* plant anchors capacity utilization at present. However, with time, plant capacity can change. New plants can be built and old plants torn down. These changes could alter the entire scale of capacity, from the number of machines in place and the amount of roofing overhead to the acreage of land underfoot. These changes in capacity could also change the number of workers toiling away. Variations in scale can affect productivity because such overall size variations open doors to different labor/capital ratios, different production schedules, and different management practices. In these matters of scale, bigness is sometimes better than smallness, and smallness is sometimes better than bigness. Then too, medium size may sometimes be best at reducing the cost per unit.

Time, the third element, has several possible influences on labor requirements. Note, for instance, that time invaded the previous discussion to distinguish the influences of capacity utilization and scale of capacity. Capacity utilization is a short-run matter because plant capacity is assumed to be fixed, while its utilization rate varies. In contrast, scale of capacity can change only in the long run, a period of time long enough to permit the variation of all resource inputs, including plant and equipment. Aside from drawing the distinction between capacity utilization and scale of capacity, time influences labor requirements in another way as well. Following the innovation of a new product, added time allows added learning by the workforce. For some products, like airliners, the lessons taught by each new unit of output can significantly reduce labor requirements for later units of output and thereby lessen labor costs per unit.

Technology, the last element, refers in this context to the science and engineering in production processes. As *hardware*, technology alters with variations in equipment design, in power sources, in materials makeup, and in other characteristics often observable to the naked eye. For example, the Japanese auto industry has relied more heavily on assembly-line robots than its U.S. competitors, and this partly explains the substantial difference in labor productivity noted earlier. As *software*, improved technology improves the skill level of workers. Higher skill levels, in turn, translate into improved productivity—lower labor input requirements and higher outputs per unit of labor input.

The ensuing sections elaborate on these several points. The next section disregards all dollar values to concentrate on physical productivity—the relationship between inputs and outputs under differing circumstances of capacity use, scale, and technology. Thereafter, dollar values are pinned on the inputs, permitting us to see how cost per unit of output dances to the tunes played by capacity use, scale, and technology.

Despite appearances, this agenda does not omit time. Time accounts for definitions of the short run, which is the context for variations in capacity use, and of the long run, which is the context for variations in scale.

The **short run** is the time period in which at least one of the firm's inputs is fixed (plant and equipment in particular).
The **long run** is a time period in which all inputs are variable (including plant and equipment).

No calendar period applying to all industries can be incorporated in these definitions. For some industries, plant and equipment might be variable within a relatively few months or years. For other industries, the time needed to achieve variability for all inputs might be very lengthy indeed. Compare grocery retailing with nuclear electric power, for instance. It typically takes only about a year to build, furnish, and stock a grocery store. In contrast, it takes 10 years to erect a nuclear power plant. The auto industry lies somewhere between these extremes. General Motors spent 2 years modifying its Fremont, California, plant to produce a new small car.

It may be helpful to think of the long run as a *planning horizon.* The input, output, and cost figures considered are *hypothetical* figures derived from "what if" situations: What if a new plant is built or an old one expanded? What if plants are scaled back or scrapped? In contrast, the input, output, and cost figures of the short run are *actual* figures. Once the type and size of equipment are frozen, as they essentially are in the short run, the monthly and quarterly experiences of the firm are solidified in the reality of immediate circumstances.

The upshot is that time forces a two-part classification of inputs:

A **fixed input** is one whose quantity cannot be changed during the period of time under consideration.
A **variable input** is one whose quantity can be changed during the relevant period.

III
Productivity

A
Short Run: Capacity Use

The physical relationship between outputs and inputs can be captured in a *total view* or a *per unit view*. The *total view* looks at *total output* as input varies. The per unit view looks at *output per unit of input* (or the inverse, input per unit of output) as input varies. The per unit view derives from the total view, so that we essentially have two instructive ways of looking at the same phenomenon.

To illustrate the short-run situation where capacity use varies, let's take auto painting as our hypothetical production process, with painted autos being the output. The main *variable inputs* are unpainted autos, paints, other raw materials, and labor time. Labor time is the most interesting of these, unpainted autos being an input that has a boring one-to-one relation to output in this case. The *fixed inputs* are a shop, paint sprayers, overhead lights, and related equipment.

1. Constant Productivity Table 23.3 gives some hypothetical production data for our auto paint-

TABLE 23.3   Output/Input Relationship: Hypothetical Data for Auto Painting, Constant Productivity

(1) Input: Workers (Per Day)	(2) Output: Total Autos Painted (Per Day)	(3) Average Product (2)/(1)	(4) Labor Requirements (1)/(2)	(5) Marginal Product ΔOutput/ΔInput
0	0	—	—	—
1 worker	2 autos	2 autos	½ worker day	2 autos
2 workers	4 autos	2 autos	½ worker day	2 autos
3 workers	6 autos	2 autos	½ worker day	2 autos
4 workers	8 autos	2 autos	½ worker day	2 autos

ing operation, assuming the simplest case—namely, *no variation in productivity as capacity use varies* (until 100 percent capacity is reached). Total labor input and total auto output occupy the first two columns. Together they represent the total view. Moreover, they represent what may be called a *production function.*

A **production function** summarizes the relationship between total inputs and total outputs assuming a given technology.

When graphed, these first two columns of Table 23.3 appear as part (a) of Figure 23.2, where the vertical axis is total output. Thus two workers per day yield four painted autos per day, three workers yield six autos, and so on. The assumption of constant productivity is reflected in the constant rate at which total output rises as input increases.

The per unit view has several variations, shown as columns (3), (4), and (5) of Table 23.3. Each of these derives from columns (1) and (2). Column (3) shows the *average product,* or the output per unit of labor input on average, or output/input.

The **average product** of an input is the firm's total output divided by the amount of input used to produce this amount of output.

Thus, for example, average product with one worker is 2/1, or two autos per day; with two workers it's 4/2, or two again; and so on. When graphed, the result is part (b) of Figure 23.2. The vertical axis of part (b) compares to that of part (a), both being quantity of output. But the vertical axis of part (b) is best thought of as output *per unit of input.*

Column (4) of Table 23.3 has the data for *labor requirements,* or input per unit of output. As we've already seen, this is the inverse of average product because it is calculated by dividing input by output.

The **input requirement** of an input is the firm's total amount of some input divided by the firm's total output.

In this case, the figure is always 1/2, which results from dividing the data of column (1) by those of (2)—e.g., 1/2, 2/4, etc. Pictorially, part (c) of Figure 23.2 does the honors in this case.

The final and in some ways the most important of the per unit figures is *marginal product,* shown in column (5) of Table 23.3 and in part (b) of Figure 23.2. Marginal product is the *jump* in total output that occurs when labor input *jumps* by one unit—one worker in this case. It shows what is happening at the margin. More formally and generally:

The **marginal product** of an input is the addition to total output due to the addition of an extra unit of that input (the quantity of other inputs being held constant).

As indicated by the jumps from one row to the next in column (2) of Table 23.3 (0 to 2 to 4 to 6 to 8), the added output of painted autos is always two per added worker. This is shown pictorially most directly in part (b) of Figure 23.2, but part (a) contains the same information. The *slope* of the total output curve in part (a) is the marginal product. This is especially noted for two jumps in input, namely, from one to two workers and from three to four workers. (The added unit of labor in this

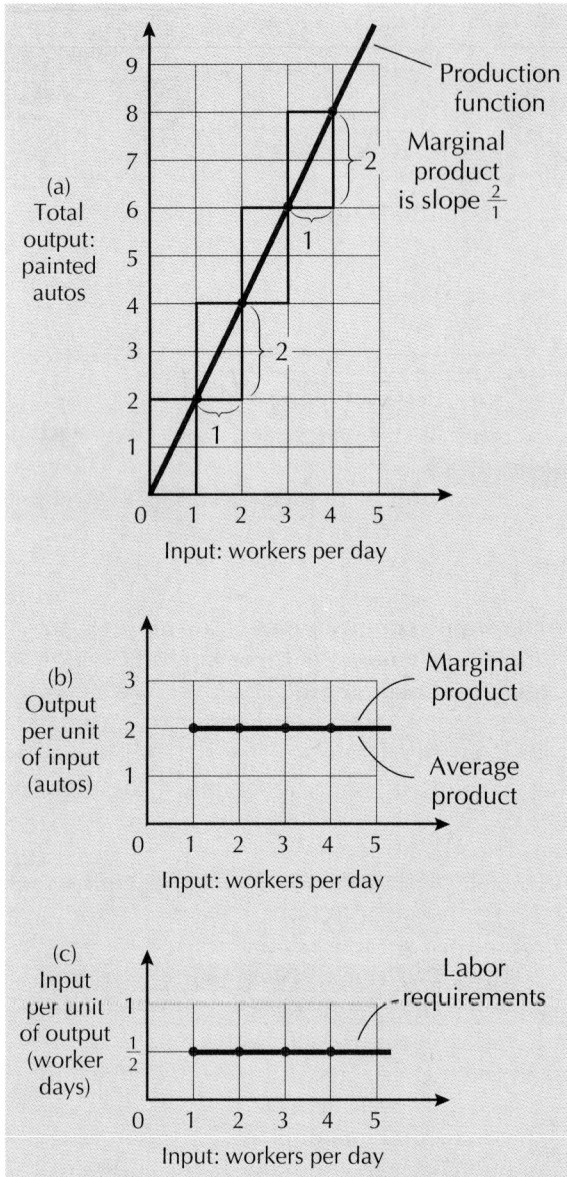

FIGURE 23.2 Output–Input Relationship, Auto Painting, Constant Productivity (Data in Table 23.3)

Part (a) shows the total view, i.e., total output of painted autos as a function of labor input. The slope of this production function is the amount of increased output associated with one added unit of input, or marginal product. Part (b) shows marginal and average product. When productivity does not change with capacity use, these two are equal and constant. Part (c) shows labor requirements, which are also constant.

example is one worker per day, but it could be one additional worker-hour, one additional person-month, or some other unit, depending on the data.)

The present assumption that productivity does *not* change causes the total output curve of part (a) to rise at a *constant rate*. Correspondingly, constant productivity causes each of the per unit relations to remain constant in parts (b) and (c) of Figure 23.2 as inputs rise, moving to the right. Varying the levels of a variable input (labor) relative to a fixed input (plant) has *no* impact on productivity in this case. Many real-world production processes display this trait, usually when the fixed input is highly divisible. A textile plant is, for instance, highly divisible. Its guts are sets of looms, each set largely independent of the others. If each set can be operated by one textile worker, one added worker brings one added set of looms on stream, adding to output the same amount of fabric as any other worker. Given the independence of each worker from the others, the productivity of each added worker can be much the same as that of the last worker when measured in, say, bolts of cloth per day per worker. Other industries experiencing constant productivity over very wide ranges of capacity use are aluminum and apparel manufacturing. However, such constant productivity can occur only when capacity is not fully used. As capacity becomes exhausted or exceeded, productivity will change. This brings us to cases of varying productivity as capacity use varies.

2. Varying Productivity Henceforth, the phrase *rising productivity* will refer to a situation where average or marginal product is rising, even though input requirements will then be falling. Conversely, *falling productivity* will describe cases of falling average and marginal product, although input requirements will then be rising. The shift toward an output orientation moves us away from our previous input orientation, but it brings us closer to prevailing economic jargon.

Figure 23.3 shows two vertical sets of diagrams, (a) for rising productivity and (b) for falling productivity. Looking first at set (a) on the left, we see several characteristics typifying *rising productivity*:

1. In the total view, total output rises at an *increasing rate* as input level rises.
2. In the per unit view, marginal product and average product both *rise* with added input. Marginal product lies *above* average product. Indeed, marginal product *must* be above average product if average prod-

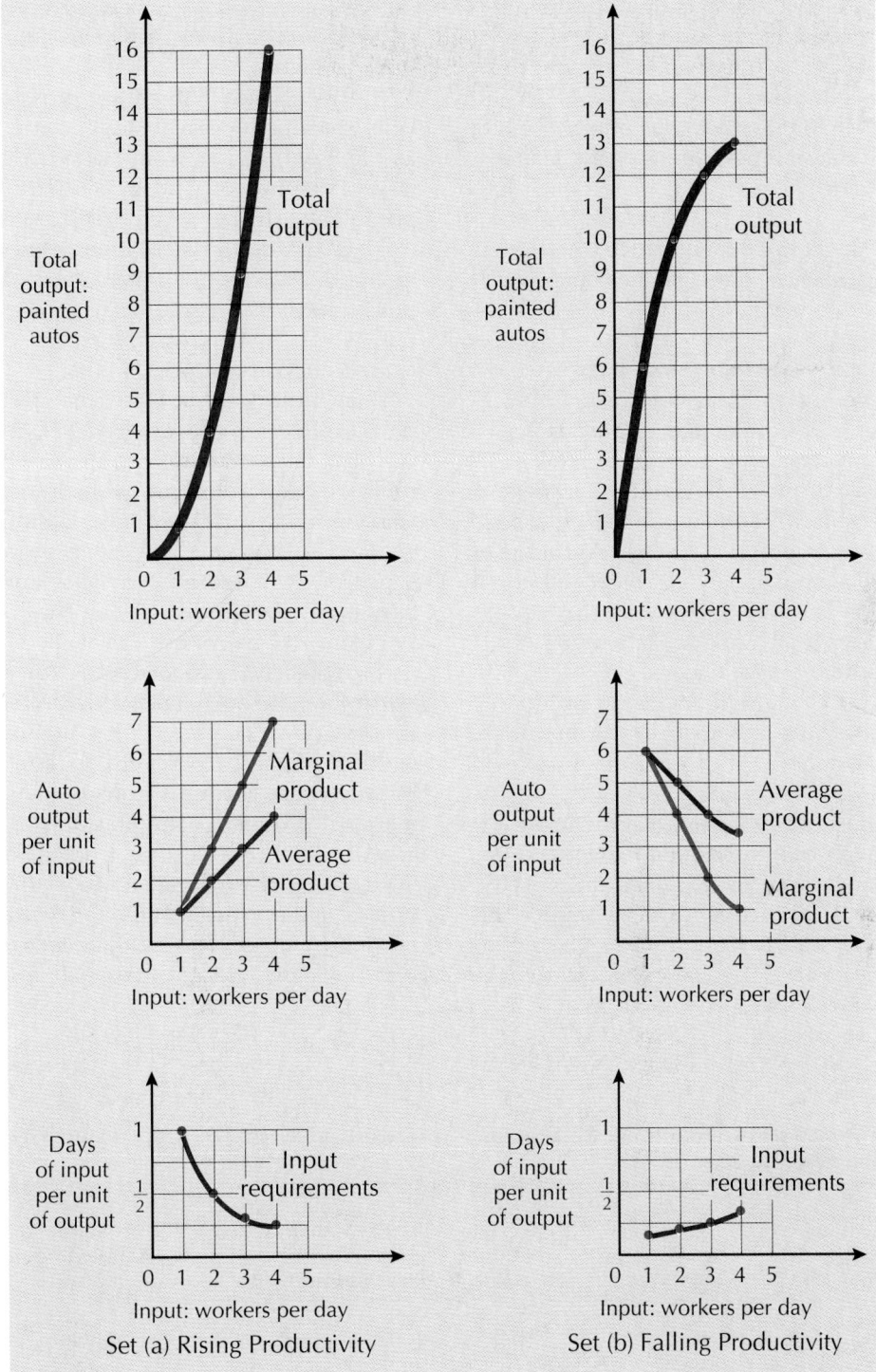

FIGURE 23.3   *Output–Input Relationship with Changing Productivity Over the Range of Inputs*

uct is to rise because marginal product is the ever higher additions to output associated with unit additions of input that lift the overall average.

3. Also in the per unit view, the bottom graph of set (a) shows input requirements *falling* as productivity rises.

Looking next at set (b) of Figure 23.3, we see that *falling productivity* has characteristics of an opposite sort:

1. In the total view, total output rises at a *decreasing rate* as input level rises.
2. In the per unit view, marginal product and average product both *fall* with added input. Marginal product lies *below* average product. In fact, marginal product *must* be below average product if average product is to fall because marginal product embodies the ever lower additions to output associated with unit additions of input that depress the overall average.
3. Finally, input requirements *rise* as productivity falls, a result shown in the bottom graph of set (b).

Which of these two cases is relevant? Conventional economic theory holds that we honor *both*. It is assumed that, given a fixed short-run capacity, productivity *at first rises* as variable inputs like labor are applied to the fixed inputs—the set (a) scenario of Figure 23.3. Thereafter, with ever high-

er levels of variable inputs employed, it is assumed that productivity eventually *falls*—the set (b) scenario of Figure 23.3.

The resulting combination of rising and then falling productivity is illustrated with data in Table 23.4 and with diagrams in Figure 23.4. In the total view of columns (1) and (2) and part (a), total output initially rises at an increasing rate, going from 0 to 1, 1 to 4, and 4 to 9 as input rises from 0 to 1, 1 to 2, and 2 to 3 units of labor. Thereafter, total output continues to rise, but at an ever decreasing rate. Pictorially, the result in part (a) of Figure 23.4 is an S-shaped curve.

The per unit view discloses the ups and downs a bit more clearly. *Average product* in column (3), which is output column (2) divided by input column (1), rises from one painted auto per day of labor input to a peak of three painted autos per worker, on average. Thereafter, average product slips from 3 to 2.8 to 2.5 as labor input increases from four to five to six workers. The arch of part (b) in Figure 23.4 captures the effect.

Next, *marginal product* is the *added* output associated with each *added* unit of labor input. Reading down column (2), it is the *row-to-row* difference. Moving from zero to one worker, for instance, raises output from zero to one, so the marginal product of the first unit of labor is $1 - 0 = 1$. Adding the second worker boosts output from one to four painted autos, so that the second unit of labor may be credited with a marginal product calculated by the difference between four and one, namely, three. Marginal product peaks at

TABLE 23.4   **Output/Input Relationship with Rising and Then Falling Productivity, Hypothetical Data**

(1) Input: Workers (per Day)	(2) Output: Total Autos Painted	(3) Average Product (2)/(1)	(4) Marginal Product Output/Input	(5) Labor Requirements (1)/(2)
0	0	—	—	—
1	1	1	$(1 - 0 =)$ 1	1/1
2	4	2	$(4 - 1 =)$ 3	1/2
3	9	3	$(9 - 4 =)$ 5	1/3
4	12	3	$(12 - 9 =)$ 3	1/3
5	14	2.8	$(14 - 12 =)$ 2	5/14
6	15	2.5	$(15 - 14 =)$ 1	6/15

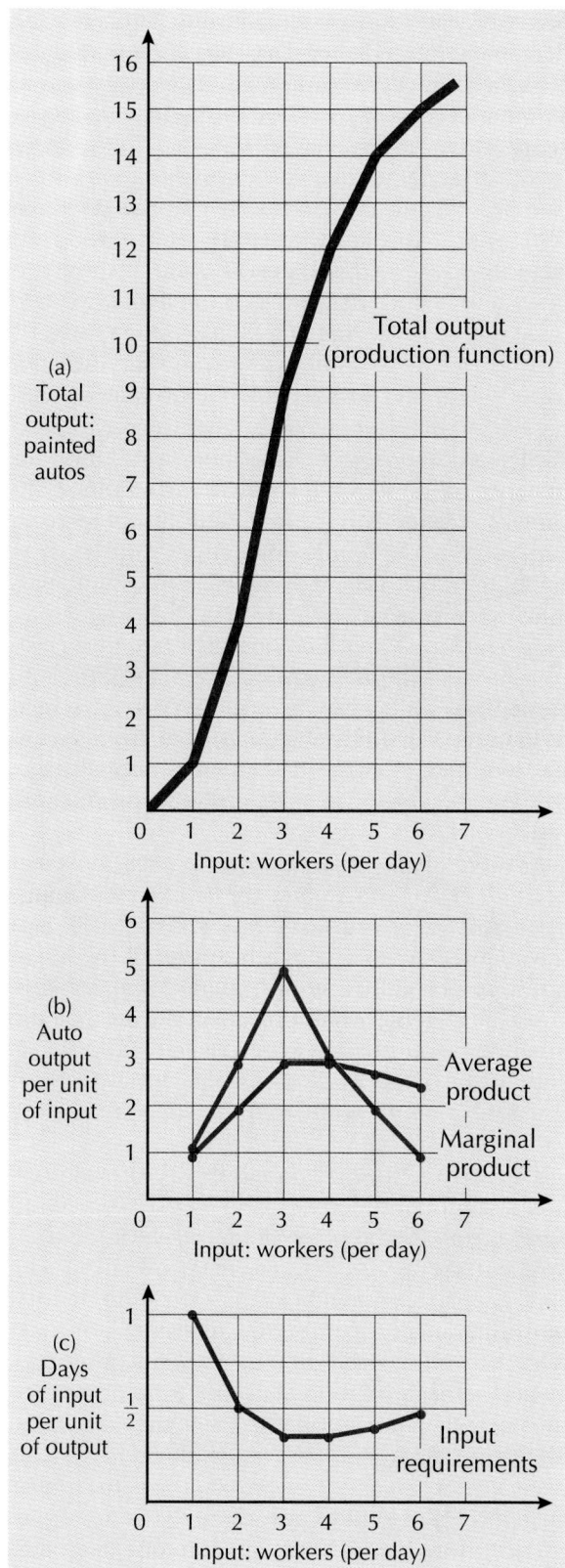

(a) Total output: painted autos

(b) Auto output per unit of input

Average product

Marginal product

(c) Days of input per unit of output

Input requirements

FIGURE 23.4 _Output–Input Relationship with Ris-_ _ing, Then Falling, Productivity (Data in Table 23.4)_

five. Note that the marginal products of three and five in this early range lie _above_ the average product. These relatively high marginal products are pulling the average up. Thereafter, marginal product falls, eventually falling below average product and thereby pulling the average down.

Expressing the pattern as input requirements results in column (5) of Table 23.4 and part (c) of Figure 23.4. When productivity is rising, labor input requirements are falling. Each painted auto then embodies less and less labor input. However, when productivity is falling, labor requirements are rising. To complete the paint jobs on the fifth, sixth, and higher-numbered cars requires more and more labor input.

3. _The Law of Diminishing Marginal Returns_ The observation that marginal product will eventually fall has been generalized into the so-called _law of diminishing marginal returns._

> The **law of diminishing marginal returns** states that if equal units of an input are added, other inputs being held fixed, the resulting additions to output will eventually decrease.

Imagine a small factory that manufactures automobile bumpers with four machines, one each for cutting, shaping, drilling, and finishing. The output of one or two workers would be quite low. They could not specialize. They would have to move materials around, as well as operate machinery. Each additional worker would add considerably to output because specialization could then occur, until eventually there would be too many workers. Once crowded conditions set in—with lines at the machines, worker interference, bumpers bumping, and idleness—added workers will add very little to bumper output. Diminishing returns will have arrived.

This law is unavoidable _under the conditions assumed._ Relaxation of those conditions relaxes its clutches, so those conditions should be explicitly underscored. First, it is assumed that _at least one input is fixed._ This is a short-run phenomenon. Second, it is assumed that _technology remains unchanged._ If technology varied with the added input, marginal product could be kept aloft, at least to a substantial degree. Third, it must be possible _to vary the proportions in which the various_ _inputs are used._ A finely divisible plant, with, for example, one worker per machine, each operating independently, would violate this last assumption over a wide range of variable input. Still, variable proportions would begin to appear at full capacity use. Hence, it seems safe to say that variable proportions seem typical of almost all plants, even if only at full capacity.

B
Long Run: Scale Changes

In the long run, _all_ inputs are variable. Scale can be increased by additions of capital capacity or decreased by subtractions. This allows diverse combinations of inputs. Labor and capital can both increase, or one can be increased given the other.

A graph of the production function generated by two inputs—labor and capital, say—would require three dimensions, one each for labor, capital, and output. Tied to the two dimensions allowed by a paper page, we must illustrate this two-input production function with the matrix of Table 23.5. The numbers inside the matrix are hypothetical outputs, say, autos painted. Movement to the right indicates greater labor input, while upward move-

TABLE 23.5 Hypothetical Production Function with Both Labor _and_ Capital Variable: Long Run

Outputs inside matrix

Units of capital input					
5	14	20	23	26	28
4	11	18	21	24	26
3	7	14	18	21	23
2	3	8	14	18	20
1	1	4	9	12	14
	1	2	3	4	5

Units of labor input

From first two columns of Table 23.4

This shows the number of units of output (inside the matrix) that a hypothetical firm can produce from various combinations of inputs. For example 3 units of labor and 2 units of capital would produce 14 units of output daily. Fourteen units would also be produced by 5 labor and 1 capital, or 2 labor and 3 capital, or 1 labor and 5 capital. Output can be maintained if, as one input is decreased, the other is increased.

ment indicates more capital inputs. Thus, moving diagonally in a northeasterly direction would occur if _both_ labor and capital inputs were increased simultaneously. Any of these three movements—rightward, upward, or northeasterly—increases total output, as indicated by the elevation of the numbers inside the matrix. If graphed in three dimensions, the form created would swoop up from the lower lefthand corner and then begin to crest at the upper righthand corner (looking somewhat like the rear half of a Volkswagen Beetle).

Holding capital input to 1 unit and varying labor input yields the bottom row of the matrix, with data from the first two columns of Table 23.4, seen earlier. As labor input rises from 4 to 5 units, for instance, output climbs from 12 to 14 units. Conversely, if labor is held to 1 unit, an increase in capital from 4 to 5 units lifts output from 11 to 14 units. In either case, the law of diminishing marginal returns begins to bite.

Several input combinations yield 14 units of output. Because capital and labor are _substitutes_ to some degree, they vary inversely as output is held at 14 units. The more labor employed, the less capital required. Conversely, the more capital used, the less need for labor in order to produce 14 units.

Substitutability of inputs provokes an important question: What combination of inputs will produce a given level of output at the lowest cost? This question is clearly a direct offspring of the larger question posed by scarcity—namely, _how_ should goods and services be produced? Note that the amount of output is not at issue. The issue is simply one of technical efficiency—least-cost production of some _given_ output when inputs are variable.

The answer that economic theory provides requires information of two kinds. First, we need to know the marginal product of each input at each level of use. Table 23.5 provides such information. The marginal product of _labor_ is the jump in total output from one cell of the matrix to the next when moving _to the right._ The marginal product of _capital_ is the _jump_ in total output from one cell to the next when moving _upward._ Second, we need to know the price (cost) of obtaining each input because the objective is to minimize the dollar cost, given the level of output.

With these items of information, one can compute *added output per dollar of added expenditure on inputs.* This is "bang for the buck," the idea being to spend dollars sequentially, beginning with the input purchase that increases output the most per price paid, followed by the next most potent purchase, followed by the next, and so on until the output objective is reached. The reasoning is like that of a consumer trying to maximize utility from a limited income or the baseball manager who places his best hitters early in the batting order.

What, then, is the added output per dollar of added input? *It is marginal product divided by the price of a unit of input.* For example, if the *price* of an added day of labor is $100, and the *marginal product* of that added day is 5 units of output, as it is in Table 23.5 when moving from 2 to 3 units of labor given 1 unit of capital input, then added output per dollar spent on labor at that point will

be:

$$\frac{5 \text{ units}}{\$100} = 0.05 \text{ unit of output per dollar}$$

Symbolically, if marginal product of labor is MP_L and price of labor is P_L, this is MP_L/P_L. For capital the symbols would be MP_C/P_C.

Table 23.6 illustrates the wisdom of using MP/P as a guide to lowest cost. The output data are borrowed from the production function of Table 23.5. Moreover, it is assumed that labor and capital are each priced at $100 per unit, so an added unit of labor or capital input would cost $100. The problem is, then, how can 14 units of output be produced at the lowest cost? The correct sequence is shown on the left of Table 23.6, an incorrect sequence on the right, each assuming an identical starting position of 1 unit of capital and 1 unit of

TABLE 23.6   Choosing the Combination of Labor and Capital That Produces 14 Units at the Lowest Cost, Assuming a Price of Labor and Capital at $100 per Unit of Input

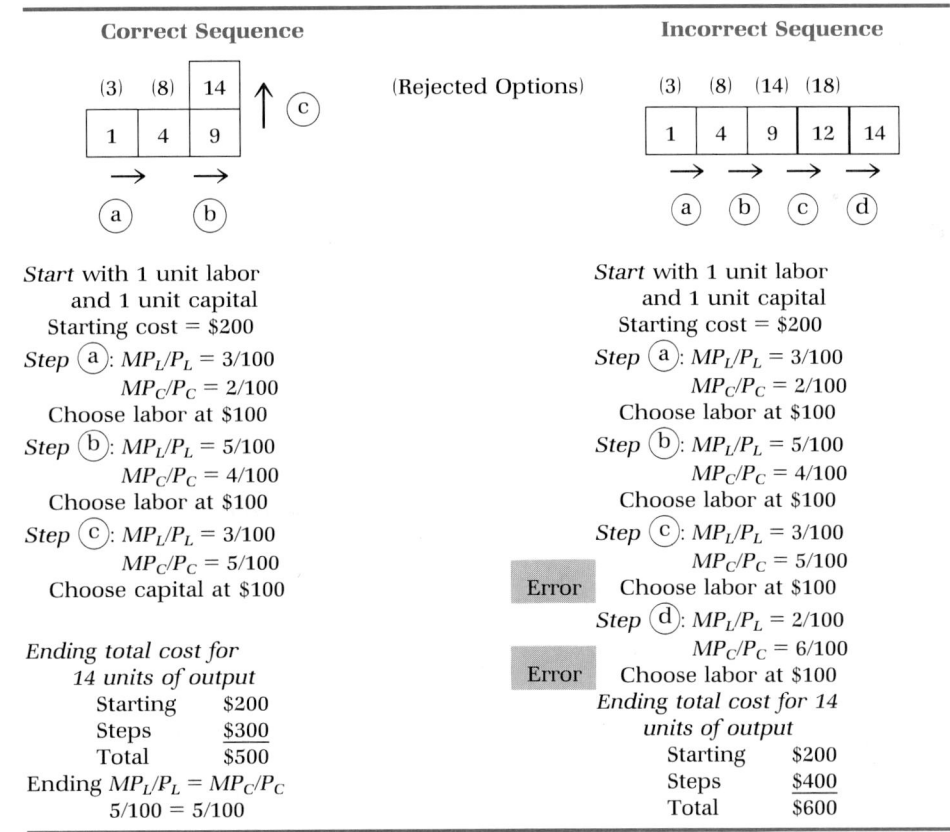

Start with 1 unit labor
and 1 unit capital
Starting cost = $200
Step (a): $MP_L/P_L = 3/100$
    $MP_C/P_C = 2/100$
Choose labor at $100
Step (b): $MP_L/P_L = 5/100$
    $MP_C/P_C = 4/100$
Choose labor at $100
Step (c): $MP_L/P_L = 3/100$
    $MP_C/P_C = 5/100$
Choose capital at $100

Ending total cost for
14 units of output
    Starting $200
    Steps $300
    Total $500
Ending $MP_L/P_L = MP_C/P_C$
    $5/100 = 5/100$

Start with 1 unit labor
and 1 unit capital
Starting cost = $200
Step (a): $MP_L/P_L = 3/100$
    $MP_C/P_C = 2/100$
Choose labor at $100
Step (b): $MP_L/P_L = 5/100$
    $MP_C/P_C = 4/100$
Choose labor at $100
Step (c): $MP_L/P_L = 3/100$
    $MP_C/P_C = 5/100$
Error   Choose labor at $100
Step (d): $MP_L/P_L = 2/100$
    $MP_C/P_C = 6/100$
Error   Choose labor at $100
Ending total cost for 14
units of output
    Starting $200
    Steps $400
    Total $600

labor. The correct choice each step of the way is to add the input yielding the greatest bang for the buck, i.e., the highest *MP/P*. The correct sequence on the left ends with a total cost of $500 for the 14 units, while the incorrect sequence on the right ends up costing $600. Note that at the end of the correct sequence $MP_L/P_L = MP_C/P_C$, or 5/100 = 5/100. This result is, indeed, a compact way to state the rule of least cost production. *The firm should obtain inputs to produce the given output such that, in the end, the added output per added dollar spent on one input is the same for all other inputs.* Symbolically,

$$\frac{MP_L}{P_L} = \frac{MP_C}{P_C} = \frac{MP_i}{P_i}$$

The incorrect sequence of Table 23.6 goes astray at step c, when the input with highest *MP/P*, capital, is rejected in favor of an added unit of labor. Note that, in the end, this incorrect sequence is lopsided by the rule of lowest cost combinations. That is, $MP_L/P_L = 2/100$ and $MP_C/P_C = 6/100$ (the 6 being the marginal product of moving from output 12 to output 18). Hence

$$\frac{MP_L}{P_L} < \frac{MP_C}{P_C}$$

This tells us that *too much* labor has been hired relative to capital. There would be more bang for the buck if capital were increased and labor released—that is, if capital were substituted for labor. The high labor intensity of the incorrect sequence would be the wise course only if labor were much cheaper than capital. If labor were priced at, say, $30 a day, the incorrect sequence would turn out to be correct.

C
Technology

Changes in technology that improve productivity *shift* the input/output relationships we've been studying. Improved technology yields more output relative to input, shifting total product, average product, and marginal product curves upward.

For example, the U.S. auto industry in recent years has adopted new production technologies in its effort to catch up with the Japanese. U.S. auto makers have been scrapping old plants, building new ones, and installing modern equipment such as robots. They have even sent American workers to Japan for training. Between 1980 and 1984, these efforts yielded substantial increases in productivity. The annual number of vehicles produced per employee nearly doubled for Ford and Chrysler, leaping from 10 to 19; the gain was somewhat less for GM. Moreover, by 1990, U.S. companies hope to adopt subassembly methods. Many auto components, like front-end sections, will arrive at the final assembly line already made up into modules. This should lift productivity still further.

■ *CHECK YOUR BEARINGS*

From a broad perspective, a firm's opportunity costs are economically most meaningful. Explicit costs, such as labor payments or raw material purchases, plus implicit costs, such as the opportunity costs of financial capital, comprise the overall opportunity cost. Subtracting these overall opportunity costs from total revenue reveals whether the firm has earned an economic profit (positive), or an economic loss (negative), or zero economic profit (normal profit).

So much for the sweeping overview. To be specific, the cost of 1 unit of output (e.g., a car) will be the product of (1) the dollar cost (price) of each unit of input times (2) the amount of input required to produce a unit of output (input/output). Alternatively, the dollar cost of each input could be divided by output per unit of input (output/input). The cost of a unit of output thus varies with physical productivity. Rising and falling productivity occurs when output/input rises and falls, which will happen with variations in capacity use, scale, time, and technological change.

We now move from productivity variations to cost variations. Dollar values are placed on the inputs and, for diagrams, our horizontal axis will be switched from inputs to outputs. Capacity use and scale are most commonly measured by output levels when output costs are the concern.

IV

Cost Behavior as a Function of Output Levels

As with productivity, the cost of producing output can be depicted in a total view or a per unit view. The total view reflects *overall* figures, such as Chrysler's $10 billion total cost in 1982. The per unit view centers on *cost per unit of output*, such as $7,000 per car. When this division of views is combined with the time division of short run and long run, a four-part subdivision of topics emerges. As shown in Table 23.7, we will take up the short-run total view first (A), followed by the short-run per unit view (B) and then finally the long-run per unit view (C). The long-run total view need not detain us.

A

Short-Run Total Costs

Three kinds of total costs occur in the short run—total fixed cost, total variable cost, and total cost. The labels *fixed* and *variable* spring from two sources—the status of inputs and the behavior of total dollar amounts in relation to output.

1. Total Fixed Cost (TFC).

Total fixed cost is the firm's total expenditure per time period for fixed inputs.

Because the quantity of fixed inputs does not, by definition, vary in the short run, total fixed cost remains unchanged regardless of the firm's level of output. Typical among a firm's total fixed costs are the costs of interest on bonds, property tax obligations, insurance on plant and equipment, and certain elements of depreciation. Another fixed cost is the opportunity cost of the firm's own money invested in plant and equipment. Combining these several costs yields a total dollar amount that is always the same no matter what the firm's rate of production. It is often called *overhead* expense.

Suppose a hypothetical firm, the Swift Bicycle Company, incurs fixed costs of $200 a day. When related to bicycle output, the resulting behavior of total fixed cost is shown in Table 23.8 and Figure 23.5. Being fixed, total fixed costs do not vary with output.

2. Total Variable Cost (TVC).

Total variable cost is the firm's total expenditure on variable inputs per time period.

A firm's output per day can increase only by greater use of variable inputs—inputs like raw materials, packaging, energy, and labor that is variable. As the amount of variable inputs rises, so too must the total expense of those inputs. Hence a firm's output and its total variable cost are always positively related. More output costs more. Less output costs less.

TABLE 23.7 Outline of the Discussion of Section IV on Cost Behavior as a Function of Output

	Total dollars view	Dollars per unit view
Short run (capacity use)	A Total fixed cost Total variable cost Total cost	B Average fixed cost Average variable cost Average total cost Marginal cost
Long run (scale size)	(Skipped)	C Long-run average cost

TABLE 23.8 Total Fixed, Total Variable, and Total Costs, Swift Bicycle Company

(1) Number of Bicycles Produced per Day	(2) Total Fixed Cost (Dollars)	(3) Total Variable Cost (Dollars)	(4) = (2) + (3) Total Cost (Dollars)
0	$200	$0	$200
1	200	70	270
2	200	130	330
3	200	180	380
4	200	220	420
5	200	300	500
6	200	420	620
7	200	574	774
8	200	760	960
9	200	990	1,190

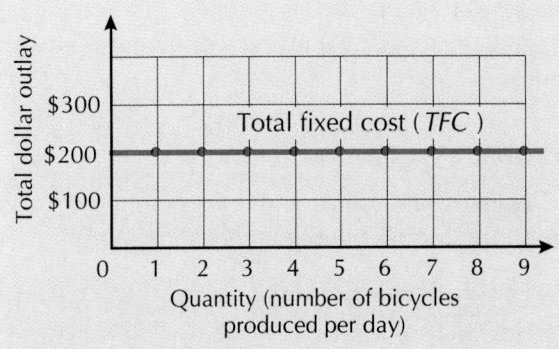

FIGURE 23.5   Total Fixed Cost of the Swift Bicycle Company (Data in Table 23.8)

The total fixed cost curve is a horizontal line because total fixed cost does not vary with output.

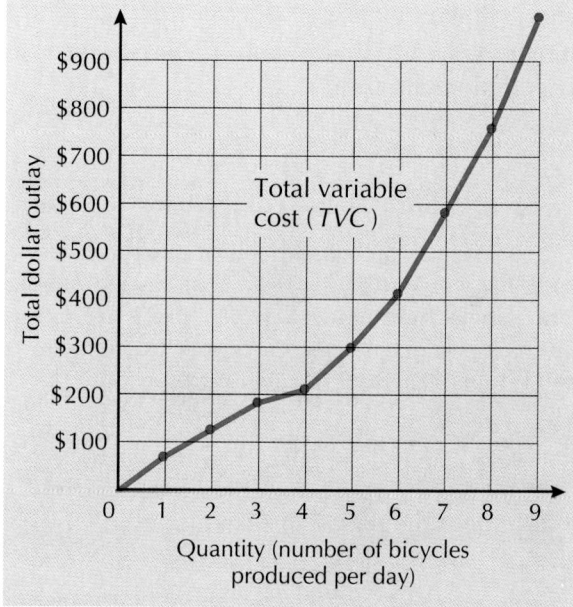

FIGURE 23.6   Total Variable Cost of the Swift Bicycle Company (Data in Table 23.8)

If productivity at first rises and then falls, the total variable cost curve at first rises at a decreasing rate and then rises at an increasing rate as output goes up. Total variable cost is the total expenditure on variable inputs.

More output *always* costs more because of the added variable inputs that add to expenses. But just *how rapidly* those costs rise is a separate issue, one that depends on productivity. In a nutshell:

1. Total variable cost rises at a *constant rate* if productivity remains *unchanged* as output rises.
2. Total variable cost rises at a *decreasing rate* if productivity *rises* as output rises.
3. Total variable cost rises at an *increasing rate* if productivity *falls* as output rises.

Table 23.8 and Figure 23.6 illustrate the decreasing and increasing cases. It is assumed that the Swift Bicycle Company experiences rising and then falling productivity as variable inputs are increasingly

applied to fixed inputs. (Such was the case previously in Figure 23.4.) As output increases from zero to four bicycles, total variable costs rise at a decreasing rate. Variable inputs rise, but input requirements per unit of output fall because of productivity gains. Thereafter, as output rises from four to nine bicycles, total variable costs rise at an increasing rate. Variable inputs rise and input requirements per unit of output also rise as the *law of diminishing returns* begins to bind and productivity falls. If productivity did not change, the total variable cost curve would rise as a straight line.

3. Total Cost

Total cost is the sum of total fixed cost and total variable cost.

When total fixed cost is added to total variable cost, the result is total cost. The last column of Table 23.8 shows the total cost of the Swift Bicycle Company as such a sum. An output of five bicycles per day, for instance, has total fixed costs of $200 and total variable costs of $300. The sum—$500— is the total cost. The top curve in Figure 23.7 plots these points of total costs. The other curves of Figure 23.7 show the components, namely, total fixed and total variable costs. Reading vertically, five bicycles per day have total variable costs of $300.

Adding the total fixed cost of $200 yields a total cost of $500. The curves of Figure 23.7 may be called total cost *functions*.

B
Short-Run Costs: Per Unit View

It is often useful to look at costs per unit of output—cost per bicycle, per car, or per sandwich. Total costs translate into unit costs in two ways. First, there are *average* costs—average fixed cost, average variable cost, and average total cost. Dividing total costs by overall output levels yields these averages. Second, there is *marginal* cost, which ignores the costs of all units except the last one produced.

1. Average Fixed Cost (AFC).

Average fixed cost is total fixed cost divided by the firm's total output.

$$\frac{TFC}{Q}$$

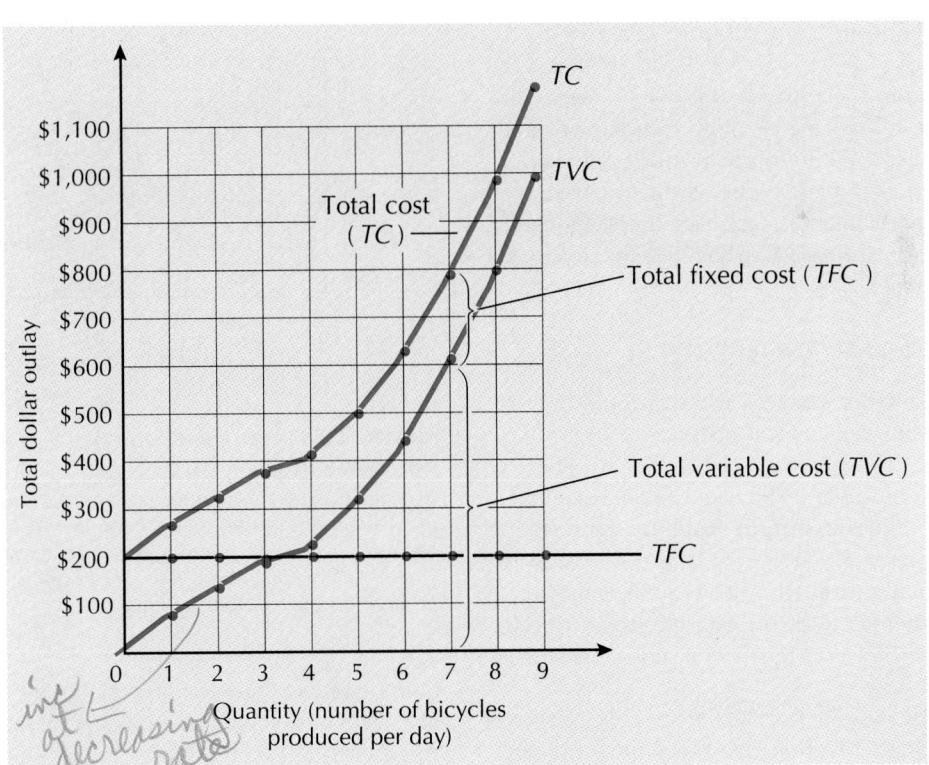

FIGURE 23.7   *Total Cost of the Swift Bicycle Company*

Total cost is the sum of total fixed cost and total variable cost. Graphically, it is the vertical addition of the two. Clearly, total cost rises because total variable cost rises.

TABLE 23.9   Average Fixed Cost, Average Variable Cost, and Average Total Cost, Swift Bicycle Company

(1) Number of Bicycles Produced per Day	(2) Average Fixed Cost ($ per Bicycle)	(3) Average Variable Cost ($ per Bicycle)	(4) Average Total Cost ($ per Bicycle)
1	$200 (= 200 ÷ 1)	$70 (= 70 ÷ 1)	$270 (= 270 ÷ 1)
2	100 (= 200 ÷ 2)	65 (= 130 ÷ 2)	165 (= 330 ÷ 2)
3	67 (= 200 ÷ 3)	60 (= 180 ÷ 3)	127 (= 380 ÷ 3)
4	50 (= 200 ÷ 4)	55 (= 220 ÷ 4)	105 (= 420 ÷ 4)
5	40 (= 200 ÷ 5)	60 (= 300 ÷ 5)	100 (= 500 ÷ 5)
6	33 (= 200 ÷ 6)	70 (= 420 ÷ 6)	103 (= 620 ÷ 6)
7	29 (= 200 ÷ 7)	82 (= 574 ÷ 7)	111 (= 774 ÷ 7)
8	25 (= 200 ÷ 8)	95 (= 760 ÷ 8)	120 (= 960 ÷ 8)
9	22 (= 200 ÷ 9)	110 (= 990 ÷ 9)	132 (= 1,190 ÷ 9)

If the total fixed cost data of Table 23.8 are used to illustrate, the result is the second column of Table 23.9. Average fixed costs fall steadily as the quantity of output rises because a fixed total dollar amount, $200, is being divided by ever larger quantities of bicycles—one, two, three, and so on. The overhead costs are being spread over more and more units of output. They fall from $200 to $100 to $67 on down.

When diagrammed, these data bend into the curve shown in Figure 23.8. Note that the vertical axis is no longer total dollars but rather dollars *per unit* (in this case, per bicycle). Note too that the label *fixed* describes constancy in the total view, not the per unit view. Average fixed costs are clearly not fixed at all.

2. *Average Variable Cost (AVC).*

Average variable cost is total variable cost divided by the firm's total output.

Column (3) of Table 23.9 gives the average variable cost of different output levels for the Swift Bicycle Company. For instance, the total variable cost of producing three bicycles is $180. Dividing 3 into $180 indicates that, on average, the variable cost is $60 per bicycle. Figure 23.9 plots this number and its brethren.

Average variable cost falls if average productivity rises. The added productivity reduces input requirements per unit of output, thereby reducing the average variable cost of output. The first several bicycles of the example are blessed by such

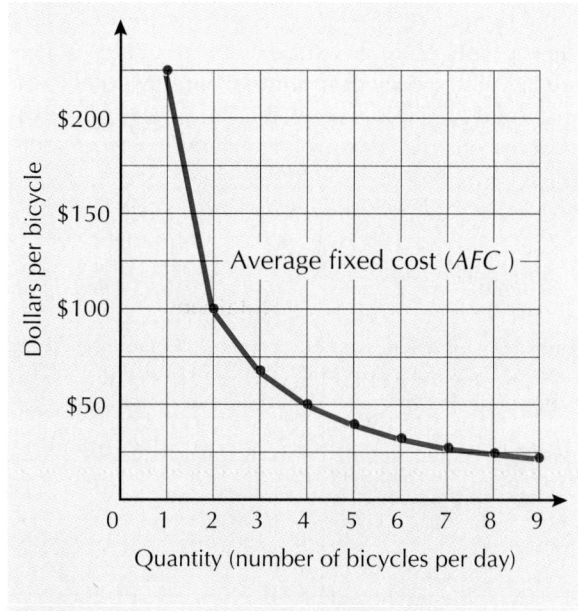

FIGURE 23.8   *Average Fixed Cost, Swift Bicycle Company (Data in Table 23.9)*

Average fixed cost is total fixed cost divided by total output. Given that total fixed cost is the same constant amount, e.g., $200 per day, average fixed cost will fall steadily as output rises. The fixed cost is "spread" over an ever larger number of units.

gains. The average variable cost of bicycles eventually rises, however, pushed up by falling average productivity. Diminishing returns set in. Input requirements per unit of output rise. In the end, average variable cost therefore heads skyward.

If there were no changes in productivity, average

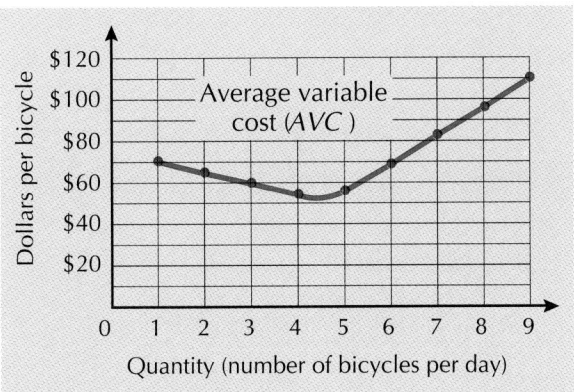

FIGURE 23.9 *Average Variable Cost, Swift Bicycle Company* (Data in Table 23.9)

Average variable cost is total variable cost divided by total output. Average variable cost falls at first—e.g., from $70 to $65 per bike. This is because productivity is rising. As the law of diminishing marginal returns grabs hold, however, average variable cost rises. AVC reaches $110 when output reaches nine bikes per day.

variable cost would not fall and then rise, as it does in Figure 23.9. Rather, it would be constant, or "fixed," at, say, $63 per bicycle. This observation underscores the fact that the label "variable" comes from events in the total view, not the per unit view. Average variable costs can be constant over a considerable range of output, but total variable costs always rise.

3. *Average Total Cost (ATC).*

   Average total cost is the sum of average fixed cost and average variable cost. It is also total cost divided by overall output.

Illustrative data appear in column (4) of Table 23.9. The calculations show Swift Bicycle's total cost being divided by quantity. But adding the average fixed cost and average variable cost of columns (2) and (3) would yield the same results. Graphically, when the average fixed cost of Figure 23.8 is added on top of the average variable cost of Figure 23.9, the result is average total cost, as shown in Figure 23.10. The vertical distance between *ATC* and *AVC* is average fixed cost. At first, average total cost falls sharply because average fixed cost falls sharply. Later, at higher levels of output, average variable cost begins to dominate, causing average total cost to rise.

4. *Marginal Cost (MC).*

   Marginal cost is the extra, or additional, cost of producing 1 more unit of output.

This also is a per unit cost concept, one crucial to two-question logic. Note that the unit of output of reference here is not the average unit, which depicts a composite of all units of some output taken together. Rather, the unit of output referred to is the *incremental, extra, or additional unit.* Marginal cost is the contribution to total cost made by each extra unit of output *individually, yet sequentially*—the first unit, second, third, fourth, and so on. Marginal cost can be calculated for each additional unit of output as the *change* in total cost occurring because of that unit. Or, more generally:

$$\text{Marginal cost} = \frac{\text{change in total cost}}{\text{change in quantity} (= 1)}$$

The data for the Swift Bicycle Company reflect changes in quantity that always equal 1, so marginal cost is calculated in Table 23.10 as the jump in total cost associated with each added unit. The first bicycle adds $70 to total cost (= $270 − $200), the second adds $60 (= $330 − $270), the third $50, and so on. Marginal cost falls at first because total cost is rising at a decreasing rate. Rising marginal productivity lies behind this result. Later, marginal cost turns upward as total cost begins to rise at an increasing rate under the influence of the law of diminishing marginal returns, with its falling productivity.

   Marginal cost is crucial to a firm's two-question logic because the key short-run issue facing the profit-minded firm is whether to produce a bit more or a bit less output. The decision hinges on the margin. Should Chrysler produce a few more cars or a few less? Should it introduce a new model or not? The answers are found in two-question logic—benefit versus cost. And the cost should be the marginal cost, as that is the cost associated with the firm's action at the margin. In Table 23.10, what is the cost of producing the seventh bicycle? It is *not* the average total cost when output is seven, previously calculated to be $111. The average total cost at that point *averages* the cost impact of *all* seven bicycles. The cost of the seventh bicycle is

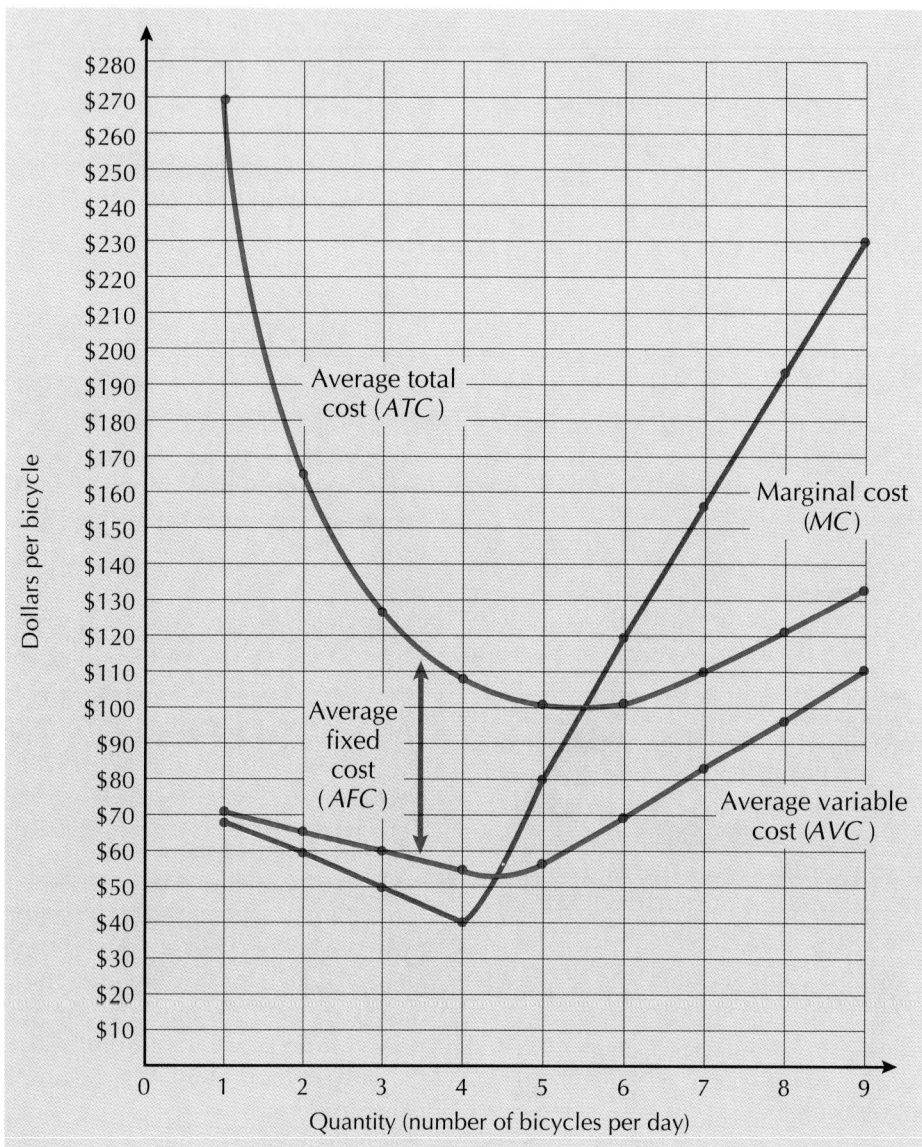

FIGURE 23.10   *The Family of Short-Run Cost Curves, Per Unit View, Swift Bicycle Company (Data in Tables 23.9 and 23.10)*

Average total cost is the sum of average fixed cost and average variable cost. Marginal cost is the addition to total cost due to the added production of one more unit of output.

$154, the marginal cost. This is the cost that enters two-question logic to test the logic of producing the seventh bicycle.

Because marginal cost is the incremental rise in total cost, and because total cost rises solely from the influence of variable cost, marginal cost has a cozy relationship with *both* average total cost and average variable cost. Figure 23.10 captures the

connections. When marginal cost lies *below* average total cost, average total cost will be *falling*. The effect is similar to what happens when your bowling average is 147 and tonight, in your marginal or additional game, you score a lowly 98. Your overall average will skid downward from 147. If tomorrow night you bowl another 98, your average will slip further. Conversely, when marginal cost lies *above*

TABLE 23.10 Marginal Cost, Swift Bicycle Company (Change in Total Cost Due to 1 More Unit of Output)

Number of Bicycles Produced per Day	Total Cost (Dollars)	Marginal Cost ($ per Bicycle)	
0	$ 200		
1	270	$ 70	(= 270 − 200)
2	330	60	(= 330 − 270)
3	380	50	(= 380 − 330)
4	420	40	(= 420 − 380)
5	500	80	(= 500 − 420)
6	620	120	(= 620 − 500)
7	774	154	(= 774 − 620)
8	960	186	(= 960 − 774)
9	1,190	230	(= 1,190 − 960)

average total cost, average total cost will be *rising*. Increments higher than the overall average will pull the average up. Assume for the sake of illustration that after your two gutter-ridden bowling scores of 98 your average stands at 139. Subsequent "marginal" scores of 170 and 182 would pull your average back up. *It follows that the marginal cost curve will always pass through the low point of the average total cost curve.* If, as is the case, *ATC* is falling when *MC*<*ATC* and *ATC* is rising when *MC*>*ATC*, then *ATC* will be bottoming out when *MC* passes through it from below. Note that *MC* can be rising while *ATC* is falling. The key is whether *MC* is *below or above ATC,* not whether *MC* is falling or rising.

Similar ties link average variable cost (AVC) and marginal cost. When *MC*<*AVC*, *AVC* will be falling. When *MC*>*AVC*, *AVC* will be rising. The upshot is that *the marginal cost curve will intersect the average variable cost curve at the latter's minimum point.*

The relationship between marginal cost and average variable cost is underscored by Figure 23.11, which also summarizes in a very general way the relationship between productivity and per unit cost behavior. Table 23.11 summarizes the several symbols and formulas of short-run costs.

Read Perspective 23B.

C
Long-Run Costs and Scale: Per Unit View

Firms operate in the short run and plan in the long run. Given the fixed inputs of the short run, the farmer decides how much wheat to plant this season, the brewer decides how much beer to brew this summer, and the auto manufacturer decides how many autos to assemble this model year. Given the opportunity to vary *all* inputs in the long run, the farmer decides whether to expand his acreage, the brewer decides whether to build another brewery, and the auto manufacturer decides whether to add assembly lines. The long run floats on planning *possibilities.*

In planning, many different scales and technologies of fixed plant can be considered hypothetical possibilities. *The long-run average cost curve* derives from a collection of these possibilities, a collection made possible because all inputs are variable in the long run. There is no distinction between fixed and variable inputs or costs.

TABLE 23.11 Summary of Short-Run Cost Symbols and Formulas

Common symbols

Q	Quantity of output
TFC	Total fixed cost
TVC	Total variable cost
TC	Total cost
AFC	Average fixed cost
AVC	Average variable cost
ATC	Average total cost
MC	Marginal cost

Standard formulas

$$TC = TFC + TVC$$

$$MC = \frac{\text{change in } TC}{\text{change in } Q} = \frac{\text{change in } TVC}{\text{change in } Q}$$

$$AFC = \frac{TFC}{Q}$$

$$AVC = \frac{TVC}{Q}$$

$$ATC = \frac{TC}{Q} = AFC + AVC$$

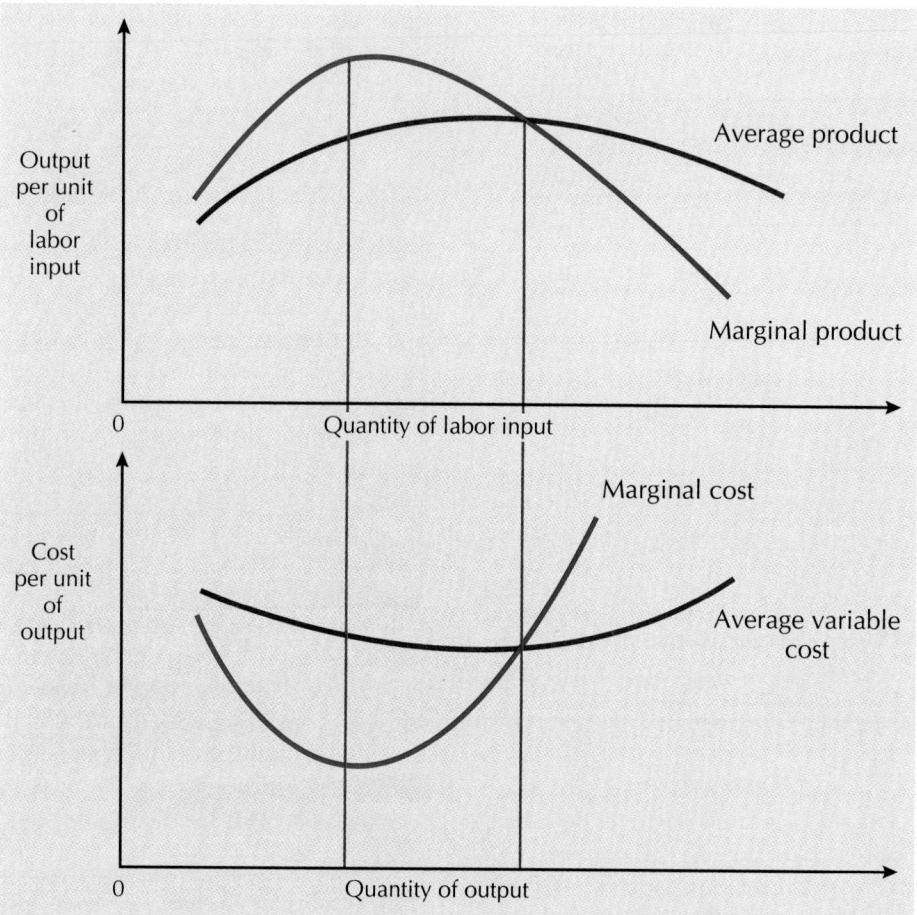

FIGURE 23.11   The Connection Between Short-Run Cost Per Unit and Productivity

Marginals and averages correspond within the general rule that rising productivity lowers the cost per unit and falling productivity raises the cost per unit. Here it is assumed that labor is the only variable input. When marginal product is at its maximum, marginal cost is at its minimum. When average product is at its maximum, average variable cost hits its minimum.

Suppose a wealthy college graduate wants to go into the business of manufacturing car seat covers. She asks engineering consultants to estimate the short-run average total costs, assuming three different technologies of production and an annual output of 200,000 seat covers. The estimates might look like ATC_1, ATC_2, and ATC_3 in Figure 23.13. Each represents a plant whose size is best suited for 200,000 units of output. Each embodies a different known technology or mix of inputs. ATC_1 clearly has the lowest-cost technology, so it would be preferred over the plants with ATC_2 and ATC_3 if 200,000 units are to be produced. Let's say, however, that while these estimates were being pre-

pared, our young entrepreneur grew skeptical. She now doubts that she can sell 200,000 seat covers annually, 100,000 being a more likely number. Subsequent estimation of the short-run average total cost, assuming an efficient output of 100,000 seat covers, yields ATC_4, also shown in Figure 23.13. Continuing the process of estimating short-run costs for different scales of output yields a collection of short-run average total cost curves. For any given level of output, only the lowest of these would be chosen, as it would minimize the cost. Hence, the long-run average cost curve is the line of points traced by the underside of these various possible short-run average cost curves. The tech-

---

PERSPECTIVE 23B
The Short-Run Costs of Producing Phonograph Records

The main costs of producing an LP record album divide neatly into fixed and variable categories. The fixed costs, which are incurred even if zero records are sold, include the artist's guarantee (if any), recording studio rental, musicians' wages, editing and mixing services, album cover design, and administrative expenses. The result is a master tape from which subsequent copies can be made. Record companies also consider promotional expenses to be fixed. The fixed cost of an album can be quite high, even hundreds of thousands of dollars if superstar artists are involved. The variable cost, which varies directly with the number of albums pressed and sold, includes outlays for vinyl plastic, labels, cardboard jackets, liners, plastic wrap, song writer's royalties, artist's royalties per record, and labor time in production and packaging. Figure 23.12 shows the costs of producing a typical record album during the mid-1970s. In the total view, $TFC = \$30,000$ while $TVC = \$12,000$ for 10,000 records, $24,000

for 20,000 records, and so on. Each additional 10,000 records adds $12,000 to total cost. In the per unit view, AVC and MC are the same at $1.20 per record because productivity is constant in this case. The amount of variable input is the same for each record, so the added cost for each added record is the same as for each of the others and the average of all taken together, namely, $1.20. When AFC is added to AVC, the result is ATC, which declines steadily under the influence of falling AFC. The more records produced, the lower the total cost *per record*. This is why record companies like to have hit records. Given a selling price, an album's profits soar once sales pass the "break-even" point.

It should be noted that studies of costs in other industries reveal linear forms similar to those of Figure 23.12. AVC and MC tend to be constant over wide ranges of output. Once full capacity is reached, however, diminishing returns set in and costs climb quickly.

---

nologies used may change with the scale, but only available technologies are considered.

The **long-run average cost curve** shows the minimum average total cost for each level of output when all inputs are variable. (Prices of inputs, e.g., wage rates, are given, as are available technologies.)

envelope curve

Although the long-run average cost curve reflects only possibilities, its shape importantly influences actualities. Three conditions carry consequences—(1) economies of scale, (2) constant returns to scale, and (3) diseconomies of scale. With all three present, the long-run average cost curve will be U-shaped, as in Figure 23.14.

1. Economies of Scale With economies of scale, bigness is better. The larger the firm—that is, the

greater the output it is capable of producing—the lower will be its long-run average cost. Added scale brings added efficiency.

If a doubling of all inputs results in more than a doubling of output, **economies of scale** provide the added efficiency.

Economies of scale can occur for a number of reasons.

1. *Specialization of labor.* As the number of workers multiplies with firm size, individual workers specialize, thereby becoming more proficient and productive. They specialize as electricians, assemblers, managers, marketers, and so on.
2. *Specialization of machinery.* Small firms must often rely on multipurpose machin-

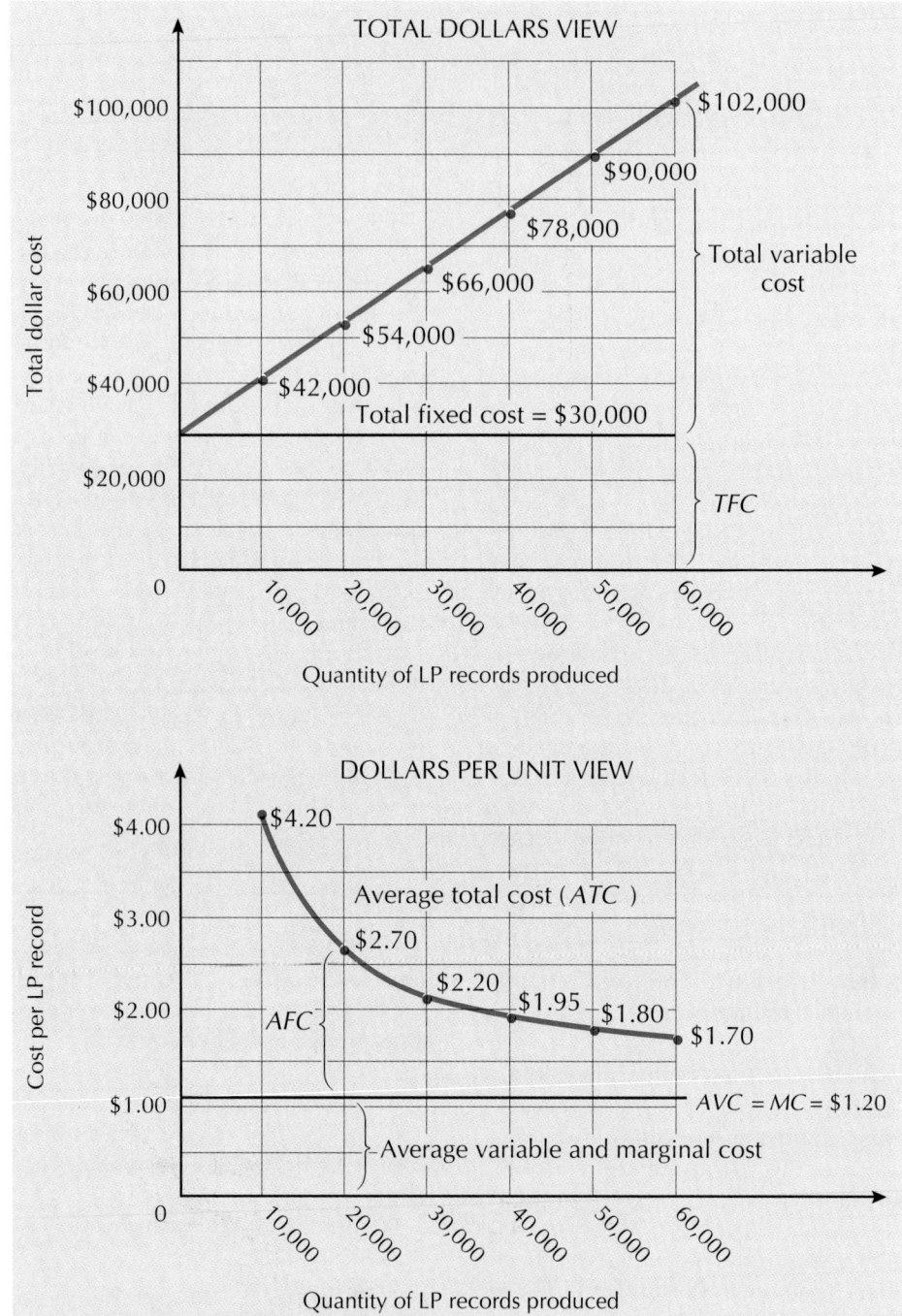

FIGURE 23.12   *The Short-Run Costs of Producing a Typical Record Album in the Mid-1970s*

(Source: Adapted from Matthew Vlahakis, "The Condition of Entry in the Phonograph Record Industry," Ph. D. dissertation, Columbia University, 1975, pp. 158–163.)

ery and equipment that does many different jobs but no one job really well. Large operations permit specialization of ma-

chinery, such as different robots or trucks or lathes for different tasks.

3. *Increased dimensions of capital.* Pipelines,

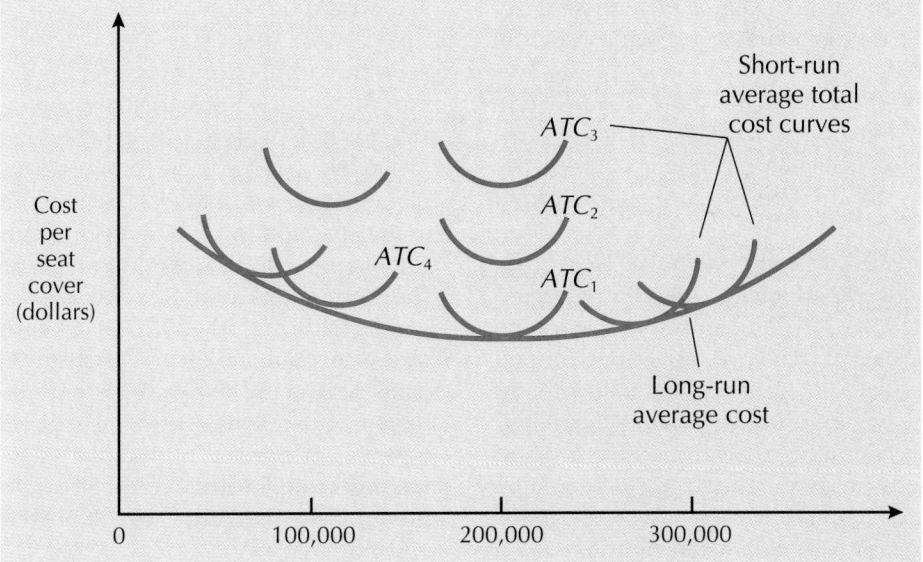

FIGURE 23.13 *Long-Run Average Cost as Derived from Short-Run Average Total Cost Options*

Long-run average cost is a hypothetical concept, derived from the minimum average cost for each level of output when all inputs can vary. ATC$_1$, ATC$_2$, and ATC$_3$ show the short-run costs that would be experienced under three alternative technologies, each geared to 200,000 units of output. ATC$_1$ would be chosen. ATC$_4$ reflects a smaller-scale operation, the best for 100,000 units of output.

tanks, ships, vats, and other such capital equipment generate economies of scale because a doubling of their surface area *more* than doubles their capacity. For example, 8-inch-diameter oil pipe costs roughly twice as much as 4-inch-diameter pipe. The 8-inch pipe has *six times* more capacity, however.

Henry Ford became famous for exploiting economies of scale in auto production. His main feat was to establish assembly line production methods, which permitted specialization of men and machinery. His insight was first applied to flywheel magneto assembly, then to motors, and finally to the entire car. As Ford said regarding motors, "The assembly of the motor, formerly done by one man, is now divided into eighty-four [specialized] operations—those men do the work that three times their number formerly did."[3] It is now estimated that full exploitation of economies

of scale requires that an auto company produce two models of about 500,000 units each, or 1 million cars per year. Technical manufacturing efficiencies are exhausted after 500,000 cars, but two models are needed as a cushion against the shocks of styling errors, gasoline shortages, and other business hazards.[4] Beyond 1 million, constant returns set in.

2. Constant Returns to Scale

If a doubling of all inputs results in a doubling of output, **constant returns to scale** prevail.

With constant returns to scale, outputs respond proportionally to inputs. A given percentage increase in all inputs produces the same percentage increase in outputs. Under such circumstances, long-run average cost neither falls nor rises. It remains constant. Evidence indicates that once

---

[3]*Henry Ford, My Life and Work,* quoted by A.D. Chandler, Jr., *Giant Enterprise* (New York: Harcourt Brace & World, 1964), p. 39.

[4]Lawrence J. White, "The Automobile Industry," in W. Adams (ed.), *The Structure of American Industry,* 6th ed. (New York: Macmillan, 1982), p. 150.

economies of scale are exhausted, constant returns to scale usually exist over a wide range of output possibilities.

The threshold where economies of scale end and constant returns to scale begin has special significance. As indicated in Figure 23.14, the name given to this threshold is fitting—*minimum efficient scale (MES)*.

An MES *plant* is one just big enough to capture all the efficiencies associated with larger *plant size*. Examples of the plant outputs needed to reach MES in several industries are shown in column (1) of Table 23.12. In beer, for instance, an MES brewery would produce about 4.5 million barrels of beer annually. Yearly output of 1 million pairs of shoes would be enough to make a shoe plant efficient.

Of course, a *firm* can have one or more plants. If a single-plant firm is just as efficient as a multi-plant firm, then the MES *firm* will be the same size as the MES plant. One firm=one plant. If, on the other hand, multiplant operations in an industry yield further efficiencies, then that industry's MES *firm* will be a multiplant firm just big enough to capture all the efficiencies associated with multiplant operations as well as single-plant operations. One firm = two or more plants. MES *firm*

size would be double or triple or some other multiple of MES plant size. Column (2) of Table 23.12 gives the number of plants required to achieve full efficiency in the industries indicated (according to the authors of these estimates). Beer companies, for instance, need three or four plants for best efficiency. Paint companies need only one.

The last column of Table 23.12 summarizes the implications of the first two columns. It reports the percentage of U.S. sales that an MES *firm* would have had in 1967. This is simply firm MES size in percentage form. According to these data, firms producing refrigerators have to be relatively big to be efficient. They have to account for as much as 20 percent of national sales. Shoe manufacturers and fabric weavers illustrate instances of the opposite sort. They do not need to be big to be efficient.

Later, the importance of MES firm size will become clear. If, as with refrigerators, a firm must be relatively big to reach the threshold where economies of scale end and constant returns begin, then efficiency dictates that only a few firms occupy the industry. If, on the other hand, relatively small firms can be efficient, as with shoe manufacturing, for example, then the industry may be populated with numerous equally efficient firms.

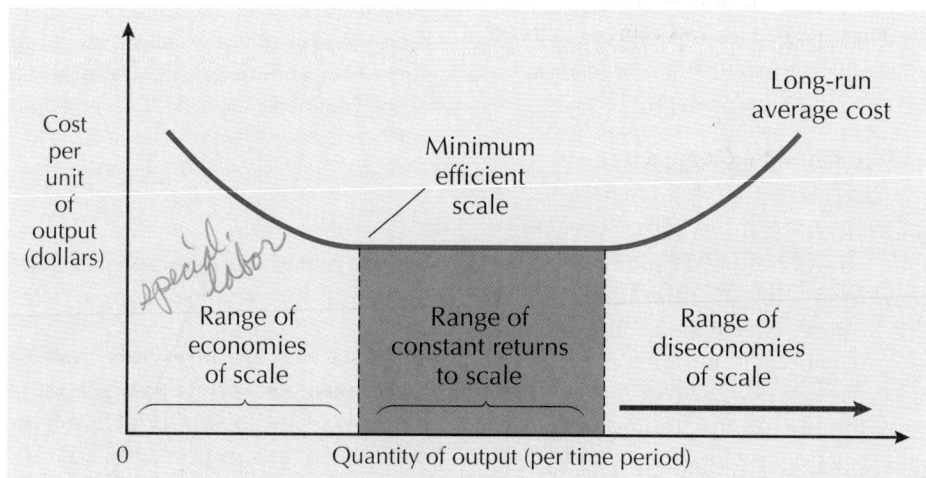

FIGURE 23.14 *Economies of Scale, Constant Returns to Scale, and Diseconomies of Scale in the Long-Run Average Cost Curve*

Economies of scale cause long-run average cost (LRAC) to fall as the scale of fixed inputs increases. Constant returns to scale imply no change in LRAC. A given percentage increase in all inputs yields the same percentage increase in outputs. Diseconomies of scale occur if added size creates inefficiencies. Such diseconomies cause LRAC to rise. With all three influences present, the LRAC curve will be U-shaped.

TABLE 23.12   MES Plant Size, Number of Plants for Firm Efficiency, and Firm
MES as a Percentage of U.S. Sales (mid-1960s)

Industry	(1) Output of MES Plant	(2) Number of Plants for MES Firm	(3) MES Firms as % of U.S. Sales
Beer brewing	4.5 million barrels per year capacity	3–4	10–14
Cigarettes	36 billion cigarettes annually	1–2	6–12
Broad-woven fabrics	37.5 million square yards annually	3–6	1
Paints	10 million gallons per year	1	1.4
Petroleum refining	200,000 barrels per day	2–3	4–6
Shoes (nonrubber)	1 million pairs per year	3–6	1
Steel	4 million short tons per year	1	3
Refrigerators	800,000 units annually	4–8	14–20
Auto batteries	1 million units annually	1	2

Source: F.M. Scherer, A. Beckenstein, E. Kaufer, R.D. Murphy, and F. Bougeon-Maassen, _The Economics of Multi-Plant Operation_ (Cambridge, Mass.: Harvard University Press, 1975), pp. 80, 336.

Diseconomies of Scale

Diseconomies of scale are present when a doubling of all inputs results in less than a doubling of output.

As the enterprise expands to monstrous size, it may well become _too_ big. If added scale reduces overall efficiency, the diseconomies will cause cost per unit of output to rise, as indicated in Figure 23.14.

The most commonly cited cause of diseconomies of scale is managerial inefficiency. As a firm's size grows, the tasks of management grow more complex. Organizational structures tend to be hierarchical or pyramidal. The chain of command has a few very powerful people at the top—owners or chief executive officers—and then descends to lower levels of ever more numerous underlings. Added size tends to add levels of authority to the organizational pyramid and human bodies to the corporate bureaucracy.

The empirical evidence on diseconomies of scale is more sketchy than that concerning economies of scale or constant returns to scale. Still, the evidence indicates that diseconomies often do arise.[5]

[5]John M. Blair, _Economic Concentration_ (New York: Harcourt Brace Jovanovich, 1972), pp. 159–173.

V

Costs as a Function of Input Prices and Technology

The preceding section looked only to output variations for variations in costs. The shackles of _ceteris paribus_ hold input prices and available technologies constant. Let's now see what happens to costs when input prices and technologies change.

A
Input Prices

Increases in wage rates, raw materials prices, interest rates, or other input prices cause a firm's costs to rise. The firm's family of cost curves will shift upward as a result. Figure 23.15 illustrates this by showing an upward shift in average total cost from ATC_0 to ATC'.

Conversely, _decreases_ in wage rates, raw material prices, or other input prices would shift a firm's cost curves down to reflect lower costs per unit of output. Figure 23.15 illustrates this possibility by showing ATC_0 falling to ATC^*.

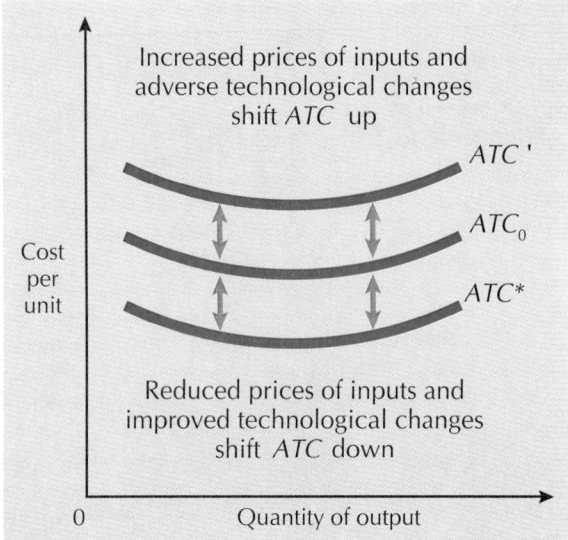

FIGURE 23.15 *The Impact of Changes in Input Prices and Production Technology*

Increases in input prices, such as a jump in worker wage rates, or adverse technological changes cause costs per unit of output to rise. Conversely, reductions in input prices or improvement in production technology cause the cost per unit of output to fall.

It is assumed in these instances that the changes in input prices are independent of the firm's level of output. By contrast, any changes in input prices that are due directly to greater levels of output would have to be incorporated in the cost curve itself, as it is a function of output. In the *short run*, for instance, added output beyond some point might require that additional workers work a night shift or overtime, each of which would boost the wage rates associated with the added output. This could be pictured by adding steps to the right-hand portion of the ATC_0 curve in Figure 23.15, not by shifting the entire curve upward.

B

Technological Change

Changes in production technologies can have a dramatic impact on cost per unit. Changes in technology that *lower productivity* cause costs to *shift upward*, as ATC_0 shifts to ATC' in Figure 23.15. Such adverse changes are relatively rare because firms usually refrain from adopting new technologies of production that elevate their costs. Such

changes can happen, however. For example, the change might improve product quality, permitting the firm's price to increase more than the cost per unit.

Advances in technology shift the firm's cost curves *downward*, as illustrated in the shift from ATC_0 to ATC^* in Figure 23.15. Perhaps the all-time best example of this concerns aluminum. Production of pure aluminum was so costly in the last century that aluminum was then a precious metal like gold. The invention of electrolytic reduction, which extracted pure aluminum from aluminum oxide rather cheaply, permitted the production of aluminum at a cost of only a few cents per pound.

GM's new asssembly plant in Orion Township, Michigan, illustrates technological changes in auto production that have cut the costs of car manufacturing. The Orion plant is home to 138 welding robots, 19 painting robots, and numerous computer-driven automated-guided vehicles (AGVs). The AGVs deliver parts to various points along the Cadillac and Oldsmobile assembly lines. After delivering the correct parts at the right time and place, they return to a computer-controlled dispatch room, where they pick up additional loads for additional runs. The AGVs are sensitive as well as hefty. They "see" people in their path, stopping until their path is clear. At full production the Orion plant turns out 270,000 cars a year using 11,000 workers—3,000 fewer workers than with the old technologies. This means that labor costs per car at Orion are more than 20 percent lower than they would be otherwise.

Note: Technological changes that boost labor productivity press unit costs *down*, while rising wage rates push unit costs *up*. This means that wage hikes will *not* raise unit costs if they are accompanied by offsetting improvements in labor productivity. A simple example illustrates. Assume that initially one worker who is paid $10 an hour can produce two auto headlights per hour. The labor cost per headlight would be $5 (= $10/2). A doubling of the wage rate to $20 per hour would double the unit labor cost to $10 per headlight (= $20/2). But this could be offset by a doubling of output per worker hour to four headlights because twice the output would then accompany the doubly higher wage. The cost per headlight would remain $5 (= $20/4).

Understanding this offsetting linkage between wages rates and productivity-improving technological change is important to understanding a firm's costs. Moreover, it is supremely important to understanding how technological change can improve economic well-being in the aggregate economy. Think about it. If people's wages can rise without raising production costs, then people's wages can rise *without* raising output prices. They can then buy more goods. The wage gains would represent *real* gains. Each hour's work would buy more real goods and services. Continued and compounded over time, the result is economic growth in the form of rising real incomes.

SUMMARY

1. Economic costs include all dollar outlays that must be received by input owners to obtain their continued commitment to a firm. Thus a firm's costs include explicit costs, which are actual payments, and implicit costs, which reflect the opportunity costs of entrepreneurs and owners.

2. Economic profit is the firm's total revenue less total opportunity costs (explicit and implicit). If economic profit is negative, entrepreneurs and owners will tend to withdraw even if accounting profit is positive. If economic profit is positive, the rewards exceed those of alternatives. If economic profit is zero, a normal profit is being earned that will keep entrepreneurs and owners contented and committed.

3. The cost (or price) of each unit of input and the productivity of inputs combine to determine the cost of outputs. The simple arithmetic is input cost multiplied by input requirement or input cost divided by output per unit of input. In the short run, inputs are fixed or variable. In the long run, all inputs are variable.

4. In the short run, productivity is determined by capacity utilization. Taking output/input as the measure of productivity, average product is total output/total input, while marginal product is the *change* in total output due to an added unit of input. Productivity may rise or remain constant over a wide range of capacity use, but it will eventually fall as capacity is exhausted because of the law of diminishing marginal returns.

5. In the long run, productivity depends on scale variation, in which all inputs can be varied to minimize the cost. The cost of a given output is minimized by equating the output per dollar of added input for all inputs, that is, $MP_L/P_L = MP_C/P_C = \cdots = MP/P$.

6. Technological change shifts the input/output relationships of the short and long run.

7. Cost behavior as a function of output levels may be studied in a three-part sequence: (A) the short-run total view, (B) the short-run per unit view, and (C) the long-run per unit view. (A) The short-run *total view* covers (1) total fixed costs, which do not vary with output, (2) total variable costs, which always rise with output, and (3) total costs, which are the sum of total fixed and variable costs. (B) Short-run *per unit* costs include *averages* of the totals obtained by dividing total fixed, total variable, and total costs by quantity. There is also *marginal cost*, the added total cost of producing an added unit of output. Marginal and average total costs eventually rise because of the law of diminishing returns. (C) Long-run average costs are the minimum short-run average total costs for each level of output when all inputs are variable. Long-run average cost falls when economies of scale prevail, remain constant with constant returns to scale, and rise with diseconomies of scale. Minimum efficient scale (MES), is the scale at which long-run average cost first reaches its lowest level.

8. When depicted as a function of output, costs rise or fall with independent changes

in input prices and production technology. Wage increases, for instance, raise the cost per unit. But productivity gains provided

by advances in technology lower the cost per unit. Wages can thus rise without increasing costs if productivity improves.

KEY TERMS

Opportunity cost
Explicit cost
Implicit cost
Accounting profit
Economic profit
Normal profit
Productivity
Short run
Long run
Fixed input
Variable input
Production function

Average product
Input requirement
Marginal product
Law of diminishing marginal returns
Total fixed cost
Total variable cost
Total cost
Average fixed cost
Average variable cost
Average total cost
Marginal cost
Long-run average cost

QUESTIONS AND PROBLEMS

1. Defective equipment allegedly causes a manufacturing plant to burn down. Two brothers own and manage the small business as a partnership. In a lawsuit against the company that produced the equipment, an accountant testifies that the fire cost the firm nothing more than the cost of the building, equipment, and inventory that were destroyed. Sales were not affected because the brothers immediately rented a similar building and managed to keep up with their orders. An economist agrees that sales did not decline, but notes that for a year after the fire the brothers had to work twice as many hours as before the fire to meet orders. She concludes that the extra labor by the partners constitutes an additional cost of $80,000. Explain why the accountant might not consider the partners' overtime work a cost.

2. John started a business that rented orchids to homeowners on a weekly basis. After one year, John closed his business and got a job in sales. Sam asked John why he did so. John explained, "I was making a profit but I was working twelve hour days. It just wasn't worth it. I'm making more in my new job and working fewer hours." On the basis of John's explanation, answer the following:
   (a) Was John's firm making an accounting profit?
   (b) Was his firm making an economic profit?
   (c) Was his firm making a normal profit?
   (d) What was the implicit cost of John's twelve hour days in the orchid business?

3. The costs per unit of producing a product may be

   the same in two countries, A and B, even if wage rates are much higher in country A. Explain.

4. Does labor productivity rise or fall when capacity utilization rises? Explain.

5. Labor productivity usually increases over time in the United States. Explain why this is to be expected in view of the factors that influence labor productivity.

6. The short run may be as long as ten years for some industries and as short as a few weeks for other industries. Explain why.

7. Explain why the law of diminishing returns is relevant only to the short run.

8. Hydrogen and oxygen are two inputs in the production process for water. Are they substitutable inputs?

9. Consumers, seeking to maximize their utility as they make spending decisions, face the same kinds of choices among final products that producers face in selecting inputs so as to minimize production costs. Compare the rule of least cost production with the decision rule that consumers use in maximizing total budget utility (from Chapter 21).

10. What is the key decision to be made in a firm's long-run planning?

11. Why are there often economies of scale in the production of a good?

12. Can a firm be "too big"? Explain.

13. Lower input prices and better technology have the same effect on average total cost curves. What do they do?

24

Product Markets: The Big Picture

In February 1982, Robert Crandall, president of American Airlines, telephoned Howard Putnam, the president of a rival airline. Locked in money-losing competition with Mr. Putnam, Mr. Crandall had a suggestion:

> Mr. Crandall: "I think it's dumb as hell . . . to sit here and pound . . . each other and neither one of us making a [word deleted] dime."
>
> Mr. Putnam: "Do you have a suggestion for me?"
>
> Mr. Crandall: "Yes, I have a suggestion for you. Raise your goddamn fares 20%. I'll raise mine the next morning."
>
> Mr. Putnam: "Robert, we . . .
>
> Mr. Crandall: "You'll make more money and I will, too."
>
> Mr. Putnam: "We can't talk about pricing."
>
> Mr. Crandall: "Oh bull—, Howard. We can talk about any goddamn thing we want to talk about."[1]

Mr. Putnam did not like discussing prices with Mr. Crandall because price fixing is illegal. Why, then, did Mr. Crandall start the discussion? Why didn't he simply raise his own prices? He apparently thought that Mr. Putnam would not voluntarily follow with similar price hikes. Mr. Putnam could therefore gain at Mr. Crandall's expense unless Mr. Crandall could engineer an *agreement* that they would *both* raise prices.

This story indicates that we are now ready to *analyze and evaluate product markets. Analysis* probes *how* product markets work and *how* firms behave in different market settings. (This is positive economics.) *Evaluation* studies *how well* markets work and *how well* firms perform for society in different market settings. (This is normative economics.)

A key motive of firms is profit maximization. We have already seen that profit is determined by revenues and costs. Furthermore, we have already seen that revenues depend on demand and that costs vary with productivity. The last three chapters have thus prepared the way.

[1]*Wall Street Journal,* February 25, 1983, p. 25, September 14, 1983, p. 2.

What remains to be seen is how revenues and costs interact. More precisely stated, *what remains is an analysis of how firms maximize their total profits (total revenues minus total costs) in various market settings, coupled with an evaluation of how well various markets consequently perform on behalf of society.* The story of Mr. Crandall and Mr. Putnam illustrates that, under certain conditions, firms may collude to maximize profits. The consequences of this for society may not be good.

Of the five basic questions—What?, How?, Who?, What's new?, and How stable?—we will be focusing on the first four. Thus, our *analysis* of firms and product markets will explore how firms, acting through markets, spin out answers to these basic questions. Our *evaluation* focuses on the desirability of the answers obtained.

The purpose of this chapter is to offer an overview—like the big picture on the box of a jigsaw puzzle. Just as the pieces of a puzzle vary in shape and color, product markets vary widely in certain critical characteristics, such as the number of firms they contain. This chapter surveys those characteristics, identifies market types according to those characteristics, and reveals firm demand curves for each type of market. The firm's view of demand is very important because that demand is what generates the firm's revenue experience, which in turn is critical to the firm's profit experience.

I

The Elements of Market Analysis and Evaluation

Take a product market—soda pop, beer, personal computers, whatever. How would you go about analyzing and evaluating that market? You would need some system. You would need (1) a catalog of the chief elements of the market and (2) a theoretical scheme tying these elements together. The process would be similar to analyzing and evaluating human health. The catalog of elements (or parts) would distinguish between the heart, lungs, stomach, and so on. The theoretical scheme would relate these elements to each other to explain how humans function.

This "modeling" of the problem helps organize your thoughts. Once understood through analysis, your health could be evaluated.

The traditional model of product markets includes four main elements, each of which has several sub-elements. Figure 24.1 presents the picture. The main elements are the *basic conditions*, *market structure*, *market conduct*, and *performance*.

The **basic conditions** are characteristics inherent in the product or its production process. In humans, these include inherited genes, male–female identity, and age. In product markets, the basic conditions could, as suggested in Figure 24.1, refer to conditions on either the demand or the supply side of the market.

On the demand side, there are important differences between *consumer goods*, like soda pop and apparel, which are bought by consumers, and *producer goods*, like crude oil or sheet steel, which are bought by business buyers such as Exxon and General Motors. Products also vary by their *elasticity of demand*—price elasticity and income elastic-

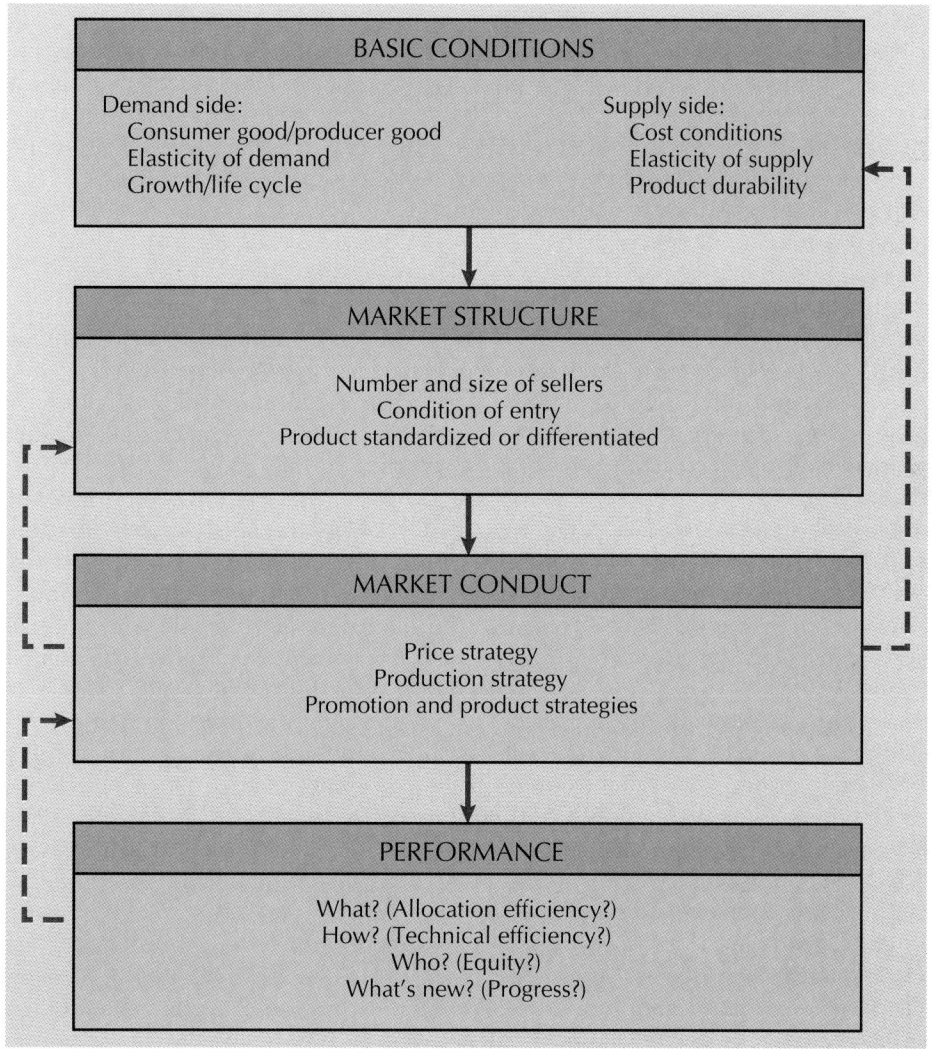

FIGURE 24.1   Elements of Product Market Analysis and Evaluation

ity, in particular. *Elasticity* measures the extent to which quantity demanded changes in response to changes in the variables affecting demand. Yet another important demand-side condition is the rate of *growth* in demand as determined largely by a product's *life cycle.*

Basic conditions on the supply side include cost conditions, elasticity of supply, and product durability. *Cost conditions* can vary in a number of ways. In the short run, the fixed costs of production, especially those associated with capital inputs, may be relatively high or low. In the long run, cost per unit of output may fall as the scale of a producing plant increases in size. These and other cost conditions are influenced by the technology of production. Nuclear production of electricity, for instance, has costs that differ from those of coal production of electricity. Another supply-side feature is the *elasticity of supply*, which is influenced by cost conditions. It measures the responsiveness of the quantity supplied to changes in price. *Product durability*, the last supply-side condition mentioned in Figure 24.1, obviously refers to a good's perishability versus durability. Breakfast cereal is perishable; TV sets are not.

Market structure *refers to certain characteristics of the market's participants and product, characteristics influencing competition.* These characteristics are fairly stable over time, but they can be changed by government policy or business efforts or new technology. They are like a person's weight or smoking habit.

Heading the brief list in Figure 24.1 is the *number and size of sellers* in the market. There may be thousands of sellers, as typified by perfect competition. At the other extreme, there may be just one seller, as in monopoly. Between these extremes lies a range of possibilities.

The condition of entry is a second major structural variable. If the condition of entry is easy, as it is under perfect competition, then newcomers may readily enter the market to compete with established sellers. If, on the other hand, entry is made difficult by cost conditions or legal barriers like patents, then established sellers are shielded against the potential competition of newcomers. Their market is insulated from upstart rivals. Between the polar cases of easy entry and impossible entry, intermediate cases cover a wide span.

Finally, Figure 24.1 mentions that products may

be either *standardized* or *differentiated.* Standardized products are the same for all sellers in the market. Farmer Smith's two-row barley is the same as Farmer Schwartz's two-row barley. In contrast, differentiated products differ among sellers. They are distinguished by trademarks, advertising image, style variation, and the like. So distinguished, each seller's offering appears different from the others, at least in the minds of buyers. Such differences may be genuine; for example, a Toyota Corolla genuinely differs from a Ford Escort. Such differences may likewise be no more than superficial or imaginary. Any two brands of grade A pasteurized-homogenized 2 percent lowfat milk, for instance, are virtually identical despite different brand images that may have from advertising.

In the case of **standardized products**, different sellers offer perfect substitutes. In the case of **differentiated products,** nonprice factors such as advertising or style influence the buyer's choice between sellers.

Read Perspective 24A.

Market conduct *refers to the actions and strategies of sellers.* It's what sellers do and pursue. It's the firms' handling of business variables—their pricing of their products, their producing outputs, promoting sales, and the like.

Price strategy entails determination of price level. Will RCA's record albums be $8.95 or $9.95, for instance? It also concerns price structure, such as the possibility that classical albums could be priced differently from rock albums. *Production strategy* chiefly determines the seller's level of output, something that is often connected closely to price strategy. *Promotion and product strategies* guide such activities as advertising, distribution, and product design. These activities are typically nonexistent or trivial in markets with standardized products. But they can be of immense significance where differentiation is an arena for competitive combat.

Performance *is the name for end results.* It refers to the market's answers to the basic economic questions raised by the problem of scarcity: What is produced in what amounts? How are goods and services produced? Who gets the goods

PERSPECTIVE 24A
Differentiated Beer

Hundreds of millions of dollars are spent each year to differentiate Budweiser, Michelob, Miller High Life, Stroh's, Old Milwaukee, and other brands of beer. Advertising accounts for most of the money spent, assuring wide familiarity for such expressions as "This Bud's for you." Packaging is also important, ranging from foil cap coverings for "super premium" beers to "30-can packs." Promotions include foot races, chili cook-offs, college festivities, and much more. What makes these enormous efforts interesting is that most people cannot taste any difference between the major brands of beer. Many "blind" taste tests prove this similarity.[2] The most brazen taste test was conducted by Schlitz and broadcast live during halftime of the NFL Super Bowl in 1981. One hundred loyal Michelob buyers drank Schlitz and Michelob from unlabeled mugs. Then, when asked to choose which beer they liked better, 50 people picked Schlitz and 50 picked Michelob. Claiming triumph, Schlitz later took out full-page ads in college newspapers to spread the news that half of these faithful Michelob drinkers "perferred Schlitz over their own beer." But here's the catch. Given two beers that taste alike, and given the law of averages, persons forced to decide between the two will normally choose 50–50. It's like a coin toss. Hence Schlitz's claim was slightly misleading. Note that no loyal Schlitz drinkers were included in the Super Bowl tests because Schlitz's spokesman would have had to explain why roughly half of those Schlitz drinkers "preferred" Michelob to Schlitz. Although the major advertised brands tend to taste alike, many unadvertised off-brands (like Anchor Steam Beer and Big Foot Beer) do not. Their differentiation is based on taste.

[2]See, e.g., R.I. Allison and K.P. Uhl, "Influence of Beer Brand Identification on Taste Perception," *Journal of Marketing Research* (August 1964), pp. 36–39; S.H. Rewoldt, J.D. Scott, and M.R. Warshaw, *Introduction to Marketing Management* (Homewood, Ill.: Richard D. Irwin, 1973), pp. 177–190.

and services? What's new, especially in terms of inventions and innovations?

Bumping into these familiar questions once again should shift your mind into an evaluative mode. To be sure, market structure and market conduct may be evaluated in terms of value judgments like freedom and fairness. For the most part, however, market structure and market conduct relate to the analytical issue of *how* a market works (and the firms in it)—*how* it goes about answering these basic economic questions of What?, How?, Who?, and What's new?. In contrast, performance addresses the issue of *how well* the market works, an issue of normative evaluation. How well does the market perform when judged by standards of allocation efficiency (What?), technical efficiency (How?), equity (Who?), and progress (What's new?)?

II
Summary of Major Market Types

Having identified the chief elements of markets, our next step is to probe their relationships. The list in Figure 24.1—basic conditions, market structure, market conduct, and performance—is not like a grocery list. It's not just a bunch of items to ponder when looking at product markets. There is more—a flow of linkages between those elements that must be understood if markets are to be understood.

In particular, the arrows of Figure 24.1 indicate the traditional theory of relationships. Traditional theory postulates a *causal flow* running from the basic conditions to market structure, from structure to market conduct, and from conduct to performance. For example, market growth and product life cycle, which are basic conditions mentioned on the demand side in Figure 24.1, greatly influence the condition of entry into a market as listed under structure. Rapid growth in demand and early stages of a product's life cycle make entry by newcomers rather easy. More than 100 firms entered the booming personal computer market during the 5 years following the introduction of Apple's innovative Apple II in 1977. Another relationship is that between the consumer good/producer good dichotomy and product differentiation. Consumer goods tend to be more sharply differentiated than producer goods. In turn, the standardized-differentiated feature of market structure strongly influences market conduct by way of promotion and product strategies. Thus structure influences conduct. And finally, in the end, structure and conduct combine to cause good or bad answers to the questions What? through What's new?.

The dashed lines of Figure 24.1 represent causal flows running in the opposite direction from those of the traditional model. Such reverse causal flows are interesting and often crucial, but we shall focus on the traditional model with stress on structure, conduct, and performance.

Theory's traditional connections between structure, conduct, and performance are most conveniently seen by an oversimplification that divides all product markets into just four fundamental types—**perfect competition, monopoly, oligopoly,** and **monopolistic competition.** Definitions of these simplified market types center on variations in market structure. One kind of market structure yields perfect competition. Another kind of market structure results in monopoly, and so on. In turn, these variations in market structure affect the way each seller in the market sees its demand curve, thereby also determining each seller's revenue perceptions. *Given different revenue perceptions from these structural variations, and given also the crucial connection between revenue and profitable conduct, these structural variations cause conduct variations. The conduct variations finally cause variations in performance by market type.* Understanding markets thus entails an appreciation of how the linkage between structure,

conduct, and performance varies across market types.

Figure 24.2 summarizes the four basic market types in terms of structure, conduct, and performance. The column headings clustered under "Structure" and "Conduct" are taken directly from Figure 24.1—that is, "Number of Firms," "Entry Condition," and so on. Those for "Performance" have been condensed, however, by using "Profit" as an overall index for both the What? and Who? questions. Broadly speaking, if firms in a market earn normal profits, which are neither so low as to injure firm owners nor so high as to lavishly enrich them, then the market is answering the What? and Who? questions pretty well. Price aligns with cost. Allocation efficiency and equity are both being served. If, however, profits are excessively high, it may signal problems regarding What? and Who?. Price then exceeds cost. Allocative efficiency does not hold because too little is being produced, and equity may also suffer because relatively rich owners may be gaining wealth at the expense of relatively poor consumers. The row headings of Figure 24.2 identify each market model—perfect competition, monopoly, oligopoly, and monopolistic competition.

Figure 24.2 can be studied both horizontally and vertically. Our later discussions in Chapters 25–28 take the horizontal approach, first tracking perfect competition's structure, conduct, and performance, then turning to monopoly's several features, and so on. Here it seems best to take the vertical approach, focusing on structure until all four market types are defined, then moving on to the conduct of each type, and concluding finally with performance. This should help to solidify such concepts as "price strategy" prior to tackling the next four chapters.

A

Structure

Notice first that in Figure 24.2 the four basic market types are distinguished by three main structural features—the number of firms in the market, the condition of entry, and the product type. Perfect competition and monopoly, the first two market types, are the extremes in these characteristics:

Market Type	Structure			Conduct			Performance		
	Number of firms	Entry Condition	Product Type	Price Strategy	Production Strategy	Promotion Strategy	Profit (What and Who?)	Technical Efficiency (How?)	Progressiveness (What's new?)
Perfect Competition	Very large number	Easy	Standardized	None	Independent	None	Normal	Good	Poor perhaps
Monopoly	One	Blocked	Perfectly differentiated	Independent		Light	Excessive	Poor perhaps	Poor perhaps
Oligopoly	Few	Impeded	Standardized or differentiated	Recognized interdependence		Moderate to heavy (if product differentiated)	Somewhat excessive	Poor perhaps	Good
Monopolistic Competition	Large number	Easy	Differentiated	Unrecognized interdependence		Moderate to heavy	Normal	Moderately good	Fair

FIGURE 24.2   Basic Market Types

1. A very large number of firms versus one.
2. Easy entry for perfect competition; blocked entry for monopoly.
3. Standardized product versus a perfectly differentiated product, that is, one without close substitutes.

Because the market types of Figure 24.2 are over-simplifications, real-world examples do not necessarily match these specifications exactly. Even so, most agricultural markets illustrate *perfect competition*. Corn farmers, cattle raisers, and other farm enterprisers number in the thousands. Entry into farming is fairly easy. And the product is standardized by both genetic makeup and grade ratings. At the other extreme, local electricity and water supply illustrate pure *monopoly*. Singular sellers are shielded from the potential competition of entrants. Moreover, their products lack close substitutes, so each monopolist has a differentiated product.

Oligopoly and monopolistic competition may be looked upon as intermediate cases, lying between perfect competition and monopoly in structural features. *Oligopoly* is closer to monopoly than to perfect competition because it is typified by few firms (as few as two or three) and by moderately difficult entry. In product type, oligopoly markets may have either standardized or differentiated products. Thus examples of oligopolies with standardized products are aluminum, steel, and sulfuric acid. Examples of differentiated oligopolies include beer, toothpaste, autos, and recorded music.

Monopolistic competition, despite its awkwardly misleading name, is closer to perfect competition than to monopoly in structure. Compare the entries in Figure 24.2. Monopolistic competition is characterized by a fairly large number of firms and fairly easy entry. These characteristics make it a first cousin to perfect competition. Where monopolistic competition and perfect competition diverge is in product type. In contrast to the standardized products of perfect competition, the products of monopolistically competitive markets are differentiated, sometimes highly differentiated. Examples of monopolistic competition include apparel, leather shoes, and many personal services like barbering and dry cleaning.

The upshot of these structural differences is that firms in different markets see different firm demand curves. We will explore them shortly.

B
Conduct

In Figure 24.2, we see that, under conduct, a *perfectly competitive* firm has no price strategy. It merely takes the price as a given, living up to its nickname of *price taker*. Its main decision variable is therefore its quantity of output, which it sets so as to maximize its profit. When setting output, the perfectly competitive firm acts independently of other sellers, as indicated in Figure 24.2. The typical chicken farmer does not merely mimic his neighbor in the number of chickens produced. The typical chicken farmer determines output by analyzing the behavior of his *own* revenues and costs in relation to various levels of his *own* output.

The *monopolist* pursues independent strategies for *both* price and output. With this observation come two questions: (1) Why is there independence in this case? (2) Why does this independence apply to *both* price and output determination? The first question is easier to answer: The monopolist need not take into account the actions of market rivals because he has no market rivals. He is a loner. The second question is answered by recognizing the implications of this position for the monopolist's demand. The monopolist's demand curve is the downward-sloping marketwide demand curve, so price and output are jointly determined. Selection of a price *necessarily* entails selection of the level of output corresponding to that price.

The price and production strategies followed by firms in the remaining markets—oligopoly and monopolistic competition—are *like* those of a monopolist in that they too are interlocked. Once a price is selected and set, the firm's level of output will automatically be set (holding constant advertising and other promotion strategies).

However, as suggested by the entries of Figure 24.2, the firms in these last two markets have price and production strategies that *differ* from those of a monopolist in one very important respect. There is interdependence among the firms in these intermediate markets. The price and output of Coca-Cola influence the price and output of Pepsi-Cola, and vice versa. The price and output of Dan's Dry Cleaners radiate into those of Laura's Laundry. In the case of *oligopoly*, this interfirm interdependence is said to be *recognized*. Coca-Cola recognizes that its price and output decisions will influence those of Pepsi-Cola. The fewness of firms is what breeds recognized interdependence in oligopolies. It also leads to the possibility of collusion, in which case firms would agree not to compete for customers. Our opening example, involving airlines, illustrates this possibility.

On the other hand, in the case of *monopolistic competition*, this interfirm interdependence is said to be *unrecognized*. Dan's Dry Cleaners does not recognize that its price and output decisions will cause ripples of reaction among its many competitors, while each of the others, in turn, fails to recognize the repercussions of their behavior. This unrecognized interdependence stems mainly from the relatively large number of firms in monopolistically competitive markets, coupled with the relatively small size of those firms. Thus the difference between the *recognized* interdependence of oligopoly and the *unrecognized* interdependence of monopolistic competition is rather like the difference between life in a sparsely populated village and life in a crowded metropolis. Neighborly nosiness causes village life to be guided by the query "What will people think?" but big city behavior goes more by the attitude "Who cares?"

As regards promotion strategy, the third element of market conduct in Figure 24.2, market structure again comes into play. Relatively little promotion activity can be expected of perfectly competitive firms or monopolists. In contrast, markets with differentiated oligopoly and monopolistic competition often display heated promotional combat. Soda pop, beer, autos, cosmetics, and many more such markets confirm this observation. Firms in these markets rely heavily on promotions to differentiate their products.

C
Performance

The quick summary that we are confined to here does greater injustice to performance than to structure or conduct. Still, the big picture is instructive.

1. Profit (What? and Who?) Note first that marketwide profits tend to be normal with perfect competition and monopolistic competition but excessive or somewhat excessive with monopoly or oligopoly. This theoretical prediction rests partly on the notion that price competition is most intense under perfect competition or monopolistic competition. Price is competed down toward cost. But note that the price is not driven down so far that profits are eliminated.

Ours is a *capitalist* economy, so profits are necessary rewards. At a bare minimum, profits must be high enough over the long run to keep firms in business. Hence the price competition of the two most competitive market types drives profits down to normal levels. Absent such competition, they could be excessive.

A key competitive force in this regard is the condition of entry. Compare the "Entry Condition" column of Figure 24.2 with the "Profit" column. When entry is easy, profits tend to be normal. When entry is blocked or impeded, as it typically is under monopoly and oligopoly, profits can be excessive or somewhat excessive. The influence of structure on performance should thus be apparent.

Traditional theory's evaluation of profit performance holds that normal profit is good and excess profit is bad. Normal profit is good because it is associated with allocation efficiency and equity. Excess profit is bad because it is associated with underallocation of resources (too little output) and inequity. Although there is much truth to these generalizations, there are important exceptions. For example, the excess profits of some oligopolists may be due to stunning innovations. Those profits would not really be excessive at all, but rather warranted reward for shouldering the heavy risks of innovation.

2. Technical Efficiency (How?) Technical efficiency requires that products be produced in the least costly fashion, without undue waste, without obsolete plants, and so on. The performance ratings of these markets in this respect follow a pattern similar to that for profit. Performance under perfect competition and monopolistic competition is said to be "good" or "moderately good," while otherwise it is said to be "poor perhaps."

Moreover, the reasoning behind these ratings is similar to the reasoning in regard to profit. The intense price competition common to perfect competition and monopolistic competition tends to *force* technical efficiency. Waste is punished with financial losses. Obsolescence is battered by bankruptcy. Matters are more relaxed under monopoly and oligopoly. There is then leeway for inefficiency.

Monopoly and oligopoly performance is qualified, however. The "poor" rating is softened by a "perhaps" that signals a mixed bag. In particular, cost conditions may be such that monopoly or oligopoly is *necessary* to achieve technical efficiency. The classic exception is "natural" monopoly. If greater and greater size means lower and lower cost per unit of output because of large economies of scale, then natural monopoly is the result. Furthermore, it is the *desired* result. Monopoly is the market structure with good performance in such instances. Less striking but similar cost situations arise to create oligopoly, *desired* oligopoly.

3. Progressiveness (What's New?) High rates of innovation and invention are generally thought to be good. Conversely, slow change and stagnation invite jeers.

Many elements influence how any given market rates over the range of possibilities. One key element is product life cycle. The early stages of a product's life cycle favor innovation and invention to an unusual degree, as VCRs and personal computers readily demonstrate. Conversely, age-old products like leather shoes and books typically offer little opportunity for vibrant change. With this and many other elements influencing progressiveness, the role of market structure is not always clear. Still, we can present some tentative generalities.

Of the several market types, perfect competition and monopoly often seem to be least progressive. Why? Part of the reason is that they represent extreme cases. Firms experiencing them either lack the resources to pour into research and development (perfect competition) or lack competitive incentives (monopoly).

Between the extremes, where oligopoly and monopolistic competition dwell, progressiveness frequently seems most spirited. Hence, Figure 24.2

rates these markets as good and fair in this respect. The explanation and evidence for these ratings are considered in detail later. Suffice it to say here that firms in these markets typically have the resources to invest in innovative projects, and they also have ample incentives.

Taking performance as a whole, Figure 24.2 illustrates that no single market type is rated best by every measure of performance. Perfect competition is rated highly on the questions of What? and Who?, but not on the question of What's new? Conversely, oligopoly often scores poorly regarding What? and Who?, but often shines in answering the question What's new? We cannot, therefore, blithely hand out white hats to identify the good guys and black hats to adorn the bad guys. Only gray hats are in order—with black bands and white feathers perhaps. Even monopoly, a market type vilified in parlor games, movies, and novels, has its occasional goodness.

This hodgepodge of performance complicates market evaluation to the point of forcing you, the reader, to look back at Figure 24.2 frequently for refresher references. Moreover, this hodgepodge complicates government policy. There is no universally ideal market type to serve as a policy goal. There is no one single policy that can treat all product markets identically. Much policy in this area thus addresses dilemmas rather than simply solving problems.

III
The Firm's View of Demand

Recall that the word _demand_ has three uses—(1) individual consumer demand, (2) marketwide demand, and (3) firm demand. We have explored individual consumer demand and marketwide demand. Now it is time for firm demand, which is best introduced by an analogy.

When you stand on the ground, the earth appears to be flat. To an astronaut walking on the moon, however, the earth looks like a round marble. Vantage point clearly matters immensely, and these are two extreme vantage points. In between,

to the pilot of a high-flying plane, the earth is neither utterly flat nor completely round. It has visible curvature.

A
Perfect Competition and Monopoly

Similarly, market structure influences the firm's view of demand because it determines the firm's vantage point. This is especially evident in the extreme cases of perfect competition and monopoly. The perfectly competitive firm sees demand much as we see the earth when standing on it— flat. In contrast, a firm that is a monopolist has a view of demand comparable to the astronaut's view of earth. The monopolist sees the entire market because it is the only firm in the market. Between these extremes, firms have intermediate views of demand.

Figure 24.3 illustrates the extreme cases of perfect competition and monopoly. The depicted market is that for broiler chickens (those laying down their lives instead of their eggs). Annual U.S. production and consumption is several billion chickens, priced at several dozen cents per pound at the farm level. A perfectly competitive firm, one farm among thousands selling broilers, would view demand as depicted in Figure 24.3(a) if the price is 40 cents a pound. The firm is a "price taker." It can sell 10,000 or 40,000 chickens without pushing the price above or below 40 cents. The firm's tiny size and standardized product rob it of any influence over the price.

If, in contrast, the market for chickens were controlled by a monopolist, that firm would see demand as depicted in Figure 24.3(b), which shows the _marketwide_ demand for broilers. Note that the vertical scale of part (b) is the same as that of part (a), namely, cents per pound. The horizontal scale of part (b) is much different, however. It measures _billions_ of chickens instead of the _thousands_ of chickens of part (a) because the overall U.S. market amounts to billions of chickens annually. The monopolist would see the billions of birds demanded in the overall market because it would be the _only seller_. The resulting marketwide demand curve and firm demand curve would have a downward

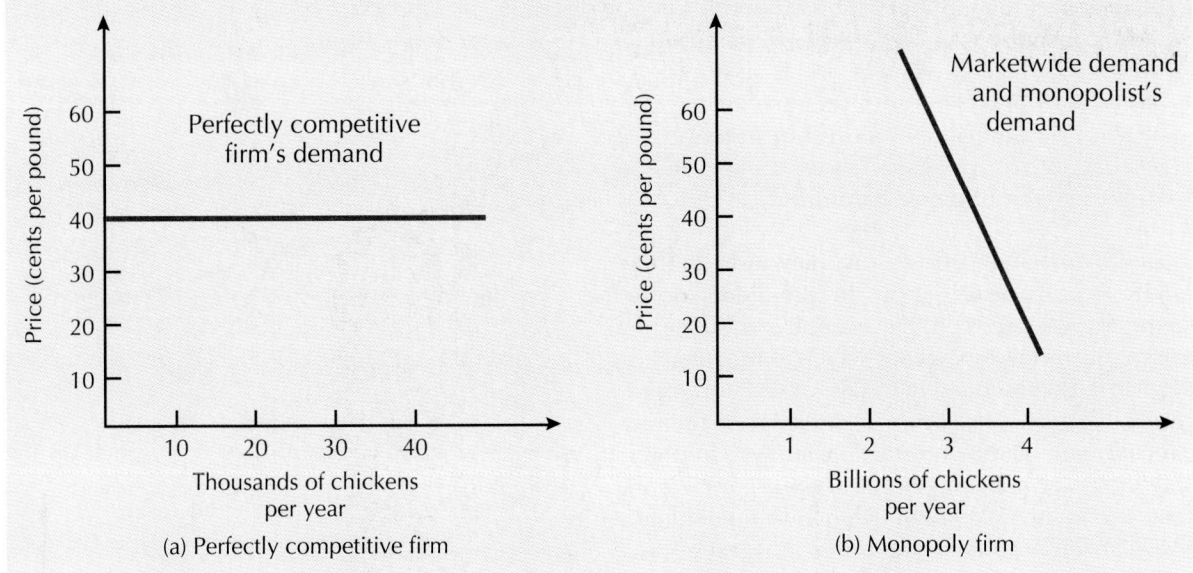

FIGURE 24.3 *A Seller's View of Demand Depends on Market Structure*

A perfectly competitive firm would confront a firm demand curve as shown in part (a) because such a firm is one of thousands, very small, and offering a product just like all other firms in the market. A monopolist would confront a firm demand curve as shown in part (b) because such a firm is the only firm in the market. In this case, firm demand and market demand are the same.

slope, as is typical of marketwide demand generally. Selecting a point on that curve, the monopolist becomes a "price maker."

B

Oligopoly and Monopolistic Competition

Firms in intermediate markets—oligopoly and monopolistic competition—experience more complexity because, theoretically, *two* possible firm demand curves are relevant to them. One we shall call the *followship demand;* the other we shall call the *nonfollowship demand.* They differ because, in these structural instances, a firm's change in price can elicit two possible reactions from rivals: Market rivals may *follow* the firm and change their prices in the same way, or they may *not follow* the firm, ignoring it instead. (Recall that it was followship that Mr. Crandall sought from Mr. Putnam in his suggestion that both airlines raise their prices.)

Accordingly, the first definition we encounter for *followship* firm demand assumes that all firms

in the market act as if in unison, each charging the same price and each altering its price up or down with the others. The firm demand curve derived from this assumption could also be called a *constant market share* demand curve because each firm maintains its market share as its price rises or falls. If, say, Firm *J* had a 7 percent market share, it would retain that 7 percent share as its price rose or fell because all other firms in the market—*K, L, M, N,* and so on—would raise or lower their prices the same as *J.*

The second definition of firm demand, *nonfollowship* demand, assumes that as the firm in question raises or lowers its price, no other firm in the market changes its price. Under this sweeping *ceteris paribus* assumption, the firm's market share *will* vary. If the firm raises its price while rival prices hold fast, it will *lose* market share to its rivals. If the firm lowers its price while rivals maintain theirs, the firm will *gain* market share, taking it away from its rivals. Hence this second firm demand curve could also be called the *varying market share* demand curve.

In oligopoly or monopolistic competition, a **firm's demand** is the set of various quantities the firm can sell at various prices, assuming either that (1) those firm prices are matched by the prices of rivals (**followship demand**), or that (2) the prices of rivals remain unchanged (**nonfollowship demand**).

Figure 24.4 shows these two demands as they might hypothetically apply to the Ford Motor Company. We simplify by assuming a single or average price for Ford's cars, which at the outset is $12,000 (with comparable prices for GM and other rivals). At this initial price, Ford sells 2.0 million cars annually. Hence we start the analysis at point s, which corresponds to this going price and quantity. Point s is on both the followship demand (*WSX*) and the nonfollowship demand (*zsy*).

Now consider a price *cut* by Ford from $12,000 to $10,000. If GM, Chrysler, and Ford's other rivals *do not* match that price reduction, the nonfollowship demand curve applies and Ford's price drops well below those rivals' prices. Many car buyers consequently switch away from the rivals to Ford, boosting Ford's market share and driving Ford's sales up to 3.5 million cars per year. This moves Ford down the nonfollowship demand curve from s to y.

On the other hand, if GM, Chrysler, and the other rivals *do* follow Ford's price cut with identical price reductions of their own, Ford will not be able to increase its market share at the expense of the others. Buyers would then have no reason to switch to Ford because *all* firms would then have lower prices, not just Ford. This would move Ford down the followship demand curve from s to x, yielding sales of 2.25 million annually, up from 2.0 initially. Ford's sales increase in this case only because sales will increase at the marketwide level in response to the lower prices that all auto firms are charging. Without the added market share that customer switching brings, however, this sales jump of 0.25 million cars is quite modest in comparison to the jump of 1.5 million associated with nonfollowship.

Consider next the consequences of a price increase by Ford from $12,000 to $14,000. If GM, Chrysler, and Ford's other rivals *do not* follow Ford with comparable increases of their own, the non-

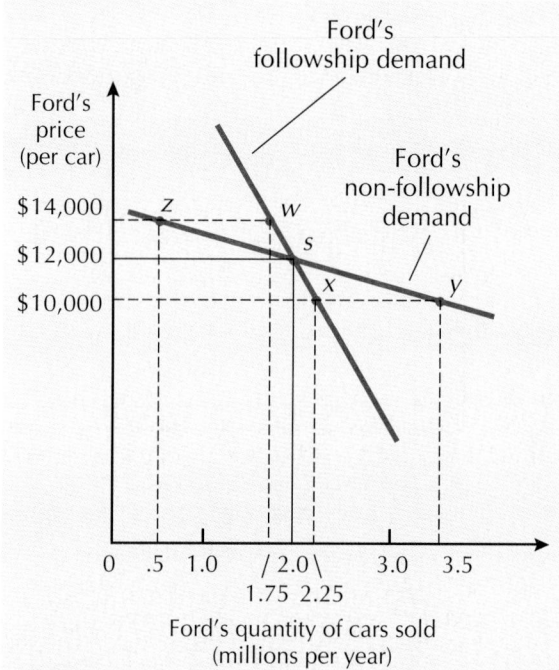

FIGURE 24.4 _Followship and Nonfollowship as They Might Apply to the Ford Motor Company_

Starting position: *Point* s *indicates the "going" price–quantity combination for the firm, $12.000 and 2.0 million units.* Price reduction: *If Ford cuts the price from $12,000 to $10,000, and General Motors and other rivals* do not *follow with matching cuts of their own, Ford can take business away from them, moving to point* y. *If rivals' price cuts* do *follow,* x *is the result. Sales increase only from higher marketwide sales. No share changes occur.* Price increase: *If Ford raises the price from $12,000 to $14,000 and others* do not *follow, Ford loses market share and sales drop to 0.5 million at point* z. *With followship, point* w *results.*

followship demand curve applies and Ford's price level ends up relatively high. This disparity in prices, with Ford on the high side, will cause many prospective Ford buyers to switch their allegiance to GM or one of the others. The switching causes Ford's quantity to shrink markedly, moving Ford up the nonfollowship demand curve from point s, with annual sales of 2.0 million, to point x, with annual sales of only 0.5 million.

If, in contrast, Ford's rivals *do* follow with matching price increases of their own, Ford's drop in sales would not be nearly as severe. It would then move up the followship demand curve from point *s* to point *w*, implying an annual quantity reduction of only 0.25 million cars, from 2.0 to 1.75 million. This drop in quantity along the followship demand curve would not be due to any brand switching away from Ford. Rather, it would be caused by reduced sales at the marketwide level once overall prices for all firms had risen.

For a general summary of Figure 24.4's message, note especially that the price elasticity of demand is much higher for the nonfollowship curve than for the followship curve. For example, the elasticity over the *sy* segment is 3.2 in comparison to the inelastic 0.65 of the *sx* segment.

This is to be expected. The nonfollowship curve reflects substantial market share changes for Ford (pluses for nonfollowed price cuts and minuses for nonfollowed price hikes). The followship curve shows no changes in Ford's market share. Its downward tilt comes solely from changes in marketwide quantities demanded as marketwide price level rises or falls. Ford gets its share of those marketwide changes.

Finally, it must be recognized that a firm in an oligopolistic or monopolistically competitive market will typically "see" either the followship curve, or the nonfollowship curve, or some combination of parts of these curves. *Except where the curves cross*, as at point *s* in Figure 24.4, *the firm cannot be on both curves at the same time*. Ford, for instance, would or would not be followed if it cut its price, so it would end up at either *x* or *y*, not both. Firms thus tend to anticipate followship or nonfollowship from their rivals. Broadly speaking, big firms tend to anticipate followship, while small firms tend to anticipate nonfollowship, but anticipation can vary with the circumstances, as we shall see in detail later.

IV
Firm Demand and the Basic Market Types

What's the payoff to the foregoing? An understanding of firm demand is crucial to an understanding of *how* markets work and *how well* they work under different structural conditions. The main early steps to understanding are as follows:

1. Structure determines the firm's view of demand.
2. The firm's view of demand determines its perceptions of revenues.
3. Revenues, when coupled with costs, determine the firm's profits. Revenues thus affect the firm's conduct as it pursues profit maximization.

We are now in a position to complete the first step. Figure 24.5 outlines the demand facing the typical firm in each of the four market categories defined earlier, namely, monopoly, oligopoly, monopolistic competition, and perfect competition. These market types are oversimplified models. So, too, are these firm demands simplified into the views of typical firms.

The main point to be made here is that market structure influences the firm's demand. To be sure, marketwide demand will also influence the firm's demand. However, the role of market structure alone is critical. Theoretically, it would be possible for marketwide demand to be essentially the *same* in every one of the four cases depicted in Figure 24.5. If so, it would look like the demand facing the monopolist in part (a). But monopoly is the only market structure that allows the typical firm to confront marketwide demand.

Two key structural conditions give *monopoly* this result. First, being the sole occupant of the market, the monopolist has a 100 percent market share. Second, the monopolist's product is, in a sense, perfectly differentiated, there being no close substitute offerings from other firms (inside or outside the market).

In the case of *oligopoly*, there are relatively few firms selling differentiated or standardized products. Fewness imparts notable size to the typical firm. Product differentiation may grant some power over price, though not to the same degree as that enjoyed by the monopolist. The typical oligopolist may thus confront either the relatively inelastic followship demand or the relatively elastic nonfollowship demand. Both demand curves are shown in Figure 24.5. However the oligopolist

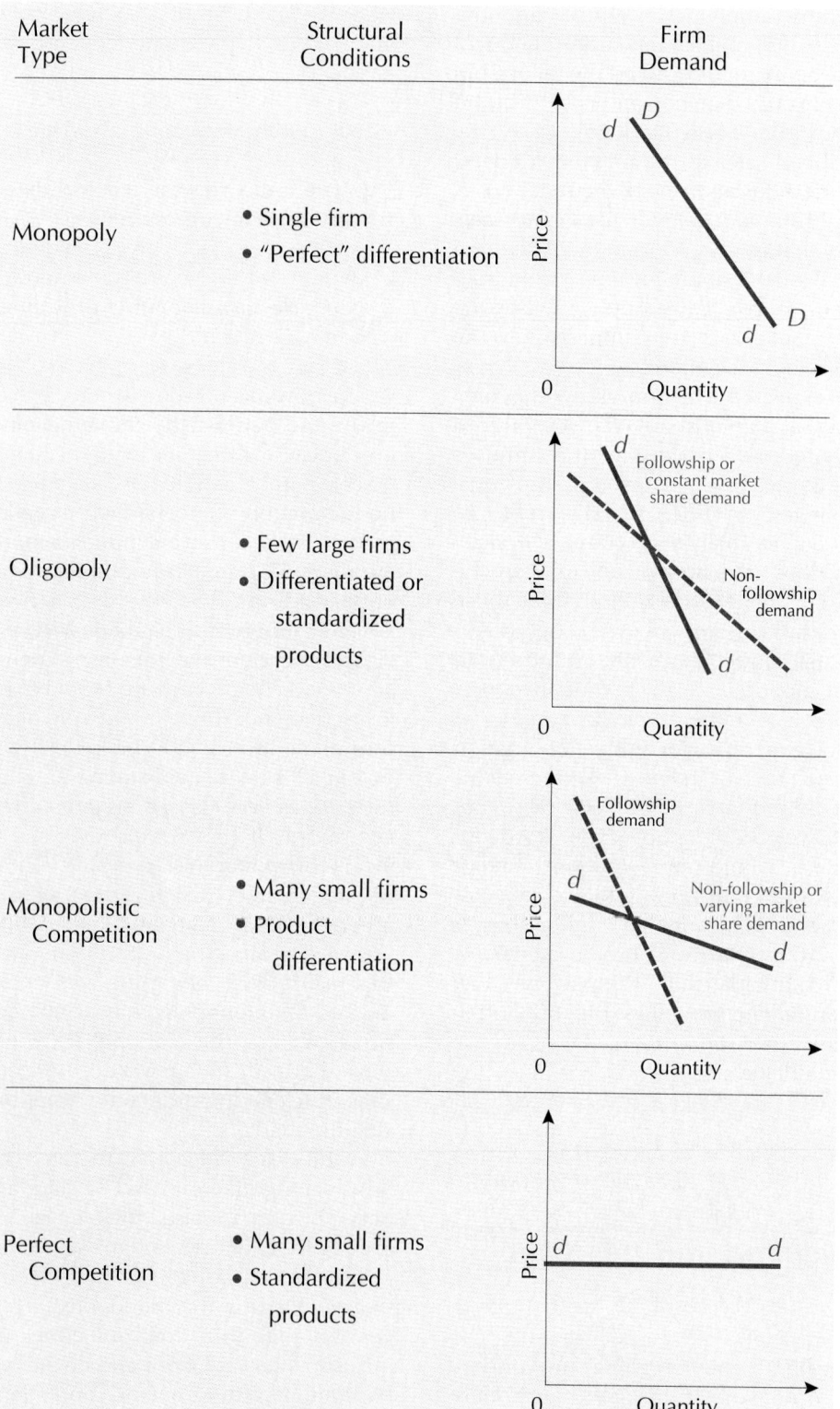

FIGURE 24.5   *Firm Demand Curves Under Different Market Structures*

cannot be on both curves simultaneously except where they intersect. Hence, either one or the other applies for different possible prices. In Figure 24.5, prominence is given to the followership demand curve in order to underscore the fact that oligopolists often recognize their interdependence. The firm recognizes that if it cuts its price, its rivals will follow with price cuts of their own. This simple characterization of the oligopolist's demand will be modified later.

The typical firm in a market with *monopolistic competition* is one among many. It has a relatively small market share and a moderately differentiated product. Accordingly, two demand curves are possible, as in the case of oligopoly. Unlike the oligopolist, however, the monopolistically competitive firm tends to ignore the possibility that its actions could influence the actions of its rivals. Interdependence is present, but it goes unrecognized because each firm feels it is too small to influence the others. Operating under this assumption, the monopolistically competitive firm will see only the nonfollowship demand curve. Figure 24.5 thus gives prominence to the nonfol-

lowship demand curve and reduces the followship demand to a dashed line. Indeed, the main feature of monopolistic competition that distinguishes it from perfect competition is product differentiation. This gives slope to its demand curve.

Under *perfect competition*, the last case illustrated in Figure 24.5, the followship demand completely disappears. Nonfollowship demand collapses into a horizontal, perfectly elastic demand. This means that the perfectly competitive firm has absolutely no power over the price. Price must be taken as given by the market, with the firm left only to decide its level of output. The structural conditions yielding this outcome were mentioned previously—namely, a multitude of relatively tiny firms producing a perfectly standardized product.

The connection between firm demand and total revenue for the case of monopoly was established earlier in Figure 22.3. The connections for the several other cases will be developed later when we explain more fully the various price and production strategies these market structures evoke.

SUMMARY

1. The main objective of the chapters that follow is to study *how* and *how well* product markets work. Product markets are complex, living creatures. They cannot be dissected on a laboratory table. Still, understanding them requires (1) a catalog of their main elements and (2) a theoretical scheme tying these elements together.

2. As shown in Figure 24.1, four main elements give product markets economic form—basic conditions, structure, conduct, and performance. (a) The *basic conditions* are characteristics inherent in the product or its production process. Consumer goods tend to differ from producer goods, for example. Elasticities of demand and supply vary across products, leaving important imprints. And so on. (b) *Structure* refers to characteristics of the market's

participants and product that influence competition. These characteristics include the number and size of sellers, the condition of entry, and the standardized or differentiated nature of the product. (c) *Conduct* comes next, covering the actions of sellers. Their strategies concerning such variables as price, production, promotion, and product design are the main items of interest here. (d) Finally, *performance* refers to economic results. These are the market's answers to the basic questions raised by scarcity—namely, What?, How?, Who?, and What's new?. The ideal answers to these questions may or may not be provided by markets.

3. Tying these several elements together by causal connections pumps life into product markets. The traditional view is that the

basic conditions influence structure. Structure, in turn, affects conduct. Finally, structure and conduct determine performance. These causal relationships emerge most clearly in a survey of four oversimplified market types. Figure 24.2 portrays these under the labels *perfect competition, monopoly, oligopoly,* and *monopolistic competition.*

4. Structural variations define these market models. At one extreme is perfect competition, with a very large number of firms, easy entry, and a standardized product. At the other extreme is monopoly, with one firm, blocked entry and a fairly distinct product. Between these extremes lie oligopoly and monopolistic competition, which typify most real world markets. Fewness of firms, impeded entry, and standardized or differentiated products typify oligopoly. Numerous firms, easy entry, and product differentiation describe monopolistic competition.

5. Figure 24.2 summarizes conduct and performance well enough. Looking behind the labels, you should appreciate the fact that structure determines the individual firm's view of demand. This perception of demand generates the firm's perception of revenue. Because profit derives in part from revenue, firms seeking to maximize their profit will conduct themselves differently according to their different percep-

tions of demand and revenue. Price strategies, for instance, run the range from *none* to *unrecognized* and *recognized interdependence* to *independence.* Finally, performance features sprout as weeds as well as roses.

6. The firm's view of demand under monopoly is the same as the marketwide demand. At the opposite extreme, the perfectly competitive firm sees demand as a horizontal (perfectly elastic) line because structure forces this firm to take the price as given.

7. In intermediate cases of oligopoly and monopolistic competition, there are two possible firm demands—(a) *followship demand,* with unity of price changes across firms that leaves market shares unchanged, and (b) *nonfollowship,* with solo price changes by the firm resulting in market share gains (price cut) or losses (price increase). The firm's followship, or constant share demand, is a percentage slice of marketwide demand. The firm's nonfollowship demand is more elastic than the followship curve because it incorporates market share changes.

8. Lastly, market structure controls firm demand because market structure varies with such conditions as firm size (firm number) and product differentiation. Refer back to Figure 24.5 for a summary of these relationships.

KEY TERMS

Basic conditions (of a market)
Market structure
Standarized products
Differentiated products
Market conduct
Performance (of a market)
Perfect competition

Monopoly
Oligopoly
Monopolistic competition
Firm's demand
Followship demand
Nonfollowship demand

QUESTIONS AND PROBLEMS

1. What characteristics identify a perfectly competitive industry? Are there any perfectly competitive industries?

2. What market structure most closely describes the typical small business owned and operated locally? Why? Give examples.

3. Interdependence is a key word in any description of the market conduct of oligopoly firms. In what ways are oligopolistic firms interdependent?

4. If there are no other firms to attract customers, why would a monopoly firm lose customers by raising its price?

5. Advertising to create brand loyalty is apparently designed to do what to a firm's non-followship demand curve?

6. Give examples of differentiated products that you buy. Give examples of standardized products that you buy. Which have been the most heavily advertised? Is this consistent with expected market conduct?

7. When do competitors become rivals?

8. Which market structure yields the best performance? Give relevant criteria for evaluation and explain why the answer is subject to debate.

25

Perfect Competition and Profit Maximizing

Who feeds more college students than anyone else? The Saga Corporation. Founded in 1948 by three students who took over the dining hall at Hobart College in New York, the company is now the food-service contractor to 420 colleges (and the owner of several restaurant chains, including Black Angus and Grandy's). Saga even runs a "college" of its own—Tailfeather University in Lewisville, Texas, where it teaches cooks how to fry chicken the Saga way. Between 1978 and 1984, Saga's profits went from an unsavory $1.5 million to a zesty $30.0 million. The man behind this rise was Chairman Charles A. Lynch, who adhered to what his employees call Lynch's law: *The rate of increase in costs should never exceed the rate of increase in revenues.*[1]

Lynch's law for maximizing profit is as old as fried chicken. In economic jargon it says: *Expand production if **marginal cost** is less than **marginal revenue** but never to the point where marginal cost exceeds marginal revenue. Stop when marginal cost equals marginal revenue.*

Marginal revenue is the added revenue from an added unit of output. Marginal cost is the added cost for an added unit of output. Now it is time to bring these key elements of a firm's experience together to explain the principles of profit maximizing. The success of Saga illustrates that these principles are broadly applicable—from college food service to posh restaurants, from perfect competition to monopoly. Even so, these principles will be explained at present only in the context of perfect competition because explaining perfect competition is the second main task of this chapter. An appendix to this chapter discusses agriculture and government policy.

[1]Kenneth Labich, "The Dean of College Cuisine Smartens Up," *Fortune*, August 6, 1984, pp. 28–32.

I
Perfectly Competitive Structure

A
The Word Competition

Economists use the word *competition* is so many different ways that qualifiers disclose meaning. Aside from *perfect competition*, there is also *imperfect competition, monopolistic competition, dynamic competition, price competition, nonprice competition,* and *workable competition.*

According to the dictionary, *competition* means a rivalry, a vying between contestants. This is the kind of competition that many firms engage in. Pepsi vies with Coke by introducing Diet Pepsi and by advertising heavily. Coke responds in kind. Economists describe such competition with various adjectives. Rivalrous competition in general, for instance, is often called *dynamic competition.* This label suggests the actions and reactions of firms over time. It stresses the rivalrous *conduct* of firms, conduct covering the entire range of business decision variables—advertising, pricing, product design, production processes, and more. It is sometimes useful to divide all these forms of dynamic competition into just two broad categories, namely, (1) price competition and (2) nonprice competition. *Price competition* covers instances where firms initiate price cuts to gain business away from rivals, thereby prompting other firms to respond with their own price cuts. *Nonprice competition* is business rivalry centering on variables other than price, such as advertising.

Perfect competition differs from dynamic competition on several counts. Whereas dynamic competition describes most *real* markets, perfect competition is best thought of as a *theoretical* model. No real-world market is perfectly competitive, although several come fairly close—in particular, those for agricultural commodities. Moreover, dynamic competition focuses primarily on competition as the rivalrous *conduct* of firms, while perfect competition stresses the competition embodied in a particular market *structure*. Note that this is merely a point of emphasis. All markets have both structure and conduct (as well as performance). However, dynamic competition revolves mainly around rivalrous conduct, while perfect competition hinges mainly on highly competitive structural conditions. Dynamically competitive firms are boldly *active*, while perfectly competitive firms are strictly *reactive*. A final point of difference concerns scope. Whereas dynamic competition can be conducted with *both price and nonprice* variables, perfect competition centers only on *price*. No perfectly competitive firm advertises on TV. No perfectly competitive firm restyles its product every year. Indeed, even though price is the only item of competition in perfect competition, price is determined by the marketwide interaction of demand and supply, not by the conscious policies of perfectly competitive firms. This lack of individual firm influence over price yields a precise definition of perfect competition.

> **Perfect competition** among sellers exists if no single seller has a perceptible influence on the market price of the good. (Perfect competition among buyers exists if no single buyer can influence price).

B
Structural Conditions and Firm Demand

What are structural conditions that prevent sellers (and buyers) from individually influencing the price? They are:

1. A very large number of sellers and buyers, each of which has a very small market share.
2. A standardized product.
3. Easy entry into and easy exit from the market.
4. Fully informed buyers and sellers.

Under these conditions, price is not determined by individual buyers and sellers, but rather by the interaction of marketwide demand and supply. As shown in Figure 25.1(a), marketwide demand for hogs, D_1, intersects marketwide supply at about 4.5 million hogs per week to generate an equilibrium price of $100 per hog. This price is taken as given by the typical firm in the market, a hog farmer. Hence the firm's view is shown in part (b), where the horizontal scale for quantity is much smaller than that for the marketwide view in part (a). The firm's demand is perfectly elastic at $100. The firm can sell seven hogs or three hogs or even no hogs a week *without influencing the price noticeably*.

The structural conditions of perfect competition dictate this result. With a *large number* of market participants, each relatively small, none individually can affect the price, just as adding or subtracting a gallon of water from a lake could not perceptibly alter the lake's water level. With a *standardized product*, the product of any one seller is exactly like the product of every other seller in the market. Hence one seller cannot raise its price relative to that of the others lest its sales vanish. With *easy entry and exit*, firms lose influence over the price in the long run because firms pricing above the marketwide level would be supplanted by new entrants, as well as by existing firms. Indeed, those trying to exercise power over the price would be forced to leave. With *fully informed buyers and sellers*, no one in the market could take advantage of ignorant souls on the opposite side of the market. All sales would occur at the market price because buyers would not knowingly pay more and sellers would not knowingly charge less.

Figure 25.1(b) thus says that the individual firm lacks influence over the price. The perfectly competitive firm's demand is d_1 at a price of $100 per hog. Note that this does *not* mean that the price is fixed at $100. Perfectly competitive prices *do* change, often frequently. When they do, the firm's demand curve shifts up or down to match each new marketwide price. If, for example, marketwide demand shifted out from D_1 to D_2 in Figure 25.1(a), the firm's demand curve would then shift up from d_1 to d_2.

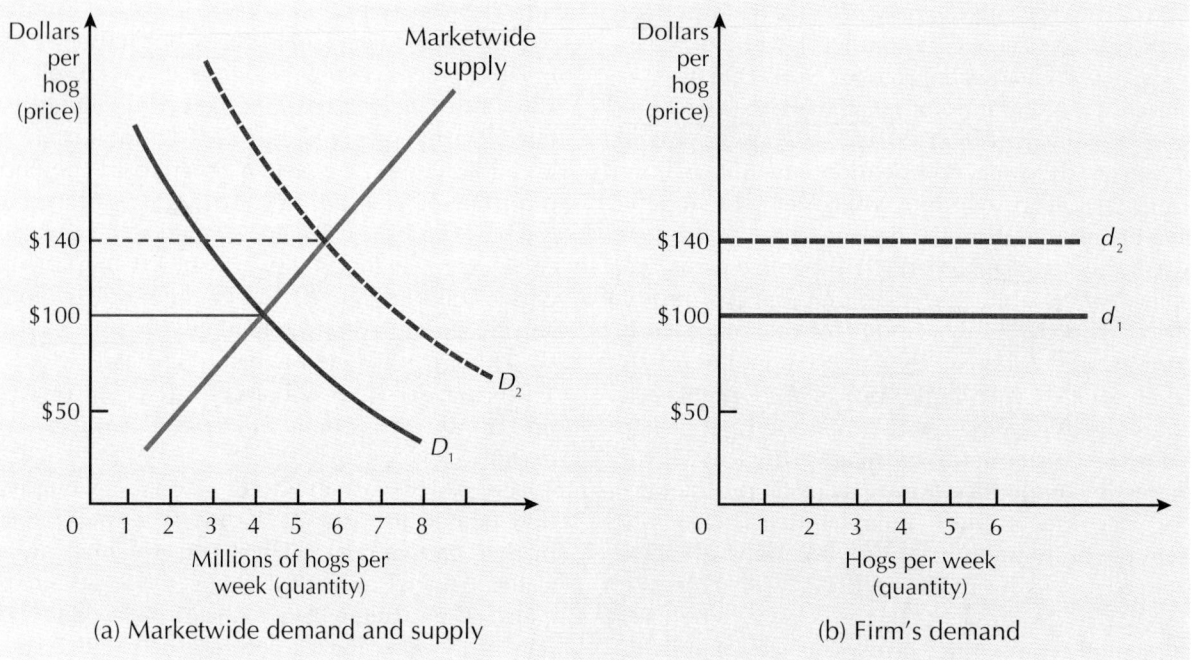

FIGURE 25.1 *Perfect Competition: Marketwide Demand and Supply Determine Firm Demand*

Under perfect competition, the marketwide forces of demand and supply generate price. Individual firms do not influence the price, so each firm views its demand as perfectly elastic, a horizontal line. Here marketwide demand D_1 generates a price of $100, resulting in the firm's demand d_1 at $100. A greater marketwide demand like D_2 would yield a higher firm demand at d_2. Notice that the quantity scale is millions for the market but single units for the firm.

C

Demand and Revenue

The fact that market structure determines the firm's view of demand is important because, in turn, the firm's view of demand yields the firm's perception of revenues, and revenues (minus costs) determine profit. Revenues may be stated in dollars per unit or total dollars. The firm's demand curve is, in fact, the per unit view because demand hinges on price, which can always be stated in dollars per unit. In Figure 25.2(a), for instance, the firm's demand curve appears anew with a vertical axis scaled in dollars per unit and a price specified at $100 *per hog* for every hog sold. In total dollars, these price/quantity combinations of firm demand become total revenue *because total revenue is price times quantity.* The total revenue associated with three hogs in Figure 25.2(a) is shown to be the

area under the demand curve, $300, because $100 × 3 = $300 per week. Part (b) of Figure 25.2 has a vertical axis scaled in total dollars, so it explicitly measures the total dollar revenue associated with each level of output. Reading vertically up from three hogs, you can see that total revenue is then $300.

Two per unit expressions of revenue (apart from price) are average revenue and marginal revenue. **Average revenue** *per unit is simply total revenue divided by total quantity.* If all units sell at the same price, average revenue *is* the price because

$$\begin{aligned}\text{Average} \atop \text{revenue} &= \frac{\text{total revenue}}{\text{quantity}} \\ &= \frac{\text{price} \times \text{quantity}}{\text{quantity}} \\ &= \text{price}\end{aligned}$$

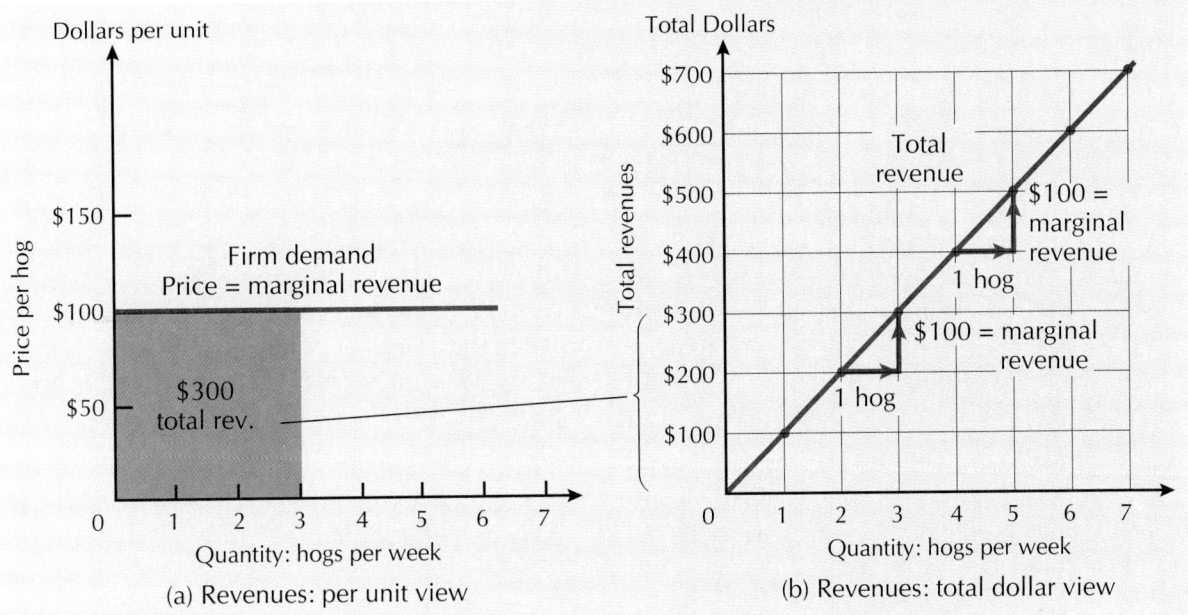

FIGURE 25.2 *Revenue as It Relates to Output for a Perfectly Competitive Firm*

In part (a) revenue per unit (per hog) is determined by the firm's demand curve, which is perfectly horizontal. Here total revenue is shown as the area under the demand curve at the given quantity, because total revenue is price times quantity. In part (b) total revenue is shown directly. It rises at a constant rate because each hog sold adds $100 to total revenue. Marginal revenue is this jump in total revenue for each hog sold, and when shown per unit terms in part (a), marginal revenue equals price.

In contrast, *marginal revenue* is the *jump* in total revenue associated with *each added individual* unit sold, the first, second, third, and so on. It is not an average across all units sold; it takes each unit individually.

> **Marginal revenue** is the added revenue associated with the sale of one more unit of output.

For a perfectly competitive firm, each added unit sold brings in added revenue equal to the price because each unit is priced the same. In Figure 25.2(b), total revenue jumps $100 with the third unit and $100 with the fifth unit. Thus, when marginal revenue is depicted on the per unit scale of part (a), it matches the price and the firm's demand curve.

> Price, average revenue, and marginal revenue are per unit revenue concepts, which for a

perfectly competitive firm are equal to each other. Total revenue, or price times quantity, is the total dollar form, and for a perfectly competitive firm it rises at a constant rate.

Read Perspective 25A.

II

Perfectly Competitive Conduct

When revenues are compared to costs over the range of possible outputs, the perfectly competitive firm can determine its profit-maximizing output. This comparison now becomes our task. To simplify, the task can be divided into a sequence of steps:

PERSPECTIVE 25A
The Hog Market

Though hypothetical, the foregoing data for hogs are actually a simplification of real data. We've assumed that a typical hog weighs 250 pounds when it leaves the farm and that the farmer gets 40 cents a pound live weight ($0.40 × 250 = $100). In 1981, hogs actually averaged 243 pounds and fetched a price of about $0.4027 per pound, or $97.86 per hog. To assume that hog raising is perfectly competitive is also an approximation, but not a misleading one. Putting 1981's data into a typical week, there were 1.78 million hogs slaughtered in the United States per week. Each farmer's output was very small by comparison. The average farm in the hog market—and there were over 450,000 hog farms—sold roughly four hogs per week. By these numbers, even a huge hog farm turning out 200 hogs per week (or 10,400 per year) would account for only 0.01 percent of the total national output. An individual farmer, even a very large one, could thus not affect the price of hogs perceptibly. During the early 1980s, the typical hog farm was also fairly small in total revenue received from hogs, getting less than $100,000. However, hog farmers typically raised crops and other livestock as well, so that their total revenues (and profits) from hogs were less than 50 percent of their overall farm revenues (and profits).[2]

[2]Sources: R.N. Van Arsdall and K.E. Nelson, *U.S. Hog Industry* (Washington, D.C.: U.S. Department of Agriculture, June 1984); *Agricultural Statistics 1982* (Washington, D.C.: U.S. Department of Agriculture, 1982).

	Total dollars view	Dollars per unit view
Short run	Step A: Firm	Step B: (1) Firm, (2) Market
Long run	(Skip)	Step C: Firm and market together

This four-part matrix reveals a pair of two-part divisions. The economics of the firm (any firm) can be considered in the short run and the long run. Moreover, we have seen two views of dollar values—the "total dollars view" and the "dollars per unit view" (although these are essentially two ways of looking at the same thing). When the time and dollar divisions are each accounted for, the result is the preceding four-way division. We will skip the long–run total dollar view in order to focus on the remaining three steps:

A. Short-run total dollars view (the firm alone).

B. Short-run dollars per unit view (1. The firm, 2. The market).

C. Long-run dollars per unit view (the firm and the market together).

A
Short-Run Total Dollars View (the Typical Firm)

1. Profit Maximizing Total profit is total revenue minus total cost. This is the profit that, in traditional theory, the firm tries to maximize because this is the profit that will give the firm's owners big homes, fancy cars, and vacation trips to Hawaii. Hence **profit maximizing** is most readily understood in the total dollar view.

Total profit is total revenue minus total cost. Total profit is maximized when this difference is greatest.

The first three columns of Table 25.1 reproduce the hypothetical revenue data for our example of a hog farmer. In particular, column (3) shows the

TABLE 25.1   Total Revenues, Total Costs, and Total Profit: Hog Farmer in the Short Run, per Week

(1) Output per Week (Hogs)	(2) Price per Hog	(3) = (2) × (1) Total Revenue (Price × Output) (Total Dollars)	(4) Total Fixed Cost (Total Dollars)	(5) Total Variable Cost (Total Dollars)	(6) = (4) + (5) Total Cost (Total Dollars)	(7) = (3) − (6) Total Profit or Loss (Total Dollars)
0	$100	$ 0	$100	$ 0	$100	−$100
1	100	100	100	40	140	− 40
2	100	200	100	60	160	40
3	100	300	100	90	190	110
4	100	400	100	140	240	160
5	100	500	100	210	310	190
6	100	600	100	300	400	200
7	100	700	100	500	600	100
8	100	800	100	750	850	−50

total revenues associated with the quantities in column (1) and the prices in column (2). Total revenue is $400 per week, for instance, when four hogs per week are sold at $100 each. Hypothetical total costs occupy the next three columns of Table 25.1. The total fixed costs of column (4) remain fixed at $100 because they cover such fixed expenses as property taxes and payments on debt. The total variable costs of column (5) rise continuously with ever greater output because they reflect expenses for variable inputs. Labor and hog feed are by far the biggest variable expenses of hog farming (with labor being more important when piglets are farrowed but feed becoming more important when those piglets mature into hogs). Together the total fixed costs of column (4) and the total variable costs of column (5) yield the total costs of column (6).

Finally, when the total costs of column (6) are subtracted from the total revenues of column (3), the result in column (7) is total dollar profit per week. At first, the profits are negative, i.e., losses. With zero output, the loss matches total fixed costs, $100, because those fixed costs pose a burden in the short run regardless of output, even zero output. As output expands, the losses turn into profits, rising to a peak of $200 per week when output is six hogs per week. Here, then, is the level of output that maximizes profit for the firm if hogs sell for $100.

The data in Table 25.1 come visually alive in Figure 25.3. Total revenue rises at a constant rate of $100 per hog. Total cost begins with $100 in total fixed cost (TFC) at zero output and thereafter rises

in accord with total variable cost (TVC). Over the range of positive profits (two to seven hogs per week), total revenue lies above total cost. The vertical difference between these two totals is total profit. Total profit rises until output is six hogs per week, where the vertical difference between total revenue and total cost is greatest. There, total revenue is $600, total cost is $400, and total profit is $200 ($600 − $400 = $200). *Here profit is maximized.* Still greater output of seven or eight hogs causes profits to shrink and turn negative.

2. Loss Minimizing   If the price fell substantially below $100, the firm might be faced with the prospect of losing money at each possible output. This unhappy prospect is depicted in Figure 25.4. Whereas before, in Figure 25.3, total revenue was generated by a price of $100 per hog, here the alternative total revenue curves of Figure 25.4 are generated by prices of $50 and $25. Total costs are the same as before, except that here they are obtained by adding total fixed costs on top of total variable costs. (Before, in Figure 25.3, total variable costs were added on top of total fixed costs.)

When the price is $50 per hog, total revenue lies beneath total cost at every level of output. Subtracting total cost from total revenue inevitably yields a negative profit, i.e., a loss. To minimize the loss, the firm should select a level of output at which the vertical difference between total revenue and total cost is *minimized*. This will minimize the negative results. In Figure 25.4, when the price is $50, an output of four hogs would achieve this aim, with losses of $40 per week:

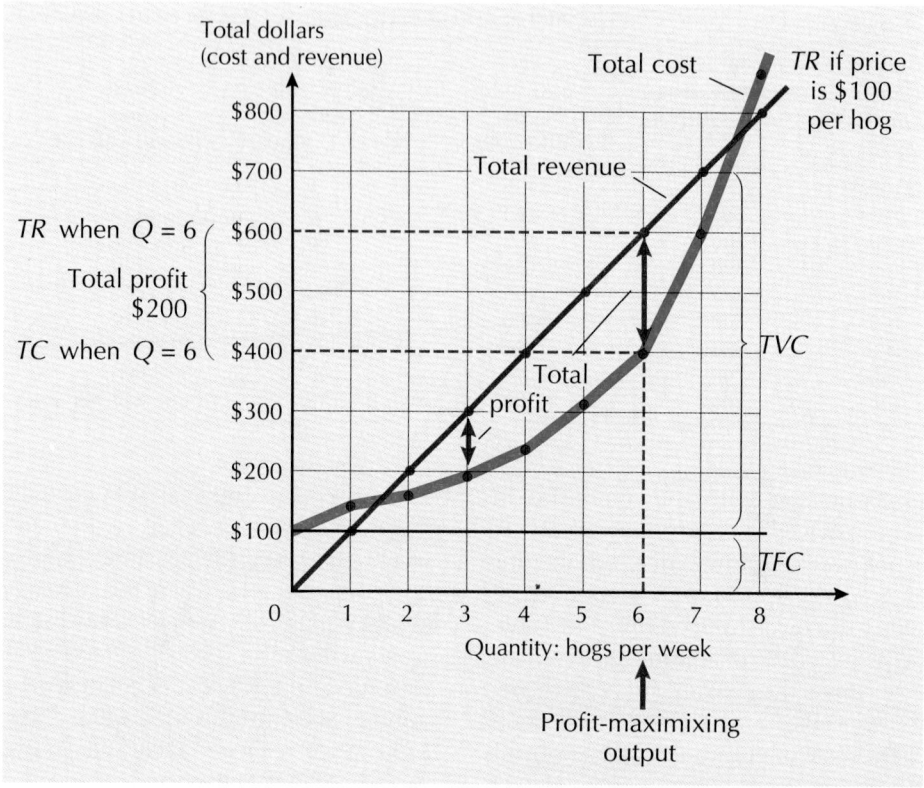

FIGURE 25.3   Short-Run Total Dollar View of Firm Profit Maximization
The profit-maximizing firm will produce where total revenue minus total cost is greatest. Here total revenue and total cost vary with output, and an output of six hogs per week maximizes the extent to which total revenue exceeds total cost. At a rate of six hogs per week, total revenue is $600, total cost is $400, and total profit is $200 (600 − 400 = 200). The data come from Table 25.1.

Quantity	Total Revenue	−	Total Cost	=	Total Profit (−Loss)
4 hogs	$200	−	$240	=	−$40

Note that this loss-minimizing output is below the profit-maximizing output of six hogs when the price is $100.

If the price plummets further to only $25 per hog, total revenue would move still further down. The losses would necessarily become greater, and the loss-minimizing output would drop still lower. Indeed, as indicated in Figure 25.4, a price of $25 would cause the firm to *shut down*, to have zero output.

The reason for this shutdown is important. Note first that the firm should *never lose more than its total fixed cost*, in this case $100 per week. That is

the amount it would lose in the short run if it chose to produce nothing at all. That is the rock bottom amount. Note second that if total revenue lies *below total variable cost*, as it does in Figure 25.4 when the price is $25 per hog, then *any output* other than zero will cause losses *greater* than the total fixed cost, greater than that rock bottom amount. To the extent that total revenue falls short of total variable costs, that uncovered portion of variable costs will be lost *as well as* all the fixed costs. To lose some total variable costs in addition to all the total fixed costs is to drop below rock bottom, shutdown losses. At zero output total revenue is zero, but so too is total variable cost. Only total fixed cost is lost.

Stated differently, the firm would be running a charity if it lost more than its fixed costs. It would be the equivalent of a soup kitchen that sold ham

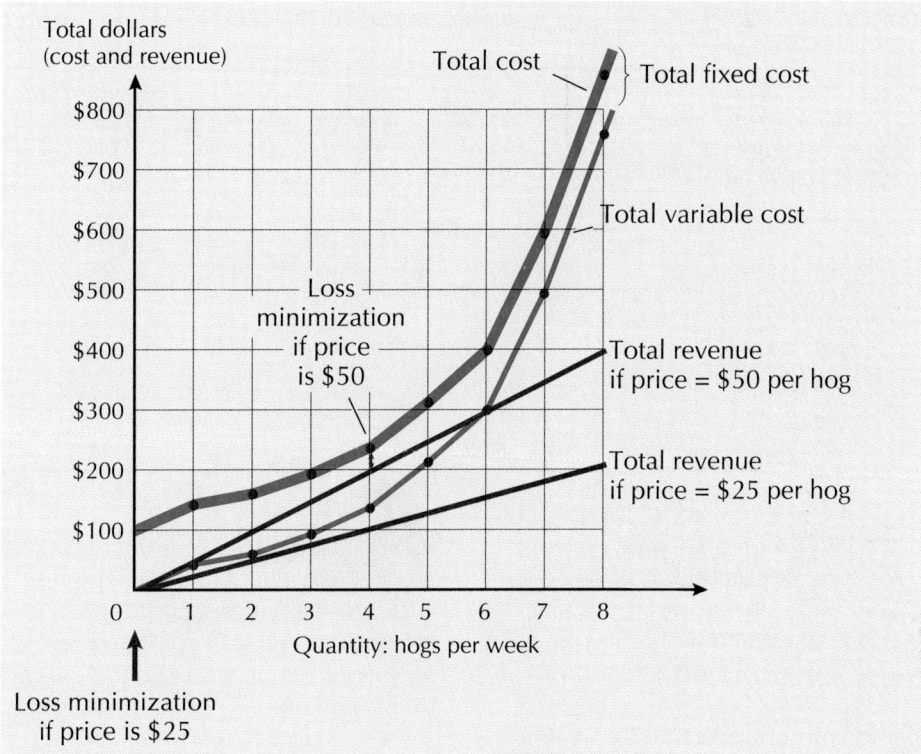

FIGURE 25.4 *Short-Run Total Dollar View of Firm Loss Minimization*

If the price at which output can be sold falls, the total revenue will shift downward. If the price slips to $50 per hog (half of what it was in Figure 25.3), there will be no level of output that yields a total revenue exceeding the total cost. Loss is inevitable. To minimize the loss when the price is $50, the firm would produce four or three hogs per week (down from six before), as that would minimize the extent to which total cost exceeds total revenue. If the price tumbles to only $25 per hog, the firm would shut down and lose its total fixed cost. The most the firm should ever lose is the total fixed cost.

sandwiches for $0.10 apiece, sandwiches whose variable costs were $0.50 apiece.

B

Short-Run Dollars Per Unit View

1. The Firm To speak in terms of $0.50 per ham sandwich is to speak in terms of dollars per unit. The short–run dollars per unit view simply converts total dollars into dollars per unit—per hog or per sandwich for instance. The objective of the firm is still the same, namely, to maximize *total dollar profit*. Moreover, the level of output that maximizes total profit in the total view will also maximize total profit in the per unit view. All that really changes is perspective. The scale of the vertical axis now changes to dollars *per unit* in order

to represent revenues and costs per unit. Two of these per unit measures—marginal revenue and marginal cost—are particularly important because they lie at the heart of the firm's two-question logic for maximizing total profit.

Profit-Maximizing Per Unit View: Table 25.2 converts the total dollar values of Table 25.1 into dollars per unit, in this case per hog. Marginal revenue in column (2) is the *addition to total revenue* that can be credited to *each* hog sold. This is the price, once again assumed to be $100 per hog, because total revenue rises by jumps of $100 (0 → $100 → $200 → $300 . . .). This marginal revenue (*MR*) is the answer to the first question of two-question logic as it applies to the firm:

Question 1: What is it worth to produce and

TABLE 25.2   Dollars per Unit: Price, Marginal Revenue, Average Costs, and Marginal Costs in the Short Run

(1) Output per Week (Hogs)	(2) Price, Marginal Revenue (Each Hog)	(3) Marginal Cost (Each Hog)	(4) = (2) − (3) Marginal Profit (Each Hog)	(5) Average Fixed Cost	(6) Average Variable Cost	(7) = (5) + (6) Average Total Cost	(8) = (2) − (7) Average Profit (Per Hog)
0	$100	—	—	—	—	—	—
1	100	$40	$60	$100.00	$40.00	$140.00	−$40.00
2	100	20	80	50.00	30.00	80.00	20.00
3	100	30	70	33.33	30.00	63.33	36.66
4	100	50	50	25.00	35.00	60.00	40.00
5	100	70	30	20.00	42.00	62.00	38.00
6	100	90	10	16.67	50.00	66.67	33.33
7	100	200	−100	14.29	71.43	85.72	14.28
8	100	250	−150	12.50	93.75	106.25	−6.25

sell each added unit of output, the first, the second, and so on?

Answer: The added revenue each sale generates: $100 for the first hog, $100 for the second, and so on.

Marginal cost in column (3) of Table 25.2 is the *addition to total cost* associated with *each* hog produced for sale. This is the change in total cost. For the first several hogs we have:

Hogs	Total Cost	Marginal Cost
Zero	$100	
1st	$140	$40
2nd	$160	$20
3rd	$190	$30

This marginal cost (*MC*) is the answer to the second question of two-question logic as it applies to the firm:

Question 2: *What does it cost to get the added revenue each unit brings*, the first unit, the second, and so on?

Answer: *The marginal cost.* The added cost that each unit incurs: $40 for the first hog, $20 for the second hog, and so on.

For a prospective unit of output, when the answer to the first question, marginal revenue, *exceeds* the answer to the second question, marginal cost, the firm *should produce that unit because it is worth*

more in added revenue than must be given up in added cost. This is true of the first hog in Table 25.2: *MR* = $100 versus *MC* = $40. It's also true of the second hog: *MR* = $100 versus *MC* = $20. And for the third hog: *MR* = $100 versus *MC* = $30. Further comparisons cause the firm to produce and sell the sixth hog per week, but *not* the seventh:

Hog	MR	MC	Produce?
4th	$100	$50	Yes
5th	$100	$70	Yes
6th	$100	$90	Yes
7th	$100	$200	No

The firm stops at the sixth hog because of two-question logic. Folks at Saga Corporation call it *Lynch's law*. Graphically, the result is shown in Figure 25.5. With dollars per unit on the vertical axis, price and marginal revenue are shown to be $100 per hog. Marginal cost lies below marginal revenue for the first through sixth hogs, then rises above marginal revenue for the seventh hog per week.

When the marginal revenue of a unit *exceeds* its marginal cost, added output *adds to total profit* because the added total revenue (*MR*) exceeds the added total cost (*MC*), and total profit is total revenue minus total cost (*TR* − *TC*). The addition to total profit that can be credited to each unit may be called *marginal profit*. It is calculated simply by subtracting from marginal revenue the marginal cost (*MR* − *MC* = Marginal profit). This is done for the hog farmer in column (4) of Table 25.2, which is column (2) minus column (3). The first hog adds

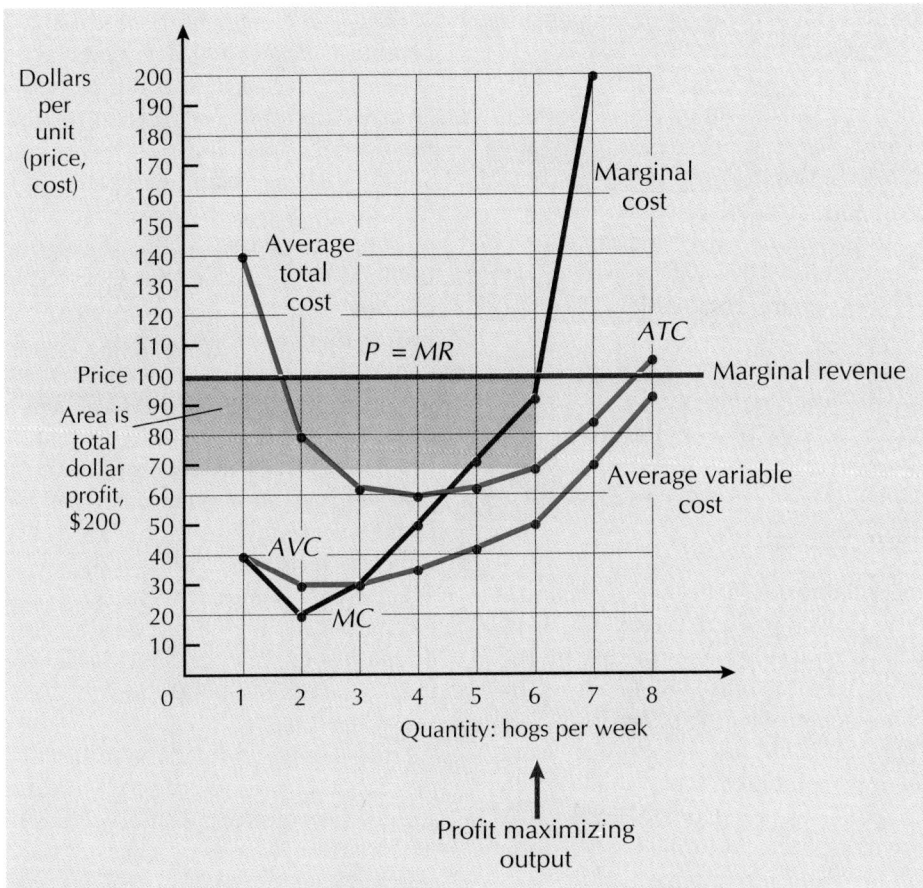

FIGURE 25.5   Short-Run Dollars Per Unit View of Firm Profit Maximizing

The vertical axis is scaled in dollars per unit (per hog). The firm will maximize its profit by increasing output as long as marginal revenue (MR) exceeds marginal (MC), which is true up to the sixth hog. Considering all six together at that point, revenue on average is P ($100), cost on average is ATC ($66.67), and profit on average is the difference, P − ATC ($33.33). Multiplying this average profit by the number of units, six, yields total profit ($200), the shaded area.

$60 to total profit ($100 − $40 = $60); the second adds $80 ($100 − $20 = $80); and so on. As output rises with the third, fourth, fifth, and sixth hogs, total profit continues to rise because these marginal profits are positive. However, total profit rises by ever smaller increments ($70, $50, $30, and $10) as marginal cost rises relative to marginal revenue. Finally, marginal cost rises above marginal revenue for the seventh hog. The seventh hog would therefore cause total profit to slip by $100, so that it should not be produced. (Note: Total dollar profit does *not* become negative with the seventh hog. It is merely lower than what it would be with the sixth. Glance back at column (7) of Table 25.1,

which shows total profit with seven hogs to be $100, down from $200 with six.)

Marginal revenue and marginal cost thus provide a rule for profit maximizing (a rule applicable to *all* firms, not just perfectly competitive firms).

The **profit maximization** rule is that a firm will maximize total profits by expanding output as long as marginal revenue (*MR*) is greater than or equal to marginal cost (*MC*). It should never add units whose marginal revenue is less than their marginal cost. In brief, *MR = MC*. This applies to all firms—monopolists, oligopolists, whatever—although their marginal revenues and marginal costs differ from those of perfectly competitive firms.

This rule applies to all firms, but its use by perfectly competitive firms yields a special result. Marginal revenue (MR) is the same as price (P) in the eyes of the perfectly competitive firm. Hence, when this firm produces to the point where marginal revenue equals marginal cost ($MR = MC$), it is also producing at the point where price equals marginal cost ($P = MC$).

Because price (P) and marginal revenue (MR) are the same for a perfectly competitive firm, this profit-maximizing firm will produce an output at which $P = MC$, as well as $MR = MC$. In brief, $P = MR = MC$.

Can the total dollar profit that is being maximized be seen in this dollars per unit view of the firm? Yes. But only through the lenses provided by the _average_ values in this per unit view because the averages take into account _all the units_ produced, not just the marginal units, and total dollar profit depends on all units combined. What is needed, in fact, is _average_ profit per unit. Once average profit per unit is known, it can be multiplied by the total number of units to yield total dollar profit.

What is _average_ profit per unit? It is _average_ revenue minus _average_ total cost. Recall that average revenue is equal to price ($TR/Q = (P \times Q)/Q = P$). Recall also that average total cost (ATC) is the total cost per unit _on average_, taking into account all units produced and all costs, fixed and variable ($TC/Q = ATC$, or $AFC + AVC = ATC$). These several amounts are shown in Table 25.2. Average revenue or price is given in column (2), while average total cost is given in column (7), the latter being the addition of average fixed cost in column (5) and average variable cost in column (6). Price _minus_ average total cost is shown in column (8), appropriately labeled "Average Profit (Per Hog)." We already know from analyzing marginal revenue and marginal cost that six hogs is the profit-maximizing output. The average profit per hog associated with six hogs is, as may be seen in column (8), $33.33 (i.e., $100 − $66.67 = $33.33). Multiplying this by the quantity of hogs yields the total dollar profit of $200 per week, that is, $6 \times \$33.33 = \$200$. This is the same total dollar profit reported earlier in Table 25.1, representing the total dollars view.

Figure 25.5 reflects these calculations. Average revenue is price, $100. Average total cost at six hogs is $66.67. The vertical distance between price (P) and average total cost (ATC) at six hogs is therefore the average profit per unit by subtraction, $100 − $66.67 = $33.33. Multiplying this vertical distance ($33.33) by the horizontal distance representing quantity (6) results in the shaded area, which is total dollar profit ($6 \times \$33.33 = \$200$). Following the $MR = MC$ rule of profit maximizing thus maximizes this area representing total dollar profit.

It may now be stressed that the firm aims to maximize _total dollar_ profit, _not_ average profit per unit. Table 25.2 and Figure 25.5 show that when the price is $100, average profit per unit would be greatest with four hogs per week ($40). But _total_ profit with four hogs is only $160 ($4 \times \$40 = \$160$), which is substantially less than the $200 _total dollar_ profit associated with six hogs per week. In other words, the hog farmer gets a camper, a college education for his kids, and other good things by maximizing his total dollar profit, not his average profit per hog.

Loss Minimization: If the price falls to $50 or $25 per hog, the question of profit maximization turns sour; it turns into a question of loss minimization. In this short-run per unit view of the situation, the rule for loss minimizing, if some loss is unavoidable, may be called the shutdown rule:

Shutdown rule: If the price falls below the average variable cost at every level of output, the firm should shut down. Otherwise, the firm should minimize its loss by following the same rule as that for profit maximization, namely expand output as long as marginal revenue is greater than or equal to marginal cost ($MR = MC$, for short) and stop thereafter.

All rules have exceptions, and the shutdown rule is an exception to the golden rule of $MR = MC$. It says that positive production might result in losses so large that they would be less if the firm shut down. Once again, the most the firm should ever lose, the rock bottom amount, is the total fixed cost. In this dollars per unit view of the firm, average variable cost constitutes the key threshold to preventing larger losses.

Consider Figure 25.6, which is the dollars per unit version of Figure 25.4. It is the same as Figure

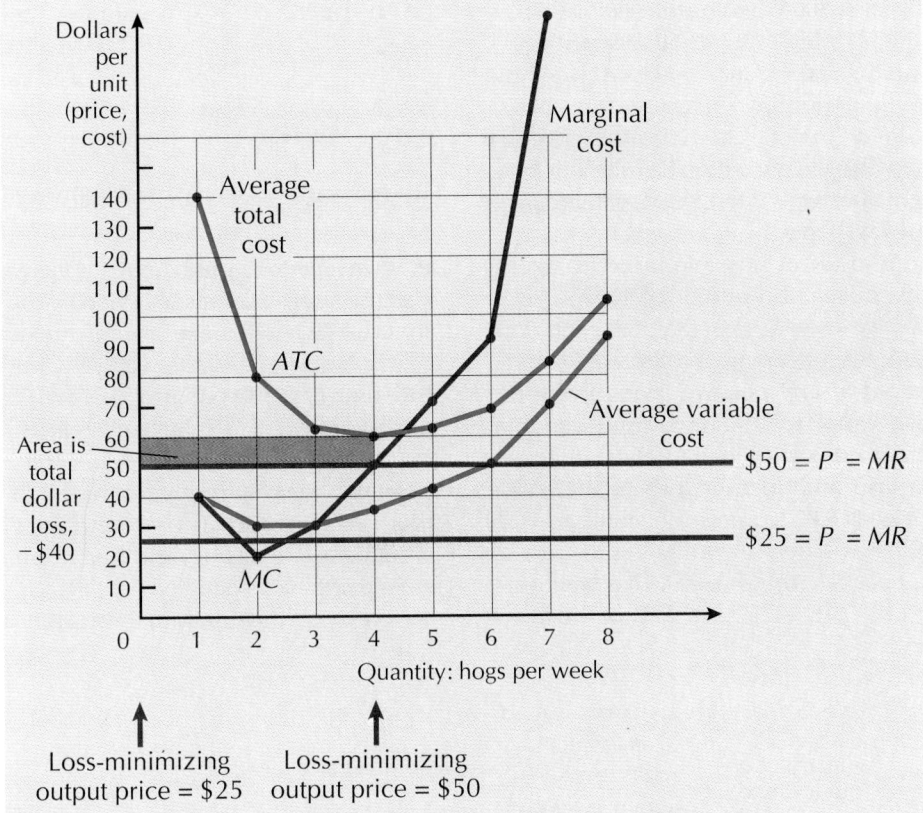

FIGURE 25.6 Short-Run Dollars Per Unit View of Firm Loss Minimizing

If the price falls to $50 per hog, it will be below ATC _at every possible output, making losses inevitable. A price of $50 is below_ ATC _but above the average variable cost,_ AVC, _so the loss will be minimized by producing each unit with marginal revenue greater than or equal to marginal cost. In brief, produce where_ MR = MC. _With P = $50, MR = MC at four hogs. If the price falls to $25 per hog, it will be below the average variable cost,_ AVC, _at every possible output. Unable to recover all variable costs, the firm would lose more than its total fixed cost if it produced any positive output. It will therefore shut down and lose only its total fixed cost._

25.5, except that the price has been lowered to $50, as one possibility, and to $25, as another. If the price is $50 per hog, price lies below average total cost (ATC) at each possible output. With revenue per unit beneath cost per unit, loss is unavoidable. However, the price of $50 is _not_ below average variable cost (AVC) at each possible output. Hence the firm will minimize the total dollar loss associated with the $50 price by producing each unit with a marginal revenue (MR) greater than or equal to its marginal cost (MC). Marginal revenue is the price, $50, and marginal cost lies below $50 until it equals it at an output of four hogs a week. Four hogs, then, is the loss-minimizing output when the price is $50.

The resulting total dollar loss is shown by the shaded area in Figure 25.6, which amounts to $40. Once again, this _total_ amount derives from the _average_ values associated with the chosen output because the average values take into account _all_ the units produced, not just the marginal units. Average revenue is $50 when the price is $50 and the output is four hogs:

$$\frac{TR}{Q} = \frac{P \times Q}{Q} = P$$

$$\frac{\$200}{4} = \frac{\$50 \times 4}{4} = \$50$$

Average total cost is $60 when output is four hogs. (See column (7) of Table 25.2.) It follows that average loss per unit is $50 − $60 = −$10. Multiplying −$10 by the total number of units, four hogs, yields a total dollar loss of −$40. The firm will continue to produce in the short run despite this loss because zero output would cause a greater loss of $100, the total fixed cost.

The second and lower possible price in Figure 25.6 is $25. This price falls not only *below* ATC, *but also below average variable cost* (AVC) *at each output.* This means that *only part* of the variable costs could be covered at any positive level of output, causing a loss equal to the uncovered variable costs *plus* total fixed costs. Since total fixed cost is the most the firm should ever lose, it will shut down if the price is $25. Numerically compare, for instance, the losses when output is 2 and zero, 2 being chosen because *MR* is near *MC* at that output:

P	Q	TR	TC	Total Loss (TR − TC).
$25	0	0	$100 (fixed)	−$100

Zero output is clearly the superior choice.

2. The Firm's Supply Curve One way to summarize the short-run per unit view of the firm is to say that the firm will maximize its total dollar profit or minimize its total dollar loss by always producing the output that equates marginal revenue and marginal cost (*MR* = *MC*), except when price (and marginal revenue) falls below average variable cost, in which case it produces nothing. A picture of this verbal summary is found in Figure 25.7(a), which generalizes beyond hog farming. Four possible prices are specified—P_1, P_2, P_3, and P_4. Each also represents a marginal revenue, namely, MR_1,

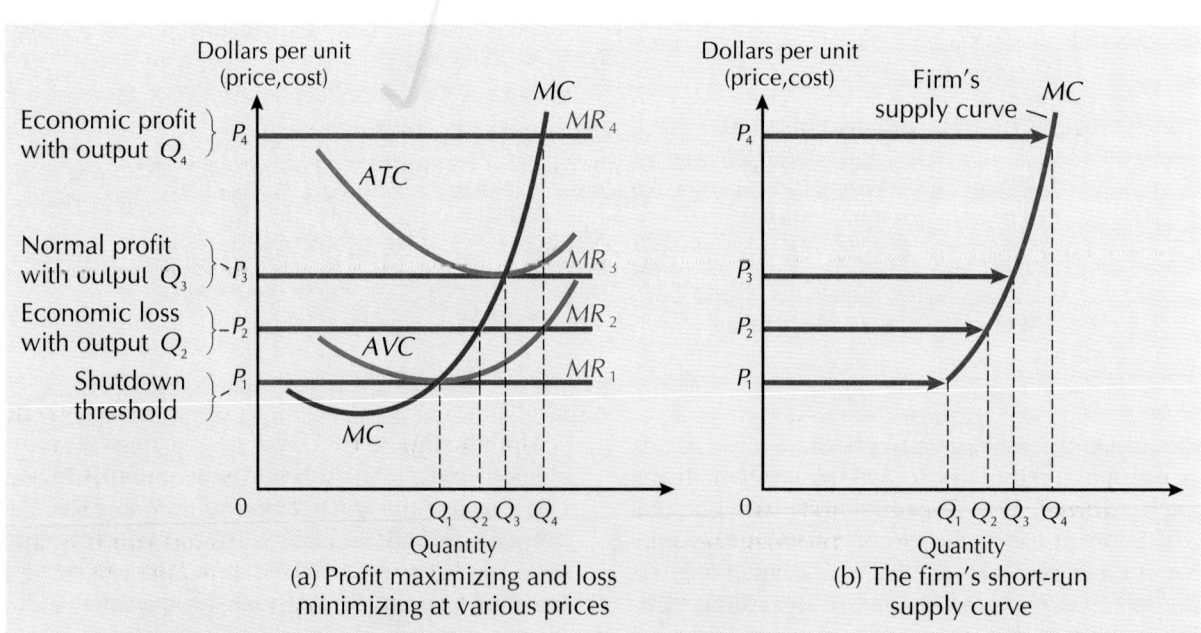

FIGURE 25.7 *Derivation of the Perfectly Competitive Firm's Short-Run Supply Curve*
The firm maximizes total dollar profit or minimizes total dollar loss by producing an output that equates marginal revenue (MR) and marginal cost (MC), except when MR falls below AVC. When MR is MR_1, output is Q_1 and on the verge of shutdown. With MR_2 the economic loss is minimized by output Q_2. With MR_3 profit maximizing yields a normal profit at Q_3, where MR_3 = ATC as well as MR_3 = MC. If the price is P_4, MR_4 yields economic profit, maximized at Q_4 output. The resulting price–quantity combinations, most clearly shown in part (b), are the firm's short-run supply curve.

MR_2, MR_3, and MR_4. The firm maximizes its total profit or minimizes its total loss by producing the level of output that equates each of these marginal revenues with marginal cost: $MR_1 = MC$ when output is Q_1; $MR_2 = MC$ when output is Q_2; $MR_3 = MC$ when output is Q_3; and $MR_4 = MC$ when output is Q_4. Note that quantity rises as price and marginal revenue rise above P_1 and MR_1. Note also that any price and marginal revenue below P_1 and MR_1 would cause the firm to shut down because P_1 and MR_1 just equal average variable cost (AVC) at Q_1. Thus P_1 and MR_1 could be considered the shutdown threshold. A lower price (and marginal revenue) would cause output to drop abruptly to zero.

The firm's efforts to maximize total profit and minimize total loss create the systematic pattern of price–quantity combinations depicted in part (b) of Figure 25.7. Below P_1, output is zero. Above P_1, price and quantity rise jointly in pairs—P_1 and Q_1, P_2 and Q_2, and so on. This sequence of pairings matches the firm's marginal cost curve in Figure 25.7(a) *insofar as price is above average variable cost* (i.e., P_1 or greater). Moreover, this sequence of price–quantity pairs is the firm's short-run supply curve because it shows how much (Q) the firm will offer for sale at each possible price (P). Indeed, the perfectly competitive firm's supply curve may be so defined.

> The perfectly competitive firm's **short-run supply curve** is that portion of its marginal cost curve extending above its average variable cost.

Before leaving Figure 25.7, the nature of the total profits and losses that the firm experiences should be clarified. You will recall how economists define profit. *Normal profit* is considered a cost because it is the amount of profit equal to the opportunity cost of a firm's owners. Earning a normal profit just keeps the firm comfortably in business.[3] *Economic profit*, then, is a profit that *exceeds* a normal profit (it results when total revenue exceeds all opportunity costs). *Economic loss*, correspondingly, is any return *less* than a normal profit (it

results when total revenue falls short of all opportunity costs).[4]

Economists typically define total dollar costs and average total costs per unit to include *all* opportunity costs, *including a normal profit*. Hence the results in Figure 25.7(a) may be more accurately described as follows. When the price is P_3 and the firm maximizes its total dollar profit by producing output Q_3, revenue per unit (P_3 and MR_3) will just equal average total cost (ATC), including in that cost a normal profit per unit. This P_3 and Q_3 result therefore embodies a normal profit, and economic profit will be zero. (In total dollars this means that total revenue equals total opportunity cost, including a total dollar normal profit.) If the price is *higher* than P_3, as it is at P_4, then the firm will be earning an *economic profit*, a profit in excess of normal profit. If, on the other hand, the price is *less* than P_3, as it is at P_2, the firm will be experiencing an *economic loss*. By these definitions, the specific amounts of total economic profit or total economic loss associated with these situations can be seen in Figures 25.5 and 25.6. The shaded area of Figure 25.5 would be a total dollar *economic profit* of $200 per week. The shaded area of Figure 25.6 would be a total dollar *economic loss* of −$40 per week.

> The firm's average total cost (ATC) includes a normal profit, so price–output combinations above ATC yield economic profits, while price–output combinations below ATC yield economic losses.
>
> *Read Perspective 23B.*

3. The Marketwide Supply Curve The perfectly competitive market is, as we have said, made up of a very large number of firms. In the short run, that number of firms—be it 5,000 or something similarly large—cannot change. The short run is a time span too brief to allow new firms to enter or old firms to leave the market. Short-run changes in marketwide supply, such as those just surveyed for farm-fed cattle, cannot therefore be due to the entry of new firms or the exit of established firms. (Established firms may produce zero output in the short run, but this is not the same as an exit

---

[3]Formally, a *normal profit* is compensation for entrepreneurial skill and financial capital that is just enough to keep the firm in business in the long run.

[4]In contrast, *accounting* profits and losses compare total revenues to *accounting* costs.

PERSPECTIVE 23B:

Cattle Producer Margins and Capacity Use

One message of Figure 25.7 is simply this: As price rises relative to average cost, perfectly competitive firms will increase output. Or, conversely, as price falls relative to average cost, perfectly competitive firms will decrease output. This latter direction of the relationship is illustrated by cattle-feeding operations among farmers in the corn belt during 1979 and 1980. A simple measure of price relative to cost for farmers feeding cattle is their *net margin*, which is the price of cattle per 100 pounds live weight minus average total cost (not including a normal profit). Between April 1979 and January 1980, this net margin for steers weighing 600 to

1,050 pounds fell from plus $16 per 100 pounds to minus $10, a drop in price relative to cost of nearly $26. The net margin then stayed negative for all but 1 month of 1980. The resulting change in output was as expected. Sales of farmer-fed cattle fell more than 8 percent, from 7.0 million head in 1979 to 6.4 million head in 1980. Moreover, rates of output varied among farmers according to their costs. Generally speaking, large farms had lower average costs than did small farms and, as reflected in Table 25.3, large farms had higher rates of capacity utilization than did small farms as of January 1980.

because the capacity and capability to produce, and the fixed costs associated with them, do not disappear in the short run.) Short-run changes in marketwide supply hinge entirely on the short-run changes in the individual supplies of the market's existing firms.

We have now seen the short-run supply curve of the typical firm in a perfectly competitive market. It matches the firm's marginal cost curve above average variable cost. Given a price (P), which is also marginal revenue (MR), the profit-maximizing firm produces a quantity that equates P to MC. Supply is the quantity offered at each possible price, and MC tracks this quantity–price relation. In turn, the *marketwide supply* is the *summation* of these individual firm quantities.

The **short-run marketwide supply curve** is the horizontal summation of the supply curves of the firms in the market, those being their MC curves above AVC.

We cannot illustrate this aggregation for the thousands of firms that would comprise a perfectly competitive market. However, Figure 25.8 illustrates the procedure for three firms, and your imagination can do the rest. The supply curves of three firms—Al's, Barb's, and Carl's—are in parts (a), (b), and (c), while marketwide supply is in part (d). At a price of P_1, Al would supply A_1, Barb would supply B_1, and Carl would supply C_1, each of which amounts to 10 units, as shown on the horizontal axes. Adding horizontally over these

TABLE 25.3 Capacity Utilization by Size of Cattle Feeding Farm, January 1980

Annual Sales, Number of Head	Average Feed Lot Capacity, Head	Animals in Stock, Percent of Capacity
20–99	113	45%
100–199	201	60
200–499	359	72
500 and over	701	83

Source: R.N. Van Arsdall and K.E. Nelson, *Characteristics of Farmer Cattle Feeding* (U.S. Department of Agriculture, August 1983), pp. 3–7.

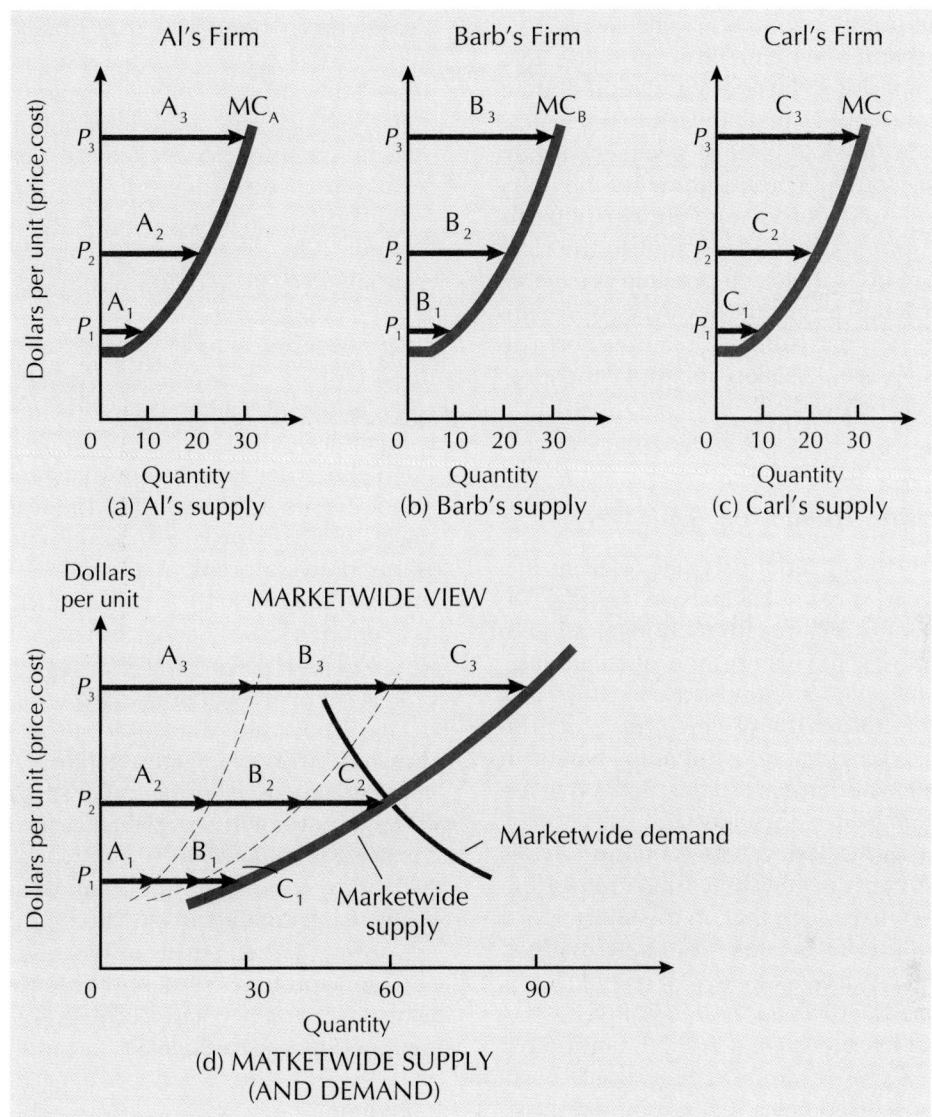

FIGURE 25.8   Short-Run Marketwide Supply as the Sum of Individual Firm Supplies (Perfect Competition)

The marketwide supply curve derives from the horizontal addition of the individual firm supply curves, shown here for only three firms. For example, at price P_2, which would be generated by the interaction of marketwide demand and supply, each firm would supply 20 units, which when added together would be 60 units of marketwide supply. If marketwide demand shifted left, driving the price down to P_1, the total would be 30. If it shifted right, raising the price to P_3, the total would be 90.

amounts yields a marketwide supply of $A_1 + B_1 + C_1$, or 30 units. If the price is higher at P_2, the individual firm supplies would be A_2, B_2, and C_2, which when summed amount to 60 units. Finally, if the price is P_3, the firms' supplies would each be 30 units, resulting in a marketwide total of 90 units.

The results for P_2 are highlighted in Figure 25.8 because they illustrate that the *actual* price observed by each firm will be determined by the interaction of supply and demand at the marketwide level. For several previous figures, we have simply created hypothetical prices. Now the source of the prevailing price may be seen.

Note also that if one of the firms in Figure 25.8, say Carl's, went out of business and exited, marketwide supply would shift to the left to reflect less output at each possible price. Conversely, if Carl stayed and if economic profits attracted the entry of new firms—say Daisy's and Ed's—then the marketwide supply curve would shift to the right to reflect more output at each possible price. Exit and entry are long-run events, however, so we cannot fully consider them until we exit the short-run context of the present section and enter the long-run context of the next.

C

Long-Run Dollars per Unit View

Although in the short run the number of firms in a competitive market cannot change, in the long run the number of firms can contract or expand with exit or entry. *Exit* is the departure of old firms (e.g., Studebaker left the auto industry in the early 1960s). *Entry* is the arrival of new firms (e.g., De-Lorean attempted entry into the auto market in the late 1970s). What causes exit or entry? What are their consequences?

As regards causes, persistent economic *losses* ($P < ATC$) will cause established firms to *exit* from the market. We have seen that, in the short run, a firm will continue to produce if it is covering at least its average variable costs ($P > AVC$). This is not good enough for its long-term viability, however. To make at least a normal profit, the firm must cover its fixed costs as well as its variable costs (including those fixed costs that are the opportunity costs to the owners). Persistent economic losses ($P < ATC$) imply that the firm is *not* covering its fixed costs, and the only way to escape the grip of those fixed costs in the long run is to go out of business. Going out of business shrinks the fixed costs to zero, as in the long run all costs are variable. The term *liquidate* is often applied to this process (a term that, as a consequence, has also come to mean "kill"). Once dead, *all* of a firm's vital signs—its revenues, costs, profits, losses, etc.,—will be zero.

Conversely, persistent economic profits ($P > ATC$) by representative firms in a market will attract entry by newcomers seeking a piece of the high-profit action. Hence, above-normal profits

cause entry when, as is true of perfect competition, entry is easy.

> In the long run, the number of firms in a perfectly competitive market can contract with exit or expand with entry. If the typical firm is sustaining economic losses ($P < ATC$), exits occur. If the typical firm is earning economic profits ($P > ATC$), entry takes place.

The *consequences* of exit and entry are just as important as their *causes*. Marketwide supply *shifts to the left with exits*, a direction of shift that will, all else equal, lift the price level *up*. In turn, the higher price level will bring to an end the economic losses that prompted the exits in the first place. In other words, exiting does not necessarily go on forever, purging the market of all firms, liquidating the lot. Rather, it continues only as long as economic losses persist, but those losses will be lessened as a consequence of the exits. The process is therefore self-adjusting.

The same holds for entry but in the opposite direction, entry being attracted by economic profits. Marketwide supply *shifts to the right with entry*, a movement that will, *ceteris paribus*, push the price level *down*. In turn, the lower price level will bring to an end the economic profits that enticed entry at the outset. Thus, entry does *not* go on forever. Rather, entry continues only as long as economic profits persist, but those economic profits will eventually disappear with the added competition entry introduces.

> Economic losses cause exits, which in turn eliminate the losses in the long run. Economic profits cause entries, which in turn eliminate the profits in the long run. Neither exit nor entry occurs in long-run equilibrium (if it were ever to arrive), and the typical perfectly competitive firm then earns a normal profit.

These causes and consequences can be illustrated in diagrams, but only by looking at the typical firm and the market simultaneously, and only by a bit of storytelling. Let's begin with exit.

1. Exit Consider Figure 25.9, which shows a typical firm in part (a) and its market in part (b). Assume at the outset that the market is at equilib-

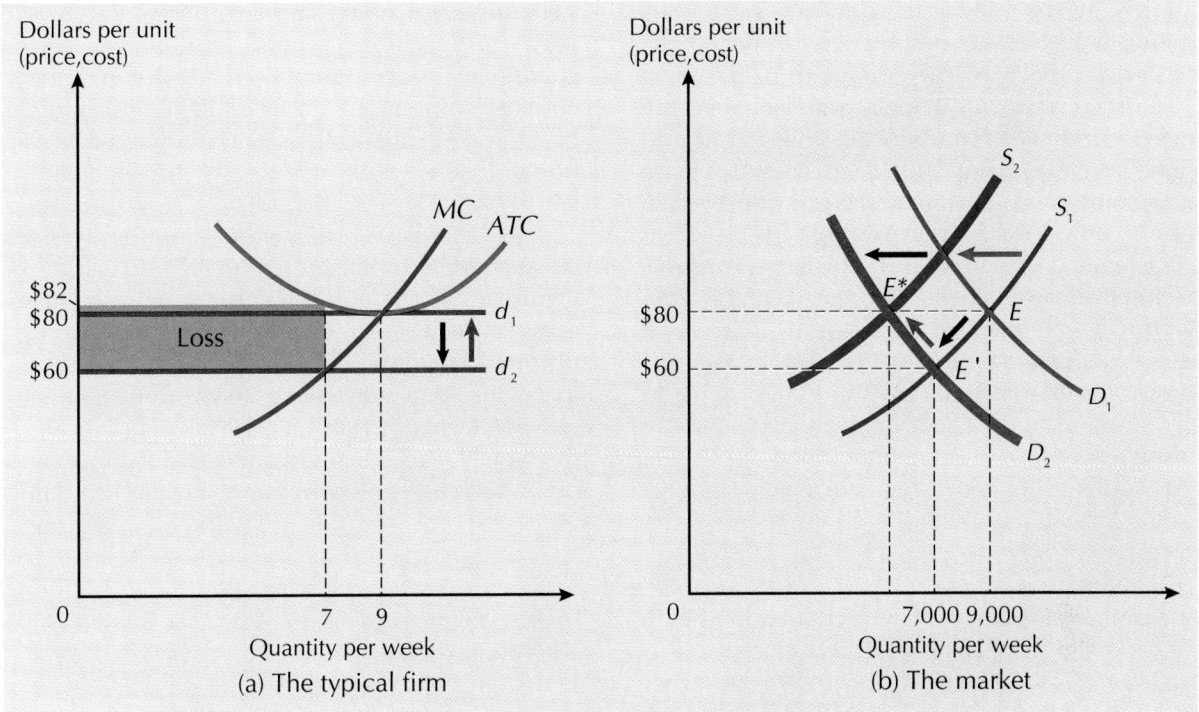

FIGURE 25.9   Loss-Induced Exit in the Long-Run Dollars Per Unit View

At the outset, marketwide demand and supply are D_1 and S_1, respectively. Their intersection created firm demand d_1, with a price and marginal revenue of $80. Equating MR = MC at nine units, the firm earns a normal profit. When marketwide demand falls to D_2, firm demand falls to d_2, or $60, which causes economic losses of −$22 per unit (−$154 total). As all firms reduce output in the short run, there is movement along the short-run supply curve, S, from E to E'. The persistent losses cause exits, shifting the entire marketwide supply from S_1 to S_2. The price rises toward $80 as movement occurs from E to E*. Once normal profit is restored, exits stop and the market is at a new and lower quantity.

rium _E_, which generates a price of $80 and an output of 9,000 units per week. The firm, one of a thousand firms, sees $80 as its demand curve d_1, and this is also its marginal revenue. Maximizing its profits by producing 9 units (1/1,000 of the marketwide total), the firm earns only a normal profit at the start.

If the product loses favor with customers, marketwide demand shifts leftward from D_1 to D_2, triggering events identified by the black arrows. The drop in demand lowers the price, prompting curtailment in the short-run supply. The firm's supply slips to 7 units as the price drops to $60 because this will equate _MR_ to _MC_ and minimize losses. With all firms curtailing supply in this way, there is movement down the short-run marketwide supply curve S_1 from E to E', which corre-

sponds to 7,000 units (1,000 × 7). The firm's economic loss _per unit_ is $P − ATC$, or $60 − $82 = −$22. Multiplying by the number of units produced, 7, reveals total dollar economic losses of −$154 (−$22 × 7).

These economic losses cause exits, with consequences indicated by the red arrows of Figure 25.9. The exits push the number of firms in the market below 1,000 and shift the supply curve to the left. The resulting movement along the new demand curve from E' toward E* raises the price from $60 toward $80. Exits will continue as long as economic losses pummel the firms. But as the price rises, these economic losses dwindle. Once normal profits are restored, the exits cease. The market arrives at a new equilibrium E*, and overall output falls. The price returns to its initial level.

2. Entry Figure 25.10 tells entry's story. The starting point is, for convenience, similar to the one before, with market demand D_1 crossing short-run market supply S_1 at point E. Here the market output is 8,000 units, the price is $80, and the typical firm, one of a thousand, takes this price as its demand, d_1, and marginal revenue. Its output of 8 units yields a normal profit.

If science discovers that the product improves the intelligence of those who eat it, market demand will shift outward from D_1 to D_2. The black arrows suggest the initial changes. The price jumps toward $108, lifting the firm's demand curve from d_1 to d_2. The firm reacts by increasing output from 8 to 10 units, which, when duplicated by 999 other firms, boosts marketwide output from 8,000 to 10,000 units. The firm moves up its MC curve to maximize profits. The market correspondingly moves along the short-run supply curve S_1 from E to E'. The firm's total economic profit at this stage will be its economic profit per unit ($P - ATC = \$108 - \$82 = \$26$) times the number of units (10)—that is, $260 (= \$26 \times 10)$.

These economic profits prompt new entry, with consequences indicated by the colored arrows in Figure 25.10. The entries lift the number of firms above 1,000 and thereby shift the marketwide supply outward to the right. The added supply lowers the price in a movement down along demand curve D_2 from E' toward E*. The lower price lowers the typical firm's demand curve and its economic profit, but entry will continue as long as economic

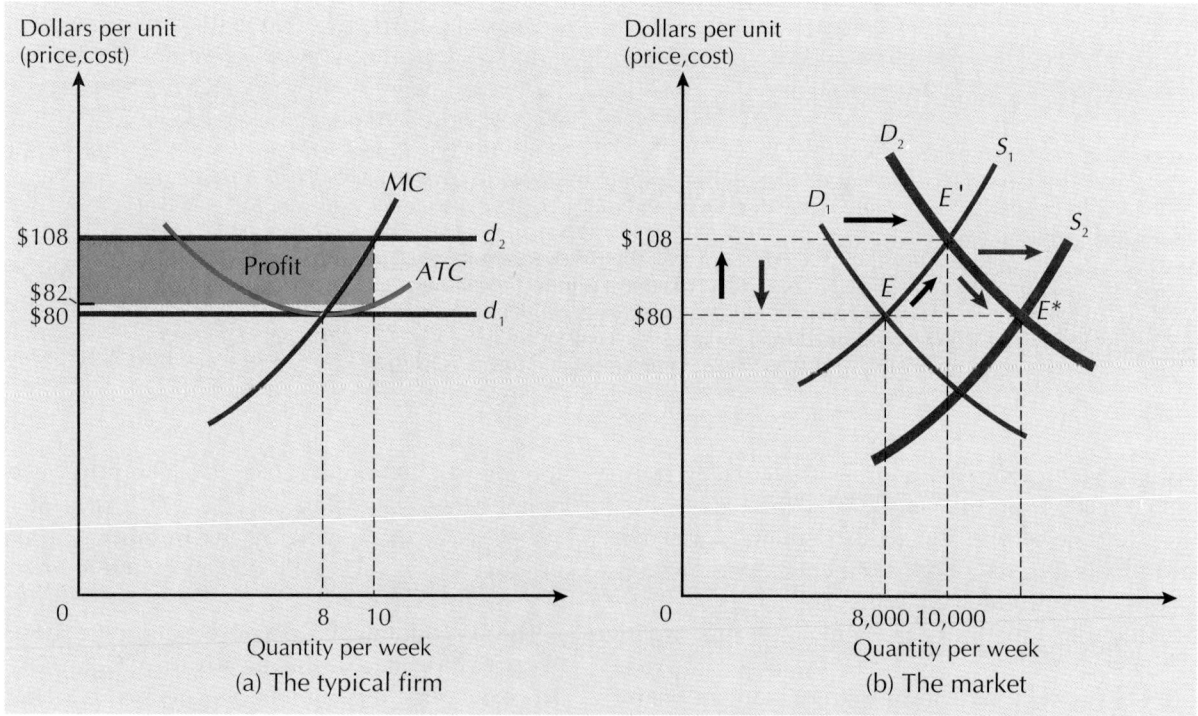

FIGURE 25.10 _Profit-Induced Entry in the Long-Run Dollars Per Unit View_

Initially, the price is $80 by the forces of marketwide demand D_1 and supply S_1. Resulting firm demand is d_1, or $80, and firm output is eight units, which equates MR = MC. When marketwide demand shifts out to D_2, the price jumps to $108, creating a higher firm demand, d_2, at $108. The firm moves up its MC curve to produce 10 units at $108, which yields economic profits ($26 per unit and $26 \times 10 = \$260$ overall). The economic profits attract new entry, causing supply to shift out from S_1 to S_2. The shift causes movement along D_2 from E' toward E*, and the price falls with the added marketwide quantity. Once the price falls to the point of eliminating the economic profit, entry stops and the firms then earn normal returns.

profits attract them. Once short-run marketwide supply reaches S_2, the economic profits are wiped out, and no further entry occurs. The market comes to rest at equilibrium E^*, with a greater quantity than before, a greater number of firms, and a price again at $80. The price gives the typical firm a normal profit, as its output returns to 8 units per week.

Read Perspective 25C.

3. Long-Run Marketwide Supply In the short run, marketwide output can contract or expand only when established firms contract or expand the use of their fixed capacities. As we have just seen, however, the long run is long enough to allow marketwide contraction or expansion through exit and entry.

> The **long-run marketwide supply curve** shows the quantities that sellers offer at different prices after the exit or entry of firms is completed.

The nature of the long-run supply curve depends on what happens to the prices of inputs (i.e., factors of production) as the market contracts or expands with exit or entry. The prices of inputs—such as, for hogs, the hourly wage rate of farm labor, the price per bushel of corn, and the price of land—are one of the two broad elements that influence a product's cost per unit, namely, (1) productivity or output/input and (2) the prices of inputs. Up to this point in this chapter, change in the first of these, productivity, has been the *sole* source of change in unit costs. As a firm's output rises from zero in the short run, average total cost falls and then rises as productivity rises and then falls. The prices of inputs have been held constant by the implicit assumption that short-run variations in market output would be too small to affect labor wages, land rents, or other input prices.

This assumption may be moderately realistic for the short run. But it can be wildly unrealistic in the long run, when exit and entry permit enormous changes in marketwide quantity, changes that would require substantial variations in inputs. Substantial changes in input requirements could obviously cause input prices to rise or fall. Adding these two possibilities to the possibility that input prices may remain constant, economic theorists

---

PERSPECTIVE 25C

Entry into the Hog Market

Between 1975 and 1980 hog production rose from a cyclical low of 69 million head for commercial slaughter to a cyclical high of over 96 million head—a jump of 40 percent. About half of the increased output came from farmers who produced hogs in both years. They were established at the start and expanded thereafter. The other half of the increase came from new entrants, some of whom were farmers in fields other than hogs and some of whom were new to farming altogether. What caused this massive entry? Hefty profits. What were its consequences? Depressed prices and profits, at least for a time. Figure 25.11 reflects both the causes and the consequences by tracing three key measures of hog-farming prosperity over these years—each based on the hog–corn price ratio, which is the price of hogs (per 100 pounds) divided by the price of a bushel of feed corn (corn being the most important cost in raising hogs). The numerous entries occurred between 1976 and 1979, when the hog–corn price ratio was so high that it exceeded the ratio that would just cover the total cost per unit, thereby yielding economic profits. Thereafter, however, the massive entry and its added output contributed to a big drop in the hog–corn price ratio. Indeed, the price dropped below the average variable costs of many hog farmers, forcing them to shut down. Profits did not then approach normal levels for most hog farmers until 1982.

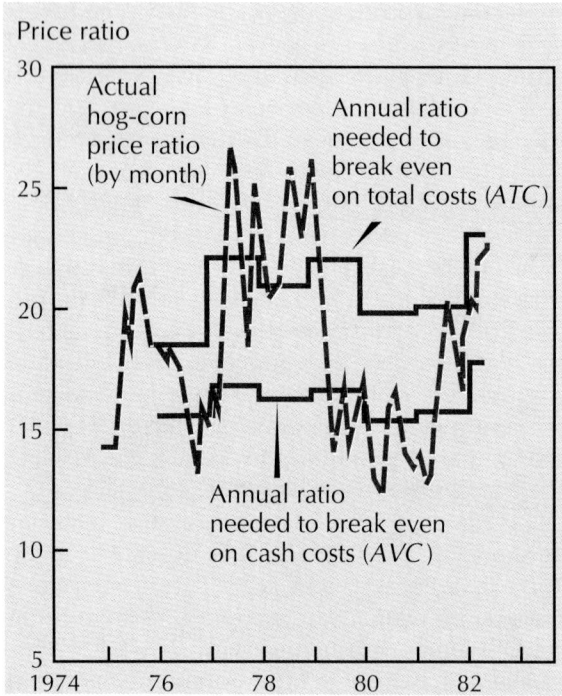

Price ratio

FIGURE 25.11   Hog–Corn Price Ratios—Actual and Needed to Break Even

Note: Estimates of cash and total costs unavailable prior to 1976. Actual hog–corn price ratio is Omaha basis. Breakeven hog–corn price ratios are for average U.S. farrow-to-finish producer. (Source: Van Arsdall and Nelson, U.S. Hog Industry. Washington, D.C.: U.S. Department of Agriculture, June 1984, p. 9.)

have identified three different long-run supply curves for competitive markets: (1) *constant-cost* long-run supply, (2) *increasing-cost* long-run supply, and (3) *decreasing-cost* long-run supply. Each of these is illustrated in a segment of Figure 25.12.

Each of these parts of Figure 25.12 posits an outward shift of market demand from D_1 to D_2, followed in the long run by the entry of new firms and a consequent shift in short-run supply from S_1 to S_2. Once demand and short-run supply are set at D_2 and S_2, respectively, a new equilibrium is established with quantity Q_2, which in each case is substantially greater than the initial quantity, Q_1. The long-run supply curve generated by the starting and ending equilibria is (1) horizontal, with no slope, (2) positively sloped, or (3) negatively sloped, depending on the behavior of input prices as

input requirements expand with the added output.

In part (a) of Figure 25.12 there is *constant-cost long-run supply*. As output expands in the long run from Q_1 to Q_2, input requirements jump, but this does not cause input prices to rise. The absence of any impact on input prices leaves the average total costs of firms in the market unaffected.

Part (b) of Figure 25.12 presents the case of *increasing-cost long-run supply*. As input requirements rise with the increase in market quantity from Q_1 to Q_2, the prices of inputs also rise. This would be especially true of scarce natural resources, like land in agriculture or crude oil in petroleum. As the prices of inputs escalate, the average total cost curve of each firm in the industry would shift upward. The upshot is that the long-run supply curve will have a positive slope in this case, something that clearly distinguishes part (b).

Finally, part (c) of Figure 25.12 depicts *decreasing-cost long-run supply*. If the greater demand for inputs necessitated by the greater outputs led to a decline in input prices, the long-run supply curve would slant downward with a negative slope. This situation is very rare, however.

4. Rents   It must be stressed that in a competitive increasing-cost industry, the average total costs of *all* producers rise as expansion occurs in the long run. This is because the prices of scarce inputs rise for all producers, not just the last ones to enter. Land is a scarce input in agriculture, so an example concerning land can be used to illustrate the point.

Iowa is home to more hogs than any other state, largely because Iowa has prime acreage for growing hog feed, mainly corn. If we assume that the short-run average total cost of producing corn is lowest in Iowa and rises with the distance from that state, then the short-run average total cost of corn would be slightly higher just south in Missouri and much higher farther south in Louisiana. We can imagine, then, long-run expansion of the corn industry beginning in Iowa, extending to Missouri, and finally, at the margin, ending up with the entry of corn farmers in Louisiana. In the process, the price of corn land would rise. Moreover, the price of corn land would differ from state to state. It would be priced highest in Iowa, where it is most productive; priced lowest in Louisiana,

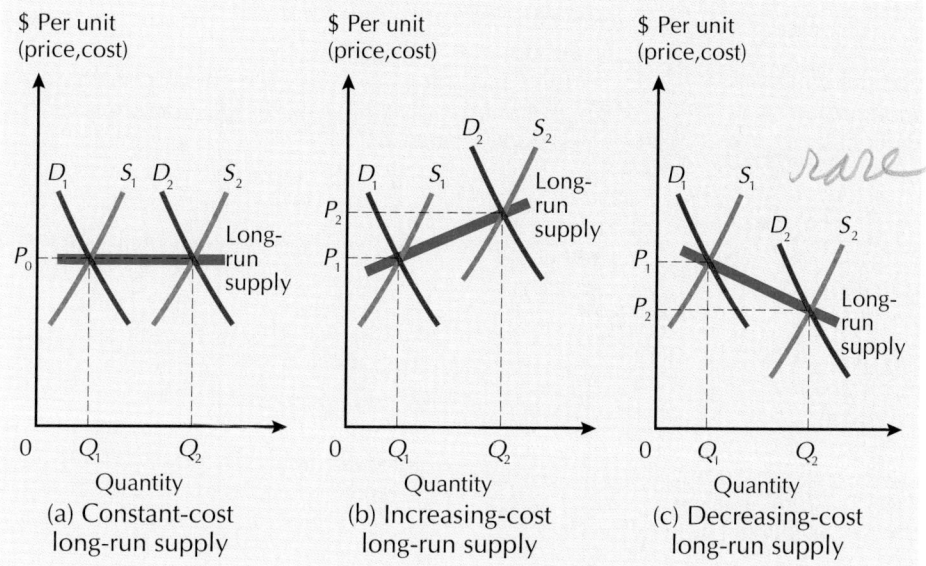

FIGURE 25.12 Long-Run Supply Curves Under Different Assumptions of Input Prices

If in each case, marketwide demand shifts outward from D_1 to D_2, followed in the long run by the entry of new firms and a consequent shift in short-run supply from S_1 to S_2, the results will differ depending on whether input prices remain constant, increase, or decrease. (a) Constant input prices permit greater output at constant average total cost per unit and constant price (P_0). Long-run supply is then horizontal. (b) Increasing input prices lead to higher average total costs per unit for each firm and the market as a whole. The long-run supply slopes upward, raising the price from P_1 to P_2. (c) Decreasing prices for inputs, if they occurred with rising output, would lower unit costs. Long-run supply has a negative slope in this case.

where it is least productive; and priced in between in Missouri. (Corn yield per harvested acre in 1982 was 127 bushels for Iowa, 110 bushels for Missouri, and 73 bushels for Louisiana.) In the long run, the premium prices paid for excellent corn land in Iowa and moderately good corn land in Missouri will hoist the average total costs per bushel in Iowa and Missouri until they match the average total cost per bushel in Louisiana, where relatively poor "marginal" corn land is used. Figure 25.13 illustrates the effect.

The premiums paid for land in Iowa and Missouri in this example are called *rents* by economists. If a farmer in Iowa did not own his land, he would lease it, paying what is popularly called a "rent," and that rent would be high to reflect the excellence of the land. To economists, the word *rent* has a broader meaning. It is a premium payment to *any* input, a payment beyond what is necessary to hire the input. It could apply to land that the farmer himself owns. The fact that Iowa's land

would still be producing corn even if it were priced lower than at present suggests that there is rent in this economic sense. The concept even applies to scarce labor. If a farm worker could be hired at $15,000 a year but is paid $17,000 because he has a way with hogs, then his rent would be $2,000.

Looking back at Figure 25.12(b), it can now be seen that the higher price, P_2, is largely absorbed by rents to scarce inputs, inputs that were producing outputs below Q_2 at prices below P_2, such as those engaged when price and output were P_1 and Q_1. Since rents rise with the price of the output, it could be said that this is a case where the price of the *output* is determining the price of the *input* rather than the reverse.

Scarcity rent is the premium paid to a scarce input above the price necessary to hire or purchase the input, the premium above the input's opportunity cost.

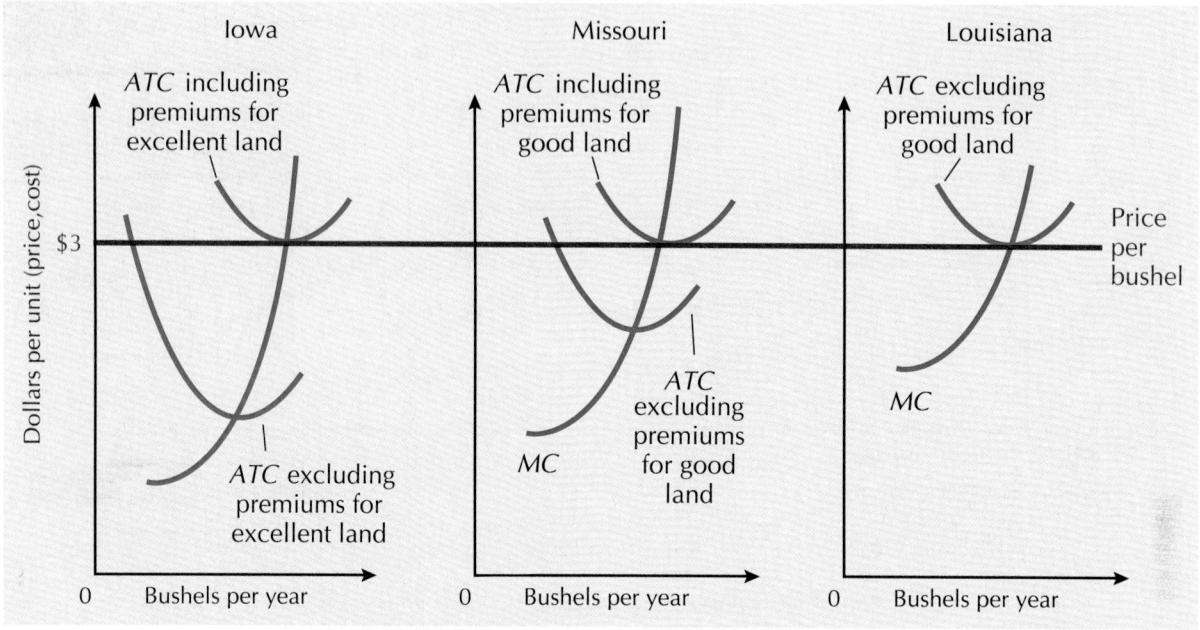

FIGURE 25.13 _Firm Average Total Costs with and without Adjustment for Premiums (Rents)_

Productivity, or output per acre, for corn is highest in Iowa and lowest in Louisiana among the states shown here. ATC for a typical farmer would therefore be lowest in Iowa and highest in Louisiana when prices for corn land are not taken into account. Including premiums for the high-priced land (Iowa) and moderate-priced land (Missouri) brings all average total costs into equality. In economic jargon, such premiums earned by owners of scarce inputs are called rents.

■ CHECK YOUR BEARINGS

This completes our analysis of _how_ a perfectly competitive market works. Structural features of the market cause the firm's demand curve to be perfectly horizontal, as the firm has no perceptible influence on the price. Accordingly, the firm's total dollar revenue will rise with output at a rate of increase constantly matching the price. In dollar per unit terms, marginal revenue and average revenue therefore equal price and correspond to the firm's demand curve. When costs are introduced, conduct may be studied from three perspectives: (a) the short-run total dollars view, (b) the short-run dollars per unit view, and (c) the long-run dollars per unit view. The firm's objective is always to maximize total dollar profit or minimize total dollar loss.

A. In the _short-run total dollars view_, this is achieved by that output yielding the greatest positive difference between total revenue and total cost $(TR - TC)$, or, in the event of losses, the lowest negative result. The firm should never lose more than its total fixed cost, the amount lost when shut down.

B. To maximize total profit in the _short-run per unit view_, a firm will expand output as long as marginal revenue (MR) is greater than or equal to marginal cost (MC). In brief, $MR = MC$. Because price (P) equals marginal revenue for the perfectly competitive firm, this implies that $P = MR = MC$ or simply that $P = MC$. The same rule applies to loss minimization unless the price falls below the average variable cost, in which case the firm shuts down. The firm's MC curve therefore becomes its short-run supply curve. Short-run marketwide supply derives from the horizontal summation of the individual firm supply curves.

C. In the _long-run per unit view_, the causes and consequences of exit and entry can be assessed. Persistent economic losses force exits, which in turn shift the short-run market supply to the left. This boosts the price and alleviates the losses until exits cease. Conversely, persistent economic profits prompt entries, which in turn shift the short-run market supply to the right. This puts downward pressure on the price until the economic profits disappear and entry ceases. In long-run equilibrium, the typical firm earns only a normal profit ($P = ATC$, as well as $MR = MC$). Scarcity rents are earned in increasing cost industries.

III

Perfectly Competitive Performance

Performance covers the four familiar microeconomic questions: *What* should be produced in what amounts? *How* should goods be produced? *Who* should get the goods? *What's new* in terms of goods, production processes, and growth? Because our society relies heavily on markets to answer these questions, we can judge the performance of markets by the answers markets provide. This is an issue of *how well* markets perform, as opposed to *how* they function.

Stated differently, an evaluation of performance is an exercise in normative economics. And the norms or ideal standards we adopt for the four basic microeconomic questions were specified in Chapter 1 in Table 1.2 p. 14).

The task before us, then, is first to identify the perfectly competitive market's answer to each of these basic questions and then to compare that answer with the ideal answer. As it turns out, the perfectly competitive market yields mixed results, so in some ways it is ideal and in other ways it is not.

A
What?

1. The Perfectly Competitive Market's Answer
As we have seen, the perfectly competitive market produces an amount corresponding to the intersection of marketwide demand and supply. Exam-

ples include 60 units in Figure 25.8(d) and Q_1 and Q_2 in Figure 25.12. This means that the competitive market is responsive to the wishes of consumers, at least to the extent that scarcity permits. If market demand shifts out, the quantity supplied increases. If, on the other hand, demand shifts back, the quantity supplied decreases. Indeed, demand may shrink to such tiny dimensions or may be so small to begin with that, given the costs, *none* of the good is produced. (Demand for chili-flavored chewing gum seems to be of this type.)

2. Comparison with the Ideal If market demand reflects the marginal social benefits of a product, and if market supply reflects the marginal social costs of producing the product, then the perfectly competitive market's answer to the What? question will be the ideal answer. In the event of external benefits, market demand would *not* reflect marginal social benefits. In the event of external costs, market supply would *not* represent marginal social costs. These and other market failures would prevent the perfectly competitive market from reaching allocation efficiency. But these problems aside, the perfectly competitive market answers the What? question nicely because it equates marginal social benefit with marginal social cost when its output corresponds to the intersection of demand and supply. In brief, $MSB = MSC$ for a product, something which takes into account *alternative products*, their marginal social benefits and marginal social costs.

An explanation for this ideal result was given earlier on pages 76–78. Now a somewhat different explanation is possible because we have since studied details of demand and supply that were previously ignored. We now know why competitive market demand reflects marginal social benefits. It shows the amounts buyers are willing to pay for each added unit of output based on the *marginal* utility or benefit obtained from each added unit in light of alternatives. It is the *addition* to total dollar benefit that can be credited to *each* unit. These amounts are scaled in dollars *per unit*, which fits the marginal measure. Moreover, we now know why competitive market supply represents marginal social costs. It shows the *added* total cost of producing *each* added unit of output under the influence of productivity and input prices, which depend on input scarcities.

Price is the key that ties marginal social benefit and marginal social cost together in equality because, at perfectly competitive output, three conditions hold:

$$MSB = P$$
$$P = MSC$$
$$MSB = P = MSC, \text{ or } MSB = MSC$$

Two-question logic on the part of buyers establishes the first of these equations, $MSB = P$. Two-question logic by sellers sets $P = MSC$. Buyers and sellers are _both_ members of society, and in the end, society's two-question logic confirms the desirability of $MSB = MSC$. Parts (a), (b), and (c) of Figure 25.14 illustrate each of these conditions. It represents one product. Alternative products should not be forgotten, however.

$MSB = P$: Assume for simplicity that there are 100 buyers with identical individual demands. The data underlying Figure 25.14(a) are then found in Table 25.4. Individual buyers value the first unit of this product at $7, the second at $6, and so on (in light of alternative products). These marginal benefits derive from the added total benefit associated with each unit (i.e., $0 \rightarrow \$7 \rightarrow \$13$, etc.), so addition over the marginals yields each total (e.g., $7 + $6 = $13 and $7 + $6 + 5 = $18). Marketwide quantities and total benefits are obtained by multiplying the individual amounts by 100. The _marginal benefits_ remain unchanged in aggregation, however, because they are the added benefits associated with _each added unit of output_. For example, the 113th unit would have a marginal benefit of $6, and each added unit between 101 and 200 would likewise yield an added benefit of $6. (Can you see in Figure 25.14 that the 87th unit would yield $7 in benefit?)

Given a marketwide price of $4 per unit, buyer-side two-question logic is as follows:

Question 1: What is the benefit of buying an added unit of this product?
Answer: The _marginal benefit_ associated with each added unit—e.g., $5 for the 233rd and $4 for the 352nd.
Question 2: What must be given up in cost to get an added unit of output?
Answer: The _price_—$4 for each.

The answer to question 1, marginal benefit, exceeds or equals the answer to question 2, price, for units 1 through 400. Hence 400 units would optimize consumer welfare given a price of $4. _In brief,_ $MSB = P$.

The _extent_ to which the answer to the first question in the logic exceeds the second, _in total,_ is called _consumers' surplus._ Consumers' surplus is the difference between the total dollar amount buyers would be _willing to pay_ for some quantity (question 1) and the amount they _actually pay_ (question 2). The total amount buyers would be willing to pay for 400 units is equal to their total benefit, $2,200. Graphically, this is the area under the market demand curve (MSB) up to 400 units, which is also the area under each of the four segments added together:

Units	Sum of MSBs
1–100	$700
101–200	600
201–300	500
301–400	400
Overall total	$2,200

TABLE 25.4 Data for Figure 25.14(a): Demand Side

	Individual Buyer			Marketwide Results (100 Buyers)	
Quantity	Total Benefit	Marginal Benefit (Demand)	Quantity	Total Benefit	Marginal Benefit (Demand)
0	0		0	0	
1	$ 7	7/1 = $7	100	$700	700/100 = $7
2	$13	6/1 = $6	200	$1,300	600/100 = $6
3	$18	5/1 = $5	300	$1,800	500/100 = $5
4	$22	4/1 = $4	400	$2,200	400/100 = $4
5	$25	3/1 = $3	500	$2,500	300/100 = $3
6	$27	2/1 = $2	600	$2,700	200/100 = $2

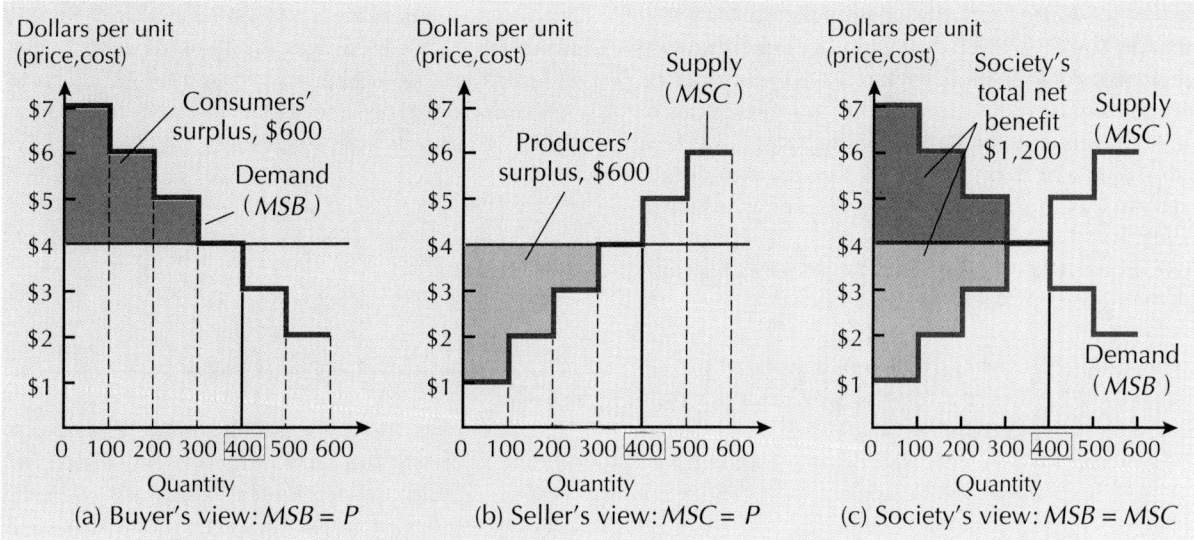

FIGURE 25.14   Allocation Efficiency Illustrated

Interaction of demand and supply at the market level establishes an equilibrium price of $4. Buyers purchase insofar as MSB is greater than or equal to the price, optimizing when MSB = P. Sellers offer output insofar as price is greater than or equal to MSC. In brief, they maximize at P = MSC. Combined, the result is MSB = MSC. This also maximizes society's total net benefit, which is the sum of consumers' surplus and producers' surplus.

The total amount that buyers actually pay to get the 400 units is price times quantity, $4 × 400 = $1,600. Subtracting this total that they actually pay from the total they would be willing to pay, $2,200 − $1,600, indicates a consumers' surplus in this case of $600.

Consumers' surplus is the difference between the total dollar amount consumers would be willing to pay and the total dollar they actually pay for a certain quantity. It is the **net** total benefit they obtain.

P = MSC: As regards the supply side in Figure 25.14(b), let's assume 100 identical firms and an increasing-cost long-run supply. Table 25.5 presents the data. The marginal cost for each firm on the left-hand side of the table derives from the change in total cost—namely, $1 for the first unit, $2 for the second, and so on (given alternative opportunities). Hence the cumulative addition of the marginal costs yields the total cost (e.g., $1 + $2 = $3 and $1 + $2 + $3 = $6). Marketwide quantities and total costs are obtained by multiplying the firms' outputs and total costs by 100. The _mar-_

TABLE 25.5   Data for Figure 25.14(b): Supply Side

Individual Seller			Marketwide Results (100 Sellers)		
Quantity	Total Cost	Marginal Cost (Supply)	Quantity	Total Cost	Marginal Cost (Supply)
0	0	—	0	0	—
1	$ 1	1/1 = $1	100	$ 100	100/100 = $1
2	$ 3	2/1 = $2	200	$ 300	200/100 = $2
3	$ 6	3/1 = $3	300	$ 600	300/100 = $3
4	$10	4/1 = $4	400	$1,000	400/100 = $4
5	$15	5/1 = $5	500	$1,500	500/100 = $5
6	$21	6/1 = $6	600	$2,100	600/100 = $6

ginal costs at the marketwide level are the same as those at the firm level, however, because they are the added total costs associated with *each added unit of output*. For example, the marginal cost of the 87th unit is $1, while that of the 231st is $3. This is due to the horizontal summation used to obtain marketwide supply, and it may be seen in Figure 25.14.

Given a marketwide price of $4 per unit, the seller's two-question logic is thus:

Question 1: What is the firms' benefit of producing and selling an added unit of output?

Answer: The *price*, $4, because that is the added revenue that would be received.

Question 2: What does it cost the firms to get the added $4 in revenue?

Answer: The *marginal cost*—$2 for the 157th unit, $3 for the 300th, and so on.

Note that the answer to question 1 exceeds or equals the answer to question 2 for outputs 1 through 400. This is profit-maximizing strategy once again. And production stops at 400 units because beyond 400 the added cost, $5, exceeds the added revenue of each unit, $4. These 400 units are the same 400 that were purchased in our demand-side analysis. *In short, P = MSC on the producers' side.*

The extent to which the answer to the first question in the logic exceeds the second for the firms, *in total*, is called *producers' surplus*, a concept similar to consumers' surplus.

Producers' surplus is the difference between the total dollar amount producers receive and the amount they must give up to cover costs, including opportunity costs. It is the net benefit going to producers after subtracting the minimum value they would have to receive in order to supply the product.

Here the total revenue received by producers (question 1) is price times quantity, $4 × $400 = $1,600. In Figure 25.14 this is the area under the price line out to 400 units. The total amount producers give up to produce this amount (question 2) is the total cost, $1,000, for 400 units. In Figure 25.14 this total cost is seen as the area under the market supply curve (*MSC*) up to 400 units, which is also the area under each of the four segments added together:

Units	Sum of MSCs
1–100	$100
101–200	200
201–300	300
301–400	400
Overall total	$1,000

Hence, comparing the total amount sellers obtain, $1,600, with the total amount they must give up, $1,000, yields a producers' surplus of $600 ($1,600 − $1,000 = $600). This is the shaded area in part (b) of Figure 25.14. (This is the scarcity rent we encountered earlier. It goes to the owners of scarce inputs like land.)

MSB = MSC: Consumers and producers together make up our society. Given that *MSB = P* for consumers and *P = MSC* for producers, it follows that, under perfect competition, *MSB = MSC* for society, as both buyers and sellers in a market see the same price, *P*.

Society's two-question logic explains why the output that yields *MSB = MSC* is the ideal output for a product:

Question 1: What is the benefit of producing an additional unit of this good?

Answer: The *marginal social benefit, (MSB)*.

Question 2: What does it cost to get an additional unit of output of this good?

Answer: The *marginal social cost (MSC)*.

A glance at part (c) of Figure 25.14 reveals that *MSB* is greater than or equal to *MSC* for each unit up to 400. That is the last unit for which *MSB = MSC*, since at that point *MSB* and *MSC* both equal $4, the price. The 401st unit and those beyond fail the test of society's two-question logic.

The ideal nature of this resulting output, 400 units, can also be seen by considering consumers' and producers' surpluses. Consumers' surplus is the *total dollar net benefit* of this output to *consumers*. Producers' surplus is the *total dollar net* _benefit_ of this output _to producers._ Total net benefit _to society_ is therefore the sum of these surpluses.

In turn, total net benefit to society can also be viewed as the _total social benefit_ of the 400 units _minus_ the _total social cost._ The data of Table 25.6 take this latter form. Quantity, total social benefit, and total social cost occupy columns (1), (2), and (3). Notice column (4) in particular, however. That is society's total dollar _net_ benefit, column (2) minus column (3). This rises until 400 units are produced and then falls thereafter. Society's total net benefit at 400 units is $1,200, which is also consumers' surplus ($600) plus producers' surplus ($600). Figure 25.14(c) identifies this result as the combined shaded areas. Equating _MSB_ and _MSC_ thus maximizes this area.

More generally, total dollar net social benefit is the area under the demand curve minus the area under the supply curve in a perfectly competitive market, as shown in Figure 25.15. At output _Q_ in this figure, _MSB_ = _MSC_ and the net total benefit are maximized. At other levels of output, the difference between total benefit and total cost would be smaller. Intuitively, this result is attractive. _Maximizing the total net benefit from this good also maximizes the welfare society obtains from using its scarce resources to produce this good as opposed to others. When the total net benefit is maximized for all goods, society maximizes the total welfare its scarce resources can provide._

The **total dollar net social benefit** is (a) consumer's surplus plus producers' surplus or (b) the area under the demand curve out to the given quantity (total benefit) minus the area under the supply curve out to the given quantity (total cost). Perfect competition maximizes this net benefit.

Regarding the What? question, the perfectly competitive market produces the ideal amount, that giving allocation efficiency.

B
How?

1. The Perfectly Competitive Market's Answer Figure 25.16 depicts the long-run equilibrium for a perfectly competitive firm. Marginal cost _(MC)_ and short-run average total cost appear as before. The _long-run_ average cost is assumed to fall as output increases from zero to _Q_ because of economies of scale. At outputs greater than _Q,_ long-run average cost is assumed to rise due to diseconomies of scale. Taken together, these several observations imply that the firm has selected its technology, its input combinations, and its scale so that the resulting cost–quantity combinations are those shown in Figure 25.16. Moreover, the firm will operate its chosen plant at point _E,_ earning a normal profit, no more and no less.

2. Comparison with the Ideal The ideal of technical efficiency would have the firm producing its output at the _lowest possible cost per unit._ The perfectly competitive results of Figure 25.16 meet this goal in two ways. The first concerns the location _of_ the average cost curves. The second relates to the location _on_ the average cost curves.

The location _of_ the average cost curves is such

TABLE 25.6   Data for Figure 25.14(c): Society's View

(1) Quantity	(2) Total Social Benefit	(3) Total Social Cost	(4) = (2) − (3) Total Net Benefit
0	0	0	—
100	$ 700	$ 100	$ 600
200	1,300	300	1,000
300	1,800	600	1,200
400	2,200	1,000	1,200
500	2,500	1,500	1,000
600	2,700	2,100	600

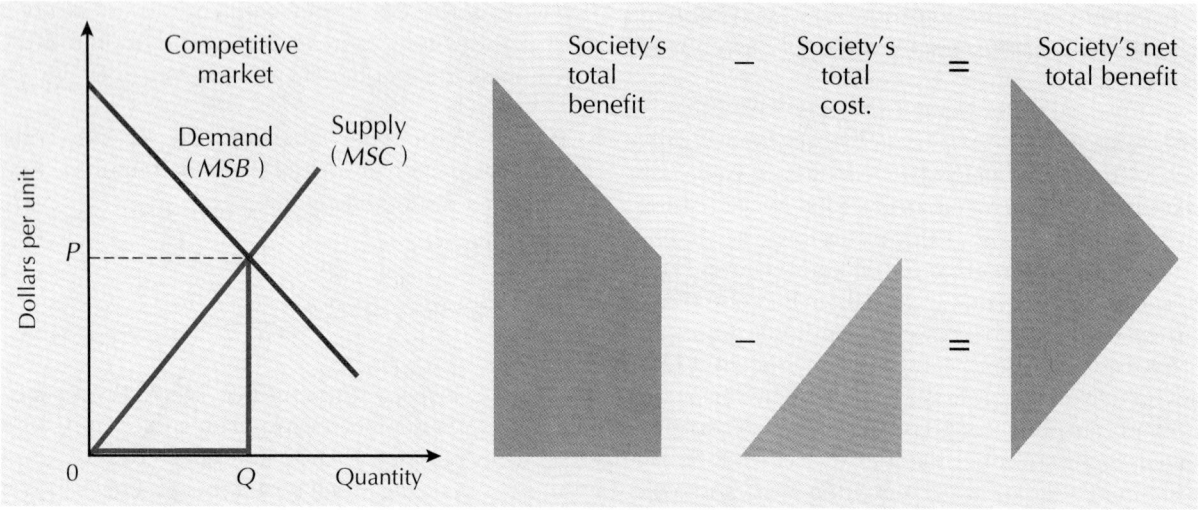

FIGURE 25.15 *Allocation Efficiency Maximizes Society's Net Social Benefit*

When the perfectly competitive market produces quantity Q at price P, the result is MSB = MSC. This maximizes the net total benefit that society obtains from using scarce inputs to produce this good as opposed to others. Net total benefit is the area under the demand curve at this output minus the area under the supply curve.

that they just touch the price line. They are therefore as low as possible while still being consistent with a normal profit. Different technologies or different input combinations would result in higher

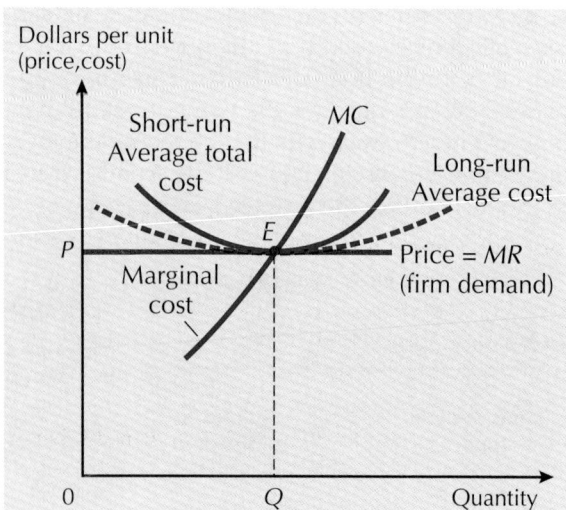

FIGURE 25.16 *Long-Run Equilibrium for the Perfectly Competitive Firm*

The perfectly competitive firm is said to be technically efficient because in long-run equilibrium it meets two criteria: (1) Its average cost curves are the lowest possible cost curves consistent with a normal profit; and (2) the firm is located on the lowest point of those curves.

short-run and long-run average costs. These and other higher cost possibilities would mean economic losses for the firm, forcing it out of business in the long run.

As regards location *on* the curves, the firm chooses point E. This further minimizes the firm's costs while maximizing its profit. In theory, then, perfect competition forces firms to minimize costs; in doing so, technical efficiency is achieved.

C
Who?

1. The Perfectly Competitive Market's Answer Those who get the goods and services produced by perfect competition are those who are willing and able to pay the market's prices. Others will not. As for income input owners would be earning competitive rates of compensation and owners of firms would only be earning normal profits.

2. Comparison with the Ideal Because there is no clearly defined ideal on this score, the perfectly competitive results look admirable partly by default. There is more, though. Whatever the actual distribution of goods and income may be, perfectly competitive markets do not, at least in theory, make matters worse. Those who get specific goods are those who want them most. Bacon goes to bacon lovers, tea to tea drinkers, and so on—all conditioned by people's income. As for income, the normal profits generated by perfect competition are a particularly attractive feature. If profits were excessively high, the owners of firms would gain at the expense of consumers. This could tilt the distribution of income in favor of the rich. But with perfect competition, profits are not, in the long run, above a level just sufficient to keep capital committed to the market.

D
What's New?

The theory of perfect competition is static, looking only at the here and now, or is a comparison of different static outcomes once long-run adjustment is assumed. It's like looking at an acorn and an oak tree without fully recognizing their connection or the growth process. As a result, technological change and growth are not central to the theory. Still, something can be said here if we draw a distinction between technological changes originating from firms *inside* the market (through invention and innovation) and those originating *outside* the market but adopted by it.

Perfectly competitive firms cannot themselves be expected to invent and innovate because they lack the large financial resources necessary to invest in risky research and development. They lack power over price and economic profits.

On the other hand, if new and proven production techniques or products are offered to competitive firms by *outside* sources (who do the inventing and innovating necessary to make them new and proven), theory and evidence indicate that perfectly competitive firms snap them up fairly quickly. This is particulary true of cost-reducing production improvements because competitive firms are constantly pressed to curtail costs. In agriculture, for instance, farmers have been quick to adopt new fertilizers, new strains of hybrid seeds, new equipment, and other innovations developed by manufacturers, government research stations, and universities. Between 1950 and 1980, the output of hogs rose from 37 to 250 pounds per hour of labor input. The output of corn jumped from 3 to 33 bushels per hour of labor input and from 39 to 100 bushels per acre. Few industries can match agriculture's amazing feats of productivity growth.

E
Qualifications (Black Clouds)

All in all, the performance of perfectly competitive markets is thus quite impressive, especially for the questions What? and How? Does this mean that we should have government vigorously impose policies to restructure every American market into one of perfect competition? Should we break up big corporations into small firms? No, because there are many problems with perfect competition. In the real world, its attainment is often impossible or, if possible, undesirable in some cases. Let's consider some problems that fit the framework of the basic questions.

1. What? The products produced by perfect competition are perfectly standardized. Between sellers there are no style variations, no distinctive brand identifications, no flavor differences. In short, there is no product differentiation. Achieving such standardized offerings is in reality often impossible. Take grocery retailing, for example. Geographic location is an important feature that differentiates one grocer from another. Nearby grocers win customer favor over more distant ones, and it couldn't be otherwise.[5]

2. How? If there happen to be substantial economies of scale in production, perfect competition may be impossible and undesirable because of cost considerations. With substantial economies of scale, bigness is better because it is cheaper. The long-run average cost curve falls over a range of output that is large compared to the quantities demanded. Local electric and telephone services are classic examples, partly because these entail direct wire connection between the seller and buyer. These are, in other words, natural monopolies. Perfect competition would be impossible in such cases.

[5]There is a more technical point that can be raised as well. If perfect competition cannot, in reality, be achieved everywhere in the economy (which it can't), then movement toward perfect competition in just some markets does not necessarily mean improvement in allocation efficiency. This "second best" of partial achievement does not guarantee gains.

3. What's New? Perfectly competitive markets may be good at *adopting* new cost-reducing technologies, but they perform rather poorly at *originating* new technologies. Ideal performance requires vigorous activity at every stage of the process of technological change—invention, innovation, and diffusion.

SUMMARY

1. A perfectly competitive market has many sellers and buyers, a homogeneous product, easy entry and exit, and fully informed participants. The firm faces a perfectly elastic demand as a result, and thus price = marginal revenue = average revenue. The firm's total revenue rises at a constant rate.

2. In the short-run total dollars view, firms maximize total profit by selecting an output yielding the greatest positive difference between total revenue and total cost (*TR* − *TC*). Minimizing negative differences also minimizes any loss, which should never exceed the total fixed cost. (These rules apply to all profit-maximizing firms.)

3. In the short-run per unit view, the firm maximizes total profit by adding output as long as marginal revenue (*MR*) is greater than or equal to marginal cost (*MC*). In brief, *MR* = *MC*. This rule will also minimize losses unless the price falls below the average variable cost (*AVC*), the situation for shutdown. (Again, these rules apply to all firms.)

4. For the purely competitive firm, price equals marginal revenue, (*P* = *MR*), so with profit maximizing, *P* = *MC*. As the price varies, the quantity varies directly, and the *MC* curve above *AVC* also serves as the firm's supply curve. Horizontal addition of firm supplies yields marketwide supply, which together with marketwide demand determines the price.

5. Firms may make economic profits or losses in the short run, but only normal profits in the long run. Persistent economic profits attract new entry, which expands the supply until the economic profit is competed away. Persistent economic losses force exits, shifting the supply back until long-run equilibrium is reached.

6. Input prices can remain stable or vary with long-run expansion, creating constant-cost, increasing-cost, or decreasing-cost long-run supply. Increasing costs create scarcity rents.

7. In theory, perfect competition provides (a) *allocation efficiency* by equating marginal social benefit and marginal social cost (*MSB* = *MSC*), a condition that also maximizes society's total dollar net benefit (the combined surpluses of consumers and producers); (b) *technical efficiency* by encouraging lowest-cost technology, input combination, scale, and capacity use; (c) substantial *equity* by returning normal profit in the long run; and (d) some limited forms of *technical progress* by fostering the adoption of low-cost innovations developed outside the market.

8. On the other hand, perfect competition is not always perfect. It often does not allow for beneficial product differentiation, substantial economies of scale, or original advances in technology. Hence it is often not a good objective for public policy.

Appendix:

Agriculture and Government Policy

Agriculture dramatically illustrates that perfect competition, or at least its closest real-world approximation, is not necessarily perfect after all. The economic problems of agriculture have fostered a huge mass of complicated government policies. Unfortunately, the case of agriculture also illustrates that government policies themselves can be seriously flawed.

We shall briefly identify two main problems facing agriculture—instability in the short run and depressed prices in the long run. A nutshell review of government policy follows.

Price and Income Instability

In the short run, wild gyrations in farm prices and farm incomes have been common. Without government intervention, the prices of many farm commodities have fluctuated hundreds of percentage points from year to year. Agriculture's approximation to perfect competition cannot, by itself, be blamed for this instability. In essence, perfect competition merely locates the price at the intersection of demand and supply. Moreover, it also merely allows short-run economic profits or losses; it does not imply violent swings from one to the other. What causes instability in agriculture, then, is not perfect competition alone, but perfect competition coupled with several factors that affect the *elasticities, shifts,* and *timing* of marketwide demand and supply.

There are two key features of *elasticities:* price inelasticity of demand and price inelasticity of supply. Marketwide demand is inelastic at the farm level partly because crops are basic staples, necessities of life. Moreover, farmers get such a small share of the consumer's food dollar (often only 17–25 percent) that price changes at the farm level are filtered into a small fraction of their size when they ultimately reach the grocery store or McDonald's, where the ultimate buyers see them. Regarding supply, short-run price inelasticity arises partly because *nature* does not respond to price changes with immediate changes in quantities produced, so farmers cannot always respond easily.

Two main factors cause erratic *shifts* of marketwide demand or supply. First, and most obviously, supply is shifted about by dramatic changes in weather, pestilence, and disease. Bumper crop conditions shift supply curves out. Natural disasters shift them back. Second, demand is pushed left and right by various forces, the most important of which lately has been swings in export demand. Normally, the output of roughly 1 out of every 3 American acres goes abroad. But this varies as foreign demand lurches about (mainly because of nature's good and bad behavior abroad).

Finally, *timing* poses problems. There is a gestation time span between agricultural inputs and outputs. For tree crops like apples and oranges, this delay can be years long. As a result, farmers cannot plant with a full knowledge of prices at harvest time. They must guess. Collective guesses that prices will be low cause supply curtailment, which in the end drives the price up. A high price may then prompt guesses that prices will be high in the future, something that encourages added supply and in the end actually depresses the price. The sequence is thus destabilizing.

Figure A illustrates the consequences of inelasticity and shifting supply. Competition pushes the price toward equilibrium points like E, E', or E^*. With a perfectly inelastic supply shifting from S_1 to S_2 and back to S_1 against inelastic demand curve D_i, the price heaves from P_1 to P_2, creating a very unhappy price pattern over time. In contrast, the same to-and-fro shifting of supply against elastic demand D_e generates a smoother price pattern over time because the price then fluctuates between P_1 and P_3 instead of between P_1 and P_2.

Depressed Prices and Incomes

If instability had been the only problem, agricultural policies could be aimed solely at price or income stabilization, but this has not been the case. These policies have also been aimed at price and income *elevation*. The problem is most starkly seen in historical statistics. In the 1930s, when present-day policies first began, average income per capita for the farm population was less than 40 percent of nonfarm income. Two decades later, farmers were only half as well off as city dwellers. Much of the problem lay in chronic output abundance, which tended to depress farm prices and incomes. Rapid productivity growth pushed crop supply curves to the right faster than demand shifted to the right with expanding consumer population and income. Supply therefore outpaced demand on average.

The low farm earnings of past decades encouraged exits. The U.S. farm population fell dramatically from 23.0 million in 1950 to only 5.6 million in 1980. In the same period, the number of farms fell by more than half. These developments bolstered the incomes of those who remained in farming, so that in 1980, median farm family income had risen

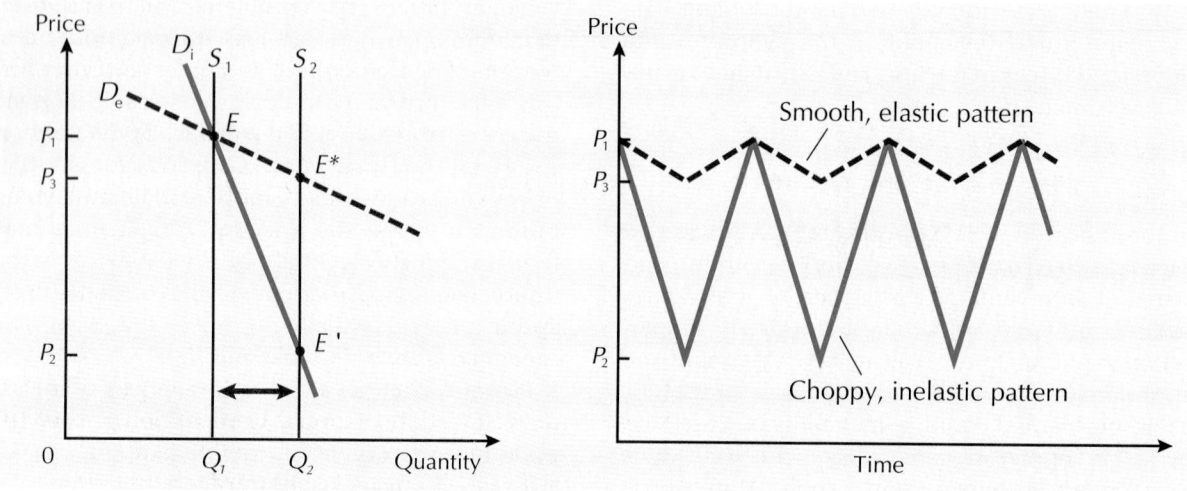

FIGURE A   Price Instability in Agriculture

Competition pushes the price toward equilibrium points like E, E*, or E'. With inelastic supply shifting between S_1 and S_2 against inelastic demand D_i, the price plummets from P_1 to P_2 and then leaps back to P_1 repeatedly. The result is a wildly unstable price pattern over time. If demand were elastic instead, like D_e, the equilibrium would vary between E and E*. Accordingly, price variation would then be relatively subdued.

to 75 percent of median *nonfarm* family income, and many farm families could claim real riches. This prosperity also affected land values, as would be predicted by the theory of rents. Adjusted for general price inflation, the average real value of an acre of farm land more than doubled between 1970 and 1980. Unfortunately, the spurt of prosperity then took a turn for the worse, and by the mid-1980s farm family incomes and land values had suffered serious setbacks. A mountain of farm debt optimistically incurred during the heady 1970s complicated problems. In 1985 more farmers faced bankruptcy than at any time since the Great Depression.

Farm Policy

Most of today's federal farm programs date from the Great Depression, when plunging crop prices put the farm economy in tatters. Legislation of the 1930s set the basic approach that endured for decades: *Regulate production and support prices.* Congress also legislated a standard to guide production regulations and price supports, namely, "parity." *Parity means that crop prices should be held high enough so that the ratio of crop prices to farmers' costs can be maintained at nearly the*

same ratio reached during the years 1910 to 1914, when farming was especially prosperous. This notion fertilized many farm programs. The federal government props up the prices of cotton, rice, corn, wheat, tobacco, and eight other commodities by storing farmers' output and granting them loans, so that they can wait for prices to rise. When prices for some crops sink below target prices, farmers are given "deficiency" payments that make up the difference between market prices and target prices. Dairy farmers enjoy their own special program, which amounts to a direct subsidy. Whatever output they cannot sell on the open market at support price levels, the government will buy automatically, paying a fixed price for milk, butter, or cheese regardless of how much it is forced to buy.

Figure B conveys the basic economics of production regulation and price support, with cotton as the example. Let's begin with *price support.* The free market price would be 50 cents a pound, as determined by the interaction of demand and supply. The corresponding quantity would be 7 billion pounds. Setting the support price at 80 cents a pound would dislodge the market from this equilibrium, with free market demand taking no more than 5 billion pounds. If the supply were

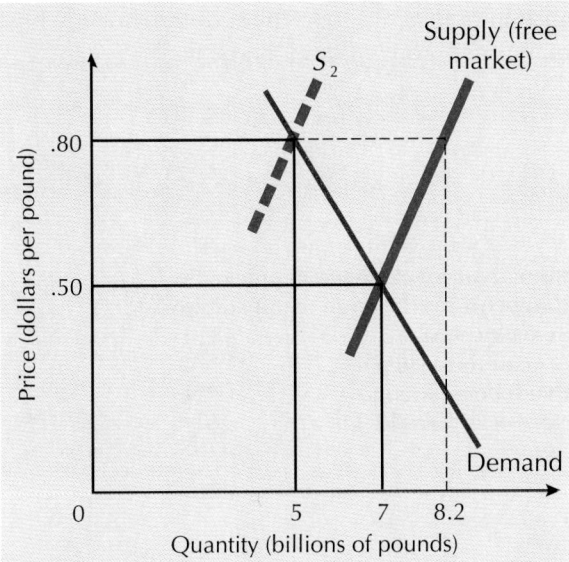

FIGURE B *Farm Price Support and Production Regulation: Cotton*

Without government intervention, the free-market price would be 50 cents a pound and output would equal 7 billion pounds. In order to lift the price to 80 cents a pound, the government could take actions common to farm policy. (1) It could buy up the surplus supply (8.2) over demand (5) at that price, which would be 3.2 billion pounds (8.2 − 5). (2) It could impose production controls to restrict the supply S₂. Idling land has been the main method used.

not officially restricted to 5 billion pounds, the government would then have to purchase all output in excess of 5 billion pounds—in this case, 3.2 billion pounds, the difference between 8.2 and 5. At a support price of 80 cents a pound, that would cost the government $2.56 billion. This subsidy would come out of taxpayers' pockets. There is also a hidden subsidy paid by consumers through a higher market price. It is $1.5 billion in this case, which is the price difference, 30 cents (80 − 50), times 5 billion pounds.

Production regulations are designed to limit the amount of surpluses the government has to buy and thereby reduce the taxpayer's burden. The hidden subsidy consumers pay remains unaffected, however, because price remains higher than it would be otherwise.[6] Looking at Figure B again, we

[6] This is not always true. Programs of direct payments, which have been tried for some crops, let the market price fall.

see that a restriction of supply to S_2 would raise the price to 80 cents a pound without the government's purchasing 3.2 million pounds of surpluses. Such supply restriction has been achieved mainly by taking land out of production—more or less land, depending on the height of the support price and the conditions of demand and supply. In some years, more than 50 million acres of farm land have been held out of commercial crop production by federal programs of supply constraint.

Aside from price supports and production regulations, there is a cornucopia of additional federal programs to aid farmers. These include credit assistance, disaster relief, loan guarantees, soil conservation subsidies, and subsidized electricity. All told, the government's aid to agriculture easily exceeded $20 billion in 1985.

Problems: Many if not most economists argue that federal farm policies should be plowed under or pruned sharply. One of the main reasons for their criticism is that these policies have produced huge distortions in the marketplace. Despite mandatory production limits and incentive programs to curb output, immense surpluses of numerous crops have developed from time to time. In 1984, for instance, Uncle Sam owned 17 billion pounds of dairy products, more than enough to meet our nation's needs for nearly 2 months (this despite large programs to eliminate the surpluses by donating milk, cheese, and butter to poor people). In 1985, tobacco warehouses from North Carolina to Kentucky were packed with 1.4 billion pounds of unwanted leaf. The government stood to lose $3 billion on this surplus tobacco. Allocation efficiency gets buried under such bulging surpluses.

A second criticism concerns the question Who?. The programs are designed so that the biggest and richest farmers get most of the benefits, a tilt that offends value judgments on equity. In 1979, for instance, farms with sales exceeding $40,000 comprised only 22 percent of all farms, but they reaped 57 percent of all government benefits. In 1983 one of the country's largest farming corporations, the J.G. Boswell Company, received over $3.7 million in subsidies.

Price supports and production controls also damage the nation's position in foreign trade. When policy increases U.S. farm prices relative to those of foreign producers, we tend to price ourselves out of world markets. Stated differently, why should a farmer export grain when he can sell it to the U.S. government for a higher price? Between 1982 and 1985, the U.S. share of the world wheat market fell from 48 to 39 percent.

KEY TERMS

Perfect competition
Average revenue
Marginal revenue
Profit maximization
Total profit
Shutdown rule
Short-run firm supply curve

Short-run marketwide supply curve
Long-run marketwide supply curve
Scarcity rent
Consumers' surplus
Producers' surplus
Net social benefit

QUESTIONS AND PROBLEMS

1. List the four structural conditions that prevent sellers from individually influencing price. Explain the importance of each condition.

2. Explain why the demand for a product produced in a perfectly competitive _market_ is downward sloping while the demand for the product of the perfectly competitive _firm_ is horizontal.

3. Describe verbally and graphically the short-run profit maximizing behavior of the perfectly competitive firm.

4. Derive the perfectly competitive firm's short run supply curve.

5. Explain the relationship between the supply curves of individual perfectly competitive firms and the supply curve of the market that they comprise. How will the entry of new firms influence market supply?

6. Economic profits will not persist in the long run in perfectly competitive firms. Explain why, both verbally and graphically.

7. Describe possible slopes for the long run supply curve in a perfectly competitive industry and explain why each might happen.

8. Explain why, in the absence of external costs and benefits, a perfectly competitive market ensures that marginal social benefits will equal marginal social costs.

9. Draw supply and demand curves for a perfectly competitive market. Assuming no external costs (or benefits), label: marginal social benefits, marginal social costs, consumer surplus, producer surplus, society's total cost, society's net total benefit.

10. Draw the long run equilibrium position for the perfectly competitive firm and explain why it is considered technically efficient.

11. Would a perfectly competitive market economy yield a "fair" income distribution? Why or why not?

12. Are perfectly competitive industries likely to experience rapid technological change?

13. What are scarcity rents and how do they relate to long-run supply curves for goods and services?

14. Describe any significant failures or flaws associated with the conduct of perfectly competitive markets.

From the appendix:

15. Agricultural markets tend to be markets in which prices change dramatically from year to year. Use graphs to assist in your explanation of this instability.

16. How are the price elasticity of demand, price elasticity of supply, and income elasticity of demand for farm products relevant to farm problems?

17. Why do production controls frequently accompany government price supports?

18. Distinguish the long run farm problem and its causes from the short run farm problem.

19. What are major criticisms of U.S. farm policy? Evaluate each from an economic perspective.

26

Monopoly and Its Regulation

Measured by assets, it was America's largest corporation, worth $155 billion. Measured by market shares, it was a colossus controlling 80 to 100 percent of the markets it occupied. And those markets amassed tens of billions of dollars in revenues annually. Little wonder, then, that on January 8, 1982, news of the company's breakup shook the country. American Telephone and Telegraph would never be the same.

AT&T was so big that the breakup took 2 years and tens of millions of dollars to complete. January 1, 1984, was the official date. Over $100 billion in assets were divested.

Now, *local parts* of the telephone business, the ones separated from AT&T, remain monopolies—those parts that provide local service, such as when you call for a carry-out pizza. *Other parts,* like long-distance service and telephone equipment, are changing from monopolies to oligopolies. One task of this chapter is to explain the breakup of AT&T—the largest corporate reorganization of all time. Why, for instance, are portions of the business still held by monopolies, while other portions are not? Your understanding hinges on an understanding of monopolies in general. The main topics of this chapter are therefore:

1. Structural conditions that define and determine monopoly.

2. Conduct of monopolies, especially pricing strategies.

3. Performance of monopolies when unregulated.

4. Regulation policy, which governs natural monopolies.

Discussion of AT&T punctuates the entire chapter. But the details of the AT&T divestiture fill a concluding appendix.

I
Monopoly Structure

A
Theoretical Pure Monopoly

Like perfect competition, *pure monopoly* is a *theoretical* model. No real markets match the theory precisely, but several are fairly close approximations—local telephone service, for instance. In other respects, pure monopoly is the exact opposite of perfect competition. Whereas perfect competition is the extreme form of competition, pure monopoly is the extreme *absence* of competition.

Pure monopoly is a market in which:
1. One firm is the seller (buyers remain numerous).
2. The good has no close substitutes.
3. Entry by new sellers is blocked.

That only *one* firm sells in a monopoly market is easy to see. The name implies this, and the famous board game of the same name is won when a player "monopolizes" all the properties. There is a problem, however, because markets vary in geographic scope. They can be local or regional, as they are for water, newspapers, and residential electricity, in which case buyers cannot deal with distant sellers. It must be stressed, then, that a monopoly market has only one firm, but there may be several different geographic markets, each with a different firm. In Los Angeles, for instance, local telephone service is supplied by Pacific Bell. In Chicago, folks do business with Ameritech. There are seven regional phone companies that sprang from AT&T's breakup. But in any given local market, there is only one supplier of local phone service.

Pure monopoly is further insulated from competition by an absence of close substitutes. Salt has no close substitute. It is therefore eligible for pure monopolization. Root beer doesn't qualify because consumers can easily switch between root beer and other soft drinks. Stated differently, a pure monopolist enjoys perfect product differentiation.

Finally, when entry is blocked, as it is in pure monopoly, *potential* competition is just as absent as actual competition. Outsiders cannot enter to vie with the monopolist.

B
Actual Monopolies

What causes actual monopolies or markets that approximate pure monopoly? There are several possible causes, each of which limits the number of firms and simultaneously raises a barrier to entry—patents, government action, control of inputs, and substantial economies of scale.

1. Patents   A firm may obtain a monopoly by having patents on a product or on the basic processes used to produce it. A *patent* is an *exclusive right* to make and sell some product, or to use some process, that is granted by the federal government for 17 years. The products or processes protected have to be *new*, however, because patents cover inventions. The idea is that patent monopolies reward inventors, thereby stimulating greater technological change than would occur otherwise.

2. Government Actions   Besides patents, other government actions, such as public ownership, licensing, or official franchising, can also create a monopoly. In the United States, mass transit systems are commonly monopolized by municipal ownership. Franchise agreements protect local cable TV companies, telephone companies, and some electricity suppliers.

3. Control of Inputs   When the production of a good requires some unique inputs, control of those inputs can cause monopoly. Before World War II, Alcoa was the sole producer of aluminum ingots in the United States. Its ownership of virtu-

ally all prime bauxite in the United States solidified its solitary position.

4. Substantial Economies of Scale   Economies of scale may be substantial, in which case bigness is best. Economies of scale cause the long-run average cost per unit to fall with larger scales of operation. If the cost per unit slides down over the entire range of market demand, there will be room for only one efficient firm in the market. Such extreme cases are called **natural monopolies.** Local telephone service, local water service, and local electricity service provide examples. Long-run average costs decline in these instances mainly because sellers supply buyers through direct physical connections—wires, pipes, and cables. Competition would require duplication of these connections, raising unit costs considerably.

Note that each of these several features—patents, government actions, control of inputs, and substantial economies of scale—has a double whammy. Each places a market in the hands of a single supplier and at the same time prevents other potential suppliers from entering the market. This implies that actual monopolies possess immense economic power, and, to be sure, they often do. On the other hand, *actual* monopolies frequently suffer weaknesses that make them less potent than the *pure* monopoly of theory. A patent, for example, can often be no more than a very fragile foundation for monopoly. Roughly 60,000 patents are granted every year, and the vast majority of them cover rather pedestrian products like A-frame bacon cookers and motorized golf carts. (A vibrating toilet seat won Patent No. 3,244,168 in 1966.) Likewise, control of rare inputs may mean little if the monopolized product has suitable substitues. In 1984 *The Wall Street Journal* reported that the market for bat guano had been "cornered" by an enterprise owning property rights to bat droppings in the three largest bat caves in the United States. Growers of "organic" vegetables (and marijuana) apparently prize bat guano highly as a fertilizer, but chemical fertilizers serve as substitutes.[1]
Read Perspective 26A.

[1]*Wall Street Journal*, July 24, 1984, pp. 1, 25.

PERSPECTIVE 26A
Long-Distance Telephone Service

Until the 1970s, AT&T enjoyed a monopoly on long-distance telephone service mainly because of substantial economies of scale. For most of this century, long-distance telecommunications required cable connections between cities. AT&T's Long Lines division laid the cable and provided the service, even for callers whose local telephone company was not owned by AT&T. With the passage of time, however, two developments eroded AT&T's natural monopoly over long-distance service. First, the demand for long-distance calling grew immensely, especially that linking major cities like Chicago and New York. Such an expansion of demand can dissipate the importance of economies of scale because such economies create monopolies only when demand is small relative to the minimum efficient scale of the firm. Second, new technologies made long-distance cables obsolete. Microwave systems, satellites, and fiberoptic wires now carry long-distance calls. Only limited economies of scale occur for these new technologies. Natural monopoly is therefore no longer warranted, and in recent years MCI, Sprint, and several other companies have begun to compete head on with AT&T. AT&T still accounts for about 80 percent of this $45 billion market, but its pure monopoly has dissolved.

Because nearly all real-world monopolies fall short of pure monopoly, it is sometimes useful to speak of *monopoly power* rather than *monopoly*. The 100 percent market share, the unique product, and the very high barriers to entry of pure monopoly permit the firm, *if unregulated,* to control the price and exclude entry. Hence *monopoly power* entails *some* price control and *some* entry exclusion, but not necessarily to the extent enjoyed by pure monopoly.

Monopoly power is the power to influence the price and deter entry.

Entry difficulties have just been given their due, but price control needs attention. We must consider the implications of monopoly market structure: What is the firm's view of demand?

C
Implications for Firm Demand

For the next several pages we shall, for the sake of clarity, focus on *pure,* unregulated monopoly. Clarity in comprehending the impact of monopoly structure on the firm's view of demand is critical because the firm's experience with demand determines its experience with revenues, and revenues, in turn, strongly influence profits.

If, as in pure monopoly, there is only one firm in the market, *then the firm's demand curve is exactly the same as the marketwide demand curve.* This is what distinguishes pure monopoly from perfect competition more than anything else.

The upper part of Figure 26.1, which comes from the data in Table 26.1, shows this coincidence of firm and marketwide demand. Figure 26.1 also depicts the resulting behavior of revenues. Recall that revenues can be represented in *dollars per unit* and *total dollars.* Demand fits the dollars per unit view because it is keyed to price, which is always in per unit terms. Hence the *upper* portion of Figure 26.1, which has a vertical axis for dollars per unit, contains demand as scheduled in columns (1) and (2) of Table 26.1. The lower portion of Figure 26.1 is tied to the upper portion by an identical quantity axis, but its vertical axis measures total dollars. It therefore depicts total revenue, which is price times quantity. Column (3) of Table 26.1 gives the underlying data, so columns (2) and (3) of the table comprise the total revenue relationship of the lower portion of Figure 26.1.

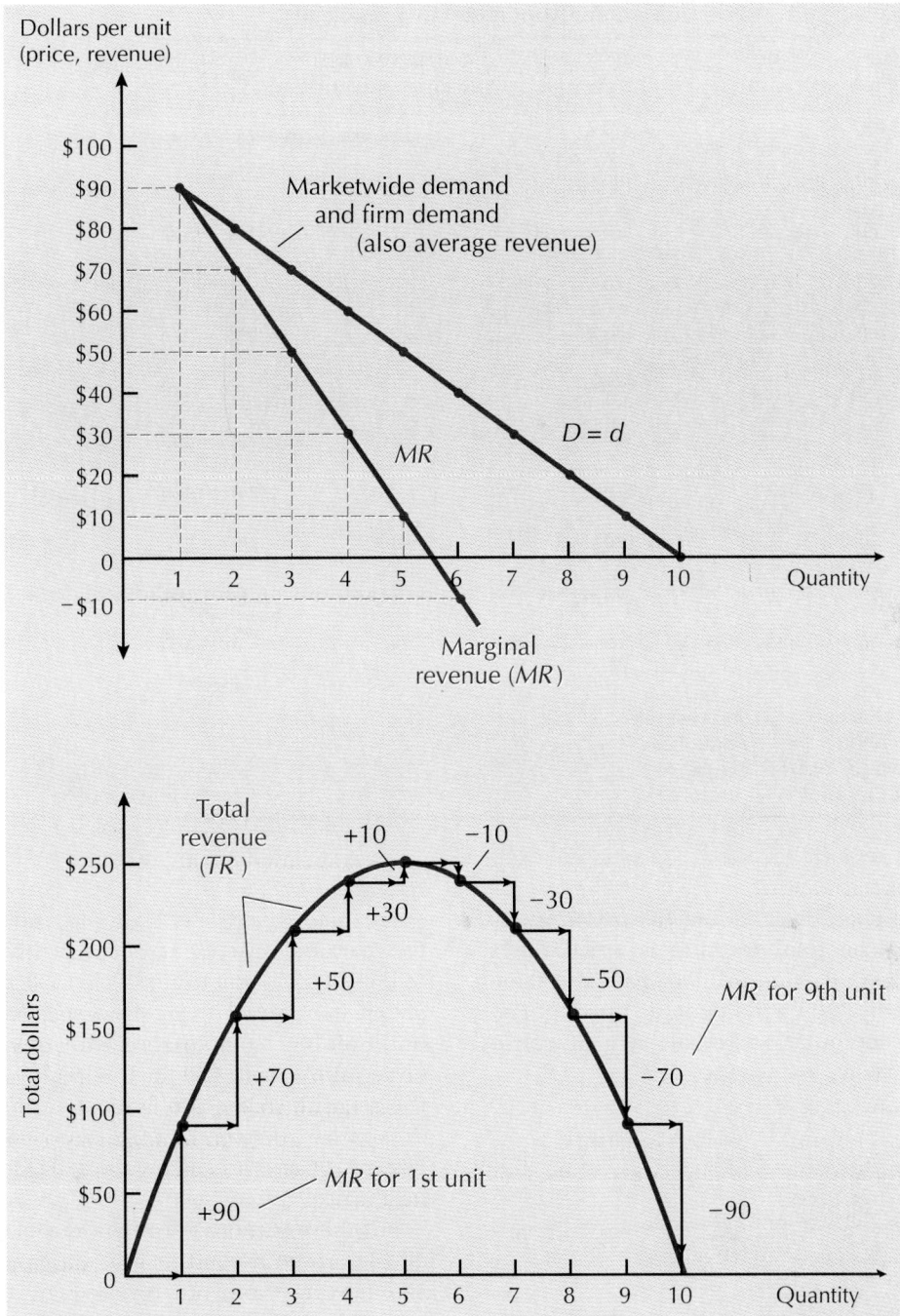

FIGURE 26.1 A Monopoly's Demand and Revenues

Firm demand matches marketwide demand in pure monopoly, as shown in the upper half of the figure, depicting dollars per unit. The demand curve is also the average revenue (TR/ Q = P). Marginal revenue, which is the change in TR associated with each unit, derives from TR in the lower half of the figure. It lies below demand and is negative for outputs greater than five units. Total revenue (TR), which is price times quantity, requires a total dollar vertical axis. It tops out at $250, which gained from five units and a price of $50.

TABLE 26.1 Revenue Data for Monopoly (Hypothetical)

(1) Price	(2) Quantity	(3) = (1) × (2) Total Revenue	(4) = Δ(3) ÷ Δ(2) Marginal Revenue	
$100	0	0		
90	1	90	90	=(90 − 0)
80	2	160	70	=(160 − 90)
70	3	210	50	=(210 − 160)
60	4	240	30	=(240 − 210)
50	5	250	10	=(250 − 240)
40	6	240	−10	=(240 − 250)
30	7	210	−30	=(210 − 240)
20	8	160	−50	=(160 − 210)
10	9	90	−70	=(90 − 160)
0	10	0	−90	=(0 − 90)

Demand schedule in Figure 26.1 ($ per unit)

Total revenue relation in Figure 26.1 (total $)

Average revenue is total revenue divided by quantity. Because total revenue is price times quantity, average revenue is once again the same as price, as indicated by the demand curve of Figure 26.1. Its computation reveals why it corresponds to price:

$$\frac{\text{Average}}{\text{revenue}} = \frac{\text{total revenue}}{\text{quantity}} = \frac{\text{price} \times \text{quantity}}{\text{quantity}} = \text{Price}$$

$$\frac{\text{Average}}{\text{revenue}} = \frac{\text{TR}}{Q} = \frac{P \times Q}{Q} = P$$

What is very important here is the behavior of *marginal revenue* under these circumstances. Marginal revenue is the *change in total revenue* associated with one more unit sold (a per unit concept). When demand slopes downward, as it does in this case, total revenue rises at a decreasing rate, reaches a peak, and then falls. Marginal revenue consequently lies beneath the demand

curve, below price. For example, Table 26.1 shows the marginal revenue associated with the first unit to be $90. This first unit sells for $90, so in *this one instance marginal revenue matches price.* The second unit has a marginal revenue of $70. Total revenue jumps from $90 for the first unit to $160 for the second, so the $70 is most easily seen as the difference between $160 and $90 ($160 − $90 = $70), and it is below the $80 price of the second unit.

But there is more here than meets the eye. Two effects are embodied in this marginal revenue of $70. Sorting them out reveals why the marginal revenue falls faster than the price. Note first that the sale of the second unit *adds* to the total revenue by an amount equal to the price of the second unit, namely, $80. However, note also that if prices for all units sold, first through last, are to be kept the same, cutting the price of the first unit from $90 to $80 to match the price of the second unit *subtracts* $10 from total revenue. The combined result is a plus $80 and a minus $10, for a *net* change in total revenue of $70:

Plus from added second unit	Minus from new price of first unit	Marginal revenue (ΔTR)
+ $80	− $10	+ $70

As the quantity rises, the plus factors shrink because the price of each added unit shrinks. At the same time, the minus factors grow because more and more items in the quantity sequence are repriced downward. Let's compare the components of marginal revenue for the third and fourth units with those in the preceding discussion for the second unit.

Unit	Plus (Price)	Minuses (Cuts)	Marginal Revenue
3rd	+$70	−$10, −$10	+$50
4th	+$60	−$10, −$10, −$10	+$30

It comes as no surprise, then, that marginal revenue eventually becomes negative when the minuses start to outweigh the pluses.

Accordingly, marginal revenue is shown on the lower portion of Figure 26.1 as the positive or negative steps that total revenue takes with each added unit. Marginal revenue is, in effect, the slope of the total revenue curve. Direct depiction of marginal revenue requires a dollars per unit scale, however, so this is done on the upper, per unit portion of Figure 26.1, where it may be seen that marginal revenue descends more rapidly than price. Comparison of the upper and lower portions is helpful.

II

Monopoly Conduct: Pricing Strategies

What pricing strategies will a pure monopoly adopt to maximize its profit? Analysis of this question has several familiar features. First, the profit to

be maximized here is once again *total dollar profit*, not profit per unit. Second, to see how the firm maximizes the total dollar profit, we can adopt two alternative views—the total dollars view, which explicitly shows the maximizing solution, and the dollars per unit view, which shows the same maximizing solution indirectly. Third, the rule of thumb for maximizing total profit in the *total dollars view* remains the same as before—namely, get the greatest positive difference between total revenue and total cost ($TR - TC$). Fourth, the rule of thumb for maximizing total profit in the *dollars per unit view* likewise reappears—namely, produce as long as marginal revenue exceeds or equals marginal cost ($MR \geq MC$). Fifth and finally, the distinction between the short run and long run stays intact, so our study of monopoly conduct follows a sequence partitioning the short run and long run across the total dollars view and the dollars per unit view:

	Total dollars view	Dollars per unit view
Short run	Step A	Step B
Long run	(Skip)	Step C

Aside from these familiar properties, we encounter novelties. One of the main ones is price discrimination.

A

Short-Run Total Dollars View

Given that total dollar profit is to be maximized, it's best to begin with the total dollars view. When the short-run total cost is added to the revenue data just reviewed, Table 26.2 and Figure 26.2 result. The short-run context entails a total *fixed* cost of $100, so *total cost* (*TC*) in column (4) of Table 26.2 is $100 when output is zero. The total dollars context uses diagrams with vertical axes notched in total dollars, so in Figure 26.2 the total cost curve intersects the vertical axis at $100. As output rises to 1 unit, 2 units, and more, the total *variable* cost rises from $0 to $35, from $35 to $50, and so on, lifting the total cost above $100 at zero output to $135,

TABLE 26.2 Monopoly Profit Maximization (Hypothetical Data)

(1) Price (P)	(2) Quantity (Q)	(3) Total Revenue (P × Q = TR)	(4) Total Cost (TC)	(5)* Total Profit (TR − TC)	(6) Marginal Revenue (MR)	(7) Marginal Cost (MC)
$100	0	0	$100	−$100	—	—
90	1	$ 90	135	− 45	$90	$35
80	2	160	150	+ 10	70	15
70	3	210	171	+ 39	50	21
60	4	240	200	+ 40	30	29
50	5	250	240	+ 10	10	40
40	6	240	285	− 45	−10	45
30	7	210	335	− 125	−30	50

*Note: If total cost includes a normal profit, then total profit is actually total economic profit.

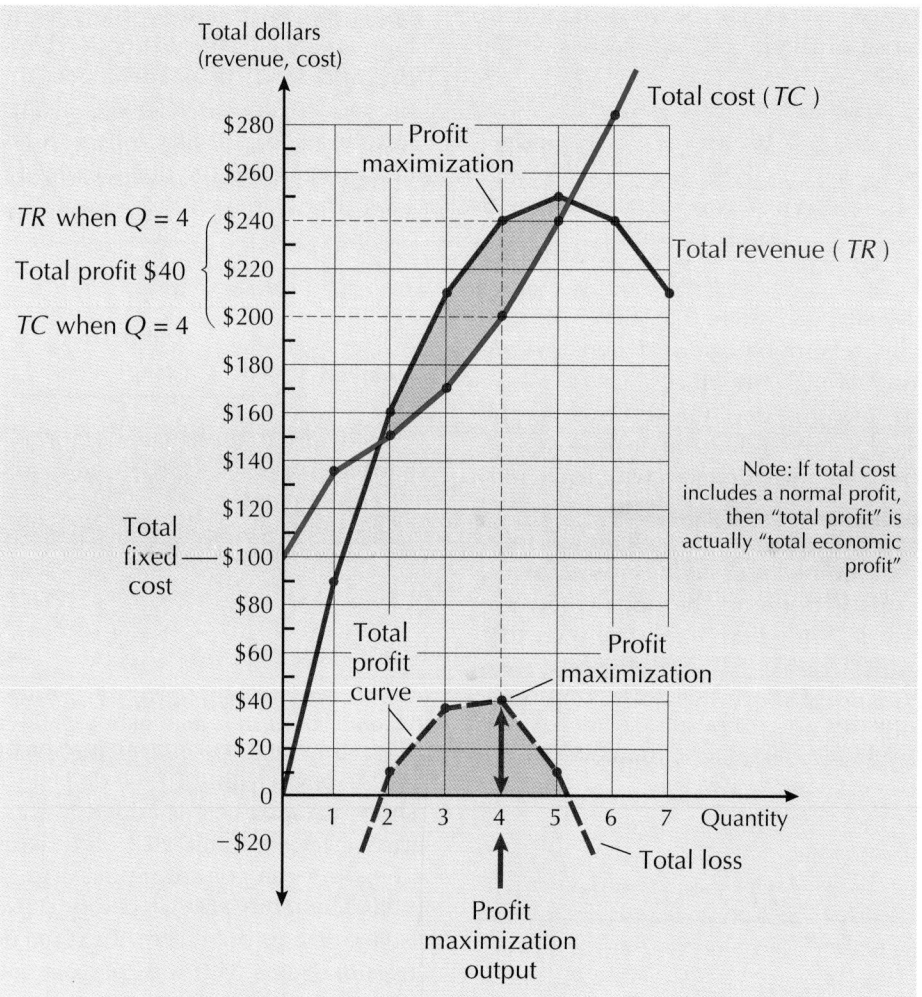

FIGURE 26.2 _Short-Run Total Dollar View of Monopoly Profit Maximization_

The profit-maximizing monopolist will produce where total revenue minus total cost is greatest. Here four units of output yield the greatest difference, TR − TC, namely, $240 − $200 = $40. The shaded areas indicate the range of positive profit (two to five units), while vertical distances measure the amounts of profit.

then to $150, and so on. Correspondingly, total revenue appears in column (3) of Table 26.2 and in the arched *TR* curve of Figure 26.2.

Total profit, the difference between total revenue and total cost $(TR - TC)$, fills column (5) of Table 26.2. $TR - TC$ is positive for units 2 through 5, a range of outputs shown by the shaded areas of Figure 26.2. Total profit rises to a peak of $40 when 4 units are produced and sold, so 4 units maximize total profit. The price associated with 4 units is $60. Total revenue (TR) is $240, while total cost (TC) is $200. Their difference, $240 − $200, yields the maximum $40 total profit.

> Total profit is maximized by achieving the greatest positive difference between total revenue and total cost $(TR - TC)$.

If total cost contains a normal profit for the opportunity cost of capital, then the total profit here is actually *economic* profit. The $40 is the amount by which the accounting profit exceeds the normal profit, which if earned would be just enough to keep capital devoted to this enterprise.

B
Short-Run Dollars Per Unit View

Converting total dollars into dollars per unit offers a different view of the same objective, maximizing total profit. One advantage of the per unit view is its explicit depiction of *price*. Since price and quantity are chained together by the monopolist's demand curve, profit maximizing is not simply an exercise in selecting the proper quantity. It is an exercise in selecting the most profitable *price– quantity combination*, and price looms most starkly in the dollars per unit view.

The principle for maximizing total profit in the per unit view hinges on two-question logic as applied by the firm. And marginal revenue (MR) and marginal cost (MC) furnish the two questions to be compared. For the example at hand, MR and MC appear in columns (6) and (7) of Table 26.2. When plotted, they form the main arteries of Figure 26.3.

> *Question 1: What is it worth* to produce an added unit?

> *Answer: The marginal revenue:* the added revenue each unit brings in: $90 for the first unit, $70 for the second, and so on.

> *Question 2: What does it cost* to get the added revenue?

> *Answer: The marginal cost:* the added cost incurred to produce each unit: $35 for the first unit, $15 for the second, and so on.

Comparing the two answers, we find for units 1 through 4 that additional units are worth *more* in added revenue than what must be given up in added cost. The total dollar profit therefore rises until it reaches a maximum at 4 units. Thereafter, two-question logic says "no" to any added production. The added worth of still more units (MR) drops below the added cost (MC), so there would be only diminished profit. The price charged to sell 4 units is $60, as read off the demand curve directly above 4 units in Figure 26.3.

> Viewing matters in terms of dollars per unit, the firm maximizes total profits by expanding output as long as MR is greater than or equal to MC. In brief, $MR = MC$. The price corresponding to that output is given by the firm's demand curve.

The total profit resulting from this strategy is found to be equal to the shaded area of Figure 26.3. Profit *per unit, on average*, at 4 units is the difference between average revenue $(P, $60)$ and average total cost $(ATC, $50)$, that is, $60 − $50 = $10. Multiplying this $10 average profit per unit by the total number of units, 4, reckons total profit at $40 ($10 × 4 = $40). Moreover, this total profit may once again be more accurately described as total *economic* profit, assuming that the costs include a normal profit.

All of the foregoing may seem very much like the short-run profit-maximizing behavior of perfectly competitive firms. And indeed it is. The two-question logic is the same. The $MR = MC$ rule is the same. And the calculation of total profit from average profit per unit is the same, namely, $(P - ATC) \times Q$ = total profit. Where, then, does the key difference between monopoly and perfect competition lie? It lies in the downward-sloping market-wide demand curve that market structure bestows

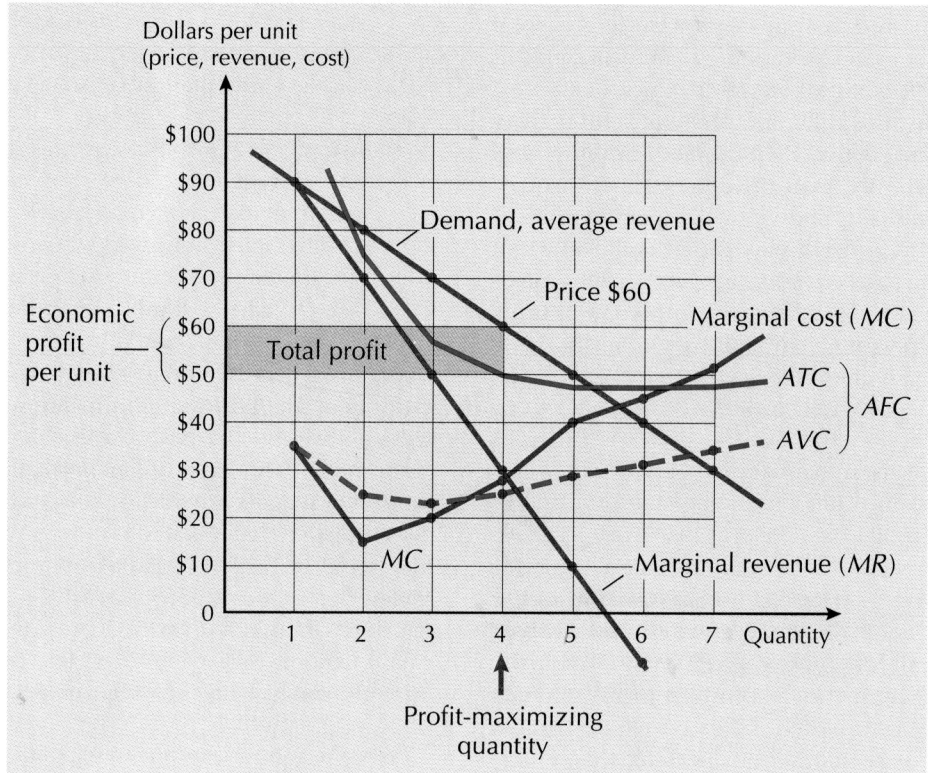

FIGURE 26.3   Short-Run Dollars Per Unit View of Monopoly Profit Maximization

To maximize total profit in the dollars per unit view, the monopolist will lower the price and expand output as long as marginal revenue (MR) is greater than or equal to marginal cost (MC). In this case, the fourth unit is the last for which MR > MC. The price corresponding to that output is given by the demand curve: $60. Profit per unit, on average, is price (average revenue) minus average total cost (ATC), i.e., $60 − $50 = $10. Multiplying average profit per unit, $10, by the number of units, four yields a total dollar profit of $40 ($10 × 4 = $40).

on the monopolist. With this demand, *marginal revenue falls below price*, which is quite a contrast to the situation of the perfectly competitive firm, for which price *equals* marginal revenue. Given that each firm maximizes its total profit by following the rule *MR = MC*, the implication is that *P* lies *above MC* for the monopolist, while *P* matches *MC* for the perfectly competitive firm. In sum:

Furthermore, it may now be seen that, unlike the perfectly competitive firm or market, the monopolist has no clearly defined supply curve. A supply curve relates the quantity supplied by sellers to the price offered. In perfect competition we saw that individual firm and marketwide supplies were reflected in marginal cost. However, this is not true of monopoly.

Market Type	Profit Maximization	Price Relative to Cost
Perfect comp.	MR = MC	P = MC
Monopoly	MR = MC	P > MC

C
Long-Run Dollars Per Unit View

Moving to the long-run context, we find another striking difference between monopoly and perfect competition. Figures 26.2 and 26.3 show the monopolist earning substantial *excess* or *economic* profit. Such a rich profit could not last in the long run under perfect competition because new entrants would be attracted, new entrants who would expand output, trim the price, and eventually compete away the economic profit. In contrast, *the economic profit of pure monopoly can persist in the long run because entry is blocked.* Economic profit would be just as attractive to newcomers here. But barriers prevent this entry into competition with the monopolist. (Or, if competitors could enter the market, they would suffer postentry losses.)

Depiction of pure monopoly in the long run is therefore rather easy. Figure 26.4 gives two examples. Part (a) depicts a monopoly earning an economic profit in the long run. Producing output Q_0 brings *MR* and *MC* into equality, maximizing the total dollar profit. Price and average revenue are P_0, while average cost per unit is C_0, so total dollar economic profit is $(P_0 - C_0) \times Q_0$. Note that in the long run, as in the short run, the monopolist does *not* raise the price indefinitely or charge the highest price it could possibly get despite its considerable power over the price. If it did raise the price flagrantly, sales would eventually disappear and not even normal profits could be captured. (In the

long run, all costs are variable, so long-run average costs are shown by *LRAC* in part (a). Still, those are hypothetical planning costs, and the firm's actual operations are always locked into some given short-run configuration. Hence, the ATC is the short-run average total cost.)

Part (b) of Figure 26.4 reveals that considerable power over the price does not necessarily ensure the monopolist an excessive economic profit. Here, in comparison to part (a), demand is weaker and the average total cost of producing the product is higher. (This might be the case for a patent monopoly on plastic shoes, in contrast to a monopoly on shoes in general.) With demand lower and costs higher, the profit-maximizing output of Q_1 gives the monopolist of part (b) no more than a normal profit, as price equals average total cost at that point ($P_1 = ATC$). Such a monopoly would be weak.

> A profit-maximizing monopoly encounters economic limits: (1) It does not charge the highest price it can possibly charge, and (2) it might not earn an economic profit.

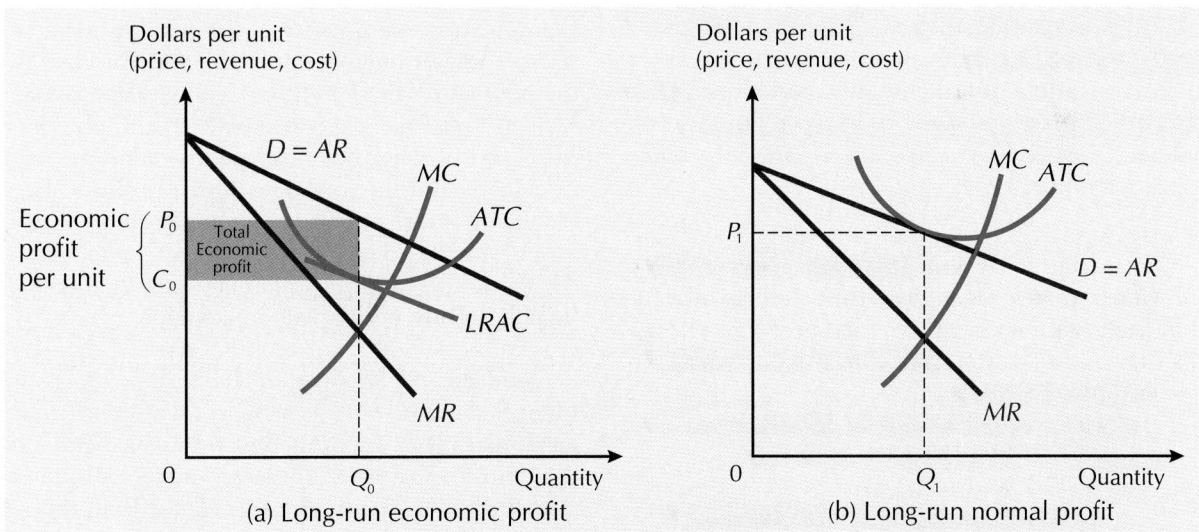

(a) Long-run economic profit

(b) Long-run normal profit

FIGURE 26.4   Long-Run Dollars Per Unit View of Monopoly

Because of barriers to entry, monopoly firms may earn economic profit in the long run. In part (a), the profit-maximizing price and output are P_0 and Q_0, a combination that brings MR into equality with MC. Total economic profit is the shaded area. Though economic profit may be typical of a pure monopoly, real world cases include weak monopolies. In part (b) costs are higher and demand lower than in part (a), with the result that profit maximizing yields no more than the normal profit embodied in ATC.

D
Price Discrimination

To this point, we've assumed that the firm charges a single price. In reality, exceptions abound. Movie theaters commonly charge lower admission prices for children and senior citizens than for others. Electric companies sell electricity at different prices to residential and industrial buyers. An airline ticket will be less costly if purchased a month early than if bought the day before your flight.

Such price differences could never exist under perfect competition. *Some degree of monopoly power must be present for these price differences to arise.* Of course, pure monopoly provides such power. And as the examples suggest, it also covers cases of monopoly power short of pure monopoly because movie theaters and airlines are not monopolies.

> **Price discrimination** occurs when a supplier sells different units of essentially the same commodity to buyers at two or more different prices for reasons not associated with different costs.

Price discrimination occasionally takes the form of quantity discounts. As an individual buys more, the price of added units falls. More commonly, different prices are charged to different buyers. To practice this type of price discrimination, four conditions must hold:

1. The seller must have some monopoly power because it must have some control over the price.
2. The seller must be able to identify different classes of buyers.
3. Different classes of buyers must have different price elasticities of demand.
4. The classes of buyers must be kept separate so that those charged low prices cannot resell to those charged high prices.

The importance of each of these conditions is underscored by Figure 26.5. Let's assume that only one firm is involved. It sells one product, each unit of which costs $3 on average (*AC*) and at the mar-

gin (*MC*). When the average cost per unit is constant over various outputs, something quite possible in the long run, $AC = MC$. This simplification allows us to focus on the key conditions.

1. Monopoly Power The downward-sloping demand curves of Figure 26-5, D_x and D_y, signal that the firm has some monopoly power. Its ability to raise or lower the price allows it to charge some buyers high prices and others low prices despite the identical cost of each unit.

2. Different Classes of Buyers Different classes of buyers are identified in Figure 26.5—Class *X* and Class *Y*. In reality, firms distinguish different classes by a wide assortment of characteristics. Age, income level, and geographic location are among the most common factors. Youngsters and old persons, for example, enjoy discounts from theaters, amusement parks, and municipal bus lines. Fees for membership in the American Economic Association, the leading society of professional economists, rise with a member's income. Some brands of beer are priced at "premium" levels in sections of the country where they have favorable brand images but are priced at "popular" levels elsewhere. Sometimes the characteristics of identification seem baffling. Airlines, for instance, try to sort out business and vacation travelers by distinguishing the length of time between departure and return, weekend stayovers, and timing of ticket purchases. Business people tend to take brief trips during weekdays and purchase their tickets on short notice. Vacation travelers, on the other hand, tend to stay away longer, usually over the weekends, and they plan far enough ahead to be able to buy tickets well in advance.

3. Different Elasticities of Demand Efforts to identify different classes of buyers would be pointless unless they had different price elasticities of demand. In Figure 26.5, Class *Y* buyers display a demand that is relatively more elastic than that of Class *X* buyers. Note, for instance, that the $3 line for *AC* and *MC* cuts the Class *X* demand curve, D_x, in the region of *inelasticity*, below the point where elasticity equals 1, while it cuts the Class *Y* demand curve, D_y, in the region of *elasticity*, above the point where elasticity equals 1. Only with such different elasticities would the seller charge differ-

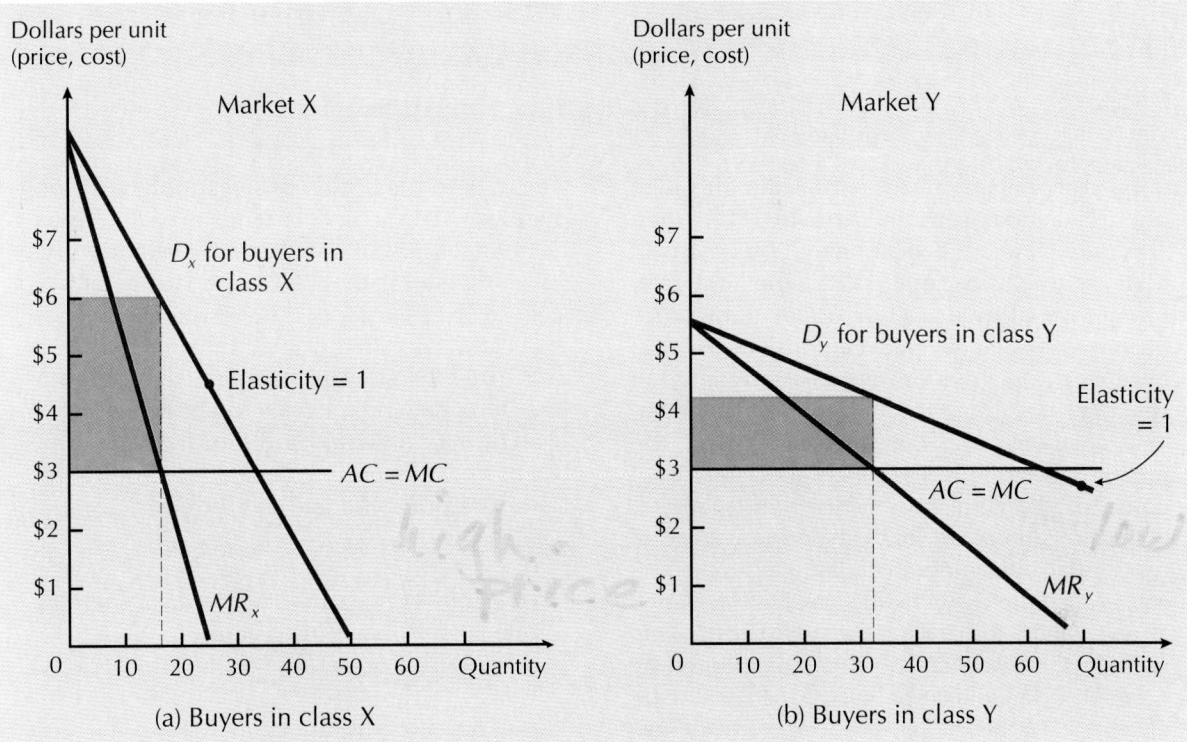

FIGURE 26.5 *Basic Price Discrimination (Two Classes of Buyers for the Same Product)*

The conditions for price discrimination are met here because (1) the downward-sloping demands grant some monopoly power; (2) class x buyers have a lower elasticity of demand than class y buyers; (3) we assume that the classes can be identified by age or geography; and (4) buyers cannot resell. When the firm profit-maximizes for each class, the price is highest to class x because of its relatively inelastic demand. The price is lowest to class y, with buyers having relatively elastic demands. Notice that this is true despite the fact that the cost in each case is $3 per unit.

ent prices. Those prices are then set so that marginal revenue equals marginal cost ($MR = MC$), the profit-maximizing standard of the per unit view. As a consequence, *those with the relatively inelastic demand pay a relatively high price, while those with the relatively elastic demand enjoy a relatively low price.* Class X buyers are thus charged $6.00 in Figure 26.5, while Class Y buyers pay $4.30.

4. Resale Not Possible Given that price discrimination entails a high price to some buyers and a low price to others, those getting the low price might be tempted to resell to those paying the high price. If Class Y buyers in Figure 26.5 could easily resell to Class X buyers, they would be buying at $4.30 and reselling at, say, $5.90, thereby earning a tidy profit of about $1.60 per unit. Such

bootlegging, or arbitrage, must be prevented to preserve price discrimination. If it's not, the various classes of buyers would tend to merge into one mass; those paying the low price would alter their demand to incorporate the demand of the high-priced class, and the high-priced class would look to the low-priced class for supplies at prices lower than those the firm is charging.

If the preceding conditions are met, *why* would a firm want to practice price discrimination? The answer is easy: profit maximization. Charging high to those relatively unresponsive to price, and charging low to those relatively responsive to price, pays off. Multiple prices multiply total dollar profits above what they would be with a single price.

Read Perspective 26B.

PERSPECTIVE 26B
Price Discrimination in Telephones

Price discrimination has permeated the telephone business from the start. In 1877, when Alexander Graham Bell launched the company that eventually became AT&T, the first telephones were leased at a price of $40 per year for business use and $20 per year for personal use. Because the telephones were *leased* rather than sold, reselling from personal customers to business customers was controlled. Moreover, the different prices reflected different elasticities of demand. In general, business demands for telecommunications are less elastic than those of residential customers because telephone service is absolutely vital to businesses (as a glance at any Yellow Pages directory will verify). This difference in elasticities has been exploited by price discrimination for over a century. One exception to this pattern concerns businesses that use telecommunications *so heavily* that they have the option of self-supplying much, if not most, of their services—businesses like the Associated Press, Dow Jones, and the TV net-

works. With the option of self-supply, their demand for AT&T's services tends to be more elastic than otherwise. Moreover, Western Union has competed with AT&T to provide some services to firms like these. The results can be seen in AT&T's so-called Telpak rates of the 1960s and 1970s. These were rates on leased, private-line, long-distance service such as would be used by a TV network. And the larger the number of lines leased in private-line bundles, the lower the price charged the buyer:

Telpak A, 51 percent discount for 12 lines
Telpak B, 64 percent discount for 24 lines
Telpak C, 77 percent discount for 60 lines
Telpak D, 85 percent discount for 240 lines.

These massive discounts to the very largest business customers could not be justified by cost differences, but they kept those customers from building their own systems or turning to Western Union.

■ *CHECK YOUR BEARINGS*

Pure monopoly gives a firm sole control of a market without worry about competition from close substitutes or potential entry. The firm's demand then coincides with marketwide demand, so the (unregulated) firm is free to set the price while barring entry. Structural conditions that are less extreme bestow monopoly power, which is a lesser ability to influence the price and deter entry. The upshot is that, in these situations, total revenue arches and marginal revenue falls below the price. In the total dollars view, total profit maximizing requires the highest positive value for $TR - TC$. In the dollars per unit view, the simple rule is $MR = MC$. With MR below P, this implies that $P > MC$ for the monopolist, and economic profits easily ensue (though not necessarily). These economic profits can persist in the long run because of

entry barriers. Monopoly also provides one of the key conditions for price discrimination—price differences for the same product from the same firm unrelated to cost variations. The conditions are (1) some monopoly power, (2) identification of different buyer classes, (3) differing demand elasticities for those classes, and (4) an absence of reselling.

III
Monopoly Performance

In ancient Greece, Aristotle complained of monopoly in the iron trade. Countless other great thinkers have also attacked monopoly. The structure and conduct of monopoly account for much of this disapproval. Monopoly centralizes power. It limits a buyer's freedom of choice. It typically raises the price well above the cost, which seems unfair.

Moving beyond structure and conduct to consideration of performance brings us again to the basic questions of What?, How?, Who?, and What's new? And here also monopoly may be criticized, especially when compared to perfect competition. Still, certain aspects of monopoly performance deserve praise, and we need to review the good as well as the bad.

A

What?

As defined previously, allocation efficiency is the ideal answer to the question of what ought to be produced and in what amounts. With allocation efficiency, scarce resources are allocated so that outputs are *just right*. In terms of total dollars, this maximizes the total net benefit society gets from each good or service. In terms of dollars per unit, this equates marginal social benefit *(MSB)* with marginal social cost *(MSC)*.

Figure 26.6, a dollars per unit view, contrasts the allocation efficiency of perfect competition in part (a) with the allocation *inefficiency* of pure monopoly in part (b). Marketwide demand, *D,* is the same in both cases, and this demand reflects marginal social benefit *(MSB)*. Note that with monopoly this demand is also the firm's demand. As regards costs, constant unit costs are assumed for simplicity. A single horizontal line represents both average cost *(AC)* and marginal cost *(MC)*. Absent external costs such as pollution, this marginal cost of production also reflects marginal social costs *(MSC)*. These constant-unit costs simplify matters by ruling out scarcity rents.

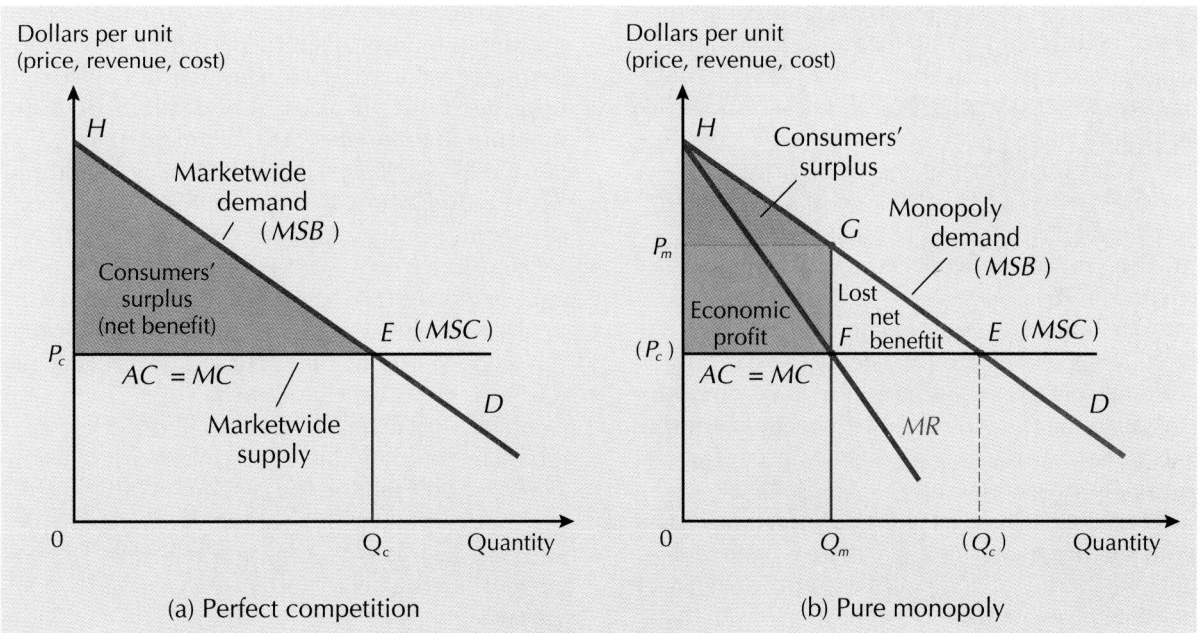

FIGURE 26.6 *Allocation Inefficiency Under Monopoly*

In answering the question "What?", perfect competition presents an amount that is just right, OQ$_c$ in part (a). This equates marginal social benefit and marginal social cost (MSB = MSC) at point E. In a total dollars view, this maximizes the total net benefit, which with constant cost is all consumers' surplus, namely, the shaded area HEP$_c$. The pure monopoly in part (b) prices higher at P$_m$ and produces less at Q$_m$ in the course of maximizing its profits, shaded area P$_m$GFP$_c$. Marginal social benefit at G is then well above marginal social cost by an amount GF (MSB > MSC). This signals that Q$_m$ is too little, and it is. Society's total net benefit is then reduced to area HGFP$_c$, which divides between producer and consumer members of society. The lost net benefit is therefore area GEF.

The two settings are thus the same. The *MSB* and *MSC* values in parts (a) and (b) are identical. The difference lies in the sharply contrasting market structures. What is produced under perfect competition? The amount OQ_c. What is produced under pure monopoly? The lesser amount, OQ_m. Correspondingly, the perfect competitive price, P_c, is well below the pure monopolist's price, P_m.

> The quantity produced under pure monopoly is lower than the perfectly competitive quantity. The monopoly price is higher than the competitive price (all else equal).

In Figure 26.6(a), perfectly competitive price and quantity, P_c and Q_c, are determined by the intersection of marketwide demand and supply at point *E*. Demand reflects the values people place on the good, or marginal social benefit *(MSB)*. Supply under perfect competition is grounded on marginal cost, which here matches marginal social cost *(MSC)*. Hence, when demand intersects supply at point *E* in part (a), marginal social benefit also equals marginal social cost *(MSB = MSC)*. This signals allocation efficiency in the dollars per unit view. Society's two-question logic confirms this. "What's it worth at the margin?" *(MSB)* exceeds "What must be given up at the margin?" *(MSC)* until point *E* is reached at output Q_c.

Expressed in total dollars, total net benefit is maximized by efficiency. The *areas* of Figure 26.6(a) tell the story. Total *net* benefit, area HEP_c, is the difference between total benefit, area HEQ_cO, and total cost, area P_cEQ_cO. In this case, given the constant unit cost, society's net benefit is entirely consumers' surplus, there being no producers' surplus from scarcity rents.

In Figure 26.6(b), pure monopoly maximizes the profit by producing OQ_m, which is clearly less than the perfectly competitive output, OQ_c and therefore also less than the allocation ideal. Q_m is the monopolist's profit-maximizing output because it equates marginal revenue *(MR)* and marginal cost *(MC)* at point *F*. Price is vertical distance OP_m or Q_mG, and total dollar economic profit emerges as the colored area P_mGFP_c.

The fact that Q_m is too little, an inefficient result, may be revealed by two routes. The dollars per unit route reveals that marginal social benefit *(MSB)* at point *G* exceeds marginal social cost *(MSC)* at point *F*, so *MSB > MSC. This is a direct*

consequence of the fact that, under monopoly, P > MR. The total dollars route reveals the total dollar loss to society. Society's total net benefit under monopoly is the combined shaded areas of part (b). This is the difference between society's total benefit (area HGQ_mO) and society's total cost (area P_cFQ_mO). A portion goes to consumers in the form of consumers' surplus (HGP_m, recalling that P_m is now the price under monopoly), while a portion goes to the monopolist in the form of economic profit (P_mGFP_c). This combined total net benefit, $HGFP_c$, is *less* than the total net benefit under competition, HEP_c, by an amount depicted in triangle *GEF*. Hence area GEF *represents society's lost total net benefit due to monopoly misallocation.*

Triangle GEF is *society's* loss, but consumers bear the brunt of it. When the monopolist raises the price above the competitive price P_c to P_m, consumers' surplus is reduced from HEP_c to HGP_m. Part of this lost consumers' surplus, P_mGFP_c, is captured by the monopoly in the form of economic profit, thereby becoming producers' surplus or monopoly rent. This may be considered a *transfer* from the pockets of consumers to the pocket of the monopoly. A second portion of lost consumers' surplus, triangle *GEF*, is *not* captured by the monopoly. It is therefore lost by both consumers and producers, both members of society. Imagine, most simply, that a school-yard bully grabs a two-scoop ice cream cone away from a little girl who has taken a few bites. The half-eaten top scoop plops to the dirty ground during the tussle. In the end, the girl gets half of the top scoop (eaten before the heist), the bully gets a one-scoop ice cream cone, and half of the top scoop is lost by society when it falls on the ground. In other words, the efficiency loss represented by triangle *GEF* is a *real* loss, just as it would be a real loss if floods wiped out a fourth of our cotton crop each year.

> When monopoly produces less than the ideal indicated by *MSB = MSC*, allocation inefficiency reduces society's net benefit.

B
How?

How does monopoly produce goods and services? Is technical efficiency achieved? Are goods produced at the lowest possible cost? Our answers contain both bad news and good news.

The *bad news* is that, shielded from the rigors of competition, a monopoly could very well have *higher costs* than would prevail under competition. The absence of competition permits a monopoly to pursue the easy life. Rather than scratch and scrape for every possible penny of cost savings, the monopolist might succumb to the temptations of luxury offices, excessive executive jets, slovenliness, disorder, delay, ineptitude, inertia, and related technical inefficiencies. In economic jargon, this is called *X-inefficiency.*

When costs rise because of slackness, mismanagement, needless spending, or other such waste, the result is **X-inefficiency.**

Theoretically, a profit-maximizing firm should seek to minimize the cost per unit in the long run. Realistically, however, since a monopoly need not maximize its profit, it need not minimize its cost. And there is no competition to *force* the monopolist to minimize its cost. The experience of Xerox illustrates this point. Xerox launched a cost-cutting drive for the *first time in its history* in 1975, after its monopoly over the copy machine market during the 1960s and early 1970s began to erode. Xerox's chairman admitted that his company was suffering from "sloppy" internal practices and corporate "fat" that had developed during the easy days of monopoly. Responding to new competitive pressures, the company fired 8,000 employees, deferred construction of a lush new headquarters, sharpened its inventory control, and scrapped plans for a new plant—all while sales grew.[2]

The *good news* is that monopoly fosters rather than retards technical efficiency when economies of scale loom large enough to justify natural *monopoly.* The monopoly in Figure 26.7(a) is a natural monopoly because the long-run average cost, $LRAC_m$, falls over nearly the entire range of demand (D). Recall that long-run average cost is the hypothetical depiction of what minimum cost per unit would be for various possible sizes of plants (or firms). The profit-maximizing monopolist of part (a) would actually build facilities that, once built, would generate short-run average total costs indicated by curve ATC_m. With the associated mar-

ginal cost depicted by MC, and with marginal revenue of MR, the profit-maximizing output and price are Q_m and P_m, respectively. Because long-run average cost declines over such a vast range relative to demand, there is no room in the industry for more than this one firm.

Let's verify this last statement in Figure 26.7(b). Let's imagine that the output of the monopoly, Q_m, is produced by two *smaller* firms, each roughly half the size of the monopolist in part (a), but each operating under the same *LRAC* conditions as the monopolist. Part (b) shows the consequences for cost per unit. The cost per unit nearly doubles from C_m up to C_o. The cost per unit *must* rise because this reduction in scale causes the average total cost to slide up the long-run average cost curve, *LRAC*, from ATC_m at the monopolist's large scale to ATC_1 for firm 1 in part (b). The addition of a second firm is shown by ATC_2 in part (b). Assuming that these two firms produce at the low point of their *ATC* curves, their combined output will match the monopolist's output of Q_m. However, this occurs at a much higher cost per unit— C_o.

We thus have a mixed answer to the question How?. Monopoly may raise the cost because of X-inefficiency. On the other hand, monopoly may lower the cost if economies of scale are large relative to demand.

C
Who?

Many of America's richest families amassed their fortunes from firms earning hefty economic profits because of monopoly power. Such was the case for the Rockefellers (Standard Oil Company of New Jersey, now Exxon), the Dukes (American Tobacco Company), and the Carnegies (United States Steel Corporation). It appears, then, that monopoly causes the distribution of income to become *less equal* than it would be under competition.

Depending on one's value judgments, this may be good or bad. In general, however, our society seems to favor greater equality over greater inequality, so this enriching aspect of monopoly performance is often condemned.

Displeasure with the treasure of monopoly goes beyond the gains of relatively wealthy owners at the expense of relatively poor consumers. It also stems from the *nature* of those gains. People can

[2]*Business Week*, April 5, 1976, pp. 60–66.

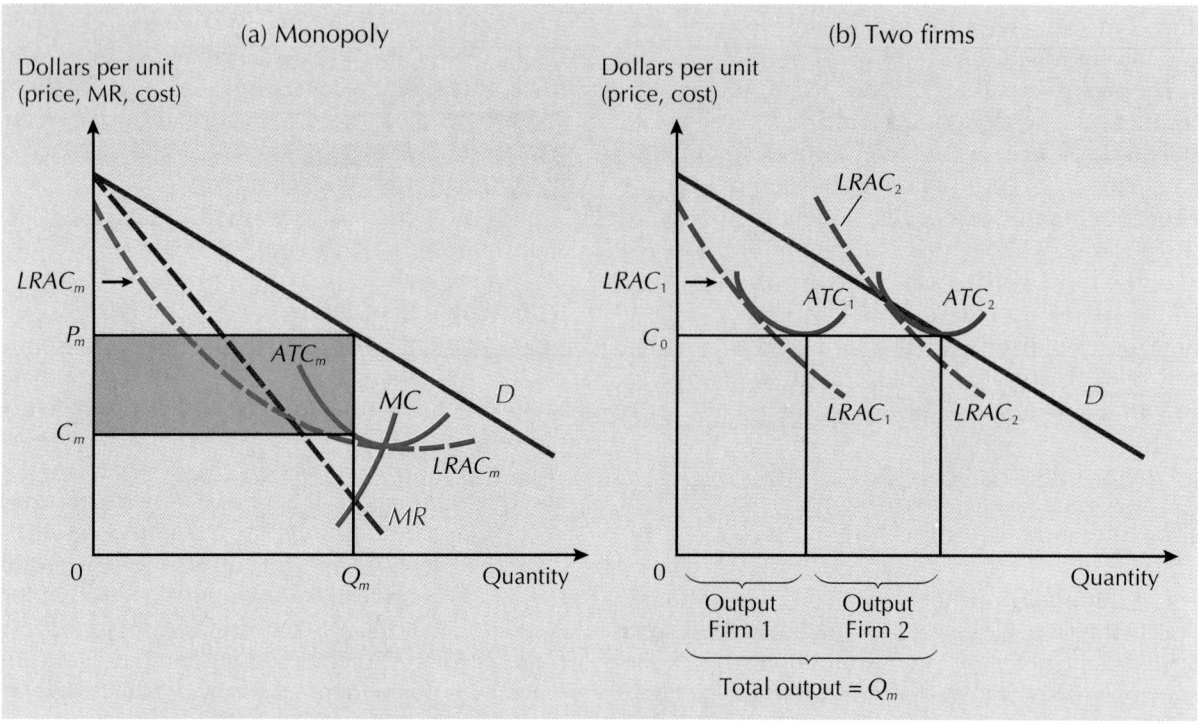

FIGURE 26.7   *Natural Monopoly and Technical Efficiency*

*If the long-run average cost falls throughout most or all of the range of marketwide demand,
as LRAC_m falls below D in part (a) above, natural monopoly is the result. Monopoly is then
more efficient technically than alternative market structures. It can produce a given output,
such as Q_m, with fewer inputs than any two or more firms. Part (b) shows the consequences
of having two firms produce output Q_m. The cost per unit rises from C_m under monopoly to
C_0. This is because the smaller scales of the two firms lift the average cost per unit up with
ATC_1 and ATC_2.*

become rich under perfect competition if they garner scarcity rents. Land owners and talented entertainers, for instance, earn scarcity rents. But,
given competition, these scarcity rents do not
stem from long-run economic profits, such as are
earned by monopoly. The persistent economic
profits of monopoly may be called *monopoly
rents.*

Monopoly rent is another name for the economic profit due to monopoly power. It is a
form of producers' surplus, but it differs from
producers' surplus that may arise under perfect competition, which is scarcity rent.

D
What's New?

Technological change seems to thrive most vigorously when firms have a blend of financial *ability*
and competitive *incentive.* Perfectly competitive
firms are weak in financial ability but strong in
competitive incentive. As a result, perfect competition is less than perfect in this regard. Pure
monopoly displays exactly opposite endowments.
It tends to be long on financial ability but short on
competitive incentive. As a consequence, the performance of monopoly is at best mixed in terms of
progressiveness.

Read Perspective 26C.

PERSPECTIVE 26C
AT&T and Technological Change

Before its breakup, AT&T was known worldwide for invention and innovation. Its Bell Laboratories in New Jersey became a preeminent research institution, especially in basic research. Over the years, scientists working there won seven Nobel Prizes and thousands of key patents in electronics, lasers, and fiber optics. On the other hand, AT&T also developed a reputation for being rather slow and stodgy when it came to applying its scientific prowess to the development of new equipment. It stayed with the basic black dial-up telephone, for instance, long after new technologies permitted improvements. Its $200 million annual budget for fundamental scientific research did not prevent AT&T from falling substantially behind Rolm, Northern Telecom, and several other companies in the production of advanced private branch exchange (PBX) equipment. (These PBXs link many phones, such as those in large offices and hotels.) Changes in regulation during the 1970s injected competition into telecommunications technology even before the breakup of AT&T, and the breakup spurred still more competition. What was competition's impact on Bell Labs? "There is [now] a sense of urgency: The time scale of introduction and production is shorter than it was in the past."[3] And the impact on telecommunications in general? "New equipment and gadgetry have proliferated—telephones with computerized memories and computers with telephones, not to mention an enormous variety of conventional telephones."[4] Competition, though not perfect competition, thus generally seems better than monopoly in this case. Monopoly performed well, but added competition has made the industry even better in this respect.

[3]*Business Week*, December 3, 1984, p. 121.

[4]*Wall Street Journal*, December 17, 1984, p. 1.

IV
Public Utility Regulation

A
Introduction

A century ago, the U.S. Congress enacted two major pieces of legislation—the Interstate Commerce Commission Act of 1887 and the Sherman Act of 1890. They embodied America's two main policy approaches to the control of monopoly: public utility regulation and antitrust. A third option—public ownership and operation of monopolies—has been tried to some extent in the United States, but it is much more popular abroad than here.

Public utility regulation *is an industrial halfway house. Private firms own and operate enterprises, while state and federal governments police their conduct and performance, telling firms what prices they may charge, what services they may offer, what profits they may earn, and what they may do in other respects.* At the federal level, such regulation started with the Interstate Commerce Commission Act.

Antitrust has many facets, but as it applies most directly to monopolies, it forces their breakup by dissolution or divestiture. Such restructuring increases the number of sellers in a market or lowers entry barriers. It attacks monopoly at its roots. This was the thrust of Section 2 of the Sherman Act, which outlawed monopolization.

In theory, each policy approach has its place. *Public utility regulation* applies most appropriately to *natural monopoly*. Such regulation accepts, even encourages, the existence of monopoly, while presumably limiting the evils and abuses of conduct and performance that monopoly power might bestow. In theory, then, public utility regulation allows society to realize the technical efficiencies of natural monopolies while checking allocation inefficiencies and income inequities, and perhaps even encouraging technical progress. In practice, the chief aim of public utility regulation is legally specified to be *prices and profits that are just and reasonable,* an aim that need not yield efficiency or equity. Electricity, local telephone service, local natural gas, and other natural monopolies are now the main subjects of such regulation.

By contrast, antitrust dissolutions would be foolish if applied to natural monopolies because such dissolutions couldn't last or would raise production costs. Antitrust, in other words, applies most appropriately to *artificial monopoly,* such as that which might derive from needlessly centralized control of scarce inputs or the acquisition of patents.

Public utility regulation, the topic of the present section, divides into two main types: overall **price level regulation** and **price structure regulation.**[5] The government bodies responsible for devising and enforcing these regulations are federal or state commissions whose members, numbering from 3 to 11, are typically appointed by the president (for federal commissions) or by the governor (for state commissions, although several states elect their commissioners). Those at the federal level, like the Interstate Commerce Commission (ICC) and Federal Communications Commission (FCC), typically specialize in the interstate commerce of certain industries, such as railroading or telecommunications. In contrast, those at the state level, like California's Public Utilities Commission and New York's Public Service Commission, have narrower geographic jurisdictions limited to *intra*state commerce but broader authority to regulate electricity, gas, and telephone prices and profits.

B
Price Level Regulation

Regulation of electric utilities started in New York in 1907 after a government study discovered that

the New York Gas and Electric Light Company sold current to residential consumers at an average price of 8.04 cents per kilowatt-hour, with some paying as much as 15 cents, while the cost of production was only 3.66 cents.[6] Unregulated price levels were too high. Hence the basic idea of price level regulation is to limit overall price levels below what they would be otherwise, while at the same time allowing the firm sufficient revenues to pay its "full" costs plus a "fair" return on the "fair" value of its capital. Stated differently, *the main objective is to strike a reasonable balance between the interests of consumers* (who should not be injured by monopoly exploitation) *and the interests of the utility investors and operators* (who should not be penalized by overzealous commissions). As a Connecticut commissioner once put it, "We're the buffer between the company and the consumer."[7]

Figure 26.8 conveys the consequences. The top diagram is a dollars per unit view. The bottom diagram, with an identical quantity axis, is the total dollars view. The *un*regulated monopoly would wind up at points U and U'. Free to maximize its profit, the unregulated monopoly would set the price at P_u and produce an output of Q_u. This combination yields a total dollar economic profit depicted by the shaded area in the top diagram and by the vertical distance $U'K$ in the bottom diagram.

Imposing price level regulation shifts the monopoly to solutions R and R'. In the dollars per unit view, the price is pressed down by regulation from P_u to P_r, where it matches the long-run average cost (*LRAC*), including a fair or normal profit. Correspondingly, output expands with the added demand to become Q_r. In the total dollars view, this price–output combination lands the firm at R', where total revenue (*TR*) equals total cost (*TC*), including a fair or normal profit.

Note that if the regulators push the price level still *lower* to P_e, the result would be a price matching the long-run marginal cost (*LRMC*). However, at E, price P_e is below average cost (*LRAC*), so the firm would then be suffering losses. The losses are most clearly seen in the total dollars view of the

---

[5] For details see, e.g., Alfred E. Kahn, *The Economics of Regulation,* Vols. I and II (New York: Wiley, 1971); K.M. Howe and E.F. Rasmussen, *Public Utility Economics and Finance* (Englewood Cliffs, N.J.: Prentice-Hall, 1982); and S.V. Berg, *Innovative Electric Rates* (Lexington, Mass.: Lexington Books, 1983).

[6] D. Anderson, "State Regulation of Electric Utilities," in J.Q. Wilson (ed.), *The Politics of Regulation* (New York: Basic Books, 1980), p. 14.

[7] *Wall Street Journal,* May 23, 1978, p. 40.

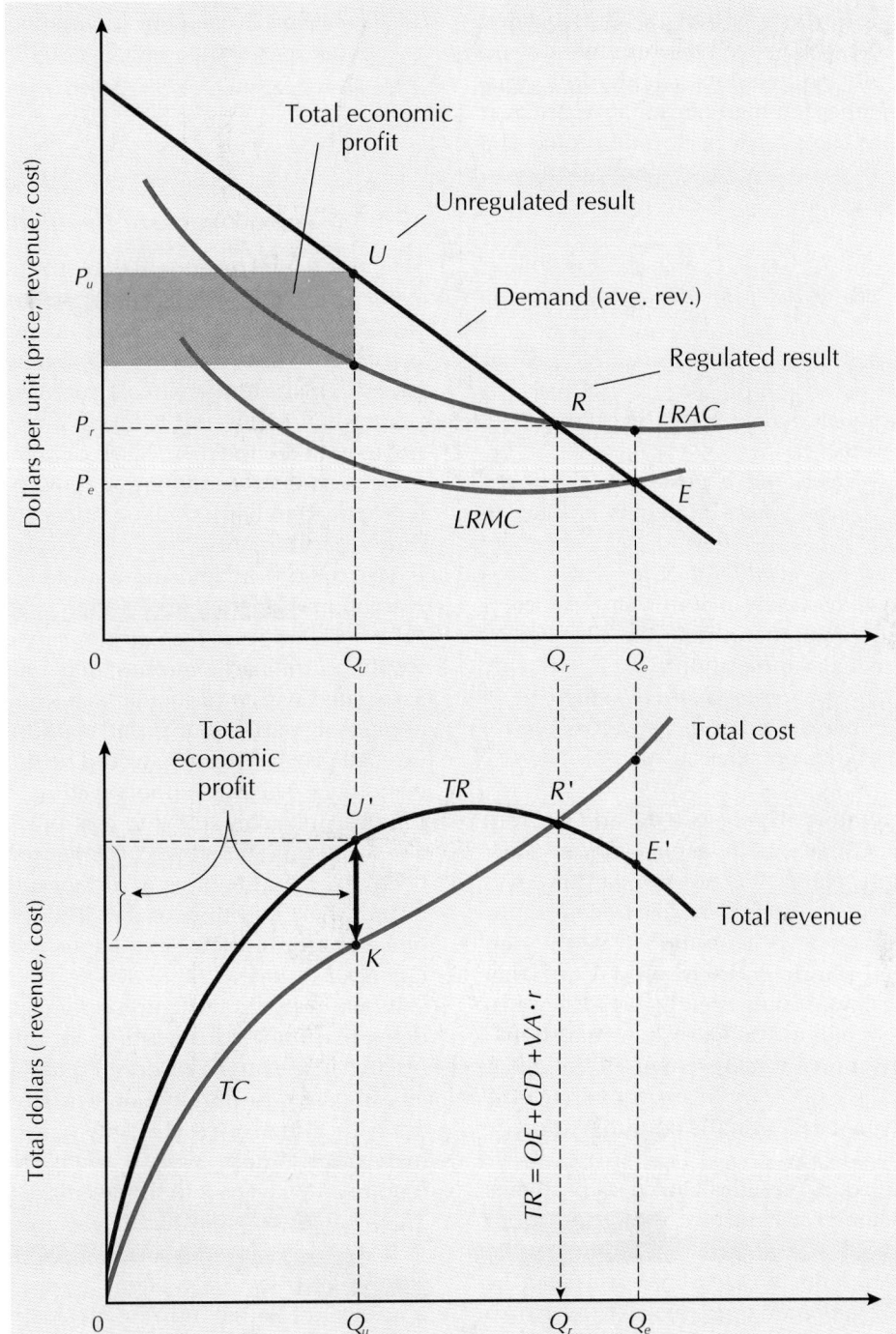

FIGURE 26.8   Price Level Regulation of Natural Monopoly

The unregulated monopolist would be at points U and U', charging a price level of P_u and producing quantity Q_u. Economic profit would be the result. Regulating to allow total revenues to equal operating expenses (OE), current depreciation (CD), plus a "fair" return on the "fair" value of the assets (VA • r) would yield solutions R and R', where the price level is P_r. and output is Q_r. If the price level were pushed still lower to P_e, the result might yield allocation efficiency because price would then equal marginal cost (LRMC). However, the firm would lose money as TR < TC.

bottom diagram, where output Q_e is associated with a total cost well above total revenue at E'.

How do utility commissions decide on a price level that is neither too high nor too low, one just high enough to allow a fair or normal profit? The reckoning is done in a total dollars context. In essence, commissions solve for TR in the following equation:

$$TR = OE + CD + VA \cdot r$$

where

TR is the annual *total revenue* the utility will be allowed.

OE is yearly *operating expenses*, including fuel costs, labor wages, materials, and taxes.

CD is *current depreciation* for the year.

VA is *value of the assets*, mainly plant, cables, conduits, equipment, and the like (less accumulated depreciation).

r is the "fair" percentage *rate of return*, including interest on bonds as well as dividend earnings on stocks.

Note that operating expenses, *OE*, and current depreciation, *CD*, are both *annual dollar flows*. Capital or asset value, *VA*, is not a dollar flow. It is the asset value on a certain date, like December 31, 1987. However, once *VA* is multiplied by the percentage rate of return, *r*, the result, $VA \cdot r$, is an annual dollar flow. Adding overall cost and return elements thus yields a total yearly flow that should be covered by annual total revenue, *TR*. In Figure 26.8, TR and $OE + CD + VA \cdot r$ are both shown by the vertical distance $R'Q_r$ in the bottom part of the figure.

This simple equation hides countless problems that commissions must resolve. Many are judgment calls, so value judgments have an influence. For example, should the costs of advertising be allowed as an operating expense? How much should the company president be paid? Should the $5 billion value of a nuclear power plant that is shut down because of a partial meltdown be allowed in the value of assets, *VA*? Is the proper rate of return, *r*, 10 percent or 15 percent or something else? (In 1983, allowed rates of return on local telephone service ranged from 7.09 percent

in Hawaii to 15.0 percent in Virginia.)

C
Price Structure Regulation

Selecting a total revenue *(TR)* is only the beginning. What about price discrimination? What specific prices should be permitted, recognizing that prices can vary with who buys, how much, and when? This issue of price structure radiates importantly. Indeed, the ICC was originally created not to regulate the price levels of railroads, despite their considerable monopoly power at the time, but instead to battle against prices that were "unduly discriminatory."

Two main principles now guide price structure regulation—cost of service and value of service. Prices based on the *cost-of-service* principle would, as the name implies, fully reflect the costs associated with a particular service or product. If applied to perfection, profit markups would not vary; all price/cost ratios would be the same for all customers. Though not followed perfectly for any utilities, approximations to cost-of-service pricing abound. Long-distance telephone calls have long been billed on the basis of distance, duration, day of the week, and time of day. The longer the distance and duration, the larger the costs and charges.

When costs do not guide pricing, elasticities of demand often do, resulting in *value-of-service* pricing. The pattern discovered earlier while discussing price discrimination exists here. Customers with a low price elasticity can be hit with a high price. Those with a high price elasticity require a low price if their patronage is to be held. The label *value of service* derives from the notion that differing elasticities signal differing values to customers. Electricity offers an enlightening example. Residential buyers of electricity have a price elasticity of about 1.0. In contrast, industrial buyers have a much higher price elasticity of around 1.7, partly because industrial buyers have the option of generating their own electricity. The prices paid by each group differ accordingly. In 1982, the average price paid by residential buyers was 6.45 cents per kilowatt-hour. That for industrial buyers was 4.66 cents per kilowatt-hour.[8] Yet these differences are apparently not "unduly disciminatory" in the eyes of regulators.

D

Problems with Regulation

Regulation has received much bad press of late, as suggested most dramatically by a recent trend toward deregulation. Some of the problems are inherent in the many unknowns and imponderables that infect even the most well-intended regulatory effort.

The situation is not helped by the disagreement among economists on many key issues concerning regulation. There is dispute, for instance, over whether regulation lowers electricity price levels significantly. Still, several regulatory problems seem to win wide agreement.

First is the problem of *regulatory lag*. As demand or cost conditions change over time, regulatory commissions respond, but only with delayed reaction. For instance, a utility's request for a price level change may take 18 months to 2 years to decide. During periods of rapid cost inflation, this lag can levy a heavy burden on utilities if substantial cost increases do not promptly show up in compensatory price increases. Delays can force the realized

---

[8]Data on elasticity: L.D. Taylor, "The Demand for Electricity: A Survey," *Bell Journal of Economics* (Spring 1975), pp. 74–110. Prices: *Statistical Abstract of the United States 1984*, p. 586. The costs for industrial buyers are, on the whole, lower than those for residential buyers, but not by the full amount of the rate difference. See, e.g., W. Primeaux, Jr., and R.A. Nelson, "An Examination of Price Discrimination and Internal Subsidization by Electric Utilities," *Southern Economic Journal* (July 1980), pp. 84–99.

profit below the allowed rate of return, making it hard for utilities to raise capital for expansion. On the other hand, regulatory lag may be less serious than many critics claim. Innovative procedures such as the "automatic pass-through" of fuel costs and the use of future "test" years to calculate costs have helped to reduce the lag.

A second and more serious problem has been the *inappropriate application* of public utility regulation. Beginning in the 1930s, for instance, federal regulation spread to cover trucking and airlines, two industries never threatened by natural monopoly. Economies of scale have not been overwhelming in trucking or airlines. Entry has always been fairly easy, especially in trucking. Yet ICC jurisdiction was extended to trucking, and the Civil Aeronautics Board (CAB) was created to control the airlines. The regulations had the effect of limiting competition in what would otherwise be competitive industries. The entry of newcomers was legally restricted. Price rivalry was smothered. Inefficient uses of equipment were condoned. Excessively high worker wages were endorsed.

Prompted by evidence of these problems, and by the urgings of economists, Congress *deregulated* trucking and air travel in the late 1970s and early 1980s. The CAB disbanded in January 1985 (its death ceremony was highlighted by a Marine bugler playing "Taps"). The ICC still exists, with limited control over railroading, but it no longer regulates trucking. The consequences for both trucking and air travel have been what economists predicted during the debate over deregulation, namely, lower prices than otherwise, entry by newcomers, greater technical efficiency, a wider variety of service offerings, and more.

SUMMARY

1. Pure monopoly is an extreme case: a single firm astride a market without any close substitutes or threat of new entry. The firm's demand curve is the down-sloping marketwide demand curve; thus, if left unregulated, the firm can freely set the price while barring entry. Monopoly power, a milder condition, is the ability to influence the price and deter entry. Given such command over demand, the monopolist's total revenue arches, and its marginal revenue falls below its price. Such is structure's impact.

2. As for conduct, profit maximizing requires

that, in the total dollars view, total revenues exceed total costs by the greatest amount (TR − TC). In the dollars per unit view, profit maximizing is achieved by lowering the price and expanding output as long as marginal revenue exceeds marginal cost (until $MR = MC$). With the marginal revenue below the price, this result places the marginal cost below the price $(P > MC)$. Any economic profit can persist in the long run because of entry's absence.

3. If conditions are favorable, still greater profit can be gained by practicing price discrimination. Those conditions are (1) some monopoly power, (2) identifiable buyer classes, (3) elasticity differences, and (4) no reselling.

4. In performance, monopoly gets a mixed review. (1) Allocation inefficiency results when monopoly prices are high and output is curbed. Society's net benefit shrinks as marginal social benefit becomes greater than marginal social cost $(MSB > MSC)$. The monopolist's grab at the consumers' surplus causes some surplus to be lost. (2) Technical efficiency may be less than ideal if X-inefficiency ensues from monopoly. On the other hand, natural monopoly would minimize costs if economies of scale loom large. (3) Economic profit, or monopoly rent, may adversely affect the income distribution. (4) Technological change may occur under monopoly, but it may be less brisk than it would be with some competitive rivalry.

5. Public utility regulation is the main policy approach to natural monopoly in the United States. The price level (profit level) is supposed to be just and reasonable for both buyers and suppliers, so total revenue is set to cover operating expenses, current depreciation, and a fair return on a fair value of the assets. In addition, the utility's price structure is considered to prevent undue price discrimination. Aside from regulatory lag, the biggest problem with public utility regulation is that it has too frequently been applied where it was not warranted. Trucking and air travel are examples of this situation.

Appendix:
Breaking Up AT&T

The splintering of AT&T can be seen most clearly as the separation of two different classes of business: _regulated_—that area of telecommunications where economies of scale foster natural monopoly and therby justify regulation, namely, local telephone service; and _deregulated_—those areas where competition can protect the public interest, namely, long-distance service and telecommunications equipment. An understanding of this division emerges from a brief review of the telecommunications system and AT&T's split.

Equipment and Connections

Four main elements comprise the telecommunications system, as shown in Figure A. (1) _Terminal equipment_ is the most visible part, as it includes the 170 million telephones we use every day. Also included are PBXs, teletypes, and computers. (2) _Local loops_ connect terminals to the rest of the system. (3) In turn, the local loops meet at a local hub known as a _central switch_, where a local call is routed from one local loop to another. (4) Long-distance calls are switched into _long lines_ for transmission to another central switch and further relay. Cables comprised these long lines until the advent of microwave and satellite systems, which now dominate the long-distance field.

Local loops and their associated central switches generate sufficient economies of scale to create a natural monopoly at the local level. Complete connection to two competing local companies would call for two local loops for each customer plus two central switches, with higher multiples for more rivals and higher costs.

Terminal equipment and long lines are quite different. AT&T strongly dominated these markets in decades past, but its monopoly was never _natural_ for terminal equipment and is _no longer natural_ in the case of long lines. Telephones are like other electronic devices—toasters or radios—and AT&T's monopoly over them and other equipment endured merely as a result of AT&T's longstanding policy of not permitting any "foreign attachments" to its service system. Given its ser-

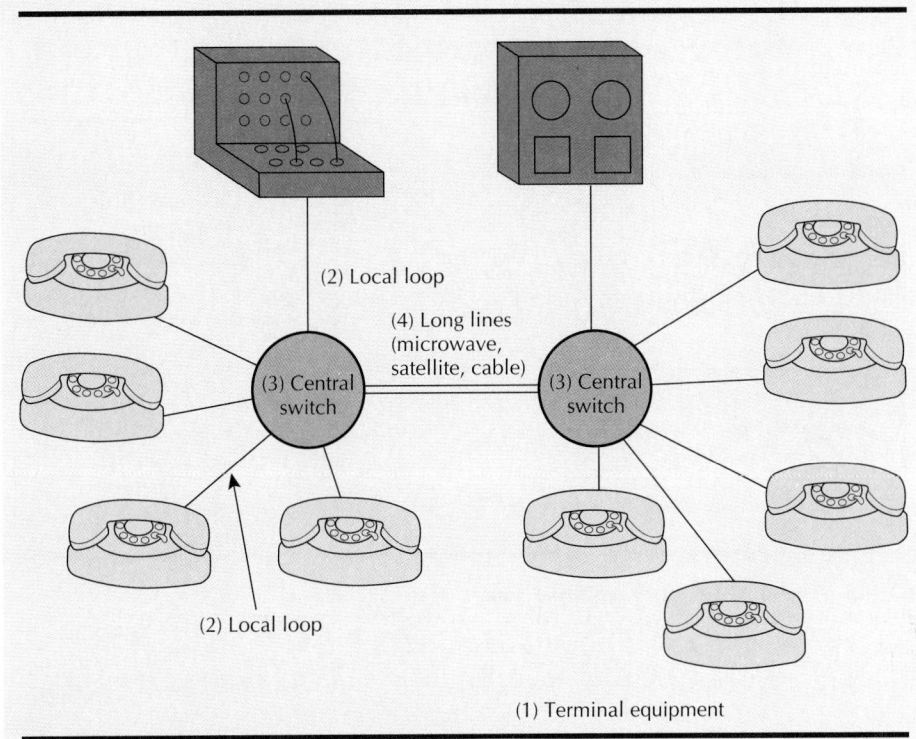

FIGURE A   The Telecommunications Network

vice monopoly, this policy also gave AT&T an equipment monopoly. As regards the long lines, substantial economies of scale prevailed when cables were the long lines. But now, microwave and satellite technologies make natural monopoly obsolete for most long-distance service. There is now room for competitors like MCI and Sprint.

AT&T: Before and After

When the old AT&T died at age 107, it controlled three branches of *national* orientation. As shown in Figure B, these were its (1) Long Lines Division, which provided long-distance service regulated by the FCC; (2) Western Electric, which manufactured all the telephones, switching gear, and other telecommunications equipment used in the AT&T system (including most of AT&T's 827 million miles of copper wire); and (3) Bell Laboratories, its research arm. AT&T also held controlling stock ownership in 22 separate "operating companies," whose main duty was to provide state-regulated *local telephone service* and whose diverse geo-

graphic names divulge that the system resembled a quilted spread, with patches of regional companies varying in size from coast to coast. These operating companies were the ones severed from AT&T by antitrust decree.

The 22 operating companies, collectively worth $117 billion in assets in 1983, were reorganized into seven separate regional companies, as shown in Figure C. These newly independent regional companies now have the local service monopolies that operate under the watchful eyes of state regulators. They can buy equipment from suppliers other than Western Electric. They can even compete with the new AT&T in certain lines of business.

The new AT&T itself has reorganized. Old branches have been renamed (Long Lines is now AT&T Communications). Entirely new branches have been formed, such as AT&T Technology Systems. And the new AT&T operates in markets that may become or already are competitive. Equipment markets illustrate this situation. By 1984 AT&T accounted for only about half of all tele-

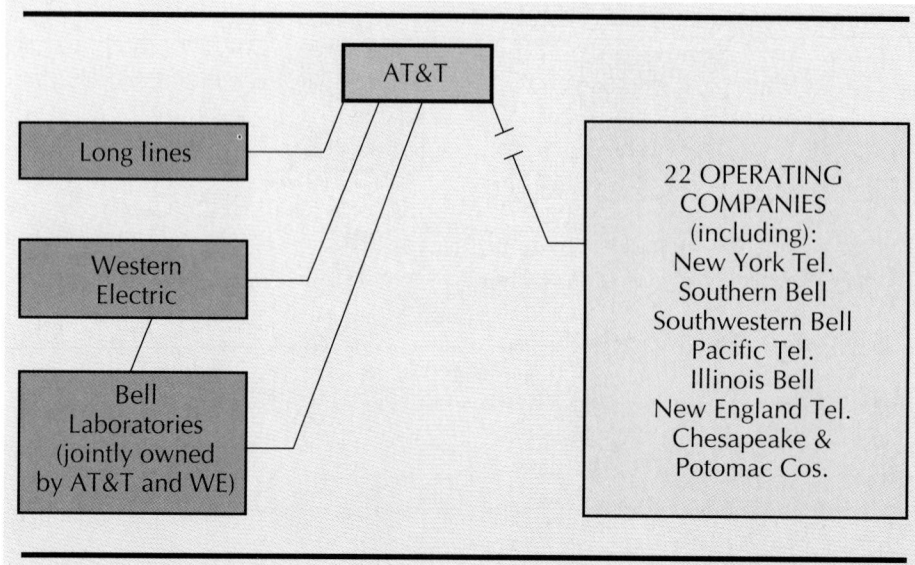

FIGURE B   Old AT&T and the Divestiture

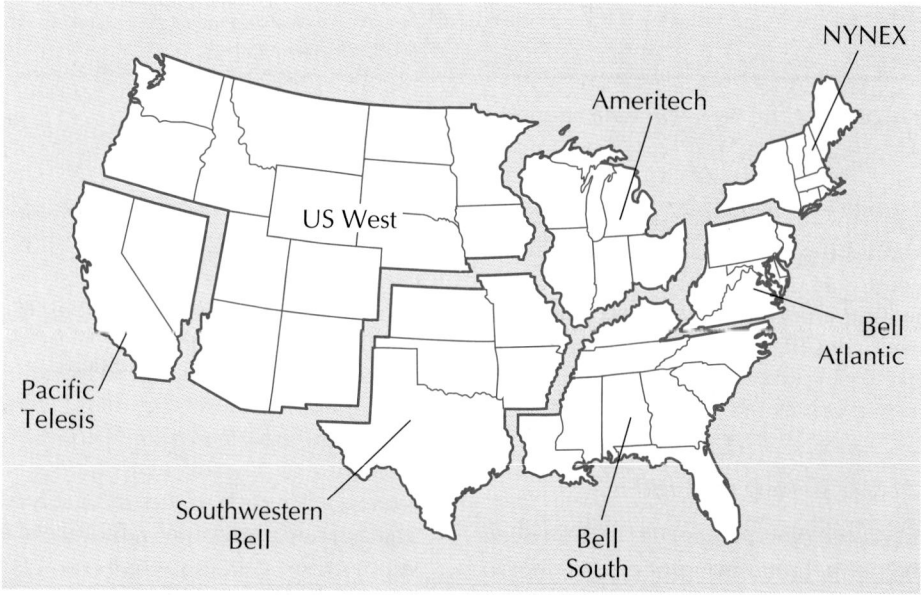

FIGURE C   The Seven Independent Regional Companies Formed from AT&T's Divestiture

phone sales and less than 30 percent of the PBX business. In markets that AT&T is newly entering, it faces even stiffer competition. IBM, for example, rebuffs its forays into the computer field. Although at this writing AT&T's long-distance operations are still subject to some regulation, it is conceivable that before long all of AT&T's activities will be in markets free of public utility regulation.

Economic Consequences

Pinpointing the effects of AT&T's breakup is complicated because regulatory changes were occurring shortly before the divestiture. Still, several observations both pleasant and unpleasant, seem possible.

On the good side, prices for long-distance service have fallen. The new competition of discount companies like MCI has contributed to this decline. Of equal and perhaps greater importance, however, is that long-distance prices in the past were held artificially high by regulation, the excess earnings being used to heavily subsidize local service prices. An estimated 37 cents of every $1 in long-distance revenue went to this subsidy. Severing local service companies from AT&T ended the subsidy. On the bad side, this meant that local phone service prices had to rise substantially once the subsidy disappeared.

A second benefit of the breakup is the faster introduction of new technologies and services mentioned previously. A drawback, however, is that these novel technologies and services are now flying at consumers from all directions. The one-stop service provided in the past had its comforts and conveniences. Consumers may now be somewhat bewildered.

Finally, competition in equipment has lowered equipment prices to both local phone companies and consumers. However, consumers must now pay more for installation and repair service.[9]

[9]For surveys of effects, see _Business Week_, (December 3, 1984), pp. 86–124; _Wall Street Journal_, (December 17, 1984), pp. 1, 22. For background on the breakup, see D.F. Greer, _Business, Government, and Society_ (New York: Macmillian, 1987), pp. 316–338; _Wall Street Journal_, November 17, 1983, pp. 1, 24–27.

KEY TERMS

Pure monopoly
Natural monopoly
Monopoly power
Price discrimination
X-inefficiency

Monopoly rent
Public utility regulation
Price level regulation
Price structure regulation

QUESTIONS AND PROBLEMS

1. Define and describe a "pure monopoly."
2. What causes actual monopolies or markets that approximate pure monopoly?
3. What is a natural monopoly? Give examples.
4. Patents create monopoly power. Should the government stop granting patents? Explain.
5. When does a firm have "monopoly power"? Does a perfectly competitive firm have any monopoly power?
6. Marginal revenue and product price are exactly equal for the perfectly competitive firm. This is not true for the pure monopolist. Why?
7. How does a pure monopolist decide how much to produce? At what price does the monopolist offer that output for sale?
8. How does the decision rule used by the pure monopolist to decide the production level compare with that of the purely competitive firm? How does the pricing decision of the pure monopolist compare with that of the purely competitive firm?
9. Why can a pure monopolist earn an economic profit in the long run while the purely competitive firm cannot?

10. What is price discrimination and why would a firm choose to sell its product at two or more different prices? What four conditions are necessary for price discrimination to be possible?
11. Vacation airline travelers, children under twelve who go to movies, and senior citizens riding municipal buses enjoy lower prices than others buying the same goods or services. What do these diverse groups have in common?
12. Allocative inefficiency results when a good is produced by a pure monopolist. Specifically, too few resources are allocated to the production of the good. Show why graphically.
13. What is X-inefficiency? Why can it happen in pure monopoly?
14. Using the same four criteria identified earlier for evaluating market performance, explain what is "bad" about a pure monopoly. Is pure monopoly ever good?
15. What is the goal of public utility regulation?
16. What were the consequences of the deregulation of trucking and air travel?

From the appendix:

17. AT&T, both before and after its breakup, is best viewed as a firm producing several different goods and services, all involved in telecommunications. The production of some of those goods and services fits the description of natural monopoly. Other areas of AT&T's production cannot (could not) be described as natural monopoly situations. Describe what goods and services AT&T produced before the breakup, under what market conditions those goods and services are produced today, and whether natural monopoly conditions apply (or applied) in each case.

27

Oligopoly and Monopolistic Competition: Price Strategies

Imagine that you manage a firm with $1 billion in sales, 25 percent of the market, and several strong rivals. How does it feel to initiate a hefty price increase when you are uncertain whether your rivals will raise their prices too? Would it feel anything like a combat Marine leading a charge? According to executives of the Du Pont Corporation, the period after announcing a major price increase is "exciting" and "very, very nerve-wracking, tense." Why? "Every time you put out a price that is higher than what competition establishes ... I guarantee you, you will take abuse."[1]

The product involved in these remarks was a gasoline additive—a lead-based antiknock compound—bought by oil refiners like Texaco and Exxon. According to these buyers, there was nothing "exciting" about Du Pont's price increases because those increases were almost always followed by those of Du Pont's rivals—the Ethyl Corporation, PPG, and the Nalco Chemical Company. According to the complaints of the buyers, "There is and never has been price competition in antiknocks."[2]

Welcome to the world of oligopoly. It's the subject of the first half of this chapter. The second half covers monopolistic competition. Most American businesses operate in these markets, so a good understanding of them is crucial. At the same time, these markets are more complex than perfect competition or monopoly. To simplify matters, this chapter focuses mainly on price competition or the *lack* of price competition. (Check the outline.)

To simplify further, we shall now drop consideration of the total dollars view and concentrate solely on the dollars per unit view in both the short and the long run. As we have seen, the total dollars view and the dollars per unit view are just two ways of looking at the same thing. To be sure, total dollars remain important. We shall therefore refer to total revenues that soar and plunge, and

[1]Testimony of DuPont executives, Federal Trade Commission, *In the Matter of Ethyl Corp. et al.*, 101 F.T.C. 425 (1983), p. 424.

[2]*Ibid.*, p. 547.

we shall continue to speak of maximizing total dollar profit. Still, we shall abandon complete total dollar depictions because we want to focus on price strategies, and price is always a per unit measure.

What of nonprice strategies like advertising, innovation, and brand proliferation? They dwell in the next chapter.

I
Oligopoly Structure

A
Overview: Conditions and Causes

Autos, beer, steel, and aluminum are oligopolies. So are the markets for toothpaste, breakfast cereal, and computers. What characteristics do these diverse markets have in common? There are several.

An **oligopoly market** may be identified by:
1. A relatively small number of firms.
2. Difficult entry.
3. A product that is either standardized (e.g., aluminum) or differentiated (e.g., beer).

The main implication of these structural conditions is that oligopolists recognize their interdependence in the market.

Recognized interdependence means that the actions of one firm will influence the actions of others in the market, and this interactive influence is recognized.

Ford, for instance, knows that its prices will influence GM and Chrysler, while, in turn, GM and Chrysler know that their prices will affect each other and Ford.

1. Fewness of Firms: Oligopoly markets contain relatively few firms, where "few" denotes a low but varying number. There may be only two firms. There may be two dozen or several score. The basic idea is that the number be low enough that the firms in the market recognize their close interdependence.

Though an interesting statistic, the number of firms in a market may often be misleading. There may be a large number, while at the same time the market is *dominated* by just a few firms. Take beer, for instance. There are over 40 brewing companies in the United States. But the vast majority of them are very small, like the Dixie Brewing Company and the Anchor Brewing Company, which account for only tiny fractions of total national output. Table 27.1 shows that in 1983 over 90 percent of national beer output was sold by just six firms, each of which marketed a family of brands.

Thus, in order to avoid the wrong impressions that the raw number of firms might give, economists use several measures of fewness that incorporate percentage shares of the market. One such measure is the *concentration ratio*.

The **concentration ratio** is the percentage of market sales accounted for by an absolute number of the largest firms in the market—for example, the top four or eight firms.

The *four-firm* concentration ratio, which is the combined market share of the top four firms, is the most common ratio in U.S. data. For example, the

four-firm concentration ratio for beer based on the data in Table 27.1 would be 77.5, which is the sum of the market shares of Anheuser-Busch, Miller, Stroh, and Heileman ($33.5 + 20.8 + 13.5 + 9.7 = 77.5$). Further examples are found in Table 27.2, which reports four-firm concentration ratios for several oligopoly industries in 1982.

As a measure of market dominance, the concentration ratio has several flaws. For example, it profiles the market at only one slice in a range of possible slices. The four-firm ratio cuts the market at four firms, for instance. This leaves blind spots. Left in the dark is the size of the number 1 firm relative to the rest, or the relative sizes of those ranked 1, 2, and 3. Different markets might have identical four-firm concentration ratios of 70, yet the leading firm in one market might have a 60 percent share, while the top-ranked firm in another might have a 30 percent share, just half as much.

To address this problem and others like it, economists have devised several alternative measures of concentration. One is the H index, so named for its inventors Herfindahl and Hirschman.

The **H index** is the sum of the squares of the percentage sizes of all firms in the market.

If, for example, there were only two firms in the market, one with a 70 percent share and the other with a 30 percent share, the H index would be

TABLE 27.1 Major U.S. Beer Companies (and Their Chief Brands) Ranked by Percentage of Nationwide Shipments, 1983

Company (Chief Brands)	Percent Share of Nationwide Shipments, 1983
Anheuser-Busch (Budweiser, Michelob, Bud Light, Busch)	33.5
Miller (Lite, Miller High Life, Meister Brau, Plank Road)	20.8
Stroh (Stroh's, Old Milwaukee, Schlitz, Schaefer)	13.5
Heileman (Old Style, Blatz, Rainier, Grain Belt, Red Label)	9.7
Coors (Coors, Coors Light, Killian's Irish Red)	7.6
Pabst (Blue Ribbon, Olympia, Hamm's, Jacobs Best)	7.1
Total for top six	92.2

Source: Beer Statistics News, various issues.

$70^2 + 30^2 = 4,900 + 900 = 5,800$. In the event of pure monopoly, the H index would be 10,000. At the opposite extreme, perfect competition would shrink the H index toward zero.

A major advantage of the H index is that, unlike the concentration ratio, it summarizes the shares of *all firms* in the market simultaneously, not just the top four or top eight. A disadvantage is that the H index is rather complicated in comparison to the simplicity of the concentration ratio. Examples of the H index are given in Table 27.2, along with the concentration ratios.

Which is better? We need not probe the question here. Each measure correlates fairly closely with the other. A high four-firm concentration ratio usually corresponds to a high H index.

In particular, a four-firm concentration ratio of 40 roughly corresponds to an H index of about 800. And markets with measures above these levels can be considered oligopolies. By this definition, approximately half of all manufacturing markets are oligopolies. Data on other sectors of the economy indicate that oligopoly typifies many markets in other sectors as well. Indeed, oligopoly markets may account for more of our gross national product than any other type of market.

What *causes* fewness of firms and moderate to high concentration? Numerous causes contribute, but we shall highlight only a few items under the general headings of chance or luck, business policies, government policies, and technicalities.

The first cause, chance or luck, is in some ways the most interesting. What do you suppose would happen, for instance, if you and 10 friends got together for an all-night gambling session? Assume that each of you brought $50 to fritter away, and that every game played was one of pure chance—bingo, perhaps—with all of you having *identical* chances of winning. What would be the distribution of money by the break of dawn? Would everyone leave with $50? The laws of probability say "no". A few of you would put together a string of lucky games. A few would lose rather regularly. The rest would roughly break even. The result: a concentration of winnings, with two of you collecting, say, half of the original funds.

Several economists argue that the same laws of probability apply to firms in markets, that pure chance explains much concentration. Empirical research verifies that chance may play a role, but research also shows that chance cannot be the whole story.

The second cause, business policies, includes activities of firms that affect market concentration. The most important business policy of this sort is merging, which brings together two or more formerly independent companies. Table 27.3 offers dramatic evidence of the effects of business mergers. The 10 firms in the table accounted for the disappearance of 577 formerly independent rivals during a period of feverish merger activity around the turn of the century. The consequences are captured in the last column of the table, which provides rough estimates of the market shares these combinations amassed. Mergers of more recent times have likewise had an impact. The oil

TABLE 27.2   Concentration Ratios and H Indexes for Selected Industries, 1982

Market	Four-Firm Concentration Ratio	H Index
Household refrigerators	94	2745
Flat glass	85	2032
Greeting cards	84	2840
Turbines (generators)	84	2602
Photographic equipment and supplies	74	2147
Aircraft engines	72	1778
Woven carpets	71	1733
Tires and inner tubes	66	1591
Primary aluminum	64	1704
Explosives	59	1307
Pet food	52	1167

Source: U.S Bureau of the Census, *1982 Census of Manufacturers, Concentration Ratios in Manufacturing,* MC82-S-7 (1986), pp. 6–48.

TABLE 27.3   Selected Major Mergers Causing High Concentration, 1895–1904

Company (or Combine)	Number of Firms Disappearing	Rough Estimate of Market Controlled (%)
U.S. Steel	170	65
U.S. Gypsum	29	80
American Tobacco	162	90
American Smelting & Refining	12	85
DuPont de Nemours	65	85
Diamond Match	38	85
American Can	64	65–75
International Harvester	4	70
National Biscuit (Nabisco)	27	70
Otis Elevator	6	65

Source: Ralph L. Nelson, *Merger Movements in American Industry 1895–1956* (Princeton, N.J.: Princeton University Press, 1959), pp. 161–162.

industry, for instance, was transformed during the early 1980s by several huge combinations. Still, U.S. antitrust policy currently curbs really massive merger-built concentration.

The third cause, government policy, includes the antitrust policy just mentioned. The government has various *antitrust laws* that can dissolve excessive concentrations of market power or prevent such concentrations from occurring in the first place. These policies, when diligently applied, thus affect concentration by holding it down. This may sound good, and it is. However, antitrust policy is not the only government policy affecting concentration. And many other policies are anticompetitive rather than procompetitive, revealing the government's ambivalence about these matters. The anticompetitive policies include *tariffs and quotas* restricting the free flow of imports and *licenses* inhibiting the entry of finance companies, banks, taxicabs, liquor stores, landscape architects, and various other professionals. The effects of these policies on concentration should be obvious. They increase it.

Fourth and finally, technicalities of various sorts influence market concentration. One such factor is the *size of the market,* as measured by the volume of business or the buyer population. Everything else being equal, small markets tend to be more concentrated than large markets. Grocery retailing and commercial banking, for instance, tend to be more highly concentrated in small towns than in big cities. Another factor is the *product life cycle.* Early in the introductory phase or very late in the declining phase of a product's life cycle, forces tend to limit the number of firms in the market. Only innovators are around at first, and only diehards are around until the very end.

2. Difficult Entry   Fewness of firms thus characterizes oligopoly. In addition, barriers to entry are important, for they help to explain why many oligopolies can earn economic, or excess, profits in the long run. Like concentration, entry barriers are a source of monopoly power.

> A **barrier to entry** is any factor that gives a market's established firms advantages over potential entrants.

When entry is easy, the advantages of established sellers are slight. When entry is difficult, as is typical of oligopoly, the advantages of established sellers are great.

What factors create barriers to entry in oligopoly? For the most part, they are the same factors that shield monopolies from entry, namely, patents, other legal barriers, control of scarce inputs, and substantial economies of scale. Each of these barriers varies in height from market to market. In the extreme case of pure monopoly they are *extremely* high, effectively blocking all entry. In the less extreme case of oligopoly they are moderately high, checking but not necessarily completely blocking new entry.

The milder influence of these entry barriers in oligopoly is most easily appreciated for patents, other legal barriers, and scarce inputs. (1) Numerous patents of varying importance can be held by a number of firms, as is now true of copy machines, electronics, and drugs. Such a situation tends to protect an oligopolistic group rather than isolate a pure monopolist. (2) Other legal barriers need not completely bar entry; they just make it difficult. Tariffs on imported steel or autos give advantages to domestic producers over foreign rivals without banning imports completely. (3) Scarce inputs usually fall into the hands of a few oligopolistic firms rather than into the clutches of a pure monopolist. This helps to explain past entry barriers to the gypsum and copper industries, for instance.

In all of these cases, the impact of the barrier is quite direct; *it raises the costs per unit experienced by potential entrants relative to the costs per unit of established firms, thereby putting entrants at a disadvantage.* The barrier effects of (4) economies of scale are more subtle. Cost again lies at the root of the problem. But it is not the overall height, or level, of the per unit cost curve that matters here. Rather it is the *shape* of the curve, the declining long-run costs with greater scale. If economies of scale are important, the only way an entrant can be efficient after entry is to build a large-scale plant. This would give the entrant the same cost per unit as established firms, implying no disadvantage. The problem is, however, *that the added output of the entrant's efficient plant may be so large relative to the market demand that, after entry, the product price will fall below the entrant's cost per unit.* In other words, there may not be room in the industry for an added seller when efficient output is large relative to existing output and demand. The situation is similar to the situation creating natural monopoly, so it could be called *natural oligopoly.*

These several entry barriers of oligopoly thus overlap those of monopoly. In addition, oligopolies have a different barrier to entry—product differentiation. In saying this, we encounter the third main structural feature of oligopoly—the dual possibilities of product type.

3. Standardized or Differentiated Products
Some oligopolists produce standardized products. In that case, different firms sell exactly the same goods. The aluminum ingots produced by Alcoa are, for instance, identical to those of Kaiser and Reynolds. Other oligopolists offer *differentiated goods.*

> **Differentiated products** differ among sellers in the same market, being distinguished by trademarks, advertising, style, service, packaging, durability, distribution, and other such nonprice features.

The key is that each seller's offering appears different from that of the others, at least in the minds of buyers.

In the next chapter, product differentiation is the main topic. Here it is only important to note that product differentiation could pose a barrier to entry. Successful entry would then depend on more than just passing tests in production. It would also require mastery of *marketing* problems, for newcomers would then have to woo customers away from established firms by advertising, packaging, style variation, and so on.

Product differentiation finds further use in this chapter when we explain the oligopolist's view of demand. Before proceeding, however, here is a case study of oligopoly structure involving a standardized product, an example that we embellish later.

Read Perspective 27A.

B
The Firm's View of Demand

What are the implications of oligopolistic structure for the firm's view of demand and its perception of revenues? Recall this chapter's opening quotations on antiknocks. When Du Pont raised its price above the going price charged by its rivals, Du Pont's executives grew tense. Why? Because the reaction of those rivals was crucial to Du Pont's resulting demand. If Ethyl, PPG, and Nalco *did not* follow Du Pont's price hike, Du Pont's demand would plummet as customers would shift their business to the others. If rivals *did* follow Du Pont with equivalent price hikes of their own, Du Pont would not lose customers to its rivals, although its demand might shrink a bit as marketwide demand would decline a little due to the overall higher

PERSPECTIVE 27A
Oligopoly in Antiknocks

Until the recent switch to lead-free gasoline, lead-based antiknock additives were used extensively to increase the octane rating of gasoline. These additives, which contain tetraethyl or tetramethyl lead, are produced by an oligopoly of chemical companies that supply gasoline refiners. Much data on the market are available from the 1970s.[3] In 1977, for instance, the sales and market shares of America's only four suppliers were as follows:

Company	Sales ($Millions)	Market Share (%)
Du Pont	$321.7	35.2%
Ethyl	316.6	34.6
PPG	152.7	16.7
Nalco	122.7	13.4
Totals	$913.6	100.0

As regards barriers to entry, they have always been substantial (and with the recent decline in lead additive sales, entry is now essentially blocked). When additives were first produced by a predecessor of the Ethyl Corporation in the 1920s, a strong patent established pure monopoly. After 1948 membership expanded to include Du Pont, PPG, and Nalco. Economies of scale helped to exclude other potential entrants. During the mid-1970s, for instance, with annual sales peaking in excess of $1 billion, all the industry's supplies were produced in just six plants. Indeed, more than 20 years have now passed since the last entry by Nalco in 1964. Finally, as regards product type, lead-based additives are identical in chemical composition, so each firm matches the others' product offerings. This homogeneity suggests standardization. However, this market illustrates that some differentiation can creep in even where it might seem impossible. These firms differentiate their offerings with a host of services. They instruct customers' employees on the safe handling of lead additives, help clean customers' weigh tanks, and develop technology that customers use in their production of leaded gasoline.

[3]Federal Trade Commission, *In the Matter of Ethyl Corp. et al.*, 101 F.T.C. 425 (1983).

---

prices. In other words, Du Pont's executives trembled a bit because Du Pont faced *two* demand curves for its antiknock compound: one that would apply if rivals *did not* follow and one that would apply if they *did*. Once Du Pont committed itself, it had to wait for its rivals' response to know which demand would in fact apply.

Two possible demand curves thus face an oligopoly firm, depending on the possible reactions of rivals—followship or nonfollowship—given a change in the firm's price. The **followship** demand curve applies if a change in price is matched by rivals. A price reduction under followship will gain added sales for the firm, but not at the expense of rivals because they will have lowered their prices too. The sales come from added *marketwide* sales, which, if distributed among all rivals like their preexisting market shares, would leave each firm's market share unchanged. Conversely, a followed price increase curtails a firm's sales in proportion to the market's loss of sales. The followship curve could therefore also be called a *constant market share* demand curve.

A set of followship demands is shown in Figure 27.1. Each part of the figure represents a different firm size but assumes the *same* marketwide demand. The followship demand *(FD)* for the Big firm is drawn on the assumption of a 60 percent market share; that for Middle assumes a 30 percent market share; and Little has a 10 percent market share. Each *FD* is a reflection of the marketwide demand underlying the illustrations. Hence the elasticity of each *FD* curve at price P_0 is the same, and each elasticity, in turn, matches marketwide elasticity. (The elasticity happens to be 1.)

Although the followship curves of Figure 27.1

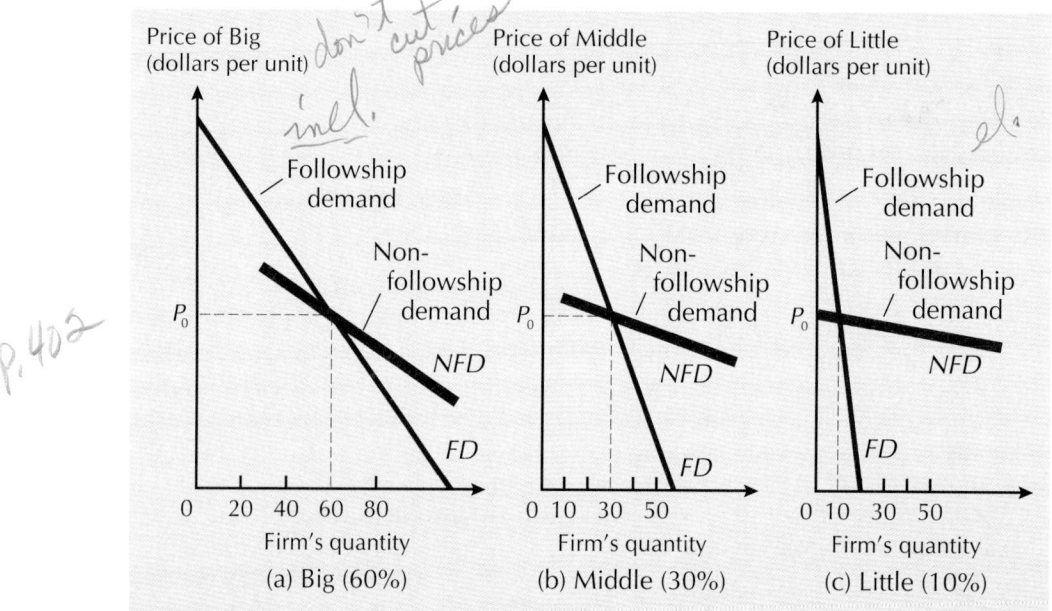

don't cut prices

inel.

p. 402

FIGURE 27.1 *Followship (FD) and Nonfollowship (NFD) Demand Curves for Three Sizes of Firms*

Marketwide demand is assumed to be the same for each case. Only the firm's market share at the initial or original price, P_0, is assumed to differ across these three cases. Part (a) shows the two demands facing Big, a firm with 60% of the market. Part (b) shows the two demands facing Middle, a moderate-sized firm with a 30% market share. Part (c) represents the view of Little, a firm with 10% of the market. It can thus be seen that the smaller the firm, the more elastic will be its NFD curve relative to its FD curve.

are identical in elasticity, such is not true of the **nonfollowship** demand curves labeled *NFD*. They vary in elasticity across firms within a given market because the assumption underlying their construction—that rivals do *not* match price changes—yields substantially different quantity results depending on firm size. Big firm's *NFD* will have an elasticity similar to that of its *FD*, though slightly higher. An unfollowed price cut below P_0 would cause customers to switch to Big. But the most Big could gain from competitors would be an additional 40 percentage points of market share, since at price P_0 Big already enjoys 60 percent. Comparing 40 to the beginning 60 implies a relatively low elasticity for Big's *NFD* curve. (Imagine the extreme case of a 95 percent market share. The *FD* and *NFD* curves would then be very close, as the firm could then capture very little additional share in the *NFD* case.) At the other extreme, an unfollowed price cut of similar amount, if made by Little, could easily double Little's sales volume,

implying that Little's nonfollowship demand curve at P_0 is highly elastic. We may therefore conclude that the smaller the firm relative to its market, the greater the divergence between its followship and nonfollowship demand curves and between their elasticities. More briefly, *the smaller the firm, the greater the elasticity of its nonfollowship demand.*

Because product differentiation also influences demand, a related conclusion holds that *the more differentiated the firm's product is, the less the divergence will be.* Consider the nonfollowship demand. If the firm raises its price and is not followed, it loses sales to rivals, but the loss will be *less* if its product is strongly differentiated because customers will continue to buy for *nonprice* reasons. Buyers made loyal by differentiation are less "switchable." Stated in terms of standardization instead of differentiation, *the more standardized the product, the greater the divergence between followship and nonfollowship demand and their elasticities.*

II

Oligopoly Conduct: Price Strategies

A

Introduction

At bottom, oligopolists' pricing strategies are variations on one theme—_recognized interdependence_. Each oligopolist recognizes interdependence with others in its market. Each knows that what it does influences rivals.

But recognized interdependence is only the beginning. Oligopolistic pricing is very complicated, with colorful contrasts of behavior from one market to the next. There are essentially three reasons for this diversity. _First, there is uncertainty_. One oligopolist can never be absolutely certain about what another in its market will do. Each firm has a choice. It can cooperate collusively with the others or strike out on its own, behaving like a maverick. Given a choice between collusive cooperation and competitive combat, there is uncertainty. Calouste Gulbenkian may have said it best when, speaking of the giant international petroleum companies, he quipped, "Oilmen are like cats; you can never tell from the sound of them whether they are fighting or making love."

Second, a wide variety of forces influence firm behavior. Besides the number of firms, barriers to entry, and product differentiation, these forces include the rate of growth, the pace of technological change, the stage of product life cycle, and the lumpiness of sales. If, for instance, sales go in large "lumpy" lots, as they do for wide-bodied jet airliners, there tends to be greater competition than if sales flow fairly evenly in small amounts per purchase, as they do for milk.

Third, firms typically diverge in position or standing within oligopoly markets. Just as there are runts in a typical litter of puppies, there are "runts" in a typical cluster of oligopolists. There is also a "top dog," plus those in between.

Let's ease ourselves into the complex subject of oligopoly pricing by exploring this last point. Why does a diversity of position or size cause complexity in pricing behavior?

Reconsideration of Figure 27.1 reveals a quick answer. Big, Middle, and Little hold their relative positions splitting the market 60, 30, and 10 percent. Let's now recall the relationship between price changes and total revenue: When a firm's demand is highly _elastic_, a price cut raises total revenue and a price increase reduces total revenue. On the other hand, when demand is _inelastic_, a price cut reduces total revenue, while a price increase lifts total revenue. (See pages 399-402 for details.) Mindful that total revenue is half of the story for maximizing total profit, we can begin to understand the varied perceptions of different firms. For example, which of the three firms in Figure 27.1 gains the most from a trip down its non-followship demand curve via price cuts below P_0? Answer: Little has the most highly elastic _NFD_. Hence it would gain the greatest percentage jump in total revenue, assuming that it could in fact move down its _NFD_. Conversely, Big has the least to gain from such behavior. We can therefore surmise from this analysis that relatively small firms are more likely to cut prices than big firms (_ceteris paribus_). Turning the issue around, we may ask which firm is most likely to gain from a price _increase_ if the _NFD_ curve applies? Answer: Big is the most likely gainer in this case because its _NFD_ curve is the least elastic of the three. Accordingly, we might expect to find relatively large firms more eager to raise prices than small firms.

This deduction that small firms tend to be price cutters while large firms lean toward loftier prices is proper. It is, however, a bit premature. We have not considered two important factors affecting its accuracy: (1) Costs are as important as revenues in determining behavior because costs as well as revenues determine profits. (2) Just as we mortals cannot be in two places at one time, the firm cannot be on more than one demand curve at any one time, except where the curves intersect. A price cut will take the firm down _either NFD or FD_, not both. A price increase is an either-or journey in the opposite direction. Because the elasticities of _NFD_ and _FD_ differ, sometimes greatly, we must discover _which_ curve the firm regards as its _actual_ demand curve under various circumstances. The firm's view of its terrain determines what steps it takes.

We shall demonstrate the significance of these additional considerations while studying four major models of oligopolistic behavior: *price leadership*, *kinked demand*, *small-firm maverick*, and *cartelization*. Very roughly, the first three hinge on the respective views of Big, Middle, and Little in Figure 27.1, while the last, cartelization, covers the possibility that all firms in the market might explicitly collude. A few words on long-run pricing round out the analysis.

B
Price Leadership

Recognized interdependence often causes oligopolistic firms to recognize the futility of cutthroat price competition and the profitability of mutual restraint or *tacit collusion*.

> **Tacit collusion** is mutual self-restraint, a parallel reluctance to compete on price (or other variables) grounded on individual understanding.

If successful, tacit collusion has its rewards—high prices and profits, perhaps nearly as high as a monopolist's.

> **Price leadership** is one way competition can be tacitly avoided. Under price leadership, prices set by a leading firm are imitated by the other firms in the market simply by self-interest, not by formal agreement.

Given the diversity of oligopolistic structures, price leadership can take many forms. The role of leader typically falls to the largest firm in the market, but it need not. Sometimes the leader is the most efficient firm. Sometimes the role of leader shifts between two firms. Likewise, variations occur in the strength of followship. In some markets, followers match the leader's price changes quickly and precisely. In others, followers delay their reactions to a leader's price changes or maintain prices that differ slightly from those of the leader.

If a price leader is always followed faithfully by its rivals, it will see only the followship demand curve (*FD*), as shown in Figure 27.2. The nonfollowship demand fades into irrelevance. Profit maximization for the leader is then very similar to that of a monopolist, except that here marginal revenue

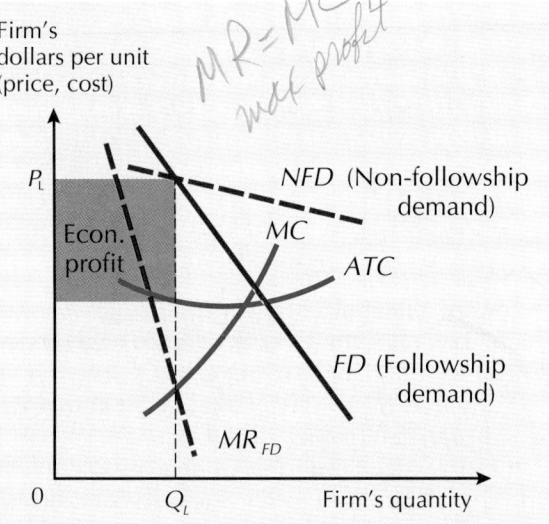

FIGURE 27.2 Price Leader's View and Profit-Maximizing Strategy

If a firm is such a strong price leader that its prices are always followed by rivals in the market, the only firm demand curve of relevance is the followship demand (FD). *The leader may then maximize its total dollar profit by equating marginal revenue associated with the followship demand* (MR$_{FD}$) *to marginal cost* (MC). *The result is a price for the leader at* P$_L$, *quantity* Q$_L$, *and an economic profit (because price* P$_L$ *is above average total cost,* ATC).

does not derive from marketwide demand. Rather, it derives from the leader's followship demand. Two-question logic applies once again. Equating this marginal revenue, *MR$_{FD}$* in Figure 27.2, with the marginal cost, *MC*, yields a profit-maximizing price and quantity at *P$_L$* and *Q$_L$*. The total dollar economic profit resulting is identified by the shaded area.

Note that this solution maximizes the *leader's* profit. It may not maximize marketwide profit or the profit of any rival firm. Rivals might prefer a higher price, but they cannot impose their wishes as long as the leader maximizes its profit with *P$_L$*. They cannot price above *P$_L$* lest they lose large chunks of market share to the leader, perhaps even to the point of going out of business. In other words, the leader's rivals might earn *higher* profits if the leader set some price other than *P$_L$* in Figure 27.2, but they nevertheless follow the leader because their profits would be *lower* if they did not. They must be content to do the best they can given the situation.[4] Still, the results for market price and output might approach those of monopoly.

Read Perspective 27B.

C
Kinked Demand

It is frequently observed that oligopoly prices tend to be rigid despite shifts of demand or changes in

[4]Generally, the advantage lies with any large firm that favors a lower price than rivals prefer because a low price attracts customers. There are exceptions, though. "In early 1980, for instance, chewing gum makers increased their wholesale prices to raise the pack of gum at retail by five cents. Wrigley, a big gum maker, at first didn't go along. Even so, retailers raised the price of Wrigley's gum by five cents a pack. They told Wrigley that a standard price on chewing gum made it easier for cashiers. . . . Finally Wrigley, too, raised its prices." *Wall Street Journal.* (Dec. 23, 1981), p. 17.

input prices. Sulfur offers an extreme example. The price of sulfur remained stuck at $18 a ton from 1926 to 1938 despite substantial swings in demand and production costs during the Great Depression. To explain this rather weird behavior and less extreme cases, economist Paul Sweezy devised the theory of kinked oligopoly demand.

Let Figure 27.4 represent a single oligopoly firm whose current price, P_0, matches that of other firms in the market. Q_0 is the firm's output, and K indicates the firm's position on its demand curves. Given these conditions, what action is best for the firm? Is it likely to slash the price, boost it, or leave it unchanged? If the firm thinks that its *price cut below P_0 will be followed*, then *below* point K the followship demand curve, *FD*, alone is relevant. The nonfollowship demand curve, *NFD*, disap-

PERSPECTIVE 27B
Price Leadership in Antiknocks

The pattern of price leadership in lead-based gasoline additives during the mid-1970s is especially interesting because the role of leader rotated between the market's two largest firms—Du Pont and Ethyl. Contracts required sellers to tell buyers *at least* 30 days in advance of changes in list prices, so Du Pont or Ethyl would typically lead the way by announcing price changes 35 to 39 days in advance. The extra days' notice gave rivals enough time to announce matching price changes, say 31 days in advance, with the result that all four firms in the market could then charge identical list prices every day of the year, even on days when price changes became effective. There were 24 price increases from 1974 to 1979, and in 20 of these the antiknock oligopolists had identical list prices effective on the same date despite the 30-day notice requirement. Figure 27.3 illustrates those increases occurring in 1976. The dates *above* the price line are the dates price changes went into effect, while those *below* it are the dates of announcement. For example, the increase from 60.5 to 62.3 cents a pound that became effective August 13, 1976, was first

announced by Du Pont on July 9, then announced by Ethyl (July 13), PPG (July 13), and Nalco (July 14). Hence when August 13, the effective date, rolled around, all four sellers hiked their prices in unison. This method permitted more than uniformity. It permitted the leader, Du Pont or Ethyl, to know *in advance* whether everyone would be following. Adjustments could be made before commitments solidified. Rather than engage in price leadership, the firms could have jousted for additional market shares by price shading. But a Du Pont document explains why outright rivalry was resisted: "An alternative strategy would be [to] attempt to hold or increase market share by selective discounting to meet competitive situations. This has been rejected because the potential earnings gain from increased shares is small compared with the risk of earnings loss through a reduction in market price which would probably result from competitive reaction."[5] In short, price leadership was more profitable than price competition.

[5]*In the Matter of Ethyl Corp. et al.,* 101 F.T.C. 425 (1983), p. 455.

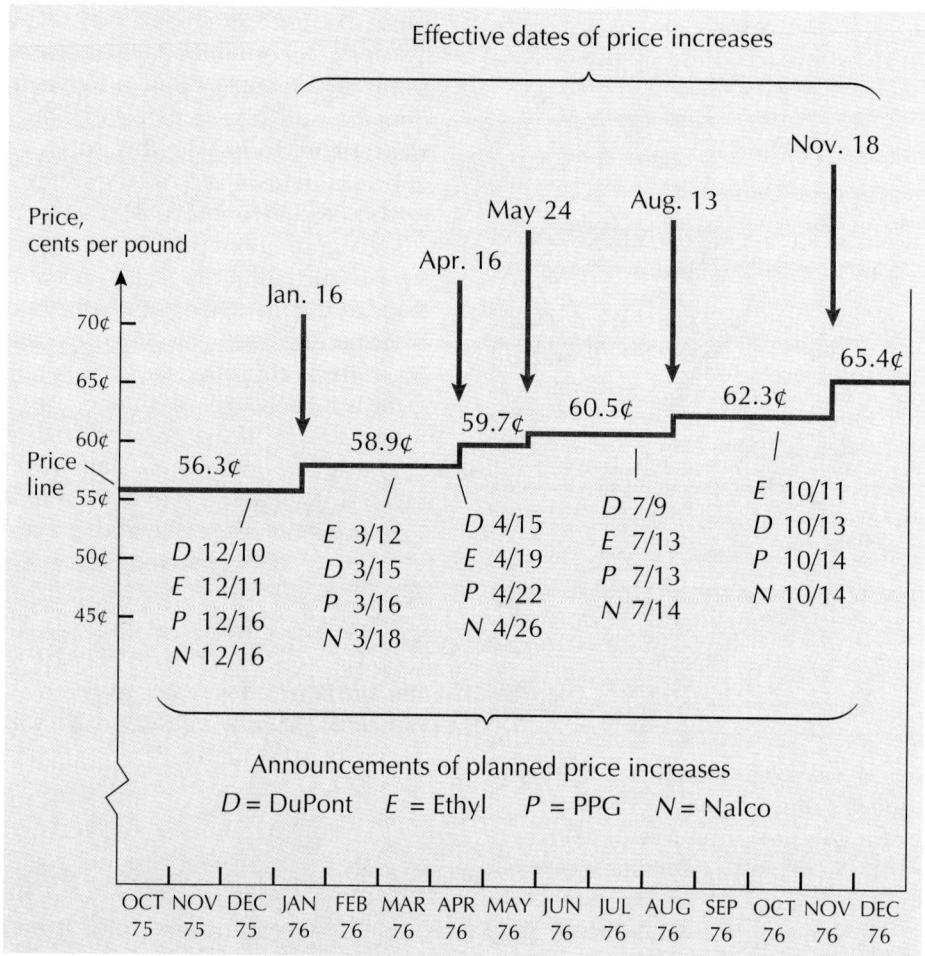

FIGURE 27.3 *History of the Price for Tetraethyl Lead Antiknock Gasoline Additive, 1976*

The typical pattern for changes in list prices during the mid-1970s was as follows: (1) Ethyl (E) or DuPont (D) gives 35- to 39 days' notice that it will increase the price. (2) The other firms match the leader, giving their customers at least 30 days' notice, as required by contract. (3) List prices are actually changed, by all firms on the very same day, so that they all charge identical prices every day of the year. [Source: In the Matter of Ethyl Corp. et al, 101 FTC 425 (1983), pp. 578–579.]

pears below *K.* Conversely, if the firm expects that its *price increase will not be followed,* then *above K* only the *NFD* curve is applicable, and the followship demand *FD* curve does the vanishing act. Considering both the downside and the upside, all that remains is a kinked demand curve.

Schizophrenic demand curves such as this put the firm in a straightjacket. Looking at these demands, you will note that a sizable price cut below P_0 would drop total revenue substantially because the *FD* curve below *K* is inelastic. Moreover, things

are just as bad in the other direction. A price increase above P_0 would likewise reduce total revenue sharply because *NFD* above *K* is highly elastic. *With total revenue tumbling from a step in either direction, the best strategy is to stand still.*

Furthermore, this rigidity of price may hold even after considering costs. If the firm in Figure 27.4 is operating under the *MR = MC* rule of profit maximization, marginal costs can vary over a spacious range without causing the firm's price to flutter from its P_0 perch because the marginal rev-

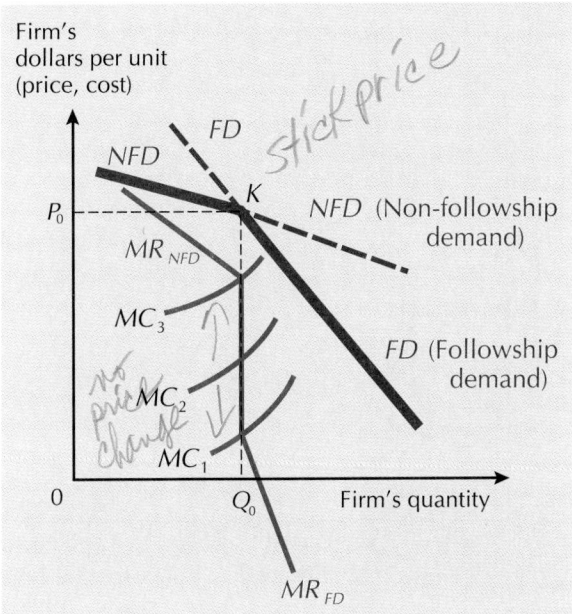

FIGURE 27.4   The Kinked Demand Oligopoly Model

The original or "going" price of the firm is P$_0$, the same price as that of other firms in the market. If this firm raises the price above P$_0$, it assumes that it will not be followed, so NFD is the applicable demand. FD disappears above P$_0$. Conversely, if this firm cuts the price, it anticipates that it will be followed, so FD is then the applicable demand. NFD vanishes below P$_0$. Because NFD is elastic and FD is inelastic where they remain "visible," total revenue would fall if the price changes substantially. Moreover, marginal cost equals marginal revenue over a wide range of cost (MC$_1$ to MC$_3$).

enue for price increases is MR_{NFD} (which derives from the *nonfollowship* demand curve above K), whereas the marginal revenue for price reductions is MR_{FD} (which derives from the *followship* demand curve below K). Marginal cost is shown to vary from MC_1 to MC_3, but it always remains equal to marginal revenue in the discontinuity between MR_{NFD} and MR_{FD}. Hence cost changes need not prompt price changes under these assumptions.

There is some truth to this theory of kinked demand and rigid prices, but that truth is mainly limited to explaining some *individual firm* behavior rather than *marketwide* behavior. For the theory to work well in explaining marketwide behavior one has to have a market in which all firms see a kink. That is, all would have to be approximately the same moderate size (say, five firms, each with one-fifth of the market), all offer nearly identical

products, and all charge exactly the same price. However, as we already know, oligopolists usually differ in size and often differ in products and prices, even within the same market. So the theory may apply to certain *individual* firms in an oligopoly without applying to all the firms.

This can be explained as follows. Consider firms like Big, Middle, and Little in Figure 27.1. Which firm is most likely to see a kinked demand? Not Big, because Big is a good candidate to act as a price leader. And as we have just seen in Figure 27.2, a genuine price leader does not see a kinked demand. Little is likewise not a good candidate for a kinked demand curve. If Little is truly small, with, say, only 1 or 2 percent of the market, then Little may be able to raise or cut its price without being followed. This would give Little a view of demand limited *only* to nonfollowship demand. Because the kink requires portions of followship demand as well as nonfollowship demand, Little would then see no kink. Thus, in general, firms like Middle are the ones most likely to see a kinked demand. *They are big enough to always be followed if they cut their price, but not big enough or well established enough as a price leader, to anticipate followship if they raise their price.* In the auto industry, for instance, Ford, a middle-sized firm, has demonstrated great reluctance to initiate either price increases or price decreases. It therefore behaves as if it sees a kink of some kind in its demand. In contrast, big GM has usually served as the price leader, while tiny AMC typically (but not always) found its price initiatives, up and down, to be ignored by the other car companies.

The kinked demand may thus apply to certain individual firms, but it probably does not apply to entire markets. Still, the theory is useful. It illustrates recognized interdependence very nicely, and it describes the situation facing many individual oligopolists rather accurately, especially those of medium stature in their markets. Their prices will not be rigid, but *they will be reluctant to initiate price changes.*

D

Small-Firm Maverick

If firms like Big often become price leaders contending with followship demands, and if firms like Middle often see kinked demands, then what behavior typifies the smallest firms that frequently populate oligopolies? Once again, diversities preclude sweeping generalities for all the little MCIs and Dixie Brewing Companies of the world. But two broad tendencies deserve mention.

First, small firms frequently incur higher costs of production than their bigger brethren. The higher costs may be *involuntary*—due to smallness in the face of economies of scale or to inferior access to inexpensive inputs. On the other hand, the higher costs could be incurred *voluntarily*—in an effort by the small firm to differentiate its product, offering higher quality, special services, or other costly features that may prove attractive to a limited segment of the market. BMW follows this strategy in autos, as does Anchor Brewing Company in beer. In either case, involuntarily or voluntarily, when a small firm incurs higher costs per unit than the market norm, it obviously must maintain its price at the market norm or charge even more (which product differentiation might permit, as is true of BMW and Anchor Brewing Company). Costs prevent aggressive price cutting in this situation.

Second, dramatically different tendencies may emerge among small firms that suffer no cost disadvantages. Demand-side conditions then leap to the fore, two conditions especially—visibility and elasticity. Assuming that its price cuts will not be followed, the small firm may see *only* its nonfollowship demand. This is particularly true if it is small enough to go largely unnoticed by the Bigs and Middles in its market; or if those Bigs and Middles are earnestly trying to maintain or elevate the price; or if the small firm can *secretly* cut its price. When the small firm assumes nonfollowship demand, the followship demand curve vanishes. As regards elasticity, we have already established in Figure 27.1 that the price elasticity of nonfollowship demand is higher for small firms than for larger rivals.

The results for many a small firm—an invisible followship demand curve and a highly elastic nonfollowship demand curve—are shown in Figure 27.5. And the implication is that *small firms often play the role of price cutters, i.e., markdown mavericks.* To see the inducement, let $6 be the small firm's initial price in Figure 27.5, a price prevailing marketwide. At $6 the firm sells 3 million units, for a total revenue of $18 million ($6 × 3 million = $18

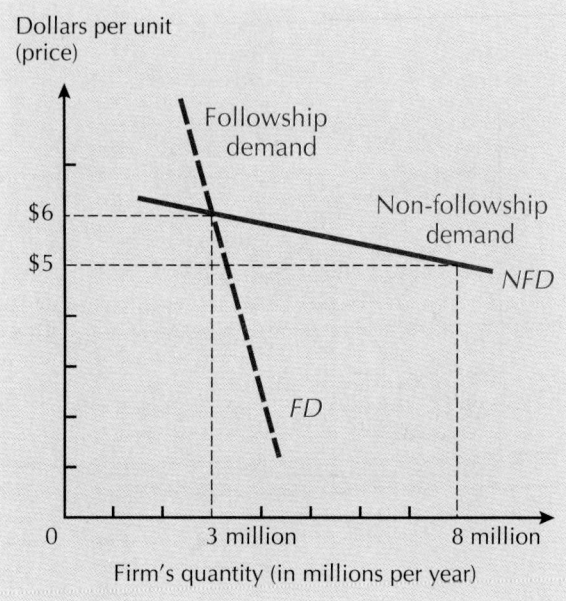

FIGURE 27.5 *Frequent View of Demand by the Small Firm in Oligopoly*

Let $6 be the firm's initial price (matching the prevailing marketwide price). If the firm assumes that its price cut to $5 will not be followed, the followship demand disappears, leaving only the nonfollowship demand. The firm than anticipates a tremendous jump in total revenue from the price cut. At a price–quantity combination of $6 and 3 million, total revenue is $18 million ($6 × 3 million). At a price of $5, total revenue is $40 million ($5 × 8 million). High elasticity propels these numbers.

million). What would happen to total revenue if the firm cut the price to, say, $5? When the firm assumes that the highly elastic nonfollowship curve applies, it anticipates a tremendous jump in total revenues as the quantity sold more than doubles. The area of the rectangle associated with $5 and 8 million units is $40 million, more than twice the starting revenue of $16 million.

Examples of small-firm price cutting are abundant, many of them associated with cyclical downturns in marketwide demand:

1. During the 15 months prior to January 1975, the United States sank into a severe recession. The auto industry cut back capacity use by close to 50 percent. Price reductions were resisted. Indeed, GM led price increases averaging $1,000 per car. Then that January, Chrysler, the smallest of

the big three, broke the ice by cutting the price as much as $400 per car under its "Car Clearance Carnival" rebate program.[6]

2. During a massive recession in 1981–1982, the airlines fought intermittent price wars. One-way coach fares between New York and California, for example, plunged from $478 to $99. Relatively small carriers such as World Airways, Air Florida, and Capitol International triggered the discounting.[7]

3. Trailways Bus Company started a campaign of fare reductions in 1981 that continued into 1982. The cuts ranged from 38 to 61 percent. Greyhound complained bitterly about "these ill-conceived fare reductions."[8]

In each of these cases, the market's leading firms eventually joined in the price cutting. This means that small firms may anticipate or hope for nonfollowship, but quite often they end up experiencing followship (partly because their price cutting causes them to become bigger). This also means that, to the extent that small firms are actively cutting prices, they are not following the market leaders, which tend to prefer price maintenance or even price hikes. A leader then becomes less of a leader.

This is not so much a paradox as a tension that occurs between the forces of competition and collusion in many oligopoly markets. The point made earlier about uncertainty bears repeating. Each firm has a choice: It can cooperate collusively or strike out on its own. The broad tendency is for big firms to perceive the inelastic followship curve. They therefore try to maintain prices and resist price combat. In contrast, the broad tendency is frequently for little firms to be seduced by the rich attractions of their elastic nonfollowship curves, even when their perceptions and hopes may not, in the end, accord with reality. They see the rewards and risks differently than big firms. A comment made by big United Airlines during the airline price war of 1981–1982 summarizes the sit-

uation: "We didn't start it. We want to stop it." Accordingly, United repeatedly attempted to lead fare increases.

Note that the reluctance of big firms to cut the price may contribute to the small firm's expectations (or hopes) that its discounting will not be followed. Moreover, the nonfollowship expectation is often borne out. In antiknock additives, the smallest two firms, PPG and Nalco, took occasional trips down their nonfollowship demand curves during the 1970s. They succeeded partly because they kept their discounts secret. They matched the leaders, Du Pont and Ethyl, in *list* price, but they shaved *transaction* prices "under the table" for a few select customers.[9]

E
Cartels

As we have seen, if structural conditions are especially favorable to cooperation, mavericks are absent and oligopolists can *tacitly collude* to maintain prices and profits. If, on the contrary, structural conditions are especially unfavorable to cooperation, mavericks abound and oligopolists *compete vigorously* on price. Tacit collusion is impossible. Formal agreements likewise cannot float. This would be true, for instance, if there were dozens of firms, none with more than 10 percent of the market, technological change periodically shook the market, and excess capacity abounded.

These are oligopolistic extremes. The tension between cooperation and competition is very clearly resolved one way or the other, depending on structural conditions. There is a middle ground, however. And it is in that middle ground that *cartel* activities flourish.

[6]*Business Week* and *Wall Street Journal*, various issues.

[7]*Wall Street Journal*, October 19, 1981, p. 6; April 28, 1982, pp. 1, 24.

[8]*Wall Street Journal*, May 12, 1982, p. 6.

[9]An element that may protect price cutters from followship is product differentiation. With product differentiation, the small firm's product is often thought to be inferior to that of its larger rivals even when it is not. If so, the small firm can underprice without denting its larger rivals' sales to the point of provoking followship. Indeed, prevailing brand images may force the small firm to discount if it is to have any sales at all. During the early 1980s, for example, Kodak had 90 percent of the film market in the United States and set prices high, while Fuji, with only about 10 percent of the U.S. market, priced 5 percent to 10 percent below Kodak. In Japan the tables were turned. There Kodak had only 12 percent of the market and priced its film well below Fuji, which held 70 percent of that market. *Forbes*, November 22, 1982, pp. 55–56.

A **cartel** is express collusion. Firms in a market explicitly agree among themselves to limit competition.

The concept includes price fixing, production quotas, and customer allocations. The collusion might be achieved through casual discussions or formal negotiations of contract agreements. Cartels may be open or secret, legal or illegal, local or international. The most famous cartel of all time, the Organization of Petroleum Exporting Countries (OPEC), is open and international.

We say that cartels frequent the middle ground between cooperation and competition because they occur most commonly when structural conditions are competitive enough to hamper tacit collusion but not so extremely competitive as to prevent all collusion. Where tacit collusion is quite feasible, cartels are unneeded. Where *any* collusion is impossible, cartels are unfeasible.

Consider just one structural variable—the number of firms in the market. All else equal and speaking generally, we should expect little cartel activity where firms are particularly few, say two or three. Tacit collusion could then work. Likewise we should expect little cartel activity where firms are particularly numerous, say 40 to 60 or so. Competition would tend to dominate in that range. Between these extremes, particularly where the number of firms ranges from 4 to 20, we should expect to find the greatest incidence of cartel activity. And empirical evidence supports this expectation.

Now it may also be seen why many cartels sputter and fail, giving way to vigorous competition. Each cartel member has some incentive to cheat or double-cross its fellow conspirators. If a double-crosser can slip down its nonfollowship demand curve (the others not following because they abide by the agreement), then lush added revenues ensue, boosting profits. Small firms have especially strong inducements because their nonfollowship demand curves are more visible to them and more elastic than those of larger colluders. Thus cartels involving numerous small firms are likely to be relatively weak.

On the other hand, many cartels have been remarkably strong and durable, lasting decades and even centuries. These more potent forms typically occur when cartelization arises as an alternative to tacit collusion and very few firms, say three to five, are involved. If a cartel is set up because tacit collusion is not working well enough to be profitable, then that cartel is probably built upon a fairly solid structural foundation. Double-crossing can then be stifled.

It must be stressed that factors other than firm number affect the incidence and strength of cartel activity. In general, *cartelization is more difficult to achieve when the market is highly unstable, when maverick behavior can be secretive, when the incentives to cheat are great, and when cartelization is illegal.* Instability may be caused by chaotic technological change or wide swings in demand. Secrecy is aided by opportunities for under-the-table discounting. Incentives to cheat are increased by excess capacity, high elasticity of marketwide demand, and large, lumpy sales. Illegality comes about by such laws as the Sherman Act, which we explore later.

F

Long-Run Pricing

Collusive pricing, be it tacit collusion or express cartelization, may raise prices and profits in the short run, but in the long run entry threatens. How do oligopolists handle this problem? Once again, there are a variety of strategies recognized in economic theory and realized in actual behavior.

One strategy goes by the label *limit pricing*. Here, oligopolists hold the price level up, but *not* so high up that entry would be attractive to potential newcomers. Limiting the price level severely limits the prospective profits of potential entrants, thereby limiting actual entry to zero. Oligopolists who practice limit pricing sacrifice short-run profits that could be earned by still higher prices, but they gain long-run profits as potential entrants are held at bay.

A contrasting strategy is *open pricing*. In this approach, oligopolists raise the price toward monopoly levels to gain extravagant profits in the short run, recognizing that entry will occur in the long run. The resulting pattern of profits over time is opposite to that of limit pricing. Present-day profits are higher, while future profits are lower than those under limit pricing.

Both limit pricing and open pricing can be found in the annals of business behavior. Sometimes firms even follow a mixed strategy, pricing *above* a level that would limit entry to zero but *below* a level that would rapidly attract hordes of newcomers. Some firms, like Kodak and Du Pont, have switched from limit pricing to open pricing as circumstances changed.[10]

G
Summary

In sum, oligopoly pricing is a mixed bag. It can be quite competitive when structural conditions cause firms to vie vigorously with sharp price cuts or sly discounts. At the opposite extreme, it can be quite noncompetitive, with tacit collusion and strong price leadership achieving results that may closely approximate those of pure monopoly. Between these polar cases, competition and cooperation can both prevail in combinations of varying composition. In this middle ground, cartelization often occurs.

The one constant in all of this variation is the following: Where market concentration is high (and other structural conditions contribute to monopoly power), prices likewise tend to be high, at least higher than they would be otherwise. This has been shown most clearly in studies comparing the prices of a given product or service in diverse geographic markets at one point in time. Products and services so studied include life insurance, bank loans, newspaper advertising space, bread, beer, and grocery retailing.[11] Results for the last of these are shown briefly in Table 27.4. The data come from a team of economists who compiled observations of the weighted average price consumers paid for a "grocery basket" filled with 94 items in 1974. Isolating the impact of concentration through statistical analysis, these economists estimated that an increase in a city's four-firm concentration ratio from 40 to 70 would raise the price of the grocery basket from $90.95 to $95.78, a jump of 5.3 percent.

[10]Don E. Waldman, *Antitrust Action and Market Structure* (Lexington, Mass.: Lexington Books, 1978), pp. 41–49, 146–149; Waldman, "The Du Pont Cellophane Case Revisited," *Antitrust Bulletin* (Winter 1980), pp. 805–830.

[11]For citations see D.F. Greer, *Industrial Organization and Public Policy*, 2nd ed. (New York: Macmillan, 1984), p. 296.

TABLE 27.4 Estimated Prices of Grocery Baskets for Different Levels of Four-Firm Concentration in City Markets, October 1974

Four-Firm Concentration Ratio	Price of a Standard Grocery Basket ($)	Percentage Above the Lowest Price
50	91.84	1.0
60	93.64	3.0

Note: The relative firm market share assumed for these estimates is 10.
Source: B.W. Marion, W.F. Mueller, R.W. Cotteril, F.E. Geithman, and J.R. Schmelzer, *The Profit and Price Performance of Leading Food Chains 1970–74*, A Study for the Joint Economic Committee, U.S. Congress, 95th Congress, 1st Session (1977), p. 66.

III
Oligopoly Performance

What are the implications of oligopoly structure and conduct for the basic questions of What?, How?, Who?, and What's new? Here we take up the questions of What?, How?, and Who? as they relate to pricing conduct. In the next chapter, we take up What's new?

A
What?

The theory of perfect competition provides the ideal answer to the question What?—namely, allocation efficiency. The theory of pure monopoly reveals how the ideal can be missed by a mile. These extremes bracket the possible performance of oligopoly, as shown in Figure 27.6. The perfectly competitive ideal is indicated by output Q_{PC}, which is associated with the equality of marginal social benefit and marginal social cost at point A ($MSB = MSC$). The pure monopoly's answer to What? yields output Q_m, which is lower than Q_{PC} because the monopolist's price, P_m, is higher than the perfectly competitive price, P_{PC}. As we have seen, the *oligopoly price* falls somewhere between these extremes, depending on the circumstances, with a general tendency to be higher as opposed to lower in this range. This means that the *oligopoly quantity* will likewise fall somewhere between

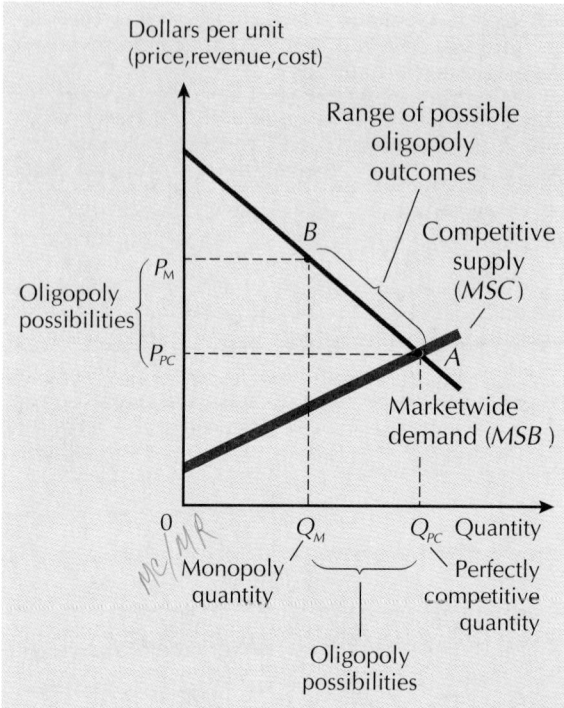

FIGURE 27.6 *Oligopoly Compared to Perfect Competition and Pure Monopoly*
The perfectly competitive price–output combination is P_{pc} *and* Q_{pc}. *Allocation efficiency is obtained because* MSB = MSC *at point A. The pure monopoly results are* P_m *and* Q_m. *Oligopoly lies between these cases.*

these extremes, with a general tendency to lie in the lower portion of the range. Oligopoly may therefore be faulted for typically producing an inefficient allocation of resources, though less seriously so than pure monopoly.

B

How?

As regards technical efficiency, oligopoly mildly mirrors monopoly once again. We find good news and bad news.

The good news is that economies of scale may be large enough that oligopoly structure is required to achieve technical efficiency. The reasoning is similar to that concerning natural monopoly, but less strictly so. Here economies of scale justify a few firms, whereas in the case of natural monopoly they warrant only one firm in the market.

The bad news is that oligopoly frequently stifles competition, with the result that X-inefficiencies may bloat costs. The best evidence of this comes from cartel case studies. A study of price fixing in three U.S. industries—gymnasium seating, rock salt, and structural steel—found cost increases of 10 to 23 percent due to cartelization.[12] A research team headed by F.M. Scherer uncovered numerous examples of excessive costs due to cartelization in Europe, including cases for cigarettes, steel, and paint.[13] In short, the typically higher prices of oligopoly may be partly due to higher costs arising from X-inefficiency.

C

Who?

If the frequently higher prices of oligopoly were due entirely to higher costs, those elevated prices would not yield excessive economic profits. They would only cover the higher costs. However, empirical research discloses that, quite frequently, oligopoly not only fosters higher prices and higher costs in comparison to competition, but also higher profits. Over 100 statistical studies have tested the relationship between market concentration and profit levels. Their measures of concentration include the four-firm concentration ratio and the H index. Their measures of profit levels similarly vary. And the vast majority of these studies find a positive relationship between concentration and profit level.[14]

To the extent that oligopoly fosters economic profit, the consequences for income distribution are similar to those of monopoly. Because owners of oligopoly firms are generally richer than their customers, these economic profits may contribute to an uneven distribution of income in the economy.

Overall, then, the performance of oligopoly as it concerns prices and outputs is mixed. It changes

[12]W. Bruce Erickson, "Price Fixing Conspiracies: Their Long-Term Impact," *Journal of Industrial Economics* (March 1976), pp. 189–202.

[13]Scherer, Beckenstein, Kaufer, and Murphy, *The Economics of Multi-Plant Operation* (Cambridge, Mass.: Harvard University Press, 1975), pp. 74–75, 168–169, 314–315.

[14]For a survey, see F.M. Scherer, *Industrial Market Structure and Economic Performance*, 2nd ed. (Chicago: Rand McNally, 1980), Chap. 9.

from one oligopoly to another and from one criteria to another. However, to the extent that oligopoly stifles competition, the results approach those of monopoly—namely, allocation inefficiency, technical inefficiency, and income inequity.

Read Perspective 27C.

IV
Monopolistic Competition: Structure

A
Introduction

The final market form confronting us—*monopolistic competition*—lies closer to perfect competition than to monopoly in all its features: structure, conduct, and performance. Habit dictates that we tackle structure first, then conduct and performance.

The term *monopolistic competition* was coined by economists Edward Chamberlin and Joan Robinson in the 1930s. The name awkwardly suggests a market whose firms possess some monopoly power yet compete vigorously. And that is precisely what we have here, as indicated by its structural definition.

With **monopolistic competition** there is:
1. A relatively large number of firms.
2. Easy entry.
3. A differentiated product.

Examples include apparel manufacturing, retailing of certain types, barber shops, printing services, and restaurants.

1. Large Number of Firms Hundreds of firms populate these markets. Moreover, each firm is relatively small. In theory, none has more than a few percentage points of market share. It's as if *every* firm in the market was a feisty little maverick, so many of small size that *unrecognized interdepen-*

TABLE 27.5 Profits in the Antiknock Business Compared to Average Profits in All Manufacturing, 1974–1977

Company	Percentage Return on Investment			
	1974	1975	1976	1977
Ethyl	32.2	36.1	49.9	42.4
Du Pont	20.6	27.5	32.2	23.7
PPG	17.7	26.7	23.4	13.1
Nalco	19.5	16.6	18.7	24.4
All manufacturing average	10.6	8.6	9.8	9.9

Source: Federal Trade Commission, *In the Matter of Ethyl et al.,* 101 F.T.C. 425 (1983), pp. 492, 586.

PERSPECTIVE 27C
Profits in the Antiknock Additive Oligopoly

An internal memo of the Ethyl Corporation characterized its antiknock additive business as a "golden goose." PPG documents disclose its pleased appraisal: "historically high returns." Table 27.5 shows why antiknock additive producers were so happy to be in that market. They were earning extremely high profits. From 1974 to 1977, the lowest rate of return on investment experienced by any of the four companies was 13.1 percent, which PPG earned in 1977. The

highest was Ethyl's 49.9 percent in 1976. The central tendency for all firms together was about 26.6 percent.

Compared to the average profits of manufacturers in general, which are given on the bottom line of Table 27.5, these numbers are fantastic. The antiknock additive business was, on the whole, more than two and a half times as profitable as manufacturing generally, a golden goose indeed.

dence prevails. Cartelization cannot take root. There is independence even though the firms may interact in rivalry.

> **Unrecognized interdependence** means that each firm acts independently of the others while interacting in rivalry.

2. Easy Entry Large economies of scale are absent from monopolistic competition. Inputs readily abound. Patents pose no problem. In these respects and others, potential entrants find little to keep them out of these markets.

3. Product Differentiation If firms are numerous and entry is easy, what is the source of monopoly power in these markets? Product differentiation. Because of brand image, flavor, style, retail location, service, or other nonprice features, monopolistic competitors have *some power over*

the price. This is the key condition that distinguishes monopolistic competition from perfect competition. Consumers do not regard the rival offerings of sellers as perfect substitutes, so they willingly pay a bit more for Brand X, for convenient store location, and the like. Still, the differences among sellers remain less than monumental. Each firm's product is a fairly close substitute for others in its market.

B
The Firm's View of Demand

As part (a) of Figure 27.7 attests, the monopolistically competitive firm sees only its nonfollowship demand curve. There may be interdependence in that one firm's actions could provoke reactions from others. But followship is ignored.

Moreover, the firm's nonfollowship curve is

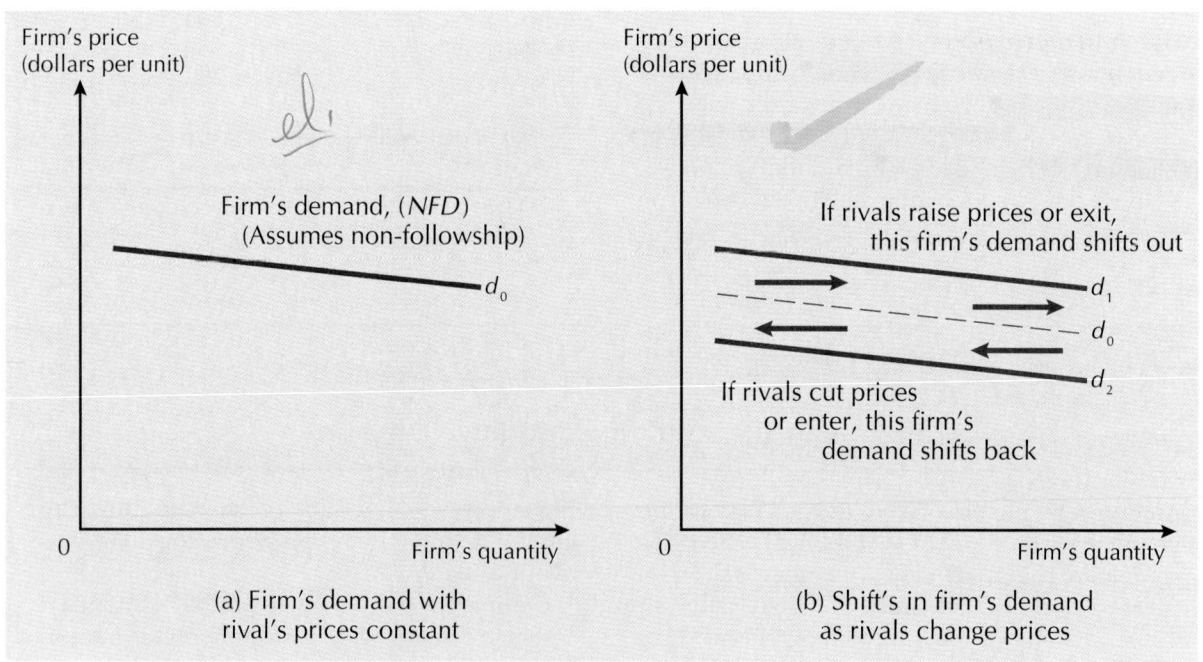

(a) Firm's demand with rival's prices constant

(b) Shift's in firm's demand as rivals change prices

FIGURE 27.7 Firm Demand: Monopolistic Competition

Part (a) depicts the monopolistically competitive firm's demand, assuming that the prices of others in the market are unchanged in response to this firm's price changes (i.e., nonfollowship, as in Figure 27.5). Part (b) illustrates the impact of rivals' actions. Because of substitution, the firm's demand shifts right when rivals raise their prices and shifts left when they cut their prices. Rival exit and entry have similar effects. Exits shift the firm's demand out; entries shift it back.

highly elastic. Small firm size relative to the market and fairly close substitute offerings cause this high elasticity. Still, the firm's demand curve is not perfectly elastic, as is a perfectly competitive firm's.

Figure 27.7 also underscores the nature of the firm's demand. The vertical axis represents *this firm's price*. As it varies in part (a) demand d_0 emerges, assuming rivals' prices remain constant. If, on the contrary, rivals' prices do change, the results are shown in part (b). An *increase* in rivals' prices would *shift this firm's demand out* to d_1, because it then gains customers at each of its possible prices. A *decrease* in rivals' prices would *shift its demand back* to d_2 as its customers switch to rivals. Thus substitutability imparts some interdependence, but it goes unrecognized.

Read Perspective 27D.

V

Monopolistic Competition: Conduct

Price conduct in these markets tends to be highly competitive in both the short and the long run. The short run is typified by short-sighted price cutting. The long run opens the door to new entry. A comment concerning the very high $495 price Lotus charged for its popular 1-2-3 program in 1985 illustrates the combined effect: "one or more companies will come out with clones and software prices will come down very fast."[16]

[16]*Wall Street Journal*, May 15, 1985, p. 1.

PERSPECTIVE 27D

Personal Computer Software: An Example of Monopolistic Competition

One of the newest markets on the economic landscape approximates monopolistic competition pretty well—personal computer software publishing. Several thousand firms produce several thousand new programs each year. The largest of these in the mid-1980s, Lotus, had about 7 percent of the $2 billion market in 1984, largely because of its popular 1-2-3 program. This share may not be tiny enough to fit the classic model of monopolistic competition perfectly, but it's small enough for illustrative purposes. As regards entry, software publishing has witnessed a swarm of new entrants during the past decade. One-person startups grounded on no more than about $10,000 in capital have been so common that it seems as if anyone can give it a shot. Perhaps the only barrier of note is product differentiation. Programs are differentiated by advertising, by distribution coverage, by computer compatibility, by speed of operation, by task performed, and by other features. Lotus, for instance, was running large advertisements in 1985 claiming in big, bold type that *"1-2-3 is to software what Sunkist is to oranges."* The consequences of all this for firm demand were discovered in a pricing experiment that the Noumenon Corporation conducted on its Intuit program. When originally priced at $395, Intuit remained on the shelves, not selling even with extensive advertising. So the firm experimented, slashing the price to $50 and then raising it $20 each week until sales ceased. It also dropped all advertising to isolate the effect of price on demand. A downward-sloping demand curve emerged in association with corresponding total revenues (see Figure 26.1 on page 505). Total revenues rose at each higher price up to $130, where they topped out. Then, at each $20 jump beyond $130, revenues were lower than at the previous price level until they shrank to zero at a price of $210.[15]

[15]*Wall Street Journal*, May 15, 1985, pp. 1, 20; *Forbes*, January 28, 1985, p. 88; *Business Week*, March 18, 1985, pp. 94–104.

A
Short-Run Price Competition

Because a monopolistic competitor has something akin to a small monopoly, it might be able to price like a monopoly, thereby earning economic profits in the short run following the two-question logic of $MR = MC$. But monopolistic competitors are also prone to price wars, or short-sighted price competition.

Figure 27.8 shows the situation as viewed by a typical monopolistic competitor. We begin with all firms in the market pricing at $65 (for a coat or a computer program, depending on the product or service). The typical firm is earning a total economic profit equal to the difference between $65 and the average total cost (*ATC*) directly below point *A* *times* the quantity it produces. Though adequate, the firm's profit would rise if it cut the

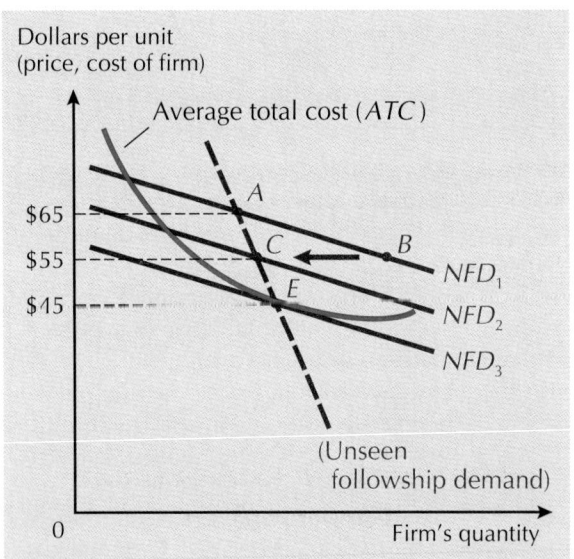

FIGURE 27.8   Short-Sighted Price Cutting Under Monopolistic Competition

At the outset, the firm is at point A, with a price matching the market price, $65. Ignoring possible followship, the monopolistic competitor tries to increase its profit by cutting the price to $55, which, if not followed, would raise its market share and place the firm at point B. This firm is typical, so the other firms see the same situation and cut the price too, placing this firm at C, a point on the unseen followship curve. An equilibrium, where further cutting is obviously not profitable, is at point E, where NFD₃ lies tangent to ATC and profits end up normal.

price to $55 without being followed by rivals. In that event, it would move down its nonfollowship demand curve, NFD_1, to a point such as *B*. Notice the very high elasticity of NFD_1. The quantity nearly doubles. So this ploy yields a substantial increase in total revenue, while declining unit costs (*ATC*) keep total costs from rising by an equal amount. However, the profit gains last only as long as rivals fail to follow, because these gains come at their expense. Their demand curves will have shifted to the left, leaving them with fewer customers, higher costs, and lower profits. To regain their former customers, these rivals also cut their prices to $55, an action that shifts the firm in Figure 27.8 from point *B* to point *C*. After cut and countercut, the result is a movement down the unseen followship demand curve from *A* to *C* and to a new nonfollowship curve, NFD_2. As the firm in Figure 27.8 is typical of all firms in the market, this descent carries all other firms with it. If our typical firm is shortsighted enough to try the same cuts again, the others will naturally follow and further downward shifts will ensue. Equilibrium is reached at point *E* with a price of $45, at which point any further price cutting takes the firm below its average total cost. Here theory posits a truce. Only normal profits (embodied in *ATC*) prevail in the end.

The key to this scenario is the inability of the small monopolistic competitor to see beyond its first step down the nonfollowship curve. Unlike a large oligopolist, the firm does not consider the inelastic followship curve. Rivals' reactions go unrecognized. The temptations of *NFD*'s high elasticity seem too attractive. The consequence is price competition.

Read Perspective 27E.

B
Long-Run Entry

If monopolistic competitors are able to escape the clutches of price competition in the short run, they may earn economic profits in the short run. However, because of easy entry, those economic profits cannot last into the long run. Newcomers thirsting after profits inject enough competition to force prices down and squeeze out the economic profits.

PERSPECTIVE 27E
A Grocery Price War

The preceding pattern may be illustrated with an example from grocery retailing, which in certain cities might qualify as monopolistically competitive. In 1975 and 1976 price wars ignited in several cities, despite the fact that industry executives decried them, saying that "price wars always hurt profits and rarely change market shares among the combatants—the supposed goal." Except for consumers, who obviously benefit, "everybody fights harder and everybody loses."[17] Here is the story of one of the bloodiest battles of this period:

> The Chicago price war, undoubtedly one of the longest and costliest in supermarket history, began abruptly. On a Saturday afternoon in April ..., the manager of a Jewel Food Store heard from a visitor that a nearby Dominick's store was changing a lot of prices. Unusual for a Saturday, the manager thought. He sent an employee to check.
>
> The employee found Dominick's aisles swarming with stock boys repricing merchandise. And all the prices were being reduced. Within

[17]"Supermarket Scrap," *Wall Street Journal*, July 19, 1976.

> minutes, Jewel employees throughout the area were scouting Dominick's stores. Their reports were startling.... Dominick's was slashing prices as much as 15% on "hundreds and hundreds" of items.
>
> On Tuesday, Jewel's response was ready. Jewel was cutting prices on 3,327 items from 2% to 30%. On Friday, National Tea announced it was reducing prices. ... Other competitors jumped in quickly.
>
> Mr. DiMatteo [the manager of Dominick's] says he thought he could batter the competition. So he ordered the price cuts. ... However, "the competition jumped in a lot faster than I thought they would," he concedes. "I thought we'd be alone for a while."[18]

Although the followship demand curve was not wholly invisible to Mr. DiMatteo, it was certainly obscure. As for the ultimate effects on market share, "*Progressive Grocer*, a trade magazine, found that 95% of the Chicago shoppers it questioned at one point during the price war said they were going to the same store they had before the battle broke out."

[18]Ibid.

Figure 27.8 can be adapted to illustrate. Suppose that established firms are able to hold the price up at $65, resulting in the short-run economic profit for the typical firm shown in Figure 27.8. This attracts entry. The new entrants divert some demand away from established firms by offering slightly lower prices, different styling, more convenient retail locations, and other features that attract customers. These diversions shift the established firm's demand down (or back) from NFD_1 to NFD_2. Entries and diversions continue until economic profits disappear and equilibrium is reached. Point E in Figure 27.8 illustrates this result. At this combination of price and output, the firm's average total cost equals its price. Entry stops.

VI
Monopolistic Competition: Performance

Figure 27.9 shows the theoretical long-run equilibrium for the monopolistic competitor after price competition and entry run their course. It summarizes several conclusions regarding performance.

A
What?

The firm's equilibrium price and quantity in Figure 27.9 are P_E and Q_E, respectively. This combi-

MSB 7MSC
produce
more

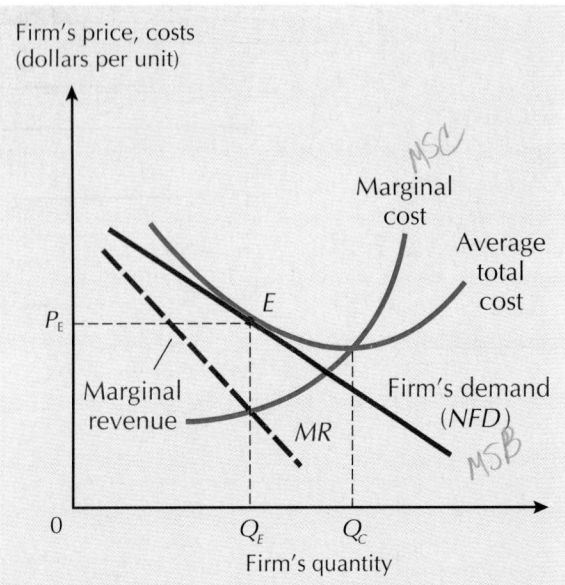

Firm's price, costs
(dollars per unit)

MSC

Marginal
cost

Average
total
cost

P_E

E

Marginal
revenue

MR

Firm's demand
(NFD)

MSB

0   Q_E Q_C

Firm's quantity

FIGURE 27.9   *Monopolistic Competitor in Long-Run Equilibrium*

Long-run equilibrium price and quantity are P_E *and* Q_E. *At* Q_E, *marginal revenue matches marginal cost for profit maximization. However, profits are normal (zero economic profit) because price matches average total cost at point E. Price is above marginal cost, raising questions about allocation efficiency. Moreover, output is below* Q_C, *which would minimize cost and secure technical efficiency. Still, the performance of monopolistic competition is usually judged superior to that of oligopoly or monopoly.*

nation brings marginal revenue and marginal cost into equality, thereby maximizing profit. Does this combination bring allocation efficiency? A quick answer is "no." Price at point *E* exceeds marginal costs. And since price reflects marginal social benefits, this result has marginal social benefits exceeding marginal costs. Recalling that allocation efficiency requires marginal social benefits to equal marginal social costs *(MSB = MSC)*; this result implies poor performance for monopolistic competition.

Still, this quick answer may be misleading. Once product varieties are allowed, as they are in the differentiated products of monopolistic competition, the norm for allocation efficiency becomes muddled. If people value variety (as they appear to do), and if each variety of the product cannot be supplied by perfect competition (as it cannot in the real world), then the *MSB = MSC* standard

seems irrelevant, too utopian. What is produced by monopolistic competition? Millions of personal computer software disks in thousands of different programs. Shirts and blouses in dozens upon dozens of different styles and brands. Economic theory has not yet reached a state of refinement where we can say that these quantities and varieties are not desirable. They may be just fine.[19]

B
How?

The typically intense competition of monopolistic competition probably holds down X-inefficiencies of the usual sort—luxurious corporate headquarters, excessive layers of management, undue spoilage or waste. This is good.

On the other hand, monopolistic competition invites criticism for its apparent excess capacity, which can be considered a form of X-inefficiency. Notice in Figure 27.9 that an output of Q_c is required to reach the low point of the average total cost curve. Q_c then defines full capacity use, as it does for a perfectly competitive firm. The firm's output, Q_E, thus falls short of low-cost, full capacity use. At least it does in theory.

Moving from theory to reality, examples of excess capacity under monopolistic competition are easy to find. But any condemnation of monopolistic competition for excess capacity must be heavily qualified for at least two reasons. First, the excess capacity is lessened by the highly elastic demand facing these firms. The higher the elasticity, the closer it approaches perfect competition and the low point on the average total cost curve. Second, excess capacity is often difficult to measure. When properly measured, it may be less serious than it seems. In retailing, for instance, capacity is needed for peak demand periods, such as weekends and holidays.

C
Who?

Theory posits zero economic profits for the monopolistic competitor. This suggests good performance—that is, no contribution to inequities in income distribution.

[19]Michael Waterson, *Economic Theory of the Industry* (Cambridge: Cambridge University Press, 1984), pp. 124–127.

Reality is a bit more complex, but it does not violently contradict theory. Within a given monopolistically competitive market, some firms may earn economic profits from especially strong customer loyalty or from unusual cost efficiency. McDonald's in fast foods and Levi's in apparel are examples. At the same time, others will be suffering economic losses. _On average,_ monopolistic competition does seem to yield no more than normal profits in the long run.

Overall, then, the performance of monopolistic competition is pretty good. Prices may be higher _and output lower than under perfect competition, but not to the degree observed for oligopoly or monopoly. Costs, too, may be a bit higher for monopolistic competition than for perfect competition, something that explains the price–output results. Softening the blow is the fact that these differences derive from product differentiation, and that, to some degree, carries benefits. Consumers value variety. Moreover, the profits of monopolistic competitors are clearly closer to the normal rates of perfect competition than to the frequently excessive rates of monopoly and oligopoly._

SUMMARY

1. Oligopoly and monopolistic competition blanket the territory between monopoly and perfect competition. And on the outer fringes of that blanket—where oligopolists are particularly powerful and monopolistic competitors are especially contentious—the results border on those for monopoly and perfect competition.

2. Few firms, difficult entry, and standardized or differentiated products characterize oligopoly. Variations in fewness are registered by concentration ratios and H indexes and are caused by luck, business policies, government policies, and economic technicalities. Established firms gain advantages over potential entrants for several reasons, including economies of scale and (occasionally) product differentiation. The upshot of oligopoly structure is a pair of demand curves for each firm, distinguished by followship or nonfollowship on the part of rivals.

3. Oligopoly price strategies revolve around recognized interdependence and the possibility of either collusion or competition. Under price leadership, prices set by a leader are aped by those of rivals. A strong leader, who is always followed, sees only its followship demand curve. The theory of kinked demand splices the upper portion of the nonfollowship curve to the lower portion of the followship curve by assuming different reactions of rivals when the firm initiates price increases or decreases. The result is a model of price rigidity that is limited by being more applicable to certain oligopoly firms (mid-sized) than to markets as a whole. The small-firm maverick, which tends to see a highly elastic nonfollowship demand curve, is the most likely price cutter in an oligopoly. Finally, cartelization may occur, in which case a market's members expressly agree not to compete in some way, usually on price. Cartelization seems most frequent under structural conditions where neither tacit collusion nor cutthroat competition dominates.

4. As for performance, oligopoly tends to raise prices toward monopoly-like levels when competition is lacking. This typically yields allocation inefficiency, allows costly X-inefficiency, and may warp the income distribution inequitably.

5. Monopolistic competition is a first cousin to perfect competition, the main difference being product differentiation. With a fairly large number of relatively small firms, interdependence goes unrecognized. So, independence prevails.

6. Vigorous price competition in the short run and easy entry in the long run typify conduct in this case. Independent attempts to maximize profit lead in the end to normal profits on average.

7. Although the price is above the marginal cost under monopolistic competition, the

key question What? may not be answered too badly. Product differentiation has its costs, but it also yields benefits. As for the question How?, excess capacity and excess differentiation expenses may create X-inefficiencies, but otherwise this market gets high marks. Finally, the issue of Who? wins hurrahs for monopolistic competition and its normal profits.

Appendix:
Prisoner's Dilemma Game Theory

Imagine that the police capture two men suspected of committing a crime together. Placed in separate interrogation rooms and not allowed to speak to each other, the prisoners are each told the following: "If *neither* of you confesses, our weak evidence will result in 1-year sentences for you both. If you *both* confess, you will both get 5-year terms. Under these circumstances, silence is in your best interest. But to encourage your confession, we will let you go free if you double-cross your partner by confessing and implicating him while he remains silent. Moreover, if he talks and you do not, we will make it very tough on you—a 7-year sentence."

This is called the *prisoner's dilemma* in an area of study known as *game theory*. Note that silence by both prisoners would be best for both together (1 year), but at the same time there are very strong incentives for each prisoner to "squeal" on the other. Freedom is a possible reward for confessing, and silence when coupled with the other's betrayal results in the stiffest penalty of all (7 years). If both prisoners cave in to the pressure, they each serve an intermediate term of 5 years. In brief, *cooperative* silence would be best for them, but the temptations for *competitive* betrayal are quite strong.

The principles behind the prisoner's dilemma nicely illustrate the tensions between collusive cooperation and competitive rivalry that arise in many oligopoly markets. Figure A illustrates this with a simple game involving you and an opponent. Rather than profits, we will use "points" for rewards in what is called a *payoff* matrix. And "co-

FIGURE A   Prisoner's Dilemma Game Matrix
You must decide whether to "cooperate" or "defect" without knowing what your opponent will do. If you both cooperate, the combined winnings are greatest (3 + 3 = 6). However, there are strong incentives to defect. If you assume that your opponent will cooperate, you would gain 5 points by defecting, which is more than the 3 points your cooperation would bring. If you assume that your opponent will defect, you will again find it in your interest to defect because that strategy pays 1 point instead of the 0 points your cooperation would bring. Your opponent will be following similar logic, so you may both defect, resulting in the lowest combined payoff (1 + 1 = 2).

operation" will be the same as holding the price up in the market, while "defection" will be shorthand for aggressive price cutting.

If you and your opponent were going to play this game only once and operate independently, there would be strong incentives for you both to defect, resulting in a payoff of only 1 point apiece even though mutual cooperation would clearly be better for you both, yielding 3 points apiece. The combined total in mutual cooperation, 6 points (3 + 3), is clearly better than the combined total in the chosen course, 2 points (1 + 1), and also better than the combined total of either of the two remaining options, 5 points (5 + 0, or 0 + 5), so the reasons behind this result are interesting. Let's explore your decision to defect.

You notice that your opponent can either cooperate or defect. If you assume that he will cooperate, your best strategy is to *defect* because your payoff is then 5 points compared to the 3 points you get by cooperating. If, on the other hand, you assume that he will defect, your best strategy is again to *defect* because your payoff is then 1 point compared to the 0 point you would get by cooperating. Hence you defect because that gives you the best result *regardless of the option chosen by your opponent.* Your opponent will follow the same line of logic because he faces the same numbers as you (only from the other side, of course). Hence you both defect despite the great rewards of cooperation.

Note, however, the constraints we imposed on the situation at the outset—namely, *independent play only once.* By dropping independence so that *collusion* to cooperate can occur (as it does with cartelization), the mutual cooperation result becomes more likely, with payoffs of 3 points apiece. Dropping the constraint of playing only one game reinforces the attraction of mutual cooperation. With only one game, the "binding" commitment of collusion can be undermined by the continued presence of one big payoff for a lone defector (5

points). With *iterated* prisoner dilemmas, where the game is repeated, cooperation by you and your opponent will be in *your individual and your mutual best interests* over the long run. This emerges from the strategy of "tit for tat," which is best in iterated games even in the absence of explicit collusion.[20] In tit for tat you do to your opponent what he has just done to you. You cooperate as long as your opponent cooperates. If he betrays you, then the next time you betray him to penalize him in retaliation. If he responds to the penalty and cooperates, you reinforce that action. You cooperate again. And so on.

"Games" among rivals in a given market tend to be of this iterated variety because business continues from month to month and year to year. Hence collusive behavior is often logical for oligopolists even when the forces favoring competitive betrayal are strong.

[20]Robert Axelrod, *The Evolution of Cooperation* (New York: Basic Books, 1984).

KEY TERMS

Oligopoly	Nonfollowship
Recognized interdependence	Tacit collusion
Concentration ratio	Price leadership
H index	Cartel
Barrier to entry	Monopolistic competition
Differentiated products	Unrecognized interdependence
Followship	

QUESTIONS AND PROBLEMS

1. An oligopoly market is dominated by a few large firms, though there may be many small firms in the market. This fact results in the use of concentration measures to indicate the extent of market dominance. Explain what concentration ratios and H indexes are. What values for these two measures indicate oligopolistic market conditions?

2. What are barriers to entry? What are the implications of high barriers to entry in a market?

3. In what sense does an oligopolistic firm face two demand curves for its product?

4. Explain why firms in an oligopolistic industry might choose to cooperate via price leadership behavior.

5. Show graphically and explain verbally why prices in an oligopolistic industry with four approximately equal sized firms might remain the same for years, despite changing cost conditions and shifting demand conditions.

6. Explain why small firms in an industry might be "mark-down mavericks."

7. What is a cartel? What conditions allow cartels to

survive for extended periods of time? What factors make long-term cartelization the exception rather than the rule?

8. Residents of small towns (populations less than 8,000) often find that furniture, groceries, and clothing in local stores are more expensive than in large cities. Explain why this might be so.

9. Compare the performance of oligopoly to that of perfect competition and pure monopoly (with respect to What?, How?, and Who?)

10. Compare the demand curve of a monopolistically competitive firm (a) to that of a perfectly competitive firm and (b) to that of a pure monopolist.

11. Evaluate the performance of monopolistically competitive firms with respect to What?, How?, and Who?

Appendix:

12. In what sense do oligopolists necessarily participate in an iterated "prisoner's dilemma" game?

28

Oligopoly and Monopolistic Competition: Nonprice Strategies

The average American guzzles 43 gallons of soda pop per year, much of it Coca-Cola. First concocted over 100 years ago, Coca-Cola has dominated the industry for most of this century, at times garnering 60 percent of total sales. The flavor of its secret formula and the draw of its advertising have made Coca-Cola a worldwide favorite. But Pepsi, its arch rival, has been climbing. After a brush with bankruptcy during the Great Depression, Pepsi lifted its market share from 10 percent in 1940 to 20 percent in 1965 to nearly 30 percent in 1985. Advertising expenditures that greatly exceeded Coke's on a per case basis and advertising themes that caught the imagination of the "Pepsi generation" lifted Pepsi into a position rivaling Coca-Cola in the $25 billion industry. Then in April 1985, the Coca-Cola Company made history when it changed the flavor of Coke, making it a little sweeter, a change that was hard for many Cokaholics to swallow. Within weeks more than 40,000 anguished Coke drinkers telephoned complaints to the company. Protest groups formed. Demonstrations were held. But Coca-Cola held fast, budgeting $100 million to tout the new taste and delighting in the fact that more than 110 million people tried new Coke during its first month on the market. Sales of new Coke soon began to fizzle, however, so 3 months after its explosive introduction, the Coca-Cola Company announced that it would resurrect the old flavor in a new brand called "Coca-Cola Classic." Pepsi claimed victory and Coca-Cola tried to cover its mistake by saying that new Coke and old Coke together would please everyone.

The saga of Coke introduces *dynamic competition*. The traditional price theory of previous chapters is largely "static." It deduces static equilibriums and compares one static equilibrium with another. It's like a lake. In contrast, much real-world competition flows through time like a river—swelling, contracting, speeding, and slowing. Dynamic competition depends on the actions and reactions of rivals during a market's unfolding history rather than on any close comparison of prices and costs on some supposedly typical day.

Moreover, we have here a dramatic demonstration that price is not the only competitive weapon. Firms rely on *marketing effort* and *product variation*, as well as price. Indeed, in many markets, marketing effort and product variation outweigh price strategy. Firms annually spend over $80 billion on advertising and introduce thousands of new products. The Coca-Cola Company accounts for about $400 million of the ad total, promoting its 18 drinks in more than 100 different packages. Similarly, Kellogg offers nearly two dozen different breakfast cereals. And sales managers for Deere & Company, a big farm equipment maker, display that firm's philosophy by wearing tie clasps with the letters *SOQ, NOP*, which stands for "sell on quality, not on price."

Our task in this chapter is to expand on these topics. Advertising and innovation are emphasized in what follows as representative features of marketing effort and product variation. Dynamic competition involves other variables, but because of our limited space, they will not be covered.

I
Identifying Dynamic Competition

A
Definition

What happens when Procter & Gamble introduces Citrus Hill orange juice, backed by a $100 million advertising budget? How do Minute Maid and Tropicana react? What happens when Apple Computer upgrades its Macintosh, offering 512K capacity instead of the old 128K? How do IBM and H-P respond? These events illustrate vigorous competition, yet they spring from markets that are not perfectly competitive at all. They illustrate *dynamic competition*.

Dynamic competition entails an independent striving for patronage by firms employing various strategies and counter-strategies, using nonprice variables as well as price in efforts to outmaneuver one another over time.

The first thing to note here is that dynamic competition does *not* rigorously require masses of firms, standardized products, or any of the other structural conditions of perfect competition. Compared to perfect competition, the *structure* of dynamically competitive markets includes many imperfections. For example, whereas the perfectly competitive firm is almost invisibly small, the theory of dynamic competition includes firms large enough to have notable identities and to have some influence over price. For another example, perfect competition assumes that buyers and sellers have perfect information, while dynamic competition assumes imperfect information. In the end, the theory of dynamic competition downplays the importance of market structure altogether. Its main focus is conduct.

Regarding *conduct*, dynamic competition could just as well be called *rivalrous competition*. Its firms vie with each other in ways not recognized by the theory of perfect competition. According to J. M. Clark, dynamic competition "includes initiatory action by a firm, responses by those with whom it deals, and responses to these responses by rival firms, to which one could add the subsequent rejoinders of the imitators."[1] Moreover, these rivalrous actions and reactions commonly involve the many *nonprice* variables that fall under the broad headings of marketing effort and product variation—namely, advertising, promotion, product design, technological innovation, and packaging. Thus a list of conduct characteristics would include the following:

1. Dynamic competition is chiefly an *activity* of sellers.
2. Dynamic competition arises out of conscious attempts by firms to devise *overall product offerings* that attract buyers.
3. As the competitive process unfolds over time, independent rivalry will result in

firms both *creating* and *responding* to new market forces, shifting product life cycles, and changing consumer tastes.

Why does *nonprice* competition take center stage in this context of dynamics? There are several reasons. Note *first* that a firm's price cuts can usually be matched immediately by rivals and may lead to ruinous price wars. Price cutting therefore often offers little competitive advantage and may even be considered suicidal. In contrast, marketing maneuvers and product innovations can reward their originators with at least temporary economic profits because they typically cannot be imitated immediately. For instance, after Miller's rousing initial success with its "Lite" beer in the 1970s, many months passed before other brewers could put out their light beers. Moreover, and *second*, firms have discovered that marketing ploys and product changes are in many cases a means of *increasing* prices (and therefore profits). Miller's Lite beer costs less to make than its regular beer because it contains fewer ingredients. Yet Miller prices Lite at or above the price of its regular brands (High Life, Meister Brau, and Milwaukee's Best). Finally, and *third*, firms have found that product differences make price discrimination, or something similar, easier than otherwise. Product differences enable market segmentation, with higher price/cost ratios for "luxury" brands in comparison to "economy" brands. Beers, for instance, are segmented into super-premiums (e.g., Michelob), premiums (e.g., Budweiser), popular-priced (e.g., Old Milwaukee), and generics or private labels. Each of America's four leading brewers has brands in each of the top three price categories, and their profit margins are much higher on their super-premium brands than on their popular-priced brands.

B

Advertising

Of all the marketing maneuvers used in dynamic competition, none is as obvious as advertising. Hundreds of advertisements pelt each of us every day—on television, radio, everywhere. Table 28.1 gives a summary of the amounts sellers spend on advertising by major media. Newspapers and tele-

---

[1]J.M. Clark, "Competition: Static Models and Dynamic Aspects," in *Readings in Industrial Organization and Public Policy* (Homewood, Ill.: Richard D. Irwin, 1958), p. 251.

TABLE 28.1   U.S. Advertising Expenditures, 1985, by Media

Medium	Billions of Dollars	Percent of Total
Newspapers	$25.2	26.6%
Magazines	5.2	5.9
Television	20.8	22.0
Radio	6.5	6.9
Direct mail	15.5	16.4
Business publications	2.4	2.5
Outdoor	0.9	1.0
Other	18.2	19.2
Total	$94.7	100.0

Source: Reprinted with permission from *Advertising Age* (May 12, 1986), p. 76. Copyright 1986 by Crain Communications, Inc.

vision clearly account for the biggest chunks of total spending.

For later purposes, it is useful to distinguish advertising that is *informative* and that which is *persuasive*, although many advertisements blend both qualities. *Informative advertising* provides facts on such matters as prices (e.g., "$50 off"), product features (e.g., front-wheel drive), ingredients (e.g., no sodium)[2] and availability (e.g., 17 models to choose from). Studies show that newspapers have a very high quotient of informative ads. This is not surprising. It's in newspapers that grocery stores disclose weekly specials, that department stores flash pictures of high-fashion apparel, and that used-car sellers identify the make, model, mileage, and equipment of their offerings. Of course, the purpose of informative advertising is not to educate consumers. The purpose of all advertising is to gain sales by *influencing* buyers. It is simply the case that some buyers of some goods and services are best influenced by information. So advertisers use information in those situations.

The purpose of *persuasive advertising* is likewise to gain sales by influencing buyers, but here exhortation is used rather than information. Exhortation commonly involves exaggeration, humor, sex, jingles, plays on insecurity, and cajolery. Moreover, it often is aimed at changing the tastes of consumers rather than merely informing consumers about how they might best satisfy their established tastes.

Economists have no theories of how persuasion works or how consumers' tastes change, but many social psychologists and marketing experts earn their living by developing such theories and testing them.[3] Since this is an economics book, we will just mention two examples of exhortative techniques that advertisers often find effective.

1. A person's attitudes and opinions are strongly influenced by groups to which he or she belongs or wants to belong. Athletes and entertainers therefore give testimonials for everything under the sun. You drink Pepsi if you want to join the "Pepsi generation."
2. Repeating a theme tends to prolong its influence, and slight variations of the repetition are advantageous. Thus, how many ways has Miller Lite said that "It tastes great"? Would you like a dime for every cowboy you've seen puffing a Marlboro?

Some media and some products lend themselves more to persuasive advertising than others. Among the media, television seems to pack an especially strong persuasive punch. This is demonstrated in extensive research showing a lack of information in TV commercials.[4] You can discover it yourself by comparing the TV and newspaper

---

[2]The very first real commercial ever to be aired over the radio was informative on ingredients. That was in the 1920's, when cigars were still rolled by hand rather than machine. The commercial: "There is no spit in Cremo cigars!" E. Barnouw, *The Sponsor* (New York: Oxford University Press, 1978) p. 25.

[3]See, e.g., S.H. Britt, *Psychological Principles of Marketing and Consumer Behavior* (Lexington, Mass.: Lexington Books, 1978).

[4]A. Resnik and B. Stern, "An Analysis of Information Content in Television Advertising," *Journal of Marketing* (January 1977), pp. 50–53.

ads of airline companies. In newspapers you're informed of airline schedules, destinations, and fare discounts. On TV you see emotive dramas depicting the "Friendly Skies of United" and hear lush choral singing of "Delta gets you there."[5]

Not all economists draw a distinction between informative and persuasive advertising. A few maintain that all advertising is informative and none of it is persuasive. Some claim that information and persuasion cannot be distinguished. Here we adopt the apparent view of most people. In one of the most extensive opinion surveys ever conducted, people were asked to rate everyday ads as to whether they were "especially annoying, enjoyable, informative, or offensive." Those for candy and soft drinks turned out to be among the least informative but the most enjoyable. Conversely,

those for agricultural supplies were the most informative but the least enjoyable.[6] Thus people in general seem to find meaningful distinctions, and we leave it up to you to agree or disagree.

Read Perspective 28A.

C

Innovation

Technological change proceeds in three main stages, each of which is risky. **Invention** comes first. It has been defined as *"the first confidence that something should work, and the first rough test that it will in fact work."*[8] It requires an *initial*

---

[5]For more on this point, see D. F. Greer, *Industrial Organization and Public Policy*, 2nd ed. (New York: Macmillan, 1984, 2nd Ed.), pp. 65–69.

[6]R. A. Bauer and S. A. Greyser, *Advertising in America: The Consumer View* (Boston: Division of Research, Graduate School of Business Administration, Harvard University, 1968), pp. 175–183, 296–97.

[8]J. Jewkes, D. Sawers, and R. Stillerman, *The Sources of Invention*, 2nd ed. (New York: Norton, 1969), p. 28.

PERSPECTIVE 28A
Coke's Image

The Coca-Cola Company has a venerable history of being one of America's premier marketers. The uproar caused by its change of flavor in April 1985 may suggest that Coke's taste is more important than its advertising image. But there is evidence to refute this conclusion. Blind taste tests reveal that at least half the populace cannot correctly identify old Coke, new Coke, and Pepsi, or taste any difference between them. Even the fellow who formed Old Cola Drinkers of America, the largest protest group spawned by Coca-Cola's change in flavor, failed repeatedly to identify (or even prefer) old Coke in blind taste tests conducted during 1985. Why then his protest and that of others? It was apparently a matter of *image*. Coke had become an American institution. "Baseball, hamburger, Coke— they're all the fabric of America." Or, as a company spokesman put it: "We had taken away more than the product Coca-Cola. We had taken away a little part of [our customers] and their

past. They said, 'You had no right to do that. Bring it back.' " The advertising themes building Coke's image over the decades have been largely persuasive. In the 1890s Coke was "The Ideal Brain Tonic." In the 1970s it was "The Real Thing." And just before its change in 1985, countless ads insisted that "Coke Is It." Thus the present combination of new Coke and Coca-Cola Classic poses an image problem. The company cannot say "Coke Are It," or "The Real Things."

As this is written, the company is trying to persuade youngsters that new Coke is for them and convince older persons that Coca-Cola Classic is their brand.[7]

[7]*Wall Street Journal*, July 18, 1985, p. 25; July 12, 1985, p. 2; July 11, 1985, pp. 2, 12, 18; May 13, 1985, p. 21; *Newsweek*, July 22, 1985, pp. 40–42; June 24, 1985, pp. 32–33; May 6, 1985, pp. 50–52; D. Greer, "Some Case History Evidence on the Advertising–Concentration Relationship," *Antitrust Bulletin* (Summer 1973), pp. 307–332; *Fortune*, August 5, 1985, pp. 44–46.

concept and _crude proof._ Thus it could be said that Xerox copy machines were "invented" on October 22, 1938, when Chester Carlson first used a crude device embodying his novel ideas to copy the message "10–22–38 Astoria."

Moving from the test lab to the market requires a second and more costly stage—**innovation**, _which is the first commercial application of an invention._ This entails refinement of the basic idea, testing prototypes, debugging, development, engineering, and initial production. The boundary between invention and innovation is often fuzzy because these innovative activities usually lead to many additional inventions. Chester Carlson's basic ideas for a copy machine won four patents between 1940 and 1944, but it was not until 1959, after more than 100 "improvement" patents for various machine designs, selenium drums, paper feeding devices, powder dispensers, and so on that the Xerox Company commercially introduced its historic 914 console copier. Still, despite the overlap between invention and innovation, they are often worth separating. "Invention is the stage at which the scent is first picked up, development the stage at which the hunt is in full cry."[9]

One measure of invention and innovation taken together is that, in 1984, U.S. firms spent $48.1 billion on research and development (R & D). This is less than their advertising outlays in the same year, but once government spending for R & D is added, the grand total for 1984 tops $90 billion, an impressive amount indeed. Still, invention and innovation would come to naught if it were not for the third and final stage—diffusion. After market introduction, innovations may flop or spread. **Diffusion**, _refers to the extent and speed of an innovation's adoption, its penetration of the marketplace, if a product, and its popularity on the plant floor, if a process._ Diffusion usually takes time and money because it can involve multitudes of producers and users. Copy machines, for example, are now produced by IBM, Kodak, Canon, Savin, Royal, and many other firms besides Xerox. Diffusion has been so extensive as to change our way of life.

It may be concluded that a full assessment of progressiveness must take account of invention, innovation, and diffusion. Each is different. Each is

crucial. Still, we must concentrate on innovation—in particular _product_ innovations as opposed to _process_ innovations. _Product innovations_ represent new products sold. They can be momentous, like copy machines, personal computers, or microwave ovens. They can also be quite trivial, like wine coolers, or chocolate-covered granola bars. Indeed, some product innovations are so trivial that they amount to little more than brand proliferation. Coke's flavor change ranks in this category of creativity.

In contrast to product innovations, _process innovations_ introduce new methods of production, like catalytic cracking of petroleum or mechanical tomato picking. The distinction between product and process innovations blurs because a product of one industry is often a process to another. Pesticides, for instance, are products for chemical companies but process inputs in the eyes of farmers. We therefore will not be too picky about drawing this last distinction.

_II_
The Effects on Firm Revenue and Cost

The motive behind advertising and innovation is no mystery. It's mainly _profit._ Also, by now there should be no mystery about what factors determine profit—_revenue_ and _cost._ What, then, is new here? The answer is simple.

Previously we have assumed that, in essence, each firm faced _given_ revenue and cost conditions. The firm's revenue opportunities were set by its demand curve, which in turn was determined by such factors as market share. Similarly, the firm's cost constraints were set by production technologies, input prices, and the like. We saw a firm's revenues and costs change _only as functions of the firm's output or scale._ We never saw those functions themselves change as a result of the firm's other possible actions. Now we will see that change. _The main reason firms engage in advertising or innovation is to **manipulate** their revenue and cost conditions so as to raise their profits or protect them from decline._

It's two-question logic once again. What is it

[9]Ibid.

worth to advertise or innovate? What does it cost to do so? It's just that these actions *alter the firm's conditions*. We begin with the manipulation of revenues as derived from changes in firm demand. Cost changes come next.

A

Lowering the Elasticity of Demand

Figure 28.1 illustrates how advertising, especially persuasive advertising, might lower a firm's elasticity of demand, thereby facilitating price increases to raise total revenue. The firm sells Brand X at a price of $4, starting at point A. Let the AB curve depict the firm's (nonfollowership) demand, assuming little or no advertising. Then let the AC curve depict demand after introduction of an aggressively financed advertising campaign that

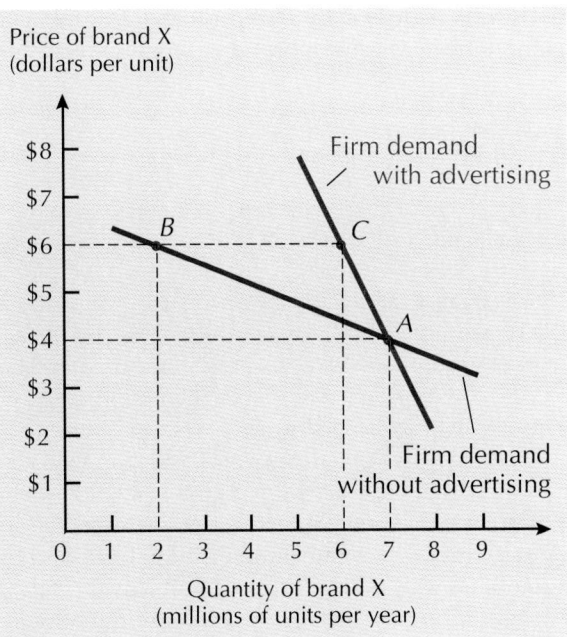

FIGURE 28.1 *Lowering the Firm's Elasticity of Demand by Persuasive Advertising*

Without advertising, the firm's demand is relatively elastic, so a price increase from $4 to $6 would move the firm from point A to point B, causing its total revenue to slide from $28 million at point A ($4 × 7 million units) to $12 million at point B ($6 × 2 million units). With advertising, elasticity is lowered, so the same price increase would move the firm from point A to point C. Total revenue in this latter case would rise from $28 million to $36 million ($6 × 6 million units).

shouts incessantly that "Brand X folks would rather fight than switch." If the price of Brand X had been raised without the new campaign from $4 to $6, the quantity would have tumbled from 7 million to 2 million units, causing total revenues (price times quantity) to *drop* from $28 million at point A ($4 × 7m) to $12 million at point B ($6 × 2m). But once most Brand X buyers are convinced that they would rather fight than switch, the same price increase from $4 to $6 trims the quantity comparatively little, from 7 million to 6 million units, and total revenues *rise* from $28 million at point A (again $4 × 7m) to $36 million at point C ($6 × 6m). The striking difference in revenue results is due to the fact that the firm's elasticity of demand is much lower with advertising than without it. Of course, the added costs of the advertising must be subtracted from the added revenues in order to calculate the added profit.

For years Taryton cigarettes relied on this very theme in their advertising. Determined-looking people peered out from billboards everywhere, saying, "I'd rather fight than switch." And they each had a black eye to prove it. More generally, Smirnoff has been particularly successful in differentiating its vodka with image advertising. And its comparatively high price apparently adds to its image as the best vodka. This is rather remarkable because vodka is a colorless, odorless, and tasteless beverage that is produced by an essentially simple, easily imitated process. Indeed, Smirnoff has been so confident about the inelasticity its image provides that at one point it *raised* its price in response to a competitor's price *cut*.[10]

A product innovation, such as an instant coffee produced by freeze drying, might have this elasticity effect on a brand's demand. More commonly, however, product innovations seem to be used to obtain related but slightly different elasticity effects. Recall that price discrimination requires different elasticities of demand among different classes of buyers, and these classes must be identified and separated. Product innovation or, more simply, brand proliferation can often be employed to achieve these effects, thereby facilitating a form of price discrimination. In 1984, for example, Gillette introduced Brush Plus, a device that dis-

[10]R. D. Buzzell, R. E. M. Nourse, J. B. Matthews, Jr., and T. Levitt, *Marketing: A Contemporary Analysis* (New York: McGraw-Hill, 1972), pp. 10–11.

penses shaving cream through a brush. The Brush Plus refill cartridge was priced one-third higher than Gillette's Foamy shaving cream in a can with an equivalent number of shaves.[11]

B
Shifting Firm Demand

Advertising and product innovation can also affect a firm's demand by *shifting* it outward. Figure 28.2 illustrates this for the case of advertising. In part (a) a successful increase in persuasive advertising for Brand Y shifts the demand curve for Brand Y out, resulting in greater sales volume. At a constant price of $4, the shift is from point M to point N. Total revenues consequently rise from $8 million at M to $16 million at N ($4 × 2m versus $4 × 4m). Profits, too, jump, provided the added costs of producing and advertising Brand Y are less than the added revenue. (Alternatively, the outward shift in

[11]*Business Week*, July 15, 1985, pp. 130–134.

Brand Y's demand would permit a higher price for Y such as at point P in Figure 28.2. This, however, would require some sacrifice in quantity.)

Part (b) of Figure 28.2 looks at this from the viewpoint of one of Brand Y's rivals. Assuming that Brand Z and Brand Y are to some degree substitutes (as are Coke and Pepsi), the favorable shift of demand to Brand Y in part (a) will shift the demand for Brand Z in part (b) to the left, lowering Brand Z's revenues. The negative shift for Z doesn't match the positive shift for Y, assuming that several other brands, say V and W, absorb part of the shock. Of course, sellers of Brands Z, V, and, W could retaliate by changing their promotional pitches or boosting their advertising outlays in response. This would cause reverse movements to those seen in Figure 28.2, but we shall ignore such gamesmanship until later.

A dramatic example of Figure 28.2 comes from the beer industry. In 1969 the Miller Brewing Company was acquired by Philip Morris, the tobacco giant, whose Marlboro brand is tops in cigarettes.

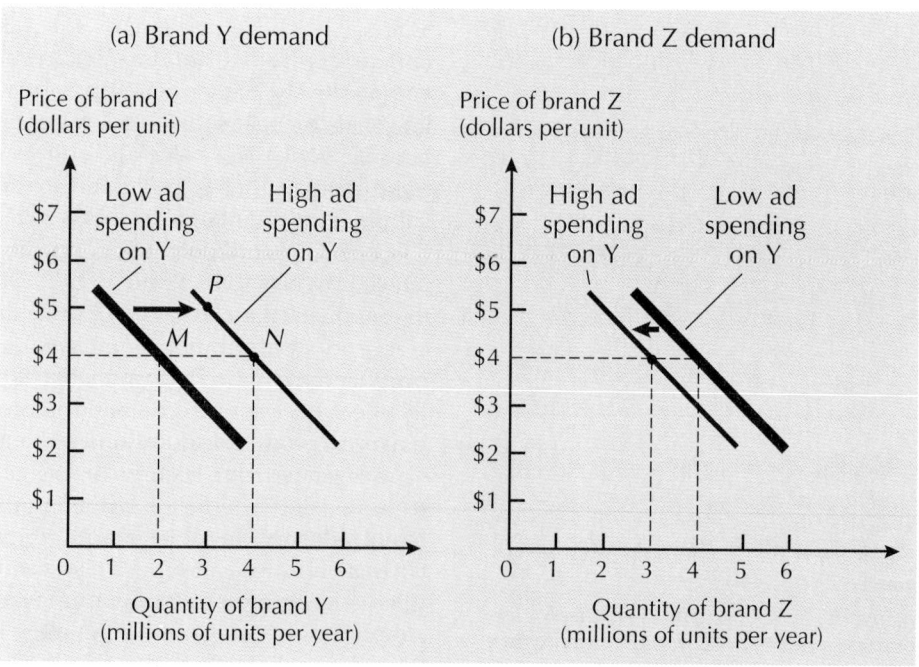

FIGURE 28.2   A Shift of Demand to Brand Y by Means of Advertising

An increase in advertising for brand Y shifts its demand to the right, doubling sales at a given price and thereby doubling revenues from $8 million (associated with point M) to $16 million (point N). Assuming that brand Z and brand Y are to some extent substitutes, this will cause the demand for brand Z (and for other substitute brands) to shift left, lowering their sellers' revenues.

At the time, Miller ranked ninth in national beer sales, with a market share of just over 4 percent. But that quickly changed after Phillip Morris aggressively escalated Miller's ad spending, changed its ad theme, and introduced some new brands. In 1971 Miller's ad spending was $2.59 per barrel compared to $0.98 for Anheuser-Busch and $1.03 for Schlitz, the first- and second-ranked companies at the time. And between 1971 and 1978, Miller's measured-media advertising outlays jumped 387 percent, apparently exceeding $260 million for the period. This, along with the other factors mentioned, caused Miller's market share to rocket from 4.5 percent in 1969 to 18.8 percent in 1978, lifting the firm into second place behind Anheuser-Busch.[12]

Product innovation can have the same effect on a firm's demand. Indeed, Miller's fantastic flight was helped immensely by its introduction of Lite during the 1970s, a low-calorie beer that now outsells Miller High Life. This example is strained by the fact that Miller was *not* the first on the market with a light beer. That distinction goes to Rheingold, which introduced Gablinger's in 1968. Still, Miller deserves some credit because it marketed the idea of a light beer better than Rheingold did. The virtues of Gablinger's were touted by fashion models and beauty queens instead of ex-athletes.

Of course, some product innovations are revolutionary—television, antibiotic drugs, and automobiles among them. In these instances, more is involved than a mere shift of the firm's demand curve. A whole new market demand curve is created.

C

Combination Effects

Sometimes firms use informative advertising in tandem with a price reduction, the advertising being used to broadcast the price cut. This can increase the firm's total revenues if the combined effect creates a new, *more highly elastic* demand curve. Figure 28.3 demonstrates. Assume that the firm starts at point *S*, with a price of $6 and a quan-

[12]D. Greer, "The Causes of Concentration in the Brewing Industry," *Quarterly Review of Economics and Business* (Winter 1981), pp. 87–106.

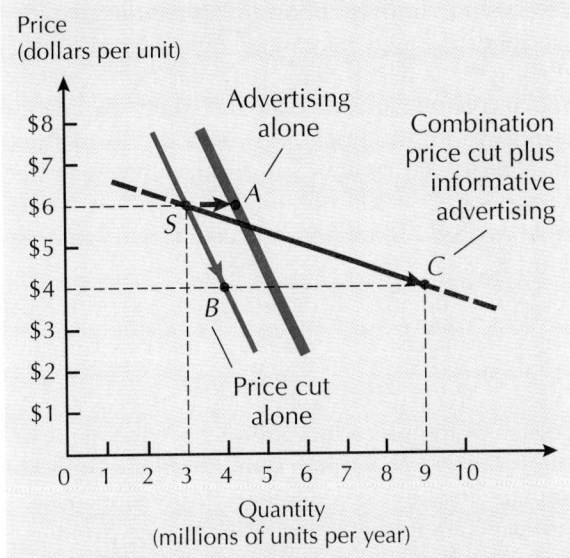

FIGURE 28.3 *Combination of the Firm's Price Cut and Informative Advertising*

It is assumed that the firm starts at point S, with a price of $6, zero advertising, and total revenues of $18 million ($6 × 3 million units). Spending to advertise, absent any other change, would shift demand rightward, moving the firm from S to A. Cutting the price, without advertising the cut, moves the firm from S to B. Neither of these moves boosts total revenues bountifully, but a combination of them does. Cutting the price from $6 to $4 and informing buyers moves the firm from S to C, doubling total revenue to $36 million at S ($4 × 9 million units).

tity of 3 million units earning $18 million in total revenue with *no* advertising. If the firm did not change the price but simply began to spend substantially on informative advertising, it might thereby move from point *S* to point *A* on a new firm demand curve to the right of the old original demand curve running through points *S* and *B*. Total revenue at *A* is $24 million, up a bit from the $18 million at point *S*. If, on the other hand, the firm simply cut the price from $6 to $4 while continuing to do without advertising, the result would be a movement from *S* to *B* along the original demand curve. Total revenue at *B* is $16 million, down from the starting total revenue.

Neither of these strategies appears very attractive to the firm, and the second one even causes total revenue to drop. However, the final possibility posed by Figure 28.3 is quite seductive. If the firm *combines* the price cut with a well-financed advertising campaign informing potential customers about the new bargain, it moves from S to C along what is in essence a new and highly elastic demand curve. Buyers, once informed, are highly responsive to the price cuts, with the result that the firm's total revenue can jump sharply. Total revenue at C is $36 million ($4 × 9m), twice as much as the $18 million associated with starting point S.

D

Lowering Costs

In each of the preceding instances, advertising or innovation _raised the firm's total revenues_ through changes in the firm's demand, promising higher profits. The alternative route to higher profits—_lower costs_—can also be traveled with advertising and innovation.

1. Advertising Figure 28.4 illustrates this possibility for informative advertising. The demand

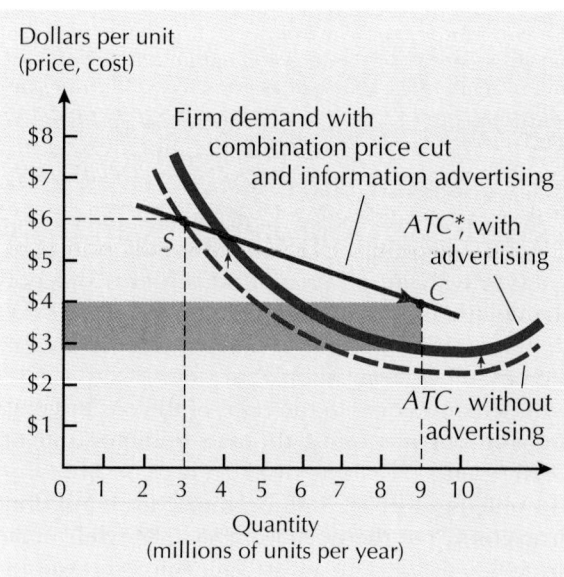

FIGURE 28.4 _Cost-Reducing Effect of Informative Advertising_

At point S, the price is $6 and the average total cost without advertising is also $6. Normal profits ensue. A strategy of cutting the price and advertising the discount moves the firm to point C, where the price of $4 is greater than the average total cost with advertising, namely, $2.90. Economic profit, even if later eliminated by imitative rivals, thus may motivate this strategy of advertised price discounting.

curve is the same as that just seen in Figure 28.3. Points S and C in Figure 28.4 correspond to points S and C in Figure 28.3, so the movement from S to C here is again caused by the firm's price reduction coupled with advertising that informs buyers of the discount. This advertising raises the firm's average total cost per unit at every level of output from ATC to ATC*. However, the greater quantity associated with the advertising—9 million units as opposed to 3 million units—moves the firm down along its cost curve because of some economies of scale. Thus the advertising causes two simultaneous changes: (1) an upward shift of the ATC curve and (2) a movement to the right down along the new ATC* curve. The _net_ result is a _drop_ in the cost per unit from $6.00 per unit at 3 million units to $2.90 at 9 million units. Moreover, _this result yields a higher profit despite the lower price and the upward shift of_ ATC. At starting point S, price and average total cost are equal, namely, $6. This grants a normal profit but nothing more. In comparison, ending point C has a price of $4. This is well above the average total cost of $2.90, including the cost of advertising at that point. Economic profits thus reward this strategy under these circumstances.

Retailing provides numerous examples of this phenomenon. On the demand side, consumers seem to respond when retailers advertise low prices. On the cost side, retailers can lower their costs through high-volume, low-overhead operations. Supermarkets like Safeway, Kroger, and Winn Dixie exploit this strategy in grocery retailing, as does Crown Books in book retailing. Systematic empirical research into this behavior is made possible by the fact that some states legally ban or heavily restrict retail advertising for some products. One such study compared the prices of eyeglasses in states that banned merchant advertising with the prices in states where merchant advertising was wholly unrestricted. The results were striking—a $20 difference in average prices in 1963. Where advertising was prohibited, eyeglasses averaged $37.48. Where advertising was unrestricted, they averaged only $17.98.[13]

2. Innovation Although our emphasis is on product innovations, cost changes are most dra-

[13]Lee Benham, "The Effect of Advertising on the Price of Eyeglasses," _Journal of Law and Economics_ (October 1972), p. 339.

matically achieved by *process* innovations. In steel making, for example, the development of continuous casting during the 1960s and 1970s replaced at least two steps in the traditional process of steel production—ingot casting and primary rolling. Molten steel was traditionally poured into ingot molds, where it then cooled into heavy ingots. These were then stored until needed, at which time they had to be reheated and rolled into semifinished shapes like slabs or billets, a stage called *primary rolling*. With continuous casting, however, molten steel now moves *directly* into these semifinished shapes. The labor cost savings have been as high as 60 percent in mills converted to continuous casting. Fuel costs are likewise down.

Figure 28.5 diagrams the consequences of these kinds of developments for innovative firms. Point *T* illustrates the profit-maximizing price and output for the firm under the old, traditional technology. Assuming the firm has some monopoly power, the price–cost combination of P_o and C_o awards the

firm some economic profit, as indicated by the small shaded rectangle. A process innovation that shifted the firm's average total cost down from *ATC* to *ATC** would enlarge those economic profits greatly. If Q_n is the profit-maximizing output after adoption of the new process technology, the cost per unit would fall from C_o to C_n and the price would slide from P_o to P_n. Multiplying the difference between the new price and new cost per unit, $P_n - C_n$, by the number of units, Q_n, yields the larger rectangle identified by point *N* on its northeastern corner. The enlarged economic profit discloses the firm's incentive for acting as an innovator.

3. Experience Curves Some of the most spectacular events in this dynamic realm of technological change are a *blend* of product innovation, process innovation, and what is called *learning by doing*. The consequences are best summarized by *experience curves* which show costs or prices falling over time, and best introduced by simple examples.

When videocassette recorders, (VCRs), were first introduced in 1975, they were priced between $1,000 and $1,400. Within 10 years, prices fell to the $200–$400 range for all but the most expensive models. Moreover, the VCRs selling for $250 in 1985 were far better than their $1,300 ancestors of 1975. They had remote control, freeze frame, search, and other fancy features.[14] If VCRs could record the history of digital watches, home computers, microwave ovens, compact laser discs, and many other products, the pattern would be the same—*prices falling steeply over time even as the product is improving.*

Of course, prices cannot fall for these new products simply because time passes. What, then, is happening? Prices are falling because *cost savings permit falls as the cumulative quantity of output increases, something that takes time.* Note the word *cumulative*. Previously we have always referred to output during some *given period of time*, such as 5 million barrels of beer *per year*. Now we are referring to total cumulative output from the time the product was first introduced, such as 87 million VCRs since their debut in 1975. Because cumulative output is partly a positive function of time (more time, more output), the cost per unit

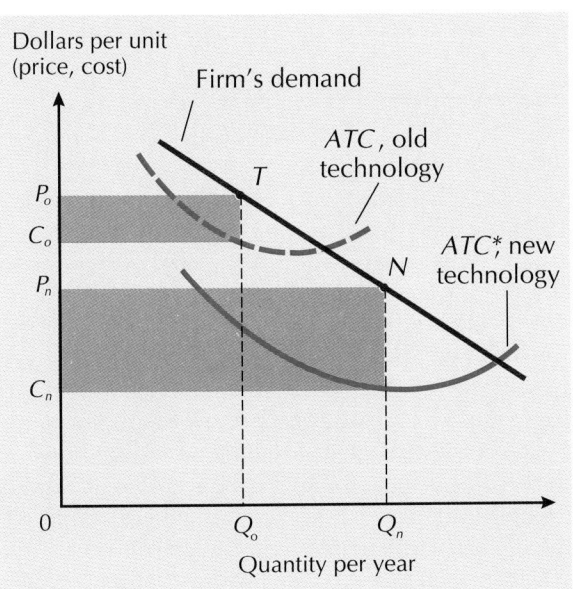

FIGURE 28.5 The Effects of a Cost-Reducing Process Innovation

The traditional production technology yields results associated with point T. The firm's optimal output is OQ_o, which is sold at price OP_0 and produced at an average cost shown by distance OC_0. Economic profits grow with a process innovation that shifts costs from ATC to ATC*. The latter's summary solution at point N is associated with output OQ_n, price OP_n, and average cost per unit OC_n.

[14]*Wall Street Journal*, July 15, 1985, p. 15.

falls with the passage of time, but not simply as a result of time.

Why does the cost per unit fall with the cumulative output of some products? There are at least two key reasons, both of which can be summarized by the word **experience**. *First, experience brings increased labor efficiency.* This is learning by doing. Labor learns better methods and greater skills at operating new machinery as cumulative output increases. Experience also includes the discovery of better ways to organize work, increasing specialization. Such effects as these are most apparent in airplane manufacturing. You can easily imagine that the labor costs of building the first Boeing 747 were much higher than those for the 36th 747 as the work changed from the novel to the repetitious. *Second, experience brings technological improvements.* As cumulative output grows, it becomes possible to shift from batch production to continuous flow production, from labor-intensive methods to automated methods. Moreover, greater cumulative output may lead to new discoveries for equipment design or materials handling, discoveries that save labor, curb waste, and conserve energy, all of which further improve efficiency.

Because experience is integral to these effects, the curves that trace declining costs and prices as a function of cumulative output are called *experience curves.* Moreover, because experience is usually most important during the early stages of a product's life cycle, experience curves are most closely associated with *product innovations,* or, more precisely, the introduction and growth phases of the product's life cycle following its innovation.

Figure 28.6 illustrates. The horizontal axis measures *both* cumulative quantity *and* time duration,

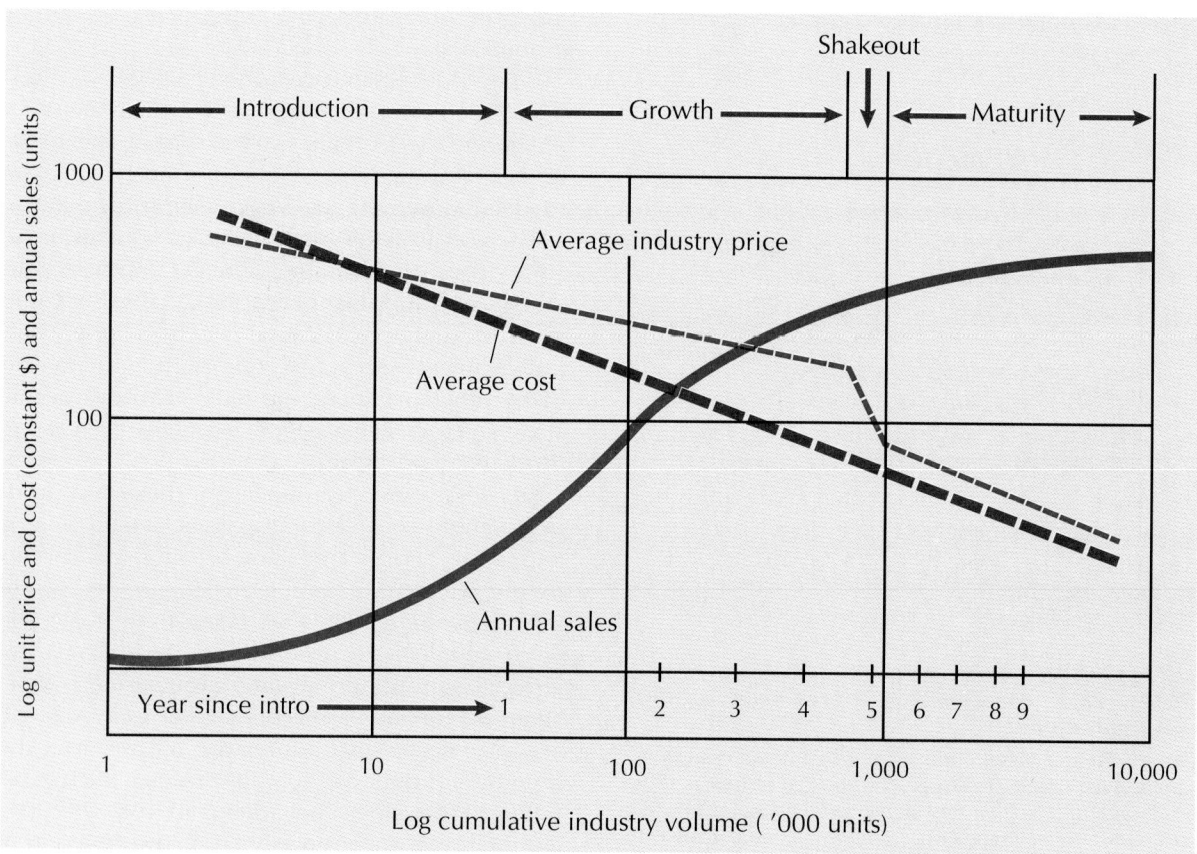

FIGURE 28.6 Product Life Cycle Stages and the Industry Price Experience Curve
(Source: G. S. Day and D. B. Montgomery, "Diagnosing the Experience Curve," Journal of Marketing, Spring 1983, p. 51.)

because cumulative volume takes time. The vertical axis also serves double duty. It measures *either* dollars per unit for price and cost *or*, alternatively, the total number of units sold annually (annual sales, *not* cumulative sales). The experience curves are the dashed lines. These negatively sloped curves show price and average cost falling as cumulative output expands over time through the early stages—introduction, growth, and so on. In turn, these stages are guaged by the positively sloped, S-shaped curve reflecting annual sales volume, a curve we "experienced" earlier when product life cycles were first discussed (pages 407-408).

Looking more closely at Figure 28.6, you will see that very early on, during introduction, the price is at its *highest* level, but it is *below* the cost in the expectation that, with time, costs will fall and in the hope that such a money-losing price will spur buyer acceptance of the product. Later, during the growth stage, the price is *lower and falling* but it exceeds the cost per unit to the point of rewarding the innovators with economic profits. Those economic profits attract competing newcomers, however, as entry is easiest during the growth phase. And these added competitors, plus some slow-down in the rise of annual sales volume, result in a shakeout as the industry moves from growth to maturity. During this shakeout, prices drop more sharply than before, approaching the average cost rather than diverging from it. Just how sharply they drop depends on such factors as the number of competitors and the abruptness of the slow-down. Also, some firms fail. Finally, in maturity, prices dance further down with costs, while allowing for some economic profit and depending on the extent to which still further experience bestows additional benefits. The overall pattern is extensively illustrated by our later discussion of personal computers.

■ CHECK YOUR BEARINGS

Marketing effort and product variation frequently play major roles in dynamic competition—the independent rivalry of firms using various strategies over time. Among marketing efforts, advertising is the most prominent. Informative advertising deals in facts, such as prices and product ingredients. Persuasive advertising exploits consumer psychology. As regards product variation,

innovation stands out. This commercialization of new ideas is preceded by invention and followed by diffusion. Other product variations can be so trivial as to be classified as brand proliferation.

These nonprice actions affect profits by *altering* the revenue and cost conditions of a firm. Revenues are altered through changes in firm demand, such as a lowering of its elasticity or a rightward shift of its location by means of persuasive advertising or product innovation. If price reductions are combined with informative advertising, the result can be a more highly elastic firm demand. On the cost side, it is possible for advertising that raises the ATC curve to reduce unit costs in the end if the added output fosters scale economies. Innovations, especially process innovations, more consistently and conspicuously contribute to cost reductions. Finally, the added experience provided by added cumulative output may cut costs during the early stages of a new product's life cycle. Learning by doing lowers labor costs. Discovery by doing prompts efficient process innovations. Experience curves for costs and prices represent the results.

Note that *from the buyers' viewpoint* advertising and innovation may be good or bad. Advertising, for instance, may raise the price or lower it. Innovation usually proves beneficial to buyers, but we've seen that brand proliferation can spawn price discrimination. Next, we study advertising and innovation in detail.

III
Advertising in Depth

Studying advertising in greater depth, we shall probe several issues. (A) What are the basic conditions causing a product's advertising to be informative or persuasive, and especially voluminous or meager? (B) What is the relationship between market concentration and advertising? (C) When does it add to or detract from allocation and technical efficiency?

A
Basic Conditions

Soda pop advertising tends to be much more persuasive and voluminous than that for farm machinery. Why? A major reason is the wide differences in buyers and products involved. Let's explore buyer types and product types in two simple dichotomies: (1) business buyers versus household consumers and (2) shopping goods versus convenience goods.

1. Business Buyers versus Household Consumers People who buy for businesses are usually well informed buyers. Indeed, professional purchasing agents for large firms specialize in buying such broad categories of goods and services as raw materials, construction, transportation, insurance, machinery, and office supplies. The most important reason for this highly developed expertise is the ability of professional buyers to spread the costs of obtaining this expertise over their large-volume purchases.

On the other hand, we have the typical American consumer, who is incompetent by comparison. He or she runs a very small-scale operation. Moreover, many of the thousands of decisions consumers make each year are terribly complex, preventing the growth of low-cost per unit expertise. The resulting ignorance often leads consumers to rely on false *cues* of product quality. Among other things, studies have shown that consumers may judge the quality of identical hosiery on the basis of scent; the quality of beer on price; the power of kitchen mixers on noise; the thickness of syrup by darkness; and the quality of tape recorders on the basis of exaggerated advertising claims.

Given the vast difference in knowledge between business buyers and household consumers, there is a vast difference in the content of the advertising typically directed at them. Opinion surveys indicate that ads for industrial materials, building materials, and manufacturing equipment are much more informative than those for cigarettes, liquor, beer, perfumes, candy, and detergents.[15]

A convenient measure of the intensity of advertising is advertising expenditure as a percentage of sales revenue. And here once again there are immense differences by type of buyer. According to detailed data from the mid-1970s, the *average* advertising outlay as a percentage of sales was 0.6 percent for producer goods (going to business buyers) and 3.6 percent for consumer goods, a six-fold discrepancy. Table 28.2 gives a few examples. Proprietary drugs like headache and cold remedies ranked number one among all products in these data, with 20.1 percent of manufacturers' sales revenues going into television, magazine, and other media advertising. In contrast, many producer goods experienced no media advertising whatever—paper board and primary copper among them. Other sales expenses, like those for salespeople in the field, point of sale displays, free samples, and trade allowances to distributors, follow a similar pattern in Table 28.2. Outlays for consumer goods exceed those for producer goods.

2. Shopping Goods versus Convenience Goods This classification applies only to consumer products. By definition:[16]

> **Shopping goods** are mainly high-priced, infrequently purchased durables. The consumer typically compares prices, quality, and style in several stores, and the purchase can be delayed. Examples include autos, refrigerators, TV sets, furniture, and apparel.

> **Convenience goods** are those with a relatively low unit price and are purchased repeatedly. Examples include food, cigarettes, beverages, drugs, and candy.

The kind of retail store carrying each of these classes of goods helps to identify them. Locating close to consumers has obvious advantages for *convenience goods retailers*, since consumers value their time and want to minimize transportation expenses. Thus, food stores, gas stations, and drug stores dot the landscape here and there, widely dispersed. In contrast, *shopping good retailers* tend to cluster together in the heart of town, along major highways, or in large shopping malls. Such clustering enables people who are in the market for a new car, stereo, or suit of clothes to shop around before they buy, comparing prices, styles, service facilities, and so forth.

The advertising *by manufacturers* of these two classes of goods differs in part because of these

---

[15]Bauer and Greyser, *Advertising in America*, pp. 296–297.

[16]Michael E. Porter, *Interbrand Choice, Strategy, and Bilateral Market Power* (Cambridge, Mass.: Harvard University Press, 1976), pp. 24–25.

TABLE 28.2   Advertising and Other Selling Expenses as a Percentage of Sales for Selected Products, Mid-1970s

Product	Media Advertising Expense	Other Selling Expense	Total Selling Expense
Low-priced consumer convenience goods			
Proprietary drugs	20.1%	15.0%	35.1%
Toiletries	13.8	14.8	28.6
Chewing gum	12.3	13.1	25.4
Distilled liquor	11.9	13.4	25.3
Breakfast cereals	10.2	9.3	19.5
High-priced consumer shopping goods			
Household vacuum cleaners	3.0%	22.2%	25.2%
Radio and TV sets	2.9	5.0	7.9
Household refrigerators	1.1	3.7	4.8
Passenger cars	0.8	1.5	2.3
Men's and Boys' suits and coats	1.0	6.0	7.0
Producer goods			
Basic steel	0.1%	1.5%	1.6%
Paper board	0.0	1.5	1.5
Gypsum products	0.5	3.3	3.8
Farm machinery	0.6	4.2	4.8
Primary copper	0.0	0.3	0.3

Source: Federal Trade Commission, *Statistical Report: Annual Line of Business Report 1975*, Table 2-7.

retailing differences. Since consumers often shop around for *shopping goods*, their physical features will be noted and are likely to be important. The retailers' role in this case is crucial, as they offer informative sales assistance and advice. Therefore the manufacturers of these goods include considerable amounts of information in their advertising. Buyers use it, hoping to learn about those important physical features. Moreover, given the prominent role of the retailers here, the manufacturers' advertising need not be as voluminous as that for convenience goods.

By comparison, the advertising of *convenience goods* tends to be both persuasive and intense. Manufacturers of convenience goods aggressively attempt to "pre-sell" consumers. This is so because consumers consider each purchase individually as rather unimportant. They therefore do not shop around. They seek no sales help from retailers. Instead they rely on the brand image that manufacturers advertise. They use convenient methods for convenience goods.

In sum, advertisements for autos, apparel, and household furnishings are rated by consumers as being generally more informative than those for foods, toiletries, and soft drinks. Ad spending pat-

terns likewise diverge. According to one study, manufacturers' average advertising as a percentage of sales was 2.1 percent for shopping goods industries and 4.7 percent for convenience goods industries.[17] Looking again at Table 28.2, you will find examples of this disparity. The first five products are consumer convenience goods. The next five are consumer shopping goods. Manufacturers of the former spend lavishly on advertising, reaching double-digit levels. Producers of the latter do not.

Table 28.3 crudely summarizes this discussion.

[17]Ibid., p. 148.

TABLE 28.3   Summary of Advertising Content and Intensity by Buyer and Product Type

Buyer and Product Type	Advertising Content	Advertising Intensity
Business buyers	Informative	Low
Household consumers	Persuasive	Moderate–high
Shopping goods*	Informative	Low
Convenience goods*	Persuasive	Moderate–high

*Applies only to consumer goods and the advertising of manufacturers.

We say *crudely* because it includes gross oversimplifications. Note, for instance, that in the first pairing, advertising aimed at household consumers is said to be persuasive. Yet the next pairings imply that much advertising aimed at consumers is informative, namely, that for shopping goods. Thus, the table merely summarizes *relative* relations. Advertising aimed at consumers is, on the whole, relatively persuasive in comparison to that aimed at business buyers. This flag of caution waved, let's continue.

B

Market Concentration and Advertising

What is the relationship between market concentration and advertising intensity? Extensive economic research indicates that it's *both* positive *and* negative in the case of consumer goods but *neither* in the case of producer goods.[18]

The explanation for producer goods is easiest, so let's begin there. Advertising intensity and market concentration appear to be *un*related to each other when business buyers occupy the demand side of the market. The apparent reason for this emerges from our earlier findings. Business buyers are knowledgeable professionals. Sellers generally advertise to them in a relatively informative, subdued way. The level of market concentration is then irrelevant.

The explanation for consumer goods is summarized in Figure 28.7, where advertising intensity varies horizontally and concentration rises vertically. The connection between advertising and market concentration is *both* positive and negative because the relationship is *nonlinear*. Research reveals that concentration and advertising intensity are *positively* related as concentration varies from low to moderate levels—the *A* to *B* or *A* to *B'* regions of Figure 28.7. Thereafter, in the range of high concentration up to pure monopoly, advertising and concentration are *negatively* related. Different data sets and research methods yield different estimates, so two versions are depicted in

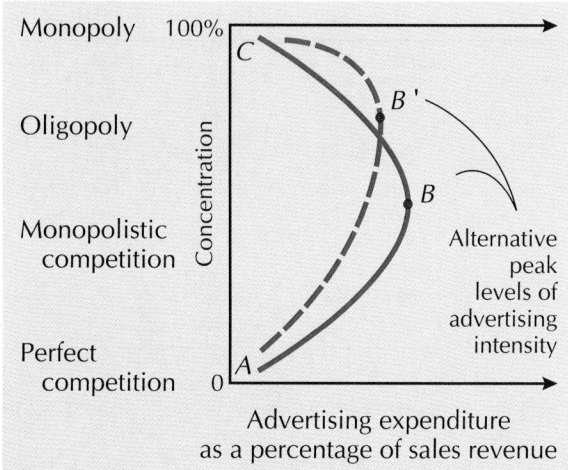

FIGURE 28.7 Advertising Intensity As It Relates to Market Concentration

Advertising expenditure as a percentage of sales revenue is generally rather low at the extremes of either very high market concentration (e.g., monopoly) or very low concentration (approaching perfect competition). In between, especially with loose-knit oligopoly, advertising is most intense. The markets for proprietary drugs, cosmetics, soda pop, detergents, beer, and breakfast cereal epitomize the relation, as all are differentiated oligopolies and among the most intense advertisers.

Figure 28.7. Moreover, intensities of differentiation effort other than advertising follow similar patterns.[19]

The vigorous advertising rivalry of moderate oligopoly (in the region of *B*) is fostered by the *gamesmanship* referred to earlier when discussing Figure 28.2. If sellers of Brand *Y* escalate outlays, shifting their demand curve to the right at the expense of rivals like Brand *Z*, sellers of Brand *Z* (and Brands *V* and *W*, too) are likely to retaliate by upping their advertising outlays in response. With *everyone's* ad outlays much higher than before, there may be no appreciable increase in marketwide demand and no large shifts of market share between the combatants. The result, then, is a burdensome ad budget for every oligopolist in the market. Yet the spending could persist. *Mutual deescalation of the spending would yield higher profits, but the firms might be stuck in high gear.*

[18]For details on what follows, see Weiss, Pascoe, and Martin, "The Size of Selling Costs," *Review of Economics and Statistics* (November 1983), pp. 668–672; Buxton, Davies, and Lyons, "Concentration and Advertising in Consumer and Producers Markets," *Journal of Industrial Economics* (June 1984), pp. 451–464.

[19]John M. Connor, "Food Product Proliferation: A Market Structure Analysis," *American Journal of Agricultural Economics* (November 1981), pp. 607–617.

Given independence, no firm could singlehandedly try to start a deescalation by cutting spending on its own without running the risk of not being followed by its rivals.

C

Advertising and Performance

The basic questions of What? and How? loom largest when tackling advertising's impact on market performance. Our measures of good and bad remain largely the same as before. Price and profit levels are again at issue regarding What?. And cost containment is the concern in regard to How?. In addition, however, advertising is quite different from anything we've seen before. We therefore include a third subject, one labeled *consumer sovereignty versus producer sovereignty.*

1. What?—Price and Profit Levels   In traditional static theory, monopoly lifts prices and profits above perfectly competitive norms, leading to a misallocation of resources. The impact of advertising may be judged the same way: Is advertising *pro*competitive or *anti*competitive for price and profit levels?

Figure 28.8 sketches the possibilities. Relation *KE* at the bottom shows prices and profits *falling* with increased advertising intensity. This would hold if advertising nourished competition and efficiency, as suggested earlier in Figures 28.3 and 28.4. Next is a pattern of neutrality, *KN,* with *no* association between these variables. Finally, *KM* traces a *rising* association that would occur if advertising contributed to monopoly power by lowering elasticities of demand, building large market shares, or creating a barrier to entry, as seen earlier in Figures 28.1 and 28.2.

Which of these possibilities emerges from empirical research? They *all* do. As circumstances vary, the results vary. Sorting out those circumstances is tricky, but the task can be simplified, at some risk of being *over*simplified, by referring back to the outline of Table 28.3. In those cases where advertising tends to be *informative,* the relationship between advertising, prices, and profits seems to be favorable *(KE)* or neutral *(KN).* This holds for *producer goods* generally, which concern professional business buyers. Among *consumer goods,* this seems to hold for *shopping*

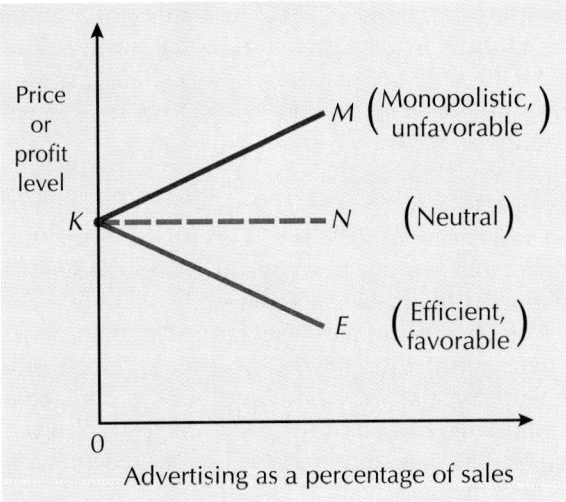

FIGURE 28.8   *Possible Relationships Between Advertising and Price or Profit Level*

Relation KN would indicate no association between advertising intensity and price or profit. If advertising furthers efficiency through better information and heightened competition, KE would be the resulting pattern. Finally, to the extent that advertising imparts monopolistic advantage to sellers, KM would arise, along with misallocation problems.

goods. It also holds for retail store advertising. Recall the example of eyeglasses.

In contrast, an unfavorably positive *KM* pattern occurs for *manufacturer* advertising of *consumer convenience goods* like detergents, soda pop, cosmetics, cigarettes, foods, and proprietary drugs. Concrete evidence appears in the price differences between advertised manufacturers' brands and unadvertised private-label brands of retailers. Clorox, for instance, is a manufacturer's brand. If you check the shelves of your nearest chain-store supermarket, say Safeway, you will also find private-label brands, like Safeway's White Magic bleach. Upon reading the labels, you'll discover that all household liquid chlorine bleaches are chemically identical—5.25 percent sodium hypochlorite plus 94.75 percent water. Hence we have here a product that is essentially the same, except for brand identification. And Clorox, the leading nationally advertised brand, is priced 30 percent or so above unadvertised private-label brands.

Other examples abound. Take acetaminophen, a popular substitute for aspirin. So-called extra-strength tablets contain 500 mg of this chemical.

Browsing at the local drugstore-chain by one of the authors in 1985 revealed the following prices for bottles of 100 extra-strength tablets: private-label brand, $2.99; Tylenol, $5.89; Anacin-3, $5.89; and Panadol, $6.59.

2. How?—Cost Levels Firms spent $94 billion on advertising in 1985. Is this excessive? Does this mean that we are burning up more productive resources than is socially desirable?

This issue arises partly because advertising is, in a sense, *forced* on buyers. Consumers don't buy advertising the way they buy books or broccoli. Could it be, then, that the economic test advertising faces is so distorted that expenditures for it are indeed excessive?

Any answer is controversial because waste or excess here cannot be measured by the level of advertising expenditures alone. Aside from the fact that, industry by industry, ad spending can be restrained or intense, the ads themselves can be informative or persuasive. When advertising is *informative*, it benefits buyers immensely and therefore tends to be more useful than wasteful. On the other hand, when advertising is *persuasive*, it probably benefits buyers very little and therefore tends to be more wasteful than useful. (How much would you be willing to pay to see another Marlboro cowboy on horseback?)

Using information content as an earmark, then, we can speculate about which advertising is excessive waste. Assisting our rough calculations is the fact that information content and spending intensity are, in general, inversely related. As summarized earlier in Table 28.3, information and low spending tend to go together, while persuasion and high spending tend to go together. More specifically, manufacturers' outlays as a percentage of sales are greatest for consumer convenience goods such as pet food, breakfast cereals, candy, chewing gum, soda pop, beer, cigarettes, distilled liquor, drugs, detergents, perfumes, and cosmetics. All are oligopolies. And their ads rate among the lowest in information content. Because TV, radio, and magazines are the main foci of these efforts, and because ad spending in these three media amounts to about 35 percent of total ad spending, it would not seem implausible that perhaps 20 to 25 percent of all advertising is economic waste. The How? question thus suffers somewhat.

3. Consumer Sovereignty versus Producer Sovereignty When the Coca-Cola Company responded to protests by resurrecting old Coke, some economists hailed the act as a demonstration that all was well with American capitalism. *Consumer sovereignty* had prevailed.

> **Consumer sovereignty** is the idea that consumers, by casting their dollar votes, determine what will and what will not be produced.

Most notions of consumer sovereignty assume that people have fixed, predetermined tastes. They know what's best for themselves. So, it's wonderful that producers dance to the tune called by consumers.

Some economists are more skeptical. They claim that *producer sovereignty* prevails. They might say that the Coca-Cola Company had molded people's tastes so completely over the decades that the company itself didn't fully realize its power. It built an institution out of flavored, sweetened, carbonated water, a product whose nutritional qualities and dental damage cannot justify consumption rates of 43 gallons per capita annually.

> **Producer sovereignty** is the notion that producers determine what is produced through their influence on consumer tastes.

These two conflicting views are crucial to the What? question. If consumers determine what is produced, allocation efficiency can be defined, and good or bad changes in output can be identified. If, on the other hand, consumers' tastes change under the influence of producers, economics can say very little about whether changes in output are good or bad because the yardstick of judgment—consumer preference—is altered in the process.

A controversy over the welfare effects of advertising thus revolves around the question of who has sovereignty—consumers or producers. *Defenders* of advertising opt for consumer sovereignty. They have several arguments: (1) Consumers are too smart ever to be persuaded to do something against their own best interests. (2) They don't even pay much attention to advertisements.

(3) When people do pay attention, ads may influence their brand selections but ads do not affect consumption patterns across products. (4) People may buy things that are bad for them, but not because of advertising. Russians consume more vodka than anyone else even though it is not promoted in the Soviet Union. *In sum*, advertising has no persuasive influence. It aids consumers in exercising their sovereignty.

Critics of advertising, on the other hand, see many signs of producer sovereignty. They muster various counterarguments: (1) Opinion polls find that 70 to 80 percent of all people surveyed agree with the statement that "advertising leads people to buy things they don't need or can't afford."[20] (2) Ads pack a persuasive punch even when people don't pay close attention to them. People can be influenced without knowing it.[21] (3) If advertising can alter brand choices, it can also alter consumption patterns, especially for nonessentials like candy. (4) The consumption of unhealthy or otherwise bad products is not completely independent of advertising, for if it were, sellers wouldn't spend millions of dollars promoting them. In sum, critics argue that advertising is not always informative. They say that it's largely persuasive—a *tool of producer sovereignty*.

Read Perspective 28B.

IV
Innovation in Depth[23]

Performance standards for innovation are much less controversial than for advertising. Innovation is a matter of What's new? So, generally, *the more, the better*. More innovation brings better products and better processes. Hence the key issue here is

simply this: What conditions encourage more as opposed to less innovation? In particular; (A) What size of firm is most innovative? (B) What level of market concentration proves most progressive?

A
Firm Size and Innovation

1. Theory Confident that big firms were more progressive than small ones, J. K. Galbraith wrote over 30 years ago that "a benign Providence . . . . has made the modern industry of a few large firms an excellent instrument for inducing technical change."[24] Such praise for bigness rests on several theoretical arguments.

1. *Absolute size:* It is claimed that big firms can better afford R&D outlays. Given the immense expense of R&D projects, small firms simply cannot put up the money.
2. *Economies of scale:* Invention and innovation often require costly specialized equipment, like wind tunnels and electron microscopes. Researchers themselves are growing ever more specialized, necessitating teamwork. Because of economies of scale, these R&D inputs are most efficiently used by big firms, or so it is argued.
3. *Risk:* Every project is a gamble. Large size enables numerous projects, so the hits can offset the misses. Risk thus lessens with added size.

Economists who doubt that bigness is better make counterclaims. Regarding the first point, they argue that although many projects are indeed costly, many are not. Some tasks cost millions of dollars, some only thousands. The range leaves ample room for smaller firms.

As for economies of scale, it is argued that R&D is a *creative* activity. The bureaucratic tangles that accompany bigness may stifle this creativity and therefore foster *in*efficiencies rather than efficiencies.

Risk, too, has been questioned as a force favoring bigness. Small firms may be able to fund only a few projects, but that need not deter them. After

---

[20]Bauer and Greyser, *Advertising in America*, p. 71; H. Becker, "Advertising Image and Impact," *Journal of Contemporary Business* (Vol. 7, No. 4, 1979), p. 84.

[21]G. J. Gorn, "The Effects of Music in Advertising on Choice Behavior: A Classical Conditioning Approach," *Journal of Marketing* (Winter 1982), pp. 94–101.

[23]This section draws heavily on F. M. Scherer, *Industrial Market Structure and Economic Performance*, 2nd ed. (Chicago: Rand McNally, 1980), chapter 15; M. I. Kamien and N. L. Schwartz, "Market Structure and Innovation: A Survey," *Journal of Economic Literature* (March 1975), pp. 1–37.

[24]John Kenneth Galbraith, *American Capitalism* (Boston: Houghton Mifflin, 1956), p. 86.

PERSPECTIVE 28B
Cigarettes Ignite Controversy

(From the _Wall Street Journal_, July 5, 1985) In Gambia, smokers who send in cigarette box tops get a chance on a new car. In Argentina, smoking commercials fill 20% of television advertising time. And in crowded African cities, billboards that link smoking and the good life tower above swelling shanty towns.

Throughout the developing world, the tobacco industry is avidly courting consumers, using catchy slogans, obvious image campaigns, and single-cigarette sales that fit a hard-pressed customer's budget. The reason is clear. As Peter Temple, a London tobacco analyst put it, the Third World "is where the growth is."

While cigarette sales decline or stagnate in many industrialized nations, some poorer countries offer rich markets. In Indonesia, per capita cigarette consumption quadrupled from 1973 to 1981. . . Kenya's consumption rises 8% annually. . . .

In pursuing Third World markets, tobacco companies operate unburdened by many of the restraints they face in the West. They generally can advertise freely on radio and television, unlike in the U.S. and European countries, and packages don't have to carry health warnings . . . .

But the Third World marketing push is controversial. Critics complain that sophisticated promotions in unsophisticated societies entice people who can't afford the necessities of life to spend money on a luxury—and a dangerous one at that.

Developing countries consume about a third of the $200 billion worth of cigarettes sold in the world each year. . . .

Sophistication is a theme running through smoking ads. In Kinshasa, Zaire, billboards depict a man in a business suit stepping out of a black Mercedes as his chauffeur holds the door. . . . Similarly, in Nigeria, promotions for cigarettes called Graduate show a university student in his cap and gown. . . .

Tobacco companies say their promotional slant is both reasonable and common. "Every cigarette manufacturer is in the image business," says Jack Prosser, a spokesman for Rothmans International PLC, a London-based tobacco company. In the Third World, he adds, "a lot of people can't understand what is written on the ads anyway. . . ."

Third World smokers often buy cigarettes one at a time and consume fewer than 20 a day. But Dr. Thompson of Zimbabwe contends that "for people who may only make $100 a month, even these smaller quantities represent a serious drain on their resources. . . . ." A study published in _The Lancet_, the British medical journal, in 1981 said people in Bangladesh spend about 20% of their incomes on tobacco. It asserted that "smoking of only five cigarettes a day in a poor household in Bangladesh might lead to a monthly dietary deficit."

It is hard to judge how smoking may be affecting Third World health, as statistics are scanty. . . . In any case, says Mr. Prosser of Rothmans, people in developing countries don't have a long enough life expectancy to worry about smoking-related problems. "You can't turn around to a guy who is going to die at age 40 and tell him that he might not live two years extra at age 70," Mr. Prosser says.[22]

[22]Steve Mufson, "Smoking Section," _Wall Street Journal_, July 5, 1985, pp. 1, 19.

all, small firms may have the most to gain from innovation. Their survival may depend on it.

In short, theories favoring large firms typically stress their _ability_ to innovate while ignoring their _incentives._ Conversely, theories favoring small firms tend to emphasize the _incentives_ of small firms while neglecting their _ability._ In the end, innovation often calls for a _blend_ of both elements, something that middle-sized firms may have more of than either the giants or the pygmies. Hence let's not forget middle-sized firms.

2. Evidence So much for theory. What are the facts? At first glance, statistics reflecting R&D effort overwhelmingly favor the big firms as being the most progressive. Aggregate R&D expenditures are tightly concentrated. About 700 companies account for well over 90 percent of all private R&D spending, and very few of them could be considered small. There is thus some truth to the claim that bigness is better.

However, these aggregate, economywide statistics exaggerate the prominence of large enterprises. For one thing, these numbers lump large and medium-sized firms together. They do not distinguish the efforts of Kodak and Polaroid or IBM and Apple. A key question, then, is this: *Within a given industry, is the effort of the largest firms greater, relative to their size, than the effort of medium-sized firms?*

The question is diagrammed in Figure 28.9. The vertical axis is R&D outlay per dollar of sales or some other measure of *relative* effort. The horizontal axis is firm size. The solid line indicates what we have just learned, namely, that the effort of really small firms is relatively small. The dashed lines indicate the possibilities among the medium-sized and large firms consistent with the aggregate statistics. If relative effort always rose with size, pattern D would prevail. Merging medium-sized firms to create big ones would then boost R&D. Next, consider pattern F. If medium-sized and large firms put forth the *same* relative effort, pattern F would occur. Nothing would be gained or lost by merging medium-sized firms. Finally, pattern G would hold if relative effort dwindled beyond the middle range. Added bigness would then be good only up to a point. Thereafter it would be bad.

In fact, numerous statistical studies indicate that patterns F and G prevail in all but a few industries. That is to say, *inventive and innovative efforts tend to increase more than proportionately with firm size only over the small to medium range* ("medium" varying from industry to industry). *For still larger firms, intensity of effort is either constant or declining with size.* Hence bigness is better for R&D effort only to a limited degree. Ultimately, it is often worse.

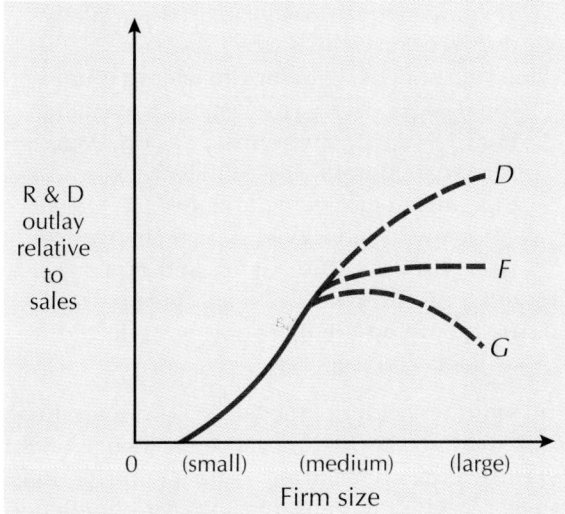

FIGURE 28.9 Relative R&D Effort and Firm Size Within a Given Industry

The solid line indicates that the relative R&D effort rises with firm size up to a point. Very small firms, as a class, are inferior to medium-sized and large firms as a combined class. The dashed lines indicate whether those gains continue with ever-larger size (D), or end in a stationary pattern of equality for medium-sized and large firms (F), or decline with ever-greater firm size (G).

A second problem with the aggregate data, and also with these results just surveyed, is that they reflect only *effort* (or input) as measured by R&D expenditures. They do not reflect the *results* (or output) of that effort, as might be measured by the number of patents awarded or the frequency of major innovations introduced. These measures of results cast still further doubt on theories that ever bigger size yields ever better performance. The relationships between firm size and these measures of results follow the F and G patterns of Figure 28.9, but in ways that are more favorable to small and medium-sized firms.

Let's illustrate these sweeping generalities on effort (input) and results (output) with several examples:

1. Royal Crown is the most innovative firm in the soft drink industry. Its credits include the first decaffeinated cola, the first use of cans, the first with 16-ounce returnable bottles, and the first to offer a diet cola. "At each stage, the industry pooh-poohs what

we consider a breakthrough, then follows our lead," says RC's vice-president.[25]

2. It was not GM, Ford, or Chrysler that innovated small cars in the United States after World War II, but rather Kaiser, Willys, American Motors, and Studebaker.[26]

3. Copy machines were developed by a small company called Haloid, which changed its name to Xerox. IBM, Kodak, and numerous other big firms were offered the opportunity to develop the invention but rejected it as being too risky.

A word of caution, however: Although huge firms may not be as innovative as theory might suppose, they do make substantial contributions, especially when the costs for project completion happen to be immense. RCA's color television and Du Pont's nylon are just two instances of large-firm innovation involving vision, risk, and voluminous cost.

Thus medium-sized firms may be the most eager and able to spur advances, but a range of sizes might be best for an industry, just as it is best for a basketball team. Because R&D projects vary in the incentives they offer and the abilities they require, a variety of firm sizes may be most innovative overall.

B

Market Concentration and Innovation

1. Theory Theories concerning market structure's impact on progress stress *rivalry* or the lack thereof. And once again, *ability* and *incentive* enter the analysis.

Ability includes the financial wherewithall to undertake expensive, risky projects. Pure monopoly (regardless of absolute firm size) would seem to supply a firm with the greatest ability because pure monopoly offers the best shot at rich economic profits. Conversely, perfectly competitive markets would seem to deprive firms of innovative abilities.

It's another story, however, regarding *incentives.* Here incentives refer not only to the prospective

---

[25]*Wall Street Journal*, May 24, 1982, p. 21; *Forbes*, August 16, 1982, pp. 50–51.

[26]L. J. White, "The American Automobile Industry and the Small Car, 1945–1970," *Journal of Industrial Economics* (April 1972), pp. 179–192.

rewards that innovation might bestow, but also to the prospective *punishments* that *non*innovation might inflict. Because monopoly markets lack rivalry, they tend to protect monopolists too much. Monopolists may therefore lack a major incentive for progress. Perfectly competitive markets, on the other hand, tend to overflow with such incentives. The vulnerability of perfectly competitive firms would presumably spur them toward experimentation if they had the ability.

All told (and oversimplifying), it appears that monopolies have a great deal of ability but very little incentive, whereas perfectly competitive firms probably have little ability but ample incentive. Thus, in theory, *neither* structural extreme is particularly conducive to progress. However, the elements blend in intermediate structures of oligopoly and monopolistic competition. These settings give firms sufficient market power to secure financial ability and also have the incentives of rivalry. *With both ability and incentive present, the intermediate levels of concentration typical of oligopoly may be the best.*

2. Evidence Research reveals a mixed picture. Numerous studies support the theory that innovation rises with concentration until oligopoly is reached and then falls as monopoly is approached (like the *ABC* pattern in Figure 28.7). These results are contradicted, however, by research showing other patterns or no relationship whatever.

Why this mishmash of empiricism? The main reason seems to be that market concentration has at best a relatively small influence on innovativeness. Other influences are far more important. In particular, some industries have much greater *potential* for progress than others. Semiconductors, computers, and chemicals have much greater potential than, say, textiles, apparel, and wood products. Semiconductors, for instance, are in the *earlier stages of their product life cycle* as compared to textiles, which have been around for centuries. This puts semiconductors on a higher plateau of progressiveness.

Any conclusions thus suffer some uncertainty. *Still, pure monopoly seems bad. Some degree of competition—obtained by no more than moderate concentration or by fairly easy entry—seems much better for technological change than monopoly or near monopoly.*

Read Perspective 28C.

PERSPECTIVE 28C

Personal Computers

The personal computer was not IBM's baby. It began as a microprocessor pioneered by the Intel Corporation in 1972. Then around 1977, with the addition of keyboards, disk drives, and other such equipment, it emerged from such tiny firms as Vector Graphic, Ohio Scientific, and Processor Technology. The most successful of these small innovators was Apple Computer, founded in 1976 by Steve Jobs and Steve Wozniak, who started in a two-car garage. Bigger companies sat on the sidelines as the market grew from a few million dollars annually in the late 1970s to well over a billion dollars annually in 1981. Apple had about 23 percent of the market that year, followed by Tandy-Radio Shack with 16 percent and Commodore with 10 percent. After 1981 the market changed explosively. Sales rocketed into a trajectory that, as shown in Figure 28.10, matches the early life cycle of many new products. Equally important, 1981 marks IBM's entry into the personal computer field. In just 2 years, IBM's market share went from 0 to 26 percent as its annual output jumped from zero to 500,000 units. IBM's famous name helped its rapid ascent. The fact that IBM established a small company within its huge corporate structure also contributed immensely:

> The task force responsible for what was to become IBM's Personal Computer was set up as an independent business unit separate from the Armonk (N.Y.) giant's bureaucratic tangle and granite-like rules. Taking the unconventional— for IBM—approach was the key to the PC's phenomenal success.... "If you're going to compete with five men in a garage, you have to do something different" than what IBM usually does, says David J. Bradley, one of the designers of the PC.[27]

Seduced by IBM's huge success and the market's breakneck growth, other large companies entered the fray in the early 1980s—ITT, Xerox, AT&T, and Zenith among them. Big and small, personal computer companies multiplied to more than 150 in 1983. The resulting competition, plus experience curve effects, pulled prices down. (IBM's prices fell about 50 percent during 1981–1984.) Firms exchanged blows with new gadgetry. (Macintosh was Apple's answer to the IBM PC.) And firms turned to television to build their images. As maturity approached and market growth began to slow in the mid-1980s, a shakeout occurred. Many firms went belly-up—Osborne, Franklin, Victor, and Gavilan, to name a few. Even Apple, the industry's most famous pioneer, underwent a series of painful adjustments that forced its founders, Jobs and Wozniak, to leave. IBM couldn't complain, however. It had amassed 35 percent of the market by 1985.

[27]*Business Week*, October 3, 1983, pp. 86, 90.

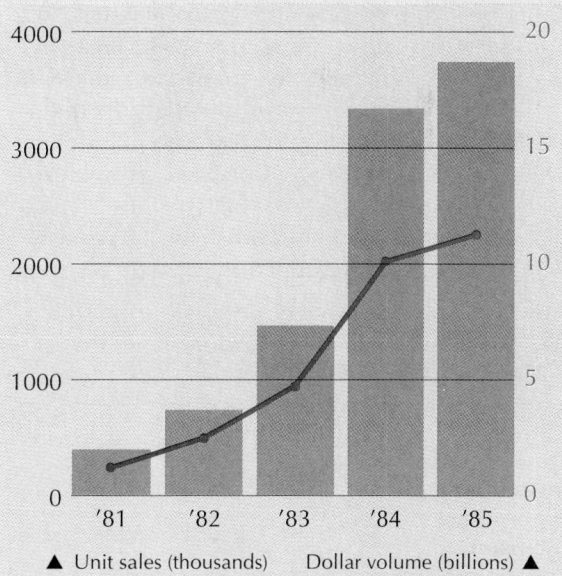

▲ Unit sales (thousands)   Dollar volume (billions) ▲

FIGURE 28.10 Personal (and Portable) Computer Annual Sales in Units and Dollar Volume, 1981–85 (*Source:* Business Week, June 24, 1985, p. 77.)

SUMMARY

1. Nonprice activities, marketing effort and product variation in particular, play a major role in dynamic competition, which is independent rivalry among firms using various strategies and counterstrategies over time.

2. Advertising is the most obvious of all marketing efforts. Informative advertising provides facts on prices, product features, and the like. Persuasive advertising relies on the exhortation of repetition, jingles, celebrity endorsements, and related ploys.

3. Innovation is a mainstay of product variation. It is the commercialization of an invention. If successful, its diffusion is quick and extensive.

4. Prospective profits fire nonprice efforts. Since profits depend on both revenues and costs, these efforts attempt to manipulate *revenues* by (a) lowering the firm's price elasticity of demand, thereby permitting price hikes or price discrimination; (b) shifting the firm's demand outward; and (c) combining informative advertising and price cuts to raise the price elasticity of demand. These efforts may lower *costs* by (a) promoting sales to exploit economies of scale; (b) improving productivity through process innovation; and (c) traveling down experience curves with added cumulative output.

5. Advertising is informative or persuasive, light or intense, depending partly on the type of buyer and the type of product. Table 28.3 summarizes for two simple dichotomies—business versus consumer buyers and shopping versus convenience goods.

6. Concentration's impact on advertising intensity varies. It has no impact for producer goods. It has a nonlinear impact for consumer goods, as seen in Figure 28.7.

7. In performance, advertising gets mixed marks. It usually promotes reasonable prices and normal profits when informative and relatively restrained (i.e., producer goods, retail store services, and shopping goods). On the other hand, it seems to raise prices and profits when persuasive and intense (i.e., consumer convenience goods). Waste is also a problem in the latter setting. On a higher plane, a debate rages on whether, or to what degree, consumers or producers are sovereigns of the marketplace.

8. Innovation itself escapes sharp controversy, but the factors fostering it do not. In general, it seems that innovative performance improves with firm size only up to a middle range and thereafter it frequently worsens. As regards market concentration, its impact is greatly weakened by other factors influencing potential technological change. Though its relevance is therefore slight, it seems that pure monopoly is bad.

KEY TERMS

Dynamic competition
Invention
Innovation
Diffusion
Experience curves

Shopping goods
Convenience goods
Consumer sovereignty
Producer sovereignty

QUESTIONS AND PROBLEMS

1. Define and describe dynamic competition. Explain why dynamic competition is primarily nonprice competition.
2. What are the goals of advertising?
3. Identify and describe the three main stages of technological change.
4. How will brand loyalty be reflected in the demand curve for a product?
5. Advertising increases costs for producers. Yet product prices sometimes tend to be lower when producers are free to advertise than when advertising is prohibited. Why?
6. Distinguish between *product* innovation and *process* innovation. What is the primary incentive for process innovation?
7. We all know at least one or two of them, and some of us may count ourselves among them—the people who rush to buy a new product as soon as it comes out. They were the first to own personal computers, VCR's, and compact disc players. Even if we aren't among these adventurous consumers, we can appreciate the fact that their enthusiasm means not only rapid success for new products but also falling prices for future buyers. Why?
8. Household purchasing decisions are usually less informed than those of businesses. Explain why. How is this fact reflected in advertisements aimed at the two groups?
9. How is the intensity of advertising for consumer goods linked to market concentration?
10. Does advertising result in higher prices and profits for firms in the industry or in lower prices and profits?
11. Discuss the relationship between firm size and innovation.

29

Antitrust and Information Policies

It was headline news. Two massive antitrust suits ended on the same day—January 8, 1982. AT&T *would be* broken up. IBM *would not be* broken up.

Both suits had been brought under Section 2 of the Sherman Act. Both companies were colossal. Both were accused of monopolization. And both spent hundreds of millions of dollars for legal defenses over many years. Yet one company was to be split asunder, while the other escaped whole. Why the contrast? The obvious answer is that each case was different, warranting different outcomes. Still, the AT&T and IBM cases had much in common, so these contrasting results illustrate a main problem of this chapter. Our antitrust policy—which concerns competition—is complex and often confusing. Hence a principal objective of this chapter is to explain U.S. antitrust policy as clearly as possible.

You will learn that antitrust policy is quite different from public utility regulation, which we discussed in Chapter 26. Under public utility regulation, competition is abandoned. Monopoly is permitted and even encouraged where it seems to be inevitable or desirable, as in cases of natural monopoly. Market decision making is then replaced by government decision making. In contrast, antitrust policy is supposed to enhance and maintain competition. Antitrust policy is the government's attempt to facilitate or strengthen the market system by keeping it free of monopolistic restraints.

Earlier, in Chapter 4, antitrust policy was described as an effort to reduce market imperfections, and monopolistic restraints are indeed imperfections. A related policy effort, but one aimed at curbing imperfections of a different sort, can be called *information policy*. This covers such things as ingredient labeling, grade rating, and deceptive advertising. These and other forms of information policy are the subject of the last segment of this chapter.

Given what we said earlier about the government's imperfections, you will not be surprised to learn that the market's imperfections have not been eradicated by these official efforts. Still, on balance, they seem to serve our economy fairly well.

I

Antitrust: Introduction

A

Problems

The basic aim of antitrust policy is to foster competition by curbing monopolistic restraints. Why? The answer is found in the main conclusions of previous chapters. Competition—not necessarily perfect competition, but competition nevertheless—is generally *good*, while monopoly power, including cartelization, is generally *bad*. The potential sins of monopoly power are serious:

1. *Reduced freedom:* Limited options for buyers, given the limited number of independently acting sellers that monopoly power entails.
2. *Allocation inefficiency:* A higher price and lower output than would occur under competition.
3. *Technical inefficiency:* Higher costs of production due to slack and sloth, plus other sorts of X-inefficiency.
4. *Inequity:* Distortions in income distribution due to excess economic profits.
5. *Poor progressiveness:* Slow invention and innovation relative to the opportunities for new technologies.

All told, monopoly power seems undesirable. There are problems, however. Our previous analysis disclosed instances where monopoly power was actually *good*.

1. *Technical efficiency:* Where economies of scale are large relative to market demand,

natural monopoly (or natural oligopoly) reduces costs.

2. *Progressiveness:* Monopoly power may occasionally encourage innovation and invention. Patents, for instance, confer monopoly power on inventors as an inducement to be progressive.

In sum, competition is not necessarily always good, and monopoly power is not necessarily always bad. This complicates matters. Further complications arise because business conduct can likewise be good or bad, depending on the circumstances. Take *tying,* for instance (also called *tie-in sales*).

> **Tying** occurs when a seller ties the sale of two products together, so that buyers must buy both products even if they want only one.

When tying is used by small firms for promotional purposes, it is innocuous and perhaps even pro-competitive. A cheap toy might be included in each box of Ralston Wheat Chex, but that would not give Ralston a monopoly over either breakfast cereals or toys. On the other hand, tying may have anticompetitive consequences. Prior to the mid-1950s, Kodak had a monopoly on photo film, and purchasers of Kodak film were required to buy Kodak's film *processing* when they bought its film. This restricted competition in the market for film processing.

B

Solutions

Given these ambiguities and complexities concerning competition, it might appear that *any* policy in this area would be hopeless. Still, U.S. policy has several features that ease these problems, although they do not eliminate them completely.

First, a certain basic orientation is helpful. The government does *not* try to enforce perfect competition in any market, or anything even approaching perfect competition. IBM recently escaped dissolution despite its considerable power. Likewise, General Motors, General Electric, General Foods, General Dynamics, and most other large "generals" have never been seriously threatened with dissolution. Huge aggregations of corporate power are thus permitted because *the orientation of the law is to curb unreasonable monopolistic restraints, and this grants much leeway to businesses.* Such is suggested by the very name of the policy—*antitrust.* Late in the last century, after 1870 in particular, numerous major industries came to be dominated by so-called trusts. The most famous of these was the Standard Oil trust, which through a combination of numerous companies and various predatory practices came to control 90 percent of the petroleum refining industry in the United States. Hence it was not a lack of perfect competition that motivated passage of the Sherman Antitrust Act in 1890. It was, rather, the awesome ascendance of giants like Standard Oil. And most of these aggregations of power have been attacked, while many less ominous ones stand untouched.

Second, and more specifically, monopoly power can be achieved or maintained in many ways, both natural and artificial. The natural ways usually reflect the *good* side of monopoly. The artificial ways usually reflect the *bad.* Hence antitrust policy avoids major conflicts with economic realities by, in effect, *exempting* natural monopolies (and natural oligopolies). The exemption of public utilities is the most obvious case. Other exemptions include those firms that attain dominance by patenting technological improvements (e.g., GE in lighting) or by simply producing a superior product at a competitive price (e.g., Boeing in commercial aircraft). As for the artificial cases, these *are* attacked for being unreasonable monopolistic restraints. If General Motors, Ford, and Chrysler attempted to merge, they would be challenged. If their executives met to fix the prices of cars, they would be prosecuted. This is because anticompetitive mergers and collusive price fixing artificially injur competition.

Third, the problem of good/bad ambiguity is eased by the fact that antitrust law has only a few flat prohibitions. It does *not* outlaw every firm with assets of over $5 billion or with a market share of over 80 percent. It does *not* ban all mergers between competing firms. Antitrust law is composed of several rather *vague statutes* that prohibit such things as monopolization and mergers, which may substantially lessen competition. In turn, these statutes are enforced by *court judgments* of cases initiated by *governmental and private plaintiffs*. The result is a rule of reason approach that is applied to most parts of the law. This approach permits courts to consider a wide variety of economic circumstances when reaching their opinions. In some cases, they consider the intent of business executives. In others, they may consider evidence of technical efficiency. The resulting flexibility allows for considerable judgment. Thus an attempt is usually made to distinguish the artificial from the natural and to weigh the procompetitive against the anticompetitive consequences. Where the rule of reason does not apply—as in collusive price fixing—the monopolistic restraint is said to be per se unreasonable and therefore automatically unlawful.

In sum, economics provides enough theory and evidence against monopolistic restraints to establish a presumption that impairments of competition are harmful. The problem is, however, that there are exceptions. And this problem is addressed by (1) a basic stance that opposes unreasonable monopolistic restraints rather than one that imposes perfect competition; (2) an attack against acts and circumstances that are artificial or contrived, and (3) a rule of reason approach to deciding specific cases in most areas of antitrust law (the major exception being collusive restraints such as price fixing, which are per se illegal).

II
Possible Objectives of Antitrust

A
Introduction

To say that antitrust policy curbs unreasonable monopolistic restraints may not be very helpful. What is meant by *unreasonable*? Or *monopolistic*? Or, indeed, *restraints*? Imagine yourself as a judge in a federal court. U.S. Justice Department attorneys file suit against, say, the IBM Corporation. Your decision of what is unreasonable or monopolistic would hinge partly on what you perceived to be the main overall *objectives* of the antitrust laws. Such objectives can be discussed now, prior

to specifying the contents of the statutes, because a knowledge of objectives aids in understanding the language of the statutes. Indeed, Congress had to have some objectives in mind before it could pass those statutes, so you should have them in mind before you read on.

Although Congress had objectives, they are not entirely clear. Different congressional supporters of antitrust legislation stressed different reasons for their support. Moreover, the legislators expressed themselves in generalities rather than specifics. Senator Sherman, father of the venerable Sherman Antitrust Act of 1890, said, "If we [in the United States] will not endure a king as a political power, we should not endure a king over the production, transportation, and sale of any of the necessaries of life."

Given the generalities of congressional voices, it is not surprising that the courts likewise speak of antitrust aims in rather sweeping terms. Here is an example from a Supreme Court ruling of the 1950s:

> *The Sherman Act was designed to be a comprehensive charter of economic liberty aimed at preserving free and unfettered competition as the rule of trade. It rests on the premise that the unrestrained interaction of competitive forces will yield the best allocation of our economic resources, the lowest prices, the highest quality and the greatest material progress, while at the same time providing an environment conducive to the preservation of our democratic political and social institutions.*[1]

B
Structure, Conduct, and Performance

Putting this matter of aims into a familiar context, we can categorize aims depending on their focus. Market structure, conduct, and performance each offer a possible focus.

1. Maintenance of Competitive Structure Antitrust could aim at maintaining competition as an end in itself. If so, this would be largely a structural goal, whose earmarks might include such features as (1) an ample number of sellers and buyers in

---

[1] *Northern Pacific Railway Co. v. United States*, 356 U.S. 1 (1958).

markets, (2) no more than moderate concentration, and (3) fairly easy entry. Conduct could also be covered by the aim of maintaining competition, with prohibitions against cartelization. Still, the emphasis here is on structure, the _mere possession_ of power.

While business power is most typically reckoned in economic terms such as concentration ratios, it may also carry political and social implications because political and social powers are often grounded in economic power. As the preceding quotation suggests, antitrust policy may provide "an environment conducive to the preservation of our democratic and social institutions."

2. Fair Conduct   The foregoing relates primarily to the mere possession of market power, not to its exercise. In contrast, aims of fair conduct relate to the _way business power is used_ rather than its mere presence. Should monopolistic sellers be allowed to engage in tying? What about 100 sellers in a market who compete vigorously among themselves but who, by collective boycotts, bar the entry of any new rivals? Is this unfair? Antitrust policy could attempt to lay down certain standards of fair business conduct that would curtail these practices without necessarily attacking market power directly.

3. Desirable Economic Performance   Because market structure and conduct greatly affect economic performance, antitrust policy could be concerned with structure and conduct _only_ insofar as they clearly produce poor economic performance, while overlooking any concentrations of power or unfair practices that have no notable effect on performance or promise potential improvements therein. Most advocates of this aim typically ignore performance as it relates to income equity or progressiveness. Rather, they argue that allocative and technical _efficiency_ should be the sole aim of antitrust.

These three possibilities being the main options, what are the actualities? Which of these aims is the target of U.S. antitrust policy as revealed in the actions of our legislatures, enforcement agencies, and courts? In fact, there is no clear-cut answer. Until fairly recently, it appears that the first two— maintenance of competitive structure and fair conduct—dominated. Of late, many commenta-

tors and several judges have argued that the sole aim of antitrust policy should be economic efficiency, a performance standard. As of 1987, the Supreme Court has nodded in the direction of efficiency, but it has refused to adopt it as the only aim. Thus, at present, there is a blend of all three aims. Such is suggested by the earlier quotation of the Supreme Court, which moves from "unfettered competition" to "the best allocation of our economic resources" and then concludes with a concern for our "democratic political and social institutions."

The alert reader might readily accept such a blend and wonder how there could ever be any sharp dispute over aims. As we have seen, success in maintaining competition and fair conduct typically bear fruits of economic efficiency (not to mention such other fruits of good performance as progressiveness and equity). Still, there are some sparks in the debate between those critics advocating only efficiency and those holding more traditional views. Those favoring efficiency want to give enormous latitude to big business. They claim that, contrary to conventional evidence, a fewness of firms usually lowers the price and expands output. They claim to have never seen a real-world example of tacit collusion. Overall, they say, we should _scrap all antitrust_ except perhaps that curbing cartels (and some of the critics claim that even cartels are no problem).[2] Hence this dispute over aims has grown into a dispute over the contents of antitrust policy. And we now turn to those contents.

III
Antitrust Statutes and Procedures

Antitrust policy is the child of three parties—(1) legislators who write the satutes, (2) plaintiffs who sue under the statutes, and (3) judges who rule on those suits in light of the statutes, thereby developing case law. In this section we tackle the first

---

[2]See, e.g., the views of Yale Brozen and Robert Bork in _Industrial Concentration and the Market System_, ed. Eleanor Fox and J. T. Halverson (section of Antitrust Law; American Bar Association, 1979), pp. 81–161.

two under headings of "Statutes" and "Procedures." Case law developments are reserved for Section IV, "Selected Antitrust Cases."

A

Statutes

The objective of maintaining free and fair competition may be found in the language of the antitrust statutes themselves—the Sherman Act of 1890 and the Clayton Act and Federal Trade Commission Act of 1914. The latter two statutes have since been amended in major ways that will be mentioned later. Conceptually, these laws have five main concerns—*collusion, monopolization, exclusionary practices, mergers,* and *unfair or deceptive practices.* (Table 29.1 offers a slightly different summary.)

1. *Collusion.* Under Section 1 of the Sherman Act, it is illegal to enter into a "contract, combination . . . , or conspiracy, in restraint of trade or commerce." This forbids cartelization to fix prices or allocate territories and bans collective boycotts.
2. *Monopolization.* Under Section 2 of the Sherman Act, it is illegal to "monopolize, or attempt to monopolize, or combine or conspire . . . to monopolize any part of trade or commerce". Despite the word "monopolize," market shares of less than 100 percent may be in violation.

3. *Exclusionary practices.* The Clayton Act, in Section 2 (as amended by the Robinson-Patman Act) and Section 3, prohibits price discrimination, exclusive dealing, tying, and related practices where the "effect may be to substantially lessen competition or tend to create a monopoly."
4. *Mergers.* Section 7 of the Clayton Act (as amended by the Celler-Kefauver Act) bans mergers that may "substantially" lessen competition.
5. *Unfair or deceptive practices.* The Federal Trade Commission Act (as amended by the Wheeler-Lea Act) makes it illegal to use "unfair methods of competition" and "unfair or deceptive acts or practices" (regardless of their impact on competition).

Because anticompetitive effects need not be shown to establish the illegality of deceptive practices, our discussion of those practices is postponed until the end of this chapter. As for the rest, it should be noted that the statutes make no special references to performance considerations. Cartel participants cannot defend themselves by claiming that their conspiracy fosters allocation efficiency. Anticompetitive mergers are not excused by the statutes even if they produce technical efficiencies. The main focus of each policy could thus be outlined as follows:

Collusion—conduct
Monopolization—structure and conduct

TABLE 29.1   The Main Antitrust Statutes

Sherman Antitrust Act (1890)
- Section 1:   Outlaws contracts and conspiracies in "restraint of trade," like price fixing.
- Section 2:   Forbids monopolization and "attempts" to monopolize.

Clayton Act (1914)
- Section 2 as amended by the *Robinson-Patman Act* (1936): Bans price discrimination that substantially lessens competition or injures particular competitors.
- Section 3:   Prohibits certain exclusionary practices, such as tying and exclusive dealing, which substantially lessen competition.
- Section 7 as amended by the *Celler-Kefauver Act* (1950): Outlaws mergers that substantially lessen competition.

Federal Trade Commission Act (1914)
- Section 1:   Establishes the Federal Trade Commission
- Section 5 as amended by the Wheeler-Lea Act (1938): Prohibits "unfair methods of competition" and "unfair or deceptive acts."

Exclusionary practices—conduct and structure

Mergers—structure

Unfair practices—conduct

B
Procedures

Action against alleged offenders of these statutes may be initiated by the U.S. Department of Justice, by the Federal Trade Commission, or by private plaintiffs. The _Justice Department_ concentrates on collusive restraints, monopolization, and mergers, filing its suits in the Federal District Courts. Most of these suits are settled without trial because of guilty pleas, _nolo contenderes_, and consent settlements. Those that are decided by trial may be appealed to a Circuit Court of Appeals and, after that, perhaps even to the U.S. Supreme Court. Since passage of the Sherman Act in 1890, the Justice Department has initiated well over 1,700 cases, and several dozens of them have reached the Supreme Court.

The _Federal Trade Commission (FTC)_ is headed by a panel of five commissioners, each appointed by the President. Unlike the Justice Department, the FTC has no direct responsibility for enforcing the Sherman Act. Rather, the Clayton Act, the Federal Trade Commission Act, and the various amendments to these statutes get most of the FTC's attention. (Still, the "unfair methods of competition" of the Federal Trade Commission Act have been interpreted to include Sherman-type offenses.) Also unlike the Justice Department, which files its cases in Federal District Courts, almost all formal FTC proceedings are started by an administrative complaint issued to one or more alleged offenders. These complaints are settled without trial by a negotiated "consent" or are tried by an administrative law judge. These events are reviewed by the full commission, whose decision on any case can be appealed to the high federal courts.

Private plaintiffs who are injured by antitrust offenders may sue them under any of the statutes except the Federal Trade Commission Act. A major motive for these suits is that private plaintiffs can be awarded amounts totaling _three times_ the proven damages. Indeed, over the last 20 years, private suits have outnumbered those of the Justice Department and the FTC combined. Most of them are filed by wholesalers or retailers who have disputes with manufacturer-suppliers, and the vast majority of them end in voluntary dismissals or pretrial settlements.

C
Remedies

Mention of treble damages brings us to remedies. Only private plaintiffs who prove their injuries can sue for treble damages. Though they lack this weapon, the Justice Department and the FTC have ample ammunition of their own. Operating under _civil_ law, the Justice Department and the FTC can address structural problems by forcing firms to break up through dissolutions or divestitures. These authorities typically solve problems of conduct by obtaining _cease and desist orders_ or _injunctions_. Moreover, and in many ways most importantly, the Justice Department may bring _criminal_ actions against those violating the Sherman Act. Heavy fines and prison sentences have greeted the most flagrant violators of Section 1 of the Sherman Act. Though possible, such penalties have very rarely been levied against Section 2 offenders, dissolution being the preferred alternative.

Why the striking contrast between Sections 1 and 2 of the Sherman Act in this matter of criminal penalties? The explanation emerges in the next section. (Sneak preview: The courts have interpreted most Section 1 violations as _per se_ offenses, while Section 2 offenses are judged by a _rule of reason_ approach.)

IV
Selected Antitrust Cases

The antitrust statutes have been land mines set by Congress and exploded by specific cases. Review of the major cases is best organized by the divisions already charted—namely, collusion, monopolization, exclusionary practices, and mergers.

Throughout the discussion, note that the courts are the main speakers here, not the Congress and not the enforcement agencies. Note further that the Supreme Court has over time developed several rules of thumb for deciding various cases. The courts do not like to engage in full-blown, open-ended economic analysis of each case. To do so would impose great burdens on everyone involved in enforcement—the defendants, the plaintiffs, and the courts. Moreover, wide-open inquiry into every case would leave business executives in the dark about what precisely was illegal. The resulting confusion could crimp business severely. Hence much of the discussion of cases centers on these various rules of thumb.

A

Collusion

The oldest and most consistently applied rule of thumb in all of antitrust is the per se rule governing collusive restraints of trade, which are outlawed by Section 1 of the Sherman Act (1890).

> **Collusive agreements** to fix prices, to allocate territories or customers, to curtail output, to boycott certain suppliers or customers are per se illegal.

This rule holds that cartel practices are, *in themselves*, unlawful. If prices are being fixed, the courts will not try to determine whether those prices are reasonable. If all sellers sell through a single sales agency and refuse to supply customers directly (outside the sales agency), they cannot defend themselves by claiming vast efficiencies for the scheme. If sellers controlling only 40 percent of the market form a cartel, the courts will not try to determine whether this 40 percent was enough to influence the whole market. In short, the courts do not consider motives, efficiencies, circumstances, effect, or the like. Acts of express collusion are automatic offenses.

The leading case establishing the per se rule was *United States v. Trenton Potteries*, decided in 1927. Twenty-three corporations producing 82 percent of the vitreous pottery fixtures (bathroom bowls, tubs, and so on) in the United States were accused of conspiring to fix prices and limit production. In their defense, they claimed that their prices were reasonable. But the Court rejected this argument, saying:

> *The aim and result of every price-fixing agreement, if effective, is the elimination of one form of competition. The power to fix prices, whether reasonably exercised or not, involves power to control the market and to fix arbitrary and unreasonable prices. . . . Agreements which create such potential power may well be held to be in themselves unreasonable or unlawful restraints. . . .* [3]

The per se rule and the offenses to which it applies are usually clear and simple. As a consequence, offenders of Section 1 frequently face criminal actions, with fines and prison sentences as possible penalties. Indeed, Section 1 accounts for almost all stints in the slammer under the antitrust laws.

The main problem arises in defining "collusive agreement." If competitors gather in smoke-filled rooms to set identical prices, that would certainly qualify. But what about price leadership or some other form of *tacit* collusion? Each rival, acting independently of others in its market, may decide not to compete on price. The courts call this *conscious parallelism*, and they have decided that this alone does not amount to an illegal collusive agreement. However, if conscious parallelism is accompanied by some added behavior, some plus factor, then the courts might well decide that a collusive agreement is present even though minutes of meetings or recordings of phone conversations are unavailable as evidence.

Read Perspective 29A.

B

Monopolization

The first thing to note about Section 2 of the Sherman Act is that it outlaws "monopolization," not "monopoly." If an innovative firm is the first to market, say, a personal computer, it will have a monopoly. But it will have a monopoly simply because it is the sole occupant of a market that it created, and it will therefore escape Section 2. If a small town of 20,000 people is too small to support more than one newspaper, that newspaper also has a monopoly, but it too would dodge prosecution. Thus a firm having monopoly thrust upon it by virtue of its economic merits or the market's

---

[3]*U.S. v. Trenton Potteries*, 272 U.S. 392, 397 (1927).

PERSPECTIVE 29A
The Electrical Equipment Cases

The electrical equipment cases are to American price fixing what Watergate is to American political corruption. The collusive activity began in the 1920s or 1930s, and by the 1950s it had spread to 20 different product lines—turbine generators, power transformers, circuit breakers, condensers, meters, insulators, and so on. Several of the largest participants, like General Electric and Westinghouse, operated and conspired in many of the markets. Smaller firms, like Moloney Electric and Wagner, were more specialized. In all, 29 firms and 44 individuals were indicted during 1960 for criminal conspiracies involving roughly $7 billion worth of business.

The collusive methods and experiences varied from product to product, from sealed-bid sales to off-the-shelf transactions, and from higher to lower levels of company management. One common thread, however, was the atmosphere of skulduggery. Code names, payphone communications, plain envelope mailings, destruction of evidence, secret meetings in out-of-the-way places (like Dirty Mary's

Roadhouse), faked expense account records, and secret market allocations all entered the plot. Perhaps the most sensational technique devised was the "phases of the moon" system for sealed-bid switchgear sales. This system automtically fixed the price each company would quote on switchgear bids, with the low price being rotated among the conspirators in a way that gave buyers the illusion of random competition. The government's criminal suits were settled under the per se rule, with seven executives serving brief terms in prison and with fines totaling $1,954,000, the bulk of which was paid by the companies. Furthermore, hundreds of private treble-damage suits tapped the treasuries of the electrical companies, yielding about $400 million for the plaintiffs. Although many rather interesting conspiracies have been uncovered since then—concerning such industries as uranium yellow cake, highway construction, and paper products—the electrical equipment conspiracies still set the standard for size, seriousness, and sensationalism in domestic American price fixing.

odd circumstances need not fear. Monopoly (the noun) is not outlawed even though it may grant a firm considerable market power. This is as it should be. If the law attacked meritorious firms (like innovators), it would stifle meritorious behavior (like innovation). If the law banned monopolies created by market circumstances (i.e., natural monopolies), there would be no sensible remedy to correct the situation. Breaking up the monopoly would probably raise costs and provide no more than a temporary pause before monopoly was reestablished.

The violation is thus expressed as a verb—to *monopolize*. This implies that offenders possess great market power, something like that of a monopoly. The law goes further, however, to require that offenders also display some drive, some active pursuit, of that power through anticompetitive

conduct. As Justice William Douglas wrote in the *Grinnell* case, the offense of monopolization "has two elements: (1) the possession of monoply power in the relevant market and (2) willful acquisition or maintenance of that power."[4]

The rule of thumb for **monopolization** calls for proof of two factors: (1) substantial market power and (2) intent.

1. Power The key index of market power is the alleged monopolizer's market share. A number of firms with market shares exceeding 80 percent have run afoul of the law. On the other hand, market shares below 60 percent seem to lie beneath the reach of the law. If a firm has a market share

[4]*U.S. v. Grinnell Corporation*, 384 U.S. 563 (1966).

between the boundaries of 80 and 60 percent, case law indicates that it occupies a gray area. It may or may not be found to possess sufficient power.

All this sounds simple enough. There is, though, a major catch. Before the market share of a firm can be calculated, there must be some definition of the "market." A firm selling $9 billion worth of some product would have 90 percent of a market defined so narrowly as to include only $10 billion in total sales, but it would have only 9 percent of a market defined broadly enough to include $100 billion in sales. Generally speaking, antitrust plaintiffs like to argue for narrowly defined markets in order to pin a large market share on any alleged monopolizer. Conversely, defendants typically argue for broadly defined markets in order to give the appearance of possessing very small market shares.

Take the case of *Du Pont*, for instance, decided in 1956.[5] The government accused Du Pont of monopolizing the market for cellophane, 75 percent of which was prodcued by Du Pont. The company defended itself by arguing that cellophane alone could not be considered the relevant market. Du Pont defined the market to include *all* flexible packaging materials—wax paper, foil, pliofilm, polyethylene, and so on—as well as cellophane. Although Du Pont produced 75 percent of all cellophane in the United States, this business amounted to only 14 percent of all flexible packaging. Hence market definition made a big difference. When the Supreme Court adopted Du Pont's definition, Du Pont won acquittal. The decisive point for the Court's majority was cross-elasticity of demand, as may be seen in its opinion:

> *If a slight decrease in the price of cellophane causes a considerable number of customers to switch to cellophane, it would be indication that a high cross-elasticity of demand exists between them; that the products compete in the same market . . . . we conclude that cellophane's interchangeability with other materials mentioned suffices to make it a part of this flexible packaging material market.*

Besides cross-elasticity of demand, the Court has relied on numerous other earmarks to define markets, including the physical characteristics of products, the end uses of products, and any unique production facilities or supply elasticities. Given the large number of possible indicators, and given the lack of clear boundaries for most markets, market definition can be messy. Thus a rule of reason.

2. Intent Even messier is the matter of intent. A monopolist's intent is not determined by subjecting its executives to psychoanalysis. Intent emerges from the firm's particular acts or its general course of action. And here there are three rather distinct periods of Section 2 interpretation, depending on what the courts have required of plaintiffs to prove intent:

1. *1890–1940:* In the early days, the Supreme Court usually held that intent could be established only with evidence of abusive conduct.
2. *1945–1970:* The *Alcoa* case of 1945 set a new standard, excusing monopolists only when power was "thrust upon" them, as if by accident. Intent could be shown by very little evidence because, according to the Court, "no monopolist monopolizes unconcious of what it is doing."
3. *1970–present:* Current policy apparently drops the *Alcoa* standard and retreats toward the early days, providing greater leniency for alleged monopolists and placing a greater burden of proof on plaintiffs.

U.S. v. Standard Oil Company of New Jersey, decided in 1911, highlights the early 1890–1940 era.[6] Standard Oil (now Exxon) was the most notorious monopolist of its time. First organized in Ohio in 1870, by 1872 it had acquired all but a few of the three dozen refineries in Cleveland. Additionally, it had garnered complete control of pipelines running from oilfields to refineries in the East. Further transportation advantages were extracted from the railroads through preferential shipping fares and rebates. From this strategic footing, Standard Oil was able to force competitors to join the combination or be driven out of busi-

---

[5]*U.S. v. E.I. DuPont de Nemours Company*, 351 U.S. 377 (1956).

[6]*U.S. v. Standard Oil Company of New Jersey*, 221 U.S. 1 (1911).

ness. As a result, the combine grew to control 90 percent of the petroleum refining industry. Under legal attack from authorities in Ohio, the company reorganized in 1899 as Standard Oil of New Jersey. The new combine continued to exact preferential treatment from railroads and to cut crude oil supplies to competing refiners. Business espionage, local price warfare, and the operation of bogus independent companies were also Standard tactics.

The Supreme Court's decision against Standard Oil emphasized intent, contrasting the tainted history of the company with what could be called "normal methods of industrial development." Dissolution of the combine followed, yielding 34 separate companies. At the time, these offspring were regionally specialized—such as Standard Oil of California (Chevron), Standard Oil of Ohio (Sohio), and Standard Oil of New York (Mobil). Thereafter they spread into each other's territories to compete. The Court's emphasis on abusive conduct in this early era is further reflected in the Court's acquittal of the U.S. Steel Corporation in 1920. Although U.S. Steel was formed through a chain of mergers involving 170 formerly independent steel companies, the Court found insufficient evidence of intent because U.S. Steel "resorted to none of the brutalities or tyrannies that the cases illustrate of other combinations."[7]

The second major era, 1945–1970, emerged from *U.S. v. Alcoa* (1945).[8] According to this ruling, intent could be demonstrated even if the alleged monopolist had not engaged in abusive or brutal conduct. Much else could also qualify to prove intent, so much else that the Court found it easier to describe innocence than guilt. According to the *Alcoa* opinion, a monopolist could escape only if its monopoly had been "thrust upon it," only if "superior skill, foresight and industry" were the basis for its success. Alcoa, which had controlled over 90 percent of the primary aluminum sales in the United States for about 50 years, did not pass this test. In the eyes of the Court, control did not simply fall into Alcoa's lap. The company blocked new entry by always anticipating increases in the demand for ingots and supplying them: "Nothing

compelled it to keep doubling and redoubling its capacity before others entered the field." Hence Alcoa was found to have violated Section 2 of the Sherman Act.

Note that this interpretation had a strong structural orientation. Conduct counted for little. Once power was proven, intent could be fairly easily demonstrated. No subsequent case went as far as *Alcoa*, but other cases of this second era clearly held that violations need "not rest on predatory practices" such as those observed in *Standard Oil*.[9]

The present era, unfolding since 1970, marks a retreat from the stringent *Alcoa* standard. Treatment of alleged monopolizers has become more lenient. Just how lenient remains unclear because the Supreme Court has not ruled on a major monopolization case for quite some time. Still, the actions of the lower courts and the enforcement authorities signal a shift in policy. Several cases involving IBM illustrate this. Let's glimpse at the government's case.

IBM has dominated the mainframe computer market for several decades. (In 1983 its market share was about 78 percent, a hefty amount compared to that of its second-ranked rival, Burroughs, which had less than 6 percent of the mainframe market.) The key question here is, how did IBM come by this power? Was it especially innovative? Did it rely on predatory practices? The answer is mixed. Its conduct was neither purely good nor brutally bad. Still, IBM's behavior was probably bad enough so that it would have run afoul of the *Alcoa* criteria. The Justice Department filed suit in 1969, alleging that a number of IBM's actions established intent, including:

1. Paper machines, whereby IBM tried to dissuade computer users from acquiring or leasing Control Data's 6600 (an advanced, truly remarkable machine) by announcing that IBM would soon have a comparable and perhaps even superior product, when in fact IBM had no such thing.
2. Tying, whereby IBM quoted a *single* price for hardware, software, and related support.

---

[7]*U.S. v. Untied States Steel Corporation,* 251 U.S. 417 (1920).

[8]*U.S. v. Aluminum Company of America,* 148 F 2d 416 (1945).

[9]*U.S. v. United Shoe Machinery Corp.,* 110 F. Supp. 295 (D. Mass, 1953), aff'd per curiam, 347 U.S. 521 (1954).

The suit proceeded under three presidents, but President Reagan's assistant attorney general withdrew the suit in January 1982, saying that he did not think IBM had committed any "serious business improprieties."[10]

Thus, power and intent form the rule of thumb for monopolization. These require a rule of reason approach, an approach open to fluctuating interpretation over time. *Most recently, the authorities have become more lenient.*

C
Exclusionary Practices

In general, exclusionary practices are the kind of conduct that would indicate intent in a monopolization case:

> **Exclusionary practices** raise barriers to new firm entry or force small established firms out of the market.

Sections 2 and 3 of the Clayton Act (as amended by the Robinson-Patman Act) prohibit several practices that could be called exclusionary in this sense. Indeed, the whole idea behind the Clayton Act, including its ban on anticompetitive mergers, is to curb *incipient* monopolization. If monopolizers could be checked early, they would be easier to control because they would then not become so bad as to require application of the Sherman Act.

The specific practices covered include price discrimination, tying, exclusive dealing, and full-line forcing. None of these is banned outright, however. Each practice is handled by its own rule of thumb, and each must substantially lessen competition before a violation is proven. This may be illustrated with tying.

If Kodak tied film processing to the sale of its film, shutterbugs could not buy Kodak film without also buying Kodak's film processing. Film would be the tying good and film processing would be the tied good. Such tying may not have anticompetitive consequences. Indeed, tying is of-

ten so efficient and convenient that the resulting ties are thought of as single products rather than separate products—e.g., shirts sold with buttons, autos with tires, and pencils with erasers. On the other hand, tying can be anticompetitive. It can sometimes raise barriers to entry in the market of the tied good or seriously disadvantage smaller tied-good competitors. Both of these effects are exclusionary.

For example, some years ago Kodak actually did tie film processing to the sale of its film. When tied, Kodak controlled *90 percent of both* of these markets. Because of a 1954 antitrust case, Kodak severed the tie, licensed its processing technology to new entrants, and agreed to substantial divestiture of its processing facilities. A flood of new film processors entered the market. With entry, Kodak's control of film processing was shattered and prices of film processing fell substantially.

Tying can thus be good or bad. The rule of thumb governing tying loosely tends to recognize this. Violations are found only when the answers to *all* the following questions are "yes":

1. Are two goods (or services) involved?
2. Does the seller possess sufficient power in the market of the *tying* good?
3. Is there substantial commerce in the *tied* good?
4. Are defenses of reasonableness absent?

Judgment informs each answer, so a rule of reason approach again applies. Even the first question, which seems easy to answer, is often difficult. For instance, are two goods involved when the Ford Motor Company insists that its radios be installed in Ford cars? Are two goods involved if IBM ties disk drives to its central processing units? As regards the second question—economic power in the tying-good market—the issue is much like that of monopolization. And the Supreme Court has found a variety of conditions providing "yes" answers, including a large market share in the tying-good market or high barriers to entry there. The need for a rule of reason approach is thus apparent. It must be noted, however, that the Court reduces the rule of reason to a per se rule when economic power in the tying good is grounded on patents. A patent on the tying good makes the tie unreasonable per se.

---

[10]*Wall Street Journal*, January 11, 1982. IBM had won several private suits, so our conclusion of a retreat rests on more than this withdrawal.

D

Mergers

1. Merger Types Corporations are like used cars. They can be bought and sold, although this may seem odd, given the billions of dollars often at stake in the buying and selling. When one corporation buys another through purchase of its assets or common stock, a *merger* results. The union of two or more direct competitors is called a *horizontal merger*. The combining companies operate in the same market, as illustrated in Figure 29.1 by the merger of Auto Company F and Auto Company G. In contrast, a *vertical merger* links companies that operate at different stages of the production-distribution process. Two vertical sequences appear in Figure 29.1, namely, steel–autos and textiles–apparel. Hence, if Textile Firm N acquired Apparel Firm Y, that would be a vertical merger. Finally, *conglomerate mergers* are all those that are neither horizontal nor vertical. The classic or pure conglomerate merger involves two firms with nothing at all in common. Figure 29.1 illustrates this by the merger of Steel Firm B and Textile Firm M. Other conglomerate mergers unite firms in dif-

ferent but related markets, such as the markets for bleach and detergents or the markets for television sets and VCRs. Of course, it is possible for a single merger to be of all three types—horizontal, vertical, and conglomerate. The huge merger between GE and RCA in 1986 was one such example. Before merging, GE and RCA competed horizontally in TV sets and other consumer electronics. They supplied each other vertically in some lines. And they were also, to some degree, pure conglomerates—GE's jet engines having nothing to do with RCA's television network, NBC.

> **Horizontal mergers** unite direct competitors. **Vertical mergers** combine firms with vertical buyer–supplier links. **Conglomerate mergers** are multimarket marriages with little or no common ground.

2. Some History American history contains four periods when merger activity reached rather astounding proportions. The *first* merger movement occurred around the turn of the century. Over the 7-year period 1897–1903, 2,864 mergers were recorded in manufacturing and mining. Horizontal

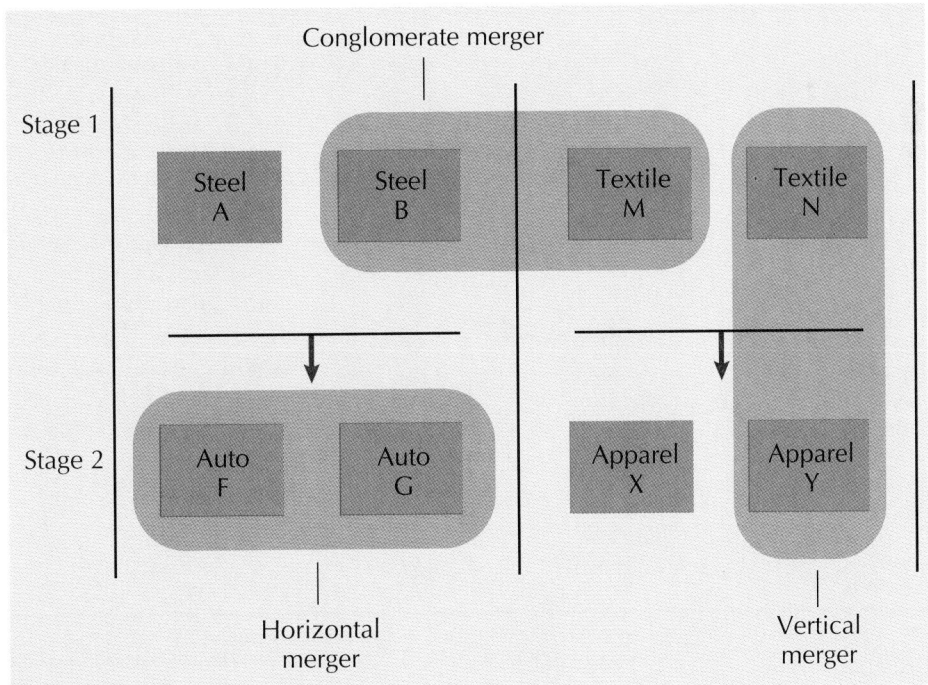

FIGURE 29.1 Types of Mergers

mergers dominated the scene, producing such giant companies as U.S. Steel, U.S. Gypsum, DuPont, American Tobacco, American Can, and National Biscuit.

The *second* wave of merger activity arose during the Roaring Twenties. From 1925 to 1930, 5,382 mergers were recorded in manufacturing and mining. During the peak year of 1929, ownership shares moved at the feverish pace of more than four mergers per business day. Horizontal mergers were again very popular, but vertical and conglomerate types rose in prominence. For example, it was during this era that General Foods was put together by the combination of Maxwell House Coffee, Jello, Birds-Eye, Baker's Chocolate, Sanka, and other major brands.

The *third* merger movement, from 1960 to 1970, topped both previous waves in frequency and scale. The FTC recorded 25,598 mergers during that decade. Slightly more than half of them were in manufacturing and mining. This sector's peak year was 1968, when 2,407 firms with more than $13 billion in assets were acquired. Conglomerate mergers clearly dominated that period.

The *fourth* great wave of merger activity, beginning about 1980, is underway as these words are written. Before looking at this present wave, however, let's pause and reflect upon the data of Table 29.2. It shows, by several measures, the extent to which the 15 largest U.S. industrial firms relied on acquisitions to achieve their size as of 1980. In other words, it estimates the influence of past history concretely. The 15 largest industrials had made a total of 483 acquisitions by 1980, the greatest number being due to ITT, with 182 (see column 1). Just how important these numbers are to each company is difficult to estimate (partly because the asset values of most of the older acquisitions are not available in public records and partly because the acquisitions occurred at different points in time, making them less than fully comparable). Still, columns (3) and (4) of Table 29.2 give two such estimates. Column (3) estimates the percentage of each firm's assets accounted for by known acquisitions after adjusting only for price inflation. (That is, a 1968 acquisition by ITT and a 1947 acquisition by U.S. Steel are made comparable to each other, and to the 1980 asset values of these respective

TABLE 29.2 Summary Acquisition History of the 15 Largest U.S. Industrials of 1980

| (1) | (2) | Value of Acquired Assets as a Percentage of Total Company Assets | |
| | | (3) | (4) |
Name of Company	Number of Acquisitions	Adjusting for Price Inflation	Adjusting for Inflation and Growth
Exxon	22	3.4%	18.6%
General Motors	18	3.1	15.9
Mobil	19	24.2	62.0
IBM	8	0.2	1.0
Texaco	22	6.2	14.6
Ford	10	6.2	44.6
Chevron	7	16.4	25.4
Std. Oil (Ill.)	18	15.8	76.3
Gulf	8	11.8	65.0
General Electric	34	0.1	0.3
Shell Oil	17	23.2	31.3
ARCO	29	47.7	74.5
ITT	182	28.3	51.1
Tenneco	55	28.6	63.9
U.S. Steel	34	42.1	—

Note: The asset value of many acquisitions is unknown for lack of data, so the estimates of columns (3) and (4) are understated. The growth-adjusted figure for U.S. Steel would be an extreme value because of the age and size of the 1901 merger.
Source: Stephen A. Rhoades, "Mergers of the 20 Largest Banks and Industrials," *Antitrust Bulletin* (Fall 1985), pp. 636–638.

companies, by converting those acquisition values into 1980 dollars.) By this measure, acquisitions accounted for very little of General Electric's size in 1980 but a lot of ARCO's size. The average is 17.2 percent for all 15 companies. Column (4) takes into account the growth of the acquired companies since acquisition, as well as inflation (assuming that their growth matched that of all companies generally). By this measure, the acquisitions gain greater importance, accounting for roughly 40 percent of the size of these largest companies, on average, as of 1980.

Now, what has happened since 1980? We happen to be in the largest merger wave of all time—a tidal wave. Figure 29.2 charts the amazing data in raw numbers and dollar values. The year 1986 alone witnessed an estimated 4,024 acquisitions, a frantic rate of more than 15 per business day. In dollar value, it appears that over 190 billion in corporate assets were acquired during that year. Moreover, the firms listed in Table 29.2 contributed to the mountain of mergers pictured in Figure 29.2. Since 1980, multi-billion-dollar acquisitions have been made by General Motors, Chevron, Texaco, Mobil, General Electric, IBM, and DuPont, adding further to their stature among the nation's largest industrial enterprises. As *Fortune* described it, the merging became "frenzied." Regarding merger types, conglomerates again dominated the scene, as they had during the 1960s. Still, horizontal mergers have made some recent gains in popularity, as indicated by such major pairings as Chevron–Gulf (oil), Texaco–Getty (oil), and LTV–Republic (steel).

The variety of merger types and the historic swings in merger frequency suggest a diversity of motives for mergers. Among these motives are a number that have very little to do with enhancing the market power of the acquiring firm. These include risk reduction through diversification, financial speculation, and personal aggrandizement for the managers of acquiring firms. A quest for economic efficiencies apparently also motivates some mergers, but empirical evidence indicates that efficiencies are realized in no more than a minority of instances. On the other hand, greater market power may be the aim of numerous mergers. And even where market power is not the principal aim, it could be a by-product of mergers based on other designs.

3. Merger Antitrust Law   Section 7 of the Clayton Act, as amended by the Celler-Kefauver Act of 1950, outlaws anticompetitive mergers. Identifying offenses proceeds by a three-part rule of thumb:

1. *Product market definition:* What product markets are involved? For example, would Coke and Budweiser be in the same beverage market if they merged? The major factors affecting the courts' definitions are similar to those in monopolization cases.
2. *Geographic market definition:* Is the market

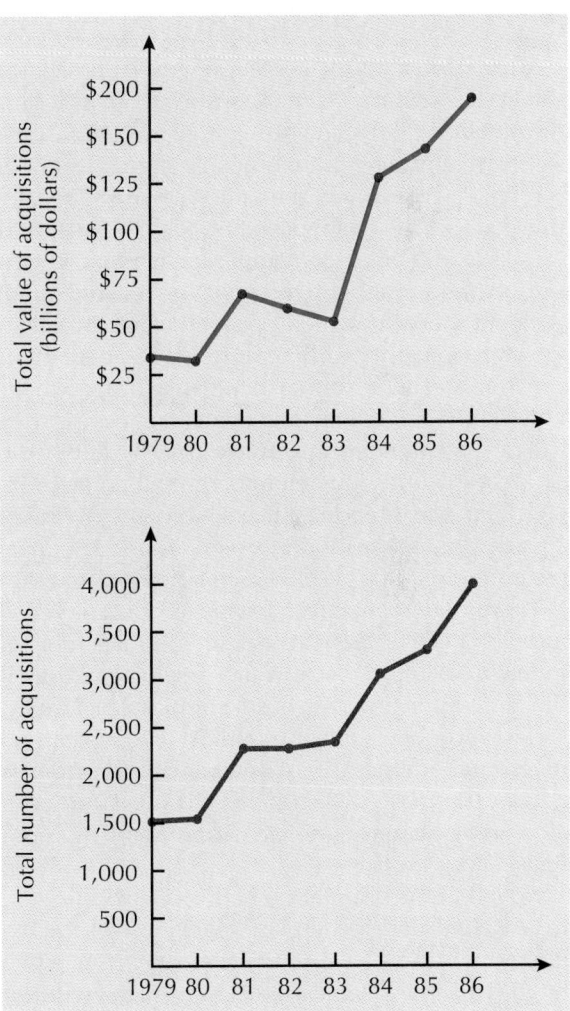

FIGURE 29.2 *The Merger Movement of the 1980s in Total Number and Dollar Value of Acquisitions (Transactions of $1 Million or More)*

(*Source:* Mergers and Acquisitions, *May–June 1987, p. 57.)*

local, regional, national, or international? Grocery retailing would be local, while the market for semiconductor chips could be international in scope.

3. _Substantial lessening of competition:_ The type of merger is crucial here. Indices for horizontal mergers include the effects of the merger on market concentration, firm ranks, and trends in market concentration. Conglomerate mergers do not raise the concentration in any single market, but the acquired firm may be a _potential_ competitor of the acquiring firm if it could easily enter the latter's markets.

Merger policy was ineffective until passage of the Celler-Kefauver Amendment of 1950. Strict interpretation of this amendment from 1950 to 1980 severely curbed horizontal mergers, mildly screened vertical mergers, and, as suggested by the massive merger movement of the 1960s, had very little impact on conglomerate mergers. Beginning in about 1980, enforcement was relaxed for all types of mergers, which probably contributed to the most recent outbreak of frenzied acquisition activity. At this writing, the Justice Department and the FTC do not challenge mergers unless they violate their merger guidelines of 1982 and 1984. These guidelines judge a horizontal merger by its effect on the H index. (Recall that the H index squares the market share of each firm in the market and adds them together.) A horizontal merger is permitted in markets having a postmerger H index of 1,000 or less. If the merger results in an H index of 1,000 to 1,800, it will be challenged only if the combining firms are of substantial size. Finally, serious trouble confronts almost all substantial horizontal mergers in markets with H indexes greater than 1,800. Treatment of vertical and conglomerate mergers is very lenient under the guidelines.

Note that the orientation of this policy is limited to lessened competition in _specific markets_. No limitations apply to absolute _firm size_. Hence two huge firms in the same market may merge without challenge if the _market itself_ is so huge that the resulting market share of the combination is relatively small. (The Chevron–Gulf merger illustrates this to some degree.) Likewise huge conglomerate firms (like GE and RCA or GM and Hughes Aircraft) may join without provoking legal challenge if they do not increase the concentration appreciably in specific markets that are already concentrated. As with monopolization, it's size _relative_ to some market that counts, not absolute size alone.

V

Debate and Assessment

No economist completely agrees with everything in our antitrust policy. Yet most seem to think that, overall, it has made a positive contribution to the economy. The Sherman Act effectively blocks collusion and curbs the grossest forms of monopolization. The Clayton Act controls several exclusionary practices and, as amended by the Celler-Kefauver Act, stands in the way of mergers that would greatly increase concentration in already highly concentrated markets.

Exactly how influential antitrust legislation has been, however, is difficult to say. Any assessment rests on judgments of what might have been had we had no policy, and such judgments are difficult. Counting cases offers little help because an effective policy would influence corporate behavior voluntarily on a daily basis. Business executives confess to feeling constrained by antitrust laws. Indeed, it is often said that Senator Sherman is an ex officio board member of every major corporation. Still, precise measures of impact are impossible.

Then there are the critics. Lately the most vocal critics are those who argue that the antitrust laws should be abolished. They attack antitrust mainly by questioning two key _premises_ underlying antitrust policy—namely, its desirability and its necessity. A vigorous antitrust policy presumes that competition is _desirable_, where competition basically means an absence of high market concentration and monopolistic restraints. Moreover, the policy also assumes that this desired degree of competition does not always occur naturally or automatically, so antitrust is _necessary_ to the maintenance of competition. Without it, monopolistic restraints would adversely affect the economy.

A
Desirability

When critics question the desirability of antitrust, they usually argue that bigness is best for achieving efficiency or technological progress. On efficiency, Yale Brozen speaks bluntly:

> concentration benefits the nation by increasing the accumulated experience and learning in large firms where these factors can increase productivity.
>
> The reason large firms are formed is similar to that that motivates almost every other reularity in commercial behavior—the incentive for efficiency.[11]

On technological change, John Kenneth Galbraith is most emphatic:

> a benign Providence . . . has made the modern industry of a few large firms an excellent instrument for inducing technical change.[12]

Of course, defenders of antitrust see things differently. They tend to accept the evidence reviewed in previous chapters indicating that, as a _general proposition_, high concentration is not especially conducive to either efficiency or progress. Further, in _particular instances_ where such is the case, they believe antitrust's rule of reason approach is flexible enough to accommodate the exceptions.

B
Necessity

Critics questioning the necessity of antitrust often concede that vigorous competition is desirable, but they see intense competition occurring naturally everywhere _without_ any governmental umpiring. They see this in dynamic innovation, in easy entry, in foreign imports, and in countless other ways. According to Harold Demsetz, for instance:

> There is ample evidence that competition is robust. There is a constant search for new ways to acquire the business of customers. When a new product is developed, imitators are rarely far behind. Resources move quickly into industries experiencing boom conditions.[13]

In this view, even cartels are little problem because the forces of competition crush them. To quote Robert Bork:

> They are fragile. Changing market conditions and the temptation to "cheat" to pick up profitable business frequently break down almost all cartels.[14]

Defenders of antitrust rebut by arguing that unacceptable tendencies to monopolize or cartelize are inevitable simply because they are profitable activities. Absent antitrust, competition may not be stamped out completely. But it would be suppressed artificially and excessively, or so it is argued.

Because the debate is fed by value judgments, it will not end any time soon. Where do you stand? Would you, for instance, favor the 1985 proposal of President Reagan's Secretary of Commerce that antitrust restraints on mergers be eliminated?

VI
Information Policies

A
Overview

The previous chapter showed the importance of buyer knowledge. Knowledge is typically greatest for professional business buyers. Conversely, knowledge is usually least for consumer buyers. Among the consequences we found that, in general:

---

[11]Yale Brozen, _Concentration, Mergers, and Public Policy_ (New York: Macmillan, 1982), pp. 82; 382.

[12]John Kenneth Galbraith, _American Capitalism_ (Boston: Houghton Mifflin, 1956), p. 86.

[13]Harold Demsetz, "The Trust Behind Antitrust," in _Industrial Concentration and the Market System_, p. 46.

[14]Robert H. Bork, "Antitrust and the Theory of Concentrated Markets," ibid., p. 85.

1. Advertising tends to be most wasteful (intense and persuasive) for consumer goods.
2. Advertising boosts prices and profits for consumer convenience goods, suggesting anticompetitive effects when buyer knowledge is weak.

In sum, real-world consumers, by not being fully informed, frequently fail to conform to the ideal. They consequently fall prey to misleading persuasion and behave inefficiently.

Evidence indicates that consumers are especially ill-informed when they buy *experience goods* as compared to *search goods*.

Search goods can be fairly well evaluated by buyers before purchase. **Experience goods** can be evaluated by buyers only after purchase, when they can be experienced.

In the case of *search goods*—like fresh fruits and vegetables, apparel, and greeting cards—consumers can judge pretty well *prior* to actual purchase whether an article is of good quality and reasonably priced. In the contrasting case of *experience goods*, utility and value can be appraised only *after* purchase. To evaluate accurately canned foods, laundry detergents, and autos, for instance, one has to try them out with ownership because they have hidden qualities at the time of purchase. Buying experience goods is made difficult by the fact that sample purchases are often costly or impossible (e.g., refrigerators or autos). Morever, experiments show that buyer judgment is distorted by the mere act of purchase (people like what they buy just because they choose it over other options). Hence, consumers tend to do best when buying search goods and worst when acquiring experience goods.

Read Perspective 29B.

PERSPECTIVE 29B
Price–Quality Correlations

The degree to which price correlates with quality across brands within a given product class is a measure of consumer knowledge. If consumers were well informed, low-quality goods could be sold only at low prices, while high-quality goods could justifiably command high prices. Thus a high positive correlation (the maximum possible being + 1.0) between price and quality for a given product would indicate wise buying behavior, whereas a low correlation (approaching zero or even turning negative) would signal that something was seriously amiss. Every study of price–quality correlations has found surprisingly low correlations, with many products producing negative coefficients. Peter C. Riesz found an average correlation of only + 0.09 for 40 packaged food products.[15] R.T. Morris and C.S. Bronson's study of 48 diverse products (including electric appliances, detergents, and auto tires) produced a mean

correlation of +0.29.[16] Alfred Oxenfeldt's computation of correlations for 35 products in 1949 is particularly instructive because his sample included numerous search goods, while other studies were essentially confined to experience goods. Oxenfeldt's results for the five products with the highest correlation and the five products with the lowest correlation are presented in Table 29.3. Note that those with the highest correlations are all search goods, whereas those with the lowest correlations are experience goods. This implies that consumers are more adept at buying search goods than experience goods.

[15]Peter C. Riesz, "Price–Quality Correlations for Packaged Food Products," *Journal of Consumer Affairs* (Winter 1979), pp. 236–247.

[16]R.T. Morris and C.S. Bronson, "The Chaos of Competition Indicated by Consumer Reports," *Journal of Marketing* (June 1969), pp. 26–34.

TABLE 29.3 Coefficients of Rank Correlation Between Brand Quality Score and Brand Price

Product	Number of Brands Tested	Coefficient of Rank Correlation
Top five (search goods)		
Boys' shirts	8	+0.82
Men's hats	30	+0.76
Women's slips (knitted)	28	+0.75
Mechanical pencils	26	+0.71
Women's slips (nonknitted)	67	+0.70
Bottom five (experience goods)		
Vacuum cleaners	17	−0.26
Biscuit mixes	10	−0.46
Hot roll mixes	3	−0.50
Waffle mixes	3	−0.50
Gingerbread mixes	6	−0.81

Source: Alfred R. Oxenfeldt, "Consumer Knowledge: Its Measurement and Extent," *Review of Economics and Statistics* (October 1950), p. 310.

Information policies thus might improve the situation if they could make consumers more like professional buyers and make experience goods more like search goods. The freshness of milk, for example, is an experience quality unless plainly disclosed on the carton, in which case it then becomes a search quality. Educating consumers on the proper use of such disclosures gives them the knowledge of professionals. The policies that most clearly serve these ends entail *standardization for price comparisons* and *information disclosure*. These policies operate on the principle of revelation. They are supposed to educate consumers, to aid them in making comparisons, and to reveal relevant product characteristics. Therefore these policies are generally *pre*scriptive and positive. Sellers are required to act in the consumers' interest.

In addition, some information policies *prohibit deceptive practices*, such as misleading advertising. These policies are *pro*scriptive and negative. Whereas policies of standardization and disclosure attempt to fill voids in the consumer's mind with correct information, prohibitions against deceptive practices attempt to prevent sellers from filling those voids with incorrect information.

Accordingly, our tour of information policies has three topics: (1) *standardization*, (2) *disclosure*, and (3) *deception*.

B
Standardization Policies

Standardization policies promote simplification or uniformity or both. Their main purpose is to aid consumers in making price comparisons.

Truth in lending (TIL) is a good example of standardization, one covering consumer credit. Before the adoption of TIL in 1969, all but a few people were unaware of how much they actually paid for credit. Their ignorance arose partly from an absence of price standardization. In computing interest rates, one lender would use the add-on method, while others would use a discount rate, or an annual percentage rate, or a monthly rate. Depending on the method, the price for the same credit could have been quoted as being 1 percent, 7 percent, 12.83 percent, or something else.

The objective of the Truth-in-Lending Law is to let consumers know exactly what the price of credit is and to let them compare the prices of various lenders. To achieve these ends, the law requires disclosure of two main things:

1. The *finance charge*, which is the amount of money paid to obtain the credit.
2. The *annual percentage rate (APR)*, which provides a simple way of comparing credit prices.

C
Disclosure Policies

Standardization policies make price comparisons easier, but they do not take into account differences in the qualities or contents of competing brands or products. The general purpose of **disclosure policies** is to help buyers identify qualities and contents.

The oldest of these policies simply provide *content disclosures.* Thus, because of the Fur Products Labeling Act of 1951, rabbit cannot be passed off as *Baltic lion* and sheared muskrat cannot be called *Hudson seal*—not at long as the FTC's agents stay awake on the job. Similarly, the Textile Fiber Products Identification Act of 1958 requires labels revealing the generic names and percentages of all fibers that go into a fabric, except those comprising less than 5 percent of the fabric. Hence *Dacron*, which is a trade name, must be identified as *polyester*, its generic name. More recently, since about 1972, the government has expanded its labeling activity so that detailed disclosures of composition are now required on the labels of most processed food products. Now you can easily learn that Campbell's Chicken Broth includes salt, yeast extract, and monosodium glutamate, as well as chicken broth.

Performance disclosures go one step further. For example, you may be told by a window sticker that a new Toyota Corolla contains a "four-cylinder, 97-cubic-inch displacement engine plus a two-barrel carburetor," but that may be difficult for you to translate into mileage performance. Beginning with 1977 models, all new cars sold in the United States have had labels disclosing the estimated number of miles they get per gallon of gas and an estimate of what annual fuel costs would be like if 15,000 miles were traveled per year. The Federal Energy Act of 1975 requires these performance disclosures on the theory that they assist efficiency comparisons. That law also requires energy efficiency ratings for major home appliances like refrigerators, freezers, and dishwashers (see Figure 29.3).

Disclosures of ingredients or specific performance may sometimes be too complex to be useful. So *grade rating* is yet another type of disclosure. This simplifies complicated quality information into an ABC format. The most active fed-

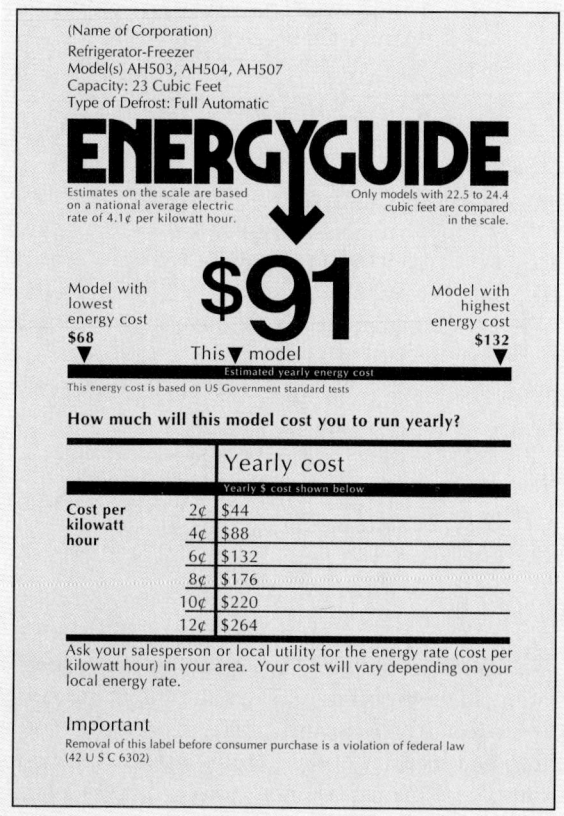

FIGURE 29.3   Energy Guide Label

eral agency in this respect is the U.S. Department of Agriculture, whose agents grade meat, eggs, butter, poultry, grain, fruits, and vegetables. (Look for the *Grade A* label on your next carton of milk.)

D
Deception Policies

In April 1972, the American Association of Advertising Agencies released the results of a poll of some 9,000 students from 177 universities and colleges. The students took a dim view of advertising. Fifty-three percent said they considered advertising believable only "some of the time."[17]

Some of those students may have wondered whether there was any policy at all controlling deceptive advertising. There is, but it is a limited policy. It prohibits, in the words of the statute, "unfair or deceptive acts or practices" (Section 5 of

[17]*Business Week*, June 10, 1972, p. 48.

the Federal Trade Commission Act, as amended by the Wheeler-Lea Act of 1938).

Note in particular the word *deceptive*. Legality here does not hinge on truth and falsity. Deception is the key—*that which is not deceptive is legal, and that which is deceptive is illegal*. The distinction has meaning. Whereas truth and falsity depend on the literal content of the advertisement, deception depends upon what goes on in the minds of people receiving the ad, the potential buyers. Hence, depending on buyers' perceptions, literal falsehood is permitted if it is not deceptive and literal truth may be attacked if it is deceptive.

To be sure, most falsehoods are deceptive and most truths are nondeceptive. But this broader view allows exceptions. Take, for example, Schlitz's promise that popping open a can of its malt liquor releases a rampaging bull. The implied claim is patently false. There is no bull. Yet no one is deceived. So the FTC does not flinch. On the other hand, considering truth that may be deceptive, Hot Wheels toy racing cars provide an example. In 1971 the FTC found deception in nonfalse television ads showing Hot Wheels cars speeding over their tracks. To the TV viewer, the cars seemed to move like bullets. But this was merely a special effect achieved by filming the cars at close range from clever angles. The representation was technically true but nevertheless misleading.

Under this criterion, then, what has been found deceptive? Since passage of the Federal Trade Commission Act in 1914, over 3,300 cases of deception have been prosecuted by the FTC, covering more classes of con artistry than we can review. Our limited samples illustrate only misleading claims of function of efficacy.

During the late 1960s, Firestone advertised that its Super Sports Wide Oval tires could "stop 25% quicker." When sued by the FTC, Firestone presented evidence that several cars with these tires traveling at 15 miles per hour *did* stop 25 percent quicker than those with ordinary tires. However, the tests were done on very-low-friction surfaces, equivalent in slickness to glare ice or waxed linoleum. Thus Wide Ovals might enable some poor soul who crashes through the end of his garage to stop short of the kitchen refrigerator. But since slippery surfaces and slow speeds are obviously not typical of highway conditions, the FTC decided that these ads were deceptive.

Another case concerns Vivarin, a tablet containing caffeine and sugar in amounts roughly equivalent to those in a half-cup of sweetened coffee. The offending ad, which ran in 1971, had a middle-aged woman speaking as if she had just discovered a sure-fire aphrodisiac:

> *One day it dawned on me that I was boring my husband to death. It wasn't that I didn't love Jim, but often by the time he came home at night I was feeling dull, tired and drowsy. [Then I began taking Vivarin.] All of a sudden Jim was coming home to a more exciting woman, me. . . . And after dinner I was wide-awake enough to do a little more than just look at television. . . .*

The usual remedy for deceptive advertising is a *cease and desist order*. This simply prohibits the offender from further practicing that which has been found unlawful.

As in the case of antitrust, the Reagan administration has substantially relaxed enforcement of regulations governing deception. Still, the law remains on the books and past cases continue to offer precedents, so a revival is possible at any time.

SUMMARY

1. Antitrust and information policies try to improve markets by reducing certain market imperfections. Antitrust attempts to foster competition, but not dogmatically. It does so by (1) opposing unreasonable monopolistic restraints rather than imposing perfect competition, (2) attacking artificial restraints, and (3) using a rule of reason approach for most areas of the law. The specific objectives of antitrust are clouded, but they seem to be a mixture of structure, conduct, and performance features.

2. Antitrust policy emerges from the actions of legislators, plaintiffs (public and private),

and the courts. Regarding the first of these, the Sherman Act outlaws collusive restraints of trade (Section 1) and monopolization (Section 2). The Clayton Act, designed to check incipient monopoly, curbs exclusionary practices (like tying) and mergers where they may substantially lessen competition. (The Robinson-Patman Act amends the Clayton Act on price discrimination, while the Celler-Kefauver Act does so for mergers.) The Federal Trade Commission Act bans unfair methods of competition and deceptive acts. The Department of Justice and the FTC serve the public as plaintiffs, supplemented by private parties. Remedies include criminal penalties for collusive restraints, dissolution for monopolization and anticompetitive mergers, and cease and desist orders for most of the remaining offenses.

3. The courts use rules of thumb to ease the burden of their task. (1) Collusive restraints like price fixing are governed by a per se rule, making them automatically unlawful. In contrast, almost all other areas of the law call for considerable judgments—a rule of reason approach. (2) Proof of monopolization requires a showing of (a) monopoly power plus (b) intent. The interpretation of intent has swung from the abusive acts required in the early decades, to the thrust-upon approach of Alcoa, and back toward abusive acts. (3) Exclusionary practices deter entry or hamper small estab-

lished firms. Different rules of thumb apply to these practices. The one for tying involves four issues, such as whether the seller has monopoly power in the tying-good market. (4) Mergers may be horizontal, vertical, or conglomerate. Of the thousands that may occur each year, only a few are challenged as being substantially anticompetitive, and these few are almost all horizontal mergers. To be successful, those challenges require product and geographic market definitions plus some showing of a possible anticompetitive effect.

4. Although most economists apparently favor antitrust in principle, if not in every particular, there is a vocal minority who favor its demise. They question the policy on its two key premises—its desirability and its necessity. They claim that bigness is best or believe that seriously adverse monopolistic restraints cannot occur.

5. Information policies address the problem of buyer ignorance. Standardization and disclosure policies—such as truth-in-lending—have the virtue of moving consumers in the direction of professional buyers and nudging experience goods in the direction of search goods. Control of deceptive practices works on the principle of prohibition rather than revelation. Deceptive advertising is subject to cease and desist orders (even if literally or technically truthful.)

KEY TERMS

Tying (tie-in sales)
Rule of reason
Per se rule
Collusive agreements
Monopolization
Exclusionary practices
Horizontal merger

Vertical merger
Conglomerate merger
Search goods
Experience goods
Standardization policies
Disclosure policies

QUESTIONS AND PROBLEMS

1. Describe the basic position of the U.S. government regarding monopoly power.
2. U.S. antitrust policy currently seems to be based on a blend of what three aims?
3. List and summarize the five main concerns of antitrust statutes.
4. Explain why the definition of the market is so important in deciding whether a firm is guilty of "monopolization."
5. What is "tying"? Why is it sometimes anticompetitive and sometimes not?
6. What is a "merger"? What are the motives for mergers?
7. Describe the primary considerations in current merger treatment. (Make clear the importance of the distinction between horizontal, vertical and conglomerate mergers.)

8. Distinguish "search goods" from "experience goods." Give examples of each.
9. Studies of price-quality correlations have generally found very weak correlations. How can this be explained? What are the implications of this for the consumer?
10. How do standardization policies benefit consumers? Provide examples of standardization policies.
11. Give examples of disclosure policies and explain their purpose.
12. Are false advertisements illegal?
13. Consider services purchased by households, such as auto repair, attorney's services, medical care, and hair styling. Do you think that the average consumer purchases services on the basis of better information than he/she purchases goods, or vice-versa? Explain.

V
Factor Markets

30

Competitive Labor Markets

In 1985, *Parade Magazine* published a list of annual earnings that varied widely:

Gary Knerr, dentist	$62,000
Leonard Goodman, software engineer	$46,000
Greg Sawrey, truck driver	$36,900
Lucy Nigh, school teacher	$31,000
Karen Gordon, secretary	$13,256

The number of jobs also varies widely by occupation. Comparing employment in 1972 and 1982, we find the number of computer specialists soaring from 276,000 to 751,000, while the number of typists slid from 1,025,000 to 942,000.

Statistics like these signal a shift of focus. The previous nine chapters studied product markets—like those for soda pop and autos. In this and the next two chapters we concentrate on *resource (or input) markets*—those for labor, land, capital, and entrepreneurship.

In many ways, this shift offers little that is new. Once again, prices and quantities get intense scrutiny, although here prices have special names:

1. Labor resources receive *wages* (or salaries).
2. Land and related natural resources receive *rent*.
3. Capital resources receive *interest*.
4. Entrepreneurial resources receive *profit*.

Once again, we will be studying demand and supply because these resource markets are like other markets: Each has a demand side and a supply side generating price–quantity results. Once again, micro two-question logic prevails. And once again, the participants in our story will be business firms and people.

Resource markets thus share many similarities with product markets. Still, a few key differences arise. For one thing, business firms and people switch roles here. To see this, look back at Figure 2.8. In product markets, households demand goods and business firms supply them. In re-

source markets, it's the reverse—businesses are on the demand side, while households are on the supply side. Businesses demand resource inputs to produce the goods and services they sell. Households supply resource inputs to earn the incomes they need to purchase those goods and services. This first difference is very important, for you must keep in mind that business firms are now the demanders, while households act as suppliers.

A second key difference concerns the basic questions raised by scarcity. The What? and What's new? questions dominated the last nine chapters. The How? and Who? questions now hold sway. How much labor will be useful to produce corn flakes and apartment houses? How much land and capital? Who gets a greater share of the economic pie—a McDonald's counter attendant or a United Airlines pilot?

In this chapter and the next, we concentrate on labor markets, saving other resource markets for later. Labor markets deserve this emphasis because of their immense importance to the economy. Labor earnings account for about 75 percent of all income earned by all households in the United States. Moreover, many of the principles learned here will also apply to other resource markets.

To introduce labor markets, we first look at those that could be considered competitive. With few exceptions, neither the buyers (firms) nor the sellers (individuals) have market power in this chapter. The market for stenographers in New York City and the market for fast-food counter attendants in Chicago are illustrative.

I
Competitive Demand and Supply: A Preview

Given our previous encounters with demand and supply, we can easily preview demand and supply in competitive labor markets. However, one preliminary step will help. Competition and market power have different implications when the firm is a *buyer* of labor inputs instead of a *seller* of goods and services.

As a *seller,* the firm sees its *demand* curve vary with competitive conditions. This is shown in parts (a) and (b) in the top half of Figure 30.1. The perfectly competitive seller in part (a) sees its demand as horizontal. By contrast, the seller with product market power in part (b) sees a downward-sloping demand because its large market share gives it some influence over the product price. (Note that the horizontal axis in part (b) is scaled in millions of units, while that of part (a) is scaled in hundreds.)

As a *buyer* of labor inputs, the firm will view its *supply* of labor differently, depending on its competitive status as an employer. This is shown by parts (c) and (d) in the bottom half of Figure 30.1. Look first at part (c). The employer is small relative to the market, hiring only a few workers among many and competing with many other employers who hire from the same pool of workers, so that firm will see its labor supply curve as perfectly horizontal. It can hire more or fewer workers without affecting the wage prevailing in the market. As marketwide conditions change, that wage rate might rise or fall, shifting the firm's supply curve up or down, but the firm itself is too small to influence the wage rate with its hiring behavior. It's a price taker. If, on the other hand, the firm has some market power in the labor market, then part (d) of Figure 30.1 applies. Such a firm would be large relative to the labor market. To increase its employee roster, it would have to attract additional workers by offering ever higher wage rates. If such a firm reduced its hiring or closed down completely, wages would fall as its workforce shrank.

A **competitive** employer in a labor market is one whose hiring is not large enough to affect the wage rate. The firm sees a **horizontal** labor supply curve.

An employer with **market power** in a labor market is one whose hiring is large enough to affect the wage rate. The firm sees an **upward-sloping** labor supply curve.

Competitive conditions among employers may depend on the type of labor employed. The federal government, for instance, has market power as an employer of atomic bomb engineers but not as an employer of secretaries, partly because the former line of work is much more specialized than the latter. Geography may also play a role because workers are not perfectly mobile. For example, the manager of a fast-food eatery in Chicago would see a horizontal supply curve for counter attendants. She could increase or decrease her staff of counter attendants by dozens without affecting the going wage of, say, $3.50 an hour. In contrast, the manager of a fast-food eatery in Fishtail, Montana, would probably have to pay higher wages to attract counter attendants, the higher wages being necessary to entice them away from other job opportunities.

In sum, competitive conditions among employers in a labor market determine each firm's view of its labor supply curve. (And, more generally, competition among buyers of any input influences each buyer's perception of the input supply.)

This summarizes supply. Now what about demand? There are firm demands and marketwide demands.

A **firm's demand curve for labor** is the relationship between the price of labor and the amount of labor hired by the firm.

The **marketwide demand curve for labor** shows the amount of labor that will be demanded in the entire market at various possible wage rates.

For reasons we will explain shortly, the *firm's* demand for labor will be downward sloping. Moreover, *marketwide* demand is likewise downward sloping because, broadly speaking, it is the horizontal summation of the demands of all firms in the labor market.

Thus, when we place the competitive buyer of labor in the context of the overall labor market, the results will resemble those shown in Figure 30.2. The firm is on the left in part (a); the market is on the right in part (b). Fast-food counter attendants are the workers involved.

Assume that the *firm,* located in a big-city shopping mall, is a franchisee of McDonald's or Burger

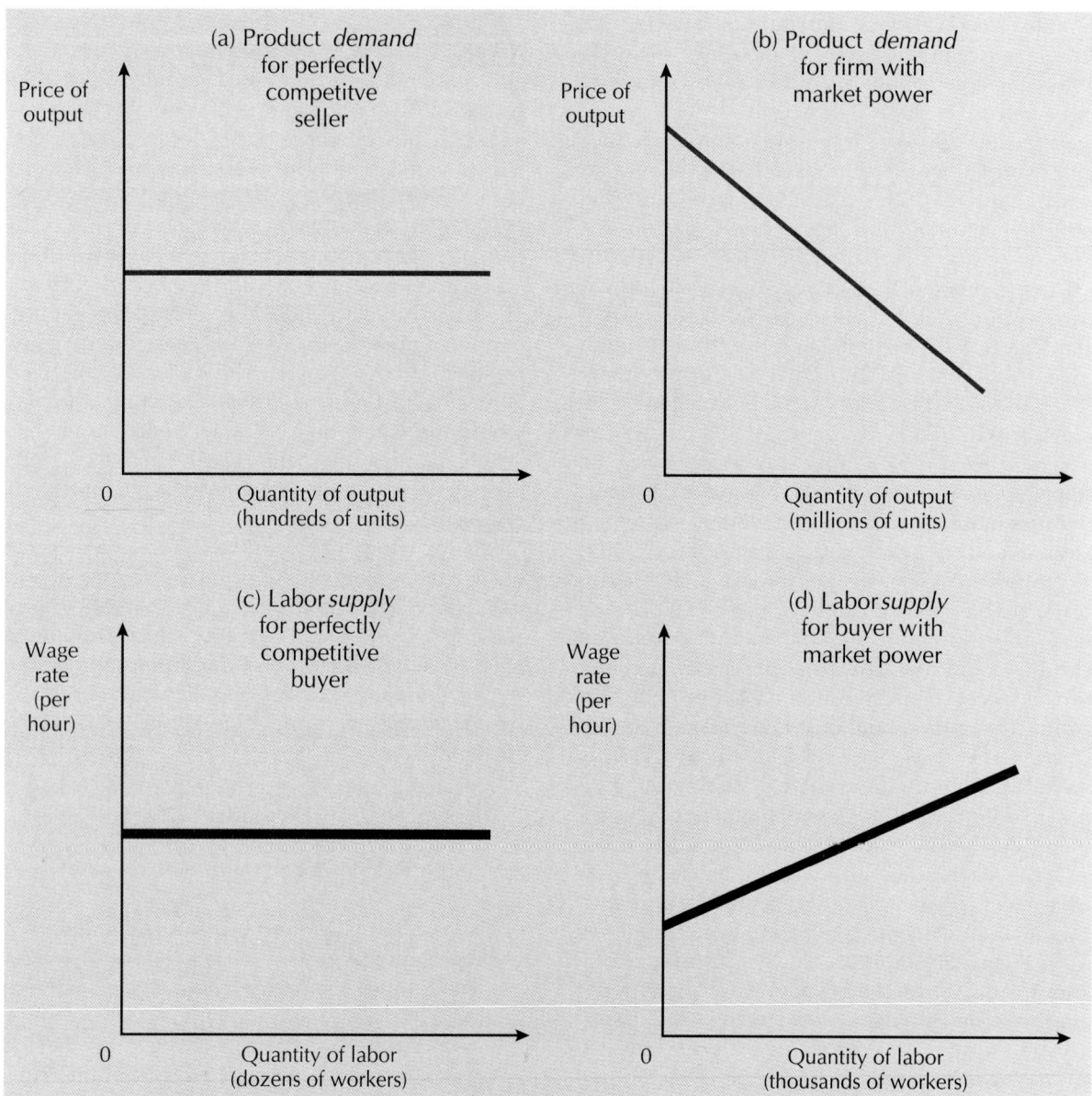

FIGURE 30.1 *Competition versus Market Power for the Firm in Product Markets and Labor Markets*

Parts (a) and (b) show that, as a seller in a product market, the firm facing perfect competition has no influence on the price, while a firm with market power does. To sell more, the latter firm lowers the price. To sell less, it raises the price. Parts (c) and (d) show the difference in competitive conditions for a firm buying labor inputs. The competitive firm sees supply as horizontal, for it can hire added workers without influencing the wage rate. The firm with market power in (d) must pay more to hire more.

King. As suggested by the small scale of the horizontal axis of Figure 30.2(a), the firm is tiny relative to the city-wide market for counter attendants. Consequently, it sees its supply of prospective counter attendants as horizontal. As a price taker,

it can hire 2 or 24 counter attendants at the going wage rate of $3.50. Exactly how many it hires depends on its demand for counter attendants. And as shown in part (a), it will hire eight. Its reasoning involves micro two-question logic. The

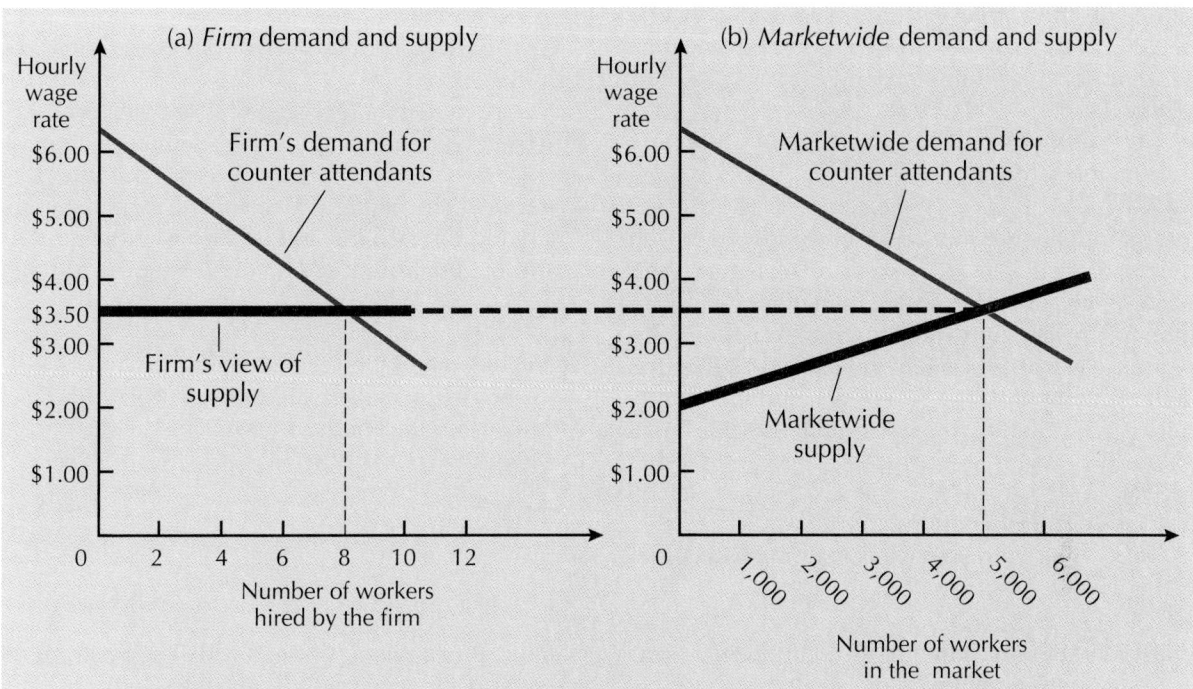

FIGURE 30.2 Demand for and Supply of Labor (Fast-Food Counter Attendants) in a Competitive Market: Firm and Marketwide Levels

This situation assumes competition on both sides of the market—demand (by the employers/buyers) and supply (by the workers/sellers). (a) The individual firm is too small to influence the wage rate, so it sees its supply as horizontal at an hourly wage of $3.50. It hires out to the point where its demand (willingness to pay) falls below $3.50, which is eight counter attendants. (b) The wage of $3.50 is set by the interaction of demand and supply at the marketwide level. The total number employed comes to 5,000.

firm's demand reflects what each worker is worth to the firm. Simultaneously, the firm's supply curve at $3.50 indicates what it costs to hire each worker. As long as added workers are worth more to the firm than the wage that must be paid to get them, they will be hired. That is true for up to eight counter attendants.

The going wage of $3.50 is determined by the interaction of demand and supply at the *marketwide* level, as shown in Figure 30.2(b). Note first the larger scale on the horizontal axis of part (b)—thousands of workers. Note second that the marketwide supply curve is upward sloping because the marketwide hiring or firing of fast-food counter attendants will affect the wage rate. This stems from the two-question logic exercised by prospective counter attendants on the supply side. What is it worth to work as a counter attendant? Answer: the wage paid. What must be given up to do so? Answer: the wages paid in alternative

work (such as bagging groceries) or the enjoyment of leisure, which, of course, has a value. The marketwide supply is upward sloping because ever higher wages paid to counter attendants will tilt the results of this two-question logic ever more in favor of being a counter attendant as opposed to being a grocery bagger or sun bather. The higher the counter attendants' wage, the greater the supply of people wanting to be counter attendants. Note next that the downward-sloping demand curves of all the firms in the market will combine to create a downward-sloping marketwide demand for this labor. Note finally that the upward-sloping supply and downward-sloping demand intersect at an hourly wage of $3.50 and an overall quantity of 5,000 counter attendants. This is the equilibrium point for this labor market.

It must be stressed that this preliminary overview assumes competition on *both* sides of the market—the workers' side and the employers' side. If on the employers' side there was only one massive firm, there would be market power of an extreme sort called *monopsony*.

> A **monopsony** is a market in which there is only one buyer.

The monopsony firm would see supply as it is at the marketwide level in part (b) of Figure 30.2. Accordingly, the wage and employment results for monopsony are quite different from those for competition. As for the workers in Figure 30.2, they too behave competitively. They act independently rather than jointly, as they would if they formed a *union*.

> A **labor union** is an organization of workers that engages in collective bargaining with the employer.

If fast-food counter attendants could form a powerful union, then that would also alter the story of Figure 30.2.

Cases of monopsony and unionization occupy the next chapter. Here we want to tackle cases with substantial competition on both sides of the labor market. And our next steps in this task are to study in detail first the demand side and then the supply side.

II
The Demand Side

A
Derived Demand

As just noted, a firm's demand curve for labor reflects labor's *worth*, or *benefit*, to the firm. What does it benefit a tomato farmer to hire a field hand? What is it worth to your local McDonald's to hire another counter attendant? A worker benefits a firm because the worker can produce an output that is valued by the firm's customers. In other words, the demand for labor is a *derived demand* because it derives from the demand for the goods and services produced by the labor. The demand for tomato pickers derives from the demand for

tomatoes. The demand for fast-food counter attendants derives from the demand for fast foods. And so on.

More generally, the demand for *any input* is a derived demand. Inputs are demanded not as ends in themselves, but for the outputs they produce. The demand for crude oil stems from the demand for gasoline and jet fuel. The demand for land results from the demand for food and housing.

> The demand for a resource input is a **derived demand** because it is derived from the demand for the goods and services the resource helps to produce.

B
Marginal Revenue Product Theory

Recognizing that a worker's worth stems from the demand for the worker's output is only the first step. It establishes that a worker is worth *something* because the worker's output is, in the end, worth something. The next question is, how much is he or she worth? And the answer is found in what economists call **marginal revenue product (MRP).**

> The **marginal revenue product (MRP)** of any resource input is the extra revenue the firm gains by using one more unit of the input (holding other inputs constant).

The theory here is simple. The worth of an added counter attendant is the added revenue that can be credited to that counter attendant, his or her marginal revenue product. If your local McDonald's hires another counter attendant and finds that, as a result, total revenue jumps by $5 an hour during the hours she works (net of other costs), then her marginal revenue product is $5. That's what she's worth.

Digging deeper, we find that worker worth, or marginal revenue product, hinges on two things—(1) the *marginal revenue* per unit of the added output produced, which with perfect competition is the *price* per unit, and (2) the *amount* of added output produced by the added input, or productivity. The words *revenue* and *product* in

---

PERSPECTIVE 30A
Professional Athletes' Earnings

Variations in the earnings of athletes illustrate these two elements. A professional athlete's income broadly depends on two things—(1) the popularity of the athlete's sport among spectators and (2) his or her skill as a performer. Let's take the first one first. In total attendance at games, total revenues, total TV viewing audience, and in other ways, baseball is much more popular than ice hockey. The average annual salaries of major league athletes in 1985 reflect this—$360,000 for the typical baseball player versus $120,000 for the typical hockey player. Similarly, professional tennis players earn more than professional badminton players of similar athletic ability, and a star basketball player like Michael Jordan can earn more playing in the

United States than in Italy. Take talent next. In baseball, Dale Murphy, Rickey Henderson, George Brett, and Jim Rice each made more than $1.5 million in 1985, well above the major league average of $360,000. The reason is obvious. These players are much more "productive" than the average baseball player. Their "output" is greater. Who among those on summer fields of green are the *least* productive? Umpires, of course, and their salaries reflect that fact. Starting pay for major league umpires in 1985 was $28,000. Old veterans got as much as $72,000 tops. Bench-sitting utility infielders did much better.[1]

[1]*Wall Street Journal*, April 8, 1985, p. 15; March, 25, 1985, p. 29; *Business Week*, August 12, 1985, pp. 40–48.

---

the phrase *marginal revenue product* suggest this. Speaking loosely, one could say that a worker's worth depends on (1) the strength of the demand for the output, its popularity, or desirability, and (2) the capability of the worker in producing that output, his or her skill or talent (given the quantity and quality of other inputs).

Read perspective 30A.

To illustrate the marginal revenue product theory of labor demand more precisely, let's explore the hypothetical data of Table 30.1. It is assumed that the firm's production function is known. It is also assumed that labor is the only variable input, so any changes in output are directly associated with changes in labor (as opposed to some other input). Columns (1) and (2) of Table 30.1 report the

TABLE 30.1   The Firm's Demand for Labor Under Perfect Competition

(1) Number of Workers per Day	(2) Total Product (Output) per Day	(3) Marginal Product of Labor $\Delta(2)/\Delta(1)$	(4) Price of Output per Unit	(5) Marginal Revenue Product (3) × (4)
0	0	—	—	—
1st	8	8	$10	$80
2nd	15	7	10	70
3rd	21	6	10	60
4th	26	5	10	50
5th	30	4	10	40

number of workers per day and the associated total outputs. With three workers, for instance, total output is 21 units. Columns (3) and (4) report the two elements that directly determine each worker's marginal revenue product. Column (3) shows the output, or productivity, that can be credited to each worker, namely, the *marginal product* of labor, which is the *change* in total output associated with each additional worker. The first worker's marginal product is 8 units per day. The second worker's is 7 units per day. And so on. The law of diminishing marginal returns holds here as elsewhere, so each successive worker hired is credited with a smaller addition to total output than the preceding worker—8, 7, 6, 5, and finally 4. (On this law see pages 426–427.) Column (4) gives the output's *price* per unit, which is assumed to be $10. The fact that the output price is $10 over the entire range of output indicates that the firm faces perfect competition in its *product* market, so price equals marginal revenue.

Finally, *marginal revenue product* is found in column (5). It is obtained by multiplying the daily output of each worker, the marginal product in column (3), by the unit price (marginal revenue) in column (4). Thus, according to Table 30.1, the firm achieves a daily output of 8 units when it hires the first worker; and because each unit is worth $10, this yields $80 in daily revenues to the firm. The first worker is worth $80 per day (*MRP*). By hiring the second worker, the firm raises its daily ouput by 7 units, each of which gains $10. So the second worker is worth $70 per day to the firm. Similarly, the increase in the firm's daily revenues from hiring the third worker is $60; the increase for the fourth is $50; and for the fifth, $40.

> Marginal revenue product (MRP) may be calculated by multiplying marginal product per unit of worker input by the marginal revenue per unit of product output (and with perfect competition, marginal revenue is the product's price).

The workers of column (1) and their marginal revenue products in column (5) are plotted in Figure 30.3, where the horizontal axis is the number of workers and the vertical axis is dollars per worker per day (a scale that can represent the daily wage rate as well as the marginal revenue prod-

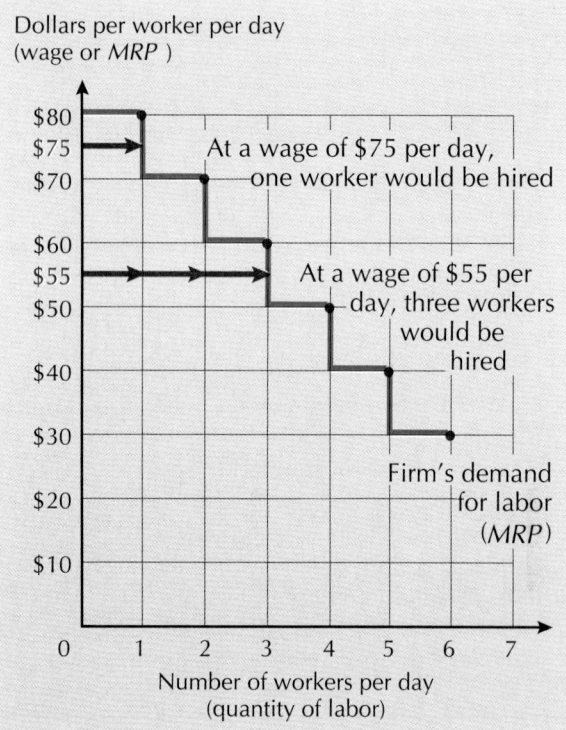

FIGURE 30.3   *The Firm's Demand for Labor Under Perfect Competition (Data in Table 30.1)*

The number of workers hired at any given wage rate is indicated by marginal revenue product. As long as marginal revenue product is greater than the wage (or equal to it), added workers will be hired.

uct). The resulting curve looks as though it could be the firm's demand curve for labor, and it is. *It shows how many workers the firm would hire at various possible daily wage rates, assuming profit maximization.* The explanation rests in the firm's two-question logic:

1. What is it worth to hire each worker? Answer: Each worker's marginal revenue product.
2. What does it cost to hire each worker? Answer: The prevailing wage rate.

Assume, for instance, that the market wage rate is $75 per worker per day, as suggested at the top of Figure 30.3. Would the first worker be hired? Yes. The first worker is worth $80 in added daily revenue (*MRP*), which exceeds the $75 daily wage that would be paid. Hiring the first worker is profitable.

Indeed, the first worker would be hired at _any_ daily wage less than $80. Would the second worker be hired? Two-question logic says "no." The second worker is worth $70 in _MRP_, which is less than the wage cost of $75 (+$70 −$75 = −$5). Thus the second worker would not be hired if the firm is maximizing its profit.

Assume next a prevailing daily wage of $55. How many workers would then be hired? The _first? Yes,_ because worth (_MRP_ = $80) exceeds the wage cost ($55). The _second? Yes,_ because worth (_MRP_ = $70) exceeds the wage cost ($55). The _third? Yes_ again. The _fourth? No,_ because the worth of the fourth worker (_MRP_ = $50) is _less_ than the wage that would have to be paid ($55). Each of the first three workers would be profitable employees, but the fourth would not.

In sum, the downward-sloping marginal revenue product curve in Figure 30.3 (and in column (5) of Table 30.1) is the collection of answers to the first question in two-question logic in this case— What is it worth to hire workers? The labor market sets various possible answers to the logic's second question—What is the wage cost? And the profit-maximizing firm will hire additional workers as long as the marginal revenue product (worth) is greater than or equal to the wage rate (cost). Once the marginal revenue product falls below the wage, the firm should not hire more labor. The general rule follows:

> The firm facing competition in the labor market will hire labor to the point where the marginal revenue product equals the wage rate (MRP = W).

Moreover:

> The MRP curve is the firm's demand curve for labor because the firm hires the number of workers at which the marginal revenue product equals the wage.

The _marketwide demand curve_ for labor is just an aggregation of the labor demanded by _all the firms_ in a particular labor market at each possible wage level. A simple horizontal summation of the individual firm demands might seem sufficient to achieve this aggregation for marketwide demand. After all, a horizontal summation of individual consumer demands for shirts yields the market-wide demand for shirts. Such a simple summation does not work here, however. This is because the demand for labor is a _derived demand,_ a demand dependent on the product's price. In explaining the individual firm's demand for labor, we could reasonably assume a _constant product price_ for the firm selling in a perfectly competitive product market. It was always $10 in the examples of Table 30.1 and Figure 30.3. However, when aggregating labor demand to the _marketwide_ level, the product price can no longer be taken as constant. Varying labor at the marketwide level will vary product output at the marketwide level, and that will alter the product price and marginal revenue product. More marketwide labor means a lower product price. Less marketwide labor means a higher product price. This is because product demand is downward sloping. Thus, _marketwide demand for labor is the horizontal summation of individual firm demands adjusted for variations in product price._

Still, the important point is that _the marketwide demand for labor will slope downward._ Moreover, if there are shifts in the labor demands of individual firms, marketwide demand will shift in the same direction.

C
Optimal Combinations of Resources

Firms use many inputs other than labor. The profit-maximizing rule for combining resources is the same for each resource. Let's assume that the firm faces perfect competition in its purchase of each input—capital equipment, land, fuel, and labor. Then the individual firm will not affect the price of these inputs. What amounts of these inputs will be used by the firm, given their prices set by market-wide conditions? The firm will acquire capital as long as the marginal revenue product of capital (MRP_C) is greater than or equal to the price of capital (P_C). The firm will acquire land as long as the marginal revenue product of land (MRP_L) is greater than or equal to the price of land (P_L). And so on. The summary rule for profitably hiring workers is, as we have seen,

$$MRP_W = P_W \qquad \text{(for workers)}$$

It follows that the firm's summary rules for maximizing profits in these other resource markets are (assuming competition as purchaser):

$$MRP_C = P_C \quad \text{(for capital)}$$
$$MRP_L = P_L \quad \text{(for land)}.$$

Notice that, with $MRP_W = P_W$, the *ratio* of these values, MRP_W/P_W, will equal 1, as for instance if $50 = 50$, then $50/50 = 1$. This leads to an alternative formation of firm profit maximizing when all inputs are considered:

$$\frac{MRP_W}{P_W} = 1 \quad \frac{MRP_C}{P_C} = 1 \quad \frac{MRP_L}{P_L} = 1$$

or, more briefly,

$$\frac{MRP_W}{P_W} = \frac{MRP_C}{P_C} = \frac{MRP_L}{P_L} = 1.$$

Under this condition, all inputs are employed in profit-maximizing amounts. Stated differently, the quantity of output the firm produces is being produced with the least costly combination of inputs whenever the preceding equation holds.

D

Shifts in Demand for Labor

What causes labor demand to shift? Given that the demand for any particular labor is its marginal revenue product (*MRP*), this question is the same as the question: "What causes MRP curves to shift?". The answer divides into two parts because marginal revenue product has two elements—product price (*P*) and marginal product (*MP*). In particular, $MRP = P \times MP$, given fixed levels of the other resources employed (and given competition in the product market, which equates price with marginal revenue). The demand for labor will thus shift with:

1. Shifts in the marketwide demand for the product that alter its price (ΔP).
2. Changes in the productivity of labor (ΔMP), which may be caused by
   a. changes in the amounts of other inputs used with labor,

b. changes in production technology,
c. changes in the inherent productivity of workers (e.g., skill level).

These two sources of shifting labor demand are summarized in Figure 30.4, the first in part (a), the second in part (b).

1. Shifts in Product Demand Because labor demand is derived from product demand, changes in product demand alter labor demand. An increase in product demand will increase product price, thereby lifting marginal revenue product and shifting the demand for labor to the right. Conversely, a decrease in product demand will decrease product price, causing marginal revenue product and labor demand to shift left. *Product demand and labor demand thus move together in the same direction*, something common sense would suggest as well as part (a) of Figure 30.4.

For a hypothetical example, imagine what would happen to the demand in Figure 30.3 if the product price in Table 30.1 fell from $10 to $5 as a result of falling product demand. It would shift left (i.e., downward) since *MRP* in column (5) of Table 30.1 would then drop by half—to $40 instead of $80, to $35 instead of $70, and so on. For a real-world example of a product price increase, the demand for domestic U.S.-produced crude oil jumped greatly during the 1970s as the price of OPEC oil soared. This drove up the price of domestic oil and the demand for oil well drillers. By 1980 drillers in Alaska were earning $90,000 a year (even young ones with only a high school education).[2]

2. Changes in Labor Productivity If the marginal product of labor changes, then the demand for that labor will change in the same direction, as suggested in part (b) of Figure 30.4. *Increases in productivity increase demand; decreases in productivity decrease demand.*

What would cause such changes in labor productivity? The amounts of other inputs used with labor—machinery and fuel, for instance—play a major role. However, this relationship between nonlabor inputs and labor is complex. Labor productivity may either *increase or decrease* as the use of nonlabor inputs rises, depending on wheth-

[2]*Wall Street Journal*, April 14, 1981, pp. 1, 15.

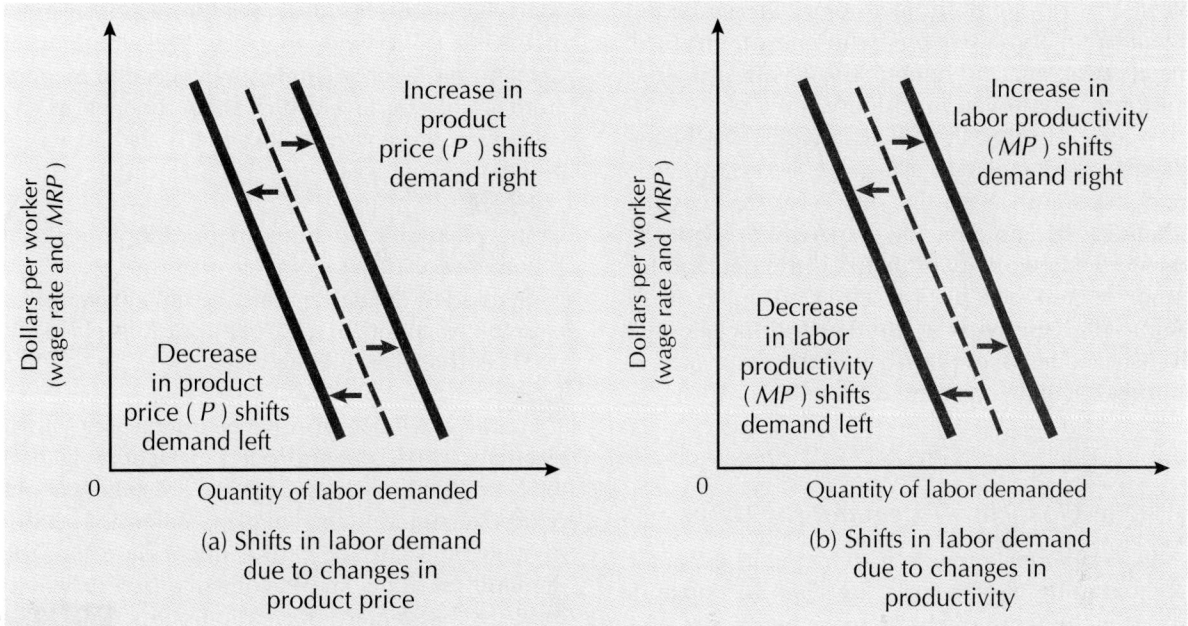

(a) Shifts in labor demand
due to changes in
product price

(b) Shifts in labor demand
due to changes in
productivity

FIGURE 30.4   _Shifts in the Demand for Labor_

The demand for labor matches marginal revenue product (MRP), _which is product price_ (P)
times the marginal product of labor (MP), _or_ MRP = P × MP. _It follows that labor demand
will shift with changes in product price and worker productivity._

er those nonlabor inputs are _complements or sub-_
stitutes for labor. If a nonlabor input is a _comple-_
ment to labor, then an _increase_ in its use will
increase the productivity of labor and thereby also
increase the demand for labor. For example, jet
fuel and airline pilots are complementary inputs.
With greater use of jet fuel, pilots can fly more people to their destinations, so pilots' marginal product increases. If, on the other hand, a nonlabor
input is a _substitute_ for labor, then an _increase_ in
its use will _decrease_ the productivity of labor and
consequently _reduce_ the demand for labor. Mechanical tomato pickers are, for instance, substitutes for human tomato pickers. Increased use of
mechanical tomato pickers would therefore decrease the demand for human tomato pickers.

The next question is, why would a firm suddenly increase the use of nonlabor inputs such as jet
fuel or mechanical tomato pickers? One major reason is obvious: _reductions in the prices of those_
nonlabor inputs. When the price of jet fuel fell substantially during the early 1980s, the demand for
airline pilots rose substantially—typical for a case
of complementary inputs. Conversely, if the price

of mechanical tomato pickers were to fall substantially, greater use of these machines would cause a
tumble in the demand for human tomato pickers
because those two inputs are substitutes.

A drop in the price of a **complementary** nonlabor input will increase the demand for labor, whereas a drop in the price of a **substi-**
tute nonlabor input will decrease the demand
for labor. (Price increases have opposite effects, respectively.)

Technological changes also shift the demand for
labor because they too change the productivity of
labor. Moreover, new discoveries of production
techniques may either increase or decrease the
demand for labor, depending on the circumstances. Usually, the demand for some workers
will fall while the demand for others rises. Take
robots and other computer-controlled factory machinery, for instance. Annual purchases of factory
automation systems doubled from $9 billion to $18
billion between 1980 and 1985. This _reduced_ the
demand for factory blue-collar labor. On the other

hand, this revolution in technology _increased_ the demand for those workers who design, produce, install, program, and operate the robots and other computer-controlled machinery.[3]

Finally, the productivity of labor can change because of changes in skill level (everything else held constant). A better skill level, as may be obtained by training or experience, typically boosts the labor demand. What is the demand for major league ball players as opposed to bush league players? What is the demand for talented eye surgeons as opposed to those who are all thumbs? The answers are obvious.

E

The Elasticity of Demand for Labor

Movement _along_ a marketwide demand curve for labor may be as important as _shifts_ in demand. And the impacts of those movements are best measured by the elasticity of demand for labor. Recall that the price elasticity of demand for a

[3]_Business Week_, June 16, 1986, pp. 100–101.

good like soda pop measures the responsiveness of buyers to changes in price. The elasticity of demand for labor is similar. It gauges the responsiveness of employers (firms) to changes in the wage rate. Moreover, its formula is also a ratio of percentage changes.

The **elasticity of demand for labor** is the percentage change in the quantity of labor demanded divided by the percentage change in the wage rate. If greater than 1, it is elastic. If less than 1, it is inelastic.

Figure 30.5 illustrates two extreme cases—high elasticity in part (a) and deep inelasticity in part (b). Note that both can occur. We are talking about particular (micro) labor markets here, not economywide labor. Hence part (a) might represent the demand for snow shovelers, while part (b) could indicate the demand for airline pilots. With high elasticity, a small percentage increase in the wage rate would cause a big drop in the quantity demanded. With very inelastic demand, wage increases could be quite large and yet not cause much decline in the quantity demanded.

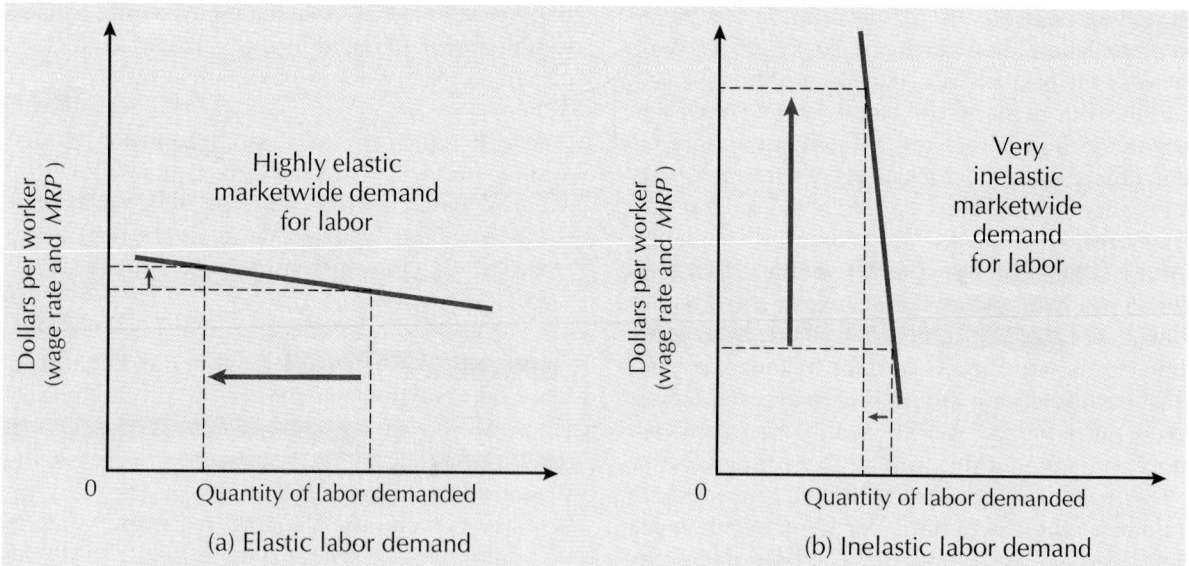

FIGURE 30.5 Variations in the Elasticity of Demand for Labor
(a) This is typically associated with highly elastic product demand, high portions of total cost going for labor, and readily available substitute inputs. (b) This is typically associated with inelastic product demand, low portions of total cost going for labor, and a lack of close substitute inputs.

What makes elasticity high or low? There are three major influences: (1) the elasticity of demand for the product that labor produces, (2) the proportion of total production costs going to workers, and (3) the availability and cost of nonlabor substitute inputs.

1. The Elasticity of Demand for the Product Produced The elasticity of labor demand is directly related to the elasticity of product demand. If demand for the product is highly elastic, then a small percentage increase in its price will cause a large percentage decrease in its quantity demanded. If this increase in product price is caused by an increase in worker wages, then the large percentage decrease in product quantity demanded will also cause a large percentage decrease in labor demanded. Working in reverse, reductions in wages that reduce product price will boost labor demand greatly if product demand is highly elastic. In sum, *high product price elasticity translates into high labor elasticity, and low product price elasticity implies low labor elasticity.*

2. Proportion of Production Costs in Labor Ponder a bag of french fries that costs $1.00 to produce, including a normal profit, and is priced at $1.00. If 10 cents of that dollar are wage costs, then a doubling of wages from 10 to 20 cents will increase the final price only *10 percent* from $1.00 to $1.10. If, however, wage costs are a much greater percentage of the total cost, 50 cents, say, then a doubling of wage costs from 50 cents to $1.00 will increase the final price by *50 percent* from $1.00 to $1.50 (*ceteris paribus*). In *both* cases, wage costs double—they increase by the *same* percentage, 100 percent. However, the ultimate percentage change in product price is quite different—10 percent versus 50 percent—depending on the proportion of total costs accounted for by labor. When the proportion is low, the ultimate effect of the wage hike on the product price is relatively slight. When the proportion is high, the ultimate effect of the wage hike on the product price is relatively large. It follows that any *particular* wage increase, such as 100 percent in this example, will have a *greater* adverse impact on the quantity of product demanded (and labor demanded), the *greater* the proportion of labor costs as a share of the total costs. *Hence, the larger the percentage of total costs accounted for by labor, the greater the elasticity of demand for labor. Conversely, the smaller the percentage of total costs accounted for by labor, the smaller the elasticity of demand for labor (ceteris paribus).*

3. The Availability of Substitute Inputs The elasticity of demand for labor is also directly related to the availability of substitute inputs. The elasticity of labor demand tends to be high when close substitutes are readily available because wage increases then readily prompt firms to shift their hiring away from labor toward the substitutes. As wages rise, substitute inputs such as capital equipment then appear *relatively* cheaper, so if they are readily available at low cost, they will be used to replace labor. And the more readily available they are, the greater the elasticity of demand for labor.

Research discloses, for instance, that the elasticity of demand for blue-collar production workers (such as assemblers and lathe operators) is greater than the elasticity of demand for white-collar nonproduction workers (such as plant managers and marketing vice-presidents). This seems to be due to the fact that capital (like robotic machinery) is generally a closer substitute for production workers than for nonproduction workers.[4]

■ **CHECK YOUR BEARINGS**

After noting that labor demand is a derived demand, we explored the firm's demand, the marketwide demand, shifts in demand, and the elasticity of demand. The demand for labor is a derived demand because it stems from the demand for the goods and services labor produces. The firm's demand for labor matches what labor is worth to the firm, or marginal revenue product. This is the change in total revenue that can be credited to an added unit of labor. For any given wage (*W*), *MRP* indicates how many workers the firm demands because the firm will hire out to the point where $MRP = W$. The marketwide demand curve is the horizontal summation of the individual firm demand curves, adjusting for changes in

[4]R. J. Flanagan, R. S. Smith, and R. G. Ehrenberg, *Labor Economics and Labor Relations* (Glenview, Ill.: Scott, Foresman, 1984), p. 92.

product price. When this $MRP = W$ rule is generalized to other inputs, the resulting rule for the firm's profit maximization and cost minimization is

$$\frac{MRP_a}{P_a} = \frac{MRP_b}{P_b} = \frac{MRP_c}{P_c} = 1$$

where a, b, and c are different inputs. Shifts in labor demand will occur because of changes in product price (ΔP) or productivity (ΔMP). As for elasticity, the elasticity of demand for labor will be higher (1) the higher the product's price elasticity of demand, (2) the larger the proportion of labor costs as a share of total costs, and (3) the more readily available are substitute inputs. Demand thus mastered, we now turn to supply.

III
The Supply Side

Earlier we glanced at the marketwide supply of a particular type of labor (fast-food counter attendants in a major city) and a competitive firm's view of supply. These aspects of labor supply are critically important. Even so, the term *labor supply* also has other applications. At the macro level, labor supply refers to the aggregate supply of all labor in the economy. This is measured by population and the overall **labor force participation rate,** which is the percentage of total population that either has a job or is looking for one. Recently, aggregate labor force participation has been about 64 percent of the populace.

Labor supply in a particular market, or **marketwide labor supply,** may be heavily influenced by the labor force participation rate of *specific population groups,* such as males or teenagers. For example, the supply of fast-food counter attendants is probably affected by the percentage of girls 16–19 years of age who are working and seeking work. Between 1960 and 1982 this rose from 39.3 to 51.4 percent, a whopping jump of 30.8 percent in just two decades. Other labor force participation rates are reported in Table 30.2. Note that the participation rate is, on the whole, greater for

TABLE 30.2 Labor Force Participation Rates, By Sex and Age, 1982

Age Group (Years)	Male	Female
16–19	56.7%	51.4%
20–24	84.9	69.8
25–34	94.7	68.0
35–44	95.3	68.0
45–54	91.2	61.6
55–64	70.2	41.8
65 and over	17.8	7.9
All ages over 16	76.7	52.6

Source: Bureau of the Census, *Statistical Abstract of the United States 1984*, p. 407.

males than females—76.7 percent versus 52.6 percent. At the same time, there is wide variation by age level. The male rate reaches a peak in the 35- to 44-year age bracket, while the female rate reaches a peak in the 20- to 24-year age bracket.

Moving to the micro-micro level, the term *labor supply* can refer to the supply behavior of an **individual**—yourself, for instance. As just suggested by the labor force participation statistics of Table 30.2, individual supply curves depend on such noneconomic variables as sex and age. They also vary with marital status, parental status, and cultural traits. Still, we shall concentrate on purely economic considerations. And after we have explored individual supply curves, we shall tackle marketwide supplies of labor in earnest. Focusing most intently on economic matters, we shall study how wage rates and labor supply are related.

A
Individual Labor Supply

Individual labor supply curves vary immensely. Still, in general, individuals respond *positively* to increases in wage rates, entering the labor force and working longer hours the higher their wages, at least up to a point. Once wages rise beyond some very high level, individuals typically respond *negatively* by reducing their working time (just as many people who win millions of dollars in state lotteries retire early). The usual result is a *backward-bending* individual labor supply curve.

Imagine that Figure 30.6 applies to you. At point *A* you currently do not have a job, the $3.50 per

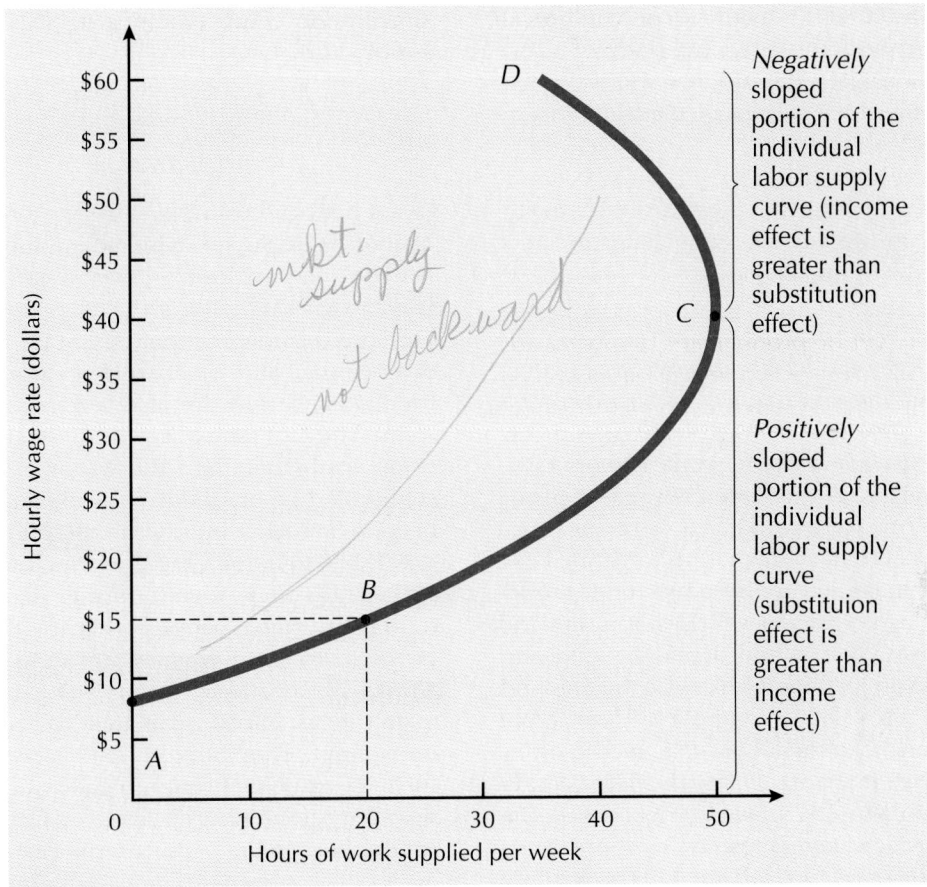

FIGURE 30.6   An Individual's Supply of Labor

As the wage rises from $5 to $40, the individual works longer hours, substituting work for leisure as not working becomes more costly. Further wage increases above $40 cause hours supplied to fall because the person will then want more leisure time to enjoy the high income.

hour you might earn as a counter attendant being too low to attract you. If you get a job offer at $15 per hour, however, you decide to cut back on college, enter the work force, and work part time, say 20 hours a week. This would place you at point *B* in Figure 30.6. Even better job offers at $25, $30, or $35 an hour cause you to quit college and work full time, these lucrative offers being too good to pass up. Indeed, at point *C* you would be working intensely, logging 50 hours a week when rewarded lavishly by $40 per hour. At still higher wage rates, though, your supply of labor begins to drop, just as it would probably drop if you suddenly won $1 million. At these towering and more luxuriant wage rates—$50 and $60 an hour—you begin to

play more tennis and golf or sail in your sloop. Although the horizontal axis in Figure 30.6 is measured in hours per week, higher wages will also encourage you to work fewer weeks per year as you take longer and more frequent vacations. Thus, in terms of hours per week and weeks per year, you begin to take more leisure time in order to enjoy your riches.

An interesting economic analysis of the labor supply of individual dentists discovered such backward-bending supply curves for both weekly hours and weeks worked per year. In 1976 dollars, the turning point for weekly hours occurred at an hourly income of $43, and the turning point for weeks per year occurred at an annual income of approximately $74,000. About 25 percent of all dentists were above these turning points.[5]

Economists explain the individual's backward-bending supply curve with particular reference to _leisure_, broadly defined.

> **Leisure** is time spent in any activity other than work in the labor force or work in the home (e.g., washing dishes).

Leisure is indeed attractive. However, _when the wage rate increases, leisure becomes_ both _less attractive and more attractive._ It becomes _less_ attractive because, as the wage level rises, it becomes more expensive not to work. The opportunity cost of leisure is the foregone wage that one could earn if one were working. So a higher wage means that leisure has a higher opportunity cost. On the other hand, leisure becomes _more_ attractive because, as the wage level rises, the demand for leisure rises. Just as the demand for lobster dinners rises with income, so likewise the demand for free time rises with income (free time to eat lobster dinners, take vacations, golf, and so on).

As wages rise in Figure 30.6 _both effects always apply._ But over the _ABC_ range of Figure 30.6, the first of these effects dominates, so the labor supply _rises_ with the wage as leisure becomes more expensive and therefore, _on balance, less_ attractive. Over the _CD_ range of Figure 30.6, the second of these effects dominates, so labor supply _falls_ with even higher wages as the demand for leisure grows and it therefore becomes, _on balance, more_ attractive.

In economic jargon, this says that leisure is like a consumption good, say autos, and price changes (wage changes) cause a **substitution effect** and an **income effect.** As wages rise, there is a tendency to _substitute_ work for leisure because the "price" of leisure rises. On the other hand, rising wages also raise _income_ levels, causing people to demand more leisure, just as higher income levels tend to create a demand for more autos. At first, when wage rates are low to moderate, the substitution effect dominates the income effect, resulting in positively sloped supply (_ABC_). After a certain point (_C_), the income effect outweighs the

[5]R.M. Scheffler and L.F. Rossiter, "Compensation Schemes and the Labor Supply of Dentists," _Quarterly Review of Economics and Business_ (Autumn 1983), pp. 29–43.

substitution effect, resulting in negatively sloped supply (_CD_).

B
Human Capital

In the previous example, the wage rate was simply offered by some anonymous employer. However, workers can influence their wage earnings by altering the skill level of the labor they supply. In particular, some occupations, such as medicine, engineering, and biochemistry, require years of training, and they are also very rewarding financially. The fact that wages in these skilled professions are higher than the wages of unskilled or semiskilled labor is not coincidental. The wages need to be higher in order to compensate individuals who enter such fields for the heavy expenses and effort they incur during many years of training. In effect, people who want to enter high-paying professions _invest_ their time, money, and diligence in near-term training because they anticipate that, in future years, they will profit by their investment. They hope to earn a high return on their investment through higher wages and salaries. The basic idea is like that of a firm investing in capital equipment—short-term cost outweighed by long-term gain. Hence, economists say that individuals are developing _human capital_ when they go to college, attend a trade school, or take on-the-job training.

> **Human capital** is the accumulation in schooling, training, and health that raises the productive capacity of people.

Figure 30.7 illustrates human capital theory as it might apply to obtaining a college degree. College has social, intellectual, and cultural benefits, of course, benefits not to be slighted. Still, for many students, the main benefit of college is the training received in such fields as business and engineering, training that will boost their incomes above what they would be without college. Thus Figure 30.7 illustrates in a simple way the economic costs and benefits of college as compared to full-time entry into the work force immediately after high school at age 18.

It is assumed that our noncollege worker could earn $20,000 per year over his or her working years

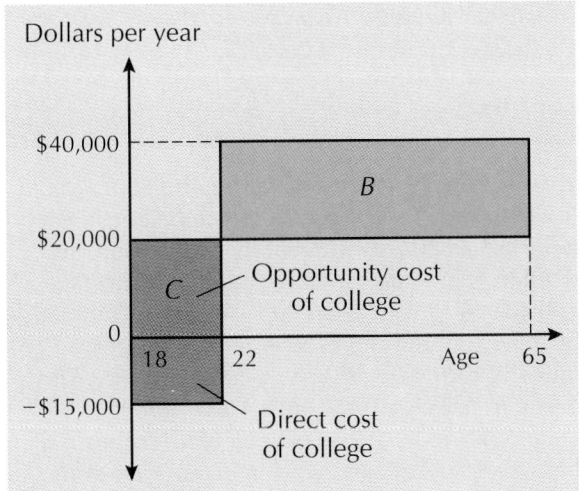

FIGURE 30.7   _The Human Capital Decision and College_

In this simple example, an individual has two choices: (1) go directly to work after high school, earning $20,000 a year from age 18 until retirement at age 65; (2) go to college, which costs $20,000 annually in the foregone wages that could be earned plus $15,000 in direct expenses such as tuition and books, the combined cost being area C. The benefit is area B, which shows the greater annual income earnings that result, in total. If area B is greater than area C, the college investment pays off economically.

until retirement at age 65. (In the real world this would actually vary with experience and seniority, but we're simplifying.) How does the financial situation of a college graduate compare to this? The near-term _costs_ are indicated by shaded area C in Figure 30.7. These costs come in two forms. First, there is the opportunity cost of not working for $20,000 a year during the 4 years of college between ages 18 and 22. Second, there are the direct, out-of-pocket costs associated with college—such as those for tuition, books, and travel to and from home. These are assumed to be $15,000 per college year. These combined costs are compared to the monetary _benefits_ indicated by shaded area B. Annually, these benefits are the amount by which the postcollege income of $40,000 exceeds the noncollege income of $20,000, namely, $20,000 ($40,000 − $20,000 = $20,000). Totaling these annual benefits over the now shorter working life span between ages 22 and 65 yields area B.

Does college pay off financially? If the benefits of

area B exceed the costs of area C, it does. If area B is smaller than area C, it does not. This is just another form of micro two-question logic. (Technically, the dollars of area B are not strictly comparable to those of area C because they come in the more distant future, and future dollars are worth less than present dollars. But the basic idea of human capital is all that's important here.)

Read Perspective 30B.

C
Marketwide Supply

As we have just seen, individuals respond positively to rising wage rates. Substitution effects encourage greater work. And the relatively high monetary rewards of skilled occupations encourage the human capital investments to supply such labor. From these influences, labor supplies in some labor _markets_ will also be positively related to wage levels in those markets. But what about the backward-bending portion of individual supply curves? That is negatively sloped. Does this raise the possibility that the labor supply at the marketwide level is also backward-bending in many instances?

The answer is "no." Positively sloped supply prevails in particular labor markets despite backward-bending individual supplies. Let's take electricians as an example to explain why. A rise in electricians' wages will cause substitution effects for _existing_ individual electricians, thereby encouraging them to supply more labor and to cut back on leisure. But that's not all. Even if income effects outweigh these substitution effects for many existing electricians, thereby causing them to work less, there will be _new entry_ induced by the higher electricians' wages. As electricians' wages rise _relative_ to those for plumbers, carpenters, and others, work as an electrician becomes more attractive than alternative work. Many who have past electrical training but are currently doing something else, like truck driving, will switch occupations and become electricians. Many veteran workers who have no electrical experience will forsake their current jobs and take up electrical training. After attaining the required human capital, they too will add to the supply of electricians. Moreover, young people searching for careers will have a greater incentive to choose electrical work

PERSPECTIVE 30B
College and Earnings

Does college *really* pay off? Various economic studies say "yes." Table 30.3, for instance, presents expected lifetime earnings as they would have appeared to typical 18-year-old men and women in 1979, assuming different degrees of educational attainment. With only a high school education, a typical male could expect to earn $1,041,000. With 4 years of college, his lifetime earnings climb to $1,392,000. The difference, $351,000, reflects the financial benefits of college for him (area *B* of Figure 30.7). The numbers for women are lower (something we take up later when discussing discrimination). Even so, the financial benefits of college for women are not pocket change: $846,000 − $634,000 = $212,000. When benefits like these

are discounted to present values and compared to costs, the payoff from a college degree is not as great as these raw numbers for men and women may suggest. But college, on average, still seems to be a good "investment." The rate of return in the 1970s was about 8.5 percent, and the return for those in college during the 1980s is forecast to be at least as good.[6] Note also in Table 30.3 that payoffs arise for even a few years of college and for postgraduate degrees.

[6]Richard Freedman, "The Overeducated American in the 1980s: A Report to the National Commission on Student Financial Assistance," *Higher Education Marketing Journal* (Summer 1983).

TABLE 30.3 Expected Lifetime Earnings of a Typical 18-Year-Old in 1979 (Year-Round, Full-Time Workers)

Education Level	Men	Women
High school completed	$1,041,000	$ 634,000
College		
1–3 years	1,155,000	716,000
4 years	1,392,000	846,000
5 years or more	1,503,000	955,000

Source: Lifetime Earnings Estimates for Men and Women in the United States: 1979 (Washington, D.C.: Bureau of the Census, 1983), p. 3.

over auto repair or other trades as the wages of electricians rise *relative* to those in other lines of work.

In sum, the marketwide supply of electricians is positively associated with the wages of electricians (holding other wages constant). The key is *relative* wages. The positive association occurs because of added supply from new entry into the occupation, as well as any positive supplies of existing electricians. These new entries may take some time, but that simply means that the long-run elasticity of supply will be greater than the short-run elasticity

of supply. (Note: The evidence cited earlier on dentists' backward-bending supply is not inconsistent with this picture because that concerned *individual* dentists.)

Read Perspective 30C.

■ CHECK YOUR BEARINGS

In broad aggregates, the supply of labor emerges from the labor force participation rate of the general populace and of specific groups. Still, wages are crucial. Among individuals, the labor supply curve is positively sloped as long as the substitution effect dominates. Also, high wages encourage individual supplies to highly skilled occupations by more than covering the costs of investment in human capital. At extremely high wages, individual supply curves may bend backward into a negative slope. Even so, the quantities of labor supplied in particular markets, such as those for electricians or barbers, will be positively related to wages in those markets.

We may conclude that in particular competitive labor markets, supply slopes upward while demand slopes downward. Let's now study supply and demand together.

PERSPECTIVE 30C
The Work and Pay of MBAs

The positive slope of the labor supply in specific markets is illustrated by the behavior of new masters of business administration (MBAs) during the early 1980s. As shown in Table 30.4, the starting salaries of MBAs in three different job areas were roughly identical in 1980. However, by 1984 the pay in investment banking had leaped ahead of the pay in financial services and manufacturing. At the same time, the percentage of new MBAs choosing investment banking rose substantially, from 6.4 to 10.0 percent, and the percentage of MBAs choosing financial services or manufacturing fell. J. Fredric Way, associate dean and director of placement at the Columbia Business School, explained it this way: "If you're 26 or 27 and the gold ring is there, you might as well grab for it."[7]

[7]*Wall Street Journal*, June 30, 1985, p. 27.

TABLE 30.4   Where New MBAs Worked and What They Earned, 1980 and 1984

Field of Choice	Average Starting Salary		Average Percentage of Graduating Class	
	1984	1980	1984	1980
Investment banking	$32,447	$22,425	10.0%	6.4%
Financial services	26,505	22,242	13.8	15.1
Manufacturing	27,655	21,609	23.0	29.2
Note: Based on surveys of 85 U.S. business schools.				

Source: The Wall Street Journal, July 30, 1985, p. 27.

IV
Demand and Supply Together

Why does a dentist earn $62,000 a year and a truck driver take home $36,900? We have seen that demand and supply each make separate contributions to an understanding of why wages differ. But a complete understanding requires that we study demand and supply together. In a freely competitive market, the equilibrium wage will be determined by the intersection of demand and supply, as indicated earlier in Figure 30.2(b). However, not all jobs are the same and not all people are the same, so demands and supplies vary from one labor market to another. Some of the chief variations follow.

A
General Variations

1. Demand Variations   Assume a fairly homogeneous supply of workers of a particular type, say new MBAs, as in the last perspective. The supply curve of these new MBAs might look like the supply curve of Figure 30.8. Despite the similarities of all new MBAs in a given year's graduating class, the salaries paid to new MBAs differ from one industry to another, as just indicated in Table 30.4. One explanation for this lies in variations of demand. If the investment banking industry has a greater demand for new MBAs than the insurance industry, then the results will be as suggested in Figure 30.8. Those employed in investment banking will earn loftier annual salaries than those in insurance, say $30,000 versus $25,000. Indeed, between 1980 and

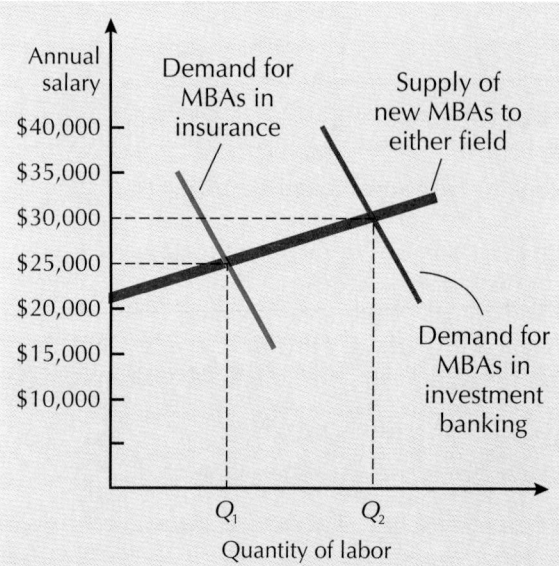

FIGURE 30.8 _Demand Variations and Income Earnings_

For a given supply, such as this hypothetical supply of newly graduated MBAs, the wage and quantity of employment will vary with variations in demand. Here the investment banking industry has a higher demand for new MBAs than the insurance industry, so the income and quantity of MBAs in investment banking are higher than those in insurance.

1984 there was a big jump in the salaries of new MBAs going into investment banking as compared to insurance (see Table 30.4). This was apparently due to a surge in demand. Investment bankers are financial experts who handle corporate mergers. And between 1980 and 1984 the number and size of corporate mergers soared. In technical jargon, the marginal revenue product of new MBAs in investment banking apparently rose substantially. With time these wage differentials would tend to shrink as more MBAs entered investment banking relative to other fields.

2. Compensating Wage Differentials Wage differentials that derive from the supply side are often due to _nonmonetary_ characteristics of jobs that attract or repel people. These characteristics therefore affect labor supplies. In general, people prefer clean jobs over dirty jobs. They like to work aboveground instead of underground. If they work outdoors, they dislike $-20°F$ temperatures. And so on. In sum, how would you like to be a fish

sniffer? (There is such a job with the U.S. Food and Drug Administration because the FDA inspects fish in order to prevent rotten catches from reaching the market.)

Given that jobs differ in nonmonetary characteristics, and given that people's preferences differ in these general ways, labor markets differ accordingly. Figure 30.9 illustrates. Assume, for simplicity, that the demand for underground coal miners and the demand for bakers are essentially identical. Hence one demand curve in Figure 30.9 illustrates the demand for either type of labor. The jobs, however, are quite different and cannot be assumed to be otherwise. Underground coal miners work in some of the dirtiest, riskiest, and bleakest conditions known. By contrast, bakers have pleasant circumstances (especially if they can eat an occasional cookie). As a result, the supply of coal miners will be less relative to the supply of bakers, and the wage that must be paid to coal miners will therefore be higher than that paid to bakers. This higher pay for nasty work conditions is called a _compensating wage differential_.

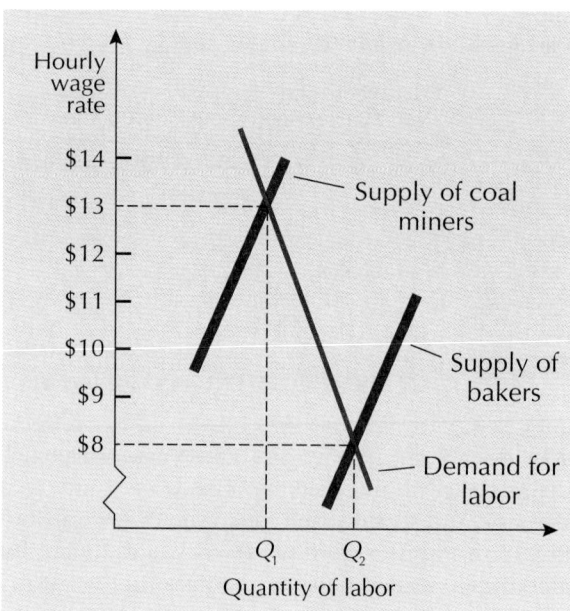

FIGURE 30.9 _Compensating Wage Differentials_

Some wage differentials are explained by nonmonetary work conditions, such as risk of injury, work environment, hours of work, and job cleanliness. Coal mining is a nasty job in comparison to baking bread, so the supply of coal miners is less (ceteris paribus) and they are consequently paid more than bakers.

Compensating wage differentials are the higher monetary rewards that must be paid to workers to compensate them for undesirable work conditions.

In the mid-1980s underground coal miners were paid over $14 an hour, on average, while bakers earned only about $9 an hour. This supports the theory of compensating wage differentials. Another, simpler example is the higher wage typically paid to those who work a night shift as compared to a day shift in what is otherwise the same job. Less well known but perhaps of even greater interest is the following: Statistical studies reveal that people typically dislike jobs lacking task variety, autonomy, intrinsic challenge, responsibility, comfort, and safety. They alter their labor supplies accordingly, as suggested in Figure 30.9.[8] Compensating wage differentials follow.

3. Noncompeting Groups   Not only do jobs differ, people also differ. In physical makeup, intellectual prowess, philosophical outlook, and training, there is a huge difference between prize fighters and college professors. Variations in the earnings of prize fighters are unlikely to affect the supply of college professors, and vice versa. These are *noncompeting groups* because the people in these groups are so strikingly different that they offer no competition to each other in the labor market. As a consequence, their income earnings can diverge greatly even in the long run. These groups also differ from the general labor force. Of *particular* note are those people who possess very rare talents or vast mental powers—such as major league athletes, computer design engineers, and top-flight investment bankers. Their labor offerings are quite scarce. Hence they can command astronomically high pay without worrying that readily available substitute supplies from other folks will compete away their rich earnings.

Noncompeting groups are groups of labor supplies differentiated by very scarce natural abilities or very scarce acquired skills, groups sufficiently different that they do not compete with each other or with labor generally.

[8]Randall K. Filer, "The Effect of Nonpecuniary Compensation on Estimates of Labor Supply Functions," *Quarterly Review of Economics and Business* (Spring, 1986), pp. 17–30.

For a contrast, consider bus drivers, taxi drivers, trash collectors, and delivery workers. These are competing groups, and they even face competition from the many people who could easily train for their jobs. Much the same could be said of salespeople of all kinds—those selling appliances, autos, stereos, and so on. These could be called *partially competing groups*.

The phenomenon of noncompeting groups helps to explain an oddity that arises when considering only compensating wage differentials as a cause of wage variations. Why is it that interesting, challenging, prestigious, clean, even *fun* jobs often pay considerably more than dull, tedious, humiliating, and dirty jobs? Why do petroleum geologists, say, earn more than trash collectors? The answer is easy. Their scarce skills place them in a noncompeting group.

To summarize the general pattern of wage determination in competitive markets, one could say that:

1. If all jobs and all people were exactly alike, there would be no wage differentials. Everyone would be paid the same.
2. Jobs differ with industry demands and nonmonetary characteristics like unpleasantness. Greater demand means a higher wage (at least temporarily). Unpleasantness results in compensating wage differentials.
3. People differ, so some with scarce skills—those in noncompeting groups—can earn substantially more than those lacking scarce skills (given a market value for those special traits). Where there is some mobility between groups, as between truck drivers of various sorts, there will be less pronounced wage differentials because of the greater competition from potential entry.

B
Minimum-Wage Law

The influence of demand and supply on the wage rate can be blocked by a **minimum wage law.** This sets a wage floor, so employers have to pay at least the minimum wage. When this law was first passed by Congress in 1938, the minimum wage was $0.25 an hour and covered only 43 percent of all workers (exempting those mainly in agriculture, retail trade, and service industries). At this writing, the minimum hourly wage under federal law is $3.35 and has been since 1981. Periodic increases to this level were necessary to keep up with general inflation. Coverage has likewise increased, standing now at well over 80 percent of the work force. (Some states have minimum wages higher than the federal level and broader coverage.)

The main intent of Congress in these efforts has been to help low-income workers by raising their wages. However, there can be serious adverse consequences for the quantity of labor hired in a competitive market. Figure 30.10 illustrates both the _wage effect_ and the _employment effect_ of the minimum wage, assuming a floor of $3.35 per hour.

Let's consider the wage level first. Notice that to have any positive impact on observed wages, the legal minimum must be _above_ the equilibrium

wage rate that would emerge from the interaction of demand and supply. In Figure 30.10 the equilibrium hourly wage would be $2.50, so the assumed minimum of $3.35 would indeed lift the observed wage in this market. In other labor markets, such as those for dentists or computer programmers, there would be no wage impact because the free-market equilibrium wage would be well above this $3.35 minimum. Hence, we can conclude that the minimum wage will directly affect only markets for unskilled, inexperienced workers. In these markets, those who retain their jobs and earn the higher minimum wage will benefit by the law. (These workers are represented by distance $0Q_1$ on the horizontal axis of Figure 30.10.)

There is a catch, however—the employment effect. Some people will lose their jobs, and they therefore suffer costs under the policy. In Figure 30.10, equilibrium employment without the minimum wage would be Q_2. Once the $3.35 minimum is set, the market will move from equilibrium point E up the demand curve to point M. In the process, employment sags from Q_2 to Q_1. The difference between these quantities $(Q_2 - Q_1)$ thus represents those who would lose their jobs as a consequence of the minimum wage legislation. (At $3.35 there is a surplus of labor supply over demand represented by the difference between Q_3 and Q_1, but only the unemployment between Q_2 and Q_1 can be directly blamed on the minimum wage.)

It should now be clear why the minimum wage law is one of the most controversial of all government economic policies. Those who favor it stress the benefits to those workers who receive higher wages. Those who oppose it stress the costs to those who are thrown out of work because of it. Indeed, numerous studies of the employment effect of the minimum wage law have been conducted, and virtually all of them show adverse employment effects in those markets where such effects could be expected—those for young, inexperienced, and unskilled workers. Of particular interest is the general finding that, on balance, each 10 percent increase in the minimum wage results in a reduction of about 1 to 3 percent in the employment of teenagers (16–19 years).[9]

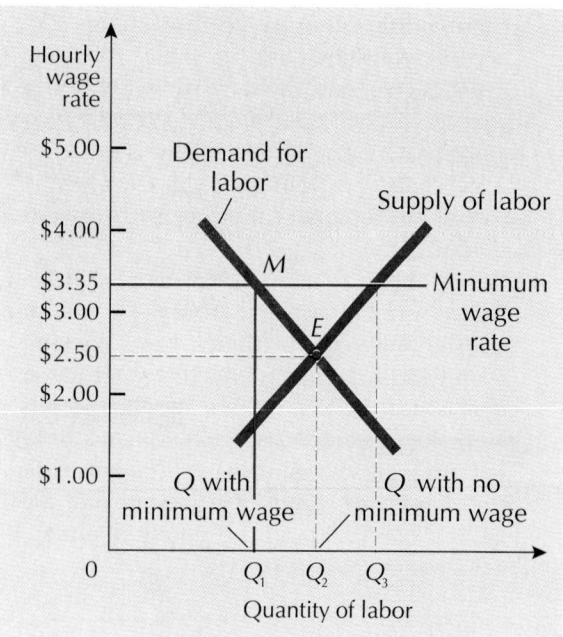

FIGURE 30.10 _Impact of the Legal Minimum Wage_
Under free market competitive conditions, the hourly wage rate would be $2.50 and Q_2 would be the quantity of labor hired. Setting the minimum wage at $3.35 prevents the market wage from falling to $2.50 and employment would be Q_1. The difference between Q_1 and Q_2 $(Q_2 - Q_1)$ would be the unemployment caused by the minimum wage, although the surplus labor supply at the minimum wage is $Q_3 - Q_1$.

[9]This 10 percent increase is in real terms relative to the price level generally. For a survey see Charles Brown, Curtis Gilroy, and Andrew Kohen, "The Effect of Minimum Wages on Employment and Unemployment," _Journal of Economic Literature_ (June 1982), pp. 487–528.

SUMMARY

1. Resource markets are similar to product markets, but in resource markets (a) firms are on the demand side while households are on the supply side, and (b) the main issues relate to the basic questions of How? and Who?

2. The competitive employer of labor sees a horizontal labor supply curve, while the employer with some monopsony power sees an upward-sloping supply curve. Firm and marketwide demands slope downward, reflecting the worth of workers.

3. Demands for inputs are derived demands.

4. The firm's demand for labor matches the marginal revenue product of labor (*MRP*), which is the extra revenue the firm gains by using one more unit of labor. *MRP may be calculated by multiplying marginal product per unit of labor times the marginal revenue per unit of output. With perfect competition in the product market, marginal revenue is price, so MRP = MP × P.*

5. The profit-maximizing firm hires labor until *MRP* equals the wage rate.

6. Marketwide demand is the horizontal summation of individual firm demands, adjusting for variations in product price.

7. With multiple inputs, the firm's rule for maximizing profit and minimizing cost is to equate the *MRP* of each input with each input's price.

8. Shifts in labor demand will occur because of changes in product price and marginal product.

9. The elasticity of demand for labor is higher (a) the higher the product's price elasticity of demand, (b) the larger the proportion of labor costs as a share of total costs, and (c) the more readily available are substitute inputs.

10. The supply of labor is determined by labor force participation rates, wages, individual preferences for work versus leisure, and investments in education and training.

11. At very high wages individual labor supply may be backward-bending, but marketwide supply will be positively sloped because of new entry into the particular labor market at higher wages.

12. Variations in market demand, nonmonetary job characteristics, and people help to explain wage variations as a function of both demand and supply. Compensating wage differentials compensate for job unpleasantness. Noncompeting groups can earn high wages because of their scarce skills.

13. The minimum wage law raises wages in unskilled markets, benefiting those who retain jobs at the higher wage. However, this also reduces employment, especially among teenagers.

KEY TERMS

Competitive employer
Horizontal labor supply curve
Market power
Upward-sloping labor supply curve
Firm's demand curve for labor
Marketwide demand curve for labor
Monopsony
Labor union
Derived demand
Marginal revenue product (MRP)
Complementary nonlabor input
Substitute nonlabor input

Elasticity of demand for labor
Market labor supply
Labor force participation rate
Individual labor supply
Leisure
Substitution effect
Income effect
Human capital
Compensating wage differentials
Noncompeting groups
Minimum wage law

QUESTIONS AND PROBLEMS

1. Distinguish product markets from resource markets. Explain how they are alike as well as how they differ.

2. What does it mean for an employer to have market power in a labor market?

3. Why is the demand for any input a "derived" demand?

4. Define "marginal revenue product" and explain why the marginal revenue product of labor declines as more and more workers are hired.

5. Assuming a competitive labor market, how will the slope of the marketwide demand curve for labor compare with the slope of the typical firm's demand curve for labor? Explain.

6. What combination of inputs will maximize profits for a firm?

7. Explain how an increase in the demand for the final product will affect the MRP curve.

8. Explain verbally and show graphically how the availability of lower-cost computers that can do the jobs of many workers in the newspaper publishing business will affect the demand for labor by that industry.

9. Explain why the elasticity of demand is lower for some kinds of labor than for others. Give one or more examples of workers whose elasticity of demand would likely be quite low.

10. Explain why an individual's labor supply curve might be backward-bending. Why is the backward section of an individual's labor supply curve likely to become relevant only if he/she is a highly skilled professional?

11. Traditional roles for males and females within the family unit lead to the accumulation of human capital by the male and the depreciation of the female's human capital. Explain why. How is this fact likely to be reflected in the two spouses' post-divorce earnings?

12. What prevents marketwide labor supply curves from bending backward like individual labor supply curves?

13. What factors explain the existence of significant wage differences across occupations?

14. Why are minimum wage laws politically popular? Show graphically why economists generally see minimum wage laws as a poor solution to the problems of unskilled workers.

31

Imperfect Labor Markets: Employer and Employee Power

With competition on both sides of a labor market, wage determination occurs automatically, impersonally. With power on both sides, bargaining forces and personalities intrude. Listen to Lee Iacocca bellowing at the auto workers' union when he sought wage cuts to help save Chrysler from bankruptcy. "Hey boys," he said, "I've got a shotgun at your head. I've got thousands of jobs available at seventeen bucks an hour. I've got none at twenty. So you better come to your senses." The union glumly took wage cuts. A few years later, however, in 1984, it was the union's turn to bluster. "Restore and More in '84," the union insisted. Wage boosts followed.[1]

Our ultimate objective in this chapter is to explore situations where employers have power (monopsony power) and employees also have power (union power). In the extreme, there is *bilateral monopoly:*

> With **bilateral monopoly** a labor market has only one buyer, an employer, and only one seller, a union.

Battles and bargaining emerge from power situations, even those less extreme than pure bilateral monopoly, such as those with a few employers (oligopsony) and less than complete unionization. Strikes, lockouts, and occasional violence are weapons in these battles.

Although tangles between labor market titans are our main interest, we shall approach that subject with brief explorations of two other possibilities—pure monopsony (with competition on the employees' side of the market) and pure unionism (with competition on the employers' side of the market).

> A **monopsony** is a market in which there is only one buyer (e.g., the employer).

A **labor union** is an organization of workers that (as a monopolistic seller) engages in collective bargaining with the employer.

I
Overview

There are two sides to any labor market—the buyers' (employers') and the sellers' (employees'). Oversimplifying, there are also two possible structures on each side—competitive and noncompetitive. This yields four possible cases, as outlined in the matrix of Figure 31.1. Case A, with competition on both sides of the labor market, is the case we covered in the previous chapter. Employers and workers are both price takers because wages are set by the competitive interaction of demand and supply. Case B has competition among workers while introducing monopsony on the employers' side of the market. Workers are once again price takers, as they once again have no power to influence the wage rate. In contrast to case A, however, the wage in case B will be set by the monopsonistic employer. In case C, with unionized labor plus competition among employers for that labor, power shifts from employers to workers. The workers, acting in unison and threatening a massive walkout, or strike, can influence the wage in this case. The employers, lacking power, behave as price takers, accepting the wage set by the union. Finally, in case D, neither employers nor workers are price takers. There is only a single employer, implying monopsony power. On the other side of the market, workers are unionized, so they likewise wield power. Here, wage determination takes on the tone of a contest—like the USC Trojans versus the UCLA Bruins in football or a python versus a panther. These images may be on target occasionally. But quite frequently the contest can also be seen as a chess match—with wile and guile deciding the outcome, plus the strong possibility of a draw rather than a clear victory for one side.

---

[1] Lee Iacocca, *Iacocca: An Autobiography* (New York: Bantam books, 1986), p. 245; *Wall Street Journal*, July 5, 1984, p. 6.

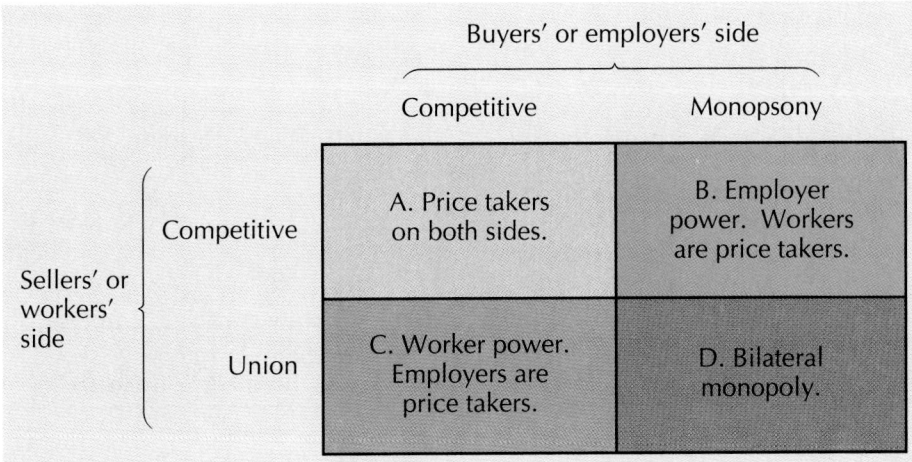

Buyers' or employers' side

	Competitive	Monopsony
Competitive	A. Price takers on both sides.	B. Employer power. Workers are price takers.
Union	C. Worker power. Employers are price takers.	D. Bilateral monopoly.

Sellers' or workers' side

FIGURE 31.1   *Four Possible Combinations of Labor Market Structure*

The basic economics of these four cases, in wage rates and employment levels, are summarized in Figure 31.2. The multipart figure allows comparison of the cases and prepares the way for later elaborations. The firm's view is on the left. The marketwide view is on the right. Case A simply repeats what we already know. Given *competition on both sides* of the labor market, wage and employment levels emerge from the equilibrium of marketwide supply and demand. By these hypothetical data, the wage is $8 per hour and employment stands at 6,000 workers. The firm, one small employer among many, considers the $8 wage as a given, so in its view the supply is horizontal at $8. Maximizing its profit, the firm hires five workers (as that is where the marginal revenue product equals the wage).

Case B in Figure 31.2 depicts pure *monopsony*. With only one employer, the firm's view will be the same as the marketwide view because the firm *is* the market. The firm therefore sees the upward-sloping marketwide supply curve. Expansion of its hiring lifts the wage rate. And as will be explained shortly, this causes the marginal cost of hiring—called the *marginal resource cost (MRC)*—to rise above the employees' supply curve. Micro two-question logic (comparing *MRC* and *MRP*) leads the monopsonist to hire 4,000 workers at an hourly wage of $6. Compare these results with those of competition in case A. Monopsony results in a *lower* wage ($6 versus $8) and a *lower* level of marketwide employment (4,000 instead of 6,000).

Case C in Figure 31.2 turns the tables. Here a *union* monopolizes the supply of labor. Employers, on the other hand, are small, numerous, and independent. Threatening a strike, the union can set an hourly wage *above* the competitive level of case A—$12 instead of $8. This alters the marketwide supply as indicated. The typical firm, as depicted on the left side of part C in Figure 31.2, takes the union wage of $12 as given and hires accordingly. Equating the wage of $12 to its marginal revenue product *(MRP)*, the firm hires two workers. Note that this is a *lower* level of firm employment than in case A because the wage is higher. Correspondingly, marketwide employment will also be *lower* in case C as compared to competitive case A—4,000 instead of 6,000. This is only one of several possible theories of union behavior, but it is common. The union willingly sacrifices some employment in order to gain greater income earnings.

Finally, in case D of Figure 31.2, we see a monopsonist pitted against a union in *bilateral monopoly*. Once again, monopsony merges the firm and the market into one. Yet, here, theory offers no clear-cut wage and employment results. Reviewing the results of cases B and C, we see that the monopsonistic employer's preferred wage is $6, while the union's preferred wage is much greater at $12. There is thus a gap. The gap opens a *range* of possible outcomes from which the actual wage will emerge, depending on the *bargaining power* of the two sides. Similarly, marketwide employment is

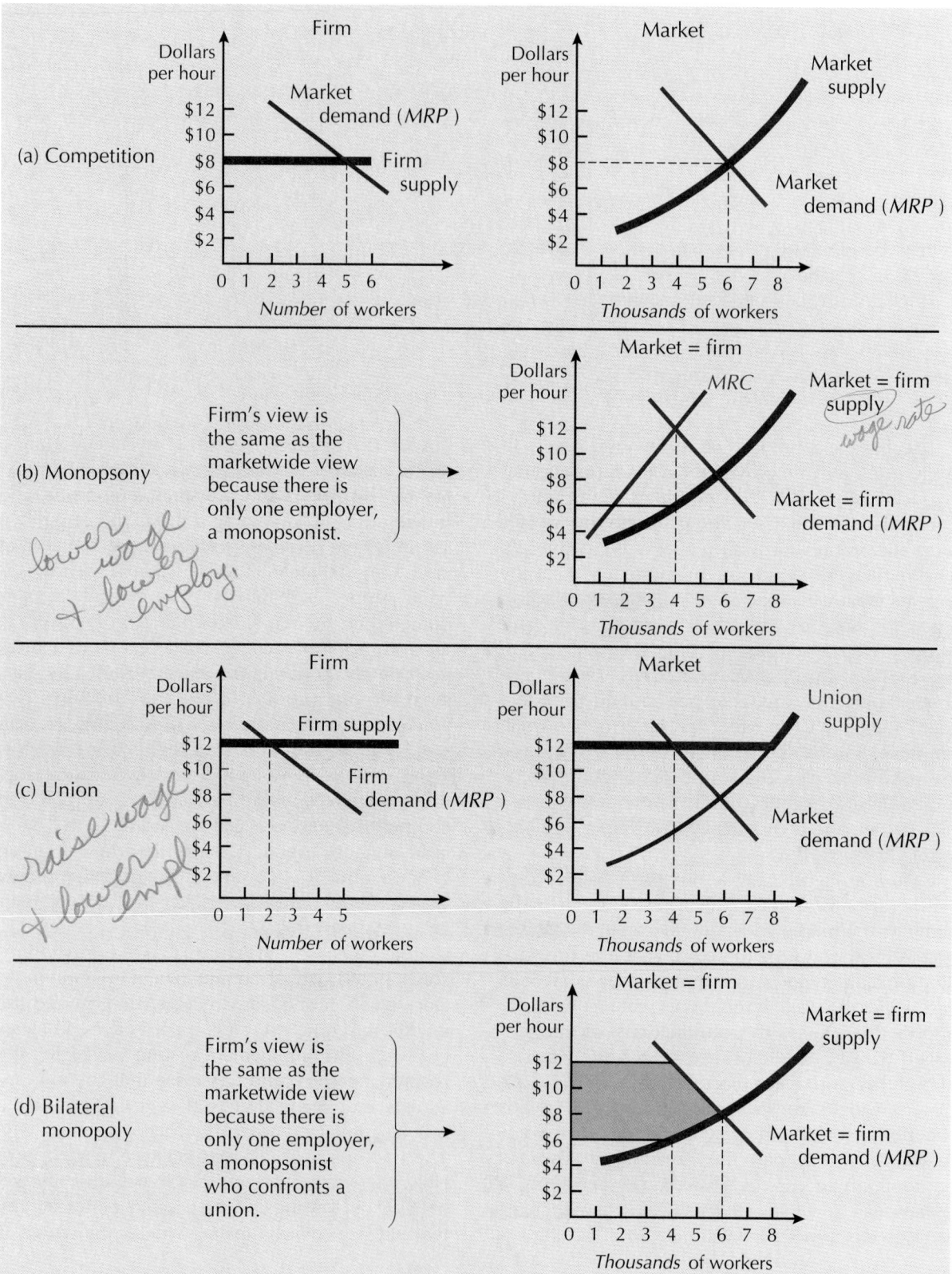

FIGURE 31.2 Summary of Four Basic Cases, Firm View on the Left and Marketwide View on the Right

theoretically indeterminate because it will depend on the wage level set by bargaining. Employment could be as high as the competitive level, 6,000 workers, if the bargained wage matched the competitive wage of $8. On the other hand, higher wages would reduce employment as dictated by the demand curve, and lower wages would reduce employment as dictated by the supply curve. Since theory gives ambiguous answers in this case of bilateral monopoly, we later heed what empirical evidence reveals about real-world outcomes.

Having considered these basic cases in a comparative cluster, we can now summarize the theoretical implications of three "imperfectly competitive" cases not covered previously—those of monopsony, unionism, and bilateral monopoly.

In comparison to the case of competition on both sides of the labor market, **monopsony** lowers the wage and employment, **unionism** raises the wage and lowers employment, and **bilateral monopoly** yields indeterminate results.

Let's now probe these cases more deeply. Because unions are important to the last two of these cases, and because unions influence more than wages and employment, we then conclude this chapter with an extensive discussion of unions.

II
Monopsony Theory

In 1984, Mazda Motors of Japan announced that it might build an auto assembly plant in Greenville, South Carolina, employing 12,000 to 14,000 workers. Everyone in Greenville celebrated gleefully, right? Wrong. A lot of people did hail the announcement, but others stewed. In particular, Eugene E. Stone III, chairman of an apparel company employing 5,000 in Greenville, decried the prospect of the Mazda plant because he said, "It would upset the wage structure for textiles." At the time, textile wages averaged $6.79 an hour. In contrast, Mazda would likely be paying about $14.00 an hour. Because of its vast influence on employment

in the Greenville area, Mazda would have to compete for textile and apparel labor, entice local workers from still other lines of work, and perhaps even attract auto workers from distant spots like Detroit, where auto assembly pays well. Hence the higher wage.[2]

In short, an employer like Mazda, hiring 12,000 to 14,000 workers in Greenville, South Carolina, would have a monopsonistic influence. Indeed, Mr. Stone, who was then hiring 5,000, already had a monopsonistic influence. Such examples are by no means rare. Oregon lumber towns and Colorado mining towns often have just one major employer. There can also be cases of *oligopsony*, where just a few employers may account for a vast number of jobs in a labor market, as brewers do in Milwaukee and aircraft manufacturers do in Seattle.

In these instances, employers are not in pure competition for labor. They do not see their labor supply as perfectly horizontal at the going, market-determined wage rate. Rather, when a firm hires a considerable portion of the total available supply of a particular type of labor, its decision to hire more or fewer workers will influence that labor's wage rate. *More hiring raises the wage. Less hiring lowers the wage.*

Table 31.1 and Figure 31.3 illustrate this with hypothetical data assuming a simple case, say, a lawyer in Sagebrush, Nevada, who is a local monopsonist in hiring legal secretaries. (Legal secretaries are a special breed, more skilled than secretaries generally.) His law firm would pay $8 an hour to the first secretary hired. In order to attract a second, the firm would have to pay $9 an hour. Columns (1) and (2) of Table 31.1 report further data in such a positive association, and these two columns taken together represent the labor supply in this market. They show the number of workers offering labor services at various hourly wages. Graphically, columns (1) and (2) form the supply curve of Figure 31.3.

Two-question logic will guide the firm's decision on how many workers to hire: What is an added worker worth? What does it cost to hire this worker? The answer to the first question is the same as we've seen before, namely, marginal revenue product (*MRP*). The answer to the second

[2]*Wall Street Journal*, July 9, 1984, p. 29.

TABLE 31.1   The Supply of Labor with Monopsony and Marginal Resource Cost (Hypothetical Data)

(1) Number of Workers Hired	(2) Wage Rate per Hour	(3) Total Labor Cost per Hour (1) × (2)	(4) Marginal Resource Cost (Δ3)
0	$ 7	$ 0	
1	8	8	$ 8
2	9	18	10
3	10	30	12
4	11	44	14
5	12	60	16

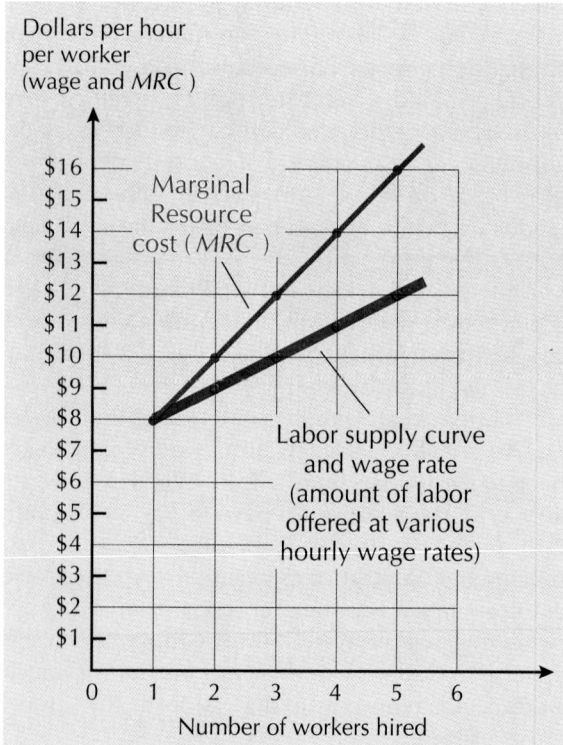

FIGURE 31.3   *Monoposony's View of Labor Supply* (Data in Table 31.1)

Under monopsony the marketwide view applies, so the labor supply curve is upward sloping. The higher the wage rate paid, the greater the labor supply. The implications for the monopsonist's cost of hiring additional workers is shown by the marginal resource cost (MRC). MRC is the added total cost of hiring an added unit of input, in this case labor. With an upward-sloping supply curve, MRC is above the supply curve and hourly wage.

question has been, under competition, the wage rate. But *under monopsony* that changes, and the relevant data are in columns (3) and (4) of Table 31.1. What must be paid when hiring an added worker is the *marginal resource cost (MRC)*, or the addition to the total labor cost that is associated with the added worker.

> **Marginal resource cost (MRC)** is the firm's extra total cost of using 1 more unit of resource input.

Under *competition*, with the wage taken as given and constant to the firm, the firm's marginal resource cost is the same as the wage rate. At, say, $5.75 an hour, the firm's total labor cost per hour would go up by $5.75 with the first worker, the second, the third, and so on. However, under *monopsony*, the wage rate is, as we've just seen, *not* constant to the firm. It rises with added workers. Hence, the marginal resource cost will be above the wage rate, as shown in columns (3) and (4) of Table 31.1 and in the *MRC* curve of Figure 31.3. The higher wages involved in attracting *additional* workers will also have to be paid to *all* workers, including those first hired at lower wages. This avoids labor unrest, charges of discrimination, and other problems that would arise if workers in essentially identical jobs were paid differently by the firm.

Note that the total hourly labor cost in column (3) of Table 31.1 is the number of workers in column (1) times the hourly wage of column (2). The *change* in total hourly labor cost, in column (4), is the marginal resource cost, or *MRC*. The first worker adds $8 to the total hourly labor cost, as it goes from $0 to $8. Hiring the second worker adds $10, as the total hourly labor cost rises from $8 to $18. Two factors contribute to this latter jump. First, the $9 paid to the second worker adds $9 to the total hourly labor cost. Second, the $1 raise paid to the first worker adds another $1. Hence, $9 + $1 = $10. Next, hiring the third worker adds $12 to the total hourly labor cost (this being $10 for the third worker's hourly wage plus $1 for each of the two preceding workers, i.e., $10 + $1 + $1 = $12). And so on. The fact that the marginal resource cost, *MRC*, lies *above* the wage rate associated with the supply curve is most clearly seen in Figure 31.3. It is this marginal resource cost, then, that

must be given up by the monopsonist when hiring additional workers.

Figure 31.4 illustrates the wage and employment results for monopsony, using our earlier data in summary Figure 31.2. The monopsonist will use two-question logic to maximize the profit. Question 1: What is it worth to hire each worker? This is shown by the firm's demand curve reflecting the marginal revenue product (*MRP*) of each worker. Question 2: What does it cost to hire each worker? The answer is, as we have just seen, the marginal resource cost (*MRC*). As long as *MRP* exceeds or equals *MRC*, as it does for workers 1 through 4,000, the monopsonist hires. If, for instance, *MRP* is $14 and *MRC* is $10, as they are for the 3,000th worker, the firm will profit by $4 when hiring that worker ($14 − $10 = $4). However, once *MRP* drops below *MRC*, the firm will begin to lose money on each

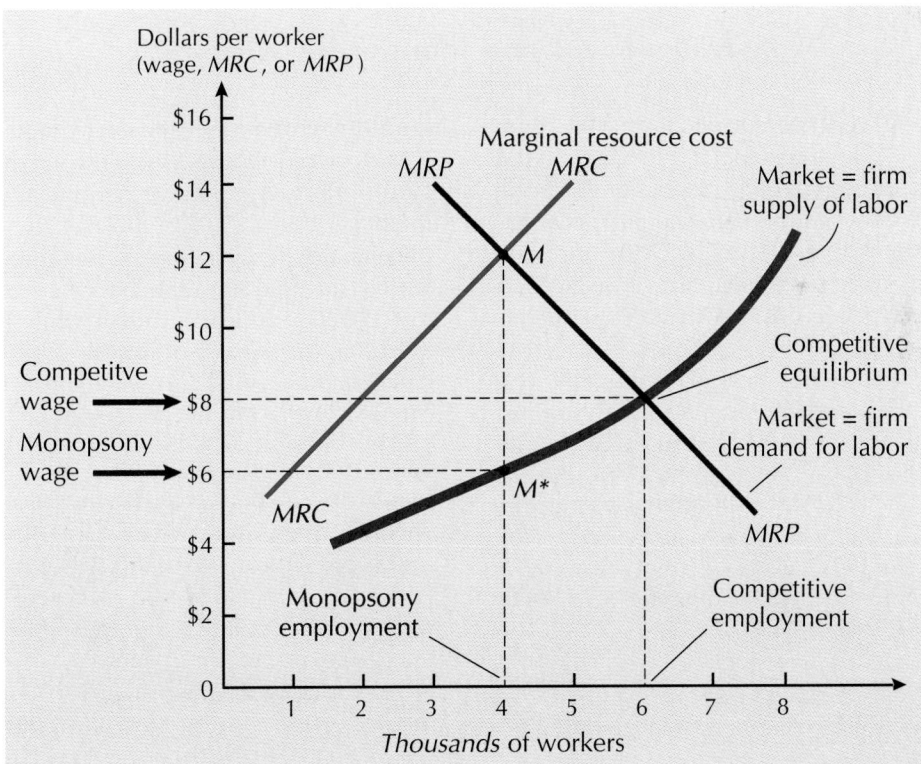

FIGURE 31.4   *Wage Rate and Employment Under Monopsony Compared to Competition*

Simple interaction of market supply and demand would determine wage and employment levels under competition. With monopsony, however, the firm is the market. The monopsonist experiences higher wages at higher employment, lifting the marginal resource cost above the labor supply curve. The monopsonist stops hiring when MRC equals MRP at point M, paying a wage of $6 and employing 4,000 workers corresponding to point M*. These levels are less than the competitive results of $8 and 6,000 workers.

additional worker. Hence, the profit-maximizing equilibrium occurs where *MRP* = *MRC*, as it does at point *M* in Figure 31.4. Employment at that point is 4,000, the number of workers that will be supplied at an hourly wage of $6, corresponding to point *M** on the marketwide labor supply curve.

The profit-maximizing firm uses added inputs until MRP = MRC. For monopsony in a labor market, MRC is above the wage rate, so MRP will be greater than the wage rate in equilibrium.

These results may be compared with those that would occur under competition. Figure 31.4 shows that with competition on both sides of the labor market, demand and supply would yield a wage of $8 an hour and an associated employment of 6,000 workers. Hence, *theory predicts a lower wage and a lower level of employment for monopsony as compared to competition.*

Read Perspective 31A.

III

Union Theory

There are two main kinds of unions in the United States, as identified in Table 31.3:

PERSPECTIVE 31A

Evidence on Low Monopsony Wages

Does the real world conform to economic theory? Table 31.2 illustrates that it often does in the case of monopsony. Those data come from the early 1960s. Other things being equal, the wages of newspaper printers in cities with only one newspaper, a monopsonist, were lower than those of newpaper printers in cities with numerous newspapers.

More recently and more sensationally, the impact of monopsony was demonstrated in 1977 when the "reserve clause" that tightly bound each baseball player to only one team was declared illegal. Moving from monopsony to the more competitive condition was like a financial grand slam home run for many ball players. Sal Bando's annual income went from $80,000 to $250,000, Don Baylor's from $35,000 to $170,000, and Joe Rudi's from $67,000 to $418,000. On average, the income of big-league ball players popped up over 40 percent in 1977, the first year without monopsony.

TABLE 31.2   Hourly Wage Rates of Newspaper Printers Under Monopsony as Compared to More Competitive Conditions, Early 1960s

Size Class of Cities Compared (Population)	Wage in Single-Newspaper Cities (Monopsony)	Wage in Multiple-Newspaper Cities (More Competitive)
Over 1 million population	No cases	$4.23
500,000–1 million	$4.00	4.08
250,000–500,000	3.90	4.02
100,000–250,000	3.71	3.89
Overall average	$3.81	$4.04

Source: John Landon, Ph.D. dissertation, Cornell University, 1968.

TABLE 31.3 Membership in Selected Industrial and Craft Unions, 1985

Industrial unions	Membership
Auto workers	1,100,000
Steel workers	1,000,000
Clothing and textile workers	355,000
Mine workers	157,000
Rubber workers	130,000
Hotel, restaurant employees	405,000

Craft unions	Membership
Carpenters	632,000
Airline pilots	34,000
Plumbers	350,000
Machinists	819,300
Painters	154,466
Sheet metal workers	140,000

Source: Business Week, May 6, 1985, pp. 102–103.

First, **industrial unions** represent the employees of a certain industry or firm, regardless of their specific tasks or skills. Second, **craft unions** represent workers who have a specific skill or occupation.

Industrial unions, like those for the auto workers and steel workers, could be called *inclusive* unions because they attempt to include all the workers in a given industry or firm among their membership. They include workers who operate machines, stock parts, inspect for product flaws, whatever. In contrast, *craft unions,* like those for pilots and plumbers, are sometimes called *exclusive* unions because they often follow restrictive membership policies. Requiring high initiation fees or long apprenticeships, craft unions sometimes try to discourage new entry into their line of work.

Simple theories of union behavior differ with regard to these different types of unions. Let's consider industrial unions first and craft unions second, assuming in both cases that there is competition on the employer's side of the market. A third possible strategy common to both types of unions will round out this section, one affecting labor demand instead of supply.

A

Industrial or Inclusive Unionism

Most unions try to gain as much membership as possible, organizing skilled, semiskilled, and even unskilled workers. This is typical of industrial unions like the United Auto Workers and the United Steel Workers of America. If an industrial union is successful in organizing nearly all the workers in an industry, it will have greater power in dealing with employers than otherwise. The union's chief weapon for wielding power is *a strike,* in which workers collectively refuse to work. With inclusive membership coverage, this can be a very potent weapon indeed. If nearly all the workers of a firm or an industry were to walk off the job, continued production would be virtually impossible. Immense losses for the firm or industry could ensue.

A **strike** occurs when all unionized employees stop work in order to persuade management to agree to union demands.

The simple theory of this case is illustrated in Figure 31.5, as drawn from our earlier cluster of cases in Figure 31.2. With competition in the market, the results would be the same as before. The hourly wage would be $8, and the associated level of competitive employment would be 6,000, as equilibrium is at point C. Now assume the creation of an inclusive union. The union imposes a higher hourly wage of $12, enforcing this wage level by threatening to strike any employer who pays less. This dramatically alters the labor supply curve for the market. With the union, market supply becomes horizontal at an hourly wage of $12 out to the point where the competitive supply curve reaches the $12 wage, point T. This says, in effect, that the industry can hire *no* workers at any wage less than $12 and as many as it wants at $12 out to the point where competitive supply takes over at point T. If the strike threat succeeds, marketwide employment at the $12 wage extends to point U on the marketwide demand curve. The move from competitive point C to union point U in Figure 31.5 lowers employment from 6,000 to 4,000 as the hourly wage rises from $8 to $12.

What does the individual firm experience in this case? The answer was indicated earlier on the left-hand side of part C in Figure 31.2. Given competition on the employer's side of the market, the firm's labor supply is always horizontal (perfectly elastic) at the going wage rate. Without the union, it would be horizontal at $8 an hour by these data.

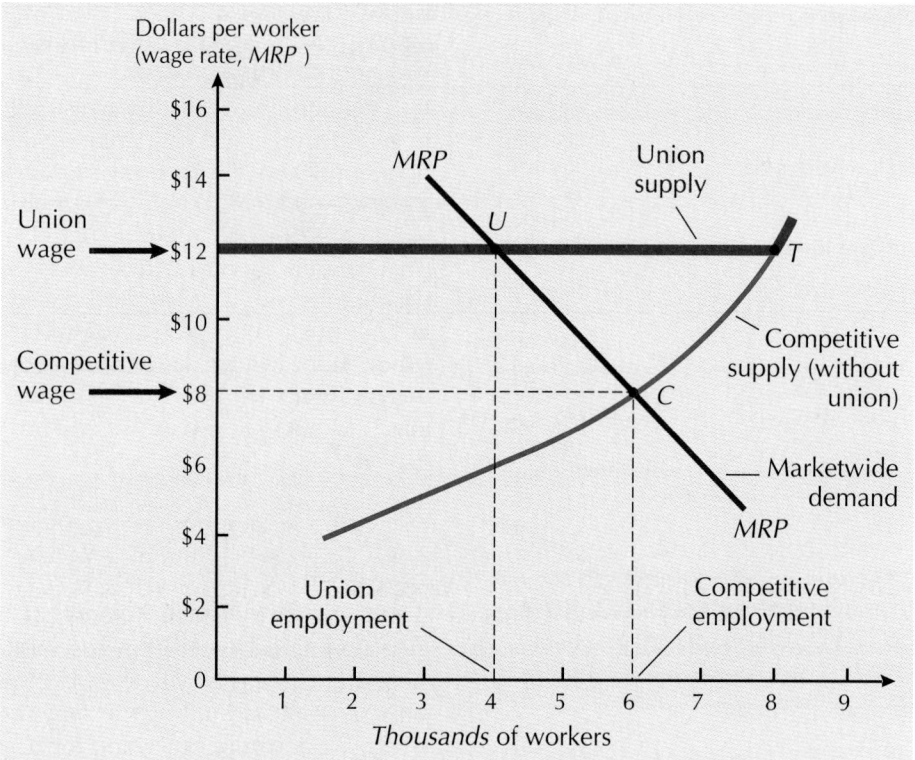

FIGURE 31.5   Industrial or Inclusive Unionism

Threatening a strike to exercise power, a union that includes virtually all of an industry's workers can set a wage $12, above the competitive wage of $8. It is like a wage floor, so with the union, the labor supply becomes horizontal at the set wage. Employers hire according to their collective demand (MRP), resulting in a level of employment below the competitive level—4,000 workers versus 6,000.

With the union, the firm's supply curve would appear horizontal at the higher $12 wage rate. This reduces the quantity of firm demand, which, of course, explains the reduced marketwide quantity of labor demanded.

B
Craft or Exclusive Unionism

Figure 31.6 illustrates the consequences of craft or exclusive unionism. Our assumed competitive equilibrium at point C remains unchanged. Now suppose an exclusive union is formed. Worker entry into the occupation is restricted, limiting the number of workers possessing the skill for this line of labor. This strategy shifts the supply of labor to the left (fewer workers at each possible wage rate). In Figure 31.6, this moves the labor market equilib-

rium from point C to point U*. As the hourly wage rises from $8 to $11, employment falls from 6,000 to 4,500.

The higher skill levels associated with craft trades assist union efforts to restrict supply in this way. The typical person on the street cannot become a professional airplane pilot, electrician, machinist, or musician overnight. Occupational preliminaries and preparations are imperative. Hence exclusionary practices in these cases have taken the form of especially high membership initiation fees, lengthy apprenticeship periods at low pay, and occasionally even quotas or fixed limits on new membership.

Some unions are assisted in their exclusionary efforts by **occupational licensing,** which is imposed by state and local government authorities. In these instances, many of which extend to nonunion occupations, a worker cannot practice his

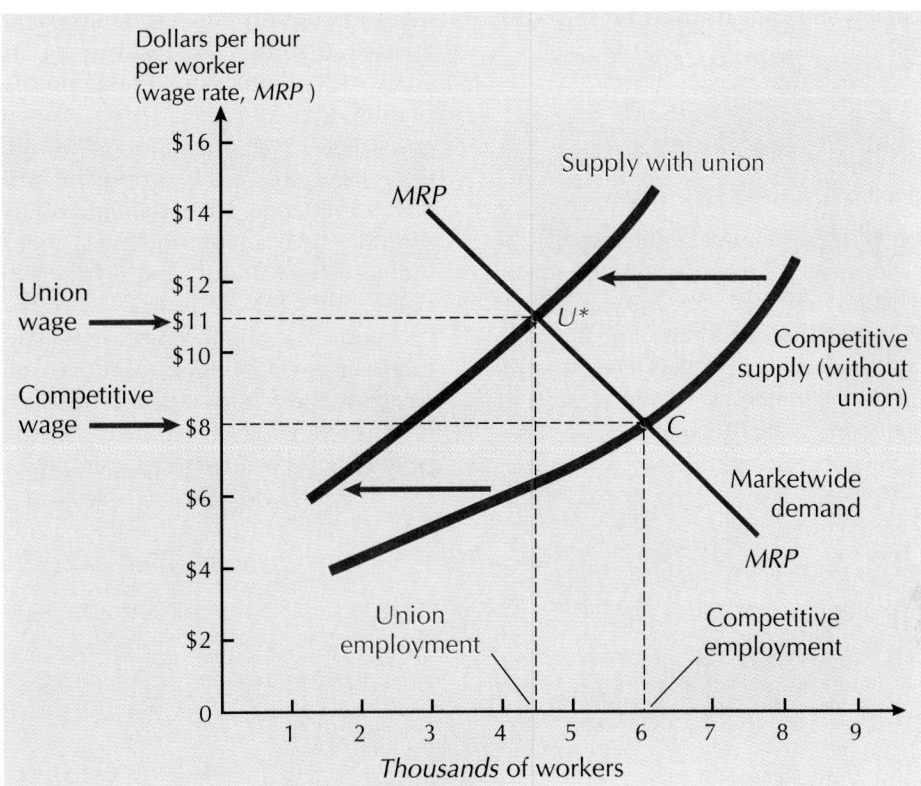

FIGURE 31.6 Craft or Exclusive Unionism

If a union can restrict entry into an occupation, it will shift the supply of labor to the left. Less labor will be offered at each wage in comparison to the competitive supply. Here the exclusive unionism raises the wage from $8 to $11 an hour. Employment drops from 6,000 to 4,500.

or her craft without first obtaining an official license. The occupations covered vary from state to state, but they include doctors, lawyers, heavy equipment operators, TV repairmen, barbers, plumbers, pilots, electricians, cosmeticians, and many more (even taxidermists, lightning rod sales people, and tree surgeons in some areas). The entry requirements imposed on workers are ostensibly designed to ensure good performance from practitioners in these occupations, so that consumers will be protected against the financial hazards of cheats and incompetents. However, these requirements are commonly established and enforced by practitioners already in the occupation—doctors for doctors, electricians for electricians, and so on. This gives current practitioners an opportunity to protect their economic interests. They often make licensing requirements for newcomers so rigorous and expensive in terms of

schooling, testing, and the like that those requirements become unduly restrictive. In short, occupational licensing, supported by unions and other professional groups, can artificially lower the labor supply, as indicated in Figure 31.6.

Notice that in both models of union behavior studied so far—inclusive and exclusive unionism—the higher wage gained by the union comes at the expense of employment, which falls. Just how far employment falls with any given increase in wages will depend on the elasticity of demand for labor. If labor demand is inelastic, then the percentage drop in employment will be *less* than the percentage increase in the wage rate. If labor demand is elastic, then the percentage drop in employment will be *more* than the percentage increase in wages. At especially high wage levels, demand is likely to become elastic, so this drop in employment indicates why unions, even quite powerful unions, would not want to hoist wages astronomically.

C

Increased Labor Demand

Labor demand is largely outside the control of labor unions because it depends on the basic forces underlying marginal revenue product, namely, product demand and productivity. Still, there are notable instances in which labor unions have been able to influence the demand side in order to gain higher wages than otherwise. This union strategy, when successful, curbs employ-

ment losses and may even allow employment increases in conjunction with wage increases.

Figure 31.7 illustrates. For comparison, the competitive equilibrium remains $8 in hourly wage and 6,000 in employment. Without union influence, labor demand is simply the *MRP* curve. With union influence, labor demand shifts to the right to *MRP**. As a consequence, the hourly wage increases to $10 and employment in the market *rises*, rather than falls, from 6,000 to 7,000.

Unions for public employees, such as policemen, firemen, school teachers, and sanitation workers, have been among the most successful unions following this strategy. Some studies show public sector unions raising employment for their

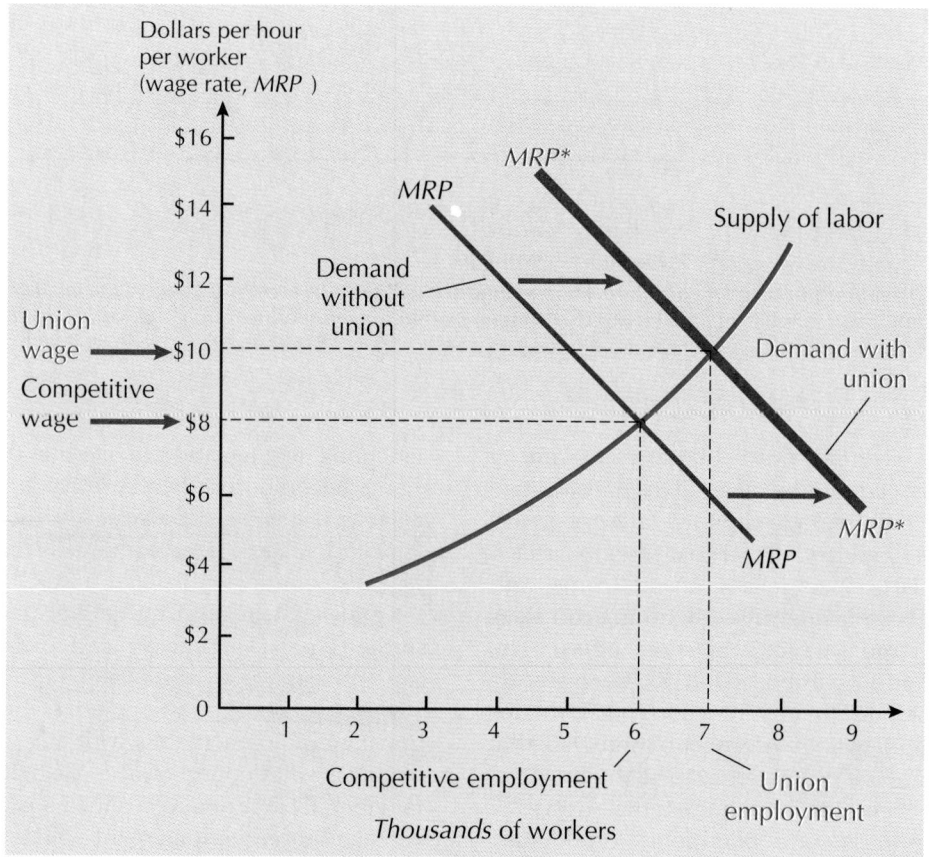

FIGURE 31.7 Unions Increasing the Demand for Labor

If the union can shift the demand for labor by altering work rules, gaining quotas on competitive imports, or the like, wages and employment both rise. Here the rightward shift in demand raises hourly wages from $8 to $10 and employment from 6,000 to 7,000 in comparison to the competitive levels.

members by as much as 10 percent.[3] The reason for this is that public sector unions can have much greater influence over employer behavior than private sector unions. Public sector unions push political buttons. They can gain greater budget expenditures for their occupational areas by lobbying legislatures, by campaigning for the election of officials friendly to their cause, and by supporting ballot initiatives. In effect, unionized government workers can thereby shift demand for their labor outward.

Examples of private sector unions influencing labor demand are more varied, and on the whole probably less impressive. Still, they do occur. The International Ladies' Garment Workers Union has from time to time advertised on national television, urging shoppers to "look for the union label." More commonly, some unions have obtained work rules that require a greater number of workers than employers would like to hire. This frequently happens when technological change reduces the need for workers and the union forestalls the resulting reduction in labor demand. Railway workers, for instance, forced railroads to operate with coal-stoking "firemen" long after the railroads switched to diesel locomotives. Musicians have obtained various work rules that leave many of them sitting idle while other musicians perform or recorded music is played. Practices such as these are called *featherbedding.*

> Make-work rules designed to increase artificially the number of workers on a particular job results in **featherbedding.**

Sometimes private sector unions follow the example set by public sector unions and attempt to influence the labor demand through politics. Governmental restrictions on imports, for example, can boost the demand for domestic unionized labor. Unions for the auto workers, steel workers, and textile workers have been among the most successful at lobbying for tariffs and quotas against imports that would reduce jobs in the United States. (By one estimate, quota restrictions on Japanese auto imports during the early 1980s created about 4,600 jobs for auto workers. Because auto prices rose with these supply restrictions, the estimated annual cost to consumers was roughly $240,000 per job created.[4])

IV
Bilateral Monopoly

Situations in which unions face numerous competitive employers, as assumed previously, are rather unusual. Union presence is more commonly associated with monopsony (or oligopsony) on the employers' side, partly because unions are easier to organize when fewer employers are involved. Indeed, we have had to strain a bit to give examples in the previous section. And those examples citing auto workers, steel workers, school teachers, and several others were not fully appropriate because employers in those markets are not fully competitive.

Once monopsony is combined with unionism, the result is, in the extreme, *bilateral monopoly.* Figure 31.8 captures the theory by combining Figure 31.4 (pure monopsony) with Figure 31.5 (inclusive unionism). As indicated by our earlier analysis, the monopsonistic employer will seek a wage of $6, which is below the competitive wage of $8. In contrast, the union will strive for a wage of $12, well above the competitive wage. A gap thus opens up between the wage targets of the two sides, $6 versus $12. What will the actual wage turn out to be? Economic theory offers no solid answer. Bargaining power and strategies become crucial. The greater the power of the employer, the lower the ultimate wage. Conversely, the stronger the union, the higher the wage. As we shall see later, the balance of power depends on many factors, such as the financial health of the employer and the current level of unemployment in the industry. The main point is that, because bargaining prevails, economic theory yields a *range* of wage possibilities instead of one certain solution.

---

[3]Richard B. Freeman, "Unionism Comes to the Public Sector," *Journal of Economic Literature* (March 1986), pp. 61–62.

[4]David G. Tarr and Morris E. Morkre, *Aggregate Costs to the United States of Tariffs and Quotas on Imports* (Washington, D.C.: Federal Trade Commission Bureau of Economics Staff Report, 1984), pp. 69–70.

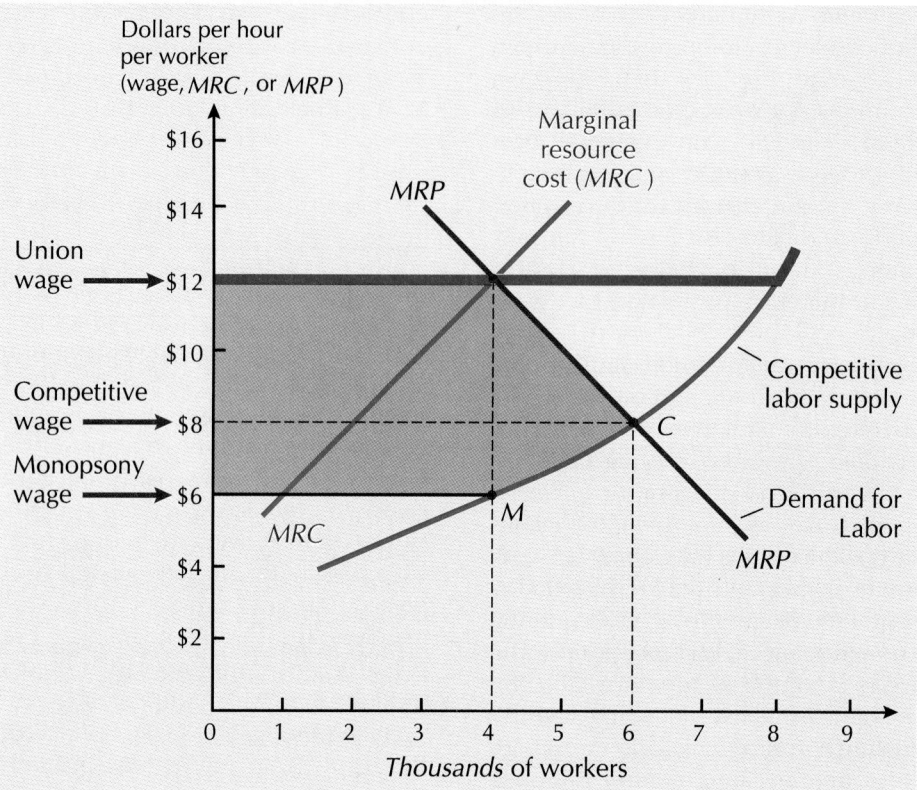

FIGURE 31.8 Bilateral Monopoly in a Labor Market

When a union confronts a monopsonist, the resulting wage could be as high as that preferred by the union ($12) or as low as that desired by the monopsonist ($6), or any amount between this range. The result is indeterminate in theory, something to be settled by bargaining. Given the wage range, employment will be set by demand or supply—demand if the wage is above the competitive rate of $8 (e.g., 5,000 at $10) or supply if the wage is below the competitive rate (e.g., 4,000 at $6).

Theory yields another, equally intriguing result here. *Once the wage is set by bargaining,* the monopsonistic employer no longer sees a divergence between the marginal resource cost (*MRC*) and the labor supply curve (wage rate), as indicated in Figure 31.8. Once the wage is set by contract agreement, variations in employment cannot affect it. The employer can hire as many workers, or as few, as he or she wants at the contractual wage (constrained only by the competitive labor supply). Hence the employer will then see the supply curve as perfectly horizontal, and the marginal resource cost will then be the same as the wage rate. If, for instance, the agreed hourly wage is $8, each extra worker always adds $8 to the total hourly labor cost. Given this situation, the employer

will hire workers out to the point where the wage equals demand (*MRP*) or where no further labor is supplied, whichever comes first. Note that in Figure 31.8 demand determines employment in the $8 to $12 range. With a wage of $10, for example, 5,000 workers would be hired. On the other hand, supply determines employment in the $8 to $6 range. Thus, *employment is likewise theoretically uncertain until the wage is set, because it depends on what that wage happens to be.*

Moreover, it can now be seen that, *in theory,* unionism need not cause a drop in employment when it engineers a wage increase, or push a labor market away from competitive results. *Given monopsony,* the introduction of a union could raise the wage *and* employment, moving the market from the monopsony result (point *M* in Figure 31.8) *toward the competitive result* (point *C* in Figure 31.8). Conversely, *given unionism*, the presence of monopsony could likewise move the market *toward competitive results* instead of away from them. In short, *bilateral monopoly can yield competitive results*. If bargaining in bilateral monopoly fixes the wage at $8 in Figure 31.8, the monopsonistic employer will see a horizontal supply curve at $8 and will, accordingly, hire out to point *C*. There, with 6,000 employees, the supply curve (horizontal at the $8 wage) meets the demand curve. There, in other words, the marginal resource cost, $8, equals the marginal revenue product, $8.

(Note: In the hypothetical examples of Figures 31.4 and 31.5, the monopsony employment and the union employment were the same, 4,000. In Figure 31.8, this brings *MRP* and *MRC* together at the union's preferred wage of $12. This need not occur. It just simplifies the analysis to do it this way.)

■ *CHECK YOUR BEARINGS*

The best review was in the earlier overview. Go back to Figures 31.1 and 31.2. Rethink their contents and the text on pages 635–637. They summarize theories of imperfect competition in labor markets (except for Figures 31.6 and 31.7).

V
Unions: Practice and Policy

We have defined unions. We have distinguished industrial and craft unions. We have also theorized about their impact on wage levels and employment. Still, many issues remain. Why do workers join unions? How are unions organized? What do unions really do?

In the following introductory section, we briefly explore matters of motivation and organization. We then focus on the two main activities of unions—(1) gaining *recognition* from employers as the legitimate representatives of workers and (2) *bargaining* with employers about wages, fringe benefits, working conditions, and the like.

A
Introduction

1. Why Unions? As workers, people naturally desire high wages, nice working conditions, and respect and fair play from the boss. They can pursue these ends by *individual action*. If a worker does not like her present job, she can quit, seeking a better job elsewhere, hopeful that some other employer is competing for good workers by offering better wages, better working conditions, and other improvements. Such individual action is, of course, highly prized in our society, where individualism and freedom are closely associated.

An alternative means of pursuing these goals is *collective action*, which is the essence of unionism. The basic idea behind unionism is that workers can often pursue their employment goals more effectively through collective action than they can through individual action.

In this connection there are, from the workers' point of view, several benefits of unionism. These can be divided into two broad categories—*monopoly* benefits and *voice* benefits. Monopoly benefits include the following:

1. Unions give workers greater bargaining power to extract higher wages than otherwise.
2. This bargaining power can also be used to extract other benefits unattainable by competitive individualism—e.g., generous retirement pensions, long paid vacations, and featherbedding work rules.
3. Unions may act more effectively in politics to obtain monopolistic governmental protection, such as occupational licensing or import quotas.

In contrast, voice benefits concern matters of fairness, security, and equity. Without a union, for instance, a firm might fire older workers just before they become eligible for pension rights. This could be considered unfair, and the collective voice of a union might be able to prevent it by actions such as these:

1. By bargaining for uniform pay scales for certain jobs, a union can achieve equal pay for equal work within a firm.

2. A union can influence the criteria for promotions, layoffs, sick leaves, and task assignments in order to achieve greater fairness.

3. A union can establish grievance procedures to handle day-to-day disputes between individual workers and management.[5]

Why, in light of these several benefits, do many workers choose *not* to unionize? These's a one-word answer—*costs*. The costs of union membership include the following:[6]

1. *Strike costs:* Threatened strikes give unions bargaining power, but actual strikes cost members lost pay.

2. *Job loss:* The higher wages extracted by unions can reduce members' employment.

3. *Loss of individualism and freedom:* Unionism often introduces greater job rigidity, reducing rewards for individual initiative and curbing variations in task assignments. Moreover, unions require dues, attendance at meetings, and other forms of support from members, thereby imposing costs and impinging on their freedom.

Because workers experience costs as well as benefits, it is possible to theorize in terms of the demand and supply of unionism. But let's move on to union organization as it prevails in the United States.

2. Union Organization Unions are organized at three levels—(1) labor federations, (2) national unions, and (3) local unions. *Labor federations* are associations of national unions. In turn, *national unions* are collections of local unions. Finally, *local unions* are the immediate, grass-roots organizations with which members deal daily.

At present, there is only one labor federation in the United States, the *American Federation of Labor and Congress of Industrial Organizations (AFL-*

CIO). The awkward name derives from the time when, between 1935 and 1955, there were two separate federations, one for craft unions, the American Federation of Labor (AFL), and another for industrial unions, the Congress of Industrial Organizations (CIO). The AFL-CIO is a voluntary association of more than 90 national unions, both craft and industrial, with a total membership of about 14 million workers. Not all national unions participate in the AFL-CIO. Still, the AFL-CIO accounts for two thirds of all union members, so it has hefty influence. That influence does not, however, extend to the tasks of gaining employer recognition or collective bargaining with employers. The AFL-CIO settles disputes between national unions, lobbies for favorable labor legislation, campaigns for friendly politicians, promotes the ideals of unionism through public relations, and engages in other activities favorable to organized labor generally.

National unions are, for our purposes, the main union organizations of interest. They comprise the chief power centers—working to gain employer recognition, negotiating labor contracts, and calling strikes. Local unions share in these responsibilities, but the main function of most local unions is to represent workers in a single plant or a single city. Local unions commonly administer labor contracts, serving members directly and personally.

B
Recognition

Assume that some employees of a firm form a union. Before the union can bargain with management, it must gain management's *recognition*. If management refuses to sit down at the bargaining table to negotiate and this refusal is legal, there is nothing the union can do except use muscle, a strike for instance, to gain the employer's recognition. But, in order to strike effectively, the union needs many members, and membership may be minimal without employer recognition. Hence, obtaining employer recognition is a crucial step in unionism.

> **Employer recognition** occurs when the employer acknowledges the union as the workers' legitimate representative for purposes of collective bargaining.

---

[5]Voice benefits are stressed by Richard B. Freeman and James L. Medoff, *What Do Unions Do?* (New York: Basic Books, 1984).

[6]Bruce E. Kaufman, *The Economics of Labor Markets and Labor Relations* (Chicago: Dryden Press, 1986), pp. 414–416.

Because of its importance, the issue of recognition is central to the history of the American labor movement and to trends in union membership. Figure 31.9 illustrates. It shows union membership in the United States as a percentage of total nonagricultural employment from 1890 to the present. Before 1935, union membership was relatively low, amounting to less than 10 percent of nonagricultural workers previous to 1910 and less than 15 percent for most of the next quarter of a century. Beginning in 1935, union membership ballooned, mainly because of the National Labor Relations Act (or Wagner Act), which was passed in 1935 and which made employer recognition much easier to obtain than before. The percentage of union membership began to slide after union organizing power was checked by the Taft-Hartley Act of 1947. That slide slowed temporarily after 1962, when workers in the public sector began to obtain recognition from their governmental employers, starting principally with the federal government. Most recently, the decline has accelerated, partly, perhaps even largely, because of growing employer resistance to union organizing efforts. Let's survey some details.

1. History Before the 1930s Prior to the 1930s, in the absence of any government policies favor-

able to unionism, employers could legally refuse recognition even if a majority of their workers wanted a union. Moreover, employers had at their command a number of weapons they could use to thwart union organizing and to resist recognition.

First, employers could simply *fire* anyone who became a union member or union advocate. This tactic, **discriminatory discharge,** was embellished by two related tactics—the yellow-dog contract and blacklisting. In **yellow-dog contracts** workers had to agree not to become union members as a condition of their employment. No contract, no job. And if a worker broke the contract by joining a union, he or she could be fined or imprisoned as well as put out of work. When **blacklisting** workers, employers circulated lists of known union members or "labor agitators" so that a union sympathizer fired by one employer would not be hired by another. This way, workers could not dodge the resistance of one employer by turning to another, not even one in a distant town. Nor could they easily shed the union stigma by quitting their union while switching employers.

A second employer weapon was the **lockout.** Here management closes down the workplace, temporarily refusing to operate. In the early years of this century, when workers were generally

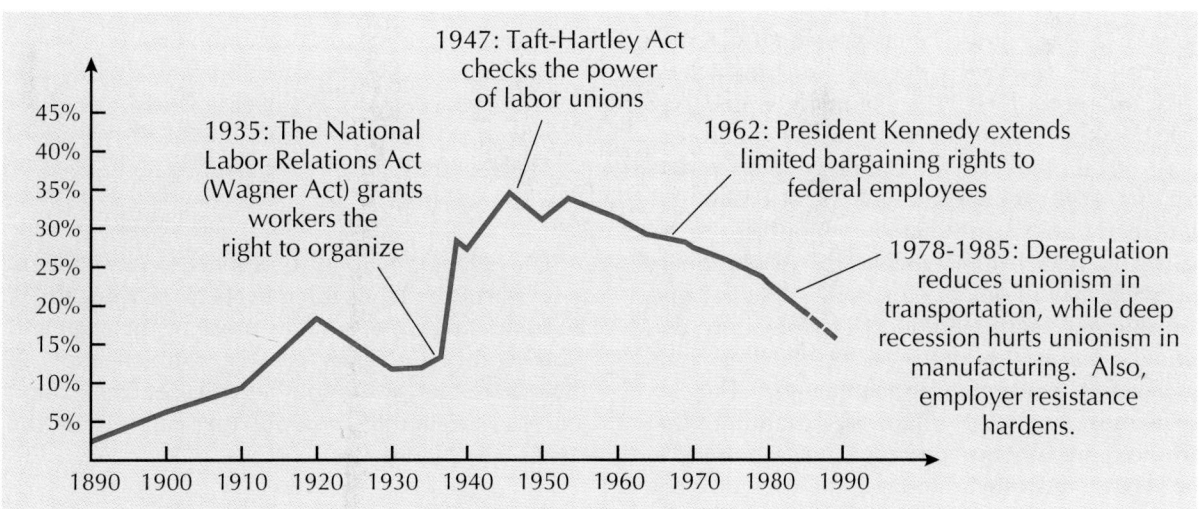

FIGURE 31.9 *Union Membership in the United States a Percentage of Nonagricultural Employment*

(Sources: Robert J. Flanagan, Robert S. Smith, and Ronald G. Ehrenberg, Labor Economics and Labor Relations. *Glenview, Ill.: Scott, Foresman, 1984, p. 334; Larry T. Adams, "Changing Employment Patterns of Organized Workers,"* Monthly Labor Review, *February 1985, pp. 25–31.)*

poorer than they are now, and lacking savings or a union strike fund, this tactic commonly imposed heavier costs on the workers than on the employers, thereby often making it an effective weapon.

Third, employers sometimes established **company unions.** These had the appearance of unions. Indeed, they often bestowed generous benefits on their members—pensions, group insurance, and social programs. Yet they were not independent unions. They were established by employers only as paternalistic shields against genuine unions. Company unions favored the interests of employers over those of workers in the event of conflict between the two.

Aside from these employer weapons, there were in those early years several *government weapons* that employers could launch on their behalf. The **injunction** proved especially potent. An injunction is a court order prohibiting certain actions, which if violated brings charges of criminal contempt of court. Although union membership itself was legal and could not be enjoined, many of the actions unions had to take to gain recognition from employers before the 1930s were regularly curbed by court injunctions. Striking, picketing, and boycotting could often be squashed in this way.

Given managements' hostility toward unions and the unfavorable legal setting, unions frequently took strong measures to gain recognition. Thus the early history of the labor movement contains instances of massive violence. A union would strike for recognition. The company would hire strikebreakers. And bloody clashes often ensued—exemplified by the Pullman strike of 1894 and the Ludlow Massacre of 1914. Frustrated, many early unions advocated communism or socialism to realize their goals. This revolutionary approach may have made matters worse because it deepened management's determination and tainted unionism in the eyes of many farmers, shopkeepers, and other noncombatants.

The most successful union organization of that turbulent era was the *American Federation of Labor (AFL)*, forerunner of today's AFL-CIO. How the AFL survived while other unions crumbled is a very interesting and important question. Its answer partly explains the basic orientation of modern American unionism (as opposed to that in Europe or elsewhere). The leadership of Samuel Gompers was vital here. Gompers, now rightly called "the father of the American labor movement," held fast to three fundamental tenets: *(1) practical business unionism, (2) political neutrality for unions, and (3) autonomy for each trade or craft.*

1. *Practical business unionism* aimed at achieving immediate bread-and-butter benefits for workers rather than overthrowing the capitalist system. Higher wages and better working conditions, not socialism or communism, were the AFL's objectives.

2. *Political neutrality for unions* meant that the AFL would not ally itself with the Democratic or Republican Party, nor would it form its own "labor" party (as unions did in Europe). Gompers believed that organized labor should support political friends and oppose political foes regardless of their party affiliation. He also favored government neutrality in labor affairs because that would have been an improvement over the government's hostility of the time.

3. *Autonomy for each trade or craft* implied craft unionism instead of industrial unionism. Strikes, threatened or actual, were the main means of getting employer recognition in those days. Gompers believed that craft unions were most potent in this regard. Their narrow occupational focus provided cohesiveness or solidarity. Moreover, the specialized skills of craft workers could not be easily replaced by strikebreakers, reducing the power of management vis-á-vis the unions.

These tenets helped to unionize more than 15 percent of the labor force by 1920. But neglect of industrial workers, such as those in the steel and auto industries, plus greater sophistication of managements' antiunion activities, caused union coverage to shrink sharply thereafter until the 1930s (see Figure 31.9).

2

History from the 1930s to the 1970s

The Great Depression triggered many government policy changes. Those in labor law were especially momentous.

First, the *Norris-LaGuardia Act* of 1932 shifted the balance of power a bit. The act outlawed yellow-dog contracts and made injunctions against union activities more difficult for employers to obtain.

Second, the *National Labor Relations Act* of 1935 (unofficially called the *Wagner Act*) shifted the balance of power immensely. The act did so in three main ways:

1. *It outlawed several of management's most potent antiunion weapons*, namely, company unions, discriminatory firings, blacklisting, and other "unfair labor practices."
2. *It required employer recognition* if a majority of workers voted to have a union represent them in collective bargaining. By law thereafter, a union receiving majority support from employees became the exclusive bargaining representative of all employees in the bargaining unit.
3. *It established the National Labor Relations Board (NLRB)* to conduct elections for union representation and to investigate, prosecute, and judge unfair labor practice charges against employers.

In short, the National Labor Relations Act set new rules for recognition. Majority rule rather than force became the means of establishing a bargaining relationship. The act has therefore been called the Magna Carta of the union movement.

The spurt in unionism after 1935 occurred mainly among industrial workers. Aside from the now greater ease of gaining recognition, industrial unions blossomed because of the *Congress of Industrial Organizations (CIO)*. Formed in 1935 by several industrial unions disenchanted by the AFL's fondness for craft unionism and its neglect of industrial workers, the CIO offered a labor federation for newly organized workers in steel, autos, rubber, and other industries.

Partly as a reaction against the burgeoning power of unions, the *Taft-Hartley Act* was passed in 1947, amending the National Labor Relations Act and tipping the balance of power back toward management. This act, in brief, gives rights to workers wishing *not* to unionize:

1. *It outlaws several union unfair labor practices* (such as coercing employees to vote for the union).

2. *It provides for decertification elections*, in which employees can vote to remove a union as their bargaining representative.
3. *It sets procedures to deal with major strikes* that might cripple the economy or endanger health and safety.
4. *It outlaws the closed shop in most industries and allows states to outlaw the union shop.*

An understanding of this last item hinges on definitions of *closed shop, union shop,* and *open shop.*

A **closed shop** requires the employer to hire only workers who are already union members.

A **union shop** gives employers freedom in hiring but requires employees to become union members after some period (usually 30 to 60 days).

An **open shop** allows employers to hire workers who are not (and need not become) union members.

Thus the Taft-Hartley Act curbed unionism when it struck down closed shops in most industries and when it expressly enabled states to pass laws banning all but the open shop. These **right-to-work laws,** which allow any employee to reject union membership, have been enacted in 20 states located primarily in the South and Southwest.

The union movement saw the Taft-Hartley Act as a setback. The downward trend in membership share following 1947 would suggest that it was. But other problems also contributed. In hopes of gaining clout and prestige for organized labor, the AFL and CIO merged to form the AFL-CIO in 1955. This helped. Shortly thereafter, though, congressional investigations—spearheaded by the McClellan Committee—discovered that leaders of the Teamsters Union had misused union funds, had embarrassing relations with the underworld, and had gained leadership positions by questionable means. In order to control union corruption, Congress passed the *Landrum-Griffin Act* in 1959. This act regulates the election of union officers, the management of union funds, and the rights of union members in dealing with their union.

During the 1960s, the union movement rebounded a bit. Most noteworthy among the historical developments was the spread of unionism in the public sector. Between 1963 and 1977, the proportion of federal employees in the executive branch covered by collective bargaining rose from 48 to 88 percent. Over the same period, membership in unions for state and local government employees more than doubled, rising from about 7 percent to roughly 17 percent of all such workers.

These gains helped to slow the slide in the share of union membership generally, but a qualifier is needed. Public sector unions are, by law, typically more limited in what they can do in comparison to private sector unions. For example, most federal employee unions can bargain over working conditions but not wages. Similarly, most states prohibit strikes by their employees.

3. Recent Membership Trends What have the 1980s wrought? The union movement lost 2.7 million members among employed workers between 1980 and 1984—a severe loss. Before the 1980s, unionism gained membership in *absolute numbers* even as its *percentage share* of employment fell because growth in the number of people employed exceeded growth in the number joining unions. During the 1980s, unionism lost in absolute numbers as well as in percentage share. And as a consequence, organized labor's percentage share plummeted during the early 1980s, falling below 20 percent for the first time in over 50 years (see Figure 31.9).

Several factors explain unions' dramatic recent decline. For one thing, unions have traditionally been especially strong in certain industries and regions of the country, and the share of overall economic activity accounted for by these strongholds has been dwindling for quite some time, even before the 1980s. Unionism has been popular in goods-producing industries like mining and manufacturing as opposed to service-producing industries like finance and insurance, yet economic growth has favored services over goods. Regionally, union strength has centered in the northern and northeastern states, while recent economic growth has especially blessed the southern and southwestern states. The unionized "rust belt" has stalled relative to the nonunion "sun belt."

In addition, increased management opposition to unions has taken a toll. By one estimate, 40 percent of organized labor's recent decline can be credited to this cause. Unfair practice charges against employers rose from 7,723 in 1960 to 31,281 in 1980. Firings of union sympathizers has, unions allege, been a main antiunion technique because, though illegal, such firings bring only light penalties against management and a single firing dampens the union ardor of many workers. In 1980, the National Labor Relations Board secured the reinstatement of 10,033 employees who had apparently suffered discriminatory discharge (up from 1,885 such reinstatements in 1960). Coincident with these developments, the percentage of decertification elections won by unions has been falling and the percentage of decertification elections lost by unions has been rising.[7] In short, this matter of employer recognition remains important.

Read Perspective 31B.

C
Collective Bargaining

Over 200,000 collective bargaining agreements are in force in the United States. What is *collective bargaining?*

> **Collective bargaining** consists of negotiations between representatives of labor and management over the terms and conditions of employment to which both parties will be bound for the duration of the labor agreement that normally results.[8]

Negotiating procedures vary widely. Some cover all workers in an industry nationally, the firms acting as a coalition. Others cover only individual firms or plants. Some negotiations occur every year, others every 2 or 3 years. The resulting agreements likewise vary immensely. Still, several generalities are possible. We shall concentrate on (1) contract contents and (2) dispute resolution.

[7]Paul Weiler, "Promises to Keep: Securing Workers' Rights to Self-Organization Under the NLRA," *Harvard Law Review* (June 1983), pp. 1769–1803.

[8]Robert J. Flanagan, Robert S. Smith, and Ronald G. Ehrenberg, *Labor Economics and Labor Relations* (Glenview, Ill.: Scott, Foresman, 1984), p. 424.

PERSPECTIVE 31B
A Union–Management Tangle

Five years ago, union workers at Ingersoll-Rand Co. made bearings in South Bend, Ind., hand tools in South Deerfield, Mass., and pneumatic tools in Athens, Pa.

Today, the bearing plant is closed, the work shifted to a nonunion factory. The hand-tool plant has been sold. And although Ingersoll-Rand still makes tools in Athens, the workers have voted to disband their union.

In the past few years, Ingersoll-Rand has moved production from union plants in the North to nonunion plants in the South. It has withdrawn from businesses, including some that were heavily unionized. And where it has had the chance, it has encouraged workers to reject their unions. The result: 30 percent of Ingersoll-Rand's U.S. production workers now are represented by unions, down from 60 per cent at the end of 1981. . . .

By law, companies aren't permitted to close plants, move production or fire workers in order to weaken a union, but they can take those steps for economic reasons. The National Labor Relations Board has ruled three times in the past decade that Ingersoll-Rand engaged in unfair labor practices, but given the company's size, its legal record at the NLRB isn't unusual.[9]

[9]*Wall Street Journal*, June 13, 1985.

1. *Contract Contents*   The main contents of collective bargaining agreements concern union security, wages and hours, fringe benefits, job security, and grievance procedures. Let's cover each.

First, *union security:* Where legal, the closed shop and the union shop are negotiable, not automatic. Hence contracts typically specify what requirements, if any, hold workers to union membership.

Second, *wages and hours:* These items are usually the guts of labor agreements. Hourly wages are specified for various jobs at various levels of worker seniority. In conjunction, the number of hours in the regular work week will be set, such as 35 or 40. And pay levels for deviations from these standard hours will be indicated, such as those for overtime and night work. The factors affecting the negotiations on these matters can be complex. They include (1) the pay scales prevailing in other industries, companies, or plants; (2) productivity changes, either past or planned; (3) the financial ability of the industry or company to pay; and (4) the rate of price inflation. In recent decades, for instance, during periods of rapid price inflation, this last item has gained increasing importance. As a result, a large percentage of workers covered by collective bargaining agreements obtained automatic *cost-of-living adjustments (COLAs),* whereby wages are increased automatically with increases in the Consumer Price Index.

Third, *fringe benefits:* As much as 30 percent of a union worker's total compensation can be in the form of fringe benefits instead of straight-time pay. These include pensions; life, accident, and health insurance; paid vacation time; and sick leave. Contracts specify the details of what fringes are granted.

Fourth, *job security:* In the event of layoffs, who goes first? Why can a worker be fired? If a worker changes departments within a company, does he or she lose seniority? These matters relate to job security. During times of high unemployment within an industry, they take on tremendous importance. In general, seniority is paramount.

Fifth, *grievance procedures:* Although contracts can be quite detailed, they cannot anticipate the many special situations that arise almost daily. Hence, over 98 percent of all major collective bargaining agreements provide for grievance procedures, which enable workers to appeal managerial decisions relating to the contract. As a typical first step, the disgruntled worker complains to the union shop steward, who talks to the worker's supervisor. In subsequent steps, the complaint is handled by ever higher levels of authority until resolution is found.

Because contract provisions are so many and varied, the negotiating process may include trade-offs between these categories. One side may give ground in one area in order to gain elsewhere. Hence, the word *bargaining* covers more than merely reaching compromises within each contract category. During negotiations in 1985, for instance, the United Auto Workers (UAW) relaxed their demands for wage increases in order to obtain a greater degree of job security. The plum in their contract with General Motors was a $1 billion program that would provide jobs to most GM workers who would otherwise be laid off because of new technology or negotiated productivity improvements.

2. Dispute Resolution Compromise and give-and-take are usually enough to arrive at a contract. Over 95 percent of all bargaining negotiations reach peaceful settlements. But some differences may persist to the point where negotiations break down. Each side then has an "ultimate" weapon. Unions may *strike*. Less commonly, employers may impose a *lockout*.

Strikes receive great attention from the news media because they can seriously disrupt the economy or inconvenience the public. Moreover, they sometimes provoke violence. On the whole, however, strikes are not as debilitating as they might seem. Between 1975 and 1981, for instance, the average amount of annual working time lost to strikes was only .16 percent, much less than the time lost to coffee breaks or goofing off. Moreover, strikes have less economic wollop when durable goods manufacturers are able to build up product inventories to sustain sales during the strike, or when the production process is so highly automated that managerial personnel can continue operations for a long time despite the walkout.

Whatever their effect on the general public, strikes can be effective for unions because they often impose severe costs on companies. In 1983, for instance, the Caterpillar Tractor Company lost over $200 million in profits while struck. On the other hand, workers likewise suffer. Each worker striking Caterpillar lost over $12,000 in income.

Indeed, some striking workers risk losing their jobs. In 1981, when the Professional Air Traffic Controllers Organization (PATCO) went on strike against the Federal Aviation Administration, President Reagan responded by firing the striking controllers and replacing them with nonunion controllers. The fact that strikes are costly to workers as well as employers helps to explain several things: (1) why the strike weapon is actually used so little; (2) why strikes often end without management surrendering to the demands of the union, resulting in a compromise on both sides; and (3) why occasionally strikes result in total union defeat. Thus, the unions' ultimate weapon is less than truly ultimate. It is a double-edged sword that can cut both ways.

VI
The Impact of Unions

Unions stir bitter controversy. Critics decry them for being too corrupt, too powerful, and too inefficient. On the other hand, defenders claim that unions should be praised for giving dignity, security, fairness, and prosperity to millions of workers who toil in their service to the economy.

The controversy comes as no surprise. Unions, as we have suggested, may have "monopoly" effects and "voice" effects. From society's point of view, these are typically "bad" and "good." Let's review the evidence on monopoly and voice effects, and then close with a brief interpretation of the findings.

A
Monopoly Effects of Unions

Evidence solidly confirms that unions have a positive effect on *members'* wages. The word *members* needs to be stressed because unions apparently do not raise the wages of workers generally. Rather, they (1) raise the wages of union members above what they would be in competitive labor markets. This (2) reduces employment in unionized sectors below what it would be otherwise, causing those left unemployed in union sectors to seek work in nonunion sectors. In turn, (3) the added supply of workers in nonunion sectors depresses nonunion wages *below* what they would be otherwise. Hence the wage impact of unions is usually measured as the *differential* between observed union wages (affected positively) and nonunion wages (affected negatively), holding other factors constant.

Estimates of the union/nonunion wage differential vary. Depending on the data, the time, and other influences, union wages exceed nonunion wages by a little or a lot. Still, the differential is *almost always positive*, attesting to the monopoly power of unions in general. Figure 31.10 illustrates the overall level of the union/nonunion wage differential from 1920 to 1980. The differential tends to rise during periods of economic sluggishness and fall during booms. Lately, the differential has

been rising despite the adverse trends in union membership. Indeed, the rising differential has contributed to those membership trends. Higher wages imply reduced employment, and reduced employment implies fewer members.[10]

Unions also have a positive impact on fringe benefits—especially pensions, vacation pay, and life, accident, and health insurance. In fact, it appears that the percentage increase in fringe benefits spending attributable to unionism exceeds the percentage increase in wages attributable to unionism. Data from the 1970s indicate the consequences. Looking only at wages, unionism

[10]Peter Linneman and Michael L. Wachter, "Rising Union Premiums and the Declining Boundaries Among Noncompeting Groups," *American Economic Review* (May 1986), pp. 103–108.

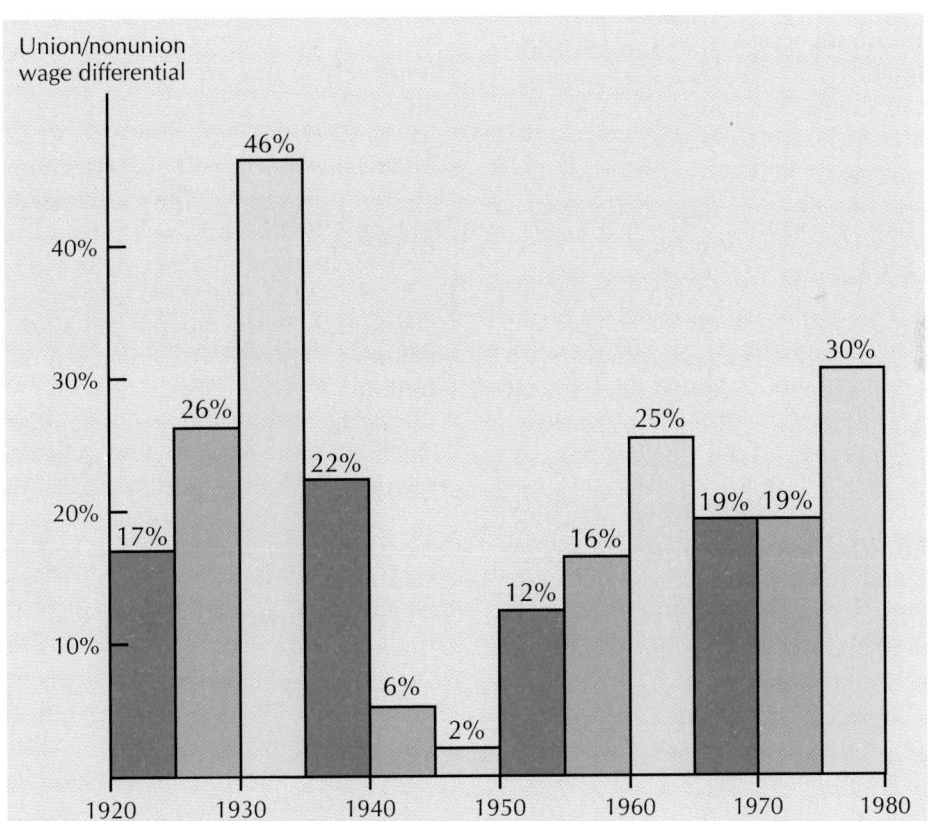

FIGURE 31.10 *Union Wage Differential Over Time*

(Source: George Johnson, "Changes Over Time in the Union/Nonunion Wage Differential in the United States." University of Michigan, February 1981, mimeographed, Table 2, as presented in Richard B. Freeman and James L. Medoff, What Do Unions Do? *New York: Basic Books, 1984, p. 53.)*

boosted worker compensation about 20 percent on average. Looking at wages *plus* fringes, unionism lifted total labor compensation 25 percent relative to nonunion workers.[11]

Productivity is yet another possible measure of monopoly effects. To the extent that unions use that power to obtain featherbedding work rules, they retard productivity. As suggested by our earlier references to railroad firemen and idle musicians, instances of this are not hard to find. Still, the available evidence is neither sufficiently abundant nor adequately clear-cut to conclude that unions, on average, reduce productivity. Consequently, a debate rages, consuming many pages of economics literature. Indeed, there is some evidence that unions often *increase* productivity rather than reduce it.[12]

Taken together, the monopoly effects of unionism explain why employers harbor hostility toward unionism. On the whole, the *profits* of unionized firms are substantially lower than those of nonunion firms.

B
Voice Effects of Unions

As Freeman and Medoff put it, the voice aspect of unionism "changes the employment relationship from a casual dating game, in which people look elsewhere at the first serious problem, to a more permanent 'marriage,' in which they seek to resolve disputes through discussion and negotiation."[13] If this is so, then unionism should reduce labor turnover. Unionism should lower worker quit rates and lengthen job tenure. Evidence indicates that it does. Holding wages and other variables fixed, Freeman and Medoff find that unionism reduces quits in the range of 31 to 65 percent,

while it increases job tenure an average of 23 to 32 percent.

Aside from worker turnover, the unions' voice also appears to affect the uniformity of wage rates within plants, firms, and industries that are unionized. Unionism tends to *equalize* the pay of similar workers across different plants and firms within industries. Moreover, unions tend to reduce the pay differential between highly paid white-collar workers and blue-collar workers.

C
Interpretation

Unionism thus creates winners and losers. Both belong to society. Hence it is not possible to reach sweeping conclusions about whether unions are good or bad from society's viewpoint. Let's review the debate in terms of the basic questions What? and Who?

Regarding What?, the monopoly effects of unionism leap to mind. Critics of unionism point out that union gains in wages and fringes lead to allocation inefficiency, just as does monopoly in product markets. These inefficiencies cost the economy $30 to $60 billion annually. Defenders of unions reply by saying that these losses are small relative to the gross national product, so we shouldn't fret over them.

Regarding Who?, the defenders of unions claim that the voice effects deserve praise. The greater equality of earnings across plants and firms secured by unions serves society's goals of equity and fairness. On the other hand, critics point out that unions increase inequality by creating a large union/nonunion wage differential. Moreover, the critics question whether the unions' equalizing, to the extent that it occurs, is really good. The wage uniformity attained by unions may stifle incentives, they say.

Whatever side you take in this debate, you must now acknowledge that unions are a prominent part of our economic landscape. Some people urge their abolition. Others want to unionize all workers. Most seem to accept the middle course taken by present policy.

---

[11]Freeman and Medoff, *What Do Unions Do?*, pp. 62–64.

[12]*Ibid.*, pp. 162–180. But for a critique, see John T. Addison, "What Do Unions Really Do?" *Journal of Labor Research* (Spring 1985), pp. 127–146.

[13]Freeman and Medoff, *What Do Unions Do?*, p. 94.

SUMMARY

1. Theory posits three main cases of labor market imperfection—monopsony, unionism, and bilateral monopoly (a combination of the first two).

2. With monopsony, there is only one employer. When there is competition on the workers' side of the market, the monopsonist sees the rising marketwide supply. Marginal resource cost (*MRC*) consequently rises above supply. Equating *MRC* with the marginal revenue product (*MRP*) to maximize profit, the monopsonist will pay a lower wage and employ fewer workers than would be the case with competition on both sides.

3. Under unionism, workers act collectively. When coupled with competition among employers, it offers several theoretical possibilities. (a) The inclusive model—typical of industrial unions—sets the wage at some minimum, enforced by threatened strike. (b) The exclusive model—typical of craft unions—shifts the labor supply to the left, thereby raising the wage. In both of these models, employment falls below the competitive level as the wage rises above the competitive level. (c) If the union can shift the demand for labor outward, it can maintain or increase employment while raising the wage rate. This is most successfully practiced by public sector unions.

4. Under bilateral monopoly, wage and employment levels are theoretically indeterminate. The employer wants a low wage. The union strives for a high wage. A gap opens. Once bargaining sets the wage, the employer's *MRC* matches the wage, so competitive results are theoretically possible here, though unlikely.

5. Unionism offers possible monopoly benefits and voice benefits to workers, encouraging membership. Monopoly benefits include higher wages, richer fringe benefits, and protection against competition. Voice benefits secure greater fairness and equity in pay, job security, and grievance procedures.

6. Still, many workers choose not to unionize. The costs include strike costs, job losses, and less individualism and freedom.

7. Union organization spans three levels: (a) labor federations, which bring national unions into association, (b) national unions, and (c) local unions.

8. Union activities center on two main issues—employer recognition and collective bargaining.

9. Recognition occurs when the employer acknowledges the union as the workers' legitimate representative. Forceful strikes were the main means of gaining recognition prior to 1935 because employers forcefully resisted unions with discriminatory discharges, blacklists, and the like. The AFL survived the hostile environment, guided by Samuel Gompers and his principles.

10. The National Labor Relations Act of 1935 tied the hands of management and tied recognition to worker elections, setting up the National Labor Relations Board to regulate employer unfair practices as well as administer the elections.

11. Membership boomed, but then began to fall as a percentage of total employment after passage of the Taft-Hartley Act of 1947. This act curbed unfair union practices, provided decertification elections, and loosened membership obligations by outlawing the closed shop and allowing states to pass right-to-work laws.

12. Aside from growth in the public sector, union membership has declined recently with shifts in economic activity (e.g., away from goods toward services) and growing employer resistance.

13. Given recognition, collective bargaining produces contracts specifying union security, wages and hours, fringe benefits, job security, and grievance procedures.

14. When collective bargaining hits an impasse, unions strike. However, strikes can be as costly to unions as they are to management, sometimes more so.
15. Empirical evidence shows that unions raise wages and fringes above nonunion levels. They are also associated with lower quit rates and longer tenure. The evidence on productivity is mixed. Whether unions are, on balance, good or bad for the economy is a much debated question.

KEY TERMS

Bilateral monopoly
Monopsony
Labor union
Unionism
Marginal resource cost
Industrial union
Craft union
Strike
Occupational licensing
Featherbedding
Employer recognition (of union)

Discriminatory discharge
Yellow-dog contract
Blacklisting
Lockout
Company union
Injunction
Closed shop
Union shop
Open shop
Right-to-work laws
Collective bargaining

QUESTIONS AND PROBLEMS

1. Compare verbally and graphically equilibrium conditions in competitive and monopsonistic labor markets.
2. Compare verbally and graphically equilibrium conditions in competitive and unionized labor markets.
3. Do you think monopsony power was more common in the 1800's than today? In your answer, consider the likely impacts of population growth, economic growth, and improvements in transportation and communication on monopsonists.
4. Does the existence of an industrial union in an otherwise competitive industry result in increased availability of jobs in the industry? Explain verbally and graphically.
5. Occupational licensing, usually defended by advocates as essential to consumer protection, is costly for the consumer. Explain why both verbally and graphically.

6. Describe methods used by unions to increase demand for their workers.
7. What are the pros and cons of belonging to a union?
8. Describe trends in union membership since the U.S. National Labor Relations Act of 1935 granted workers the right to organize. What factors explain these trends?
9. Explain the importance to unionism of:
   (a) the Norris-Laguardia Act of 1932
   (b) the National Labor Relations Act of 1935
   (c) the Taft-Hartley Act of 1947
   (d) the Landrum-Griffin Act.
10. What issues are typically addressed in the contracts that result from collective bargaining?
11. Discuss the importance of the strike weapon to unions.
12. Who wins and who loses when unions enter an industry?

32

Land, Capital, and Entrepreneurship

After Bill Gates dropped out of Harvard University, no one hired him. He didn't care though. He had other things in mind. Gates started a small company of his own in 1975, a company called Microsoft that made and marketed personal computer software. Microsoft did very well, and in March 1986 the company went "public," which meant that stock ownership shares would no longer be held privately by Gates and a few others. New shares of stock were issued. Gates kept 45 percent of them, while most of the rest were sold to the public. Offered at $21 apiece, the shares zoomed to $35.50 on the stock market. Going public thus put a market value of $350 million on the 45 percent stake Gates retained. At age 30 this young entrepreneur became one of America's 100 richest men.[1]

Among resource inputs, land, capital, and entrepreneurship can be as intriguing as labor. Table 32.1 indicates that the rent, interest, and profit generated by these inputs, taken together, account for only about 26 percent of all national income. Yet these inputs are supremely important. Relying on labor alone, we would still be a Stone Age society.

In some ways the markets for land, capital, and entrepreneurship are very similar to those for labor. Each has a derived demand reflecting the input's contribution to output and the value of

[1]*Fortune*, July 21, 1986, pp. 23-33.

that output (i.e., marginal revenue product). Moreover, business firms are the demand-side buyers. As for the supply side, it is again occupied directly or indirectly by households.

These are oversimplifications of what actually happens. The entrepreneurial services of Bill Gates, for example, were not really "demanded" by any established firm. Like many entrepreneurs, Gates created the demand while also filling the supply. Still, these simplifications aid learning.

The biggest difference between labor markets and those for other resources is time. A Burger King counter attendant works by the hour. Burger King's obligations are therefore brief. So are the counter attendant's. In contrast, a firm may purchase a building that lasts for decades, placing it on land with availability that could be clocked in eons. Such durability leads to long-term obligations and complicates the firm's two-question logic. What is an industrial site worth? Or a new brewery that may occupy it? The worth of these inputs cannot be measured solely by their contributions to output this year or next. Their contributions run deeply into the future, and calculating what they are worth must take this into account. That is done through *capitalization*, which converts a time stream of monetary values into a single, present-time dollar amount. Notice, for instance, what was said earlier about Bill Gates. His stake in Microsoft was valued at $350 million in 1986. He was *not* paid a salary of $350 million in 1986. In

TABLE 32.1   National Income by Type, 1984

Type of Income	Percent Share	Billions of Dollars
Compensation to employees	73.4%	$2,173
Rental income of persons	2.1	63
Net interest	9.6	284
Proprietors income*	5.2	154
Corporate profits	9.7	286
Total	100.0%	$2,960

*Note: Proprietors' income actually includes much that could be considered labor income because it includes remuneration for the labor services of farmers and other small business owners.

Source: *Statistical Abstract of the United States 1986* (Washington, D.C.: U.S. Department of Commerce, 1985), pp. 436–438.

fact, the total sales revenues of Microsoft did not exceed $200 million annually at the time. The common stock ownership shares of Microsoft, those held by Gates and the public, were worth a great deal because the time stream of expected profits that they would yield was "capitalized" into a single, present-day value or price.

This matter of capitalization is postponed until the end of the chapter. Meanwhile, our measures of worth—prices, revenues, and costs—can all be stated in terms of annual rates, such as the annual percentage rate of interest when referring to capital. Moreover, it will simplify matters if we touch no more than lightly on the "real" stuff involved here—such as Gates's ingenuity in designing the PC-DOS system or Anheuser-Busch's huge brewery in St. Louis. We will concentrate on financial reflections of what is happening in the concrete. Doing so, we will tackle each resource and its remuneration as well as capitalization.

I
Land and Rent

A
Economic Rents

In everyday language the word *rent* indicates payment for something used temporarily, such as an apartment or a U-Haul trailer. As with several other words, however, economists give this one a special meaning, best signified by adding the qualifier *economic*.

> **Economic rent** is a payment to any resource input above the price required to obtain the quantity supplied.

Stated technically, an *economic rent* is a payment to any factor of production—land, labor, or capital—beyond its opportunity cost or the forgone value of its next most productive use. In everyday language, this is more like a bonus payment than a rental payment.

Note that labor can receive an economic rent as well as any other resource. Reggie Jackson illustrates this nicely. In 1986 he earned $975,000 from

the California Angels. When asked by a news reporter why he played baseball, he said, "A lot of it is the money, but I'd be playing if I was making $150,000."[2] Reggie's economic rent that year would thus be the *difference* between the $975,000 he was actually paid and the $150,000 minimum he would have to be paid to play baseball, namely, $825,000. Indeed, it is probably safe to say that most of the earnings of most professional athletes, movie stars, best-selling novelists, and captains of industry are economic rents. Workers in general also commonly earn economic rents, but not by as much.

Although economic rents commonly flow to nearly all resource suppliers, different types of economic rents arise in different circumstances. One type of economic rent is associated with land—namely, *pure* economic rent.

B
Pure Economic Rent

A **pure economic rent** is a return to a factor of production that has a *perfectly inelastic supply curve*. Perfectly inelastic supply occurs when the quantity supplied is fixed, so that the quantity offered neither rises nor falls with variations in the price paid for the resource.

Land surface, in the aggregate, illustrates pure economic rent. The aggregate supply of land surface is fixed in a freely available amount from nature, so its return is characterized as a pure economic rent. Note the qualifications *surface* and *aggregate*. Earlier we defined land to include all natural resources—including water, coal, and oil. Here we refer only to terrain, which may have value as a field for crops, as a range for livestock, or as a location for factories, offices, stores, schools, or dwellings. In the *aggregate*, the United States has nearly 2.5 billion acres of land. Given political boundaries, this amount is set by nature. Although lake drainage, landfill, and other human efforts may alter this amount a bit, it is not really going to change in response to variations in the amount of money paid to those who own the land, even if that amount of money should happen to fall to zero.

Figure 32.1 explains. Let's simplify by assuming

[2]*Newsweek*, March 31, 1986, p. 15.

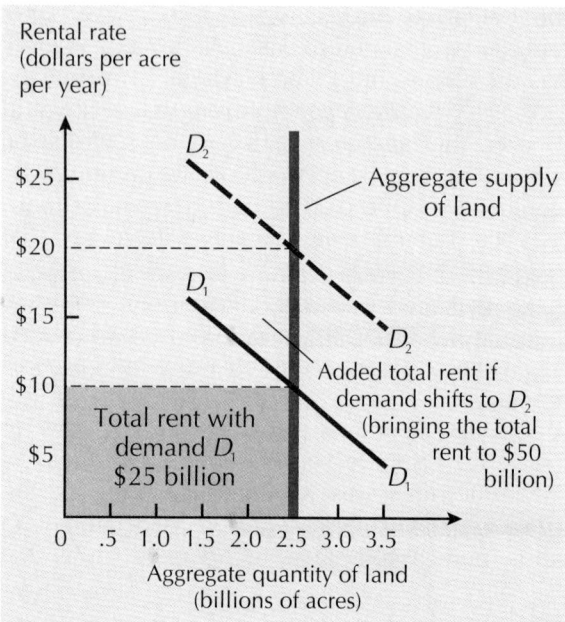

FIGURE 32.1 *Pure Economic Rent and the Aggregate Supply of Land*

The aggregate supply of land is fixed at 2.5 billion acres (a round number for the United States). The demand reflects the marginal revenue product of land. With demand D_1, the equilibrium rental rate would be $10 per acre per year, which, when multiplied by the number of acres, 2.5 billion, yields a total annual rent of $25 billion. Population growth might shift the demand to D_2, in which case the rental rate would be $20 and the total rental income would be $50 billion.

that all users of land lease their land from landlord-owners by paying an annual *rental rate*. Users could, of course, buy the land they need, but the purchase price would reflect the capitalized value of the land over time, and we wish to postpone capitalization until later. The rental rate can be measured in dollars per acre per year. Let's also assume that this annual rental rate can be averaged over all the different parcels of land that make up the aggregate supply of land, the parcels of crop land in Iowa as well as the parcels of factory land in Ohio.

How much in rental rate would land users be willing to pay land owners, looking at the matter in this aggregated way? The question may be rephrased as: *What is the demand curve for land in the aggregate?* The answer, as pictured in Figure 32.1, hinges on elements we have considered be-

fore. The demand for land is derived from the demand for the products and services land helps to produce. Demand for land thus reflects its *marginal revenue product (MRP)*, that is, the estimated value of the annual flow of services that land provides. This varies inversely with quantity, so demand slopes downward. Given the supply of other resource inputs like labor and capital, the marginal revenue product of land would fall with any increase in its aggregate quantity. Conversely, land's marginal revenue product would rise with any decrease in aggregate quantity. Assume that present aggregate demand is indicated by curve D_1D_1 in Figure 32.1.

Imagining variations in the aggregate quantity of land helps one to see the downward slope of demand. (Imagine Florida flooding as the polar ice caps melt from the greenhouse effect.) However, the *aggregate supply of land* is actually fixed by nature, so it is not responsive to price. (Nature might flood Florida, but not because of a fall in the rental rate for land, not even if that rental rate fell to zero.) Hence, in Figure 32.1, the aggregate supply curve of land is shown to be perfectly inelastic. It rises vertically at 2.5 billion acres (the round number for total U.S. acreage).

Given a demand of D_1D_1, the equilibrium rental rate for land in Figure 32.1 will be the rental rate that equates the quantity demanded with the fixed quantity supplied, namely, $10 per acre per year. Total annual rental income of land owners would then be indicated by the shaded area, which is the $10 rental rate times the total number of acres, 2.5 billion, or $25 billion.

The nature of pure economic rent and its blessings for land owners can also be seen in changes. What would happen in Figure 32.1 if the aggregate demand for land shifted upward from D_1D_1 to D_2D_2? Quantity supplied would not budge. So the rental rate on land would rise proportionately with the upward shift in demand, doubling from $10 per acre per year to $20 per acre per year. Doubling the rental rate would also double the total annual rental income of land owners, increasing it from $25 billion to $50 billion. Such shifts in demand occur with population and income growth, which raise the demand for food, apparel, ground transportation, housing, and other products and services that heavily influence the derived demand for land.

C

Rents on Parcels of Land

Different parcels of land capture widely varying rents. Moving from the *aggregate* demand and supply of Figure 32.1 to the demand and supply of *particular parcels* of land is easy because each parcel of land is itself fixed in supply. Any particular acre of land is 4,840 square yards. It does not expand to 7,000 square yards as its rental value rises.

Figure 32.2 illustrates for two hypothetical parcels of land—a particular patch of urban land in Trenton, New Jersey (part a), and a particular patch of range land in Wyoming (part b). The demand for the parcel in New Jersey is substantially greater than the demand for the parcel in Wyoming. Hence the rental rate and total rental income of the former are much greater than those of the latter.

One major determinant of demand for a particular parcel is its *location*. If you were seeking a site for a supermarket, for instance, you would be willing to pay more rent for a parcel of land in Trenton, New Jersey, than for one on the prairies of Wyoming. The grocery sales revenues that can be gained from the parcel in Trenton are much greater than those that would be gained in wide-open Wyoming. Hence the marginal revenue product of the Trenton site would be much greater, and its demand is correspondingly greater. (Transportation costs are a key to such variations in location value. Low-cost transportation conditions foster higher rents, while high-cost transportation conditions foster lower rents. In this example of a supermarket, the transportation costs of 1,000 shoppers would obviously be much lower in the urban setting than in the rural setting.)

Physical features likewise influence the economic rents of particular parcels. Soil fertility, subsoil drainage, mineral content—these and many more physical features determine the productivity of particular parcels of land and therefore the pure economic rents they gain for their owners.

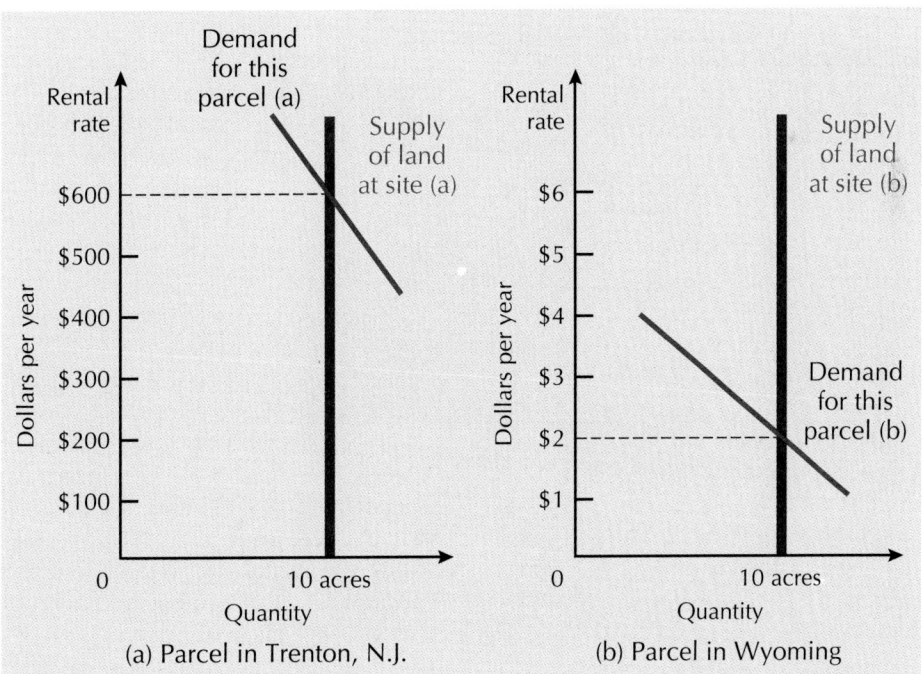

FIGURE 32.2 *Demands for Different Parcels of Land and the Resulting Rents*

Specific parcels of land are fixed in supply. Variations in the demand for them then determine the rental incomes they generate. Here location is a key influence. Demand for the urban parcel in part (a) is much greater than demand for the prairie parcel in part (b).

In sum, a **pure economic rent** is a return to a factor of production that is perfectly inelastic in supply (as is true of land in the aggregate or of particular parcels).

It must be stressed that the pure economic rents we have been discussing accrue to land in its natural condition. Improvements in land—such as those in fertility and drainage—also influence the demand for particular parcels because they improve productivity. However, such improvements are capital investments. As such, their supply is not perfectly inelastic. Higher payments for land improvements will induce a greater supply of improvements. Higher payments for land *itself* do not induce greater supply.

D
Rents and the Allocation of Land

From what has been said, land rents may seem to serve no useful economic function. Land is a free gift of nature, so these pure economic rents cover no real costs. Pure economic rents, especially jumps in them, may therefore be regarded as unearned windfalls to those who happen to own land.

Despite appearances, however, economic rents serve the function of allocating parcels of land to their most productive uses, thereby fostering economic efficiency. Even when rents are regarded as windfalls by land owners who gain from the free gifts of nature, they are regarded as *costs* by those

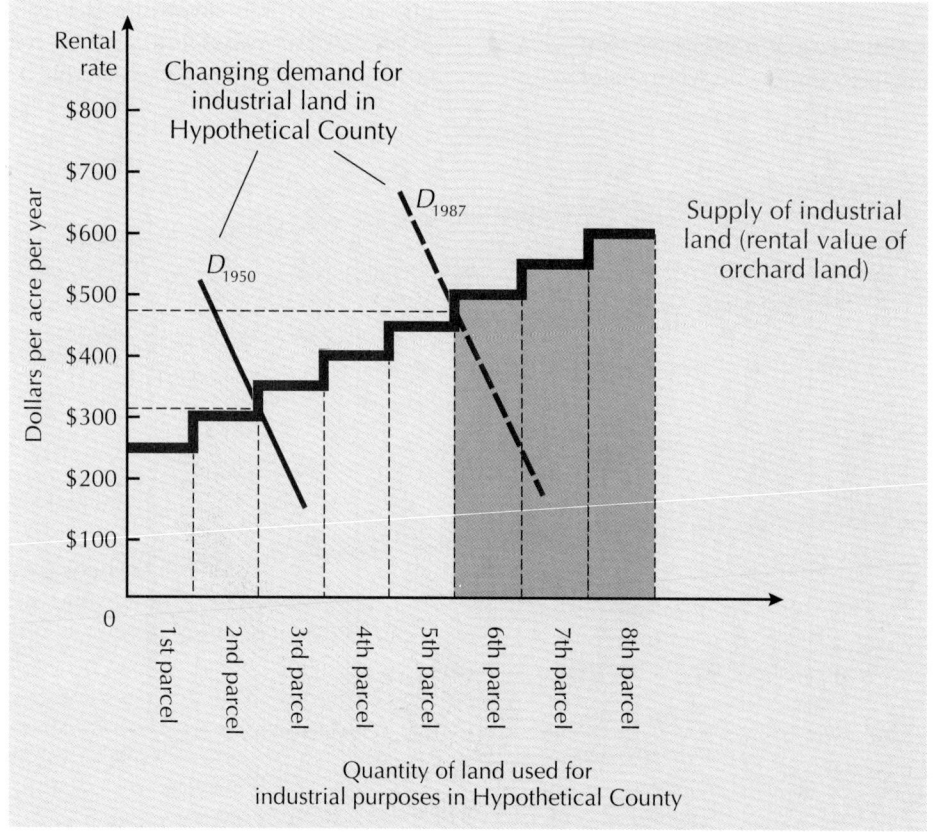

FIGURE 32.3   Rents Allocate Land Among Alternative Uses

Assuming only two uses for the eight parcels that make up Hypothetical County, rental rates will allocate the land between those uses. Supply is the rental value of each parcel used as orchard. As industry demand shifts, industrialists are increasingly willing to pay a rent that attracts land to industry.

using the land to produce goods and services. As *user costs*, rents allocate parcels of land to different uses.

To illustrate this, the collection of parcels that comprise Hypothetical County are arranged in Figure 32.3. Assume that each parcel has only two possible uses—industry and orchard. Historically, the orchards came first, and the rental values of the parcels when thus used for fruit are indicated in steps, from least fruitful to most fruitful, moving from left to right. Industrialists wanting to hire land for factory sites would have to pay a rental rate for each parcel that exceeded the orchard rental rate. Hence their willingness to pay would be indicated by their industrial demand, and the land owners' willingness to supply land for industrial use would be indicated by the various rental values of the parcels when used as orchards. Figure 32.3 shows that industrial demand in 1950, as indicated by D_{1950}, was relatively low, so only two parcels, those least fruitful for orchard crops, went to industrial use at a rental rate of $310 per acre. With industrial demand shifting out to D_{1987}, the third through fifth parcels are also allocated to industrial use, and the equilibrium rental rate for industrial land rises to $470 per acre. As of 1987, then, rental rates allocate five parcels to industries and three parcels to orchards. If industrial demand shifted further, with willingness to pay rents rising above $600 for all the acreage in the eight parcels, then all the parcels would be converted to industrial use.

Read Perspective 32A.

II

Capital and Interest

Two hundred thousand years ago, when humanity lived hand-to-mouth, capital and interest did not exist because the future did not exist, at least not in the minds of people. The advent of agriculture brought with it more than greater food consumption. It also brought an extended concept of time. Looking beyond the immediate moment, people started doing two things we now take for granted—borrowing and lending. Today, the borrowing and lending of financial capital—like com-

---

PERSPECTIVE 32A

Henry George and Land Taxes

In 1879, Henry George published a book, *Progress and Poverty*, which outsold the most popular novels of the day. In this book, George defined economic rent as a functionless surplus. Land owners gain substantial rents, he wrote, not because they do anything productive for society, but only because they happen to own land whose supply falls short of demand at a zero price. If most of these pure economic rents were taxed away by government, the aggregate supply of land would not be altered and the distribution of wealth might be improved. Indeed, George argued that a tax on the economic rent of land could replace all other taxes, thereby becoming known as a *single tax*.

In theory, George's argument is strong. In theory, a functionless surplus can be taxed without loss of economic efficiency. This element of truth boosted the book's popularity. However, George's views have been sharply criticized on practical grounds. Although the aggregate supply of land is indeed fixed, land improvements are not. So, in practice, almost any such tax would probably discourage improvements. Moreover, economic rental rates allocate land to alternative uses, and George's tax could play havoc with that function of economic rents. Finally, critics point out that the cost of government has grown so big that a single tax on land rent would not be enough. Other tax revenues would surely be needed.

mercial paper and corporate bonds—reflect conditions in the market for real capital, because real capital goods—buildings, machines, dams, and so on—link the present and the future. Similarly, the interest rate paid by borrowers and earned by lenders is more than just the price paid for financial capital. It's like a rope that ties the future to the present and the present to the future.

Who are the lenders and borrowers? Complexities of today's capital markets tend to hide their identities. Financial institutions, like banks and life insurance companies, act as intermediaries between ultimate lenders and borrowers. The ultimate _lenders_ in the economy are _savers,_ whose savings take many forms—savings accounts, certificates of deposit, pension contributions, life insurance premiums, and more. The ultimate _borrowers_ are _investors,_ whose investments primarily include buildings, factories, warehouses, and machinery but could also be considered to include investments in education (student loans) and housing (mortgage loans). Hence it may be helpful if subsequently we occasionally refer to saver-lenders on the one hand and investor-borrowers on the other.

A
Roundabout Production and Interest

Real capital inputs arise with _roundabout production._

In **roundabout production,** real capital inputs are produced and used in order to produce greater amounts of consumption goods in the future.

For example, without roundabout production, humans would have the same relationship to fruit that chimpanzees do. They would simply pluck whatever bananas or apples were available in the wild and eat them. With roundabout production, however, humans clear and level the land, plant orchards, raise dams or drill wells for irrigation water, build equipment for spraying, picking, and transporting the fruit, and construct canneries for processing fruit that is not eaten fresh. Notice that this roundabout approach to obtaining fruit requires abundant real capital inputs—land im-

provements, machinery, water works, and so on—plus the time needed to produce those capital inputs. These are costs. Yet there is good reason to incur these costs for real capital. The payoff can be huge. The output of fruit is much greater than that provided directly by nature alone.

At bottom, what happens here is very simple. Present consumption is reduced in order to release resources that build capital inputs. In turn, these capital inputs increase future production and consumption. There is a sacrifice of present consumption for greater future consumption, linked by roundabout production.

Consumers and producers are both active in this story, and the _interest rate_ guides their actions. Here's a summary. _Consumers_ must curtail current consumption in order to free resources for the production of capital inputs. They do this by becoming saver-lenders in the market for financial capital. Their reward for curbing current consumption is the _interest_ they earn on the money they save and lend. Hence, _the interest rate induces saver-lenders to delay their gratification._ People generally like to have goods and services now rather than later. Interest compensates them for postponing their consumption. If real interest is, say, 8 percent per year, postponed consumption will allow 8 percent more consumption after a year.

Producers, on the other hand, pay the interest rate to saver-lenders because they act as investor-borrowers. To producers, the interest rate is a cost rather than a benefit. But _producers are willing to pay that interest cost to the extent that the capital goods financed by the borrowing actually increase future output because that increased output then more than covers the cost._ Take investments in office automation, for instance. A complete system with computer hardware, software, wired networks, and training can cost $6,000 per user and many millions of dollars per company. Yet there is payoff potential. In 1985, the Westinghouse Electric Corporation bought an $8.8 million system from Data General for its salespeople in 70 offices to take orders, check inventories, manage appointment calendars, and the like. Aside from greater efficiency, Westinghouse planned to have its salespeople do more "cold calling" of prospective buyers than before. As a result, according to a company executive, they expected to "get a 2½-to-1 annual payback" on the investment.[3]

Interest may thus be defined from two points of view—that of the saver-lender or of the investor-borrower:

> **Interest** is the price a saver-lender receives for an amount saved or loaned, measured as a percentage of the amount. **Interest** is also the price an investor-borrower pays for a loan.

If, for instance, you receive $8 for every $100 of savings kept for a year at your local bank, the interest is 8 percent annually.

Observed interest rates vary, depending on the nature of the borrower and the type of loan. A one-person taxi company might have to pay 12 percent interest on a bank loan in order to buy a taxi. A huge corporation like General Motors may issue bonds that pay 9 percent to lenders. The variety is thus immense, but several generalizations usually hold.

1. *Risk:* Interest rates tend to vary directly with the riskiness of the loan; the greater the risk, the higher the interest rate (*ceteris paribus*).
2. *Maturity:* The time taken to repay the loan will often influence the interest rate. In general, the longer the maturity of the loan, the higher the interest rate (*ceteris paribus*).
3. *Size of loan:* The costs of granting a loan—that is, the costs of credit review, contract completion, and collections—are to some extent fixed costs. In dollars, they do not vary proportionately with the amount of money lent. Because fixed-dollar costs will fall as a percentage of the amount lent, so too the interest rate tends to fall as the size of the loan increases (*ceteris paribus*).

These factors help to explain variations in interest rates for *particular* loans, at a particular time, under particular circumstances. They do not explain why interest rates in 1986 were *generally* lower than they were in 1980, or why they might be

[3]*The Wall Street Journal,* April 8, 1985, pp. 1, 15.

generally higher in Britain compared to the United States. To understand variations in the *general* or *average* level of interest rates, we must explore the market for loanable funds, its demand and supply sides broadly defined.

B
Determination of the Interest Rate

Because the interest rate is the *price* paid for the use of loanable funds, it is determined like other prices—by demand and supply. Those on the demand and supply sides of the market for loanable funds have already been identified as borrowers and lenders, thus helping to identify the market itself.

> **The market for loanable funds** registers the demands of all borrowers and the supplies of the lenders, thereby determining the price of debt capital.

Figure 32.4 converts these words into a hypothetical diagram, with the interest rate on the vertical axis and the quantity of loanable funds on the horizontal axis. The demand and supply curves have familiar features, and their interaction establishes an equilibrium at point *E*, with the interest rate at 10 percent and the quantity of loanable funds at $300 billion.

1. The Demand for Loanable Funds The demand curve for loanable funds shows the quantity of loanable funds demanded by borrowers at each interest rate. These borrowers include households, the government, and businesses. And, as suggested by the downward slope of the demand curve in Figure 32.4, these three sources of demand desire a greater quantity of loanable funds at a lower rate of interest than at a higher rate of interest. The reason for the negative relationship between price and quantity in this case is most readily seen for *households* as they demand loanable funds to help buy homes, autos, appliances, and college educations. During 1984–85, for instance, the average rate on all home mortgage loans fell from about 13 percent to 12 percent, and housing starts consequently rose from an annual

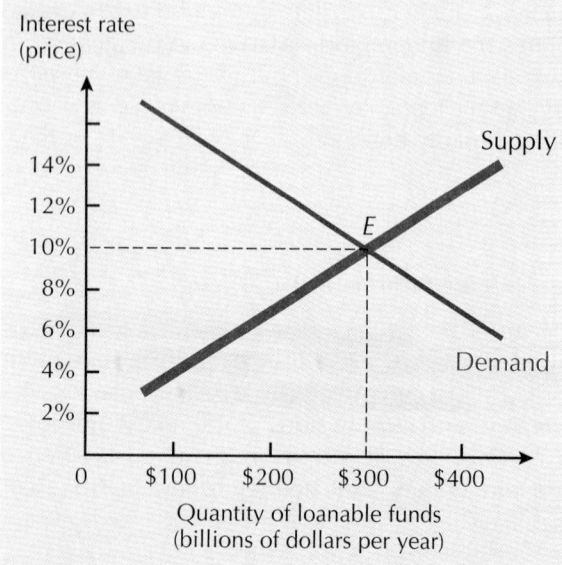

FIGURE 32.4 *The Market for Loanable Funds*

The demand curve shows the quantity of loanable funds that would be demanded by borrowers at various possible interest rates. The supply curve shows the quantity of loanable funds that would be offered by lenders at various possible interest rates. At an interest rate of 10 percent the quantities demanded and supplied are equal, establishing an equilibrium at point E.

rate of 1,550 to 1,900.[4] A lower interest rate on loans for expensive durables may be considered to be, in effect, a lower price for the durable goods themselves.

The *government* demands loanable funds in order to build highways, schools, sewage treatment plants, water facilities, and other public works. This demand apparently also varies inversely with the interest rate.

The demand of *businesses* is likewise downward sloping with the interest rate, and this relationship is especially pertinent here because of our focus on capital inputs. Business firms demand loanable funds in order to invest in capital goods like factories, warehouses, office buildings, computers, and machine tools. To see the linkage between the interest rate and the demand for loanable funds for this purpose, we need to consider (1) the rate of return on capital investment and (2) the firm's array of capital investment projects.

[4]*Business Week*, June 24, 1985, p. 41.

Consider first the *rate of return on capital investment*. This is the marginal revenue product of the capital investment, measured as an annual percentage of the total value of the investment. Suppose, for example, that a firm can drill a water well for $100,000. The well saves the firm the expense of trucking water to its factory year after year indefinitely into the future. Assume that these savings amount to $20,000 per year (which savings are calculated after covering any costs of pumping and well maintenance). The rate of return on this capital investment is 20 percent because 20,000/100,000 = 0.20. (A return that lasted only a short while, like 5 years, would be calculated differently. But this example of a permanent return shows the basic idea.) This particular project is thus "worth" 20 percent per year in rate of return. If the interest cost of loanable funds is anything *less* than this 20 percent, say 10 percent, then borrowing to undertake the project would be wise and profitable. If, however, the interest cost of loanable funds is *more* than this, say 25 percent or more, then the firm should not borrow to undertake the project.

Now consider the firm's *array of capital investment projects*. Each firm typically has a variety of capital investment projects that it could undertake—such as building an additional factory, replacing some old machinery, or installing new telecommunications equipment. When these are ranked by their percentage rates of return, from highest to lowest, they form an array that, in effect, becomes the firm's demand curve for loanable funds. Figure 32.5 illustrates. Four projects, *A* through *D*, are arrayed by their rates of return, 20 percent through 5 percent. If the interest cost of loanable funds was greater than 20 percent, none of these projects would be undertaken. At lower interest costs, more and more projects would be undertaken as the rate of return becomes greater than the interest cost. At an interest cost of 10 percent, Figure 32.5 shows projects *A*, *B*, and *C* to be profitable, but project *D* would be rejected. To return to our earlier example of office automation, the Pillsbury Company invested $2.5 million and $3.0 million on new office equipment during 1983 and 1984, respectively, but curbed such spending substantially in 1985. Explaining this curtailment of capital spending in 1985, a Pillsbury spokesman said, "We've taken advantage of all the easy oppor-

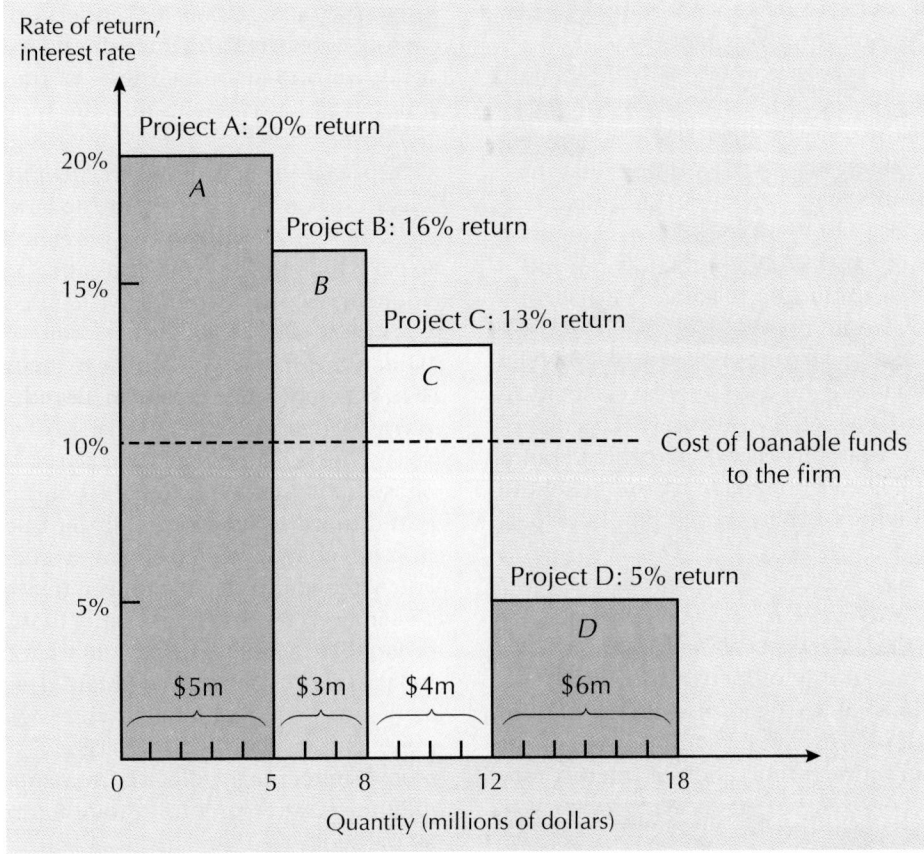

FIGURE 32.5 *The Firm's Demand for Loanable Funds*

Here a firm's capital investment projects are arrayed from highest rate of return (A) to lowest rate of return (D). The firm will borrow loanable funds only for those projects with rates of return that exceed the interest cost of loanable funds. For example, projects A, B, and C would be undertaken if the cost is 10 percent. The rates of return thus determine the firm's demand for loanable funds.

tunities, and we're finding fewer and fewer major opportunities to invest in office technology."[5]

In sum, a profit-maximizing firm will borrow to undertake investments only when the rate of return exceeds the interest cost of funds. The lower the interest rate, the larger the quantity of loanable funds the firm will demand, as then a larger number of capital investments qualify.

2. The Supply of Loanable Funds The supply curve for loanable funds shows the quantity of loanable funds offered by saver-lenders at various

[5]*Wall Street Journal*, April 8, 1985, p. 15.

possible average interest rates. Who are these potential saver-lenders? They are members of the same broad groups that comprise the demand side of the market for loanable funds—namely, households, the government, and businesses. Household saving has averaged about 4 percent of Gross National Product in recent years. Business saving, by far the largest source of supply, comes from retained earnings. As for the government, state and local governments have been savers of modest but good repute (with savings amounting to roughly 1.3 percent of GNP in recent years). The federal government, on the other hand, has been a "negative" saver for quite some time because of its big deficits. Combining all sources, and subtracting these negative amounts for the federal government, overall savings hovered at around 14 percent of GNP during the early 1980s.

In general, the quantity of loanable funds supplied is positively related to the interest rate. Loanable funds are therefore not like land. The quantity supplied is responsive to the price. Just how responsive is unclear, however. Empirical evidence indicates that much saving is aimed at achieving some fixed objective, such as funding 4 years of college tuition or placing $150,000 in a retirement nest egg. This sort of fixed-objective saving is not very responsive to interest rates. Even so, there is apparently enough interest elasticity in other saving to produce the positively sloped supply. Overall, for example, each 1 percentage point increase in real interest seems to boost household savings by roughly 0.3 percentage points of personal income.

3. Shifts in Demand and Supply A number of forces _other than the interest rate_ influence the demand for and supply of loanable funds. When these forces change, they cause shifts in the demand and supply of loanable funds, shifts that alter the equilibrium combination of interest rate and quantity. For example, revolutionary developments in technology that increase the productivity of capital inputs tend to shift the demand for loanable funds outward to the right (or upward), as businesses then seek to borrow more credit at each possible interest rate. A major influence on the supply side of the market is the Federal Reserve System, which manages the money supply by influencing the supply of loanable funds. An expansive, or "easy," monetary policy shifts the supply of loanable funds outward to the right (or down). A restrictive, or "tight," monetary policy shifts the supply of loanable funds back to the left (or up).

A variable that shifts _both_ demand _and_ supply simultaneously, a variable that has been especially active over the last two decades, is the rate of price inflation in the overall economy. A loan is the temporary use of money. Money is handed from the lender to the borrower at an _early time_. Money payments are then made from the borrower to the lender at _later times_, payments covering the original amount lent plus interest. Inflation disrupts the process because it lowers the value of money

over time. To compensate lenders and to properly charge borrowers, the interest rate must be adjusted upward to align the values of the early money granted by lenders with the later money repaid by borrowers.

Suppose, for example, that _without_ any price inflation, you would be willing to lend $100 to your neighbor for 1 year at 10 percent interest. You expect him to pay you $110 after 12 months, so your sacrifice is rewarded by 10 percent more purchasing power after a year's wait. Consider next what interest you would have to charge in order to gain the same 10 percent increase in purchasing power _with_ a price inflation of, say, 20 percent per year. The dollars repaid after 1 year will then purchase _20 percent less_ in goods and services compared to the dollars originally lent, so keeping the interest charge at 10 percent would inflict upon you a _loss_ in purchasing power. In _real_ terms, $110 1 year later has much less value than the $100 lent originally, a value closer to $90 than to $100 when inflation is 20 percent. To obtain the same reward as before, you must charge your neighbor the 10 percent rate you would charge with no inflation _plus_ a percentage rate that _matches_ the rate of inflation, 20 percent, for a total interest charge of 30 percent.

Now, from your neighbor's viewpoint, a similar adjustment occurs. If in the absence of price inflation he would like to borrow at 10 percent interest, he will be just as willing to borrow at 30 percent interest in the event inflation is running prices up at a rate of 20 percent per year.

Figure 32.6 shows the consequences of these considerations for lenders and borrowers generally, assuming a more moderate 6 percent annual rate of price inflation. Without inflation, equilibrium is at E_1 and the interest rate is 10 percent. With inflation of 6 percent, the lenders' supply curve and the borrowers' demand curve both shift up by 6 percentage points, establishing a new equilibrium interest rate of 16 percent at point E_2. Because the shifts in the two curves are proportionate, there is no change in the equilibrium quantity of loanable funds. That remains at $300 billion. (Alternatively, we could say that inflation shifts supply to the left, from S_1 to S_2, as lenders become less willing to lend at each given interest rate, while at the same time it shifts demand to the right, from

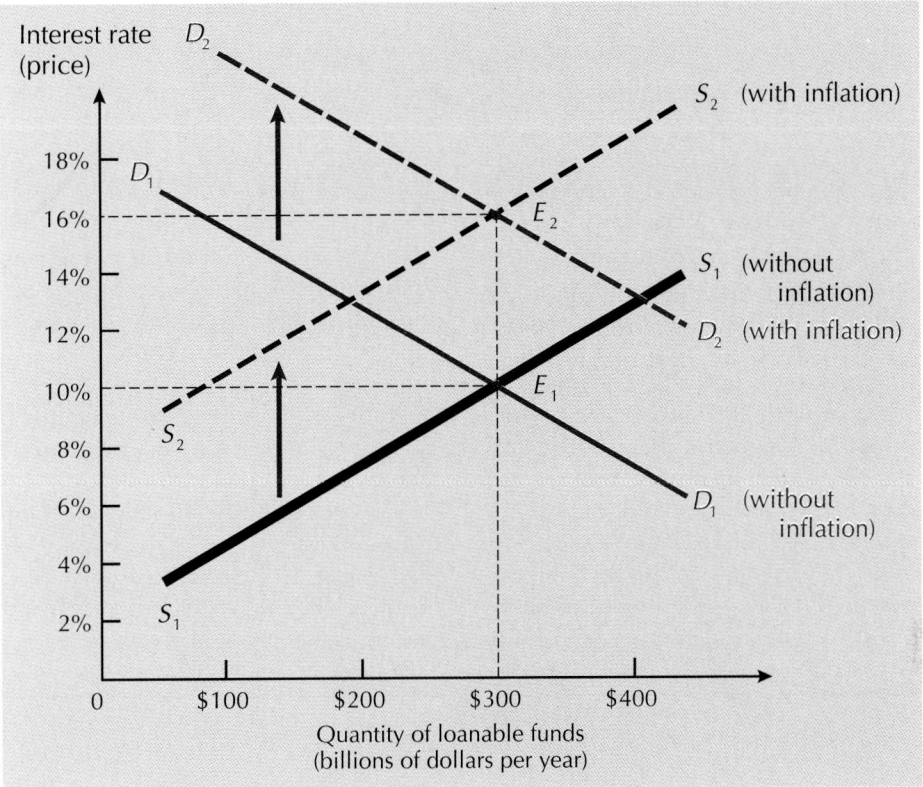

FIGURE 32.6 *Shifts of Demand and Supply Due to Inflation*

If the equilibrium rate of interest is 10 percent without inflation, then steady inflation at 6 percent per year will cause both the demand for and the supply of loanable funds to shift upward by 6 percent. The new equilibrium interest rate, 16 percent, reflects these inflation adjustments.

D_1 to D_2, as borrowers become more eager to borrow at each given interest rate. The combined shifts lift equilibrium interest by the rate of inflation.)

These observations point up the importance of distinguishing the *nominal* and the *real* rate of interest. The **nominal interest rate** *is that stated on loan contracts,* such as the annual percentage rate (APR), specified on consumer loans and credit card agreements. The **real interest rate** *is the nominal interest rate minus the anticipated annual rate of price inflation.* This reflects the fact that, as suggested in Figure 32.6, the nominal rate, or observed market interest rate, will be the sum of the real interest rate plus the rate of price inflation.

Read Perspective 32B.

III

Entrepreneurship and Profit

Entrepreneurs are everywhere. Among today's college students, entrepreneurs seem to be especially common. The Association of Collegiate Entrepreneurs, a clearinghouse for entrepreneurial ideas, started with 7 member colleges in 1983 and gained more than 170 by 1985. The financial experiences of collegiate entrepreneurs are, moreover, no different from those of entrepreneurs traditionally. Whatever the product or service—be it flowers for dances or underwear printed with school crests—some collegiate entrepreneurs earn

PERSPECTIVE 32B
Nominal and Real Interest Rates

Table 32.2 gives some estimated examples of nominal and real interest rates for selected years over the period 1970–85. Anticipated rates of price inflation in column (1) are measured by the rate of inflation during the previous year (a crude but convenient measure). Clearly, inflation jumped around substantially. The nominal interest rates of column (2) likewise leap about, beginning with 6.39 percent, rising to 14.03 percent, and then finally tumbling back to 7.99 percent. Moreover, these ups and downs in nominal interest correspond to those for price inflation, as if the changes in price inflation were causing the changes in nominal interest (or the rate of inflation was a component of the nominal rate of interest.) The implications of these patterns are found in the estimated *real interest rates* of column (3), which are the nominal interest rates minus the anticipated inflation rates. Real interest does vary over the period, but it varies much less dramatically than nominal interest. Between 1970 and 1981, for instance, the nominal rate rose 7.64 percentage points, from 6.39 to 14.03 percent, while at the same time the real rate rose only 2.74 percentage points, from 2.09 to 4.83 percent. Clearly, the nominal rate in this comparison is responding to the rise in inflation from 4.3 to 9.2 percent. You can do your own comparisons for 1981–85, when inflation fell sharply.

TABLE 32.2   Simple Examples of Price Inflation, Nominal Interest Rates, and Real Interest Rates, 1970–85

Year	(1) Anticipated Price Inflation (%)*	(2) Nominal Interest Rate (%)†	(3) Real Interest Rate (2) − (1) = (3)
1970	4.3	6.39	2.09
1979	7.4	10.07	2.67
1981	9.2	14.03	4.83
1985	3.8	7.99	4.19

*Rate of price inflation during the previous year, as measured by the GNP deflator.

†Average annual interest rate on a 3-month U.S. government Treasury bill.

Source: Statistical Abstract of the United States 1986 (Washington, D.C.: U.S. Department of Commerce, 1985), pp. 469, 505.

princely profits, while others lose their shirts.[6]

In Chapter 1, we identified entrepreneurship as a blend of economic leadership and imagination. In particular, entrepreneurs (1) *combine and coordinate* the other inputs—labor, land, and capital—to produce some good or service; (2) *accept the main risks* of loss that threaten businesses in light of uncertainties; and (3) *engage in innovation* by introducing new products, new services, and new production processes. Given the critical importance of these several functions to the economy, entrepreneurship can be considered a fourth factor of production along with labor, land, and capital. However, entrepreneurship cannot be measured as easily as these other inputs. Leader-

[6]Karen Blumenthal, "On Campuses, Making Dean's List Comes Second to Making a Profit," *Wall Street Journal*, April 4, 1985, p. 35.

ship and imagination cannot be calibrated precisely, so there is no way to determine a price per unit of entrepreneurship. Still, most economists seem to agree that, elusive though entrepreneurship may be, its main reward is *profit*.

In Chapter 23, we distinguished between *normal profit* and *economic profit*. When firms earn a *normal profit*, total revenues cover all explicit and implicit costs, no more and no less. Explicit costs include payments to workers, materials suppliers, and credit suppliers. Implicit costs include the opportunity costs of capital and labor supplied by owners and entrepreneurs. In other words, a normal profit is normal compensation for entrepreneurial skill and ownership capital. It's like a cost, so it is an implicit cost. Any profit exceeding this normal profit is an *economic profit*.

The relationship between these profits and entrepreneurship is a subject of debate among economists. Economists agree that entrepreneurship is a scarce, indispensable ingredient in production. They also agree that entrepreneurship is compensated by profit. Beyond these basics, however, we find much disagreement. A key unsettled question is this: *What causes economic profit, as distinct from normal profit?*

The answer we favor has two divisions, one for normal profit and another for economic profit. First, *normal profit* could be considered *a return to basic enterprise ownership*. To the extent that financial capital is part of this basic ownership, it is a capital commitment very much like that involved in owning a low-risk government bond. To the extent that entrepreneurial effort is part of this basic ownership, the effort resembles routine management—that is, rudimentary hiring and firing, simple scheduling, ordinary marketing, and so on. One way to imagine these conditions for firms in general would be to imagine an entire economy in which there is (1) very little difficulty in coordinating the contributions of the other inputs— labor, land, and capital; (2) very little risk, partly because of this easy management responsibility but mainly because of a lack of uncertainty; and (3) very little innovation. This would be a very dull, static, predictable economy, one in which normal profits would be the monotonous norm.

By implication, then, *economic profits* are associated with entrepreneurship of a more lively sort in a more lively world, one much more like the real world. In this context, economic profits are rewards for three activities that typify entrepreneurship at its best, namely, *rewards for (1) especially efficient management, (2) acceptance of risk, and (3) successful innovation.* Another source of economic profit is *(4) monopoly power.* We'll consider each of these in turn.

A
Profit and Especially Efficient Management

Perhaps the most obvious source of economic profit is unusually efficient management. Formulas for good management abound. They appear in countless business textbooks. Some of them even make their appearance in this book (remember $MC = MR$?). Yet these many formulas fail to tell the whole story. If they did, there would be no poorly managed companies. (But there are many.) If they did, firms could not be characterized as having "corporate cultures" or distinct "management styles." (But they can be so characterized.) If formulas were the whole story, there would be very little for *Business Week* and the *Wall Street Journal* to report about the personalities of the people who head our major corporations. (But they do report on them, people like Lee Iacocca and Ross Perot being among their favorite subjects.)

In other words, excellent management entails undefinable qualities and requires special leadership talents. When asked to explain his company's persistent success, John G. Smale, chief executive of the Procter & Gamble Corporation (Tide, Crest, etc.), once said:

> *I think another part of our advantage is an intangible thing, the principles that the company operates by, the fact that we try to do the right thing. It's important to our kind of people that they're comfortable with the character of the organization they're working with.*[7]

In short, managements that are for some reason better than the norm usually earn profits that are above the norm. Indeed, economic profits act as an incentive for managerial excellence.

[7]Cynthia Hutton, "America's Most Admired Corporations," *Fortune*, January 6, 1986, p. 20.

B
Profit and Risk

The economy is constantly changing, with shifts in population, scientific discoveries, business cycles, tax law amendments, and many other developments. These changes make the future uncertain and thereby foster risk. Moreover, risk is inherent in some activities, such as oil exploration. Entrepreneurs bear most of these risks. Hence much economic profit can be considered a reward for risk acceptance.

What happens is somewhat like gambling. Among all entrepreneurs, some gain rich economic profits, some break even, and some, usually the majority, suffer economic losses. Oil exploration illustrates the point nicely because stories of fantastic profits made from a few remarkable oil wells are familiar to everyone. What tends to be overlooked, however, is that these enormous profits are, in the aggregate, largely offset by losses experienced on many thousands of unpublicized exploratory wells that turn out to be dry losers. (One dry hole, drilled in 1983, cost $1.6 billion because it required the construction of an artificial island in the Beaufort Sea off the northern coast of Alaska, a very hostile environment.) Assume, for instance, that one successful oil well makes $10 million in economic profit for a "wildcat" entrepreneur. This $10 million can easily be offset by 10 other wells, each costing $1 million, that are dry holes.

In theory, the economic losses that risk imposes on entrepreneurs should not fully offset the economic profits they, as a group, happen to earn. They should, in other words, earn economic profits on balance. Whether this theory holds in the real world is, however, unclear.

C
Profit and Innovation

Innovation is the act of putting a new idea into practical commercial use. The new ideas are usually inventions of one kind or another, like fiber optics or personal computers, but they can also be new forms of business organization, fresh procedures for production, or novel methods of product distribution. Thus the supermarket is as much an innovation as the ballpoint pen or the computer software created by Bill Gates.

Innovation, when successful, is a third source of economic profit for entrepreneurs because it gives innovators temporary advantages over their rivals. If the innovation is a new product or new production process, the temporary advantage may be based on patents, which legally grant 17-year monopolies. Once patents expire, rivals may imitate the innovator, providing competition that adds to the quantity supplied, presses the price down, and thereby eventually shrinks the economic profits earned by the innovator. Even where patents are not involved, innovators get a jump on their rivals merely by being innovative. Imitation often takes appreciable time. For example, it was over a year before GM and Chrysler responded to Ford's innovative Mustang, and it took quite a while before IBM challenged Apple's success in personal computers. These lags give innovators short-term powers that generate economic profits.

D
Profit and Monopoly Power

All three sources of economic profit discussed so far—special efficiency, risk acceptance, and innovation—serve socially desirable functions. Since economic profits provide incentives, entrepreneurial energies are aimed at achieving extraordinary efficiencies, overcoming the long odds of risky ventures, and introducing innovations that contribute to economic growth and change. Good performance in these several respects fosters good performance in answering three of the basic questions arising because of scarcity—What?, How?, and What's new?

As we have seen, however, economic profit can come from monopoly power as well as from these laudable sources (Chapter 26). In many instances, such monopoly power may be natural because of economies of scale or especially scarce resource inputs. To the extent that economic profits arise in such instances, they may be considered inevitable, something neither worthy of praise nor deserving of condemnation. On the other hand, there are instances when such monopoly power stems from artificial actions, such as cartelization or merging. The economic profits entrepreneurs earn under these circumstances serve no useful purpose. Indeed, they may even be considered dysfunctional in some ways. If entrepreneurs invest their scarce time and talents in building artificial monopolies rather than searching out efficiencies, bearing risks, or fathering fresh innovations, then the economy will clearly be less well off than it would be otherwise.

Read Perspective 32C.

IV
Capitalizing Income Streams

Bill Gates came to be worth $350 million in 1986. Why? That is how much people at the time would have been willing to pay for his stake in the Microsoft Corporation if he had been willing to sell—

that is, the price per share times the number of shares. How much would you be willing to pay for a share of Microsoft stock today? More generally, how much would you be willing to pay to acquire some other asset representing the inputs discussed in this chapter, say a share of GM common stock, or a debt instrument of the Coca-Cola Company, or a parcel of land in Indiana? The answer in all these cases clearly depends on the stream of annual earnings you could reasonably expect to gain from the asset, those annual earnings called *rents* in the case of land, *interest* in the case of borrowed funds (debt), and *profit* in the case of enterprise ownership. One thing should be crystal clear. The *higher* the rents or interest payments or

---

PERSPECTIVE 32C
Thomas Alva Edison: Entrepreneur

Thomas Edison is, of course, famous for his many inventions—the incandescent lamp, phonograph, alkaline storage battery, electric generators, electric motors, and motion pictures among them. His 1,093 patents outnumber those of any other individual. What is less well known about Edison is that he was a very active entrepreneur. Moreover, his many entrepreneurial efforts generated economic profits and losses that can be attributed to risk taking, innovation, and monopolization. In the area of monopolization, for instance, Edison helped establish the Motion Picture Patents Company in 1908. This was, in essence, a cartel of all the principal parties in the motion picture industry of the time. As an innovator, Edison, through his many companies, was a pivotal character in first providing electricity to New York City, in first manufacturing phonographs, light bulbs, and many other electronic devices, and in first testing the commercial feasibility of electric railroads. Indeed, Edison's efforts at invention focused entirely on prospective innovations. "Anything that won't sell," he once said, "I don't want to invent. Its sale is proof of utility, and utility is success." As for risk, Edison often seemed to revel in it. The consequences were

sometimes catastrophic, for he suffered immense failures as well as huge triumphs. One of his biggest losses, running into millions of dollars, occurred in connection with his effort to commercialize a process of magnetic iron ore separation. Over a 2-year period, one failure was heaped on another. Machinery repeatedly broke down. Product quality never quite came up to the necessary standards. Bad weather hampered development. And so on. Yet Edison persisted. In other areas he had succeeded so often where others had failed that he could not easily give up on this project. Finally, however, abandonment was forced upon him. He ran out of money.

Henry Ford, Andrew Carnegie, and John D. Rockefeller were contemporaries of Edison. Their vast fortunes lasted well enough to influence American business history and to enrich their heirs lavishly for many generations down to the present. In contrast, there is no Edison family fortune today. Edison collided with the dark side of risk too often and too seriously.[8]

---

[8]Robert Conot, *A Streak of Luck* (New York: Bantam Books, 1980).

profits you could expect, the _more_ you would be willing to pay to acquire the assets generating those income streams.

Let's now be more precise. You should be willing to pay an amount approximated by the **present value** of the income stream that the asset generates. Because others seeking to be land owners, lenders, and enterprise owners would likewise be willing to pay an amount approximated by the present value of the income stream, the actual price of the asset will be greatly influenced by this present value. The price therefore _capitalizes_ the anticipated future stream of income amounts into one lump-sum amount. For example, Microsoft's stock was initially offered at $21 per share but was quickly bid up to $35 per share, which meant that high anticipated Microsoft earnings were capitalized into the price of the stock. Since anticipated earnings represent **future values,** we have here three main items needing calculations—namely, _present values, future values,_ and _capitalization._

A
Present Values Converted to Future Values

Let's begin by converting present values into future values, as that operation is already familiar to you. If you have $1,000 today, its _present value_ is, by definition, $1,000. If you place it in a 1-year certificate of deposit at your local bank and it earns annual interest of 6 percent, then after 1 year that $1,000 has a _future value_ of $1,000 _plus_ interest, or $1,060. Arithmetically, the calculation is this:

$$\$1{,}060 = \$1{,}000 + \$1{,}000 \times 0.06$$

or

$$\$1{,}060 = \$1{,}000(1 + 0.06)$$

Symbolically, let
PV = present value
FV = future value
r = rate of interest expressed as a fraction of 1 (so that 6 percent = 0.06)

The formula for finding 1-year future values can therefore be generalized:

$$FV_1 = PV(1 + r)$$

If the certificate of deposit had a 2-year maturity and the interest is compounded annually, then

the 2-year future value would be the 1-year future value extended for another year. Arithmetically, the preceding example becomes:

$$\$1{,}123.60 = \$1{,}060(1 + 0.06)$$

or

$$\$1{,}123.60 = \$1{,}000(1 + 0.06) \times (1 + 0.06)$$

or

$$\$1{,}123.60 = \$1{,}000(1 + 0.06)^2$$

Symbolically, this last expression for the 2-year future value can be written:

$$FV_2 = PV(1 + r)^2$$

By extension, any present value, PV, can be converted into a future value, FV, t years from now by the formula:

$$FV_t = PV(1 + r)^t$$

Taking $(1 + r)$ up to the t power is called _compounding_ because you are earning interest on the interest. The result can be, as John Maynard Keynes said, "magic" if many years and a healthy rate of interest are involved. For example, $1,000 invested at 12 percent would be worth $9,646 after 20 years and $83,522,266 after 100 years.

B
Converting Future Values to Present Values

How would you find the present value of some lump-sum future value? Easy. Just run the foregoing logic and formulas in reverse. To obtain the present value, PV, of a _1-year_ future value, FV_1, divide through by $(1 + r)$ so that

$$PV = \frac{FV_1}{(1 + r)}$$

Specifically, the present value of $1,000 earned 1 year from now, using a 6 percent rate of interest, would be

$$\$943 = \$1{,}000/(1.06)$$

It should now be clear that a dollar now and a dollar a year from now are not worth the same.

Before, *multiplication* with interest made present values worth *more* as future values. Here, *division* with interest makes future values worth *less* as present values. Converting a *2-year* future value into a present value is done similarly:

$$PV = \frac{FV_2}{(1 + r)^2}$$

The present value of $1,000 paid 2 years hence at 6 percent interest thus becomes

$$\$890 = \frac{\$1,000}{(1 + 0.06)^2}$$

More generally, for a lump-sum payment *t* years from now,

$$PV = \frac{FV_t}{(1 + r)^t}$$

So much for the present value of a *single lump-sum* future amount of money. What about the present value of a *stream* of future values coming in over a number of years (*T*)? Assets like land, loanable funds, and corporate ownership usually yield a series of future values rather than some single future value. This added step is straightforward because the present value (*PV*) of such a *series* of future values ($FV_1, FV_2, FV_3, \ldots, FV_T$) would be the *addition* of what would otherwise be single lump-sum future values. Symbolically, we thus have

$$PV = \frac{FV_1}{(1 + r)} + \frac{FV_2}{(1 + r)^2} + \ldots + \frac{FV_T}{(1 + r)^T}$$

or, generalizing and using the symbol for summation, Σ,

$$PV = \sum_{t = 1}^{T} \frac{FV_t}{(1 + r)^t}$$

Table 32.3 illustrates the computation involved, assuming a stream of future values equaling $1,000 each year over 5 years discounted with a 6 percent rate of interest. Notice from column (4) that the present value of a lump-sum $1,000 1 year from now is $943 (as reported earlier), and the present value of a lump-sum $1,000 2 years from now is $890 (as also reported earlier). When these and the other present values are added together at the bottom of column (4), the result, $4,212, is the present value of the 5-year *stream* when discounted at 6 percent interest. Without conversion, without discounting, the stream of earnings would be worth $5,000, as shown at the bottom of column (2) in Table 32.3.

Because the interest rate enters the denominator of the formula, higher interest rates cause the present value of a stream of future values to become smaller. For example, discounting with an interest rate of 10 percent reduces the $1,000 stream of future values in Table 32.3 to $3,791 (and with an interest rate of 20 percent it becomes only $2,991).

If the stream of annual earnings an asset yields, $\Sigma \, FV_t$, extends out into the indefinite future, *forever* as it were, then the formula for present value collapses into a very easily remembered ratio:

$$PV = \frac{FV_t}{r}$$

Such an asset is called a *perpetuity*. If, for example, a parcel of land can be expected to yield rental payments of $100,000 per year indefinitely, then

TABLE 32.3 The Present Value of an Annual Stream of $1,000 Earnings for 5 Years, Discounted at 6 Percent

(1) Period	(2) Future Value (Payment)	(3) $(1 + 0.06)^t$	(4) Present Value $\$1,000/(1.06)^t$
1st year	$1,000	1.060	$ 943
2nd year	1,000	1.124	890
3rd year	1,000	1.191	840
4th year	1,000	1.262	792
5th year	1,000	1.338	747
Totals (Σ)	$5,000		$4,212

when assessed at 10 percent interest, its present value would be $1 million:

$$\frac{\$100,000}{0.10} = \$1,000,000$$

This means that you should be willing to pay $1 million for this piece of property if the next best alternative investment open to you would yield a 10 percent permanent return. (If the actual price of the property was $1.3 million, you would put your money in that next best alternative investment.)

C

Capitalization

The process that discounts expected future earnings by the interest rate to convert those future earnings into a present value is called **capitalization.** When the *market* does the conversion—i.e., the land market, loanable funds market, or stock market—then this capitalization process results in a *current price* for the asset. When, for instance, the stock market capitalized the expected future earnings of Microsoft on a per-share basis once Microsoft went public in 1986, that capitalized value became $35 per share (making Bill Gates's shares worth $350 million).

Such capitalizations also cause *changes* in the market prices of assets. For example, assume that you bought 1,000 acres of scrubby desert land for $1 an acre some time ago, the total purchase price then being $1,000. Now what happens to the market value of your land when a government irrigation project is completed, allowing you (or anyone else) to farm the land, thereby earning an *additional $200* per acre above its old earnings (net of all other costs) for the indefinite future? The present value *per acre*, assessed at 10 percent, would *grow* by $2,000. This is because, by the formula for perpetuities:

$$PV = \$200/0.10 = \$2,000$$

Once the added earnings are thus capitalized into the value of your land, your 1,000 acres are worth $2 million more than what you paid for them. You have become a multi-millionaire almost overnight. If you farm the land yourself, you now earn a fantastic rate of return:

$$\frac{\$200 \text{ (earnings per acre)}}{\$1 \text{ (investment cost per acre)}} = 20,000\%$$

If you sell the land to someone else, you "cash in" on the capitalized value. Note that when someone else pays you $2,000 per acre to get the newly added $200 per acre per year, *this person's rate of return is just a normal rate of return:*

$$\frac{\$200 \text{ (earnings per acre)}}{\$2,000 \text{ (cost per acre)}} = 0.10 \text{ or } 10\%$$

Hence the *real* way to make money is the way Bill Gates did. Get in on the ground floor. Be holding an asset when its value *changes* because of a jump in its prospective earnings. When the jump in earnings is capitalized into a present value, or price, by the market, you can then boast of booming bucks. (Of course, it works on the downside, too. Reduced earnings, when capitalized into reduced asset values, can cause you to *lose* a bundle.)

Alternatively, you can grow wealthy by buying assets owned by people holding pessimistic views about the future earning power of those assets. The price will be low because the present value will be underestimated. Once the true earning power becomes known, you can sell the assets at a much higher price than you paid. The catch is this: Other bright, energetic people will be searching for such bargains in competition with you. This competition tends to lift asset prices through capitalization and lower your prospective earnings toward normal levels. Hence, if you choose this course, you will need lots of good luck.

Read Perspective 32D.

SUMMARY

1. Land, capital, and entrepreneurship receive rent, interest, and profit, respectively. These earnings comprise about 24 per-

cent of national income, and these resources are in many ways more important than their income share would suggest.

PERSPECTIVE 32D

Lotteries and Values

Speaking of luck, in September 1986, California newspapers carried headlines that Elsie Hopkins of San Diego had won *$4.23 million* in the state's lottery. Although the headlines said $4.23 million, the fine print said that Elsie would get 20 annual installments of $169,400 each after the lottery paid 20 percent of the total for federal income taxes on Elsie's behalf. Let's check this. It is true that the 20 installments and the tax add up to $4.23 million. But did Elsie *really* win $4.23 million? No, not when computed in present value. Why would Elsie be interested in present value? Why might she try to sell the stream of future installments in order to get a present value lump sum? She was 85 years old, that's why.[9] In fact, state lotteries throughout the country routinely misrepresent the value of big-money prizes by failing to convert future values into present values. A top prize of $50,000 a year for 20 years is *not* the same as $1 million. At 5 percent interest it is actually $654,266, and at 10 percent interest it is actually no more than $468,246. If, instead of $50,000 for 20 years, you actually did win $1 million *today*, you could buy a tax-free municipal bond paying, say, 10 percent interest. You could then spend the interest—$100,000 per year—and at the end of 20 years you would still have your $1 million!

[9]"A $4.23 million winner," *San Jose Mercury News*, September 14, 1986, p. 16.

---

2. Economic rent is like a bonus. It is a payment to any resource input above the price required to obtain the quantity supplied.

3. Land, in the aggregate, receives a pure economic rent, because the supply is fixed, or perfectly inelastic.

4. Variations in location and physical features cause rents for specific parcels of land to vary. In turn, these variations in rents guide the allocation of parcels to different uses, because rents are costs to users of land.

5. Real capital inputs permit roundabout production, which increases output through growth. However, real capital inputs require curtailed current consumption. Financial capital, as reflected in the market for loanable funds, translates the curtailed current consumption into the real capital inputs.

6. With roundabout production real output is increased in the long run, thereby providing the gains to reward saver-lenders for their delayed gratification and to allow the investor-borrowers to cover their credit costs. Financially, these rewards and costs are measured by the interest rate, which links the present and future.

7. The interest on *particular* transactions varies with risk, maturity, and loan size.

8. More generally, average interest is determined by the interaction of demand and supply in the market for loanable funds.

9. Changes in the general level of interest rates occur with shifts in demand and supply in the market for loanable funds. Price inflation shifts both, raising the nominal rate of interest by an amount roughly equal to the anticipated rate of inflation. The real rate (nominal rate less inflation) is steadier.

10. Normal profits cover a return to basic enterprise ownership and entrepreneurship reflecting routine management.

11. Economic profits reward more exciting entrepreneurship—namely, that associated with (a) especially efficient management, (b) risk acceptance, and (c) successful innovation.

12. Economic profit serves a useful purpose as a stimulant to the preceding functions of entrepreneurship. Economic profit associated with monopoly serves no social purpose.

13. The process that discounts expected future earnings by the interest rate to convert those earnings into a present value is called _capitalization._ When the markets for land, capital, and entrepreneurship do this conversion, it results in a current price for the asset. Changes in future earnings can therefore cause huge changes in the present values and prices of these assets.

KEY TERMS

Economic rent
Pure economic rent
Roundabout production
Interest
Market for loanable funds

Nominal interest rate
Real interest rate
Future value
Present value
Capitalization

QUESTIONS AND PROBLEMS

1. Land surface rents are pure economic rents. Explain why.
2. Doomsayers in the U.S. have periodically forecast starvation for masses of Americans, noting the rapid rate at which farmland is being converted to parking lots. Explain the economic considerations being ignored by these doomsayers.
3. Explain the basis for rural/urban price differentials in land surface.
4. Why does the demand curve for loanable funds slope down?
5. Distinguish between real and nominal interest rates. Which are more volatile?
6. Why does a change in the inflation rate shift _both_ the demand and supply curves for loanable funds?

7. How is the use of capital in the production process linked to the market for loanable funds?
8. What are the causes of economic profits?
9. John Smith files suit against Jamestown Company. On 1 January 1989, his attorney, Ms. Rolfe, negotiates a settlement with the company's attorney. If Mr. Smith agrees to drop his suit, the company will pay either of the following to Mr. Smith:
   (a) a lump sum of $50,000 on 15 January 1989;
   (b) a lump sum of $9,000 on 15 January 1989 and future payments of $7,000 on 15 January in each of the next eight years.

Assuming that the payments are nontaxable and that Mr. Smith can earn about 6% (after taxes) each year on any lump sum payment he receives, should he choose alternative (a) or alternative (b)?

VI

Selected Topics In Microeconomics

33

Poverty, Inequality, and Discrimination

Consider the case of Beatrice Halsey Bell, a 59-year-old woman who lives with her infant grandson on an income of $147 a month near North Wilkesboro, North Carolina: "I buys the cheapest stuff I can find," she says. "I can get four spaghetti for a dollar. Now crackers, I can get two boxes for one dollar. . . . I make kraut, pickled beans, and pickled beets."[1]

Consider next the case of Caroline Rose Hunt Schoellkopf, the 63-year-old daughter of H. L. Hunt, who struck it rich in Texas oil during the early 1930s. Mrs. Hunt Schoellkopf has seen her massive inheritance grow into a fortune worth about $1.3 billion. Besides oil, her vast holdings include a chain of superluxury hotels in places like Beverly Hills. Says she: "The hotels are not the whim of a rich woman, but a calculated real estate investment."[2]

These cases illustrate the *personal distribution of income*, which is the subject of this chapter. The personal distribution differs from the *functional distribution of income* that held our attention in previous chapters. The *functional distribution* is the division of national income among the owners of various resources—the income shares going to wages, rents, interest, and profits. In contrast, the *personal distribution* is the division of national income among the poor and the rich and those in the middle class, between men and women, and between whites and minorities—regardless of the sources of those earnings (be they labor, land, capital, or entrepreneurship).

A little over 20 years ago, President Lyndon Johnson declared "War *on* Poverty," instigating hefty increases in spending for the poor. Now there seems to be a "War *over* Poverty," a noisy debate over what should be done. We shall see why this is so. Poverty is still with us despite great government efforts.

As regards discrimination, our second major topic, controversy abounds there as well. Policies started just over 20 years ago have been subjected to increasingly shrill dispute. One side argues that discrimination is not a problem (or no longer a problem) worthy of vigorous government policies. The other side claims that discrimination remains a national disgrace, a problem that requires "affirmative action" if objectives of equity are to be achieved.

I

Poverty and Inequality

A

How Are Poverty and Inequality Defined and Measured?

In the early 1960s, you could drive through the South and see children with distended stomachs who were clearly starving. Likewise, you could easily spot many homeless people wandering the streets of our biggest cities. Now, after $20 billion has been spent annually for food programs and extensive housing subsidies, these problems are less severe but still with us. Recent estimates indicate that several hundred Americans die of starvation each year and about 2 million people lack homes for shelter.[3]

People lacking the bare essentials of food or shelter could be considered poor in an *absolute* sense. They do not have the goods and services necessary for basic well-being. An alternative definition of poverty adopts a *relative* approach. It says that a person is poor when his or her income falls substantially below the average income of those in society. Relative to other Americans of typical means, the homeless and starving obviously fare pretty badly.

We shall survey statistics drawn from definitions of both sorts—*absolute* and *relative*. However, it should be recognized at the outset that, in reality, these approaches tend to blend. What is considered essential in the absolute approach is, in the

---

[1] "New Poor Find Holes in the Social Security Net," *San Jose Mercury News*, January 27, 1986, p. 2A.

[2] "The Forbes Four Hundred," *Forbes*, October 25, 1985, p. 115.

[3] *The Wall Street Journal*, March 9, 1984, p. 12.

end, heavily influenced by the standard of living provided by the typical income that is key to the relative approach. For example, what would you consider essential if a person or family is to avoid poverty in an absolute sense? A black-and-white television? A telephone? A meal at a fast-food restaurant at least once a week? When asked, a solid majority of Americans who were surveyed thought that these were important enough that people on welfare should be given sufficient assistance to enable them to afford these purchases.[4] However, an absolute standard drawn up in the days of George Washington would certainly have excluded these as frivolous luxuries.

In brief, a definition of poverty would refer to a *shortage of income.* Attempts to identify what is meant by *shortage* have led to two approaches:

An **absolute definition** specifies a poverty-line income based on the amount needed to buy essential goods and services.

A **relative definition** specifies a poverty-line income at some minimum level relative to other, higher incomes.

In turn, attempts to specify what is meant by *income* lead to three broad approaches—(1) income *before* any government intervention affecting the distribution of income, (2) income *after* accounting for government cash transfers, and (3) income *after* accounting for government cash transfers *and in-kind* assistance.

Pretransfer Income: The first of these income concepts can be called *pretransfer income* or *free-market income,* because it reflects what people would earn from the market system absent official intervention. Direct observations of these earnings are impossible to obtain today because the government intervenes in a big way, presently transferring over $400 billion annually from taxpayers to recipients of various kinds. Social security alone tops $180 billion annually. Crude estimates of what people would earn in the absence of all transfers can be obtained by subtracting their transfer income from their total income. What is left is a pretransfer market income. However, this

[4]*Washington Post National Weekly Edition,* September 23, 1985, p. 38.

can be no more than a very rough estimate of market income in the absence of transfers. If actually deprived of those transfers, people would probably boost their market earnings by working more than they presently do.

Income After Cash Transfers: The poverty statistics published by the federal government are based on incomes that include earnings from **cash transfers** as well as earnings from resource markets. These cash transfers include such things as social security retirement benefits, disability pensions, and unemployment compensation to those who are temporarily out of work.

Income After Cash and In-Kind Transfers: Much aid to the poor takes the form of **in-kind transfers.** These are actual goods and services—such as the food purchased with food stamps and the medical services granted under Medicaid. Although all economists agree that these in-kind transfers increase the economic well-being of those who receive them, there is much debate over how they should be accounted for and the extent to which they should be added to money income for purposes of defining poverty. Hence we will review income figures with and without in-kind transfers.

When these three possible measures of income are aligned with the two measures of shortage identified earlier, we have six relevant measures—*absolute* measures of poverty before any transfers, after cash transfers, and after all transfers (including in-kind aid), plus *relative* measures of poverty under the same three definitions of income.

1. The Absolute Approach   A 1955 survey found that the average family spent about one-third of its income on food. So during the 1960s, when the War on Poverty began, the government set its poverty-line income at three times the cost of a cheap but nutritionally sound diet. Since then the official poverty-line income has been adjusted for family size and price inflation. In 1986, for instance, a family of four whose income fell below $11,000 was said to be in poverty. (For a one-person family the threshold was $5,360 in 1986, and for a six-person family it was $14,760.)

How many Americans fall below this absolute poverty line? Figure 33.1 shows statistics for our three different definitions of income in 1983. The pretransfer poverty rate that year was 24.2 percent,

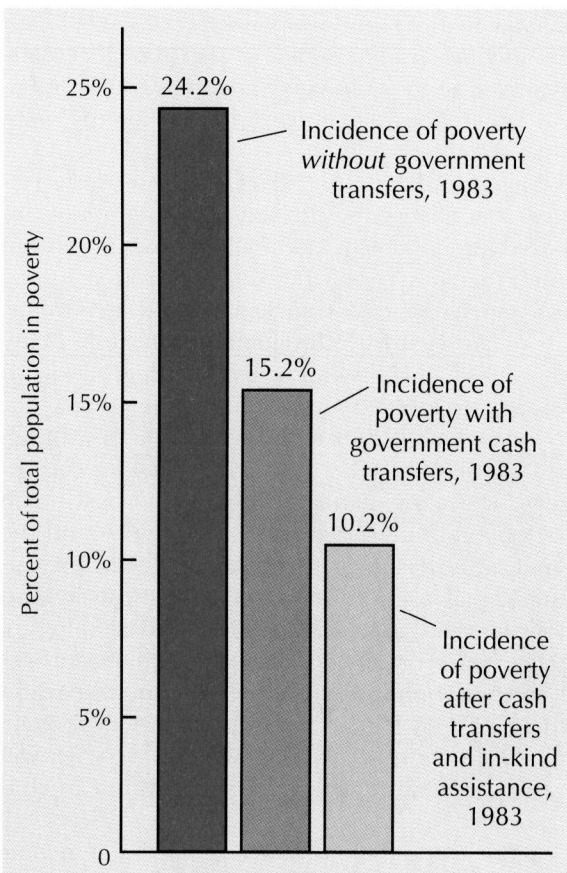

FIGURE 33.1 *Incidence of Poverty Using the Official Absolute Definition, 1983 Data, by Different Degrees of Government Intervention*

(Sources: Sheldon Danziger and Peter Gottschalk, "On Losing Ground," Challenge, *May–June 1985, p. 34; Sheldon Danziger, Robert Haveman, and Robert Plotnick,* Focus. *University of Wisconsin; Institute for Research on Poverty, Summer 1985, p. 2.)*

meaning that 24.2 percent of the population fell below the poverty threshold when only their market earnings are counted as income. (That's 56.6 million people.) Once cash transfers are included in income, counting social security benefits and the like, the incidence of poverty in the United States drops substantially to 15.2 percent (or 35.6 million people). Finally, once in-kind assistance is also accounted for, the incidence of poverty drops still further to 10.2 percent in 1983 (or roughly 23.9 million people).

What has been the long-term *trend* in poverty measured absolutely? Very few data are available before 1960. But those sparse data indicate a sub-

stantial downward trend over this century. In 1930, it appears that perhaps half of all Americans were below the absolute poverty line as now defined. This is a pretransfer *and* a posttransfer estimate simply because there were no government transfers of any significance at that early date. It is interesting to compare this 50 percent pretransfer and posttransfer rate to the more recent rates of Figure 33.1 because such a comparison summarizes the long-run trend. Whereas in 1930 market earnings put roughly half of the population in poverty, the crude estimate now is about 24 percent, a huge drop. Economic growth can be credited with this great achievement, because growth tends to lift the real income of the populace generally, thereby lifting many of the less fortunate members of society above the absolute poverty line. Once cash transfers are included in the calculation, poverty drops from 50 percent to about 15 percent, an even more impressive result than the one provided by the market system alone. After adding in-kind assistance, the long-term drop is even steeper—50 percent in 1930 to about 10 percent in 1983.

The data between 1930 and today are spotty before 1960. For example, estimates of posttransfer poverty around 1950 range from 30 to 40 percent, depending on the source.[5] However, data since 1960 are more abundant. Figure 33.2 illustrates this by showing absolute poverty in percentage terms and in number of persons, based on money income after cash transfers, from 1960 to 1985. These data reflect the tail end of the long-run downward trend just summarized. Moreover, they show annual swings in the poverty rate triggered by serious recessions. Most important, Figure 33.2 shows a recent rise in the poverty rate since 1980, such that the 14 percent poverty rate of 1985 was about the same as the rate nearly 20 years earlier in 1967. Two developments explain this recent rise in poverty after many decades of decline—(1) the recession of 1981–82, the worst since the Great Depression, and (2) substantial cutbacks in federal assistance under the Reagan administration.

In sum, great strides have been made against absolute poverty in the United States until recently. The rates for the mid-1980s (e.g., 24 percent pre-

[5]"The Level and Trend in Poverty," *Social Security Bulletin* (April 1986), p. 25; Christopher Jenks, "How Poor Are the Poor?" *New York Review of Books*, May 9, 1985, p. 42.

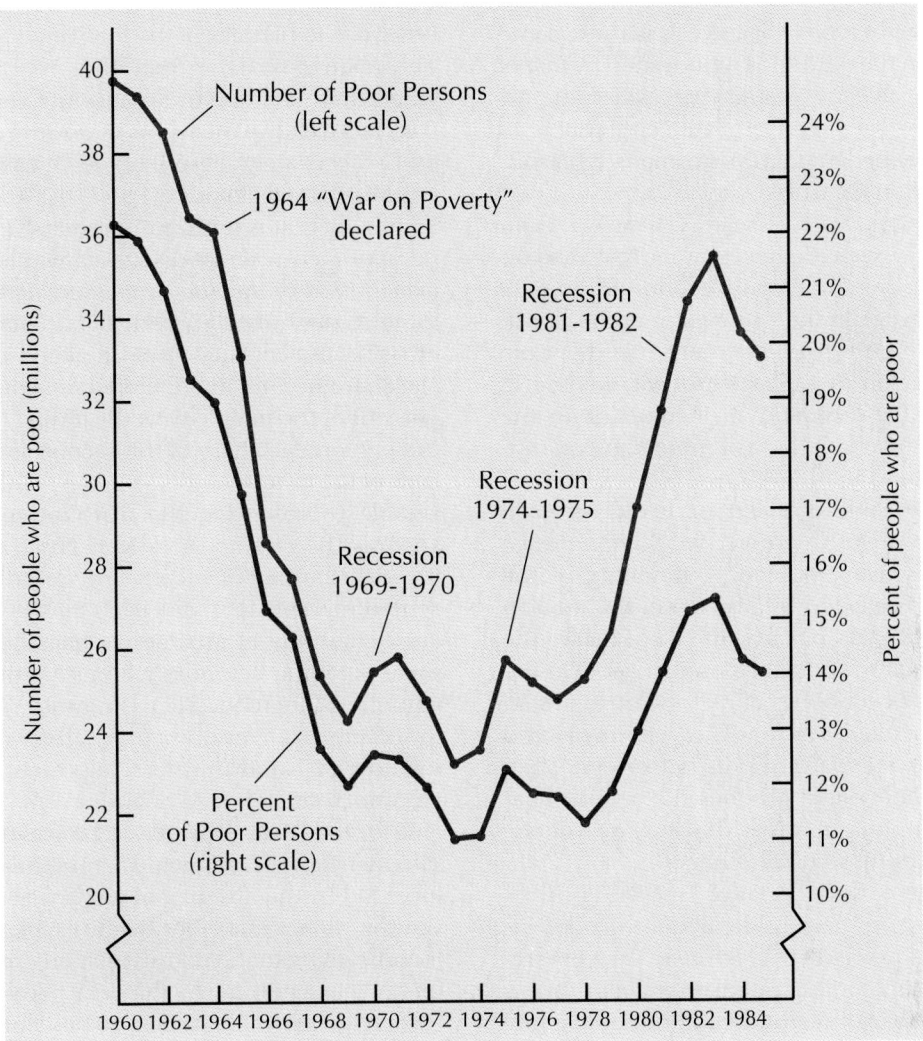

FIGURE 33.2   _Recent Trend in U.S. Poverty_

This figure shows the recent trend in poverty as defined in official U.S. government statistics—the number and percentage of people below the poverty line after taking account of all cash transfers. (Source: Economic Report of the President 1986, _p. 286;_ The Wall Street Journal, _August 27, 1986, p. 5.)_

transfer, 15 percent posttransfer cash, and 10 percent posttransfer in kind for 1983) are way below the rates of 1930 (roughly 50 percent pre- and posttransfer). Economic growth and government policy can both be credited.

2. _The Relative Approach_ In 1986 millions of Americans linked hands in a 4,152-mile human chain spanning the country. This "Hands Across America" campaign helped feed the hungry. If we were to line up _everyone_ across the country in

order of their family income earnings, placing the very richest in the East and the very poorest in the West, we would then have a basis for calculating several _relative_ measures of poverty.

One such measure would draw the poverty line at some set percentage of the median family income. Median family income would be the income earned by the family in the very middle of the countrywide lineup of all families. This is _not_ the average family income, which would be the total aggregate income divided by the number of families, but it is a type of average. It is the income of the family in the middle as determined by half of the number of all families. Many specialists in poverty economics say that a family income that is 40 percent of the median family income is a reasonable poverty line measure.

What distinguishes this relative measure from the absolute measure? Note that as real median income rises over time with economic growth, there is *no change* in the proportion of the populace in *relative* poverty *unless* there is at the same time a change in the *distribution* of income (a reduction in the *inequality* of income), with the very poorest experiencing rising incomes *relative* to those around the median level. For example, if real median income doubled (as it did between 1950 and 1980), relative poverty would *not change* if *all* incomes also doubled. A doubling of the incomes of those below 40 percent of the median and those above this poverty line would leave the proportions below and above unchanged. On the other hand, a doubling of all incomes *would* reduce the incidence of poverty when measured by an *absolute* standard (representing food, shelter, etc.). Economic growth does not reduce relative poverty unless it raises the incomes of the poor *relative* to those of all others.

One problem with relative measures thus emerges. They are heavily dependent on the income level of the *society of reference*. Take Beverly Hills as a society to illustrate this concept. By an absolute standard, it might be that not one family in Beverly Hills, California, is poor. However, there are quite a number of families in that town earning less than 40 percent of the *median in Beverly Hills*. The relative measure may thus report "poverty" when there is none in an absolute sense.

In fact, relative measures of poverty are perhaps more accurately described as measures of **inequality** rather than of poverty. A measure of inequality that is more comprehensive than the 40 percent measure just discussed would look at *the distribution of income over all income groups*. If, for instance, we returned to our line of people crossing the country and calculated the percentage share of total national income going to the 20 percent of the people with the lowest income, and the percentage share of the second lowest 20 percent of the people, and so on, the results would be a table representing the distribution of income such as the one in Table 33.1. Three estimates of the distribution of income by quintiles are presented in Table 33.1, one each for the three different definitions of income we have been working with—income before any government transfer in column (1), income after cash transfers (and taxes) in column (2), and income after all transfers, including in-kind transfers (and taxes), in the last column. (Data for each definition are not yet available for the 1980s, so Table 33.1 refers to the 1970s.) The distribution of income across quintiles is very lopsided in the absence of any government intervention. Column (1) shows only 0.6 percent of total income going to the poorest 20 percent of the population, in contrast to the 48.2 percent share of income going to the richest 20 percent of the population. The inequality is reduced by the more equal distribution of column (2), which incorpo-

TABLE 33.1   Distribution of Total Income Going to Different Segments of the Population, Ranked by Fifths (Data from the 1970s)

Ranking by Quintile	(1) Before Any Government Intervention	(2) After Cash Transfers (and Taxes)	(3) After All Transfers (and Taxes)
Lowest 20%	0.6%	6.5%	12.6%
Second 20%	8.0	12.1	16.1
Third 20%	16.4	16.9	18.4
Fourth 20%	26.7	24.6	20.9
Highest 20%	48.2	39.8	31.9
Total	100.0%	100.0%	100.0%

Source: G. William Hoagland, "The Effectiveness of Current Transfer Programs in Reducing Poverty." (Washington, D.C.: Congressional Budget Office, 1980), p. 19; Edgar K. Browning, "The Trend Toward Equality in the Distribution of Net Income," *Southern Economic Journal*, (July 1976), p. 919. Numbers may not sum to total due to rounding.

rates cash transfers (plus taxes). It is reduced still further in the estimates of column (3), which accounts for in-kind transfers as well as cash transfers.

A handy way to depict such measures of inequality is with the **Lorenz curve,** so named for its inventor, Max Otto Lorenz. Figure 33.3 illustrates with hypothetical data. Both axes are scaled in percentages, with maximum possible values of 100 percent. The axes are therefore bounded to form a square of 100 percent dimensions. Our line-up of people is shown on the horizontal axis as a *cumulative* percentage, beginning with the poorest on the left (in the West) and ending with the richest on the right (in the East). The vertical axis represents the *cumulative* percentage of total income earned by these people, starting at zero and ending at 100 percent. If each 20 percent of the population had exactly 20 percent of the income, the cumulative percentages would rise along the *diagonal*, rising first to point *x*, where the "poorest" 20 percent of the people would be getting 20 percent of the income, then rising to point *w*, where the "poorest" 40 percent of the people would be getting 40 percent of the income, and so on (60:60 and 80:80) until all incomes and all people were accounted for (100:100). The diagonal is thus a *line of perfect equality.* With inequality, as actually occurs, the Lorenz curve bows out, away from the line of equality. For example, if in reality the poorest 20 percent of the populace gets only 5 percent of the total income, the Lorenz curve moves through point *y* in Figure 33.3. Further unequal accumulations in Figure 33.3 lead to point *z*, where 80 percent of the population, cumulating from the poorest, are shown to receive 55 percent of the income (leaving 45 percent for the enjoyment of the top 20 percent). *The greater the inequality, the further the Lorenz curve diverges from the line of equality.*

This last observation is illustrated in Figure 33.4, which is based on the real-world data of Table 33.1. Note, however, that the data in Table 33.1 are not cumulated, whereas by necessity they are cumulated in Figure 33.4. The dashed-line Lorenz curve, depicting the income distribution before any government intervention, displays the greatest degree of inequality, being farthest from the diagonal line of equality. As first cash transfers and then in-kind transfers are taken into account, the income earnings of the poor rise relative to those of the rich, shifting the Lorenz curve toward the line of equality.

What about *trends* over time in these relative measures? The long-term trend does reveal some increased equality (reduced inequality), but not as much as might be suggested by the very large changes observed earlier in the absolute measures. The reason for the smaller effect here is fairly clear. Oversimplifying, there are *two* factors at work on the absolute measures—growth and government. Here, with the relative measure, there is essentially only *one* main factor at work—government. Economic growth enlarges the absolute size of the income pie without greatly altering the relative percentages in its slices. Government, on the other hand, with its extensive activities of tax and transfer, effectively *redistributes* income from the rich to the poor, thereby achieving greater equality of income shares than would otherwise occur. It reslices the pie, and as government has engaged in ever more extensive transferring over time, it has

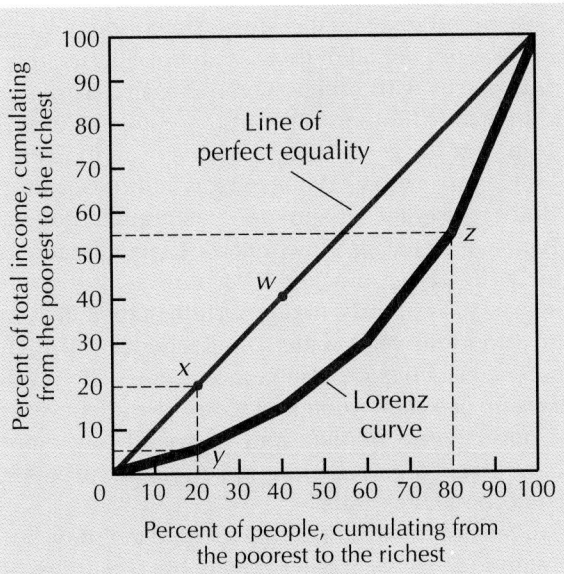

FIGURE 33.3   The Lorenz Curve

The Lorenz curve depicts the degree of inequality in the income distribution. If all incomes were equal, each 20 percent of the population would receive 20 percent of the income, placing society on the diagonal line of equality, as illustrated by points x and w. With inequality, the poorest 20 percent of the population receives less than 20 percent of the income, say, 5 percent (as at y). The poorest 80 percent receives, say, 55 percent (as at z).

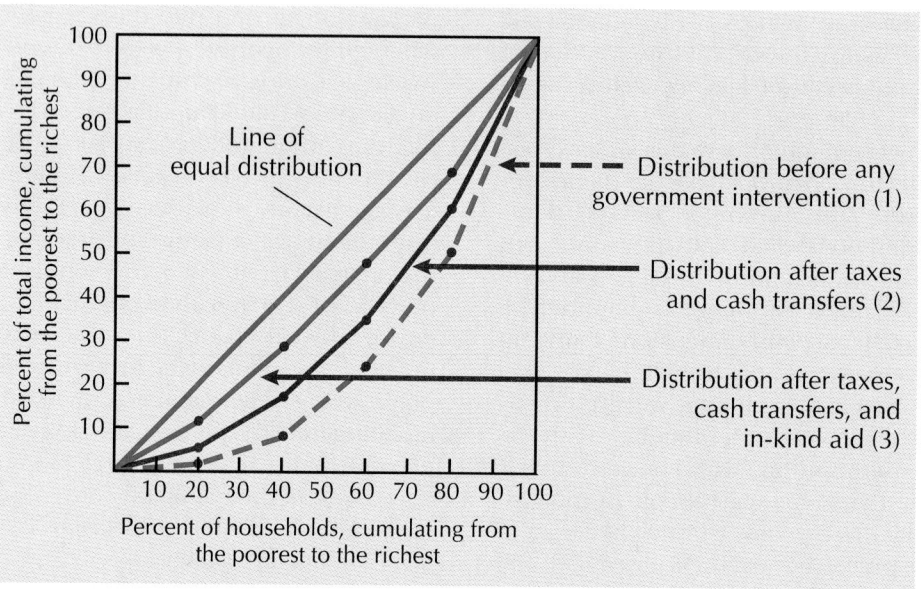

FIGURE 33.4 *Lorenz Curves Depicting the Degree of Inequality Before and After Government Interventions, 1970s*

(Source: See Table 33.1.)

shifted America's actual Lorenz curve toward the line of equality. Stated differently, Figure 33.4 serves double duty. Besides showing the current effects of government, it gives a faint representation of what has happened *over time*, as a result of *changes* in government policy, because in the long run the government has become ever more active in redistributing income.

Using a *relative* measure that sets the poverty threshold at 44 percent of the median income, researchers have recently found posttransfer poverty falling 10 percent over the 30 years from 1949 to 1979. This is a much smaller drop in poverty than the 68 percent drop in poverty over the same years when measured *absolutely* by a fixed standard of living.[6]

3. Mobility and Wealth: Two Qualifications
Two qualifications modify the impression left by the foregoing discussion. One brightens the statistical picture of poverty. The other darkens it.

The brightener qualification, which makes the grip of poverty seem less severe than suggested previously, is **income mobility.** If those who are poor at any one time are only *temporarily* poor,

then their plight is only temporary. They are not condemned to a squalid life at the bottom year in and year out, for all of their existence. Rather, they trade places with others who themselves slip into poverty only temporarily and then out. For example, one of the major determinants of an individual's income is age. When one is either a young adult or a senior citizen, one has a much greater chance of suffering a low income than a person in the 30 to 60 age bracket. Yet youngsters and old persons also spend a major portion of their lives in those middle years when their chances of high income earnings are well above average. If, in the extreme case, *everyone* had to endure a few years of poverty and *nobody* had to spend any more than those few years in poverty, the problem would be less serious.

In fact, there is substantial income mobility, but not enough to wash the problem away. Studies of posttransfer cash income experience indicate that approximately 25 percent of all Americans fall below the poverty line at some time in their lives. Most of the resulting spells of poverty are quite short. Nearly 45 percent of them end within 1 year. On the other hand, it is also true that, of those who are below the poverty line on some given date, say May 1, 1986, more than 50 percent will be in a peri-

[6]*Social Security Bulletin* (April 1986), p. 26.

od of poverty lasting 10 years or more.[7] So income mobility does not eliminate the problem.

Our second qualification, the one that darkens the picture a bit, concerns wealth. The foregoing discussion concerns annual *income*, not *wealth*. **Wealth** *is comprised of financial assets like savings accounts, common stocks and bonds, or real assets like real estate, oil reserves, and gold.* Although data on wealth are sketchier than data on annual income, it seems quite clear that the distribution of American wealth is much *less equal* than the distribution of income. As indicated in Figure 33.5, which reports data from 1983, the richest 0.5 percent of all households enjoy 26.9 percent of all the wealth in the United States. The richest 10 percent of all households—those with wealth exceeding $206,340 in 1983, hold over 67 percent of all wealth. Comparing these statistics with those for income in Table 33.1, we find a much sharper inequality here in wealth.

[7]Mary Jo Bane and David T. Ellwood, "Slipping Into and Out of Poverty," *Journal of Human Resources* (Winter 1986), pp. 1–23. See also Greg J. Duncan, *Years of Poverty, Years of Plenty* (Ann Arbor: Survey Research Center, University of Michigan, 1984).

B

What Are the Causes of Poverty?

Individual incomes differ for many reasons, some of which were suggested earlier.

1. *Work intensity:* Other things being equal, those who work longer hours or put more effort into each hour of work tend to earn higher incomes than others.
2. *Work ability:* Given the importance of productivity to wages, differences in ability affect differences in income earnings (although ability is often difficult to measure).
3. *Compensating wage differentials:* Hazardous or otherwise unpleasant working conditions can influence income differences.
4. *Luck:* As everyone knows, many rags-to-riches stories center on good luck, while many riches-to-rags stories hinge on bad luck.
5. *Inherited wealth:* This is a form of luck. According to *Forbes* magazine, fewer than half of the 400 very richest people in the

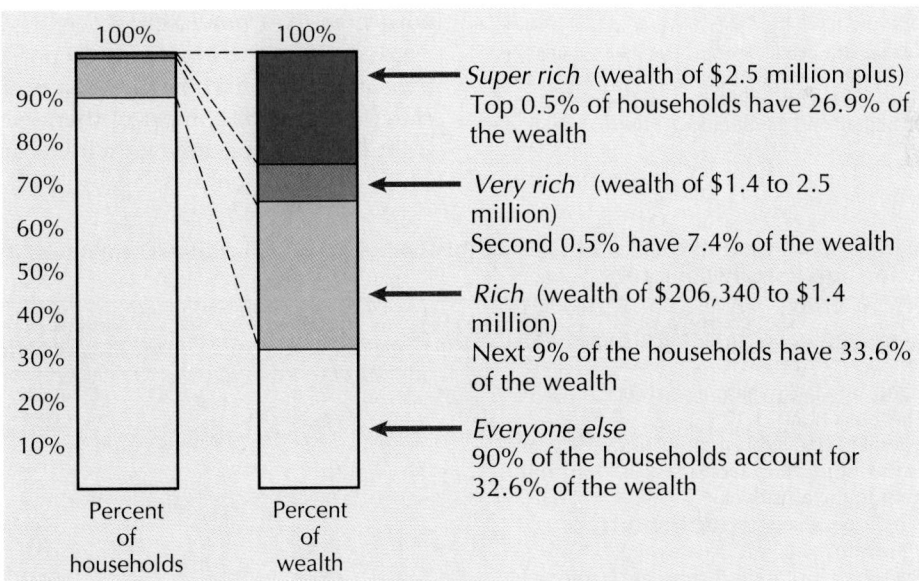

FIGURE 33.5 _Distribution of Wealth in the United States, 1983_

(Source: Joint Economic Committee, U.S. Congress, 1986, as reported in The Wall Street Journal, *August 22, 1986, p. 6. Note: Early numbers from this source showed an even greater concentration of wealth. Here are the "conservative" estimates understating the degree of inequality in 1983.)*

United States built their fortunes on their own, without any "significant inheritances" (165 people, to be exact, in 1985).[8]

6. *Risk taking:* As seen in our earlier discussion of entrepreneurship, risk taking is often rewarded by stupendous incomes.

Although these factors go a long way toward explaining individual differences in income, thereby explaining much *relative inequality,* they do not adequately explain *absolute poverty.* Those at the very bottom of the heap have several characteristics that more thoroughly identify the causes of their plight. *In particular, there appear to be three major elements that explain poverty in the United States—(1) no work, (2) low human capital, and (3) discrimination against women and minorities.* We shall discuss each in turn, using Tables 33.2 and 33.3 to illustrate the main points. Both tables report data on estimated *pretransfer* poverty. That is, they count only market incomes because market incomes are the most telling about causes.

1. Work/Not Work   Table 33.2 identifies the chief characteristics of those households with pretransfer incomes that fell below the official absolute poverty line in 1976. Almost half of all such

[8]"The Forbes Four Hundred," *Forbes,* October 28, 1985, p. 127. By the way, the total estimated net worth of the 1985 *Forbes* 400 was $134 billion, an amount exceeding the GNP of Switzerland ($100 billion) and Saudi Arabia ($108 billion). Ibid., p. 206.

households, 46.8 percent, were headed by people 65 years of age and over. Another 12.2 percent were headed by disabled people. In neither of these cases—old age or disability—are people expected to work. Hence a solid majority of the pretransfer poor, almost 59.0 percent by these data, do not and cannot be expected to work.

Quite a number of other poor households, 6.8 percent in Table 33.2, are headed by women with children under 6. Here, too, a lack of work explains the poverty. Several decades ago, these women would not be expected to work. Now, greater expectations of work are placed on these single mothers of very young children. Even so, for most, the child-care expenses that working would require are probably too great, relative to the incomes offered, to warrant working.

Adding these households to the aged and disabled yields a total of 65.8 percent who are poor mainly because of the work/not work distinction. Adding nonworking students to this class as well—another 5.2 percent—puts the percentage of nonworkers at 71 percent, although students are clearly the least worrisome of the nonworkers because they will soon work for large financial rewards. *In sum, the work/not work distinction seems to explain roughly 70 percent of all cases of poverty in the United States.*

What about the remaining 30 percent who slip beneath the official absolute poverty line? As indicated in Table 33.2, most of them work, but they work *less* than full-time for a full year. Hence lack

TABLE 33.2   **Characteristics of Households with Market (Pretransfer) Incomes Below the Poverty Line, 1976**

Description of Household	Number (Millions)	Percentage of the Poor
Aged head (65 years and over)	9.76	46.8%
Disabled head	2.54	12.2
Female head with a child under 6 years	1.41	6.8
Household head working less than full time for a full year*	2.59	12.4
Single person working less than full-time for a full year	1.88	9.0
Persons working full-time for a full year	1.58	7.6
Students	1.09	5.2
All pretransfer poor households	20.85	100.0%

*Includes male heads and female heads without children under 6.

Source: Focus, Winter 1981-1982, Vol. 5, No. 2, p. 7. (*Focus* is published by the Institute for Research on Poverty, University of Wisconsin-Madison.)

of work helps to explain most of these remaining cases as well. Here, however, is where low human capital and discrimination begin to have an impact as causes of poverty.

2. Low Human Capital   Table 33.3 reports only on nonaged, able-bodied heads of households, so it is quite different from Table 33.2. It shows the *incidence* of pretransfer poverty for certain segments of the nonaged, able-bodied population. In other words, it reports the percentage of each identified group earning less from market sources than a poverty-level income. Reading the table vertically, from top to bottom in each column, you will see that more education uniformly lowers the incidence of poverty for both sexes and for whites and nonwhites. Look, for instance, at the "some college" numbers. The pretransfer poverty rate for white males with some college, 2.6 percent, is 76 percent lower than the rate for elementary school dropouts, 10.8 percent. *In sum, poverty rises dramatically among the nonaged able-bodied as education level falls.*

3. Discrimination   Viewed horizontally, Table 33.3 indicates that discrimination may be considered a third major source of poverty. The pretransfer poverty rate for nonwhites is much greater than that for whites, among both men and women, and at each level of educational attainment. On average, for instance, the poverty rate for nonwhite men is 32 percent greater than it is for white men in these data. The discrepancies between men and women are even more striking. The poverty rate for white women is 6.6 times greater than that for white men, averaging over all educational classes. We will see shortly that discrimination cannot explain the entire extent of these huge differences between races and sexes. Factors other than discrimination also contribute. Still, it can be concluded that *discrimination against blacks and women fosters a greater incidence of poverty for households headed by these two groups than would otherwise occur.*

C
What Are the Policies?

President Johnson's War on Poverty brought a hefty expansion of government antipoverty policies that Johnson hoped would create a "Great Society." However, as the years passed, the critics multiplied, arguing that we could not solve these problems by "throwing money" at them. During the early 1980s this critical view became official government policy, as indicated in this 1982 statement by President Ronald Reagan: "With the coming of the Great Society, government began eating away at the underpinnings of the private enterprise system. The big taxers and big spenders in Congress had started a binge that would slowly change the nature of our society and, even worse, it threatened the character of our people."

Notice that both *taxes* and *spending* enter Reagan's remarks. Our discussion of policy shall cover both.

TABLE 33.3   Predicted Incidence of Market Income (Pretransfer) Poverty Among Nonaged, Able-Bodied Household Heads, 1978

Level of Education	White Male	Nonwhite Male	White Female	Nonwhite Female
Elementary school dropouts	10.8%	14.7%	50.1%	72.2%
High school dropouts	6.8	12.7	52.2	65.0
High school graduates	3.2	4.7	24.9	37.7
Some College (1–3 years)	2.6	3.0	16.0	22.7

Source: Focus, Winter 1981-1982, Vol. 5, No. 2, p. 8. (*Focus* is published by the Institute for Research on Poverty, University of Wisconsin-Madison.)

1. Taxes and Income Inequality Taxes can influence income distribution by their impact on after-tax income. Taxes may be *progressive, proportional*, or *regressive*. A tax is *progressive* if, *as a percentage of income*, the tax burden *rises* as income rises. The reference to a percentage of income needs stress because a tax burden can rise in absolute dollars as well as a percentage of income, and it is the latter that really counts here. If, for example, someone with an annual income of $20,000 pays $5,000 in taxes while someone else with an annual income of $40,000 pays $12,000 in taxes, the tax system is progressive because $5,000 is 25 percent of $20,000, while $12,000 is 30 percent of $40,000. As income doubles, the tax bill more than doubles. This is shown in Table 33.4, which also illustrates proportional and regressive taxation. There it may be seen that a tax is *proportional* if, as a percentage of income, the tax liability *remains unchanged* as income rises. Finally, a tax is *regressive* if, as a percentage of income, the tax burden *falls* as income rises. In this last case, the poor pay more than the rich as a percentage of income.

A tax is **progressive, proportional,** or **regressive** depending on whether the ratio of tax to income (percentage rate) rises, remains unchanged, or falls as income rises.

The tax rate of greatest relevance here is the *effective tax rate*. To calculate the **effective tax rate**, *the taxpayer's total tax bill is divided by his or her total income*. According to effective tax rates, then, is the U.S. tax system progressive, proportional, or regressive? If the tax system is progressive, it helps redistribute income from the rich to the poor. If it is regressive, it does the reverse, saddling the poor more than the rich. If it is proportional, the tax system has a neutral impact on income distribution.

TABLE 33.4 Illustrations of Progressive, Proportional, and Regressive Taxes

	Income Level	
Type of Tax	**$20,000**	**$40,000**
Progressive tax	$5,000 (25%)	$12,000 (30%)
Proportional tax	$5,000 (25%)	$10,000 (25%)
Regressive tax	$5,000 (25%)	$ 8,000 (20%)

Unfortunately, an exact answer to this question is very difficult to obtain because it is very difficult to estimate who pays certain taxes. One especially tricky tax is the corporate profits tax. Do corporate stockholders pay in reduced dividends, or do corporate customers pay in higher product prices? It's not clear who pays. Given uncertainties such as this, researchers vary their approaches.

Perhaps the best approach is the one reflected in Figure 33.6, which comes from a Brookings Institution study of the issue for 1980. The horizontal axis is the cumulative array of people, from poor to rich, running left to right, as before. The vertical axis is the percentage of total income these people paid in taxes of all kinds—local, state, and federal—for an overall effective tax rate. Two estimated tax distributions are shown. One makes the most progressive assumptions possible about who pays those taxes of uncertain incidence. The other makes the least progressive assumptions. In the end, Joseph Pechman, who authored the study, concludes that "*the tax system has very little effect on the distribution of income.*" Under either set of assumptions, *the tax burden is very close to being proportional.*[9] *If it is at all progressive, it is only slightly so.* The redistributive effects of government therefore come mainly from the *spending side* of the government's fiscal activities, not the tax side.

2. Spending Programs and Poverty Given that poverty has a variety of causes, it follows that there should be a variety of spending policies to assist the poor. For the vast majority of the poor who cannot work or cannot be expected to work, the principal aim of policy should simply be transfers to lift income. For those suffering temporary job loss but with a bright future, some sort of temporary relief would seem appropriate. For those who can be expected to work but who earn poverty-level incomes because of low education or weak skills, training and employment programs would offer the best hope.

To a large degree, this desired variety has been realized in actual policies, which may be placed in the four main classes to be described and outlined in Table 33.5—*(1) social insurance, (2) cash welfare, also called public assistance, (3) in-kind transfers,*

[9]Joseph Pechman, *Who Paid the Taxes, 1966–1985?* (Washington, D.C.: Brookings Institution, 1985), p. 4.

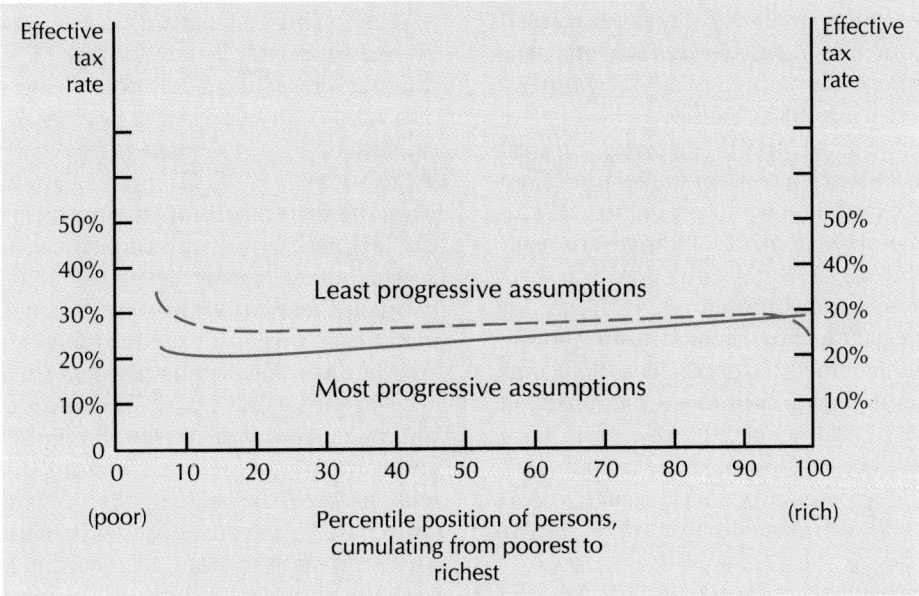

FIGURE 33.6 *Effective Rates of All Taxes Combined Under the Most and Least Progressive Assumptions of Incidence, 1980*

(Source: Joseph A. Pechman, Who Paid the Taxes, 1965–85? *Washington, D.C.: Brookings Institution, 1985, p. 4.)*

TABLE 33.5   Programs Assisting the Poor by Type, Mid-1980s

Program	Average Number of Monthly Recipients (in Millions)	Dollars per Month per Recipient
Social insurance (1985)		
Social Security (OASDI)	37.1	$421
Unemployment insurance	2.9	466
Medicare	17.9	218
Cash welfare, or public assistance (1985)		
Aid to Families with Dependent Children (AFDC)	10.9	$119
Supplemental Security Income (SSI)	3.8	202
In-kind transfers (1984)		
Medicaid	21.9	$143
Food stamps	22.4	50
School lunch programs	12.1	18
Energy assistance	8.5	20
Employment programs (1984)		
Jobs and training	2.5	$137
Head Start	0.4	225

Sources: Social Security Bulletin (June 1986), pp. 5–19; *Statistical Abstract of the United States, 1986* (Washington, D.C.: U.S. Department of Commerce, 1985), p. 357.

and (4) employment programs. It must be stressed that, aside from the elderly and disabled, only about half of those below the poverty line receive any government assistance. Moreover, because of this and also because of the relatively modest amounts of assistance going to recipients each month, these government transfer programs lift no more than about 60 percent of the pretransfer poor out of poverty.

Social Insurance: The premiums you pay for auto insurance entitle you to compensation in the event of a fender bender, regardless of your income or wealth. Programs of _social insurance_ are similar. People and corporations contribute through payroll taxes. These taxes establish eligibility as well as funding for benefits once the need arises due to old age, disability, or some similar predicament.

Social security, officially known as Old-Age, Survivors, and Disability Insurance (OASDI), is the most sweeping of these programs. It helps replace income that is lost when a worker retires in old age, becomes severely disabled, or dies. Coverage is nearly universal, so the total amount of money involved is immense—over $180 billion annually. Two thirds of the aged rely on social security for more than half of their income. The other one third includes old people who are pretty well off financially because social security is not limited to the poor.

Complementing social security with coverage just as sweeping is _Medicare_, which started in 1965 and has since grown to cost more than $40 billion annually. This program provides medical care mainly for old people drawing social security.

Unemployment insurance provides temporary benefits to regularly employed people hit by involuntary unemployment (who are able and willing to take suitable jobs but cannot get them). Funded by a uniform national payroll tax levied on firms with eight or more workers, the system is primarily run by state governments, which set the amount and duration of benefits, collect contributions, process claims, determine eligibility, and pay benefits. Benefits normally amount to about 50 percent of the workers' usual wage.

Although these social insurance programs cover many more people than those who are poor, they contribute immensely to reducing posttransfer poverty. This is because they are keyed to events—such as old age—that explain much poverty. Well over half of all pretransfer poor people over age 65 are lifted out of poverty by social security alone.[10]

Cash Welfare: Recipients of _cash welfare_ must pass a _means test._ This is to say, unlike social security recipients, these folks must have incomes and assets below certain levels in order to qualify because these programs are designed to provide direct cash support only for the needy.

Aid to Families with Dependent Children (AFDC) is by far the largest and most controversial of these programs. The typical AFDC family is headed by a young mother of two small children (with no adult male present). Because this is a federal–state program rather than strictly federal, monthly benefits vary from state to state. In 1986 they ranged from $118 for a family of three in Alabama to $740 in Alaska. The overall national median was $346 per month for a family of three.

Supplemental Security Income (SSI) ranks second among cash welfare programs, with benefits totaling more than $11 billion in 1985. Sixty-five percent of the SSI population are blind or otherwise disabled. The rest are over age 65. Aside from eligibility requirements keyed to disability or age, recipients must also have incomes below $4,032 per year (as of 1986), including incomes from any source—social security, relatives, whatever. As indicated in Table 33.5, 3.8 million persons were receiving federal SSI payments averaging $202 per month in the mid-1980s.

In-Kind Transfers: Means-tested _in-kind transfers_ covering a variety of goods and services go to approximately 60 percent of all poor households (as defined absolutely). The market value of these noncash benefits came to $51.5 billion in 1984, of which $33.3 billion was for the largest of these programs—_Medicaid._ The Medicaid program provides federal funds to states to help them cover the costs of medical care and services for low-income persons through direct payments to physicians, hospitals and others.

Second in magnitude is the _food stamp_ program, which gives households coupons redeemable at grocery stores. The amounts vary with

---

[10]Sheldon Danziger, "Budget Cuts as Welfare Reform," _American Economic Review_ (May 1983), pp. 65–70.

income and household size. The maximum bene-fit, $268 for a family of four, is set to provide mini-mum nourishment, and only 18 percent of all food stamp recipients get the full amount. Other in-kind programs offer free school lunches, energy assistance, and housing subsidies of various sorts.

Employment Programs: Long-term solutions to the poverty problem among those who are able-bodied and nonaged lie in *job training and em-ployment* rather than income maintenace. Hence there are several programs designed to move peo-ple off welfare rolls onto payrolls. For example, federal funds provided under the Job Training Partnership Act of 1982 go to training programs approved by state governors and private industry councils. Aside from assisting the disadvantaged, these programs also assist dislocated workers. Dis-located workers have not been poor in the past, but they may fall into poverty because they have lost their jobs due to plant closings and perma-nent layoffs, and they have little chance of return-ing to their old jobs. Though not a job training program, Head Start is mentioned in Table 33.5 as an example of the special education programs available to poor children. Preschool youngsters get attention here, the idea being that early educa-tional achievements will help build human capital.

Overall, it should be stressed that very little transfer assistance, only about 5 percent of the total, is cash welfare going to able-bodied people. Further, most of these people are in the AFDC pro-gram, with average benefits of only a few hundred dollars a month per family and with children mak-ing up the majority in the typical family. This is contrary to the impression many people seem to have about the government's policies.

Read Perspective 33.

D
Problems with Policies: Equity versus Efficiency

On any given day, about 400 people in the United States are waiting for liver transplants because available livers are very scarce. Some die while waiting. How should the livers that are available be allocated? Economic *efficiency* would require that price be the only criterion. Those willing and able to pay the price—which typically runs $100,000 and often runs $500,000 per transplant—would get their liver transplants. Others would not. How-ever, is this solution *equitable?* It means that rich retired bank presidents and superwealthy Arabian oil sheiks flown in from abroad would get trans-plants, while poor, otherwise healthy, 25-year-olds would be left at death's door simply because of financial considerations.[11]

[11]Richard Koenig, "As Liver Transplants Grow More Com-mon, Ethical Issues Multiply," *Wall Street Journal*, October 14, 1986, pp. 1, 26.

PERSPECTIVE 33
The Trend in Transfer Spending

Cash welfare not only amounts to very little when compared to other transfer spending, its share of total transfer spending has been falling. This may be inferred from Figure 33.7, which contains other messages as well. It shows the major categories of transfer expenditures as a percentage of GNP in 1960, 1970, 1980, and 1984. Note that social insurance transfers grew more rapidly than GNP even during the Reagan years of the 1980s. In-kind transfers burgeoned dur-ing the War on Poverty of the 1960s, doubled as a percentage of GNP during the 1970s, and then merely held steady during President Reagan's efforts to curb spending in the 1980s. In con-trast to these cases, expenditures on cash wel-fare in 1984 were about the same as they were in 1960 as a percentage of GNP. A main reason for this is that Reagan's efforts at curtailment have been more successful in this area of cash wel-fare than in any other area. Indeed, the median value of AFDC benefits, per family, fell 33 per-cent in real terms between 1972 and 1985.

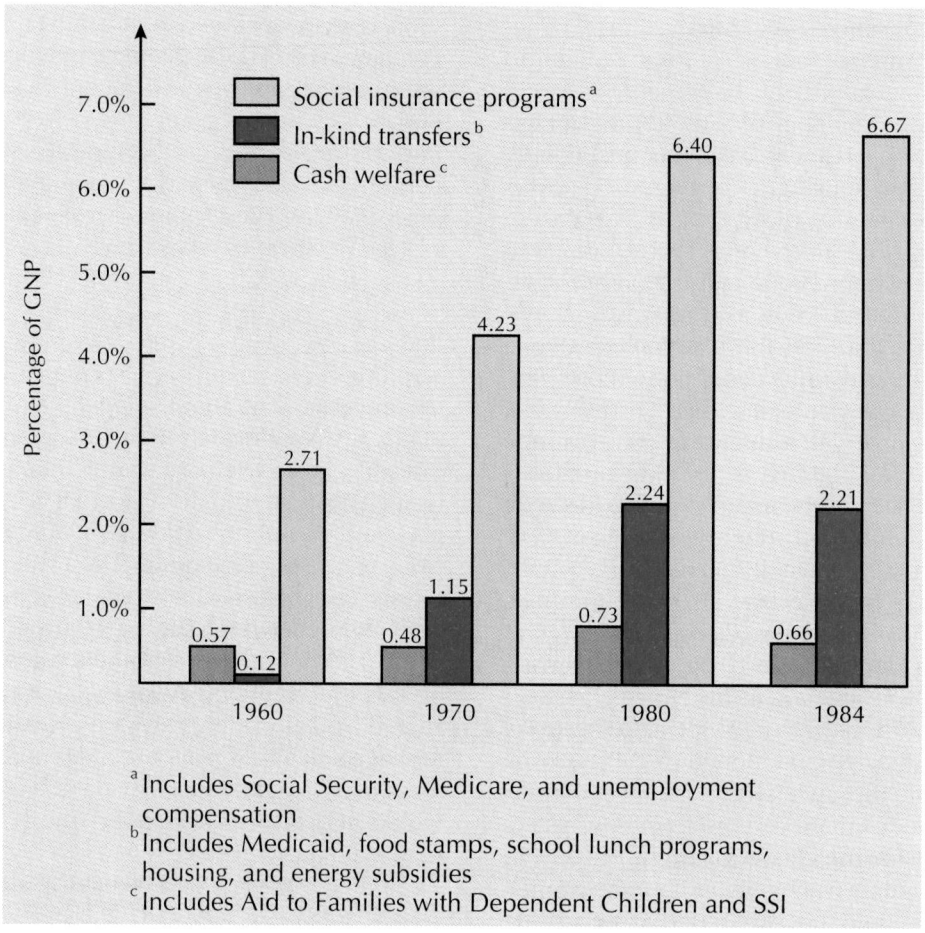

FIGURE 33.7 *Transfer Expenditures as a Percentage of GNP, 1960–84*
(*Sources:* Social Security Bulletin; Statistical Abstract of the United States.)

This example of liver transplants illustrates the clash between efficiency and equity that frequently arises in poverty policy. Efficiency requires that goods and services go to those willing and able to pay the full price, while equity often says that they should go to those in greatest need. Efficiency is fostered when incomes go to the most diligently deserving, as measured by the labor market, not to those who are merely disadvantaged. Assistance to the poor violates this last principle of efficiency in two ways. First, *those who pay* the cost of the transfers are taxed more heavily than otherwise. This reduces their incentive to work by reducing their financial rewards. Second, *those who receive* transfers may also experience disincentives to work. Uncle Sam's helping hand may promote laziness and encourage lasitude.

A common metaphor to describe the efficiency/equity trade-off is the *sliced pie*. The government attempts to achieve greater equity by reslicing the national income pie, taxing Mary Moneybags $1,000 in order to assist Nancy Needy. However, in the process, inefficiencies arise, causing the pie to shrink, so in the end Nancy Needy does not get $1,000 but rather something less, like $700. In the extreme, *equal* slices of a small pie might mean *less* pie for the poor than *unequal* shares of a larger pie. That would be an especially sharp trade-off, as inefficiency would then get an especially large bite of the pie.

Because disincentives among the poor *recipients* of assistance are most frequently the focus of poverty policy critics, we shall focus on them here. The problems can be considered under two headings—(1) dependency and (2) the negative income tax.

1. Dependency

The dependency argument says that government poverty policies *create* poverty rather than *cure* it. People are naturally lazy, always wanting something for nothing. Hence, if they are given handouts, the poor will remain poor and the nonpoor will shirk work to join them. One widely quoted critic of recent policy put it this way: "We tried to provide more for the poor and produced more poor instead."[12] His solution? Eliminate all social programs except unemployment insurance for the working-aged population.

Defenders of poverty policy respond to this criticism in various ways.[13] Here we only note a few statistics on mobility that fail to support the view that dependency is caused by the welfare system itself. A study of 5,000 American families during the decade 1969–78 revealed that, of those who received any welfare during those 10 years, 19 percent did so for less than 2 years and another 34 percent did so for 3 to 7 years. Moreover, it was found that the typical recipient of welfare was victimized by some dramatic event—like severe injury, divorce, or the death of a spouse.[14] On the whole, welfare is thus treated more like a temporary cushion than a permanent lounge chair by those who benefit by it.

2. Negative Income Tax

Means-tested transfers such as Aid to Families with Dependent Children (AFDC) have long been criticized for discouraging the work effort among those who fall below the minimum income levels specified in the means test. Whereas the simple dependency argument says that poverty policy encourages and even creates poverty, the alleged problem here is that the policy discourages work among those who happen to be in poverty for whatever reason.

---

[12]Charles Murray, *Losing Ground: American Social Policy, 1950–1980* (New York: Basic Books, 1984).

[13]See, for example, Sheldon Danziger and Peter Gottschalk, "The Poverty of Losing Ground," *Challenge* (May–June 1985), pp. 32–38; Christopher Jencks, "How Poor Are the Poor?," *New York Review of Books*, May 9, 1985, pp. 41–49.

[14]Data from the University of Michigan's Institute for Social Research, reprinted in the *Washington Post National Weekly Edition*, April 23, 1984, p. 38.

In essence, the problem is this: A strict means-test approach pays recipients only insofar as their income falls below some minimum guaranteed level. Once recipients are below that level, added work earnings will cause the transfer benefits to be reduced by like amounts, thereby discouraging work. The reductions in transfer payments are like an *implicit tax of 100 percent* on all added income earnings below the guaranteed minimum income.

Figure 33.8 illustrates this, assuming a guaranteed minimum income of $7,000 for the recipient family. With zero income earnings (pretransfer), the government would pay $7,000 in transfer income to provide the minimum. As pretransfer income rises to $1,000 from odd jobs, transfer income is reduced by $1,000 so that total income after transfer remains at $7,000. With training and further work effort the recipient might be able to boost his or her earned, pretransfer income to $6,000. But there is no incentive to do so if transfer income is reduced to $1,000, still leaving income after transfer at $7,000. Only as earned income before transfer rises above $7,000 (on the horizontal axis) does the income after transfer also rise to reward the earnings effort.

Part of the justification for this approach to income support has been that such support was *not* keyed to income alone. Rather, the aid was *categorical.* Cash welfare was to be strictly limited to those who were short of income and *not expected to work,* namely, the aged, the blind, the disabled, and single parents of small children. Unfortunately, this categorical approach leads to certain inefficiencies of its own. In particular, it requires extensive bureaucratic procedures and abundant government personnel to sort out those who meet the categorical qualifications from those who do not. How blind is "blind"? Who is actually "disabled"? And so on. Another main feature of the categorical approach has been its in-kind benefits of food, medical care, and the like. A broader approach would simply and always give money, which the poor could spend as they please.

Eyeing this scene of disincentives and disjointedness, many critics have argued in favor of a **negative income tax** program. *This would provide sliding-scale income assistance uncategorically, according only to simple standards of economic need. Given an approach linked to income level*

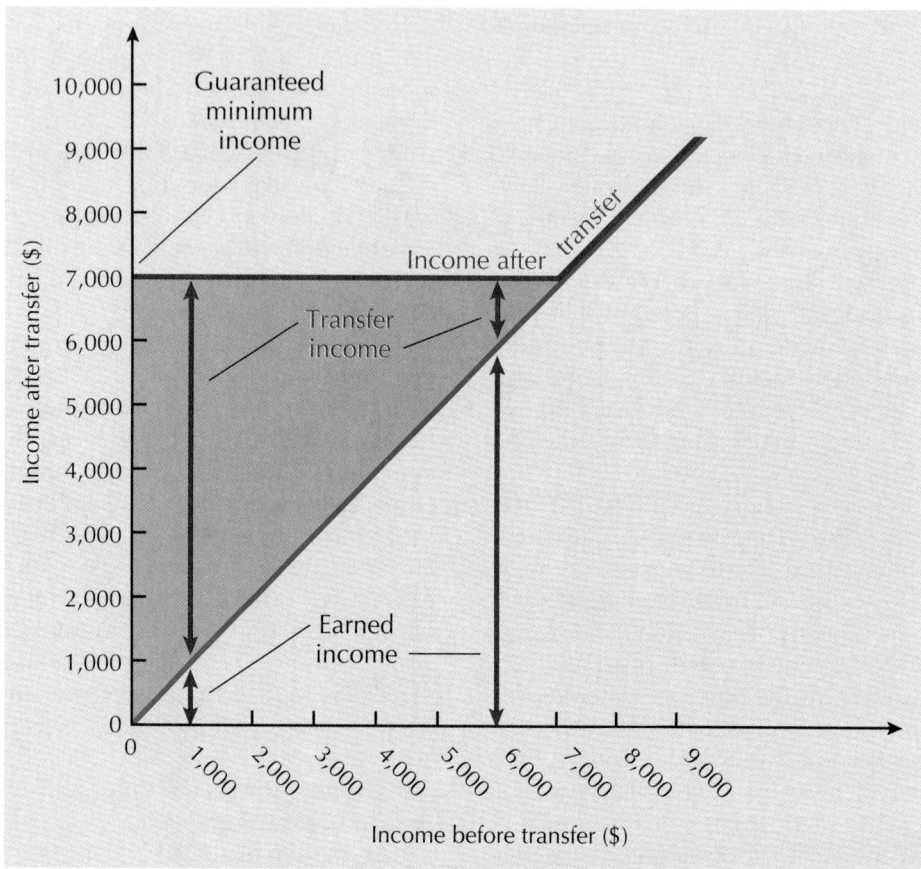

FIGURE 33.8   *Possible Disincentive Effect of Means-Tested Transfers*

The 45⁰ line rising from the origin shows earnings in the absence of transfers. If $7,000 is set as the minimum income for this family, transfer income amounts to $7,000 when earned income is zero. However, if earnings cause transfers to fall at an implied 100 percent tax rate, then $1,000 in earnings reduces the transfer by $1,000 to $6,000. Earnings of $6,000 reduce the transfer to $1,000. With $7,000 in income after the transfer over all levels of earnings below $7,000, there is no incentive to work in that range.

alone, dispensing only money benefits, and universally applied to all potentially poor people, it could be appended to the income tax system. It would pay money out as well as take it in, hence the name *negative income tax.*

Figure 33.9 illustrates. A guaranteed minimum after-transfer income of $7,000 is again assumed, just as in Figure 33.8. A zero pretransfer income would therefore prompt $7,000 in negative income tax payments *from* the government *to* the poor recipient. As *pretransfer* income rises above zero, *posttransfer* income also rises because the worker is allowed to retain $33.33 of every $100 earned on jobs. For example, in Figure 33.9, pretransfer earnings of $3,000 result in a total posttransfer income

of $8,000 because the worker's transfer income is reduced by $2,000, from $7,000 to $5,000. The combination of $3,000 earned income and $5,000 transfer income yields the total posttransfer income of $8,000. In other words, there is an implicit tax of 66.66 percent here instead of the 100 percent implicit tax of Figure 33.8. This 66.66 percent implicit tax is rather hefty, so the financial rewards for work are still stunted. But the disincentive for those in poverty is hardly as severe as with the 100 percent implicit tax. Moreover, the negative income tax permits abandonment of the categorical approach, thereby allowing much government red tape to be cut.

The foregoing is theory. In practice, the negative

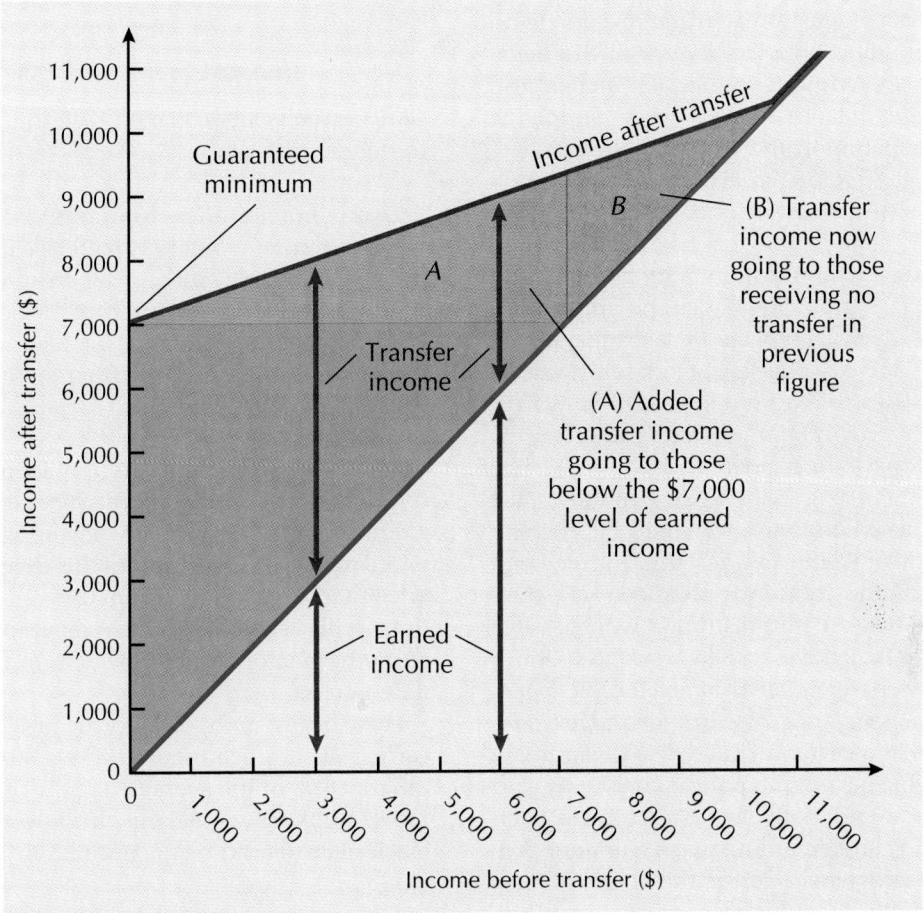

FIGURE 33.9 *Negative Income Tax Program*

Here all additions to earned income raise the income after transfer, even those earnings below the guaranteed minimum income of $7,000. Every added $3,000 reduces the transfer income by $2,000, so here the implicit tax rate on earnings below the minimum is 66.6 percent. At earnings of $3,000, for instance, the transfer income is $5,000 ($8,000-$3,000) instead of $7,000, as it is at zero earnings (or as it is in Figure 33.8).

income tax will probably never win adoption. Why? Two main reasons: First, these theoretical effects were tested by extensive experiments for over two decades. People were actually offered cash assistance uncategorically under several alternative implicit tax rates. Their behavior was then monitored carefully. The results showed that, on balance, the incentive effects of the negative income tax were *actually unfavorable.* People worked less, on balance.

Part of the explanation for these unfavorable results can be seen in Figure 33.9. Notice areas *A* and *B,* which represent regions of *added expenditure* and therefore *added receipts* in comparison

to the transfer spending of Figure 33.8, without the negative income tax. Given a guaranteed post-transfer minimum of $7,000, these added expenditures occur as a positive slope is built into the line depicting "Income After Transfer," this slope being necessary to reduce the implicit tax below 100 percent. Some expenditures, area *A,* are added transfers given to those with earned incomes below the minimum. The rest, area *B,* will be transfer incomes going to those *not* receiving any transfer income under the strict means test of Figure 33.8. Both of these added expenditures have disincentive effects.

A second reason why work fell among recipients

in the negative income tax experiments centers on the universal, noncategorical nature of the negative income tax. Without the *inconvenience* and *embarrassment* that are presently part of applying to and participating in the welfare system, negative income tax recipients are apparently much more willing to quit work and go on the dole. Under the present policy, for instance, the time between filing an application and getting food stamps is generally 30 days. Once the application is processed, a person repeatedly faces the stigma of paying the grocery checkout clerk with welfare vouchers instead of real money. In other words, there are some *noneconomic* factors that heavily influence people's incentives. Under the negative income tax there is a right to real money. This apparently proves attractive to would-be idlers.

The negative income tax has thus never been fully adopted, and its future prospects are dim. However, the Reagan administration won passage of other work incentives called *workfare*. Under **workfare,** *a welfare recipient can be forced to perform public service work in return for welfare benefits.* No work, no welfare. The idea is to eliminate "freebees" while giving the poor a chance to gain job experience and skills. The states have been responsible for implementing these workfare programs. Some programs, such as the one in Massachusetts, seem to be quite successful, others less so.

How long workfare will last, and how successful it will ultimately be, are at present unknown. However, one thing is certain. There is a substantial trade-off between efficiency and equity in the area of poverty policy. Because the trade-off poses a dilemma rather than an easily solvable problem, the debate over what to do about poverty will continue as long as poverty exists.

II

Discrimination

The aim of antidiscrimination policies is not to curb poverty. The aim is to reduce *inequity*. Still, poverty is associated with labor market discrimination, so the policies covered in this section overlap those just discussed.

A
Measurement and Extent

Conceptually, labor market discrimination is easy to define:

> **Labor market discrimination** occurs when one group of workers is paid less than another for the same work, or when some workers are prevented from entering particular occupations, getting training, or winning promotion because of some characteristic irrelevant to job performance.[15]

Actually measuring the extent of labor market discrimination is much more difficult. Blacks and women earn substantially lower incomes than white males, but only part of this difference can be attributed to discrimination. Differences in education, skills, age, work time, geographic location, and other factors also contribute to these income differences.

Let's begin with blacks. In 1983 black males earned an average income of $11,501, which was roughly 61% of the average income of white males, $18,823. Broadly speaking the lower earnings of black males could be accounted for as follows:

1. *Education:* If blacks on average brought educational backgrounds to the labor market equal to those of whites in both quantity (years of schooling) and quality (school equipment, teacher competence, etc.), the earnings gap would be reduced by about half.
2. *Experience and geography:* If in addition to educational equality, blacks were like whites in skills, age composition, geographic distribution, and all other such factors, the gap would be reduced further by one fourth.
3. *Labor market discrimination:* By implication, the remaining gap represents racial bias. Blacks would gain some eight to ten percentage points relative to white earnings if labor market discrimination were eliminated.

[15]Henry J. Aaron and Cameran M. Lougy, *The Comparable Worth Controversy* (Washington, DC: Brookings Institution, 1986), p. 18.

To summarize, roughly one half of the black/white earnings differential can be pinned on educational differences alone. One fourth can be attributed to all other measurable characteristics. And one fourth is left to be explained by labor market discrimination.[16]

In 1927 a New York City apparel manufacturer advertised for help by offering "White Workers $24; Colored Workers $20." Such blatant wage discrimination is now a thing of the past, thanks partly to legal changes. Today discrimination appears mainly as _occupational_ discrimination (where certain occupations are not fully open to blacks) or as _employment_ discrimination (where blacks have less chance of being hired). For example, blacks are underrepresented in such high-paying occupational categories as craftsmen and managers, while being overrepresented in relatively low-paying occupations like service work.

As regards women versus men, the unadjusted gap in earnings is similar to that between blacks and whites. _Women, on average, earn only about 60 percent of what men earn in the labor market._ Accounting for education, experience, hours of work, and similar variables, the differences between men and women are reduced but the gap remains. The extent of the discrepancy is indicated in Figure 33.10, which shows the expected lifetime earnings for year-round, full-time workers by age, educational attainment, and sex (in 1979). Note especially that women with 4 years of college earn less than men with only a high school education, a differential that prevails at every age level. Once all variables like education, hours of work, and experience are taken into account—all variables, that is, except occupational differences—the gap between men and women is reduced by about half, _to the point where women earn approximately 80 percent of what men earn on average._

The remaining 20 percent difference between men and women is due to two factors—(1) labor market discrimination against women and (2) voluntary occupational choice by women. Each of these factors is important, but the exact contribution of each is uncertain because they both lead to substantial differences in the "genders" of occupations. For example, 35 percent of all white females in the labor market are clerical workers compared to 6 percent of all white males. On the other hand, 21 percent of all white males are craftsmen, a rate of occupational incidence 10 times greater than the 2 percent rate for white females. To some extent these immense differences appear to be a matter of taste or voluntary preference, especially as they may relate to the family responsibilities of females. For example, many women apparently choose to become elementary school teachers because the work schedule in hours and months allows them to give their children greater care than would otherwise be possible. Even so, discrimination is also probably important. Do women really prefer to be airline flight attendants instead of pilots to the lopsided degree we see in the skies? Probably not. Or, to return to elementary schools, discrimination may explain why men make up a hugely disproportionate number of school principals, while women comprise a disproportionate number of teachers.

B

Trends Over Time

According to census data analyzed by James P. Smith and Finis R. Welch, the income gap experienced by blacks, as big as it is at present, has been falling over the past five decades. Table 33.6 summarizes their findings. In 1940 the average income of full-time black male workers was only 43.3 percent of that of full-time white male workers. In 1980 blacks were earning 72.6 percent as much as whites by these data.

TABLE 33.6   Average Income of Black Full-Time Male Workers as a Percentage of White Full-Time Male Income, 1940–80

Year	Black Income as a Percentage of White Income
1980	72.6%
1970	64.4
1960	57.5
1950	55.2
1940	43.3

Source: James P. Smith and Finis R. Welch, _Closing the Gap: Forty Years of Economic Progress for Blacks_ (Santa Monica, Calif.: Rand Corp., 1986), p. 5.

---

[16]Bradley R. Schiller, _The Economics of Poverty and Discrimination_, 4th ed. (Englewood Cliffs, NJ: Prentice-Hall, 1984), pp. 148–150.

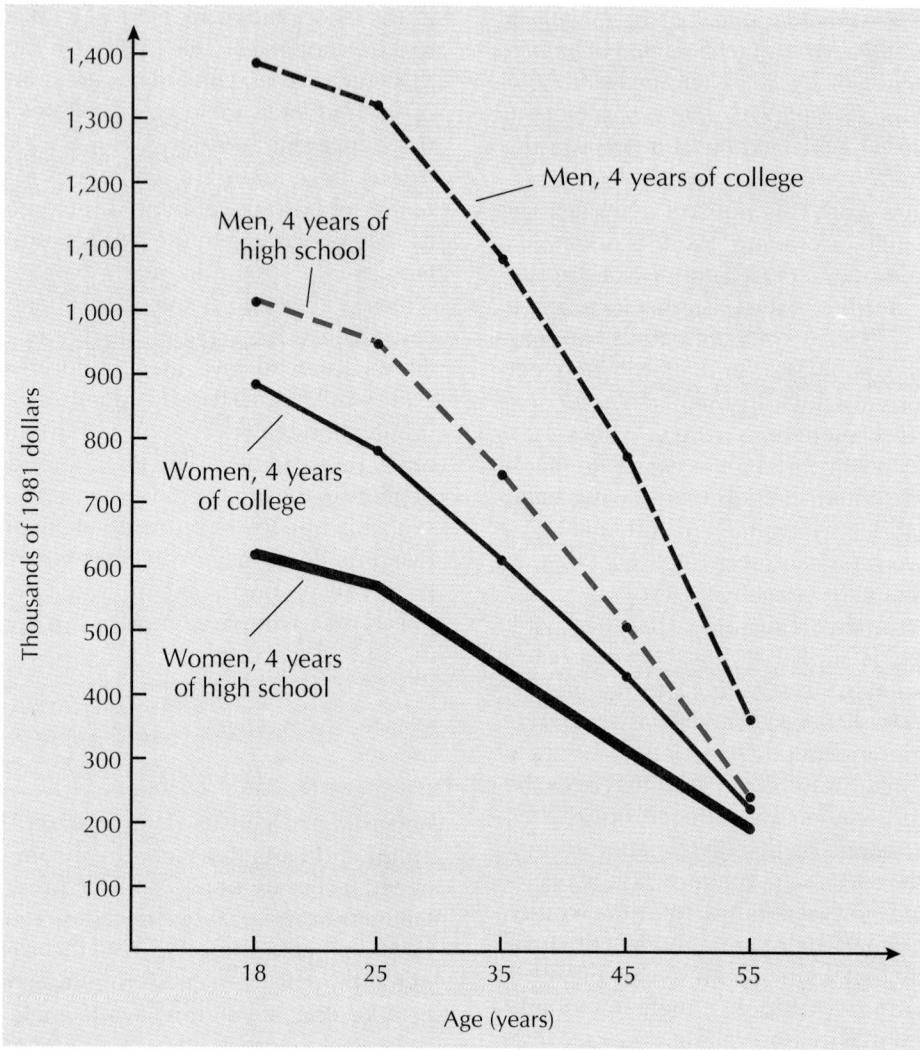

FIGURE 33.10   *Expected Lifetime Earnings in 1979 for Year-Round, Full-Time Workers by Years of School Completed, Age Groups, and Sex*

(*Source: U.S. Department of Commerce, Bureau of the Census*, Lifetime Earnings for Men and Women in the United States: 1979, *Series P-60, No. 139, 1983, p. 3.*)

The major explanation for this dramatic long-run improvement lies in the major changes that have occurred among blacks in years of educational attainment, school quality, and geographic relocation. For example:

In 1980, a typical black male had a year and a half less schooling than the average white male worker. A majority of black men in 1980 were high school graduates. Forty years earlier, white men had 3.7 years more schooling than did black male workers with whom they competed in the labor market. The

typical 1940 black worker had completed only 4.7 years of schooling.[17]

The long-term trend for women has been similarly favorable, although evidence of this is more difficult to detect than in the case of blacks. If one looks at the gap between male and female average earnings *unadjusted* for any changes in the char-

[17]James P. Smith and Finis R. Welch, *Closing the Gap: Forty Years of Economic Progress for Blacks* (Santa Monica; Calif.: Rand, Corp., 1986), p. x.

acteristics of working women, one will find very little change in income differentials over time, as indicated in the first column of Table 33.7. These unadjusted numbers are somewhat misleading, however, because they fail to take into account the *huge* increase in labor force participation among women during this century. *In 1900, fewer than 2 of every 10 women were working or seeking work. By 1983, more than 6 in 10 were working or seeking work. This is one of the most important social changes in the American economy during this century.* These immense changes in labor force participation distort the trend in women's earnings relative to those of men. Once adjustments are made to correct for the effects of changing labor force participation, it appears that since 1920, women's earnings have been *rising* relative to those of men, as shown in the last column of Table 33.7. Indeed, much of the increase in labor force participation among women can be explained by the fact that women's earnings have been improving relative to men's earnings over the long haul. With women's wages going up, the number of women working has increased.

C

Antidiscrimination Policy and Controversy

Some of the improvements just reviewed may be credited to antidiscrimination policies. Moreover, policy may help foster further improvements in the future. We shall focus on (1) equal employment opportunity policy generally and (2) affirmative action.

TABLE 33.7 **Average Wage of Women as a Percentage of Men's Wages, 1920–80**

Year	Female Wage as a Percentage of Male Wage *Unadjusted* for Labor Force Participation Changes	Female Wage as a Percentage of Male Wage *Adjusted* for Labor Force Participation Changes
1980	60	53
1950	63	48
1920	63	43

Source: James P. Smith and Michael P. Ward, *Women's Wages and Work in the Twentieth Century* (Santa Monica, Calif.: Rand Corp., 1984), p. xiii.

1. Equal Employment Opportunity Prompted by massive demonstrations and violent riots, the Civil Rights Act was enacted in 1964. Under Title VII of the act, firms, unions, apprenticeship programs, and employment agencies are prohibited from discriminating against any individual on the basis of race, color, sex, or national origin. As amended in 1972 the act applies to all employers with 15 or more employees, including educational institutions and state and local governments.

The Equal Employment Opportunity Commission (EEOC) enforces Title VII for most businesses. An independent agency composed of five commissioners, the EEOC presses its formal legal proceedings with suits in federal courts, securing such remedies as worker reinstatement, back pay, and affirmative action. In addition, a certain class of firms receives special attention—namely, those firms that do business with the federal government as contract suppliers. Legal authority for action against federal contractors rests on an executive order promulgated by President Johnson in 1965 and adhered to by subsequent presidents. Under this order, federal contractors are required to take affirmative action not to discriminate and to develop affirmative action plans, including goals and timetables, that make earnest efforts to correct for past deficiencies in minority and female employment. These regulations are significant because they cover 30 million workers in about 200,000 firms with federal contracts.

2. Affirmative Action Mention of **affirmative action** raises the question of how this differs from *equal employment opportunity.* The original idea behind the Civil Rights Act of 1964 was to give minorities and women the right to *equal opportunity,* not the right to a job. The duty of employers thereafter was to give no consideration whatever to race, color, sex, or religion.

However, *affirmative action* evolved. Among federal contractors it became routine. Among others it became a remedy to correct for past discrimination. In any case, affirmative action can mean a variety of things, but it basically entails *preferential treatment for women and minorities instead of strict neutrality.* At a low level, affirmative action occurs when employers make special efforts to recruit minorities and women or to help them acquire training. Posting job vacancy notices in black schools or black churches that were previously ignored illustrates these possibilities. At a higher level of intensity, employers set goals and timetables against which to measure their efforts. Such goals might specify certain percentages of minorities and women in various job classifications, but they need not be considered mandatory. Finally, affirmative action could, in its most aggressive form, include quota systems, which assign slots in hiring, training, or promoting minorities and women in some fixed proportion to the slots assigned to unprotected job candidates, white males in particular. *In brief, equal opportunity pursues equity in procedures, whereas affirmative action pursues equity in results.*

Not surprisingly, affirmative action has become very controversial. Those *favoring* strong affirmative action tend to stress fairness in results set against a backdrop of regrettable history:

> *It is fundamental that civil rights without economic rights are mere shadows.*
> —Judge Charles R. Weiner

In contrast, those *opposing* affirmative action stress fairness in procedures and impracticalities:

> *Under the present bureaucratic formulation, affirmative action is, in reality, affirmative discrimination.*
> —Senator Jesse Helms

Siding with the latter view, the Reagan administration made some movement toward abandoning goals and timetables for federal contractors. Apparently little will change, however. Polls indicate that most major businesses will continue to use goals and timetables even if they become wholly voluntary.[18] One apparent reason for this support is that goals and timetables are much less stringent than quotas, while at the same time boosting overall employee morale.[19]

[18.]Anne B. Fisher, "Businessmen Like to Hire by the Numbers," *Fortune*, September 16, 1985, p. 28.

[19.]Jonathan S. Leonard, "What Promises Are Worth: The Impact of Affirmative Action Goals," *Journal of Human Resources* (Winter 1985), pp. 3–20.

SUMMARY

1. An absolute definition of poverty specifics a poverty-line income based on the amount needed to buy essential goods and services.
2. A relative definition specifies a poverty-line income at some minimum level relative to other, higher incomes (such as the median income).
3. The income of reference in any definition of poverty can be (a) pretransfer income (which is market earnings before any government transfer), or (b) income after cash transfers (including social security benefits, AFDC assistance, and the like), or (c) income after cash and in-kind transfers (adding food, medical care, and the like).
4. By the absolute approach adopted for government statistics, 24, 15, and 10 percent of the population was in poverty in 1983, according to the preceding three definitions, respectively Also, the long-

term trend is down substantially. Taking into account the influences of both economic growth and government policy, poverty has fallen from about 50 percent of the population in 1930 to about 10 percent today.
5. Relative approaches measure inequality more than poverty as such. Reductions in inequality are obtained with cash and in-kind transfers, as indicated in Table 33.1 and in the Lorenz curves of Figure 33.4. As for the time trend, economic growth has had little effect on inequality, so almost all such changes can be credited to government policy.
6. Considerations of income mobility brighten this picture of poverty, while considerations of wealth distribution, which is much more unequal than income distribution, darken the picture.
7. Work intensity, work ability, compensat-

ing wage differentials, luck, inherited wealth, and risk taking affect the personal income distribution generally. Poverty is explained mainly by (a) inability to work or unavailability of work, (b) low human capital, and (c) discrimination against women and minorities.

8. Among government policies, taxes have very little influence on income distribution because, in general, they are proportional rather than regressive or progressive. Spending plays the chief role in several forms: (a) social insurance programs like social security and unemployment insurance, (b) cash welfare, mainly AFDC and SSI, (c) in-kind transfers, such as food stamps and medical aid, and (d) employment programs that offer training and job placement services. In growth over time and in present financial magnitude, the social insurance programs are by far the most important.

9. The tax burden of financing these programs discourages work among the nonpoor, while the transfer benefits create work disincentives among the poor. Improvements in *equity* thus tend to create *inefficiencies*, leading to a trade-off. The negative income tax is a proposal that lessens the dilemma in theory but apparently does not do so in practice.

10. Labor market discrimination in wages, occupational choice, training, and promotion adversely affect women and minorities. This shows up in lower average earnings for blacks and women as compared to white men, but the exact gap is unknown. It may be 10 percent for blacks and 5 to 15 percent for women, due primarily to occupational discrimination.

11. The earnings of women and minorities have been rising relative to those of white males, chiefly because of various long-term improvements in education among the disadvantaged.

12. Equal opportunity policy in its simplest and least vigorous form ensures *procedural* fairness for women and minorities. Affirmative action goes further to show various degrees of favoritism toward women and minorities in the hope of fostering some kind of fairness in *results*. Nonmandatory goals and timetables are the most common forms of affirmative action among large corporations. They are controversial, but they will probably persist.

KEY TERMS

Absolute definition of poverty
Relative definition of poverty
Pretransfer income
Cash transfers
In-kind transfers
Inequality
Lorenz curve
Income mobility
Wealth

Progressive tax
Regressive tax
Proportional tax
Effective tax rate
Negative income tax
Workfare
Labor market discrimination
Affirmative action

QUESTIONS AND PROBLEMS

1. Explain the two general approaches to defining poverty and why they give different answers to questions about the incidence of poverty.

2. Explain how government welfare programs that provide cash transfer payments or in-kind transfers to the needy complicate the specification of a poverty-line income level.

3. Explain the purpose of the Lorenz curve.

4. Will people who are poor in the U.S. today remain poor for the rest of their lives?

5. Distinguish between wealth and income. Can wealth be seen as a cushion that lessens suffering for those with low incomes?

6. What causes poverty in the U.S. today? What data are relevant in answering this question?

7. Do existing tax laws in the U.S. today significantly redistribute income?

8. Describe the "safety net" of programs funded by government in the U.S. to assist the poor.

9. Outline the efficiency versus equity conflict associated with government poverty policies.

10. What happened in actual experiments with the use of a negative income tax to alleviate poverty?

11. Define labor market discrimination. Why is it difficult to measure the impact of discrimination on wages for blacks, females, or other victims?

12. How large is the gap between the earnings of white males and black males? Between white males and white females? What factors other than discrimination are involved?

13. What did the Civil Rights Act of 1964 do? What is the EEOC?

14. What is "affirmative action" and what is its purpose?

34

Public Choice and Government

In 1984, government policies limited the amount of steel shipped to the United States from Japan and other foreign countries. This caused U.S. steel production to be greater than it would have been otherwise. Approximately 9,000 steelworkers therefore had jobs because of the government. Without restrictions against imports, those 9,000 steelworkers would have been working as auto mechanics or insurance salesmen or perhaps not working at all. This makes the government's action seem good—9,000 jobs saved, high-paying jobs, too, worth as much as $45,000 a year in wages and fringe benefits for each steelworker.

There was a big catch, however. Each of those jobs cost U.S. consumers an estimated $750,000 per year. Altogether the jobs cost about $6.8 billion. The benefit of steelworkers' jobs was thus very costly in the form of higher prices for steel products (like autos and refrigerators). Comparing the annual wage of $45,000 per steelworker with the annual consumer cost of $750,000 per job saved, it would have been much cheaper to freely allow steel imports. In principle, each of the steelworkers put out of work by free trade could have been paid $100,000 annually from tax revenues for just loafing, and society would have come out ahead by about $650,000 per job. Much the same could be said about thousands of jobs in meatpacking, automobiles, and other industries shielded from imports.[1]

How can this be? How can several thousand steelworkers, meatpackers, auto workers, and others gain at the great expense of many millions of consumers? It happens in other areas of government activity as well—e.g., farm price supports, wasteful defense spending, and excess water projects. Relatively few people routinely capture big benefits at the cost of millions of others. Explaining this is one of the main objectives of this chapter. It is but one aspect of this chapter's general theme—government decision making on economic matters.

Other chapters have shown that as a servant of society, the market system can occasionally be a very clumsy maid. This chapter demonstrates that there are also serious problems with government decision making. As a servant of society, the government often behaves no better than a lazy butler. Hence, it may not be wise to have the government act whenever the market falters. The government's solution may be worse than the market's problem. In the end, then, society must sometimes choose between two imperfect alternatives. If so, it should pick the less injurious servant—the market or the government—depending on the situation. The trick in assigning tasks is to decide what is right for the clumsy maid and what can be handled by the lazy butler.

I

Review of Government Tasks

In Chapter 4, we identified a number of tasks that might be best for government. One set of tasks relates to *market maintenance*. When performing these tasks, the government helps the market mechanism perform better than it otherwise would. The government makes *procedural* contributions. Government facilitates the market system by maintaining the key elements of the exchange process—property rights, money, and contracts. A contract, for instance, is just an empty promise unless the government stands ready to enforce it. To further assist markets procedurally, the government also has policies that maintain competition and keep buyers and sellers well informed.

Beyond matters of market maintenance, the government is sometimes called upon because the market system seems *incapable* of obtaining satisfactory *results*. Such incapacities prevent the market from yielding good answers to the basic questions of What?, How?, Who?, What's new?, and How stable? In the case of *public goods*, for

---

[1]As of 1984, the consumer cost per job saved in meatpacking was $160,000, and in auto manufacturing it was $105,000. These estimates are the work of Gary Hufbauer and Howard Rosen of the Institute for International Economics (*Fortune*, May 11, 1987, p. 125).

instance, the market is incapable of providing correct answers to the question of what will be produced. The ideal answer to the What? question is allocation efficiency, where society gains the greatest net benefit possible from each of its scarce resources, whether that use is to produce autos or defense weapons or whatever. In the case of public goods, the market fails by causing an underallocation of resources to the production of such goods. Too little national defense would therefore be provided by the free market because national defense is a public good. While allocation problems lead to such inefficiencies, *distribution problems* divert us from ideals of equity, problems of *slow technological change* hamper progress, and *stabilization problems* like high unemployment arise. (See Table 4.1 for a list of cases where the market system apparently needs official help.)

The normative objectives of government policies vary because of this variety of problems. Efficiency, equity, progress, and stability are all desirable ends that the government may wish to promote. By the same token, there is a wide variety of tasks that the government can reasonably be called upon to perform. Spending to provide for national defense and regulating to curb air pollution illustrate the diversity of government policies. Is there any element common to all the policies that are most properly pursued by governments? Do economic activities that best fit the government, instead of the market, share some common feature? Indeed, they do. And that common feature was suggested in our earlier definition of *government.*

Government is the process within a group for making and enforcing decisions.

The key word is *group.* Unlike market decision making, which can be highly individualized, government decision making is mainly group decision making. Decisions are reached collectively, by group participation, and they are then implemented by various means of enforcement. *Thus, in summary, government is most needed (and most justified) where group, or collective, decision making is needed.*

Although this collectivity is true of all the major areas of government policy identified earlier—external costs, external benefits, antitrust policy,

money supply management for stability, and so on—it is most clearly illustrated for *public goods.*

A **public good** benefits everyone, and excluding people from those benefits is either impossible or costly.

The market can handle *private goods*, like coffee and soda pop, because people consume them *individually.* When you drink a cup of coffee, no one else gets the benefits, only you. If you want to get some, you pay for it, and you get it. If you don't want any coffee, you don't pay for it and you don't get it. Paying and getting are linked to each individual's strength of demand, ranging from zero to dozens of cups a day.

Such is not true of public goods because they are consumed *collectively* by many people simultaneously. National defense, the classic case of a public good, cannot be parceled out in small pieces, permitting a lot more to hawks than to doves. Everyone gets the same amount. Clean air is also a public good, and the gap between paying and getting that causes markets for public goods to fail can best be illustrated by an example concerning air pollution control.

Imagine a new invention—an auto pollution control device that would clean up the air in your city *if* every car owner paid $300 to install it. Would you and everyone else scurry to buy one? Probably not. Two possibilities decrease your desire: (1) the possibility that you pay your $300 for clean air but hardly anyone else does, in which case you lose $300 because the air remains dirty, or (2) the possibility that even though you do not buy the device, almost everyone else does, in which case you get clean air without paying a dime (you are a *free rider*). Hence, you do not pay. Neither do most other people for the same reasons. And with very few people paying, the market provides *too little* of the public good (clean air).

Under such circumstances, collective decision making is needed. The market fails for public goods because the tie between paying and receiving is broken. But the government can establish such a tie through its powers of enforcement.

To continue with the example of auto pollution, imagine further that a measure is put on the ballot for the next election, which, if passed, would officially _require_ purchase of the $300 pollution control device by everyone who owns a car. It could be that this measure passes by an _overwhelming majority_ (e.g., 97.3 percent of the people vote "yes"), even though very few people (e.g., only 0.2 percent) would have purchased such a device voluntarily in the free market. Why the difference with the vote? The collective decision-making process, backed by enforcement, forges a direct link between paying and getting. Each person in the majority _is_ willing to pay _if everyone else is also going to pay_ because all persons are then assured that, when they pay, they actually get what they pay for, namely, clean air. This example not only illustrates how government decision making can often be superior to market decision making, it illustrates that the coercive power of government is not always to be dreaded. Aside from its use in curbing criminal activities, the threat of official force may be something that people occasionally wish to impose upon themselves. Coercion is often necessary for the implementation of decisions reached collectively.

The focus of this chapter is thus _collective decision making_. Such decision making centers on the activities of voters, senators, governors, congressmen, bureaucrats, and other people involved with governmental processes.

> **Collective decision making** is nonmarket decision making carried on by voters, politicians, civil servants, and others associated with the government.

A specialized branch of economics that studies collective decision making has grown briskly in recent decades. This area of study has come to be called the _theory of public choice_ because it focuses on the public sector rather than the private sector.

> The **theory of public choice** analyzes collective decision making (mainly that of the government).

As we probe the theory of public choice, you will see that it is an interesting blend of political science and economics.

II
The Market versus the Government: Similarities and Differences

An understanding of public choice theory depends partly on an appreciation of the similarities and differences that arise in government, as opposed to market, decision making. We begin with the similarities and then turn to the differences.

A
Similarities in Market and Government Decision Making

Market and government decision making are in many ways quite similar. Four similarities deserve special mention: (1) _scarcity_ is dealt with by both, (2) _self-interest_ motivates both sets of decision makers, (3) the results of both procedures may be judged by how well they satisfy individual preferences, i.e., _consumer sovereignty_, and (4) both the market and the government can be studied in _positive and normative_ ways.

1. Scarcity What are the decisions in government decision making? Stripped to essentials, they are decisions concerning the basic questions arising from scarcity, namely, What?, How?, Who?, What's new?, and How stable? When the government decides that 6 percent of our GNP will be spent on defense, it is partially answering the What? question. When Uncle Sam taxes workers and gives the funds to the retired elderly drawing social security, the Who? question is clearly at issue. Thus market and government decision making share a fundamental feature: They both serve society by handling the questions raised by scarcity.

2. Self-Interest What are the motives of those who participate in government decision making—the voters, senators and congresspeople, the bureaucrats, and others? It might be tempting to think that everyone involved in public choice is trying to further the public's interest. Such behavior would require altruism. And this altruism would frequently require substantial sacrifices. Altruistic voters might favor measures that raise their taxes in order to provide for the poor. Altruistic administrators, such as the head of the central bank and members of the president's cabinet, might work long hours in government for salaries that are small fractions of the money they could earn in the private sector. Altruistic congresspeople or senators might favor the interests of the entire nation over the narrow interests of their individual districts or states.

There are, to be sure, many actual instances of such altruistic behavior in the public sector. In the extreme, for instance, military personnel sometimes volunteer for dangerous assignments out of a sense of duty to their country. However, the theory of public choice is grounded on the assumption that public sector decision makers are like private sector decision makers in this regard. *It is assumed that all people usually act in their own self-interest—people in the public sector as well as those in the private sector.* James Buchanan, a leading public choice theorist, put it this way:

Like business people, politicians and bureaucrats are concerned primarily with private interests, not public interest. So we shouldn't be confident that government will protect us against greedy private interests because it has greedy private interests, too. Its interest is in enhancing its power, protecting its perks and getting reelected.[2]

The notion that people in government are not angels is very old. Our founding fathers made essentially the same assumption when they wrote into the Constitution a system of checks and balances. This system, which divides power, was designed to check and balance the private self-interests of government officials, politicians especially. Moreover, this notion of self-interested motivation is not without some solid factual foundations. Reflect back on the steelworker statistics reported at the outset of this chapter. If public officials always acted solely in the public interest, how could that import protection policy pass?

[2]James M. Buchanan, "Interview," *Forbes*, November 17, 1986, p. 108.

Later it will be shown that government decision making actually turns on a *mix* of private self-interest and perceived public interest. For our discussion of public choice theory, however, we shall temporarily assume that public sector people are concerned primarily with private self-interest.

3. Consumer Sovereignty The normative objective of *public* choice theory is essentially the same as that of *private* choice theory—namely, satisfying the preferences of people in society. When defining allocation efficiency, economists assume that consumer sovereignty is the normative ideal. Consumer sovereignty rests on two propositions: (1) the psychological assumption that people's preferences are essentially given and unchanging and (2) the normative belief that those preferences ought to be fully respected and satisfied within the bounds of scarcity. Stated differently, normative evaluation of private sector decision making assumes that people (1) really know their preferences and that (2) those preferences should be honored.

The theory of public choice applies this notion to government decision making. As applied here, it might best be called *citizens' sovereignty* instead of *consumers' sovereignty*. Whatever the label, though, the underlying principles are the same: (1) people have solid preferences (for public goods, say, as well as private goods), and (2) those preferences ought to be satisfied as far as possible. This rules out paternalism. It also implies that the individual preferences of citizens should not be replaced by some vague overarching goal such as service to a religion or to international Marxism. Thus, our earlier criteria of efficiency and equity can reapply here as normative ideals.

4. Positive and Normative Study Note that the second preceding point was *positive*. The theory of public choice assumes that, as a *factual matter*, voters and government officials act in their own self-interest. In contrast, the third preceding point was *normative*. It stated that, ideally, government officials *ought to be* furthering the preferences of the populace—especially to achieve efficiency and equity. Ideally, officials ought to do this even if it requires sacrifices.

These observations lead to a final similarity between government and market decision making. They are both open to positive and normative study. They each have observable and desirable aspects. Indeed, to a large extent, the theory of public choice is a recent positive revolt against the old normative theories of government intervention. The old normative theories looked upon government policies as rational collective responses to those problems that clearly warranted official attention—problems such as external costs, public goods, and monopoly. According to these theories, the government acted only, or primarily, when it *should* act. In contrast, the new positive theory of public choice postulates a real world where certain self-interested entities (such as labor unions and business firms) offer votes, campaign financing, and other important means of political support to self-interested politicians. In turn, the politicians have government doing all it *can* (not just what it should do) for these several narrow self-interests.

B

Differences in Market and Government Decision Making

There are probably more differences between market and government decision making than similarities. The differences to be discussed may be identified as follows: (1) collective action versus individual action, (2) voting process versus spending process, (3) coercion versus voluntarism, (4) redistribution versus no redistribution, and (5) agency versus direct decision making.

1. Collective Action versus Individual Action Government decision making is mainly *collective*. In contrast, market decision making is mainly *individual*. As we have seen, this means that government decision making can provide public goods, whereas market decision making cannot. Indeed, the government decision-making process itself could be thought of as a public good.

By its nature, collective action can occur without the direct connection between paying and receiving that typifies individual action in the private sector. The government provides national defense free to everyone. The government can act collectively even where such public goods are *not*

involved, as when it gives out free school lunches, financed by general tax revenues. Such collective provision is simply not possible in market decision making because the market almost always relies on a direct connection between paying and receiving. (We say "almost always" because there are exceptions. Radio and TV programs, for instance, are broadcast free because they are indirectly subsidized by the sale of advertised goods.)

2. Voting Process versus Spending Process In government decision making, people's preferences are expressed primarily by *voting*. On the other hand, people's preferences in market decision making are expressed chiefly by *spending* money. Differences arise, then, because voting is, by nature, less flexible as a means of expressing preferences in comparison to spending money. With voting, it is usually *one person, one vote*. With spending, it is essentially a system of *one dollar, one "vote,"* and people may therefore "vote" more than once in the market. This fundamental difference results in two other differences.

First, with just a single vote to cast for any government issue or candidate, an individual has *no way* of expressing his or her *intensity* of feeling. For example, you might strongly favor a policy of compulsory refundable deposits for beverage containers as a way of reducing litter. If a proposal for such a deposit system is put on the ballot, you have only *one* vote, just like another person who does not care one way or the other. In contrast, you can easily express your intensity of preference when spending money in the market. If you crave soda pop, you may buy dozens of cans of it a day. If you loathe it, you spend nothing.

Second, voting preferences are usually implemented by *majority rule*, whereas spending preferences are implemented by *proportional rule*. With majority rule, the option that wins a majority is the one chosen. The alternatives, because of their minority support, never see the light of day. With the proportional rule of marketplace spending, mixed outcomes are possible. Indeed, they are typical. The minority portion of people wanting lemon-lime flavored soda pop will be satisfied along with the vast majority that prefers cola-flavored soda pop. Even tiny proportions can be supplied—with ginger ale and cream soda, for instance.

3. _Coercion versus Voluntarism_   Federal, state, and local governments can rely on force to obtain public compliance with their economic actions. Sometimes the element of force is subtly hidden, but it is present nevertheless. To build a local park, for instance, the government uses its power of taxation. Imprisonment is a possible penalty for those not paying taxes. In contrast, the market system does not rely on coercive measures. Rather, it runs on free and voluntary exchange.

4. _Redistribution versus No Redistribution_   Because of the distinguishing features of the government just mentioned, especially coercion, the government can redistribute incomes or wealth. The market mechanism cannot do so. By definition, redistribution implies that some people gain at others' expense. The market system cannot easily accommodate gains and losses. A free and voluntary exchange in a market implies that _both_ parties to the exchange benefit by it. If they do not, the exchange cannot occur. The market cannot make someone give up something for another person's gain. Because the market is completely inactive here and the redistributions of charity are considered inadequate, our government engages extensively in redistribution. It uses its power to take wealth and income from some people for the benefit of others.

5. _Agency versus Direct Decision Making_   In the market, most people make their own decisions. You decide for yourself whether to buy some new shoes or to save for a VCR. There are exceptions, as when parents decide which breakfast cereal their children will eat and when doctors decide which prescription drugs are best for their patients. These are instances where _agency_ is at work because one person is acting as the _agent_ of another. But these exceptions are relatively few. Direct decision making typifies market decision making. In contrast, agency is typical of government decision making. Your representatives in Congress decide for you how much should be spent on battleships and missiles. Your governor decides on your behalf whether or not to veto legislation that would expand the highway system.

Because the people in government are not the same as citizens at large, there is some uncertainty regarding whom these government agents are acting for. Is it really the average Mr. and Mrs. John Q. Public? Is it big business or big labor that the agents most frequently assist? Is it those in education or the military? The theory of public choice assumes that government agents act for others in such ways as to further their own, the agents', self-interest. The "others" may therefore vary—from citizens to campaign contributors to special interest lobbyists. Thus official agents attend to their own interest, but this often requires attention to the interests of others.

III
Ideal Collective Choice Conditions

A
Introduction

As stated just a while ago, and also in Chapter 1, our study of government decision making divides into normative and positive realms. Normative analysis covers ideal, or desired, decision making. Positive analysis considers realities. In addition, another division distinguishes between choice procedures and choice results. _Procedures_ are the rules or mechanics of decision making. _Results_ are the outcomes. Altogether, then, we have a four-part division of subjects (as first outlined in Figure 1.1):

Observed choice procedures (positive)
Observed choice results (positive)
Desired choice procedures (normative)
Desired choice results (normative)

For purposes of orientation, let's briefly illustrate each.

> _Observed choice procedures:_ **Majority rule** is a very common procedure. A two-thirds rule or **unanimous rule** is used only rarely. By popular vote we elect senators and congressmen to serve as our representatives in Washington, D.C., senators for 6-year terms and congressmen for 2-year terms.
> _Observed choice results:_ The import restrictions discussed at the outset of this chapter

are instances of observed choice results. Your annual income tax payment is another.

Desired choice procedures: For many decisions, unanimous rule might be more desirable than majority rule. It may also be argued that, in Congress, each spending measure should include specification of the taxes that would be raised to finance the appropriation. (Note that these normative statements concerning procedures use words like *should* and *more desirable*, signaling that value judgments arise here.)

Desired choice results: Allocation efficiency, equity, and full employment are highly prized results. Government policies to achieve them are therefore good.

Now, at this point, we wish to concentrate on *desired choice procedures*. However, before discussing desired procedures, it is important to recognize the role of *desired choice results*. In general, the normative theory of public choice judges procedures by whether or not they produce desirable results. In particular, a desirable voting rule is one that yields allocation efficiency, equity, or stability when the market fails to achieve these ends. *Allocation efficiency is served when the benefits of some government action exceed its costs. Equity is served when the rich do not gain at the expense of the poor. Macro-stability is served by full employment and price stability.*

B
Ideal Conditions (No Agency)

In theory, collective decision making can often achieve these ends of efficiency, equity, and stability if it occurs under ideal conditions. Ideal conditions should hold for two key steps in government decision making—preference articulation and preference aggregation. We shall explore both. In doing so, we shall for the moment consider only direct democracy, where people themselves vote on issues rather than relying on representatives. This, in other words, temporarily assumes away agency.

1. Ideal Preference Articulation Accurate expression of citizens' preferences is crucial. The

only sure way of identifying the presence of a problem is to have citizens voice their preferences. Voting is our chief means of preference articulation. And several ideal voting conditions foster accurate preference articulation.

First, accurate articulation requires *full participation*. This means that all people affected by some policy must vote for or against it. In some cases, this is obviously not possible or practical. We cannot reliably hear from future generations or the insane. We do not allow children to vote even when issues affect them greatly. Still, the basic idea behind full participation is highly desirable. Nearly everyone should have a vote and use it when his or her fate is at stake.

Second, *full information* is desirable. This requires that all participants be completely knowledgeable about policy options. For each voter to cast a ballot in his or her self-interest, each must know the benefits and costs he or she would feel—issue by issue. Those expecting their benefits to exceed their costs will vote "yes." Those expecting their costs to exceed their benefits will vote "no." This requirement of full knowledge is difficult to meet because of the horrendous complexities and huge number of policies created by our modern world. Even experts cannot typically tell us where taxes will bite or the degree of injury caused by cholesterol in our food. Still, we are dealing with ideals here.

2. Ideal Preference Aggregation (Voting Rules)
Majority rule, where one vote over 50 percent is decisive, seems as sacred as mom and apple pie. Yet it cannot, in general, be considered the ideal voting rule because it gives the majority an opportunity to exploit the minority. This means that majority rule allows propositions to pass that have social costs much greater than social benefits, thereby violating standards of efficiency. In contrast, a *unanimous rule* would, in theory, prevent such inefficient results, while at the same time allowing passage of measures that are efficient.

Table 34.1 illustrates how majority rule may result in inefficient government action for a public good. A five-person community is the setting. An open park is proposed that would benefit everyone. Although all benefit, each person benefits differently, as indicated by the column for benefits in Table 34.1. Al, for instance, loves parks and would

TABLE 34.1 The Benefits and Costs of a Public Good (Park) for a Five-Person Community (per Year)

Person	Dollar Value of Benefits to Each Person	Tax Cost Imposed on Each Person	Net Benefit (+) or Net Cost (−) for Each Person	Vote
Al	$130	$100	+$ 30	Yes
Barb	120	100	+ 20	Yes
Carl	110	100	+ 10	Yes
Dan	20	100	− 80	No
Eve	10	100	− 90	No
Totals	$390	$500	−$110	Yes

benefit by this one greatly. Eve is more of an indoors type, and she therefore would benefit less. Altogether, society's total benefit would be $390 (per year), which falls short of the total cost by $110. Hence, by standards of efficiency, the park should *not* be built. It *will* be built, however, if it is put on the ballot in a proposition that divides the cost equally among all members of the community and if the majority rules. Equally divided, the cost would be $100 per person. When each person compares this $100 cost with his or her perceived benefit, three people realize a positive net benefit (+) and two have a net cost (−), as shown in the last column of numbers. Accordingly, the vote would be 3 to 2 *in favor* of the park, despite its inefficiency. On the whole, society suffers a net cost of −$110.

Under a unanimous rule, the park proposal would fail. If *all five members* of the community had to vote "yes" for the measure to pass, it would be doomed. Given the data of Table 34.1, Dan and Eve would resoundingly vote "no," ensuring defeat. The proponents of the park—Al, Barb, and Carl—might try to rewrite the measure, shifting

more of the cost to themselves and away from Dan and Eve. But there is no assignment of cost burden that would yield "yes" votes from all. *Whatever the distribution of costs, there will always be at least one person for whom the cost exceeds the benefit because, overall, the total cost to society exceeds the total benefit. Hence, under unanimous rule, there will always be at least one "no" vote to defeat the inefficient ballot measure.*

Tables 34.2 and 34.3 illustrate the theoretical principle that *unanimous* rule allows passage of efficient propositions, while, as just shown, it prevents passage of inefficient ones. Recall that society's total benefit exceeds its total cost for efficient actions, something true of the propositions in Tables 34.2 and 34.3. The setting here is the same five-person community as before. Now, however, the proposed public good is annual mosquito control. A nearby swamp teems with those bloodthirsty bugs, and annual pesticide treatment would bring abatement benefits to everyone. The dollar value of these benefits, as each individual perceives them, is just to the right of their name in the tables. Al is apparently thick-skinned and out

TABLE 34.2 The Benefits and Costs of a Public Good (Mosquito Control) for a Five-Person Community

Person	Dollar Value of Benefits to Each Person	Tax Cost Imposed on Each Person	Net Benefit (+) or Net Cost (−) for Each Person	Vote
Al	$ 50	$100	−$ 50	No
Barb	70	100	− 30	No
Carl	200	100	+ 100	Yes
Dan	180	100	+ 80	Yes
Eve	330	100	+ 230	Yes
Totals	$830	$500	+$330	Yes

TABLE 34.3 Benefits and Costs of a Modified Mosquito Control Measure for the Community

Person	Dollar Value of Benefits to Each Person	Tax Cost Imposed on Each Person	Net Benefit (+) or Net Cost (−) for Each Person	Vote
Al	$ 50	$ 40	+$ 10	Yes
Barb	70	60	+ 10	Yes
Carl	200	120	+ 80	Yes
Dan	180	110	+ 70	Yes
Eve	330	170	+ 160	Yes
Totals	$830	$500	+$330	Yes

of town for much of the summer because he would be willing to pay only $50 for mosquito control. Eve has characteristics of an opposite order because abatement would benefit her immensely, by $330.

The individuals' benefits remain the same for both Table 34.2 and Table 34.3. What changes is the distribution of the $500 total cost. A ballot measure that distributes the cost equally, at $100 apiece, is shown in Table 34.2. With that distribution, Al and Barb would have costs that exceed their benefits, so they would vote "no." These "no" votes would block passage under unanimous rule, but they would not be enough to block passage under majority rule. A majority of Carl, Dan, and Eve have positive net benefits with the distribution of costs in Table 34.2, so they would carry the day.

Although a unanimous rule would torpedo Table 34.2's measure with its equal cost distribution, a unanimous rule would bring passage of a rewritten measure that distributed the costs more heavily to those benefiting greatly (Carl, Dan, and Eve) and less heavily to those benefiting only slightly (Al and Barb). This is done in Table 34.3. With each individual then expecting a positive net benefit, each votes "yes," and the measure in Table 34.3 passes unanimously.

Conclusion on the theory of voting rules: Majority rule lacks discretion. It allows passage of both inefficient and efficient measures. In contrast, unanimous rule blocks inefficient measures while allowing passage of efficient measures.

This theoretical endorsement of unanimity is only theoretical. The practical problems of actually using a unanimous rule are huge. How can we learn each individual's preference for a proposi-

tion (to tailor the cost burden) when it is in the interest of each to get a free ride, to keep that preference hidden, given the public good nature of the decision? Moreover, won't some egocentric nitwit take the opportunity to play last holdout against all other voters just to gain media notoriety? In reality, few if any decisions could ever be made under a rule of unanimity.[3]

Moreover, unanimous rule can claim perfection _only_ when applied to policies involving the allocation of resources (the What? question). Policies that deliberately redistribute income to achieve some greater degree of equality (the Who? question) cannot be decided under unanimous rule because those policies necessarily hurt some people while helping others. Unanimous procedures would be hopeless in such instances (assuming voters avoid sacrifices by voting only in their own self-interest). Thus it could be argued that truly ideal procedures would require different voting rules for different types of policies: a unanimous rule for allocation improvements and a majority rule for equity adjustments.[4] But theoretical problems remain, even for mixed procedures.

3. Ideal Tax Expenditure Ties: Earmarked Financing Nearly a century ago, Knut Wicksell, an outstanding Swedish economist, proposed an ideal for government spending procedures. He argued that every expenditure proposal should be accompanied by a specific tax measure that would yield the necessary funding. This procedure con-

[3]James M. Buchanan, _The Demand and Supply of Public Goods_ (Chicago: Rand McNally, 1968), pp. 94–95.

[4]Dennis C. Mueller, _Public Choice_ (Cambridge: Cambridge University Press, 1979), pp. 223–225, 263–270.

trasts sharply with what actually happens. Typically, tax proposals are not tied to spending measures. Instead, public expenditures are usually financed out of _general revenues_, and these, in turn, are raised by general taxes on the population. Such a separation of spending and tax financing can lead to what is called _fiscal illusion_. People can incorrectly think that they are overtaxed or undertaxed. At the same time, government can incorrectly overspend or underspend. Usually, the biases created by incorrect perceptions seem to lead to a combination of overspending and undertaxing, with the result that budget deficits abound. As James Buchanan explains:

Elected politicians enjoy going back to their constituents and saying: I voted to bring you this program that will benefit us here, this harbor, or we clean this river, or this defense program. So they enjoy voting on spending programs. They don't enjoy going back to voters and saying: Look, I have to raise your taxes. So there is a proclivity for them to create deficits.[5]

The ideal of tying the means of tax funding to any proposed expenditure can be called _earmarked financing_.

Read Perspective 34A.

[5]Buchanan, "Interview," _Forbes_, November 17, 1986, p. 108.

PERSPECTIVE 34A
Inefficiency in Government Decision Making

The ideal conditions outlined previously do not, of course, hold in reality. Before turning to a detailed discussion of the imperfections and failures of reality, it may be instructive to explore briefly an example of the adverse benefit-cost results that actually occur. A major water project, the Colorado-Big Thompson Project, was recently analyzed by Charles Howe to determine its benefits and costs from 1938 through 1980. Moreover, the benefits and costs were calculated for two alternative geographic areas—the nation as a whole (society as a whole) and the region served by the project directly (Colorado). Table 34.4 shows the estimates. National benefits amounted to $209.3 million, mainly from irrigation, electricity generation, and water recreation. Regional benefits were much higher, at $874.8 million. How could regional benefits exceed national benefits? Wouldn't all benefits to a region also benefit the nation because the region is part of the nation? Not necessarily. When a canning plant moves from, say, California to Colorado as a result of the project, Colorado thinks of it as a benefit, a gain. California, however, suffers a loss. Thus, nationally, California's loss exactly offsets Colorado's gain. Over $600 million of Colorado's

benefits were of this type, so national benefits fell far short of Colorado's benefits. As for costs, they were of opposite orders. National costs were $550.7 million, while Colorado's costs were only $107.9 million. Project costs were much higher nationally because federal taxes paid for the project's construction and most of its operation. In addition, the project added substantially to the salinity of the Colorado River, thereby imposing pollution costs on downstream states in the Lower Colorado River Basin, such as Arizona and California, which are, of course, part of the nation but not part of the project's home region. Comparing the benefits and costs in the last column of Table 34.4, it appears that, nationally, the benefits were considerably smaller than the costs, resulting in a net cost of −$341.4 million. In contrast, there was a huge net benefit of +$766.9 million for Colorado because Colorado perceived benefits that were not benefits to the nation as a whole, and also because Colorado paid little of the total cost burden. _It thus becomes clear why public works projects that, from the national point of view, are extremely inefficient and wasteful may nevertheless receive strong political support from local politicans and interest groups._

TABLE 34.4 Estimated Benefits and Costs for the Colorado-Big Thompson Water Project, 1938–80 (in 1960 Dollars)

Area	Benefits ($ Millions)	Costs ($ Millions)	Net Benefits (+) Net Costs (−) ($ Millions)
National (United States)	$209.3	$550.7	−$341.4
Regional (Colorado)	$874.8	$107.9	+$766.9

Source: Charles W. Howe, "Project Benefits and Costs from National and Regional Viewpoints: Methodological Issues and Case Study of the Colorado-Big Thompson Project," _National Resources Journal_ (Winter 1987), p. 20.

IV

Government Imperfections and Failures (with Agency)

The Colorado-Big Thompson Project illustrates the presence of government imperfections and failures:

Government imperfections and failures arise when government action causes economic inefficiency, or violates norms of equity, or creates macroinstabilities.

Some imperfections and failures were noted during our discussion of ideal circumstances. For example, we acknowledged that spending measures are typically passed without earmarked financing. Furthermore, the possible inefficiencies of majority rule were demonstrated in our discussion of Table 34.1. Now we tackle problems in detail, concentrating especially on difficulties that arise from representative decision making. Mischief arises in the gap separating government agents and the populace. The troubles consist of (A) rational ignorance, (B) median voters, (C) bundle purchases, (D) special interest effects, (E) logrolling or vote trading, and (F) short time horizons.

Earlier we identified situations where the majority might exploit the minority, resulting in problems of inefficiency or inequity. _Now we shall identify instances where the minority can exploit the majority, causing the same problems._ Minorities outdid majorities in trade protection for steel and the Colorado-Big Thompson Project.

A

Rational Ignorance

Only 38 percent of the adult population of the United States voted in the federal election of 1986. That year was a nonpresidential election year, with federal contests only for Congress. Voter participation is usually better for presidential elections, but not much better. In 1980 and 1984 only about 55 percent of all voting-age adults cast votes for president. The odd consequences of these low turnouts are shown in Table 34.5. Ronald Reagan's

TABLE 34.5 Votes for Ronald Reagan During the Presidential Elections of 1980 and 1984

Election Year	Reagan Votes in Total Number (Millions)	Reagan Votes as a Percentage of Voting for President	Reagan Votes as a Percentage of the Adult Population
1980	43.9	50.7%	27.9%
1984	54.5	58.8%	32.0%

Source: Statistical Abstract of the United States 1986 (U.S. Department of Commerce, 1985), pp. 240, 256.

43.9 million votes in 1980 and his 54.5 million in 1984 were each enough to give him a _majority of those who were actually voting._ But those vote totals were just _small minorities_ of the country's entire voting-age population. In 1980, for instance, Reagan was put into office by only 27.9 percent of all those who could have voted if they had so wanted.

These low numbers show clear violations of the ideal of full participation. Still, as low as they are, they might be considered high according to public choice theory. If people acted strictly in their own self-interest, they would vote only when the anticipated benefits of voting exceeded the costs of voting. In fact, the anticipated _benefits_ of voting in government elections are ordinarily quite small to any individual—infinitesimally small. This is so because an individual voter has almost no chance of influencing the outcome. He or she is very unlikely to cast the one vote that carries an election. By comparison, the individual's _costs_ are usually quite high—for the time taken to study candidates and issues, for the time spent casting a ballot, for the transportation expenses, and so on. With individual costs exceeding benefits in this way, it would be rational for people to abstain from voting and to remain ignorant of public affairs. Hence, the name for this problem is _rational igno-rance._

> **Rational ignorance** arises when, by individual benefit-cost criteria, it is not in people's self-interest to become actively involved in government affairs.

Although according to rational calculations no one would vote, tens of millions of people actually do. This is the _paradox of voting._ The paradox is resolved once it is acknowledged that when it comes to voting, people may not act in a narrowly self-interested manner. They may act out of patriotism or altruism. Whatever the case, not enough people overcome their rational ignorance to prevent a problem of low participation. Because of rational ignorance, minorities of the populace can put politicians into office. (Moreover, because of rational ignorance, surprisingly few people can correctly name their senators, congressperson, governor, and mayor.)

B

The Median Voter in the Two-Party System

Why does your vote, or any one else's, have such a tiny probability of affecting the outcome of an election? A chief reason is that in a two-party system operating under majority rule, the one voter who really holds sway is the _median voter,_ the one in the middle who tips the balance one way or the other. If outcomes were set proportionately, so that many minority parties could gain representation in legislatures (as they do in European parliaments), then this would not be the case. However, with majority rule in a two-party system such as ours, the winner takes all. The majority winner is the one who, at the very least, attracts the vote of half the electorate plus one, the "one" being the median voter.

An important result then follows. The median voter, in theory, becomes very powerful. The two candidates, Republican and Democratic, will typically try to win the median voter's favor. In so doing, they will tend to adopt middle-of-the-road positions on the issues. At least they will give the temporary appearance of being close to the center. In the end, the two candidates for any given office, president for instance, typically begin to sound very much alike, especially as election day approaches.

> The **median voter** is the one in the middle who decides a majority-rule election and who therefore heavily influences the positions that politicians take on issues.

Figure 34.1 explains this statement. Assume that voters can be arrayed from most "liberal" on the left to most "conservative" on the right. The vertical distance indicates the number of voters at each position. Relatively few voters would hold extreme beliefs in this scale of things. Most would hold "moderate" views, while leaning a bit to the liberal left or conservative right, depending on their political preferences. The result would be a frequency distribution of voters that would look like the bell-shaped normal distribution of statistics. Figure 34.1 shows this distribution in three different ways. Parts (a), (b), and (c) indicate voting results for that distribution, depending on the position

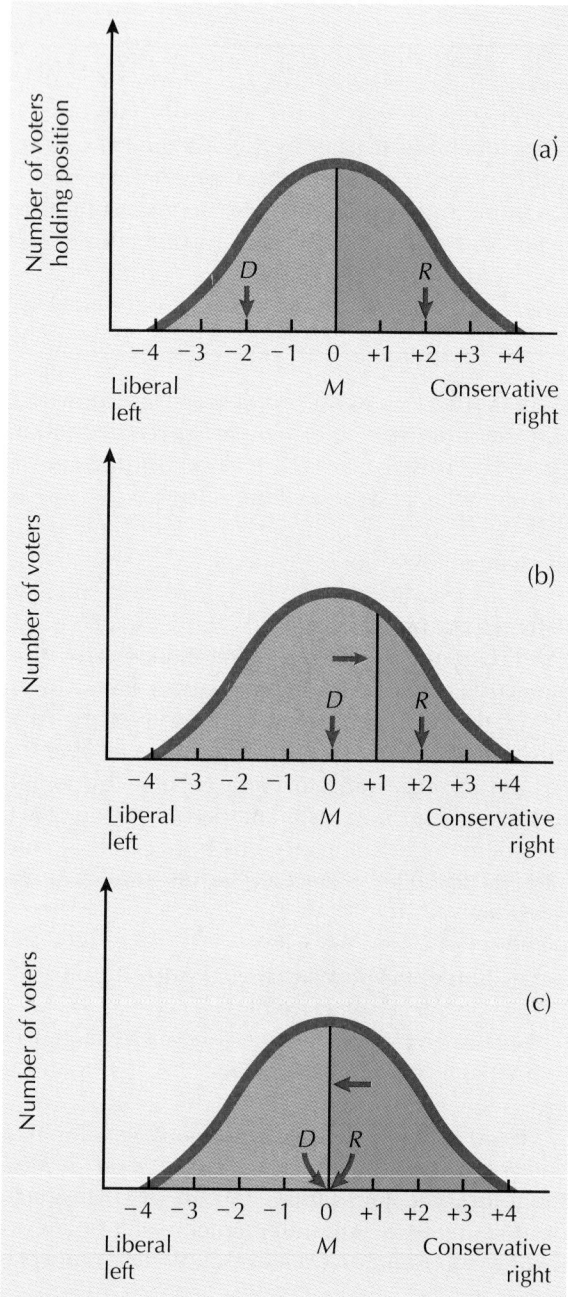

FIGURE 34.1 *The Power of the Median Voter Under Majority Rule in a Two-Party System*

in showing who is closest to whom, the horizontal axis is scaled with fictional distances from the zero origin—(−) to the left and (+) to the right. With people voting for the closest candidate, they will always split the distance between the candidates when the two candidates are separated on the political spectrum.

Part (a) of Figure 34.1 indicates what might happen in the beginning, before the median voter's power is realized. D maintains a middle position among liberals at −2 on the left, while R takes a middle position among conservatives on the right at +2. Being equally distant from the center at 0, they split the overall vote between them 50–50. The median voter, M, will be undecided. When pressed to vote, he or she will perhaps toss a coin to decide.

Assume that from this toss-up in part (a) of Figure 34.1, candidate D is the first to discover that he or she can improve the chance of winning by shifting his or her position on the issues to become more conservative. Moving toward the center to gain the vote of median voter M, D stops at zero. D retains the support of everyone to the left, from 0 to −4, while adding those closer to him or her than to R on the right, from 0 to +1. This is because D and R always split the distance evenly between them when voters vote for the nearest candidate. In part (b), then, D would always win by a landslide.

However, R can adopt the same strategy. In part (c) of Figure 34.1, R recognizes that he or she can move left to 0 from +2 and retain all voters on the right while at the same time recapturing the support of those located between +1 and 0. In the end, both D and R occupy positions in the middle of the spectrum near M. Both sound very much alike on the issues. And, in theory, the vote tally is likely to be very close.

This theory of the median voter seems to explain events fairly well much of the time. For example, during the election campaign of 1980, Ronald Reagan, who was quite conservative, shifted his position on issues almost daily to appear moderate to the voters. His shifting became especially rapid as election day approached and the polls forecasted a very tight race with incumbent President Jimmy Carter. Occasionally, Republicans and Democrats have selected extremist candidates, like Barry Goldwater and George Mc-

each candidate takes on the political spectrum. D represents the Democratic candidate and R the Republican. M is the median voter. Finally, keep in mind that people will vote for the candidate *closest* to them on the left-right continuum. To assist

Govern. After lopsided losses to opposing moderates, each party successfully shifted back to support moderates in subsequent elections. Nixon followed Goldwater for the Republicans in 1968. Carter followed McGovern for the Democrats in 1976.

C

Bundle Purchases

When grocery shopping, you can fill your shopping cart with the exact mix of brands and goods you like. You can choose Coca-Cola over Carnation Milk and Wheat Chex instead of eggs. You can "customize" the cluster of commodities you buy.

Ideally, citizens should be able to exert their influence on government decisions much the same way—separately, issue by issue, favoring this position while opposing that one. Actually, however, such is not the case. Because elected representatives act as our agents on almost all issues, the political process works in bundles, which are very imprecise.

> **Bundle purchases** occur when people must vote for a single political "agent" who holds views on many issues.

As James Gwartney and Richard Stroup explain, voters must select a legislator or president or governor composed of a bundle of political "goods" and tax "prices":

> _The voter either gets the bundle of political goods offered by candidate A or the bundle offered by candidate B. Often, neither of these bundles of political goods represents what a specific consumer (voter) would like to have. The political consumer does not have the freedom to "shop around," buying some goods from any of several suppliers. He is forced to accept the bundle favored by the majority coalition._[6]

Indeed, numerous voters may strongly _disagree_ with candidate A's position on, say, trade protec-

[6]James Gwartney and Richard Stroup, _Microeconomics: Private and Public Choice_, 2nd ed. (New York: Academic Press, 1979), p. 445.

tion for the steel industry, yet feel compelled to vote for her anyway because they like A's solid commitment to pollution abatement and parkland preservation. Once in office, A may then be able to act against the best interests of the majority on the issue of steel industry protection. As a bundle, she is less vulnerable to replacement than she would be otherwise.

D

Special Interest Effects

Why would any politician adopt a position contrary to the general public interest? How can water projects like Colorado-Big Thompson get passed? Special interest effects help to explain.

> **Special interest effects** occur when subgroups of voters (especially minorities like farmers or steelworkers) have more political influence than their proportionate share.

Preference articulation and aggregation are, in reality, heavily influenced by a few thousand interest groups. These groups are typically formed by people who share some common economic interest—such as the Association of American Railroads, American Petroleum Institute, AFL-CIO, American Bar Association, or United Steelworkers of America. There are also _issue groups_ that spring up around specific issues, such as the Environmental Defense Fund and the National Organization for Women. It is in these interest groups that we find the most politically active people and business firms.

Much public policy furthers _neither_ economic efficiency _nor_ greater equity, and a major explanation for this government failure lies in special interest politics. When the benefits of a policy are concentrated among relatively few, and the costs are spread widely in little bits throughout society, then special interests who benefit will have the advantage of being able to mobilize particularly well-organized, vociferous support in favor of passage, while rational ignorance silences the many who bear the cost. Thus, for years, economists have pointed out that quota and tariff protection against imports is inefficient. They have argued that restrictive licensing of barbers and other service personnel is anticompetitive and costly to the public. They have also questioned the wisdom of most water projects. Yet these policies and many more like them abound because special interest groups exploit the mismatch between concentrated benefits and diffuse costs.

When a policy carries an opposite distribution of benefits and costs, with benefits spread thinly and costs concentrated thickly, the problem is reversed. Then the cost side typically has the more powerful interest group representation. The overall benefits of a policy may greatly exceed the costs, but that policy's chances of passage are reduced to the extent that the benefits go in small amounts to vast numbers of people, while the costs fall heavily on relatively few, who can loudly voice their special interest. Disparities such as this apparently explain why environmental protection policies are delayed until crisis conditions arise. The immediate costs of such policies fall most heavily on businesses, which, compared to citizens, are few in number and readily mobilized. The benefits are spread diffusely to everyone.

Read Perspective 34B.

E
Logrolling, or Vote Trading

Sometimes representatives of two or more different special interest minorities may engage in _logrolling, or vote trading,_ to form majorities that win passage of special interest measures. For instance, a senator representing one special interest will say to another representing a different special interest, "If you vote for my special interest, I'll vote for yours." In this way, a senator from Utah may gain support for Utah water projects by voting in favor of military bases in Texas and tobacco subsidies for North Carolina (and vice versa for the latter interests regarding Utah).

> **Logrolling** is the exchange of political favors, such as votes in vote trading, to win passage of legislation.

F
Short Time Horizons

With **short time horizons** politicians tend to discount heavily the distant future and stress near-term appearances.

Elections are life-and-death matters to politicians. Evidence shows that they often change their behavior as election day approaches (much like smokers who quit after learning that they have lung cancer). Add to these observations the fact that elections occur rather frequently, as often as every 2 years for a member of the U.S. House of Representatives, and it is easy to see why elected officials tend to have limited time horizons.

The policy consequences of their shortsighted outlook are fairly easy to see. Government policies with high _short-run costs_ compared to large _future benefits_ will tend to be voted down, leading to inaction. The instincts of the political process are therefore not generally geared to squirreling away nuts against hard winters. As a result, crisis conditions regularly arise and seem necessary to spur action in such areas as environmental protection and product safety.

Conversely, when _benefits_ are concentrated in the _near term_ and _costs_ are concentrated in the _distant future,_ shortsightedness has the opposite effect. Action tends to be hasty or excessive. This deficiency is especially evident for macroeconomic policies. The benefits of reduced unemployment and sprightly prosperity can be obtained in the short run by expansive government policies like deficit spending and rapid money supply growth. But the long-run cost of these policies is inflation. Another example is direct wage–price control to check inflation. The short-run benefit of quick price stability is bought at the long-run cost of inefficiencies in product markets and inequities in labor markets. Historically, "stabilization" policies that were not really stabilizing in the long run preceded the presidential elections of 1964, 1968, 1972, and 1976.

V
Ideology: Boon or Bane?

The preceding discussions were based on the fundamental assumption of most public choice theory—namely, that all people involved in government decision making attempt to further their private self-interest. Efforts to advance the public interest, motivated by patriotism, altruism, or such, were assumed away. However, as we have

---

PERSPECTIVE 34B
Campaign Financing and Policy Lobbying

Of course, special interest groups do not voice their interests merely by writing letters to elected representatives or calling them on the phone. They attempt to gain favor and influence among politicians by contributing money to finance election campaigns and lobbying vigorously. _Political action committees (PACs)_ are the campaign contribution arms of special interests groups. They donated a total of $111.1 million to those running for seats in the U.S. Senate and House of Representatives during the federal election of 1984. Figure 34.2 divides these PACs into four main types, depending on the special interest, and shows the distribution of money from each type between Democratic and Republican candidates. Clearly, business corporations are the largest single source of PAC money, followed by trade associations (which are collections of businesses and professional groups, such as the American Bankers Association and the American Medical Association). All business interests taken together thus accounted for approximately $65.9 million, or nearly 60 percent of the total PAC money. In their choice of party, corporations strongly favored Republicans, while trade associations divided their contributions more evenly between Republicans and Democrats. Labor unions ranked third, with total contributions of $26.0 million, almost all of which went to Democrats. Finally, the "other" category includes "issues" and "ideological" groups. Although each of these interest groups probably concentrated its contributions on the candidates of one party, as an aggregate their money was fairly evenly split between Democrats and Republicans.

Apart from these election efforts, _lobbying_ is the most important activity of special interest groups. **_Lobbying_** _is the attempt to sway lawmakers and other officials to side with whatever special interest the lobbyist happens to represent._ It is often called _influence peddling._ Lobbyists, many of whom are former government officials, serve their special interest clients in a wide variety of ways. Among other things, they write drafts of favorable legislation that will be introduced by friendly congresspeople; stir up grass-roots support for a client's initiatives on Captiol Hill; hire university professors and other experts to testify at hearings in favor or in opposition to some proposed legislation; gather information about an issue; build coalitions by bringing together lobbying groups that share similar interests; and, of course, meet with legislators to remind them of the generous campaign support they have received in the past from the special interest group.

Interestingly, lobbying itself has become a big business, with large firms staffed by many lobbyists serving numerous clients. Perhaps one day we will witness the spectacle of lobbyists lobbying for _their_ special interests. According to _Fortune,_ "Lobbying. . . . has become such established, highly paid, big-league stuff that new players are flocking to the game. In the halcyon days of yore, highpriced lawyers from blue-chip Washington firms dominated the field. No more. Public relations outfits have begun clambering onto the turf."[7]

[7]Anna Cifelli Isgro, "Pricey Lobbyists Who Do It All," _Fortune,_ July 20, 1987, p. 72.

---

already seen in the paradox of voting, the self-interest assumption of behavior cannot be the whole story. If it were, no one would overcome rational ignorance to vote, to attend political rallies, and so on.

One problem with a broader assumption that

allows for public-interest motives is the absence of any clear definition of what is in the "public interest." When a policy that promotes efficiency also causes inequities, what is in the public interest? When a policy that reduces income inequality and curbs discrimination against blacks also en-

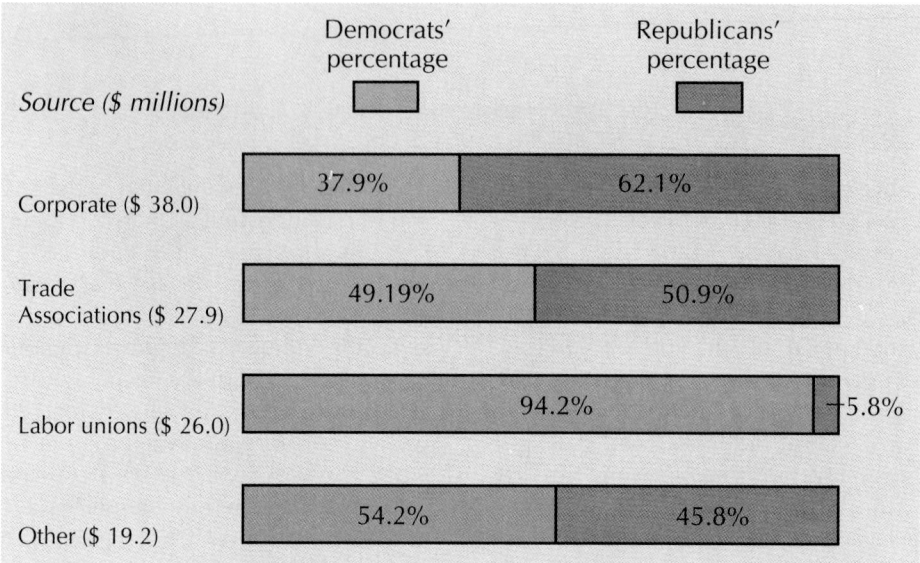

FIGURE 34.2   Contributions to Congressional Campaigns (House and Senate) by Political Action Committees (PACs) by Type of Committee and Party of Candidate, 1984
(*Source:* Statistical Abstract of the United States 1986 *(U.S. Department of Commerce)*, p. 258.)

croaches upon individual freedom, what is in the public interest? When a health policy protects a few dozen people against early death but costs $2 billion, what is in the public interest? More generally, what is patriotism when it comes to economic policy? Is it anything like altruism?

Although this uncertainty of definition is a problem, it is not completely crippling. Economists who study public-interest motives have successfully used the notion of *ideology* to broaden the analysis of government decision making beyond the confines of assumed private self-interest.

An **ideology** is a set of beliefs and value judgments about the nature of the world and ways to improve it.

As indicated at the end of Chapter 4 and summarized here in Figure 34.3, conservatives and liberals espouse substantially different ideologies (while moderates occupy the middle ground). *Conservatives*, in general, tend to think of humans as being inherently materialistic, wholly rational creatures, who are very competent in making all the right choices to further their own economic interests. To allow full expression to these traits,

the value judgment that should be given priority over all others is freedom (often defined by conservatives as the absence of government). Efficiency also ranks high with conservatives. These views are consistent with conservative beliefs about the market and the government. The market is marvelous in almost every way, for if left undisturbed by the government it furthers freedom and efficiency. In contrast, the government is the conservatives' despair. Its flaws are innate and serious, so it is to be avoided.

Liberals, on the other hand, believe that humans display weaknesses and needs that are uncharacteristic of the conservatives' perception of human nature. Indeed, liberals argue that paternalism has its place. Among liberal value judgments, equity often outranks freedom or efficiency, although the latter two are not completely disregarded. (Also, liberals define freedom to include freedom from hunger and illness.) Liberals look upon the market with favorable eyes, but they are quick to see its imperfections and failures. They therefore support government policies for such things as antitrust, environmental protection, and poverty relief more vigorously than conservatives. This support for government policies that would be denounced by

	Summary of conservative views	Summary of liberal views
Views of human nature	People are inherently materialistic, rational, and competent.	People are often fallible and need to cooperate.
Basic value judgments	Freedom outweighs all other values. Efficiency ranks high.	Equity is stressed along with freedom and efficiency.
Regard for the market	The market works amazingly well for all the basic questions (What? etc.).	The market suffers imperfections and failures in many instances.
Regard for the government	The government is tyrannical, flawed, and meddlesome. It should be avoided.	The government serves society fairly well, correcting the markets' flaws.

FIGURE 34.3 Summary of Conservative and Liberal Ideologies As They Relate to Economic Matters

(Sources: See, for example, Robert B. Carson, Microeconomic Issues Today, Alternative Approaches (New York: St. Martin's Press, 1980); Benjamin Ward, The Ideal Worlds of Economics (New York: Basic Books, 1979); Milton Friedman, Capitalism and Freedom (Chicago: University of Chicago Press, 1962).

conservatives is consistent with the liberals' generally favorable view of government. According to liberals, democratic government is not tyrannical or especially harmful.

These nutshell descriptions of conservative and liberal views are oversimplified, and many conservatives and liberals would disagree with some of the characterizations. Still, they serve to identify the two prevailing ideologies of those involved in public choices and to bracket the moderates who hold beliefs that blend these two. They identify two broad views of the "public interest." Altruistic behavior is often aimed at furthering these ideologies.

If these ideologies are in fact important to government decision making, then private interest would not fully account for political behavior. For example, a proposed law that would favor the oil interests in Texas might nevertheless be opposed by a Texas senator because it conflicts with the senator's conservative views. Table 34.6 illustrates the point more concretely. Data on the voting behavior of senators from five states are shown. If economic private interests were all that mattered, both senators from the same state should vote pretty much the same because the economic interests of their constituents would be the same. However, Table 34.6 shows dramatically different

TABLE 34.6 The Influence of Ideology on Voting Behavior in the U.S. Senate: Crude Oil Price Regulation, 1970s

State and Senators	Liberal Senator		Conservative Senator	
	Liberal Rating	Pro-Regulation Voting Percent	Liberal Rating	Pro-Regulation Voting Percent
Idaho				
Church	91.7	100.0		
McClure			3.3	15.7
New York				
Javits	87.9	91.7		
Buckley			3.7	6.7
Utah				
Moss	65.6	92.9		
Garn			6.9	7.7
North Dakota				
Burdick	69.4	66.7		
Young			3.2	25.0
Wyoming				
McGee	63.0	39.4		
Hansen			2.8	6.2

Source: Joseph P. Kalt, _The Economics and Politics of Oil Price Regulation_ (Cambridge, Mass.: MIT Press, 1981), pp. 262–264.

voting by senators depending on ideology. The "Liberal Rating" of each senator was compiled by Americans for Democratic Action from votes on social issues (such as abortion, pornography, and capital punishment), as well as on economic issues. Accordingly, the first senator mentioned for each state is identified as a liberal, while the second senator mentioned is a conservative. Their voting behavior is measured by how often during the 1970s they voted in favor of regulating crude petroleum prices and production—how often, measured as a percentage of the 36 opportunities that arose during the period. (For example, 24 pro-regulation votes out of 36 possible votes would yield a voting index of 24/36 = 66.7 percent, as in the case of Senator Burdick of North Dakota.) It may thus be seen that, despite a strong similarity of private interests, liberal Senator Church of Idaho consistently voted in favor of government regulation, while his colleague from Idaho, conservative Senator McClure, voted against it in almost every instance. A similar sharp contrast holds for New York, where liberal Senator Javits voted 91.7 percent of the time in favor of regulation, while conservative Senator Buckley voted against it all but 6.7 percent of the time. The contrasts for Utah, North Dakota, and Wyoming are similar, though less extreme (partly because, strictly speaking,

Senators Moss, Burdick, and McGee might be considered moderates instead of liberals).

The influence of ideology has been analyzed for congressional voting on many issues besides petroleum regulation—including coal strip mining, environmental protection, loan guarantees to a troubled Chrysler Corporation, occupational safety, farm policy, and import protection.[8] The evidence that ideology does have a substantial influence is overwhelming. Indeed, it is often the single most important variable explaining congressional voting behavior. Economic variables are also important. But it seems that a senator's ideology (as revealed, for instance, in his or her vote on the death penalty, sex education, and school prayer), frequently has greater accuracy in predicting how the senator will vote on coal strip-mining regulation than economic information about coal mining in the senator's home state. It must be concluded, therefore, that _political behavior is governed by a mixture of private-interest and public-interest motives. Economic consequences and ideological con-_

[8]James B. Kan and Paul H. Rubin, _Congressmen, Constituents, and Contributors_ (Boston: Martinus Nijhoff, 1982); Joseph P. Kalt and Mark A. Zupan, "Capture and Ideology in the Economic Theory of Politics," _American Economic Review_ (June 1984), pp. 279–300; and Peter Navarro, _The Policy Game_ (Lexington, Mass: Lexington Books, 1984).

victions both play important roles in government policy formulation.

This is a positive observation. What about the normative question: Is this good or bad? You may judge for yourself, for value judgments—your ideology—will largely determine your answer.

SUMMARY

1. Government decision making, like market decision making, can be subjected to economic analysis.

2. The tasks government is called upon to perform include market maintenance (e.g., contract enforcement and antitrust), correction for market failures (e.g., public goods), and redistribution. Government is needed most where group or collective decision making is required.

3. Collective (government) decision making is nonmarket decision making by voters, politicians, civil servants, and others associated with government. The theory of public choice analyzes collective decision making.

4. Market and government decision making are alike in that (a) scarcity is dealt with by both, (b) private self-interests motivate both sets of decision makers, (c) the results of both procedures may be judged by how well they satisfy individual preferences of those in society, i.e., consumer and citizen sovereignty, and (d) both the market and the government can be studied in positive and normative ways.

5. Government decision making differs from market decision making (a) by being collective action instead of individual action, (b) by registering people's preferences through voting instead of spending, (c) by being coercive, (d) by dealing in redistribution, and (e) by relying more heavily on agency representation of individuals rather than on direct individual action.

6. Ideally, there should be full participation and full information. Unanimous rule for allocation decisions is also desirable (but impractical). Earmarked financing would ideally tie taxes to spending measures.

7. Actually, government imperfections and failures occur, causing economic inefficiency, problems of inequity, and macroinstabilities.

8. The reasons for these imperfections and failures include (a) rational ignorance, (b) median voter influence under two-party, majority-vote procedures, (c) bundle purchases of political agents, (d) special interest effects, (e) logrolling and vote trading, and (f) short time horizons.

9. Government decision making is heavily influenced by ideologies, which are sets of beliefs and value judgments about the nature of the world and ways to improve it. Liberal and conservative ideologies are especially important to economic decision making. See Figure 34.3 for a summary of those views.

KEY TERMS

Government
Public good
Collective decision making
Theory of public choice
Majority rule
Unanimous rule
Government imperfections and failures
Rational ignorance

Median voter
Bundle purchases
Special interest effects
Lobbying
Logrolling
Short time horizons
Ideology

QUESTIONS AND PROBLEMS

1. What is (are) the primary goal(s) of the politician? Do politicians have the same motives as consumers?

2. What are the political implications when the benefits of a possible government action are concentrated and costs are spread across many taxpayers?

3. When is a government decision a good one?

4. How does government decision-making differ from private decision-making?

5. Explain the difference between majority rule and unanimous rule. What are the problems with each from both theoretical and practical perspectives?

6. Explain what earmarked financing involves. Would a policy of earmarked financing be a good and politically feasible solution to the growing U.S. budget deficit? Why?

7. How many people vote in U.S. presidential elections? Why do so few people vote? Why do so many people vote?

8. Why is it so often difficult to discern meaningful differences among candidates' positions in U.S. elections?

9. What are major flaws in the government decision-making process in the U.S.?

10. Why is Congress shortsighted? What might be some solutions to this problem?

11. Is it liberal or conservative to focus on individual freedoms? Are civil rights activists liberals or conservatives? Why? Are advocates of the legal right to have an abortion liberals or conservatives? Why? Could you argue that advocates of legalized abortions are conservatives rather than liberals?

35

Environment and Energy

During the 1960s and 1970s, America stumbled from crisis to crisis. For example, the Cuyahoga River, which runs through Cleveland, caught fire and burned out of control in 1969—a consequence of 155 tons of chemical, oil, and acid wastes being dumped into the river every day. Nearby, Lake Erie was dying. Nitrate and phosphate pollution fed huge algae blooms, which consumed dissolved oxygen and pushed the lake into accelerated eutrophication. Overall in 1971, water pollution killed 73 million fish. Poor air quality also caused problems. During the mid-1970s, Los Angeles suffered "very unhealthful" and "hazardous" air on 1 out of every 3 days. Nationwide, emissions of carbon monoxide, hydrocarbons, and nitrogen oxide in 1970 were more than double their level 30 years earlier.

Energy problems also appeared. In the winter and spring of 1973–74, gasoline grew especially scarce because of an Arab oil embargo against the United States. Further oil disruptions followed in the late 1970s. Long lines at service stations resulted, testing the tempers of motorists and even triggering some violence. Likewise, natural gas shortages occurred during several especially harsh winters, closing factories and schools in the Midwest and Northeast.

The environmental problems caused some pessimistic people to predict that civilization would soon be throttled by the excess dirt and poison. Others claimed that energy shortages would do us in, that we were foolishly burning up our future too hastily. Still others were predicting that environment and energy problems would *combine* to cause catastrophe. After all, the two are related. Our combustion of coal and oil fouls the air, while at the same time depleting fuel supplies that future generations could use.

Fortunately, events of the 1980s have disproven the gloomiest predictions. Alarm has lessened. Still, complete complacency is not warranted. Some energy and environmental problems persist. Hence the purpose of this chapter is to put these past and present problems and their possible solutions into an economic perspective. One of our main messages is that economics contributes tremendously to an understanding of these topics. It helps to identify problems and assess policies.

I
Environment

A
The Problems

1. What Is Pollution?   As previous chapters reveal, scarcity imposes production trade-offs between, say, autos and airplanes or chicken dinners and hamburgers. Costs always seem to accompany benefits. Hence the old economic axiom: "There is no such thing as a free lunch."

In nature, there is likewise no such thing as a free lunch. Nature's laws of conservation of mass and energy tell us that we never really "consume" anything. When we use minerals, fuels, gases, and other materials, we merely change their form, extract their services, and push them around a bit. When ultimately discarded as trash, sewage, exhaust, or other waste, they do not disappear. They remain in our environment.

Our environment—the air, water, and land— serves us in three ways. First, it provides a *habitat*, that is, life support surroundings. Destruction of our habitat or the habitat of other creatures is not merely inconvenient or uncomfortable, it is deadly. Second, the environment provides natural *resources* useful for the production of goods and services. River water, for instance, quenches thirst, yields fish, floats transport, and irrigates crops. It can also be a convenient place to dump sewage, and this waste reception is also a resource service. Third, environmental *amenities* make life pleasant. Swimming, boating, fishing, skiing, hiking, and sightseeing illustrate the possibilities for enjoyment.

In a physical sense, pollution occurs whenever humans alter the environment. *In an economic* sense, **pollution** _occurs when one use of the environment diminishes other possible uses of value to humanity._ Typically, resource exploitation injures habitat and amenity uses, as when use of the atmosphere for an exhaust repository creates smog that kills people and blots out beautiful sunsets. However, pollution also occurs when one resource use hurts another resource use, as when strip mining interferes with farming, for example. Pollution is, in short, a problem of scarce environmental capabilities relative to human demands. Misuse is the same as misallocation; _there is too much pollution when the environment is used excessively for waste disposal relative to other, cleaner endeavors._

> **Pollution** occurs when one use of the environment, waste disposal in particular, diminishes other valuable uses, including other resource uses, as well as habitats and amenities.

Wastes dumped into the air are certainly the most obvious pollutants. These include particulates from soot and hydrocarbons from fossil fuels. One air pollutant attracting especially intense attention is sulfur dioxide (SO_2), which comes mainly from coal combustion and which contributes to acid rain, thereby killing trees, other vegetation, and fish. Over 20 million tons of SO_2 are thrown into our atmosphere every year.

Water pollutants can be either _degradable_ or _nondegradable._ Once in the water, degradable pollutants change through chemical and biological processes. They are, in fact, subject to nature's self-cleansing capabilities as long as they are not overly concentrated by excessive emissions. Domestic sewage (like wildlife sewage) is among these degradable wastes, along with the organic wastes of food canneries.

Nondegradable pollutants do not change in the water, or change only very slowly. Mercury, lead, cadmium, polychlorinated biphenyls (PCBs), and DDT persist long after emission. They can be directly poisonous or more deviously dangerous. Some, like DDT, can concentrate in animals highly placed in nature's food chain, harming their reproductive capabilities or doing other damage.

Mention of these hazards brings to mind the broader problem of toxic substances. There are some 30,000 hazardous waste disposal sites in the United States. Hundreds, perhaps thousands, of them emit acutely poisonous substances like benzidene, trichloroethylene, methylene chloride, and PCBs. Contaminated soil and water result. When humans are exposed to that contamination they may suffer cancer, genetic alteration, neurological damage, and sterility.

2. What Causes Pollution? Are the managers of America's corporations deranged criminals who deliberately pour SO_2, carbon monoxide, PCBs, and other pollutants into our environment in order to damage property, kill wildlife, and harm people? Is that what causes pollution? Or does moral degeneration lie at the heart of the problem—a diminishing sense of respect and responsibility among people toward nature and toward their fellow human beings? Or is the problem due to technology? Would it go away if we could somehow magically do away with all the modern chemicals and production processes that threaten our air, water, and soil?

Simple reflection raises doubts about these possible explanations. For example, the notion that a criminal conspiracy is the cause does not hold up given the fact that virtually _everyone_ is a polluter, not just our industrial chieftains. We pollute when we drive our cars, litter the landscape, or run our record players on electricity generated by coal combustion. As for technology, it should be recognized that pollution has been a problem for ages, even in simpler times. Today carbon monoxide is an unsavory waste product of transportation. In the past, horse manure was the menace. To be sure, some polluters do act in a criminal manner (like those who recklessly dump toxic wastes). Moreover, it must be admitted that technology has spawned some pollutants of intense danger (like plutonium). But the best general explanation of what causes pollution appears to lie elsewhere— in the economics of external costs.

External costs can arise in the process of production or consumption. In production, firms must pay internal or private costs for labor, materials, energy, and the like. Other costs go unpaid, however. Firms impose these external costs on outsiders, as when steel manufacturers pump soot and noxious gas into the atmosphere, damaging crops, injuring people's health, and doing other injury. If external parties could bill the steel companies for the property damage, the hospital costs, and the lost wages when work is missed, then these and similar costs would be internalized. Once internalized, these costs would alter producer behavior. Production would be cleaner. But these costs are not internalized, so problems arise. As regards consumption, such costs occur when those who consume goods and services harm or irritate others. Auto travel, for instance, emits carbon monoxide that triggers angina attacks among pedestrians and emits the makings of smog.

External costs are those costs (or harms) experienced by people other than the firm

producing the good or the person consuming it.

Figure 35.1 illustrates the problem as it relates to production, using hypothetical data for steel. Assuming perfect competition, the market would yield an equilibrium output of 60 million tons of steel and an equilibrium price of $120 per ton. This equates marginal _private_ benefit (demand) and marginal _private_ cost (supply), each of which is $120 at this output of 60 million tons. However, _society's_ costs and benefits are out of whack because producers are imposing on other people external costs of $40 per ton of steel produced (and those others are members of society). Thus, at

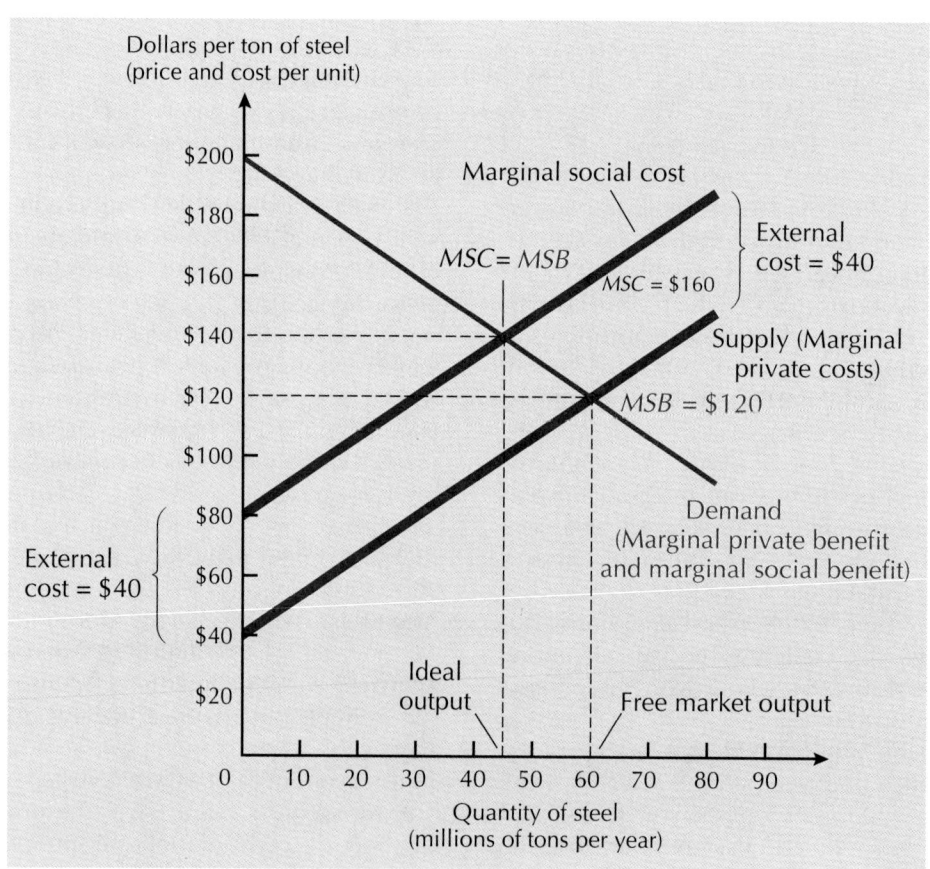

FIGURE 35.1 _External Costs and the Problem of Pollution_
A purely competitive market's demand and supply reflect marginal private benefits, MPB (demand), and marginal private costs, MPC (supply), as these are what buyers and sellers experience. In the free market, MPB = MPC. However, with external costs (here $40 per ton), the free market output is too much and the marginal social cost, MSC, exceeds the marginal social benefit by the amount of the external cost.

60 million tons of output, marginal *social* benefit, *MSB*, is \$120, as indicated by the demand curve. Marginal *social* cost, *MSC*, on the other hand, is \$160 at that level of output, which is the sum of the marginal private cost (\$120, as indicated by the supply curve) and the external cost (\$40 per ton).

The fact that marginal social cost exceeds marginal social benefit at 60 millions tons (*MSC* > *MSB*) signals an overallocation of resources to the production of steel, i.e., too much. The What? question receives a bad answer from the free market in this case. Too much output is resulting in too much pollution. If output could be reduced in Figure 35.1 to 45 million tons, the pollution would be reduced and marginal social benefit would then equal marginal social cost (at \$140 per ton). Note that, in addition, the price would rise as output falls. The price rises by \$20, which is less than the full amount of the external cost (\$40) because demand is downward sloping. The higher price may irritate consumers, while among producers the lower level of output will mean plant closings and unemployment. These burdens of adjustment will ease with time, however, and they *should* be undertaken to improve the long-run, permanent condition of the economy and the environment.

The reason external costs are imposed on others is fairly obvious. Profit-maximizing firms will try to minimize their own costs. And it is less costly to dump raw industrial wastes into nearby rivers and lakes than it is to process those wastes into harmless substances or to dispose of them in permanently sealed containers. Similarly, it is cheaper to expel sulfur oxides into the atmosphere than it is to wash coal free of sulfur before burning or to scrub the smoke to remove SO_2.

B

Pollution Policies

1. Introduction and Overview There are many possible approaches to environmental policy; moral suasion, direct regulation, emission taxes, marketable permits, and subsidies are the most prominent. All of these have been tried at one time or another both here and abroad.

Our experience with **moral suasion,** for instance, includes publicity campaigns featuring cartoon characters who urge us not to be "litter bugs" or who chirp "give a hoot, don't pollute." *The idea is to persuade people not to pollute.* Although some ardent environmentalists have faith that the rest of us can someday be converted to their staunch ethical views and clean behavior, moral suasion has had little impact to date. For reasons outlined in the previous section, the basic problem is not really one of morality. A competitive firm would simply go out of business if, in a fit of moral conviction, it undertook the necessary expenses to abate its pollution while its rivals did not. Moral suasion does have a place, however, as do practically all of these policy options. It works best during temporary crises, when the danger is immediate and readily apparent to all (like serious smog attacks).

The approach tried most extensively in the United States has been **direct regulation.** *This is control by decree.* And this is the major method of U.S. government intervention in areas of product and job safety, as well as environmental protection. Such regulation requires two major classes of official activity—(1) standard setting and (2) enforcement for compliance. The first involves drawing the line between permissible and not permissible behavior. The second is, in effect, a process of checking up to see if anyone is stepping over the line into forbidden territory. Sanctions then discourage violations. Details of regulation will be taken up shortly.

Although regulation is the mainstay of U.S. policy, many economists argue that a *tax* or **emission fee** approach is superior. *The basic idea here is to change behavior for the better by imposing perpetual monetary inducements, such as the market provides. Polluters would pay a tax geared to the extent of their pollution.* More pollution means more taxes. Nonpolluters would not have to pay. For example, SO_2 emissions could be taxed at a rate of \$300 for every ton emitted into the atmosphere. This would discourage such emissions.

Another policy alternative much favored by economists would rely on **marketable permits.** *Under this approach, polluters may produce only as many tons of pollution as allowed by the official permits that they have purchased, and the supply of those permits would be limited according to considerations of health, property protection, and other such standards of environmental cleanliness.*

For example, 10,000 permits, each allowing 10 tons of SO_2 emissions for a 1-year period, might be sold by the government to producers located in the state of Ohio. Although permits of a traditional type are presently used in connection with the regulatory approach, the marketable permits suggested here would differ in two ways: (1) They would be marketable, that is, transferable among polluters for a price. (2) They would limit the aggregate amount of emissions in a geographic area more rigorously.

Finally, **abatement subsidies** conclude this brief survey of policies. Whereas taxes goad, subsidies entice. _With subsidies, the government pays polluters to abate by covering part or all of the costs they incur to stem their pollution._ A main problem with subsidies aimed at private industry is that, unlike direct regulation or taxation, subsidies disguise the costs of abatement. Subsidies gain abatement without raising product prices to reflect the costs of abatement. Hence consumers do not confront the true social costs of production, including the costs of cleanliness. As a result, consumers are not encouraged to shift their purchases from high-pollution products to low-pollution products. Society's misallocation of resources may therefore persist under the subsidy approach. For this and other reasons, subsidies have been used sparingly in the United States. They have been used to clean up abandoned toxic waste disposal sites and to finance municipal sewage treatment facilities. But that is about all.

2. Regulation: Some Details The environmental laws passed by Congress fill over 400 pages with fine print. The policy pronouncements of the Environmental Protection Agency (EPA) fill thousands of pages more. The staff of the EPA has exceeded 10,000 in some years. Environmental regulation is, in other words, an official undertaking of huge magnitude and baffling complexity. Here we can do no more than outline what is involved, illustrating that outline with some examples.

Table 35.1 provides the outline. It shows the two major divisions of the regulatory approach mentioned earlier—_standard setting_ and _enforcement for compliance_. It then goes on to indicate several subdivisions of each of these activities.

Regulatory **standard setting** breaks down into two major subcategories—(1) broad standards and (2) narrow standards. _Broad standards_ are usually set by Congress in order to give guidance to the enforcement agencies (the EPA in particular) and to the courts, which may ultimately rule on regulations. These broad standards are often vague, referring to such objectives as "swimmable"

TABLE 35.1   Outline of Major Activities in Environmental Regulation

Activity	Purpose	Examples
A. _Standard setting_		
1. Broad standards	To set goals and limits for regulators.	"Swimmable" rivers, "safe" drinking water.
2. Narrow standards	To set goals and limits for polluters.	Auto emissions of carbon monoxide not to exceed 3.4 grams per mile.
B. _Enforcement for compliance_		
1. Certification or permit	To approve firms' intentions and give guidance.	Engine design "W" approved; construction permit granted.
2. Sample testing	To monitor regulated firms' activities.	Smokestack emissions measured.
3. Field surveillance (optional)	To double-check compliance and catch "mistakes."	Semiannual inspection of autos in use.
4. Remedies	To bring violators into line.	Force recall of autos; fine violators.

water. Sometimes they are a bit more specific. In any event, polluters cannot be prosecuted for violating these broad standards because they are too broad. The standards that actually apply to specific polluters and trigger charges of violation are the _narrow standards_. These are typically specific emission standards rather than sweeping objectives for ambient conditions. When firms go bad, they violate these emission standards.

Regulatory **enforcement,** the second major division of Table 35.1, entails several steps to attain and maintain compliance. Such enforcement is necessary, just as traffic police must enforce speed limits. _Certification or permits_ is an early step in such enforcement. This gives prior approval to a firm's plans. Without certification, for example, an auto company might build a plant that produces auto engines that are eventually banned from the market. The losses could run into tens of millions of dollars. With official certification of prototype engines prior to their actual production, this problem can be avoided. _Sample testing_ monitors the compliance of products as they come off the assembly line or assesses the compliance of plant operations while the plant is active. Smokestack emission sampling is one example. _Field surveillance_ serves as a final backup. Autos can be tampered with after sale or their abatement equipment can break down too quickly. Hence, in many areas with serious air pollution, autos are regularly checked for their on-the-road compliance. Field surveillance may also detect special problems, like spills of oil or toxic substances. Finally, _remedies_ round out enforcement efforts. These provide inducements, for they may include harsh penalties, and even jail in some circumstances. More generally, they take the form of product recalls, temporary plant closures, modest fines, and other such actions as may bring violators into line.

Read Perspective 35A.

C

Evaluation

1. Physical Achievements The EPA was established in 1970, and most of the major statutes for present regulatory policy were enacted in the early 1970s. Enough time has therefore passed to allow an evaluation of regulation. And, overall, it seems to have been a qualified success. The suc-

cess is especially apparent in statistics on physical trends in pollution.

Table 35.2 illustrates the situation for the major air pollutants. Before 1970, the tonnage of nationwide emissions was rising for every major pollutant except particulates, and particulates were closer to holding steady than they were to being in sharp decline. After 1970 and the advent of present policies, the annual emissions of all major air pollutants except nitrogen oxide fell. For example, annual emissions of particulates dropped from 18.0 million tons in 1970 to 6.9 million tons in 1983, a decrease of 62 percent. Over the same period, sulfur oxide emissions fell 26 percent, hydrocarbons 26 percent, and carbon monoxide 31 percent. Partial success could even be claimed for nitrogen oxide emissions, which have remained basically unchanged since 1970. It is fairly clear that environmental policy substantially curbed their rate of increase even though policy cannot be credited with achieving a great reduction. Similar reversals of upward trends or reductions have occurred for water pollutants. After extensive study of physical trends for both air and water pollution, the General Accounting Office concluded:

> Overall there has been progress toward meeting established goals. The air is significantly cleaner, more waste water now receives the required level of treatment and most drinking water meets national standards. The job, however, is far from complete.[1]

The story concerning toxic substances is less rosy because their dangers are in many instances on the rise. The use of herbicides is nearly double what it was in 1970. Disposal or containment of nuclear wastes is still a problem. The entire town of Times Beach, Missouri, had to be abandoned in the early 1980s because of PCB contamination. And so on. Still, even in this bleak area of toxics there is much good news to report. Residues of several toxic chemicals found in human tissue— like DDT, dieldrin, and beta-benzene hexachloride—are down since 1970. Toxic residues in fish and fowl are also down. And usage of hazardous pesticides has fallen since 1970.

[1]U.S. General Accounting Office, _Cleaning Up the Environment: Progress Achieved but Major Unresolved Questions Remain,_ Vol. 1 (Washington, D.C.: 1982), p. 5.

PERSPECTIVE 35A
Air Pollution Regulation

Each item in the foregoing outline of regulation may be illustrated in a summary of air pollution regulations.

Broad standards: The broad standards set for air pollution mainly take the form of *primary* ambient air quality standards (where *ambient* indicates the air outside rather than the air in workplaces or homes). These broad standards were set by the EPA in order to protect human health, and they are stated as thresholds. For example, the level of particulates is not supposed to exceed 75 micrograms per cubic meter of air as an annual average. The level of sulfur oxides is not supposed to exceed 365 micrograms per cubic meter of air in any 24-hour period.

Narrow standards: Specification of the emission limits applying to particular polluters (in the hope of achieving the broad standards) is the task of narrow standards. These vary depending on whether the source of pollution is stationary (e.g., factories) or mobile (e.g., trucks). Among *stationary sources* there is further variation depending on the area and on whether a new source or an old source is involved. In general, the typical narrow standard calls for a certain percentage of abatement from all sources of a given class, guided mainly by technological possibilities and ambient air conditions. For example, in areas of New York, New Jersey, and Connecticut that do not meet the broad ambient ozone standard, controls call for 40 to 50 percent reductions in the amounts of hydrocarbons emitted by 15 categories of stationary sources. Among *mobile sources*, cars are the most important, and since 1981 their emission limits have been the following number of grams per mile: carbon monoxide, 3.40; hydrocarbons, 0.41; and nitrogen oxide, 1.00.

Certification and permits: Certification applies importantly to autos. The companies have prototype vehicles checked and certified by the EPA prior to manufacturing and marketing. Stationary sources need permits. Before a new petroleum refinery can be built, for example, its owners must obtain a pollution permit that sets emission limits and grants operating clearance.

Sample testing: Samples of autos are tested as they come off the assembly line. For stationary sources, there are stack tests, source inspections, and opacity readings, with the largest plants receiving most of the monitoring.

Field surveillance: Cars are supposed to meet standards for their first 50,000 miles. To ensure such continued compliance and to prevent owners from tampering with pollution control equipment, nearly 30 states conduct tests of operating vehicles in areas with serious pollution, such as Los Angeles and Denver.

TABLE 35.2 National Air Pollution Emission Estimates by Pollutant, 1940–83 (Millions of Metric Tons per Year)

Year	Particulates	Sulfur Oxides	Nitrogen Oxides	Hydro-carbons	Carbon Monoxide
1940	22.4	18.0	6.7	17.7	79.4
1950	24.2	20.3	9.3	20.3	84.8
1960	20.9	20.0	12.8	23.3	87.5
1970	18.0	28.2	18.1	27.0	98.3
1980	8.3	23.2	20.3	22.3	75.0
1983	6.9	20.8	19.4	19.9	67.6

Source: Environmental Quality 1984 (Washington, D.C.: Council on Environmental Quality), pp. 584–585.

2. The Benefit-Cost Ideal

2. The Benefit-Cost Ideal We used the phrase *qualified success* in the previous section for two main reasons. First, as indicated in these physical trends, the wayward ways of some substances continue unabated, and there is still much to be done about those displaying a favorable trend. Second, when evaluated by *economic* criteria instead of purely *physical* criteria, the record of regulatory policy is far from sparkling. In particular, statistics of physical achievements such as those in Table 35.2 reveal nothing about the economic benefits and costs of environmental policy. And many economists criticize present policy for violating benefit-cost standards even though it might be credited with achieving considerable success by physical criteria.

If benefit-cost analysis served as a guide for environmental policy, it would further the objective of economic efficiency (good answers to the What? and How? questions). One of the chief conclusions to emerge from such benefit-cost analysis is that, *for most pollutants, complete abatement would not be desirable.* Weighing the benefits and costs of abatement, as illustrated by the hypothetical data in Figure 35.2, explains why. Moving from left to right on the horizontal axis indicates greater levels of abatement, starting with zero abatement and ending with removal of all 20 million tons of SO_2 from the atmosphere. The marginal costs of abatement rise with ever-higher abatement, those costs reflecting expenses for equipment, employees to maintain and operate the equipment, and so on. At the same time, abatement brings benefits in the form of *reduced costs of pollution* (reduced property damage, less human illness, and so on). As abatement proceeds, however, these benefits *at the margin* dwindle, as indicated by the downward-sloping marginal benefit curve in Figure 35.2. Note, for instance, that elimination of the last 2 million tons of SO_2, moving from 18 to 20 million tons, is assumed to yield no benefits whatever. (Stated differently, movement in the opposite direction, from right to left, indicates greater pollution, with the marginal cost of pollution, the straight line, rising after the first 2 million tons of SO_2, which do no damage.) In moving from zero abatement at the origin to the right, two-question logic says that abatement should stop after eliminating 12 million tons of SO_2. At that point, the marginal benefits equal the marginal costs. Added

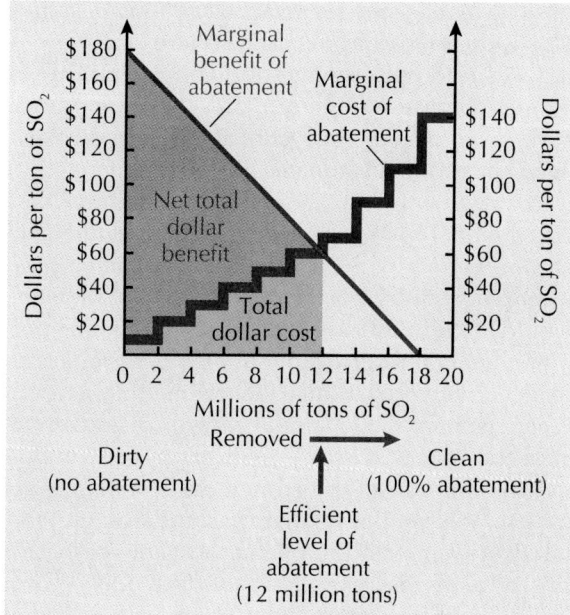

FIGURE 35.2 Benefit-Cost Analysis of Abatement

Moving from left to right, the marginal cost of abatement rises and the marginal benefit of abatement falls. They are equal at 12 million tons of abatement, which is the efficient level, the one that maximizes the net total benefit. Total benefit at this point is the entire area under the MB curve ($1,440 million). The difference is the net benefit ($1,020 million).

benefits of further abatement, as indicated by the marginal benefit curve, would fall below the marginal costs of abatement. Indeed, at the extreme, abatement of the last 2 million tons of SO_2 would cost a total of $280 million (2 million tons times a cost of $140 per ton) and would yield *no* benefits to society at all. With 12 million tons of abatement, society's net benefit will be maximized. The difference of total dollar benefits less total dollar costs will be as large as possible, as suggested by the triangular shaded area of Figure 35.2.

So much for *theory.* In *practice,* the marginal benefits and marginal costs associated with environmental regulations cannot be accurately estimated. In some cases it is possible to estimate, albeit rather crudely, the *total* benefits and *total* costs, even when the *marginal* values defy calculation. In these cases it appears that environmental regulations sometimes yield total benefits that exceed total costs, while in other instances the reverse seems to hold. An example of the former positive result is the removal of lead from gasoline. This reduces lead in the atmosphere and thereby reduces lead poisoning in humans (which causes mental damage in children and high blood pressure in adults, thereby contributing to strokes). According to EPA estimates, the overall benefits of lead abatement were about $7,474 million in 1987 and the total costs were only $558 million, for a _net_ annual benefit of $6,916 million.[2] Conversely, an example of total costs exceeding total benefits would be the effort to abate other automobile pollution generally (nitrogen monoxide, carbon monoxide, and hydrocarbons). According to one set of recent estimates, the annual benefits of auto emission control could not possibly exceed $8.3 billion in 1984 dollars. Yet the annual costs of equipping cars to achieve the regulatory standards are certainly greater than $10 billion. A major reason for this adverse discrepancy is the fact that control costs apply to _all_ cars _everywhere_ in the United States, while control benefits are obtained mainly in a limited number of areas where auto pollution is especially troublesome—such as Los Angeles, Denver, Pittsburgh, and New York City.[3]

One of the main problems in actually applying benefit-cost analysis is the difficulty of predicting the favorable _physical effects_ that may follow abatement efforts. For example, some years ago, when a ban on saccharin was being debated, one expert estimated that its removal would save 1,200 lives per million persons exposed; another said 450 lives per million; and yet another (sponsored by an industry group) predicted a saving of only 1 life per _billion_ persons exposed. A serious problem also arises when the benefit-cost analyst tries to place a _dollar value_ on the human lives saved by abatement. At present, the favored method for estimating the value of human lives relies on data from the labor market. Risky jobs pay higher wages (_ceteris paribus_), because there is a _compensating wage premium_ for the risk. However, estimates of this risk premium vary depending on the data, the model specification, and other technical details. The resulting values of human life vary widely,

from less than $1 million to over $5 million. This range does not inspire confidence that accuracy can be achieved.

These problems, together with others, contribute to great uncertainty. For example, one expert found that the annual benefits of controlling air pollution from stationary sources ranged from $1.8 billion to $14.4 billion (in 1978 dollars).[4] Still, benefit-cost analysis is often helpful even if uncertain.

3. _Cost Effectiveness_ Although it is difficult to conduct a complete benefit-cost analysis of any environmental policy, it is often possible to tell whether a policy is **cost effective.** When assessing cost effectiveness, economists take whatever benefits that may be obtained as _given_, or _fixed_, without trying to express them in dollar values. For example, in this approach the dollar benefits of cutting SO_2 emissions by, say, 13.5 million tons need not be calculated. With **cost effectiveness,** the objective is _to achieve the stated target of physical abatement (and its associated benefits) in the most efficient, lowest-cost way._ It is like trying to minimize the costs, including the opportunity costs, of traveling from Seattle to Atlanta without asking what benefits may be gained from the trip.

The easiest way to understand cost effectiveness is by what may be called the _array_ approach. Table 35.3 and Figure 35.3 illustrate this, using simple hypothetical data. Assume that "muck" can be abated from four possible sources in your state—sources _A_, _B_, _C_, and _D_, as indicated in column (1) of Table 35.3. Assume further that the marginal cost of abatement is constant over all units of abatement from each source individually, as indicated by the average (and marginal) cost of abatement in column (4), which is the total cost in column (3) divided by the total number of units of abatement in column (2) of Table 35.3. (See also the flat steps of cost per pound in Figure 35.3.) If the target level of abatement happens to be 11 million pounds of muck, then the cost-effective solution would be found by, first, ordering the sources from lowest cost per pound of muck removed to highest—that is, _B_, _D_, _C_, and _A_, as shown by the numbers of column (4) and the steps of Figure 35.3—and, second,

[2]U.S. Council on Environmental Quality, _Environmental Quality 1984_ (Washington, D.C.: 1986), p. 235.

[3]Robert W. Crandall, Howard K. Gruenspecht, Theodore E. Keeler, and Lester B. Lave, _Regulating the Automobile_ (Washington, D.C.: Brookings Institution, 1986), pp. 85–116.

[4]_Environmental Quality 1979_ (Washington, D.C.: U.S. Council on Environmental Quality, 1979), p. 654.

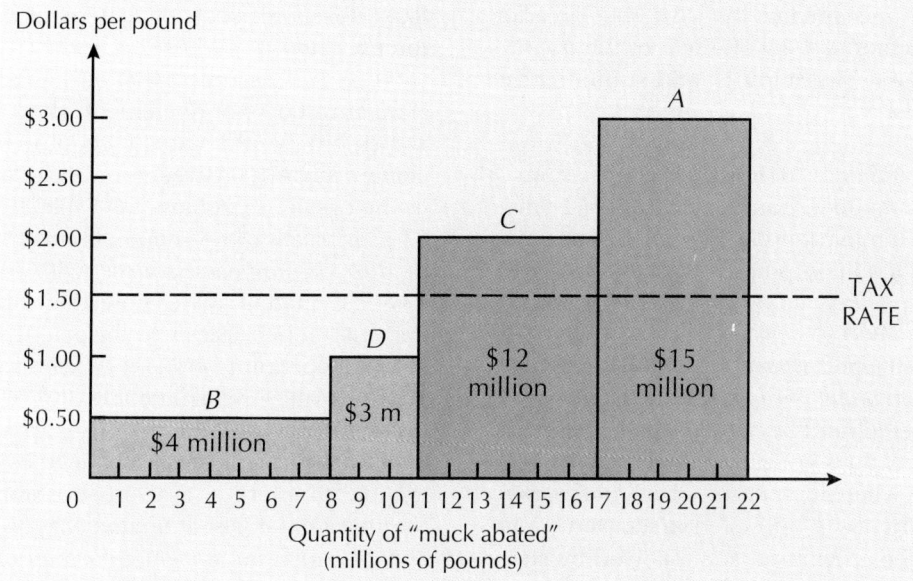

FIGURE 35.3 *Cost-Effective Abatement of "Muck"*

To achieve a target of 11 million pounds of abatement in a cost-effective way would require, according to these data, full abatement from sources B and D . They have the lowest cost per unit and the second lowest cost, as indicated in column (4) of Table 35.3. No fraction of abatement from another source is needed.

TABLE 35.3 Cost-Effective Abatement of "Muck"

(1) Source	(2) Pounds of Possible Abatement (Millions)	(3) Total Cost of Full Abatement by Source (Millions of Dollars)	(4) = (3)/(2) Cost per Pound of Abatement (Dollars)
A	5	$15	$3.00
B	8	4	0.50
C	6	12	2.00
D	3	3	1.00
Totals	22	$34	

proceeding to implement abatement until the target of 11 million pounds is reached. Full abatement from sources *B* and *D* together is enough in this case, and no fraction of abatement from higher-cost sources *C* and *A* is required. The *total* cost of achieving the 11 million pounds of abatement by this approach is $7 million, which is a combination of $4 million in cost for source *B* ($0.50 per pound × 8 million pounds) and $3 million for source *D* ($1.00 per pound × 3 million pounds).

No other combination can hit the target abatement for less cost. Assume, for instance, that instead each source is required to abate by 50 percent (the uniform percentage approach common to regulation, although 50 percent is not always the number used in regulation). The target of 11 million pounds would then be reached because the total muck coming from these four sources is 22 million pounds, one half of which is 11 million pounds. The total dollar cost of this 50 percent approach would be $17 million, which is *more than double* the cost-effective amount. This can be calculated by multiplying the cost per unit for each source (column 4) by one half of the quantities of abatement (in column 2) and summing the results. That is:

Source *A:* 2.5 million pounds × $3.00 = $7.5m
Source *B:* 4.0 million pounds × $0.50 = $2.0m
Source *C:* 3.0 million pounds × $2.00 = $6.0m
Source *D:* 1.5 million pounds × $1.00 = $1.5m
Total $17.0m

It may be concluded that a regulatory approach that calls for an equal percentage cutback from all sources will usually not *be cost effective.* Stated differently, society does not eliminate the most muck for the buck when it requires equal percentage abatement. The array approach discussed previously is like the array approach followed by baseball managers. When they set their team's batting order, baseball managers always place the best hitters early in the lineup and the worst hitters late. A team has 27 outs per game (3 × 9 innings), and this approach will maximize the hitting power of the team, given those 27 outs.

One of the greatest advantages of a tax policy or marketable permit policy, in comparison to a regulatory policy, is that either of these two alternatives tends to be cost effective, whereas regulation does not. The cost effectiveness of the tax approach is illustrated by introducing a tax rate of $1.50 per pound of muck into the analysis of Figure 35.3. If those who pollute must pay $1.50 for each pound of muck emitted, then it would be wise for sources *B* and *D* to abate fully. The cost of abatement for *B* is $0.50 per pound, which is much less than the tax of $1.50 per pound without abatement. Source *B* will therefore minimize cost by abating. Source *D* compares an abatement cost of $1.00 per pound to the tax of $1.50 and reaches the same conclusion. For source *C*, however, it is cheaper to pollute and pay $1.50 per pound than it is to abate and pay expenses of $2.00 a pound. The cost of the total tax bill is $9 million ($1.50 × 6 million pounds), which is much less than the $12 million total cost of abatement. Source *A* would likewise pollute and pay the tax, comparing the tax rate of $1.50 per pound with its unit cost of abatement, $3.00 per pound. In sum, an emission tax tends to be cost effective because it *automatically* focuses the abatement effort on low-cost abaters

first, those with costs of abatement that fall below the tax rate.

When it is assumed that each source has constant unit costs of abatement, then cost-effective abatement would usually require that low-cost abaters abate 100 percent and others not at all (as in the previous problem for Table 35.3 and Figure 35.3). In reality, the marginal costs of abatement *tend to rise for each source*, with the result that low-cost abaters abate more than high-cost abaters, but not necessarily to the extent of an extreme split, 100 percent versus 0 percent.

In this more realistic context of rising marginal costs for each source, the array approach to cost effectiveness leads to varying degrees of abatement among polluters of a given substance, such that *the marginal costs of abatement for one polluter should equal the marginal costs of abatement for every other polluter.* That is, the marginal costs of abatement should be the same for all abaters (of that specific pollutant in the area). If these marginal costs are not equal, then lower *total* costs for society could be achieved by *expanding abatement* where marginal costs are relatively *low* and *curtailing abatement* where marginal costs are relatively *high.* This will lower the total costs of abatement until the expanding abatement of low-cost abaters raises their marginal costs to meet the falling marginal costs of the high-cost abaters. A tax or emission fee policy tends to be cost effective because polluters will abate to the point where their marginal costs equal the tax rate. And if the tax rate is the same for all polluters, then their marginal costs of abatement will, in the end, also be the same. Marketable permits tend to be cost effective for a related reason.

It must be stressed that the *amount of abatement* attained under emission taxes or marketable permits could be *exactly the same* as under the present regulatory approach. The cost savings we have identified for these alternatives do not occur because of less physical abatement. They occur because the *same* physical abatement is achieved at less total cost.

Read Perspective 35B.

Partly because emission taxes and marketable permits tend to be cost effective, there is greater reliance on them now than there was 15 years ago. Several states now impose mandatory deposits on beverage containers, following the lead of Oregon,

PERSPECTIVE 35B
SO₂ and Cost Effectiveness

The impact of regulation on the costs of SO_2 abatement at coal-fired electric power plants illustrates the foregoing points. As of 1979, regulated abatement of SO_2 from power plants in the northeastern United States resulted in widely varying marginal costs of abatement. The lowest marginal cost of abatement was $3 per ton of SO_2, while the highest was $3,623 per ton. Imagine expanding abatement by 1 ton at a cost of $3 while contracting abatement by 1 ton at a savings of $3,623. The difference, $3,620 ($3,623 − $3), signals the extent of the regulatory inefficiency and the huge potential gains from a cost-effective result. Indeed, by one esti-

mate, a shift to cost-effective SO_2 abatement in the Northeast would yield cost savings of 49.7 percent, or $932.9 million dollars, in comparison to the costs of regulation in 1979. Related savings for other regions were as follows: Great Lakes, $473.0 million; Midwest, $3.8 million; South, $380.8 million; and West, $161.5 million. The overall total savings for the United States were estimated to be $1,952 million. These savings could occur with *no change* in the amount of abatement.[5]

[5] F. M. Gollop and M. J. Roberts, "Cost Minimizing Regulation of Sulfur Emissions," *Review of Economics and Statistics* (February 1985), pp. 81–90.

---

which passed a *bottle bill* in the early 1970s. This is, in effect, a tax approach. If you pollute by tossing out your bottles, you lose the deposit. If you don't pollute, you don't pay. As regards marketable permits, an *offset* program has emerged among stationary sources of air pollution in areas that have not attained the broad standards set by regulation. New factories can be built in these areas if their added pollution is offset by reduced pollution from old established sources, and the reductions can be purchased by those building new factories from those owning old factories. The purchased reductions therefore become, in effect, purchased permits. Large efficiencies have been found for both beverage container deposits and offsets, running into hundreds of millions of dollars annually.

Although cost effectiveness is perhaps the most attractive feature of emission taxes and marketable permits, economists favor them for other reasons as well. It is argued, for instance, that compared to direct regulation, these alternative approaches (1) require less technical knowledge among government bureaucrats for implementation, (2) require less meddling in the internal affairs of business enterprises, and (3) encourage greater innovation

and invention for the discovery of improved abatement technologies.

■ *CHECK YOUR BEARINGS*

To summarize, this evaluation of past environmental protection policies has stressed the apparent advantages of emission taxes or marketable permits in comparison to the current policy mainstay—direct regulation. Perhaps the greatest advantage would be improved efficiency through cost effectiveness. Still, direct regulation has had its considerable, if qualified, successes. In the end, it may be that the true policy ideal would be some *mix* of the several possible policies. Regulation, for instance, might work best for very hazardous toxic substances that require nearly 100 percent control. Criminal penalties may be needed in these instances, and 100 percent control erases issues of who abates how much to achieve cost effectiveness. Taxes might work best for degradable water pollutants like simple organic wastes. And so on. Indeed, in this mixed scheme even moral suasion and subsidies cannot be ruled out. They, too, might have a place.

II

Energy

A

The Problems

Perhaps more midnight oil has been burned over the last two decades than Middle Eastern oil. So much has been written about energy, so many debates have centered on energy, and so many government officials, business people, and academics have fretted over energy in recent times that late-night hours of work on the issue seem to have become the norm. Congress, for example, spent more time in the 1970s wrangling over the deregulation of natural gas than it has spent on any other issue in recent history except perhaps tax reform. Indeed, energy problems have even found their way into the plots of major motion pictures, such as *Road Warrior*. Here we shall focus on three main energy problems that we can identify by self-descriptive labels—(1) environmental pollution, (2) dangerous dependency, and (3) supply shrinkage.

1. Environmental Pollution   As suggested earlier, environmental and energy problems overlap. Pollution is a major by-product of energy production and consumption. A U.S. senator put it this way: "Airborne pollutants, concentration of nuclear wastes, oil spills, thermal pollution from power plants, extensive modifications of the landscape by the increased construction of transmission lines, refineries, pumped storage facilities, and marine transmission facilities are illustrative causes of environmental problems related to energy production and use."[6]

Details concerning air pollution underscore the difficulties. Energy combustion in transportation, industry, electric power generation, and other areas account for the vast bulk of all air pollution. By individual pollutant, the numbers are staggering: 98.7 percent of all sulfur oxides are due to energy combustion; 88.8 percent of all nitrogen oxides; 76.0 percent of all carbon monoxide; 64.4 percent of all hydrocarbons; and 57.9 percent of all particulates.

On the ground, strip mining illustrates the problem. By the late 1970s, approximately 65 percent of U.S. coal production came from surface mining, up from 19 percent immediately after World War II. Moreover, roughly 90 percent of all western coal is strip-mined, and most of our coal reserves lie in the West. In the future, coal could very likely become the single most important U.S. energy resource to replace our dwindling oil supplies because the United States is to coal what Saudi Arabia is to oil. Yet:

> The strip mining of coal requires an unusually large amount of inputs from the environment. The most obvious impact of surface mining is the complete removal of the stripped land from non-mining uses. The unsightliness of stripped land degrades surrounding property values, as well as scenic and recreational qualities. Strip mining can also cause extensive damage to hydrologic systems through sedimentation and silting of rivers and streams and/or through the drainage of acidic waste from mine operations.[7]

2. Dangerous Dependency   In 1970, U.S. domestic production of oil reached a peak and began to decline. Domestic demand did not fall with domestic production. As a result, oil imports more than doubled as a percentage of U.S. consumption, quickly climbing from close to 20 percent in 1970 to well over 40 percent in 1977. Nearly three quarters of those imports came from members of the Organization of Petroleum Exporting Countries (OPEC), so during the late 1970s OPEC accounted for roughly 30 percent of all the oil consumed in the United States. Since then, U.S. oil imports have fallen as a percentage of total domestic consumption, but they still run in the 30 percent range. Likewise, our dependence on OPEC oil has diminished, but in the mid-1980s OPEC still accounted for about 13 percent of total U.S. consumption.

Our growing dependence on outside suppliers in recent decades means increased vulnerability. Oil is absolutely crucial to our modern economy. Its importance to transportation, manufacturing, agriculture, and other key sectors of the economy

---

[6.] Richard B. Mancke, *The Failure of U. S. Energy Policy* (New York: Columbia University Press, 1974), p. 43.

[7.] Joseph P. Kalt, "The Costs and Benefits of Federal Regulation of Coal Strip Mining," *Natural Resources Journal* (October 1983), p. 894.

cannot be exaggerated. So dependence on others for our supplies, dependence especially on Middle Eastern countries, raises very serious risks of supply disruptions and price escalations:

> For the industrial nations to continue to depend on Middle Eastern oil in the way current trends indicate means heavy reliance on a region of high political tension and risk. In the last three decades, the Middle East has been subjected to a dozen wars, a dozen revolutions, and innumerable assassinations and territorial disputes. Dependence reinforces the twin vulnerabilities—interruption of supplies and major price increases.[8]

The problem first became apparent in late 1973 and early 1974. Prompted by an outbreak of war between Israel and several Arab nations, the Arab members of OPEC ceased supplying the United States by imposing an oil embargo. Oil shortages ensued, and the price of OPEC oil thereafter quadrupled from $3 to $12 a barrel. A second major shock occurred during 1979–80 after the fall of the Shah of Iran. Again, supplies were disrupted and prices soared, rising from $20 a barrel to over $35 a barrel in a matter of months. During the mid-1980s our fortunes were reversed by a glut of foreign oil, much of it coming from non-OPEC sources like Mexico, Britain, and Norway. But the problem of foreign dependency continues, and given the drop in domestic supply, it is not likely to go away anytime soon.

3. Supply Shrinkage   A third major energy problem, one related to the dependency problem, is the shrinkage in fuel supply over time. This applies not just to oil but to all fossil fuels generally, including natural gas and coal. Moreover, our reference to "time" here is meant to signal a special concern for future generations as well as present ones. Fossil fuels are nonrenewable resources; once they are burned up, they are gone forever.

Just how long these nonrenewable energy resources will last is uncertain. Their duration depends on such variables as the rate of consumption, the rate of discovery, and the costs of extraction. Of our fossil fuels, oil is certainly the most precariously placed at the moment. By some esti-

mates the United States is likely to run out of oil completely, or very nearly so, sometime around the year 2010, give or take 5 years. The signals of this depletion are already present. Annual production is declining despite record-high levels of drilling activity in recent times. Our output per well and output per mile of drilling effort have slid appreciably and are likely to continue downward because, after more than a century and hundreds of thousands of wells drilled, the U.S. oil mining industry is, in essence, dying. Abroad, the numbers are not as bleak. Still, some projections of worldwide supply availabily do not go much beyond the year 2060.

This problem can be judged by two criteria—efficiency and equity. Assuming there will be no magical changes in technology, _efficiency_ requires that, compared to present generations, future generations will get _a smaller quantity_ of these nonrenewables and will pay _higher prices_ for them. This is true even with eventual reliance on such renewable substitutes as solar power. Note, however, that, as a matter of _equity_, less quantity and higher prices may mean that future generations are being unfairly treated despite the achievement of efficiency. The problem is thus a sticky one.[9]

B
Energy Policies

1. Objectives   Problem identification helps to guide policy prescription. These energy problems— (1) environmental pollution, (2) dangerous dependency, and (3) supply shrinkage—would be eased if policies could further three main objectives, namely, _reduced demand, expanded supply, and greater substitution of renewable alternatives for fossil fuels._

Curbing the demand for energy, especially for combustible fossil fuels, would tend to alleviate all three problems. With fewer barrels of oil and fewer tons of coal going up in flames, there would be fewer exhaust emissions damaging the atmosphere, fewer ships carrying vulnerable imports from the Middle East, and fewer concerns that we are depriving future generations of what is right-

---

[8]Robert Stobaugh and Daniel Yergin, _Energy Future_ (New York: Vintage Books, 1983), p. 5.

[9]See, for example, Tom Tietenberg, _Environmental and Natural Resource Economics_ (Glenview, Ill.: Scott, Foresman, 1984), pp. 110–130, 416–434.

fully theirs in terms of resource endowments.

Encouraging the expansion of supplies would help to reduce the problem of dangerous dependency. This is particularly true of *domestic* supplies, because expansion of these supplies would, for obvious reasons, permit us to cut our reliance on precarious foreign supplies. Expansion of foreign supplies would also help because this usually entails increased output from fairly safe sources (like Britain and Norway) as well as risky sources. Safe foreign sources may not reduce our dependency, but they certainly help to reduce the danger that comes with relying on risky sources. Unfortunately, expanded supplies may worsen the problem of environmental pollution. Also, to the extent that expanded supplies shift resource availabilities away from future generations toward present generations, they also worsen the problem of supply shrinkage.

Greater substitution of renewable resource alternatives for fossil fuels would address all three problems. Here the most important factor is technological change, and the most promising prospects concern various forms of solar power. With photovoltaics, for instance, silicon cells convert the sun's daily radiation directly into electricity. And with greater reliance on the sun, our problems of pollution, dependency, and shrinkage are likely to be at least partially solved.

2. Past Policies and the Objectives A thorough review of past energy policies would fill a book—indeed, several books. We lack the space (and energy) for such a review, but a selective survey, organized around the policy objectives just discussed, is certainly in order.

Contraction of Demand: One of the major justifications for the 55-mile-per-hour speed limit when it was first introduced was the fuel savings that reduced speed would achieve. This and numerous other policies have been tried as a means of curbing energy demand. Here are some further examples: (1) From July 1979 to April 1980, federal regulations specified that, during the winter, temperatures in most commercial and industrial buildings could not be heated to more than 65°F and, during the summer, could not be cooled to less than 78°F. (2) Energy efficiency ratings for major appliances are now disclosed to consumers on information tags in the hope that consumers

will buy energy misers. (3) In 1975, Congress imposed corporate average fuel economy standards on auto manufacturers. Under these regulations, each auto producer was required to achieve an average gasoline mileage rating of 18 miles per gallon for all of its autos by the 1978 model year and 27.5 miles per gallon by the 1985 model year.

Expansion of Supply: Domestic supplies of oil were encouraged during the 1950s and 1960s by quotas that limited imports. Favorable tax breaks, such as depletion allowances, also boosted domestic supplies for many decades in the past. Recent policy efforts that fit this category include the Reagan administration's efforts to hasten the offshore drilling of oil and the onshore mining of coal.

Substitution Away from Fossil Fuels: During the 1970s and early 1980s, the federal government promoted the development of solar power by granting very favorable tax advantages to people who used solar energy. Solar equipment was, in effect, subsidized. Of much greater duration and monetary importance is the federal government's support of nuclear power. From below-cost charges for nuclear fuel enrichment to massive research projects and legal limits on the liability of plant owners in the event of damaging accidents, the government has nurtured the nuclear industry with huge subsidies. From 1955 to 1984, those subsidies amounted to roughly $30 billion.

C

Evaluation

Criticism of energy policies has not been in short supply. Indeed, it sometimes seems that for every bureaucrat in the Department of Energy there is at least one economist who believes that we would all be better off if Washington, D.C., were strip-mined into oblivion.

The basic complaint of most critics is that the free market should be expected to solve or alleviate the three major problems outlined earlier—environmental pollution, dangerous dependency, and supply shrinkage. The market would do so principally by curtailing demand and expanding supply, as was needed over recent decades and may be needed in the future, using the incentive of *higher price levels* to achieve both results.

Take the demand side, for example, particularly the policy of minimum gas mileage standards for automobiles mentioned earlier. Between 1973 and 1984, the average gas mileage of autos sold in the United States did increase substantially, from 14.1 to 26.6 miles per gallon. However, it is doubtful that the government's fuel efficiency standards can be given much credit for this achievement. Higher fuel prices seem to have played a major role. The real price of gasoline rose 34 percent over the same period, and careful analysis of the relationship between price and miles-per-gallon performance indicates that the "automobile producers' increase in fuel economy is about what one should have expected given the rise in gasoline prices since 1973."[10]

An example from the supply side is revealed in Figure 35.4. The basic relationship between market price and supply is positive, especially in extractive industries like petroleum and coal mining. Higher prices mean higher output, without any

aid from government subsidies. Figure 35.4 shows the trend in the price of crude oil in the United States from 1970 to 1986 together with a key measure of supply activity—the number of wells drilled in the United States for oil exploration or production (and also for natural gas, as the two often go together). Drilling activity clearly climbs and falls as the price of oil goes up and down. A critic of supply-side policies might very well ask why government promotion should be necessary when the free market works as well as is suggested by Figure 35.4.

Indeed, critics of government policy can go further. Not only can the free market perform quite well in energy, even beautifully; in the eyes of many economists, government is seen as the *problem*, not the solution. Why have shortages occurred? Why have there been lines at gas stations? Why have domestic supplies of natural gas fallen short of apparently excessive demands? Why have oil imports been running uncomfortably high in recent decades?

Critics contend that, for both petroleum and

[10]Crandall, et al., *Regulating the Automobile*, p. 139.

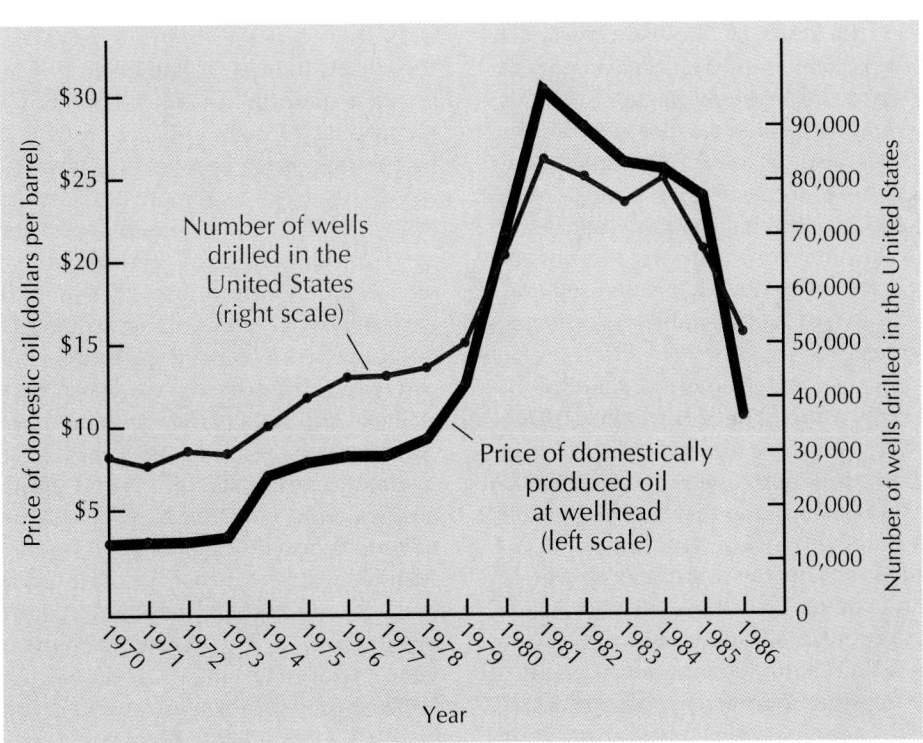

FIGURE 35.4 *The Price of Oil and Drilling Activity in the United States, 1970–86*
(*Sources:* Monthly Energy Review, *various issues.*)

natural gas, the main cause of these problems during the 1970s was governmentally imposed price ceilings. Price ceilings on natural gas (in the field or at the well head) began in the late 1950s when the Federal Power Commission (now the Federal Energy Regulatory Commission) was given the power to impose them in a Supreme Court case interpreting the Natural Gas Act of 1938. During the 1960s, the average wellhead price of natural gas was allowed to rise slightly from 14.0 to 16.7 cents per 1,000 cubic feet. During the 1970s, the average regulated price jumped sharply from 17.1 to 114.4 cents per 1,000 cubic feet. Still, the price level did not rise quickly enough or high enough to avert shortages. Official rationing of the scarce supplies during several periods in the 1970s was the result.

Price control in oil started when President Nixon imposed a temporary price freeze on all commodities in August 1971. It graduated to flexible formal control in the general wage–price regulations that followed, and then finally persisted after controls on other commodities ended in 1974. Why the continued price controls on oil? In the winter of 1973–74 the price of OPEC oil skyrocketed, pulling up the price of domestic oil in its wake and raising problems of inflation and equity. In equity, for instance, a freely rising price for domestic oil would have caused a massive transfer of income from domestic oil consumers to domestic oil producers—a transfer that would have ranged from $10 to $20 billion per year. Still, regardless of the initial justifications, the consequences in reduced supply relative to demand were the same as in natural gas, namely, shortages of various degrees.

The price controls for both natural gas and oil evolved into very complicated, multilevel price programs. In 1977, for example, "old" oil was priced at $5.19 a barrel, "new" oil went for $11.22 a barrel, and third-tier oil made up of stripper well output and imports was free of controls at $13.59. Although these price controls were very complex, their basic implications for supply, demand, and the interaction of supply and demand can be seen in Figure 35.5, which simplifies the story greatly. Demand and supply are shown in conventional forms. With perfect competition and an absence of government regulation, demand and supply would be in equilibrium at point *E*, with price level

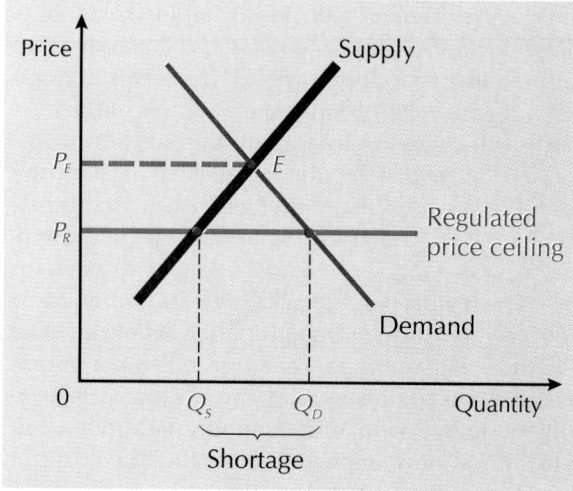

FIGURE 35.5 *Price Ceilings and Shortages*

Under free market conditions, demand and supply would be in equilibrium at point E *and price* P_E *would result. A price ceiling below* P_E *at* P_R *would reduce the supply to* Q_S *and boost the demand to* Q_D. *Because demand then exceeds supply, a shortage develops.*

P_E prevailing. A government-imposed price ceiling beneath equilibrium price P_E, such as the one indicated by price P_R in Figure 35.5, would curb the supply to level Q_S and boost the demand to Q_D. Because quantity demanded then exceeds quantity supplied, a hefty shortage results, as indicated by the difference between Q_D and Q_S.

This shortage was more evident for natural gas than it was for crude oil because there were no price controls on imported oil, only on domestic oil. With freedom to import oil, oil imports could for the most part fill domestic demand (the exceptions occurring during embargoes). There was a catch here, however. With controls creating an artificial shortage of *domestic* oil that was alleviated by greater reliance on *imported* oil, the price control program for oil caused another problem besides shortages. It caused the United States to rely *more heavily on foreign oil* than it would have without price controls. Imports, in other words, tended to fill the gap pictured in Figure 35.5, thereby aggravating the problem of dangerous dependency on foreign oil.

The problems of shortage and import dependency associated with legal price ceilings are now a matter of past history because phased price decontrol has occurred for both oil and gas, beginning during Carter's presidency. Many other policies remain in place, however, and some of them rate as poorly among critics as price controls. On the other hand, there are some policies that enjoy rather wide and enthusiastic support. Let's close this evaluation, then, with a brief look at two such policies—(1) the gas guzzler tax and (2) the strategic petroleum reserve.

If improved fuel efficiency for autos was deemed to be a desirable national objective (to check demand and reduce dependency), what would be a better way to achieve that aim than direct regulation of the auto companies, with fines for failure to meet miles-per-gallon standards? Many economists support a *gas guzzler tax*. And such a tax is now in place. For the 1986 model year, cars with gas mileage of 22.5 miles per gallon or better were exempt from the tax. Below this level, the tax per car went up as the mileage went down, reaching $1,500 for a car with mileage in the 16.5 to 17.5 range and topping out at $3,850 for a car that achieved less than 12.5 miles per gallon. The basic idea is obvious. A tax on low-mileage cars encourages the purchase of high-mileage cars. Economic incentives much like market incentives are at work, and cumbersome regulations can be avoided.

If our dependence on foreign oil is unnerving enough to bring forth calls for some kind of policy, what policy might be economically superior to, say, subsidized expansion of domestic production? Many economists praise the *strategic oil reserve*. This program uses huge underground salt domes located along the Gulf Coast to store mil-

lions of barrels of crude oil in an easily accessible way. One billion barrels of oil in storage was the original target, set in 1976. But that target has been missed. In 1985, with reserves standing at 500 million barrels, government purchases for the reserves were suspended. If imports were completely cut off, the 500 million barrels would fully replace them for about 100 days. Support for the strategic petroleum reserve among economists can be measured by the fact that most studies of the optimal size of such a reserve recommended an amount exceeding 1 billion barrels, double what we now have.

All in all, then, recent public policy has made some contributions to solving the problems outlined earlier. Additional contributions, perhaps even greater ones, can be credited to *de*regulation that has allowed energy prices to rise. A nice summary measure of the demand-side impact of recent policies and price increases is this: The amount of energy required to produce a real dollar of GNP in the United States dropped more than 25 percent between 1973 and 1986. Roughly one half of this improvement is due to newly achieved energy efficiency in capital and durable goods, such as more efficient cars, refrigerators, and air conditioners; more heat recovery in industrial processes; and greater use of insulation in homes and buildings. The other half of the improvement can be explained by various changes in behavior, such as keeping lights turned off when not in use and shifting demand to low-energy goods and services, especially services.

SUMMARY

1. Pollution occurs when one use of the environment, waste disposal in particular, detracts from other valuable uses, including resource uses other than waste disposal, as well as habitats and amenities. There is *too much* pollution when the environment is used excessively for waste disposal relative to other, cleaner endeavors.
2. The definition of *too much* depends on benefits and costs. Ideally, marginal social benefits should equal marginal social costs. External costs prevent this from occurring. External costs cause a problem because they are experienced by people

other than the firm producing the good or the person consuming it.
3. Pollution policies include moral suasion, direct regulation, emission taxes, marketable permits, and subsidies.
4. Direct regulation is the main U.S. policy for environmental protection. It entails, first, *standard setting*—both broad standards to guide the authorities and narrow standards to guide the regulated firms in specific behavior. Standards often result in uniform percentage abatement. Second, *enforcement for compliance* is also required,

which involves certification or permits, sample testing, field surveillance, and remedies.

5. Direct regulation has been judged a qualified success. Physical measures of air and water pollution indicate substantial improvement since 1970. Toxic waste regulation has mixed results, but it too has achieved good marks.

6. Regulation can be criticized for not passing tests of economic benefit and cost. On the other hand, complete and accurate benefit-cost analyses are very difficult to conduct in practice.

7. Cost effectiveness attempts to achieve benefits in the lowest-cost way, where those benefits are assumed to be given or fixed by policy (rather than variable, as in benefit-cost analysis). Direct regulation, especially that requiring equal percentage abatement from various sources, is not cost effective in comparison to emission taxes or marketable permits.

8. Emission taxes and marketable permits allegedly have other advantages over direct regulation besides cost effectiveness, namely, lower information requirements, less meddling in business affairs, and greater encouragement for innovation.

9. Energy is associated with three main problems—(a) environmental pollution, (b) dangerous dependency, and (c) supply shrinkage. The fact that most air pollution derives from fuel combustion illustrates the first problem. Dangerous dependency arises because so much of our oil is imported, and much of those imports come from uncertain Middle East sources. Supply shrinkage refers to the long-run depletion of fossil fuels and the potential problems for future generations.

10. These problems would be eased by reduced demand, expanded supply, and greater substitution of renewable alternatives for fossil fuels. Past and present policies attempting to achieve these ends include regulations of auto gas mileage, quotas limiting oil imports, and subsidies for solar and nuclear alternatives.

11. Critics of energy policies claim that the free market performs quite well. Price increases, for instance, simultaneously curtail demand and boost supply. By contrast, government policies—price ceiling regulations especially—have been a problem, not a solution. Still, some policies seem to have been beneficial on balance. The gas guzzler tax and the strategic oil reserve illustrate the positive possibilities.

KEY TERMS

Pollution
External costs
Moral suasion
Direct regulation
Emission fee

Marketable permits
Abatement subsidies
Regulatory standard setting
Regulatory enforcement
Cost effectiveness

QUESTIONS AND PROBLEMS

1. What is pollution and why does it happen?
2. Would pollution happen if polluters had to pay the costs to others of their pollution?
3. Is moral suasion effective in preventing pollution?
4. Indicate the range of values assigned to human life on the basis of wage premiums paid to workers who do risky jobs. Do you consider it morally repulsive to assign a dollar value to human life? Is it ethical to take steps to prevent the loss of life only if the lives saved are worth more than the costs involved? Can you think of decisions in areas other than pollution control that force people to decide how much should be spent to prolong human life?
5. Compare the cost effectiveness of a tax policy with that of a regulatory policy.

6. Why is energy a topic that is closely linked to that of pollution?
7. Show graphically and explain verbally why government price ceilings cause shortages, discourage production, and increase the quantity of a product demanded by consumers.
8. What happens in a free market to the price of a product that becomes increasingly scarce (its supply shrinks)? What happens to the quantity consumed? What responses are likely from producers if the market price for a product rises over the years? What responses are likely from consumers if the market price rises over the years? What are the implications of these market responses for the future of fossil fuels?

VII

International Economics and Comparative Economic Systems

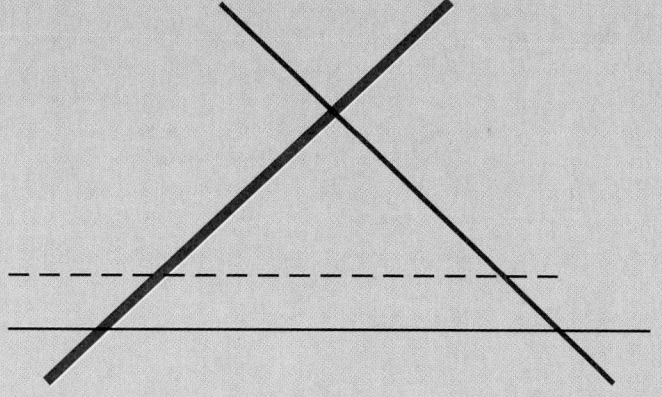

36

International Trade

It's time to throw open the doors and examine U.S. trade and financial relations with other countries. These transactions are large and growing. In this chapter we consider U.S. trade. In the next chapter we examine the international monetary system and U.S. financial relations with other countries.

U.S. international trade has been growing rapidly in recent years. In 1987 imports of goods and services from abroad totaled $424.1 billion, 9.5 percent of the GNP, compared to $39.9 billion, 3.9 percent of the GNP in 1970. Growth in imports has been strong both for consumer goods, such as foreign cars, cameras, TVs, shoes, and clothing, and for raw materials, such as petroleum and steel.

Exports have grown as well, from $42.5 billion in 1970 (4.2 percent of GNP) to $252.9 billion in 1987 (5.6 percent of GNP). Still, it can be seen from these figures that imports have risen faster than exports. The result is a huge *balance of trade deficit* (excess of imports over exports), about which more will be said in the next chapter.

I

The Composition of U.S. Foreign Trade

Even with the rapid growth in foreign trade, the United States remains a far less open economy than many other industrialized countries, where *openness* means the degree of dependence on foreign trade. This can be seen from Table 36.1, which shows imports and exports as a percentage of GNP for a number of countries.

The United States, because of its large size, varied resource base, and location (far from most other industrialized countries), is least dependent on foreign trade. At the other extreme, Belgium and the Netherlands, which are small, centrally located countries, have the highest ratios of foreign trade to GNP.

Table 36.2 indicates where our imports come from and where our exports go. The majority of our imports (62 percent) come from other industrialized countries. Canada, Japan, and Western Europe together account for 60 percent of our imports. Oil imports from OPEC are a large item in the import column (8 percent). The "Other Countries" category in the table also includes some countries with which we have substantial trade, in particular, Latin American countries and the Philippines.

On the export side, trade shares are roughly similar. About two thirds of our trade is with other industrialized countries. Canada, Japan, and Western Europe provide the market for a little over 60 percent of our exports. Western Europe and Canada have somewhat higher shares of our exports than of our imports. Japan has a strikingly smaller share of our exports compared to our imports. This reflects the fact that we have a large trade deficit with Japan.

Table 36.3 shows the composition of our imports and exports across different product types. We import substantial amounts of petroleum. We also import substantial amounts of each of the other categories in the table. The large item in the "Other" category is also indicative of the broad range of our imports. Our exports are more concentrated in a few product categories (though these are broad categories). Industrial supplies and materials together with capital goods (excluding automobiles) account for about 60 percent of exports, automobiles about 10 percent, and agriculture products 17 percent.

In the rest of this chapter, we consider two questions concerning U.S. foreign trade.

1. What determines trade patterns? Why do we import and export the goods we do? More fundamentally, why do nations trade with one another? We will see that they trade because trade makes both nations better off than they would be if they depended only on production at home.
2. This last being the case, why do nations restrict foreign trade? The United States, for example, has a complex array of **tariffs,** which are taxes on foreign goods. We have

TABLE 36.1   Imports and Exports as a Percentage of GNP, Selected Countries*

	Imports (Percentage of GNP)	Exports (Percentage of GNP)
United States	8.9	5.4
Canada	22.8	26.8
Japan	11.8	14.7
United Kingdom	23.1	20.7
France	19.9	17.9
Italy	23.9	20.8
West Germany	23.3	26.2
Netherlands	47.0	49.7
Belgium†	69.0	64.6
Norway	25.2	34.3

*Data are for either 1984 or 1985.
†including Luxembourg.
Source: _Economic Report of the President_, 1987.

TABLE 36.2   U.S. Imports and Exports by Area, 1984

	Share of U.S. Imports (%)	Share of U.S. Exports (%)
Industrial countries		
Canada	20.7	24.1
Japan	18.0	10.6
Western Europe	21.6	26.8
Australia, New Zealand and South Africa	1.7	3.6
Other countries (except Eastern Europe)		
OPEC	8.0	6.2
Other countries	29.3	26.5
Eastern Europe	0.7	2.2
	100.0	100.0

Source: _Economic Report of the President_, 1986.

TABLE 36.3   Composition of U.S. Exports and Imports, 1984

Imports ($ Billions)	
Petroleum and products	57.5
Industrial supplies and materials	67.0
Capital goods except automotive	61.2
Automotive	57.2
Other	91.1
Total	334.0

Exports ($ Billions)	
Agricultural	38.3
Industrial supplies and materials	56.3
Capital goods except automotive	73.7
Automotive	22.3
Other	29.2
Total	219.9

Source: _Economic Report of the President_, 1986. Figures may not sum to the total due to rounding.

also set up a number of nontariff barriers to trade such as **quotas,** which are limits on the amount of imports of certain goods. If trade is mutually beneficial to nations, why restrict it?

II
Why Nations Trade

Nations trade with each other for the same reason households or, at a broader level, states within the United States trade with each other. They trade because, by specializing in producing those goods and services where they are most efficient, selling them, and with the proceeds buying goods in the production of which they are less efficient, they increase their standard of living.

A
The Law of Comparative Advantage

At the level of the household, the rationale for specialization and trade was explained by Adam Smith in the *Wealth of Nations* over 200 years ago:

> *The taylor does not attempt to make his own shoes, but buys them of the shoemaker. The shoemaker does not attempt to make his own clothes, but employs a taylor. The farmer attempts to make neither the one nor the other, but employs those different artificers. All of them find it for their interest to employ their whole industry in a way in which they have some advantage over their neighbours, and to purchase with a part of its produce, or what is the same thing with the price of a part of it, whatever else they have occasion for.[1]*

Extending this logic to the foreign trade of nations, Smith wrote:

> *What is prudent in the conduct of every private family, can scarce be folly in that of a great kingdom. If a foreign country can supply us with a commodity cheaper than we ourselves can make it, better buy it of them with some part of the produce of our own industry, employed in a way in which we have some advantage.[2]*

Smith here is making an early statement of the *law of comparative advantage*, which was explained in Section 2.IV.A. Comparative advantage is the ability to produce a good or service relatively cheaply, where by "cheaply" is meant *with a low opportunity cost*.[3]

The **law of comparative advantage** states that individuals, companies, regions, or nations can gain by specializing in the production of goods and services that they produce relatively cheaply and exchanging those for other goods and services that are relatively expensive for them to produce.

In Chapter 2 the law of comparative advantage was illustrated for two states (Mississippi and Kansas). Now we adapt that analysis to trade between two countries: England and France. In our example, in addition to considering only trade possibilities between these two countries, we will assume that there are only two goods, namely, food and clothing. Moreover, as in Chapter 2, although we assume that opportunity costs differ between England and France, we assume that they are constant in each country, i.e., independent of the level of production of each good.

Figure 36.1 illustrates a hypothetical set of production possibilities for the two countries. For England (part a), we see that maximum clothing production, assuming no food is produced, is 30 units (point A). Moving down the production-possibilities frontier, as food is produced in increasing amounts, clothing output falls by 10 units per 10-unit increase in food output. We move, for example, from point A to point B, where food output has risen from 0 to 10 and clothing output has fallen from 30 to 20. Maximum output of food (no clothing production) is 30 units. For England, then, the opportunity cost of each 10 units of food is −10 units of clothing; for each unit of food, the opportunity cost is −1 unit of clothing. Looked at in reverse, the opportunity cost of each 10 units of clothing is −10 units of food; each 1 clothing equals −1 food.

For France (part b), the production-possibilities frontier indicates that maximum clothing output (no food production) is 40 units (point F) and maximum food production (no clothing production) is 80 units (point J). In between, moving down the production-possibilities frontier, food production can be increased by 20 units per 10-unit decline in clothing production. Moving, for example, from point F to point G, food output rises from 0 to 20 units, while clothing output falls from 40 to 30 units. The opportunity cost of each 20 units of food is −10 units of clothing; the opportunity cost of 1 unit of food is −1/2 unit of clothing. This compares with an opportunity cost of −1 unit of clothing for 1 unit of food in England. *France therefore has a comparative advantage in food production.* France can produce food relatively cheaply (at a low opportunity cost) in comparison to England.

---

[1]Adam Smith, *The Wealth of Nations* (New York: Random House, 1937), p. 424.
 [2]Ibid.
 [3]Recall from Chapter 2 that the opportunity cost of a product is the other products given up because resources are used to make that product.

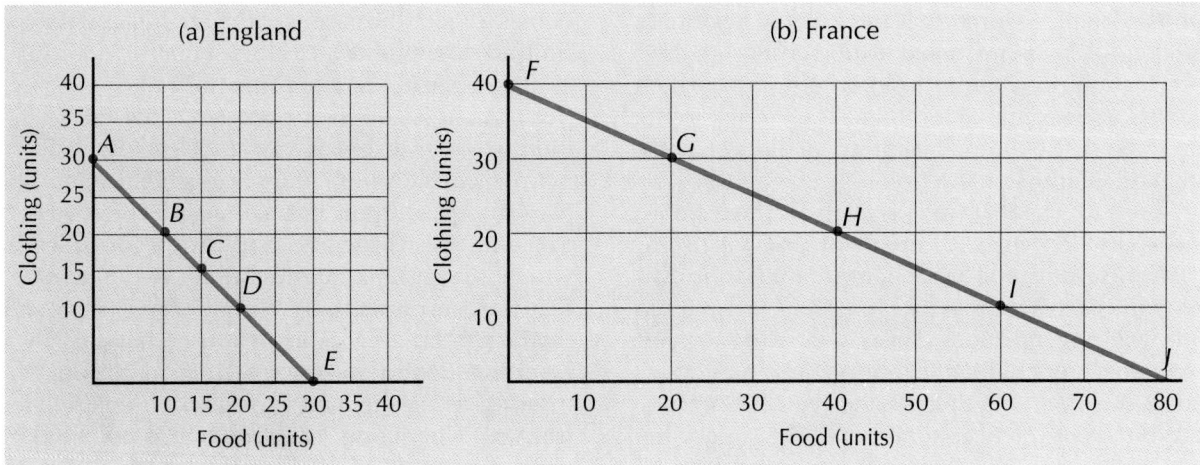

FIGURE 36.1 *Production-Possibilities Frontier for England and France*

Part (a) shows the production-possibilities curve for England. If no food is produced (point A), 30 units of clothing can be produced. For each unit of food produced, 1 fewer unit of clothing can be made. The opportunity cost of each unit of food is −1 unit of clothing. The production-possibilities curve for France is shown in part (b). If no food is produced (point F), 40 units of clothing can be produced. For each unit of food produced, the production of clothing falls by ½ unit. For France the opportunity cost of each unit of food is −½ unit of clothing. France has a comparative advantage (lower opportunity cost) in food production.

Considering things in reverse, however, for each unit of additional clothing produced in France, 2 fewer units of food can be produced. In France the opportunity cost of producing clothing is −2 units of food. In England, for each additional unit of clothing produced, only 1 fewer unit of food is produced; the opportunity cost of clothing is −1 unit of food. England therefore has a comparative advantage in the production of clothing.

Now consider moving in the opposite direction (e.g., from *G* to *F*) along France's production-possibilities frontier. To produce 10 more units of clothing, France must give up 20 units of food. For France the opportunity cost of 1 unit of clothing is −2 units of food. In England it is −1 unit of food. *England has a comparative advantage in producing clothing.*

These cost conditions for England and France are summarized in Table 36.4. It is because of cost differences in the two countries that opportunities for trade emerge.

B

The Gains from Trade

Trade need not emerge. In the extreme case, one or both nations may simply prohibit trade. Or one

or both may put such high tariffs on imported goods that trade will become unprofitable and stop. In the no-trade case, each country will pick a point along its production-possibilities frontier shown in Figure 36.1. The precise point chosen will depend on the relative preferences of the people for food and clothing. To illustrate the gains from trade, let us compute combined consumption of food and clothing for this no-trade case for each country and then show how the economic welfare of *both* countries can be improved through trade.

Assume that the English, beginning at point *A*, proceed (politely in a queue) down their production possibilities frontier to point *C* and find this the optimal point for the no-trade case. Their consumption therefore is 15 units of clothing and 15

TABLE 36.4   Cost Conditions, England and France

England	France
Cost of 1 unit of clothing = 1 unit of food	Cost of 1 unit of clothing = 2 units of food
Cost of 1 unit of food = 1 unit of clothing	Cost of 1 unit of food = ½ unit of clothing

758

units of food. Assume that the French, beginning at point *J*, proceed (more exuberantly) up their production-possibilities frontier to point *I*, which we assume is optimal for them. The French in the no-trade case end up consuming 10 units of clothing and 60 units of food.

Now suppose that trade is allowed. If we ignore transportation costs, the price of food relative to that of clothing will be equalized across the two countries. This follows because, for example, no one will give up more clothing for English food than for French food (ignoring product differences—which, with English and French food, may not be a very good assumption). This one price will, in general, be between the relative prices of the two goods in the separate countries in the absence of trade. The relative prices depend, in turn, on the relative costs of production of the two goods in each country.

In our example, this means that with trade the "world" (English and French) price of food relative to that of clothing will be between 1 clothing

equals 1 food (the relative price in England for the no-trade case) and 1 clothing equals 2 food (the relative price in France for the no-trade case). Suppose that this common price is 1 clothing = 1 1/2 food or, in reverse, 1 food = 2/3 clothing.

Now consider the trade possibilities for England, as illustrated in part (a) of Figure 36.2. If England specializes in clothing production, in which it has a comparative advantage (at point *A*), the English can export clothing at the price 1 clothing = 1 1/2 food. This is a better deal than diverting English resources to food production (moving along England's production-possibilities frontier), where only 1 unit of food is obtained by giving up 1 unit of clothing. In Figure 36.2(a), by trading, the English can move along the line AA', which lies outside their production-possibilities frontier.

One possible outcome with trade is a move to point *C**, where England trades 12 units of clothing to France and receives 18 units of food in return (1 clothing = 1 1/2 food, so 12 clothing = 18

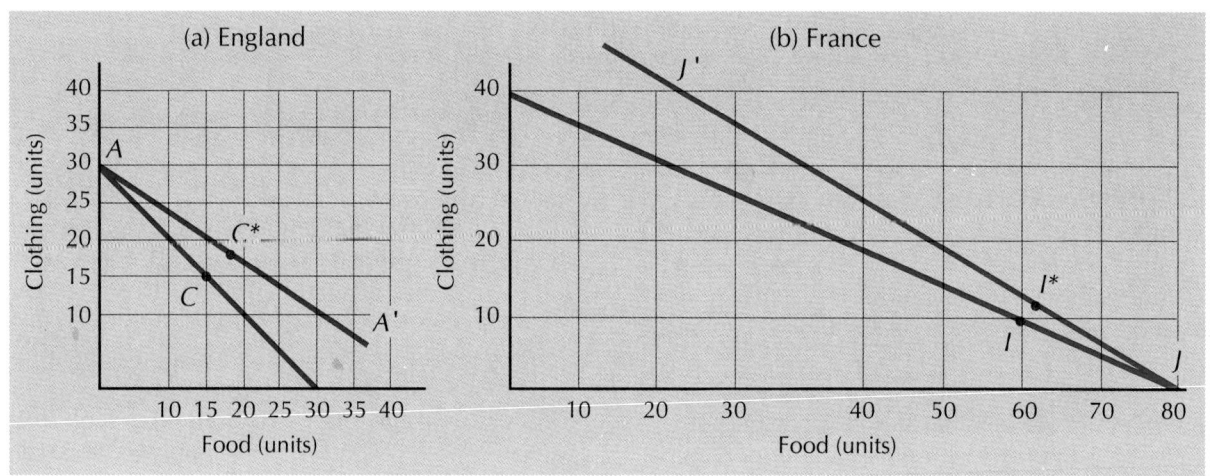

FIGURE 36.2   The Gains from Trade

In part (a), point C illustrates the no-trade position for England where 15 units of clothing and 15 units of food are both produced and consumed. Point I in part (b) shows the no-trade position for France where 60 units of food and 10 units of clothing are both produced and consumed.

With trade and the assumed "world" (meaning both England and France) price of 1 clothing = 1.5 food. England could produce only clothing and trade for food along schedule AA'. England could produce 30 units of clothing, for example, and trade 12 units of clothing for 18 units of food. England then moves to point C (18 clothing, 18 food), where it is better off than at C (15 clothing, 15 food). France would also benefit from this trade. France could produce only food (80 units) and export 18 units of food to England in return for 12 units of clothing. France would move along schedule JJ' to point I*, where it is better off (62 food, 12 clothing) than at I (60 food, 10 clothing).*

Both countries gain from trade.

food). At point C^*, England consumes 18 units of clothing (30 units produced minus the 12 exported to France) and 18 units of food (imported from France). At C, which we assumed was the point chosen in the no-trade case, England consumed (and produced) 15 units of clothing and 15 units of food. England clearly gains from trade.

What about France? If France specializes in food production, where it has a comparative advantage, it will produce 80 units of food. If, as we just assumed, it exports 18 units of food to England, it would have 62 units of food left and 12 units of clothing imported from England.

In terms of Figure 36.2, by trading with England at a price of 1 clothing = 1 1/2 food, France moves up line JJ' to point I^*. This trade-off is preferable to diverting French resources to clothing production, as was done in the no-trade case (the movement along the production-possibilities frontier from J to I). France also benefits from exploiting its comparative advantage. At I^* the French consume 12 units of clothing and 62 units of food, compared to 10 units of clothing and 60 units of food at I in the no-trade case.

Production and consumption totals for England and France for the case where there is no trade and for the case where they do trade are summarized in Table 36.5. Clearly, both countries benefit from trade. We have made a number of simplifying assumptions in our example, but our result is a quite general one. *Countries will benefit if they concentrate production on products where they have a comparative advantage and trade for those goods where they have a comparative disadvantage.* Adam Smith was correct on the advantages of specialization for nations, as well as for tailors and shoemakers.

C
Absolute versus Comparative Advantage

Notice that if we assume that France and England use the same amount of land and labor, then in our example France is more efficient in the production of *both* food and clothing. If both countries specialize in food production, France would produce 80 units compared to 30 for England. If both specialize in clothing production, France would produce 40 units compared to 30 for England. France, then, has an *absolute advantage* relative to England in the production of both goods, meaning that it produces both goods more efficiently. Still, we found that France benefits from trade. France is better off specializing in the activity where it has a comparative advantage—the area where its absolute advantage is greatest—food production.

To see why this is so, consider the case of a lawyer who is also an expert typist. In fact, the lawyer is a better typist than her secretary. She has an absolute advantage over her secretary both in the practice of law and in typing, though presumably a greater absolute advantage in the former. Would the lawyer maximize her net income by doing her own typing or by specializing in the practice of law and paying her secretary to do her typing?

III
Patterns of International Trade

From the principle of comparative advantage, we see *why* nations trade. Here we ask, why do they trade *what* they trade? How are trade patterns

TABLE 36.5 The Gains from Trade

	Without Trade		
	England	**France**	**Total Combined**
Clothing	15	10	25
Food	15	60	75
	With Trade		
	England	**France**	**Total Combined**
Clothing	18	12	30
Food	18	62	80

determined? Why, for example, does Japan export so many cars, Taiwan so many textiles, the United States so many agricultural products?

A
The Heckscher-Ohlin Theory

The modern theory of trade patterns among nations was developed by the Swedish economists Eli Heckscher and Bertil Ohlin early in the twentieth century.

According to the **Heckscher-Ohlin theory,** a country will tend to export goods the production of which requires relatively large amounts of factors of production that it has in abundance. A country will tend to import goods that require relatively large amounts of factors of production that are relatively scarce in the country. Factors of production include capital (plant and equipment) and labor, as well as land and other natural resources.

The Heckscher-Ohlin theory predicts, for example, that Taiwan, with an abundance of semi-skilled labor, will tend to export products such as textiles, which use a large quantity of such labor. Still a developing country, Taiwan would import sophisticated industrial equipment. The United States, with an abundance of fertile land and capital, will tend to export (among other things) agricultural goods produced by a highly mechanized technology. The United States might be expected to import goods the production of which requires a large amount of unskilled labor. Perhaps the clearest application of the theory is to the case of natural resources. Saudi Arabia, with a huge quantity of oil under its desert, exports oil. With its small population, it imports goods whose production requires labor. In fact, Saudi Arabia imports labor in the form of visiting workers from Yemen, Egypt, and other countries.

The Heckscher-Ohlin theory is not in conflict with the principle of comparative advantage. Rather, this theory is an explanation of why countries have the comparative advantages they do. A country can produce certain goods with relatively low opportunity costs (has a comparative advantage in those goods) because production of these goods requires large quantities of the factors of production that the country has in abundance.

The Heckscher-Ohlin theory also leads to an understanding of the fundamental reason why nations trade. They trade because the goods they produce can move from country to country more easily than the factors of production that produce them.

Trace back the logic that leads to this conclusion. Nations trade because they have comparative advantages in different goods. They have different comparative advantages because they have different endowments of factors of production. But if factors of production were quite mobile internationally, they could simply flow between countries. If labor were relatively scarce in some country, one would expect the wage level to be higher than where labor is abundant.

With a high degree of labor mobility, workers would flow into the labor-scarce country. This is exactly what happens *within* countries. To some extent, it happens among countries. The movement of workers to Saudi Arabia from Egypt and Yemen, as mentioned previously, is one example. The flow of Mexican workers to the United States is another. International flows of labor are, however, subject to many restrictions, both natural (e.g., language barriers) and governmental (e.g., immigration quotas). Trade in products between labor-scarce and labor-abundant countries substitutes for the migration of labor.

Similarly, with capital and especially natural resources (how would you export climate or fertile soil?), trade substitutes for factor movements in a world of diverse factor endowments.[4]

B
Other Explanations of Trade Patterns

Differing factor endowments, and therefore differing comparative advantages, explain much but not all trade among nations. Some other explanations of trade are as follows:

1. Differentiated Products A significant amount of trade occurs within product categories. In Table 36.3, for example, we saw that the United States

[4]To convince yourself that trade substitutes for generally more difficult factor movements, consider the following case, where the factor is more mobile than the "product." Master French chefs produce excellent food, but if frozen and shipped from Paris to New York, the food would lose its distinctive quality. Therefore, many French restaurants in New York import French chefs.

imported $57.2 billion worth of automobiles in 1984, but also exported $22.3 billion worth. Clearly, we don't have both a comparative disadvantage *and* a comparative advantage in the same product. But automobiles are *differentiated products*. A Ford is not a Toyota. A Ferrari is not a Cadillac.

One explanation for trade in differentiated products is that domestic producers concentrate on the mass market and thus on the majority taste in products. Imports, then, satisfy the minority taste. In the 1950s and 1960s in the United States, the majority taste was for comparatively large cars that were not particularly fuel-efficient. These were the cars Detroit auto makers produced. If you were in the minority and wanted a small car, you might buy a Volkswagen imported from Germany.

2. Economies of Scale   Another explanation for trade is *economies of scale*. Economies of scale are increases in efficiency that come as the size of an enterprise increases. For some products, economics of scale are so important that a few firms will come to dominate the worldwide industry. The wide-body jet industry, for example, is an industry where, given the size of the market, only a few firms can produce at cost-efficient levels. Current competitors for this market are the U.S. firms Boeing, McDonnell-Douglas, and Lockheed, as well as the joint European venture Airbus. Eventually experts expect only two or, at most, three firms to succeed. Airlines in all other countries will then import wide-bodied airplanes.

3. Technology Gaps   A final explanation for trade patterns relates to technological change. Most of the development of new production technologies takes place in highly developed countries. They therefore gain *temporary* comparative advantages in the production of goods that use these new technologies. Often the technological advances are protected by patents. During this early period following a technological advance, the highly developed countries will export products that are made with the new technology to less developed countries. Eventually, the less developed countries will employ the new technology, stop importing the products from the developed countries, and perhaps start exporting them.

Trade due to technology gaps is compatible with the Heckscher-Ohlin theory because such trade is due to temporary comparative advantages.

The new element in the technology gap explanation is the changing pattern of comparative advantages explaining changing trade patterns over time.

IV

Trade Restrictions

If there are important gains from trade among nations, why do almost all nations restrict international trade? Most economists oppose such restrictions. In one survey, 97 percent of economists polled believed that trade restrictions lowered general economic welfare. Why do politicians who enact trade restrictions not take economists' advice?

In this section, we examine several types of trade restrictions. In the next sections, we will examine the arguments for and against such restrictions.

A

Tariffs

Among the most important trade restrictions are tariffs. Tariffs are taxes on traded goods. Tariffs may be levied on either imports or exports, but import tariffs are far more common. The tariff may be a percentage of the value of the good (e.g., 10 percent) or a fixed sum (e.g., $5 per item).

Figure 36.3 illustrates the economic effects of an import tariff, using the example of a tariff on shoes. In the figure, D^d and D^s are the *domestic* demand and supply curves for shoes, respectively. In the absence of international trade, the equilibrium price and quantity would be at the intersection of these curves. The price would be $30 per pair; the quantity would be 60 million pairs (point E).

The solid horizontal line (*WP*) in the figure gives the price of shoes on the world market—the price at which we can import shoes. This price is assumed to be $10. Domestic demand is assumed to be a small enough part of the total world market so that this price does not depend on the amount we import. If there were free trade (no restrictions), the quantity of shoes demanded would be 100 million pairs (point B). This demand would be satisfied by 20 million pairs produced domestically (point *A* along the domestic supply curve) and by 80 million pairs of imported shoes (the distance *AB* in the figure).

Now suppose a 50 percent tariff is levied on shoe imports. The price of shoes inclusive of the tariff will be $15. The domestic quantity demanded will fall from 100 to 90 million pairs (point *D*). The quantity supplied domestically will rise from 20 to 30 million pairs (point *C*). Consequently, shoe imports will fall from 80 to 60 million pairs (the distance *CD*).

One cost of the tariff is that consumers pay more and buy fewer shoes. This is partially offset by the benefit to domestic producers from a higher price for their product. The government also gains revenues from the tariff, $300 million in our example ($5 × 60 million pairs of imported shoes). Overall, however, economic welfare will in general decline because the tariff causes resources to move to the shoe industry, where the domestic cost of additional production exceeds the world price. These resources could be used more productively in sectors where we have a comparative advantage—the point of Section II.

no good ti gain

B
Quotas

An import quota is a direct quantitative limit on imports of a commodity. Steel imports, for example, could be limited to 15 million tons per year. In many respects, quotas have the same effects as tariffs. The reduction in imports after a quota is enacted will raise the domestic price of the product. Consumers will pay a higher price and buy less of the product. Domestic resources will be diverted from more productive uses to the industry protected by the quota. Overall economic welfare will in general be reduced.

One difference between a quota and a tariff concerns the effect on government revenues. Revenue is collected with a tariff. With a quota, whether or not any revenue is raised depends on how

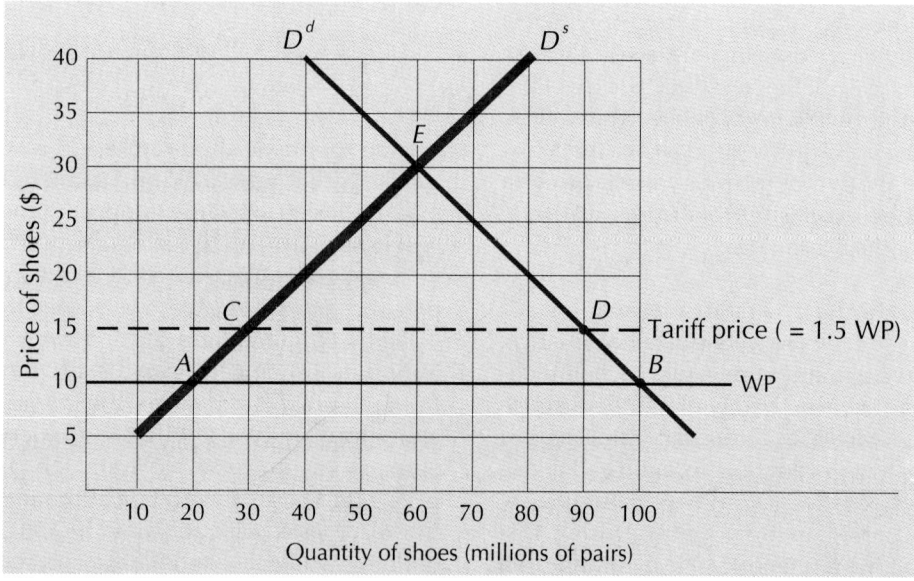

FIGURE 36.3   *The Effects of a Tariff*

The figure illustrates the effect of a tariff on shoes. If there are no restrictions to trade, anyone can buy shoes at the world price of $10 per pair. Total demand for shoes will be 100 million pairs (point B on the domestic demand curve for shoes, D^d). Domestic production of shoes will be 20 million pairs (point A on the domestic supply schedule for shoes, D^s). Imports will be 80 million pairs (distance AB).

A $5 per pair tariff on imported shoes will raise the price to $15. The quantity demanded will fall to 90 million pairs (point D on D^d). As the price rises, domestic production of shoes will rise to 30 million pairs (point C on D^s). Imports will fall to 60 million pairs.

licenses to import are distributed. Since imports are being restricted to below the free trade level and the price of the good has risen, there will be competition for such licenses. If the government auctions off the licenses to the highest bidders, then government revenue will rise. Often, however, governments have used other schemes to distribute licenses (e.g., give them to political supporters or friends and relatives). In the latter case, no revenue is raised by a quota.

Another difference between a tariff and a quota concerns the effect of changing demands in the two cases. If demand rises, for example (the D^d curve in Figure 36.3 shifts to the right), with a tariff the domestic price will remain the same (the world price plus the tariff) and increased demand will be satisfied by more imports. This cannot happen with a quota, since a quota fixes the quantity of imports. With a quota the domestic price must rise, and any increase in demand must be satisfied by more (relatively inefficient) domestic production. A quota is therefore a more inflexible trade restriction than a tariff.

C
Other Trade Restrictions

In recent years, rather than impose tariffs or quotas on some categories of imports, the United States has negotiated agreements with other countries, which voluntarily limit their exports to us. For several years prior to 1986, for example, there was a voluntary restriction on Japanese automobile exports to the United States. Voluntary export restrictions have the political advantage of appearing less like an attack on other countries' trade with us than do quotas, although in practice they are far from voluntary. Also, relative to a quota, a voluntary export restriction is more palatable to foreign exporters, since they (or their government) receive the benefit of the higher prices for their goods in the United States that result from the restrictions. This follows because, instead of import licenses being distributed by the U.S. government, there would be export licenses distributed by the foreign (e.g., Japanese) government.

In addition to those regulations discussed so far, there are other regulations that serve as trade restrictions, although they often ostensibly serve other purposes. Some safety and health regu-

lations are, for example, designed in ways that discourage imports. (The French prohibit advertisements of Scotch whiskey. Is the purpose to discourage alcohol consumption or to protect the domestic wine industry from competition?) *Read Perspective 36A.*

V
Why Nations Restrict Trade

We return here to the question of why nations enact trade restrictions and forgo some of the potential gains from trade. Are they shooting themselves in their collective foot? If so, why? Or are there real-world considerations that are neglected in the economists' arguments for free trade and that may justify trade restrictions? Let us start with the latter line of explanation for the prevalence of tariffs and other trade barriers.

A
Some Legitimate Economic Arguments for Trade Restriction

There are some factors left out of the analysis of Section II, the consideration of which can lead to legitimate economic arguments for trade restrictions.

1. Terms of Trade Effects In considering the effects of a tariff, we assumed that the country imposing the tariff was a small enough part of the world market so that the world price of the imported good would be unaffected by the tariff. For a large country such as the United States, this may not be correct. For a large country, the imposition of a tariff will, as it reduces the U.S. demand for the imported good, lower *total* world demand substantially. This will cause the world price of the import to *fall*.

This fall in the price of imports relative to the price of the goods that the United States exports is called an improvement in the U.S. **terms of trade.** Basically, an improvement in our terms of trade means that we benefit by getting more imports for a given amount of exports—in this case, due to a decline in the price of imports. When the improve-

PERSPECTIVE 36A

The Consumer Cost of U.S. Trade Restraints

In the mid-1980s, the average tariff rate on U.S. imports was only 4.4 percent. But in addition to tariffs, there were important quota and voluntary agreements with other countries to limit their exports to us. The most important import restraints are on textiles, sugar, steel, and, until recently, automobiles. There are less important tariff or nontariff restraints on trade in dairy and meat products, mushrooms, tobacco, fruit juices, clothspins, motorcycles, books, magazines, gasohol, and cookware.

A study by the Federal Reserve Bank of New York computed the cost to consumers of the most important restraints.[5] Table 36.6 shows the *lower*, more conservative, estimates of these costs for the year 1984. Even so, the cost is high, a total of $16 billion. The higher estimate was $21.5 billion. For a middle-income consumer (income range, $18,700–$23,400), using the lower cost estimates, the cost of trade restrictions was the equivalent of having to pay a 10 percent income tax surcharge (an extra 10 percent income tax). For a low-income consumer, the cost was equivalent to a 23 percent income tax surcharge.

The loss in overall economic welfare is less than the cost to consumers, since there are gains to the producers, and, where the barriers are tariffs, gains in government revenue, but the figures in Table 36.6 do indicate that U.S. trade restrictions impose a substantial cost on the general public. Moreover, as an instrument of government policy, they are equivalent to a *regressive* tax—one that falls proportionately

[5]Susan Hickok, "The Consumer Cost of U.S. Trade Restraints," Federal Reserve Bank of New York *Quarterly Review* (Summer 1985), pp. 1–12.

TABLE 36.6   Consumer Cost of Major U.S. Trade Restrictions

Protected Industry	Annual Consumer Cost ($ Billions)
Clothing	$8.5
Sugar	$1
Steel	$2
Automobiles	$4.5

Source: Hickok, "Consumer Cost of U.S. Trade Restraints," Federal Reserve Bank of New York *Quarterly Review* (Summer 1985), pp. 1–12.

ment in a large country's terms of trade is taken into account along with the other effects of imposing a tariff, general economic welfare *may* increase in a large country that imposes a tariff.

There is a serious limitation, however, to the ability of a country to exploit this terms-of-trade effect. If, for example, welfare in the United States improves because we impose a tariff due to the terms-of-trade effect, our gains come totally at our trading partners' expense. Their terms of trade have worsened. They will have a strong incentive to retaliate by instituting tariffs of their own. If they do, they can reverse the movement of the terms of trade. The effect will be that *both* countries are then worse off relative to a free trade position. The terms of trade are improved for neither country, and both lose some of the gains from trade because of the tariffs.

In the extreme case, attempts to gain a terms-of-trade advantage via tariffs can lead to tariff wars where nations raise tariffs repeatedly, seriously hindering world trade and consequently world-wide economic welfare.

2. Economies of Scale, Developing Technologies, and Strategic Concerns

Important recent research on trade policy emphasizes the interaction of economies of scale and developing technologies as factors that lead to *strategic* considerations in a nation's trade policy.[6] Let us use an example to illustrate the type of argument made in this literature.

The jumbo jet aircraft industry was cited previously as an example of an industry with significant economies of scale.[7] Due to the huge research, development, and design costs, to be efficient a firm must produce on a large scale. Given the world demand for jumbo jets, the industry will support only a few firms. Those firms will then be able to make profits above the normal rate of return due to lack of competition.

Suppose you are a planning minister in France. You would like to see a French firm succeed in this market. That way, the higher than average profits would go to French citizens. You would also know that as aircraft technology changes, French technology will develop faster if France is one of the nations designing and producing jumbo aircraft. The French will be *learning by doing*. If, on the other hand, the industry becomes dominated by U.S. firms, France will fall behind technologically and it will become harder to compete in the future. Further assume that in a free trade situation, the French today would not be able to compete with U.S. technology. A French firm would *not* be one of the two or three that would ultimately dominate the industry.

If France put a sufficiently high tariff on the importation of jumbo jets, the French producer would have the whole domestic market. With that advantage, the French firm may be able to produce on a large enough scale (with a lower cost) to compete with U.S. firms in world markets. Moreover, in time, due to *learning by doing*, as mentioned previously, French technology may develop to the point where the tariff can be removed.

This is, of course, only an example, but recent research in this area provides a number of situations in which deviations from a free trade policy may increase a nation's economic welfare. As in the jumbo jet case, one reason is economies of scale, which lead to situations where only a few firms will dominate the market and make high profits. Here nations are competing to develop such firms. Tariffs may help in the competition. Again, as in the jumbo jet case, ongoing changes in technology may make it in a country's interest to protect industries with a tariff while they develop the technological expertise to compete in world markets.

There are limitations, however, on the potential gains to a nation from strategic trade policies. One limitation is retaliation. The French may gain by a tariff to protect their aircraft industry, but suppose the United States, the United Kingdom, West Germany, and Japan all do the same. Each country then ends up with small, inefficient production, and all are likely to lose relative to a free trade outcome.

Another difficulty with strategic trade restrictions is that the government must identify potential winners among its industries. In the jumbo jet case, it is possible that the French firm will not be competitive in world markets even with a guaranteed domestic market. The French will then just end up paying high prices for inefficiently produced planes. Critics of strategic trade restriction doubt that governments have the ability to pick a winning industrial mix and prefer to let the market perform that function.

Read Perspective 36B.

B

Shooting Ourselves in the Foot?

Trade barriers aimed at improving a large country's terms of trade and those for the strategic reasons just discussed explain only a small portion of actual trade restrictions. This is true because actual trade restrictions are as prevalent in small countries for which tariffs will not affect their terms of trade. (They are too small a part of the market for a

---

[6]See, for example, the papers in Paul Krugman, *Strategic Trade Policy and the New International Economics* (Cambridge, Mass.: MIT Press, 1986).

[7]Recall that economies of scale are increases in the efficiency of production and therefore decreases in unit cost that come as a result of increases in the size of an enterprise.

PERSPECTIVE 36B
Japanese Strategic Trade Policy

Japan is an often-cited example of a nation that has successfully pursued a strategic trade policy. The Japanese Ministry of International Trade and Industry (MITI) targets various industries in which Japan might develop an international competitive position. Capital is channeled to these industries to finance investment in new technologies. Tariff or nontariff barriers are erected to protect the domestic market for Japanese firms. Cooperative strategies (collusion) among firms are also allowed.

Protection of the domestic market allows firms to produce at high enough levels to benefit from economies of scale. Cooperation rather than competition among domestic firms results in high domestic prices and profits for the firms on domestic sales. This enables firms to sell at lower prices on the international market.

An example of the success of such a trade policy is the Japanese television receiver industry. The Japanese market was protected by a tariff of 20 to 30 percent in the 1950s and 1960s, while Japanese firms invested in new technologies. Firms were allowed to fix domestic prices cooperatively. The major firms in the industry—Matsushita, Sony, Sanyo, Hitachi, Mitsubi-

shi, Toshiba, and Sharp—dominated the domestic market, together producing 100 percent of the monochrome and 99 percent of the color TV sets.

With this profitable base, the Japanese began to compete successfully in the world market. In the United States, for example, the Japanese share of the monochrome market rose from 0.8 percent in 1962 to 25 percent in 1977. The Japanese share of the U.S. market for color sets rose from 3 to 37 percent between 1967 and 1977.

The effect of Japanese competition on U.S. television producers was disastrous. Employment in the industry fell by 65 percent between 1966 and 1975. Twenty-one of 26 U.S. firms left the industry.[8] How a nation such as the United States should respond when other nations employ strategic trade restrictions is one of the most difficult issues in international economic policymaking.

---

[8]This description of Japanese policy in the television industry is based on Kozo Yamamura, "Caveat Emptor: The Industrial Policy of Japan," in Paul Krugman, ed., *Strategic Trade Policy and the New International Economics* (Cambridge, Mass.: MIT Press, 1986).

---

tariff-induced change in their demand to change the world price of goods.) Moreover, actual tariffs and other trade restrictions are not most prevalent in industries where there are economies of scale and rapidly changing technologies. They are more likely to be found in older declining industries than in new and vibrant ones.

We must look for additional explanations for trade restrictions, and these are not to be found among arguments showing that such restrictions increase the general level of economic welfare. They are rather to be found in the effects that trade restrictions have on specific groups of industries and workers and in the political process that leads to the success of such groups in enacting legisla-

tion to foster their interests, *even though the general economic welfare will be hurt.*[9]

Protection from foreign competition will enable firms in an industry to produce more and to sell at a higher price. In our hypothetical example of the shoe industry, imposition of a tariff raises output from 20 to 30 million pairs and raises the price

---

[9]Another argument for trade restriction is that we need to protect domestic industries that produce goods vital to national defense. Even if tariffs for this purpose lower general economic welfare, they are argued to be necessary for national security. This argument is correct as far as it goes. (We wouldn't want to import all our tanks from the Soviet Union.) This rationale for tariffs applies, however, only to a narrow range of strategic goods and explains relatively few real-world trade restrictions.

from $10 to $15. Clearly, there are considerable potential benefits to the workers and owners of firms in the shoe industry.

In our example, however, the country is unable to affect its terms of trade, and there are no strategic considerations such as those discussed in the previous section. The tariff will not raise general economic welfare. On the contrary, the loss to consumers due to a higher price, and therefore lower shoe consumption, will exceed the gain to shoe producers. An important point to note, however, is that the loss to any individual consumer is small—a few dollars extra for shoes each year—while the gains to owners and workers are likely to be substantial. Some of the workers will, for example, not be employed in the shoe industry without the tariff.

Owners of firms, their trade associations, and unions of workers treatened by foreign competi-

tion will expend considerable money and energy lobbying legislators for protection. Legislators from states where such industries are located will have to support their position. (A North Carolina or South Carolina senator who espoused free trade in textiles would not be a senator for long.) Coalitions will form between different industry groups seeking protection. Against these interests will be the much less vocally represented interests of consumers. The outcome in many cases— though by no means all—has been some degree of protection for many industries, whether by tariffs, quotas, or voluntary export limits negotiated with our trading partners.

In the 1980s, as the volume of imports has surged, the pressure for protection has grown. To date the Reagan administration has successfully opposed most protectionist initiatives.

SUMMARY

In this chapter we have examined U.S. international trade—its patterns, the reason for those patterns, and the rationales for trade restrictions.

1. We began by examining the size of U.S. foreign trade. The volume of exports and imports has risen rapidly in recent decades. Still, foreign trade accounts for a much smaller portion of GNP in the United States than in other industrialized countries.

2. The reasons why nations trade were seen to lie in the benefits that come from specialization. Like individuals and localities, nations gain by producing those goods where they have comparative advantages and buying from others those goods where they have comparative disadvantages.

3. The most important factors determining trade patterns among nations, as explained by the Heckscher-Ohlin theory, are relative factor endowments. A country can produce certain goods with relative efficiency (have a comparative advantage in those goods) because production requires large quantities of factors of production

that the country has in abundance. Countries will therefore tend to export goods whose production requires large amounts of their relatively abundant factors of production. They will import goods whose production requires large amounts of their scarce factors of production.

4. The last sections of this chapter explained the types of restrictions countries impose and the reasons they impose them. Valid economic arguments for trade restriction include attempts to improve a large country's terms of trade and restrictions for strategic reasons (capitalizing on economies of scale and promoting technological change). Most trade restrictions, however, are not explained by these motives. Instead, they seem explainable by the significant gains a particular trade restriction may give to a certain group, which will work to enact the restriction, compared to the small loss imposed on any individual as a result of an individual trade restriction.

KEY TERMS

Tariffs

Quotas

Law of comparative advantage

Absolute advantage

Heckscher-Ohlin theory

Terms of trade

QUESTIONS AND PROBLEMS

1. To what extent is the U.S. dependent upon foreign trade?
2. Where do U.S. imports come from? Where do U.S. exports go?
3. List some goods and services that the U.S. exports and imports.
4. Consider a hypothetical world with only two countries, each producing the same two goods. Could one country have an absolute advantage in both goods? Could one country have a comparative advantage in both goods?
5. The Heckscher-Ohlin theory predicts that countries will export what goods? Explain why immigration restrictions make international trade more important to economic efficiency.
6. Which groups in an economy win and which lose when an import tariff is imposed on textiles? Which

of these groups are more likely to send lobbyists to Washington to represent their position to members of Congress?

7. Do existing trade restrictions exist because of legitimate arguments that the nation as a whole is better off with these restrictions? Are there any legitimate arguments to this effect?
8. The Purewater Textile Plant in Shelburn, South Carolina, announces that it will close in one month and a thousand employees will lose their jobs. You are campaigning for the Presidency and need to win votes in that state. Knowing that textile workers blame "cheap" foreign imports for their plight, what policy positions might you state without compromising your concern for the welfare of the nation as a whole? Could you advocate higher tariffs or the imposition of import quotas on textiles?

37

Exchange Rates and the International Monetary System

An exchange rate between currencies is the price of one currency in terms of the other. The price of the British pound in terms of the U.S. dollar on February 24, 1988, for example, was $1.76 ($1.76 = 1 pound); the price of the French franc was 17 U.S. cents; and the price of the West German mark was 54 U.S. cents. The determination of exchange rates among currencies is a baffling subject to many, including some world leaders. Witness the following exchange between former President Richard Nixon and his chief of staff, Robert Haldeman.

> "You get the report that the British floated the pound?" Haldeman asked.
> "No, I don't think so," Nixon replied.
> "They did."
> Mr. Nixon brushed aside the British pound. "I don't care about it," he said. "Nothing we can do about it." Haldeman continued anyway. "It's too complicated for me to get into," the President insisted.
> He had even less time for the Italian lira.
> "Burns [then Federal Reserve Board Chairman Arthur Burns] is concerned," Haldeman reported, "about speculation about the lira."
> "Well, I don't give a (expletive deleted) about the lira," the President answered. (Watergate Tapes, June 23, 1972)

But exchange rates and other questions about the international monetary system are important to us as purchasers of foreign products, as workers for companies that compete in world markets, and as travelers to other countries.

In this chapter, we examine the factors that determine the rate of exchange between the dollar and other national currencies. We see that the way in which the exchange rate is determined depends upon the **international monetary system** set up by the nations of the world. We begin by explaining how the U.S. government keeps track of foreign economic transactions via the **balance of payments accounts.**

I

The U.S. Balance of Payments Accounts

Exchanges between the dollar and other currencies take place when U.S. residents want to purchase foreign goods or assets, as well as when foreign residents want to purchase U.S. goods and assets. A look at the nature of these transactions between the United States and other countries is a first step in studying how the relative values of national currencies are determined. The U.S. balance of payments accounts summarize our foreign economic transactions.

On one side of the accounts, all earnings from the foreign activities of U.S. residents and the U.S. government are recorded as credits, whereas on the other side, expenditures abroad are reported as debits. A point to notice is that, by the usual principles of double-entry bookkeeping, each credit must be matched by an equal debit, and vice versa. Each expenditure on foreign goods, for example, must be financed somehow; the source of financing is recorded as a credit. A first conclusion, then, before we even look at the numbers, is that if *all* transactions are counted, the balance of payments always balances.

We will, however, want to consider subcategories of our foreign transactions, and for such subcategories there is no reason to believe that receipts from abroad will equal earnings from abroad. In recent years, for example, expenditures on our merchandise exports by foreign residents (a credit in our balance of payments) have fallen far short of our expenditures on imported goods (a debit in our balance of payments). This *deficit* in our **merchandise trade balance** has been a matter of concern, for reasons to be discussed.

Table 37.1 summarizes the U.S. balance of payments accounts for 1986.

TABLE 37.1   U.S. Balance of Payments, 1986 (Billions of Dollars)

	Credit (+)	Debit (−)	Balance (−) Deficit (+) Surplus
Current account			
Merchandise exports (+) and imports (−)	224.4	−368.7	−144.3
Service transactions (net) _ins, finance_	18.6		
Transfers (net) _pensions_		−15.7	
Current account balance			−141.4
Capital account			
Capital inflows (+) and outflows (−)*	178.7	−96.3	
Capital account subbalance			+82.4
Statistical discrepancy			+23.9
Official reserve transactions			
Reduction in U.S. official reserve assets			0.4
Increase in foreign official assets in the United States			34.7
Total official reserve transactions			35.1

autonomous

central bank

finance deficit   _$ = reserve currency_

*Includes increases in U.S. government foreign assets other than official reserve assets.
Source: Federal Reserve Bulletin, January 1988, p. A53.

A

The Current Account

The first group of items in the table are what are called **current account** transactions. Among these, the first items listed are _merchandise exports and imports_, to which we have just referred. Examples of merchandise exports are the sale of a U.S. computer system to a British firm or the sale of U.S. grain to the Soviet Union. Purchases of Japanese cars, German cameras, or Honduran bananas by U.S. residents are examples of U.S. imports. In 1986, U.S. merchandise imports exceeded exports by $144.3 billion. We had a merchandise trade deficit of that amount.

The next category in the table is imports and exports of _services_. In the table we enter only the net value of such transactions. Examples of transactions in the service category are financial, insurance, and shipping services. Also in this category are dividends and interest earned by U.S. residents from their assets abroad (a credit) and interest and dividends paid to foreign residents who hold U.S. assets (a debit). The net item in the table, $18.6 billion, indicates that in 1986 we exported more of such services than we imported. The last transactions in the current account are _net transfers_. Recorded here are private and government transfer payments made between the United States and other countries. Such payments

include U.S. foreign aid payments (a debit) and private or government pension payments to persons living abroad (a debit). Any such transfer to a U.S. resident from abroad would be a credit on this line.

If we stop or draw the line at this point, we can compute the _current account balance_. The table indicates that in 1986 the current account was in deficit by $141.4 billion. Merchandise imports exceeded exports by more than the surplus in the services category, and further, there was a net debit in the transfers category. Overall, just considering current account transactions, U.S. residents spent over $141 billion more abroad than was earned.

B

The Capital Account

The next entries in the table record **capital account** transactions. Capital inflows (credits) are purchases of U.S. assets by foreign residents. Such capital inflows include purchases by foreigners of U.S private or government bonds, stocks, and bank deposits. Additionally, foreign direct investments in the United States, such as Honda's building of a plant in Ohio, are capital inflows in the balance of payments. Purchases by U.S. residents of financial assets or direct investments in foreign countries are capital outflows (debits) in the balance of payments. As can be seen from the table, capital inflows exceeded capital outflows by $82.4 billion in 1986.

An important point to note is that foreign purchases of our assets represent, in large part, U.S. borrowings from foreign residents. In 1986, for example, the inflow of capital in Table 37.1 included over $8 billion of foreign purchases of U.S. government securities (government borrowing from abroad) and over $70 billion of foreign purchases of private U.S. securities (private, primarily business, borrowing from abroad).[1] From the table, it can be seen that in 1986 a huge current account deficit, due to the excess of merchandise imports over merchandise exports, was, in effect, financed, for the most part, by borrowing from abroad.

The next item in the table is the *statistical discrepancy*. Not all international transactions are properly recorded, and the statistical discrepancy, or error and omissions term, is the amount that must be added to make the total balance of payments balance, what might be called an official *fudge factor*.

C

Official Reserve Transactions

Let us stop here and examine the point we have now reached in considering U.S. foreign economic transactions. Suppose we draw a line below the statistical discrepancy.

All the items above the line represent international economic transactions undertaken by private U.S. residents or the U.S. government for some independent motive. By this we mean a motive other than the effect the transaction will have on the balance of payments, or, as we see presently, on the value of the U.S. dollar relative to other currencies. A U.S. resident buys a Japanese car or a share of stock in a German company because he prefers them to their domestic counterparts. The U.S. government may give foreign aid to another

government to stabilize the political situation in that country. All the items above the line are what, from the point of view of the balance of payments accounts, can be termed *autonomous* or independently motivated transactions.

The official reserve transactions below this line are, in contrast, carried out by central banks, either the U.S. Federal Reserve System or foreign central banks (e.g., the Bank of England or West German Bundesbank) in pursuit of international policy objectives. Here we simply explain the nature of these transactions. The motivation for them is explained later in the chapter.

The first item below the statistical discrepancy in Table 37.1 is the *reduction in U.S. official reserve assets*. In 1986 U.S. official reserve assets *decreased* by 0.4 billion. Official reserve assets are holdings of gold, special drawing rights (a reserve asset created by the International Monetary Fund),[2] and foreign currency holdings. The reduction of $0.4 billion in 1986 indicates that we used this amount of our official reserves to finance other expenditures abroad. Reductions in U.S. official reserve assets are a credit in the balance of payments.

The next and last item in the balance of payments table is the *increase in foreign official assets in the United States*. Foreign central banks hold a portion of their reserve assets in the form of dollars. Dollars are an important reserve asset because the dollar is commonly used in international transactions and because of the central role the dollar has played in the international monetary system since World War II. If foreign central banks buy dollars, that is a credit in our balance of payments (a capital inflow), since they are investing in the United States.[3] In 1986, foreign central banks increased the amount of official reserve assets held in the United States by $34.7 billion, hence the positive item in this line of our balance of payments accounts.

---

[1]The term *securities* refers to bonds, which are long-term assets, as well as short term assets. An example of the latter are 3-month U.S. Treasury *bills*.

[2]The International Monetary Fund is an agency that was set up near the end of World War II to administer the international monetary agreements signed at that time. These agreements, the Bretton Woods agreements, are discussed in Section VII. Special drawing rights will also be discussed further.

[3]They need not hold actual U.S. currency. After buying the dollars, they can use them to purchase U.S. government or private securities.

II

The Foreign Exchange Market

The demand for foreign currencies by domestic residents is called the demand for **foreign exchange**. The foreign exchange market is the market in which national currencies are traded for one another. It is in this market, for example, that U.S. residents sell dollars to purchase foreign exchange (foreign currencies). In the United States, the central market for foreign exchange is composed of a number of brokers and bank foreign exchange departments in New York.

To see the link between the balance of payments accounts and transactions in the foreign exchange market, we begin by recognizing that all expenditures by U.S. residents on foreign goods, services, or assets and all foreign transfer payments (debits in the balance of payments accounts) also represent demands for foreign currencies, i.e., demands for *foreign exchange*. The U.S. resident buying a Japanese car pays for it in dollars, but the Japanese exporter will expect to be paid in yen. So dollars must be exchanged for yen in the foreign exchange market. To take another example, if a U.S. resident wants to buy a share of stock on the London stock exchange, a broker must convert the buyer's dollars into British pounds before actually making the purchase. *Thus the total U.S. residents' expenditures abroad represents a demand for foreign exchange.* Looked at from the point of view of the dollar, we can also state that the *total foreign expenditure of U.S. residents represents an equal supply of dollars in the foreign exchange market.*

Conversely, all foreign earnings of U.S. residents reflect equal earnings of foreign exchange. American exporters, for example, will expect to be paid in dollars, and to buy our goods, foreigners must sell their currency and buy dollars. *Total credits in the balance of payments accounts are then equal to the supply of foreign exchange or, what is the same thing, the demand for dollars.*

It is in the foreign exchange market that exchange rates among national currencies are determined. Having come this far in the book, it will come as no surprise that the supply of and demand for foreign exchange are important in the determination of exchange rates, which are, after all, relative prices of currencies. Consequently, prior to discussing exchange rate determination, it will be useful to construct explicit demand and supply curves for the foreign exchange market. As we do so in the next two sections, we will make some simplifying assumptions that will carry over to our later analysis.

III

The Demand for Foreign Exchange

The demand curve for foreign exchange and the supply curve in the next section exclude official reserve transactions by central banks. For the moment, we assume that such transactions do not exist. In the jargon of international economics, we assume that central banks do not *intervene* in the foreign exchange market.

Another simplification is to assume that there are only two countries: the United States, whose domestic currency is the dollar, and West Germany, with the mark as the domestic currency. Germany here represents the rest of the world. This two-country assumption enables us to define *the* exchange rate in a simple manner. Once exchange rate determination between two currencies is understood, the extension to a multicountry world is not difficult.

The exchange rate in this simple situation is the relative price of the two currencies, which we will express as the price of the mark in terms of U.S. dollars or cents. If, for example, the price of the mark is twenty-five cents ($0.25) then 0.25 dollar trades for 1 mark; at fifty cents ($0.50) the exchange rate (price of the mark) is *higher*, and 0.50 dollar equals 1 mark. It is important to keep in mind as we go along that with the exchange rate expressed this way, *a rise in the exchange rate means that the price of the foreign currency (foreign exchange) has gone up; the value of the U.S. dollar has declined. Conversely, a fall in the exchange rate is a fall in the price of foreign currency and therefore a rise in the value of the dollar.*

A

The Exchange Rate and the Demand for Foreign Exchange

Figure 37.1 shows the demand curve for foreign exchange (D^{fe}) plotted with the exchange rate (cents per mark) on the vertical axis. Remember that all foreign expenditures by U.S. residents (imports, purchases of foreign assets, and foreign transfers) are demands for foreign exchange. As drawn in the figure, the demand curve is downward sloping, indicating that as the exchange rate (price of foreign currency) *falls*, the quantity of foreign exchange (foreign currency) demanded *rises*. This is because a fall in the price of foreign currency will decrease the cost *in terms of dollars* of purchasing foreign goods.

Suppose, for example, you were considering purchasing a German camera that cost 400 marks. If the exchange rate is 50 cents = 1 mark, the camera would cost $200. At a lower exchange rate (price of foreign currency) of 25 cents = 1 mark, the same camera would cost only $100. We would

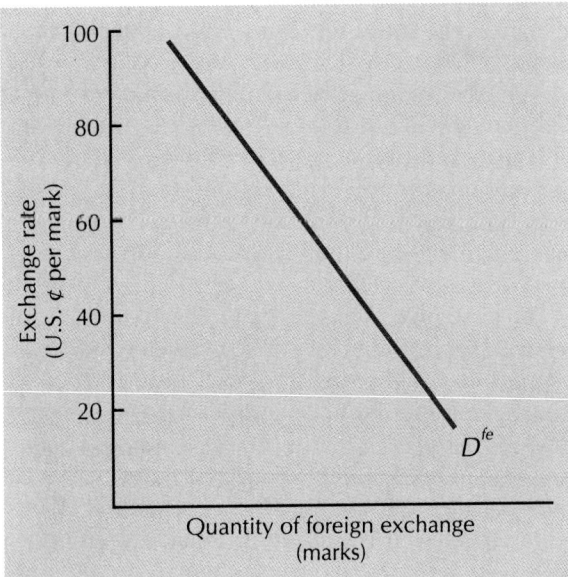

FIGURE 37.1 *The Demand Curve for Foreign Exchange*

The demand curve for foreign exchange (D^{fe}) shows the quantity of foreign exchange (marks) demanded for each value of the exchange rate. The curve is downward sloping, reflecting the fact that the quantity of foreign exchange demanded declines as the exchange rate (price of foreign exchange) rises.

expect U.S. residents to purchase more cameras and other German goods and therefore demand more foreign exchange (marks) at the lower exchange rate.

What about the demand for foreign exchange for the purchase of foreign assets and for foreign transfers? With respect to the latter, there seems to be no reason for a definite relationship between the amount of foreign transfers and the exchange rate. It is not clear what effect the change in the exchange rate would have on foreign aid programs, pension payments to persons living abroad, or gifts to foreign residents. In the case of purchases of assets (e.g., securities or shares of stock), a fall in the exchange rate will, as in the case of imported goods, reduce the price in dollars of foreign assets. The fall in the exchange rate will, however, also result in a proportional fall in the interest or dividend earnings from the foreign asset, again measured in dollars.

Consider, for example, a German security that costs 1,000 marks and pays interest of 100 marks per year. At an exchange rate of 50 cents = 1 mark, the security will cost $500 and pay interest of $50 or 10 percent. At the lower exchange rate of 25 cents = 1 mark, the security will cost $250 and pay interest of $25, again 10 percent. Since the foreign asset pays the same interest rate in both cases, we would not expect the demand for foreign assets to depend on the level of the exchange rate. The downward slope of the demand curve for foreign exchange therefore results only from the fact that imports rise as the exchange rate falls.

B

Other Influences on the Demand for Foreign Exchange

Changes in the level of the exchange rate result in changes in the quantity of foreign exchange demanded—movements along the D^{fe} curve. In this subsection we examine factors that shift the demand curve for foreign exchange—factors that change the demand for foreign exchange for a given level of the exchange rate.

1. Expected Changes in the Exchange Rate
Previously we saw that the demand for foreign assets does not depend on the *level* of the exchange rate. A factor that does strongly affect

the demand for foreign assets is an *expected* change in the exchange rate. To see why, consider the foreign security (costing 1,000 marks) just discussed. If you purchased the foreign security at the beginning of a year when the exchange rate was 50 cents = 1 mark, consider what happens if over the year the exchange rate falls to 25 cents = 1 mark. You paid $500 for the security. If you sell it at the end of the year, when the exchange rate is 25 cents (= 1 mark), you will get back $250; even with the interest you earn, your overall return will be negative. On the other hand, if the exchange rate had risen, you would make a profit (in addition to the interest earned) on the sale of the security. We see then that *expected declines in the exchange rate will make foreign assets less desirable. Conversely, expected increases will make foreign assets more desirable*.

Figure 37.2 illustrates the effect of an expected *fall* in the exchange rate. The demand curve for foreign exchange shifts to the left from D_0^{fe} to D_1^{fe}. The demand for foreign assets, and hence for foreign exchange, falls because foreign assets become less desirable when their *dollar* value is expected to decline.

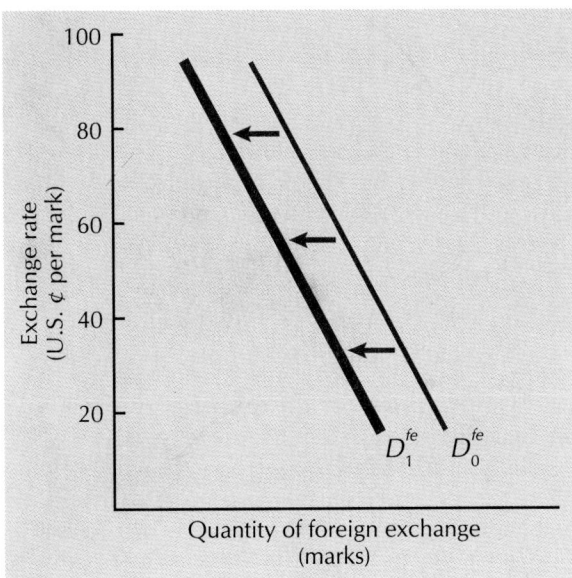

FIGURE 37.2 A Shift in the Demand for Foreign Exchange

An expected fall in the exchange rate makes foreign assets less desirable relative to U.S. assets. The demand for foreign exchange (for use in buying foreign assets) declines.

2. Domestic GNP Changes in domestic (U.S.) *gross national product* (GNP) shift the demand curve for foreign exchange. An increase in domestic GNP (total output) increases the demand for foreign exchange and shifts the demand curve to the right. This follows because as domestic output and therefore income rises, domestic consumer purchases increase. Part of this increase in consumer purchases is increased purchases of imported goods (more Japanese VCRs, Belgian chocolates, and French perfume). Also, increased domestic output requires increases in imported materials (e.g., more imported oil). Conversely, a reduction in domestic output, during a recession, for example, results in a decline in the demand for foreign exchange. The demand curve for foreign exchange shifts to the left.

3. The Price Level Another factor affecting the demand curve for foreign exchange is the level of domestic (U.S.) *prices relative to foreign prices*. A rise in the domestic price level for a given value of the foreign price level makes domestic products more expensive relative to foreign products (Chevrolets versus Volkswagens). U.S. residents are led to substitute imports for purchases of domestic goods. The demand curve for foreign exchange shifts outward as U.S. residents purchase more foreign exchange in order to purchase more imported goods. Conversely, a rise in the foreign price level for a given U.S. price level makes imports more expensive. The demand curve for foreign exchange shifts back to the left.

4. Interest Rates The last major influence on the demand for foreign exchange that we consider is the level of domestic interest rates relative to foreign interest rates. A *rise* in domestic (U.S.) *interest rates relative to foreign interest rates* makes domestic securities more attractive relative to foreign securities. The demand for foreign exchange therefore declines as investors shift funds from foreign securities to U.S. securities to take advantage of the higher interest rates. The U.S. demand curve for foreign exchange therefore shifts to the left if U.S. interest rates rise relative to foreign interest rates. Alternatively, if U.S. interest rates fall relative to foreign interest rates, the U.S. demand curve for foreign exchange shifts out to the right.

■ *CHECK YOUR BEARINGS*

Before going on to consider the supply side of the foreign exchange market, we summarize the influences on the demand for foreign exchange.

A fall (rise) in the exchange rate increases (decreases) the quantity of foreign exchange demanded due to an increased (decreased) demand for imported goods.

An *expected* decline (rise) in the exchange rate makes foreign assets less (more) attractive, relative to domestic assets and decreases (increases) the demand for foreign exchange.

A rise (fall) in domestic GNP increases (decreases) the demand for foreign exchange because as the domestic economy expands (contracts), the demand for imports rises (falls).

A rise (fall) in the domestic price level relative to the foreign price level increases (decreases) the demand for foreign exchange because it increases (decreases) the demand for imports.

A rise (fall) in domestic interest rates relative to foreign interest rates decreases (increases) the demand for foreign exchange because investors shift funds into domestic (foreign) assets.

Be sure you understand the economic reasoning for each of these effects.

IV
The Supply of Foreign Exchange

To understand the factors that determine the supply of foreign exchange, begin by recognizing that our supply of foreign exchange is the *foreign demand for dollars*. In our two-country world, our supply of foreign exchange (marks) is the German demand for foreign exchange (dollars). The factors that determine our supply of foreign exchange will be those that affect the German demand for foreign exchange. These are the same influences as those that determine U.S. demand for foreign exchange, except that they are now considered from the foreigner's perspective.

A
The Exchange Rate and the Supply of Foreign Exchange

Figure 37.3 shows the U.S. supply of foreign exchange curve (S^{fe}). The supply curve is upward sloping because a rise in the exchange rate makes our exports cheaper to German residents, causing them to import more from us. To do so, they buy more dollars and, therefore, the quantity of marks supplied rises. Recall that the exchange rate is the price of marks in terms of dollars; with a rise in the exchange rate, the Germans get *more* dollars per mark.[4] This is why our exports become cheaper to them.

---

[4]Note, however, that because they can get more dollars for each mark, it is *possible* that they supply fewer marks even though they buy more dollars. In drawing the supply curve upward sloping, we assume that the German demand for our exports rises sufficiently to cause them to spend more marks on our goods.

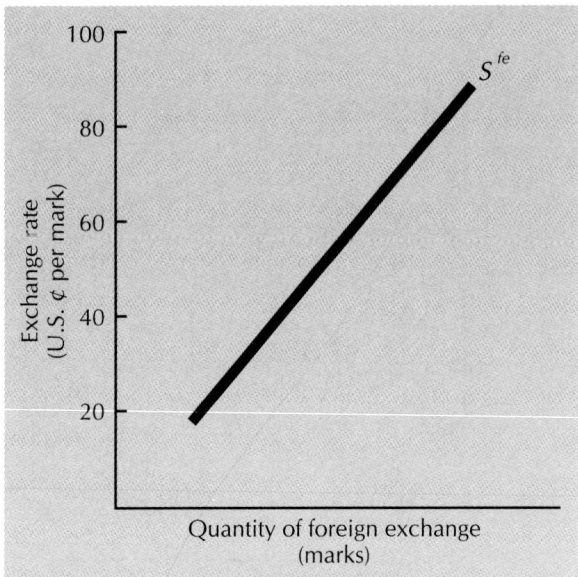

FIGURE 37.3   The Supply of Foreign Exchange

The supply curve for foreign exchange (S^{fe}) shows the quantity of foreign exchange (marks) supplied at each value of the exchange rate. The curve is upward sloping, indicating that the quantity of foreign exchange supplied rises as the exchange rate (the price of foreign exchange) rises.

B *all supply shift rt*

Other Influences on the Supply of Foreign Exchange

Other factors that affect the supply of foreign exchange are those that shift the supply curve. They change the supply of foreign exchange for a given exchange rate.

1. Expected Changes in the Exchange Rate We saw that an expected fall in the U.S. exchange rate made German assets (e.g., securities) less desirable and U.S. assets more desirable. Therefore the U.S. demand for foreign exchange fell as U.S. residents purchased fewer foreign assets. Conversely, the supply of foreign exchange increases as a result of an expected fall in the exchange rate, as German residents also switch to U.S. assets.[5] German residents would switch to the U.S. asset because if the U.S. exchange rate is expected to fall, this means that the dollar is expected to rise relative to the mark. This effect of an expected fall in the exchange rate is illustrated in Figure 37.4. The supply of foreign exchange curve (S^{fe}) shifts to the right from S^{fe}_0 to S^{fe}_1.

2. German GNP A rise in GNP in Germany increases the incomes of German residents and they increase consumer purchases, including purchases of U.S. exports (their imports). This shifts the supply of foreign exchange curve to the right as the Germans supply more foreign exchange (demand more dollars) to buy our goods.

3. The Price Level A rise in the German price level relative to the U.S. price level causes German residents to switch from purchases of German goods to U.S. goods. They therefore supply more foreign exchange (buy more dollars). The supply of foreign exchange curve shifts to the right.

4. The Interest Rate A fall in the German interest rate relative to the U.S. interest rate causes German residents to respond by switching from German securities to U.S. securities. The result is a shift to the right in the supply of foreign exchange curve as the Germans buy the dollars needed to buy our securities.

[5]U.S. residents who already hold foreign assets would also sell some of them, buy dollars, and switch to U.S. assets. This would further increase the supply of foreign exchange.

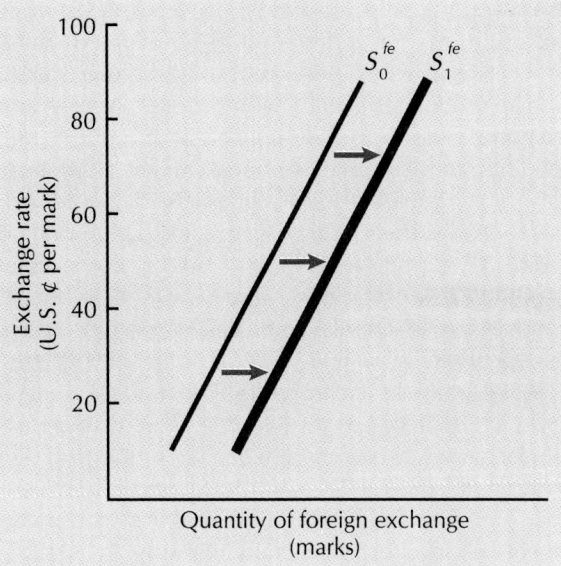

FIGURE 37.4 A Shift in the Supply of Foreign Exchange

An expected fall in the exchange rate (price of marks) makes foreign (German) assets less desirable relative to U.S. assets. The supply of foreign exchange increases as dollars are purchased to, in turn, buy U.S. assets.

■ CHECK YOUR BEARINGS

To see if you understand the factors that determine the supply of foreign exchange, try to explain the effects of changes in the opposite direction in the factors just considered; that is, explain how the supply of foreign exchange is affected by:

An expected rise in the U.S. exchange rate (price of the mark).

A fall in the German domestic price level relative to the U.S. price level.

A fall in German GNP.

A rise in the German interest rate relative to the U.S. interest rate.

V

Exchange Rate Determination: A Flexible Exchange Rate

In the previous section, we assumed that central banks did not *intervene* in the foreign exchange market—there were no official reserve transactions. All transactions in that market were autonomous (or independently motivated) ones. In this case, we would expect the exchange rate to move to clear the market, to equate supply and demand. Figure 37.5 depicts such an equilibrium position in the foreign exchange market. With supply and demand curves given by S_0^{fe} and D_0^{fe}, respectively, the market-clearing exchange rate (at point E) will be 40 cents (= 1 mark). A system of exchange rate determination where there is no central bank intervention is a **flexible exchange rate system** or, as it is sometimes called a *floating rate* system. An exchange rate system is a set of international rules governing the setting of exchange rates. A completely flexible or floating rate system is a particularly simple set of rules for central banks to follow; they do nothing to directly affect the level of their exchange rate.

In a flexible exchange rate system, the exchange rate responds to the forces of supply and demand. Movements in the exchange rate are caused by shifts in the supply and demand curves in the foreign exchange market, shifts which, in turn, are due to the factors discussed in the previous two sections. Let's look at two examples.

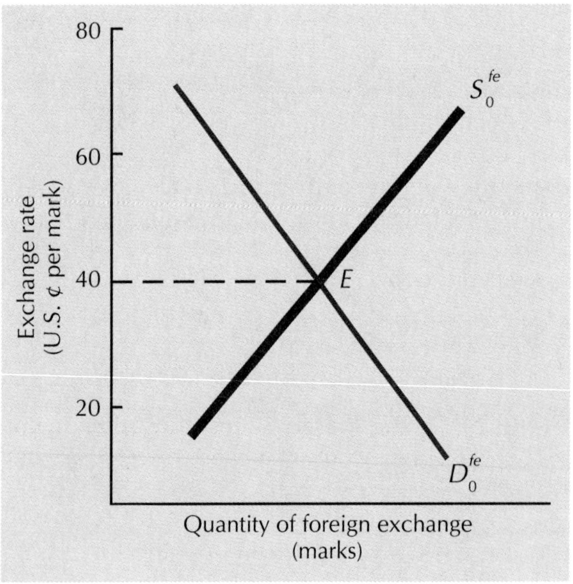

A

Effect of a Rise in the U.S. Price Level

Suppose that due to U.S. macroeconomic policy—for example, an expansion of the U.S. money supply—the U.S. price level rose relative to the German price level. As discussed in the previous two sections, the direct effects of this rise would be twofold. U.S. demand for German imports would rise, because they have become relatively less expensive, while German demand for our now more expensive exports would drop. The effect of this in the foreign exchange market is shown in Figure 37.6. The demand curve shifts to the right from D_0^{fe} to D_1^{fe}. (We buy more marks to buy more imports.) The supply curve shifts to the left from S_0^{fe} to S_1^{fe}. (Germans supply fewer marks to buy fewer of our exports.)

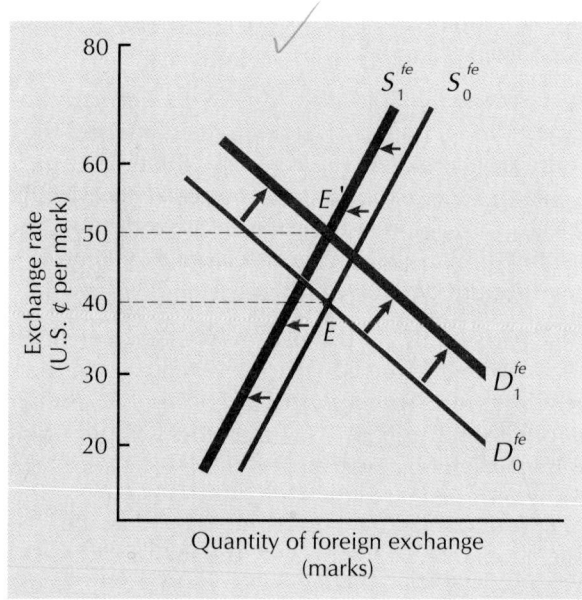

FIGURE 37.6   The Effect of a Rise in the U.S. Price Level

A rise in the U.S. price level relative to the German price level increases the U.S. demand for imports; the demand curve for foreign exchange shifts out to the right (from D_0^{fe} to D_1^{fe}). The rise in the U.S. price level also reduces the German demand for U.S. exports; the supply of foreign exchange curve shifts to the left (from S_0^{fe} to S_1^{fe}). With a flexible exchange rate, the equilibrium exchange rate rises, from 40 to 60 cents.

FIGURE 37.5   Exchange Rate Determination: Flexible Exchange Rate

In a flexible exchange rate system, the exchange moves to equate supply and demand in the foreign exchange market. With the supply and demand curves governed by S_0^{fe} and D_0^{fe}, the equilibrium exchange rate is 40 cents (= 1 mark) at point E.

At the initial exchange rate of 40 cents (= 1 mark), there is now an *excess demand* for foreign exchange. In a flexible exchange rate system, the exchange rate (price of the mark) will rise to clear the market. In Figure 37.6 we assume that the exchange rate rises from 40 cents (= 1 mark) to 50 cents (= 1 mark). We move from point E to point E'.

The rise in the exchange rate causes a decline in the quantity of imports demanded by U.S. residents because the *dollar price* of German goods is higher at the higher exchange rate. Also, the quantity of U.S. exports demanded by German residents rises because with the rise in the exchange rate (value of the mark), our exports become cheaper to them. A rise in the exchange rate to 50 cents is just sufficient to return the foreign exchange market to equilibrium, with demand equal to supply.

B

Effect of a Rise in the U.S. Interest Rate

Next, consider the effect of a rise in the U.S. interest rate relative to the German interest rate, caused, for example, by a restrictive U.S. monetary policy that lowers the U.S. money supply. Initially, suppose that the supply and demand curves in the foreign exchange market are given by S_0^{fe} and D_0^{fe} in Figure 37.7. The initial equilibrium exchange rate is 40 cents (= 1 mark).

The rise in the U.S. interest rate makes U.S. securities more attractive relative to German securities. As investors buy more U.S. securities the supply of foreign exchange curve (demand for dollars) shifts to the right (from S_0^{fe} to S_1^{fe}). As investors purchase fewer German securities, the demand for foreign exchange (marks) curve shifts to the left (from D_0^{fe} to D_1^{fe}). The effect of these shifts is a *fall* in the U.S. exchange rate. In Figure 37.7, the exchange rate is assumed to fall from 40 cents (= 1 mark) to 30 cents (= 1 mark). We move from point E to point E''.

We could consider further examples of events that would lead to adjustments in the exchange rates—changes in foreign or domestic GNP or changes in expectations about exchange rate movements, for example. But the preceding examples bring out the central point: *in a system of flexible exchange rates, market forces expressed*

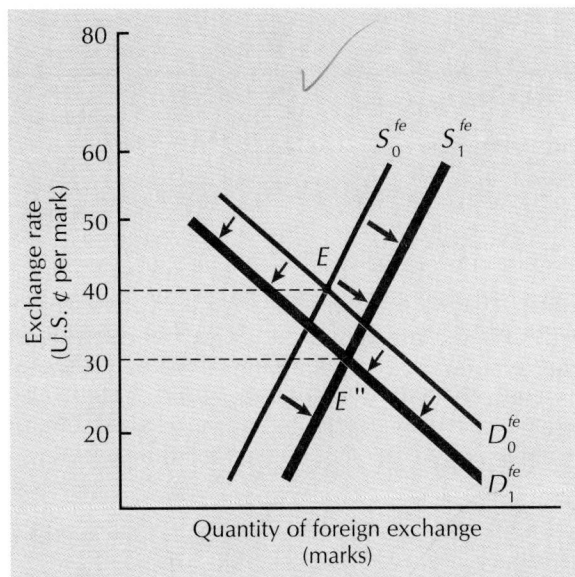

FIGURE 37.7   *The Effect of a Rise in the U.S. Interest Rate*

A rise in the U.S. interest rate of interest relative to the German rate of interest makes U.S. securities more attractive to German securities. As investors buy more U.S. securities, the U.S. supply of foreign exchange curve shifts to the right (from S_0^{fe} to S_1^{fe}). As investors buy fewer German securities, the U.S. demand for foreign exchange curve shifts to the left (from D_0^{fe} to D_1^{fe}). With a flexible exchange rate, the equilibrium exchange rate falls from 40 to 30 cents (we move from point E to point E'').

through supply and demand in the foreign exchange market determine a nation's exchange rate.

C

Greater Exchange Rate Flexibility

In the 1970s, the United States and other major industrialized countries moved toward greater flexibility in exchange rates. Still, the current exchange rate system is not one of *complete* exchange rate flexibility. To various degrees during the 1970s and 1980s, central banks, including the U.S central bank, have intervened in the foreign exchange market to affect their exchange rates. In the next section, we consider exchange rate systems where central banks do intervene in foreign exchange markets: a *fixed rate system* and a *managed floating rate system*.

VI

Exchange Rate Determination: A Fixed Exchange Rate or a Managed Float

As noted previously, an exchange rate system is a set of rules organizing exchange rate determination. In a *fixed* exchange rate system or a *managed float,* where central banks intervene in foreign exchange markets, the exchange rate system also specifies which assets are to be used as official reserve assets (the assets used for intervention).

A   *1945-1971*
Fixed Exchange Rates

An example of a fixed exchange rate system was the post–World War II *Bretton Woods system.* The international monetary agreements that comprised this system were negotiated near the end of the war at Bretton Woods, New Hampshire. The *International Monetary Fund (IMF)* was set up to administer the system.

According to the rules of the system, the United States was to set a par value for the dollar in terms of gold. Originally this par value was $35 per ounce of gold. The United States agreed to maintain convertibility between the dollar and gold at the fixed price. This meant that the United States would buy or sell gold at $35 per ounce. Other countries that adhered to the system—and this eventually included all the major free market economies—agreed to maintain convertibility with the dollar and other currencies, but not with gold. This meant, for example, that the British central bank would buy or sell dollars at a fixed price, originally $2.80 equal to 1 pound, but was not committed to buy or sell gold at any price. Notice that every country fixing the value of its currency relative to the dollar fixes the value of each currency relative to every other currency (e.g., if 1 pound = $2.80 and 1 German mark = $0.40, then 1 pound = 7 marks). The Bretton Woods system was one of fixed rates for all adherents to the agreement.

The dollar was central to the system, and dol-

lars, along with gold, were the major reserve assets that central banks held for international transactions. Later (in 1967) another reserve asset, special drawing rights (SDRs) at the IMF, were added. SDRs are essentially a form of "paper gold," a world currency unit for use by central banks.

1. Pegging the Exchange Rate   To see how a central bank maintains a fixed exchange rate— what is called *pegging* its exchange rate—let us go back to our two-country example, where we used Germany as representative of the rest of the world.[6] In this case, pegging the exchange rate means maintaining a fixed price of the mark, which we assume to be 40 cents = 1 mark. The working of the foreign exchange market with this fixed exchange rate is illustrated in Figure 37.8.

We assume that the official fixed exchange rate of 40 cents (= 1 mark) is below the market-clearing rate, assumed to be 50 cents. In such a situation, the dollar is said to be *overvalued* and the mark is said to be *undervalued,* meaning that if exchange rates were flexible (market determined), the value of the mark would rise while that of the dollar would fall. What prevents this from happening in a fixed exchange rate system such as the Bretton Woods system?

Here is where central bank intervention comes in. If the United States were committed to maintaining an exchange rate of 40 cents = 1 mark, the U.S. central bank must stand ready to enter the foreign exchange market and buy or sell marks at that rate. In the situation depicted in Figure 37.8, with the official exchange rate below the equilibrium rate, there is an excess demand for foreign exchange (marks), shown as XD_{fe} in the figure. To keep the exchange rate from rising, the U.S. central bank must supply marks (foreign exchange), i.e., it must exchange marks for dollars in the foreign exchange market.

Alternatively, the German central bank might be the one to intervene. This bank would supply marks (sell marks and buy dollars) to satisfy the

---

[6]We discuss the pegging of exchange rates here as if a country maintains an *exact* exchange rate. Such precision is not, in fact, possible. The Bretton Woods system allowed for a range of 1 percent in either direction from the par value. Pegging meant keeping the currency value in this narrow range.

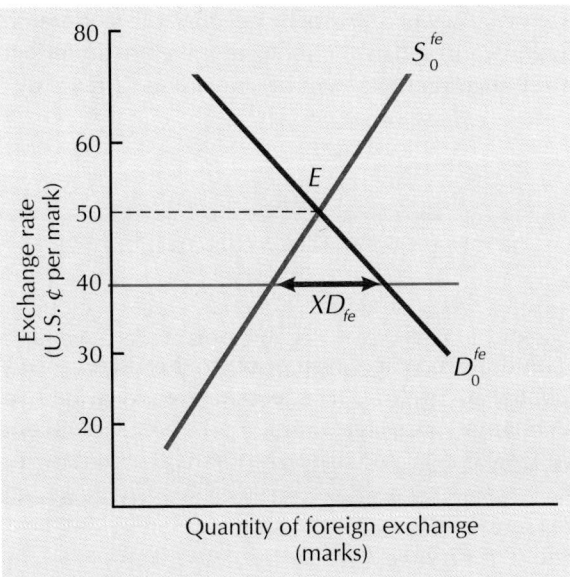

FIGURE 37.8   Pegging the Exchange Rate

The official par value of the exchange rate is 40 cents (= 1 mark). This is below the equilibrium (or market) clearing rate of 50 cents at point E. There is therefore an excess demand for foreign exchange (marks), shown as XD_{fe}. To maintain the official exchange rate, either the U.S. or the German central bank must intervene in the foreign exchange market and supply this quantity of foreign exchange.

excess demand for marks and keep the price of the mark at the official exchange rate of 40 cents.

2. Implications of Intervention   There are two points to note concerning central bank intervention. The first concerns the effect on the U.S. balance of payments as a result of intervention in the foreign exchange market. Suppose it is the U.S. central bank that intervenes. Where does it get the marks that it sells to keep the exchange rate (price of the mark) from rising? (The Germans would be quite upset if we just printed some up.) Our central bank must use up its international reserve assets to buy marks from the German central bank in order to sell them in the foreign exchange market. This would show up in Table 37.1 as a reduction in U.S. official reserve assets.

If, alternatively, the German central bank supplied the marks directly in the foreign exchange

market to satisfy the U.S. excess demand for foreign exchange, it would end up with increased holdings of dollars. In the U.S. balance of payments (Table 37.1), this would show up as an increase in foreign official assets in the United States. The sum of these two items (a reduction in U.S. official reserve assets and an increase in foreign official assets in the United States) equals the U.S. balance of payments *deficit*. This is a deficit because it is the amount by which our spending abroad (demand for foreign exchange) exceeds our earnings from abroad (supply of foreign exchange), taking account of only autonomous transactions (those reflected in the D^{fe} and S^{fe} curves). This deficit must be financed by central bank intervention if the official exchange rate is to be maintained.

Conversely, if, at the official exchange rate, the supply of foreign exchange exceeds the demand (there is an excess supply of foreign exchange), a country will have a surplus in the balance of payments. In this case, earnings from sales to foreign residents that produce the supply of foreign exchange exceed U.S. residents' expenditures abroad. When this is true for the United States, our official reserve assets increase or foreign official reserve assets in the United States decrease.

The second point to note about central bank intervention is that countries that must intervene continually to finance deficits will run out of official reserve assets. In our example, it is clear that if the United States financed its deficits by reductions in U.S. official assets, it would eventually exhaust its reserve holdings. But what if the deficit were financed by the German central bank, increasing its reserve assets in the United States by buying dollars? If the Germans continued to hold dollars, it would not affect our reserves. Under the Bretton Woods agreement, however, if they wished, the Germans could request that the U.S. buy back the dollars, using reserve assets (gold and SDRs). If they do, our reserves then fall.

To an extent, the United States was able to run continual balance of payments deficits during the Bretton Woods period because foreign central banks did not ask us to buy back dollars they had acquired in foreign exchange market interventions. At first, they did not do so because they wanted the dollars, which served as a reserve asset for them. (Remember, they were committed to maintaining the convertibility between their currency and the dollar.) Later on they did not ask us to redeem our dollars because they knew we couldn't do it; foreign dollar holdings far exceeded our reserves. This situation contributed to the collapse of the system, as we will see.

Countries other than the United States, Belgium for example, could not run persistent deficits without losing their reserves more quickly. Since their currency, the Belgian franc, was not used as a reserve asset, other central banks would expect the Belgian government to buy back quickly the francs they obtained in foreign exchange market intervention. To do so, Belgium would have to use up its official reserves (gold, SDRs, and U.S. dollars).

■ CHECK YOUR BEARINGS

Let us summarize our discussion of exchange rate determination with fixed exchange rates:

1. A fixed exchange rate system is one where exchange rates are set at official par values by international monetary agreement. The agreement also specifies the assets that serve as official reserve assets.

2. Countries agree to defend those values by intervening in foreign exchange markets.

3. Intervention by a country with an excess demand for foreign exchange (an overvalued currency and a balance of payments deficit) will deplete that country's official reserve assets. Countries cannot have persistent deficits without running out of official reserve assets.

B
A Managed Float

A *managed,* or *dirty, float* contains elements of a flexible exchange rate system (the float part) and a fixed rate system (the managed part). For a country with a managed float, the exchange rate is allowed to move in response to market forces. At times, however, the central bank does intervene to prevent *undesirable* or *disruptive* movements in the exchange rate. The question of how an undesirable or disruptive movement in the exchange

rate has been defined in practice, and therefore when central banks choose to intervene in foreign exchange markets, will be considered presently.

VII
The Current Exchange Rate System

The Bretton Wood system of fixed exchange rates collapsed in 1971. The current world system of exchange rate determination is best described as a managed float for major industrialized countries. Developing nations often have fixed exchange rate systems, although some allow exchange rate flexibility of varying degrees.

A
Current Exchange Rate Arrangements

Table 37.2 gives details of the exchange rate arrangements (or systems) for many of the countries of the world. Countries that have an entry in the column labeled "Exchange Rate Pegged to" have fixed exchange rates. These are primarily developing countries. What they peg their currency to varies from country to country, as can be seen from the table.

The major industrialized European countries, as well as Canada, Japan, and the United States, all have entries in the "Exchange Rate Otherwise Determined" column, meaning that they do not have a pegged exchange rate. The major continental European countries (see table footnote 7) are members of the European Monetary System. They do peg their exchange rates relative to one another, but these rates float as a group relative to other world currencies. Britain, Canada, Japan, and the United States all have a floating exchange rate, but it is a managed float in that they all intervene at times in the foreign exchange market.

Table 37.2 also shows the exchange rate for each currency as of March 31, 1988. For countries with a fixed rate, the rate given is the price of the foreign currency unit to which the exchange rate is pegged (e.g., for Benin, which pegs to the French franc (F), the exchange rate is expressed as 50

Benin francs = 1 French franc). Otherwise the exchange rate is expressed as the price of the U.S. dollar in terms of the domestic currency (e.g., approximately 1.35 Australian dollars = 1 U.S. dollar).

B

How Much Managing? How Much Floating?

In a managed float, central banks intervene in foreign exchange markets to prevent undesirable or disruptive movements in their exchange rates. Otherwise their exchange rates float. In the 1970s and 1980s, the degree to which the major industrialized countries intervened in the foreign exchange market varied significantly.

In the United States during the 1970s, there were frequent interventions in the foreign exchange market by the U.S. central bank. For example, in November 1978 there was a massive support program for the price of the dollar coordinated by the U.S. government. In 1981 the Reagan administration announced that there would be central bank intervention only when necessary to prevent disorder in the foreign exchange market initiated by crisis situations following events such as the shooting of President Reagan, the assassination of Egypt's President Sadat, or the declaration of martial law in Poland. Following this shift in the interpretation of what constituted a disruptive movement in the exchange rate, there was a marked decline in U.S. intervention in the foreign exchange market. During the first Reagan administration, there were periods of several quarters in which _no_ intervention took place.

Even in the absence of U.S. central bank intervention, the price of the dollar does not float freely with the current exchange rate system. This is true because foreign central banks buy or sell dollars to influence the price of their currencies relative to the dollar. For example, in 1981, 1984, and 1986, European central banks sold dollars from their reserve holdings to slow the rise in the price of the dollar, which would have meant a fall in the price of their currencies (a rise in their exchange rate relative to the dollar). More recently, in 1987 and 1988, foreign central banks intervened and _bought_

dollars in order to halt the fall of the dollar. In 1987 and early 1988 the U.S. Federal Reserve System also intervened to prop up the value of the dollar (keep the U.S. exchange rate from rising).

C

The Breakdown of the Bretton Woods System

We see from Table 37.2 that the current international monetary system is quite disorganized. Some call it a _nonsystem_ and suggest a new Bretton Woods-type conference to reorganize it. How did this disorganization come about? In other words, what process led to the breakdown of the Bretton Woods fixed exchange rate system?

Central to the Bretton Woods system was the set of fixed exchange rates and the key currency role of the dollar. Par values set for currencies were not assumed to be fixed for all time; the Bretton Woods system was to be one of adjustable pegs. A country was to be able to change its exchange rate if it found that there was a _fundamental disequilibrium_ in its balance of payments.

In fact, adjustments in exchange rates proved extremely difficult. Countries with persistent surpluses were under no pressure to revalue their currencies. Countries with persistent deficits found it politically difficult to devalue, since a decline in the value of the currency was taken as a sign of the failure of a government's economic policy. Also, rumors that a currency was to be devalued led to waves of speculation against the currency, as speculators sold the currency with an eye to buying it back after it had been devalued. Because of these difficulties in making adjustments in the par values of currencies, over the Bretton Woods period some countries (e.g., Great Britain) developed chronic balance of payments deficits and others (e.g., Germany) chronic surpluses.

Most damaging to the system, the United States developed into a chronic deficit country, an indication that the dollar was overvalued. To devalue the dollar—which, since the dollar was convertible into gold at the fixed par value, meant a rise in the price of gold—presented special difficulties because of the key currency role played by the dol-

TABLE 37.2   Exchange Rates and Exchange Arrangements, March 31, 1988

Member (currency)	Exchange Rate Pegged to[1]	Exchange Rate[1]	Exchange Rate Otherwise Determined[2,3]
Afghanistan (afghani)[4]	$	50.60	
Algeria (dinar)[4]	bskt	5.2971	
Antigua and Barbuda (EC$)[5]	$	2.70	
Argentina (austral)[4]			5.275
Australia (dollar)			1.35355
Austria (schilling)	bskt	11.661	
Bahamas, The (dollar)[4]	$	1.00	
Bahrain (dinar)[6]			0.376
Bangladesh (taka)[4]	bskt	31.50	
Barbados (dollar)	$	2.0113	
Belgium (franc)[4,7]			34.7225
Belize (dollar)	$	2.00	
Benin (franc)	F	50.00	
Bhutan (ngultrum)	Re	1.00	
Bolivia (boliviano)			2.29
Botswana (pula)	bskt	1.6935	
Brazil (cruzado)[8,9]			113.98(3/30)
Burkina Faso (franc)	F	50.00	
Burma (kyat)	SDR	8.50847	6.13316
Burundi (franc)	SDR	181.60	130.903
Cameroon (franc)	F	50.00	
Canada (dollar)			1.2341
Cape Verde (escudo)	bskt	68.465	
Central African Republic (franc)	F	50.00	
Chad (franc)	F	50.00	
Chile (peso)[4,8,9]			244.57
China (renminbi)[4]			3.7221
Colombia (peso)[9]			280.09
Comoros (franc)	F	50.00	
Congo (franc)	F	50.00	
Costa Rica (colón)[4]			73.45
Côte d'Ivoire (franc)	F	50.00	
Cyprus (pound)	bskt	0.449944	
Denmark (krone)[7]			6.4075(3/30)
Djibouti (franc)	$	177.721	
Dominica (EC$)[5]	$	2.70	
Dominican Rep. (peso)			4.96
Ecuador (sucre)[4,10]	$		
Egypt (pound)[4]			0.70
El Salvador (colón)[4,10]	$		
Equatorial Guinea (franc)	F	50.00	
Ethiopia (birr)	$	2.07	
Fiji (dollar)	bskt	1.43947	
Finland (markka)[11]	bskt	3.994	
France (franc)[7]			5.625
Gabon (franc)	F	50.00	
Gambia, The (dalasi)			6.3950
Germany, Fed. Rep. of (deutsche mark)[7]			1.6593
Ghana (cei)[4]			260.00
Greece (drachma)			132.80
Grenada (EC$)[5]	$	2.70	
Guatemala (quetzal)[4]	$	1.00	
Guinea (franc)			445.00
Guinea-Bissau (peso)			974.29
Guyana (dollar)[4]	$	10.00	
Haiti (gourde)	$	5.00	
Honduras (lempira)	$	2.00	
Hungary (forint)	bskt	47.5843	
Iceland (króna)			38.90
India (rupee)[12]			12.953506
Indonesia (rupiah)			1660.00
Iran, Islamic Rep. of (rial)	SDR	92.30	66.5326
Iraq (dinar)	$	0.310857	
Ireland (pound)[7]			0.619694
Israel (new sheqel)	bskt	1.5596	
Italy (lira)[7]			1230.90
Jamaica (dollar)			5.48
Japan (yen)			125.40
Jordan (dinar)	SDR	0.387754	0.279505
Kenya (shilling)	bskt	17.02718	
Kiribati (dollar)	A$	1.00	
Korea (won)			746.20
Kuwait (dinar)	bskt	0.27318	
Lao People's Dem. Rep. (kip)[4]	$	10.00	
Lebanon (pound)			363.50
Lesotho (loti)[4]	R	1.00	
Liberia (dollar)	$	1.00	
Libya (dinar)[13]	SDR	0.383929	0.276747
Luxembourg (franc)[4,7]			34.7225
Madagascar (franc)[9]			1266.45
Malawi (kwacha)	bskt	2.4795	
Malaysia (ringgit)[11]	bskt	2.5638	
Maldives (rufiyaa)			8.50
Mali (franc)	F	50.00	
Malta (lira)	bskt	3.1255	
Mauritania (ouguiya)[10]			
Mauritius (rupee)	bskt	12.7903	
Mexico (peso)[4,10]			
Morocco (dirham)			7.95315
Mozambique (metical)	$	454.50	
Nepal (rupee)	bskt	21.90	
Netherlands (guilder)[7]			1.8630
New Zealand (dollar)			1.51057
Nicaragua (new córdoba)[4]	$	10.00	
Niger (franc)	F	50.00	
Nigeria (naira)			4.1925
Norway (krone)	bskt	6.29(3/30)	
Oman (rial Omani)	$	0.3845	
Pakistan (rupee)			17.6440
Panama (balboa)	$	1.00	
Papua New Guinea (kina)	bskt	0.88285	
Paraguay (guarani)[4,10]	$		
Peru (inti)[4]	$	33.00	
Philippines (peso)			21.016
Poland (zloty)	bskt	380.00	
Portugal (escudo)[9]			136.526
Qatar (riyal)[6]			3.64
Romania (leu)	bskt	13.96	
Rwanda (franc)	SDR	102.71	74.0364
St. Kitts and Nevis (EC$)[5]	$	2.70	
St. Lucia (EC$)[5]	$	2.70	
St. Vincent (EC$)[5]	$	2.70	
Sao Tome and Principe (dobra)	bskt	72.083	
Saudi Arabia (riyal)[6]			3.745
Senegal (franc)	F	50.00	
Seychelles (rupee)	SDR	7.2345	5.21484

Member (currency)	Exchange Rate Pegged to[1]	Exchange Rate[1]	Exchange Rate Otherwise Determined[2,3]
Sierra Leone (leone)	$	28.0702	
Singapore (dollar)	$	2.0069(3/30)	
Solomon Islands (dollar)	bskt	2.03293	
Somalia (shilling)	$	100.00	
South Africa (rand)[4]			2.12549
Spain (peseta)			111.433(3/30)
Sri Lanka (rupee)			30.8975
Sudan (pound)[4]	$	4.50	
Suriname (guilder)	$	1.785	
Swaziland (lilangeni)	R	1.00	
Sweden (krona)[14]	bskt	5.878	
Syrian Arab Rep. (pound)[4]	$	11.225	
Tanzania (shilling)	bskt	93.7303	
Thailand (baht)	bskt	25.15	
Togo (franc)	F	50.00	
Tonga (pa'anga)	A$	1.00	
Trinidad and Tobago (dollar)	$	3.61575	
Tunisia (dinar)			0.808709
Turkey (lira)[15]			1223.25
Uganda (new shilling)	$	60.00	
United Arab Emirates (dirham)[6]			3.671
United Kingdom (pound)			0.531971
United States (dollar)			1.00
Uruguay (new peso)			317.00
Vanuatu (vatu)	bskt	102.45	
Venezuela (bolívar)[4,10]	$		
Viet Nam (new dong)[4,10]	$		
Western Samoa (tala)	bskt	2.05973	
Yemen Arab Rep. (rial)	$	9.76	
Yemen, People's Dem. Rep. (dinar)	$	0.345399	
Yugoslavia (dinar)			1437.62
Zaïre (zaïre)			162.00
Zambia (kwacha)	$		8.00
Zimbabwe (dollar)	bskt	1.71615	

$	U.S. dollar	bskt	Currency basket other than SDR
F	French Franc	Re	Indian rupee
R	South African rand	A$	Australian dollar

Source: *IMF Survey*

[1] Rates and arrangements as reported to the Fund and in terms of currency units per unit listed; rates determined by baskets of currencies are in currency units per U.S. dollar.

[2] Market rates in currency units per U.S. dollar.

[3] Under this heading are listed those members that describe their exchange rate arrangements as floating independently or as adjusting according to a set of indicators (see footnote 9) and certain other members whose exchange arrangements are not otherwise described in this table. In addition, U.S. dollar quotations are given for the currencies that are pegged to the SDR and for those that participate in the European Monetary System (see footnote 7).

[4] Member maintains dual exchange markets involving multiple exchange arrangements. The arrangement shown is that maintained in the major market. A description of the member's exchange system as of December 31, 1986 is given in the *Annual Report on Exchange Arrangements and Exchange Restrictions, 1987.*

[5] East Caribbean dollar.

[6] Exchange rates are determined on the basis of a relationship to the SDR, within margins of ± 7.25 percent. However, because of the maintenance of a relatively stable relationship with the U.S. dollar, these margins are not always observed.

[7] Belgium, Denmark, France, the Federal Republic of Germany, Ireland, Italy, Luxembourg, and the Netherlands are participating in the exchange rate and intervention mechanism of the European Monetary System and maintain maximum margins of 2.25 percent (in the case of the Italian lira, 6 percent) for exchange rates in transactions in the official markets between their currencies and those of the other countries in this group.

[8] Member maintains a system of advance announcements of exchange rates.

[9] Exchange rates adjusted according to a set of indicators.

[10] Exchange rate data not available.

[11] The exchange rate is maintained within margins of ± 2.25 percent.

[12] The exchange rate is maintained within margins of ± 5 percent on either side of a weighted composite of the currencies of the main trading partners.

[13] The exchange rate is maintained within margins of ± 7.5 percent.

[14] The exchange rate is maintained within margins of ± 1.5 percent.

[15] The central bank establishes its selling rate daily and the buying rate is set at ½ of 1 percent below the selling rate. Commercial banks must use the central bank's selling rate, but are free to set their own buying rate.

lar within the Bretton Woods system. But the growing deficits in the U.S. balance of payments were creating a glut of dollars on the market. The problem became acute in the late 1960s and especially in 1971. Throughout the 1960s, the United States had had balance of payments deficits. As long as such deficits were not too large, foreign central banks were willing to hold the dollars created by them, since (as explained previously) the dollar served as a reserve currency. In this process, as described in Section VI, foreign central banks intervened in the foreign exchange market. They sold their currency, obtained dollars, and held them as an official reserve asset. Such dollar reserves, which constituted claims on the United States, rose from $21.0 billion in 1960 to $38.5 billion in 1968. To some extent, the deficits of the 1960s were also financed by a decline in U.S. official reserve assets. The U.S. official gold stock fell from $17.8 billion in 1960 to $10.9 billion in 1968.

In the late 1960s, the U.S. balance of payments position worsened. Severe inflationary pressure developed in the United States as a result of government spending on the Vietnam War, which was not adequately financed by increased taxes. This increased inflation worsened the U.S. balance of payments in the following way. We have seen how a rise in the domestic price level relative to the foreign price level increases the demand for foreign exchange (as domestic residents shift from domestic goods to imports) and decreases the supply of foreign exchange (as foreign residents shift demand away from our exports). In a flexible exchange system, as we have also seen, this leads to a rise in the exchange rate. In a fixed exchange rate system, it leads to an excess demand for foreign exchange and a balance of payments deficit (excess of expenditures abroad over earnings from abroad). Central banks must intervene to prevent the rise in the exchange rate. This was the process set in motion by the rise in the U.S. inflation rate in the late 1960s; our price level was rising relative to foreign price levels. By 1971 our balance of payments deficit had risen to $29.8 billion, much of it being financed by foreign central bank purchases of dollars (increases in their reserve assets).

Foreign central banks could not continue to absorb so many dollar reserves. Nor could they demand payment from the United States in gold, since the U.S. gold stock had fallen to $10.9 billion by 1968. The glut of dollars and the presumption that eventually the dollar would have to be devalued led to a lack of confidence in the dollar as an asset.

In 1972 the dollar was devalued and the price of gold increased to $38. A new set of par values for other IMF member currencies was established. Attempts to defend the new set of par values collapsed, however, by 1973. Again a surge of inflation in the United States and a loss of confidence in the dollar were proximate causes of the problems in maintaining a set of fixed currency values.

VIII
Fifteen Years of a Managed Float

How has the system of managed floating for the world's major currencies worked? How has the dollar fared? On the latter question, Figures 37.9 and 37.10 trace the course of the dollar from two perspectives. Figure 37.9 plots the U.S. exchange rate measure as the price of the mark for the years since 1973. Recall that the exchange rate is the price of foreign currency, so a rise in the exchange rate means a *fall* in the value of the dollar relative to a foreign currency, in this case the German mark.

Figure 37.10 reverses the perspective and plots a measure of the *value of the dollar* in terms of the other currencies. Also, here we use a broader measure of foreign currencies, an average of our trading partners with weights that reflect the importance of these other countries in our trade. In this figure, an upward movement in the plotted line represents a *rise* in the value of the dollar relative to the foreign currencies (a fall in the U.S. exchange rate).

Looking at either Figure 37.9 or 37.10, the time path of the value of the dollar breaks into three phases, which could be called the dollar's fall (1976–80), rise (1981–85), and fall again (1985–87).

A
The Dollar in Decline (1976–80)

Between 1976 and 1980, the U.S. exchange rate (measured by the price of the mark) rose by 39 percent (the dollar fell 39 percent relative to the mark). Viewed from the standpoint of the value of

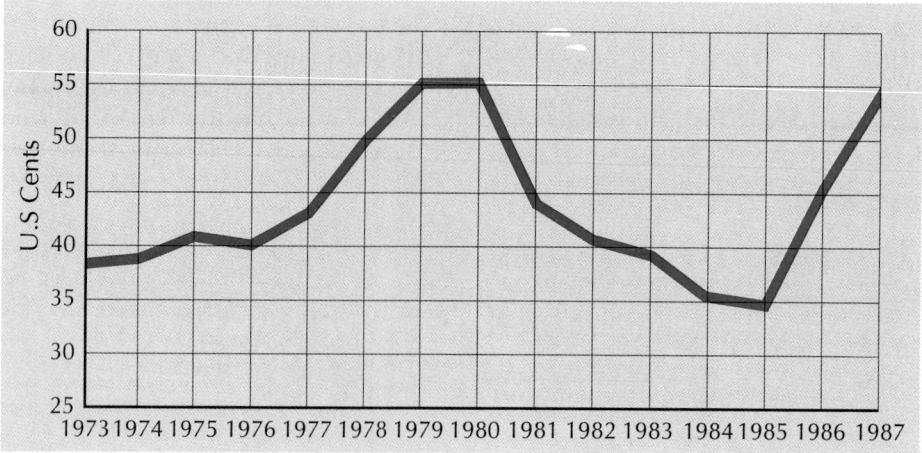

FIGURE 37.9 *Price of the German Mark (in U.S. Cents)*

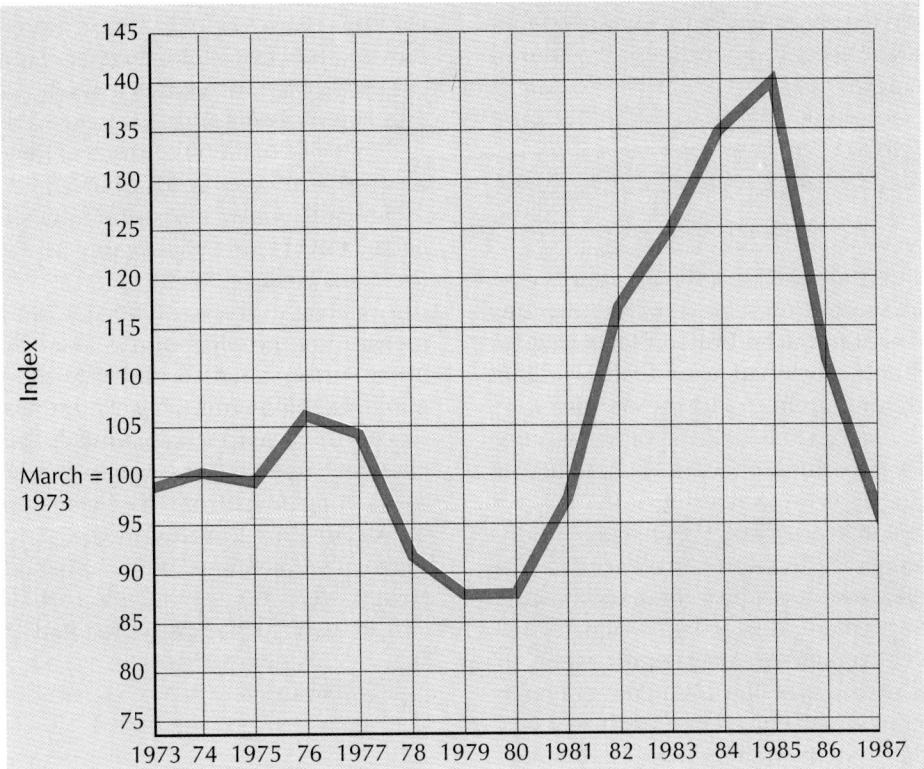

FIGURE 37.10 *Value of the U.S. Dollar*

the dollar relative to the broader weighted set of foreign currencies, the dollar also declined, but by a more modest 17 percent.

What caused the decline in the value of the dollar in this period? In Section V we saw that in a flexible exchange rate system a rise in the domestic price level relative to the foreign price level causes a country's exchange rate to rise (the value of its currency to fall). This follows because as domestic prices rise relative to foreign prices, the supply of foreign exchange falls (exports fall) and the demand for foreign exchange rises (imports rise). With this excess demand for foreign exchange, the exchange rate must rise to clear the foreign exchange market (see Figure 37.6).

One plausible explanation for the fall in the value of the dollar (rise in the U.S. exchange rate) between 1976 and 1980 is that U.S. domestic policies were more inflationary than those of Germany and several other of our important trading partners. The U.S. domestic price level was increasing relative to that of Germany and other important

trading partners. This explanation is consistent with the fact that the dollar fell most relative to the currencies of the countries that had the least inflation during the period (e.g., 39 percent relative to the German mark and 54 percent relative to the Swiss franc). The dollar fell less relative to countries whose inflation rates were closer to ours and even *rose* relative to some countries with higher inflation rates than ours. (The dollar, for example, rose 24 percent relative to the Italian lira.)[7]

It is true that the U.S. exchange rate was not completely flexible during these years. There was a managed float and, as discussed previously, the U.S. central bank did intervene frequently in the foreign exchange market in the 1970s. Still, during the 1970s and parts of the 1980s, while intervention by the U.S. and foreign central banks may have affected the exchange rate over short periods, over

[7]The Swiss and German inflation rates for 1975–80 were 2.3 and 4.1 percent, respectively. The U.S. inflation rate was 8.9 percent, while the Italian inflation rate was 16.3.

periods of several years such as those we are considering, market forces determined the movements of exchange rates.

B

The Super Dollar (1981–85)

Beginning in 1981, the dollar reversed course and began to rise sharply in value relative to other major currencies, as can be seen in Figure 37.10. This meant that our exchange rate *fell* over this period, as can be seen from Figure 37.9. Between 1980 and the peak in the dollar's value in early 1985, the mark fell from a price of 55 cents (fewer than 2 per dollar) to 31 cents (more than 3 per dollar), a drop of 44 percent. Against the trade-weighted average of foreign currencies (Figure 37.10), the dollar rose by 64 percent. In early 1985, pictures of Superman with a dollar sign on his chest began to appear on magazine covers. In Britain, there was fear of the ultimate economic disgrace: the pound sterling falling to a value less than the dollar.[8] What explains this phenomenal rise in the value of the dollar?

The U.S. inflation rate declined in the early 1980s, so that the forces that had been causing the dollar to fall were no longer at work. But inflation rates in other countries also fell in the 1980s, so a lower U.S. inflation rate does not seem to have been the main cause of the rise in the value of the dollar.

Still, as in the 1970s, many economists do see domestic macroeconomic policies as the cause of the changing value of the dollar. In the early 1980s, U.S. policy was characterized by an expansionary fiscal policy (see Section IV of Chapter 4), as evidenced by the large federal budget deficits of the period. Monetary policy was, for the most part, restrictive during these years. The result of a restrictive monetary policy and the financing needs caused by the budget deficit was that the U.S. interest rate was high relative to foreign interest rates during the early 1980s.

As we saw in Sections III and IV of this chapter, a rise in the U.S. interest rate relative to foreign inter-

[8]In fact, the value of the pound fell from $2.33 in 1980 to a low of $1.05 in February 1985.

est rates causes both domestic and foreign investors to shift from foreign financial assets to U.S. assets. To buy our financial assets, investors must first buy dollars, and the increased demand for dollars will push up the price of the dollar—push down the price of foreign currencies.

Our previous analysis also indicates that an *expected* fall in the exchange rate (rise in the value of the dollar) makes U.S. financial assets more attractive relative to foreign assets. A German investor, for example, would buy U.S. financial assets now because he expects the dollar to rise relative to the mark, enabling him to sell the asset later and receive more marks. In buying dollars (to buy U.S. financial assets), the German investor would be *speculating* on a future rise in the dollar's value. As the dollar rose in value in the early 1980s, such speculative buying of dollars pushed its value up further. Near its peak value in early 1985, speculation in favor of the dollar seemed to be the *only* factor explaining its rise.

Read Perspective 37A.

C

The Dollar's Slide (1985–87)

In October 1985, the finance ministers of five of the largest free market economies (the so-called G-5, or group of five) met at the Plaza Hotel in New York. At the meeting they agreed jointly to intervene in the foreign exchange market to bring down the value of the dollar. The central banks in these countries would do so by selling dollars from their reserve stocks (buying their own currencies) in the foreign exchange market, therefore increasing the supply of dollars (reducing the supply of foreign currencies) and driving the price of the dollar down.

Other factors were driving down the value of the dollar as well. Just as speculative buying of dollars had contributed to the rise of the dollar, with fear of central bank intervention and other signs of weakness, speculative selling began in 1986 to contribute to the dollar's fall. The dollar had risen so high that few believed its value was sustainable. Additionally, as the economic expansion in the United States slowed, monetary policy here became less restrictive and the U.S. interest rate fell.

PERSPECTIVE 37A
The World's Largest Debtor

To say that foreigners purchased our assets is to say that we borrowed from abroad. The federal government raises funds, for example, by selling bonds. When those bonds are purchased by foreign investors, they become part of our external (foreign) debt. U.S. corporations raise funds for investment by selling bonds and stocks (equities). If these are sold to foreign investors, they are also part of our external debt. Interest and dividends must be paid to foreign investors by both the government and U.S. corporations.

During the 1980s, foreign investors greatly increased their holdings of U.S. assets. U.S. investors did continue to buy foreign assets, but not as fast as foreign investors bought U.S. assets. As a result, our net investment position (U.S. holdings of foreign assets minus foreign holdings of our assets) went from one of a net creditor nation to that of a net debtor. This transition is charted in Figure 37.11. By the end of 1986, foreign holdings of our assets (our debt) exceeded U.S. holdings of foreign assets by $264

billion. The United States had become the world's largest debtor.

Should we worry? While few see cause for panic, many observers are concerned about the size of the U.S. external debt. The debt is still relatively small compared to the size of the U.S. economy. At the end of 1986, it was less than 7 percent of GNP. This compares to an external debt of 50 percent of GNP or more for large debtors among developing nations such as Brazil, Argentina, and Mexico. But one worrisome feature is the *rapid growth* in the U.S. net debtor position that can be seen in Figure 37.11. Estimates are that by the end of the 1980s the U.S. external debt will reach $500 billion, requiring interest payments of $35 billion annually. Another concern is that foreign investors will at some point pull out of U.S. assets. If there were a large *sudden shift* to foreign assets, our exchange rate would rise rapidly (as investors sold dollars) and our interest rate would rise (as firms and the government sought domestic lenders).

Relative to those of some European countries, U.S. financial assets were no longer so attractive.

By 1987, relative to the weighted average of foreign currencies (Figure 37.10), the value of the dollar had fallen 32 percent from its peak in 1985. In February the finance ministers met again, this time in Paris, and reached what has been called the *Louvre Accord*. They decided that the dollar had fallen far enough. They agreed to use foreign exchange market intervention to try to maintain their exchange rates within ranges around their then current values. At first these efforts were not successful and the value of the dollar continued to fall throughout 1987. In 1988, however, as central bank intervention continued, the value of the dollar stabilized.

IX
The Merits of Exchange Rate Flexibility

At the beginning of the previous section, two questions were posed: How has the dollar fared in the period of increased exchange rate flexibility, and how well has the system performed overall? We turn now to the latter question.

There are essentially two views on the performance of the exchange rate system since the collapse of the Bretton Woods system of fixed exchange rates. The first is that, given the strains to which the world economy was exposed during the

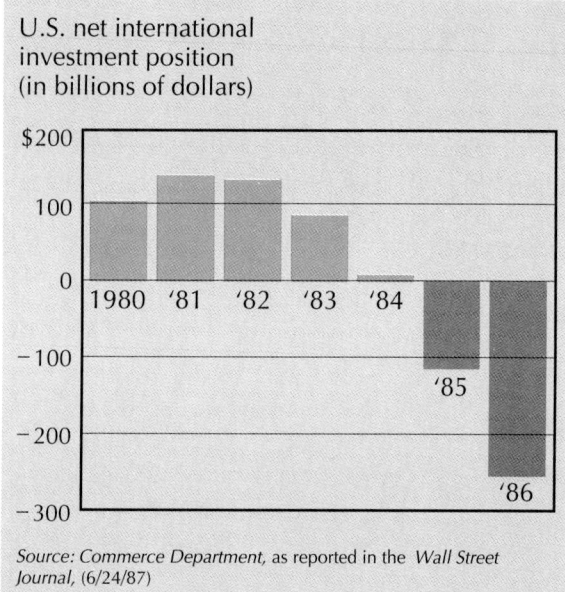

U.S. net international
investment position
(in billions of dollars)

Source: Commerce Department, as reported in the Wall Street Journal, (6/24/87)

FIGURE 37.11 **U.S. External Debt**

unstable and inflationary 1970s and during the recession and slowdown of inflation in the 1980s, the system of managed floating has worked well—not flawlessly, but well.

Others disagree, find the system unsatisfactory, and want a return to a system where major countries fix the value of their currencies. Some would like to see another Bretton Woods-style conference to establish a formal system of fixed exchange rates. A proposal with more widespread support is that countries should less formally announce **target zones** for their exchange rates and then intervene in the foreign exchange market to maintain the exchange rate within that range. The target zone might be varied every 6 months or every year, as circumstances require. The target zone proposal would formalize the type of agreement embodied in the *Louvre Accord*. Advocates of target zones for exchange rates see them as part of a program of *policy coordination* among the major industrialized nations. As nations jointly agree on target zones for exchange rates, advocates of this approach believe that they will agree on coordinated domestic monetary and fiscal policies.

Advocates of a formal or informal system to fix exchange rates (or ranges for exchange rates) argue that without such a mechanism exchange rates are too volatile—with damaging effects on the world economy. Swings in currency values such as those in the dollar in recent years pose large domestic adjustment problems. The large rise in the value of the dollar in the early 1980s, as foreigners bought dollars to, in turn, purchase U.S. financial assets, made U.S. exports expensive in foreign countries. Consequently, our exports declined and employment in the export industries suffered. The rise in the dollar also lowered import prices here. As a consequence, U.S. demand for imported goods (e.g., Japanese cars, VCRs, and TVs, German cameras, French wines, and Belgian chocolates) soared in the early 1980s—again with jobs lost in U.S. industries that competed against the imports.

By 1985, the U.S. trade deficit had climbed to $134 billion and the competitiveness of U.S. industry was a major issue. Then, as the value of the dollar fell—a fall that was especially sharp relative to the Japanese yen—foreign countries, particularly Japan, began to experience contractions in their export industries. The recovery of U.S. export- and import-competing industries began but was slow. Advocates of moving back toward fixed exchange rates argue that in this way such costly and painful adjustments can be avoided.

Defenders of the current system do not deny that exchange rates have been volatile, both in the short run (e.g., day-to-day variations) and in the long run, nor do they deny that there have been adjustment costs due to the large shifts in currency values that have occurred during the post-1973 period. They believe, however, that such swings are inevitable as long as countries pursue different domestic policies and therefore have diverging inflation rates, GNP growth rates, and interest rates. Moreover, such divergent policies seem inevitable because different governments have different domestic goals. Also, defenders of exchange rate flexibility argue that the system has helped the world economy to absorb shocks such as the huge rise in oil prices during the 1970s, which would have resulted in balance of payments crises in a system of fixed exchange rates. Overall, defenders of the current system (or nonsystem) argue, "If it ain't broke, don't fix it."

SUMMARY

In this chapter we discussed the monetary side of U.S. international economic activities. The main points covered were as follows:

1. The U.S. balance of payments accounts keep track of U.S. international economic transactions. The *current account* records imports and exports of goods and services, as well as international transfers. The *capital account* records capital inflows (purchases of U.S. assets by foreign residents) and capital outflows (purchases of foreign assets by U.S. residents). In recent years, the United States has had a large current account deficit balanced by a large capital account surplus. A final category of transactions in the balance of payments is *official reserve transactions*. These are purchases or sales of international reserve assets by the U.S. or foreign central banks. The aim of such transactions is to affect the U.S. exchange rate.

2. The exchange rate, expressed as the price of foreign currencies (foreign exchange) in terms of dollars, is determined in the foreign exchange market, where national currencies are traded for each other.

3. The U.S. demand for foreign exchange (ignoring official reserve transactions by central banks) is the U.S. demand for foreign currencies to be used to buy foreign goods, services, and assets. The quantity of foreign exchange demanded depends negatively on the exchange rate (the price of foreign exchange). The demand for foreign exchange also depends on expected future changes in the exchange rate, the U.S. GNP, the U.S. price level relative to foreign price levels, and U.S. interest rates relative to foreign interest rates.

4. The U.S. supply of foreign exchange (again ignoring official reserve transactions by central banks) is the foreign demand for U.S. dollars. The quantity of foreign exchange supplied depends positively on the exchange rate (the price of foreign exchange). The U.S. supply of foreign exchange also depends on future expected changes in the exchange rate, foreign GNP levels, foreign price levels relative to the U.S. price level, and foreign interest rates relative to U.S. interest rates.

5. In a *flexible exchange rate* system there is no intervention in the foreign exchange market by central banks. The exchange rate is determined by the supply of and demand for foreign exchange.

6. In a *fixed exchange rate* system, central banks do intervene in foreign exchange markets to *peg* their exchange rate at an agreed-upon *par value*. The Bretton Woods system set up at the end of World War II is an example of a fixed exchange rate system.

7. Since the collapse of the Bretton Woods system early in the 1970s, exchange rate determination for the major industrialized countries is best described as a *managed float*. For a country with a managed float, the exchange rate is at times allowed to move in response to market forces. At other times, however, the central bank does intervene in the foreign exchange market to prevent undesirable movements in the exchange rate.

8. During the period of managed floating, the time path of the value of the dollar breaks into three phases: a period when the dollar's value fell substantially (the U.S. exchange rate rose) (1976–80), a period when the value of the dollar rose sharply (1981–85), and another period of decline in the dollar's value (1985–87).

9. There is a controversy over the performance of the current system (or nonsystem) of exchange rate determination. Some believe that the system has worked tolerably well, considering the strains on the world economy in the 1970s and 1980s. Others believe that excessive volatility of exchange rates under the managed float has had large economic costs. They argue for more stability of exchange rates, achieved either through a return to fixed exchange rates or a less rigid system of *target zones* for exchange rates.

KEY TERMS

International monetary system
Balance of payments accounts
Merchandise trade balance
Current account
Capital account
Foreign exchange

Flexible exchange rate system
Intervention in foreign exchange markets
Fixed exchange rate system
Managed float
Bretton Woods system
Target zones

QUESTIONS AND PROBLEMS

1. If the U.S. balance of payments must balance, how can there be trade deficits?
2. What are capital inflows and how do they affect (a) the current account balance and (b) the capital account balance?
3. Who are the sellers in foreign exchange markets? Who are the buyers? Where is the U.S. foreign exchange market centered?
4. What is meant by central bank "intervention" in the foreign exchange market?
5. When an American buys a Swiss security whose price and yield are in francs, that American bears an exchange rate risk that she would not bear with a U.S. security. Explain why.
6. Explain why each of the following would shift the demand curve for foreign exchange to the right (an increase) and increase the exchange rate, ceteris paribus:
   (a) growing confidence that the value of the dollar (the domestic currency) will fall in foreign exchange markets;
   (b) rapid growth in domestic GNP;
   (c) a rise in domestic prices relative to foreign prices;
   (d) a drop in domestic interest rates relative to foreign interest rates.
7. In the U.S., the government has sometimes set price ceilings in product markets; similarly, it has set price floors for some products. Under the Bretton Woods system, the dollar was pegged (or fixed) in value relative to other currencies. How does pegging the value of a currency compare to setting a price ceiling or a price floor? Are the results the same? Explain.
8. Are exchange rates in the world today fixed or floating? Explain.
9. When and why did the Bretton Woods system collapse?
10. Explain why policy coordination among major industrialized nations would be essential in maintaining stable exchange rates over time.

38

Other Places, Other Systems, Other Problems

This book has analyzed the way that free-market economies function, problems they face, and policies designed to solve these problems. The focus has been on the problems that confront wealthy, highly industrialized economies such as those of the United States, Japan, and Western Europe. But most people don't live in countries with such economies.

Figure 38.1 shows a map of the world, with countries divided into five categories. The industrial market economies comprise a relatively small fraction (about 15 percent) of the world's population. The low- and middle-income economies, which are together called the **developing countries**, contain the bulk (roughly 70 percent) of the world's population. What is more, since the population growth rate is over three times higher in the developing than in the industrial countries, a growing proportion of the world's population will be living in these lower-income countries in the future.

Another category in Figure 38.1 is the East European **nonmarket economies.** In these **socialist** countries, the state owns the major nonhuman factors of production (capital and land), and central planning for the most part substitutes for markets as a means of allocating resources. Some of the developing countries are also nonmarket economies.

The final group in Figure 38.1 is the high-income oil exporters. These countries are in some respects like the developing countries, but their oil revenues provide them with a high standard of living.

One reason for focusing on the industrial market economies is that most of you readers live in one. A second justification, however, is made clear by Figure 38.2. This figure shows the countries of the world sized in proportion to their share of world output, measured by GNP. Even though two thirds of the world's population lives in the developing countries, over half of world production takes place in the industrial market economies.

In this chapter, we consider special features of developing economies and nonmarket socialist economies. We also look briefly at particular features of the high-income oil-exporting economies. These are very broad subjects, and we can deal only with a few of the most important points.

I

The Developing Countries

The central problem facing developing countries is poverty. Table 38.1 shows some basic statistics about conditions in developing and industrial countries. The table gives figures for population, the level of per capita GNP, the average annual growth rate in per capita GNP for 1965–85, and life expectancy. The developing countries are divided into three categories—upper-middle, lower-middle, and low-income—on the basis of their per capita income.

The table shows considerable differences in economic conditions even among the developing countries. Per capita income in Venezuela is more than 25 times higher than in Ethiopia and 20 times higher than in Bangladesh. Poverty is much more severe in the poorest countries, where most of the population exists at a bare subsistence level. In Ethiopia, for example, nearly 1 million people died from famine in 1984–85. Even in developing countries where income is not as low as in Ethiopia or Bangladesh, much of the population lives in extreme poverty; life expectancy is much lower than in the industrial countries (see the last column of Table 38.1); infant mortality rates are high; and educational opportunities are severely limited.

The income gap between the developing and industrial countries is huge. This is true even if the most extreme cases are avoided. GNP per capita in West Germany, for example, is more than 10 times greater than that in Turkey, 20 times greater than that in Indonesia, and 40 times greater than that in India.

The poverty problem is made worse by the extreme inequality of income distribution in the developing countries, inequality greater than that in the industrial countries. In Brazil, for example, the wealthiest 10 percent of the population receive 50.6 percent of the total income, in Peru 42.9 percent, and in Argentina 32.5 percent. Comparable figures for the United States, the United Kingdom, and West Germany are 23.3 percent, 23.4 percent, and 24.0 percent, respectively. With more income (and wealth) concentrated in the hands of the wealthiest group, the poverty of most of the people in developing countries is even greater than the per capita GNP figures indicate.

The low standard of living is a problem in a broader sense than the unsatisfactory material conditions in which most of the world's population now lives. Economic development would enrich the lives of the world's poor in other ways as well. In the words of one development economist:

The advantage of economic growth is not that wealth increases happiness, but that it increases the range of human choices. . . . The case for economic growth is that it gives man greater control over his environment, and thereby increases his freedom.[1]

II

Barriers to Economic Growth

Why are some nations poor and others rich? European countries were the first to experience industrialization, and with it sustained economic growth. However, just when and how the growth process began is a complex question:

It certainly began in Western Europe, though just where and when, whether in eighteenth, seventeenth or sixteenth century Britain or in the city states of Renaissance Italy or in the monasteries from the tenth century onward, depends on which aspect of the emergence of modern civilization one regards as crucial, the Industrial Revolution, the Newtonian view of the physical world, the rise of capitalism and

the Protestant ethic, or the very notion of rational and empirical enquiry.[2]

Development in Western Europe was a process with social, religious, philosophical, and political as well as economic aspects.

Countries that underwent this development process at a later date often did so to compete with and protect themselves from the industrial countries. Japan, for example, consciously pursued economic development in the late nineteenth century to increase its national power and ward off the industrial Western "barbarians." Recently, competition with unfriendly neighboring states has spurred economic development in South Korea and Taiwan.

If the forces that lead to economic development are varied and complex, what about the causes of underdevelopment? Why are some nations poor? In discussing conditions in developing countries, economists often refer to the **vicious circle of poverty,**

For example, a poor man may not have enough to eat; being underfed, his health may be weak; being physically weak, his working capacity is low, which means that he is poor, which in turn means that he will not have enough to eat, and so on. A situation of this sort, relating to a country as a whole, can be summed up in the trite proposition: "a country is poor because it is poor."[3]

To be more specific, let's examine more closely the linkages in this vicious circle of poverty as it pertains to some of the poorest nations.

There are three central elements in the process of economic development: **capital formation, technological advances,** and **growth in human capital.** Each of these presents significant barriers for poorer countries.

A
Capital Formation

Capital formation leads to growth because with more capital, in the form of buildings and ma-

[2]Ibid., p. 10.

[3]Ragnar Nurkse, *Problems of Capital Formation in Underdeveloped Countries* (New York: Oxford University Press, 1953), p. 4.

[1]Quoted from H. W. Arndt, *Economic Development: The History of an Idea* (Chicago: University of Chicago Press, 1987), p. 177.

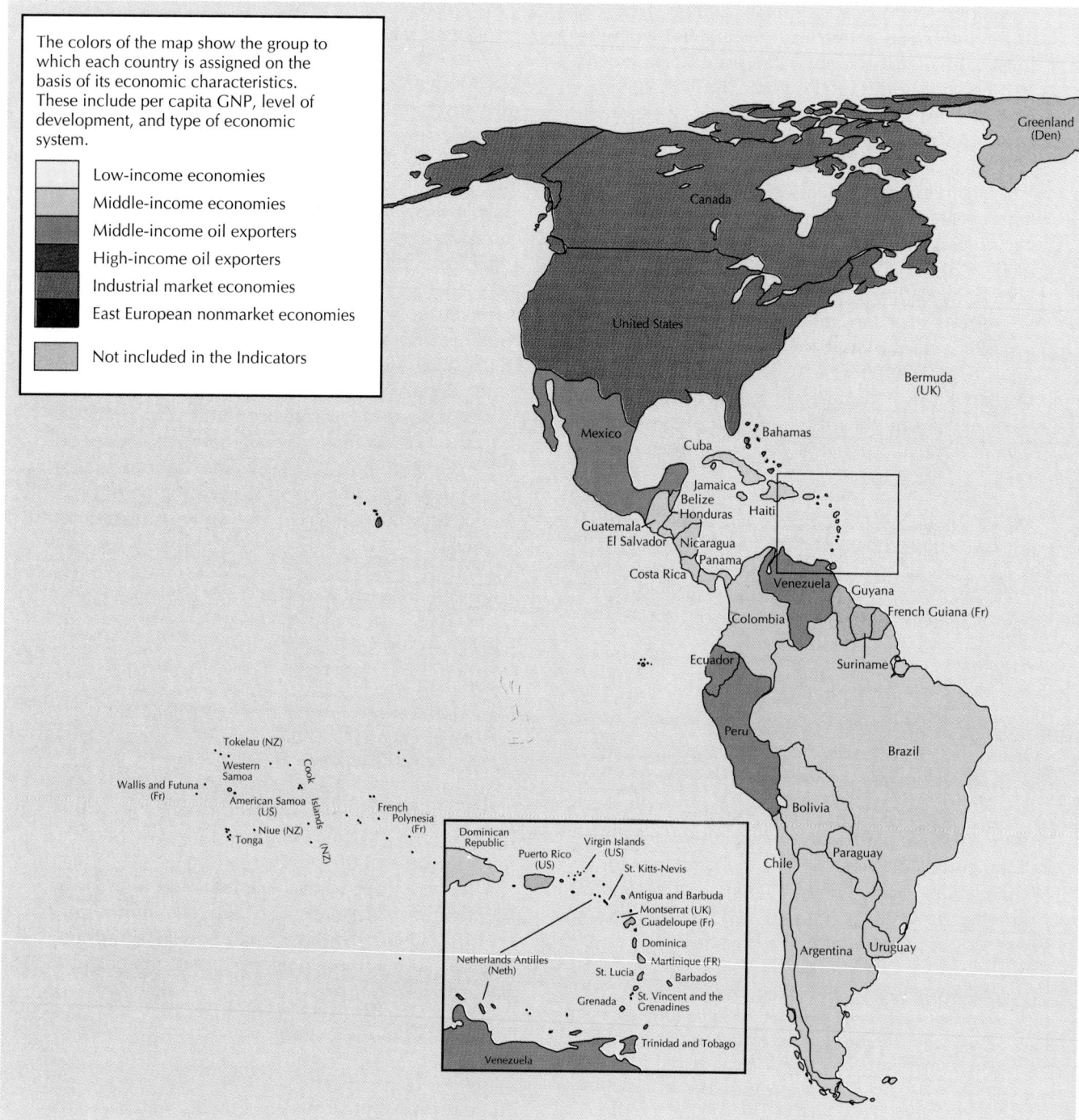

The colors of the map show the group to which each country is assigned on the basis of its economic characteristics. These include per capita GNP, level of development, and type of economic system.

- Low-income economies
- Middle-income economies
- Middle-income oil exporters
- High-income oil exporters
- Industrial market economies
- East European nonmarket economies

- Not included in the Indicators

FIGURE 38.1   Groups of Economies

(*Source: World Development Report 1984, published for The World Bank by Oxford University Press. © 1984 by the International Bank for Reconstruction and Development/The World Bank*)

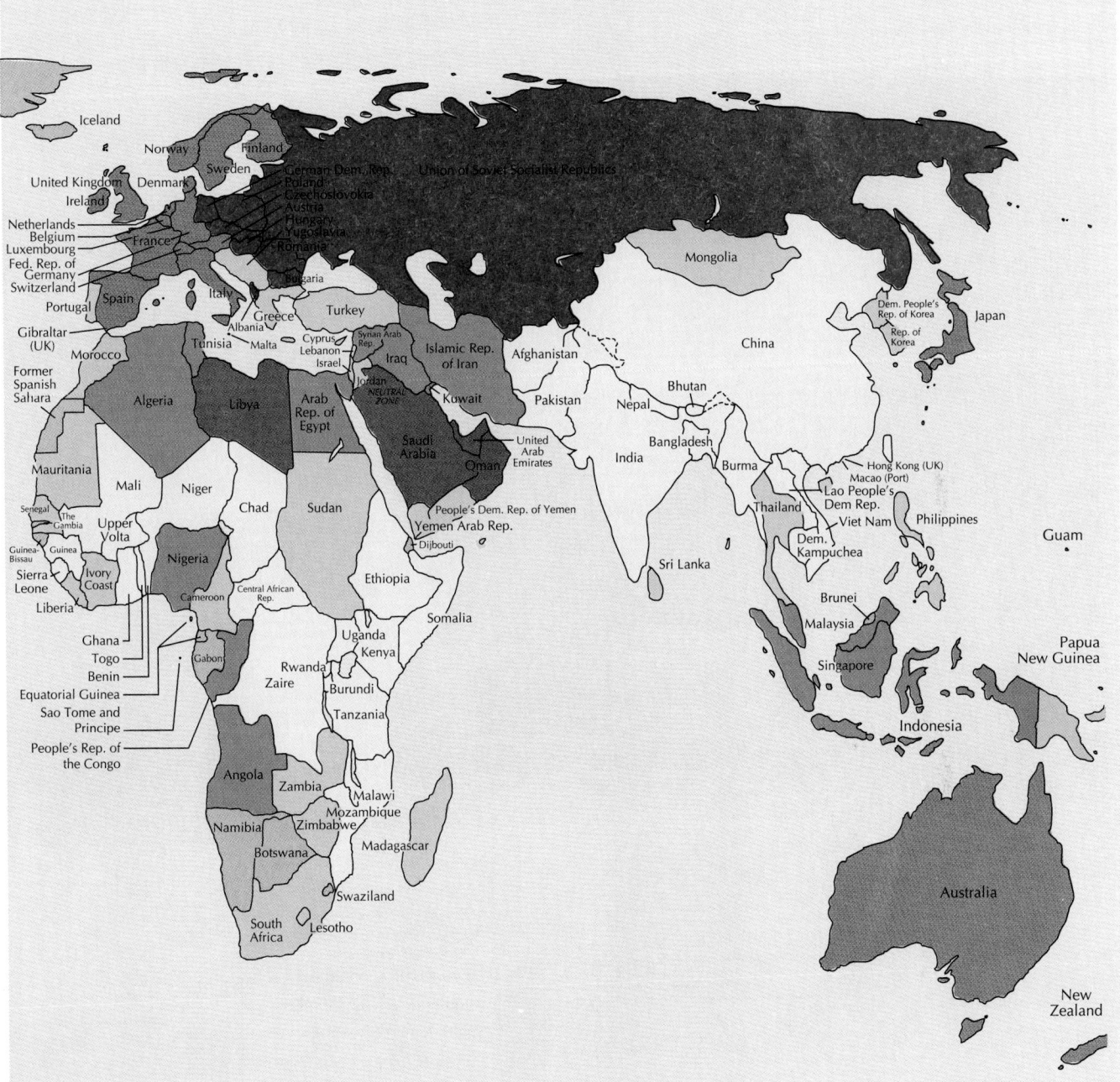

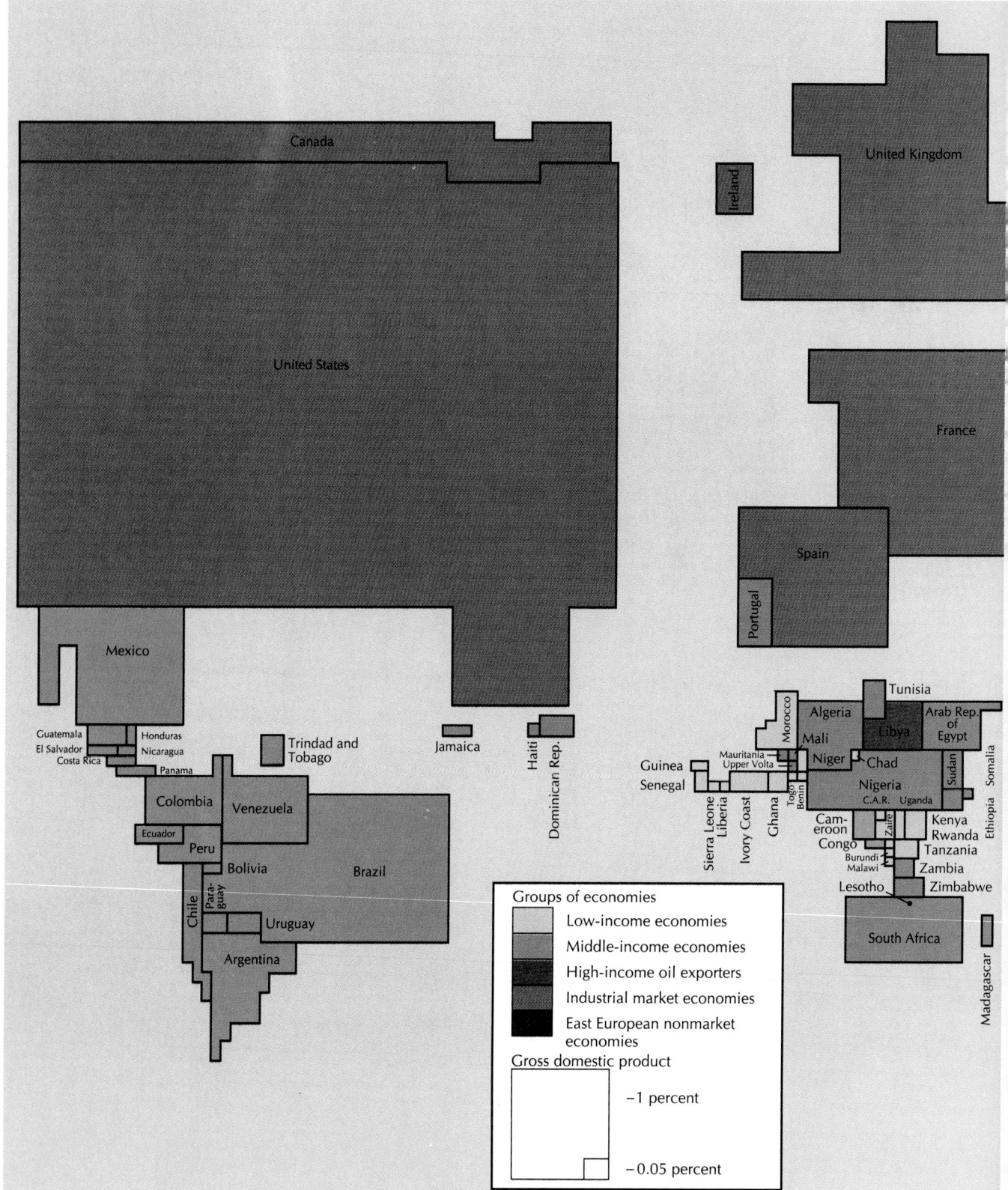

FIGURE 38.2   Distribution of Product Among Selected Countries, 1982

(Source: World Development Report 1984, published for The World Bank by Oxford University Press. © 1984 by the International Bank for Reconstruction and Development/The World Bank)

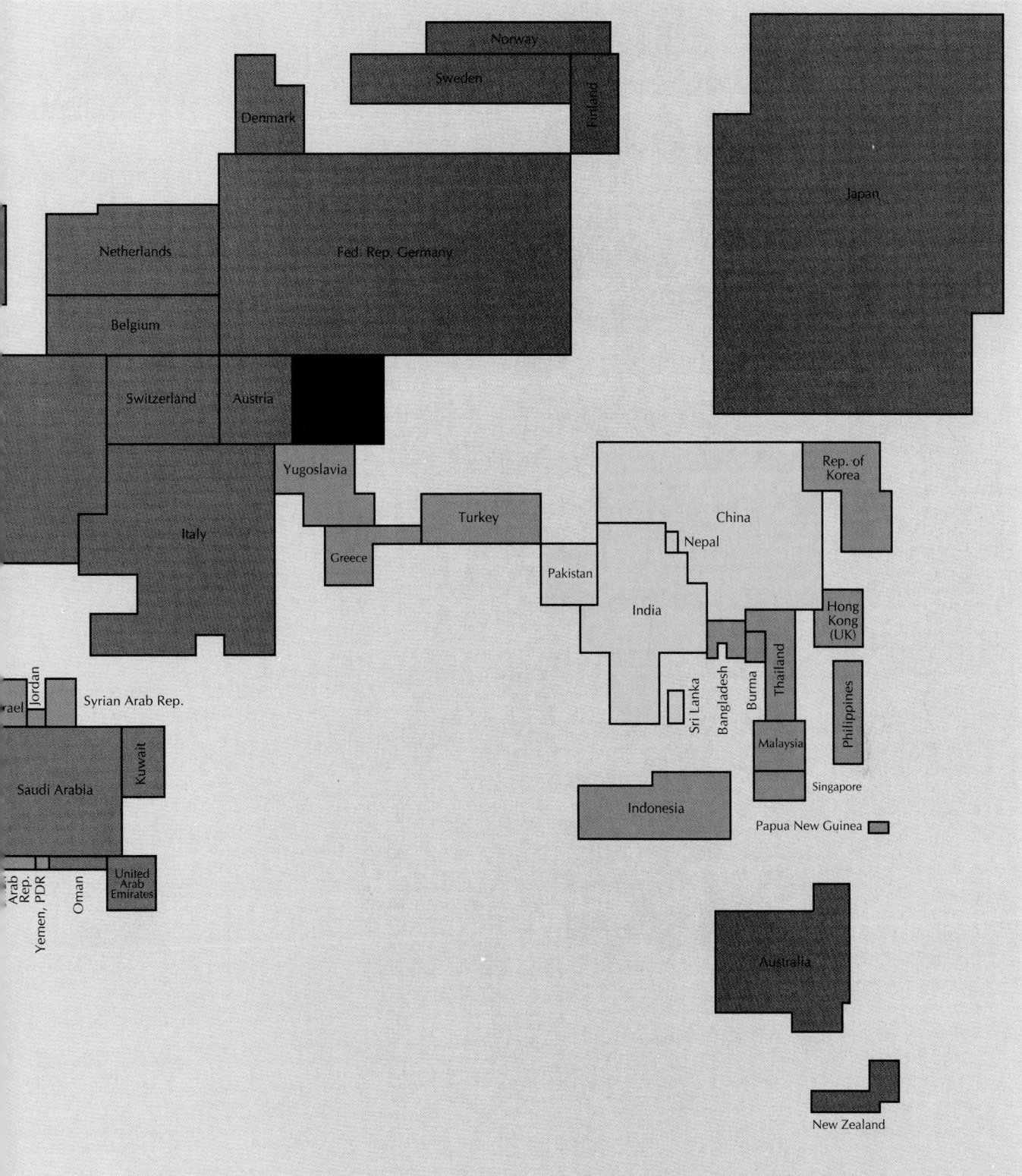

TABLE 38.1   Basic Indicators

Country	Population (Millions), 1985	GNP Per Capita		Life Expectancy; Years, 1985
		Level ($), 1985	Growth Rate, 1965–85	
Industrialized Market Economies				
United States	239.3	16,690	1.7	76
Switzerland	6.5	16,370	1.4	77
Norway	4.2	14,370	3.3	77
Canada	25.4	13,680	2.4	76
Sweden	8.4	11,890	1.8	77
Japan	120.8	11,200	1.8	77
W. Germany	61.0	10,940	2.7	75
Australia	15.8	10,820	2.0	78
France	55.2	9,540	2.8	78
United Kingdom	56.5	8,460	1.6	75
Italy	57.1	6,520	2.6	77
Developing Countries				
Upper-Middle-Income				
Venezuela	17.3	3,080	3.5	70
Korea	41.1	2,150	6.6	69
Argentina	30.5	2,130	0.2	70
Panama	2.2	2,100	2.5	72
Mexico	78.8	2,080	2.7	67
Malaysia	15.6	2,000	4.4	68
Portugal	10.2	1,970	3.3	74
Uruguay	3.0	1,650	1.4	72
Brazil	135.6	1,640	4.3	65
Lower-Middle-Income				
Colombia	28.4	1,320	2.9	65
Tunisia	7.1	1,090	4.0	63
Turkey	50.2	1,080	2.6	64
Cameroon	10.2	810	3.6	55
Thailand	51.7	800	4.0	64
Nigeria	99.7	800	2.2	59
Nicaragua	3.3	770	−2.1	59
Egypt	48.5	610	3.1	61
Philippines	54.7	580	2.3	63
Indonesia	162.2	530	4.8	55
Low-Income				
Zambia	6.7	390	−1.6	52
Pakistan	96.2	380	2.6	51
Ghana	12.7	380	−2.2	53
China	1040.3	310	4.8	69
Sudan	21.9	300	n.a.	48
Kenya	20.4	290	1.9	54
India	765.1	270	1.7	56
Madagascar	10.2	240	−1.9	52
Burma	36.9	190	2.4	59
Zaire	30.6	170	−2.1	51
Mali	7.5	150	1.4	46
Bangladesh	100.6	150	0.4	51
Ethiopia	42.3	110	0.2	45

n.a. = figures not available.

Source: World Development Report (New York: Oxford University Press, 1987), pp. 202–03.

chines, labor is more productive; there is more output per worker. But capital formation requires investment. Investment, in turn, requires saving—an excess of current output above current consumption. Poor countries, where consumption is already low, find it difficult to forgo consumption in order to free resources for investment.

B
Technological Advances

Economic growth in the industrial countries went hand in hand with technological advances. New techniques of production, from steam power in the eighteenth century to computerized robots in the twentieth century, contributed to increases in output per worker. While it is true that developing countries need only adapt, not invent, modern production methods, advancement even using existing technologies runs into the same difficulty as capital formation—it requires funds for investment. Moreover, the poorer nations must find production methods suitable to their own economies, mostly with abundant unskilled labor, not to the developed economies, which have more capital and skilled labor.

C
Growth in Human Capital

Economists use the term _human capital_ to describe the skills and educational level of a work force. As the work force becomes better educated and more highly skilled, output per worker rises. For poorer countries, with masses of unskilled, largely agricultural workers, developing human capital also requires scarce investment funds. Funds are needed to build schools, train teachers, or finance overseas education. Poorer countries also need basic health and nutrition programs just to achieve a healthy work force.

The vicious circle of poverty now becomes more clear: _Poor nations lack the funds to invest in capital formation, technological advance, and the development of human capital. But without such investment, they remain poor._

D
Population Growth

Another barrier to growth in per capita income for many developing countries is rapid population growth. Table 38.2 shows population growth rates

TABLE 38.2 Annual Rates of Population Growth (Percent)

	1965–80	1980–85	1985–2000
Industrialized Market Economies			
United States	1.0	1.0	0.6
Canada	1.3	1.1	0.7
Sweden	0.5	0.1	0.0
Japan	1.2	0.7	0.4
W. Germany	0.3	−0.2	−0.2
France	0.7	0.6	0.4
Developing Countries			
Venezuela	3.5	2.9	2.6
Korea	1.9	1.5	1.2
Mexico	5.2	2.6	2.2
Brazil	2.5	2.3	1.8
Thailand	2.7	2.1	1.6
Nigeria	2.5	3.3	3.4
Egypt	2.4	2.8	2.2
Indonesia	2.3	2.1	1.8
Pakistan	3.1	3.1	2.7
China	2.2	1.2	1.3
Kenya	3.9	4.1	4.0
India	2.3	2.2	1.8
Zaire	2.8	3.0	3.0
Bangladesh	2.7	2.6	1.3

Source: World Development Report (New York: Oxford University Press, 1987), pp. 254–55.

in selected periods for some of the countries in Table 38.1. The table also includes population projections for the rest of this century.[4]

The difference between population growth rates in the industrial and developing countries is striking. Population growth in the industrial countries has been slow in recent decades and is slowing further. In some of these countries, projected population growth rates for the rest of the century are negative; the population is projected to decline.

In developing countries, current population growth rates (1980–85) are, on average, more than three times higher than those in the industrial countries. For the low-income countries, population growth rates are four times as high as in the industrial countries. Projections for the rest of the century do show a slowdown in population growth in many, though not all, of the developing countries. Among the poorer nations, China and India, already the world's most populous, have had the greatest success in slowing the rate of population growth.

The still relatively high projected population growth rates for developing countries means that their populations will increase substantially by the year 2000. For example, the population of Bangladesh is projected to rise from 101 million in 1985 to 141 million in 2000, Egypt's from 49 to 67 million, and Nigeria's from 100 to 163 million. Even in India, where growth has slowed, the population is projected to increase from 765 million to just under 1 billion in the same period.

The cause of the high rate of population growth in developing countries is clear. The growth rate in population is the difference between the birth rate (measured, for example, as the number of births per 1,000 population) and the death rate (number of deaths per 1,000). In Western Europe and in other countries that industrialized early, birth rates were high in the initial stages of development and death rates fell gradually as nutrition and health care improved. As a result, the population grew. Then, as these countries became more affluent and childhood death rates fell, the birth rate declined sharply. More affluent industrial economies were also more urban and less agricultural. Children that were an asset on a farm were expensive in cities. And with fewer childhood deaths,

fewer births were necessary to ensure that the desired number of offspring would survive. As the birth rate fell and the death rate more or less stabilized, population growth rates declined in industrial countries.

In developing countries, the death rate has also fallen as nutrition has improved and medical advances have been imported from the industrial countries. Diseases such as smallpox, typhoid, and cholera have been all but wiped out within a generation. However, the economic adjustment that gradually reduced the birth rate in the industrial countries has only begun to occur. The result—birth rate relatively constant, death rate down sharply, and population growth rate up sharply.

The consequences of rapid population growth in developing countries are also clear. Just to keep per capita income (or more generally overall living standards) constant, these countries must have substantial economic growth. If the projections in Table 38.2 prove correct, Kenya, for example, must have average growth in GNP of 4.0 percent per year *just to maintain the current level of GNP per capita*—another linkage in the vicious circle of poverty.

Read Perspective 38A.

III
Strategies for Development

Can the vicious circle be supplanted by a virtuous circle that produces development? Many strategies have been put forth for development. They can be broken down into those that aim for **balanced growth** in all sectors of the economy and those that call for **unbalanced growth** led by the development of several *strategic* sectors.

A
Balanced Growth

Balanced growth means that investments are made in many sectors (capital goods, consumer durable goods, agriculture), so that all sectors grow more or less together. Adherents to balanced growth favor this approach because they believe that all (or many) sectors must grow before each

---

[4]The projections were made by the *World Bank*, an international agency that promotes economic development.

PERSPECTIVE 38A

Debt Problems of Developing Countries

A large foreign debt further complicates economic development in many countries, as shown in Table 38.3. The last two columns in the table show the debt service burden, which consists of interest and repayment of principal, measured as a percent of both GNP and exports. The need to use so large a fraction of export earnings for debt service means that, after imports of consumer goods and basic materials are taken into account, little is left for imports of capital goods needed for investment. Note that the debt problem is especially severe for some Latin American countries.

can find a market for its products. Consider the situation in a poor country if only one sector, say, investing to build a shoe factory, is developed.[5] If the country is very poor, the market for the shoes may be too small. The factory itself will generate income for its workers, but only a small portion of that income will be used to purchase shoes. Where will the demand come from?

If, in contrast, a number of factories are built to produce shoes, automobiles, steel, packaging, textiles, and other goods, then income from each will supply demand for the others. Advocates of balanced growth believe that such widespread development plans are most likely to succeed.

[5]Nurske, *Problems of Capital Formation*, chapter 1.

Balanced growth plans have several common elements:

1. They emphasize foreign aid in the form of grants or loans. In the early stages of development, such funds are useful because enterprises in developing countries may not be profitable enough to attract private capital from abroad.
2. The government of the developing country also has a role in the investment process. An investment in one sector (e.g., the shoe industry) benefits other sectors by enlarging the domestic market. This is an *external* benefit that does not go to the private investor in the shoe industry. Private investors will therefore invest *less* than is opti-

TABLE 38.3   Foreign Debt of Selected Developing Countries, 1985

	Total External Debt (Billions of Dollars)	Debt Service as a	
		Percent of GNP*	Percent of Exports*
Burma	3.1	2.8	51.4
Indonesia	35.7	6.1	25.1
Philippines	26.2	4.9	19.5
Egypt	24.3	8.5	33.6
Nigeria	18.3	5.5	32.1
Chile	20.2	14.7	44.1
Brazil	106.7	4.9	34.8
Mexico	97.4	8.5	48.2
Argentina	48.4	n.a.	n.a.
Venezuela	32.1	n.a.	n.a.

*Figures are for servicing only long-term debt.

n.a. = figures not available.

Source: World Development Report (New York: Oxford University Press, 1987), p. 236.

mal for the country as a whole because they will not take account of this external benefit. The government must provide subsidies or invest directly, so that the socially optimal level of investment is reached.

3. Advocates of balanced growth often (but not always) favor *protection* from foreign competition by tariffs and/or quotas on imports. Protection allows a process of **import substitution** whereby the output of the new domestic industries (e.g., shoes) replaces previously imported goods. This enlarges the domestic market and improves the profitability of the new industries.[6]

B
Unbalanced Growth

Critics argue that the balanced growth approach is an escapist solution to the difficulties of development. One development economist, Albert Hirschman, describes this escapism as follows:

> *How many a western traveler to an underdeveloped country has been bewildered and dismayed by the ubiquitous poverty and inefficiency, by the immensity of the task, and by the interlocking vicious circles! The temptation is strong then to leave all this backwardness alone and to dream of an entirely new type of economy where, in the words of the poet, "toute est ordre and beauté!"*[7]

In Hirshman's view, those who favor the balanced growth approach say that the poor countries should be like the industrial countries, with many built-up sectors all interacting.

But critics who favor unbalanced growth consider this unrealistic because, with scarce investment funds, meaningful industrialization in many sectors is not possible. Instead, these critics argue that a few *strategic sectors* should be developed to act as *engines of growth*. These sectors will create *constructive disequilibria* that spill over eventually

---

[6]Development economists, however, generally favor protection only in the early stages of industrialization. They also stress that protection itself, without adequate and well-designed investment, will not aid development.

[7]Albert O. Hirschman, *The Strategy of Economic Development* (New Haven, Conn.: Yale University Press, 1958), p. 52.

to other sectors. Building railroads in the United States in the nineteenth century, for example, created opportunities for exporting agricultural products, as well as a demand for iron and steel.

Some strategies for unbalanced growth consist of developing export sectors of the economy. Countries such as Singapore and Taiwan, for example, began by developing the textile and other manufacturing industries to export to the West. Income from these industries created domestic demand and funds of investment in industries for home consumption. Japan's post–World War II recovery was similarly based on **export-led growth.**

IV
The Role of the Industrial Countries

How do the industrial countries fit into strategies for development of the poorer countries? *Aid* and *trade* are the two main roles for the industrialized countries.

A
Foreign Aid

We have noted that in the balanced growth strategy, aid from the industrial countries was a requirement for the high level of investment needed to develop many sectors simultaneously. Foreign aid also has a role in the unbalanced growth strategy. Here the problem is mobilizing large amounts of funds for one sector. Foreign aid is one way to make available a large block of capital for a few sectors—to "enable and embolden a country to set out on the path of unbalanced growth."[8]

Foreign aid from the industrial nations has been substantial, totaling $37 billion in 1986. Table 38.4 shows overall aid to developing countries from a number of industrial countries in 1965 and 1986 as a percent of the donor country's GNP. Table 38.5 shows aid received in 1985 by a number of developing countries, also as a percent of GNP.

TABLE 38.4   Aid to Developing Countries as a
Percent of Donor's GNP 1965, 1986

	1965	1986
Italy	0.10	0.40
Belgium	0.60	0.48
United Kingdom	0.47	0.33
Netherlands	0.36	1.00
France	0.76	0.72
Australia	0.53	0.49
W. Germany	0.40	0.43
Denmark	0.13	0.89
Japan	0.27	0.28
Sweden	0.19	0.88
Canada	0.19	0.48
Norway	0.16	1.20
Switzerland	0.09	0.30
United States	0.58	0.23

Source: World Development Report (New York: Oxford University Press, 1987), p. 242.

TABLE 38.5   Receipts of Foreign Aid (Percent of
Recipient's GNP), 1985

Ethiopia	15.1
Bangladesh	7.1
Mali	34.9
Mozambique	9.2
Zaire	7.5
Burma	5.1
Niger	19.8
India	0.7
Somalia	14.5
Kenya	7.9
China	0.4
Senegal	12.2
Pakistan	2.2
Zambia	15.4
Bolivia	6.2
Morocco	7.5
Indonesia	0.7
Philippines	1.5
Egypt	6.1
Turkey	0.3
Colombia	0.2
Brazil	0.1
Malaysia	0.8
Mexico	0.1
Argentina	0.1

Source: World Development Report (New York: Oxford University Press, 1987), p. 244.

On the donor side, a notable feature is the rise in foreign aid in recent years from Scandinavia (Norway, Sweden, and Denmark) and the Netherlands. All these countries come close to or exceed the 1.0 percent of GNP target called for by the developing

countries. In contrast, foreign aid from the United States declined from a little over one half of 1 percent of GNP in 1965 to less than one quarter of 1 percent in 1986.

On the recipient side, foreign aid was substantial for the poorer African countries: 34.9 percent of GNP for Mali, 15.1 percent for Ethiopia, and 19.8 percent for Niger. For the large Asian countries (India and China) and for the middle-income developing countries (all those below Zambia in the table), foreign aid is a less significant percent of GNP.

B
Trade

The years from the late 1940s to the early 1970s saw generally stable growth and falling trade barriers, mostly tariffs, in the industrial countries. This provided the developing countries with a growing market for their exports. Those countries that had chosen export-led growth strategies benefitted the most.

Circumstances since 1973 have been less favorable, however. Growth in the industrial countries has been slower and less stable. Moreover, as this sluggish growth has led to higher unemployment, many industrial countries have become more *protectionist*. They have increased barriers to trade with both developing and other industrial countries.

Trade with industrial countries has been a vital engine of growth for many developing countries in the post–World War II period. Growing protectionist sentiment in the United States and other industrial countries is a serious threat to the development plans of the poorer countries.

V
Developing Economies: Concluding Comments

Valid generalizations about developing countries are difficult. Their experiences are extremely diverse. What does stand out is that relative political stability and avoidance of prolonged wars are important for successful economic development. The histories of Lebanon, Uganda, Vietnam, and

Cambodia demonstrate the disastrous economic effects of civil strife and lengthy wars.

On the question of the best development strategy, evidence to date favors export-led growth. This is true in the sense that countries strongly oriented to exports such as Hong Kong, Korea, and Singapore have had very rapid growth. Even those only moderately export oriented have fared better than countries that have followed development strategies that focus predominantly on production for the domestic market.[9] Whether this advantage will persist in the future depends in large part on the trade policies of the *industrial* countries. Will the move toward protectionism persist or will there be a reversal to the trade liberalization of the earlier post–World War II period?

Read Perspective 38B.

VI
Nonmarket Economies

Economies in the United States, Western Europe, and Japan are predominantly **capitalist** (or free-enterprise) systems. A capitalist system, as defined

---

[9]See the discussion and table in *World Development Report, 1987* (New York: Oxford University Press, 1987), chapter 5.

in Chapter 3, is one in which the means of production (capital and land) are privately owned and operated for profit. In addition, the economic activities of people and businesses are coordinated by markets. Under pure capitalism, the market system is completely free of government intervention except for money matters, contracts, and protection of private property. In fact, what we call market or free-enterprise economies are not that free. Governments in the Western economies interfere with the market mechanism through policies aimed at affecting resource allocation, income distribution, and other aspects of economic performance. The Western economies are *mixed*, not *pure*, capitalist systems. Still, markets are the *main* means of regulating economic activity.

The communist (or socialist) economies are *nonmarket* economies. The Soviet Union and the Eastern European economies are industrialized (or semiindustralized) communist systems. China, Cuba, North Korea, Vietnam, and Angola are examples of communist systems in developing economies.

In a communist (or socialist) system, the means of production are owned by the state. Some markets still function, but government planning has largely replaced the market mechanism. Currently, however, many of these countries are experimenting with reforms that allow a greater role for

---

Perspective 38B
The High-Income Oil Exporters

Some of the developing countries have large amounts of oil. These countries benefitted from the high oil prices of the 1970s but found it hard to adjust to the falling oil prices of the 1980s. Countries in this category include Mexico, Indonesia, Venezuela, Nigeria, Iraq, and Iran. Other high-income oil exporters—Libya, Saudi Arabia, Kuwait, and the United Arab Emirates—have much smaller populations. As a result, they rank with the industrial countries in per capita income. Still, in other respects their economies are underdeveloped. Table 38.6 provides some data on their economic situations.

The basic economic problem for the rich oil

exporters is how to use the revenues from oil to finance development plans for their economies. Saudi Arabia, for example, has invested in expensive industrial projects (steel mills, oil refineries), construction projects (roads, port facilities), and in domestic education. The economic problems of the high-income oil exporters are compounded by global politics. The Arab states have been caught up in the war between Iran and Iraq. Libya's development plans have been secondary to the military and diplomatic adventures of its leader, Colonel Muammar Qaddafi.

TABLE 38.6 High-Income Oil Producers, Basic Indicators

	Population (Millions, 1985)	GNP Per Capita (Level, 1985, US$)	Oil Exports as Percent of Total	Life Expectancy
Libya	3.8	7,170	98	60
Saudi Arabia	11.5	8,850	98	62
Kuwait	1.7	14,480	95	72
United Arab Emirates	1.4	19,270	95	70

Source: World Development Report (New York: Oxford University Press, 1987), p. 203.

markets, a point to which we return after we describe the workings of a planned communist system.

A

A Planned Economy: The Soviet Example

We will use the Soviet economy as an example of a planned communist system. The Soviet Communist Party came to power in Russia in 1917. While there had been some industrialization in Russia between 1860 and 1914, the economy was far less developed than those of Western Europe. V. I. Lenin, the first leader of the Soviet Communist Party, at first permitted a good deal of free-market activity and private property. But beginning in the mid-1920s and more dramatically after Joseph Stalin became the party's leader (after Lenin's death in 1924), economic activity came under state control.

Stalin accomplished rapid industrialization of the Soviet economy. Agriculture was collectivized, with some 25 million rural households forced to merge into collective farms. The state then exploited the collectives to provide the funds for investment in industry, particularly in capital goods and defense. This exploitation took the form of the state buying agricultural products at artificially low prices and selling to the collectives industrial products at artificially high prices. Some agricultural output was exported, and some went to feed the growing numbers of urban industrial workers. Soviet peasants, not surprisingly, resisted this forced collectivization but were ruthlessly suppressed. In the Ukraine, collectivization led to a massive famine, but Stalin continued to export grain in order to provide funds for industrialization. It is estimated that over 10 million Soviet peasants died during collectivization.

Soviet industrialization has been guided by a series of 5-year plans administered by an increasingly complex bureaucracy. As it functions today, the planning process begins with the Soviet Council of Ministers, which sets broad economic goals. These are passed down to *Gosplan*, the State Planning Committee, which converts them into a detailed plan for output goals for various sectors of the economy. The plan also sets input requirements for these sectors, including required labor inputs. These output and input requirements are then sent to various ministries, to local and regional planning committees, and eventually to the individual state enterprises that are responsible for meeting the production goals. State planning also extends to agriculture, foreign trade, banking and finance, and the setting of prices and wages. Overall the planning bureaucracy sets production targets for some 70,000 items and over 200,000 prices. It's no easy job to replace the market as an allocative device.

Table 38.7 shows estimates of annual GNP growth for the Soviet Union over selected intervals. Note that in terms of output growth, the Soviet system has been successful, although growth rates have slowed since the mid-1970s. Soviet GNP is second in size (overall, not per capita) only to that

TABLE 38.7 Estimated Soviet GNP Growth

Years	Annual GNP Growth (Percent)
1929–52	6.7
1953–65	6.1
1966–70	5.3
1971–75	3.8
1976–80	2.7
1981–85	2.4

Source: World Development Report (New York: Oxford University Press, 1987)

of the United States. The Soviet economic system has not, as many Western observers have predicted over the years, collapsed because of the inherent inefficiency of state planning.

However, the Soviet model of development has costs that do not show up in figures for output growth. One cost is the result of skewing industrialization toward heavy capital goods and defense industries. Not until the 1960s did state planning place much emphasis on production of consumer goods, beyond the essential minimum. This has meant that the standard of living for Soviet households has risen much less rapidly than has Soviet GNP.

A second, more fundamental cost has been that state control of the economy in the Soviet Union has proceeded hand in hand with state control of other aspects of individuals' lives. The Soviet Union is a totalitarian state, meaning that most aspects of life are controlled by authoritarian means. Under Stalin, state action was more brutal than under his successors, but individuals have much less freedom of choice under the Soviet system than in the Western industrial nations. Of course, basic Western freedoms never existed in Russia. The point is that in the West, as private enterprise economies developed, so did democratic institutions and growing individual freedom. In the course of Soviet state-controlled economic development, whether inevitably or not, no such process took place.

B
Soviet Economic Reforms

Mikhail Gorbachev's rise to the leadership of the Soviet Union in 1985 led to the policy of _glasnost_, meaning openness of public disclosure. In the economic sphere Gorbachev called for _perestroika_, which means restructuring. Parts of the restructuring are a series of policies to boost worker morale, reduce absenteeism, and stem the growing problems due to alcoholism.

A second, more important set of policies are aimed at decentralization of economic decision making and a greater role for the market in resource allocation. Included in this program are the election of plant managers in many state-owned enterprises and placing state enterprises on a self-financing basis. This latter shift means

that investment will flow to those state enterprises that are profitable rather than to those chosen by planning committees. State enterprises have also been allowed to buy and sell goods abroad without going through the Trade Ministry. These enterprises can then keep part of the foreign currency they earn through such sales to purchase foreign equipment. Additionally, joint ventures between Soviet and foreign firms are now being encouraged.

Some private enterprise is being allowed. Privately owned restaurants have been permitted to compete with those owned by the state. Individuals have been permitted to sell services. For example, carpenters or plumbers can take on private work and drivers can use their own automobiles as taxis.

The aim of all of these policies is to promote efficiency through competition and thus to reverse the trend toward slower growth in the Soviet economy (see Table 38.7).

Other communist countries have also instituted reforms in recent years that allow a larger role for markets. China has pursued such a course since 1978. Hungary is offering tax incentives for firms and workers. All these countries want to improve the communist system, not replace it with capitalism. Nor do their leaders intend to relinquish their monopoly on political power.

VII
Middle Roads

A Soviet system of nearly complete state ownership of the means of production is at the opposite end of the spectrum from a private-enterprise, capitalist economy such as that of the United States. Other countries have adopted economic systems that are between these extremes. Some distinctive examples will now be considered.

A
The Swedish Welfare State

Sweden has an economic system where most production is by private enterprise. The government, however, intervenes in the economy to a much greater extent then in the United States to influence the distribution of income. Tax rates are higher and transfer payment programs much more generous than in the United States. The government also intervenes directly to maintain high employment. Firms are subsidized to keep workers on the payroll when output drops. Government jobs are also provided for those who cannot find work in the private sector.

B
Yugoslavia's Worker Management

The communist regime in Yugoslavia split with the Soviet Union in the late 1940s. Thereafter, Yugoslavia adopted a system of worker-managed enterprises. The means of production are owned by the state, but worker councils at the individual enterprises make most production decisions. Prices are for the most part market determined.

C
French Indicative Planning

In the French economic system, most production is by private enterprise (though there is more state ownership than in the United States), but the government has an extensive _central planning_ function. The government's role in this _indicative_ planning approach is to bring together representatives of labor, management, and technical experts to develop a coordinated plan for economic growth. Targets for the steel industry are, for example, set to be consistent with other industries' demand for steel products. The planning process is voluntary, but the government can use taxes and subsidies to steer economic activity to its desired targets if necessary.

The systems in Sweden, Yugoslavia, and France provide more of a role for the government than that of the United States, but also more of a role for markets than the Soviet economic system.

SUMMARY

1. In this chapter we examined the economies of developing countries and the non-market economies of the Soviet Union and other communist countries.

2. The central problem facing the developing countries is poverty. Developing countries, especially the lowest-income countries, are often said to suffer from the vicious circle of poverty. Their poverty makes it difficult to achieve the capital formation and technological advances that have been central to growth in the industrial countries. Poverty also makes it difficult for developing countries to invest in education, which would result in increased worker productivity. High rates of population growth often complicate the process of eliminating poverty.

3. Two strategies have been proposed for development. One aims at _balanced growth_ in all sectors of the economy. The second proposes _unbalanced growth_ in a few strategic sectors to lead the way in the development process. Unbalanced growth strategies often aim at export-led growth.

4. Industrial countries can help the developing countries by providing foreign aid and buying their exports. Foreign aid has been a significant portion of GNP for some of the poorest countries. On the trade side, the interval between the late 1940s and the mid-1970s was one of trade liberalization and growth in the industrial countries. The market for the exports of developing countries therefore expanded over this period. Since the mid-1970s, circumstances have been less favorable. Growth has been less stable in many industrial countries, and barriers to trade have increased.

5. Some industrial and developing economies are _nonmarket economies_. In communist economic systems, such as that of the Soviet Union, the state owns the means of production. State planning substitutes for the market as the mechanism for allocating resources.

6. Under Stalin and his successors, the Soviet Union achieved rapid industrialization under communism. There was, however, a tremendous human cost to the collectivization of agriculture that was part of the Soviet development plan. Soviet economic development was also accompanied by the growth of the totalitarian, one-party state.

7. After Gorbachev came to power in 1985, the Soviet Union began a series of economic reforms aimed at decentralization of economic decisionmaking and a greater role for the market in resource allocation. China and several of the East European economies are pursuing similar restructuring programs.

8. A number of countries, including Sweden, Yugoslavia, and France, have sought a middle road between a mostly free market system and a centrally planned economy. The role of government in these economies is more extensive than in the U.S. economy but less pervasive than in the Soviet Union.

Nobel Prize-winning economist George Stigler has written that the goal of the economist "is to understand this economic world in which we live and the other ones which a thousand reformers of every description are imploring and haranguing us to adopt." This book has provided a first look at the breadth of the terrain of economics. We hope it leads you to further exploring.

KEY TERMS

Developing countries
Nonmarket economies
Vicious circle of poverty
Capital formation
Technological advances
Growth in human capital

Balanced growth
Unbalanced growth
Import substitution
Export-led growth
Capitalist economies

QUESTIONS AND PROBLEMS

1. Explain some of the *barriers to growth* faced by the poorer developing countries.

2. How do the causes and barriers to escape from poverty for individuals within the U.S. compare with the causes and barriers to escape from underdevelopment by other countries?

3. What factors are involved in the high population growth rates typical in developing countries?

4. How is the external debt problem of some developing countries linked to their efforts to achieve economic growth?

5. Explain the controversy among development economists regarding the best path toward economic growth for an underdeveloped country.

6. How does economic growth in the industrial countries spur economic development in the underdeveloped countries?

7. Since the 1920's, the Soviet Union has been primarily a nonmarket economy. The free market is not permitted to determine most product prices and quantities sold. How are product prices and quantities sold determined?

8. Discuss and evaluate the following statement: Free market economies, by their very nature, promote individual freedom; central planning necessarily restricts individual freedom.

Glossary

A

Abatement subsidies are payments by the government to polluters to cover the cost of reducing pollution.

An **absolute definition of poverty** specifies a poverty-line income based on the amount needed to buy essential goods and services.

Accounting profit is the firm's revenues less explicit accounting costs. (If negative, it's an accounting loss.)

Affirmative action entails preferential treatment for women and minorities instead of strict neutrality. For example, affirmative action occurs when employers make special efforts to recruit minorities and women or to help them acquire training.

Aggregate demand is the sum of the demands for current output by each of the buying sectors of the economy: households, businesses, the government, and foreign purchasers of exports.

The **aggregate demand curve** measures the demand for total output at each value of the aggregate price level.

The **aggregate supply curve** is the macroeconomic analogue to the individual market supply curve, which shows the output forthcoming at each level of product price. The aggregate supply curve shows the total output firms will supply at each value of the aggregate price level.

Allocation efficiency requires that marginal social benefit equal marginal social cost.

Antitrust laws make it illegal to monopolize a market. These laws also forbid other anticompetitive practices such as *price fixing*.

Automatic stabilizers are changes in taxes and government transfer payments that occur when the level of income changes. They help stabilize the economy.

Autonomous expenditures are expenditures which are largely determined by factors other than current income.

The **autonomous expenditure multiplier** gives the change in equilibrium output per unit change in autonomous expenditures (e.g., government spending).

Average fixed cost is total fixed cost divided by the firm's total output.

The **average product** of an input is the firm's total output divided by the amount of input used to produce this amount of output.

Average revenue per unit is total revenue divided by total quantity.

Average total cost is the sum of average fixed cost and average variable cost. It is also total cost divided by overall output.

Average variable cost is total variable cost divided by the firm's total output.

B

The **balanced-budget multiplier** gives the change in equilibrium output that results from a one-unit increase or decrease in *both* taxes and government spending.

Balanced growth means that investments are made in many sectors (capital goods, consumer durable goods, agriculture), so that all sectors grow more or less together.

A **barrier to entry** is any factor that gives a market's established firms advantages over potential entrants.

811

Barter is the direct exchange of goods and services without money.

With **bilateral monopoly** a labor market has only one buyer, an employer, and only one seller, a union.

When **blacklisting** workers, employers circulated lists of known union members or "labor agitators" so that a union sympathizer fired by one employer would not be hired by another.

The stockholders elect a **board of directors** to represent their views to management, a board that meets only occasionally such as once a month.

The **Board of Governors of the Federal Reserve** is composed of seven members (governors) appointed by the President of the United States with the advice and consent of the Senate for a term of 14 years. One member of the board is appointed chairman.

The **Bretton Woods system** was a pegged exchange rate system set up at the end of World War II.

C

Capital refers to durable inputs which themselves have been produced in the past. It includes office buildings, factories, machinery, equipment, roads, bridges, trucks, trains, and other such materials used in production.

Capitalism is an economic system in which the means of production are privately owned and operated for profit. In addition, the economic activities of people and businesses are coordinated by free markets through contractual exchanges.

Capital formation is growth in the stock of plant and equipment.

A **capital gain** is the increase in the market value of any asset above the price originally paid. The capital gain is realized when the asset is actually sold.

Capital goods are capital resources like factories, machinery, and railroads used to produce other goods.

A **capital loss** is the decrease in the market value of any asset below the price originally paid. The capital loss is realized when the asset is actually sold.

Capitalization is the process that discounts expected future earnings by the interest rate to convert those future earnings into a present value.

A **cartel** is express collusion. Firms in a market explicitly agree among themselves to limit competition.

The expression **ceteris paribus** means "other things being constant."

Choice procedures are decision-making mechanisms, whereas **choice results** are the decisions themselves.

A **closed shop** requires the employer to hire only workers who are already union members.

Collective bargaining consists of negotiations between representatives of labor and management over the terms and conditions of employment to which both parties will be bound for the duration of the labor agreement that normally results.

Collective decision making is nonmarket decision making carried on by voters, politicians, civil servants, and others associated with the government.

Collusive agreements are illegal agreements to fix prices, allocate territories or customers, curtail output, or to boycott certain suppliers or customers.

A **common stock** of a corporation is a piece of paper that gives an ownership share in the company.

In a **communist** (or socialist) system, the means of production are owned by the state. Some markets still function, but government planning has largely replaced the market mechanism.

A **comparative advantage** is the ability to produce a good or service relatively cheaply (with a low opportunity cost).

Compensating wage differentials are the higher monetary rewards that must be paid to workers to compensate them for undesirable work conditions.

The **concentration ratio** is the percentage of market sales accounted for by an absolute number of the largest firms in the market — for example, the top four or eight firms.

Conglomerate mergers are multimarket marriages with little or no common ground.

Constant returns to scale mean that increasing all inputs by a certain proportion (e.g., 100 percent) will cause output to rise by the same proportion (e.g., 100 percent).

Consumer sovereignty is the idea that consumers, by casting their dollar votes, determine what will and what will not be produced.

Consumers' surplus is the difference betwen the total dollar amount consumers would be willing to pay and the total dollar amount they actually pay for a certain quantity. It is the *net* total benefit they obtain.

Consumption is the household sector's demand for output for current use. *Consumption expenditures* consist of purchases of durable goods (e.g., autos and televisions), nondurable goods (e.g., food and newspapers), and services (e.g., haircuts and taxi rides).

The **consumption function** is the Keynesian relationship between income and consumption.

A **contract** is the binding element of any market exchange. It is a commercial promise that the government will enforce.

Convenience goods are those with a relatively low unit price and are purchased repeatedly. Examples include food, cigarettes, beverages, drugs, and candy.

A **corporation** is a firm created by a government charter. The law grants certain powers, privileges, and liabilities separate from those of the individual stockholder-owners.

Corporate bonds are formal IOUs that require the corporation to pay a fixed sum of money (interest payment) annually until maturity and then, at maturity, a fixed sum of money to repay the initial amount borrowed (principal).

The **CPI** measures the retail prices of a fixed "market basket" of several thousand goods and services purchased by households.

Craft unions represent workers who have a specific skill or occupation.

The **cross-price elasticity of demand** for J with respect to K is the percentage change in the quantity of J divided by the percentage change in the price of related good K.

The **cyclical deficit** is the portion of the federal deficit that results from the economy being at a low level of economic activity.

Cyclical unemployment results from fluctuations in the level of economic activity and consequent fluctuations in industry demand for workers.

D

Debt instruments are claims against money income at a specified interest rate. They are assets to those who hold them.

The demand for a resource input is a **derived demand** because it is derived from the demand for the goods and services the resource helps to produce.

A **demand schedule** or **demand curve** shows the various quantities of a good or service that buyers would purchase at various possible prices during some time period (*ceteris paribus*).

The **deposit multiplier** gives the increase in bank deposits per unit increase in bank reserves.

Depository institutions are financial intermediaries whose main liabilities are deposits. These depository institutions include commercial banks, savings and loan associations, mutual savings banks, and credit unions.

Depreciation is the portion of the capital stock that wears out each year.

Differentiated products differ among sellers in the same market, being distinguished by trademarks, advertising style, service, packaging, durability, distribution, and other such nonprice features.

Diffusion refers to the extent and speed of an innovation's adoption, its penetration of the marketplace, if a product, and its popularity on the plant floor, if a process.

The **discount rate** is the interest rate the Federal Reserve charges on loans to banks.

Diseconomies of scale are present when a doubling of all inputs results in *less* than a doubling of output.

Disposable income is personal income less personal tax payments.

Dynamic competition entails an independent striving for patronage by firms employing various strategies and counter-strategies, using nonprice variables as well as price in efforts to outmaneuver one another over time.

E

Economic models (1) simplify reality and (2) demonstrate relationships among variables.

Economic rent is a payment to any resource input above the price required to obtain the quantity supplied.

Economic profit is the firm's revenues less total opportunity costs. (If negative, it's an economic loss.)

Economies of scale are present when a doubling of all inputs result in output *more* than doubling.

The **effective tax rate** is the taxpayer's tax bill divided by her or his total income.

Elasticity measures the magnitude of change in demand. It shows the responsiveness of the quantity demanded to changes in the price of the good, or to changes in other variables determining demand, such as income or the prices of related goods.

Employer recognition occurs when the employer acknowledges the union as the workers' legitimate representative for purposes of collective bargaining.

Equilibrium is a state of balance between conflicting forces. In the market, balance occurs when the quantities demanded and supplied are equal.

An **establishment** is a physical place of business activity. It can be a factory, assembly plant, retail store, warehouse, office building, or some other facility.

An **exchange rate** is the value of one country's currency in terms of foreign currencies.

An **exchange rate system** is a set of rules organizing the determination of exchange rates among currencies.

Experience goods can be evaluated by buyers only after purchase, when they can be experienced.

An **explicit cost** (or *accounting cost*) is incurred when the firm makes an actual payment.

Externalities also called *spillovers*, are effects of production or consumption that help or harm bystanders, neighbors, or others not directly involved. **External benefits** are benefits gained by people other than those directly involved in some production or consumption activity. **Ex-** ternal costs are costs borne by people other than those directly involved in some production or consumption activity.

F

The **factors of production** are labor, land, capital, and entrepreneurship.

The **fallacy of composition** occurs when one incorrectly assumes that what is true for an individual is also true for a group.

The **fallacy of false cause** occurs when one incorrectly deduces causality from mere association.

The **fallacy of misplaced blame** occurs when the individual is blamed for problems that are the fault of the system, or, conversely, when the system is blamed for problems that are the fault of the individual.

The **Federal Reserve System** (Federal Reserve for short) is composed of 12 regional Federal Reserve banks and the Board of Governors located in Washington.

Financial intermediaries are institutions that accept funds from savers and make loans to ultimate borrowers (e.g., firms).

A **firm** is a business organization that owns and/or operates one or more establishments.

Fiscal stabilization policy is the use of government spending and tax policies to affect the level of economic activity.

A **fixed input** is one whose quantity cannot be changed during the period of time under consideration.

Frictional unemployment is unemployment due to the time workers spend between jobs and to the time entrants or reentrants to the labor force need to find jobs.

G

Government is the process within a group for making and enforcing decisions. Public government can claim a monopoly on the legitimate use of physical force within a given territory.

Government imperfections and failures arise when government action causes economic inefficiency, or violates norms of equity, or creates macroinstabilities.

Government purchases of goods and services are the part of current output that goes to the government sector—the federal government as well as state and local governments.

Government spending refers to government outlays for purchases, transfer payments, and subsidies.

Government subsidies lie somewhere between purchases and transfers in both character and effect. In simplest form, the government subsidizes by paying part of the cost of some favored private sector's production or consumption activity.

The **Gramm-Rudman Act** mandated a move to a balanced budget in steps over 5 years, by *automatic* spending cuts if Congress failed to balance the budget by legislation.

Gross National Product (GNP) is a measure of all currently produced final goods and services.

H

The **H index** is the sum of the squares of the percentage sizes of all firms in the market.

According to the **Heckscher-Ohlin theory,** a country will tend to export goods the production of which requires relatively large amounts of factors of production that it has in abundance. A country will tend to import goods that require relatively large amounts of factors of production that are relatively scarce in the country. Factors of production include capital (plant and equipment) and labor, as well as land and other natural resources.

Horizontal mergers unite direct competitors.

Human capital is the accumulation of investments in schooling, training, and health that raises the productive capacity of people.

I

An **ideology** is a set of beliefs and value judgments about the nature of the world and ways to improve it.

Imperfect competition occurs when there are (1) few sellers or buyers, (2) nonstandardized, differentiated products, (3) barriers to new entry, or (4) poorly informed buyers or sellers.

An **implicit cost** is incurred when a valued alternative is forgone. Explicit costs plus implicit costs equal the firm's overall opportunity costs.

The **implicit GNP deflator** is an index of the prices of goods and services included in GNP.

Indirect business taxes are general sales and excise taxes.

Induced expenditures are expenditures that are determined primarily by current income.

Industrial unions represent the employees of a certain industry or firm, regardless of their specific tasks or skills.

Inflation is an increase in the general level of prices.

Innovation is the first commercial application of an invention.

Interest is the price a saver-lender receives for an amount saved or loaned, measured as a percentage of the amount. Interest is also the price an investor-borrower pays for a loan.

Invention has been defined as "the first confidence that something should work, and the first rough test that it will in fact work."

Investment is the part of GNP purchased by the business sector plus residential construction.

L

Labor comprises the physical energy, manual skill, and mental ability that humans apply to the production of goods and services.

Labor market discrimination occurs when one group of workers is paid less than another for the same work, or when some workers are prevented from entering particular occupations, getting training, or winning promotion because of some characteristic irrelevant to job performance.

A **labor union** is an organization of workers that engages in collective bargaining with the employer.

Land is a shorthand term that refers to all of nature's gifts—air, water, sunshine, forests, wildlife, and minerals, as well as soil surfaces.

The **law of comparative advantage** states that

individuals, companies, regions, or nations can gain by specializing in the production of goods and services that they produce relatively cheaply and exchanging them for other goods and services that they produce relatively expensively.

The **law of demand** says that the price of a good and the quantity demanded vary inversely (or negatively) when other factors are held constant.

The **law of diminishing marginal returns** states that if equal units of an input are added, other inputs being held fixed, the resulting additions to output will eventually decrease.

The **law of diminishing marginal utility** states that, as a person consumes more and more of a given commodity, the marginal utility of the commodity eventually declines.

The **law of supply** states that the price of a good and the quantity supplied vary directly (or positively) when other factors are held constant.

Legal reserve requirements specify that banks must hold a certain percentage (fraction) of deposits either in the form of vault cash (currency) or as deposits at regional Federal Reserve Banks. They are what are called *fractional reserve requirements*.

Leisure is time spent in any activity other than work in the labor force or work in the home (e.g., washing dishes).

With **limited liability** the amount an owner-shareholder of a corporation can lose in the event of bankruptcy is limited to the amount paid to purchase an ownership stake in the corporation.

Lobbying is the attempt to sway lawmakers and other officials to side with whatever special interest the lobbyist happens to represent. It is often called influence peddling.

A **lockout** occurs when management closes down the workplace temporarily and refuses to operate.

Logrolling is the exchange of political favors, such as votes in vote trading, to win passage of legislation.

The **long run** is a time period in which all inputs are variable (including plant and equipment).

The **long-run average cost curve** shows the minimum average total cost for each level of output when all inputs are variable. (Prices of inputs, e.g., wage rates, are given, as are available technologies.)

The **long-run marketwide supply curve** shows the quantities that sellers offer at different prices after the exit or entry of firms is completed.

The **Lorenz curve** is a device for depicting a measure of income inequality.

M

M1 is the narrowest of the money supply measures in the United States. It consists of currency plus *checkable* deposits. Two other measures, M2 and M3, are broader. They include all the components of M1 plus some additional bank deposits that have no or only limited provisions for checks.

Macroeconomics is the study of economics in the large. It covers aggregate economic performance.

A **managed float** for a country's exchange rate is a system where at some times the exchange rate is allowed to respond to market forces, while at other times the central bank *intervenes* to influence the exchange rate.

Marginal is a term commonly used by economists to mean "additional." For example, if this week you have already had three hamburgers, the benefits of a fourth would be the marginal benefits.

Marginal cost is the extra, or additional, cost of producing one more unit of output.

The **marginal product** of an input is the addition to total output due to the addition of an extra unit of that input (the quantity of other inputs being held constant).

The **marginal propensity to consume (MPC)** is the increase in consumption per unit increase in disposable income.

The **marginal propensity to save (MPS)** is the increase in saving per unit increase in disposable income.

Marginal resource cost (MRC) is the firm's extra total cost of using one more unit of resource input.

Marginal revenue is the added revenue associated with the sale of one more unit of output.

The **marginal revenue product (MRP)** of any resource input is the extra revenue the firm gains by using one more unit of the input (holding other inputs constant).

The **marginal tax rate** is the rate paid on each additional dollar earned from an activity.

The **marginal utility** of a good is the additional satisfaction a consumer derives from consuming one additional unit of that good.

A **market** is an organized process by which buyers and sellers exchange goods and services, usually for money.

Market conduct refers to actions and strategies of sellers. It's what sellers do and pursue.

The **market for loanable funds** registers the demands of all borrowers and the supplies of the lenders, thereby determining the price of debt capital.

Market structure refers to certain characteristics of the market's participants and product, characteristics influencing competition.

The **median voter** is the one in the middle who decides a majority-rule election and who therefore heavily influences the positions that politicians take on issues.

Microeconomics is the study of economics in the small. It covers personal choice, firm behavior, and individual markets.

A **minimum wage law** sets a wage floor; employers have to pay at least the minimum wage.

Under **mixed capitalism** the government is quite active, owning large amounts of public property, correcting market imperfections, and influencing answers to the basic questions What?, How?, Who?, What's new?, and How stable?.

The **monetary base** is equal to currency held by the public plus bank reserves.

Monetary policy is the central bank's use of control of the money supply and interest rates to influence the level of economic activity.

Money is whatever is commonly accepted as payment in exchange for goods and services (and payment of debts and taxes).

The **money multiplier** gives the increase in the money supply per unit increase in the monetary base.

Monopolistic competition is characterized by a fairly large number of firms and fairly easy entry. These characteristics make it a first cousin to perfect competition. Where monopolistic competition and perfect competition diverge is in product type. In contrast to the standardized products of perfect competition, the products of monopolistically competitive markets are differentiated, sometimes highly differentiated.

Monopoly power is the power to influence price and deter entry.

Monopoly rent is another name for the economic profit due to monopoly power. It is a form of producers' surplus, but it differs from producers' surplus that may arise under perfect competition, which is scarcity rent.

A **monopsony** is a market in which there is only one buyer.

N

National income is the sum of the earnings of all factors of production that come from current production.

A **natural monopoly** occurs if the cost per unit slides down over the entire range of market demand. There will be room for only one efficient firm in the market.

Natural rates of output, employment, and therefore unemployment, in the monetarist model are determined by *real* supply-side factors: the capital stock, the size of the labor force, and the level of technology. In our simple model, the natural rates of output, employment, and unemployment are the classical equilibrium levels of these variables (unemployment being confined to frictional and structural forms).

A **negative income tax** program would provide sliding-scale income assistance uncategorically, according only to simple standards of economic need. Given an approach linked to income level alone, dispensing only money benefits, and universally applied to all potentially poor people, it could be appended to the income tax system. It would pay money out as well as take it in, hence the name negative income tax.

Nominal (or money) GNP is gross national product measured in current dollars.

The **nominal interest rate** is that stated on loan contracts, such as the annual percentage rate (APR), specified on consumer loans and credit card agreements.

Noncompeting groups are groups of labor suppliers differentiated by very scarce natural abilities or very scarce acquired skills, groups sufficiently different that they do not compete with each other or with labor generally.

Nonmonetary assets are substitutes (e.g., stocks and bonds) for holding wealth in the form of money.

A **normal profit** is compensation for entrepreneurial skill and financial capital that is just enough to keep that skill and capital from leaving a firm and going into other productive activities. It is the opportunity cost of a firm's owners.

Normative economic analysis could be considered economic policy analysis. It requires making value judgments to rank alternative outcomes or procedures.

O

Oligopoly is closer to monopoly than to perfect competition because it is typified by few firms (as few as two or three) and by moderately difficult entry. In product type, oligopoly markets may have either standardized or differentiated products.

The **open market** is the market of dealers in government securities in New York City.

The **Open Market Committee** is composed of 12 voting members: the 7 members of the Board of Governors and 5 of the presidents of regional Federal Reserve Banks. Presidents of the regional banks serve on a rotating basis, with the exception of the president of the Federal Reserve Bank of New York, who is vice chairman and a permanent voting member of the committee.

Open market operations are purchases and sales of government securities in the open market by the Federal Reserve. Open market operations are the primary tool for control of the monetary base.

The **opportunity cost** of an action is the value of the best forgone alternative.

P

A **partnership** is a firm whose ownership is shared by a fixed number of proprietors.

Patents give inventors legal monopoly rights for 17 years, with the prospect of large profits, thereby promoting private R&D efforts.

Perfect competition exists if (1) There are many buyers and sellers, who each account for only a small share of the business. (2) The product is standardized, or homogeneous, so that sellers offer identical products. (3) The entry of newcomers into the market is easy. (4) All buyers and sellers are well informed about prices, qualities, product availabilities, and other pertinent facts.

Personal income is the national income accounts measure of the income received by persons from all sources.

The **Phillips curve** is the schedule showing the relationship between the unemployment and inflation rates.

Pollution occurs when one use of the environment, waste disposal in particular, diminishes other valuable uses, including other resource uses, as well as habitats and amenities.

Positive economic analysis attempts to determine verifiable relationships among economic variables.

Potential GNP (output) is the level that would be reached if productive resources (labor and capital) were being used at benchmark high levels.

A **preferred stock** grants a fixed prior claim on profits (ahead of common stock).

Price ceilings exist when the government outlaws any price above a specified maximum.

Price discrimination occurs when a supplier sells different units of essentially the same commodity to buyers at two or more different prices for reasons not associated with different costs.

Price elasticity of demand measures the responsiveness of the quantity demanded to changes in the price of the good. In particular, it is the percentage change in quantity divided by the percentage change in price.

Price elasticity of supply is the percentage change in quantity supplied divided by the percentage change in price.

Price floors exist if by law the price cannot fall below some set level.

A **price index** measures the aggregate price level relative to a chosen base year.

Price leadership is one way competition can be

tacitly avoided. Under price leadership, prices set by a leading firm are imitated by the other firms in the market simply by self-interest, not by formal agreement.

The **principle of increasing cost** says that the opportunity cost rises as more of a particular commodity is produced.

Producer sovereignty is the notion that producers determine what is produced through their influence on consumer tastes.

Producers' surplus is the difference between the total dollar amount producers receive and the amount they must give up to cover costs, including opportunity costs. It is the net benefit going to producers after subtracting the minimum value they would have to receive in order to supply the product.

The theory of **product life cycles** proposes that products pass through four distinct phases: introduction, growth, maturity, and decline.

A **production function** summarizes the relationship between total inputs and total outputs assuming a given technology.

The **production-possibilities frontier** shows the greatest combinations of goods that can be produced with (1) limited resources, (2) given technology, and (3) maximum potential resource use. It shows the choices open to society and those denied by scarcity at a particular point in time.

Productivity refers to the relation between resource inputs and product outputs. It is expressed as inputs required per unit of output (input/output) or outputs per unit of input (output/input).

The **profit maximization** rule is that a firm will maximize total profits by expanding output as long as marginal revenue (MR) is greater than or equal to marginal cost (MC). It should never add units whose marginal revenue is less than their marginal cost. In brief, $MR = MC$. This applies to all firms—monopolists, oligopolists, whatever—although their marginal revenues and marginal costs differ from those of perfectly competitive firms.

Public choice is the application to macroeconomic policy-making of the microeconomic theory of how decisions are made.

A **public good** is a good that benefits everyone;

excluding people from those benefits is either impossible or costly.

Public utility regulation is an industrial halfway house. Private firms own and operate enterprises, while state and federal governments police their conduct and performance, telling firms what prices they may charge, what services they may offer, what profits they may earn, and what they may do in other respects.

A **pure economic rent** is a return to a factor of production that has a *perfectly inelastic supply curve*. Perfectly inelastic supply occurs when the quantity supplied is fixed, so that the quantity offered neither rises nor falls with variations in the price paid for the resource.

Q

The **quantity theory of money** is the classical theory stating that the price level is proportional to the quantity of money. In the monetarist version the quantity theory is a theory of nominal GNP.

R

Rational expectations are expectations formed on the basis of all available relevant information concerning the variable being predicted. Moreover, economic agents are assumed to use available information intelligently; that is, they understand the relationships between the variables they observe and the variables they are trying to predict.

Rational ignorance arises when, by individual benefit-cost criteria, it is not in people's self-interest to become actively involved in government affairs.

Real GNP measures aggregate output in constant-valued dollars from a base year.

The **real interest rate** is the nominal interest rate minus the anticipated rate of price inflation.

A **recession** is a period when economic activity declines significantly relative to potential output, but less severely than in a depression such as that of the 1930s.

Recognized interdependence means that the

actions of one firm will influence the actions of others in the market, and this interactive influence is recognized.

A **relative definition** specifies a poverty-line income at some minimum level relative to other, higher incomes.

The **required reserve ratio** is the percentage of deposits banks must hold as reserves.

Right-to-work-laws allow any employee to reject union membership. Such laws have been enacted in 20 states, primarily in the south and southwest.

In **roundabout production,** real capital inputs are produced and used in order to produce greater amounts of consumption goods in the future.

S

Scarcity rent is the premium paid to a scarce input above the price necessary to hire or purchase the input, the premium above the input's opportunity cost.

Shopping goods are mainly high-priced, infrequently purchased durables. The consumer typically compares prices, quality, and style in several stores, and the purchase can be delayed. Examples include autos, refrigerators, TV sets, furniture, and apparel.

The **short run** is the time period in which at least one of the firm's inputs is fixed (plant and equipment in particular).

The **slope of a curved line** at a particular point is the same as the slope of the straight line that is tangent to that point.

The **slope of a straight line** is the ratio of the vertical change to the corresponding horizontal change while moving to the right along the horizontal axis (the ratio of the rise over the run).

A **sole proprietorship** is a business firm owned directly by one person (without the legal device of incorporation).

Special interest effects occur when subgroups of voters (minorities like farmers or steelworkers especially) have more political influence than their proportionate share.

Standardization policies typically promote simplification or uniformity or both. Their main purpose is to aid consumers in making price comparisons.

A **strike** occurs when all unionized employees stop work in order to persuade management to agree to union demands.

The **structural deficit** is the part of the federal deficit that would exist even if the economy were at its potential level of output.

Structural unemployment, like frictional unemployment, originates in the dynamic nature of the product and job mix in the economy, but structural unemployment lasts longer.

A **substitute good** is one that can be used instead of another.

A **supply schedule** or *supply curve* shows the various quantities of a good or service that sellers would offer for sale at various possible prices during some time period (*ceteris paribus*).

T

Tacit collusion is mutual self-restraint, a parallel reluctance to compete on price (or other variables) grounded on individual understanding.

Target zones for exchange rates are ranges within which policymakers would try to maintain their currency's value. The target zones would be jointly set by major industrialized nations.

Tariffs are taxes on imported goods.

A **tax** is *progressive, proportional,* or *regressive* depending on whether the ratio of tax to income (percentage rate) rises, remains unchanged, or falls as income rises.

Technical efficiency requires that a given output be produced at the lowest cost possible. This implies no wasted resources, no wasted motion, and no use of obsolete technology. Also, the resource combination used is most economic.

Technological change includes changes in technological knowledge (e.g., ways to employ robots in the production process), as well as new knowledge about how to organize businesses (managerial strategies).

Technology is the set of scientific methods and materials designed to achieve industrial or commercial objectives.

Total cost is the sum of total fixed cost and total

variable cost. **Total fixed cost** is the firm's total expenditure per time period for fixed inputs. **Total variable cost** is the firm's total expenditure on variable inputs per time period.

The U.S. **trade deficit** is the excess of U.S. imports over U.S. exports.

Tying occurs when a seller ties the sale of two products together, so that buyers must buy both products even if they want only one.

U

Unbalanced growth is a development strategy that emphasizes growth in a few key (strategic) sectors.

The **unemployment rate** expresses the number of unemployed persons as a percent of the labor force.

A **union shop** gives employers freedom in hiring but requires employees to become union members after some period (usually 30 to 60 days).

Unrecognized interdependence means that each firm acts independently of the others while interacting in rivalry.

Utility is the satisfaction people feel as a result of consuming goods and services.

V

A **variable input** is one whose quantity can be changed during the relevant period.

The **velocity of money** is the rate at which money *turns over* in GNP transactions during a given period, i.e., the average number of times each dollar is used in GNP transactions.

Vertical mergers combine firms with vertical buyer-supplier links.

W

Wealth is comprised of financial assets like savings accounts, common stocks and bonds, or real assets like real estate, oil reserves, and gold.

Under **workfare,** a welfare recipient can be forced to perform service work in return for welfare benefits.

X

X-inefficiency occurs when costs rise because of slackness, mismanagement, needless spending, or other waste.

Y

In **yellow-dog contracts** workers had to agree not to become union members as a condition of their employment. No contract, no job. And if a worker broke the contract by joining a union, he or she could be fined or imprisoned as well as put out of work.

Index

A

IV MICRO PRODUCT MARKETS